THE CAMBRIDGE HANDBOOK OF PERSONALITY DISORDERS

This *Handbook* provides both breadth and depth regarding current approa‌
understanding, assessment, and treatment of personality disorders. The five ‌
book address etiology; models; individual disorders and clusters; assessment; and treatment. A comprehensive picture of personality pathology is supplied that acknowledges
the contributions and missteps of the past, identifies the crucial questions of the present,
and sets a course for the future. It also follows the changes the *Diagnostic and Statistical
Manual of Mental Disorders* (DSM-5) has triggered in the field of personality disorders.
The editors take a unique approach where all chapters include two commentaries by
experts in the field, as well as an author rejoinder. This approach engages multiple
perspectives and an exchange of ideas. It is the ideal resource for researchers and
treatment providers at all career stages.

CARL W. LEJUEZ is the Interim Provost and past Dean of Liberal Arts & Sciences at the
University of Kansas, where he is also a professor in the Department of Psychology. He
served as founding editor of the journal *Personality Disorders: Theory, Research, and
Treatment.*

KIM L. GRATZ is Professor and Chair of the Department of Psychology at the University
of Toledo, Ohio. She has received awards from the National Education Alliance for
Borderline Personality Disorder and the North American Society for the Study of
Personality Disorders.

THE CAMBRIDGE HANDBOOK OF PERSONALITY DISORDERS

Edited by

Carl W. Lejuez
University of Kansas

Kim L. Gratz
University of Toledo

CAMBRIDGE
UNIVERSITY PRESS

CAMBRIDGE
UNIVERSITY PRESS

University Printing House, Cambridge CB2 8BS, United Kingdom

One Liberty Plaza, 20th Floor, New York, NY 10006, USA

477 Williamstown Road, Port Melbourne, VIC 3207, Australia

314–321, 3rd Floor, Plot 3, Splendor Forum, Jasola District Centre,
New Delhi – 110025, India

79 Anson Road, #06–04/06, Singapore 079906

Cambridge University Press is part of the University of Cambridge.

It furthers the University's mission by disseminating knowledge in the pursuit of
education, learning, and research at the highest international levels of excellence.

www.cambridge.org
Information on this title: www.cambridge.org/9781108424349
DOI: 10.1017/9781108333931

© Cambridge University Press 2020

First published 2020

Printed in the United Kingdom by TJ International Ltd. Padstow Cornwall

A catalogue record for this publication is available from the British Library.

Library of Congress Cataloging-in-Publication Data
Names: Lejuez, Carl W., editor. | Gratz, Kim L., editor.
Title: The Cambridge handbook of personality disorders / edited by Carl W. Lejuez,
 Kim L. Gratz.
Description: Cambridge ; New York, NY : Cambridge University Press, 2020. |
 Includes bibliographical references and index.
Identifiers: LCCN 2019038700 (print) | LCCN 2019038701 (ebook) | ISBN 9781108424349
 (hardback) | ISBN 9781108440097 (paperback) | ISBN 9781108333931 (epub)
Subjects: LCSH: Personality disorders–Handbooks, manuals, etc.
Classification: LCC RC554 .C33 2020 (print) | LCC RC554 (ebook) | DDC 616.85/81–dc23
LC record available at https://lccn.loc.gov/2019038700
LC ebook record available at https://lccn.loc.gov/2019038701

ISBN 978-1-108-42434-9 Hardback
ISBN 978-1-108-44009-7 Paperback

Contents

PART III INDIVIDUAL DISORDERS AND CLUSTERS

Figures

Tables

Contributors

Madelaine Abel, *Department of Psychology, University of Kansas, USA*

Elizabeth Allison, *Psychoanalysis Unit, University College London, UK*

Emily B. Ansell, *Department of Biobehavioral Health, The Pennsylvania State University, USA*

Arnoud Arntz, *Department of Clinical Psychology, University of Amsterdam, Netherlands*

Bo Bach, *Center for Personality Disorder Research, Slagelse Psychiatric Hospital, Denmark*

R. Michael Bagby, *Departments of Psychiatry and Psychology, University of Toronto, Canada*

Arielle Baskin-Sommers, *Department of Psychology, Yale University, USA*

Anthony Bateman, *Department of Clinical, Educational and Health Psychology, University College London, UK*

Theodore P. Beauchaine, *Department of Psychology, The Ohio State University, USA*

Joseph E. Beeney, *Department of Psychiatry, University of Pittsburgh, USA*

Chloe F. Bliton, *Department of Psychology, Pennsylvania State University, USA*

Marina A. Bornovalova, *Department of Psychology, University of South Florida, USA*

Robert F. Bornstein, *Department of Psychology, Adelphi University, USA*

Philippe Boursiquot, *Department of Psychiatry and Behavioural Neurosciences, McMaster University, Canada*

Sarah J. Brislin, *Department of Psychology, Florida State University, USA*

Nicole M. Cain, *Graduate School of Applied and Professional Psychology, Rutgers, The State University of New Jersey, USA*

William Calabrese, *Department of Psychiatry, Icahn School of Medicine at Mount Sinai, USA*

Chloe Campbell, *Psychoanalysis Unit, University College London, UK*

W. Keith Campbell, *Department of Psychology, University of Georgia, USA*

Michael Carnovale, *Department of Psychology, University of Toronto Scarborough, Canada*

Chi C. Chan, *Department of Psychiatry, Icahn School of Medicine at Mount Sinai & James J. Peters Veterans Affairs Medical Center, Mental Illness Research, Education, and Clinical Center (MIRECC), USA*

Shou-An Ariel Chang, *Department of Psychology, Yale University, USA*

Alexander L. Chapman, *Department of Psychology, Simon Fraser University, Canada*

Michael Chmielewski, *Department of Psychology, Southern Methodist University, USA*

Alexandria M. Choate, *Department of Psychology, University of South Florida, USA*

Fiona Choi, *Department of Psychiatry, University of British Columbia, Canada*

Alex S. Cohen, *Department of Psychology, Louisiana State University, USA*

Lindsey C. Conkey, *Department of Psychological and Brain Sciences, University of Massachusetts Amherst, USA*

Christopher C. Conway, *Department of Psychology, Fordham University, USA*

Sheila E. Crowell, *Department of Psychology, University of Utah, USA*

Patrick T. Davies, *Department of Psychology, University of Rochester, USA*

Sindes Dawood, *Department of Psychology, Pennsylvania State University, USA*

Barbara De Clercq, *Department of Developmental, Personality and Social Psychology, Ghent University, Belgium*

Filip De Fruyt, *Department of Developmental, Personality and Social Psychology, Ghent University, Belgium*

Katherine L. Dixon-Gordon, *Department of Psychological and Brain Sciences, University of Massachusetts Amherst, USA*

C. Emily Durbin, *Department of Psychology, Michigan State University, USA*

Elizabeth A. Edershile, *Department of Psychology, University of Pittsburgh, USA*

Chloe M. Evans, *Department of Psychology, University at Buffalo, The State University of New York, USA*

Luis C. Farhat, *Department of Psychiatry, University of Sao Paulo Medical School, Brazil*

Haya Fatimah, *Department of Psychology, University of South Florida, USA*

Janine D. Flory, *Department of Psychiatry, Icahn School of Medicine at Mount Sinai & James J. Peters Veterans Affairs Medical Center, NY, USA*

Peter Fonagy, *Division of Psychology and Language Sciences, University College London, UK*

Andrea L. Gold, *Department of Psychiatry and Human Behavior, Warren Alpert Medical School of Brown University, and Pediatric Anxiety Research Center, Emma Pendleton Bradley Hospital, USA*

Andrea M. Gorrondona, *Department of Psychology, University of Tennessee Knoxville, USA*

Nathan T. Hall, *Department of Psychology, Pennsylvania State University, USA*

Michael N. Hallquist, *Department of Psychology, Pennsylvania State University, USA*

Erin A. Hazlett, *Department of Psychiatry, Icahn School of Medicine at Mount Sinai & James J. Peters Veterans Affairs Medical Center, Mental Illness Research, Education, and Clinical Center (MIRECC), USA*

Anna Darre Hector, *Department of Psychology, Wesleyan University, USA*

Ashley C. Helle, *Department of Psychological Sciences, University of Missouri, USA*

Nora H. Hope, *Department of Psychology, Simon Fraser University, Canada*

Christopher J. Hopwood, *Department of Psychology, University of California, Davis, USA*

Christopher D. Hughes, *Graduate School of Applied and Professional Psychology, Rutgers, The State University of New Jersey, USA*

Kerry L. Jang, *Department of Psychiatry, University of British Columbia, Canada*

Amber M. Jarnecke, *Department of Psychiatry & Behavioral Sciences, Medical University of South Carolina, USA*

Parisa R. Kaliush, *Department of Psychology, University of Utah, USA*

Laurence Y. Katz, *Department of Psychiatry, University of Manitoba, Canada*

John G. Kerns, *Department of Psychological Sciences, University of Missouri, USA*

Laura E. Kessler, *Department of Psychiatry, Icahn School of Medicine at Mount Sinai, New York, NY, & James J. Peters Veterans Affairs Medical Center, Mental Illness Research, Education, and Clinical Center (MIRECC), USA*

Thanh Le, *Department of Psychology, Louisiana State University, USA*

Nicole Legg, *Department of Psychology, University of Victoria, Canada*

Mark F. Lenzenweger, *Department of Psychology, The State University of New York at Binghamton & Department of Psychiatry, Weill Cornell Medical College & Personality Disorders Institute, The New York-Presbyterian Hospital, USA*

Kenneth N. Levy, *Department of Psychology, Pennsylvania State University, USA*

Klaus Lieb, *Department of Psychiatry and Psychotherapy, University Medical Center Mainz, Germany*

Scott O. Lilienfeld, *Department of Psychology, Emory University, USA, & Melbourne School of Psychological Sciences, University of Melbourne, AUS*

Madison Links, *Department of Psychiatry and Behavioural Neurosciences, McMaster University, Canada*

Paul S. Links, *Department of Psychiatry and Behavioural Neurosciences, McMaster University, Canada*

Patrick Luyten, *Department of Clinical, Educational and Health Psychology, KU Leuven and University College London, Belgium & UK*

Donald R. Lynam, *Department of Psychological Sciences, Purdue University, USA*

Jenny Macfie, *Department of Psychology, University of Tennessee Knoxville, USA*

David K. Marcus, *Department of Psychology, Washington State University, USA*

Kristian E. Markon, *Department of Psychology, University of Iowa, USA*

Maria Martin Lopez, *Department of Psychiatry, Icahn School of Medicine at Mount Sinai, USA*

Kibby McMahon, *Department of Psychiatry and Behavioral Science, Duke University, USA*

Lars Mehlum, *National Centre for Suicide Research and Prevention, University of Oslo, Norway.*

Neil A. Meyer, *Department of Psychology, Oklahoma State University, USA*

Joshua D. Miller, *Department of Psychology, University of Georgia, USA*

Jiwon Min, *Department of Psychology, Oklahoma State University, USA*

Stephanie N. Mullins-Sweatt, *Department of Psychology, Oklahoma State University, USA*

Madeline G. Nagel, *Department of Psychology, Washington State University, USA*

Inga Niedtfeld, *Department of Psychosomatic Medicine and Psychotherapy, Central Institute of Mental Health, Medical Faculty Mannheim, Heidelberg University, Germany*

Samantha K. Noose, *Department of Psychology, University of Tennessee Knoxville, USA*

Christian Paret, *Department of Psychosomatic Medicine and Psychotherapy, Central Institute of Mental Health, Medical Faculty Mannheim, Heidelberg University, Germany*

Joel Paris, *Department of Psychiatry, McGill University, Canada*

Christopher J. Patrick, *Department of Psychology, Florida State University, USA*

M. Mercedes Perez-Rodriguez, *Department of Psychiatry, Icahn School of Medicine at Mount Sinai, USA*

Paul A. Pilkonis, *Department of Psychiatry, University of Pittsburgh School of Medicine, USA*

Aaron L. Pincus, *Department of Psychology, Pennsylvania State University, USA*

Marc N. Potenza, *Department of Psychiatry, Child Study Center, Department of Neuroscience, Yale School of Medicine, & Connecticut Mental Health Center, USA*

Jennifer Presnall-Shvorin, *War Related Illness and Injury Study Center (WRIISC), VA New Jersey Health Care System, USA*

Julie Prud'homme, *Department of Psychology, University of Victoria, Canada*

Whitney R. Ringwald, *Department of Psychology, University of Pittsburgh, USA*

Shireen L. Rizvi, *Graduate School of Applied and Professional Psychology, Rutgers, The State University of New Jersey, USA*

Michael J. Roche, *Department of Psychology, Penn State Altoona, USA*

Elsa Ronningstam, *Department of Psychiatry, Harvard Medical School and McLean Hospital, USA*

Nina L. J. Rose, *Department of Psychiatry, Icahn School of Medicine at Mount Sinai & James J. Peters Veterans Affairs Medical Center, Mental Illness Research, Education, and Clinical Center (MIRECC), USA*

M. Zachary Rosenthal, *Department of Psychiatry and Behavioral Science, Duke University, USA*

Tiffany Russell, *Department of Psychiatry, Harvard Medical School and McLean Hospital, USA*

Sarah B. Rutter, *Department of Psychiatry, Icahn School of Medicine at Mount Sinai, USA*

Nicholas Salsman, *School of Psychology, Xavier University, USA*

Charles A. Sanislow, *Department of Psychology, Wesleyan University, USA*

Shannon Sauer-Zavala, *Department of Psychology, Boston University, USA*

Christian Schmahl, *Department of Psychosomatic Medicine and Psychotherapy, Central Institute of Mental Health, Medical Faculty Mannheim, Heidelberg University, Germany*

Alison M. Schreiber, *Department of Psychology, Pennsylvania State University, USA*

Lori N. Scott, *Department of Psychiatry, University of Pittsburgh School of Medicine, USA*

Martin Sellbom, *Department of Psychology, University of Otago, NZ*

Carla Sharp, *Department of Psychology, University of Houston, USA*

Leonard J. Simms, *Department of Psychology, University at Buffalo, The State University of New York, USA*

Susan C. South, *Department of Psychological Sciences, Purdue University, USA*

Jutta Stoffers-Winterling, *Department of Psychiatry and Psychotherapy, University Medical Center Mainz, Germany*

Morgan J. Thompson, *Department of Psychology, University of Rochester, USA*

Mayson Trujillo, *Department of Psychology, Southern Methodist University, USA*

Jacqueline Trumbull, *Department of Psychiatry, Icahn School of Medicine at Mount Sinai, USA*

Brianna J. Turner, *Department of Psychology, University of Victoria, Canada*

Peter Tyrer, *Centre for Psychiatry, Imperial College, UK*

Brandon T. Unruh, *Department of Psychiatry, Harvard Medical School and McLean Hospital, USA*

Daniel H. Vaccaro, *Department of Psychiatry, Icahn School of Medicine at Mount Sinai & James J. Peters Veterans Affairs Medical Center, Mental Illness Research, Education, and Clinical Center (MIRECC), USA*

Eric M. Vernberg, *Department of Psychology, University of Kansas, USA*

Robert D. Vlisides-Henry, *Department of Psychology, University of Utah, USA*

Igor Weinberg, *Department of Psychiatry, Harvard Medical School & McLean Hospital, USA*

Brandon Weiss, *Department of Psychology, University of Georgia, USA*

Thomas A. Widiger, *Department of Psychology, University of Kentucky, USA*

Trevor F. Williams, *Department of Psychology, University at Buffalo, The State University of New York, USA*

Sherry E. Woods, *Department of Psychological and Brain Sciences, University of Massachusetts Amherst, USA*

William C. Woods, *Department of Psychology, University of Pittsburgh, USA*

Aidan G. C. Wright, *Department of Psychology, University of Pittsburgh, USA*

Leila Z. Wu, *Department of Psychology, Pennsylvania State University, USA*

Kristin P. Wyatt, *Department of Psychiatry and Behavioral Science, Duke University, USA*

Shirley Yen, *Department of Psychiatry and Human Behavior, Warren Alpert Medical School of Brown University and Massachusetts Mental Health Center/Beth Israel Deaconess Medical Center, USA*

Preface

The most recent version of the *Diagnostic Manual of Mental Disorders* (5th ed.; DSM-5; American Psychiatric Association [APA], 2013) characterizes personality disorders (PDs) as developing through a complex interaction of environmental influences (including family, peer, societal, and cultural influences) and inherited characteristics. PDs involve a way of thinking, feeling, and behaving that differs from cultural expectations, impairs functioning, and largely endures over time. Although there is still much to be learned about how these processes unfold, our evolving knowledge is crucial for future advancements in understanding, defining, assessing, and treating PDs.

PDs represent a significant challenge for those who suffer from these disorders and for society more broadly. PDs also present a wide array of challenges for researchers and treatment professionals who work in this area. The willingness to take on these challenges has led to a proliferation in recent decades of research examining both PDs and personality processes across a continuum from normal to pathological functioning. Research across multiple disciplines has played an important role in this regard, spurring advances in our understanding of basic mechanisms underlying personality pathology, as well as the development of novel assessment, prevention, and treatment strategies. With the elimination of the multiaxial classification system in DSM-5, PDs are no longer relegated to Axis II and distinguished from other disorders that had previously occupied Axis I. Rather, the classification of PDs alongside other disorders has clarified their clinical relevance and highlighted the importance of further research in this area.

This considerable progress has also led to difficult and sometimes highly charged questions that are now shaping the future of research and clinical endeavors in the PDs. These questions include the relative contribution of biological and environmental factors to the development of personality pathology, the stability of PD diagnoses and personality pathology over time, the meaning and implications of heterogeneity across PDs and even within individual PDs, and the most effective treatments for PDs. However, the most widely recognized and debated controversy in the field came to the forefront during the lead-up to the DSM-5. This controversy focused on the conceptualization of PDs and the question of whether the longstanding categorical approach to the diagnosis of PDs should be replaced by a dimensional approach or a hybrid of the two approaches. After considerable (and sometimes contentious) debate, the decision was made to keep the main body of the diagnostic system categorical and add a hybrid dimensional-categorical approach to a separate section of the DSM-5 (with the idea that this hybrid approach could play a more significant role in the primary diagnostic system in future iterations). Now more than five years since the publication of the DSM-5, there are important questions regarding how best to navigate the growing disparity between the large amount of emerging research on dimensional approaches to personality pathology and the largely exclusive focus on categorical diagnoses in the DSM-5.

In considering how best to advance research on the etiology, underlying mechanisms, assessment, and treatment of PDs and personality pathology more broadly, this is an ideal time to take stock of current research in this area and review both recent progress and needed future directions for advancing our understanding of the pathogenesis and treatment of PDs. This perspective serves as the impetus for this handbook and the selection of chapters that provide coverage of more basic and foundational principles and processes at the core of personality pathology, in addition to cutting-edge research on the diagnostic categories that currently make up the PDs. We also have endeavored to pay equal attention to the basic and applied developments in the field, with the goal of informing both research and treatment.

Part I: Etiology includes chapters covering neurobiology, genetics, environmental/sociocultural factors, and developmental considerations. **Part II: Models** includes chapters covering the controversies surrounding classification and diagnosis with specific chapters from categorical, dimensional, and interpersonal perspectives. **Part III: Individual Disorders and Clusters** includes chapters covering each cluster along with specific chapters on borderline PD and psychopathy/antisocial PD for which a larger body of specific theory and research is available. **Part IV: Assessment** includes chapters covering categorical and dimensional assessment approaches as well as the use of assessment to target underlying mechanisms. Finally, **Part V: Treatment** includes chapters covering pharmacological therapies, as well as cognitive behavioral, psychodynamic/psychoanalytic, trait-based, and brief therapeutic approaches. Together, these chapters provide a comprehensive picture of personality pathology that acknowledges the contributions and missteps of the past, identifies the thorny and crucial questions of the present, and sets a course for the future.

One positive outcome of the controversy surrounding the conceptualization of PDs that emerged in the years leading up to the publication of DSM-5 is the recognition of the importance of multiple voices in shaping and sharing what we know about PDs. With that in mind, an innovative feature of this handbook is that each chapter forms the basis of a set of scientific documents that introduce multiple perspectives and greater nuance than afforded by a single chapter alone. Specifically, each chapter is accompanied by two commentaries from leading experts in the field, as well a final rejoinder from the original chapter authors. The goal of this approach was to recognize and facilitate the importance of multiple perspectives in a manner that provides a deeper connection to the material for readers. This approach mirrors a signature feature of the American Psychological Association journal, *Personality Disorders: Theory, Research, and Treatment* (PDTRT), one that has been adopted for several recent special issues by the *Journal of Personality Disorders*. This approach has been invaluable to the PD field over the past ten highly impactful years and we believe it has translated well to this handbook.

To further increase the impact of this novel approach, we have also strategically sought to provide diversity of thought in our selection of authors for the chapters/rejoinders and commentaries. In addition to ensuring wide representation of different perspectives and areas of expertise, we were cognizant of the importance of featuring fresh perspectives. Thus, although our handbook includes many of the more senior names in the field, we have also intentionally sought out mid-career and early-career scholars whose work is clearly driving the future of the field.

As we reflect on the complicated, rich, and impactful history of the study and treatment of PDs, we endeavored to pull together a series of manuscripts that both acknowledge that history and begin to point us in the new directions that will mark the future of PDs. We believe that these contributions will clarify the ongoing controversies in this field and provide a comprehensive framework for resolving debate, guiding future research, and developing clinical innovations as the field of PDs moves forward.

Carl W. Lejuez, PhD
Interim Provost
Professor, Department of Psychology
University of Kansas

Kim L. Gratz, PhD
Professor and Chair, Department of Psychology
University of Toledo

PART I ETIOLOGY

1 Neuroimaging in Personality Disorders

CHI C. CHAN, DANIEL H. VACCARO, NINA L. J. ROSE, LAURA E. KESSLER, AND ERIN A. HAZLETT

Advances in neuroimaging methods have provided a window into the brain *in vivo* and have been critical to the understanding of the neural substrates and brain circuits involved in psychiatric disorders. In personality disorders, neuroimaging techniques have been used to examine mechanisms underlying the disturbances in interpersonal relations, affect regulation, impulsivity, and cognitive processes seen in these disorders.

Structural neuroimaging techniques provide static anatomical information about the brain. Early neuroimaging studies used computed tomography (CT), which combines multiple X-ray images taken from different angles to produce cross-sectional images or "slices" of anatomy. Studies that used CT primarily examined ventricular size and ventricle-brain ratios. CT studies then gave way to magnetic resonance imaging (MRI), a technique that does not involve harmful radiation but uses powerful magnetic fields and radio waves to create images that surpass CT in spatial resolution. MRI provides greater soft tissue contrast and anatomical detail. The development of diffusion tensor imaging (DTI) provided a measure of white matter tract coherence by measuring the diffusion characteristics of water molecules along the axon. The scalar unit that is most often used in DTI studies is fractional anisotropy (FA), which quantifies the degree to which diffusion is directionally constrained. In general, lower FA is a putative measure of decreased white matter integrity.

Functional neuroimaging methods provide information on the neural substrates and circuits involved in brain functioning while the individual is at rest or performing a behavioral task. Positron emission tomography (PET) and single photon emission computed tomography (SPECT) track the path of a radiolabeled ligand to measure metabolic processes in tissues and organs. The radiotracer to use depends on the physiological system of interest to the study. For example, fluorodeoxyglucose (^{18}FDG) is a glucose-analog radiotracer commonly used in PET studies, and its uptake is a proxy for glucose metabolism. Functional magnetic resonance imaging (fMRI) noninvasively measures the brain's blood oxygen level dependent (BOLD) signal as a proxy for neural activity. Spatially separate brain regions are considered "functionally connected" if their BOLD signals are temporally correlated, and the degree of functional connectivity can be compared between groups.

A comprehensive review of the literature is beyond the scope of this chapter; therefore, the most robust and relevant structural and functional neuroimaging findings in personality disorders will be discussed. In keeping with the current categorization of personality disorders in the DSM-5, we primarily discuss studies that specifically include individuals diagnosed with a personality disorder, and at times supplement with those that only characterize the possession of a level of a trait (e.g., psychometric schizotypy, impulsivity). Due to the scarcity of literature in many of the personality disorders and to allow for a deeper analysis in the space provided, this chapter will focus on schizotypal personality disorder, borderline personality disorder, and antisocial personality disorder as hallmark examples and will conclude with direction for how this literature can move forward to include the full range of personality disorders.

SCHIZOTYPAL PERSONALITY DISORDER

Schizotypal personality disorder (SPD) is characterized by pervasive interpersonal deficits, cognitive-perceptual distortions, and eccentric behavior resulting in impaired functioning (American Psychiatric Association, 2013). It is the Cluster A personality disorder that has received the most research attention in the area of neuroimaging, due to its relationship with schizophrenia as part of the schizophrenia spectrum. SPD shares genetic, phenomenological, and neurobiological features with schizophrenia (Siever & Davis, 2004), but without the frank psychosis and more severe cognitive and functional difficulties. Similar to schizophrenia, individuals with SPD exhibit impairments in multiple cognitive domains, particularly working memory and processing speed (McClure, Harvey, Bowie, Iacoviello, & Siever, 2013). SPD is considered the prototypical schizophrenia-spectrum disorder as it falls in the middle of the spectrum and allows for the study of protective and vulnerability factors for psychosis, without the confounds associated with schizophrenia such as chronic psychosis, recurrent institutionalization, and long-term antipsychotic use. Many of the studies were driven by findings in schizophrenia with the aim of determining how brain abnormalities in SPD are similar to or different from those observed in schizophrenia.

Structural Neuroimaging

MRI studies in schizophrenia consistently report volume reductions in the temporal and frontal lobes (Shepherd, Laurens, Matheson, Carr, & Green, 2012), making these areas a particular focus in SPD. One of the most robust findings in SPD is reduced gray matter volume in the lateral temporal lobe, particularly in the superior temporal gyrus (e.g., Dickey et al., 1999; Goldstein et al., 2009; Takahashi et al., 2010) and in its component parts including Heschl's gyrus (Dickey et al., 2002) and planum temporal (Kawasaki et al., 2004; Takahashi et al., 2006). Volume reduction has also been reported in the middle (Asami et al., 2013; Hazlett et al., 2014; Koo et al., 2006) and inferior temporal gyri (Asami et al., 2013; Downhill et al., 2001). Many of the reported findings were predominantly in the left hemisphere (Fervaha & Remington, 2013; Hazlett, Goldstein, & Kolaitis, 2012) where language processing is localized. Indeed there is evidence that reduced temporal volumes are associated with odd speech (Dickey et al., 2003), as well as greater overall SPD symptom severity (Goldstein et al., 2009) and negative symptoms (Asami et al., 2013).

Medial temporal lobe volume reductions have been reported in the posterior fusiform gyrus (Takahashi et al., 2006), hippocampus (Dickey et al., 2007; Suzuki et al., 2005), insula and entorhinal cortex (Yoneyama et al., 2003), and amygdala (Suzuki et al., 2005). Furthermore, reduction of the normal hemispheric asymmetry has been found in the middle and inferior temporal gyri (Chan et al., 2018), while increased asymmetry was found in the parahippocampal gyrus (Dickey et al., 1999). Follow-up studies show that volume reduction in regions of the temporal lobe remains stable in SPD over approximately three years, whereas there is progressive deterioration in the early phase of schizophrenia (Takahashi et al., 2010, 2011). Individuals with SPD seem to share temporal lobe abnormalities with schizophrenia, but they are generally less severe, widespread, and progressive.

In contrast to temporal lobe findings, the frontal lobe appears to be less affected in SPD than in schizophrenia. Although volume reduction has been reported in the right superior prefrontal (Koo et al., 2006) and left inferior frontal regions (Kawasaki et al., 2004), these abnormalities are less severe than the widespread volume reduction in medial and lateral frontal cortex seen in schizophrenia

(Kawasaki et al., 2004). Furthermore, Yoneyama et al. (2003) did not find any differences in orbitofrontal and medial frontal regions. Interestingly, studies have reported increased volume in the dorsolateral prefrontal cortex (Hazlett, Buchsbaum, Haznedar, et al., 2008; Suzuki et al., 2005) and the inferior frontal lobe (Matsui et al., 2008). The relatively mild, negative, or opposite frontal lobe findings in SPD compared with schizophrenia serve as the basis for the theory that temporal lobe abnormalities contribute to the clinical and cognitive symptoms of SPD while a preserved frontal lobe is a protective factor against the development of frank psychosis (Hazlett, Buchsbaum, Haznedar, et al., 2008; Siever & Davis, 2004). Indeed, temporal lobe volume reductions have been shown to predict SPD group membership and severity of symptoms, while greater sparing and larger volume of frontal lobe regions such as the dorsolateral prefrontal cortex were associated with better outcomes, including less severe symptoms in SPD (Hazlett et al., 2014).

Subcortical areas have received less research attention. In the anterior cingulate, some studies have found no difference in SPD compared with healthy controls (Goldstein et al., 2009; Haznedar et al., 2004), while schizophrenia patients showed reduced volume (Takahashi et al., 2002). However, one study (Hazlett, Buchsbaum, Haznedar, et al., 2008) found smaller cingulate gray matter volume in areas of the anterior cingulate and dorsal posterior cingulate. There is also evidence in SPD of reduced volume of white matter fibers that connect the frontal lobe and thalamus (Suzuki et al., 2004) and shortened length of the interthalamic adhesion, a band of tissue connecting bilateral thalamic masses (Takahashi et al., 2008). In the thalamus, SPD individuals show reduced volume in the pulvinar (which has temporal lobe projections), while schizophrenia patients show reduced volume in both the pulvinar and mediodorsal nuclei (which has frontal lobe projections; Byne et al., 2001).

In addition to abnormalities in cortical volume, evidence also suggests disrupted neural connectivity in schizophrenia based on DTI studies that report lower fractional anisotropy (FA), a putative measure of white matter integrity, in white matter tracts that connect cortical regions (Ellison-Wright & Bullmore, 2009; Kubicki et al., 2007; Wheeler & Voineskos, 2014). Lener et al. (2015) conducted a DTI study comparing individuals with schizophrenia, SPD, and healthy controls. They found a spectrum pattern in which FA was highest in controls, intermediate in SPD, and lowest in schizophrenia in the inferior longitudinal fasciculus (temporal-occipital tract) and the genu of the corpus callosum. Results of later studies also support these findings in SPD (Sun et al., 2016; Zhang et al., 2017). The uncinate fasciculus (a frontotemporal white matter tract) has also been shown to have lower FA bilaterally in SPD relative to healthy controls (Gurrera et al., 2007; Nakamura et al., 2005), which was associated with greater cognitive and clinical symptoms (Nakamura et al., 2005). In contrast, the cingulum bundle (with prefrontal, parietal, and temporal lobe con-nections) and the anterior limb of the internal capsule (thalamo-frontal tract) showed lower FA in the schizo-phrenia patients but not in the SPD individuals (Lener et al., 2015), which supports previous negative findings in these tracts in SPD (Hazlett, Collazo, et al., 2012; Naka-mura et al., 2005).

Taken together, structural neuroimaging studies indi-cate volume reduction of the temporal lobe and decreased structural integrity in white matter tracts in SPD. These abnormalities resemble those seen in schizophrenia, albeit to a lesser extent and may represent a vulnerability to schizophrenia which manifest in the attenuated subthres-hold psychotic symptoms of SPD. Frontal lobe volume reductions are relatively minimal in SPD and there is even evidence of increased frontal lobe volume, which may be a protective factor against psychosis.

Functional Neuroimaging

Complementary to findings in brain structure, neuroima-ging studies have also found abnormal brain function in SPD. Mirroring the structural findings in the frontal and temporal lobe, Buchsbaum et al. (2002) reported that SPD patients exhibited reduced glucose metabolism in the tem-poral lobe that was intermediate between schizophrenia and healthy controls, whereas they did not exhibit reduc-tion in metabolic rates in the frontal lobe and the cingu-late. It is important to note that the schizophrenia and SPD patients were neuroleptic-naïve or neuroleptic-free at the time of the study, reducing the confound of medica-tion status. Similarly, Thompson et al. (2014) did not find an increase in prefrontal dopamine receptor availability as seen in schizophrenia (Abi-Dargham et al., 2002). In the striatum, individuals with SPD show increased glucose metabolism compared with healthy controls and schizo-phrenia patients, which was associated with fewer psychotic-like symptoms and may be protective against psychosis (Shihabuddin et al., 2001).

In response to various tasks, individuals with SPD exhibit abnormalities in activation of structures in frontal and temporal lobes, thalamus, basal ganglia, and limbic system. Compared to healthy controls, SPD patients show increased activation in the superior temporal gyrus when passively processing tones, which was associated with greater odd speech and impaired verbal learning (Dickey et al., 2008). In a study comparing healthy controls, SPD, and borderline personality disorder groups, the SPD group demonstrated the highest overall peak activation in the amygdala when viewing unpleasant, neutral, and pleasant pictures (Hazlett, Zhang, et al., 2012). Hazlett and col-leagues (Hazlett, Buchsbaum, Zhang et al., 2008) found that both patients with schizophrenia and individuals with SPD utilized frontal-striatal-thalamic (FST) circuitry inef-ficiently during a sensorimotor gating task: schizophrenia patients did not recruit the FST enough during task-

relevant stimuli, and SPD patients allocated excessive FST resources during task-irrelevant auditory stimuli. In contrast to abnormal increased activation during sensory and affective tasks, working memory tasks reveal decreased activation in SPD in frontal and parietal regions (Koenigsberg et al., 2005) and in the superior temporal gyrus, frontal regions, and insula (Vu et al., 2013).

Along with distinct brain regions found to be abnormal in schizophrenia and SPD, there is also evidence of dis-ruptions in the ongoing intrinsic neural activity in the brain. The default mode network (DMN) is a network of brain areas that are activated during rest, when the brain is not actively engaged in any cognitive tasks. It is com-posed of a widely distributed network of regions where activity is in temporal synchrony (Raichle et al., 2001). Research has shown altered DMN functional connectivity in schizophrenia that correlates with clinical features (Huang et al., 2010; Rotarska-Jagiela et al., 2010). Two studies have reported significant differences in resting state functional connectivity between SPD and healthy controls. Zhang et al. (2014) first showed that resting state functional connectivity was increased in the bilateral superior temporal gyrus and striatum, and decreased in frontal regions, consistent with previous research showing similar resting-state hypofrontality in schizophrenia (Garrity et al., 2007; Hill et al., 2004). Zhu et al. (2017) examined functional connectivity in the precuneus, a functional hub of the DMN, and found abnormal connect-ivity with medial and lateral temporal regions. Moreover, lower connectivity between the precuneus and parahippo-campus was associated with increased schizotypal symp-toms. These results are similar to schizophrenia research by Kraguljac, White, Hadley, Reid, and Lahti (2014) who reported deficits in resting state functional connectivity between the precuneus and hippocampus.

Functional neuroimaging studies are consistent with structural MRI findings of attenuated temporal lobe abnormalities in SPD relative to schizophrenia. Individ-uals with SPD show decreased temporal lobe glucose metabolism while glucose metabolism and dopamine receptor availability in the frontal lobe appear to be normal. SPD is also marked by increased brain activation during auditory, affective, and sensory processing, which may be associated with cognitive and clinical symptoms. There may also be disruptions in the intrinsic neural net-work connectivity that support cognitive functions char-acterized by hyperconnectivity of the temporal regions, hypoconnectivity in frontal regions, and aberrant patterns of increased and decreased connectivity in the precuneus.

Conclusions for Neuroimaging Studies in SPD

Studying SPD as a schizophrenia-spectrum disorder pro-vides a unique opportunity to understand vulnerability and protective factors from the psychosis in schizophre-nia. A fairly consistent pattern of findings is that temporal lobe abnormalities in SPD are similar to those in schizophrenia but less marked, while SPD seems to show relative sparing of the frontal lobe abnormalities that is characteristic of schizophrenia. The literature generally supports the notion that the relatively less marked abnormalities in the frontal lobe may be protective against the development of frank psychosis (Buchsbaum et al., 1997; Siever & Davis, 2004). Firm conclusions are difficult to draw from the functional neuroimaging literature given the relatively small number of studies and variety of tasks used. However, there appears to be abnormal functional connectivity and brain activation to sensory, affective, and working memory tasks that involve both increased and decreased activation/connectivity. These results suggest inefficient recruitment of brain regions that may be associated with the clinical symptoms and cognitive impairments in SPD.

Additional studies that directly compare SPD, schizophrenia, and healthy controls are needed to understand brain abnormalities across the schizophrenia spectrum. At the same time, new studies that involve other personality disorders as comparison groups will help delineate the specificity of SPD abnormalities. For example, Goldstein et al. (2009) reported that individuals with SPD had smaller superior temporal gyrus volume than healthy controls as well as individuals with borderline personality disorder. Functional neuroimaging findings would benefit from replication using more homogeneous methodology. SPD is a difficult-to-recruit population given the relatively low base rate, their non-treatment-seeking nature, and increased resources necessary to establish the pervasive patterns of personality dysfunction for accurate diagnosing. As a result, many studies are limited by small sample sizes, which may be addressed by multi-site collaborations. Using neuroimaging methods to understand the vulnerability and protective neural mechanisms that underlie SPD may provide neural targets for treatment and prevention efforts in the schizophrenia spectrum.

BORDERLINE PERSONALITY DISORDER

Individuals with borderline personality disorder (BPD) exhibit a pervasive pattern of instability of personal relationships, self-image, affects, and marked impulsivity (American Psychiatric Association, 2013). This disorder is associated with increased suicide risk (Oldham, 2006) and a high prevalence of childhood adversity (Zanarini et al., 1997). BPD is recognized as having a multifaceted etiology that stems from an interaction of genetic and environmental factors (Leichsenring, Leibing, Kruse, New, & Leweke, 2011). Of all the personality disorders, BPD is the most studied in terms of neuroimaging methods examining the neurobiology. These studies have largely focused on identifying the neural circuitry associated with affect dysregulation and behavioral impulsivity, which involves limbic and prefrontal regions of the brain.

Structural Neuroimaging

BPD was initially derived from noticing a group of patients who were on the "border" between neurosis and psychosis (Kernberg, 1967). As such, early studies focused on comparing schizophrenia and BPD (Gunderson & Singer, 1975) or so-called borderline personality organization (Kernberg, 1967). However, CT studies did not find ventricular enlargement in BPD that was characteristic of schizophrenia (Lucas, Gardner, Cowdry, & Pickar, 1989; Schulz et al., 1983). More recently, MRI studies have reported morphological abnormalities in various structures considered to be implicated in the affective dysregulation and impulsivity symptoms of BPD. Individuals with BPD show reduced hippocampus and amygdala volume (Nunes et al., 2009; Ruocco, Amirthavasagam, & Zakzanis, 2012; Schulze, Schmahl, & Niedtfeld, 2016) with an average of 13 percent and 11 percent reductions, respectively (Ruocco et al., 2012). Furthermore, these changes are not a result of psychotropic medication status, comorbid depression, posttraumatic stress disorder (PTSD), or substance use disorder (Ruocco et al., 2012). Because these structures are involved in the regulation of emotions and behavior during stress (Daniels, Richter, & Stein, 2004; Gregg & Siegel, 2001), they may be neurobiological correlates for some of the symptoms and characteristics associated with BPD such as aggression, affective dysregulation, emotional outbursts, and difficulties in social relationships. For example, smaller hippocampus volumes have been linked to greater intrusion and hyperarousal symptoms (Irle, Lange, & Sachsse, 2005) and increased hospitalization and aggressive behavior (Zetzsche et al., 2007).

The anterior cingulate cortex (ACC) is of particular interest in BPD given its role in cognitive and emotional processing. The dorsal portion has interconnections with prefrontal and motor areas, and is implicated in modulation of attention and executive functions; the anterior portion has connections with limbic regions and orbitofrontal cortex (among other areas) and is involved in affective functions such as emotion regulation and motivation (Bush, Luu, & Posner, 2000). BPD individuals show smaller ACC volume (e.g., (Hazlett et al., 2005; Minzenberg, Fan, New, Tang, & Siever, 2008; Soloff et al., 2012), which was found to be associated with increased parasuicidal behavior and impulsivity (Whittle et al., 2009). Other frontal lobe regions with connections to the ACC and implicated in modulation of emotional and cognitive activity have also been shown to be smaller in BPD, including the frontal lobe as a whole (Lyoo, Han, & Cho, 1998), dorsolateral prefrontal cortex (Brunner et al., 2010), and orbital frontal cortex (Brunner et al., 2010; Chanen et al., 2008; Tebartz van Elst et al., 2003).

Volumetric abnormalities also have been reported in other regions, including reduction of the middle temporal gyri and inferior frontal gyrus, and greater volume in the supplementary motor area, cerebellum, and middle frontal gyrus (Schulze et al., 2016). A study by Soloff et al. (2012) comparing individuals with BPD with and without a history of a suicide attempt found that attempters had diminished gray matter concentration in the middle inferior orbitofrontal cortex, insular cortex, fusiform gyrus, and parahippocampal gyri. Directly comparing BPD with SPD patients and healthy controls, Goldstein et al. (2009) reported that the BPD patients did not exhibit the volume reduction in the superior temporal gyrus that was observed in the SPD patients.

A number of white matter structures are also affected in BPD. The corpus callosum (CC) is a large fiber bundle connecting the two hemispheres of the brain. FA in the CC has been shown to be lower in BPD compared with healthy controls (Carrasco et al., 2012; Gan et al., 2016), and may be associated with increased suicidal behavior (Lischke et al., 2017). Individuals with BPD also show decreased FA in the fornix, a bundle of white matter fiber in the limbic system that is implicated in memory (Gan et al., 2016; Maier-Hein et al., 2014; Whalley et al., 2015), which was found to be associated with greater symptom severity, for example, avoidance of abandonment and affective instability (Whalley et al., 2015). Reduced FA in the fornix appears to be specific to BPD when compared with a group of mixed psychiatric diagnoses (Maier-Hein et al., 2014). Findings in the cingulum and the uncinate fasciculus are mixed. Specifically examining these two tracts, Lischke et al. (2015) found lower FA in the uncinate fasciculus but not the cingulum while Whalley et al. (2015) found the opposite, that is, lower FA in portions of the cingulum but not the uncinate fasciculus.

Several studies have examined white matter microstructure in the frontal cortex, an area considered to be important for emotion regulation and behavioral control. Decreased FA has been found in orbitofrontal areas in BPD (Carrasco et al., 2012) and anterior frontal regions in BPD with self-injurious behaviors (Grant et al., 2007), but not in inferior frontal regions (Rusch et al., 2007). Other findings in BPD include abnormalities in association fibers that connect cortical regions in the same hemisphere. New et al. (2013) examined healthy adults, healthy adolescents, adults with BPD, and adolescents with BPD. They reported decreased inferior longitudinal fasciculus (ILF) FA in BPD adolescents compared with their healthy peers, but no difference in the two adult groups. Healthy adolescents had higher ILF FA than all of the other groups. Given that FA in the ILF develops in an inverted "U" shape as it increases through adolescence and decreases in adulthood (Hasan et al., 2010), the findings suggest that peak FA normally seen in adolescence is not achieved in those with BPD. Reduced white matter integrity has also been found in the inferior frontal occipital fasciculus (Ninomiya et al., 2018) and uncinate fasciculus (Lischke et al., 2015), although New et al. (2013) only found reductions in the adolescent and not the adult BPD group.

Taken together, individuals with BPD show significantly reduced volume of limbic regions involved in behavioral and emotional responses, including the hippocampus, amygdala, and anterior cingulate cortex. Moreover, these abnormalities may be associated with BPD symptom severity including suicidal behavior. There is also evidence of reduced volume in prefrontal areas involved in the modulation of cognitive and affective processing. Some studies in adolescents have found decreased frontal lobe volume but not amygdala or hippocampal volume (Brunner et al., 2010; Chanen et al., 2008), suggesting that structural alterations in limbic regions may not be present in the early stage of the BPD illness. White matter structural integrity appears to be reduced in the corpus callosum, limbic areas (e.g., fornix), frontal regions, and cortical association fibers, with some evidence that these abnormalities may be specific to BPD as opposed to other clinical disorders (Maier-Hein et al., 2014), or to adolescents with BPD as opposed to adults (New et al., 2013).

Functional Neuroimaging

The functioning of the serotonin system is of particular interest in BPD given its role in impulsive behavior (Coccaro, 1992), as impulsivity is a core feature of BPD. Pharmacologic challenge studies consistently show altered response to serotonergic stimulation in fronto-limbic areas and circuitry in BPD (Soloff, Meltzer, Greer, Constantine, & Kelly, 2000), BPD with comorbid intermittent explosive disorder patients (New et al., 2007), and individuals with major depressive disorder (MDD) and comorbid BPD (Oquendo et al., 2005). Interestingly, symptom improvement in aggression with a selective serotonin reuptake inhibitor (SSRI) appears to correspond to increased glucose metabolism in cingulate and orbital frontal cortex, suggesting that SSRIs normalize prefrontal cortex metabolism in impulsive aggressive patients with BPD (New et al., 2004). There is also evidence of sex differences in the serotonergic system functioning in BPD. For example, only males exhibited decreased glucose uptake in the left temporal lobe in response to serotonergic stimulation (Soloff, Meltzer, Becker, Greer, & Constantine, 2005), only female BPD subjects show greater binding in medial temporal and occipital cortex than males when compared with same-gender controls (Soloff, Chiappetta, Mason, Becker, & Price, 2014), and BPD traits are more closely associated with serotonin binding in females than males (Soloff et al., 2014).

Given the heightened emotional reactivity and difficulty in emotion regulation observed in BPD, the majority of task-based fMRI studies have focused on emotion processing using a wide range of methods. Individuals with BPD exhibit prolonged or enhanced amygdala activity when viewing or anticipating emotional stimuli (Hazlett, Zhang, et al., 2012; Kamphausen et al., 2013; Scherpiet et al., 2014), engaging in a cognitive task while being distracted by emotional stimuli (Holtmann et al., 2013; Jacob et al., 2013; Krause-Utz et al., 2012), and engaging in social cognitive tasks (Frick et al., 2012; Mier et al., 2013). Furthermore, there appears to be increased functional connectivity between the amygdala and other brain regions, including the rostral anterior cingulate (Cullen et al., 2011) and right dorsomedial prefrontal cortex and hippocampus (Krause-Utz et al., 2014) during processing of emotional stimuli. Individuals with BPD show hyper-responsivity to negative stimuli in the amygdala and hippocampus (Schulze et al., 2016), and this response is eliminated by medication use (Ruocco, Amirthavasagam, Choi-Kain, & McMain, 2013; Schulze et al., 2016). Physical pain also appears to produce deactivation in the amygdala (Niedtfeld et al., 2012; Schmahl et al., 2006) and anterior cingulate gyrus (Schmahl et al., 2006) in BPD patients, which may explain the use of self-injurious behavior to manage emotions. There is also enhanced activity in the posterior cingulate gyrus and insula, and decreased activity in the dorsolateral prefrontal cortex (Ruocco et al., 2013; Schulze et al., 2016).

To better understand the symptoms of emotional dysregulation and impulsivity in BPD, researchers have examined the neural substrates underlying top-down control of affective responses. Areas of the prefrontal cortex exert inhibitory control over limbic structures (Rosenkranz & Grace, 2002). One study found that under conditions of behavioral inhibition in the context of negative emotion, reduced ventromedial prefrontal activity in BPD patients was associated with measures of decreased self-reported constraint (Silbersweig et al., 2007). BPD patients also showed increased amygdala and ventral striatum activity, which was associated with greater self-reported negative emotion. These results suggest enhanced sensitivity of the amygdala and difficulty recruiting frontal regions to inhibit limbic responses. When provoked to aggression, BPD patients with intermittent explosive disorder responded more aggressively behaviorally and exhibit increased glucose metabolism in orbitofrontal cortex and amygdala compared with healthy controls (New et al., 2009). This suggests a hypersensitivity to provocation in BPD with intermittent explosive disorder. While it was thought that decreased orbitofrontal cortex activity promotes aggression, there is likely a complex relationship between the orbitofrontal cortex and amygdala (Blair, 2004).

Self-injurious behavior is frequently observed in BPD and has led to attempts at understanding the function of self-harm and brain reactions to physical pain. Niedtfeld et al. (2012) showed that when BPD patients experienced physical pain while viewing emotional pictures, they demonstrated enhanced negative connectivity (i.e., a greater negative correlation) between limbic and medial and dorsolateral prefrontal regions than healthy controls. Therefore, physical pain may enhance the ability of the prefrontal cortex to inhibit the limbic system in BPD, attenuating the hyperactivation in limbic areas.

Dialectical behavior therapy (DBT) is a cognitive behavioral treatment that heavily targets maladaptive behaviors associated with BPD, including self-injurious acts. Niedtfeld et al. (2017) showed that DBT weakened amygdala deactivation in response to physical pain during negative emotional stimuli. This indicates DBT may modulate the effectiveness of self-injurious behaviors to decrease emotion dysregulation, suggesting the potential to replace self-harm acts with more adaptive coping strategies. Additionally, DBT has been shown to decrease activity in the posterior cingulate and insula in response to negative stimuli (Schnell & Herpertz, 2007) and to improve amygdala habituation to unpleasant pictures, which was associated with improved self-reported difficulties with emotion regulation (Goodman et al., 2014). Using an imaging-genetics approach, recent work suggests that amygdala habituation deficiency to unpleasant pictures is modulated by a brain-derived neurotrophic factor genotype in healthy controls and BPD patients (Perez-Rodriguez et al., 2017). Identifying genetically modulated neural biomarkers that contribute to emotion processing and habituation abnormalities holds promise for developing novel therapeutic targets for BPD.

Individuals with BPD show altered default mode network, with complex patterns of increased and decreased activity in areas of the cingulate cortex, prefrontal cortex, and precuneus (Amad & Radua, 2017; Visintin et al., 2016). However, overlap between PTSD and BPD, as well as heterogeneity in BPD, make it difficult to draw strong conclusions about specific disturbances in the DMN (Amad & Radua, 2017). Other forms of network disturbance reported include decreased inter-network connectivity of the central executive network involved in cognitive control and increased inter-network connectivity of the salience network involved in emotion-related activity (Doll et al., 2013), although another study found differences in network connectivity between BPD and bipolar disorder, but not BPD and controls (Das, Calhoun, & Malhi, 2014).

Studies examining seed-based analysis of resting state functional connectivity have reported increased amygdala connectivity with a cluster consisting of the insula, orbitofrontal cortex, and putamen (Krause-Utz et al., 2014), decreased amygdala connectivity with right ventral anterior cingulate cortex and orbital frontal cortex (Baczkowski et al., 2017), disturbed connectivity mainly distributed in the frontotemporal and limbic lobes that was not correlated with clinical symptoms (Lei et al., 2017), and increased functional connectivity from the noradrenergic locus coeruleus to the anterior cingulate cortex, which was positively correlated with the degree of motor impulsivity (Wagner et al., 2018).

In summary, functional neuroimaging studies reveal that BPD is associated with altered serotonin system functioning in fronto-limbic regions of the brain. Limbic structures including the amygdala and hippocampus are hyper-responsive to emotional and negative stimuli and show increased connectivity to other brain regions.

However, medication and physical pain appears to deactivate the amygdala, which may explain symptom improvement with medication in some individuals and the use of self-injurious behavior by BPD patients to manage emotions. Increased limbic activity concurrent with reduced prefrontal region activity suggest enhanced emotional responsivity and difficulty recruiting frontal regions to inhibit limbic responses. Dialectical behavior therapy also appears to work by decreasing neural activity to unpleasant stimuli. Furthermore, the evidence suggests that there is altered resting state activity in the default mode network characterized by both increased and decreased activity in a number of frontal and limbic brain regions.

Conclusions for Neuroimaging Studies in BPD

Neuroimaging studies in BPD have focused on frontal and limbic regions considered to be implicated in the emotion dysregulation and impulsivity characteristics of the disorder. The predominant theory is that there is a failure of prefrontal areas to appropriately modulate limbic regions. Empirical evidence indicates that individuals with BPD exhibit a combination of reduced volume and increased activity in the amygdala and anterior cingulate cortex. Volume reduction has also been consistently found in the hippocampus and dorsolateral and orbital regions of the frontal lobe. Furthermore, there is altered structural connectivity characterized by decreased structural integrity in interhemispheric and fronto-limbic white matter tracts including the corpus callosum and fornix. Functional neuroimaging suggests that individuals with BPD demonstrate altered serotonergic system functioning, exaggerated reactivity in frontal and limbic areas in reaction to emotional stimuli, and disruptions in resting state network connectivity.

The BPD neuroimaging literature is limited by methodological differences. While some studies use BPD samples with comorbid conditions such as intermittent explosive disorder (New et al., 2007) and attention deficit hyperactivity disorder (Rusch et al., 2010), other studies exclude for comorbidities (Grant et al., 2007). The heterogeneous nature of BPD and its high comorbidity with other conditions including anxiety, mood, impulse control, and substance use disorders (Lenzenweger, Lane, Loranger, & Kessler, 2007) make it difficult to disentangle potential confounds. For example, different combinations of hippocampal, anterior cingulate cortex, and amygdala volume loss are also frequently found in posttraumatic stress disorder (Kuhn & Gallinat, 2013), bipolar disorder (Altshuler, Bartzokis, Grieder, Curran, & Mintz, 1998; Haldane & Frangou, 2004), major depressive disorder (Frodl, Meisenzahl, Zetzsche, Born, et al., 2002; Frodl, Meisenzahl, Zetzsche, Bottlender, et al., 2002; Lange & Irle, 2004) and women with a history of severe abuse (Stein, Koverola, Hanna, Torchia, & McClarty, 1997). Furthermore, a study by Brunner et al. (2010) found that both adolescents

with BPD and a clinical control group with mixed psychiatric diagnoses had reduced dorsolateral prefrontal cortex volume compared with healthy controls, suggesting that these brain changes are not specific to BPD. Still, other studies have found decreased hippocampal (Irle et al., 2005; Weniger, Lange, Sachsse, & Irle, 2009) and amygdala (Weniger et al., 2009) volume in BPD patients regardless of comorbid PTSD, suggesting that PTSD is not necessary for these changes. White matter abnormalities have also been shown to be specific to BPD when compared with a mixed psychiatric group (Maier-Hein et al., 2014).

A history of childhood trauma is common in individuals with severe mental illness, and a positive relationship between reported childhood trauma and greater volume reduction in the hippocampus and amygdala has been reported across BPD studies (Brambilla et al., 2004; Driessen et al., 2000; Rusch et al., 2003; Schmahl et al., 2003; Tebartz van Elst et al., 2003). Therefore, it is possible that childhood trauma as an environmental factor may in part underlie the neuropathology of BPD and other disorders with similar neurobiological markers. Future neuroimaging studies may wish to examine individuals with childhood trauma and the nature of their differential trajectory to later clinical presentations or lack thereof. Moreover, while there is empirical support for frontal and limbic abnormalities in BPD, this conceptualization does not seem to account for the range of findings in other neural substrates and circuitry. Further investigation into other relevant neural circuitry implicated in cognitive and affective processing would further our understanding of BPD. Finally, more studies that examine neural changes following pharmacological or psychosocial intervention are needed to shed light on mechanisms of change with intervention.

ANTISOCIAL PERSONALITY DISORDER

Individuals with antisocial personality disorder (ASPD) exhibit pervasive disregard for the rights of others, beginning in childhood and continuing into adulthood (American Psychiatric Association, 2013). The current DSM-5 diagnostic criteria for ASPD is heavily based on observable behaviors such as repeated unlawful activity, lying, physical fights, and failure to honor financial responsibility. However, underlying personality structures such as manipulativeness, callousness, lack of empathy, and deceitfulness are alternative models for ASPD that are often used by researchers. The construct of psychopathy is frequently associated with ASPD, and is characterized by marked emotional deficits in guilt and remorse, callousness, and socially deviant behaviors. The most widely used measured of psychopathy is the Hare Psychopathy Checklist – Revised (Herve, Hayes, & Hare, 2003) with score cutoffs used for a categorical determination of "psychopathy" that vary depending on clinical and research purposes. While psychopathy and ASPD are sometimes viewed as being interchangeable, their diagnostic criteria and measurement instruments render them overlapping but distinct. Most individuals high in psychopathy would likely meet criteria ASPD but not all individuals with ASPD are psychopaths (Ogloff, 2006). There is a small number of neuroimaging studies that use samples with a clearly defined ASPD diagnosis derived from clinical interview, but most studies focus on distinct characteristics of ASPD, such as antisocial behavior (e.g., violence, aggression) and traits (e.g., callousness, psychopathy). This method expands our understanding of various antisocial behaviors but at the same time, introduces heterogeneity in sample characteristics. Furthermore, while prevalence of ASPD in the general population is estimated to be 1 percent in females and 3 percent in males (Coid, Yang, Tyrer, Roberts, & Ullrich, 2006), prevalence in prisons has been estimated to be 21 percent in females and 47 percent in males (Fazel & Danesh, 2002). As such, many studies include males involved in the legal system. The present section will focus on studies of individuals clinically diagnosed ASPD supplemented by information from studies of antisocial behaviors and traits.

Structural Neuroimaging

The most common brain area of focus for neuroimaging studies in individuals with antisocial behavior is the frontal lobe implicated in the regulation of impulse and aggression, although some studies have also examined the temporal lobe. A meta-analysis of structural and functional neuroimaging studies of broadly defined antisocial behavior (e.g., psychopathy, violence, aggression, criminal offenders) found reduced structure and function in the right orbitofrontal cortex, left dorsolateral prefrontal cortex, and right anterior cingulate cortex (Yang & Raine, 2009). Raine, Lencz, Bihrle, LaCasse, and Colletti (2000) found that individuals with a DSM diagnosis of ASPD had reduced prefrontal gray matter volume of 11 percent compared with a control group. Individuals with ASPD have been shown to have reduced cortical thickness in the orbitofrontal and lateral frontal cortex, as well as the insula, middle temporal gyrus, and bank of the superior temporal sulcus (Jiang et al., 2016), and thinner cortex in these regions was associated with less impulse control (Jiang et al., 2016). Research in psychopathy has fairly consistently found reduced gray matter volume in the temporal lobe including the amygdala (Yang, Raine, Narr, Colletti, & Toga, 2009), hippocampus (Laakso et al., 2001), superior temporal gyrus (Muller, Sommer, et al., 2008), and anterior temporal cortex (de Oliveira-Souza et al., 2008). In a review by Blair (2010) of four studies (De Brito et al., 2009; de Oliveira-Souza et al., 2008; Muller, Gansbauer, et al., 2008; Tiihonen et al., 2008) that used voxel-based morphology, an automated technique that reduces subjectivity in image processing, three of the four found

structural abnormalities in the orbitofrontal cortex and insula and all four found abnormalities in the superior temporal cortex.

The meta-analysis by Yang and Raine (2009) on broadly defined antisocial behavior did not find any moderating effects of violence or comorbidity on prefrontal cortex volume. However, it is important to note that some studies designed to tease apart effects from comorbid conditions have found significant effects. For example, medial frontal cortical thinning was found to be specific to violent individuals with ASPD when compared with nonviolent and violent individuals with ASPD or schizophrenia (Narayan et al., 2007). A study of violent offenders with ASPD and psychopathy, violent offenders with ASPD but no psychopathy, and healthy non-offenders reported that only violent offenders with ASPD and psychopathy exhibited reduced gray matter volume bilaterally in the dorsolateral prefrontal cortex and temporal poles (Gregory et al., 2012). Duration of alcoholism and years of education may also account for volume reductions in the frontal cortex in ASPD (Laakso et al., 2002). One study (Schiffer et al., 2011) contrasted four groups of males: violent offenders with substance use disorders (SUD), violent offenders without SUD, non-offenders with SUD, and non-offenders without SUD. They found that greater volume in multiple mesolimbic areas including the nucleus accumbens, amygdala, and caudate, as well as smaller volume in the insula, were specific to violent offenders and that reduced gray matter volumes in the frontal lobe were specific to those with SUD.

DTI studies reveal that disruption in white matter tracts across association pathways that connect cortical areas of the same hemisphere are found in individuals with broadly defined antisocial behavior (Waller, Dotterer, Murray, Maxwell, & Hyde, 2017). These tracts include the uncinate fasciculus, cingulum, inferior fronto-occipital fasciculus, inferior longitudinal fasciculus, and superior longitudinal fasciculus. Furthermore, individuals clinically diagnosed with ASPD exhibit decreased white matter integrity in the frontal lobes bilaterally and the left posterior portion of the brain (Sundram et al., 2012). Jiang and colleagues (Jiang, Shi, Liu, et al., 2017) investigated 20 individuals with ASPD and no other personality disorder compared with 23 healthy controls. They found abnormalities in the bilateral superior longitudinal fasciculus, left superior corona radiate, and inferior fronto-occipital fasciculus, which were associated with greater self-reported impulsivity and risky behavior. There is also some evidence of reduced coherence of the corpus callosum and projection fibers that connect cortical and subcortical centers (e.g., internal capsule, corona radiata) in ASPD (Sundram et al., 2012) and women with conduct disorder (Lindner et al., 2016). As with the MRI studies, there is evidence that white matter structural abnormalities may be associated with comorbid psychopathy; for example, lower FA in the uncinate fasciculus was observed in incarcerated males with psychopathy relative to those without psychopathy (Motzkin, Newman, Kiehl, & Koenigs, 2011).

In summary, individuals with ASPD or antisocial behaviors exhibit decreased volume in the frontal regions including the orbitofrontal cortex and dorsolateral prefrontal cortex, as well as medial and lateral temporal lobes. Additionally, there is decreased integrity in a number of white matter tracts that connect cortical regions in the same hemisphere of the brain. Importantly, there may be significant effects of comorbid conditions, particularly psychopathy and substance use, in these structural abnormalities.

Functional Neuroimaging

Among studies that included a clinical diagnosis, Goyer et al. (1994) did not find any difference between ASPD and controls on frontal cortex metabolism during an auditory discrimination task (while finding differences between BPD and controls). However, Kuruoğlu et al. (1996) showed that among patients with alcoholism who had ASPD versus those with other personality disorders including dependent PD, narcissistic PD, and paranoid PD, those with ASPD had significantly reduced regional cerebral blood flow in the frontal cortex.

Serotonin system functioning is implicated in impulsive aggression and has been investigated in ASPD. In a sample of individuals with a history of violent aggression who also met criteria for ASPD or conduct disorder and healthy controls, Meyer et al. (2008) found that lower serotonergic receptor binding potential in the dorsolateral prefrontal cortex, orbitofrontal cortex, anterior cingulate, and medial temporal cortex was associated with more severe impulsivity in the group with violent aggression. Furthermore, abnormalities in serotonin system functioning in non-callous individuals with high impulsive aggression were found to be associated with greater childhood adversity (Rylands et al., 2012). Monoamine oxidase-A (MAO-A) metabolizes amine neurotransmitters implicated in aggressive behavior, such as serotonin. MAO-A level was found to be lower in ASPD compared with healthy controls in the orbitofrontal cortex, ventral striatum, prefrontal/anterior cingulate cortex, thalamus, and hippocampus (Kolla, Matthews, et al., 2015). In ASPD, lower MAO-A level in the ventral striatum has been associated with greater self-reported impulsivity (Kolla, Dunlop, et al., 2015; Kolla et al., 2016) and more risky performance on a gambling task (Kolla, Dunlop, et al., 2015).

The majority of fMRI studies in ASPD have been conducted by a group of researchers at China's Central South University. They report a number of activation abnormalities, including decreased resting state activity in the orbitofrontal cortex, temporal pole, inferior temporal gyrus, and cerebellum (Liu, Liao, Jiang, & Wang, 2014), and increased activity in the occipital cortex and inferior

temporal gyrus (Tang, Jiang, Liao, Wang, & Luo , 2013). Studies of resting state functional connectivity have found increased functional connectivity within the default mode network (Tang et al., 2016) but uncoupling between the default mode network and the attention network (Tang et al., 2013) in individuals with ASPD. Jiang and colleagues (Jiang, Shi, Liao, et al., 2017) used whole-brain network analysis and reported that brain networks in ASPD are less functionally integrated, less modular, and less connected within and between modules, particularly in the fronto-parietal control network. In ASPD, greater connectivity between the striatum and dorsomedial prefrontal cortex, as well as between the striatum and hippocampus, were associated with less impulsivity (Kolla et al., 2016).

Task-based fMRI studies in individuals with ASPD have revealed greater activation of the dorsolateral prefrontal cortex, anterior cingulate cortex, and inferior parietal lobe when lying (Jiang et al., 2013). While this study did not have a control group, these areas are consistent with regions implicated in cognitive control and working memory involved in deception (Christ, Van Essen, Watson, Brubaker, & McDermott, 2009). Interestingly, the investigators rated capacity for deceitfulness based on a clinician administered personality interview. They found that increased clinical ratings of capacity for deceitfulness were associated with decreased contrast in the fMRI between truth and lie conditions. This result suggests that individuals with ASPD who are skilled at lying or lie frequently may require less cognitive effort to lie.

Taken together, the literature suggests that individuals with ASPD have serotonergic system function abnormalities that are associated with symptoms of impulsive aggression. Furthermore, individuals with ASPD have altered resting state brain activity and functional connectivity, including in the default mode network and central executive network. For individuals with ASPD and high capacity for deception, there is less evidence of differential activity in brain areas implicated in cognitive control when lying versus truth-telling.

Conclusions for Neuroimaging Studies in ASPD

Neuroimaging studies in ASPD are scarcer than in other PDs. However, studies on antisocial behavior, albeit broadly defined, have provided additional information on brain abnormalities associated with behaviors and characteristics of individuals with ASPD. ASPD has been demonstrated to be heterogeneous (Poythress et al., 2010), and comorbid conditions such as psychopathy and substance use have been shown to affect brain structure (Gregory et al., 2012; Schiffer et al., 2011). Nevertheless, there is consistent evidence that individuals with ASPD exhibit volume reduction and cortical thinning in areas of the prefrontal cortex including orbitofrontal and dorsolateral prefrontal regions. They also show volume reduction in temporal lobe structures including the amygdala, hippocampus, superior temporal gyrus, and insula. White matter structure compromise is demonstrated in the uncinate fasciculus as well as a number of commissural, association, and projection fibers. These structural abnormalities may be associated with the increased impulsivity and risky behaviors characteristic of ASPD. Functional imaging studies suggest that individuals with ASPD have decreased cerebral blood flow in the frontal cortex, and that there is pre- and post-synaptic serotonergic system dysfunction. There appears to be decreased resting state functional activity in frontal, temporal, and cerebellar regions, but increased activity in the occipital cortex. Alterations in brain network functional connectivity in the dorsal attention network and the fronto-parietal control network may also be implicated.

A major challenge for future studies is to disentangle effects associated with ASPD from those resulting from comorbid conditions. Well-designed studies that compare and contrast groups with and without certain characteristics (e.g., psychopathy) and comorbid conditions (e.g., substance use) would help advance this endeavor. Furthermore, some characteristics of ASPD, particularly impulsivity, are also present in other conditions such as bipolar disorder, borderline personality disorder, and substance use disorders. The NIH's Research Domain Criteria approach (Insel et al., 2010) suggests that it will be important for future studies to examine whether the underlying neural circuitry involved is common across these disorders.

OVERALL SUMMARY AND FUTURE DIRECTIONS

Neuroimaging research examining the neurobiology of personality disorders is not as plentiful compared with studies of other psychiatric illnesses. Yet, it is clear that research in this area has been fruitful. Studies characterize SPD as having a pattern of decreased temporal lobe volume and white matter tract integrity, dysfunctional striatal dopamine activity, and inefficient recruitment of brain areas during task performance. These findings are similar to schizophrenia, albeit to a lesser degree, suggesting neurobiological vulnerability to schizophrenia. In contrast, the relatively intact frontal lobe may be a protective factor against frank psychosis. The most promising findings in BPD suggest that a diminished top-down control of affective responsivity, which likely involves decreased activity, size, and/or functional connectivity of prefrontal cortex regions combined with increased limbic activity, may underlie the affective hyper-responsivity observed in this disorder. In addition, neuroimaging findings point to a role for serotonin in this affective disinhibition and dysregulation. Findings in ASPD implicate volume reduction in the prefrontal and temporal lobes, as well as white matter structural abnormalities in the impulsivity seen in this disorder. There is also emerging evidence of decreased activity in frontal regions and altered brain network functional connectivity in the attention network and the fronto-parietal control networks.

Several brain regions appear to be implicated in all three of the personality disorders covered in this chapter, particularly the prefrontal cortex, temporal lobe, limbic regions, and a number of white matter tracts. Therefore, the *pattern* of abnormalities can provide key information on the neural basis of each personality disorder. For example, while SPD appears to be predominantly associated with abnormalities in temporal and striatal regions, BPD and ASPD share alterations in prefrontal and limbic regions. This is consistent with the impulsivity and aggression that are common to both BPD and ASPD and that places them in the same cluster. However, the limbic hyperactivity seen in BPD is not consistently found in ASPD. Additional studies that directly compare personality disorders with each other are needed to clarify shared and distinct neurobiological mechanisms. One promising avenue may be a transdiagnostic approach that examines the neurobiological basis of personality constructs across personality disorders. Given the emerging dimensional conceptualization of personality disorders, future studies should investigate the domains (i.e., negative affect, detachment, antagonism, disinhibition, and psychoticism) of the multidimensional personality trait model in the Emerging Measures and Models of the DSM-5. Additionally, since SPD is frequently used to better understand vulnerability and protective factors for schizophrenia, more studies including longitudinal designs are needed that directly compare SPD and schizophrenia.

It will be important for future research to establish consensus on methodology in personality disorders research, such as which tasks to use that best elicit psychological constructs of interest. The heterogeneous methodology currently used likely contributes to inconsistent findings and limits the ability to draw strong conclusions. Also, careful consideration of sample characteristics, including sample size, gender, and particularly comorbid conditions will help identify moderating factors that contribute to variance. Finally, many studies fail to find direct correlations between neuroimaging abnormalities and specific symptoms, which is likely due to the complexity of the mechanisms by which brain abnormalities result in the behaviors associated with personality disorders. Continued development of integrated theories and use of rigorous methods that can infer causality will provide a better understanding of the neural mechanisms underlying personality pathology.

ACKNOWLEDGMENT

This work was supported in part by the Mental Illness Research, Education, and Clinical Center at the James J. Peters VA Medical Center, Bronx, NY and a VA Research Career Scientist Award to Dr. Hazlett (IK6 CX001738–01).

REFERENCES

Abi-Dargham, A., Mawlawi, O., Lombardo, I., Gil, R., Martinez, D., Huang, Y., . . . Laruelle, M. (2002). Prefrontal dopamine D1 receptors and working memory in schizophrenia. *Journal of Neuroscience, 22*(9), 3708–3719.

Altshuler, L. L., Bartzokis, G., Grieder, T., Curran, J., & Mintz, J. (1998). Amygdala enlargement in bipolar disorder and hippocampal reduction in schizophrenia: An MRI study demonstrating neuroanatomic specificity. *Archives of General Psychiatry, 55* (7), 663–664.

Amad, A., & Radua, J. (2017). Resting-state meta-analysis in borderline personality disorder: Is the fronto-limbic hypothesis still valid? *Journal of Affective Disorders, 212*, 7–9.

American Psychiatric Association. (2013). *Diagnostic and Statistical Manual of Mental Disorders* (5th ed.). Arlington, VA: American Psychiatric Publishing.

Asami, T., Whitford, T. J., Bouix, S., Dickey, C. C., Niznikiewicz, M., Shenton, M. E., . . . McCarley, R. W. (2013). Globally and locally reduced MRI gray matter volumes in neuroleptic-naive men with schizotypal personality disorder: Association with negative symptoms. *JAMA Psychiatry, 70*(4), 361–372.

Baczkowski, B. M., van Zutphen, L., Siep, N., Jacob, G. A., Domes, G., Maier, S., . . . van de Ven, V. (2017). Deficient amygdala-prefrontal intrinsic connectivity after effortful emotion regulation in borderline personality disorder. *European Archives of Psychiatry and Clinical Neuroscience, 267*(6), 551–565.

Blair, R. J. (2004). The roles of orbital frontal cortex in the modulation of antisocial behavior. *Brain and Cognition, 55*(1), 198-208.

Blair, R. J. (2010). Neuroimaging of psychopathy and antisocial behavior: A targeted review. *Current Psychiatry Reports, 12*(1), 76–82.

Brambilla, P., Soloff, P. H., Sala, M., Nicoletti, M. A., Keshavan, M. S., & Soares, J. C. (2004). Anatomical MRI study of borderline personality disorder patients. *Psychiatry Research, 131*(2), 125–133.

Brunner, R., Henze, R., Parzer, P., Kramer, J., Feigl, N., Lutz, K., . . . Stieltjes, B. (2010). Reduced prefrontal and orbitofrontal gray matter in female adolescents with borderline personality disorder: Is it disorder specific? *NeuroImage, 49*(1), 114–120.

Buchsbaum, M. S., Nenadic, I., Hazlett, E. A., Spiegel-Cohen, J., Fleischman, M. B., Akhavan, A., . . . Siever, L. J. (2002). Differential metabolic rates in prefrontal and temporal Brodmann areas in schizophrenia and schizotypal personality disorder. *Schizophrenia Research, 54*(1–2), 141–150.

Buchsbaum, M. S., Trestman, R. L., Hazlett, E., Siegel, B. V., Jr., Schaefer, C. H., Luu-Hsia, C., . . . Siever, L. J. (1997). Regional cerebral blood flow during the Wisconsin Card Sort Test in schizotypal personality disorder. *Schizophrenia Research, 27* (1), 21–28.

Bush, G., Luu, P., & Posner, M. I. (2000). Cognitive and emotional influences in anterior cingulate cortex. *Trends in Cognitive Sciences, 4*(6), 215–222.

Byne, W., Buchsbaum, M. S., Kemether, E., Hazlett, E. A., Shinwari, A., Mitropoulou, V., & Siever, L. J. (2001). Magnetic resonance imaging of the thalamic mediodorsal nucleus and pulvinar in schizophrenia and schizotypal personality disorder. *Archives of General Psychiatry, 58*(2), 133–140.

Carrasco, J. L., Tajima-Pozo, K., Diaz-Marsa, M., Casado, A., Lopez-Ibor, J. J., Arrazola, J., & Yus, M. (2012). Microstructural white matter damage at orbitofrontal areas in borderline personality disorder. *Journal of Affective Disorders, 139*(2), 149–153.

Chan, C. C., Szeszko, P. R., Wong, E., Tang, C. Y., Kelliher, C., Penner, J. D., . . . Hazlett, E. A. (2018). Frontal and temporal cortical volume, white matter tract integrity, and hemispheric asymmetry in schizotypal personality disorder. *Schizophrenia Research, 197*, 226–232.

Chanen, A. M., Velakoulis, D., Carison, K., Gaunson, K., Wood, S. J., Yuen, H. P., . . . Pantelis, C. (2008). Orbitofrontal, amygdala and hippocampal volumes in teenagers with first-presentation borderline personality disorder. *Psychiatry Research, 163*(2), 116–125.

Christ, S. E., Van Essen, D. C., Watson, J. M., Brubaker, L. E., & McDermott, K. B. (2009). The contributions of prefrontal cortex and executive control to deception: Evidence from activation likelihood estimate meta-analyses. *Cerebral Cortex, 19*(7), 1557–1566.

Coccaro, E. F. (1992). Impulsive aggression and central serotonergic system function in humans: An example of a dimensional brain–behavior relationship. *International Clinical Psychopharmacology, 7*(1), 3–12.

Coid, J., Yang, M., Tyrer, P., Roberts, A., & Ullrich, S. (2006). Prevalence and correlates of personality disorder in Great Britain. *British Journal of Psychiatry, 188*, 423–431.

Cullen, K. R., Vizueta, N., Thomas, K. M., Han, G. J., Lim, K. O., Camchong, J., . . . Schulz, S. C. (2011). Amygdala functional connectivity in young women with borderline personality disorder. *Brain Connectivity, 1*(1), 61–71.

Daniels, W. M., Richter, L., & Stein, D. J. (2004). The effects of repeated intra-amygdala CRF injections on rat behavior and HPA axis function after stress. *Metabolic Brain Disease, 19*(1–2), 15–23.

Das, P., Calhoun, V., & Malhi, G. S. (2014). Bipolar and borderline patients display differential patterns of functional connectivity among resting state networks. *NeuroImage, 98*, 73–81.

De Brito, S. A., Mechelli, A., Wilke, M., Laurens, K. R., Jones, A. P., Barker, G. J., . . . Viding, E. (2009). Size matters: Increased grey matter in boys with conduct problems and callous-unemotional traits. *Brain, 132*(Pt 4), 843–852.

de Oliveira-Souza, R., Hare, R. D., Bramati, I. E., Garrido, G. J., Ignacio, F. A., Tovar-Moll, F., & Moll, J. (2008). Psychopathy as a disorder of the moral brain: Fronto-temporo-limbic grey matter reductions demonstrated by voxel-based morphometry. *NeuroImage, 40*(3), 1202–1213.

Dickey, C. C., McCarley, R. W., Voglmaier, M. M., Frumin, M., Niznikiewicz, M. A., Hirayasu, Y., . . . Shenton, M. E. (2002). Smaller left Heschl's gyrus volume in patients with schizotypal personality disorder. *American Journal of Psychiatry, 159*(9), 1521–1527.

Dickey, C. C., McCarley, R. W., Voglmaier, M. M., Niznikiewicz, M. A., Seidman, L. J., Demeo, S., . . . Shenton, M. E. (2003). An MRI study of superior temporal gyrus volume in women with schizotypal personality disorder. *American Journal of Psychiatry, 160*(12), 2198–2201.

Dickey, C. C., McCarley, R. W., Voglmaier, M. M., Niznikiewicz, M. A., Seidman, L. J., Hirayasu, Y., . . . Shenton, M. E. (1999). Schizotypal personality disorder and MRI abnormalities of temporal lobe gray matter. *Biological Psychiatry, 45*(11), 1393–1402.

Dickey, C. C., McCarley, R. W., Xu, M. L., Seidman, L. J., Voglmaier, M. M., Niznikiewicz, M. A., . . . Shenton, M. E. (2007). MRI abnormalities of the hippocampus and cavum septi pellucidi in females with schizotypal personality disorder. *Schizophrenia Research*, 89(1–3), 49–58.

Dickey, C. C., Morocz, I. A., Niznikiewicz, M. A., Voglmaier, M., Toner, S., Khan, U., ... McCarley, R. W. (2008). Auditory processing abnormalities in schizotypal personality disorder: An fMRI experiment using tones of deviant pitch and duration. *Schizophrenia Research*, 103(1–3), 26–39.

Doll, A., Sorg, C., Manoliu, A., Woller, A., Meng, C., Forstl, H., ... Riedl, V. (2013). Shifted intrinsic connectivity of central executive and salience network in borderline personality disorder. *Frontiers in Human Neuroscience*, 7, 727.

Downhill, J. E., Jr., Buchsbaum, M. S., Hazlett, E. A., Barth, S., Lees Roitman, S., Nunn, M., ... Siever, L. J. (2001). Temporal lobe volume determined by magnetic resonance imaging in schizotypal personality disorder and schizophrenia. *Schizophrenia Research*, 48(2–3), 187–199.

Driessen, M., Herrmann, J., Stahl, K., Zwaan, M., Meier, S., Hill, A., ... Petersen, D. (2000). Magnetic resonance imaging volumes of the hippocampus and the amygdala in women with borderline personality disorder and early traumatization. *Archives of General Psychiatry*, 57(12), 1115–1122.

Ellison-Wright, I., & Bullmore, E. (2009). Meta-analysis of diffusion tensor imaging studies in schizophrenia. *Schizophrenia Research*, 108(1–3), 3–10.

Fazel, S., & Danesh, J. (2002). Serious mental disorder in 23000 prisoners: A systematic review of 62 surveys. *Lancet*, 359(9306), 545–550.

Fervaha, G., & Remington, G. (2013). Neuroimaging findings in schizotypal personality disorder: A systematic review. *Progress in Neuro-Psychopharmacology & Biological Psychiatry*, 43, 96–107.

Frick, C., Lang, S., Kotchoubey, B., Sieswerda, S., Dinu-Biringer, R., Berger, M., ... Barnow, S. (2012). Hypersensitivity in borderline personality disorder during mindreading. *PLoS ONE*, 7(8), e41650.

Frodl, T., Meisenzahl, E. M., Zetzsche, T., Born, C., Groll, C., Jager, M., ... Moller, H. J. (2002). Hippocampal changes in patients with a first episode of major depression. *American Journal of Psychiatry*, 159(7), 1112–1118.

Frodl, T., Meisenzahl, E., Zetzsche, T., Bottlender, R., Born, C., Groll, C., ... Moller, H. J. (2002). Enlargement of the amygdala in patients with a first episode of major depression. *Biological Psychiatry*, 51(9), 708–714.

Gan, J., Yi, J., Zhong, M., Cao, X., Jin, X., Liu, W., & Zhu, X. (2016). Abnormal white matter structural connectivity in treatment-naive young adults with borderline personality disorder. *Acta Psychiatrica Scandinavica*, 134(6), 494–503.

Garrity, A. G., Pearlson, G. D., McKiernan, K., Lloyd, D., Kiehl, K. A., & Calhoun, V. D. (2007). Aberrant "default mode" functional connectivity in schizophrenia. *American Journal of Psychiatry*, 164(3), 450–457.

Goldstein, K. E., Hazlett, E. A., New, A. S., Haznedar, M. M., Newmark, R. E., Zelmanova, Y., ... Siever, L. J. (2009). Smaller superior temporal gyrus volume specificity in schizotypal personality disorder. *Schizophrenia Research*, 112(1–3), 14–23.

Goodman, M., Carpenter, D., Tang, C. Y., Goldstein, K. E., Avedon, J., Fernandez, N., ... Hazlett, E. A. (2014). Dialectical behavior therapy alters emotion regulation and amygdala activity in patients with borderline personality disorder. *Journal of Psychiatric Research*, 57, 108–116.

Goyer, P. F., Andreason P. J., Semple W. E., Clayton, A. H., King, A. C., Compton-Toth, B. A., ... Cohen, R. M. (1994). Positron-emission tomography and personality disorders. *Neuropsychopharmacology*, 10(1), 21–28.

Grant, J. E., Correia, S., Brennan-Krohn, T., Malloy, P. F., Laidlaw, D. H., & Schulz, S. C. (2007). Frontal white matter integrity in borderline personality disorder with self-injurious behavior. *The Journal of Neuropsychiatry and Clinical Neurosciences*, 19(4), 383–390.

Gregg, T. R., & Siegel, A. (2001). Brain structures and neurotransmitters regulating aggression in cats: Implications for human aggression. *Progress in Neuro-Psychopharmacology & Biological Psychiatry*, 25(1), 91–140.

Gregory, S., ffytche, D., Simmons, A., Kumari, V., Howard, M., Hodgins, S., & Blackwood, N. (2012). The antisocial brain: Psychopathy matters. *Archives of General Psychiatry*, 69(9), 962–972.

Gunderson, J. G., & Singer, M. T. (1975). Defining borderline patients: An overview. *American Journal of Psychiatry*, 132(1), 1–10.

Gurrera, R. J., Nakamura, M., Kubicki, M., Dickey, C. C., Niznikiewicz, M. A., Voglmaier, M. M., ... Seidman, L. J. (2007). The uncinate fasciculus and extraversion in schizotypal personality disorder: A diffusion tensor imaging study. *Schizophrenia Research*, 90(1–3), 360–362.

Haldane, M., & Frangou, S. (2004). New insights help define the pathophysiology of bipolar affective disorder: Neuroimaging and neuropathology findings. *Progress in Neuro-Psychopharmacology & Biological Psychiatry*, 28(6), 943–960.

Hasan, K. M., Kamali, A., Abid, H., Kramer, L. A., Fletcher, J. M., & Ewing-Cobbs, L. (2010). Quantification of the spatiotemporal microstructural organization of the human brain association, projection and commissural pathways across the lifespan using diffusion tensor tractography. *Brain Structure and Function*, 214(4), 361–373.

Hazlett, E. A., Buchsbaum, M. S., Haznedar, M. M., Newmark, R., Goldstein, K. E., Zelmanova, Y., ... Siever, L. J. (2008). Cortical gray and white matter volume in unmedicated schizotypal and schizophrenia patients. *Schizophrenia Research*, 101(1–3), 111–123.

Hazlett, E. A., Buchsbaum, M. S., Zhang, J., Newmark, R. E., Glanton, C. F., Zelmanova, Y., ... Siever, L. J. (2008). Frontal-striatal-thalamic mediodorsal nucleus dysfunction in schizophrenia-spectrum patients during sensorimotor gating. *NeuroImage*, 42(3), 1164–1177.

Hazlett, E. A., Collazo, T., Zelmanova, Y., Entis, J. J., Chu, K. W., Goldstein, K. E., ... Byne, W. (2012). Anterior limb of the internal capsule in schizotypal personality disorder: Fiber-tract counting, volume, and anisotropy. *Schizophrenia Research*, 141(2–3), 119–127.

Hazlett, E. A., Goldstein, K. E., & Kolaitis, J. C. (2012). A review of structural MRI and diffusion tensor imaging in schizotypal personality disorder. *Current Psychiatry Reports*, 14(1), 70–78.

Hazlett, E. A., Lamade, R. V., Graff, F. S., McClure, M. M., Kolaitis, J. C., Goldstein, K. E., ... Moshier, E. (2014). Visual-spatial working memory performance and temporal gray matter volume predict schizotypal personality disorder group membership. *Schizophrenia Research*, 152(2–3), 350–357.

Hazlett, E. A., New, A. S., Newmark, R., Haznedar, M. M., Lo, J. N., Speiser, L. J., ... Buchsbaum, M. S. (2005). Reduced anterior and posterior cingulate gray matter in borderline personality disorder. *Biological Psychiatry*, 58(8), 614–623.

Hazlett, E. A., Zhang, J., New, A. S., Zelmanova, Y., Goldstein, K. E., Haznedar, M. M., ... Chu, K. W. (2012). Potentiated amygdala response to repeated emotional pictures in borderline personality disorder. *Biological Psychiatry*, 72(6), 448–456.

Haznedar, M. M., Buchsbaum, M. S., Hazlett, E. A., Shihabuddin, L., New, A., & Siever, L. J. (2004). Cingulate gyrus volume and metabolism in the schizophrenia spectrum. *Schizophrenia Research*, 71(2–3), 249–262.

Herve, H. F., Hayes, P. J., & Hare, R. D. (2003). Psychopathy and sensitivity to the emotional polarity of metaphorical statements. *Personality and Individual Differences*, 35(7), 1497–1507.

Hill, K., Mann, L., Laws, K. R., Stephenson, C. M., Nimmo-Smith, I., & McKenna, P. J. (2004). Hypofrontality in schizophrenia: A meta-analysis of functional imaging studies. *Acta Psychiatrica Scandinavica*, 110(4), 243–256.

Holtmann, J., Herbort, M. C., Wustenberg, T., Soch, J., Richter, S., Walter, H., ... Schott, B. H. (2013). Trait anxiety modulates fronto-limbic processing of emotional interference in borderline personality disorder. *Frontiers in Human Neuroscience*, 7, 54.

Huang, X. Q., Lui, S., Deng, W., Chan, R. C., Wu, Q. Z., Jiang, L. J., ... Gong, Q. Y. (2010). Localization of cerebral functional deficits in treatment-naive, first-episode schizophrenia using resting-state fMRI. *NeuroImage*, 49(4), 2901–2906.

Insel, T., Cuthbert, B., Garvey, M., Heinssen, R., Pine, D. S., Quinn, K., ... Wang, P. (2010). Research Domain Criteria (RDoC): Toward a new classification framework for research on mental disorders. *American Journal of Psychiatry*, 167(7), 748–751.

Irle, E., Lange, C., & Sachsse, U. (2005). Reduced size and abnormal asymmetry of parietal cortex in women with borderline personality disorder. *Biological Psychiatry*, 57(2), 173–182.

Jacob, G. A., Zvonik, K., Kamphausen, S., Sebastian, A., Maier, S., Philipsen, A., ... Tuscher, O. (2013). Emotional modulation of motor response inhibition in women with borderline personality disorder: An fMRI study. *Journal of Psychiatry & Neuroscience*, 38(3), 164–172.

Jiang, W., Li, G., Liu, H., Shi, F., Wang, T., Shen, C., ... Shen, D. (2016). Reduced cortical thickness and increased surface area in antisocial personality disorder. *Neuroscience*, 337, 143–152.

Jiang, W., Liu, H., Liao, J., Ma, X., Rong, P., Tang, Y., & Wang, W. (2013). A functional MRI study of deception among offenders with antisocial personality disorders. *Neuroscience*, 244, 90–98.

Jiang, W., Shi, F., Liao, J., Liu, H., Wang, T., Shen, C., ... Shen, D. (2017). Disrupted functional connectome in antisocial personality disorder. *Brain Imaging and Behavior*, 11(4), 1071–1084.

Jiang, W., Shi, F., Liu, H., Li, G., Ding, Z., Shen, H., ... Shen, D. (2017). Reduced white matter integrity in antisocial personality disorder: A diffusion tensor imaging study. *Scientific Reports*, 7, 43002.

Kamphausen, S., Schroder, P., Maier, S., Bader, K., Feige, B., Kaller, C. P., ... Tuscher, O. (2013). Medial prefrontal dysfunction and prolonged amygdala response during instructed fear processing in borderline personality disorder. *The World Journal of Biological Psychiatry*, 14(4), 307–318, S301–304.

Kawasaki, Y., Suzuki, M., Nohara, S., Hagino, H., Takahashi, T., Matsui, M., ... Kurachi, M. (2004). Structural brain differences in patients with schizophrenia and schizotypal disorder demonstrated by voxel-based morphometry. *European Archives of Psychiatry and Clinical Neuroscience*, 254(6), 406–414.

Kernberg, O. (1967). Borderline personality organization. *Journal of the American Psychoanalytic Association*, 15(3), 641–685.

Koenigsberg, H. W., Buchsbaum, M. S., Buchsbaum, B. R., Schneiderman, J. S., Tang, C. Y., New, A., ... Siever, L. J. (2005). Functional MRI of visuospatial working memory in schizotypal personality disorder: A region-of-interest analysis. *Psychological Medicine*, 35(7), 1019–1030.

Kolla, N. J., Dunlop, K., Downar, J., Links, P., Bagby, R. M., Simpson, A., & Meyer, J. (2015). Ventral striatum monoamine oxidase-A is associated with ventral striatum functional connectivity in antisocial personality disorder: A PET/FMRI study. *Biological Psychiatry*, 77(9), 366s–366s.

Kolla, N. J., Dunlop, K., Downar, J., Links, P., Bagby, R. M., Wilson, A. A., ... Meyer, J. H. (2016). Association of ventral striatum monoamine oxidase-A binding and functional connectivity in antisocial personality disorder with high impulsivity: A positron emission tomography and functional magnetic resonance imaging study. *European Neuropsychopharmacology*, 26(4), 777–786.

Kolla, N. J., Matthews, B., Wilson, A. A., Houle, S., Bagby, R. M., Links, P., ... Meyer, J. H. (2015). Lower monoamine oxidase-A total distribution volume in impulsive and violent male offenders with antisocial personality disorder and high psychopathic traits: An [C-11] harmine positron emission tomography study. *Neuropsychopharmacology*, 40(11), 2596–2603.

Koo, M. S., Levitt, J. J., McCarley, R. W., Seidman, L. J., Dickey, C. C., Niznikiewicz, M. A., ... Shenton, M. E. (2006). Reduction of caudate nucleus volumes in neuroleptic-naive female subjects with schizotypal personality disorder. *Biological Psychiatry*, 60(1), 40–48.

Kraguljac, N. V., White, D. M., Hadley, J., Reid, M. A., & Lahti, A. C. (2014). Hippocampal-parietal dysconnectivity and glutamate abnormalities in unmedicated patients with schizophrenia. *Hippocampus*, 24(12), 1524–1532.

Krause-Utz, A., Elzinga, B. M., Oei, N. Y., Paret, C., Niedtfeld, I., Spinhoven, P., ... Schmahl, C. (2014). Amygdala and dorsal anterior cingulate connectivity during an emotional working memory task in borderline personality disorder patients with interpersonal trauma history. *Frontiers in Human Neuroscience*, 8, 848.

Krause-Utz, A., Oei, N. Y., Niedtfeld, I., Bohus, M., Spinhoven, P., Schmahl, C., & Elzinga, B. M. (2012). Influence of emotional distraction on working memory performance in borderline personality disorder. *Psychological Medicine*, 42(10), 2181–2192.

Kubicki, M., McCarley, R., Westin, C. F., Park, H. J., Maier, S., Kikinis, R., ... Shenton, M. E. (2007). A review of diffusion tensor imaging studies in schizophrenia. *Journal of Psychiatric Research*, 41(1–2), 15–30.

Kuhn, S., & Gallinat, J. (2013). Gray matter correlates of posttraumatic stress disorder: A quantitative meta-analysis. *Biological Psychiatry*, 73(1), 70–74.

Kuruoğlu, A. C., Arikan, Z., Vural, G., Karataş, M., Araç, & Işik, E. (1996). Single photon emission computerised tomography in chronic alcoholism: Antisocial personality disorder may be associated with decreased frontal perfusion. *British Journal of Psychiatry*, 169(3), 348–354.

Laakso, M. P., Gunning-Dixon, F., Vaurio, O., Repo-Tiihonen, E., Soininen, H., & Tiihonen, J. (2002). Prefrontal volumes in habitually violent subjects with antisocial personality disorder and type 2 alcoholism. *Psychiatry Research*, 114(2), 95–102.

Laakso, M. P., Vaurio, O., Koivisto, E., Savolainen, L., Eronen, M., Aronen, H. J., ... Tiihonen, J. (2001). Psychopathy and the posterior hippocampus. *Behavioural Brain Research*, 118(2), 187–193.

Lange, C., & Irle, E. (2004). Enlarged amygdala volume and reduced hippocampal volume in young women with major depression. *Psychological Medicine*, 34(6), 1059–1064.

Lei, X., Zhong, M., Liu, Y., Jin, X., Zhou, Q., Xi, C., ... Yi, J. (2017). A resting-state fMRI study in borderline personality disorder combining amplitude of low frequency fluctuation, regional homogeneity and seed based functional connectivity *Journal of Affective Disorders, 218*, 299–305.

Leichsenring, F., Leibing, E., Kruse, J., New, A. S., & Leweke, F. (2011). Borderline personality disorder. *Lancet, 377*(9759), 74–84.

Lener, M. S., Wong, E., Tang, C. Y., Byne, W., Goldstein, K. E., Blair, N. J., ... Hazlett, E. A. (2015). White matter abnormalities in schizophrenia and schizotypal personality disorder. *Schizophrenia Bulletin, 41*(1), 300–310.

Lenzenweger, M. F., Lane, M. C., Loranger, A. W., & Kessler, R. C. (2007). DSM-IV personality disorders in the National Comorbidity Survey Replication. *Biological Psychiatry, 62*(6), 553–564.

Lindner, P., Savic, I., Sitnikov, R., Budhiraja, M., Liu, Y., Jokinen, J., ... Hodgins, S. (2016). Conduct disorder in females is associated with reduced corpus callosum structural integrity independent of comorbid disorders and exposure to maltreatment. *Translational Psychiatry, 6*(1), e714.

Lischke, A., Domin, M., Freyberger, H. J., Grabe, H. J., Mentel, R., Bernheim, D., & Lotze, M. (2015). Structural alterations in white-matter tracts connecting (para-)limbic and prefrontal brain regions in borderline personality disorder. *Psychological Medicine, 45*(15), 3171–3180.

(2017). Structural alterations in the corpus callosum are associated with suicidal behavior in women with borderline personality disorder. *Frontiers in Human Neuroscience, 11*, 196.

Liu, H., Liao, J., Jiang, W., & Wang, W. (2014). Changes in low-frequency fluctuations in patients with antisocial personality disorder revealed by resting-state functional MRI. *PLoS ONE, 9*(3), e89790.

Lucas, P. B., Gardner, D. L., Cowdry, R. W., & Pickar, D. (1989). Cerebral structure in borderline personality disorder. *Psychiatry Research, 27*(2), 111–115.

Lyoo, I. K., Han, M. H., & Cho, D. Y. (1998). A brain MRI study in subjects with borderline personality disorder. *Journal of Affective Disorders, 50*(2–3), 235–243.

Maier-Hein, K. H., Brunner, R., Lutz, K., Henze, R., Parzer, P., Feigl, N., ... Stieltjes, B. (2014). Disorder-specific white matter alterations in adolescent borderline personality disorder. *Biological Psychiatry, 75*(1), 81–88.

Matsui, M., Suzuki, M., Zhou, S. Y., Takahashi, T., Kawasaki, Y., Yuuki, H., ... Kurachi, M. (2008). The relationship between prefrontal brain volume and characteristics of memory strategy in schizophrenia spectrum disorders. *Progress in Neuro-Psychopharmacology & Biological Psychiatry, 32*(8), 1854–1862.

McClure, M. M., Harvey, P. D., Bowie, C. R., Iacoviello, B., & Siever, L. J. (2013). Functional outcomes, functional capacity, and cognitive impairment in schizotypal personality disorder. *Schizophrenia Research, 144*(1–3), 146–150.

Meyer, J. H., Wilson, A. A., Rusjan, P., Clark, M., Houle, S., Woodside, S., ... Colleton, M. (2008). Serotonin(2A) receptor binding potential in people with aggressive and violent behaviour. *Journal of Psychiatry & Neuroscience, 33*(6), 499–508.

Mier, D., Lis, S., Esslinger, C., Sauer, C., Hagenhoff, M., Ulferts, J., ... Kirsch, P. (2013). Neuronal correlates of social cognition in borderline personality disorder. *Social Cognitive and Affective Neuroscience, 8*(5), 531–537.

Minzenberg, M. J., Fan, J., New, A. S., Tang, C. Y., & Siever, L. J. (2008). Frontolimbic structural changes in borderline personality disorder. *Journal of Psychiatric Research, 42*(9), 727–733.

Motzkin, J. C., Newman, J. P., Kiehl, K. A., & Koenigs, M. (2011). Reduced prefrontal connectivity in psychopathy. *Journal of Neuroscience, 31*(48), 17348–17357.

Muller, J. L., Gansbauer, S., Sommer, M., Dohnel, K., Weber, T., Schmidt-Wilcke, T., & Hajak, G. (2008). Gray matter changes in right superior temporal gyrus in criminal psychopaths: Evidence from voxel-based morphometry. *Psychiatry Research: Neuroimaging, 163*(3), 213–222.

Muller, J. L., Sommer, M., Dohnel, K., Weber, T., Schmidt-Wilcke, T., & Hajak, G. (2008). Disturbed prefrontal and temporal brain function during emotion and cognition interaction in criminal psychopathy. *Behavioral Sciences & The Law, 26*(1), 131–150.

Nakamura, M., McCarley, R. W., Kubicki, M., Dickey, C. C., Niznikiewicz, M. A., Voglmaier, M. M., ... Shenton, M. E. (2005). Fronto-temporal disconnectivity in schizotypal personality disorder: A diffusion tensor imaging study. *Biological Psychiatry, 58*(6), 468–478.

Narayan, V. M., Narr, K. L., Kumari, V., Woods, R. P., Thompson, P. M., Toga, A. W., & Sharma, T. (2007). Regional cortical thinning in subjects with violent antisocial personality disorder or schizophrenia. *American Journal of Psychiatry, 164*(9), 1418–1427.

New, A. S., Buchsbaum, M. S., Hazlett, E. A., Goodman, M., Koenigsberg, H. W., Lo, J., ... Siever, L. J. (2004). Fluoxetine increases relative metabolic rate in prefrontal cortex in impulsive aggression. *Psychopharmacology (Berl), 176*(3–4), 451–458.

New, A. S., Carpenter, D. M., Perez-Rodriguez, M. M., Ripoll, L. H., Avedon, J., Patil, U., ... Goodman, M. (2013). Developmental differences in diffusion tensor imaging parameters in borderline personality disorder. *Journal of Psychiatric Research, 47*(8), 1101–1109.

New, A. S., Hazlett, E. A., Buchsbaum, M. S., Goodman, M., Mitelman, S. A., Newmark, R., ... Siever, L. J. (2007). Amygdala-prefrontal disconnection in borderline personality disorder. *Neuropsychopharmacology, 32*(7), 1629–1640.

New, A. S., Hazlett, E. A., Newmark, R. E., Zhang, J., Triebwasser, J., Meyerson, D., ... Buchsbaum, M. S. (2009). Laboratory induced aggression: A positron emission tomography study of aggressive individuals with borderline personality disorder. *Biological Psychiatry, 66*(12), 1107–1114.

Niedtfeld, I., Kirsch, P., Schulze, L., Herpertz, S. C., Bohus, M., & Schmahl, C. (2012). Functional connectivity of pain-mediated affect regulation in borderline personality disorder. *PLoS ONE, 7*(3), e33293.

Niedtfeld, I., Schmitt, R., Winter, D., Bohus, M., Schmahl, C., & Herpertz, S. C. (2017). Pain-mediated affect regulation is reduced after dialectical behavior therapy in borderline personality disorder: A longitudinal fMRI study. *Social Cognitive and Affective Neuroscience, 12*(5), 739–747.

Ninomiya, T., Oshita, H., Kawano, Y., Goto, C., Matsuhashi, M., Masuda, K., ... Akiyoshi, J. (2018). Reduced white matter integrity in borderline personality disorder: A diffusion tensor imaging study. *Journal of Affective Disorders, 225*, 723–732.

Nunes, P. M., Wenzel, A., Borges, K. T., Porto, C. R., Caminha, R. M., & de Oliveira, I. R. (2009). Volumes of the hippocampus and amygdala in patients with borderline personality disorder: A meta-analysis. *Journal of Personality Disorders, 23*(4), 333–345.

Ogloff, J. R. P. (2006). Psychopathy/antisocial personality disorder conundrum. *Australian and New Zealand Journal of Psychiatry, 40*(6–7), 519–528.

Oldham, J. M. (2006). Borderline personality disorder and suicidality. *American Journal of Psychiatry, 163*(1), 20–26.

Oquendo, M. A., Krunic, A., Parsey, R. V., Milak, M., Malone, K. M., Anderson, A., ... John Mann, J. (2005). Positron emission tomography of regional brain metabolic responses to a serotonergic challenge in major depressive disorder with and without borderline personality disorder. *Neuropsychopharmacology, 30* (6), 1163–1172.

Perez-Rodriguez, M. M., New, A. S., Goldstein, K. E., Rosell, D., Yuan, Q., Zhou, Z., ... Hazlett, E. A. (2017). Brain-derived neurotrophic factor Val66Met genotype modulates amygdala habituation. *Psychiatry Research, 263,* 85–92.

Poythress, N. G., Edens, J. F., Skeem, J. L., Lilienfeld, S. O., Douglas, K. S., Frick, P. J., ... Wang, T. (2010). Identifying subtypes among offenders with antisocial personality disorder: A cluster-analytic study. *Journal of Abnormal Psychology, 119* (2), 389–400.

Raichle, M. E., MacLeod, A. M., Snyder, A. Z., Powers, W. J., Gusnard, D. A., & Shulman, G. L. (2001). A default mode of brain function. *Proceedings of the National Academy of Sciences USA, 98*(2), 676–682.

Raine, A., Lencz, T., Bihrle, S., LaCasse, L., & Colletti, P. (2000). Reduced prefrontal gray matter volume and reduced autonomic activity in antisocial personality disorder. *Archives of General Psychiatry, 57*(2), 119–127; discussion 128–129.

Rosenkranz, J. A., & Grace, A. A. (2002). Cellular mechanisms of infralimbic and prelimbic prefrontal cortical inhibition and dopaminergic modulation of basolateral amygdala neurons in vivo. *Journal of Neuroscience, 22*(1), 324–337.

Rotarska-Jagiela, A., van de Ven, V., Oertel-Knochel, V., Uhlhaas, P. J., Vogeley, K., & Linden, D. E. (2010). Resting-state functional network correlates of psychotic symptoms in schizophrenia. *Schizophrenia Research, 117*(1), 21–30.

Ruocco, A. C., Amirthavasagam, S., Choi-Kain, L. W., & McMain, S. F. (2013). Neural correlates of negative emotionality in borderline personality disorder: An activation-likelihood-estimation meta-analysis. *Biological Psychiatry, 73*(2), 153–160.

Ruocco, A. C., Amirthavasagam, S., & Zakzanis, K. K. (2012). Amygdala and hippocampal volume reductions as candidate endophenotypes for borderline personality disorder: A meta-analysis of magnetic resonance imaging studies. *Psychiatry Research, 201*(3), 245–252.

Rusch, N., Bracht, T., Kreher, B. W., Schnell, S., Glauche, V., Il'yasov, K. A., ... van Elst, L. T. (2010). Reduced interhemispheric structural connectivity between anterior cingulate cortices in borderline personality disorder. *Psychiatry Research, 181*(2), 151–154.

Rusch, N., van Elst, L. T., Ludaescher, P., Wilke, M., Huppertz, H. J., Thiel, T., ... Ebert, D. (2003). A voxel-based morphometric MRI study in female patients with borderline personality disorder. *NeuroImage, 20*(1), 385–392.

Rusch, N., Weber, M., Il'yasov, K. A., Lieb, K., Ebert, D., Hennig, J., & van Elst, L. T. (2007). Inferior frontal white matter microstructure and patterns of psychopathology in women with borderline personality disorder and comorbid attention-deficit hyperactivity disorder. *NeuroImage, 35*(2), 738–747.

Rylands, A. J., Hinz, R., Jones, M., Holmes, S. E., Feldmann, M., Brown, G., ... Talbot, P. S. (2012). Pre- and postsynaptic serotonergic differences in males with extreme levels of impulsive aggression without callous unemotional traits: A positron emission tomography study using C-11-DASB and C-11-MDL100907. *Biological Psychiatry, 72*(12), 1004–1011.

Scherpiet, S., Bruhl, A. B., Opialla, S., Roth, L., Jancke, L., & Herwig, U. (2014). Altered emotion processing circuits during the anticipation of emotional stimuli in women with borderline personality disorder. *European Archives of Psychiatry and Clinical Neuroscience, 264*(1), 45–60.

Schiffer, B., Muller, B. W., Scherbaum, N., Hodgins, S., Forsting, M., Wiltfang, J., ... Leygraf, N. (2011). Disentangling structural brain alterations associated with violent behavior from those associated with substance use disorders. *Archives of General Psychiatry, 68*(10), 1039–1049.

Schmahl, C., Bohus, M., Esposito, F., Treede, R. D., Di Salle, F., Greffrath, W., ... Seifritz, E. (2006). Neural correlates of antinociception in borderline personality disorder. *Archives of General Psychiatry, 63*(6), 659–667.

Schmahl, C. G., Elzinga, B. M., Vermetten, E., Sanislow, C., McGlashan, T. H., & Bremner, J. D. (2003). Neural correlates of memories of abandonment in women with and without borderline personality disorder. *Biological Psychiatry, 54*(2), 142–151.

Schnell, K., & Herpertz, S. C. (2007). Effects of dialectic-behavioral-therapy on the neural correlates of affective hyperarousal in borderline personality disorder. *Journal of Psychiatric Research, 41*(10), 837–847.

Schulz, S. C., Koller, M. M., Kishore, P. R., Hamer, R. M., Gehl, J. J., & Friedel, R. O. (1983). Ventricular enlargement in teenage patients with schizophrenia spectrum disorder. *American Journal of Psychiatry, 140*(12), 1592–1595.

Schulze, L., Schmahl, C., & Niedtfeld, I. (2016). Neural correlates of disturbed emotion processing in borderline personality disorder: A multimodal meta-analysis. *Biological Psychiatry, 79*(2), 97–106.

Shepherd, A. M., Laurens, K. R., Matheson, S. L., Carr, V. J., & Green, M. J. (2012). Systematic meta-review and quality assessment of the structural brain alterations in schizophrenia. *Neuroscience & Biobehavioral Reviews, 36*(4), 1342–1356.

Shihabuddin, L., Buchsbaum, M. S., Hazlett, E. A., Silverman, J., New, A., Brickman, A. M., ... Siever, L. J. (2001). Striatal size and relative glucose metabolic rate in schizotypal personality disorder and schizophrenia. *Archives of General Psychiatry, 58* (9), 877–884.

Siever, L. J., & Davis, K. L. (2004). The pathophysiology of schizophrenia disorders: Perspectives from the spectrum. *American Journal of Psychiatry, 161*(3), 398–413.

Silbersweig, D., Clarkin, J. F., Goldstein, M., Kernberg, O. F., Tuescher, O., Levy, K. N., ... Stern, E. (2007). Failure of frontolimbic inhibitory function in the context of negative emotion in borderline personality disorder. *American Journal of Psychiatry, 164*(12), 1832–1841.

Soloff, P. H., Chiappetta, L., Mason, N. S., Becker, C., & Price, J. C. (2014). Effects of serotonin-2A receptor binding and gender on personality traits and suicidal behavior in borderline personality disorder. *Psychiatry Research: Neuroimaging, 222*(3), 140–148.

Soloff, P. H., Meltzer, C. C., Becker, C., Greer, P. J., & Constantine, D. (2005). Gender differences in a fenfluramine-activated FDG PET study of borderline personality disorder. *Psychiatry Research, 138*(3), 183–195.

Soloff, P. H., Meltzer, C. C., Greer, P. J., Constantine, D., & Kelly, T. M. (2000). A fenfluramine-activated FDG-PET study of borderline personality disorder. *Biological Psychiatry, 47*(6), 540–547.

Soloff, P. H., Pruitt, P., Sharma, M., Radwan, J., White, R., & Diwadkar, V. A. (2012). Structural brain abnormalities and suicidal behavior in borderline personality disorder. *Journal of Psychiatric Research, 46*(4), 516–525.

Stein, M. B., Koverola, C., Hanna, C., Torchia, M. G., & McClarty, B. (1997). Hippocampal volume in women victimized by childhood sexual abuse. *Psychological Medicine, 27*(4), 951–959.

Sun, Y., Zhang, L., Ancharaz, S. S., Cheng, S., Sun, W., Wang, H., & Sun, Y. (2016). Decreased fractional anisotropy values in two clusters of white matter in patients with schizotypal personality disorder: A DTI study. *Behavioural Brain Research, 310*, 68–75.

Sundram, F., Deeley, Q., Sarkar, S., Daly, E., Latham, R., Craig, M., ... Murphy, D. G. (2012). White matter microstructural abnormalities in the frontal lobe of adults with antisocial personality disorder. *Cortex, 48*(2), 216–229.

Suzuki, M., Zhou, S. Y., Hagino, H., Takahashi, T., Kawasaki, Y., Nohara, S., ... Kurachi, M. (2004). Volume reduction of the right anterior limb of the internal capsule in patients with schizotypal disorder. *Psychiatry Research, 130*(3), 213–225.

Suzuki, M., Zhou, S. Y., Takahashi, T., Hagino, H., Kawasaki, Y., Niu, L., ... Kurachi, M. (2005). Differential contributions of prefrontal and temporolimbic pathology to mechanisms of psychosis. *Brain, 128*(Pt 9), 2109–2122.

Takahashi, T., Kawasaki, Y., Kurokawa, K., Hagino, H., Nohara, S., Yamashita, I., ... Kurachi, M. (2002). Lack of normal structural asymmetry of the anterior cingulate gyrus in female patients with schizophrenia: A volumetric magnetic resonance imaging study. *Schizophrenia Research, 55*(1–2), 69–81.

Takahashi, T., Suzuki, M., Zhou, S. Y., Nakamura, K., Tanino, R., Kawasaki, Y., ... Kurachi, M. (2008). Prevalence and length of the adhesio interthalamica in schizophrenia spectrum disorders. *Psychiatry Research, 164*(1), 90–94.

Takahashi, T., Suzuki, M., Zhou, S. Y., Tanino, R., Hagino, H., Niu, L., ... Kurachi, M. (2006). Temporal lobe gray matter in schizophrenia spectrum: A volumetric MRI study of the fusiform gyrus, parahippocampal gyrus, and middle and inferior temporal gyri. *Schizophrenia Research, 87*(1–3), 116–126.

Takahashi, T., Suzuki, M., Zhou, S. Y., Tanino, R., Nakamura, K., Kawasaki, Y., ... Kurachi, M. (2010). A follow-up MRI study of the superior temporal subregions in schizotypal disorder and first-episode schizophrenia. *Schizophrenia Research, 119*(1–3), 65–74.

Takahashi, T., Zhou, S. Y., Nakamura, K., Tanino, R., Furuichi, A., Kido, M., ... Suzuki, M. (2011). A follow-up MRI study of the fusiform gyrus and middle and inferior temporal gyri in schizophrenia spectrum. *Progress in Neuro-Psychopharmacology & Biological Psychiatry, 35*(8), 1957–1964.

Tang, Y., Jiang, W., Liao, J., Wang, W., & Luo, A. (2013). Identifying individuals with antisocial personality disorder using resting-state FMRI. *PLoS ONE, 8*(4), e60652.

Tang, Y., Long, J., Wang, W., Liao, J., Xie, H., Zhao, G., & Zhang, H. (2016). Aberrant functional brain connectome in people with antisocial personality disorder. *Scientific Reports, 6*, 26209.

Tebartz van Elst, L., Hesslinger, B., Thiel, T., Geiger, E., Haegele, K., Lemieux, L., ... Ebert, D. (2003). Frontolimbic brain abnormalities in patients with borderline personality disorder: A volumetric magnetic resonance imaging study. *Biological Psychiatry, 54*(2), 163–171.

Thompson, J. L., Rosell, D. R., Slifstein, M., Girgis, R. R., Xu, X., Ehrlich, Y., ... Siever, L. J. (2014). Prefrontal dopamine D1 receptors and working memory in schizotypal personality disorder: A PET study with [(1)(1)C]NNC112. *Psychopharmacology (Berl), 231*(21), 4231–4240.

Tiihonen, J., Rossi, R., Laakso, M. P., Hodgins, S., Testa, C., Perez, J., ... Frisoni, G. B. (2008). Brain anatomy of persistent violent

offenders: More rather than less. *Psychiatry Research: Neuroimaging, 163*(3), 201–212.

Visintin, E., De Panfilis, C., Amore, M., Balestrieri, M., Wolf, R. C., & Sambataro, F. (2016). Mapping the brain correlates of borderline personality disorder: A functional neuroimaging meta-analysis of resting state studies. *Journal of Affective Disorders, 204*, 262–269.

Vu, M. A., Thermenos, H. W., Terry, D. P., Wolfe, D. J., Voglmaier, M. M., Niznikiewicz, M. A., ... Dickey, C. C. (2013). Working memory in schizotypal personality disorder: fMRI activation and deactivation differences. *Schizophrenia Research, 151*(1–3), 113–123.

Wagner, G., Krause-Utz, A., de la Cruz, F., Schumann, A., Schmahl, C., & Bar, K. J. (2018). Resting-state functional connectivity of neurotransmitter producing sites in female patients with borderline personality disorder. *Progress in Neuro-Psychopharmacology & Biological Psychiatry, 83*, 118–126.

Waller, R., Dotterer, H. L., Murray, L., Maxwell, A. M., & Hyde, L. W. (2017). White-matter tract abnormalities and antisocial behavior: A systematic review of diffusion tensor imaging studies across development. *NeuroImage: Clinical, 14*, 201–215.

Weniger, G., Lange, C., Sachsse, U., & Irle, E. (2009). Reduced amygdala and hippocampus size in trauma-exposed women with borderline personality disorder and without posttraumatic stress disorder. *Journal of Psychiatry & Neuroscience, 34*(5), 383–388.

Whalley, H. C., Nickson, T., Pope, M., Nicol, K., Romaniuk, L., Bastin, M. E., ... Hall, J. (2015). White matter integrity and its association with affective and interpersonal symptoms in borderline personality disorder. *NeuroImage: Clinical, 7*, 476–481.

Wheeler, A. L., & Voineskos, A. N. (2014). A review of structural neuroimaging in schizophrenia: From connectivity to connectomics. *Frontiers in Human Neuroscience, 8*, 653.

Whittle, S., Chanen, A. M., Fornito, A., McGorry, P. D., Pantelis, C., & Yucel, M. (2009). Anterior cingulate volume in adolescents with first-presentation borderline personality disorder. *Psychiatry Research, 172*(2), 155–160.

Yang, Y., & Raine, A. (2009). Prefrontal structural and functional brain imaging findings in antisocial, violent, and psychopathic individuals: A meta-analysis. *Psychiatry Research, 174*(2), 81–88.

Yang, Y. L., Raine, A., Narr, K. L., Colletti, P., & Toga, A. W. (2009). Localization of deformations within the amygdala in individuals with psychopathy. *Archives of General Psychiatry, 66*(9), 986–994.

Yoneyama, E., Matsui, M., Kawasaki, Y., Nohara, S., Takahashi, T., Hagino, H., ... Kurachi, M. (2003). Gray matter features of schizotypal disorder patients exhibiting the schizophrenia-related code types of the Minnesota Multiphasic Personality Inventory. *Acta Psychiatrica Scandinavica, 108*(5), 333–340.

Zanarini, M. C., Williams, A. A., Lewis, R. E., Reich, R. B., Vera, S. C., Marino, M. F., ... Frankenburg, F. R. (1997). Reported pathological childhood experiences associated with the development of borderline personality disorder. *American Journal of Psychiatry, 154*(8), 1101–1106.

Zetzsche, T., Preuss, U. W., Frodl, T., Schmitt, G., Seifert, D., Munchhausen, E., ... Meisenzahl, E. M. (2007). Hippocampal volume reduction and history of aggressive behaviour in patients with borderline personality disorder. *Psychiatry Research, 154*(2), 157–170.

Zhang, Q., Shen, J., Wu, J., Yu, X., Lou, W., Fan, H., ... Wang, D. (2014). Altered default mode network functional connectivity in schizotypal personality disorder. *Schizophrenia Research, 160* (1–3), 51–56.

Zhang, T., Wang, D., Zhang, Q., Wu, J., Lv, J., & Shi, L. (2017). Supervoxel-based statistical analysis of diffusion tensor imaging in schizotypal personality disorder. *NeuroImage, 163,* 368–378.

Zhu, Y., Tang, Y., Zhang, T., Li, H., Tang, Y., Li, C., ... Wang, J. (2017). Reduced functional connectivity between bilateral precuneus and contralateral parahippocampus in schizotypal personality disorder. *BMC Psychiatry, 17*(1), 48.

1a A Clinically Relevant Neuroscience for Personality Disorders: Commentary on Neuroimaging in Personality Disorders

JOSEPH E. BEENEY

One of my favorite graduate school professors liked to ask a provocative question about the increasing emphasis placed on neuroscience in Psychiatry and Clinical Psychology: "What from all of this work has influenced our clinical practice at all?" A nice variation of this question was, "What has clinical neuroscience produced that a therapist in the community could use?" These were meant to be rhetorical questions. I think the answer was supposed to be "nothing." Still, I took the question as a serious, if humbling, challenge. Neuroscience is a fascinating, exciting field in its own right. Yet, I would guess for most clinical researchers, when we wrap up our careers and look back on our contributions, we want to see some work that is unambiguously relevant to clinical practice. So, "How does this inform clinical practice at all?" is a refrain to which I return. The chapter by Chan, Vaccaro, Rose, Kessler, and Hazlett (this volume) on "Neuroimaging in Personality Disorders" provides an opportunity for each of us to use this lens to interpret what the field has produced so far in the clinical neuroscience of personality disorders (PDs). At the same time, it is a chance to note the limitations of our approaches as an opening to find methods that might bring us closer to unambiguous relevance for clinical practice.

The National Institute of Mental Health (NIMH) declared an historic shift prior to the new millennium by calling the 1990s the "decade of the brain" – a development my graduate professor found irksome. However, in the 1990s, researchers began to develop an understanding of the brain that should matter a great deal to clinical researchers. During the decade, researchers began to understand that the brain is much more plastic and malleable than previously thought. Our experiences, even in adulthood, shape our neurocircuitry (Holtmaat & Svoboda, 2009) and these neural alterations are partly the result of epigenetic changes in gene expression (Houston et al., 2013). For researchers focused on identifying risk factors, prevention, or treatment approaches, these findings seem to place the human brain as the critical mediator between experience and psychopathology or health. As a consequence, there has been an enormous increase in structural and functional MRI studies. And at the same time, it can be difficult to see the clinical relevance of all of this work. Some even refer to these efforts as phrenology with better pictures (e.g., Uttal, 2002).

So, what might a neuroscience of PDs that informs clinical practice look like? It might tell us something about the mechanisms of the disorder, help us to carve out the boundaries between and commonalities across disorders, or maybe tell us how medication or psychotherapy work. The biggest obstacle for a clinically relevant neuroscience study is less-than-ideal research design. Study design is critical in how clearly we can interpret results. Poor design is likely much more frequently a function of practical issues (e.g., recruitment, limited funding), rather than researcher skill. Still, clinically relevant findings can be derived from studies that are less than perfect, if they are placed in the context of a network of findings. In addition, studies using network-based approaches and performance-based tasks can help with the interpretation that leads to clinical relevance.

CAN STUDIES OF STRUCTURAL MORPHOLOGY BE CLINICALLY RELEVANT?

Identifying the neural mechanisms specific to a disorder that are distinct from other disorders is a major goal of clinical neuroscience. Yet, few studies provide unambiguous information on mechanisms specific to PDs. Researchers commonly employ a design in which people diagnosed with a PD are compared to people with no mental health difficulties. With multiple studies, this design can help generate a picture of differences in brain structure. But these are differences between people with no mental health difficulties and a group that is distinct in endless ways, in addition to having a specific clinical diagnosis. Drawing conclusions regarding specific abnormalities from such studies is problematic.

For instance, as Chan et al. (this volume) note, abnormal temporal lobe volumes may play a role in schizotypal PD (SPD) and psychotic symptoms. At the same time, it is unclear whether these differences are actually due to abnormalities specific to SPD, or simply having any mental health diagnosis or experience common to many mental health disorders (e.g., trauma). On the other hand, some of the studies the authors review that compare diagnostic near neighbors provide more compelling information, though these studies also have limitations. Several reports have compared people with SPD and schizophrenia, generally finding, on average, that there are differences between these two groups in terms of temporal lobe brain volumes, and that specific symptoms are related to temporal lobe abnormalities. In terms of brain structure, SPD resembles a less severe version of schizophrenia. However, it is possible other disorders may resemble a less severe version of schizophrenia when compared in this way. Temporal lobe abnormalities have been found in numerous disorders including autism, attention deficit/hyperactivity disorder, and psychopathy (Calhoun, Maciejewski, Pearlson, & Kiehl, 2008; Kobel et al., 2010; Lombardo et al., 2010).

Providing more context to these findings seems to provide a more compelling picture. We may know little that's definitive, but the network of studies focusing on different levels of inquiry (e.g., genes, brain structure and function, phenomenology) does seem to be coherent. SPD and schizophrenia appear to share genetic risk. Similar brain pathology is observed in both disorders. Symptoms are similar in both disorders and the degree of temporal lobe abnormality is commonly associated with severity of symptoms (e.g., odd speech; Rosell, Futterman, McMaster, & Siever, 2014). In other words, combining multiple sources of information seems to support the idea of a schizophrenia spectrum in which the temporal lobe is critically involved. Even better evidence for the role of the temporal lobe in schizophrenia-spectrum symptoms could be garnered from studies that compare SPD and schizophrenia with other severe disorders (e.g., bipolar disorder, borderline personality disorder). Studies comparing severe disorders could rule out the possibility that severity of mental health diagnosis is driving the results (some studies already show differences between schizophrenia and bipolar disorder; e.g., Calhoun et al., 2008).

A network of results based in genetics, brain structure, and phenomenology provides clinically relevant information about diagnosis and prognosis. These results indicate that though a categorical boundary between SPD and schizophrenia may be useful for communicating severity, these are disorders that may be differentiated only by degrees of severity. In addition, as a starting point, these results suggest that the pharmacological and psychosocial interventions that are effective for treating other schizophrenia-spectrum disorders may be relevant for SPD. This is particularly important because there are is little research on treatment for SPD (Rosell et al., 2014).

NETWORK APPROACHES TO FUNCTIONAL NEUROIMAGING

Up until the past decade, studies of functional brain activation tended to focus on differences in neural activation for specific brain regions. Recently, as Chan et al. (this volume) note, researchers have emphasized neural networks over regions (Bressler & Menon, 2010; Bullmore, Bullmore, Sporns, & Sporns, 2009). Research suggests the idea that a brain region performs a specific cognitive function in isolation is untenable. Rather, the brain is organized into distinct but interacting networks (Sporns, 2012). A single region may support different aspects of cognition or emotion depending on the network with which it is coactive. Ideally, such a shift in perspective and analysis could aid in the ongoing problem of interpreting functional brain activation. Activation of the amygdala may be related to any of the multitude of psychological functions the amygdala has been found to participate in. At the same time, if evidence generated from neural connectivity models indicates that amygdala activation co-occurs with that of the anterior insula, dorsal anterior cingulate, ventral striatum, and medial temporal lobe (e.g., hippocampus), this coactivation constrains our interpretation somewhat. These regions are part of the salience network (Menon, 2015), a neural network that filters and amplifies stimuli that has biological or learned value. Thus, amygdala activation in this instance might plausibly be interpreted as contributing to this process.

As indicated by Chan et al. (this volume), most fMRI studies of PDs have used a regional approach; yet, studies that did not necessarily focus on neural networks, or use a connectivity-based approach, have provided results highly suggestive of the activation of a neural network. The evidence is imperfect, but the combination of regional activations, task, and design can decrease the ambiguity of our interpretations. Again, the integration of multiple sources of data is helpful for this goal. For instance, Silbersweig and colleagues (Silbersweig et al., 2007) found that individuals diagnosed with BPD evidenced less activation in the ventromedial PFC (vmPFC) and increased activation in the limbic and reward systems when trying to inhibit behavior, particularly in the presence of negative emotional stimuli. The vmPFC and its connections to limbic and reward systems supports social and emotional behavior. Other studies have found this circuit is central to tasks in which participants need to inhibit a proponent response in the face of emotional stimuli (e.g., Kanske & Kotz, 2011). Among non-clinical participants, inhibiting such responses appears to be due to increased connectivity between the vmPFC and amygdala and down-regulation of amygdala activity. Individuals diagnosed with BPD appear to struggle with this process, made clear because the researchers used a performance-based task in which the people with BPD do not perform as well. Mixing these behavioral results with the neuroimaging data, the Silbersweig study suggests that negative emotion is detrimental to response inhibition because individuals with

BPD fail to regulate limbic and reward systems in the face of emotional stimuli. Again, this finding could be used to inform treatment. The context that is provided both by the activation of a relevant neural network, along with the context provided by well-designed performance-based tasks, aids in the interpretation of these findings and increases their clinical relevance.

NEW NOSOLOGY, NEW NEUROSCIENCE?

The diagnostic definition of personality disorders is also currently undergoing revision (Bender, Morey, & Skodol, 2011). The promise of any new diagnostic system is greater diagnostic clarity that can aid in clinical relevance. Researchers have often pointed to the limitations of our classification models as a major impediment to translating advances in neuroscience to the clinical realm. There is currently extensive empirical work being done to develop a nosology of personality disorders (and mental health disorders, generally) that do not have the same problems of within-diagnosis heterogeneity, comorbidity across disorders, low reliability and artificial categorical structure of the current system (Hopwood et al., 2011; Insel et al., 2010; Kotov et al., 2017). The promise of such efforts is that we may have better ability to understand the neural mechanisms of symptoms that are present in multiple disorders in the current system (e.g., impulsivity), but are not always present within two people with the same disorder.

Chan et al. (this volume) focus their chapter on categorical diagnosis, likely because the field has yet to shift in a substantial way towards a more dimensional approach to personality disorders. At the same time, perhaps we should begin to envision what neuroscience research might look with a more dimensional approach to PDs. This could include questioning how a dimensional view affects interpretability of results to focus on transdiagnostic symptoms and the neural circuits from which these symptoms manifest, as suggested by the Research Domain Criteria (RDoC; Insel et al., 2010) approach promoted by NIMH. Moreover, this raises important questions about how a review of relevant research regarding symptom domains and brain circuits from an RDoC point of view might provide different understanding of more basic phenomena and/or clinical implications compared to that provided from a categorical perspective.

The alternative DSM-5 model for personality disorders is also an effort to move to a more dimensional diagnostic approach. The alternative model prescribes a dimensional assessment of self (identity and self-direction) and interpersonal disturbance (empathy and intimacy), followed by evaluation of pathological personality traits (negative affectivity, detachment, antagonism, disinhibition, and psychoticism). Afterward, a categorical diagnosis is determined (antisocial, avoidant, borderline, narcissistic, obsessive-compulsive, schizotypal, or personality

disorder-trait specified). This model combines a determination of severity of dysfunction (self and interpersonal dysfunction) with assessment of extreme elevations on the five-factor model of personality. Each of these constructs and diagnoses has at least a small body of neuroscience literature. It is important to evaluate whether our current literature suggests such an approach will bring greater clarity and clinical utility to our structural and functional neuroscience of PDs. At the same time, there seems to be an opportunity to consider how the existing neuroscience of PDs can inform this model.

CONCLUSION

The field of clinical neuroscience continues to advance in ways that may yield exciting new understanding of the character of personality disorders and effective approaches to treatment. Statisticians are rapidly developing new methods and tools for conducting connectivity analyses (e.g., Gates, Molenaar, Hillary, & Slobounov, 2011; Wang, Zuo, & He, 2010). Some researchers are using longitudinal designs to map neural and symptom changes over time, while others are identifying neural changes following successful psychotherapy. At the same time, these and other advances offer the possibility of improved interpretability of our findings, which generally translates into increased clinical relevance. We may not win over my skeptical professor, but we increase the possibility he may find something in the neuroscience literature that is directly applicable to his psychotherapy practice.

REFERENCES

Bender, D. S., Morey, L. C., & Skodol, A. E. (2011). Toward a model for assessing level of personality functioning in DSM-5, part I: A review of theory and methods. *Journal of Personality Assessment*, 93(4), 332–346.

Bressler, S. L., & Menon, V. (2010). Large-scale brain networks in cognition: Emerging methods and principles. *Trends in Cognitive Sciences*, 14(6), 277–290.

Bullmore, E., Bullmore, E., Sporns, O., & Sporns, O. (2009). Complex brain networks: Graph theoretical analysis of structural and functional systems. *Nature Reviews Neuroscience*, 10 (3), 186–198.

Calhoun, V. D., Maciejewski, P. K., Pearlson, G. D., & Kiehl, K. A. (2008). Temporal lobe and "default" hemodynamic brain modes discriminate between schizophrenia and bipolar disorder. *Human Brain Mapping*, 29(11), 1265–1275.

Gates, K. M., Molenaar, P. C. M., Hillary, F. G., & Slobounov, S. (2011). Extended unified SEM approach for modeling event-related fMRI data. *NeuroImage*, 54(2), 1151–1158.

Holtmaat, A., & Svoboda, K. (2009). Experience-dependent structural synaptic plasticity in the mammalian brain. *Nature Reviews Neuroscience*, 10(9), 647–658.

Hopwood, C. J., Malone, J. C., Ansell, E. B., Sanislow, C. A., Grilo, C. M., McGlashan, T. H., ... Morey, L. C. (2011). Personality assessment in DSM-5: Empirical support for rating severity, style, and traits. *Journal of Personality Disorders*, *25*(3), 305–320.

Houston, I., Peter, C. J., Mitchell, A., Straubhaar, J., Rogaev, E., & Akbarian, S. (2013). Epigenetics in the human brain. *Neuropsychopharmacology*, *38*(1), 183–197.

Insel, T., Cuthbert, B., Garvey, M., Heinssen, R., Pine, D. S., Quinn, K., ... Wang, P. (2010). Research Domain Criteria (RDoC): Toward a new classification framework for research on mental disorders. *American Journal of Psychiatry*, *167*(7), 748–751.

Kanske, P., & Kotz, S. A. (2011). Conflict processing is modulated by positive emotion: ERP data from a flanker task. *Behavioural Brain Research*, *219*(2), 382–386.

Kobel, M., Bechtel, N., Specht, K., Klarhöfer, M., Weber, P., Scheffler, K., ... Penner, I. K. (2010). Structural and functional imaging approaches in attention deficit/hyperactivity disorder: Does the temporal lobe play a key role? *Psychiatry Research: Neuroimaging*, *183*(3), 230–236.

Kotov, R., Krueger, R. F., Watson, D., Achenbach, T. M., Althoff, R. R., Bagby, R. M., ... Zimmerman, M. (2017). The Hierarchical Taxonomy of Psychopathology (HiTOP): A dimensional alternative to traditional nosologies. *Journal of Abnormal Psychology*, *126*(4), 454–477.

Lombardo, M. V., Chakrabarti, B., Bullmore, E. T., Sadek, S. A., Pasco, G., Wheelwright, S. J., ... Baron-Cohen, S. (2010). Atypical neural self-representation in autism. *Brain*, *133*, 611–624.

Menon, V. (2015). Salience network. In A. Toga (ed.), *Brain Mapping: An Encyclopedic Reference* (Vol. 2, pp. 597–611). New York: Academic Press.

Rosell, D. R., Futterman, S. E., McMaster, A., & Siever, L. J. (2014). Schizotypal personality disorder: A current review. *Current Psychiatry Reports*, 16: 452.

Silbersweig, D., Clarkin, J. F., Goldstein, M., Kernberg, O. F., Tuescher, O., Levy, K. N., ... Stern, E. (2007). Failure of fronto-limbic inhibitory function in the context of negative emotion in borderline personality disorder. *American Journal of Psychiatry*, *164*(12), 1832–1841.

Sporns, O. (2012). From simple graphs to the connectome: networks in neuroimaging. *NeuroImage*, *62*(2), 881–886.

Uttal, W. R. (2002). Précis of the new phrenology: The limits of localizing cognitive processes in the brain. *Brain and Mind*, 3 (2), 221–228.

Wang, J., Zuo, X., & He, Y. (2010). Graph-based network analysis of resting-state functional MRI. *Frontiers in Systems Neuroscience*, *4*, 16.

1b Methodological Advancements Needed in Neuroimaging Research on Personality Disorders: Commentary on Neuroimaging in Personality Disorders

SHOU-AN ARIEL CHANG AND ARIELLE BASKIN-SOMMERS

Personality disorders (PDs) are among the costliest psychiatric conditions (Lenzenweger, Lane, Loranger, & Kessler, 2007; Soeteman, Roijen, Verheul, & Busschbach, 2008). They are chronic and pervasive conditions that have a severe personal, social, and financial impact. As Chan and colleagues (this volume) outline in "Neuroimaging in Personality Disorders," the use of neuroimaging seeks to pinpoint mechanisms underlying several forms of PDs (e.g., schizotypal personality disorder [SPD], borderline personality disorder [BPD], and antisocial personality disorder [ASPD]). Neuroimaging methods, such as magnetic resonance imaging (MRI) or diffusor tensor imaging, identify structural and functional abnormalities associated with these PDs. Some neural abnormalities appear common across disorders, and others appear unique to each disorder.

Substantial progress has been made in characterizing neural abnormalities related to PDs through the use of neuroimaging methods. The chapter from Chan et al. (this volume) on "Neuroimaging in Personality Disorders" nicely lays out the current empirical foundation of neuroimaging in PDs. While not an explicit focus in their chapter, their review does unearth two issues plaguing neuroimaging research on PDs. First, in the studies covered in their review, most rely on a region of interest (ROI) approach that is limited in several important ways. Second, the tasks used in many of the studies covered in their review are too broad to specify a precise mechanism. Together, these two issues limit progress in understanding the variety of potential neural mechanisms that underlie PDs and the ability to link those mechanisms to pathological behavior. To unlock the full potential of neuroimaging methods to increase our clinical understanding of PDs, researchers must implement more advanced methods and use precise tasks that contextualize the behavior of those affected by PDs. Thus, the goal of this commentary is to provide a deeper dive into each of these limitations touched on less explicitly by Chan et al. (this volume), building towards suggestions for how to advance the neuroscience of PDs.

The continued reliance on a region of interest (ROI) approach (i.e., extracting signals from pre-specified regions; Poldrack, 2007) is a significant issue that limits our identification of broader dysfunctions that may cut across regions or the interplay between regions that yield complex behavioral dysfunctions. There are advantages to using an ROI approach, such as statistical control, theory testing, and functional exploration (Poldrack, 2007); however, a key criticism of the ROI approach is that many tasks evoke activation beyond ROIs, making it difficult to interpret the functional specificity of any particular ROI (Friston, Rotshtein, Geng, Sterzer, & Henson, 2006).

The limitations of the ROI approach for research on PDs is highlighted in a recent study cited in Chan et al. (this volume) by Holtmann and colleagues (2013). In this study, BPD patients and healthy controls (HC) completed a modified Eriksen Flanker during which task-irrelevant neutral and fearful faces were presented. Holtmann et al. (2013) identified several *a priori* ROIs, including the amygdala and dorsal anterior cingulate cortex, to compare between BPD patients and HC. Examination of a key contrast, fear versus neutral faces, revealed that the only ROI differentiating BPD patients and HC was the dorsal anterior cingulate.

First, in terms of *a priori* ROIs, one could question the inconsistency between this study and several other studies noting amygdala activation abnormalities in BPD patients versus HC (van Zutphen, Siep, Jacob, Goebel, & Arntz, 2015). However, the validity of ROIs is dependent on their context-sensitivity, making task demands an important factor to consider when identifying ROIs. Studies showing amygdala activation differences between BPD patients and HC often are in the context of direct viewing of emotional content, and not when this content is used as an irrelevant distractor, as was done in the Holtmann et al. (2013) study. Therefore, identification of ROIs must be based on context in order to appropriately constrain interpretation of the presence or absence of any effect.

Second, several regions, including the precuneus, distinguished BPD patients versus HC (see Holtmann et al., 2013, table 8 for full list). The precuneus has been implicated in self-related mental representations (Cavanna & Trimble, 2006). Combined with the dorsal anterior cingulate finding, it is possible that compared to HC, BPD patients recruit more neural resources to engage in self-referential evaluative processing of emotion content, regardless of task relevance, and that dorsal anterior cingulate hyperactivation is not simply a reflection of enhanced "executive functions" used to "compensate" for the processing of emotion content. Consideration of patterns of activation beyond ROIs is essential in order to accurately capture and interpret the complexity of neural abnormalities as they relate to PDs. To be clear, an ROI approach is not inherently problematic. However, clear interpretation of the patterns of ROI activation and their meaning is very difficult, especially when tasks are used that fail to discriminate mechanisms.

Beyond issues specific to ROI, neuroimaging studies in PDs also are hindered by the fact that many rely on tasks that measure functions broadly, and lack the necessary precision needed to identify a specific mechanism. Often tasks such as viewing emotional images or Go/No-Go are used to assess emotional and executive function, respectively, in research on PDs. These tasks engage broad processes, but tend to lack the specificity in design (e.g., condition manipulations) to identify the exact mechanisms underlying dysfunction. For example, face processing studies involve recording brain activity while participants evaluate faces on a particular dimension (e.g., emotional expression, gender, trustworthiness). Many mechanisms underlie face processing, including attending to the image, integrating visual information, and potentially selecting or inhibiting a response to the face (Jehna et al., 2011). Therefore, dysfunction in face processing could be due to narrowed attention to a specific part of the face (e.g., only looking at the mouth), an inability to process the face as a whole (e.g., difficulty integrating parts of the face), and/or overarousal, amongst other possibilities.

In fact, SPD, BPD, and ASPD all are associated with difficulty in face processing tasks, particularly when it comes to evaluating emotional expressions (SPD; Dickey et al., 2011; ASPD; Dolan & Fullam, 2006; BPD; Domes et al., 2008; Schönenberg & Jusyte, 2014). However, the reason(s) why individuals with these disorders show difficulty on this type of task is likely different. By using broad face processing tasks, we are left in the dark about the cause of the difficulties in these tasks and are falling into the trap of conflating behavior (e.g., face processing dysfunction) with mechanism (i.e., the cause of the dysfunction). As an example of an approach that attempts to narrow down the mechanism underlying face processing dysfunction, an emotion recognition task could include a condition with uninstructed viewing of faces and a condition with an explicit attentional cueing to the eyes to see if the resulting difference in emotion recognition accuracy or brain activity is due to atypical attention rather than emotion processing more broadly. Disambiguating mechanism from behavior is not only important for

understanding mechanisms within a specific personality disorder, but also for distinguishing among PDs. Phenotypically, many PDs share overlapping symptomology (e.g., interpersonal difficulties); and, in order to understand what is driving this symptomology within and across PDs, more precise tasks are needed.

Related to the issues of relying on ROIs and using broad tasks in the study of PDs, several methodological advancements are needed to further the state of research on PDs. First, researchers should combine neuroimaging with other measures, such as genetic data or behavioral measures, in order to create a profile or "fingerprint" of different PDs (Brazil, van Dongen, Maes, Mars, & Baskin-Sommers, 2018). For example, Chan et al. (this volume) outline a wealth of research evidencing abnormalities in structural, functional, and resting state brain activity in PDs. These measures could be combined with genetic and/or behavioral (e.g., task performance, neuropsychological assessments, real-world indicators) data in order to identify latent profiles classifying individuals based on common and unique associations among these variables (Uludağ & Roebroeck, 2014; Wolfers, Buitelaar, Beckmann, Franke, & Marquand, 2015; see Chan et al.'s BPD imaging-genetics example). This "fingerprinting" approach even could leverage the ROI approach by combining these region activations with other measures to better contextualize our understanding of the contribution of this activation. Building a profile of biological and behavioral dimensions and their interrelationships could prove to be especially fruitful in distinguishing PDs, as it is unlikely that one specific mechanism underlies each distinct personality disorder.

Second, researchers could implement more advanced methods, such as computational modeling and newer imaging methods to further clarify the mechanisms driving symptomology in PDs. Computational psychiatry aims to break down cognitive functions, such as attention or action selection into smaller cognitive operations. This approach necessitates the implementation of more precise tasks for the study of neural function in PDs. For instance, Behrens, Hunt, Woolrich, and Rushworth (2008) leverage models of reinforcement learning to show that individuals learn about reward probability from a social informant in the same manner as when learning from personal experience. When combined with functional MRI data, they show that distinct anatomical structures are involved in encoding learning from a social informant versus learning from personal experience. Of note, SPD, BPD, and ASPD all are associated with atypical reinforcement learning (BPD; Bornovalova, Lejuez, Daughters, Zachary Rosenthal, & Lynch, 2005; ASPD; Glenn & Yang, 2012; Gregory et al., 2015; Schuermann, Kathmann, Stiglmayr, Renneberg, & Endrass, 2011; SPD; Waltz, Frank, Robinson, & Gold, 2007). If applied to individuals with PDs, this method would allow for greater precision in relating neural abnormalities to behavior by delineating whether a deficit in reinforcement learning is broad or whether the deficit in reinforcement learning is specific to a particular domain (e.g., social, reward, punishment).

Another example of more advanced methods that could help refine our understanding of neural function in PDs is the use of graph theory. Broadly, graph theory moves beyond traditional connectivity analyses, which measure the association between two regions, to estimate how well and in what manner neural regions communicate with one another (Bullmore & Sporns, 2009). As noted by Chan et al. (this volume), all PDs show abnormal structural and functional connectivity. For example, in both SPD and BPD there are alternations in default mode network connectivity and in ASPD disruptions in fronto-parietal control network connectivity is evident. Graph theory could be advantageous for studying PDs, as it moves past quantifying the ability of regions to communicate and specifies the quality of that communication by estimating the amount of time or energy required to transfer information from one part of the network to any other part of the network. The application of graph theory in future research might be useful for clarifying in what ways information processing is disrupted in PDs.

SUMMARY

The chapter by Chan et al. (this volume) provides a thorough review of the current state of neuroimaging research in PDs, and a base from which researchers can build to design precise tasks isolating underlying mechanisms of dysfunction, combine methods to create "fingerprints" of PDs, and apply more advanced neuroimaging methods and analyses to identify distinct and overlapping mechanisms underlying PDs symptomology. It is essential that researchers strive to link neural mechanisms to behavior in order to inform precision in assessment and the development of targeted treatments.

REFERENCES

Behrens, T. E., Hunt, L. T., Woolrich, M. W., & Rushworth, M. F. (2008). Associative learning of social value. *Nature*, *456*(7219), 245–249.

Bornovalova, M. A., Lejuez, C. W., Daughters, S. B., Zachary Rosenthal, M., & Lynch, T. R. (2005). Impulsivity as a common process across borderline personality and substance use disorders. *Clinical Psychology Review*, *25*(6), 790–812.

Brazil, I. A., van Dongen, J. D. M., Maes, J. H. R., Mars, R. B., & Baskin-Sommers, A. R. (2018). Classification and treatment of antisocial individuals: From behavior to biocognition. *Neuroscience & Biobehavioral Reviews*, *91*, 259–277.

Bullmore, E., & Sporns, O. (2009). Complex brain networks: Graph theoretical analysis of structural and functional systems. *Nature Reviews Neuroscience*, *10*(3), 186–198.

Cavanna, A. E., & Trimble, M. R. (2006). The precuneus: A review of its functional anatomy and behavioural correlates. *Brain*, *129* (3), 564–583.

Dickey, C. C., Panych, L. P., Voglmaier, M. M., Niznikiewicz, M. A., Terry, D. P., Murphy, C., ... McCarley, R. W. (2011). Facial emotion recognition and facial affect display in schizotypal personality disorder. *Schizophrenia Research*, *131*(1), 242–249.

Dolan, M., & Fullam, R. (2006). Face affect recognition deficits in personality-disordered offenders: Association with psychopathy. *Psychological Medicine*, *36*(11), 1563–1569.

Domes, G., Czieschnek, D., Weidler, F., Berger, C., Fast, K., & Herpertz, S. C. (2008). Recognition of facial affect in borderline personality disorder. *Journal of Personality Disorders*, *22*(2), 135–147.

Friston, K. J., Rotshtein, P., Geng, J. J., Sterzer, P., & Henson, R. N. (2006). A critique of functional localisers. *NeuroImage*, *30*(4), 1077–1087.

Glenn, A. L., & Yang, Y. (2012). The potential role of the striatum in antisocial behavior and psychopathy. *Biological Psychiatry*, *72*(10), 817–822.

Gregory, S., Blair, R. J., ffytche, D., Simmons, A., Kumari, V., Hodgins, S., & Blackwood, N. (2015). Punishment and psychopathy: A case-control functional MRI investigation of reinforcement learning in violent antisocial personality disordered men. *The Lancet Psychiatry*, *2*(2), 153–160.

Holtmann, J., Herbort, M. C., Wustenberg, T., Soch, J., Richter, S., Walter, H., ... Schott, B. H. (2013). Trait anxiety modulates fronto-limbic processing of emotional interference in borderline personality disorder. *Frontiers in Human Neuroscience*, *7*, 54.

Jehna, M., Neuper, C., Ischebeck, A., Loitfelder, M., Ropele, S., Langkammer, C., ... Enzinger, C. (2011). The functional correlates of face perception and recognition of emotional facial expressions as evidenced by fMRI. *Brain Research*, *1393*, 73–83.

Lenzenweger, M. F., Lane, M. C., Loranger, A. W., & Kessler, R. C. (2007). DSM-IV personality disorders in the National Comorbidity Survey Replication. *Biological Psychiatry*, *62*(6), 553–564.

Poldrack, R. A. (2007). Region of interest analysis for fMRI. *Social Cognitive and Affective Neuroscience*, *2*(1), 67–70.

Schönenberg, M., & Jusyte, A. (2014). Investigation of the hostile attribution bias toward ambiguous facial cues in antisocial violent offenders. *European Archives of Psychiatry and Clinical Neuroscience*, *264*(1), 61–69.

Schuermann, B., Kathmann, N., Stiglmayr, C., Renneberg, B., & Endrass, T. (2011). Impaired decision making and feedback evaluation in borderline personality disorder. *Psychological Medicine*, *41*(9), 1917–1927.

Soeteman, D. I., Roijen, L. H.-v., Verheul, R., & Busschbach, J. J. (2008). The economic burden of personality disorders in mental health care. *Journal of Clinical Psychiatry*, *69*(2), 259–265.

Uludağ, K., & Roebroeck, A. (2014). General overview on the merits of multimodal neuroimaging data fusion. *NeuroImage*, *102*, 3–10.

van Zutphen, L., Siep, N., Jacob, G. A., Goebel, R., & Arntz, A. (2015). Emotional sensitivity, emotion regulation and impulsivity in borderline personality disorder: A critical review of fMRI studies. *Neuroscience & Biobehavioral Reviews*, *51*, 64–76.

Waltz, J. A., Frank, M. J., Robinson, B. M., & Gold, J. M. (2007). Selective reinforcement learning deficits in schizophrenia support predictions from computational models of striatal-cortical dysfunction. *Biological Psychiatry*, *62*(7), 756–764.

Wolfers, T., Buitelaar, J. K., Beckmann, C. F., Franke, B., & Marquand, A. F. (2015). From estimating activation locality to predicting disorder: A review of pattern recognition for neuroimaging-based psychiatric diagnostics. *Neuroscience & Biobehavioral Reviews*, *57*, 328–349.

1c Illustrating the Value of Neuroimaging Studies Using the Example of Affect Regulation: Author Rejoinder to Commentaries on Neuroimaging in Personality Disorders

CHI C. CHAN, DANIEL H. VACCARO, NINA L. J. ROSE, LAURA E. KESSLER, AND ERIN A. HAZLETT

Commentaries from Chang and Baskin-Sommers (this volume) as well as Beeney (this volume) cogently highlight limitations of current methods in neuroimaging research on personality disorders and suggest approaches that would further specify neural mechanisms and increase clinical relevance. Both commentaries noted the need to incorporate multiple sources of evidence from neuroimaging, genetics, and behavioral data and the need to examine patterns of brain activation in addition to individual regions of interest (ROIs). Here, we use examples from the study of affect regulation to illustrate how these methods combined with a transdiagnostic approach could advance neurobiological understanding of personality pathology.

A large body of research implicates serotonin in affect regulation (Hariri & Holmes, 2006), and a common polymorphism in the serotonin transporter gene (5-HTTLPR) has downstream effects that modulate serotoninergic activity at the synapse. However, studies and meta-analyses have reported conflicting findings on whether the 5-HTTLPR short allelic variant is associated with affect regulation traits such as neuroticism or harm avoidance (Munafò, Clark, & Flint, 2005; Sen, Burmeister, & Ghosh, 2004), or whether there is any significant genetic effect at all on either trait (Munafò et al., 2009). One challenge is the difficulty in detecting the modest effect of a single common polymorphism on a highly complex phenotype.

Neuroimaging data can serve as an endophenotype to bridge the gap between genes and behavior, as endophenotypes are thought to be more closely related to genotype than distant behavioral phenotype. The 5-HTTLPR polymorphism may account for up to 10 percent of the variance in responsivity of the amygdala, a brain region highly involved in emotion processing (Munafò, Brown, & Hariri, 2008), but a more recent meta-analysis revealed no such effect (Bastiaansen et al., 2014). Going beyond individual ROIs and examining brain connectivity patterns provide important insight into potential mechanisms. Studies report that 5-HTTLPR short allele variant carriers have reduced amygdala–anterior cingulate cortex coupling (Pezawas et al., 2005), increased amygdala–insula coupling (Klucken et al., 2015), and increased amygdala–prefrontal cortex coupling (Madsen et al., 2016). Importantly, while structure and function of individual regions were unrelated to self-reported harm avoidance, amygdala–anterior cingulate cortex *functional connectivity* accounted for about 30 percent of the variance in the trait (Pezawas et al., 2005). Additionally, increased neuroticism was associated with decreased functional connectivity of the amygdala with other brain regions (Madsen et al., 2016).

Applying these methods to the study of emotion regulation in personality disorders requires further consideration of within-disorder heterogeneity and cross-disorder overlap. For example, 5-HTTLPR appears related to the number of BPD symptoms (Hankin et al., 2011) and individual affective symptoms (Maurex, Zaboli, Ohman, Asberg, & Leopardi, 2010), but not the diagnosis of borderline personality disorder as a whole (BPD; Calati, Gressier, Balestri, & Serretti, 2013). On the other hand, neurobiological studies on affective instability across clinical disorders including BPD converge on the role of the amygdala and its functional connectivity with other brain regions (Broome, He, Iftikhar, Eyden, & Marwaha, 2015).

Research on the neurobiology of affect regulation demonstrates the utility of combining multiple units of analysis with a dimensional approach, consistent with the Research Domain Criteria framework as suggested by Beeney. Together with neural network analyses that appreciate the complexity of the brain, these methods hold promise for illuminating the neurobiology of personality pathology. The alternative DSM-5 model for personality disorders can guide investigation of clinically relevant constructs that directly inform treatment development.

REFERENCES

Bastiaansen, J. A., Servaas, M. N., Marsman, J. B. C., Ormel, J., Nolte, I. M., Riese, H., & Aleman, A. (2014). Filling the gap: Relationship between the serotonin-transporter-linked polymorphic region and amygdala activation. *Psychological Science*, *25*(11), 2058–2066.

Broome, M. R., He, Z., Iftikhar, M., Eyden, J., & Marwaha, S. (2015). Neurobiological and behavioural studies of affective instability in clinical populations: A systematic review. *Neuroscience & Biobehavioral Reviews*, *51*, 243–254.

Calati, R., Gressier, F., Balestri, M., & Serretti, A. (2013). Genetic modulation of borderline personality disorder: Systematic review and meta-analysis. *Journal of Psychiatric Research*, *47* (10), 1275–1287.

Hankin, B. L., Barrocas, A. L., Jenness, J., Oppenheimer, C. W., Badanes, L. S., Abela, J. R. Z., . . . Smolen, A. (2011). Association between 5-HTTLPR and borderline personality disorder traits among youth. *Frontiers in Psychiatry*, *2*, 6.

Hariri, A. R., & Holmes, A. (2006). Genetics of emotional regulation: The role of the serotonin transporter in neural function. *Trends in Cognitive Sciences*, *10*(4), 182–191.

Klucken, T., Schweckendiek, J., Blecker, C., Walter, B., Kuepper, Y., Hennig, J., & Stark, R. (2015). The association between the 5-HTTLPR and neural correlates of fear conditioning and connectivity. *Social Cognitive and Affective Neuroscience*, *10*(5), 700–707.

Madsen, M. K., McMahon, B., Andersen, S. B., Siebner, H. R., Knudsen, G. M., & Fisher, P. M. (2016). Threat-related amygdala functional connectivity is associated with 5-HTTLPR genotype and neuroticism. *Social Cognitive and Affective Neuroscience*, *11*(1), 140–149.

Maurex, L., Zaboli, G., Ohman, A., Asberg, M., & Leopardi, R. (2010). The serotonin transporter gene polymorphism (5-HTTLPR) and affective symptoms among women diagnosed with borderline personality disorder. *European Psychiatry: The Journal of the Association of European Psychiatrists*, *25*(1), 19–25.

Munafò, M. R., Brown, S. M., & Hariri, A. R. (2008). Serotonin transporter (5-HTTLPR) genotype and amygdala activation: A meta-analysis. *Biological Psychiatry*, *63*(9), 852–857.

Munafò, M. R., Clark, T., & Flint, J. (2005). Does measurement instrument moderate the association between the serotonin transporter gene and anxiety-related personality traits? A meta-analysis. *Molecular Psychiatry*, *10*(4), 415–419.

Munafò, M. R., Freimer, N. B., Ng, W., Ophoff, R., Veijola, J., Miettunen, J., . . . Flint, J. (2009). 5-HTTLPR genotype and anxiety-related personality traits: A meta-analysis and new data. *American Journal of Medical Genetics Part B: Neuropsychiatric Genetics*, *150B*(2), 271–281.

Pezawas, L., Meyer-Lindenberg, A., Drabant, E. M., Verchinski, B. A., Munoz, K. E., Kolachana, B. S., . . . Weinberger, D. R. (2005). 5-HTTLPR polymorphism impacts human cingulate-amygdala interactions: A genetic susceptibility mechanism for depression. *Nature Neuroscience*, *8*(6), 828–834.

Sen, S., Burmeister, M., & Ghosh, D. (2004). Meta-analysis of the association between a serotonin transporter promoter polymorphism (5-HTTLPR) and anxiety-related personality traits. *American Journal of Medical Genetics Part B: Neuropsychiatric Genetics*, *127B*(1), 85–89.

2 Issues and New Directions in Personality Disorder Genetics

KERRY L. JANG AND FIONA CHOI

Where do the personality disorders come from? Are they passed down from parent to child or are they shaped by exposures to formative events, such as a dysfunctional relationship with one's mother or a bump on the head? The role of nature and nurture on the development of personality and its disorders has been central in the field since personality types were first described (Torgersen, 2009). The history of the genetics of personality is very much the history of psychiatric genetics in general, so much so that triumphs and failures searching for the etiology of schizophrenia or bipolar disorder, are little different from the triumphs and failures searching for the etiology of personality disorder. Indeed, in the context of any history of psychiatric genetics, one can simply exchange the name of the disorder with another and the history is little different.

This state of affairs is perplexing given that several major psychiatric disorders from schizophrenia to autism and the major traits of personality and personality disorder types are among the most heritable of genetically complex medical illnesses. Indeed, one of the most replicable findings in psychiatric genetics are from studies comparing identical to fraternal twin similarities on personality disorders and traits showing that heritable factors account for half of the observed differences. However, 30 years of psychiatric genetics research demonstrate that high heritability does not necessarily facilitate identifying specific genetic causes and to date the history of psychiatric genetics is largely a story of non-replicated discoveries and unrealized expectations.

Why hasn't high heritability made it easier to find the putative genes? One possible explanation is the "bandwagon effect." Personality and personality disorder researchers have been quick to adopt the latest advances in genetics methodology, be they twin and adoption studies to estimate heritability, linkage and association studies looking for single gene effects, or now using high throughput single nucleotide pair (SNP) analyses to identify a multitude of genes. Indeed, it would seem that the failure to identify putative genes was very much attributed to the gene finding technique or concepts of gene function

rather than the result of overlooking fundamental issues in personality disorder research that are likely behind the inability to identify specific genes. For example, how personality function is measured, either as a typology (e.g., diagnostic category as found in the DSM or ICD systems) or a continuum (e.g., dimensional model embodied in personality trait models), and any imprecision introduced by the chosen personality measure will affect the ability of any genetic association to be found. Current measurement issues and their effect on the hunt for genes has become a bit of a hackneyed subject with some of the key issues being discussed a decade ago and continuing to this day (e.g., Cloninger, 2012; Jang & Vernon, 2018; Livesley, 2008; Reichborn-Kjennerud, 2008).

Indeed, the measurement issue is so alive that the new DSM-5 has attempted to integrate the categorical and dimensional models into a functional hybrid that capitalizes on the strengths of each approach by using the strengths of one approach to mitigate the weakness of the other. Only time will tell if this has been successful. More immediately, with the creation of this hybrid model does this mean that genetics research must stop and retool to use this system, or wait until the validity and functionality of the new system is understood? Quite simply, the answer is "no." It's not just a simple question of measurement and waiting for the best available measure. Rather, genetics research can continue but to progress will require a rephrasing of the fundamental questions of what the purpose of genetics research is and where it is best applied. The purpose of the present chapter is to explore this "rephrasing" and to begin by revisiting the *raison d'être* of genetics research.

WHAT IS THE PURPOSE OF GENETICS RESEARCH?

The primary purpose of genetics research has been to identify putative gene(s) underlying a somewhat vaguely defined group of symptoms. That is a very narrow focus and quite to the contrary, genetics research has a role beyond gene hunting. For example, genetics can help refine how we measure and define personality disorder concepts regarding diagnoses or measurement. For example, determining which personality behaviors are *pleiotrophic* – that is, influenced by the same or different genetic influences – is useful to refine which behaviors are actually central to a diagnostic category or trait structure. Similarly, determining which personality disorder concepts and other mental illnesses are influenced by a common genetic basis highlights the interrelationships between personality and other conditions such as schizophrenia, and helps us understand why something such as schizotypal personality disorder exists and how it is related to schizophrenia. Perhaps the role of genetic research has nothing to do with genes at all, but rather its most useful function is to highlight the role of the environment, such as the influence of learning, observation, and the impact of environmental conditions that impinge on and shape behavior.

Broadening the fundamental research question also brings to light issues that need to be considered as part of this research, and this chapter discusses four encumbrances that we believe impact the advancement of genetic research on the personality disorders. The focus of the research question will shift as each is discussed. The four encumbrances are (1) the development of grand theories of personality, (2) issues of measurement that continue to beset the field, (3) limitations of genetics research, and (4) the obsession with genetics as a whole. We do not think that dealing with these interrelated issues warrants a wholesale revolution, but rather a shift in perspective that takes the best of the thinking and research extant while opening new avenues of investigation that *bypasses* the worst of it.

The Problem of Grand Theories

Gordon Allport (1937, p. 48) wrote, "personality is something and personality does something . . ." that outlined the central task for personality psychologists. Hence personality psychologists have attempted to fulfill his famous dictum by developing an empirically based unified model of personality that integrated all the rich ideas of psychoanalytic theorizing without the introspective methods. The eventual approach adopted was the *lexical model* that essentially took every word in the English dictionary that describes personality, had people rate themselves and others on these words using a Likert-type scale, and subjected the ratings to factor analysis. Factor analysis of the inter-correlations between these ratings extracted the common variance that defined basic traits, such as neuroticism or extraversion that are considered to exist in every individual, and individual differences were accounted for by the extent to which a person exhibited each of the traits.

However, debate soon ensued over the correct number of traits such as the famous debate over the "Big Five" – Neuroticism, Extraversion, Openness to Experience, Agreeableness, or Conscientiousness (Goldberg, 1990; McCrae & John, 1992) or the "Gigantic Three" – Neuroticism, Extraversion, and Psychoticism (Eysenck, 1994). The debate between the Big Five and Gigantic Three was eventually reconciled when both were shown to be compatible and the models just represented different levels of analysis (Draycott & Kline, 1995). This spurred debate over the existence of a general factor for personality, akin to Spearman's general intelligence factor, g, extracted from cognitive ability data. Whether or not there is a general factor or only independent personality factors was really an artifact of factor analysis methods used to analyze the data, such as allowing factors to become inter-correlated (oblique versus orthogonal rotations) or factor extraction techniques, such as principal components that seeks to maximize the first factor, for example. The most important thing to recognize in personality research is that the measure used to develop the grand model focused largely on the normal range of function.

Similar issues were mirrored in the personality disorder research with one important difference caused by having its origins in the medical model that preferred to classify behavior into *typologies* as opposed to traits. Categories of personality disorder were created using prototypical patients whom clinicians agreed exhibited the symptoms indicative of the personality disorder under consideration. This led to a number of categories, such as borderline PD, schizotypal PD, and so on. A problem soon emerged that the diagnostic criteria often overlapped between categories. For example, symptoms of anxiety are a feature of many categories and the degree of overlap on symptoms across categories fueled revisions of the DSM or ICD with the collapsing or creation of new categories. As a result, multiple diagnoses were assigned to patients to cover all of their symptoms and the silliness of it all reached a head when categories such as "personality disorder not otherwise specified" were included to provide a diagnosis for someone who could not be classified. All of this comes as little surprise given that the creation of new categories was a decidedly political affair usually decided by a committee of experts, and ratified by vote at a convention. Moreover, the focus on disorder also defined the primary range of behaviors under study that were clinically significant forms of behavior without clear understanding of when normal behavior became abnormal. Instead, a broad criterion of whether or not a behavior interfered with daily activities was used.

A rapprochement between the two solitudes occurred when new scales of personality disorders began to emerge that embraced the content and dimensionality of personality function in its entirety (Trull & Widiger, 2013; Widiger, 2007). The scales were created using modern psychometric methods and techniques, and whose content was validated and reliability of measurement established by robust research programs in general population and clinical samples. A large body of research also exists that documents their relationship to existing measures of personality such as the NEO-PI-R and EPQ-R, and the well-understood diagnostic categories of the DSM-IV all on clinical and general population samples. Indeed, this body of research began to frame the need for a revision of the DSM-IV categories for the then upcoming DSM-5 – but that is another story (Franić, Borsboom, Dolan, & Boomsma, 2014; Widiger & Lowe, 2008). At last, a unified grand theory began to emerge that could explain what personality is and what it does.

Genetics research, particularly twin research was fundamental in supporting a grand theory because it showed that personality disorder concepts were related to one another because they were influenced by a common set of genetic factors to justify and define the broad concepts and trait domains (see Jang & Vernon, 2018 for a review). This research supported the idea that personality function is best conceptualized as a continuum of normal and extreme range behaviors. Furthermore, heritability analyses supported the hierarchical structure of traits into higher and lower order levels (viz., the Big Five or Gigantic Three debate) by showing that more specific lower order traits show some shared genetic influence and form into fewer broader traits, but a great deal of the variability observed in them remained unique to each facet (Mõttus, Kandler, Bleidorn, Riemann, & McCrae, 2017; Torgersen et al., 2012).

However, in terms of identifying actual loci, the broad nature of each trait – even facet traits that encompassed a range of behaviors – has made gene hunting impossible (Cloninger, 1987; Munafò et al., 2009; Verweij et al., 2010). The usual explanation for the failure included a range of methodological issues including but not limited to small sample size, identification of the wrong neurotransmitter or loci, and/or the use of an inappropriate instrument for measurement. We would argue that the more pressing problem lies with an overly broad and behaviorally complex phenotype. Perhaps the way forward is to move beyond research targeting broad concepts in the search for the grand theory, and instead shifting the focus of genetic research onto highly specific behaviors and emotions related to summative personality constructs of the grand theory. The work in *personality nuances* captures this idea. For example, two individuals may have the same high score on a measure of sensation seeking. However, one person may engage in skydiving while the other prefers horror movies. What accounts for these differences in *expression* – skydiving versus horror movies – is what might be central to new genetics research.

Do genes play a role in the differential expression of sensation seeking as opposed to genes underlying sensation seeking *per se*? Personality nuances represent a meaningful level of the trait hierarchy below facets that correspond roughly to single items (or groups of very similar items) in a facet scale (see McCrae, 2015). For example, bitterness and touchiness may be different nuances of angry hostility, a facet of neuroticism. Nuances may specify either the eliciting situation (e.g., fear of heights as a source of anxiety or inability to accept criticism as source of anger) or the characteristic response to a range of situations (e.g., a nervous tic as an expression of anxiety across different circumstances or feeling offended as a result of criticism of any kind). As such, nuances could be potentially more useful in understanding individuals and their differences.

Indeed, in a sample of twins, personality nuances operationalized from the NEO-PI-R showed good psychometric rank order stability of .72 and validity, and a significant heritable basis on average of 52 percent (Mõttus et al., 2017). Taking this a step further, Mohammad and Kiritchenko showed that fine affect or emotion categories such as excitement, guilt, yearning, and admiration are significant indicators of personality such as the Big Five (Mohammad & Kiritchenko, 2013) and conducting genetic analyses on the emotions associated with each of the main personality traits may be more informative. Finding the genes for what makes a person feel "keen," "helpless," "timid," or "guilty" would be far more informative and clinically significant than the gene for neuroticism which these emotions predict.

The Problem of Measurement

No measure of personality function is perfectly reliable or has a large body of convergent and discriminative validity. These issues are to be distinguished from breadth of personality concepts discussed above, but instead focus on fundamental issues of how personality disorders are measured. Simply put, re-highlight the simple principle learned by all statistics students – "garbage in, garbage out" or GIGO. Research on the mainstream personality measures, be they Eysenck's EPQ or Costa and McCrae's NEO-PI-R for example, all converge to some consistent results – that there are three or five major traits, they are related to each other in predictable ways, and that the measures themselves have acceptable levels of reliability, validity, and stability. Such features are less so with personality disorder diagnoses. If the measure of the phenotype has fundamental psychometric problems, it will affect the veracity of any genetic study that it is based upon. This state of affairs is particularly so in the case of the personality disorders whose measurement and conceptualization has been a matter for debate for decades and does not appear to have been resolved with the DSM-5, whose changes remain debatable (Oldham, 2015).

Unfortunately, the long-running issues relevant to personality disorder diagnoses (Jang, Livesley, & Vernon, 1998) culminating with the wholesale and controversial changes made to the classification of personality disorders in the DSM-5 (e.g., Wakefield, 2016) has set back genetic research because those changes were not done solely to enhance reliability and validity. Rather, the decision to continue with suboptimal medical diagnostic categories was to provide health insurance companies with easy to bill conditions. Furthermore, the changes contained in the DSM-5 throw a wrench into new genetics research. A would-be researcher is directly confronted by this problem when deciding what measures to include in the next research grant proposal. Does one include the DSM-5 criteria as primary measures, perhaps include the DSM-IV criteria, a self-report dimensional measure of personality function, and for similar inclusiveness, a measure of the Big Five personality traits as well? The inclusion of measures would be less about including the most reliable and valid measures – those with the best psychometric difficulties – but those that will please the grant reviewer! Genetic researchers will have to decide whether the extent of the changes to the phenotype will mean starting all over again using the new measures, or ignoring these measures. It begs the question of just what do we do the genetics on?

THE FUTURE: BACK TO THE PHENOTYPE

Perhaps it is time the genetic research into personality move entirely away from traditional diagnostic approaches or responses to self-report questionnaires. Gottesman and Gould (2003) suggested focusing on "endophenotypes" – a biological marker that may contain a useful link between genetic sequences and behavioral disorders – and that these biological markers can parse behavioral symptoms into more stable phenotypes with a clear genetic connection. The definition of an endophenotype is the ensemble of measurable components in the pathway from distal genotype to psychiatric "disease" that fills the "invisible" gap between them. Individual endophenotypes refer to any one measure that contributes to specifying the pathway from genes to mental disorder. The task ahead is to identify potential endophenotypes for the personality disorders. For example, Siever (2005) suggested that some clinical dimensions of PDs, such as affective instability, impulsivity, aggression, emotional information processing, cognitive disorganization, social deficits, and psychosis, lend themselves to the study of corresponding endophenotypes. The propensity toward aggression can be evaluated by multiple methods including psychometric measures, interview, laboratory paradigms, neurochemical imaging, and pharmacological studies. These suggest that aggression is a measurable trait that may be related to a reduction in serotonergic activity. Hyper-responsiveness of the amygdala and other limbic structures could be related to affective instability, while structural and functional brain alterations underlie the cognitive disorganization in psychotic-like symptoms of schizotypal personality disorder.

Ruocco, Amirthavasagam, and Zakzanis (2012) evaluated whether the magnitude of volume reductions in the amygdala and hippocampus was associated with BPD. Volumetric magnetic resonance imaging results from 11 studies comprising 205 patients with BPD and 222 healthy controls were examined using meta-analytic techniques. Patients showed an average 11 and 13 percent decrease in the size of the hippocampus and amygdala, respectively. No attenuation of volumetric differences was detected in patients being treated with psychotropic medications; and comorbid depression, posttraumatic stress disorder, and substance use disorders were unrelated to volumetric decreases in either structure.

Ruocco and Carcone (2016) reviewed the literature on the neurobiology of borderline personality disorder (BPD), identifying 146 articles in three broad research areas: neuroendocrinology and biological specimens; structural neuroimaging; and functional neuroimaging. Based on the consolidation of results from these studies, they suggest an integrative model to account for interactions among endogenous stress hormones, neurometabolism, and brain structures and circuits involved in emotion and cognition. They concluded that genetics research could profitably incorporate endophenotypes, and gene × environment interaction research that focuses on the expression of genes in response to environmental stressors given that multiple neurobiological systems interact to produce the complex clinical phenotype of the disorder. These include interconnections between hormones, neuropeptides, brain metabolites, neurotransmitter receptors, white matter pathways, gray matter volumes, and neural activity associated with emotion, cognition, and the sense of self (Ruocco & Carcone, 2016).

The studies highlighted above represent a classic approach to finding endophenotypes for personality disorders. However, what is emerging in the literature is the use of "intermediate endophenotypes" such as personality traits as endophenotypes for other major disorders. This trend in the research is occurring because certain personality traits seem to be overrepresented in people with specific disorders. For example, Ersche and colleagues (2012) identified anxious-impulsiveness and studied personality and cognitive dysfunction as endophenotypes for drug dependence. These types of studies are interesting in their attempt to find the genes for another disorder that identifies potential genes underlying a related set of personality traits and functions! It is perhaps within these constellations of traits that the genes may be best identified, as opposed to the previously adopted approach examining traits individually and out of context; or arbitrary groupings that are not observed together in a clinical (i.e., real-world) setting.

A good example of personality traits as the endophenotype for a clinical syndrome is the study by Savitz, Van Der Merwe, and Ramesar (2008). This study used personality endophenotypes for a genetic association analysis of bipolar affective disorder (BPAD). They reasoned that various personality traits are overrepresented in people with BPAD and their unaffected relatives, and these traits may constitute genetically transmitted risk factors or endophenotypes of the illness (Qiu, Akiskal, Kelsoe, & Greenwood,

2017; Savitz et al., 2008). Seven different personality questionnaires comprising 19 subscales were administered to 31 European American families with BPAD ($n = 241$). Ten of 19 personality traits showed significant evidence of heritability and were selected as candidate endophenotypes. The 3' untranslated region repeat polymorphism of the dopamine transporter gene (*SLC6A3*) was associated with scales measuring Self-Directedness and Negative Affect. The short allele of the serotonin transporter gene (*SLC6A4*) promoter polymorphism showed a trend toward association with higher Harm Avoidance and Negative Affect. The *COMT* Val[158]Met polymorphism was weakly associated with Spirituality and Irritable Temperament.

This brief review shows that endophenotypes can take many forms. Where might the search for endophenotypes go next? Kraus (2013) suggests that one direction might be to delve deeper and examine cellular function:

One thing that early gene–personality work overlooked is that a lot has to happen to allow DNA to code for specific hormones/neuropeptides that then have to act at the cellular level to subsequently influence personality. In short, *genes need to be expressed at a cellular level* in order to influence personality, and so one place where a genetic researcher might want to look to examine gene influences on personality is at this expression – that is, what genes are being unzipped by RNA, so that specific hormones/proteins are produced?

Middeldorp and colleagues (Middeldorp, Ruigrok, Cath, Van Dyck, and Boomsma, 2002) indicated that research on non-human subjects may provide some exciting leads. Research on honeybees is suggestive of the potential of examining RNA (ribonucleic acid) to predict behavior. In this work, mRNA (messenger ribonucleic acid) abundance has been shown to be a significant predictor of behavioral transitions of honeybees from hive workers to foragers (Whitfield, Cziko, & Robinson, 2003). Human work in this domain is an exciting area of future research. However, other investigators such as Paris (2011) remain much less enthusiastic about the utility of endophenotypes. The identification and use of endophenotypes are associated with the assumption that mental processes are reducible to activity at a neuronal level.

The Problem of Behavioral Genetic Methods

The vast majority of the genetic research on personality disorders has largely been based on the analysis of twin similarities. Specifically the comparisons between identical (monozygotic, or MZ) and fraternal (dizygotic, or DZ) twin pairs are used to estimate heritability – the proportion of the observed variability on a measure directly attributable to genetic differences between individuals. The primary reason for the popularity of twin studies is that this method can handle quantitative measures typical of personality research and uses model fitting to test a broad array of questions. However, the largely singular focus on twin research suggests that two or more decades

since this research began, the research using twins needs to take some new directions for progress in the field to be made.

Most twin studies use data obtained from reared-together twins because of the relative ease of finding a large representative sample, although there are several variations of the basic design, such as twins reared apart and family-of-twin designs (see Plomin, DeFries, & McClearn, 1990). A correlation coefficient (e.g., Pearson's *r*) indexes the similarity of twins. Greater MZ to DZ similarity is directly attributable to the two-fold greater genetic similarity of MZ to DZ twins, assuming all other things being equal. This is because MZ twins share all of their genes, whereas DZ twins share only half on average.

As a simple way to understand the logic of the twin study, if $r_{MZ} = .42$ and $r_{DZ} = .25$, the proportion (%) to which the individual differences observed on a measure is due to genetic differences, or the "heritability coefficient," is estimated as:

$$\text{Heritability} (h^2) = 2(r_{MZ} - r_{DZ}) = 2(.42 - .25)$$
$$= .34(100\%) = 34\%$$

The heritability coefficient, h^2, estimates genetic influences from all sources: additive genetic influences (A or the extent to which genotypes "breed true" from parent to offspring) and genetic dominance (D or genetic effects attributable to the interaction of alleles at the same locus, which results in a phenotype that is not exactly intermediate in expression as would be expected between pure breeding homozygous individuals).

Two environmental effects are also estimated. Common or shared environmental influences (c^2 or C) are defined as those that make members of a family similar to one another (i.e., result in familial resemblance), whereas non-shared environmental factors (e^2 or E) are those which make members of a family different from one another (i.e., result in differences between family members). It is important to note that it is not that the experience of the environment itself that is shared or not shared, but how these factors influence the resemblance of family members. The non-shared environment term also includes measurement error as this also lowers familial resemblance in a random way. It follows then that:

$$c^2 = 2\,r_{DZ} - r_{MZ} = 2(.25) - .45 = .05(100\%) = 5\% \quad \text{and}$$

$$e^2 = 1.0 - h^2 - c^2 = 1.0 - .34 - .05 = .64(100\%) = 64\%$$

The basic twin method has been translated into path-analytic models (see Neale & Cardon, 1992). Path models are extremely flexible in that they are able to analyze data from different populations and response formats (including diagnostic categories), and have generated an explosion of studies over the past two decades.

Heritability estimates generated using path analytic methods or by the simple equations above are predicated on the same assumptions that imparts imprecision into the estimates. One of the principal assumptions is that greater MZ to DZ similarity on a measured trait is due to genetic factors because MZ twins share all of their genes and DZ twins only half. However, this only holds if the environments of the MZ twins do not cause them to be more similar than DZ twins. That is, the greater MZ twin similarity may not be due to the fact that parents of MZ twin pairs treat their twins (e.g., dressing alike) more similarly than parents of DZ twins. This is known as the "assumption of equal environments" or EEA. Traditionally the test that the assumption holds is by rating the similarity of MZ and DZ twin environments and showing there are no significant differences. For example, when twins are being tested they are asked to complete measures that assess the degree to which they were often dressed alike, went to the same schools, and so on. MZ and DZ agreement or concordance rates on these items are compared and if differences are found (suggesting that the environments of MZ and DZ twins are not the same), then the affected twin similarity variables are correlated with the dependent measure(s) to determine whether they account for a significant proportion of the variance. It has been suggested that environmental similarity between twins does not have much of an impact on trait similarity (Felson, 2014), and that the *interaction* of sociocognitive variables in *response* to different environmental conditions such as trauma, being dressed alike, or medical treatments should be the focus (Fosse, Joseph, & Richardson, 2015). A correction for these effects is made by estimating the standardized residual from the regression of the twin similarity on these sociocognitive variables on the personality variables prior to genetic analyses, which may lead to some changes in heritability estimates and our interpretation of them (Fosse et al., 2015).

A second consideration is that twin studies require a relatively large number of twin pairs to have adequate power to detect genetic and environmental influences with any certainty (see Neale, Eaves, & Kendler, 1994). Many of the largest studies have established population-based twin registries where all of the twin pairs in a population are identified by birth records. Other large studies have used volunteer samples drawn from a population. With either method the question remains – are there sufficient numbers of twin pairs with personality disorders to actually study the genetics of personality disorders? Unlike studies of normal personality where everyone is assumed to have some kind of personality – it is difficult to recruit a large sample of twins who have a clinically significant personality disorder. Approximately 32 out 1000 people are twins (about 3 percent of the general population), and if the prevalence of DSM-IV personality disorder itself is 9.1 percent (Lenzenweger, Lane, Loranger, & Kessler, 2007), and the same paper reports prevalence rates for specific diagnoses such as borderline personality disorder at 1.4 percent and antisocial personality disorder 0.6 percent, few affected pairs would be recruited into any study. Twin studies attempt to recruit as large samples as possible using a wide variety of recruitment methods that

range from using hospital or church birth records to media advertisements. A recent issue of *Twin Research and Human Genetics* (Hur & Craig, 2013) lists the world's major twin studies and despite the size of some of the samples, suitable numbers of twin pairs with personality disorder would not be found.

To get around the problem, the threshold liability model of disease is evoked that assumes that personality function exists on a continuum of normal range and extreme behavior, and that biological and environmental factors are assumed to affect a person's position on the continuum in a particular way. Under the threshold liability model of disease, the number of individuals in a population falling into each range on a continuum of behavior – *normal range*, *spectrum*, and *disorder* – is determined by the amount, or "dosage," of genetic and environmental influence. The model is multifactorial in nature and assumes that several genes and environmental effects combine to create an individual's susceptibility. This suggests that patients differ from non-patients only in the number of pathogenic genetic and/or environmental events or experiences to which they have been exposed.

The threshold liability model is readily modified to explain disorders that exhibit clear discontinuities in the expression of pathology as seen with bimodal distributions of behavior. Under this variant of the model, the same multifactorial causes are still exerting an influence that creates much of the measured variability between individuals, with the addition of one or more significant genetic (e.g., specific gene variant for example) and/or environmental causes (e.g., traumatic experience or exposure) that creates the patient group. The threshold liability model is also important because it explains why the pattern of responses of general population subjects to items assessing PD and symptoms of psychopathology is similar to those of clinical samples (e.g., Jackson & Messnick, 1962; Livesley, Jackson, & Schroeder, 1992; Livesley, Schroeder, Jackson, & Jang, 1998). As such, behavioral genetic research is designed to estimate the extent to which the vulnerability or dosage is attributable to genetic causes by comparing greater genetic similarity of relatives for a phenotype as compared to unrelated individuals.

The other important factor is the importance of the content of a measure used reflecting the continuum of phenotypic expression. If not, the study will be a reflection of the restricted range of behaviors covered by the measures. If a study uses a measure of personality disorders where few indicate that they display behaviors as described in the measure, then the study is not really examining what the measure purports to assess. The solution is to measure personality function in as many ways as possible so that the range of behavior in all its forms and minutiae are covered. With the use of multiple measures, it is imperative that the relationship between the measures is understood – that is, they are related to each other in predictable ways. Moreover, the terms of the threshold liability model of disease in genetics show that genes underlie any observed relationship between the scales as well. In this way, one is assured that the measures are indeed measuring the same constructs in different ways (viz., multi-trait, multi-method matrix) and that the same genetic and environmental factors account for the observed relationships. The degree to which two measures are influenced by a common genetic (pleiotropy) and environmental influences are readily computed from MZ and DZ twin correlations and indexed by the genetic correlation (r_G) and environmental correlation (r_E), which vary from −1.0 to 1 and are interpreted like any correlation coefficient.

Even a measure that reflects the widest range of the behavior in question does not move research forward because it still requires that sufficient twin pairs fall into the extreme range. Few studies report the range of response or numbers of individuals who fall into the extreme range and thus it is not clear if the model is valid and studies of personality disorder may just be studies of normal personality! Another way to approach the problem is to turn the threshold liability model of genetics upside down. Normally, the threshold liability model begins with the phenotype and makes assumptions about gene dosage. A more useful approach may be to start with the genes themselves to see if they are associated with our measures or conceptions of disorder.

For example, the recent use of genomic-relatedness-matrix residual maximum likelihood (GREML) analysis has been producing new insights into the genetic architecture of personality. GREML works by looking at how very low levels of relatedness, as determined from number of shared variants across the genome, account for similarity in phenotype across traditionally unrelated individuals. In other words, GREML allows the estimation of the total genetic heritability of a trait by taking into account all gene variants available in a data set, without identifying the specific gene variants making up this heritability.

Recent GREML studies of different personality traits have been able to confirm underlying genetic heritability. For example, in a sample of 12,000 unrelated individuals, common single-nucleotide polymorphisms (SNPs) accounted for 6 percent of the variance in neuroticism and 12 percent in the case of extraversion (Vinkhuyzen et al., 2012). The only other study that we are aware of reporting GREML estimates for personality traits found that genetic variants explained 7 percent of the variance in harm avoidance, 10 percent in novelty seeking, and 8 percent in persistence (but no variance in reward dependence) in a sample of 8000 individuals (Verweij et al., 2012). The use of this approach prevents reliance on twins and allows researchers to study directly unrelated individuals with personality disorder diagnoses increasing the chances of obtaining a sufficiently large sample. Moreover, given that certain SNPs are accounting

for much lower estimates of heritability on the measures suggests that the method and results can be used to decompose the personality function phenotypes into "nuances" that predict actual behavior as discussed earlier.

The Problem of Not Seeing the Forest Through the Trees

A common answer to the question of "why do we want to find the genes for _____*FILL IN THE BLANK HERE*___" is because of the general belief that genes cause a behavior and/or an illness. Finding the genes for a condition is important because the liability genes could be manipulated to ameliorate disease. As we stated in the opening of the chapter, this is the *raison d'être* of genetics research and has become its guiding principle. However, this was done at the cost of ignoring a host of concepts important to human beings such as time, development, critical periods, interactions with genes, and that genes may be a protective factor and not always a liability. This is odd because so much of psychology and psychiatry is about these processes but our estimates of heritability are often single point estimates on measures that summarize behavior over a lifetime. It's time to seriously incorporate how life transitions, events, and role changes can affect both average slopes in personality traits and individual differences in personality maturation and change (Bleidorn et al., 2010; Bleidorn, Kandler, & Caspi, 2014; Hopwood et al., 2011).

These ideas resonate with Gottlieb's (1984) themes including: (a) the agency of organisms in constructing their environments (Odling-Smee, Laland, & Feldman, 2003); (b) plasticity of development (West-Eberhard, 2003); (c) the role of phenotypic plasticity in the genesis of evolutionary novelty (Kirschner & Gerhart, 2005); and (d) the deeply contextual character of biological information. These themes not only echo and support many of Gottlieb's own arguments, but also extend the "developmental point of view" into new domains.

A serious consideration of these issues is vital for the genetics of personality disorders to progress. Recent research on intelligence, actually called the "new genetics of intelligence" can contribute some key ideas to personality disorder research. For example, thousands of single-nucleotide polymorphisms are required to account for the heritability of intelligence because the effect sizes of SNP associations are very small. The new genetics of intelligence relies on the combination of thousands of these SNP effects in a genome-wide polygenic score (GPS), also applicable to complex traits in personality research (Plomin & von Stumm, 2018). Intelligence or cognitive ability have always been considered to run in families with the assumption that this family resemblance was due to nurture, which we defined earlier as "shared family environmental influence." Siblings were thought to be similar in intelligence because they grew up in the same environment and twin and adoption studies consistently support this assumption, but only until adolescence. After adolescence, the effect of shared family environmental influence on intelligence is negligible, which means that family environments have very little effect on individual differences in the long run. Under the normal range of environmental influence, in the absence of extremes of neglect or abuse, family resemblance for intelligence is due to nature rather than nurture (Briley & Tucker-Drob, 2013).

Kandler and Papendick (2017) have taken these issues into account in studying the genetics of personality disorder by introducing three perspectives of how quantitative behavior genetic modeling can broaden our knowledge about the etiology of personality differences, stability, and change. First, based on the data from 14 cross-sectional, 13 longitudinal, and 3 cross-sequential studies, they illustrate age trends of the genetic and environmental contributions to individual differences in five personality trait dimensions: neuroticism, extraversion, openness, agreeableness, and conscientiousness. Second, they demonstrate estimates of the stability of genetic and environmental differences in personality traits across time and different age groups using the data from 16 longitudinal studies. Finally, they visualize age trends of the genetic and environmental contributions to the stability of personality differences over the life course. In the context of these three perspectives, there is an explanation of the implications that these trends may have for the interplay between genetic and environmental sources during different stages of life and how they can deepen our understanding of personality development across the lifespan (Kandler & Papendick, 2017).

Perhaps the reason why it has been difficult to identify genes is because their effects are only "activated" by exposure to specific environmental triggers, an effect known as "gene × environment interaction." One of the most investigated genes is the serotonin transporter gene (SLC6A4, also known as 5-HTT), which has been the focus of many personality studies. As far back as 2003, Caspi and colleagues showed that the 5-HTTLPR polymorphism does not show a main effect on depression, but the s-allele increases the risk of depression once an individual is exposed to one or more life events. However, two meta-analyses, including 5 and 14 studies respectively, yielded no evidence for an effect of 5-HTTLPR in interaction with life events on depression (Munafò, Durrant, Lewis, & Flint, 2009; Risch et al., 2009). Subsequently, these meta-analyses were critiqued for having given too much weight to the studies reporting null findings that employed poorer measurement of life events (Caspi, Hariri, Holmes, Uher, & Moffitt, 2010).

Middeldorp and colleagues (Middeldorp et al., 2010) tested for an interaction effect involving 5-HTTLPR on a sample of 1155 twins and their parents and siblings from 438 families, using a detailed measure of life events. They found a significant main effect of number of life events on anxious depression and neuroticism, especially when these were experienced in the past year. No interaction with 5-HTTLPR was found for number of life events either experienced across the lifespan or across the past year, supporting the findings of the meta-analyses. It might be more useful to focus on the joint effect of several genes that are, for example, part of the same biological pathway in interaction with the environment.

The idea of analyzing several polymorphisms simultaneously was tested by Heck and colleagues (2009). They reasoned that previous studies that only examined one or a few polymorphisms within single genes neglected the possibility that the genetic associations might be more complex, comprising several genes or gene regions. As such, they performed an extended genetic association study analyzing 17 serotonergic (SLC6A4, HTR1A, HTR1B, HTR2A, HTR2C, HTR3A, HTR6, MAOA, TPH1, TPH2) and dopaminergic genes (SLC6A3, DRD2, DRD3, DRD4, COMT, MAOA, TH, DBH), which have been previously reported to be implicated with personality traits. One hundred ninety-five SNPs within these genes were genotyped in a sample of 366 general population participants (all European American), and they conducted a replication on an independent sample of a further 335 participants. Personality traits in both samples completed the German version of Cloninger's Tridimensional Personality Questionnaire (TPQ). From 30 SNPs showing associations at a nominal level of significance, two intronic SNPs, rs2770296 and rs927544, both located in the HTR2A gene, withstood correction for multiple testing. These SNPs were associated with Novelty Seeking. The effect of rs927544 could be replicated for the Novelty Seeking subscale Extravagance, and the same SNP was also associated with Extravagance in the combined samples. Their results show that HTR2A polymorphisms modulate facets of novelty-seeking behavior in healthy adults, suggesting that serotonergic neurotransmission is indeed involved in this phenotype.

Similarly, Derringer and colleagues (Derringer et al., 2010) led a consortium of researchers in an examination of a collection of SNPs associated with dopamine in prior research and subsequently examined associations between this collection of SNPs and sensation-seeking behavior. The findings were promising: Taking into account all the SNPs associated with sensation-seeking behaviors as an aggregate, dopamine genes worked in concert to explain around 6.6 percent of variation in sensation-seeking behavior. This approach is appealing because it involves conceiving of genes and personality not as simple one-to-one relationships, but instead as complex systems of genes that work in concert to express a personality trait.

The importance of including critical periods for development is demonstrated by a number of studies that show when personality traits become more or less stable. Hopwood et al. (2011) investigated the patterns and origins of personality trait changes from ages 17 to 29 using three waves of Multidimensional Personality Questionnaire data provided by twins. Results suggest that (a) trait changes were more profound in the first relative to the second half of the transition to adulthood; (b) traits tend to become more stable during the second half of this transition, with all the traits yielding retest correlations between .74 and .78; (c) negative affectivity declined over time and constraint increased over time; minimal change was observed on agentic or communal aspects of positive affectivity; and (d) both genetic and non-shared environmental factors accounted for personality changes (Hopwood et al., 2011). Overall, these genetically-informed results support a life-course perspective on personality development during the transition to adulthood.

CONCLUSION

The genetics of personality disorders will remain an active area of research and we hope this targeted chapter will provide some new ideas for the next phase of research. The genetics of personality disorders has been very much a "top-down" approach, where research begins with an imperfect phenotype and the search for genes underlying that imperfect phenotype. Is it any wonder the search for personality disorder liability genes (and environmental causes) have been so unsuccessful.

In this chapter we argue that it is time to switch gears in the study of the genetics of personality disorders by turning how we have currently thought about personality functioning upside down. For starters, the focus must shift from trying to find the genes associated with broad and inclusive psychological concepts and psychiatric typologies such as sensation seeking to the psychological processes of explaining behavioral choices associated with these broad concepts – such as when someone chooses horror movies over skydiving. The nuances of personality as opposed to broad traits and concepts are an avenue of genetics research that may lead to fruitful discoveries. Along these same lines, finding genes underlying the biological process associated with behavior, the so-called "endophenotypes," is worth continued exploration simply because, like in the case of personality nuances, focus on the broad concepts has not been successful.

Of particular note are new methods that do not rely on traditional twin studies and incorporating considerations around developmental periods as opposed to point estimates is another shift worth following up. The true value of future genetic research lies with how they offer the promise to better understand actual behavior and not simply social constructs that make up current diagnostic systems.

It is an exciting time to be working in personality disorders.

REFERENCES

Allport, G. (1937). *Personality: A Psychological Interpretation*. New York: Holt, Rinehart & Winston.

Bleidorn, W., Kandler, C., & Caspi, A. (2014). The behavioural genetics of personality development in adulthood: Classic, contemporary, and future trends. *European Journal of Personality*, 28(3), 244–255.

Bleidorn, W., Kandler, C., Hülsheger, U. R., Riemann, R., Angleitner, A., & Spinath, F. M. (2010). Nature and nurture of the interplay between personality traits and major life goals. *Journal of Personality and Social Psychology*, 99(2), 366–379.

Briley, D. A., & Tucker-Drob, E. M. (2013). Explaining the increasing heritability of cognitive ability across development. *Psychological Science*, 24(9), 1704–1713.

Caspi, A., Hariri, A. R., Holmes, A., Uher, R., & Moffitt, T. E. (2010). Genetic sensitivity to the environment: The case of the serotonin transporter gene and its implications for studying complex diseases and traits. *American Journal of Psychiatry*, 167, 509–527.

Cloninger, C. R. (1987). A systematic method for clinical description and classification of personality variants. *Archives of General Psychiatry*, 44, 573–588.

Cloninger, R. (2012). Genetics of personality disorders. In J. I. Nurnberger & W. H. Berrettini (Eds.), *Principles of Psychiatric Genetics* (pp. 316–323). Cambridge University Press.

Derringer, J., Krueger, R. F., Dick, D. M., Saccone, S., Grucza, R. A., Agrawal, A., ... Schuckit, M. A. (2010). Predicting sensation seeking from dopamine genes: A candidate-system approach. *Psychological Science*, 21(9), 1282–1290.

Draycott, S. G., & Kline, P. (1995). The big three or the big five—the EPQ-R vs the NEO-PI: A research note, replication and elaboration. *Personality and Individual Differences*, 18(6), 801–804.

Ersche, K. D., Turton, A. J., Chamberlain, S. R., Müller, U., Bullmore, E. T., & Robbins, T. W. (2012). Cognitive dysfunction and anxious-impulsive personality traits are endophenotypes for drug dependence. *American Journal of Psychiatry*, 169, 926–936.

Eysenck, H. J. (1994). The big five or giant three: Criteria for a paradigm. In C. F. Halverson, Jr., G. A. Kohnstamm, & R. P. Martin (Eds.), *The Developing Structure of Temperament and Personality from Infancy to Adulthood* (pp. 37–51). Hillsdale, NJ: Lawrence Erlbaum Associates.

Felson, J. (2014). What can we learn from twin studies? A comprehensive evaluation of the equal environments assumption. *Social Science Research*, 43, 184–199.

Fosse, R., Joseph, J., & Richardson, K. (2015). A critical assessment of the equal-environment assumption of the twin method for schizophrenia. *Frontiers in Psychiatry*, 6, 62.

Franić, S., Borsboom, D., Dolan, C. V., & Boomsma, D. I. (2014). The big five personality traits: Psychological entities or statistical constructs? *Behavior Genetics*, 44(6), 591–604.

Goldberg, L. R. (1990). An alternative "description of personality": The big-five factor structure. *Journal of Personality and Social Psychology*, 59(6), 1216–1229.

Gottesman, I. I., & Gould, T. D. (2003). The endophenotype concept in psychiatry: Etymology and strategic intentions. *American Journal of Psychiatry*, 160, 636–645.

Gottlieb, G. (1984). Evolutionary trends and evolutionary origins: Relevance to theory in comparative psychology. *Psychological Review*, 91(4), 448–456.

Heck, A., Lieb, R., Ellgas, A., Pfister, H., Lucae, S., Roeske, D., ... Ising, M. (2009). Investigation of 17 candidate genes for personality traits confirms effects of the HTR2A gene on novelty seeking. *Genes, Brain and Behavior*, 8, 464–472.

Hopwood, C. J., Donnellan, M. B., Blonigen, D. M., Krueger, R. F., McGue, M., Iacono, W. G., & Burt, S. A. (2011). Genetic and environmental influences on personality trait stability and growth during the transition to adulthood: A three-wave longitudinal study. *Journal of Personality and Social Psychology*, 100 (3), 545–556.

Hur, Y. M., & Craig, J. M. (2013). Twin registries worldwide: An important resource for scientific research. *Twin Research and Human Genetics*, 16(1), 1–12.

Jackson, D. N., & Messnick, S. (1962). Response styles on the MMPI: Comparison of clinical and normal samples. *Journal of Abnormal and Social Psychology*, 65, 285–299.

Jang, K. L., Livesley, W. J., & Vernon, P. A. (1998). A twin study of genetic and environmental contributions to gender differences in traits delineating personality disorder. *European Journal of Personality*, 12(5), 331–344.

Jang, K. L., & Vernon, P. A. (2018). Genetics. In W. J. Livesley (Ed.), *Handbook of Personality Disorders: Theory, Research, and Treatment* (pp. 177–195). New York: Guilford Press.

Kandler, C., & Papendick, M. (2017). Behavior genetics and personality development: a methodological and meta-analytic review. In J. Specht (Ed.), *Personality Development Across the Lifespan* (pp. 473–495). London: Academic Press.

Kirschner, M. W., & Gerhart, J. C. (2005). *The Plausibility of Life: Resolving Darwin's Dilemma*. New Haven: Yale University Press.

Kraus, M. W. (2013). Do genes influence personality? *Psychology Today*, July 11. Retrieved from www.psychologytoday.com/gb/blog/under-the-influence/201307/do-genes-influence-personality.

Lenzenweger, M. F., Lane, M. C., Loranger, A. W., & Kessler, R. C. (2007). DSM-IV personality disorders in the National Comorbidity Survey Replication. *Biological Psychiatry*, 62(6), 553–564.

Livesley, W. J. (2008). Research trends and directions in the study of personality disorder. *Psychiatric Clinics of North America*, 31 (3), 545–559.

Livesley, W. J., Jackson, D. N., & Schroeder, M. L. (1992). Factorial structure of traits delineating personality disorders in clinical and general population samples. *Journal of Abnormal Psychology*, 101, 432–440.

Livesley, W. J., Schroeder, M. L., Jackson, D. N., & Jang, K. L. (1994). Categorical distinctions in the study of personality disorder: Implications for classification. *Journal of Abnormal Psychology*, 103(1), 6–17.

McCrae, R. R. (2015). A more nuanced view of reliability: Specificity in the trait hierarchy. *Personality & Social Psychology Review*, 19, 97–112.

McCrae, R. R., & John, O. P. (1992). An introduction to the five-factor model and its applications. *Journal of Personality*, 60(2), 175–215.

Middeldorp, C. M., Ruigrok, P., Cath, D. C., Van Dyck, R., and Boomsma, D. I. (2002). Candidate genes for mood disorders in humans: A literature review. *American Journal of Human Genetics*, 114, 768.

Middeldorp, C. M., Slof-Op, M. C. T., Landt, S. O., Medland, S. E., van Beijsterveldt, C. E., Bartels, M., ... Boomsma, D. I. (2010). Anxiety and depression in children and adults: Influence of serotonergic and neurotrophic genes? *Genes, Brain and Behavior*, 9, 808–816.

Mohammad, S. M., & Kiritchenko, S. (2013). Using nuances of emotion to identify personality. Paper presented at the ICWSM Workshop on Computational Personality Recognition. Retrieved from http://arxiv.org/abs/1309.6352.

Mõttus, R., Kandler, C., Bleidorn, W., Riemann, R., & McCrae, R. R. (2017). Personality traits below facets: The consensual validity, longitudinal stability, heritability, and utility of personality nuances. *Journal of Personality and Social Psychology*, 112 (3), 474–490.

Munafò, M. R., Durrant, C., Lewis, G., & Flint, J. (2009). Gene–environment interactions at the serotonin transporter locus. *Biological Psychiatry*, 65, 211–219.

Munafò, M. R., Freimer, N. B., Ng, W., Ophoff, R., Veijola, J., Miettunen, J., ... Flint, J. (2009). 5-HTTLPR genotype and anxiety-related personality traits: A meta-analysis and new data. *American Journal of Medical Genetics Part B: Neuropsychiatric Genetics*, 150B(2), 271–281.

Neale, M. C., & Cardon, L. R. (1992). *Methodology for Genetic Studies of Twins and Families*. London: Kluwer.

Neale, M. C., Eaves, L. J., & Kendler, K. S. (1994). The power of the classical twin study to resolve variation in threshold traits. *Behavior Genetics*, 24(3), 239–258.

Odling-Smee, F. J., Laland, K. N., & Feldman, M. W. (2003). *Niche Construction: The Neglected Process in Evolution*. Monographs in Population Biology, vol. 37. Princeton: Princeton University Press.

Oldham, J. M. (2015). The alternative DSM-5 model for personality disorders. *World Psychiatry: Official Journal of the World Psychiatric Association (WPA)*, 14(2), 234–236.

Paris, J. (2011). Endophenotypes and the diagnosis of personality disorders. *Journal of Personality Disorders*, 25, 260–268.

Plomin, R., DeFries, J. C., & McClearn, G. E. (1990). *Behavioral Genetics: A Primer* (2nd ed.). New York: Freeman.

Plomin, R., & von Stumm, S. (2018). The new genetics of intelligence. *Nature Reviews Genetics*, 19, 148–159.

Qiu, F., Akiskal, H. S., Kelsoe, J. R., & Greenwood, T. A. (2017). Factor analysis of temperament and personality traits in bipolar patients: Correlates with comorbidity and disorder severity. *Journal of Affective Disorders*, 207, 282–290.

Reichborn-Kjennerud, T. (2008). Genetics of personality disorders. *Psychiatric Clinics of North America*, 31(3), 421–440.

Risch, N., Herrell, R., Lehner, T., Liang, K. Y., Eaves, L., Hoh, J. ... Merikangas, K. R. (2009). Interaction between the serotonin transporter gene (5-HTTLPR), stressful life events, and risk of depression: A meta-analysis. *Journal of the American Medical Association*, 301, 2462–2471.

Ruocco, A. C., Amirthavasagam, S., & Zakzanis, K. K. (2012). Amygdala and hippocampal volume reductions as candidate endophenotypes for borderline personality disorder: A meta-analysis of magnetic resonance imaging studies. Psychiatry Research, 201(3), 245–252.

Ruocco, A. C., & Carcone, D. (2016). A neurobiological model of borderline personality disorder. *Harvard Review of Psychiatry*, 24(5), 311–329.

Savitz, J., Van Der Merwe, L., & Ramesar, R. (2008). Personality endophenotypes for bipolar affective disorder: a family-based genetic association analysis. *Genes, Brain and Behavior*, 7(8), 869–876.

Siever, L. J. (2005). Endophenotypes in the personality disorders. *Dialogues in Clinical Neuroscience*, 7(2), 139–151.

Torgersen, S. (2009). The nature (and nurture) of personality disorders. *Scandinavian Journal of Psychology*, 50 (6), 624–632.

Torgersen, S., Myers, J., Reichborn-Kjennerud, T., Røysamb, E., Kubarych, T. S., & Kendler, K. S. (2012). The heritability of Cluster B personality disorders assessed both by personal interview and questionnaire. *Journal of Personality Disorders*, 26(6), 848–866.

Trull, T. J., & Widiger, T. A. (2013). Dimensional models of personality: The five-factor model and the DSM-5. *Dialogues in Clinical Neuroscience, 15*(2), 135–146.

Verweij, K. J., Zietsch, B. P., Medland, S. E., Gordon, S. D., Benyamin, B., Nyholt, D. R., ... Wray, N. R. (2010). A genome-wide association study of Cloninger's Temperament scales: Implications for the evolutionary genetics of personality. *Biological Psychology, 85*(2), 306–317.

Verweij, K. J., Yang, J., Lahti, J., Veijola, J., Hintsanen, M., Pulkki-Råback, L., ... Zietsch, B. P. (2012). Maintenance of genetic variation in human personality: Testing evolutionary models by estimating heritability due to common causal variants and investigating the effect of distant inbreeding. *Evolution: International Journal of Organic Evolution, 66*(10), 3238–3251.

Vinkhuyzen, A. A. E., Pedersen, N. L., Yang, J., Lee, S. H., Magnusson, P. K. E., Iacono, W. G., ... Wray, N. R. (2012). Common SNPs explain some of the variation in the personality dimensions of neuroticism and extraversion. *Translational Psychiatry, 2*(4), e102.

Wakefield, J. (2016). Diagnostic issues and controversies in DSM-5: Return of the false positives problem. *Annual Review of Clinical Psychology, 12*, 105–132.

West-Eberhard, M. J. (2003). *Developmental Plasticity and Evolution*. New York: Oxford University Press.

Whitfield, C. W., Cziko, A.-M., & Robinson, G. E. (2003). Gene expression profiles in the brain predict behavior in individual honey bees. *Science, 302*(5643), 296–299.

Widiger, T. A. (2007). Dimensional models of personality disorder. *World Psychiatry: Official Journal of the World Psychiatric Association (WPA), 6*(2), 79–83.

Widiger, T. A., & Lowe, J. R. (2008). A dimensional model of personality disorder: Proposal for DSM-V. *Psychiatric Clinics of North America, 31*(3), 363–378.

2a   Four Key Areas for Further Investigation: Commentary on Issues and New Directions in Personality Disorder Genetics

WILLIAM CALABRESE, MARIA MARTIN LOPEZ, JACQUELINE TRUMBULL,
SARAH B. RUTTER, AND M. MERCEDES PEREZ-RODRIGUEZ

Jang and Choi's chapter "Issues and New Directions in Personality Disorder Genetics" (this volume) provides a cogent review of research in personality disorder genetics, heritability, endophenotypes, and assessment measures for personality disorders (PDs), while also offering guidance for how to shift our perspective on the field such that future research is unencumbered by "top-down" nosologies. The following commentary highlights four issues in the field. First, future research should focus on harnessing advances in PD assessment instead of relying on politically derived diagnostic systems. This focus includes growing knowledge on the hierarchical structure of PD traits and psychopathology, as well as research in moment-to-moment, *in vivo*, personality dynamics. Second, research needs to advance our understanding of the role of the environment and account for common pathway models, critical periods, development, and better defined environmental exposures. Third, more research and data are clearly needed in PD genetics to arrive at conclusions similar to what has been drawn from schizophrenia and mood disorder genetics research. Fourth, this research ought to have an eye towards refining treatment targets for PDs.

We wholeheartedly agree that research in PD genetics should not wait for a revised diagnostic system and instead we argue for quite the opposite. Our diagnostic systems need to better reflect the state of the science. Markon (2013) takes this point further in his review of how scientific developments have actually been impeded by "authoritative nosologies" and he argues that the scientific literature should "speak for itself" in order to better reflect the "epistemological pluralism" inherent to the field of psychopathology research. The chapter by Jang and Choi (this volume) effectively represents this "bottom-up" pluralistic discourse for identifying the most valid and useful foci of study in PD genetics. Specifically, the authors do well to highlight the importance of "personality nuances" in order to get away from the overly broad PD categories which are

too distal from genetics and fraught with measurement issues (e.g., low stability, high comorbidity, high heterogeneity). Their review of research echoes the sentiment of NIMH's Research Domain Criteria (RDoC) to understand how genes impact patterns of behavior by elucidating all of the mechanisms in between, like how mRNA affects neuropeptide development, which affects cellular function, which affects neurobiological functioning (i.e., endophenotypes), which affects personality nuances and dynamics (i.e., intermediate endophenotypes), which then lead to broader traits, trait constellations, and disorders. Fortunately, PD genetics research does not need to wait for an updated RDoC or DSM as advancements in personality research are progressing independent of these systems and offer guidance for how to direct translational research from genetics to behavior.

THE NEED TO HARNESS ADVANCES IN PSYCHOPATHOLOGY STRUCTURE AND PERSONALITY DYNAMICS

As an example of "bottom-up" pluralistic discourse, the Hierarchical Taxonomy of Psychopathology (HiTOP; Kotov et al., 2017) consortium has recently integrated and synthesized the quantitative research on the organization of psychopathology, which is a more comprehensive model compared to RDoC and offers "clearer phenotypes" for basic research. The consortium proposes six primary spectra: internalizing (or negative affectivity), thought disorder (or psychoticism), disinhibited externalizing, antagonistic externalizing, detachment, and somatoform. Research in this area has shown that these spectra underlie both personality and general psychopathology, which helps to explain their frequent co-occurrence. This model is akin to what is presented in DSM-5's Section III Alternative Model of Personality Disorder (AMPD). A measure of this model, the Personality Inventory for DSM-5 (PID-5; Krueger, Derringer, Markon, Watson, & Skodol, 2012) has been constructed and well tested and offers exciting opportunities for standardized assessment of trait facets

---

The 2nd, 3rd, and 4th authors all contributed equally as 2nd author

or "nuances" (e.g., deceitfulness vs. manipulativeness). Researchers examining the neurobiology of PD have begun to integrate this model, a noteworthy example being Mancke, Herpertz, and Bertsch's (2015) multidimensional model of reactive aggression in borderline personality disorder (BPD), which includes five biobehavioral dimensions which they link to multiple levels of analysis, from neurochemistry to the DSM-5 AMPD. One example is their dimension of threat hypersensitivity, which is associated with enhanced perception of anger to ambiguous faces, enhanced P100 amplitude to facial emotions, prefrontal-limbic imbalance, low oxytocinergic activity, and can be linked to the trait facet of hostility in the DSM-5 AMPD. A natural next step in this body of research would be to examine the role of genetic factors in this chain from neurochemistry to hostility and BPD reactive aggression, more broadly.

To explore the complex role of genetics in the development and maintenance of PDs, future research can harness advances in personality "dynamics" (i.e., how personality manifests in different situations). There are emerging models that describe moment-by-moment personality and interpersonal processes which can help researchers move beyond the broader PD traits and categories. We refer readers to a recent review by Hopwood (2018) where he presents an interpersonal scheme (Pincus, Hopwood, & Wright, in press) that describes how "recursive within-situation" interpersonal patterns (e.g., motives, perceptions) lead up to the stable between-situation patterns of personality traits and disorders. He also reviews emerging models that can help to explain how personality manifests in different situations and changes over time, which would be very beneficial in PD genetics research given the push to better understand how we, and our genome, interact with our environment over time to lead to disorder. Wrzus and Roberts' (2017) TESSERA model describes how triggers lead to expectancies, which lead to states and state expressions, and reactions. It would be interesting to study how genes affect each part of this model, as well as the learning processes that occur as a result of reinforcing/punishing reactions that can eventually lead to pathological personality patterns. Wessels, Zimmermann, and Leising's (2016) version of the SORKC model (i.e., stimuli, organism, response, and subsequent consequences) highlights the difference between our internal perceptions and the external world of situations, responses, and consequences. Other models include Back et al.'s (2011) PERSOC framework that describes the interplay between personality and social relationships, DeYoung's (2015) theory of how cybernetic goals lead to actions, and Fleeson and Jayarwickreme's (2015) Whole Trait Theory, which describes how social-cognitive mechanisms lead to personality states related to the Big Five model, which coincides well with the HiTOP spectra. All of these models can help to connect the "intermediate endophenotypes" (i.e., traits) with endophenotypes and the environment.

THE NEED TO HARNESS ADVANCES IN MODELING AND MEASUREMENT OF THE ENVIRONMENT

Jang and Choi (this volume) provide an excellent review of gene–environment interaction research in personality traits. To continue moving this literature forward, it is important to take into account that "the phenotype [...] is more than the sum of the genetics and the environmental parts" (Derefinko & Widiger, 2016, p. 232; Hyde et al., 2016; Viding & McCrory, 2012). This does not alter the importance of gene–environment interaction, but merely ensures that we are clear on the nature of the phenotype so as to truly understand the gene expression being presented. As delineated by Franić et al. (2013), truly assessing the gene–environment to phenotype connection requires modeling of how genetic and environmental effects act on latent variables to cause differences in observed traits given that genetic and environmental latent variables themselves represent the effects of many unidentified influences (i.e., effect of unknown number of genes, environmental factors corresponding to unknown number of unmeasured environmental influences). In this regard, the common pathway model has proven valuable, which looks at influences of additive genetic (A), shared environmental (C), and individual-specific environmental (E) sources on item covariation mediated by a latent variable (Franić et al., 2013; Rosenström et al., 2017). Unlike independent pathway models of the past, the common pathway model assumes that genes and environment are affected and in turn influence an intermediate phenotype, which can further influence the criteria being studied.

The purpose of the common pathway model is to differentiate the contribution of genetic versus environmental effects between diagnostic items, and to provide an additional analysis of the independent pathway model which looks more deeply at the influence of multiple genetic and environmental factors on distinct sources of between-person variation (Rosenström et al., 2017). The common pathway model estimates A, C, and E components separately for each of the latent factors while the independent pathway model estimates separate latent factors for each of the modeled components. Despite the importance of explicitly comparing the two models, examining the common pathway model is crucial given that it makes an explicit assumption of the phenotypic latent variable model with regards to the sources of item covariation meaning "a latent variable model cannot hold unless the corresponding common pathway model holds" (Franić et al., 2013, p. 409). The common pathway model allows us to more explicitly delineate the nature of the intermediate endophenotypes and move towards incorporating modern measures and models of personality pathology which will dictate how we understand and conceptualize our genetic findings and may guide us in the right direction of uncovering the appropriate genes.

While not specific to PD research, another key challenge of gene–environment studies is the need for standardization and optimization of measures of environmental influences ("the exposome") (Miller & Jones, 2014). Although genetics and genomics researchers have made significant efforts to standardize their measures and analytic tools, the same cannot be said yet of studies focused on environmental exposures (Steckling et al., 2018), and environmental protective factors (i.e., "positive" environments) are particularly understudied. Several large initiatives are taking place in both the European Union and the USA to advance exposome research. For example, a major goal of the National Institute of Environmental Health Sciences (NIEHS) Strategic Plans is to "promote exposome research and create a blueprint for incorporating exposure science into human health studies."

In terms of design, PD genetics research would do well to follow studies in schizophrenia and depression in adopting objective measures of environmental factors and looking at transdiagnostic features of personality disorders, such as impulsivity, aggression, and neuroticism (Bulbena-Cabre, Bassir Nia, & Perez-Rodriguez, 2018). Regarding the lack of measures on environmental factors, Rauthmann et al. (2014) addressed this issue and constructed a taxonomy of situations called the "Situational Eight DIAMONDS" model, which includes Duty, Intellect, Adversity, Mating, pOsitivity, Negativity, Deception, and Sociality. This model could help to guide PD genetics researchers to the "psychologically important situations" that are most relevant in gene–environment interactions giving rise to pathological personality patterns.

THE NEED FOR LARGER SAMPLES

Another problem that has impeded progress in PD genetics research is the lack of samples that are sufficiently large to support finer-grained conclusions. Creating larger biobanks that would allow for some of these more complex analyses would be beneficial, as would designing studies with specific theoretical models in mind. For example, the Differential Susceptibility framework suggests that certain genes make an individual more susceptible to the environment and therefore have a for-better or for-worse effect (Assary, Vincent, Keers, & Pluess, 2018). Perez-Perez and colleagues (2018) recently used this model to examine the impact of positive and negative life events in neuroticism and FKBP5. FKBP5 encodes a binding protein for FK506, and promotes regulation of the hypothalamic-pituitary-adrenal (HPA) axis through inhibition of glucocorticoid receptor activity (Perez-Perez et al., 2018).

THE NEED FOR TREATMENT TARGETS

Our last piece of commentary pertains to the need to direct PD genetics research towards identifying appropriate treatment targets, which Jang and Choi (this volume) discuss in terms of the "raison d'être" of genetics research. This is particularly important since there are no FDA-approved pharmacological treatments for highly disabling PDs such as borderline personality disorder. Several key steps are needed to elucidate the genetic mechanisms of personality disorders. First, the genetic risk variants or loci need to be identified (e.g., through large-scale genome-wide association studies, GWAS, deep sequencing, etc.); second, the potential causal gene (or genes) need to be identified; third, studies need to elucidate the mechanism through which the causal genes exert their effect on susceptibility to PD, most likely at critical periods during development. These breakthroughs can lead to the discovery of therapeutic interventions grounded on the neurobiology of PD, which may be more efficacious than the currently available treatments, which target symptoms but not the core etiopathology of the disorders.

ETHICAL ISSUES

As technology in genetic modification progresses faster than ever (e.g., Clustered Regularly Interspaced Short Palindromic Repeats [CRISPR]), the scientific community and society, in general, will be faced with serious moral issues. For instance, if genetic testing determines that an infant could be at risk for patterns of affective instability, given a set of conditions, how do we proceed?

This commentary has aimed to highlight the complexity of how PD likely develops through interactions between variables across various levels of analysis (e.g., genes, endophenotypes, intermediate endophenotypes, environment) across time. Given this complexity, it seems clear that, in this instance, genetic modification would create a "ripple effect" that would have unfathomable consequences. However, advances in PD gene–environment research could help to identify how to influence human development to foster prevention of future PD. If a child tests as having a predisposition for affective instability, then caretakers and therapists can work to create an environment and a set of conditions that could either alter the development of related traits or mitigate the effects of these traits. Ideally, as research in PD genetics becomes more refined, so will our treatment recommendations. For example, more refined models may allow us to predict the cascade of effects and interactions that eventually lead to PD. This information could put greater demand on preemptive and disease-modifying treatment to hopefully lower the prevalence of PD and ameliorate the suffering of individuals diagnosed with a PD.

REFERENCES

Assary, E., Vincent, J. P., Keers, R., & Pluess, M. (2018). Gene–environment interaction and psychiatric disorders: Review and future directions. *Seminars in Cellular and Developmental Biology*, 77, 133–143.

Back, M. D., Baumert, A., Denissen, J. J. A., Hartung, F. M., Penke, L., Schmukle, S. C., ... Wrzus, C. (2011). PERSOC: A unified framework for understanding the dynamic interplay of personality and social relationships. *European Journal of Personality*, 25, 90–107.

Bulbena-Cabre, A., Bassir Nia, A., & Perez-Rodriguez, M. M. (2018). Current knowledge on gene–environment interactions in personality disorders: An update. *Current Psychiatry Reports*, 20, 74.

Derefinko, K. J., & Widiger, T. A. (2016). Antisocial personality disorder. In S. H. Fatemi & P. J. Clayton, (Eds.), *The Medical Basis of Psychiatry* (pp. 229–245). New York: Springer.

DeYoung, C. G. (2015). Cybernetic big five theory. *Journal of Research in Personality*, 56, 33–58.

Fleeson, W., & Jayawickreme, E. (2015). Whole trait theory. *Journal of Research in Personality*, 56, 82–92.

Franić, S., Dolan, C. V., Borsboom, D., Hudziak, J. J., van Beijsterveldt, C. E. M., & Boomsma, D. I. (2013). Can genetics help psychometrics? Improving dimensionality assessment through genetic factor modeling. *Psychological Methods*, 18, 406–433.

Hopwood, C. J. (2018). Interpersonal dynamics in personality and personality disorders. *European Journal of Personality*, 32, 499–524.

Hyde, L. W., Waller, R., Trentacosta, C. J., Shaw, D. S., Neiderhiser, J. M., Ganiban, J. M., ... Leve, L. D. (2016). Heritable and nonheritable pathways to early callous-unemotional behaviors. *American Journal of Psychiatry*, 173, 903–910.

Kotov, R., Krueger, R. F., Watson, D., Achenbach, T. M., Althoff, R. R., Bagby, R. M., ... Zimmerman, M. (2017). The hierarchical taxonomy of psychopathology: A dimensional alternative to traditional nosologies. *Journal of Abnormal Psychology*, 126, 454–477.

Krueger, R. F., Derringer, J., Markon, K. E., Watson, D., & Skodol, A. E. (2012). Initial construction of a maladaptive personality trait model and inventory for DSM-5. *Psychological Medicine*, 42, 1879–1890.

Mancke, F., Herpertz, S. C., & Bertsch, K. (2015). Aggression in borderline personality disorder: A multidimensional model. *Personality Disorders: Theory, Research, and Treatment*, 6, 278–291.

Markon, K. E. (2013). Epistemological pluralism and scientific development: An argument against authoritative nosologies. *Journal of Personality Disorders*, 27, 554–579.

Miller, G. W., & Jones, D. P. (2014). The nature of nurture: Refining the definition of the exposome. *Toxicological Sciences*, 137 (1), 1–2.

Perez-Perez, B., Cristobal-Narvaez, P., Sheinbaum, T., Kwapil, T. R., Ballespi, S., Pena, E., ... Barrantes-Vidal, N. (2018). Interaction between FKBP5 variability and recent life events in the anxiety spectrum: Evidence for the differential susceptibility model. *PLoS ONE*, 13, e0193044.

Pincus, A. L., Hopwood, C. J., & Wright, A. G. C. (in press). The interpersonal situation: An integrative framework for the study of personality, psychopathology, and psychotherapy. In J. F. Rauthmann, D. Funder, & R. Sherman (Eds.), *The Oxford Handbook of Psychological Situations*. Oxford: Oxford University Press.

Rauthmann, J. F., Gallardo-Pujol, D., Guillaume, E. M., Todd, E., Nave C. S., Sherman, R. A., ... Funder, D. C. (2014). The Situational Eight DIAMONDS: A taxonomy of major dimensions of situation characteristics. *Journal of Personality and Social Psychology*, 107, 677–718.

Rosenström, T., Ystrom, E., Torvik, F. A., Czajkowski, N. O., Gillespie, N. A., Aggen, S. H., ... Reichborn-Kjennerud, T. (2017). Genetic and environmental structure of DSM-IV criteria for antisocial personality disorder: A twin study. *Behavior Genetics*, 47, 265–277.

Steckling, N., Gotti, A., Bose-O'Reilly, S., Chapizanis, D., Costopoulou, D., De Vocht, F., ... Sarigiannis, D. A. (2018). Biomarkers of exposure in environment-wide association studies: Opportunities to decode the exposome using human biomonitoring data. *Environmental Research*, 164, 597–624.

Viding, E., & McCrory, E. J. (2012). Genetic and neurocognitive contributions to the development of psychopathy. *Developmental Psychopathology*, 24, 969–983.

Wessels, N. M., Zimmermann, J., & Leising, D. (2016). Toward a shared understanding of important consequences of personality. *Review of General Psychology*, 20, 426–436.

Wrzus, C., & Roberts, B. W. (2017). Processes of personality and development in adulthood: The TESSERA framework. *Personality and Social Psychology Review*, 21, 253–277.

Highlighting the Value of Dimensional Conceptualizations and Environmental Influences: Commentary on Issues and New Directions in Personality Disorder Genetics

SUSAN C. SOUTH AND AMBER M. JARNECKE

In their chapter, Jang and Choi (this volume) highlight the challenges of using behavior and molecular genetics methods to understand the etiology of personality disorders (PDs). We resonate with much of what they said, including the measurement difficulties that plague the PD field. We would argue, and have previously argued, that the bulk of findings from behavior genetics research support a dimensional conceptualization of PDs (South & DeYoung, 2013). We assert here that continued refinement of the phenotype (PDs) is necessary to maximize the utility of genetics methods. Further, we argue in line with Jang and Choi (this volume), that for PDs the best use of genetics methods might be to understand *environmental* influences. Examining how the environment shapes the expression of genes presents a much greater opportunity for translating findings into efficacious prevention and intervention efforts.

PERSONALITY DISORDER: WHAT IS THE PHENOTYPE?

As Jang and Choi (this volume) briefly review, the PDs classified in the current, Fifth Edition of the *Diagnostic and Statistical Manual* (DSM-5; American Psychiatric Association, 2013) are exactly the same as they were in the Fourth Edition of the manual (American Psychiatric Association, 2000). They are plagued by multiple problems that make the study of these phenotypes difficult and therefore produce estimates in genetics research that might not be reliable or valid. Each PD, as outlined in DSM-5 Section II, is diagnosed according to a group of heterogeneous criteria that delineate maladaptive behaviors, thoughts, and feelings. The threshold needed for diagnosis is not based on scientific understanding and the criteria across the PDs are often overlapping if not identical (e.g., Widiger & Trull, 2007). Dissatisfaction with the multitude of problems with the DSM-IV PDs led to a proposed shift toward a dimensional conceptualization, but this proposal was abandoned (Krueger & Markon,

2014) and left as an alternative model in DSM-5 Section III (i.e., an appendix for future study).

The Section III DSM alternative model of personality disorders (AMPD) defines personality dysfunction using self- and interpersonal problems (Criterion A) that are associated with pathological personality traits (Criterion B; American Psychiatric Association, 2013). A dimensional trait model of five higher-order PD domains (and 25 lower-order facets) builds organically on the decades of research demonstrating associations between the categorical DSM PDs and the Five Factor Model (FFM) facets and domains (e.g., Widiger, 2011). Indeed, this trait model looks much like the maladaptive ends of four of the five domains of the FFM. There is substantial overlap between the AMPD domains and the FFM domains (Thomas et al., 2013). Neuroticism from the FFM maps on to Negative Affectivity, extreme Introversion on to Detachment, low Agreeableness on to Antagonism, and low Conscientiousness on to Disinhibition; Psychoticism in the DSM-5 model does not seem to align with the Openness domain of the FFM.

One study demonstrated that all three conceptualizations of PDs (i.e., Section II DSM, AMPD, and FFM) can be captured by five common latent factors/domains (Negative Affect, Detachment, Psychoticism, Disinhibition, Antagonism) in a structural model (Wright & Simms, 2014). Given the difficulties of defining and measuring PDs, these refined phenotypes may represent constructs of interest for geneticists. In fact, there is now a consortium of scientists dedicated to revising the conceptualization and classification of psychopathology broadly, along the lines of latent domains of psychopathology that capture covariance among different forms of pathology (Kotov et al., 2017). There is a growing interest in including PDs in these models but this has extended to the genetics literature more slowly.

Much of the extant literature supports a dimensional conceptualization of PDs, and therefore a ripe place for genetics research moving forward is to study the AMPD. The AMPD can be operationalized using the Personality Inventory for DSM-5 (PID-5; Krueger, Derringer, Markon,

Both authors contributed equally to this work.

Watson, & Skodol, 2012). To our knowledge, only two studies have examined the heritability of the AMPD domains. Genetic variance on a shortened, Norwegian version of the PID-5 ranged from .25 (Psychoticism) to .37 (Detachment; South et al., 2017). In an adult US twin sample, Wright and colleagues (Wright, Pahlen, & Krueger, 2017) found that additive genetic influences on the facet scales from the full PID-5 ranged from .25 (Callousness, Irresponsibility) to .48 (Distractibility).

These heritability estimates suggest that more of the "action" is at the lower-order facet level. This makes sense, as the facets are more likely to be homogeneous and thus "purer" constructs (Smith, McCarthy, & Zapolski, 2009). Two individuals with the same score on a measure of neuroticism may have very different profiles along the neuroticism facets. As Jang and Choi (this volume) state, "Perhaps the way forward is to cease to do research on broad concepts." If we take this argument to its logical conclusion, we might suggest that all work on genetics be done at the item (i.e., "nuance") level. This may be too fine-grained an analysis, as the complexity of endorsing a particular item/behavior/nuance on any given day may render interpretation of resulting genetic and environmental influences near impossible.

Instead, we need a better sense of what constitutes "disorder" when considering PDs. For instance, narcissistic PD has been included in every version of the DSM, but there are still healthy debates in the field about the core features of the disorder (Miller, Lynam, & Campbell, 2016; Wright, 2016). If we are to move to a system that looks like the AMPD in DSM-5 Section III, then we will need to elucidate what makes a person's thoughts, feelings, and behaviors *disordered* (rather than eclectic, quirky, or idiosyncratic). Some might argue that disorder is inherent in demonstrating extreme levels of maladaptive traits; whereas others might suggest that the way forward for PD research is to focus on Criterion A – identifying when a collection or profile of maladaptive traits becomes maladaptive according to the presence of a deficit or functional impairment (see Widiger et al., 2019). This is not simply a thought exercise, but a necessity for understanding the roots of personality pathology. Until we clarify the phenotype, genetics researchers will not be able to maximize all of their tools to understand the etiology of PDs.

GENETIC METHODS TO UNDERSTAND ENVIRONMENTAL INFLUENCES

As Jang and Choi (this volume) mention, the genetics of PDs are understudied relative to normal personality or other forms of psychopathology. The extant literature suggests that PDs, although heritable, tend to show lower heritability than normal personality traits, and estimates range substantially depending on the PD in question or whether dimensional or categorical conceptualizations and measurements are used (Jang, Livesley, Vernon, & Jackson, 1996; Kendler

et al., 2008; Reichborn-Kjennerud, 2010). The few candidate, association, and genome-wide association studies (GWAS) of PDs have identified specific genes or single nucleotide polymorphisms (SNPs) associated with PDs; however, in general, findings from studies using these methods fail to replicate unless very large sample sizes are used (Marigorta, Rodríguez, Gibson, & Navarro, 2018). The genetics field as a whole has recently turned to polygenic risk score or genome-based restricted maximum likelihood (GREML) methods. To date, there are no studies that use these methods to examine PDs. It is likely that GREML studies will find lower heritability of PDs than twin and adoptions studies because the heritability estimates using GREML are derived from a subset of genes; however, these GREML estimates may provide a lower bound of genetic variance that is not conflated with the assumptions of behavioral genetics studies (e.g., assumption of equal environments).

If nothing else, genetics research has showcased the complex relationship between genes and mental health disorders. This has moved the field forward in terms of generating new methodologies that hope to get us closer to understanding how genes relate to phenotypes. Although valuable, uncovering the relationship between genes and PDs using sample-specific, point estimates captured at a cross-section of time is limited in its utility. Thus, our position is aligned with what Jang and Choi (this volume) argue: maybe the story behind genetics research is less about finding all of the genes that contribute to PDs and more about focusing on the role of the environment.

One way to focus on the environment is by using twin and other family studies. Some may question the continued need for these types of quantitative behavior genetic methods when molecular genetic research is becoming more affordable, efficient, and widely available. We would argue that there are many reasons to continue using these methods. Use of twin and family studies provides estimates of genetic variance, common environmental variance (i.e., contexts that make twins similar to one another), and unique environmental variance (i.e., contexts that make twins different from each other). Examining the environmental variance components offers a starting point for understanding what type of contexts give way to PDs and helps to generate hypotheses about environments that may contribute to the expression of a PD (e.g., childhood socioeconomic status, which may make twins more similar, versus unique trauma exposure, which may make twins less similar).

In addition, researchers can examine how PDs share genetic and environmental variance with other phenotypes, such as normal personality or other forms of psychopathology. This may help tease apart the nature of comorbidity, for instance, along the lines of quantitative structural modeling of phenotypes as described above. Finding that the patterns of shared genetic variance between PDs and other forms of psychopathology differ from patterns of environmental variance (e.g., Kendler et al., 2011) will highlight the relative genetic and environmental contributions that give way to the comorbidity.

Modeling of twin and family data is also flexible enough to make use of longitudinal designs so that *both* genetic and environmental variance and covariance can be examined over time (e.g., Bornovalova et al., 2013).

Another important way that biometric modeling can elucidate environmental effects on PDs is through study of gene–environment (G×E) interaction. These models allow researchers to investigate how a putatively environmental context, such as childhood abuse or dating violence, moderates genetic *and* environmental variance, in essence exploring how the environment impacts the expression of PDs (at one point in time and across the life course). G×Es have been explored broadly in the field of genetics, and particularly in behavior genetics investigations, over the last few decades. However, there have been relatively few behavior genetics studies of PDs that examine G×E and even fewer molecular genetics studies of PDs that include G×E. The lack of research in this area may be due, in part, to the fact that very few genetics studies include measures of PDs.

In the absence of direct measures of PDs, we can use G×E to examine how environmental variables impact the expression of endophenotypes presumed to be associated with PDs (e.g., production of proteins, neurotransmitter pathways, normal personality traits, affective responses). Moving forward this work will be important regardless of where future genetic studies of PDs take us. Uncovering the role of environment on endophenotypes may have even greater clinical utility than examining how environment impacts the genetic expression of the PD itself. That is, knowing how environment impacts the expression of a neurotransmitter pathway or affective responding may improve our ability to detect which populations respond best to treatment.

SUMMARY

Behavior genetics research can offer much more than finding the genes that contribute to PDs. The heritability of personality, normal or maladaptive, will never reach 100 percent; the environment does have an impact on the variation in individual differences. Further, the environment most undoubtedly has a role on how genetic influences on PDs are expressed. Moving forward, we must challenge our conceptualization of what genetics research is and what it can do. We also argue for a refocusing of behavior and molecular genetics: back to the phenotype. By bringing our focus to the phenotype under study, greater strides will be made in understanding both genetic and environmental contributions to dysfunction in the characteristic patterns of how we think, feel, and behave.

REFERENCES

American Psychiatric Association. (2000). *Diagnostic and Statistical Manual of Mental Disorders* (4th ed., Text Revision). Washington, DC: American Psychiatric Association.

American Psychiatric Association. (2013). *Diagnostic and Statistical Manual of Mental Disorders* (5th ed.). Arlington, VA: American Psychiatric Publishing.

Bornovalova, M. A., Hicks, B. M., Iacono, W. G., & McGue, M. (2013). Longitudinal twin study of borderline personality disorder traits and substance use in adolescence: Developmental change, reciprocal effects, and genetic and environmental influences. *Personality Disorders*, 4(1), 23–32.

Jang, K. L., Livesley, W. J., Vernon, P. A., & Jackson, D. N. (1996). Heritability of personality disorder traits: A twin study. *Acta Psychiatrica Scandinavica*, 94(6), 438–444.

Kendler, K. S., Aggen, S. H., Czajkowski, N., Røysamb, E., Tambs, K., Torgersen, S., ... Reichborn-Kjennerud, T. (2008). The structure of genetic and environmental risk factors for DSM-IV personality disorders: A multivariate twin study. *Archives of General Psychiatry*, 65(12), 1438–1446.

Kendler, K. S., Myers, J. M., & Keyes, C. L. (2011). The relationship between the genetic and environmental influences on common externalizing psychopathology and mental well-being. *Twin Research and Human Genetics: The Official Journal of the International Society for Twin Studies*, 14(6), 516–523.

Kotov, R., Krueger, R. F., Watson, D., Achenbach, T. M., Althoff, R. R., Bagby, R. M., ... Zimmerman, M. (2017). The hierarchical taxonomy of psychopathology: A dimensional alternative to traditional nosologies. *Journal of Abnormal Psychology*, 126, 454–477.

Krueger, R. F., Derringer, J., Markon, K. E., Watson, D., & Skodol, A. E. (2012). Initial construction of a maladaptive personality trait model and inventory for DSM-5. *Psychological Medicine*, 42, 1879–1890.

Krueger, R. F., & Markon, K. E. (2014). The role of the DSM-5 personality trait model in moving toward a quantitative and empirically based approach to classifying personality and psychopathology. *Annual Review of Clinical Psychology*, 10(1), 477–501.

Marigorta, U. M., Rodríguez, J. A., Gibson, G., & Navarro, A. (2018). Replicability and prediction: Lessons and challenges from GWAS. *Trends in Genetics*, 34(7), 504–517.

Miller, J. D., Lynam, D. R., & Campbell, W. K. (2016). Measures of narcissism and their relations to DSM-5 pathological traits: A critical reappraisal. *Assessment*, 23(1), 3–9.

Reichborn-Kjennerud, T. (2010). The genetic epidemiology of personality disorders. *Dialogues in Clinical Neuroscience*, 12(1), 103–114.

Smith, G. T., McCarthy, D. M., & Zapolski, T. C. B. (2009). On the value of homogenous constructs for construct validation, theory testing, and the description of psychopathology. *Psychological Assessment*, 21(3), 272–284.

South, S. C., & DeYoung, N. J. (2013). Behavior genetics of personality disorders: Informing classification and conceptualization in DSM-5. *Personality Disorders: Theory, Research, and Treatment*, 4(3), 270–283.

South, S. C., Krueger, R. F., Knudsen, G. P., Ystrom, E., Czajkowski, N., Aggen, S. H., ... Reichborn-Kjennerud, T. (2017). A population based twin study of DSM-5 maladaptive personality domains. *Personality Disorders: Theory, Research, and Treatment*, 8(4), 366–375.

Thomas, K. M., Yalch, M. M., Krueger, R. F., Wright, A. G. C., Markon, K. E., & Hopwood, C. J. (2013). The convergent structure of DSM-5 personality trait facets and five-factor model trait domains. *Assessment*, 20(3), 308–311.

Widiger, T. A. (2011). Integrating normal and abnormal personality structure: A proposal for DSM-V. *Journal of Personality Disorders, 25*(3), 338–363.

Widiger, T. A., Bach, B., Chmielewski, M., Clark, L. A., DeYoung, C., Hopwood, C. J., ... Thomas, K. M. (2019). Criterion A of the AMPD in HiTOP. *Journal of Personality Assessment, 101*(4), 345–355.

Widiger, T. A., & Trull, T. J. (2007). Plate tectonics in the classification of personality disorder: Shifting to a dimensional model. *American Psychologist, 62*(2), 71–83.

Wright, A. G. C. (2016). On the measure and mismeasure of narcissism: A response to 'Measures of narcissism and their relations to DSM-5 pathological traits: a critical reappraisal'. *Assessment, 23*(1), 10–17.

Wright, A. G. C., & Simms, L. J. (2014). On the structure of personality disorder traits: Conjoint analyses of the CAT-PD, PID-5, and NEO-PI-3 trait models. *Personality Disorders: Theory, Research, and Treatment, 5*(1), 43–54.

Wright, Z. E., Pahlen, S., & Krueger, R. F. (2017). Genetic and environmental influences on Diagnostic and Statistical Manual of Mental Disorders-Fifth Edition (DSM-5) maladaptive personality traits and their connections with normative personality traits. *Journal of Abnormal Psychology, 126*(4), 416–428.

2c Questioning Current Directions in Personality Disorder Genetics: Author Rejoinder to Commentaries on Issues and New Directions in Personality Disorder Genetics

KERRY L. JANG AND FIONA CHOI

Our chapter focused on issues surrounding the search for the genes underlying personality disorder, and the excellent commentaries provided further depth of thought to move this search forward. We believe together these three pieces provide a useful summary of where the field is going. In our rejoinder, we would like to take a different approach and raise the uncomfortable question of whether where we are going is where we should be going.

Turkheimer, Petterson, and Horn (2014) wrote a very interesting paper that turned our understanding of genetics upside down. They contend that the null hypothesis (H_0) geneticists have been working from is not the correct one. Our work is predicated that $H_0 = 0$, that is, genetic influences do not exist; and that the alternative hypothesis (H_1) is that genetic effects do exist and are significantly greater than zero. However, they suggest that the null hypothesis that we should be trying to reject is that genetic effects do exist ($H_0 > 0$) and that the alternative ($H_1 = 0$) is what we should be trying to find support for. This reversal of what H_0 and H_1 are has significant implications for the approach we take.

If we assume that genetic effects are an inexorable part of personality function ($H_0 > 0$) we have to think about what genes do. Typically, genes have been thought of in terms of liability – a risk factor – for the development of personality disorder. Our job has been to find these genes and develop ways to mitigate their expression using biochemical methods or identifying triggers, such as exposures to specific environments and experiences that would turn the liability on or off. Under the new null hypothesis ($H_0 > 0$) genetic influences are seen *less* as a liability, but instead as the fundamental building blocks to normal personality. As such, they confer protective factors against the influences of the environmental stressors. Genetic influences are not a liability but a reflection of the stability of consistent and characteristic behavior – the very definition of personality – and as the bulwarks against the ever changing landscape of environmental and experiential influences that bombard and impinge upon us every day.

It is when the environmental influences overwhelm genetic bulwarks that disorders develop and are maintained. From this perspective, the research focus thus shifts to the environment and identifying those aspects that are instrumental in the development of personality disorder. To date, environmental research has typically focused on models of gene–environment moderation/interaction and correlation (e.g., Carpenter, Tomko, Trull, & Boomsma, 2013; Jafee & Price, 2007) that attempt to identify environmental factors that activate liability genes. The most recent papers also focus on the notion of a genetic liability that is turned off and on by exposure (Bulbena-Cabre, Bassir Nia, & Perez-Rodriguez, 2018; Gescher et al., 2018). The point is that perhaps there are no liability genes – personality disorder genes are rather protective factors and personality disorder is when these genetic defenses are overwhelmed by environmental stressors. Perhaps some of our research focus might be productively directed at understanding what these factors are. Are these overwhelming influences a response to specific traumatic events? Perhaps they develop because of small cumulative events such as parenting practices that exist over time? Are personality disorders the result of a lifetime of observational activity as to what works and what does not? The nature of human experience and how maladaptive behaviors are maintained and supported deserve a second examination and it may mean a return to reconsider foundational ideas about personality such as those discussed by Gordon Allport or Sigmund Freud. Speaking of Gordon Allport (1937), he wrote that personality is something and personality does something. Returning to his famous dictum in the light of our failure to find any genes for personality disorder suggests that the biological basis of personality as reflected in the genes protects us from the vagaries of the environment and is not a liability at all. The inability to find liability genes just might be the most important contribution of genetics research in this field.

REFERENCES

Allport, G. (1937). *Personality: A Psychological Interpretation*. New York: Holt, Rinehart & Winston.

Bulbena-Cabre, A., Bassir Nia, A., & Perez-Rodriguez, M. M. (2018). Current knowledge on gene–environment interactions in personality disorders: An update. *Current Psychiatry Reports, 20*, 74.

Carpenter, R. W., Tomko, R. L., Trull, T. J., & Boomsma, D. I. (2013). Gene–environment studies and borderline personality disorder: A review. *Current Psychiatry Reports, 15*, 336.

Gescher, D. M., Kahl, K. G., Hillemacher, T., Frieling, H., Kuhn J., & Frodl, T. (2018). Epigenetics in personality disorders: Today's insights. *Frontiers in Psychiatry, 9*, 579.

Jaffee, S. R., & Price, T. S. (2007). Gene–environment correlations: A review of the evidence and implications for prevention of mental illness. *Molecular Psychiatry, 12*, 432–442.

Turkheimer, E., Pettersson, E., & Horn, E. A. (2014). Phenotypic null hypothesis for the genetics of personality. *Annual Review of Psychology, 65*, 515–540.

3 Environmental and Sociocultural Influences on Personality Disorders

BRIANNA J. TURNER, JULIE PRUD'HOMME, AND NICOLE LEGG

Personality disorders (PDs) affect approximately 9–16 percent of the population, or about one in eight adults (Grant et al., 2004; Lenzenweger, Lane, Loranger, & Kessler, 2007; Torgersen, Kringlen, & Cramer, 2001; Trull, Jahng, Tomko, Wood, & Sher, 2010). Despite their prevalence, PDs are under-researched and their causes remain poorly understood. Diagnostic frameworks caution clinicians to evaluate a person's characteristic ways of thinking, feeling, and behaving in relation to that person's culture of origin in order to arrive at an appropriate PD diagnosis (American Psychiatric Association [APA], 2013; World Health Organization [WHO], 2010). Yet, large-scale studies regarding environmental and sociocultural factors and personality pathology are only recently emerging, and minimal guidance is provided on how culture should be accounted for in diagnostic decisions. This chapter provides an overview of how environmental and sociocultural factors contribute to the development, expression, and maintenance of PDs, and considers how cultural considerations could be better reflected in research and clinical practice.

At the outset, we note that current definitions of PDs are rooted in Western biomedical traditions (Fabrega, 1994), and there is ongoing debate regarding the validity and utility of many PD diagnoses as cross-cultural or universal entities (Mulder, 2012; Ryder, Dere, Sun, & Chentsova-Dutton, 2014). Indeed, some authors argue that diagnostic nosologies such as the *Diagnostic and Statistical Manual of Mental Disorders* (DSM; APA, 2013) and the *International Statistical Classification of Diseases* (ICD; WHO, 2010) must be viewed as cultural products (Alarcón & Foulks, 1995a, 1995b; Chen, Nettles, & Chen, 2009). With this broad perspective in mind, our chapter attempts to synthesize extant research in a manner that acknowledges the role of culture in how we define and understand sociocultural and environmental influences on PDs. Our chapter begins with a review of studies that have sought to quantify the impact of environmental and sociocultural influences on PDs. Next, we consider theoretical models that explain when and how environmental and sociocultural factors influence PD symptoms. We then review empirical evidence regarding specific types of environmental and sociocultural factors associated with PDs, and conclude with recommendations for future research, evolving diagnostic models, and clinical practice.

HOW MUCH DO ENVIRONMENTAL AND SOCIOCULTURAL FACTORS CONTRIBUTE TO PERSONALITY DISORDERS?

Logically, the first step in understanding *how* environmental and sociocultural factors impact PDs is to establish *that* such factors play a role in their onset and maintenance. In this section, we will review two types of studies that test this premise: behavioral genetic twin and sibling studies, and cross-national and community epidemiological studies. Both types of research inform the scope of environmental and sociocultural contributions to the development, expression, and maintenance of PDs.

Behavioral Genetic Studies

Large-scale heritability studies of PDs have only recently been undertaken, allowing researchers to quantify the relative contributions of genetic versus environmental influences on PDs. A major population-based study of 2794 Norwegian twins estimated that between 20 percent and 55 percent of the variability in PDs is attributable to genetic variation, whereas 59–80 percent of the variability is attributable to environmental influences[1] (Kendler et al., 2008; see also Kendler, Myers, Torgersen, Neale, & Reichborn-Kjennerud, 2007; Reichborn-Kjennerud et al., 2007; Torgersen et al., 2008). These ranges roughly align with studies that have estimated environmental contributions to borderline PD (40–58 percent; Amad, Ramoz, Thomas, Jardri, & Gorwood, 2014; Distel et al., 2008;

---

[1] Note that measurement error is included in estimates of environmental influence.

Kendler, Myers, & Reichborn-Kjennerud, 2011) and anti-social PD (50–59 percent; Rhee & Waldman, 2002; Tuvblad & Beaver, 2013). However, in the Norwegian twin study, environmental factors made the smallest contribution to antisocial and borderline PDs, and the largest contribution to schizotypal, paranoid, schizoid, and narcissistic PDs (Kendler et al., 2008). Further, although most environmental contributions were disorder-specific, a structural model identified three common environmental influences that loosely correspond to the clusters of PDs defined in the DSM-IV (Kendler et al., 2008). For instance, all four Cluster B disorders share a common environmental factor that accounts for 25–41 percent of their variance, whereas 35–45 percent of the variance was accounted for by disorder-specific environmental influences (Torgersen et al., 2008). Environmental influences on PDs have also been linked to normative personality traits, such as neuroticism and disinhibition (Kendler et al., 2011). Thus, twin and sibling studies suggest that environmental factors substantially contribute to variance in PDs.

One consistent but surprising finding to arise from behavioral genetic research is that shared environments (i.e., influences that make siblings similar, such as being reared in the same family and community) make only small to negligible contributions to PDs, whereas unique, non-shared environmental influences (i.e., influences that make siblings who are reared together dissimilar) and measurement error explain the majority of variability in PDs (Kendler et al., 2008). On its face, this finding seems to conflict with many psychological theories that emphasize the role of shared family environments in the development of PDs (e.g., Clarkin, Lenzenweger, Yeomans, Levy, & Kernberg, 2007; Fonagy & Bateman, 2008; Smith Benjamin, 2005). However, a few caveats should be considered before concluding that family environments are unimportant for PDs. First, power calculations estimate that large samples, between 725 and 7000 twin pairs, are required to disentangle passive gene–environment correlations and accurately estimate shared environmental influences (see Martin, Eaves, Kearsey, & Davies, 1978). So far, most twin studies of personality pathology fall far short of this requirement (see Carpenter, Tomko, Trull, & Boomsma, 2013). Second, environmental exposures are often measured retrospectively and imprecisely, or are inadequately scaled, which has made estimation of specific shared environmental contributions difficult (Carpenter et al., 2013), and attempts to classify important sources of shared or non-shared contribution have largely been unsuccessful (Neiderhiser, Reiss, & Hetherington, 2007; Plomin, Asbury, & Dunn, 2001). Given that variance due to measurement error is also contained in estimates of non-shared environmental influences, some researchers have suggested that the larger contribution of non-shared relative to shared environments may be due to transient, measurement-occasion variance and difficulty in reliably assessing PDs (Burt, McGue, Carter, & Iacono, 2007;

Perry, 1992; Turkheimer, 2000). Contrary to this suggestion, however, recent longitudinal studies have found that non-shared environmental factors explained about 30–50 percent of stable variability in PDs across ten-year intervals (Gjerde et al., 2015; Reichborn-Kjennerud et al., 2015), supporting their prospective importance.

Notable, negligible contributions of shared environments have been identified in behavioral genetic studies of normative personality traits, cognitive abilities, and other psychological disorders, making this pattern a rule rather than an exception in the field of psychology (see Plomin et al., 2001; Turkheimer, 2000). With the previous caveats in mind, our best evidence from recent large-scale twin studies suggests that familial aggregation of PDs occurs primarily due to shared genetic vulnerability for broader personality traits (e.g., neuroticism, rigidity), and that most of the environmental contributions to PDs occur due to processes that differ between siblings (i.e., non-shared influences). In light of these results, researchers have emphasized that environmental contributions to PDs might be best conceptualized by the diathesis–stress, or gene–environment, model, wherein environmental influences have the greatest impact when interacting or co-occurring with temperamental or genetic vulnerabilities (e.g., Jaffee et al., 2005; Tuvblad, Grann, & Lichtenstein, 2006). Future attempts to disentangle the relative contributions of environmental versus genetic factors to personality pathology should attempt to account for such cumulative and interactive effects in their design and analysis.

Cross-National and Demographic Comparisons

Cross-national, national, and representative community studies compare the prevalence of personality pathology across demographic groups to elucidate factors that may place an individual at higher risk for developing or expressing personality pathology. Before considering the results of this research, we note two cautions. First, it is important to remember that personality traits and disorders vary more widely within than between cultures (e.g., McCrae & Terracciano, 2005). Even purportedly large cultural differences, such as individualistic versus collectivistic orientations, have been found to be more modest than initially theorized (Oyserman, Coon, & Kemmelmeier, 2002). Thus, the largest sources of variance in PDs are still expected to be idiographic. Second, there is an important dilemma in epidemiological research concerning how best to balance methodological standardization to ensure comparability of results across samples with the use of culturally-informed, emic designs (see Calliess, Sieberer, Machleidt, & Ziegenbein, 2008; Ryder et al., 2014). Unfortunately, there is no easy way to resolve this dilemma. The prevalence studies reviewed below adopt DSM or ICD definitions of PDs and use well-validated but potentially Western-centric assessment instruments (e.g., the *International Personality Disorder Examination* [IPDE; Loranger et al., 1994], the *Structured Interview for DSM-IV Personality* [Pfohl, Blum, & Zimmerman, 1997]).

With respect to cross-national comparisons, national studies demonstrate that PDs can be reliably detected in clinical samples across Western and non-Western countries (Benjet, Borges, & Medina-Mora, 2008; Dereboy, Güzel, Dereboy, Okyay, & Eskin, 2014; Gawda & Czubak, 2017; Loranger et al., 1994; Pedersen & Simonsen, 2014; Rossier & Rigozzi, 2008; Suliman, Stein, Williams, & Seedat, 2008; Yang et al., 2000; Zhong & Leung, 2009); these results counter the idea that PDs are entirely culture-bound syndromes. Differences in the prevalence of PDs between non-Western and Western countries are difficult to ascertain, however, given the wide range of prevalence estimates obtained across methodologies (e.g., clinical versus community samples; screening questionnaires versus interviews; see de Bernier, Kim, & Sen, 2014; Ryder et al., 2014). A recent systematic review of PD prevalence in Asian countries, for instance, found that prevalence estimates in community samples ranged from 1.8–4.4 percent among Chinese adults to 24 percent among Taiwanese and Indian adults without histories of suicide attempts (de Bernier et al., 2014). In clinical samples, estimates ranged from 1–7 percent among psychiatric inpatients and outpatients when PDs were assessed via clinical judgment to 30–50 percent of psychiatric patients and up to 87 percent of suicidal inpatients assessed via structured diagnostic tools (de Bernier et al., 2014). Similar methodological differences have been identified in studies conducted in Western countries (Lyons, Jerskey, & Genderson, 2011), suggesting that firmer conclusions regarding cross-national differences will require consideration of the research methodology used to generate the national prevalence estimates.

To our knowledge, only one major cross-national *comparison* of PD prevalence has been conducted (Huang et al., 2009).[2] The World Mental Health Surveys, conducted in 13 countries (Colombia, Lebanon, Mexico, Nigeria, China, South Africa, the USA, Belgium, France, Germany, Italy, Netherlands, and Spain), found that the prevalence of PDs ranged from around 2–3 percent (Western Europe and Nigeria) to 7–8 percent (Colombia and the USA; Huang et al., 2009). Neither regional nor country-income differences appear to account for the national variation in PD prevalence estimates (Huang et al., 2009). Although there is some evidence to suggest that the prevalence of PDs may vary cross-culturally, it is still unclear what processes might account for these differences.

Representative community surveys can also be used to compare demographic subgroups, elucidating potential environmental or sociocultural contributors to PDs. Community surveys are especially important as they overcome clinical biases that arise due to differential patterns of service use. Representative surveys show that PDs tend to be stratified by gender, age, ethnicity, and socioeconomic status. Specifically, PDs are more common in people who are younger (especially Cluster B disorders), who have lower educational attainment, who have lower annual incomes or are unemployed (especially schizotypal, borderline, and avoidant PDs), who have never married or are divorced, separated, or widowed (especially Cluster A and C disorders), who are living alone (especially Cluster A and C disorders), and who live in urban centers (Coid, Yang, Tyrer, Roberts, & Ullrich, 2006; Dereboy et al., 2014; Grant et al., 2004; Huang et al., 2009; Lenzenweger et al., 2007; Samuels et al., 2002; Torgersen et al., 2001; Trull et al., 2010). Cluster A disorders are also more prevalent among people who experience multiple indices of social deprivation (i.e., high school education or lower, living alone, living in the urban center of a city; see Torgersen, 2012). Whether these demographic factors represent a cause or consequence of personality pathology remains unclear.

Evidence for gender differences in PDs is decidedly mixed. Some studies find higher prevalence of PDs in men versus women (Coid et al., 2006; Huang et al., 2009; Samuels et al., 2002; Suliman et al., 2008; Trull et al., 2010), whereas others find equivalent rates between genders (Lenzenweger et al., 2007; Torgersen et al., 2001). There is some consensus that antisocial, narcissistic, and schizoid PDs are more prevalent in men, whereas histrionic, avoidant, and dependent PDs are more common among women (see Oltmanns & Powers, 2012; Torgersen, 2012 for recent reviews), but results do not always support this pattern. Results are especially inconsistent with respect to the gender distributions of paranoid, borderline, and obsessive-compulsive PDs, with some studies showing higher prevalence of these disorders in women (Grant et al., 2004; Oltmanns, Rodrigues, Weinstein, & Gleason, 2014), others showing no gender difference (Coid et al., 2006; Lenzenweger et al., 2007; Torgersen et al., 2001), and one study finding a higher prevalence of obsessive-compulsive PD in men (Oltmanns et al., 2014). Borderline PD may be over-represented among women in clinical samples, but is more evenly distributed in the general population (Skodol & Bender, 2003). The only PD that has demonstrated consistent gender difference in prevalence is antisocial PD, which is about three to five times more common in men versus women (see Cale & Lilienfeld, 2002). Additional explanations for gender differences will be considered later in this chapter. It is worth noting, however, that gendered patterns in PDs correspond to differences in normative personality traits, with higher sensation seeking, disinhibition, and assertiveness in men, and higher neuroticism

---

[2] Although Loranger et al. (1994), on behalf of the World Health Organization, sought to validate the reliability and validity of the IPDE across 11 countries, this study used clinical rather than community samples and was not intended to examine the prevalence of PDs cross-nationally.

and agreeableness in women (see Lynam & Widiger, 2007).

Mixed findings are also apparent when ethnic groups are compared. A recent meta-analysis suggested that white adults are slightly but significantly more likely to be diagnosed with PDs compared to black adults, although this difference may reflect regional differences (UK vs. USA) and be limited to clinical samples and settings (McGilloway, Hall, Lee, & Bhui, 2010). Differences between white adults and both Asian and Hispanic adults were not identified, but relatively few studies could be included in these analyses. In the USA, a nationally representative survey showed that rates of PDs were highest among American Indian/Alaskan Natives, followed by black non-Hispanic, Hispanic, white non-Hispanic, and finally Asian/Native Hawaiian/Other Pacific Islander adults (Trull et al., 2010). In terms of specific disorders, white Americans experienced higher rates of obsessive-compulsive PD, whereas black, Hispanic, and Native Americans experienced higher rates of schizoid and paranoid PDs (Grant et al., 2004). Avoidant and antisocial PDs were more common among Native Americans, and histrionic PD was more common among black Americans, relative to white Americans (Grant et al., 2004). Borderline PD was most common among Native American men, and least common among Asian women (Grant et al., 2008). In a large treatment-seeking sample of American adults, borderline PD was more common among Hispanic patients, and schizotypal PD was more common among black patients, relative to white patients (Chavira et al., 2003).

Apparent differences in PD prevalence must be interpreted in light of systemic differences in the experiences of racial/ethnic groups. For instance, whereas Cluster A PDs are more commonly diagnosed among black Americans (e.g., Chavira et al., 2003; Gibbs et al., 2013), several authors express concern that this difference reflects pathologization and misinterpretation of normative cultural mistrust that arises when black individuals, as well as other minorities, experience pervasive discrimination, prejudice, and trauma (Gibbs et al., 2013; Whaley, 1997). A similar effect might occur for recent immigrants and refugees whose unfamiliarity with the local language, institutions, and norms may evoke apprehension, withdrawal, and a sense of distrust that can be mistaken for paranoid or schizoid PD (Calliess et al., 2008), or who may report problems with identity, feelings of emptiness, and fears of abandonment that could be mistaken for borderline PD (Alarcón & Foulks, 1995a). Likewise, prisoners, older adults, and people with hearing impairments and other disabilities may exhibit habitual fearfulness, mistrust, antagonism, or acquiescence that must be carefully assessed before concluding it reflects personality pathology (Ryder, Sunohara, & Kirmayer, 2015).

Recent studies suggest that socioeconomic status is a better predictor of risk than race/ethnicity (De Genna & Feske, 2013; Iacovino, Jackson, & Oltmanns, 2014), but that race/ethnicity can influence symptom expression. For instance, whereas white Americans with borderline PD reported greater emotional instability, self-injury, and suicidality, Hispanic and black Americans with borderline PD reported more cognitive symptoms such as emptiness, identity instability, and dissociation (Selby & Joiner, 2008). Considering these findings, it is apparent that multiple social factors must be taken into account to accurately understand racial/ethnic and other demographic differences, and that invariance of symptoms should not be assumed.

WHEN AND HOW DO ENVIRONMENTAL AND SOCIOCULTURAL FACTORS CONTRIBUTE TO PERSONALITY DISORDERS?

Numerous theoretical models have sought to explain when and how environmental and sociocultural factors can predispose an individual to, or perpetuate, personality pathology. We first examine theories that focus on familial and interpersonal contributions to PDs, and then examine theories that focus on broader cultural contributions to PDs.

Environmental Theories of PDs

Biosocial Theory. Linehan's (1993) biosocial theory of borderline PD emphasizes the role of early family environments in the development of PD symptoms, and of later interpersonal contexts in perpetuating symptoms through adolescence and adulthood. According to the biosocial theory, emotion dysregulation is a core feature of borderline PD. This emotion dysregulation arises due to transactions between *invalidating environments* that ignore, reject, punish, or trivialize emotional experiences or expressions, and *biological predispositions* to heightened emotional sensitivity, reactivity, and behavioral disinhibition. According to this model, a lack of fit between the child's emotional sensitivity and caregivers' responses to emotions creates a vicious cycle that alternately punishes and reinforces intense emotional expressions. Ultimately, a child learns that only extreme emotional reactions are likely to garner a desired response from caregivers, but these same reactions are judged as unwarranted and unacceptable. As a result, the child does not learn how to label, control, or tolerate emotional experiences in a way that is acceptable to others, nor does she or he learn to resolve problems that contribute to overwhelming emotional experiences. Over time, these interactions become *transactional*, with biological and environmental factors constantly influencing one another to escalate the pattern of extreme emotional expression and invalidating responses. Invalidation of emotional experience and expression continues to perpetuate borderline PD symptoms in adolescence and adulthood, exacerbating problems in emotion labeling and modulation. As such, these individuals are not able to change their behavior to meet the demands of the environment or the environment itself, perpetuating the chronic emotional and behavioral difficulties that characterize borderline PD.

Attachment Theories. According to Bowlby's (1982) attachment theory, infants must develop secure relationships with a primary caregiver for successful social-emotional development. Early attachment failures or disruptions have cascading consequences for emotional, cognitive, and interpersonal development via *internal working models* that are based on early experiences with caregivers. One way of understanding how early childhood experiences relate to personality pathology is through the concept of *attachment styles* (Ainsworth, Blehar, Waters, & Wall, 1978). Children with anxious-ambivalent styles feel extreme distress when their caregivers leave their surroundings and exhibit continued distress and contact-seeking behaviors upon reunion with their caregivers. These children are more vulnerable to experiencing anxiety and frustration (Sroufe, 2005), which may increase risk for avoidant, obsessive-compulsive, dependent, borderline, or histrionic PDs (Meyer & Pilkonis, 2005). Children with anxious-avoidant styles are not overly distressed when caregivers leave their surroundings, and tend to actively ignore or avoid reuniting with the caregiver following separation. As such, these children tend to experience difficulties in empathy, hostility, and anger (Sroufe, 2005), which may increase risk of antisocial, narcissistic, schizoid, or paranoid PDs later in life (Meyer & Pilkonis, 2005). Children with disorganized-disoriented styles engage in contradictory and inconsistent behaviors with their caregivers. This style is associated with dissociation and emotion dysregulation (Sroufe, 2005), which may increase risk for schizotypal and borderline PDs (Meyer & Pilkonis, 2005).

Attachment can also be understood as a *process* that impacts brain development, self and emotion regulation, adaptive interpersonal skills, and adult personality (Sroufe, 2005), and thus has natural implications for understanding PDs (Levy, 2005). Applying this research to PDs, Gunderson's (2007) attachment theory of borderline PD argues that early attachment difficulties, especially development of a disorganized-ambivalent style, result in pervasive interpersonal hypersensitivity, which is viewed as a cardinal phenotype of borderline PD. Similarly, Fonagy and Bateman's (2008) theory posits that early attachment disruptions impair the development of *mentalization* (i.e., the ability to accurately perceive and understand the mental states of oneself and others), which results in emotion dysregulation, dissociation, and a disorganized sense of self.

Interpersonal Theories. Interpersonal theories of PDs (see Pincus & Hopwood, 2012) originated with the work of Harry Stack Sullivan (1953), who defined personality as recurring patterns of real and imagined interpersonal interactions. According to Stack Sullivan, all interactions are characterized by basic needs for security and self-esteem (later related to *communion* and *agency* by

Wiggins [1991]), which may be realized or frustrated in each interaction. Frustration of these motives can result in self-dysregulation (e.g., incoherent sense of self, unstable self-esteem, and difficulty differentiating the self from others), affective dysregulation (e.g., difficulty modulating emotional states, tendency to experience too much or too little of some emotions), and interpersonal or "field" dysregulation (e.g., difficulty initiating or maintaining intimacy, lack of empathy; Pincus & Hopwood, 2012). According to interpersonal theories, personality pathology arises when security and self-esteem motives are chronically frustrated due to a child's temperamental vulnerability and a *toxic learning environment*, which prevents the child from achieving developmental *copy processes* that are crucial to healthy interpersonal functioning (Smith Benjamin, 2005). Repeated interpersonal frustration and failure to achieve adaptive copy processes result in *parataxic distortions*, or mental representations of interactions that do not match objective representations. When parataxic distortions become chronic, they manifest as rigid and extreme patterns of interpersonal and self-protective behaviors that are commonly observed in PDs. Like other theories summarized in this section, interpersonal theories view personality pathology as arising from an interaction between temperamental vulnerability and adverse early environments, which leads to enduring problems of thinking, feeling, and behaving that, over time, become self-reinforcing (see Pincus & Hopwood, 2012).

Psychodynamic Theories. Psychodynamic theories also emphasize caregiver–infant interactions in accounting for the development of PDs. Early caregiving experiences are said to influence children's *object relations*, or mental representations of the self and others (Clarkin et al., 2007). Children who experience abusive, unresponsive, neglectful, or intrusive caregivers may develop negative, disorganized, inconsistent, or overvalued models of the self and others, resulting in identity diffusion. Negative caregiving experiences can also result in impairments in ego development, which, in turn, impact judgment, planning, and the development of mature versus immature defense mechanisms. Particularly influential among the psychodynamic theories of PD have been Kernberg's (1975) and Kohut's (1977) theories.

Kernberg's object-relations theory (1975; see also Clarkin et al., 2007) argues that early associations between the self, caregiver, and emotions, called *self-object-affect triads*, form the basis for later motivational drives. Beginning around age 3, polarized "good" and "bad" representations are gradually integrated to form more complete representations of the self and others. Among individuals who develop PDs, however, normal development is arrested, resulting in a failure to adequately integrate positive and negative triads. Such failures lead to a vulnerable sense of self and an over-reliance on *splitting* (in which positive and negative images of the self and others cannot be reconciled or simultaneously experienced), *projective identification*, and *dissociation* as defense mechanisms later in life. In borderline PD, splitting involves rapid and chaotic shifts between idealized and devalued self-concepts and appraisals of others in response to intense aggressive impulses the ego cannot handle. In narcissistic PD, relationships with others are viewed as a means of gaining external validation and reflection of the idealized self-concept to protect against criticism that could expose the devalued self-concept.

According to Kohut's theory (1977), children need accurate *mirroring* of their emotions by caregivers to overcome natural helplessness and develop a *sense of mastery*. Accurate parental mirroring fosters development of positive identity and emotion regulation abilities. In contrast, when parents provide inadequate or inaccurate mirroring, children develop a pathological fear of losing their sense of self. In narcissistic PD, inadequate or inaccurate mirroring results in a poorly developed self-concept that is highly vulnerable to threat, as shown by the individual's sensitivity to criticism, pervasive sense of shame, and need for continued mirroring to label, tolerate, and regulate emotion. In borderline PD, insufficient soothing from caregivers results in a pervasive sense of emptiness, lack of organized self-concept, and hypersensitivity to abandonment.

Sociocultural Theories of PDs

Paris' Integrated Sociocultural-Historical Theory. Paris' (1997, 2003) integrated sociocultural-historical theory argues that generation-cohort effects and cross-cultural differences in personality pathology support the idea that sociocultural norms affect the distribution, expression, and pathologization of PDs. For instance, the dramatic rise in violent crimes in the USA and UK since the Second World War might suggest that cultural norms have shifted to encourage more impulsive, aggressive, and disruptive behaviors in modern society (Paris, 1997, 2003; Rutter & Smith, 1995), resulting in an increased prevalence of Cluster B disorders (Widiger & Bornstein, 2002). Paris articulates three factors that contribute to sociocultural and historical trends: *symptom banks*, *social cohesion*, and *social capital* (Paris & Lis, 2013). The "symptom bank" describes the ways in which psychological distress is likely to be expressed in a given cultural group or historical period (Shorter, 1997). For instance, whereas somatization and conversion symptoms were prevalent during the nineteenth century, self-injury, repetitive suicidal behaviors, and externalizing behaviors may be increasing in modernized Western societies (Paris, 1997; Rutter & Smith, 1995). Shifts in symptom expression are also mediated via *social contagion*, which describes direct and indirect transmission of symptomatic expressions, and *social sensitivity*, which describes how likely a person is to respond symptomatically to distress evoked by social change (Paris & Lis, 2013).

Paris (1997, 2014) additionally argues that recent cultural shifts are increasing the rate and severity of psychological distress due to changes in *social capital* and *social cohesion*. Declines in social capital can be traced to declining engagement in traditional social institutions such as marriage, family, religion, and volunteerism, resulting in increasingly less connection, trust, and goodwill among group members. As social capital deteriorates, the buffering role of traditional social structures erodes, increasing risk for psychopathology. Moreover, as traditional roles are less strongly prescribed, many youth experience greater difficulties navigating social role choice and consolidating positive identities. The ever-increasing pace of change, particularly with regard to technological advancements, undermines continuity of norms across generations, as the norms of previous generations are no longer supplied or useful. Moreover, as social cohesion declines and less trust is placed in authority figures, community leaders, and family traditions, there are fewer avenues through which to teach and enforce prosocial behavior. Social networks become less stable, allowing more pathological peer groups to form. Together, these changes promote a kind of "cultural narcissism" that encourages self-promotion, autonomy, instant gratification, and competitive success, exacerbates externalizing behavior, and elevates the prevalence of maladaptive personality traits and Cluster B PDs (Paris, 2014). Changes in symptom banks, social capital, and social cohesion associated with modernization can thus explain why some cultural and demographic groups may be more vulnerable to personality pathology than others.

Gender Role Theory. According to gender role theory, the socially- and culturally-constructed nature of gender role expectations, identities, and behavior strongly influence personality (Spence & Helmreich, 1978; Wood & Eagly, 2012). Gendered role expectations are rooted in biological differences, reinforced by implicit and explicit socialization, and internalized as gender identities (Wood & Eagly, 2012). These gendered roles can be organized according to agentic/instrumental traits and communal/expressive traits (Spence & Helmreich, 1978). Agentic/instrumental traits, including dominance, assertiveness, independence, and competitive success, are commonly encouraged in boys and men. Communal/expressive traits, including selflessness, warmth, emotional sensitivity, and amiability, are commonly encouraged in girls and women. Gender role theory posits that, because of society's gendered socialization of children, PDs that represent agentic/instrumental traits (i.e., narcissistic and antisocial PDs) should be more common in men, whereas PDs that represent communal/expressive traits (i.e., dependent, histrionic, and borderline PDs) should be more common in women. Additionally, non-conformity to gender role expectations (e.g., women with higher agentic/instrumental traits; men with higher communal/expressive traits) may be viewed as more pathological or atypical in cultures with extreme or rigid gender role expectations. As such, clinicians should carefully evaluate cultural contexts and their own expectations when assessing potentially gendered trait expressions.

The convergence between PD descriptions and gender roles has led some authors to question whether apparent gender differences in PDs reflect true differences in prevalence, or whether diagnostic criteria artificially inflate PD diagnoses or pathologize behavior based on gender stereotypes (Bjorklund, 2006; Kaplan, 1983). At least three scenarios are possible in this regard: according to the *clinician/assessment bias hypothesis*, men and women with equivalent pathology exhibit similar symptoms but these expressions are interpreted differently by clinicians; according to the *criterion bias hypothesis*, the criteria for each PD are rooted in definitions of adaptive functioning that more closely align with one gender role than the other, reflecting inherent gender bias; and, finally, according to the *cultural relativity hypothesis*, men and women express the same underlying pathology differently, but clinicians who are unaware or insensitive to these differences may misdiagnose the underlying problem (Widiger, 1998).

Although the debate regarding the tenability of these hypotheses is far from resolved, research has shed some light on their plausibility. Consistent with the clinician/assessment bias hypothesis, studies have found that although diagnostic criteria and normative personality traits were rated and interpreted similarly by clinicians, a fictional patient was more likely to receive a diagnosis of histrionic PD if described as female, but more likely to be diagnosed with antisocial PD if described as male (Ford & Widiger, 1989; Samuel & Widiger, 2009). However, in more recent studies, a fictional client was no more likely to receive a borderline PD diagnosis compared to a diagnosis of posttraumatic stress, major depressive, or generalized anxiety disorders based on the individual's noted gender (Cwik, Papen, Lemke, & Margraf, 2016; Woodward, Taft, Gordon, & Meis, 2009). Inconsistent with the criterion bias hypothesis, studies show that clinicians do not rate criteria associated with "feminine" PDs (e.g., histrionic, dependent) as more or less severe, impairing, or abnormal than those associated with "masculine" PDs (e.g., antisocial; Funtowicz & Widiger, 1999; Morey, Warner, & Boggs, 2002), and that these criteria do not show gender bias in their associations with severity or impairment in clinical (Boggs, Morey, Skodol, Shea, & Sanislow, 2005) or non-clinical samples (Jane, Oltmanns, South, & Turkheimer, 2007; Morey et al., 2002). Consistent with the cultural relativity hypothesis, some authors suggest that diagnostic criteria may not adequately capture symptoms of antisocial PD as expressed in women versus men (Cale & Lilienfeld, 2002; Sprague, Javdani, Sadeh, Newman, & Verona, 2012). However, until broader issues related to gender biases are resolved (see Widiger, 1998), the latter hypothesis will remain difficult to test.

Critical Cultural Theory. Critical theorists note that the current diagnostic criteria for PDs are rooted in Western notions of the self that emphasize autonomy, independence, and individual agency, rather than concepts of the self that emphasize interdependence and socially determined behavior (Chen et al., 2009; Fabrega, 1994).

Emerging research shows that behaviors that are considered maladaptive in one culture may not be problematic in others. For instance, shyness and withdrawal correlate with poor emotional and social outcomes in Australia and the USA; however, these traits are not associated with impairments and predict good adjustment in China and Korea (Chen & Stevenson, 1995; Kim, Rapee, Ja Oh, & Moon, 2008). Moreover, students living in Boston, Massachusetts (an independent-orientated region) with more of a collectivistic orientation experienced more anxiety and depression than their individualistic-oriented peers, whereas students living in Istanbul (an interdependent-oriented region) with a more individualistic orientation reported more paranoid thinking, narcissism, impulsivity, and antisociality compared to their collectivistic-oriented peers (Caldwell-Harris & Ayçiçegi, 2006). Thus, certain aspects of PDs may be culturally bound, as personality traits may only be problematic when a person's cultural orientation does not fit with the demands and values of the culture in which he or she is embedded.

At the same time, cultural anthropologists note that some PD concepts, especially psychopathy and antisociality, are recognized across diverse cultural groups, including the Alaskan Inuit and Nigerian Yoruba, and thus may be considered culturally universal (Cooke, 2009; Murphy, 1976). Moreover, the Big Five personality traits have been found to characterize personality constructs and structure in Western and non-Western cultures, using both etic and emic approaches (e.g., Allik, 2005; Rossier & Rigozzi, 2008; Terracciano & McCrae, 2006; Yang & Bond, 1990). Thus, there is some reason to believe that certain personality constructs may be culturally translatable. Nevertheless, cultural context and goodness of fit must be considered in assessing the possible functional implications of these traits.

WHAT TYPES OF SOCIOCULTURAL OR ENVIRONMENTAL INFLUENCES INCREASE RISK FOR PERSONALITY DISORDERS?

Given that such a large percentage of the variance in PDs is attributable to environmental influences (Kendler et al., 2008), the next question to consider is exactly what *types* of environments increase an individual's risk for developing or expressing a PD. Before summarizing putative environmental and sociocultural risk factors for PDs, we wish to emphasize that the vast majority of people with these experiences do not go on to develop PDs, and some people with PDs do not experience *any* of the stressors listed below. In other words, these environmental and sociocultural experiences are *neither necessary nor sufficient* to cause PDs, but they may elevate risk when they interact with temperamental or genetic vulnerabilities.

Early Childhood Adversity and Developmental Trauma. People with PDs are significantly more likely to report childhood adversity, abuse, and trauma, relative to people without PDs (Afifi et al., 2011; Battle et al., 2004; Björkenstam, Ekselius, Burström, Kosidou, & Björkenstam, 2017; Widom, Czaja, & Paris, 2009). This result has been robustly supported across categorical and dimensional conceptualizations of PDs (see Hengartner, Ajdacic-Gross, Rodgers, Müller, & Rössler, 2013) for a broad range of childhood adversities, from parental separation (Lahti et al., 2012), to physical and sexual abuse (Johnson, Cohen, Brown, Smailes, & Bernstein, 1999; Widom et al., 2009), to war-related trauma (Munjiza, Britvic, Radman, & Crawford, 2017), and using both retrospective and prospective designs (e.g., Cutajar et al., 2010; Johnson et al., 1999; Widom et al., 2009). Childhood abuse or neglect is associated with a four-fold increase in the odds of developing a PD (Johnson et al., 1999), with a dose–response relationship between the total number of adverse events and symptom severity (Bandelow et al., 2005; Björkenstam et al., 2017; Distel et al., 2011).

Some evidence suggests that different types of adversities may be associated with specific PDs. Specifically, sexual abuse is associated with paranoid, schizotypal, borderline, avoidant, dependent, and obsessive-compulsive PDs; physical abuse is associated with antisocial PD; and emotional neglect is associated with histrionic and borderline PDs (Lobbestael, Arntz, & Bernstein, 2010). Further, although childhood emotional neglect has been found to be most strongly associated with avoidant and paranoid PDs, as well as Cluster A PD symptom severity, physical neglect is most strongly associated with schizotypal PD, as well as cluster A symptom severity (Johnson, Smailes, Cohen, Brown, & Bernstein, 2000).

Unsurprisingly, gene–environment interactions play an important role in this relationship. For instance, physical maltreatment was associated with a 2 percent increase in conduct problems among children at low genetic risk, but a 24 percent increase among children at high genetic risk (Jaffee et al., 2005). Whereas genetic influence explained more variance in antisocial behavior among individuals raised in socioeconomically advantaged environments, shared environmental influences explained more variance in antisocial behaviors among individuals raised in disadvantaged environments (Tuvblad et al., 2006). Adopted children of parents with antisocial PD who were exposed to caregiver conflict, divorce, psychopathology, physical maltreatment, or low social status were much more likely to develop conduct problems, relative to genetically-vulnerable but environmentally-unexposed peers (Cadoret, Yates, Troughton, Woodworth, & Stewart, 1995).

The over-representation of early adversity and developmental trauma in PD populations has led some authors to propose that certain PDs could be conceptualized as a type of posttraumatic stress disorder (see Lewis & Grenyer, 2009). However, these proposals remain controversial, as not all individuals with a PD have experienced developmental trauma or adversity (Bandelow et al., 2005; Gunderson & Sabo, 1993). Nonetheless, early childhood adversity is one of the most robust environmental correlates of PDs.

Stressful Life Events. The association between adversity, trauma, and personality pathology is not limited to childhood experiences. Adolescents and adults with PDs experience more daily hassles and stressful events than do their peers without PDs (Stepp, Pilkonis, Yaggi, Morse, & Feske, 2009; Tessner, Mittal, & Walker, 2011). Stressful life events such as divorce and job loss predicted borderline PD features in genetically vulnerable individuals, and traumatic events such as sexual assault predicted elevated borderline PD features even in those who are genetically less vulnerable (Distel et al., 2011). Among Vietnam veterans, traumatic experiences during combat were associated with more antisocial behaviors later in life, even after controlling for childhood adversity (Barrett et al., 1996). This evidence suggests that environmental stressors continue to play a role in PDs through adulthood.

Parenting Styles and Parental Psychopathology. Parenting plays a key role in emotional, behavioral, and cognitive development; thus, it is no surprise it has also been linked to PDs. Early studies based on Baumrind's parenting style typology (i.e., neglectful, permissive, authoritative, authoritarian) have linked permissive and authoritarian parenting styles to narcissistic traits (Watson, Little, & Biderman, 1992), authoritarian parenting to antisocial traits (Farrington, 1993), and authoritative parenting styles to low psychopathology (Baumrind, 1966). More recent studies of specific parenting behaviors find that personality pathology is negatively associated with parental warmth and monitoring, and positively associated with psychological control, harsh punishment, and rejection (Horton, Bleau, & Drwecki, 2006; Huang et al., 2014; Stravynski, Elie, & Franche, 1989; Wetzel & Robins, 2016). Coercive communication cycles that escalate aggression and emotional arousal via negative reinforcement are theorized to play an especially important role in the development of antisocial traits (Snyder, Schrepferman, & St. Peter, 1997).

Although theoretical models posit that specific parenting profiles might be associated with different types of personality pathology (e.g., authoritarian, overprotective parenting is predicted to elevate risk for dependent PD; rejecting, dismissive parenting is predicted to elevate risk for avoidant PD; see Widiger & Bornstein, 2002), few studies have directly tested these assumptions. One recent longitudinal study showed that low parental warmth was associated with elevated risk of paranoid, schizoid, schizotypal, antisocial, borderline, and avoidant PDs in early to middle adulthood, whereas harsh parental punishment was associated with later paranoid, schizotypal, and borderline PDs (Johnson, Cohen, Chen, Kasen, & Brook, 2006). Poor parental supervision was most strongly associated with borderline and paranoid PDs, and Cluster B symptom severity (Johnson et al., 2000). A dose–response relationship is also evident, with more problematic parenting behaviors linked to greater likelihood of personality pathology (Johnson, Cohen, Chen, et al.,

2006). Similar associations with parenting style are also evident when personality pathology is assessed dimensionally (De Clercq, Van Leeuwen, De Fruyt, Van Hiel, & Mervielde, 2008).

Combinations of different parenting profiles might exert even stronger effects on personality pathology than specific parenting behaviors considered in isolation. The combination of low warmth, low supervision, and high rejection/hostility by parents is particularly strongly associated with conduct problems and antisocial behavior (Hoeve et al., 2009), whereas the combination of maternal inconsistency and over-involvement is associated with borderline PD in adolescents (Bezirganian, Cohen, & Brook, 1993).

Parental psychopathology is also associated with elevated risk of personality pathology among children (McLaughlin et al., 2012; Schuppert, Albers, Minderaa, Emmelkamp, & Nauta, 2012). This is not surprising given that parental psychopathology is associated with many of the maladaptive parenting behaviors summarized above (Johnson, Cohen, Kasen, Ehrensaft, & Crawford, 2006). Studies increasingly highlight intergenerational cycles between psychopathology and parenting behaviors that maintain PDs in families (Infurna et al., 2016; Smith & Farrington, 2004).

Peer Relationships. Peer experiences, including rejection, humiliation, and bullying (e.g., Alden, Laposa, Taylor, & Ryder, 2002) and social contagion (e.g., Paris, 1997), are theorized to play a role in PDs, but few studies have tested these proposals. Delinquent peer groups have been consistently linked to antisocial behavior in adolescence and later adulthood (Dishion, Nelson, Winter, & Bullock, 2004; Dishion & Tipsord, 2011), but whether similar effects occur for other PD symptoms is relatively unknown.

Neighborhoods and Communities. Evidence regarding neighborhood- and community-level factors that elevate risk for PDs is sparse. Walsh and colleagues (2013) showed that residing in a high-risk neighborhood (defined by the median household income and the proportion of households or individuals in the area who were receiving public assistance, unemployed, and living below the poverty line) was associated with more severe PD symptoms, particularly for individuals with low socioeconomic status. These results are consistent with previous studies showing that neighborhood deprivation and community solidarity have an important impact on children's emotional and behavioral problems (Caspi, Taylor, Moffitt, & Plomin, 2000), as well as violent crime and antisocial behavior (Sampson, Raudenbush, & Earls, 1997). These factors merit increased attention in future studies.

WHERE TO FROM HERE? CONCLUSIONS, IMPLICATIONS, AND FUTURE DIRECTIONS

Summary and Conclusions

Although research investigating environmental and sociocultural contributions to personality pathology is still relatively new, tentative conclusions may be drawn. Both empirical and theoretical accounts underscore that environmental and sociocultural factors are integral to the development, expression, and maintenance of PDs. Non-shared environmental influences – those that account for differences between siblings – are estimated to account for 50–89 percent of the variance in PD prevalence, whereas shared influences seem to play a lesser role. Community studies highlight an elevated prevalence of PDs among those who are socially disadvantaged, including those who have lower income and educational attainment and who live in more urban and high-risk neighborhoods; however, whether these demographic features are causes, correlates, or consequences of personality pathology requires further investigation. Cross-national and cross-cultural comparisons suggest that, although we should be very cautious in assuming universality with respect to diagnostic entities, basic constructs underlying normative and maladaptive personality may have cross-cultural validity and utility. The expression, meaning, and impact of specific personality traits and behaviors may differ across gender roles, historical periods, and cultural groups. Thus, understanding the implications of personality traits for a person's social, occupational, and emotional functioning requires interpreting symptoms and traits through an environmental and cultural lens.

Implications for Practice

Applying current diagnostic guidelines for PDs requires grappling with assumptions of cultural universality versus relativity to determine whether behaviors are sufficiently persistent and pathological to merit a PD diagnosis. Clinical errors can result from adopting either assumption dogmatically. Using one's own culture as a reference or, alternatively, applying broad cultural stereotypes to evaluate a client's behavior, can lead clinicians to over-pathologize behaviors that are culturally normative or under-pathologize behaviors that are clinically significant. Clinicians should be mindful of their cultural competency and seek consultation, training, and supervision as required. Experiences of immigration and acculturation, gendered expectations for behavior, disabilities, marginalization, and discrimination can all influence symptom presentation and interpretation. Treatment planning should consider cultural issues, including patterns of help-seeking behavior and possible adaptations to treatment. Whereas current psychotherapeutic interventions naturally flow from environmental theories (e.g., Smith Benjamin 2005; Fonagy & Bateman, 2008; Linehan, 1993), sociocultural theories demand a different sort of intervention, and these systemic efforts deserve attention.

Future Directions

A number of future research endeavors can improve our understanding of the environmental and sociocultural factors that influence PDs. As noted above, cross-national comparative studies using similar methodologies may help clarify the prevalence of PDs across different countries, and within different cultural groups in the same country. At the same time, studies that adopt culturally informed assessments of PDs are crucial for understanding how distinct cultures and environments shape PD symptoms, expressions, and definitions. Prospective cohort studies will help to untangle possible generational and historical trends in personality pathology that have rarely been examined. Finally, incorporating clearly operationalized measurements of environmental and sociocultural factors in future PD studies will improve our ability to quantify and understand these effects.

One issue that deserves special consideration is the growing push for dimensional conceptualizations of personality pathology. An alternative dimensional model of PD diagnosis is included in Section III of the DSM-5 (APA, 2013), and similar models are expected to appear in the ICD-11 (WHO, 2010). Although some concerns remain regarding the clinical feasibility and utility of this approach, we believe that the field will increasingly move toward dimensional conceptualizations of personality pathology in the coming years. What would such a shift mean for understanding the role of sociocultural and environmental factors in personality pathology? As described above, many of the specific environmental and sociocultural correlates of PDs have already been validated against corresponding normative or maladaptive traits, and many theoretical models initially arose from dimensional conceptualizations of personality, suggesting excellent potential for translation. In terms of clinical practice, it is noteworthy that aside from borderline, antisocial, and unspecified PD, most categorical PD diagnoses are rarely used in most countries (Tyrer, Crawford, Mulder, & ICD-11 Working Group, 2011), potentially pointing to their limited cross-cultural utility. Given emerging evidence that the Big Five traits can be reliably assessed in diverse cultural contexts, a shift toward dimensional diagnosis of personality pathology based on maladaptive traits could improve the cross-cultural validity of PD nosology and stimulate cross-cultural research. Such a shift would require substantial effort to establish the reliability, validity, and utility of both the dimensional model and its assessment instruments, but we believe the time is right for such work. An alternative or intermediate step might be to reduce PD diagnoses into broader domains (e.g., anxious/dependent, antagonistic/aggressive, withdrawn/isolated, obsessive/rigid, and psychopathic/antisocial; Mulder, 2012); however, this may not adequately address issues of comorbidity that are frequently encountered in clinical practice.

Whether or not the field adopts dimensional models for clinical practice, increasing efforts to establish the cross-cultural structure, reliability, and validity of dimensional assessments of personality pathology is a vital step in advancing knowledge of environmental and sociocultural influences on PDs. Expanding research efforts to investigate the meaning and impact of personality constructs within distinct and intersecting cultural groups is a crucial and needed direction for future research. Moreover, future research should address limitations of previous studies by increasing the use of representative samples, prospective and repeated measurement designs of environmental influences and personality pathology, as well as standardized operationalizations of environmental influences. Cultural influences, which are largely assumed in current designs, would benefit from more explicit and nuanced measurement. Together, these efforts would substantially enhance our understanding of why some people develop PDs and how we can prevent them.

REFERENCES

Afifi, T. O., Mather, A., Boman, J., Fleisher, W., Enns, M. W., MacMillan, H., & Sareen, J. (2011). Childhood adversity and personality disorders: Results from a nationally representative population-based study. *Journal of Psychiatric Research, 45*(6), 814–822.

Ainsworth, M. D. S., Blehar, M. C., Waters, E., & Wall, S. (1978). *Patterns of Attachment: A Psychological Study of the Strange Situation*. New York: Psychology Press.

Alarcón, R. D., & Foulks, E. F. (1995a). Personality disorders and culture: Contemporary clinical views (Part A). *Cultural Diversity and Mental Health, 1*(1), 3–17.

Alarcón, R. D., & Foulks, E. F. (1995b). Personality disorders and culture: Contemporary clinical views (Part B). *Cultural Diversity and Mental Health, 1*(2), 79–91.

Alden, L. E., Laposa, J. M., Taylor, C. T., & Ryder, A. G. (2002). Avoidant personality disorder: Current status and future directions. *Journal of Personality Disorders, 16*(1), 1–29.

Allik, J. (2005). Personality dimensions across cultures. *Journal of Personality Disorders, 19*(3), 212–232.

Amad, A., Ramoz, N., Thomas, P., Jardri, R., & Gorwood, P. (2014). Genetics of borderline personality disorder: Systematic review and proposal of an integrative model. *Neuroscience & Biobehavioral Reviews, 40*, 6–19.

American Psychiatric Association [APA]. (2013). *Diagnostic and Statistical Manual of Mental Disorders* (5th ed.). Arlington, VA: American Psychiatric Publishing.

Bandelow, B., Krause, J., Wedekind, D., Broocks, A., Hajak, G., & Rüther, E. (2005). Early traumatic life events, parental attitudes, family history, and birth risk factors in patients with borderline personality disorder and healthy controls. *Psychiatry Research, 134*(2), 169–179.

Barrett, D. H., Resnick, H. S., Foy, D. W., Dansky, B. S., Flanders, W. D., & Stroup, N. E. (1996). Combat exposure and adult psychosocial adjustment among U.S. Army veterans serving in Vietnam, 1965–1971. *Journal of Abnormal Psychology, 105*(4), 575–581.

Battle, C. L., Shea, M. T., Johnson, D. M., Zlotnick, C., Zanarini, M. C., Battle, C. L., ... Morey, T. H. (2004). Childhood maltreatment associated with adult personality disorders: Findings from the Collaborative Longitudinal Personality Disorders Study. *Journal of Personality Disorders, 18*(2), 193–211.

Baumrind, D. (1966). Effects of authoritative parental control on child behavior. *Child Development, 37*(4), 887–907.

Benjet, C., Borges, G., & Medina-Mora, M. E. (2008). DSM-IV personality disorders in Mexico: Results from a general population survey. *Revista Brasileira de Psiquiatria, 30*(3), 227–234.

Bezirganian, S., Cohen, P., & Brook, J. S. (1993). The impact of mother–child interaction on the development of borderline personality disorder. *American Journal of Psychiatry, 150*(12), 1836–1842.

Björkenstam, E., Ekselius, L., Burström, B., Kosidou, K., & Björkenstam, C. (2017). Association between childhood adversity and a diagnosis of personality disorder in young adulthood: A cohort study of 107,287 individuals in Stockholm County. *European Journal of Epidemiology, 32*(8), 721–731.

Bjorklund, P. (2006). No man's land: Gender bias and social constructivism in the diagnosis of borderline personality disorder. *Issues in Mental Health Nursing, 27*(1), 3–23.

Boggs, C. D., Morey, L. C., Skodol, A. E., Tracie Shea, M., & Sanislow, C. A. (2005). Differential impairment as an indicator of sex bias in DSM-IV criteria for four personality disorders. Recommended Citation. *Psychological Assessment Personality Disorders: Theory, Research, and Treatment, 17*(41), 492–496.

Bowlby, J. (1982). *Attachment and Loss, Volume 1: Attachment* (2nd ed.). New York: Basic Books.

Burt, S. A., McGue, M., Carter, L. A., & Iacono, W. G. (2007). The different origins of stability and change in antisocial personality disorder symptoms. *Psychological Medicine, 37*(1), 27–38.

Cadoret, R. J., Yates, W. R., Troughton, E., Woodworth, G., & Stewart, M. A. (1995). Genetic–environmental interaction in the genesis of aggressivity and conduct disorders. *Archives of General Psychiatry, 52*(11), 916–924.

Caldwell-Harris, C. L., & Ayçiçegi, A. (2006). When personality and culture clash: The psychological distress of allocentrics in an individualist culture and idiocentrics in a collectivist culture. *Transcultural Psychiatry, 43*(3), 331–361.

Cale, E. M., & Lilienfeld, S. O. (2002). Sex differences in psychopathy and antisocial personality disorder: A review and integration. *Clinical Psychology Review, 22*(8), 1179–1207.

Calliess, I., Sieberer, M., Machleidt, W., & Ziegenbein, M. (2008). Personality disorders in a cross-cultural perspective: Impact of culture and migration on diagnosis and etiological aspects. *Current Psychiatry Reviews, 4*(1), 39–47.

Carpenter, R. W., Tomko, R. L., Trull, T. J., & Boomsma, D. I. (2013). Gene–environment studies and borderline personality disorder: A review. *Current Psychiatry Reports, 15*(1), 336.

Caspi, A., Taylor, A., Moffitt, T. E., & Plomin, R. (2000). Neighborhood deprivation affects children's mental health: Environmental risks identified in a genetic design. *Psychological Science, 11*(4), 338–342.

Chavira, D. A., Grilo, C. M., Shea, M. T., Yen, S., Gunderson, J. G., Morey, L. C., ... Mcglashan, T. H. (2003). Ethnicity and four personality disorders. *Comprehensive Psychiatry, 44*(6), 483–491.

Chen, C., & Stevenson, H. W. (1995). Motivation and mathematics achievement: A comparative study of Asian-American, Caucasian-American, and East Asian high school students. *Child Development, 66*(4), 1215–1234.

Chen, Y., Nettles, M. E., & Chen, S.-W. (2009). Rethinking dependent personality disorder. *Journal of Nervous and Mental Disease, 197*(11), 793–800.

Clarkin, J. F., Lenzenweger, M. F., Yeomans, F., Levy, K. N., & Kernberg, O. F. (2007). An object relations model of borderline pathology. *Journal of Personality Disorders, 21*(5), 474–499.

Coid, J., Yang, M., Tyrer, P., Roberts, A., & Ullrich, S. (2006). Prevalence and correlates of personality disorder in Great Britain. *British Journal of Psychiatry, 188*, 423–431.

Cooke, D. J. (2009). Understanding cultural variation in psychopathic personality disorder: Conceptual and measurement issues. *Neuropsychiatrie, 23*, 64–68.

Cutajar, M. C., Mullen, P. E., Ogloff, J. R. P., Thomas, S. D., Wells, D. L., & Spataro, J. (2010). Psychopathology in a large cohort of sexually abused children followed up to 43 years. *Child Abuse & Neglect, 34*(11), 813–822.

Cwik, J. C., Papen, F., Lemke, J.-E., & Margraf, J. (2016). An investigation of diagnostic accuracy and confidence associated with diagnostic checklists as well as gender biases in relation to mental disorders. *Frontiers in Psychology, 7*, 1813.

de Bernier, G., Kim, Y., & Sen, P. (2014). A systematic review of the global prevalence of personality disorders in adult Asian populations. *Personality and Mental Health, 8*, 264–275.

De Clercq, B., Van Leeuwen, K., De Fruyt, F., Van Hiel, A., & Mervielde, I. (2008). Maladaptive personality traits and psychopathology in childhood and adolescence: The moderating effect of parenting. *Journal of Personality, 76*(2), 357–383.

De Genna, N. M., & Feske, U. (2013). Phenomenology of borderline personality disorder: The role of race and socioeconomic status. *Journal of Nervous and Mental Disease, 201*(12), 1027–1034.

Dereboy, C., Güzel, H. S., Dereboy, F., Okyay, P., & Eskin, M. (2014). Personality disorders in a community sample in Turkey: Prevalence, associated risk factors, temperament and character dimensions. *International Journal of Social Psychiatry, 60*(2), 139–147.

Dishion, T. J., Nelson, S. E., Winter, C. E., & Bullock, B. M. (2004). Adolescent friendship as a dynamic system: Entropy and deviance in the etiology and course of male antisocial behavior. *Journal of Abnormal Child Psychology, 32*(6), 651–663.

Dishion, T. J., & Tipsord, J. M. (2011). Peer contagion in child and adolescent social and emotional development. *Annual Review of Psychology, 62*, 189–214.

Distel, M. A., Middeldorp, C. M., Trull, T. J., Derom, C. A., Willemsen, G., & Boomsma, D. I. (2011). Life events and borderline personality features: The influence of gene–environment interaction and gene–environment correlation. *Psychological Medicine, 41*(4), 849–860.

Distel, M. A., Trull, T. J., Derom, C. A., Thiery, E. W., Grimmer, M. A., Martin, N. G., ... Boomsma, D. I. (2008). Heritability of borderline personality disorder features is similar across three countries. *Psychological Medicine, 38*(9), 1219–1229.

Fabrega, H. (1994). Personality disorders as medical entities: A cultural interpretation. *Journal of Personality Disorders, 8*(2), 149–167.

Farrington, D. P. (1993). Childhood origins of teenage antisocial behavior and adult social dysfunction. *Journal of the Royal Society of Medicine, 86*(1), 13–17.

Fonagy, P., & Bateman, A. (2008). The development of borderline personality disorder: A mentalizing model. *Journal of Personality Disorders, 22*(1), 4–21.

Ford, M. R., & Widiger, T. A. (1989). Sex bias in the diagnosis of histrionic and antisocial personality disorders. *Journal of Consulting and Clinical Psychology, 57*(2), 301–305.

Funtowicz, M. N., & Widiger, T. A. (1999). Sex bias in the diagnosis of personality disorders: An evaluation of the DSM-IV criteria. *Journal of Abnormal Psychology, 108*(2), 195–201.

Gawda, B., & Czubak, K. (2017). Prevalence of personality disorders in a general population among men and women. *Psychological Reports*, *120*(3), 503–519.

Gibbs, T. A., Okuda, M., Oquendo, M. A., Lawson, W. B., Wang, S., Thomas, Y. F., & Blanco, C. (2013). Mental health of African Americans and Caribbean blacks in the United States: Results from the National Epidemiological Survey on Alcohol and Related Conditions. *American Journal of Public Health*, *103*(2), 330–338.

Gjerde, L. C., Czajkowski, N., Røysamb, E., Ystrom, E., Tambs, K., Aggen, S. H., … Knudsen, G. P. (2015). A longitudinal, population-based twin study of avoidant and obsessive-compulsive personality disorder traits from early to middle adulthood. *Psychological Medicine*, *45*(16), 3539–3548.

Grant, B. F., Chou, S. P., Goldstein, R. B., Huang, B., Stinson, F. S., Saha, T. D., … Ruan, W. J. (2008). Prevalence, correlates, disability, and comorbidity of DSM-IV borderline personality disorder: Results from the Wave 2 National Epidemiologic Survey on Alcohol and Related Conditions. *Journal of Clinical Psychiatry*, *69*(4), 533–545.

Grant, B. F., Hasin, D. S., Stinson, F. S., Dawson, D. A., Chou, S. P., Ruan, W. J., & Pickering, R. P. (2004). Prevalence, correlates, and disability of personality disorders in the United States: Results from the National Epidemiologic Survey on Alcohol and Related Conditions. *Journal of Clinical Psychiatry*, *65*(7), 948–958.

Gunderson, J. G. (2007). Disturbed relationships as a phenotype for borderline personality disorder. *American Journal of Psychiatry*, *164*(11), 1637–1640.

Gunderson, J. G., & Sabo, A. N. (1993). The phenomenological and conceptual interface between borderline personality disorder and PTSD. *American Journal of Psychiatry*, *150*(1), 19–27.

Hengartner, M. P., Ajdacic-Gross, V., Rodgers, S., Müller, M., & Rössler, W. (2013). Childhood adversity in association with personality disorder dimensions: New findings in an old debate. *European Psychiatry*, *28*(8), 476–482.

Hoeve, M., Dubas, J. S., Eichelsheim, V. I., van der Laan, P. H., Smeenk, W., & Gerris, J. R. M. (2009). The relationship between parenting and delinquency: A meta-analysis. *Journal of Abnormal Child Psychology*, *37*(6), 749–775.

Horton, R. S., Bleau, G., & Drwecki, B. (2006). Parenting Narcissus: What are the links between parenting and narcissism? *Journal of Personality*, *74*(2), 345–376.

Huang, J., Napolitano, L. A., Wu, J., Yang, Y., Xi, Y., Li, Y., & Li, K. (2014). Childhood experiences of parental rearing patterns reported by Chinese patients with borderline personality disorder. *International Journal of Psychology*, *49*(1), 38–45.

Huang, Y., Kotov, R., de Girolamo, G., Preti, A., Angermeyer, M., Benjet, C., … Kessler, R. C. (2009). DSM-IV personality disorders in the WHO World Mental Health Surveys. *British Journal of Psychiatry*, *195*(1), 46–53.

Iacovino, J. M., Jackson, J. J., & Oltmanns, T. F. (2014). The relative impact of socioeconomic status and childhood trauma on black–white differences in paranoid personality disorder symptoms. *Journal of Abnormal Psychology*, *123*(1), 225–230.

Infurna, M. R., Fuchs, A., Fischer-Waldschmidt, G., Reichl, C., Holz, B., Resch, F., … Kaess, M. (2016). Parents' childhood experiences of bonding and parental psychopathology predict borderline personality disorder during adolescence in offspring. *Psychiatry Research*, *246*, 373–378.

Jaffee, S. R., Caspi, A., Moffitt, T. E., Dodge, K. A., Rutter, M., Taylor, A., & Tully, L. A. (2005). Nature × nurture: genetic vulnerabilities interact with physical maltreatment to promote conduct problems. *Development and Psychopathology*, *17*(1), 67–84.

Jane, J. S., Oltmanns, T. F., South, S. C., & Turkheimer, E. (2007). Gender bias in diagnostic criteria for personality disorders: An item response theory analysis. *Journal of Abnormal Psychology*, *116*(1), 166–175.

Johnson, J. G., Cohen, P., Brown, J., Smailes, E., & Bernstein, D. P. (1999). Childhood maltreatment increases risk for personality disorders during early adulthood. *Archives of General Psychiatry*, *56*(7), 600–606.

Johnson, J. G., Cohen, P., Chen, H., Kasen, S., & Brook, J. S. (2006). Parenting behaviors associated with risk for offspring personality disorder during adulthood. *Archives of General Psychiatry*, *63*(5), 579–587.

Johnson, J. G., Cohen, P., Kasen, S., Ehrensaft, M. K., & Crawford, T. N. (2006). Associations of parental personality disorders and axis I disorders with childrearing behavior. *Psychiatry: Interpersonal and Biological Processes*, *69*(4), 336–350.

Johnson, J. G., Smailes, E. M., Cohen, P., Brown, J., & Bernstein, D. P. (2000). Associations between four types of childhood neglect and personality disorder symptoms during adolescence and early adulthood: Findings of a community-based longitudinal study. *Journal of Personality Disorders*, *14*(2), 171–187.

Kaplan, M. (1983). A woman's view of DSM-III. *American Psychologist*, *38*(7), 786–792.

Kendler, K. S., Aggen, S. H., Czajkowski, N., Røysamb, E., Tambs, K., Torgersen, S., … Reichborn-Kjennerud, T. (2008). The structure of genetic and environmental risk factors for DSM-IV personality disorders: A multivariate twin study. *Archives of General Psychiatry*, *65*(12), 1438–1446.

Kendler, K. S., Myers, J., & Reichborn-Kjennerud, T. (2011). Borderline personality disorder traits and their relationship with dimensions of normative personality: A web-based cohort and twin study. *Acta Psychiatrica Scandinavica*, *123*(5), 349–359.

Kendler, K. S., Myers, J., Torgersen, S., Neale, M. C., & Reichborn-Kjennerud, T. (2007). The heritability of cluster A personality disorders assessed by both personal interview and questionnaire. *Psychological Medicine*, *37*(5), 655–665.

Kernberg, O. F. (1975). *Borderline Conditions and Pathological Narcissism*. Lanham, MD: Jason Aronson Inc.

Kim, J., Rapee, R. M., Ja Oh, K., & Moon, H.-S. (2008). Retrospective report of social withdrawal during adolescence and current maladjustment in young adulthood: Cross-cultural comparisons between Australian and South Korean students. *Journal of Adolescence*, *31*(5), 543–563.

Kohut, H. (1977). *The Restoration of the Self*. University of Chicago Press.

Lahti, M., Pesonen, A.-K., Räikkönen, K., Heinonen, K., Wahlbeck, K., Kajantie, E., … Eriksson, J. G. (2012). Temporary separation from parents in early childhood and serious personality disorders in adult life. *Journal of Personality Disorders*, *26*(5), 751–762.

Lenzenweger, M. F., Lane, M. C., Loranger, A. W., & Kessler, R. C. (2007). DSM-IV personality disorders in the National Comorbidity Survey Replication. *Biological Psychiatry*, *62*, 553–564.

Levy, K. N. (2005). The implications of attachment theory and research for understanding borderline personality disorder. *Development and Psychopathology*, *17*(4), 959–986.

Lewis, K. L., & Grenyer, B. F. S. (2009). Borderline personality or complex posttraumatic stress disorder? An update on the controversy. *Harvard Review of Psychiatry*, *17*(5), 322–328.

Linehan, M. M. (1993). *Diagnosis and Treatment of Mental Disorders: Cognitive-Behavioral Treatment of Borderline Personality Disorder*. New York: Guilford Press.

Lobbestael, J., Arntz, A., & Bernstein, D. P. (2010). Disentangling the relationship between different types of childhood maltreatment and personality disorders. *Journal of Personality Disorders*, 24(3), 285–295.

Loranger, A. W., Sartorius, N., Andreoli, A., Berger, P., Vuchheim, P., Channabusavanna, S. M., ... Regier, D. A. (1994). The international personality disorder examination: The World Health Organization/Alcohol, Drug Abuse, and Mental Health Administration International Pilot Study of Personality Disorders. *Archives of General Psychiatry*, 51, 215–224.

Lynam, D. R., & Widiger, T. A. (2007). Using a general model of personality to understand sex differences in the personality disorders. *Journal of Personality Disorders*, 21(6), 583–602.

Lyons, M. J., Jerskey, B. A., & Genderson, M. R. (2011). The epidemiology of personality disorders: findings, methods and concepts. In M. T. Tsuang, M. Tohen, & P. B. Jones (Eds.), *Textbook of Psychiatric Epidemiology* (pp. 401–434). New York: John Wiley & Sons.

Martin, N. G., Eaves, L. J., Kearsey, M. J., & Davies, P. (1978). The power of the classical twin study. *Heredity*, 40(1), 97–116.

McCrae, R. R., & Terracciano, A. (2005). Personality profiles of cultures: Aggregate personality traits. *Journal of Personality and Social Psychology*, 89(3), 407–425.

McGilloway, A., Hall, R. E., Lee, T., & Bhui, K. S. (2010). A systematic review of personality disorder, race and ethnicity: Prevalence, aetiology and treatment. *BMC Psychiatry*, 10(1), 33.

McLaughlin, K. A., Gadermann, A. M., Hwang, I., Sampson, N. A., Al-Hamzawi, A., Andrade, L. H., ... Kessler, R. C. (2012). Parent psychopathology and offspring mental disorders: Results from the WHO World Mental Health Surveys. *British Journal of Psychiatry: The Journal of Mental Science*, 200(4), 290–299.

Meyer, B., & Pilkonis, P. A. (2005). An attachment model of personality disorders. In M. Lenzenweger & J. F. Clarkin (Eds.), *Major Theories of Personality Disorder* (2nd ed., pp. 231–281). New York: Guilford Press.

Morey, L. C., Warner, M. B., & Boggs, C. D. (2002). Gender bias in the personality disorders criteria: An investigation of five bias indicators. *Journal of Psychopathology and Behavioral Assessment*, 24(1), 55–65.

Mulder, R. T. (2012). Cultural aspects of personality disorder. In T. A. Widiger (Ed.), *The Oxford Handbook of Personality Disorders* (pp. 260–274). New York: Oxford University Press.

Munjiza, J., Britvic, D., Radman, M., & Crawford, M. J. (2017). Severe war-related trauma and personality pathology: A case-control study. *BMC Psychiatry*, 17(1), 100.

Murphy, J. M. (1976). Psychiatric labeling in cross-cultural perspective. *Science*, 191(4231), 1019–1028.

Neiderhiser, J. M., Reiss, D., & Hetherington, E. M. (2007). The Nonshared Environment in Adolescent Development (NEAD) project: A longitudinal family study of twins and siblings from adolescence to young adulthood. *Twin Research and Human Genetics: The Official Journal of the International Society for Twin Studies*, 10(1), 74–83.

Oltmanns, T. F., & Powers, A. D. (2012). Gender and personality disorders. In T. A. Widiger (Ed.), *The Oxford Handbook of Personality Disorders* (pp. 206–218). New York: Oxford University Press.

Oltmanns, T. F., Rodrigues, M. M., Weinstein, Y., & Gleason, M. E. J. (2014). Prevalence of personality disorders at midlife in a community sample: Disorders and symptoms reflected in interview, self, and informant reports. *Journal of Psychopathology and Behavioral Assessment*, 36(2), 177–188.

Oyserman, D., Coon, H. M., & Kemmelmeier, M. (2002). Rethinking individualism and collectivism: Evaluation of theoretical assumptions and meta-analyses. *Psychological Bulletin*, 128(1), 3–72.

Paris, J. (1997). Social factors in the personality disorders. *Transcultural Psychiatry*, 34(4), 421–452.

Paris, J. (2003). Personality disorders over time: Precursors, course and outcome. *Journal of Personality Disorders*, 17(6), 479–488.

Paris, J. (2014). Modernity and narcissistic personality disorder. *Personality Disorders: Theory, Research, and Treatment*, 5(2), 220–226.

Paris, J., & Lis, E. (2013). Can sociocultural and historical mechanisms influence the development of borderline personality disorder? *Transcultural Psychiatry*, 50(1), 140–151.

Pedersen, L., & Simonsen, E. (2014). Incidence and prevalence rates of personality disorders in Denmark: A register study. *Nordic Journal of Psychiatry*, 68(8), 543–548.

Perry, J. C. (1992). Problems and considerations in the valid assessment of personality disorders. *American Journal of Psychiatry*, 149(12), 1645–1653.

Pfohl, B., Blum, N. S., & Zimmerman, M. (1997). *Structured Interview for DSM-IV Personality: SIDP-IV*. Washington, DC: American Psychiatric Press.

Pincus, A. L., & Hopwood, C. J. (2012). A contemporary interpersonal model of personality pathology and personality disorder. In T. A. Widiger (Ed.), *The Oxford Handbook of Personality Disorders* (pp. 372–398). New York: Oxford University Press.

Plomin, R., Asbury, K., & Dunn, J. (2001). Why are children in the same family so different? Nonshared environment a decade later. *Canadian Journal of Psychiatry*, 46(3), 225–233.

Reichborn-Kjennerud, T., Czajkowski, N., Neale, M. C., Ørstavik, R. E., Torgersen, S., Tambs, K., ... Kendler, K. S. (2007). Genetic and environmental influences on dimensional representations of DSM-IV cluster C personality disorders: A population-based multivariate twin study. *Psychological Medicine*, 37(5), 645–653.

Reichborn-Kjennerud, T., Czajkowski, N., Ystrøm, E., Ørstavik, R., Aggen, S. H., Tambs, K., ... Kendler, K. S. (2015). A longitudinal twin study of borderline and antisocial personality disorder traits in early to middle adulthood. *Psychological Medicine*, 45(14), 3121–3131.

Rhee, S. H., & Waldman, I. D. (2002). Genetic and environmental influences on antisocial behavior: A meta-analysis of twin and adoption studies. *Psychological Bulletin*, 128(3), 490–529.

Rossier, J., & Rigozzi, C. (2008). Personality disorders and the five-factor model among French speakers in Africa and Europe. *Canadian Journal of Psychiatry*, 53, 534–544.

Rutter, M., & Smith, D. J. (1995). *Psychosocial Problems in Young People*. Cambridge University Press.

Ryder, A. G., Dere, J., Sun, J., & Chentsova-Dutton, Y. E. (2014). The cultural shaping of personality disorder. In F. T. L. Leong, L. Comas-Diaz, G. C. N. Hall, V. C. McLloyd, & J. E. Trimble (Eds.), *APA Handbook of Multicultural Psychology, Volume 2: Applications and Training* (pp. 307–328). Washington, DC: American Psychological Association.

Ryder, A. G., Sunohara, M., & Kirmayer, L. J. (2015). Culture and personality disorder. *Current Opinion in Psychiatry*, 28(1), 40–45.

Sampson, R. J., Raudenbush, S. W., & Earls, F. (1997). Neighborhoods and violent crime: A multilevel study of collective efficacy. *Science*, 277(5328), 918–924.

Samuel, D. B., & Widiger, T. A. (2009). Comparative gender biases in models of personality disorder. *Personality and Mental Health*, 3, 12–25.

Samuels, J., Eaton, W. W., Bienvenu, O. J., Brown, C., Costa Jr., P. T., & Nestadt, G. (2002). Prevalence and correlates of personality disorders in a community sample. *British Journal of Psychiatry*, 180(6), 536–542.

Schuppert, H., Albers, C. J., Minderaa, R. B., Emmelkamp, P. M., & Nauta, M. H. (2012). Parental rearing and psychopathology in mothers of adolescents with and without borderline personality symptoms. *Child and Adolescent Psychiatry and Mental Health*, 6 (1), 29.

Selby, E. A., & Joiner, T. E. (2008). Ethnic variations in the structure of borderline personality disorder symptomatology. *Journal of Psychiatric Research*, 43(2), 115–123.

Shorter, E. (1997). *A History of Psychiatry*. New York: Wiley Blackwell.

Skodol, A. E., & Bender, D. S. (2003). Why are women diagnosed borderline more than men? *Psychiatric Quarterly*, 74(4), 349–360.

Smith, C. A., & Farrington, D. P. (2004). Continuities in antisocial behavior and parenting across three generations. *Journal of Child Psychology and Psychiatry, and Allied Disciplines*, 45(2), 230–247.

Smith Benjamin, L. (2005). Interpersonal theory of personality disorders: the structural analysis of social behavior and interpersonal reconstructive therapy. In M. F. Lenzenweger & J. F. Clarkin (Eds.), *Major Theories of Personality Disorder* (2nd ed., pp. 157–230). New York: Guilford Press.

Snyder, J., Schrepferman, L., & St. Peter, C. (1997). Origins of antisocial behavior. *Behavior Modification*, 21(2), 187–215.

Spence, J. T., & Helmreich, R. L. (1978). *Masculinity & Femininity: Their Psychological Dimensions, Correlates, and Antecedents*. Austin, TX: University of Texas Press.

Sprague, J., Javdani, S., Sadeh, N., Newman, J. P., & Verona, E. (2012). Borderline personality disorder as a female phenotypic expression of psychopathy? *Personality Disorders*, 3(2), 127–139.

Sroufe, L. A. (2005). Attachment and development: A prospective, longitudinal study from birth to adulthood. *Attachment & Human Development*, 7(4), 349–367.

Stack Sullivan, H. (1953). *The Interpersonal Theory of Psychiatry*. New York: W. W. Norton.

Stepp, S. D., Pilkonis, P. A., Yaggi, K. E., Morse, J. Q., & Feske, U. (2009). Interpersonal and emotional experiences of social interactions in borderline personality disorder. *Journal of Nervous and Mental Disease*, 197(7), 484–491.

Stravynski, A., Elie, R., & Franche, R.-L. (1989). Perception of early parenting by patients diagnosed avoidant personality disorder: A test of the overprotection hypothesis. *Acta Psychiatrica Scandinavica*, 80(5), 415–420.

Suliman, S., Stein, D. J., Williams, D. R., & Seedat, S. (2008). DSM-IV personality disorders and their axis I correlates in the South African population. *Psychopathology*, 41(6), 356–364.

Terracciano, A., & McCrae, R. R. (2006). Cross-cultural studies of personality traits and their relevance to psychiatry. *Epidemiologia E Psichiatria Sociale*, 15(3), 176–184.

Tessner, K. D., Mittal, V., & Walker, E. F. (2011). Longitudinal study of stressful life events and daily stressors among adolescents at high risk for psychotic disorders. *Schizophrenia Bulletin*, 37(2), 432–441.

Torgersen, S. (2012). Epidemiology. In T. A. Widiger (Ed.), *The Oxford Handbook of Personality Disorders* (pp. 186–205). New York: Oxford University Press.

Torgersen, S., Czajkowski, N., Jacobson, K., Reichborn-Kjennerud, T., Røysamb, E., Neale, M. C., & Kendler, K. S. (2008). Dimensional representations of DSM-IV cluster B personality disorders in a population-based sample of Norwegian twins: A multivariate study. *Psychological Medicine*, 38(11), 1617–1625.

Torgersen, S., Kringlen, E., & Cramer, V. (2001). The prevalence of personality disorders in a community sample. *Archives of General Psychiatry*, 58(6), 590–596.

Trull, T. J., Jahng, S., Tomko, R. L., Wood, P. K., & Sher, K. J. (2010). Revised NESARC personality disorder diagnoses: Gender, prevalence, and comorbidity with substance dependence disorders. *Journal of Personality Disorders*, 24, 412–426.

Turkheimer, E. (2000). Three laws of behavior genetics and what they mean. *Current Directions in Psychological Science*, 9(5), 160–164.

Tuvblad, C., & Beaver, K. M. (2013). Genetic and environmental influences on antisocial behavior. *Journal of Criminal Justice*, 41(5), 273–276.

Tuvblad, C., Grann, M., & Lichtenstein, P. (2006). Heritability for adolescent antisocial behavior differs with socioeconomic status: Gene–environment interaction. *Journal of Child Psychology and Psychiatry*, 47(7), 734–743.

Tyrer, P., Crawford, M., Mulder, R., & ICD-11 Working Group for the Revision of Classification of Personality Disorders. (2011). Reclassifying personality disorders. *The Lancet*, 377(9780), 1814–1815.

Walsh, Z., Shea, M. T., Yen, S., Ansell, E. B., Grilo, C. M., McGlashan, T. H., . . . Gunderson, J. G. (2013). Socioeconomic status and mental health in a personality disorder sample: The importance of neighborhood factors. *Journal of Personality Disorders*, 27(6), 820–831.

Watson, P. J., Little, T., & Biderman, M. D. (1992). Narcissism and parenting styles. *Psychoanalytic Psychology*, 9(2), 231–244.

Wetzel, E., & Robins, R. W. (2016). Are parenting practices associated with the development of narcissism? Findings from a longitudinal study of Mexican-origin youth. *Journal of Research in Personality*, 63, 84–94.

Whaley, A. L. (1997). Ethnicity/race, paranoia, and psychiatric diagnoses: Clinician bias versus sociocultural differences. *Journal of Psychopathology and Behavioral Assessment*, 19(1), 1–20.

Widiger, T. A. (1998). Invited essay: Sex biases in the diagnosis of personality disorders. *Journal of Personality Disorders*, 12(2), 95–118.

Widiger, T. A., & Bornstein, R. F. (2002). Histrionics, dependent, and narcissistic personality disorders. In H. E. Adams & P. B. Sutker (Eds.), *Comprehensive Handbook of Psychopathology* (pp. 509–531). Boston: Kluwer Academic Publishers.

Widom, C. S., Czaja, S. J., & Paris, J. (2009). A prospective investigation of borderline personality disorder in abused and neglected children followed up into adulthood. *Journal of Personality Disorders*, 23(5), 433–446.

Wiggins, J. S. (1991). Agency and communion as conceptual coordinates for the understanding and measurement of interpersonal behavior. In D. Cicchetti & W. M. Grove (Eds.), *Thinking Clearly about Psychology: Essays in Honor of Paul E. Meehl* (pp. 89–113). Minneapolis, MN: University of Minnesota Press.

Wood, W., & Eagly, A. H. (2012). Biosocial construction of sex differences and similarities in behavior. In J. M. Olson & M. P. Zanna (Eds.), *Advances in Experimental Social Psychology* (Vol. 46, pp. 55–123). Burlington, VT: Academic Press.

Woodward, H. E., Taft, C. T., Gordon, R. A., & Meis, L. A. (2009). Clinician bias in the diagnosis of posttraumatic stress disorder and borderline personality disorder. *Psychological Trauma: Theory, Research, Practice, and Policy*, *1*(4), 282–290.

World Health Organization [WHO]. (2010). *International Statistical Classification of Diseases and Related Health Problems* (10th ed.). Geneva: WHO Press.

Yang, J., McCrae, R. R., Costa, P. T., Yao, S., Dai, X., Cai, T., & Gao, B. (2000). The cross-cultural generalizability of Axis-II constructs: An evaluation of two personality disorder assessment instruments in the People's Republic of China. *Journal of Personality Disorders*, *14*(3), 249–263.

Yang, K., & Bond, M. H. (1990). Exploring implicit personality theories with indigenous or imported constructs: The Chinese case. *Journal of Personality and Social Psychology*, *58*(6), 1087–1095.

Zhong, J., & Leung, F. (2009). Diagnosis of borderline personality disorder in China: Current status and future directions. *Current Psychiatry Reports*, *11*(1), 69–73.

3a Evidence for Caregiver Factors Proposed by Attachment and Biosocial Theories in the Development of Personality Disorders: Commentary on Environmental and Sociocultural Influences on Personality Disorders

JENNY MACFIE, SAMANTHA K. NOOSE, AND ANDREA M. GORRONDONA

Turner and colleagues have written a thoughtful and comprehensive overview of theory and research across a vast literature: environmental and sociocultural influences on the development of personality disorders (PDs). They review behavioral genetics studies and studies on the prevalence of PDs in different countries and from different socioeconomic backgrounds. They describe a wide variety of theories of how PDs develop, and review environmental risk factors from early childhood adversity to the quality of communities. Our commentary, focusing on borderline PD (for which there is the most research), extends this work in two ways. First, we propose an overarching theory of environmental and sociocultural influences on the development of PDs. Second, we add empirical support for two of the theories that Turner and colleagues present: attachment and biosocial theories. In this way, we aim to identify processes underlying the development of PDs that may be the focus of interventions.

ECOLOGICAL SYSTEMS THEORY

Maladaptive and inflexible patterns of behavior, thinking, and inner experience that endure over time characterize PDs (American Psychiatric Association, 2013). Although we do not diagnose PDs until adolescence or early adulthood, they have their origins much earlier. The authors report findings from behavioral genetics studies of twins that derive a percentage for how much genes versus the environment contribute to the development of PDs. As they point out, genes are important, a unique environment is important, and a shared environment (e.g., by siblings) is less so. However, the behavioral genetics model has limitations as a developmental theory because it sets up an artificial dichotomy between nature and nurture. Development results from a *relationship* between the environment and genes, rather than from the two components separately. This relationship consists of ongoing bi-directional influences across levels of analysis: genetic activity, neural activity, behavior, and the environment (Gottlieb, 2003; Gottlieb & Halpern, 2002; Gottlieb & Lickliter, 2007).

A developmental theory that encompasses the breadth of environmental and sociocultural influences on the development of PDs and the importance of bi-directional interactions is Bronfenbrenner's ecological systems theory (Bronfenbrenner, 1979). Bronfenbrenner proposes that, to understand child development, we need to examine the contexts within which it occurs. The child and his or her biology/genetic predispositions interact directly with proximal influences (e.g., caregivers, siblings, schools), which are themselves influenced by more distal factors (e.g., economic, political, sociocultural). As the authors note, current evidence suggests that proximal environmental influences are more significant than more distal sociocultural influences. We therefore turn to empirical evidence in support of interactions between the child and his or her caregiving environment proposed by attachment and biosocial theories.

THE ROLE OF REPRESENTATIONAL MODELS LINKING EARLY CAREGIVING TO THE DEVELOPMENT OF PDS

As Turner and colleagues report, attachment theory posits that mental representations of self and other, termed internal working models, develop in the context of the infant–caregiver relationship and are carried forward to inform future relationships (Bowlby, 1973). Thus, a secure attachment developed in infancy with a primary caregiver resulting from sensitive and responsive care is thought to result in representations of the self as worthy of care and others as trustworthy. Disorganized infant attachment, on the other hand, results from maltreatment by caregivers or from caregivers who have suffered recent losses of their own attachment figures (Barnett, Ganiban, & Cicchetti, 1999; van Ijzendoorn, Schuengel, & Bakermans-Kranenburg, 1999). Disorganized attachment may disrupt the development of representations of self and other. For example, both a child's experience of trauma (including maltreatment) and the attachment figure's experience of a loss within two years of the child's birth predicted borderline PD (Liotti & Pasquini, 2000). When an infant is frightened by his or her caregiver or sees the caregiver frightened him or herself due to having experienced a recent loss, the infant has nowhere to turn for comfort or to soothe distress. There is no strategy that the infant can employ to cope: expressing attachment needs directly (secure attachment), exaggerating them (anxious-resistant attachment), or minimizing them (avoidant attachment) does not make it more likely that the caregiver will respond to the infant's distress. Approach/avoidance motivations towards the caregiver collide, leaving the infant frozen in distress, unsoothed, dissociated, and dysregulated (Main & Solomon, 1990).

What is the empirical evidence in support of mental representations or internal working models derived from the infant–caregiver relationship in the development of PDs? In a sample of first time mothers at high risk due to poverty, with most being single parents, disorganized infant–mother attachment at 12–18 months was associated with the development of borderline PD symptoms in early adulthood (Carlson, Egeland, & Sroufe, 2009). Moreover, disturbed representations of the self, coded from children's narratives at ages 8 and 12 (e.g., involving intrusive violence, unresolved guilt or fear, bizarre images related to the self), mediated this relationship. Findings thus support an interaction between the environment in the form of caregiving and the child's representations of self and other in the development of a PD (Carlson et al., 2009).

Moreover, a second study using the same sample found that social behavior and representations of relationships (assessed three times between childhood and adolescence) mediated the relationship between early caregiving quality (including disorganized attachment at 12–18 months and observations of parenting at 12–42 months) and PD symptoms at age 28. Furthermore, there were significant interactive pathways between children's representations and their behavior over time. Thus, children's representations affected their behavior and vice versa, and both mediated the relationship between early caregiving and PD symptoms in adulthood (Carlson & Ruiz, 2016). These findings extend evidence for a relationship between the child's mental representations and the environment from borderline PD to PDs more generally.

THE ROLE OF BIOLOGY LINKING EARLY CAREGIVING TO THE DEVELOPMENT OF PDS

The authors also propose Linehan's biosocial theory to describe how the environment might influence the development of PDs, specifically borderline PD. The biosocial theory posits that emotion dysregulation is developed and maintained by the interaction between an individual's biological predispositions (e.g., emotional reactivity, trait impulsivity) and invalidating environments that prevent a child from learning how to respond adaptively to strong emotions (Crowell, Beauchaine, & Linehan, 2009; Linehan, 1993). In the longitudinal study reviewed above

(Carlson et al., 2009), both temperamental (e.g., emotionality at 30 months, infant activity at 6 months) and environmental factors (e.g., maltreatment from 12–18 months, disorganized attachment at 12–18 months, maternal hostility at 42 months, maternal life stress from 3 to 42 months, and family/father disruption from 1 to 18 years) were associated with borderline PD symptoms in early adulthood. However, this study did not test interactions between temperamental and environmental factors.

One line of research that has examined the interaction between temperament (i.e., emotional reactivity) and environment in the development of borderline PD is Stepp and colleagues' research on adolescent girls. For example, Stepp and colleagues (Stepp, Scott, Jones, Whalen, and Hipwell, 2016) found that mother-reported family adversity predicted an increase in girls' borderline PD symptoms from age 16 to 18, and strengthened the relationship between girls' negative emotional reactivity during a conflict discussion task with their mothers and the girls' borderline PD symptoms (Stepp et al., 2016). Furthermore, using the same sample, Dixon-Gordon and colleagues (Dixon-Gordon, Whalen, Scott, Cummins, & Stepp, 2016) found a stronger association between girls' negative emotional reactivity and borderline PD symptom severity when high maternal problem-solving during the conflict discussion task was combined with low maternal support/validation. Conversely, when high maternal problem-solving was combined with high levels of support/validation during this task, the relationship between girls' negative emotional reactivity and borderline PD symptoms was significantly reduced (Dixon-Gordon et al., 2016). These findings suggest that maternal skill at problem-solving is not sufficient for buffering the potential negative consequences of emotional reactivity among adolescent girls. Rather, mothers (or other primary caregivers) need to combine problem-solving with support, sensitivity, and validation of their adolescents' distress. Notably, biological data support these results. Specifically, when the girls listened to audio recordings of their mothers criticizing, praising, or giving neutral feedback, greater pupillary reactivity in response to maternal criticism predicted increasing levels of borderline PD symptoms over the 18-month period. Alternatively, lower pupillary reactivity predicted more rapid improvement of borderline PD symptoms over the same 18-month period (Scott, Zalewski, Beeney, Jones, & Stepp, 2017). These findings further demonstrate the relevance of both a temperamental emotional vulnerability and an invalidating environment in the development of borderline PD.

IMPLICATIONS FOR INTERVENTIONS

There are several effective treatments for PDs that flow from environmental theories as noted by Turner et al. (Bateman & Fonagy, 2001, 2008; Levy et al., 2006; Linehan, 1993). We add two more here. The key term in "internal working models" is "working." Bowlby theorized that, to be maximally helpful, representational models of self and other need to change to reflect changing circumstances (Bowlby, 1973). However, in PDs, models of self and other do not change, but remain fixed and applied indiscriminately across situations. Informed in part by attachment theory's emphasis on representational models, Young's schema therapy extends cognitive behavioral therapy to address maladaptive models developed from adverse experiences in childhood, including a sense of the self as defective and others as untrustworthy (Young, 1994). Indeed, total scores on the Young Schema Questionnaire correlated highly with a corresponding total score for PD symptoms (Schmidt, Joiner, Young, & Telch, 1995). Furthermore, the mistrust/abuse schema was significantly associated with paranoid PD, whereas the insufficient self-control/self-discipline schema was significantly associated with borderline PD (Schmidt et al., 1995).

In addition to working with individuals who have PDs, it is helpful to work with their families (i.e., the context in which the PD developed). One example of an intervention using the biosocial model as a framework is the Family Connections program (Hoffman et al., 2005), which seeks to better inform family members of individuals with borderline PD about the symptoms their loved one is struggling with and how to help manage them using dialectical behavior therapy skills (Linehan, 1993). Interventions such as the Family Connections program can help family members intervene at the environmental level, potentially minimizing invalidation that would otherwise further escalate and perpetuate the symptoms of individuals with borderline PD.

REFERENCES

American Psychiatric Association. (2013). *Diagnostic and Statistical Manual of Mental Disorders* (5th ed.). Arlington, VA: American Psychiatric Publishing.

Barnett, D., Ganiban, J., & Cicchetti, D. (1999). Maltreatment, negative expressivity, and the development of type D attachments from 12 to 24 months of age. *Monographs of the Society for Research in Child Development*, 63(3), 97–118.

Bateman, A., & Fonagy, P. (2001). Treatment of borderline personality disorder with psychoanalytically oriented partial hospitalization: An 18-month follow-up. *American Journal of Psychiatry*, 158, 36–42.

Bateman, A., & Fonagy, P. (2008). 8-Year follow-up of patients treated for borderline personality disorder: Mentalization-based treatment versus treatment as usual. *American Journal of Psychiatry*, 165, 631–638.

Bowlby, J. (1973). *Attachment and Loss, Volume 2: Separation*. New York: Basic Books.

Bronfenbrenner, U. (1979). *The Ecology of Human Development*. Cambridge, MA: Harvard University Press.

Carlson, E. A., Egeland, B., & Sroufe, L. A. (2009). A prospective investigation of the development of borderline personality symptoms. *Development and Psychopathology*, 21(4), 1311–1334.

Carlson, E. A., & Ruiz, S. K. (2016). Transactional processes in the development of adult personality disorder symptoms. *Development and Psychopathology*, 28(3), 639–651.

Crowell, S. E., Beauchaine, T. P., & Linehan, M. M. (2009). A biosocial developmental model of borderline personality: Elaborating and extending Linehan's theory. *Psychological Bulletin*, 135(3), 495–510.

Dixon-Gordon, K. L., Whalen, D. J., Scott, L. N., Cummins, N. D., & Stepp, S. D. (2016). The main and interactive effects of maternal interpersonal emotion regulation and negative affect on adolescent girls' borderline personality disorder symptoms. *Cognitive Therapy and Research*, 40(3), 381–393.

Gottlieb, G. (2003). On making behavioral genetics truly developmental. *Human Development*, 46(6), 337–355.

Gottlieb, G., & Halpern, C. T. (2002). A relational view of causality in normal and abnormal development. *Development and Psychopathology*, 14(3), 421–435.

Gottlieb, G., & Lickliter, R. (2007). Probabilistic epigenesis. *Developmental Science*, 10(1), 1–11.

Hoffman, P. D., Fruzzetti, A. E., Buteau, E., Neiditch, E. R., Penney, D., Bruce, M. L., ... Struening, E. (2005). Family connections: A program for relatives of persons with borderline personality disorder. *Family Process*, 44(2), 217–225.

Levy, K. N., Meehan, K. B., Kelly, K. M., Reynoso, J. S., Weber, M., Clarkin, J. F., & Kernberg, O. F. (2006). Change in attachment patterns and reflective functioning in a randomized control trial of transference-focused psychotherapy for borderline personality disorder. *Journal of Consulting and Clinical Psychology*, 74, 1027–1040.

Linehan, M. M. (1993). *Cognitive-Behavioral Treatment of Borderline Personality Disorder*. New York: Guilford Press.

Liotti, G., & Pasquini, P. (2000). Predictive factors for borderline personality disorder: Patients' early traumatic experiences and losses suffered by the attachment figure. *Acta Psychiatrica Scandinavica*, 102(4), 282–289.

Main, M., & Solomon, J. (Eds.) (1990). *Procedures for Identifying Infants as Disorganized/Disoriented during the Ainsworth Strange Situation*. University of Chicago Press.

Schmidt, N. B., Joiner, T. E., Young, J. E., & Telch, M. J. (1995). The Schema Questionnaire: Investigation of psychometric properties and the hierarchical structure of a measure of maladaptive schemas. *Cognitive Therapy and Research*, 19(3), 295–321.

Scott, L. N., Zalewski, M., Beeney, J. E., Jones, N. P., & Stepp, S. D. (2017). Pupillary and affective responses to maternal feedback and the development of borderline personality disorder symptoms. *Development and Psychopathology*, 29(3), 1089–1104.

Stepp, S. D., Scott, L. N., Jones, N. P., Whalen, D. J., & Hipwell, A. E. (2016). Negative emotional reactivity as a marker of vulnerability in the development of borderline personality disorder symptoms. *Development and Psychopathology*, 28(1), 213–224.

van Ijzendoorn, M. H., Schuengel, C., & Bakermans-Kranenburg, M. J. (1999). Disorganized attachment in early childhood: Meta-analysis of precursors, concomitants, and sequelae. *Development and Psychopathology*, 11(2), 225–249.

Young, J. E. (1994). *Cognitive Therapy for Personality Disorders: A Schema-Focused Approach* (rev. ed.). Sarasota, FL: Professional Resource Press/Professional Resource Exchange.

3b Towards a Family Process Perspective on Typical and Maladaptive Personality Characteristics: Commentary on Environmental and Sociocultural Influences on Personality Disorders

PATRICK T. DAVIES AND MORGAN J. THOMPSON

In their excellent review of the environmental and genetic underpinnings of personality disorders, Turner, Prud'-homme, and Legg provide compelling evidence that environmental parameters account for a substantial portion of individual differences in personality psychopathology. Moreover, early experiences with forms of family adversity (e.g., maltreatment, parenting difficulties, parental separation) were identified as risk factors for offspring personality difficulties. However, at this early stage of research, little is known about how and why these family characteristics increase the risk for various personality disorders. Towards addressing this gap, family process frameworks in developmental psychopathology aim to delineate the diversity of mechanisms and pathways underlying associations between family adversity in childhood and the subsequent emergence and course of patterns of maladaptation (e.g., Jouriles, McDonald, & Kouros, 2016; Repetti, Robles, & Reynolds, 2011). Thus, the aim of our commentary is to selectively illustrate how the synthesis of family process models with the personality disorder literature may serve as a heuristic for addressing these scientific barriers.

Delineating the mechanisms underlying family risk factors may be particularly valuable as a guide in reformulating approaches to characterizing mental health and illness. We believe that future progress will be facilitated by shifting from prevailing diagnostic (e.g., DSM-5, ICD) and syndrome (e.g., distinctions between internalizing and externalizing symptoms) approaches to dimensional frameworks of personality like the Five Factor Model (FFM; Bagby & Widiger, 2018; De Fruyt & De Clercq, 2014; Widiger, De Clercq, & De Fruyt, 2009). Although a detailed discussion is beyond the scope of this commentary, FFM distinguishes between different facets and gradations of adaptation and maladaptation in personality attributes across the Big Five personality traits. FFM enjoys stronger empirical support than prevailing frameworks (see Turner et al., this volume) and provides a more integrative characterization of both typical and atypical functioning. Moreover, from a family process perspective, FFM may be superior in its ability to carve nature at its joints in ways

that elucidate distinctive precursors, pathways, and mechanisms underlying psychopathology (e.g., Krueger, Tackett, & MacDonald, 2016). Therefore, although part of our commentary will describe the larger body of research using prevailing taxonomies, we also address how dimensional frameworks like FFM may offer greater leverage in advancing an understanding of family processes.

DEFENSIVE MECHANISMS AS MEDIATORS OF EARLY FAMILY ADVERSITY

In elaborating on the premise that safety and security are central mechanisms underlying the etiology and course of personality pathologies, Turner and colleagues provide a thoughtful analysis of how distinctive patterns of attachment insecurity may mediate associations between exposure to specific forms of family difficulties and DSM-5 personality pathology. However, attachment is not the only defensive behavioral system that is designed to protect against harm (Bowlby, 1969). As a goal of the attachment system, maximizing accessibility to and support from caregivers is often not possible in garnering protection from harm because attachment figures are frequently physically unavailable (e.g., in the context of some sibling or peer conflicts) or are, themselves, the sources of the threat (e.g., in the context of parent–child or interparental conflict). Therefore, according to emotional security theory, the social defense system (SDS) is another distinct defensive module that organizes biobehavioral responses to threat in many types of family and interpersonal contexts (Davies & Martin, 2013). In contrast to the attachment system goal of maximizing caregiver protection, the SDS is designed to defuse threat in social contexts through several action tendencies that include heightened perceptual sensitivity to danger cues, fear, vigilance, freezing, fight and flight, camouflaging, and social de-escalation behaviors.

Just as there are different strategies for attempting to regulate accessibility to the caregiver in the attachment system, children adopt distinct ways of defusing interpersonal danger in the SDS. These distinctive profiles of responding to threatening family events are proposed to develop from specific histories of exposure to family adversity and, in turn, have unique implications for children's psychological adjustment. For example, whereas the dominant pattern of responding is designed to directly defeat the source of threat (e.g., parents) in stressful family contexts (e.g., in parent–child or interparental conflict) through coercive and controlling behaviors, the mobilizing pattern serves to actively manage threat and opportunities for accessing social resources through dramatic displays of distress, submissive and appeasing behaviors, and solicitation of sympathy and alliances. Mobilizing responses are proposed to develop from recurrent exposure to family negativity and enmeshment, and parental psychological control and conditional warmth. In contrast, the dominant strategy is posited to be an adaptive solution to contending with parental vulnerability (e.g., depression), disengagement, and collapses in parental power as authority figures (Davies, Martin, & Sturge-Apple, 2016).

Consistent with theory emphasizing their unique developmental implications, a mobilizing profile has been shown to predict subsequent increases in children's extraversion, internalizing symptoms, externalizing difficulties, and self-regulation problems. In comparison, children with more dominant responses to family conflict specifically evidenced greater externalizing problems and extraversion over time (Davies, Martin, Sturge-Apple, Ripple, & Cicchetti, 2016). Although this research provides some support for specificity in the mental health outcomes of the two different response patterns, prevailing diagnostic frameworks are limited in their ability to distinguish between the hypothesized sequelae of the different ways of defusing threat in the family. For example, although greater extraversion is an outcome shared by mobilizing and dominant patterns of responding, these response patterns are proposed to result in distinct forms of extraversion that can be more precisely parsed in FFM. More specifically, agentic extraversion characterized by confidence, ambition, and sensation-seeking is proposed to develop from dominant responses to threat, whereas affiliative extraversion reflected in warmth, sociability, and intimacy is theorized to be rooted in mobilizing response patterns (e.g., DeYoung, Weisberg, Quilty, & Peterson, 2013). Likewise, personality traits of impulsivity and emotion instability are proposed to undergird higher levels of externalizing sequelae of mobilizing responses, whereas higher externalizing symptoms associated with dominant response patterns may be more specifically reflected in aggressive, combative, and manipulative FFM personality attributes (Davies, Martin, Sturge-Apple et al., 2016; Widiger et al., 2009).

APPROACH MECHANISMS AS MEDIATORS OF EARLY FAMILY ADVERSITY

Family process models have also underscored how children's early experiences of adversity may alter patterns of behavioral reactivity to environmental resources in ways that have significant consequences for their personality. For example, life history theory proposes that children's implicit processing of harsh and unpredictable family contexts calibrates fast life history strategies that prepare individuals for the likelihood of facing threatening, uncertain, and impoverished environmental conditions in future developmental periods (Belsky, Schlomer, & Ellis, 2012). Fast life history strategies are specifically characterized by immediate, opportunistic, live-for-today, responses that prioritize quick acquisition of rewards and a short-term temporal perspective that focuses on the here and now rather than the long term. Thus, these responses are posited to have an adaptive function of increasing accessibility to social and material resources in unreliable and harsh environments.

Although research has documented early family unpredictability and harshness as predictors of some markers of fast life history strategies (e.g., Belsky et al., 2012), little is known about the implications of this unfolding cascade for personality development. Dimensional personality approaches may address this gap by providing more nuanced characterizations of the developmental tradeoffs of these strategies. On the benign side of the personality continuum, the bold nature of fast life history strategies may coalesce into FFM tendencies to be more assertive, self-assured, strong, and tough. However, developmental costs for personality characteristics may be reflected in impairments in approach-oriented behavioral systems that regulate exploration and affiliation (Davies, Martin, & Sturge-Apple, 2016). For example, the underlying goal of the exploratory system is to acquire basic survival materials through familiarity and mastery of the physical world. Impairments in this system resulting from fast life history strategies may be manifested in personality dispositions of carelessness, aimlessness, closed-mindedness, and disinterest. By comparison, the goal of the affiliative system is to gain access to survival materials through acquisition of social skills and, ultimately, the formation and maintenance of cooperative alliances. Thus, fast life history disruptions to the affiliative system may be reflected in manipulative, exploitative, combative, and callous personality attributes.

SOURCES OF HETEROGENEITY IN FAMILY RISK

Turner and colleagues also provide compelling evidence that a large part of the variability in personality disorders is attributable to non-shared environmental influences. Within family process models, a central task is to understand why children in the same family respond so differently to similar family risk by identifying genetic, physiological, and phenotypical attributes of children that moderate the pathways between family characteristics and personality adjustment and psychopathology (e.g., Plomin, 2011; Rutter, Moffitt, & Caspi, 2006). For example, at the physiological level of analysis, an emerging corpus of research points to the promise of examining parasympathetic nervous system (e.g., respiratory sinus arrhythmia), sympathetic nervous system (e.g., pre-ejection period), and hypothalamic-pituitary-adrenal axis (e.g., cortisol) functioning as possible moderators of associations between forms of family adversity and children's psychopathology (e.g., Beauchaine, 2012; Hinnant, Erath, Tu, & El-Sheikh, 2016; Obradovic, 2012). Likewise, although genes that organize a wide array of different physiological systems may serve to alter the impact of family experiences on children's adjustment, research has been particularly focused on documenting the moderating role of dopaminergic and serotonergic genes in contexts of family risk (Belsky & Beaver, 2011; Cicchetti & Rogosch, 2012). Finally, defined as temporally stable styles of behavior with constitutional roots, children's temperamental attributes (e.g., negative emotionality, effortful control) may also serve as moderators by altering their sensitivity to family risk factors (Hentges, Davies, & Cicchetti, 2015; Liu, Zhou, Wang, Liang, & Shi, 2018).

As Turner and colleagues note, personality disorder research has predominantly interpreted the moderating role of child attributes in diathesis-stress frameworks. However, differential susceptibility theory (DST) has recently proposed that many temperamental, physiological, and genetic factors that have, in the past, been identified as diatheses may be "plasticity" or "susceptibility" factors (Belsky & Pluess, 2016). Consistent with diathesis-stress models, DST predicts that children with susceptibility attributes will exhibit greater psychological problems when exposure to family stress is high. However, because "susceptibility" is defined as greater plasticity in a "for better or for worse" fashion, DST maintains that children with "susceptibility" attributes profit more from supportive parenting contexts. Given the complementary focus of DST on how children with susceptibility attributes may thrive in supportive rearing contexts, fair tests of the relative viability of the two models will require: (a) simultaneous assessments of both cohesive and adverse family parameters; and (b) use of personality approaches like the FFM that capture both benign (e.g., cooperative) and impairing (e.g., docile, meek) dimensions of personality traits (e.g., agreeableness). In addition, more precisely identifying the forms of moderating effects of child attributes in models of family risk is just one part of a larger scientific process that will require creative syntheses of moderation and mediation to advance knowledge on the family processes involved in personality adjustment and maladjustment. For example, mediated moderation models will be useful in understanding how and why associations between family characteristics and personality dimensions are stronger or weaker for children with specific genetic, physiological, or temperamental attributes (e.g., Brody et al., 2012; Hentges et al., 2015).

CONCLUSION

Family process and personality psychopathology approaches have developed in relative isolation from each other. Therefore, the goal of this commentary was to illustrate how the synthesis of these two areas of inquiry may advance an understanding of the origins and course of typical and atypical personality characteristics in mutually informative ways. Progress in integrating these approaches will be facilitated by the delineation of mediational pathways involving specific family risk factors, children's responses to threats, challenges and opportunities, and assessments of both typical and maladaptive personality traits. Complex blends of mediator and moderator models will further facilitate the identification of the multiplicity of processes and pathways linking family adversity with personality sequelae.

REFERENCES

Bagby, R. M., & Widiger, T. A. (2018). Five factor model personality disorder scales: An introduction to a special section on assessment of maladaptive variants of the five factor model. *Psychological Assessment*, 30, 1–9.

Beauchaine, T. P. (2012). Physiological markers of emotion and behavior dysregulation in externalizing psychopathology. *Monographs of the Society for Research in Child Development*, 77, 79–86.

Belsky, J., & Beaver, K. M. (2011). Cumulative-genetic plasticity, parenting, and adolescent self-regulation. *Journal of Child Psychology and Psychiatry*, 52, 619–626.

Belsky, J., & Pluess, M. (2016). Differential susceptibility to environmental influences. In D. Cicchetti (Ed.), *Developmental Psychopathology, Volume 2: Developmental Neurosciences* (3rd ed., pp. 59–106). New York: Wiley.

Belsky, J., Schlomer, G. L., & Ellis, B. J. (2012). Beyond cumulative risk: Distinguishing harshness and unpredictability as determinants of parenting and early life history strategy. *Developmental Psychology*, 48(3), 662–673.

Bowlby, J. (1969). *Attachment and Loss, Volume 1: Attachment.* London: Hogarth Press.

Brody, G. H., Chen, Y. F., Yu, T., Beach, S. R. H., Kogan, S. M., Simons, R. L., ... Philibert, R. A. (2012). Life stress, the dopamine receptor gene, and emerging adult drug use trajectories: A longitudinal, multilevel, mediated moderation analysis. *Development and Psychopathology*, 24, 941–951.

Cicchetti, D., & Rogosch, F. A. (2012). Gene × environment interaction and resilience: Effects of child maltreatment and serotonin, corticotropin releasing hormone, dopamine, and oxytocin genes. *Development and Psychopathology*, 24, 411–427.

Davies, P. T., & Martin, M. J. (2013). The reformulation of emotional security theory: The role of children's social defense in developmental psychopathology. *Development & Psychopathology*, 25, 1435–1454.

Davies, P. T., Martin, M. J., & Sturge-Apple, M. L. (2016). Emotional security theory and developmental psychopathology. In D. Cicchetti (Ed.), *Developmental Psychopathology, Volume 1: Theory and Methods* (3rd ed., pp. 199–264). New York: Wiley.

Davies, P. T., Martin, M. J., Sturge-Apple, M., Ripple, M. T., & Cicchetti, D. (2016). The distinctive sequelae of children's coping with interparental conflict: Testing the reformulated emotional security theory. *Developmental Psychology, 52,* 1646–1665.

De Fruyt, F., & De Clercq, B. (2014). Antecedents of personality disorder in childhood and adolescence: Toward an integrative developmental model. *Annual Review of Clinical Psychology, 10,* 449–476.

DeYoung, C. G., Weisberg, Y. J., Quilty, L. C., & Peterson, J. B. (2013). Unifying the aspects of the big five, the interpersonal circumplex, and trait affiliation. *Journal of Personality, 81,* 465–475.

Hentges, R. F., Davies, P. T., & Cicchetti, D. (2015). Temperament and interparental conflict: The role of negative emotionality in predicting child behavior problems. *Child Development, 86,* 1333–1350.

Hinnant, J. B., Erath, S. A., Tu, K. M., & El-Sheikh, M. (2016). Permissive parenting, deviant peer affiliations, and delinquent behavior in adolescence: The moderating role of sympathetic nervous system reactivity. *Journal of Abnormal Child Psychology, 44,* 1071–1081.

Jouriles, E. N., McDonald, R., & Kouros, C. D. (2016). Interparental conflict and child adjustment. In D. Cicchetti (Ed.), *Developmental Psychopathology, Volume 4: Risk, Resilience, and Intervention* (3rd ed., pp. 608–659). New York: Wiley.

Krueger, R. F., Tackett, J. L., & MacDonald, A. (2016). Toward validation of a structural approach to conceptualizing psychopathology: A special section of the *Journal of Abnormal Psychology. Journal of Abnormal Psychology, 125,* 1023–1026.

Liu, S., Zhou, N., Wang, Z., Liang, X., & Shi, J. (2018). Maternal life stress and subsequent Chinese toddlers' social adjustment: The moderating role of inhibitory control. *Journal of Child and Family Studies, 27*(2), 412–420.

Obradovic, J. (2012). How can the study of physiological reactivity contribute to our understanding of adversity and resilience processes in development? *Development and Psychopathology, 24,* 371–387.

Plomin, R. (2011). Commentary: Why are children in the same family so different? Non-shared environment three decades later. *International Journal of Epidemiology, 40,* 582–592.

Repetti, R. L., Robles, T. F., & Reynolds, B. (2011). Allostatic processes in the family. *Development and Psychopathology, 23,* 921–938.

Rutter, M., Moffitt, T. E., & Caspi, A. (2006). Gene–environment interplay and psychopathology: Multiple varieties but real effects. *Journal of Child Psychology and Psychiatry, and Allied Disciplines, 47,* 226–261.

Widiger, T. A., De Clercq, B., & De Fruyt, F. (2009). Childhood antecedents of personality disorder: An alternative perspective. *Development and Psychopathology, 21,* 771–791.

3c Moving Contextual Personality Research Forward: Author Rejoinder to Commentaries on Environmental and Sociocultural Influences on Personality Disorders

BRIANNA J. TURNER, JULIE PRUD'HOMME, AND NICOLE LEGG

Macfie, Noose, and Gorrondona (this volume) and Davies and Thompson (this volume) have provided thoughtful commentaries that significantly expand on both the theoretical and empirical considerations regarding sociocultural and environmental influences on personality and personality disorders that we provided in our chapter. In our rejoinder, we wish to highlight three key directions for research and clinical work that emerge from our chapter and the subsequent commentaries.

UNDERSTANDING THE IMPORTANCE OF EARLY ENVIRONMENTS

Both Davies and Thompson's and Macfie and colleagues' excellent commentaries highlight the importance of early caregiving environments in organizing personality development. In their review of the social defense system and differential susceptibility theories, Davies and Thompson underscore the utility of adopting a contextual approach to understanding personality. For instance, behavioral responses that are adaptive in one context may be less functional or appropriate in other contexts. Similarly, temperaments or traits that are associated with increased risk in some contexts may produce substantial benefits in others. Thus, researchers and clinicians must be careful to consider both the early developmental contexts in which traits or response styles developed and their function within evolving contexts across development. In a related vein, Macfie and colleagues point to Bronfenbrenner's ecological systems theory to remind readers of the importance of considering dynamic interactions between multiple levels of environmental influence and personality development. Both commentaries thus highlight the importance of bringing a contextually-informed, dynamic perspective to research and clinical care, while also emphasizing the crucial role of early environments in personality psychopathology.

An additional direction that Davies and Thompson and Macfie and colleagues each highlight is the importance of expanding our understanding of the *developmental pathways* that link early caregiving experiences to prospective personality pathology. Macfie and colleagues review several longitudinal studies that have adopted just such an approach. Davies and Thompson expertly note that an increased focus on mediated moderation models will advance our understanding of how person–environment transactions unfold and connect early caregiver influences to personality pathology. Moreover, as Macfie and colleagues observe, there is also a need to expand our consideration of interactions between family processes and individual cognitive and emotional systems in personality research, as well as in our assessment and treatment of personality disorders. Studies in this area may spur early intervention and prevention efforts by highlighting foundational processes that could be targeted in treatment.

TESTING INTERACTIVE AND TRANSACTIONAL MODELS

One area we would like to revisit from our chapter is our consideration of biological versus environmental contributions to personality disorders. As Macfie and colleagues note, it is important to avoid a false dichotomy between these contributions given robust evidence of their transactional relationship. Increasingly, research is identifying the bi-directional interactions between biological factors (e.g., genes, biomarkers, predisposing heritable characteristics) and environments (see Macfie et al., this volume). Coupling an interactive (e.g., gene by environment) approach with the dimensional models of personality discussed below may help move the field beyond examining biomarkers that are specific to a single disorder and toward a broader understanding of the dynamic underpinnings of personality pathology.

EXPANDING THE USE OF DIMENSIONAL MODELS OF PERSONALITY PATHOLOGY

The movement toward dimensional models of personality pathology is an overarching theme within our chapter, the responding commentaries, and research within the field of personality disorders. We wholeheartedly agree with Davies and Thompson's suggestion that a move toward dimensional frameworks, such as the Five-Factor Model (Bagby & Widiger, 2018; De Fruyt & De Clercq, 2014), may facilitate more rapid advances in our understanding of the developmental pathways that underlie adaptive and maladaptive expressions of personality traits. Dimensional approaches favor the conceptualization of personality traits as continuously distributed across gradations of intensity, severity, or rigidity. The use of dimensional models has important advantages for moving contextual personality disorder research forward. For instance, dimensional models may facilitate cross-cultural research, as cultural differences in definitions of maladaptiveness can be more explicitly acknowledged and incorporated into research designs (e.g., Chen & Stevenson, 1995; Kim, Rapee, Ja Oh, & Moon, 2008). Furthermore, dimensional models may lend themselves to lifespan and developmental perspectives, which, in turn, can spur important research on the interactions of early environments, sociocultural contexts, and biological contributions to personality pathology. Finally, moving toward a dimensional approach to personality disorders may help align research with existing clinical theories that emphasize early development and reinforcement of maladaptive coping strategies or response styles, internal working models or schema, and interpersonal dynamics in their etiological explanations of personality pathology. Studies grounded in a dimensional perspective may also inform interventions that could be applied and adapted across facets of personality pathology, similar to the transdiagnostic approaches that have been developed for other disorders (e.g., Barlow et al., 2010; Ehrenreich-May & Chu, 2013).

REFERENCES

Bagby, R. M., & Widiger, T. A. (2018). Five factor model personality disorder scales: An introduction to a special section on assessment of maladaptive variants of the five factor model. *Psychological Assessment, 30*, 1–9.

Barlow, D. H., Ellard, K. K., Fairholme, C. P., Farchione, T. J., Boisseau, C. L., Allen, L. B., & Ehrenreich-May, J. T. (2010). *Unified Protocol for Transdiagnostic Treatment of Emotional Disorders*. New York: Oxford University Press.

Chen, C., & Stevenson, H. W. (1995). Motivation and mathematics achievement: A comparative study of Asian-American, Caucasian-American, and East Asian high school students. *Child Development, 66*(4), 1215–1234.

De Fruyt, F., & De Clercq, B. (2014). Antecedents of personality disorder in childhood and adolescence: Toward an integrative developmental model. *Annual Review of Clinical Psychology, 10*, 449–476.

Ehrenreich-May, J., & Chu, B. C. (2013). *Transdiagnostic Treatments for Children and Adolescents: Principles and Practice*. New York: Guilford Press.

Kim, J., Rapee, R. M., Ja Oh, K., & Moon, H.-S. (2008). Retrospective report of social withdrawal during adolescence and current maladjustment in young adulthood: Cross-cultural comparisons between Australian and South Korean students. *Journal of Adolescence, 31*(5), 543–563.

4 Personality Pathology in Youth

CARLA SHARP AND BARBARA DE CLERCQ

INTRODUCTION

Despite the acknowledgment that personality disorder onsets in adolescence (American Psychiatric Association, 1987, 1994, 2000, 2013), the assessment, diagnosis, and treatment of personality pathology in children and adolescents were regarded as highly controversial until very recently (Chanen, 2015; Sharp, 2016; Shiner & Tackett, 2014). Concerns over the clinical management of personality pathology in youth have focused on the belief that personality in youth is too unstable to justify the diagnosis of personality disorder; uncertainty whether the diagnosis of personality disorder in youth was endorsed by psychiatric nomenclature; beliefs about the normative nature of certain features of personality pathology (e.g., impulsivity, affective instability, or identity disturbances) specifically in adolescence; and worries regarding the demarcation between symptoms of personality pathology and symptoms of internalizing and externalizing disorders. Clinicians have also expressed significant worry over the possibility that labeling an adolescent with a personality disorder may be stigmatizing. Concerns over many of these beliefs have been laid to rest due to accumulating empirical evidence challenging these assumptions. Importantly, researchers and clinicians working in this area have noted that it is unlikely that a person wakes up on her or his eighteenth birthday with a personality disorder, and that turning a blind eye to personality pathology in youth was potentially perpetuating a stigma surrounding this type of pathology, which has been shown to be as treatable and "syndrome-like" as traditional Axis I disorders (Chanen, Sharp, Hoffman, & Global Alliance for Prevention and Early Intervention for Borderline Personality Disorder, 2017; Zanarini, Frankenburg, Reich, & Fitzmaurice, 2012).

However, certain controversies remain. As may be observed throughout this handbook, a longstanding tension in describing and understanding personality pathology continues to be a focus of discussion also in the developmental psychopathology of personality (Tackett, Herzhoff, Balsis, & Cooper, 2016) – that is, the tension between a categorical and dimensional approach to phenomenology. There are many reasons why a categorical approach like the DSM system has served adult psychopathology reasonably well (Krueger & Markon, 2014); for instance, the fact that by the time that categorical diagnoses were introduced in the DSM-III, enough research had been conducted on these categories to minimally justify a categorical approach (Hudziak, Achenbach, Althoff, & Pine, 2007). This is, however, not true for child and adolescent psychopathology, which has a much shorter empirical research history despite rich theoretical and clinical foundations (Hinshaw, 2017). Several unique features of child and adolescent pathology necessitate a dimensional approach (Hudziak et al., 2007), especially where personality pathology is concerned (De Clercq, Decuyper, & De Caluwé, 2014). First, psychopathology manifests differently across development, demonstrating either homotypic or heterotypic continuity. For instance, externalizing behavior in an 8-year-old may include oppositional and aggressive behavior, but may morph into moodiness and substance use in adolescence. Second, behavior that is considered typical or adaptive in one developmental period may be considered atypical or maladaptive in another. A dramatic emotional melt-down may, for instance, be considered typical for a 2-year-old, but indicative of underlying pathology in a 10-year-old. Third, whereas assessment in adults is over-reliant on self-report, the assessment of psychopathology in children and adolescents, for obvious reasons, has to include multiple sources of information (parents, teachers, and children themselves; De Fruyt & De Clercq, 2014); however, research shows modest agreement between sources on problem behaviors (De Los Reyes, Thomas, Goodman, & Kundey, 2013). A child may therefore be considered above clinical threshold from one perspective, but not another, thereby calling into question the usefulness of categorical approaches to assessment and diagnosis in children and adolescents. In short, then, due to multiple sources of variance in child and adolescent psychopathology, quantitative differences (rather than qualitative, categorical differences) may be more informative in youth.

Notwithstanding these obvious advantages, the reality in most clinical settings is that of a categorical approach to assessment, diagnosis, and treatment (Hudziak et al., 2007). Moreover, a categorical nosology is still very much in place for adult personality disorders (see DSM-5 Section II) (Herpertz et al., 2017), and a developmentally informed dimensional system of personality pathology (as well as most other disorders) in children and adolescents is yet to be developed for the DSM. It must be noted, however, that the alternative dimensional model of personality disorders in DSM-5 (AMPD) has abandoned the traditional age limit, thus leaving room for research on its validity in younger age groups. Indeed, in order to "dimensionalize" DSM personality disorders (i.e., facilitate the inclusion of a quantitative axis that can take developmentally specific sources of variance into account; Hudziak et al., 2007), the validity and reliability of well-researched DSM-based adult personality constructs must be evaluated in youth to determine their value in this population. In parallel, dimensional conceptualizations derived from trait-based approaches to personality pathology must be tested in youth. In this chapter, we review research on child and adolescent personality pathology that has emerged from both these perspectives with the goal of exploring whether the knowledge gained from these perspectives could provide complementary evidence in support of the idea of adolescence as a sensitive period for the development and manifestation of personality pathology.

A few limitations of our review should be mentioned at the outset. First, although a rich literature has developed on the phenomenology and course of maladaptive personality traits dimensionally defined, the translation into clinical utility has not yet taken place; thus, information on the prevalence, etiology, and treatment of personality pathology in youth, dimensionally defined, is lacking. We will therefore discuss the prevalence, etiology, and treatment of personality pathology in youth from categorically defined studies, whereas the phenomenology and course of youth personality disorder will include evidence from both the categorical and dimensional perspectives.

Second, for both practical and substantive reasons, the current chapter will mostly focus on borderline personality pathology (BPP), especially when discussing personality pathology from a categorical perspective. Whereas a dimensional perspective makes it easier to cover the full spectrum of personality pathology in one chapter, the coverage of ten discrete personality disorders in one chapter is hard to achieve. Fortunately, most of the research on categorically-defined youth personality pathology has focused on borderline personality disorder (BPD; Sharp & Fonagy, 2015; Shiner & Tackett, 2014). Therefore, sections on categorically defined personality pathology will focus mostly on this disorder. We do not, however, consider this practical constraint catastrophic – which bring us to the substantive rationale for focusing on BPP.

Although more research is obviously needed on other manifestations of personality pathology (that is, other PDs) in youth, recent factor analytic work at the level of both the disorder (Jahng et al., 2011; Nestadt et al., 1994; Nestadt et al., 2006) and the item/criterion (e.g., Sharp et al., 2015; Wright, Hopwood, Skodol, & Morey, 2016), have called into question the discrete nature of PDs, suggesting that the covariation between PDs and/or their symptoms is not explained by ten underlying discrete disorders. This evidence has led to suggestions – consistent with early theories of personality pathology (Kernberg, 1967) – that BPP may represent the common features shared by all personality pathology (Clark, Nuzum, & Ro, 2017; Sharp et al., 2015; Sharp & Wall, 2017). Clark, Nuzum, and Ro (2017) argue for BPP as a possible indicator of general personality impairment *severity*, such that PD severity is defined as a latent construct that can be modeled with four indicators: within-PD comorbidity, problematic course/prognosis of both PD and comorbid clinical syndromes, PD-associated psychosocial dysfunction, and features of DSM-5-II BPD. In contrast, but not mutually exclusive, Sharp and colleagues (Sharp, Vanwoerden, & Wall, 2018; Sharp & Wall, 2017) argue for BPP as an indicator of *general maladaptation in self–other function*; i.e., of all the PD criteria, BPD criteria most closely capture problems in self-definition, self-reflection, identity, self-determination, and relatedness with others. In time, empirical research will clarify the subtle nuances within these distinctions; however, the point is that BPP appears to be indicative of general personality dysfunction and, as such, allows for the generalization of BPD research, at least to some extent, to personality pathology in general. We think this is especially justified for an understudied area such as youth personality pathology, where there seems to be some urgency in translating research findings into preliminary and useful guidance for clinicians who wish to interrupt further perpetuation of the stigma associated with PD.

Finally, we also wish to clarify another important point when considering the categorical–dimensional debate. For the purposes of this chapter, when we talk about PD categorically defined, we use the *constructs* developed by the categorically-informed DSM to talk about personality pathology – in this case BPD. However, within the boundaries of the BPD construct, we may also talk about BPD symptoms dimensionally assessed with, for instance, the help of self-report measures. In contrast, when we talk about PD dimensionally defined, we refer to the dimensions that emerge empirically when personality pathology items are factor analyzed. This represents a more bottom-up approach to defining personality pathology because the DSM-based structure of ten categorically defined PDs is not imposed top-down on covariation structures. Instead, underlying dimensions (or factors) that account for covariation among personality pathology items are allowed to emerge empirically.

PHENOMENOLOGY, ASSESSMENT, AND CONSTRUCT VALIDITY PERSONALITY PATHOLOGY IN YOUTH FROM A CATEGORICAL PERSPECTIVE

With the above broader context in mind, we can now consider the definition of Section II BPD and evaluate the evidence in support of its construct validity from studies conducted in youth. The DSM defines BPD as characterized by affective instability, chronic feelings of emptiness, inappropriate or intense anger, stress-related paranoia or dissociative symptoms, fear of abandonment, unstable or intense interpersonal relationships, identity disturbance, impulsivity, and self-injurious behaviors. DSM-based BPP has been operationalized and assessed through both interview-based and self-report measures in youth. Both sources of evidence will be reviewed below.

Studies Using Interview-Based Measures

Whereas adult tools, most notably the Structured Clinical Interview for DSM-IV Axis II Personality Disorders (SCID; First, Spitzer, Gibbon, & Williams, 2002), have been used in youth samples (e.g., Chanen, Jovev, et al., 2008), there has been an attempt in recent years to develop more developmentally sensitive interview-based tools. These have included, for instance, the Childhood Interview for Borderline Personality Disorder (Zanarini, 2003) which has been evaluated for its psychometric properties in both clinical and community samples (Sharp, Ha, Michonski, Venta, & Carbone, 2012; Zanarini et al., 2011). Specifically, Sharp and colleagues (Sharp, Ha, et al., 2012), used a confirmatory factor analytic approach to examine the internal factor structure of the nine CI-BPD items in a sample of 254 inpatient adolescents and found support for a unidimensional factor structure, indicating that the DSM-IV criteria of BPD constitute *a coherent combination of symptoms* in adolescents, including adequate coefficients of internal consistency and high inter-rater agreement between self- and parental reports. CI-BPD diagnoses were further significantly related to clinician diagnosis and to two questionnaire-based measures of BPD, i.e., the PAI-BOR (Morey, 2007) and the BPFSC (Crick, Murray-Close, & Woods, 2005). The CI-BPD was also able to distinguish those who self-harmed and those who showed poor emotion regulation from those who did not, further underscoring its clinical utility.

In another study (Michonski, Sharp, Steinberg, & Zanarini, 2013) – this time in a large, population-based sample (n = 6,339) of young adolescents from the United Kingdom (ages 11 to 12), item response theory (IRT) was used to investigate the extent to which each BPD criterion (as assessed in the CI-BPD) contributed to variability in the latent borderline trait. A *single underlying dimension* adequately accounted for covariation among the BPD criteria. Each criterion was found to be discriminating to a degree comparable to what has been reported in adult studies. BPD criteria were most informative within a range of severity of BPD pathology between +1 and +3 standard units, suggesting good discrimination at the more severe end of the latent trait. Five criteria were found to exhibit differential item functioning (DIF) between boys and girls. However, DIF balanced out for the total interview score, supporting the use of the total CI-BPD score to identify youth with possible personality pathology.

Additional interview-based measures of DSM-based BPD that have been validated for use in adolescents include the MSI-BPD (Zanarini et al., 2003), which was validated in at least two studies (Chanen, Jovev, et al., 2008; Noblin, Venta, & Sharp, 2013), and the Borderline Personality Disorder Severity Index-IV-adolescent and parent versions (BPDSI-IV-ado/p; Schuppert, Bloo, Minderaa, Emmelkamp, & Nauta, 2012). Findings suggest that both the MSI-BPD and the BPDSI-IV-ado/p are valid and reliable instruments for the assessment of BPD symptom severity in adolescents.

Studies Using Self-Report Measures

DSM-based BPP has also been operationalized in several self-report measures for assessing BPD in youth – either as part of omnibus psychopathology measures or BPD-specific measures. Using standard criteria for measure evaluation (that is, the AERA, APA, NCME Standards for Educational and Psychological Testing (American Psychiatric Association, 1999), studies have demonstrated strong psychometrics for these measures, further bolstering the notion that "adult-like" BPD can be reliably assessed and operationalized in youth. For instance, Morey (2007) adapted the adult Personality Assessment Inventory (PAI) borderline subscale (PAI-BOR) and provided norms for the assessment of BPP in adolescents. This subscale was recently evaluated in two high-risk samples, an inpatient sample of adolescents and justice-involved adolescents (Venta, Magyar, Hossein, & Sharp, 2018). The purported four-factor structure of the PAI-BOR did not hold, suggesting that covariation in BPD symptoms in youth is not accounted for by four underlying factors as suggested by earlier studies of the PAI-BOR, but by one general factor. However, the scale showed good internal consistency (*alpha* = .88, .82, respectively) and good diagnostic accuracy (AUC = 0.834) for predicting a BPD diagnosis (via structured interview).

In a further extension of DSM-defined BPD, Crick et al. (2005) adapted the PAI-BOR subscale for use in children and adolescents, resulting in the Borderline Personality Features Scale for Children (BPFSC). The BPFSC has shown excellent criterion validity (Chang, Sharp, & Ha, 2011), as well as concurrent validity (Sharp, Mosko, Chang, & Ha, 2011). A parent version was adapted and also demonstrated good psychometric properties (Sharp et al., 2011). Recently, the original 24-item measure has been shortened through IRT to an 11-item version (BPFSC-11; (Sharp, Steinberg, Temple, & Newlin, 2014) to improve its item effectiveness. Factor analyses demonstrated a uni-dimensional factor structure and excellent criterion validity in the form of sensitivity and specificity in an independent clinical sample. In summary, using standard criteria for measure evaluation, adequate psychometrics for the BPFSC or BPFSC-11 have now been demonstrated for samples in Denmark (Bo et al., 2017), Italy (Fossati, Sharp, Borroni, & Somma, 2019), and Canada (Haltigan & Vaillancourt, 2016), with several studies in other countries underway (Mexico, Spain, China, Germany, France, and Portugal). Other omnibus or more circumscribed self-report measures of Section II-defined BPD with demonstrated construct validity include the Minnesota Borderline Personality Disorder Scale (Bornovalova, Hicks, Patrick, Iacono, & McGue, 2011; Rojas et al., 2014), the Minnesota Multiphasic Personality Inventory– Adolescent version (Archer, Ball, & Hunter, 1985), and the Borderline Personality Questionnaire (Chanen, Jovev, et al., 2008).

Informant Discrepancies

The use of multiple sources of information (i.e., self, informant, or clinician report) when assessing or diagnosing PDs is important given the longstanding view of PDs as relatively pervasive and persistent across contexts (American Psychiatric Association, 2013), as well as the deficits in self-reflective capacities inherent in the disorders (American Psychiatric Association, 2013; Hopwood, Wright, Ansell, & Pincus, 2013). The importance of multi-informant designs in younger age groups can be additionally understood from the finding that younger people are more sensitive to response styles (Soto, John, Gosling, & Potter, 2008) when providing self-reports, or may provide less reliable answers due to immature meta-cognitive abilities or language skills (Achenbach, McConaughy, & Howell, 1987). Although research is not extensive in this area, a couple of studies of youth personality pathology have been conducted, albeit using non-DSM-based tools of personality pathology (Tackett, 2011; Tromp & Koot, 2008). These studies have shown that inter-rater agreement varies across traits, potentially due to differences in observability, as reflected in higher agreement for more externalizing versus internalizing traits. From a DSM-perspective, Wall, Sharp, Ahmed, Goodman, and Zanarini (2017) found high diagnostic concordance for adolescent BPD between inpatient adolescents and their parents on the Revised Diagnostic Interview for Borderlines (DIB-R; Zanarini et al., 1998) and the CI-BPD (Zanarini, 2003). Sharp et al. (2011) also found significant but modest concordance in a community sample of parent and child reports on the Borderline Personality Features Scale (BPFSC). Given research that informant report discrepancies are often statistically and clinically significant if

appropriately interpreted (De Los Reyes et al., 2013), latent class analyses (LCA) were recently used to evaluate the clinical significance of parent- versus self-report concordance or divergence of DSM-based BPD symptoms in a large sample of inpatient adolescents (Wall, Ahmed, & Sharp, 2018). LCA identified three classes of parent–adolescent dyads: two convergent classes demonstrating BPFS-P and BPFS-C agreement at a moderate and high level and a divergent class consisting of dyads reporting clinically significant scores on the BPFS-P but clinically negligible BPFS-C scores. Both convergent classes evidenced higher rates of psychiatric severity and less access to internal resources to protect against the effects of psychopathology (i.e., emotion regulation and experiential acceptance).

Together, these studies suggest that personality pathology, as exemplified here with BPD studies, can be measured through either adolescent- or parent-report, and support the particular clinical utility of symptoms with high inter-rater agreement. However, these studies also point to important sources of variability based on the source of the report and recommend the use of multiple sources in the assessment of youth personality pathology. Also, discrepancies across informants may represent meaningful content to discuss with parents (or teachers) and the child in order to evaluate to what extent these discrepancies actually represent context-specific or transient maladaptive manifestations rather that personality disturbances (De Clercq, 2018).

Comorbidity

Similar to adult BPD, adolescent BPD demonstrates high comorbidity with both internalizing and externalizing disorders, ranging from 50 percent in the Children in the Community study (Cohen, 2008) to 86 percent in a clinical sample (Speranza et al., 2011). Similarly, Chanen, Jovev, and Jackson (2007) found significantly higher rates of comorbidity in adolescents with BPD, compared to adolescents with either no PD or no disorder, and Ha, Balderas, Zanarini, Oldham, and Sharp (2014) reported elevated rates of mood (70.6 percent), anxiety (67.3 percent), and externalizing (60.2 percent) disorders in adolescent inpatients with BPD relative to non-BPD psychiatric controls (39.2 percent, 45.5 percent, 34.4 percent, respectively). Adolescents with BPD also showed significantly higher scores on dimensional measures of internalizing and externalizing psychopathology than psychiatric controls, as well as significantly higher likelihood of meeting criteria for complex comorbidity (as defined by Zanarini et al. [1998] as any mood or anxiety disorder plus a disorder of impulsivity). Recent studies have also demonstrated in both adults (Eaton et al., 2011; James & Taylor, 2008) and adolescents (Sharp, Elhai, Kalpakci, Michonski, & Pavlidis, 2014) that whereas BPD appears to be a confluence of both internalizing and externalizing pathology (i.e., loaded onto both internalizing and externalizing latent factors; Roysamb et al., 2011), enough variance remains *uncaptured* by these latent factors to suggest that BPD cannot be fully explained by these pathologies. Taken together, this evidence suggests that although BPD is neither an internalizing disorder (Akiskal et al., 1985) nor a female expression of antisocial PD (Paris, 1997), it likely represents a confluence of internalizing and externalizing problems; that is, the construct of BPD contains characteristics of both internalizing and externalizing disorders, while still retaining its independence as a separate disorder. Elsewhere, it has been argued that personality pathology constitutes a qualitatively different type of pathology on the severity continuum between internalizing/externalizing pathology on the one hand and psychotic disorders on the other (Sharp et al., 2018; Sharp & Wall, 2017).

Summary: Construct Validity

A considerable amount of work (of which we presented only a representative sample) has been done to evaluate the construct validity of adult-like BPD in adolescence operationalized through interview-based and self-report measures. The framework suggested by the AERA, APA, and NCME (American Psychiatric Association, 1999) for organizing evidence to evaluate construct validity includes five categories of evidence, each varying in their importance according to how test scores are used. These include (1) evidence based on test content (i.e., themes, wording, and format of the items, questions, guidelines for administration and scoring, and the like), (2) evidence based on response processes (i.e., the fit between the latent constructs of the test and the detailed nature of performance by the examinee and conduct of the examiner), (3) evidence based on internal structure (i.e., the degree to which the relationships among the component parts of the test conform to the hypothesized constructs), (4) evidence based on relations to other (external) variables (i.e., the relationships between test scores and variables external to the test, including developmental variables and scores on other tests of similar and dissimilar constructs), and (5) evidence based on consequences of testing (i.e., the intended and unintended outcomes of the use or application of a test). In this section of the paper, we provided evidence in support of all of these categories, suggesting that BPP tools capture something about adolescent function that is scientifically sound and clinically useful. As a field, we can name the construct captured by these measures whatever we want. What we cannot do, however, is ignore the fact that standard approaches to assessing the validity of tools support the downward extension of the DSM-based conceptualizations of BPD to adolescent populations. Overall, this evidence justifies the use of the BPP construct in younger age groups in a similar way as it

has been conceived in adults, although phenomenologically speaking it should be mentioned that the more acute symptoms of BPD, such as self-harm and excessive risk taking behaviors, are often more explicitly seen in adolescents than adults (Kaess, Brunner, & Chanen, 2014). The developmental difference in the phenotypic manifestation of these symptoms may be understood in the context of reduced self-control in adolescence and the linear increase in impulse control from late adolescence to early adulthood, as will be outlined later in this chapter. This finding is important, as it points to the necessity of age-specific norms for the diagnosis of BPP in younger age groups.

PERSONALITY PATHOLOGY IN YOUTH FROM A TRAIT PERSPECTIVE

Conceptually, evidence on developmental manifestations of personality pathology from a trait approach has grown from two perspectives, including a general trait as well as a specific maladaptive trait perspective. Both viewpoints conceptualize antecedents of personality pathology as dimensional constructs, but differ in their focus on the trait continuum. The strength of such trait perspectives lies in their fundamental dimensional approach to PDs, enabling the description of young individuals on a set of trait vulnerabilities that are much more dynamic compared to a static and formal PD diagnosis (Clark, 2007; De Fruyt & De Clercq, 2014, Skodol et al., 2005). Conceptualizing a PD condition in terms of concrete and workable traits also reduces the stigma associated with a PD diagnosis and offers welcome leads to clinicians who aim to effectuate change in daily functioning (De Clercq, 2018). Indeed, a trait profile is always generated from characteristic daily behavior, cognitions, and emotions, hence facilitating communication and appropriate therapeutic goal-setting. Moreover, the hierarchical conceptualization of most trait taxonomies enables the targeting of very specific trait vulnerabilities at the facet-level (Bach, Markon, Simonsen, & Krueger, 2015), which provides a clinically feasible way to fine-tune perspectives, especially in younger age groups. Finally, a dimensional trait perspective allows one to assess personality pathology in line with the fundamental nature of the pathology. The schizotypal PD, for example, is traditionally considered a unitary construct (American Psychiatric Association, 2013), whereas multiple sources of evidence have outlined its multidimensional nature, including both positive and negative schizotypal traits already observable during adolescence (Verbeke, De Clercq, Van der Heijden, Hutsebaut, & Van Aken, 2017).

As the PD field is currently moving toward an increased familiarity with the DSM-5 alternative model for personality pathology (AMPD; Krueger, Derringer, Markon, Watson, & Skodol, 2012), it may be informative to indicate that this section of the chapter is situated at the Criterion B trait-assessment of PDs and will review evidence on the validity of traits for conceptualizing personality pathology in younger age groups. According to the latest DSM-5 AMPD standards, however, the diagnostic process of a PD requires an additional assessment of self and interpersonal processes (Criterion A; American Psychiatric Association, 2013). These are traditionally not described as separate components in trait models (Tackett et al., 2016), although some debate exists as to the extent to which these self and interpersonal dysfunctionalities are already intertwined within the trait scores (Widiger et al., 2019). As the answer to this question should result from continuing empirical exploration, this section will exclusively focus on the trait-level description of personality pathology in younger age groups.

From a general trait perspective, convincing evidence has shown that early individual differences in Emotional Stability, Extraversion, Imagination/Openness, Agreeableness, and Conscientiousness as represented by the Five-Factor Model (Costa & McCrae, 1992) are meaningfully related to each of the DSM-based PDs (De Clercq & De Fruyt, 2003; De Clercq, De Fruyt, & Van Leeuwen, 2004) in a largely similar way as has been demonstrated for adults (Saulsman & Page, 2004; Widiger, Trull, Clarkin, Sanderson, & Costa, 2002). Beyond these trait associations at the level of the categorical PD scale, Tackett et al. (2016) have recently provided an impressive review of the evidence in support of Five-Factor Model equivalents of the main developmental clinical features of PDs. This review indicates that for each of the ten DSM-based PDs, the most prominent phenotypic PD symptoms in youth can be translated into either higher- or lower-order level trait aspects. This evidence accentuates that a significant amount of the variability in personality pathology can be traced back to individual differences in the main building blocks of personality, implying that children at the extremes of these traits are at increased risk for developing a less adaptive or pathological personality. Whereas some traits reflect shared underlying dispositional components across different disorders, other traits are rather unique vulnerabilities for specific PD symptomatology.

For example, just like in adults, low Emotional Stability is a significant trait component for almost all DSM-based PDs assessed in youth, whereas high Openness to Experiences is a unique correlate for schizotypal personality pathology. It is important to understand these shared versus unique developmental trait correlates to gain insight into not only the trait-based nature of different manifestations of PD symptoms, but the nomological net of personality pathology in youth, as well as to increase our understanding of comorbidity and the overall dimensional nature of psychopathology.

Although the validity of this general trait perspective on personality pathology has been convincingly demonstrated across age, it has been argued that the extremes of general trait measures may not always assess the richness of personality pathology (Clark, 2007). From this perspective, it is exactly at these extremes that a more

specific maladaptive trait perspective was elaborated by more narrowly defining a set of maladaptive traits considered to capture early manifestations of personality pathology in the most comprehensive way. Work in this area can be understood from top-down approaches, translating relevant adult PD traits into developmentally appropriate equivalents, such as the childhood borderline pathology construct (Chang et al., 2011; Crick et al., 2005), childhood psychopathy (Frick & Hare, 2001; Hare, 2003; Lynam, 1997) or the core trait of Narcissism (Thomaes, Stegge, Bushman, Olthof, & Denissen, 2008). Not surprisingly, this maladaptive trait perspective has been particularly elaborated for traits characteristic of Cluster B PDs. This can be explained by the fact that Cluster B pathology is socio-demographically seen more frequently in younger ages (Bernstein et al., 1993; Widiger & Costa, 2013), partly because of the heavy acting-out behavior that is easily observed by others and also because the seriously impairing character of Cluster B pathology results in more frequent and quicker health-care seeking behavior or forced mental health care (Chanen et al., 2007; Krabbendam et al., 2015; Winsper et al., 2015).

Beyond the work focusing on these more narrowly defined maladaptive traits, a subgroup of researchers has attempted to construct omnibus taxonomies of early personality pathology. Independent from each other, these researchers found an underlying maladaptive trait structure parallel to the well-established structure in adults (Widiger & Simonsen, 2005). From a likely similar top-down approach, the SNAP-Y (Linde, Stringer, Simms, & Clark, 2013) and the DAPP-BQ-A (Tromp & Koot, 2008) resulted from modifications of their adult counterparts for use in younger age groups, and showed adequate psychometric properties, including construct and criterion validity. In addition, the SNAP-Y showed meaningful relations with the MMPI-A (Butcher et al., 1992), one of the most commonly used DSM-based measures of adolescent personality pathology (Archer & Newsom, 2000). Also, the recently released adult DSM-5 PID-5 measure (Krueger et al., 2012), including 25 trait facets along a similar five dimensional higher-order trait structure, can be reliably and validly used in younger age groups with both a non-referred (De Clercq et al., 2014) and referred (De Caluwé, Verbeke, van Aken, van der Heijden, & De Clercq, 2019; Somma et al., 2016) status. Several authors have pointed to the potential of the latter instrument for a more official developmentally appropriate assessment of personality pathology at a young age (Sevecke, Schmeck, & Krischer, 2014; Shiner & Allen, 2013), as it is the first instrument integrated within DSM-5 that is built upon the well-established five major building blocks of personality that account for individual differences in trait characteristics from middle childhood onwards (Shiner & DeYoung, 2013).

From an age-specific bottom-up approach, De Clercq and colleagues (De Clercq, De Fruyt, Van Leeuwen, & Mervielde, 2006) constructed an omnibus measure (the

Dimensional Personality Symptom Itempool; DIPSI) for early maladaptive traits, initially structured in the traits of Emotional Dysregulation, Introversion, Disagreeableness, and Compulsivity, and later amended with an item-set representing a fifth factor of Oddity (Verbeke, De Caluwé, & De Clercq, 2017; Verbeke & De Clercq, 2014). Interestingly, these bottom-up and top-down measures for youth were developed by independent research groups following different strategies, but proved to have significant and meaningful interrelationships (Kushner, Tackett & De Clercq, 2013), hence underscoring their construct validity.

Given the comprehensiveness of the content covered by omnibus measures, these taxonomies can be readily used to construct and examine age-specific PD constructs, such as the childhood borderline construct (De Clercq et al., 2014), childhood psychopathy (Decuyper, De Bolle, De Fruyt, & De Clercq, 2011), schizotypal pathology (Verbeke, et al., 2017), or PD-related constructs, such as the Dark Triad (De Clercq, Hofmans, Vergauwe, De Fruyt, & Sharp, 2017). The construction of such childhood PD trait constructs is interesting from a conceptual point of view, but their validity should not be assumed before extensive empirical exploration has underscored their value for understanding developmental antecedents of personality pathology. As outlined by Tackett et al. (2016), these constructs should be the starting point, rather than the end, and their relevance should always be mirrored against the developmental principles and empirical evidence on the course of personality pathology from early age onwards. Although these developmental processes through which early trait vulnerabilities are shaped into consolidated patterns of personality pathology are complex and cannot be entirely defined by a set of principles or theoretical assumptions, they are important to consider, as they may unravel some of the density of childhood development and create guidelines for early assessment and intervention programs.

THE DEVELOPMENTAL COURSE OF YOUTH PERSONALITY PATHOLOGY

Longitudinal evidence has convincingly demonstrated that both stability and change characterize the developmental course of personality pathology (Tackett et al., 2016), which is underscored by both categorical as well as dimensional oriented (trait) studies. Overall, mean-level change can be understood from the *maturation principle*, reflecting the natural growth process toward adaptation in terms of more Emotional Stability (or less Emotional Dysregulation), more Agreeableness (or less Antagonism), and more Conscientiousness (or less Disinhibition) as children achieve more emotion regulation skills, impulse control, moral reasoning, and empathy with increasing age. The timing of this age-related decline, however, may vary across disorders. Core symptoms of borderline pathology, for example, have been demonstrated to increase in adolescence, peak in early adulthood, and then decline (Arens et al., 2013; Chanen & Kaess, 2012), whereas core Disinhibited traits such as Impulsivity generally tend to start to decline from 10 years of age (Steinberg et al., 2008). Some studies also showed differences between traits in the pace of natural change over time (De Clercq, Van Leeuwen, Van den Noortgate, De Bolle, & De Fruyt, 2009; Durbin et al., 2016; Van den Akker, Dekovic, Asscher, & Prinzie, 2014). Introversion, for instance, appears to show less mean-level change over time, suggesting the relative stability of Introverted- like traits throughout childhood compared to other basic maladaptive traits. In a related vein, the balance of evidence on borderline pathology traits suggests that whereas impulsive-type symptoms do reduce over time, affective-type symptoms, which include negative affect and feelings of emptiness, are more likely to persist (Meares, Gerull, Stevenson, & Korner, 2011).

Although the maturation principle is believed to be universal, some individuals do not experience an age-related decline in personality pathology symptoms. For instance, in the Children in the Community study, one-fifth of the sample of youth showed an increase in PD symptoms over the decade from mid-adolescence to early adulthood (Cohen, Crawford, Johnson, & Kasen, 2005). Moreover, remission from a categorical diagnosis of BPD does not imply that remitted patients are healthy (Wright, Zalewski, Hallquist, Hipwell, & Stepp, 2016). As with adults, poor functional outcomes persist for years in individuals who showed borderline features in adolescence, including increased risk for substance use and mood disorders, interpersonal problems, poorer quality of life, higher levels of general distress (Crawford et al., 2008; Winograd, Cohen, & Chen, 2008), higher service utilization (Cailhol et al., 2013), and increased rates of pain, physical illness, and mortality over time (Chen et al., 2009). Krueger (2005) has suggested in this regard that categorically assessed remission often simply implies a shift towards a different disorder, because time and environmental context may change the phenotypic expression of an underlying trait vulnerability, whereas the trait itself remains rather stable. Indeed, the categorical stability of BPD is modest in both adolescents and adults (Chanen et al., 2004; Skodol et al., 2005; Zanarini et al., 2011), whereas the stability for dimensionally assessed BPD appears to be somewhat higher (Bornovalova, Hicks, Iacono, & McGue, 2009; Chanen et al., 2004; Cohen et al., 2008). Independent from age-related mean-level changes, convincing meta-analytical evidence has shown a high *rank-order stability* of traits (Roberts & DelVecchio, 2000), pointing at the stability of a child's trait position relative to her or his peer group, and suggesting that vulnerable children remain vulnerable over time compared to others. Whereas rank-order stability for personality pathology has been shown to be moderate, it still appears to be more stable than common internalizing and externalizing psychopathology (Cohen et al., 2005; De Clercq et al.,

2009). Together, these data point to the possibility that a subgroup of youngsters fail to follow the normative decline in maladaptive trait features, and may become "stuck" in adolescence. Presumably, many of these adolescents already manifested more explicit maladaptive behaviors compared to their peers in terms of frequency or intensity, although trajectories of a *steady increase* and thus a later onset of pathology have also been observed. We will return to the mechanisms that may account for these developmental delays or deviating pathways later.

Beyond the principles of maturation and rank-order stability, several studies have also underscored longitudinal measurement invariance of borderline symptomatology from adolescence onwards (Haltigan & Vaillancourt, 2016; Vanwoerden, Garey, Ferguson, Temple, & Sharp, revise and resubmit; Wright, Zalewski, et al., 2016). These studies are important against the background of other longitudinal studies on borderline pathology, which have shown that levels of borderline features increase until mid-adolescence and then level out through adulthood (Chanen & Kaess, 2012). Put differently, the prospective course of borderline pathology reported in the literature appears to be reflective of true (mean level) changes and not due to reporting biases, thus pointing to possible *homotopic continuity* of DSM-based borderline symptoms at least throughout adolescence. Personality pathology appears to provide additional explanatory value above and beyond other traditional Axis I disorders as well as other PDs in predicting current psychosocial functioning (Chanen et al., 2007) and suicidal outcomes (Sharp, Green, Venta, Pettit, & Zanarini, 2012).

PREVALENCE

As a reminder to the reader, we will be focusing mostly on BPD (most often categorically defined) going forward, as coverage of all PDs is beyond the scope of this chapter and most empirical work in prevalence, etiology, and treatment has been carried out on narrowly defined BPD. In adults, BPD occurs in approximately 1–3 percent of the general population (Leichsenring, Leibing, Kruse, New, & Leweke, 2011; Lenzenweger, 2008). Whereas few population-based studies of BPD exist for children and adolescents, early studies reported high rates of BPD in community studies, with values ranging from 11 percent (Bernstein et al., 1993) to 26.7 percent (Chabrol et al., 2002).[1] Two recent reports estimated prevalence using different scoring algorithms in a large birth cohort of 6330 British children 11 years of age (the Avon Longitudinal Study of Parents and Children; ALSPAC study) and found a prevalence of 3.27 percent (Zanarini et al., 2011)

and of 0.006 percent (Michonski et al., 2013), respectively. Other reports have estimated point prevalence for adolescents in the community at around 1 percent in the USA (Johnson, Cohen, Kasen, Skodol, & Oldham, 2008; Lewinsohn, Rohde, Seeley, & Klein, 1997) and 2 percent in China (Leung & Leung, 2009), and cumulative prevalence at 3 percent (Johnson et al., 2008). The picture in clinical populations is more concerning, with reported rates of 11 percent in outpatients (Chanen et al., 2004), 33 percent (Ha et al., 2014) and 43–49 percent in inpatients (Levy et al., 1999). The take-home message from these data is that, like the phenomenology discussed above, prevalence rates for BPD appear to be comparable between adults and adolescents.

ETIOLOGY OF YOUTH PERSONALITY PATHOLOGY

Increasing etiological evidence suggests that various manifestations of psychopathology, including personality pathology, evolve from a more general genetically-based propensity to psychopathology (Caspi et al., 2014; Kotov et al., 2017; Lahey et al., 2012), which is partly reflected in a large common growth factor of early trait pathology (De Clercq, 2018; De Clercq et al., 2017; Wright, Zalewski, et al., 2016). Although there is some evidence for significant homotypic continuity of early internalizing versus externalizing tendencies toward either internalizing or externalizing trait outcomes (Luby, Si, Belden, Tandon, & Spitznagel, 2009; Mesman & Koot, 2001, Snyder, Young, & Hankin, 2016), adult personality pathology as currently structured in the DSM-5 does not result from phenotypically-similar trait antecedents at a more lower-level trait operationalization, at least not before adolescence. Indeed, from the principle of trait crystallization (Shiner, 1998), it was recently shown that the discriminatory power of youth maladaptive traits for conceptually related outcomes becomes significant only from mid-adolescence onwards (De Clercq et al., 2017). As outlined later in this chapter, this finding is important because it signifies that adolescence in particular can be considered a sensitive developmental period in which specific configurations of personality pathology are shaped. These specific manifestations of personality pathology may thus flow from either steady-high trajectories of childhood trait vulnerabilities, or result from increasing trajectories of maladaptive traits as a consequence of recurrent failures in achieving developmental milestones (De Clercq et al., 2017).

Personality pathology does not, of course, evolve exclusively from child factors, as multiple environmental factors, as well as child × environmental processes, also contribute to PD outcomes. Two main developmental theories of BPD, for example, agree that an interaction of genetic predispositions and environmental stressors is likely at play (Gunderson & Lyons-Ruth, 2008; Sharp & Fonagy, 2015). Marsha Linehan's biosocial theory

---

[1] We would like to note at this point that in some of the older studies, prevalence estimates may have been inflated due to the use of measures that were not validated for youth at that time, hence increasing the chance that normative turmoil was presented as BPD symptoms.

(Crowell, Beauchaine, & Linehan, 2009; Linehan, 1993) suggests that BPD results from biological predispositions manifesting themselves under stress from an invalidating environment. However, due to varying thresholds of sensitivity among children, even the most well-intentioned of families can create an environment that, to a sensitive child, is perceived as invalidating. This can lead to some instances of people with BPD reporting highly stressful or traumatic childhoods that may not agree with reports from other sources, such as parents or siblings. Growing up in an environment experienced as invalidating, a child will begin to believe that her or his feelings and thoughts do not matter, ultimately hindering the capacity to recognize and label emotions, both within the self and in others. Overall, Linehan's theory posits that BPD represents dysfunction in how an individual experiences and regulates emotions, with all symptoms stemming from this deficit. The emotional instability, anger, and self-destructive impulsivity observed in BPD are all manifestations of the inability to effectively regulate unpleasant internal experiences. Similarly, Peter Fonagy's mentalization model of BPD (Fonagy & Bateman, 2008; Fonagy & Luyten, 2009, 2016) suggests that an interaction between a constitutional vulnerability to emotional distress and disruptions in attachment relationships may account for the development of the disorder. This combination of risk factors leads to hyper-responsiveness of attachment systems, resulting in deficits in mentalizing, or the ability to understand the internal experiences of others and the self, especially when experiencing stress or emotional arousal, and ultimately impeding the development of the self.

These developmental theories provide an important framework for studying the correlates and causes of personality pathology. Indeed, research in the genetics of personality pathology as well as its neurobiology in youth is emerging (see Goodman, Perez-Rodriguez, & Siever, 2014 for a review). For instance, Belsky et al. (2012) examined borderline-related features in 1116 pairs of twins aged 12. The correlation for BPD traits between MZ twins were found to be .66 compared to .29 for DZ twins. Genetic factors were found to account for 66 percent of the variance in borderline traits, suggesting very similar heritability for adolescents compared to adults. Bornovalova et al. (2009) found that borderline traits were moderately heritable, with average heritability across age of approximately .3–.5. Developmentally, heritability appeared to increase from ages 14 and 18. Importantly, this study also showed that both stability and change of BPD traits were influenced profoundly by genetic factors, and modestly, but increasingly, by non-shared environmental factors, underscoring the etiological significance of young people progressively selecting their own environment. Developmentally-specific manifestations of biologically-based etiological factors are also apparent from volumetric and functional neuroimaging studies conducted in youth. Structural imaging research has demonstrated volume reduction in the fronto-limbic network in

adolescents with BPD, including the orbitofrontal cortex (Brunner et al., 2010; Chanen, Velakoulis, et al., 2008), the anterior cingulate cortex (Goodman et al., 2011), and the amygdala and hippocampus (Chanen, Velakoulis, et al., 2008).

Of course, the most robust evaluation of the developmental models of personality pathology would be biology × environmental studies (Sharp & Kim, 2015). A nice example is provided by a study using a twin design (Bornovalova et al., 2013). Temperamental traits of behavioral disinhibition or externalizing (EXT; impulsivity and inability to inhibit undesirable actions) and negative emotionality or internalizing (INT; predisposition to experience depression, anger, and anxiety) were evaluated for their interaction with child abuse (CA) to predict borderline traits over time. Three causal models were tested: a direct causal model (CA → BPD); a diathesis stress model (INT/EXT × CA → BPD), and a genetic mediation model where the CA–BPD association was better accounted for by common genetic risk factors (i.e., INT, EXT, or additive INT and EXT psychopathology could account for genetic or environmental influences common to CA and BPD). The authors found the strongest support for a genetic mediation model where the association between exposure to traumatic events and BPD may be better accounted for by common genetic influences rather than the former causally influencing the latter.

RECONCILING CATEGORICAL AND DIMENSIONAL APPROACHES OF YOUTH PERSONALITY PATHOLOGY: SHARED PERSPECTIVES ON THE SENSITIVE PERIOD OF ADOLESCENCE

In the above sections, we have covered the research on phenomenology, comorbidity, course, prevalence, and etiology of personality pathology in youth, specifically borderline pathology. In reflecting on its content, certain conclusions can be drawn that point to adolescence as a sensitive period for the development of personality pathology, regardless of whether one takes a categorical or dimensional perspective in defining personality pathology. First, adult-like personality pathology has its onset in adolescence. Second, rank-order stability of personality pathology is moderately stable in children and adolescents and increases with age. Third, it appears that the discriminatory power of youth maladaptive traits for conceptually related outcomes becomes significant only from mid-adolescence onwards, suggesting the crystallization of early manifestations of personality pathology during adolescence. What accounts for this crystallization? Here and elsewhere (Sharp & Wall, 2017; Sharp et al., 2018), it has been argued that, if internalizing and externalizing pathology is left untreated and in the context of biological vulnerability and stressful life events, we can observe the manifestation of personality pathology in its adult-like form because it is during adolescence that an agentic, self-determining author of the self emerges (McAdams & Olson, 2010). Although the development of self begins as early as infancy, identity formation has long been understood to be a key developmental achievement of adolescence (Erikson, 1950). In contrast to other related self-concepts, identity is defined as the way in which an individual makes sense of or meaning from her or his self-concept (McLean & Pratt, 2006). Thus, identity is often studied with autobiographical narratives in which people are evaluated in their ability to integrate their autobiographical past and imagined future in a coherent way (McAdams & McLean, 2013). The complex process of reflecting and integrating disparate pieces of information across multiple domains of functioning is a meta-cognitive capacity that does not emerge until adolescence (Sebastian, Burnett, & Blakemore, 2008; Shaw et al., 2008; Somerville et al., 2013). Adolescents expand their social lives to include peers and romantic partners, offering additional data points that need integration. Cognitively, they are able to handle perspective-taking, but the task of integrating multiple self-hypotheses is a complex process that can be easily disrupted (Harter, 1999). The developmental toll of these transformations in self–other relatedness (individuation) appears to impose a heavy burden on some youngsters and their families. Whereas most adolescents grow out of the normative inter- and intra-personal conflict, confusion, distress, and instability in self-representation, others do not (Sharp & Rossouw, 2019). We suggest that it is this group of adolescents who do not show the normative decline in maladaptive traits, but whose internalizing and externalizing problems mature into a disturbance of identity, which may be conceptualized as part of the core of personality dysfunction (Hopwood et al., 2013; Sharp et al., 2018) as represented in Criterion A of Section III of the DSM-5 (American Psychiatric Association, 2013).

EARLY INTERVENTION, TREATMENT, AND PREVENTION

The question then arises whether early manifestations of personality pathology can be effectively treated and whether full-blown personality pathology can be prevented. The well-established evidence on maturation effects, rank-order stability, and a-specificity of youth trait pathology is important in several ways for those who aim to translate empirical findings into good practice. First, maturational evidence suggests we should refrain from diagnosing children at a very young age, as many of these early problematic behaviors are transient in nature and will likely turn into normative tendencies with increasing age. Relatedly, a specific personality disorder diagnosis cannot be justified throughout childhood given the a-specific predictive validity of early maladaptive traits. On the other hand, and based upon the same evidence, it is clear that overall trait vulnerabilities are traceable in

younger age groups and that especially high-scoring children should be the focus of early intervention, given the differential continuity and that maturation effects are generally linear in nature. Because of the a-specificity of childhood trait vulnerability, however, early interventions should not be built around disorder-specific protocols, but should explicitly target the traits that have proven to be the shared underlying liabilities for later PDs. From this perspective, youth with explicit manifestations of the BPD symptom cluster may be the target group par excellence, given that across PDs, BPD is the only disorder that comprehensively covers an overall pathology factor with meaningful correlates of impairment across various life domains.

However, central to the notion of early intervention and prevention, and consistent with a more dimensional approach to conceptualizing personality pathology, is the well-known fact that the threshold for distinguishing patients with and without PDs is arbitrary and there is no strict demarcation between "cases" and "non-cases" (Clark, 2007; Herpertz et al., 2017); as such, there is also no distinct point of "onset" (Chanen & Thompson, 2018). With no distinct point of onset, early intervention (defined as intervention at an early stage of disease progression) is justified either by preventing the onset of new cases (indicated prevention) or through case identification and early treatment, which involves formal diagnosis and intervention using DSM-based approaches. Chanen and Thompson (2018) identified several empirically informed principles when considering early intervention for personality pathology. First, due to issues of comorbidity (discussed earlier), as well as the fact that the relation between early manifestations of personality pathology and PD in adulthood are neither specific nor linear, personality pathology cannot be considered separate from other psychopathology. Rather, psychopathology must be viewed as a system, rather than a category. This allows for the consideration of phenotypic (e.g., trait-based; symptom-based), endophenotypic (e.g., neurobiology), and contextual factors to be considered over time in deciding which services to provide to a young person. This approach is represented in a "clinical staging" framework to assessment and diagnosis (Chanen, Berk, & Thompson, 2016), defined as a pragmatic, heuristic, and transdiagnostic integrative framework to the assessment of individual patients, emphasizing identification of risk factors for persistence or deterioration of symptoms or problems, rather than just focusing on the initial onset of disorder. Interventions are selected that are proportionate to the phase and stage of disorder, such that they may be simpler and more benign during early stages of disorder, increasing in intensity with disorder progression, and adapted for co-occurring psychopathology as the severity and comorbidity begin to increase over the course of disorder progression (Chanen & Thompson, 2018).

At higher levels of severity, clinicians may turn to evidence-based approaches for treating personality pathology in adolescence. Again, we review here randomized-controlled trials (RCTs) conducted for BPD in adolescence, as we are not aware of RCTs conducted for other PDs in adolescents. The most compelling evidence in support of not only the mentalization-based model of adolescent BPD, but also the efficacy of a mentalization-based treatment approach, was derived from an RCT conducted by Rossouw and Fonagy (2012). In this study, 80 adolescents (85 percent female) consecutively presenting to mental health services with self-harm and comorbid depression were randomly allocated to either Mentalization-Based Therapy – Adolescents (MBT-A) or Treatment as Usual (TAU). Adolescents were assessed for self-harm, risk-taking, and mood at baseline and at 3-month intervals until 12 months. Their attachment style, mentalization capacity, and BPP were also assessed at baseline and at the end of the 12-month treatment. Results indicated that MBT-A was more effective than TAU in reducing self-harm and depression. This superiority was explained by improved mentalization and reduced attachment avoidance and reflected improvement in emergent BPD symptoms and traits.

Several other evidence-based intervention programs have been evaluated for DSM-based BPD, including Cognitive Analytic Therapy (Chanen, Jackson, et al., 2009; Chanen & McCutcheon, 2013; Chanen, McCutcheon, et al., 2009) and Dialectical Behavior Therapy (DBT) (Mehlum et al., 2012). DBT synthesizes a change orientation from behavior therapy with an acceptance orientation from Zen philosophy to target the emotion dysregulation, distress tolerance, and interpersonal difficulties in BPD. DBT has been evaluated in adolescents with non-suicidal self-injury (NSSI) and two BPD criteria in Norway (Mehlum et al., 2012), adolescents with a history of NSSI and suicide attempts in New Zealand (Cooney et al., 2012), and adolescents with bipolar disorder (Goldstein, Axelson, Birmaher, & Brent, 2007). Of the three studies, the Norwegian study was the most BPD-relevant and had the most rigorous study design and demonstrated a significant decrease in NSSI in DBT but not in Enhanced Usual Care condition. In addition, DBT resulted in greater improvements in BPD symptoms and depression.

Other approaches being used in adolescents, but for which RCTs have not yet been conducted, include Transference-Focused Therapy (Normandin, Ensink, Yeomans, & Kernberg, 2014), Systems Training for Emotional Predictability and Problem Solving (Harvey, Blum, Black, Burgess, & Henley-Cragg, 2014), and Emotion Regulation Individual Therapy for Adolescents (Bjureberg et al., 2017).

SUMMARY AND CONCLUSION

In this chapter, we reviewed the evidence in support of the phenomenology, assessment, diagnosis, etiology, course, and treatment of personality pathology in youth – from both a categorical and dimensional perspective. Consistent with recent views on the categorical–dimensional debate (Sharp & Wright, 2018), this review highlights significant commonalities in conclusions drawn from the traditions underlying categorical versus dimensional approaches. Most pertinent in this regard is the evidence in support of adolescence as a unique developmental period for the crystallization of personality pathology. Many questions remain unanswered, however. For instance, whereas theoretically-driven mechanisms have been suggested to account for developmental crystallization of personality pathology (e.g., narrative identity), research will have to demonstrate that early manifestations of personality pathology morph into adult-like personality through such mechanisms. Whether these mechanisms mirror Criterion A function beyond that of Criterion B function, and whether Criterion B function is sufficient to capture crystallization of maladaptive traits into a disorder that was not crystallized already in pre-adolescence should be clarified. Either way, consistent with the recent position statement by the Global Alliance for the Prevention and Early Intervention for Borderline Personality Disorder (Chanen et al., 2017), the studies reviewed in this chapter form part of the proliferation of knowledge about personality pathology in adolescents and emerging adults ("youth") over the past two decades that provides a firm basis for establishing early diagnosis and treatment ("early intervention") for threshold and subthreshold personality pathology, and represent the continuation of research in this vibrant area.

REFERENCES

Achenbach, T. M., McConaughy, S. H., & Howell, C. T. (1987). Child/adolescent behavioral and emotional problems: Implications of cross-informant correlations for situational specificity. *Psychological Bulletin, 101*, 213–232.

Akiskal, H. S., Chen, S. E., Davis, G. C., Puzantian, V. R., Kashgarian, M., & Bolinger, J. M. (1985). Borderline: An adjective in search of a noun. *Journal of Clinical Psychiatry, 46*(2), 41–48.

American Psychiatric Association. (1987). *Diagnostic and Statistical Manual of Mental Disorders* (Revised 3rd ed.). Washington, DC: American Psychiatric Association.

American Psychiatric Association. (1994). *Diagnostic and Statistical Manual of Mental Disorders* (4th ed.). Washington, DC: American Psychiatric Association.

American Psychiatric Association. (1999). *Standards for Educational and Psychological Testing*. Washington, DC: American Educational Research Association.

American Psychiatric Association. (2000). *Diagnostic and Statistical Manual of Mental Disorders* (4th ed., Text Revision). Washington, DC: American Psychiatric Association.

American Psychiatric Association. (2013). *Diagnostic and Statistical Manual of Mental Disorders* (5th ed.). Arlington, VA: American Psychiatric Publishing.

Archer, R. P., Ball, J. D., & Hunter, J. A. (1985). MMPI characteristics of borderline psychopathology in adolescent inpatients. *Journal of Personality Assessment, 49*(1), 47–55.

Archer, R. P., & Newsom, C. R. (2000). Psychological test usage with adolescent clients: Survey update. *Assessment*, 7, 227–235.

Arens, E. A., Stopsack, M., Spitzer, C., Appel, K., Dudeck, M., Volzke, H., ... Barnow, S. (2013). Borderline personality disorder in four different age groups: A cross-sectional study of community residents in Germany. *Journal of Personality Disorders*, 27(2), 196–207.

Bach, B., Markon, K., Simonsen, E., & Krueger, R. F. (2015). Clinical utility of the DSM-5 alternative model of personality disorders. *Journal of Psychiatric Practice*, 21(1), 3–25.

Belsky, D. W., Caspi, A., Arseneault, L., Bleidorn, W., Fonagy, P., Goodman, M., ... Moffitt, T. E. (2012). Etiological features of borderline personality related characteristics in a birth cohort of 12-year-old children. *Development and Psychopathology*, 24 (1), 251–265.

Bernstein, D. P., Cohen, P., Velez, C. N., Schwab-Stone, M., Siever, L. J., & Shinsato, L. (1993). Prevalence and stability of the DSM-III-R personality disorders in a community-based survey of adolescents. *American Journal of Psychiatry*, 150(8), 1237–1243.

Bjureberg, J., Sahlin, H., Hellner, C., Hedman-Lagerlof, E., Gratz, K. L., Bjarehed, J., ... Ljotsson, B. (2017). Emotion regulation individual therapy for adolescents with nonsuicidal self-injury disorder: A feasibility study. *BMC Psychiatry*, 17. doi:10.1186/s12888-017-1527-4

Bo, S., Sharp, C., Beck, E., Pedersen, J., Gondan, M., & Simonsen, E. (2017). First empirical evaluation of outcomes for mentalization-based group therapy for adolescents with BPD. *Personality Disorders*, 8(4), 396–401.

Bornovalova, M. A., Hicks, B. M., Iacono, W. G., & McGue, M. (2009). Stability, change, and heritability of borderline personality disorder traits from adolescence to adulthood: A longitudinal twin study. *Development and Psychopathology*, 21(4), 1335–1353.

Bornovalova, M. A., Hicks, B. M., Patrick, C. J., Iacono, W. G., & McGue, M. (2011). Development and validation of the Minnesota Borderline Personality Disorder Scale. *Assessment*, 18(2), 234–252.

Bornovalova, M. A., Huibregtse, B. M., Hicks, B. M., Keyes, M., McGue, M., & Iacono, W. (2013). Tests of a direct effect of childhood abuse on adult borderline personality disorder traits: A longitudinal discordant twin design. *Journal of Abnormal Psychology*, 122(1), 180–194.

Brunner, R., Henze, R., Parzer, P., Kramer, J., Feigl, N., Lutz, K., ... Stieltjes, B. (2010). Reduced prefrontal and orbitofrontal gray matter in female adolescents with borderline personality disorder: Is it disorder specific? *NeuroImage*, 49(1), 114–120.

Butcher, J. N., Williams, C. L., Graham, J. R., Archer, R. P., Tellegen, A., & Ben-Porath, Y. S. (1992). *Minnesota Multiphasic Personality Inventory – Adolescent (MMPI-A): Manual for Administration, Scoring, and Interpretation*. Minneapolis: University of Minnesota Press.

Cailhol, L., Jeannot, M., Rodgers, R., Guelfi, J. D., Perez-Diaz, F., Pham-Scottez, A., ... Speranza, M. (2013). Borderline personality disorder and mental healthcare service use among adolescents. *Journal of Personality Disorders*, 27(2), 252–259.

Caspi, A., Houts, R. M., Belsky, D. W., Goldman-Mellor, S. J., Harrington, H., Israel, S., ... Moffit, T. E. (2014). The p factor: One general psychopathology factor in the structure of psychiatric disorders? *Clinical Psychological Science*, 2(2), 119–137.

Chabrol, H., Chouicha, K., Montovany, A., Callahan, S., Duconge, E., & Sztulman, H. (2002). Troubles de la personnalité dans un echantillon non clinique d'adolescents [Personality disorders in a nonclinical sample of adolescents]. *Encéphale: Revue de psychiatrie clinique biologique et thérapeutique*, 28(6 Pt 1), 520–524.

Chanen, A. M. (2015). Borderline personality disorder in young people: Are we there yet? *Journal of Clinical Psychology*, 71(8), 778–791.

Chanen, A. M., Berk, M., & Thompson, K. (2016). Integrating early intervention for borderline personality disorder and mood disorders. *Harvard Review of Psychiatry*, 24(5), 330–341.

Chanen, A. M., Jackson, H. J., McCutcheon, L. K., Jovev, M., Dudgeon, P., Yuen, H. P., ... McGorry, P. D. (2009). Early intervention for adolescents with borderline personality disorder: Quasi-experimental comparison with treatment as usual. *Australian and New Zealand Journal of Psychiatry*, 43(5), 397–408.

Chanen, A. M., Jackson, H. J., McGorry, P. D., Allot, K. A., Clarkson, V., & Yuen, H. P. (2004). Two-year stability of personality disorder in older adolescent outpatients. *Journal of Personality Disorders*, 18(6), 526–541.

Chanen, A. M., Jovev, M., Djaja, D., McDougall, E., Yuen, H. P., Rawlings, D., & Jackson, H. J. (2008). Screening for borderline personality disorder in outpatient youth. *Journal of Personality Disorders*, 22(4), 353–364.

Chanen, A. M., Jovev, M., & Jackson, H. J. (2007). Adaptive functioning and psychiatric symptoms in adolescents with borderline personality disorder. *Journal of Clinical Psychiatry*, 68(2), 297–306.

Chanen, A. M., & Kaess, M. (2012). Developmental pathways to borderline personality disorder. *Current Psychiatry Reports*, 14 (1), 45–53.

Chanen, A. M., & McCutcheon, L. (2013). Prevention and early intervention for borderline personality disorder: Current status and recent evidence. *British Journal of Psychiatry Supplement*, 54, s24–s29.

Chanen, A. M., McCutcheon, L. K., Germano, D., Nistico, H., Jackson, H. J., & McGorry, P. D. (2009). The HYPE clinic: An early intervention service for borderline personality disorder. *Journal of Psychiatric Practice*, 15(3), 163–172.

Chanen, A., Sharp, C., Hoffman, P., & Global Alliance for Prevention and Early Intervention for Borderline Personality Disorder (2017). Prevention and early intervention for borderline personality disorder: A novel public health priority. *World Psychiatry*, 16(2), 215–216.

Chanen, A. M., & Thompson, K. N. (June 2018). Early intervention in personality disorder. *Current Opinion in Psychology*, 21, 132–135.

Chanen, A. M., Velakoulis, D., Carison, K., Gaunson, K., Wood, S. J., Yuen, H. P., ... Pantelis, C. (2008). Orbitofrontal, amygdala and hippocampal volumes in teenagers with first-presentation borderline personality disorder. *Psychiatry Research*, 163(2), 116–125.

Chang, B., Sharp, C., & Ha, C. (2011). The criterion validity of the Borderline Personality Feature Scale for children in an adolescent inpatient setting. *Journal of Personality Disorders*, 25(4), 492–503.

Chen, H., Cohen, P., Crawford, T. N., Kasen, S., Guan, B., & Gorden, K. (2009). Impact of early adolescent psychiatric and personality disorder on long-term physical health: A 20-year longitudinal follow-up study. *Psychological Medicine*, 39(5), 865–874.

Clark, L. A. (2007). Assessment and diagnosis of personality disorder: Perennial issues and an emerging reconceptualization. *Annual Review of Psychology*, 58, 227–257.

Clark, L. A., Nuzum, H., & Ro, E. (2017). Manifestations of personality impairment severity: Comorbidity, course/prognosis, psychosocial dysfunction, and 'borderline' personality features. *Current Opinion in Psychology*, 21, 117–121.

Cohen, P. (2008). Child development and personality disorder. *Psychiatric Clinics of North America*, 31(3), 477–493.

Cohen, P., Chen, H., Gordon, K., Johnson, J., Brook, J., & Kasen, S. (2008). Socioeconomic background and the developmental course of schizotypal and borderline personality disorder symptoms. *Development and Psychopathology*, 20(2), 633–650.

Cohen, P., Crawford, T. N., Johnson, J. G., & Kasen, S. (2005). The children in the community study of developmental course of personality disorder. *Journal of Personality Disorders*, 19(5), 466–486.

Cooney, E., Davis, K., Thompson, P., Wharewera-Mika, J., Stewart, J., & Miller, A. L. (2012). Feasibility of comparing dialectical behavior therapy with treatment as usual for suicidal and self-injuring adolescents: Follow-up data from a small randomized controlled trial. Paper presented at the Association of Behavioral and Cognitive Therapies 46th Annual Convention, National Harbor, MD.

Costa, P. T., & McCrae, R. R. (1992). *Professional Manual: Revised NEO Personality Inventory (NEO-PI-R) and NEO Five-Factor-Inventory (NEO-FFI)*. Odessa, FL: Psychological Assessment Resources.

Crawford, T. N., Cohen, P., First, M. B., Skodol, A. E., Johnson, J. G., & Kasen, S. (2008). Comorbid Axis I and Axis II disorders in early adolescence: Outcomes 20 years later. *Archives of General Psychiatry*, 65(6), 641–648.

Crick, N. R., Murray-Close, D., & Woods, K. (2005). Borderline personality features in childhood: A short-term longitudinal study. *Development and Psychopathology*, 17(4), 1051–1070.

Crowell, S. E., Beauchaine, T. P., & Linehan, M. M. (2009). A biosocial developmental model of borderline personality: Elaborating and extending Linehan's theory. *Psychological Bulletin*, 135(3), 495–510.

De Caluwé, E., Verbeke, L., van Aken, M., van der Heijden, P. T., & De Clercq, B. (2019). The DSM-5 trait measure in a psychiatric sample of late adolescents and emerging adults: Structure, reliability, and validity. *Journal of Personality Disorders*, 33(1), 101–118.

De Clercq, B. (2018). Integrating developmental aspects in current thinking about personality pathology. *Current Perspectives in Psychology*, 21, 69–73.

De Clercq, B., & De Fruyt, F. (2003). Personality disorder symptoms in adolescence: A five-factor model perspective. *Journal of Personality Disorders*, 17(4), 269–292.

De Clercq, B., De Fruyt, F., & Van Leeuwen, K. (2004). A "little-five" lexically based perspective on personality disorder symptoms in adolescence. *Journal of Personality Disorders*, 18(5), 479–499.

De Clercq, B., De Fruyt, F., Van Leeuwen, K., & Mervielde, I. (2006). The structure of maladaptive personality traits in childhood: A step toward an integrative developmental perspective for DSM-V. *Journal of Abnormal Psychology*, 115(4), 639–657.

De Clercq, B., Decuyper, M., & De Caluwé, E. (2014). Developmental manifestations of borderline personality pathology from an age-specific dimensional personality disorder trait framework. In C. Sharp & J. L. Tackett (Eds.), *Handbook of Borderline Personality Disorder in Children and Adolescents* (pp. 81–94). New York: Springer.

De Clercq, B., Hofmans, J., Vergauwe, J., De Fruyt, F., & Sharp, C. (2017). Developmental pathways of childhood dark traits. *Journal of Abnormal Psychology*, 126(7), 843–858.

De Clercq, B., Van Leeuwen, K., Van den Noortgate, W., De Bolle, M., & De Fruyt, F. (2009). Childhood personality pathology: Dimensional stability and change. *Development and Psychopathology*, 21(3), 853–869.

Decuyper, M., De Bolle, M., De Fruyt, F., & De Clercq, B. (2011). General and maladaptive personality dimensions and the assessment of callous-unemotional traits in adolescence. *Journal of Personality Disorders*, 25, 681–701.

De Fruyt, F., & De Clercq, B. (2014). Antecedents of personality disorder in childhood and adolescence: Toward an integrative developmental model. *Annual Review of Clinical Psychology*, 10, 449–476.

De Los Reyes, A., Thomas, S. A., Goodman, K. L., & Kundey, S. M. A. (2013). Principles underlying the use of multiple informants' reports. *Annual Review of Clinical Psychology*, 9, 123–149.

Durbin, E. C., Hicks, B. M., Blonigen, D. M., Johnson, W., Iacono, W. G., & McGue, M. (2016). Personality trait change across late childhood to young adulthood: Evidence for nonlinearity and sex differences in change. *European Journal of Personality*, 30, 31–44.

Eaton, N. R., Krueger, R. F., Keyes, K. M., Skodol, A. E., Markon, K. E., Grant, B. F., & Hasin, D. S. (2011). Borderline personality disorder co-morbidity: Relationship to the internalizing-externalizing structure of common mental disorders. *Psychological Medicine*, 41(5), 1041–1050.

Erikson, E. (1950). *Childhood in Society*. New York: Norton.

First, M. B., Spitzer, R. L., Gibbon, M., & Williams, J. B. W. (2002). *Structured Clinical Interview for DSM-IV TR Axis I Disorders, Research Version, Patient Edition (SCID-I/P)*. New York: Biometrics Research, New York State Psychiatric Institute.

Fonagy, P., & Bateman, A. (2008). The development of borderline personality disorder: A mentalizing model. *Journal of Personality Disorders*, 22(1), 4–21.

Fonagy, P., & Luyten, P. (2009). A developmental, mentalization-based approach to the understanding and treatment of borderline personality disorder. *Development and Psychopathology*, 21(4), 1355–1381.

Fonagy, P., & Luyten, P. (2016). A multilevel perspective on the development of borderline personality disorder. In D. C. Cicchetti (Ed.), *Developmental Psychopathology, Volume 3: Risk, Disorder, and Adaptation* (3rd ed., pp. 726–792). New York: Wiley.

Fossati, A., Sharp, C., Borroni, S., & Somma, A. (2019). Psychometric properties of the Borderline Personality Features Scale for Children-11 (BPFSC-11) in a sample of community dwelling Italian adolescents. *European Journal of Psychological Assessment*, 35, 70–77.

Frick, P. J., & Hare, R. D. (2001). *The Antisocial Process Screening Device*. Toronto: Multi-Health Systems.

Goldstein, T. R., Axelson, D. A., Birmaher, B., & Brent, D. A. (2007). Dialectical behavior therapy for adolescents with bipolar disorder: A 1-year open trial. *Journal of the American Academy of Child and Adolescent Psychiatry*, 46(7), 820–830.

Goodman, M., Hazlett, E. A., Avedon, J. B., Siever, D. R., Chu, K. W., & New, A. S. (2011). Anterior cingulate volume reduction in adolescents with borderline personality disorder and co-morbid major depression. *Journal of Psychiatric Research*, 45(6), 803–807.

Goodman, M., Perez-Rodriguez, M., & Siever, L. (2014). The neurobiology of adolescent-onset borderline personality disorder. In C. Sharp & J. L. Tackett (Eds.), *Handbook of Borderline Personality Disorder in Children and Adolescents* (pp. 113–128). New York: Springer.

Gunderson, J. G., & Lyons-Ruth, K. (2008). BPD's interpersonal hypersensitivity phenotype: A gene-environment-developmental model. *Journal of Personality Disorders, 22*(1), 22–41.

Ha, C., Balderas, J. C., Zanarini, M. C., Oldham, J., & Sharp, C. (2014). Psychiatric comorbidity in hospitalized adolescents with borderline personality disorder. *Journal of Clinical Psychiatry, 75*(5), e457–e464.

Haltigan, J. D., & Vaillancourt, T. (2016). Identifying trajectories of borderline personality features in adolescence: Antecedent and interactive risk factors. *Canadian Journal of Psychiatry, 61* (3), 166–175.

Hare, R. D. (2003). *Manual for the Hare Psychopathy Checklist* (2nd ed.). Toronto, ON: Multi-Health Systems.

Harter, S. (1999). *The Construction of the Self: A Developmental Perspective*. New York: Guilford Press.

Harvey, R., Blum, N., Black, D. W., Burgess, J., & Henley-Cragg, P. (2014). Systems Training for Emotional Predictability and Problem Solving (STEPPS). In C. Sharp & J. L. Tackett (Eds.), *Handbook of Borderline Personality Disorder in Children and Adolescents* (pp. 415–430). New York: Springer.

Herpertz, S. C., Huprich, S. K., Bohus, M., Chanen, A., Goodman, M., Mehlum, L., … Sharp, C. (2017). The challenge of transforming the diagnostic system of personality disorders. *Journal Personality Disorders, 31*(5), 577–589.

Hinshaw, S. P. (2017). Developmental psychopathology as a scientific discipline: a 21st-century perspective. In T. P. Beauchaine & S. P. Hinshaw (Eds.), *Child and Adolescent Psychopathology* (pp. 3–32). New York: Wiley.

Hopwood, C. J., Wright, A. G., Ansell, E. B., & Pincus, A. L. (2013). The interpersonal core of personality pathology. *Journal of Personality Disorders, 27*(3), 270–295.

Hudziak, J. J., Achenbach, T. M., Althoff, R. R., & Pine, D. S. (2007). A dimensional approach to developmental psychopathology. *International Journal of Methods in Psychiatric Research, 16*, S16–S23.

Jahng, S., Trull, T. J., Wood, P. K., Tragesser, S. L., Tomko, R., Grant, J. D., … Sher, K. J. (2011). Distinguishing general and specific personality disorder features and implications for substance dependence comorbidity. *Journal of Abnormal Psychology, 120*(3), 656–669.

James, L. M., & Taylor, J. (2008). Revisiting the structure of mental disorders: borderline personality disorder and the internalizing/externalizing spectra. *British Journal of Clinical Psychology, 47*(Pt 4), 361–380.

Johnson, J. G., Cohen, P., Kasen, S., Skodol, A. E., & Oldham, J. M. (2008). Cumulative prevalence of personality disorders between adolescence and adulthood. *Acta Psychiatrica Scandinavica, 118*(5), 410–413.

Kaess, M., Brunner, R., & Chanen, A. (2014). Borderline personality disorder in adolescence. *Pediatrics, 134*(4), 782–793.

Kernberg, O. (1967). Borderline personality organization. *Journal of the American Psychoanalytic Association, 15*(3), 641–685.

Kotov, R., Krueger, R. F., Watson, D., Achenbach, T. M., Althoff, R. R., Bagby, R. M., … Zimmerman, M. (2017). The Hierarchical Taxonomy of Psychopathology (HiTOP): A dimensional alternative to traditional nosologies. *Journal of Abnormal Psychology, 126*(4), 454–477.

Krabbendam, A. A., Colins, O. F, Doreleijers, T. A. H., van der Molen, E., Beekman, A. T. F., & Vermeiren, R. R. J. M. (2015). Personality disorders in previously detained adolescent females: A prospective study. *American Journal of Orthopsychiatry, 85*, 63–71.

Krueger, R. F. (2005). Continuity of Axes I and II: Toward a unified model ofpersonality, personality disorders, and clinical disorders. *Journal of Personality Disorders, 19*, 233–261.

Krueger, R. F., Derringer, J., Markon, K. E., Watson, D., & Skodol, A. E. (2012). Initial construction of a maladaptive personality trait model and inventory for DSM-5. *Psychological Medicine, 42*, 1879–1890.

Krueger, B., & Markon, K. E. (2014). The role of the DSM-5 personality trait model in moving toward a quantitative and empirically based approach to classifying personality and psychopathology. *Annual Review of Clinical Psychology, 10*, 1–25.

Kushner, S., Tackett, J. L., & De Clercq, B. (2013). The joint hierarchical structure of adolescent personality pathology: Converging evidence from two approaches to measurement. *Journal of the Canadian Academy of Child and Adolescent Psychiatry, 22*, 199–205.

Lahey, B. B., Applegate, B., Hakes, J. K., Zald, D. H., Hariri, A. R., & Rathouz, P. J. (2012). Is there a general factor of prevalent psychopathology during adulthood? *Journal of Abnormal Psychology, 121*(4), 971–977.

Leichsenring, F., Leibing, E., Kruse, J., New, A. S., & Leweke, F. (2011). Borderline personality disorder. *Lancet, 377*(9759), 74–84.

Lenzenweger, M. F. (2008). Epidemiology of personality disorders. *Psychiatric Clinics of North America, 31*(3), 395–403.

Leung, S. W., & Leung, F. (2009). Construct validity and prevalence rate of borderline personality disorder among Chinese adolescents. *Journal of Personality Disorders, 23*(5), 494–513.

Levy, K. N., Becker, D. F., Grilo, C. M., Mattanah, J. J., Garnet, K. E., Quinlan, D. M., … McGlashan, T. H. (1999). Concurrent and predictive validity of the personality disorder diagnosis in adolescent inpatients. *American Journal of Psychiatry, 156*(10), 1522–1528.

Lewinsohn, P. M., Rohde, P., Seeley, J. R., & Klein, D. N. (1997). Axis II psychopathology as a function of Axis I disorders in childhood and adolescence. *Journal of the American Academy of Child and Adolescent Psychiatry, 36*(12), 1752–1759.

Linde, J. A., Stringer, D., Simms, L. J., & Clark, L. (2013). The Schedule for Nonadaptive and Adaptive Personality for Youth (SNAP-Y): A new measure for assessing adolescent personality and personality pathology. *Assessment, 20*(4), 387–404.

Linehan, M. M. (1993). *Cognitive-Behavioral Treatment of Borderline Personality Disorder*. New York: Guilford Press.

Luby, J. L., Si, X., Belden, A. C., Tandon, M., & Spitznagel, E. (2009). Preschool depression: Homotypic continuity and course over 24 months. *Archives of General Psychiatry, 66*, 897–905.

Lynam, D. R. (1997). Capturing the fledging psychopath in a nomological net. *Journal of Abnormal Psychology, 106*(3), 425–438.

McAdams, D. P., & McLean, K. C. (2013). Narrative identity. *Current Directions in Psychological Science, 22*(3), 233–238.

McAdams, D. P., & Olson, B. D. (2010). Personality development: Continuity and change over the life course. *Annual Review of Psychology, 61*, 517–542.

McLean, K. C., & Pratt, M. W. (2006). Life's little (and big) lessons: Identity statuses and meaning-making in the turning point narratives of emerging adults. *Developmental Psychology*, *42*(4), 714–722.

Meares, R., Gerull, F., Stevenson, J., & Korner, A. (2011). Is self disturbance the core of borderline personality disorder? An outcome study of borderline personality factors. *Australian and New Zealand Journal of Psychiatry*, *45*(3), 214–222.

Mehlum, L., Ramberg, M., Tørmoen, A., Haga, E., Larsson, B., Stanley, B., … Grøholt, B. (2012). Dialectical behavior therapy for adolescents with recent and repeated suicidal and self-harm behavior: A randomized controlled trial. Paper presented at the Association of Behavioral and Cognitive Therapies 46th Annual Convention, National Harbor, MD.

Mesman, J., & Koot, H. (2001). Early preschool predictors of preadolescent internalizing and externalizing DSM-IV diagnosis. *Journal of the American Academy of Child and Adolescent Psychiatry*, *40*, 1029–1036.

Michonski, J. D., Sharp, C., Steinberg, L., & Zanarini, M. C. (2013). An item response theory analysis of the DSM-IV borderline personality disorder criteria in a population-based sample of 11- to 12-year-old children. *Personality Disorders: Theory, Research, and Treatment*, *4*(1), 15–22.

Morey, L. C. (2007). *Personality Assessment Inventory: Adolescent Professional Manual*. Odessa, FL: Psychological Assessment Resources.

Nestadt, G., Eaton, W. W., Romanoski, A. J., Garrison, R., Folstein, M. F., & McHugh, P. R. (1994). Assessment of DSM-III personality structure in a general-population survey. *Comprehensive Psychiatry*, *35*(1), 54–63.

Nestadt, G., Hsu, F. C., Samuels, J., Bienvenu, O. J., Reti, I., Costa, P. T., Jr., & Eaton, W. W. (2006). Latent structure of the Diagnostic and Statistical Manual of Mental Disorders, Fourth Edition personality disorder criteria. *Comprehensive Psychiatry*, *47* (1), 54–62.

Noblin, J. L., Venta, A., & Sharp, C. (2013). The validity of the MSI-BPD among inpatient adolescents. *Assessment*, *21*(2), 210–217.

Normandin, L., Ensink, K., Yeomans, F., & Kernberg, O. F. (2014). Transference-focused psychotherapy for personality disorders in adolescence. In C. Sharp & J. L. Tackett (Eds.), *Handbook of Borderline Personality Disorder in Children and Adolescents* (pp. 333–359). New York: Springer.

Paris, J. (1997). Antisocial and borderline personality disorders: Two separate diagnoses or two aspects of the same psychopathology? *Comprehensive Psychiatry*, *38*(4), 237–242.

Roberts, B. W., & DelVecchio, W. F. (2000). The rank-order consistency of personality traits from childhood to old age: A quantitative review of longitudinal studies. *Psychological Bulletin*, *126*(1), 3–25.

Rojas, E. C., Cummings, J. R., Bornovalova, M. A., Hopwood, C. J., Racine, S. E., Keel, P. K., … Klump, K. L. (2014). A further validation of the Minnesota Borderline Personality Disorder Scale. *Personality Disorders*, *5*(2), 146–153.

Rossouw, T. I., & Fonagy, P. (2012). Mentalization-based treatment for self-harm in adolescents: A randomized controlled trial. *Journal of the American Academy of Child and Adolescent Psychiatry*, *51*(12), 1304–1313.

Roysamb, E., Kendler, K. S., Tambs, K., Orstavik, R. E., Neale, M. C., Aggen, S. H., … Reichborn-Kjennerud, T. (2011). The joint structure of DSM-IV axis I and axis II disorders. *Journal of Abnormal Psychology*, *120*(1), 198–209.

Saulsman, L. M., & Page, A. C. (2004). The five-factor model and personality disorder empirical literature: A meta-analytic review. *Clinical Psychology Review*, *23*(8), 1055–1085.

Schuppert, H. M., Bloo, J., Minderaa, R. B., Emmelkamp, P. M., & Nauta, M. H. (2012). Psychometric evaluation of the Borderline Personality Disorder Severity Index-IV: Adolescent version and parent version. *Journal of Personality Disorders*, *26*(4), 628–640.

Sebastian, C., Burnett, S., & Blakemore, S. J. (2008). Development of the self-concept during adolescence. *Trends in Cognitive Sciences*, *12*(11), 441–446.

Sevecke, K., Schmeck, K., & Krischer, M. (2014). The dimensional-categorical hybrid model of personality disorders in DSM-5 from an adolescent psychiatric perspective - criticism and critical outlook. *Zeitschrift für Kinder- und Jugendpsychiatrie und Psychotherapie*, *42*(4), 279–283.

Sharp, C. (2016). Bridging the gap: The assessment and treatment of adolescent personality disorder in routine clinical care. *Archives of Disease in Childhood*, *102*(1), 103–108.

Sharp, C., Elhai, J. D., Kalpakci, A., Michonski, J., & Pavlidis, I. (2014). Locating adolescent BPD within the internalizing-externalizing spectrum. Manuscript submitted for publication

Sharp, C., & Fonagy, P. (2015). Practitioner review: Emergent borderline personality disorder in adolescence: Recent conceptualization, intervention, and implications for clinical practice. *Journal of Child Psychology and Psychiatry*, *56*(12), 1266–1288.

Sharp, C., Green, K., Venta, A., Pettit, J., & Zanarini, M. C. (2012). The incremental validity of borderline personality disorder relative to major depressive disorder for suicidal ideation and deliberate self-harm in adolescents. *Journal of Personality Disorders*, *26*(6), 927–38.

Sharp, C., Ha, C., Michonski, J., Venta, A., & Carbone, C. (2012). Borderline personality disorder in adolescents: Evidence in support of the Childhood Interview for DSM-IV Borderline Personality Disorder in a sample of adolescent inpatients. *Comprehensive Psychiatry*, *53*(6), 765–774.

Sharp, C., & Kim, S. (2015). Recent advances in the developmental aspects of borderline personality disorder. *Current Psychiatry Reviews*, *17*(21), 1–9.

Sharp, C., Mosko, O., Chang, B., & Ha, C. (2011). The cross-informant concordance and concurrent validity of the Borderline Personality Features Scale for Children in a sample of male youth. *Clinical Child Psychology and Psychiatry*, *16*(3), 335–349.

Sharp, C., & Rossouw, T. (2019). Borderline personality pathology in adolescence. In A. Bateman & P. Fonagy (Eds.), *Handbook of Mentalizing in Mental Health Practice* (2nd ed., pp. 281–300). Washington, DC: American Psychiatric Association.

Sharp, C., Steinberg, L., Temple, J., & Newlin, E. (2014). An 11-item measure to assess borderline traits in adolescents: Refinement of the BPFSC using IRT. *Personality Disorders*, *5*(1), 70–78.

Sharp, C., Vanwoerden, S., & Wall, K. (2018). Adolescence as a sensitive period for the development of personality disorder. *Psychiatric Clinics of North America*, *41*(4), 669–683.

Sharp, C., & Wall, K. (2017). Personality pathology grows up: Adolescence as a sensitive period. *Current Opinion in Psychology*, *21*, 111–116.

Sharp, C., & Wright, A. (2018). Editorial: Personality pathology is what personality pathologists do. *Current Opinion in Psychology*, 21, iv–vii.

Sharp, C., Wright, A. G. C., Fowler, J. C., Frueh, B. C., Allen, J. G., Oldham, J., & Clark, L. A. (2015). The structure of personality pathology: Both general ('g') and specific ('s') factors? *Journal of Abnormal Psychology*, *124*(2), 387–398.

Shaw, P., Kabani, N. J., Lerch, J. P., Eckstrand, K., Lenroot, R., Gogtay, N., … Wise, S. P. (2008). Neurodevelopmental trajectories of the human cerebral cortex. *Journal of Neuroscience*, 28(14), 3586–3594.

Shiner, R. L. (1998). How shall we speak of children's personalities in middle childhood? A preliminary taxonomy. *Psychological Bulletin, 124*, 308–332.

Shiner, R. L., & Allen, T. A. (2013). Assessing personality disorders in adolescents: seven guiding principles. *Clinical Psychology Science and Practice, 20*(4), 361–377

Shiner, R. L., & DeYoung, C. G. (2013). The structure of temperament and personality traits: A developmental perspective. In P. D. Zelazo (Ed.), *The Oxford Handbook of Developmental Psychology, Volume 2: Self and Other* (pp. 113–141). New York: Oxford University Press.

Shiner, R. L., & Tackett, J. L. (2014). Personality disorders in children and adolescents. In E. J. Mash & R. A. Barkley (Eds.), *Child Psychopathology* (3rd ed., pp. 848–896). New York: Guilford Press.

Skodol, A. E., Gunderson, J. G., Shea, M. T., McGlashan, T. H., Morey, L. C., Sanislow, C. A., … Stout, R. L. (2005). The Collaborative Longitudinal Personality Disorders Study (CLPS): Overview and implications. *Journal of Personality Disorders, 19*(5), 487–504.

Snyder, H. R., Young J. F., & Hankin, B. L. (2016). Strong homotypic continuity in common psychopathology: Internalizing-, and externalizing-specific factors over time in adolescents. *Clinical Psychology and Science, 5*, 98–110.

Somerville, L. H., Jones, R. M., Ruberry, E. J., Dyke, J. P., Glover, G., & Casey, B. J. (2013). The medial prefrontal cortex and the emergence of self-conscious emotion in adolescence. *Psychological Science, 24*(8), 1554–1562.

Somma, A., Fossati, A., Terrinoni, A., Williams, R., Ardizzone, I., Fantini, F., … Ferrara, M. (2016). Reliability and clinical usefulness of the personality inventory for DSM-5 in clinically referred adolescents: A preliminary report in a sample of Italian inpatients. *Comprehensive Psychiatry, 70*, 141–151.

Soto, C. J., John, O. P., Gosling, S. D., & Potter J. (2008). The developmental psychometrics of big five self-reports: Acquiescence, factor structure, coherence, and differentiation from ages 10 to 20. *Journal of Personality and Social Psychology, 94*, 718–737.

Speranza, M., Revah-Levy, A., Cortese, S., Falissard, B., Pham-Scottez, A., & Corcos, M. (2011). ADHD in adolescents with borderline personality disorder. *BMC Psychiatry, 11*, 158.

Steinberg, L., Albert, D., Cauffman, E., Banich, M., Graham, S., & Woolard, J. (2008). Age differences in sensation-seeking and impulsivity as indexed by behavior and self-report: evidence for a dual systems model. *Developmental Psychology, 44*, 1764–1778.

Tackett, J. L. (2011). Parent informants for child personality: Agreement, discrepancies, and clinical utility. *Journal of Personality Assessment, 93*(6), 539–544.

Tackett, J. L., Herzhoff, K., Balsis, S., & Cooper, L. (2016). Toward a unifying perspective on personality pathology across the lifespan. In D. C. Cicchetti (Ed.), *Developmental Psychopathology, Volume 3: Risk, Disorder, and Adaptation* (3rd ed., pp. 1039–1078). New York: Wiley.

Thomaes, S., Stegge, H., Bushman, B., Olthof, T., & Denissen, J. (2008). Development and validation of the Childhood Narcissism Scale. *Journal of Personality Assessment, 90*, 382–391.

Tromp, N. B., & Koot, H. M. (2008). Dimensions of personality pathology in adolescents: Psychometric properties of the DAPP-BQ-A. *Journal of Personality Disorders, 22*(6), 623–638.

Van den Akker, A. L., Dekovic, M., Asscher, J., & Prinzie, P. (2014). Mean-level personality development across childhood and adolescence: A temporary defiance of the maturity principle and bidirectional associations with parenting. *Journal of Personality and Social Psychology, 107*, 736–750.

Vanwoerden, S., Garey, L., Ferguson, T., Temple, J., & Sharp, C. (2019). Borderline Personality Features Scale for Children-11: Measurement invariance over time and across gender in a community sample of adolescents. *Psychological Assessment, 31*(1), 114–119.

Venta, A., Magyar, M., Hossein, S., & Sharp, C. (2018). The psychometric properties of the Personality Assessment Inventory–Adolescent's Borderline Features Scale across two high-risk samples. *Psychological Assessment, 30*(6), 827–833.

Verbeke, L., De Caluwé, E., & De Clercq, B. (2017). A five-factor model of personality pathology precursors. *Personality Disorders: Theory, Research, and Treatment, 8*, 130–139.

Verbeke, L., & De Clercq, B. (2014). Integrating oddity traits in a dimensional model for personality pathology precursors. *Journal of Abnormal Psychology, 123*, 598–612.

Verbeke, L., De Clercq, B., Van der Heijden, P., Hutsebaut, J., & Van Aken, M. A. G. (2017). The relevance of schizotypal traits for understanding interpersonal functioning in adolescents with psychiatric problems. *Personality Disorders: Theory, Research, and Treatment, 8*(1), 54–63.

Wall, J., Ahmed, Y., & Sharp, C. (2018). Parent–adolescent concordance in borderline pathology and why it matters. *Journal of Abnormal Child Psychology, 47*(3), 529–542.

Wall, K., Sharp, C., Ahmed, Y., Goodman, M., & Zanarini, M. C. (2017). Parent–adolescent concordance on the Revised Diagnostic Interview for Borderlines (DIB-R) and the Childhood Interview for Borderline Personality Disorder (CI-BPD). *Personality and Mental Health, 11*(3), 179–188.

Widiger, T. A., Bach, B., Chmielewski, M., Clark, L. A., DeYoung, C., Hopwood, C. J., … Thomas, K. M. (2019). Criterion A of the AMPD in HiTOP. *Journal of Personality Assessment, 101*(4), 345–355.

Widiger, T. A. & Costa, P. T. (2013). *Personality Disorders and the Five-Factor Model of Personality* (3rd ed.). Washington, DC: American Psychological Association.

Widiger, T. A., & Simonsen, E. (2005). Alternative dimensional models of personality disorder: Finding a common ground. *Journal of Personality Disorders, 19*(2), 110–130.

Widiger, T. A., Trull, T. J., Clarkin, J. F., Sanderson, C., & Costa, P. T. (2002). A description of the DSM-IV personality disorders with the five-factor model of personality. In P. T. Costa, Jr. & T. A. Widiger (Eds.), *Personality Disorders and the Five-Factor Model of Personality* (2nd ed., pp. 89–99). Washington, DC: American Psychological Association.

Winograd, G., Cohen, P., & Chen, H. N. (2008). Adolescent borderline symptoms in the community: Prognosis for functioning over 20 years. *Journal of Child Psychology and Psychiatry, 49*(9), 933–941.

Winsper, C., Marwaha, S., Lereya, S. T., Thompson, A., Eyden, J., Singh, S. P. (2015). Clinical and psychosocial outcomes of borderline personality disorder in childhood and adolescence: A systematic review. *Psychological Medicine, 45*, 2237–2251.

Wright, A. G. C., Hopwood, C. J., Skodol, A. E., & Morey, L. C. (2016). Longitudinal validation of general and specific structural features of personality pathology. *Journal of Abnormal Psychology, 125*(8), 1120–1134.

Wright, A. G., Zalewski, M., Hallquist, M. N., Hipwell, A. E., & Stepp, S. D. (2016). Developmental trajectories of borderline personality disorder symptoms and psychosocial functioning in adolescence. *Journal of Personality Disorders, 30*(3), 351–372.

Zanarini, M. C. (2003). *The Child Interview for DSM-IV Borderline Personality Disorder*. Belmont, MA: McLean Hospital.

Zanarini, M. C., Frankenburg, F. R., Dubo, E. D., Sickel, A. E., Trikha, A., Levin, A., & Reynolds, V. (1998). Axis I comorbidity of borderline personality disorder. *American Journal of Psychiatry, 155*(12), 1733–1739.

Zanarini, M. C., Frankenburg, F. R., Reich, D. B., & Fitzmaurice, G. (2012). Attainment and stability of sustained symptomatic remission and recovery among patients with borderline personality disorder and Axis II comparison subjects: A 16-year prospective follow-up study. *American Journal of Psychiatry, 169*(5), 476–483.

Zanarini, M. C., Horwood, J., Wolke, D., Waylen, A., Fitzmaurice, G., & Grant, B. F. (2011). Prevalence of DSM-IV borderline personality disorder in two community samples: 6,330 English 11-year-olds and 34,653 American adults. *Journal of Personality Disorders, 25*(5), 607–619.

Zanarini, M. C., Vujanovic, A. A., Parachini, E. A., Boulanger, J. L., Frankenburg, F. R., & Hennen, J. (2003). A screening measure for BPD: The McLean Screening Instrument for Borderline Personality Disorder (MSI-BPD). *Journal of Personality Disorders, 17*(6), 568–573.

4a Toward the Integration of Developmental Psychopathology and Personality Pathology Perspectives: Commentary on Personality Pathology in Youth

ERIC M. VERNBERG AND MADELAINE ABEL

Sharp and De Clercq (this volume) summarize several major issues in applying concepts and knowledge derived from the study of personality disorders (and personality pathology) in adults to children and adolescents. The most compelling arguments in favor of incorporating these concepts and knowledge include (1) recognition that some clinical features and diagnostic symptoms of personality disorders and pathology in adults begin to emerge during adolescence, and (2) that the extensive body of research on the identification and treatment of personality disorders in adults may inform efforts focused on the early identification and treatment of nascent personality pathology in adolescence before a more severe and intransigent personality disorder emerges. A number of challenges to synthesizing and integrating knowledge from a personality pathology perspective to adolescents are also noted and discussed.

The authors focus on efforts to measure and treat borderline personality pathology (BPP) among children and adolescents to illustrate potential benefits and challenges of applying a personality pathology framework in research and intervention. They note difficulties that arise when using interview-based tools validated with adults (such as the SCID modules for assessing personality disorders in DSM-IV) with adolescents, and describe efforts to validate and refine more developmentally-sensitive interviews for assessing BPP. Important points from their summary include that BPP as measured in these alternative interviews tends to have a unidimensional factor structure and may be an indicator of the presence and severity of a more general personality pathology, rather than borderline personality disorder (BPD) per se. This point of view fits well with other lines of research suggesting that the self-system generally becomes more differentiated, domain-specific, and stable over the course of adolescence and emerging adulthood (e.g., Rosen, 2016). Similarly, research on the MMPI-A often suggests that this downward extension of the MMPI for adults tends to provide an index of an adolescent's current distress and impairment, rather than a measure of the more discrete dimensions of personality that are typically found among adults (Baer, Wetter, &

Berry, 1992). In other words, the underlying dimensions of personality (and personality pathology) found in adults may not yet have emerged in children and adolescents, although difficulties indicative of more general personality pathology may be discernible.

In their discussion of dimensional versus categorical approaches for measuring BPP and BPD among youth, Sharp and De Clerq argue that there is stronger empirical support for taking a dimensional approach to assessing BPP. Whether or not current measures of BPP for youth indicate BPD specifically or severity of overall personality pathology, symptoms of personality pathology in adolescents may be present without reaching full diagnostic criteria for a personality disorder and still cause functional impairment and indicate increased risk for developing a personality disorder in adulthood. At a practical level, if researchers and clinicians are able to accurately identify and address severe behavioral symptoms related to personality pathology *without* these youth receiving a diagnosis, there may be no additional benefit to the personality disorder diagnosis for children or adolescents. Symptoms may still be treated even without the diagnosis. In fact, many of the commonly used treatment manuals for youth are symptom specific, rather than focused on diagnoses directly (e.g., Chorpita & Weisz, 2009). Conversely, the authors suggest that a categorical approach to BPD may be more realistic in clinical practice settings in which assessment and treatment planning are often constrained by the categorical presence or absence of a diagnosis.

Regardless, accurate diagnosis of a personality disorder among youth may be difficult due to the overlap between many BPP symptoms and traits common to other youth mental health problems. The strong covariance of symptoms across disorders may increase the likelihood of false positives. Moreover, it is often hard to tease apart the underlying causes of symptoms of various youth mental health disorders. For example, distinguishing between oppositional or disruptive behaviors that may be due to anxiety, neurodevelopmental disorders that interfere with social understanding (such as autism spectrum disorder), or antisocial traits can be challenging, and comorbidity rates are often high among children. Thus, we must consider if there is an actual benefit to the BPD diagnosis, particularly when there are other means through which children can receive appropriate accommodations and services without the BPD label. The overall trend in clinical child and adolescent psychology toward developing transdiagnostic interventions that address specific problem behaviors and distress may make questions related to categorical diagnoses (including personality disorders) less relevant over time (McHugh, Murrary, & Barlow, 2009). At the same time, it is worth noting that the effort to identify and validate transdiagnostic intervention strategies and techniques is sometimes misunderstood to imply that a specific problem behavior (such as oppositional or disruptive behavior) would be addressed in the same manner regardless of diagnosis. Instead, an idiographic clinical case formulation of the underlying processes (both internal and environmental) that contribute to the emergence and maintenance of a specific problem behavior for a specific child or adolescent guides the selection of intervention approaches (e.g., Chu, 2012). In this context, more valid and reliable measures of personality pathology in children and adolescents could be extremely helpful in guiding clinical case formulation and decision-making.

It is also important to comment on the need for greater understanding of developmental pathways and processes that distinguish between maturation-related rises and declines in patterns of thoughts, emotions, and behaviors that appear similar to personality pathology versus symptom trajectories that presage the emergence of a personality disorder in adulthood. As the authors highlight, BPP symptom trajectories are likely influenced by the interplay of personal characteristics (including neurobiological vulnerabilities) and environmental factors. Longitudinal research using a combination of person-centered and variable-centered analytic strategies, such as latent growth mixture modeling (Muthén & Muthén, 2000), to identify common trajectories of BPP symptoms from childhood through adolescence may help elucidate why some youth with elevated BPP develop BPD later in life whereas others do not. For example, the severity of early symptoms and the presence of certain symptom patterns over time (e.g., high, stable levels versus normative decline), either alone or in combination with key environmental factors (e.g., prolonged exposure to invalidating environments or otherwise disrupted attachment relationships), may predict eventual diagnosis of BPD. As suggested by the authors and others (e.g., Crowell, Kaufman, & Lenzenweger, 2013), there may be multiple developmental pathways that lead to BPD.

In many ways, concepts emerging from a developmental psychopathology perspective fit well with both categorical and dimensional approaches to understanding personality pathology. For example, Sharp and De Clercq note the utility of the concepts of homotypic and heterotypic

continuity for understanding how an underlying core form of psychopathology may result in different clusters and types of symptoms at different points in development during childhood and adolescence. The extensive body of research on the emergence and persistence of disruptive and antisocial behavior from early childhood through adolescence (and into adulthood) shows that manifestations of an underlying conduct disorder emerge early in life and continue into adulthood for a subset of children. The neurobiological vulnerabilities and environmental risk factors that contribute to this early-onset and persistent pattern of antisocial and disruptive behavior are increasingly well-documented. The diagnostic criteria for conduct disorder in DSM-5 (American Psychiatric Association, 2013) include a specifier to indicate if the individual shows a persistent pattern of limited prosocial emotions such as lack of remorse or guilt, shallow or deficient affect, or a callous lack of empathy for or concern about the feelings of others. These persistent, trait-like characteristics of conduct disorder in children and adolescents overlap considerably with diagnostic criteria for antisocial personality disorder (ASPD) and the presence of conduct disorder with onset before the age of 15 years old is one of the diagnostic criteria for ASPD. Although Sharp and De Clerq use BPP/BPD to illustrate their perspective on personality pathology in youth, many of their points are relevant to attempts to synthesize the substantial bodies of research on the emergence of conduct disorder among children and ASPD among adults. Indeed, in the case of childhood-onset conduct disorder, manifestations of a persistent underlying personality pathology seem to be present at an even younger age than described by Sharp and De Clerq in their discussion of BPP (e.g., White, Moffitt, Earls, Robins, & Silva, 1990).

It is not difficult to accept the notion that some children and adolescents may have early manifestations of persistent patterns of thoughts, emotions, and behavior characteristic of (or similar to) personality pathology. The bigger challenge is to integrate and synthesize research conducted predominantly with adults from a personality pathology perspective with the increasingly robust research conducted with children and adolescents from a developmental psychopathology perspective. There is clearly an ongoing debate about how to reconcile the categorical diagnostic system represented by DSM with the more dimensional approaches used in much of the research on developmental psychopathology. Would it be useful to allow adolescents (or children) to receive a personality disorder diagnosis? In a diagnostic system already fraught with overlapping diagnostic criteria and the frequent diagnosis of multiple co-occurring conditions among children and adolescents, it is difficult to imagine how this would be helpful. However, there seems to be potential value to applying concepts and knowledge derived from the study of personality pathology to clinical case formulation and treatment planning for children and adolescents. In our opinion, a number of concepts from a personality pathology perspective have already been incorporated into research with children and adolescents from a developmental psychopathology perspective (e.g., Crowell et al., 2013). Additional translation and synthesis of concepts and knowledge derived from personality pathology and developmental psychopathology perspectives could be very helpful. Sharp and De Clercq's work represents a good model for this effort.

REFERENCES

American Psychiatric Association. (2013). *Diagnostic and Statistical Manual of Mental Disorders* (5th ed.). Arlington, VA: American Psychiatric Publishing.

Baer, R. A., Wetter, M. W., & Berry, D. T. (1992). Detection of underreporting of psychopathology on the MMPI: A meta-analysis. *Clinical Psychology Review, 12,* 509–525.

Chorpita, B. F., & Weisz, J. R. (2009). *MATCH-ADTC: Modular Approach to Therapy for Children with Anxiety, Depression, Trauma, or Conduct Problems.* Satellite Beach, FL: PracticeWise.

Chu, B. C. (2012). Translating transdiagnostic approaches to children and adolescents. *Cognitive and Behavioral Practice, 19,* 1–4.

Crowell, S. E., Kaufman, E. A., & Lenzenweger, M. F. (2013). The development of borderline personality and self-inflicted injury. In T. E. Beauchaine & S. P. Hinshaw (Eds.), *Child and Adolescent Psychopathology* (2nd ed., pp. 577–609). Hoboken, NJ: Wiley.

McHugh, R. K., Murray, H. W., & Barlow, D. H. (2009). Balancing fidelity and adaptation in the dissemination of empirically-supported treatments: The promise of transdiagnostic interventions. *Behaviour Research and Therapy, 47,* 946–953.

Muthén, B., & Muthén, L. K. (2000). Integrating person-centered and variable-centered analyses: Growth mixture modeling with latent trajectory classes. *Alcoholism: Clinical and Experimental Research, 24,* 882–891.

Rosen, K. S. (2016). Adolescent identity and the consolidation of the self. In K. Rosen, *Social and Emotional Development: Attachment Relationships and the Emerging Self* (pp. 278–330). New York: Palgrave Macmillan.

White, J. L., Moffitt, T. E., Earls, F., Robins, L., & Silva, P. A. (1990). How early can we tell? Predictors of childhood conduct disorder and adolescent delinquency. *Criminology, 28,* 507–535.

4b A Developmental Psychopathology Perspective on the Emergence of Antisocial and Borderline Personality Pathologies across the Lifespan: Commentary on Personality Pathology in Youth

THEODORE P. BEAUCHAINE

An unfortunate consequence of restricting personality disorder (PD) diagnoses to those 18 years of age and older is a literature in which developmental precursors are understudied and at times undervalued. As Sharp and De Clercq (this volume) note, most efforts to understand PD development extend adult criteria downward to adolescence. These studies demonstrate that PDs exist among teens, and predict functional impairment into adulthood (e.g., Bornovalova, Hicks, Iacono, & McGue, 2013). Other studies, also summarized by Sharp and De Clercq, evaluate structural relations among PD symptoms in large samples of teens. These studies demonstrate similar patterns of PD co-occurrence and relations to Big Five personality traits as seen in adults.

Studies that identify onset age and expression of adult PD symptoms are necessary and important, but they provide limited understanding of *etiopathophysiology*—the complex and interactive determinants of psychopathology across the lifespan. Such determinants include genetic, neural, environmental, and cultural factors that transact with one another to eventuate in psychopathology, often beginning many years before symptom onset (e.g., Cicchetti, 1993; Sroufe & Rutter, 1984). For developmental psychopathologists, specifying etiopathophysiology is of utmost importance because it ultimately increases treatment efficacy by identifying mechanistic targets for prevention and intervention (Beauchaine, Neuhaus, Brenner, & Gatzke-Kopp, 2008). Given modest effectiveness and high drop-out rates for PD interventions delivered in adulthood (e.g., Kliem, Kröger, & Kosfelder, 2010), targeting developmental mechanisms may be essential toward reducing the extensive burden of PDs on individuals, their families, and broader social systems (Beauchaine, Hinshaw, & Bridge, 2019).

In this commentary, I present a model of antisocial and borderline PDs that describes how heritable vulnerabilities interact with environments across childhood and

adolescence to affect neurodevelopment and eventuate in adult impairment. My description is necessarily brief; further details are available in our extended writings (Beauchaine, Hinshaw, & Bridge, 2019; Beauchaine, Klein, Crowell, Derbidge, & Gatzke-Kopp, 2009; Beauchaine, Zisner, & Sauder, 2017; Crowell, Beauchaine, & Linehan, 2009). Points of particular emphasis include (1) the *complexity* of psychopathology across development and levels of analysis; (2) the importance of *multifinal* outcomes – most notably ASPD for males versus BPD for females – for those reared in similar family contexts; and (3) the need to consider compromised *neuromaturation* of frontal brain regions implicated in self- and emotion-regulation in any developmental model of ASPD and BPD.

THE INORDINATE COMPLEXITY OF PSYCHOPATHOLOGY

Two related goals of our research group are to elucidate neurobiological vulnerabilities to psychopathology *without* engaging in biological reductionism (Beauchaine & Constantino, 2017), and to specify how emotional processes, which ordinarily motivate adaptive social behavior, become disrupted in various forms of psychopathology (Beauchaine & Zisner, 2017). Over the last decade, it has become clear that neurobiological vulnerabilities to psychopathology are profoundly more complex than imagined a generation ago (Beauchaine, Constantino, & Hayden, 2018). At the same time, it has also became clear that emotion dysregulation is a *transdiagnostic* feature of psychopathology, and characterizes both ASPD and BPD (Beauchaine, 2015; Beauchaine et al., 2017; Crowell et al., 2009; Gratz, Dixon-Gordon, Breetz, & Tull, 2013). Although full articulation of these points would require extensive review, Figure 4.b.1 depicts the complexity of ASPD and BPD development from preschool to adulthood.

Several important points emerge from Figure 4.b.1. First, *trait impulsivity*, a highly heritable temperamental/personality attribute that characterizes *both* ASPD and BPD (as noted by Sharp and De Clercq), arises from

Preparation of this chapter was supported by Grant DE025980 from the National Institute of Mental Health, and by the National Institutes of Health Science of Behavior Change (SoBC) Common Fund.

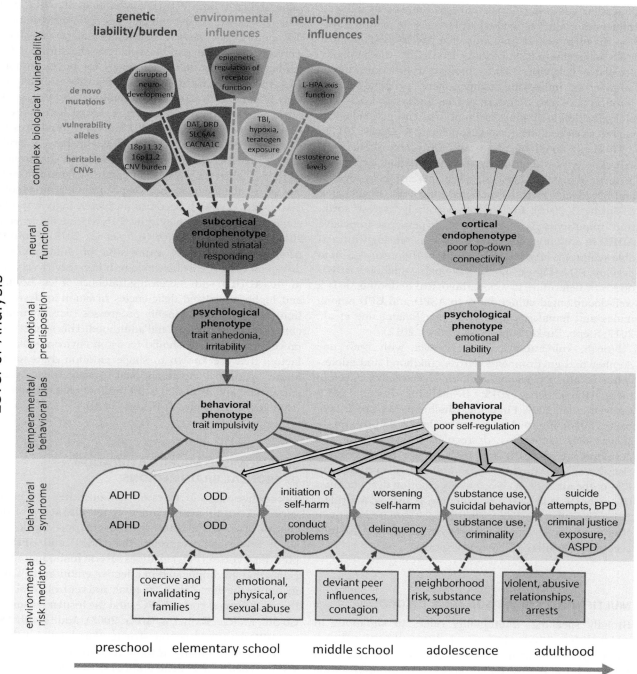

Figure 4.b.1 A neurodevelopmental model of ASPD and BPD. See text for details.

multiple determinants, including genetic burden (e.g., normal allelic variation, de novo mutations), environmental influences (e.g., brain injury, epigenetic regulation of neurotransmitters), and neuro-hormonal functions (e.g., circulating testosterone levels) (for reviews, see Beauchaine & Constantino, 2017; Gatzke-Kopp, 2011). Notably, few of these influences are necessary or sufficient to result in functional impairment. Rather, they interact in unique combinations across individuals to confer neural vulnerability. Only a decade ago, psychopathologists were

still searching for single genes to explain psychopathology. Now, it is well understood that single vulnerability alleles account for very little variance in behavioral phenotypes. For example, over 8300 single nucleotide polymorphisms (SNPs) – almost all of very small effect size – are needed to explain half of the phenotypic variance in schizophrenia liability across the population (Ripke et al., 2013). This of course includes schizotypal PD.

Second, none of these neurobiological vulnerabilities affect behavior directly. Rather, complex combinations of genetic, neuro-hormonal, and environmentally induced influences confer individual differences in neural function. In turn, neural functions give rise to psychological traits and states (e.g., anhedonia, irritability) that motivate impulsive behaviors. Thus, biological functions affect behavior by influencing temperament, personality, and emotion. PDs can therefore not be understood solely at biological levels of analysis; emotional and psychological factors must be considered (Beauchaine & Zisner, 2017).

Third, as noted by Sharp and De Clercq, behavioral expressions of vulnerability to psychopathology change in form across the lifespan, often increasing in severity and broadening across functional outcomes (Beauchaine & Cicchetti, 2016). In its developmentally "purest" form, trait impulsivity is expressed as hyperactive-impulsive ADHD in preschool, but progresses to increasingly intractable symptoms across development for those who go on to develop PDs (Figure 4.b.1). Although childhood ADHD does not determine psychopathological endpoints, it is a well-documented vulnerability to ASPD and BPD among males and females, respectively (see Beauchaine et al., 2017; Stepp, Burke, Hipwell, & Loeber, 2012).

Fourth, vulnerability traits interact with both one another and environments across childhood and adolescence to affect behavior, including personality development (Beauchaine, 2015; Beauchaine et al., 2017; Crowell et al., 2009; Finucane, Challman, Martin, & Ledbetter, 2016). Figure 4.b.1 describes how *both* trait impulsivity *and* emotion dysregulation contribute to development of ASPD and BPD. As we have reviewed elsewhere, trait impulsivity is unlikely to eventuate in PDs in the absence of co-occurring emotion dysregulation (Beauchaine et al., 2017; Beauchaine, Hinshaw, & Bridge, 2019; Crowell et al., 2009). Thus, models that include main effects of impulsivity *or* emotion dysregulation do not fully account for ASPD or BPD development.

MULTIFINALITY IN PERSONALITY DISORDERS

Broadly speaking, multifinality refers to situations in which different individuals reach distinct functional endpoints given similar initial vulnerabilities. As depicted in Figure 4.b.1 and reviewed initially by our group a decade ago (Beauchaine et al., 2009), ASPD and BPD provide a compelling example of multifinality given that (1) they share genetic and temperamental vulnerabilities (e.g., Lyons-Ruth et al., 2007), (2) males with ASPD and females with BPD are often reared in the same families (e.g., Goldman, D'Angelo, & DeMaso, 1993), and (3) similar environmental influences – both familial and extra-familial – are associated with development of both PDs (e.g., Lyons-Ruth, 2008).

In the bottom panels of Figure 4.b.1, circles represent behavioral progression of early life vulnerability (ADHD) to BPD for females (light gray) and ASPD for males (dark gray). As noted above, ADHD is a documented

vulnerability to both PDs (Beauchaine et al., 2017; Stepp et al., 2012). Rectangles indicate common environmental risk factors that *mediate* developmental progression to increasingly severe pathology across the lifespan (e.g., self-harm for girls and delinquency for boys). Although these risk factors, including coercive/invalidating families, early life abuse, deviant peer affiliations, and exposure to substances of abuse, cannot be reviewed here, they are well characterized in the ASPD and BPD literatures (see Beauchaine et al., 2017; Beauchaine, Hinshaw, & Bridge, 2019; Crowell et al., 2017). According to our developmental model, when these environmental risk factors accumulate across the lifespan, they shape and maintain emotion dysregulation, which becomes an increasingly important etiological factor in emerging PDs (Beauchaine et al., 2017; Crowell et al., 2009; Gratz et al., 2013). From this perspective, behavioral expression of vulnerability is driven more by highly heritable trait impulsivity very early in life (ADHD), with increasing influence of less heritable and highly socialized deficiencies in emotion dysregulation as PD development progresses across middle-childhood, adolescence, and adulthood. This suggests that prevention programs should focus on environmental risk factors that are known to shape emotion dysregulation *before* patterns of emotional responding become entrenched and extend to extra-familial relationships (see Beauchaine, Hinshaw, & Bridge, 2019).

COMPROMISED NEUROMATURATION OF FRONTAL BRAIN REGIONS

Twenty-five years of research demonstrates the importance of cortical neural function for efficient executive control, associative learning, and emotion regulation – all of which are compromised in ASPD and BPD. The prefrontal cortex (PFC) includes several functional subdivisions that are implicated in effective emotion regulation, including the dorsolateral, medial, and ventrolateral PFCs, the orbitofrontal cortex (OFC), and the insular cortex (e.g., Goldin, McRae, Ramel, & Gross, 2008). Adults with ASPD and BPD demonstrate both structural and functional compromises across many of these regions (e.g., Krause-Utz, Winter, Niedtfeld, & Schmahl, 2014; Yang & Raine, 2009). Although specific findings are beyond the scope of this commentary, ASPD and BPD are associated with smaller cortical volumes and deficient top-down frontal control over emotion, as assessed by functional connectivity.

Importantly, frontal regions are the last parts of the brain to develop fully, and are exquisitely sensitive to environmental insults. Ordinarily, prefrontal structures continue to mature into the mid-20s (Gogtay et al., 2004). However, frontal neuromaturation is compromised among delinquent and antisocial males (De Brito et al., 2009; Yang & Raine, 2009). Furthermore, children who are reared in contexts of poverty, neglect, and abuse – some of the very risk factors that facilitate development of ASPD and BPD (see Figure 4.b.1) – show cortical volumes that are nearly 10 percent smaller than those of their peers, and exhibit abnormal functional activity during associative learning into adulthood (Birn, Roeber, & Pollak, 2017; Hair, Hanson, Wolfe, & Pollak, 2015).

In some of our most recent work, we have found both reduced cortical volumes and altered neural function in the OFC among adolescent girls who were recruited for severe self-harm (Beauchaine, Sauder, Derbidge, & Uyeji, 2019; Sauder, Derbidge, & Beauchaine, 2016). As shown in Figure 4.b.1, self-harm is a precursor to BPD for many who develop the disorder (see Beauchaine, Hinshaw, & Bridge, 2019). These findings suggest that neural correlates of BPD are already emerging among teens who are at risk for the disorder, and also suggest compromised neurodevelopment, as seen in delinquent boys (De Brito et al., 2009).

As outlined above, overall impairment increases across development as neural vulnerability to emotion dysregulation accrues and adds to existing impairment imparted by heritable trait impulsivity. Evidence that (1) environmental enrichment has positive effects on cortical neuromaturation (e.g., Blair, 2016), and (2) effective intervention can improve frontal function (e.g., Beauchaine, Zisner, & Hayden, 2019) suggests the importance of targeted prevention for high-risk children. It is my hope that by taking a developmental psychopathology perspective and specifying etiopathophysiology, more effective prevention programs can be formulated that target mechanisms of PD development directly.

REFERENCES

Beauchaine, T. P. (2015). Future directions in emotion dysregulation and youth psychopathology. *Journal of Clinical Child and Adolescent Psychology, 44,* 875–896.

Beauchaine, T. P., & Cicchetti, D. (2016). A new generation of comorbidity research in the era of neuroscience and the Research Domain Criteria. *Development and Psychopathology, 28,* 891–894.

Beauchaine, T. P., & Constantino, J. N. (2017). Redefining the endophenotype concept to accommodate transdiagnostic vulnerabilities and etiological complexity. *Biomarkers in Medicine, 11,* 769–780.

Beauchaine, T. P., Constantino, J. N., & Hayden, E. P. (2018). Psychiatry and developmental psychopathology: Unifying themes and future directions. *Comprehensive Psychiatry, 87,* 143–152.

Beauchaine, T. P., Hinshaw, S. P., & Bridge, J. A. (2019). Nonsuicidal self-injury and suicidal behaviors in maltreated girls with ADHD: The case for targeted prevention in preadolescence. *Clinical Psychological Science, 7,* 643–667.

Beauchaine, T. P., Klein, D. N., Crowell, S. E., Derbidge, C., & Gatzke-Kopp, L. M. (2009). Multifinality in the development of personality disorders: A biology × sex × environment interaction model of antisocial and borderline traits. *Development and Psychopathology, 21,* 735–770.

Beauchaine, T. P., Neuhaus, E., Brenner, S. L., & Gatzke-Kopp, L. (2008). Ten good reasons to consider biological processes in

prevention and intervention research. *Development and Psychopathology, 20,* 745–774.

Beauchaine, T. P., Sauder, C. L., Derbidge, C. M., & Uyeji, L. L. (2019). Self-injuring adolescent girls exhibit insular cortex volumetric abnormalities that are similar to those observed in adults with borderline personality disorder. *Development and Psychopathology.* Advance Online Publication.

Beauchaine, T. P., & Zisner, A. (2017). Motivation, emotion regulation, and the latent structure of psychopathology: An integrative and convergent historical perspective. *International Journal of Psychophysiology, 119,* 108–118.

Beauchaine, T. P., Zisner, A. R., & Hayden, E. P. (2019). Neurobiological mechanisms of psychopathology and treatment action. In T. H. Ollendick, S. W. White, & B. A. White (Eds.), *The Oxford Handbook of Clinical Child and Adolescent Psychology* (pp. 699–722). New York: Oxford University Press.

Beauchaine, T. P., Zisner, A. R., & Sauder, C. L. (2017). Trait impulsivity and the externalizing spectrum. *Annual Review of Clinical Psychology, 13,* 343–368.

Birn, R. M., Roeber, B. J., & Pollak, S. D. (2017). Early childhood stress exposure, reward pathways, and adult decision making. *Proceedings of the National Academy of Sciences USA, 114,* 13549–13554.

Blair, C. (2016). Developmental science and executive function. *Current Directions in Psychological Science, 25,* 3–7.

Bornovalova, M. A., Hicks, B. M., Iacono, W. G., & McGue, M. (2013). Longitudinal twin study of borderline personality disorder traits and substance use in adolescence: Developmental change, reciprocal effects, and genetic and environmental influences. *Personality Disorders: Theory, Research, and Treatment, 4,* 23–32.

Cicchetti, D. (1993). Developmental psychopathology: Reactions, reflections, projections. *Developmental Review, 13,* 471–502.

Crowell, S. E., Beauchaine, T. P., & Linehan, M. (2009). A biosocial developmental model of borderline personality: Elaborating and extending Linehan's theory. *Psychological Bulletin, 135,* 495–510.

Crowell, S. E., Butner, J., Wiltshire, T. J., Munion, A. K., Yaptangco, M., & Beauchaine, T. P. (2017). Evaluating emotional and biological sensitivity to maternal behavior among depressed and self-injuring adolescent girls using nonlinear dynamics. *Clinical Psychological Science, 5,* 272–285.

De Brito, S. A., Mechelli, A., Wilke, M., Laurens, K. R., Jones, A. P., Barker, G. J., ... Viding, E. (2009). Size matters: increased grey matter in boys with conduct problems and callous-unemotional traits. *Brain, 132,* 843–852.

Finucane, B., Challman, T. D., Martin, C. L., & Ledbetter, D. H. (2016). Shift happens: Family background influences clinical variability in genetic neurodevelopmental disorders. *Genetics in Medicine, 4,* 302–304.

Gatzke-Kopp, L. M. (2011). The canary in the coalmine: Sensitivity of mesolimbic dopamine to environmental adversity during development. *Neuroscience and Biobehavioral Reviews, 35,* 794–803.

Gogtay, N., Giedd, J. N., Lusk, L., Hayashi, K. M., Greenstein, D., Vaituzis, A. C., ... Thompson, P. M. (2004). Dynamic mapping of human cortical development during childhood through early adulthood. *Proceedings of the National Academy of Sciences USA, 101,* 8174–8179.

Goldin, P. R., McRae, K., Ramel, W., & Gross, J. J. (2008). The neural bases of emotion regulation: Reappraisal and suppression of negative emotion. *Biological Psychiatry, 63,* 577–586.

Goldman, S. J., D'Angelo, E. J., & DeMaso, D. R. (1993). Psychopathology in the families of children and adolescents with borderline personality disorder. *American Journal of Psychiatry*, *150*, 1832–1835.

Gratz, K. L., Dixon-Gordon, K. L., Breetz, A., & Tull, M. (2013). A laboratory-based examination of responses to social rejection in borderline personality disorder: The mediating role of emotion dysregulation. *Journal of Personality Disorders*, *27*, 157–171.

Hair, N. L., Hanson, J. L., Wolfe, B. L., & Pollak, S. D. (2015). Association of child poverty, brain development, and academic achievement. *JAMA Pediatrics*, *169*, 822–829.

Kliem, S., Kröger, C., & Kosfelder, J. (2010). Dialectical behavior therapy for borderline personality disorder: A meta-analysis using mixed-effects modeling. *Journal of Consulting and Clinical Psychology*, *78*, 936–951.

Krause-Utz, A., Winter, D., Niedtfeld, I., & Schmahl, C. (2014). The latest neuroimaging findings in borderline personality disorder. *Current Psychiatry Reports*, *16*, 438.

Lyons-Ruth, K. (2008). Contributions of the mother–infant relationship to dissociative, borderline, and conduct symptoms in young adulthood. *Infant Mental Health Journal*, *29*, 203–218.

Lyons-Ruth, K., Holms, B., Sasvari-Szekely, M., Ronai, Z., Nemoda, Z., & Pauls, D. (2007). Serotonin transporter polymorphism and borderline or antisocial traits among low-income young adults. *Psychiatric Genetics*, *17*, 339–343.

Ripke, S., O'Dushlaine, C., Chambert, K., Moran, J. L., Kähler, A. K., Akterin, S., ... Multicenter Genetic Studies of Schizophrenia Consortium. (2013). Genome-wide association analysis identifies 13 new risk loci for schizophrenia. *Nature Genetics*, *45*, 1150–1159.

Sauder, C. L., Derbidge, C. M., & Beauchaine, T. P. (2016). Neural responses to monetary incentives among self-injuring adolescent girls. *Development and Psychopathology*, *28*, 277–291.

Sroufe, L. A., & Rutter, M. (1984). The domain of developmental psychopathology. *Child Development*, *55*, 17–29.

Stepp, S. D., Burke, J. D., Hipwell, A. E., & Loeber, R. (2012). Trajectories of ADHD and ODD as precursors of borderline personality disorder symptoms in adolescent girls. *Journal of Abnormal Child Psychology*, *40*, 7–20.

Yang, Y., & Raine, A. (2009). Prefrontal structural and functional brain imaging findings in antisocial, violent, and psychopathic individuals: A meta-analysis. *Psychiatry Research*, *30*, 81–88.

4c Bridging Diverging Perspectives: Author Rejoinder to Commentaries on Personality Pathology in Youth

BARBARA DE CLERCQ AND CARLA SHARP

The respective commentaries by Vernberg and Abel and Beauchaine provide unique perspectives on the developmental aspects of personality pathology. Vernberg and Abel took issue with some of the basic views espoused in our review, and appear to challenge the value of the assessment and diagnosis of personality pathology in adolescents. Beauchaine, on the other hand, did not challenge the basic premise of our review, but complemented it by providing important information on the biological aspects of personality pathology in youth. Given the complementary nature of the Beauchaine commentary, we spend our allotted word limit addressing the Vernberg and Abel commentary. However, we urge readers to seriously consider Beauchaine's outstanding model of the etiopathophysiology of personality pathology, as we fully agree that much more research should focus on increasing our understanding of the biological mechanisms underlying the development of personality pathology. We thank the writers of both commentaries for their thoughtful and insightful input.

Vernberg and Abel agree with us that borderline personality disorder (BPD) may be an indicator of severity of general personality pathology (Criterion A function), rather than BPD *per se*. In turn, we agree with Vernberg and Abel that this view fits well with research showing that the self-system becomes more differentiated, domain-specific, and stable over the course of adolescence into early adulthood (Rosen, 2016; Sharp, Vanwoerden & Wall, 2018; Sharp & Wall, 2018b). However, we disagree with Vernberg and Abel that "the underlying dimensions of personality (and personality pathology) found in adults may not yet have emerged in children and adolescents." Vernberg and Abel suggest that behavioral (especially externalizing) symptoms appear early on in childhood and adolescence, and that these symptoms can be treated "without these youth receiving a diagnosis [of personality pathology]." The first part of their thesis (that personality dimensions observed in adults have not yet emerged in youth) seems to negate more than a decade of research, including meta-analytic evidence, demonstrating the existence of underlying trait dimensions in children and

adolescents that are the same as in adults, both in terms of structure, content, and course over time (although some stability parameters differ slightly in younger age groups; for a review, see Tackett, Herzhoff, Balsis, & Cooper, 2016). Doubting the existence of these traits (and their structure) seems thus unjustifiable.

The second part of their thesis brings into focus an important conceptual issue regarding the difference between clinical and personality related symptoms, or – as defined in earlier editions of the DSM – between Axis I and II disorders. Vernberg and Abel clearly equate symptoms of internalizing and externalizing disorders with personality pathology symptoms, and suggest that an actual screening for BPD adds no additional value since practitioners can merely focus on treating internalizing and externalizing symptoms. At a taxonomic level, however, we believe there is no need to contrast personality disorder conceptualizations with the traditional clinical approach of conceptualizing symptomatology in terms of internalizing–externalizing spectra. Already more than 15 years ago, a seminal publication (Krueger, 2005), followed by many others (e.g., Kotov et al., 2017; Krueger & Eaton, 2015), clearly showed that Axis I and II show a very similar empirical structure and can thus be represented from a unified perspective (Krueger, 2005). Indeed, the internalizing–externalizing spectra are by far the most empirically validated structural features accounting for all manifestations of psychopathology, including BPD (which is underscored by both trait and clinical psychologists). The point we aimed to make in our call for early detection of BPD, however, is that it is the co-occurrence and interplay of specific symptoms in BPD in particular that guide the cascading process of maladaptation from early adolescence onwards and lead to destructive outcomes. As BPD is thus more than a sum of its symptoms, looking at each of these symptoms individually from established internalizing–externalizing measures (as Vernberg and Abel suggest) would not adequately capture the dynamics between symptoms that largely account for the downward spiral of BPD functioning. To strengthen their argument, the authors refer to the descriptive review of Chorpita and

Weisz (2009) to point out how therapeutic elements have been shown to be effective across RCTs for a number of individual symptoms in youth. Yet, precisely by referring to this review, the authors accentuate that even studies on transdiagnostic interventions focus solely on individual symptoms, providing no guidelines to clinicians on how exactly to treat youth who suffer from multiple symptoms, as always seen in BPD. Only by recognizing the subgroup of youth that suffers from the co-occurrence of multiple symptoms across both the internalizing and the externalizing spectra will BPD symptomatology in youth receive the clinical attention that it deserves. It is also worth noting that effective treatment components for internalizing versus externalizing symptoms differ heavily in the Chorpita and Weisz paper, which actually makes it a big challenge to treat BPD youth using transdiagnostic interventions only. A focused screening of BPD provides the necessary holistic picture of a young individual, which is particularly important given increasing evidence that the BPD constellation of symptoms does not necessarily represent a direct antecedent of adult BPD, but rather speaks to an overall vulnerability for maladaptive outcomes.

From an assessment perspective, these borderline phenotypic manifestations may be described along the traditional clinical perspective, or by using a trait conceptualization. Either way, we believe it is important to consider the construct of "personality functioning" as conceptualized in Criterion A of the DSM-5 AMPD (American Psychiatric Association, 2013). Whereas the exact definition of Criterion A is still a question of debate (Sharp & Wright, 2018), with some arguing that Criterion A can be readily observed in the general trait structure (Widiger et al., 2019), Criterion A may also be interpreted as an avenue for "going beyond traits." Whether Criterion A is seen mainly as a measure of severity or impairment (Clark, Nuzum, & Ro, 2017) or as a more psychodynamic construct delineating process-oriented aspects of personality pathology that lies at a different level of explanation than the behavioral phenotype (Bender & Skodol, 2007; Fonagy, Gergely, Jurist, & Target, 2002; Kernberg, 1967; Sharp & Wall, 2018a), it offers a view of how traits interact with each other and with environmental factors to result in a level of functioning that is – from a trait perspective – closely aligned to the self-concept (defined by McCrae & Costa [1996] as a distinct mental construct that develops from characteristic maladaptations, the objective biography, and underlying basic dispositional tendencies). From the perspective of both internalizing–externalizing symptoms and trait personality pathology, the self-concept is conceptually differentiable from the internalizing/externalizing/trait symptoms themselves. We therefore see the developmental mapping of maladaptive Criterion A function as an important next step in further elucidating the developmental process of personality pathology.

REFERENCES

American Psychiatric Association. (2013). *Diagnostic and Statistical Manual of Mental Disorders* (5th ed.). Arlington, VA: American Psychiatric Publishing.

Bender, D. S., & Skodol, A. E. (2007). Borderline personality as a self–other representational disturbance. *Journal of Personality Disorders, 21*(5), 500–517.

Chorpita, B. F., & Weisz, J. R. (2009). *MATCH-ADTC: Modular Approach to Therapy for Children with Anxiety, Depression, Trauma, or Conduct Problems.* Satellite Beach, FL: PracticeWise.

Clark, L. A., Nuzum, H., & Ro, E. (2017). Manifestations of personality impairment severity: Comorbidity, course/prognosis, psychosocial dysfunction, and 'borderline' personality features. *Current Opinion in Psychology, 21*, 117–121.

Fonagy, P., Gergely, G., Jurist, E. L., & Target, M. (2002). *Affect Regulation, Mentalization, and the Development of Self.* New York: Other Press.

Kernberg, O. (1967). Borderline personality organization. *Journal of the American Psychoanalytic Association, 15*(3), 641–685.

Kotov, R., Krueger, R. F., Watson, D., Achenbach, T. M., Althoff, R. R., Bagby, R. M., . . . Zimmerman, M. (2017). The Hierarchical Taxonomy of Psychopathology (HiTOP): A dimensional alternative to traditional nosologies. *Journal of Abnormal Psychology, 126*(4), 454–477.

Krueger, R. F. (2005). Continuity of axes I and II: Toward a unified model of personality, personality disorders, and clinical disorders. *Journal of Personality Disorders, 19*(3), 233–261.

Krueger, R. F., & Eaton, N. R. (2015). Transdiagnostic factors of mental disorders. *World Psychiatry, 2*, 27–29.

McCrae, R. R., & Costa, P. T., Jr. (1996). Toward a new generation of personality theories: Theoretical contexts for the five-factor model. In J. S. Wiggins (Ed.), *The Five-Factor Model of Personality* (pp. 51–78). New York: Guilford Press.

Rosen, K. (2016). *Social and Emotional Development: Attachment Relationships and the Emerging Self.* Basingstoke: Palgrave Macmillan.

Sharp, C., Vanwoerden, S., & Wall, K. (2018). Adolescence as a sensitive period for the development of personality pathology. *Psychiatric Clinics of North America, 41*(4), 669–83.

Sharp, C., & Wall, K. (2018a). Invited commentary on Hopwood: Maladaptive interpersonal signatures as "re-descriptions" of Criterion B. *European Journal of Personality.*

Sharp, C., & Wall, K. (2018b). Personality pathology grows up: Adolescence as a sensitive period. *Current Opinion in Psychology, 21*, 111–116.

Sharp, C., & Wright, A. (2018). Editorial: Personality pathology is what personality pathologists do. *Current Opinion in Psychology, 21*, iv–vii.

Tackett, J. L., Herzhoff, K., Balsis, S., & Cooper, L. (2016). Toward a unifying perspective on personality pathology across the lifespan. In D. C. Cicchetti (Ed.), *Developmental Psychopathology, Volume 3: Risk, Disorder, and Adaptation* (3rd ed., pp. 1039–1078). New York: Wiley.

Widiger, T. A., Bach, B., Chmielewski, M., Clark, L. A., DeYoung, C., Hopwood, C. J., . . . Thomas, K. M. (2019). Criterion A of the AMPD in HiTOP. *Journal of Personality Assessment, 101*(4), 345–355.

PART II MODELS

5 Controversies in the Classification and Diagnosis of Personality Disorders

JOEL PARIS

HOW PERSONALITY DISORDERS ENDED UP WITH THREE DIFFERENT DIAGNOSTIC SYSTEMS

Researchers studying personality disorders (PDs) are currently facing a situation in which there are three separate methods of classifying these disorders: two in DSM-5 (American Psychiatric Association, 2013) and one in ICD-11 (Tyrer, Crawford, Mulder, & Blashfield, 2011). If one were to consider the Research Domain Criteria (RDoC; Insel et al., 2010) as another alternative, there would be four.

This dilemma reflects the problem of defining complex psychopathological constructs that describe symptoms, traits, and psychosocial dysfunction. It also reflects long-standing disagreements as to whether PDs can be considered categories in much the same way as medical illnesses, or whether they reflect extreme and pathological variants of normal traits that can be scored dimensionally (Widiger, 2007). Behind this problem lies still another question: is there any real difference, other than levels of functioning, between personality traits and PDs?

Most experts have agreed that the system used in DSM-IV, describing ten categories of disorders (as well as a "not otherwise specified" diagnosis), was unsatisfactory. However, they could not agree on how to replace it. Discussions of how best to proceed have focused on three main questions. The first is whether there is enough data to support a different set of categories. The second is whether we should define PDs as endpoints on a continuous spectrum describing personality trait variations. A third is whether a hybrid model that combines both approaches would be preferable.

These questions have long divided the research community. Traditionally, psychiatrists, reflecting their medical background, have tended to prefer a categorical classification, and clinical psychologists have generally followed their lead (Jablensky, 2016). However, over the past few decades, an influential group of researchers trained in trait psychology have begun to argue that categories are artificial, emphasizing the absence of any sharp boundaries between trait variations and diagnosable disorders (Widiger, 2007). This view is supported by a large body of research, both in community and clinical samples (Krueger and Bezdjian, 2009). Support for the continuity of traits and disorders also comes from a large body of behavioral genetic research (Livesley, Jang, & Vernon, 1998). Nonetheless, it remains unclear as to whether trait dimensions can account for the prominent symptoms seen in some PDs, especially the borderline category (Herpertz et al., 2017).

Research on PD diagnoses has been active for several decades. As of 2017, Medline lists over 11,000 articles and PsychInfo lists 19,000 articles. Three diagnostic categories tend to dominate the literature. For borderline PD, 5800 articles are listed on Medline and 10,000 are listed on PsychInfo; for antisocial PD, both Medline and PsychInfo list over 5000 articles. (When psychopathy is added to antisocial, Medline lists over 9000, whereas PsychInfo lists over 22,000, indicating that research on these traits is more frequent than research on the related PD diagnosis.) Schizotypal PD is third in frequency, with 2400 papers on Medline, and 3900 on PsychInfo. However, many of these publications are clinical reports, and only about half are retained if one limits the search using the term "research."

Thus, most PD research has focused on the categories of borderline PD and antisocial PD. Such a large body of research is usually based on the assumption, supported by the structure of the DSM, that the categories of borderline and antisocial PD are entities as coherent as major depression or schizophrenia. However, even the most well-established diagnoses in psychiatry lack precise boundaries. For example, it is difficult to separate sadness from depression (Horwitz & Wakefield, 2007) or alcohol use from abuse (McArdle, 2008). This issue is particularly relevant for antisocial and borderline PD categories. Yet, despite this challenge, it is equally true that these two diagnostic categories are as readily recognizable to clinicians as most other diagnoses in current use. Thus, in these ways, the concerns specific to differentiation of categories seem to be largely a focus in the research literature and far less of a concern among clinicians.

THE DSM CATEGORICAL SYSTEM

PDs, categorically defined, are listed in all diagnostic systems of mental disorders. In the DSM system, the most major changes came with the 3rd edition (American Psychiatric Association, 1980), which included, for the first time, borderline PD and narcissistic PD.

One problem was that the original DSM system had no formal description of what defines a PD. This definition only came with DSM-IV (American Psychiatric Association, 1994), which introduced, for the first time, overall criteria for diagnosing a PD. The definition focuses on an enduring pattern of inner experience that affects cognition, mood, interpersonal functioning, and impulsivity.

The ten-category system of diagnosis listed in DSM-IV has been retained in Section II of DSM-5. However, a serious problem lies with the fact that, as Zimmerman and colleagues showed (Zimmerman, Rothschild, & Chelminski, 2005), about half of patients who meet overall criteria for a PD do not fit into any of these categories. Thus, about half of all patients with PDs end up being diagnosed as "not otherwise specified" (NOS), or, in the terminology of DSM-5, "unspecified." This lack of precision is a serious problem for the categorical system, and suggests that a different method of classification is required.

A second problem with the ten DSM categories is that there has been almost no research on most of them. Although obsessive-compulsive and avoidant PDs were included in the Collaborative Longitudinal Personality Disorders Study (CLPS; Gunderson et al., 2011), they have not been studied in detail, and there is even less research on schizoid, paranoid, and dependent PDs. The large database on borderline and antisocial PDs is a striking exception, and helps to explain the resistance of researchers interested in these conditions to replacing them with dimensional scores. Given that abandoning these categories would make thousands of past research studies irrelevant, it might make more sense (or, at least, would be least disruptive) to reduce the number of categories by eliminating those that lack an evidence base.

PDs are most likely to attract research when they create serious clinical problems. In borderline PD, patients frequently present to emergency rooms and display clinically important symptoms. In antisocial PD, research has been stimulated by the forensic system and by social concerns about containing criminal behavior. The other eight PD categories in DSM-5 could probably be removed without dramatic impact on research or clinical practice.

Another approach would be to make use of the three "clusters" described in DSM-5: Cluster A for "odd" PDs: Cluster B for dysregulated PDs, and Cluster C for anxious PDs (Zimmerman et al., 2005). But yet again, there is a dearth of research specifically focusing on these constructs.

Turning to the specific categories in Cluster A, schizotypal PD has a relatively small research literature, although one recent review quoted 79 publications (Rossell, Futterman, McMaster, & Siever, 2014). Many follow the ICD system in viewing this condition as better placed in the schizophrenic spectrum. Research on the related categories of schizoid and paranoid PDs is rather scant, and some research reports have combined all three diagnoses together (Esterberg, Goulding, & Walker, 2010). Given that one of the earlier iterations of the DSM-5 system proposed doing just that, combining these categories might be reconsidered.

Turning to Cluster B, histrionic PD is mainly of historical interest in that it derives from the concept of "hysteria" (Novalis, Araujo, & Godinho, 2015). On the other hand, the relatively new diagnosis of narcissistic PD has recently been enriched by a body of research on narcissistic traits (Campbell & Miller, 2011), and although the full disorder has not been well researched, the construct of pathological narcissism seems to be clinically useful.

In Cluster C, research on avoidant PD is thin, although the CLPS study (Gunderson et al., 2011) found that like other PDs, one tends to observe improvements over time. Also, avoidant PD overlaps with generalized social anxiety in both phenomenology and genetic risk (Reichborn-Kjennerud et al., 2007). It is therefore possible that these conditions might benefit from the same treatment methods. Much of the work on dependent PD has come from one research group (Beitz & Bornstein, 2010). Very little has been published on obsessive-compulsive PD, other than the CLPS study, which found some degree of improvement over time.

Findings that PD categories tend to overlap, particularly within clusters, raise the question as to whether we actually need ten of them. This argument, made several decades ago by Tyrer and Alexander (1979), proposed that four categories (i.e., sociopathic, passive-dependent, anankastic, and schizoid) could be sufficient. However, as problems with most categories proved difficult to resolve, Tyrer et al. (2011) recommended dealing with overlap by replacing them with ratings on five trait domains (i.e., asocial, emotionally unstable, obsessional [anankastic], anxious/dependent, and dissocial).

Up to now, the International Classification of Diseases, 10th edition (World Health Organization, 1992) has also used a categorical system for the diagnosis of PD that is in many respects similar to the DSM. But, as the date for publication of ICD-11 approaches, this system may be abandoned (or at least greatly modified) to allow for dimensional assessment of traits and disorders.

DIMENSIONAL SYSTEMS

Trait psychologists, schooled in psychometrics, study personality by developing self-report questionnaires that are reliable, have external validity, and can be scored dimensionally. This approach to measuring psychopathology does not apply only to PDs. In many diagnoses, there is no sharp demarcation between traits and disorders, as is clearly the case for depression (Angst and Merikangas, 1997; Horwitz & Wakefield, 2007) and anxiety (Lang and McTeague, 2009; Horwitz & Wakefield, 2012). Even in psychosis, one sees patients who fall in a space between diagnosable illness and trait variation (Potuzak, Ravichandran, Lewandowski, Ongur & Cohen, 2014). This approach to the measurement of psychopathology goes back several decades. Moreover, neurobiological studies of mental disorders show that biomarkers tend to correlate with dimensional measurements, but only rarely with categorical diagnoses (Caspi, Houts, Belsky, & Moffitt, 2014).

These findings influenced the editors of DSM-5 to hope, at least initially, to make *all* diagnosis in psychiatry dimensional (Kupfer & Regier, 2011). Because they saw PDs as the poster child for this change, Kupfer and Regier instructed the committee in charge of PD classification to develop a dimensional system.

This approach could draw on a rich literature in trait psychology that has been studying dimensional approaches to personality and psychopathology for decades. Hans Eysenck (1967), a pioneer in this field, attempted to describe all trait variations and mental disorders as admixtures of two broad factors: Neuroticism and Extraversion – later adding a third he called "Psychoticism" (which would be better labeled as impulsivity).

Building on the first two of these dimensions, the most intensively researched trait system, the Five-Factor Model (FFM), was developed (Costa & Widiger, 2013). Its broad domains (Neuroticism, Extraversion, Agreeableness, Conscientiousness, and Openness to Experience) have been the basis of thousands of research studies. The FFM has been supported by a majority of trait psychologists, has been shown to have cross-cultural validity, and helps to account for variance in personality traits (Costa & Widiger, 2013). That is why the FFM became by far the most frequently used system of its kind.

One might have thought that the American Psychiatric Association would have adopted the well-researched FFM to describe PDs and their underlying traits. However, they did not. One reason may be that in contrast to the usual method of psychiatric assessment, which relies on ratings by expert clinicians, the FFM is based on scores from self-report questionnaires. Another reason could be that the FFM, validated in normal populations, was not considered to do as good a job with psychopathology as with normal variation. Thus, the DSM-5 committee on PDs ended up striking out in a new direction and developing a new dimensional system.

PERSONALITY DISORDERS IN DSM-5

An oncologist I know was very surprised when I told him that the final form of DSM-5 was determined, not by generally agreed upon facts, but by the vote of a committee. But voting may be the only way to proceed when the facts are unclear or unavailable. Many scientific domains have struggled with the problem of fuzzy categories. Biologists have argued for decades about how best to classify species. Even the astronomical community was required to vote on whether Pluto should remain a planet or be demoted to a dwarf planet.

The problem is that a decision of a scientific committee can be determined by the opinions and biases of its members. For this reason, the DSM-5 committee on PD diagnosis consisted of a mixture of experts who favored categories and those who favored dimensions. Its chair, Andrew Skodol (then at Columbia) had been one of the researchers in the CLPS study, but was receptive to a directive to produce a dimensional system.

The initial proposals of the committee were published on the web for commentary. The result was a compromise between the two camps. The group developed a "hybrid system" in which some categories were retained, but were built entirely from trait profiles (American Psychiatric Association, 2013). Thus, each category is not, as in previous editions, diagnosed using a list of criteria that can only be rated as present or absent, but is derived from a characteristic pattern of traits that can be scored. The original draft proposed to reduce the number of categories from the ten in DSM-IV to five: antisocial/psychopathic, avoidant, borderline, obsessive-compulsive, and schizotypal. Not coincidentally, these were also the five categories studied in CLPS.

As drafts of the DSM-5 proposals were published on the internet, the system went through several iterations. Originally, there were five categorical diagnoses, but at one point a sixth, narcissistic PD, was added. This change was due to the views of a strong lobby of investigators who did not want to see the diagnosis disappear. Thus, narcissistic PD remained in the magic circle of categories that could be constructed from trait profiles.

These results were the outcome of a number of political compromises that led to a split in the committee. Two members (John Livesley of Canada and Roel Verheul of the Netherlands), who had hoped for a fully dimensional system, considered the hybrid model to be incoherent and resigned from the committee in protest.

As the deadline for publication of DSM-5 approached in 2013, a decision was needed. In the end, the American Psychiatric Association determined that the proposed changes were too radical to make with a relatively small evidence base (Silk, 2016). Once again by vote, the Board of Trustees moved the hybrid system to Section III of the manual, containing diagnostic constructs that require more research. It has since been described as an "alternative" system for diagnosis.

One might have thought that the decision of the APA not to adopt the hybrid system would have made its eventual success less likely, which is what I thought at the time (Paris, 2013), but that is not what happened. Instead, its advocates considered the decision to be only a temporary setback that could be overcome by publishing more research. Under the leadership of the University of Minnesota psychologist Robert Krueger, co-editor of the *Journal of Personality Disorders* and a member of the DSM-5 committee, over 300 research studies using the alternative system were published between 2013 and 2017. Most of these studies were carried out by trait psychologists who have a strong investment in making PD diagnoses dimensional (Krueger & Markon, 2014). The goal of their program is to remove the old PD categories and replace them entirely with the alternative system (often referred to in these research publications by its supporters as the "DSM-5 system").

DSM-5 was given an Arabic rather than a Roman numeral so that it could be revised, as DSM-5.1 and 5.2 without having to wait another 19 years for the next manual. This expectation could be viewed as either visionary or overly optimistic. In the past, some researchers have been unhappy when changes in the DSM came too soon, requiring them to use new constructs and new instruments.

The five trait domains in the model (negative affectivity, detachment, antagonism, disinhibition vs. compulsivity, and psychoticism) have a resemblance to previous schemata in trait psychology, particularly the FFM. However, this system, when applied to clinical practice, is not scored by self-report but by clinical ratings. This raises the question of whether clinicians, even when trained to rate personality traits, can produce scores that are reliable and that have external validity.

In the alternative model, all PD patients are rated on five personality trait domains. The first four (negative affectivity, detachment, antagonism, disinhibition vs. compulsivity), resemble the FFM. The fifth domain, psychoticism, does not appear in most trait models because it describes problems that are less common in community populations. (Unlike the similar term used by Eysenck, this domain describes a tendency to have psychotic symptoms.) However, it was considered necessary to use this construct to describe PD patients, some of whom have quasi-psychotic experiences.

The alternative system offers a more precise definition of PDs than was found in DSM-IV, focusing on pathology affecting self (identity and self-direction) and interpersonal relations (empathy or intimacy). Ratings involve a series of stages and procedures: (1) Is impairment in personality functioning present? (2) If present, rate the level of impairment in self and interpersonal functioning. (3) Is one of the six defined types present? (4) If so, record the type and the severity of impairment. (5) If not, is the PD trait specified or unspecified? (6) One can record the PD trait specified (PDTS), identify and list the trait domain(s) that are applicable, and record the severity of impairment. (7) If a PD is present and a detailed personality profile is desired, one can evaluate the trait facets. (8) If neither a specific PD type nor PDTS is present, the PD is unspecified, but one can evaluate trait domains and/or trait facets. At each of these steps, clinicians are asked to use a Likert scale (from 1 to 5) for scoring.

Each of these ratings requires judgment calls to determine what is normal, what is extreme, and what is truly dysfunctional. One might ask whether busy clinicians can carry out such a demanding procedure. Research has already shown that most clinicians ignore the precise instructions of the DSM system for diagnosis (First, Bhat, Adler, Dixon, & Goldman, 2014), and that these ratings reflect a global impressionistic opinion.

The work of the committee also produced a self-report measure that can be used to aid diagnosis. This is the Personality Inventory for PID-5 (Krueger, Derringer, Markon, Watson, & Skodol, 2012), which can assess the five trait domains and 25 maladaptive personality trait facets of the DSM-5 alternative system. This 220-item inventory has also been abbreviated to 100 items (PID-5-BF; Al-Dajani, Tralnick, & Bagby, 2016; Maples et al., 2015). It is offered for clinical use in monitoring change in patients, but will probably be mainly used as a research instrument.

Let us summarize the current impact of the alternative DSM-5 system. At this point, the model is shaping the current direction of research, but is not yet being used in clinical practice. The clinical community remains more comfortable with categories, which are a strong tradition in medicine and clinical psychology. Also, even if the alternative model is fully adopted in future versions of DSM-5, it will take time to be accepted. Krueger and Markon (2014) blame conservative political forces for this situation, seeing the categorical model as unscientific and the dimensional model as progressive and empirically based. This view has also been supported by Zachar and First (2015), who see the transition to what might be included in "DSM-5.1" as just a matter of time.

Few will disagree that the categorical model used in previous editions of DSM is outdated. What we do not know is how a drastic change in the conceptualization and assessment of PDs would affect clinical practice. We know from research that PDs are often misdiagnosed or entirely ignored (Zimmerman et al., 2005). Putting them in Axis II, as was done in DSM-III and DSM-IV, only made the situation worse, as clinicians were likely to write "Axis II, deferred" in their assessments of patients, allowing them to focus on the disorders they thought they knew how to treat. What would be the effect if PDs were the only diagnoses in the manual to be dimensionalized? Might this make ignoring personality pathology easier? And, if so, would patients with PDs suffer from not being assessed adequately? We just do not know. Finally, since patients these days expect a diagnosis and often look these up on the web, how would this system affect patient education and compliance with treatment?

THE INTERNATIONAL CLASSIFICATION OF DISEASES (ICD) SYSTEM

The DSM system is not the official classification of mental disorders. By treaty, almost all countries accept the International Classification of Diseases (ICD), published by the World Health Organization (1992), as the standard. The coding of disorders in DSM always allows for direct translation into an ICD equivalent. However, whereas DSM predominates in North America, in other parts of the world, the ICD system is used.

Previous editions of this manual, such as ICD-10 (World Health Organization, 1992), described categories generally similar to those in the DSM, with a few exceptions. Specifically, borderline PD was a subcategory of "emotionally unstable" PD, and narcissistic PD was never included as a diagnosis.

While controversies about the DSM system were getting international press coverage, WHO quietly and systematically prepared its own revised classification, the ICD-11. The preliminary plans for this system have been published on the web. Once again, PDs are a test case for adopting a dimensional system of diagnosis. This project was led by the British psychiatrist Peter Tyrer, who has also been a co-author of most of the preparatory research.

The proposed system for ICD-11 (Tyrer et al., 2011) asks clinicians to rate personality dysfunction on a five-point scale (none, difficulty only, mild, moderate, severe). There are no PD categories, but the manual instructs clinicians to rate patients on five trait domains (asocial, emotionally unstable, obsessional [anankastic], anxious/dependent, and dissocial). This procedure is much simpler than the alternative DSM-5 model, as there are fewer decision points. It is not known whether these five domains closely track the five domains of the DSM-5 alternative model. Further, although the procedures are much simpler than DSM-5's alternative system, it is not known whether busy clinicians can be trained to make reliable ratings.

The most radical aspect of the ICD-11 proposal, and a point of departure from both the DSM-5 alternative system and the ICD system as a whole, is to eliminate *all* categorical diagnoses of PDs. One advantage of making diagnoses on the basis of a trait profile is that so many cases do not fit any of the existing categories. On the other hand, one can question the logic of dimensionalizing PDs while leaving other potentially dimensional constructs, such as anxiety and depression, as a set of categories. And, again, one can question whether the forensic community would accept the complete disappearance of antisocial personality and psychopathy in favor of a high score on a dissocial domain, and whether clinicians (or researchers) would be satisfied giving patients previously diagnosed with BPD high scores on scales of negative emotions and disinhibition. Since any revolution in diagnostic systems can be problematic, one needs to ask what strength of evidence is required to justify drastic change. At this writing, a proposal is under negotiation to produce a compromise that would not eliminate the best-researched categories (Herpertz et al., 2017).

DIAGNOSING BORDERLINE PERSONALITY DISORDER

BPD is common in the community, affecting somewhat less than 1 percent of the population (Lenzenweger, Lane, Loranger, & Kessler, 2007). It is also the most familiar category of PD in clinical practice; Zimmerman et al. (2005) found that about 5 percent of all outpatients meet criteria for this disorder. Like all PDs, BPD is associated with an abnormal sense of self and problems in interpersonal relations. However, unlike other PD categories, it has a highly symptomatic clinical presentation. Thus, BPD is not a classically egosyntonic PD, but is associated with a wide range of egodystonic symptoms (Zanarini et al., 1998), including chronically low and/or unstable mood, a range of impulsive behaviors, and micropsychotic symptoms.

These features help to explain why the diagnosis of BPD is often missed in practice. Zimmerman and Mattia (1999) found that only half of patients meeting DSM criteria for this disorder are recognized in outpatient clinics. Often, clinicians focus on abnormalities of mood, leading them to prescribe antidepressants. It is easy to view these patients as suffering from major depression if one ignores the mood swings that characterize BPD (Gunderson & Phillips, 1991). This is an example of why it is important to recognize BPD. Both Cochrane (Binks et al., 2006) and the National Institute for Health and Care Excellence (NICE, 2009) concluded from meta-analyses that antidepressants are of little value in this clinical population.

It is also very common to see BPD patients who have been diagnosed by previous clinicians as having bipolar disorder. This is due to the current popularity of the concept of a bipolar spectrum that could be used to account for the mood symptoms seen in BPD (Paris, 2012). However, few patients with BPD ever have hypomanic episodes (Paris, Gunderson, & Weinberg, 2007). Instead, they have mood instability with prominent anger and shifts in mood that usually last a few hours and are highly sensitive to environmental adversities. The pattern of daily (or hourly) mood instability does not support viewing BPD as a subclinical form of bipolarity, nor does data drawn from family history, biological markers, or outcome (Paris et al., 2007). Unfortunately, when patients with BPD are misdiagnosed as having bipolar disorder, they can be prescribed lithium or anticonvulsant mood stabilizers – neither of which has been shown to be effective for this population (Binks et al., 2006; National Institute for Health and Care Excellence, 2009).

Another diagnostic issue in BPD is the separation from psychotic disorders. It is not widely known that about half of all patients with BPD experience auditory hallucinations at some time in the course of their illness (Schroeder, Fisher, & Schafer, 2013). These symptoms are usually related to stress and emotion dysregulation, and when they have these experiences, patients almost always recognize that the voices they have heard are imaginary. One also sees brief psychotic episodes in BPD patients that can require psychopharmacological intervention (Zanarini et al., 1998).

Another source of misdiagnosis in BPD occurs when clinicians focus on problems with attention and consider them to suffer from attention deficit hyperactivity disorder (ADHD) (Paris, Bhat, & Thombs, 2015). However, to diagnose ADHD in adults, one needs a childhood history of these symptoms. Moreover, difficulties with attention can be associated with a wide range of disorders. Olfson and colleagues (Olfson, Blanco, & Greenhill, 2013) have shown that the prescription of stimulants in office practice to patients of all kinds has become much more frequent in recent years. Further, even if patients with BPD report benefit from taking these agents, it should be kept in mind that they also often support a focus on tasks in people without psychopathology, and there is no evidence that they have specific value in the treatment of BPD (Binks et al., 2006).

Given that BPD is associated with symptoms that overlap with many other mental disorders, one often sees misdiagnosis. This would not be a problem if alternative models still generated a similar category. But if we were to remove the category of BPD entirely, and replace it with a trait profile, patients might not benefit from the body of research demonstrating that there are specific therapies that work in this population (Zanarini, 2009). Thus, eliminating the diagnosis of BPD could have real consequences for effective management.

DIAGNOSING ANTISOCIAL PD AND PSYCHOPATHY

Mental health clinicians do not often see patients with antisocial PD, who comprise only 3–4 percent of the PDs seen in practice (Zimmerman et al., 2005). However, almost 50 percent of prisoners meet criteria for this disorder (Fazel & Danesh, 2002), making it one of the most common in forensic settings. Antisocial PD is one of the few categories in the DSM that requires a childhood onset (in this case, of conduct disorder). And, because more than a quarter of children with conduct disorder will develop antisocial PD in adulthood (Zoccolillo, Pickles, Quinton, & Rutter, 1992), many of these patients will have been evaluated by child psychiatrists or psychologists.

Antisocial PD has been described in all editions of the DSM, and was also in previous editions of the ICD, using the label dissocial PD. There is an older literature describing a related construct of *psychopathy*, which describes patients with a lack of anxiety or fear and a bold interpersonal style (Hare & Neumann, 2008). Some experts consider psychopathy to be a more severe form of ASPD (Coid & Ullrich, 2010). Others see it as a different diagnosis entirely (Hart & Hare, 1996). Although psychopathy was at one point considered to be a variant of antisocial PD in preparing the DSM-5, it is not included as a specifier in the alternative model of PDs.

Although there is little evidence for effective treatment of antisocial PD, it is still important to make the diagnosis. Since this condition is marked by impulsive and dysregulated behaviors, some of these patients could be considered to have bipolar disorder, and receive medications designed for bipolarity.

PDS, PERSONALITY, AND NORMALITY

The diagnosis of PDs in DSM-5 and ICD-11 requires clinical judgment. At what point are we seeing variations in personality traits that lie within the limits of normality versus a disorder that can clearly be viewed as pathological? If trait psychologists are correct in seeing disorders as exaggerated traits, then the cutoff point must be arbitrary.

In fact, all categories of mental disorder have unclear boundaries (Frances, 2013). Thus, diagnostic constructs are subject to "concept creep" (Haslam, 2016), in which they tend to expand over time. One good example concerns narcissistic PD, for which some researchers have described another type of pathology called "vulnerable narcissism" (Dickinson & Pincus, 2003) to describe patients who are not grandiose but highly sensitive to criticism.

In a critique of overly expansive diagnostic constructs, Frances (2013) pointed out that mental disorders cannot be diagnosed without demonstrating functional impairment and/or distress. Thus, no matter how striking a trait profile is in any patient, they should not receive a PD diagnosis unless these characteristics are producing distress or a notable loss of functioning.

WHAT IS NEEDED TO CREATE A VALID DIAGNOSTIC SYSTEM FOR PDS?

Much ink has been spilled in the categorical–dimensional debate, giving the impression to outsiders that PD researchers are a fractious lot. However, both ways of diagnosing these disorders have advantages and disadvantages. At this point, we just do not know enough to resolve the issue. Without a more detailed understanding of the etiology of PDs, classifying them can only be provisional.

The current controversies about diagnosing PDs are reminiscent of the classical tale of the blind men and the elephant. DSM-5 and other diagnostic systems face similar problems in determining the boundaries of other disorders whose causes remain unclear, including schizophrenia, bipolar disorder, depression, and substance dependence (Paris, 2013). And, whereas the RDoC system has the ultimate goal of developing an etiologically based classification, it is many decades from that goal. Moreover, reducing complex mental phenomena to brain circuitry may turn out to be an impossible mission (Paris & Kirmayer, 2016).

When we know more about why people develop PDs, we will be in a better position to develop a scientific classification. Until then, it is probably best to be pragmatic. As Zimmerman et al. (2005) have shown, PDs, in spite of their high clinical prevalence, are being missed or ignored by many clinicians. At this point, it could be a priority to settle on a single system that, even if flawed, is simple enough to be user-friendly in practice.

CONCLUSIONS

In summary, the following conclusions seem warranted:

1. The categorical system in DSM-5 is poorly validated, but describes at least two categories of great clinical significance (borderline and antisocial PDs).
2. Dimensional systems proposed for the classification of PDs can be validated by their relationship to trait profiles, but have uncertain clinical utility.
3. The alternative (hybrid) system proposed in Section III of DSM-5 is an attempt to combine the benefits of the categorical and dimensions approaches, but is currently too complex for routine clinical use.
4. The question of which system for the diagnosis of PDs is best remains unsettled, as there are advantages and disadvantages associated with all options.
5. The problem could be eventually illuminated by a better understanding of the etiology of PDs.

REFERENCES

Al-Dajani, N., Tralnick, T. M., & Bagby, R. M. (2016). A psychometric review of the Personality Inventory for DSM-5 (PID-5): Current status and future directions. *Journal of Personality Assessment, 98*, 62–81.

American Psychiatric Association. (1980). *Diagnostic and Statistical Manual of Mental Disorders* (3rd ed.). Washington, DC: American Psychiatric Association.

American Psychiatric Association. (1994). *Diagnostic and Statistical Manual of Mental Disorders* (4th ed.). Washington, DC: American Psychiatric Association.

American Psychiatric Association. (2013). *Diagnostic and Statistical Manual of Mental Disorders* (5th ed.). Arlington, VA: American Psychiatric Publishing.

Angst, J., & Merikangas, K. (1997). The depressive spectrum: Diagnostic classification and course. *Journal of Affective Disorders, 45*, 31–39.

Beitz, K., & Bornstein, R. F. (2010). Dependent personality disorder. In J. F. Fisher & W. T. Dononhue (Eds.), *Practitioner's Guide to Evidence Based Psychotherapy* (pp. 230–237). New York: Springer.

Binks, C. A., Fenton, M., McCarthy, L., Lee, T., Adams, C. E., & Duggan, C. (2006). Psychological therapies for people with borderline personality disorder. *Cochrane Database of Systematic Reviews* [Article CD005652].

Campbell, W. K., & Miller, J. D. (Eds.) (2011). *Handbook of Narcissism and Narcissistic Personality Disorder*. New York: Wiley.

Caspi, A., Houts, R., Belsky, D. W., & Moffitt, T. E. (2014). The p factor: One general psychopathology factor in the structure of psychiatric disorders? *Clinical Psychological Science, 2*, 119–137.

Coid, J., & Ullrich, S. (2010). Antisocial personality disorder is on a continuum with psychopathy. *Comprehensive Psychiatry, 51*, 426–433.

Costa, P. T., & Widiger, T. A. (Eds.) (2013). *Personality Disorders and the Five Factor Model of Personality* (3rd ed.). Washington, DC: American Psychological Association.

Dickinson, K. A., & Pincus, A. L. (2003). Interpersonal analysis of grandiose and vulnerable narcissism. *Journal of Personality Disorders, 17*, 188–207.

Esterberg, M. A., Goulding, S. M., & Walker, E. F. (2010). Cluster A personality disorders: Schizotypal, schizoid and paranoid personality disorders in childhood and adolescence. *Journal of Psychopathology and Behavioral Assessment, 32*, 515–528.

Eysenck, H. J. (1967). *The Biological Basis of Personality*. Springfield, IL: Charles C. Thomas.

Fazel, S., & Danesh, J. (2002). Serious mental disorder in 23000 prisoners: A systematic review of 62 surveys. *Lancet, 359*(9306), 545–550.

First, M. B., Bhat, V., Adler, D., Dixon, L., & Goldman, B. (2014). How do clinicians actually use the Diagnostic and Statistical Manual of Mental Disorders in clinical practice and why we need to know more? *Journal of Nervous and Mental Disease, 202*, 841–844.

Frances, A. (2013). *Saving Normal*. New York: HarperCollins.

Gunderson, J. G., & Phillips, K. A. (1991). A current view of the interface between borderline personality disorder and depression. *American Journal of Psychiatry, 148*, 967–975.

Gunderson, J. G., Stout, R. L., McGlashan, T. H., Shea, T., Morey, L. C., Grilo, C. M., ... Skodol, A. E. (2011). Ten-year course of borderline personality disorder: Psychopathology and function from the Collaborative Longitudinal Personality Disorders Study. *Archives of General Psychiatry, 68*, 827–837.

Hare, R. D., & Neumann, C. S. (2008). Psychopathy as a clinical and empirical construct. *Annual Review of Clinical Psychology, 4*, 217–246.

Hart, S. D., & Hare, R. D. (1996). Psychopathy and antisocial personality disorder. *Current Opinion in Psychiatry, 9*, 129–132.

Haslam, N. (2016). Concept creep: Psychology's expanding concepts of harm and pathology. *Psychological Inquiry, 27*, 1–17.

Herpertz, S. C., Huuprich, S. K., Bohus, M., Chanen, A., Goodman, M., Mehlum, L., ... Sharp, C. (2017). The challenge of transforming the diagnostic system of personality disorders. *Journal of Personality Disorders, 31*, 577–589.

Horwitz, A. V., & Wakefield, J. C. (2007). *The Loss of Sadness: How Psychiatry Transformed Normal Sorrow into Depressive Disorder*. New York: Oxford University Press.

Horwitz, A. V., & Wakefield, J. C. (2012). *All We Have to Fear: Psychiatry's Transformation of Natural Anxieties into Mental Disorders*. New York: Oxford University Press.

Insel, T. R., Cuthbert, B., Garvey, M., Heinssen, R., Pine, D. S., Quinn, K., ... Wang, P. (2010). Research domain criteria (RDoC): Toward a new classification framework for research on mental disorders. *American Journal of Psychiatry, 167*, 748–751.

Jablensky, A. (2016). Psychiatric classifications: Validity and utility. *World Psychiatry, 15*, 26–31.

Krueger, R. F., & Bezdjian, S. (2009). Enhancing research and treatment of mental disorders with dimensional concepts: Toward DSM-V and ICD-11. *World Psychiatry, 8*, 306–310.

Krueger, R. F., Derringer, J., Markon, K. E., Watson, D., & Skodol, A. E. (2012). Initial construction of a maladaptive personality trait model and inventory for DSM-5. *Psychological Medicine, 42*, 1879–1890.

Krueger, R. F., & Markon. C. (2014). The role of the DSM-5 personality trait model in moving toward a quantitative and empirically based approach to classifying personality and psychopathology. *Annual Review of Clinical Psychology, 10*, 477–501.

Kupfer, D. J., & Regier, D. A. (2011). Neuroscience, clinical evidence, and the future of psychiatric classification in DSM-5. *American Journal of Psychiatry, 168*, 172–174.

Lang, P. J., & McTeague, L. M. (2009). The anxiety disorder spectrum: Fear imagery, physiological reactivity, and differential diagnosis. *Anxiety, Stress, & Coping, 22,* 5–25.

Lenzenweger, M. F., Lane, M. C., Loranger, A. W., & Kessler, R. C. (2007). DSM-IV personality disorders in the National Comorbidity Survey Replication. *Biological Psychiatry, 62,* 553–556.

Livesley, W. J., Jang, K. L., & Vernon, P. A. (1998). Phenotypic and genetic structure of traits delineating personality disorder. *Archives of General Psychiatry, 55,* 941–948.

Maples, J. L., Carter, N. T., Few, L. R., Crego, C., Gore, W. L., Samuel, D. B., & Markon, K. E. (2015). Testing whether the DSM-5 personality disorder trait model can be measured with a reduced set of items: An item response theory investigation of the personality inventory for DSM-5. *Psychological Assessment, 27,* 1195–1210.

McArdle, P. (2008). Use and misuse of drugs and alcohol in adolescence. *British Medical Journal, 337,* 46–50.

National Institute for Health and Care Excellence. (2009). *Borderline Personality Disorder: Recognition and Management* (NICE Clinical Guideline No. 78). Retrieved from www.nice.org.uk/guidance/CG78/

Novalis, F., Araujo, A., & Godinho, P. (2015). Historical roots of histrionic personality disorder. *Frontiers in Psychology, 6,* 1463–1467.

Olfson, M., Blanco, W., & Greenhill, L. L. (2013). Trends in office-based treatment of adults with stimulants in the United States. *Journal of Clinical Psychiatry, 74,* 43–50.

Paris, J. (2012). *The Bipolar Spectrum: Diagnosis or Fad?* New York: Routledge.

Paris, J. (2013). Anatomy of a debacle: Commentary on "Seeking clarity for future revisions of the personality disorders in DSM-5." *Personality Disorders: Theory, Research, & Treatment, 4,* 377–378.

Paris, J., Bhat, V., & Thombs, B. (2015). Is adult ADHD being over-diagnosed? *Canadian Journal of Psychiatry, 60,* 324–328.

Paris, J., Gunderson J. G., & Weinberg, I. (2007). The interface between borderline personality disorder and bipolar spectrum disorder. *Comprehensive Psychiatry, 48,* 145–154.

Paris, J., & Kirmayer, L. (2016). The NIMH research domain criteria: A bridge too far. *Journal of Nervous and Mental Diseases, 204,* 26–32.

Potuzak, M., Ravichandran, C., Lewandowski, K. E., Ongur D., & Cohen, B. (2014). Categorical vs dimensional classifications of psychotic disorders. *Comprehensive Psychiatry, 53,* 1118–1129.

Reichborn-Kjennerud, T., Czajkowski, N., Torgersen, S., Neale, M. C., Orstavki, R. E., & Kendler, K. S. (2007). The relationship between avoidant personality disorder and social phobia: A population-based twin study. *American Journal of Psychiatry, 164,* 1722–1728.

Rossell, D. R., Futterman, S. E., McMaster, A., & Siever, L. J. (2014). Schizotypal personality disorder: A current review. *Current Psychiatry Reports, 16,* 452–460.

Schroeder, K., Fisher, H. L., & Schafer, I. (2013). Psychotic symptoms in patients with borderline personality disorder: Prevalence and clinical management. *Current Opinion in Psychiatry, 26,* 113–119.

Silk, K. R. (2016). Personality disorders in DSM-5: A commentary on the perceived process and outcome of the proposal of the Personality and Personality Disorders Work Group. *Harvard Review of Psychiatry, 24,* 309–310.

Tyrer, P., & Alexander, J. (1979). Classificiation of personality disorder. *British Journal of Psychiatry, 135,* 163–167.

Tyrer, P., Crawford, M., Mulder, R., & Blashfield, R. (2011). The rationale for the reclassification of personality disorder in the 11th revision of the International Classification of Diseases (ICD-11). *Personality and Mental Health, 5,* 246–259.

Widiger, T. A. (2007). Dimensional models of personality disorder. *World Psychiatry, 6,* 79–83.

World Health Organization. (1992). International Statistical Classification of Diseases and Related Health Problems *(10th revision, ICD-10).* Geneva: World Health Organization.

Zachar, P., & First, M. B. (2015). Transitioning to a dimensional model of personality disorder in DSM 5.1 and beyond. *Current Opinion in Psychiatry, 28,* 66–72.

Zanarini, M. C. (2009). Psychotherapy of borderline personality disorder. *Acta Psychiatrica Scandinavica, 120,* 37–41.

Zanarini, M. C., Frankenburg, F. R., Dubo, E. D.. Sickel, A. E., Trikha, A., & Levin, A. (1998). Axis I comorbidity of borderline personality disorder. *American Journal of Psychiatry, 155,* 1733–1739.

Zimmerman, M., & Mattia, J. (1999). Differences between clinical and research practices in diagnosing borderline personality disorder. *American Journal of Psychiatry, 156,* 1570–1574.

Zimmerman, M., Rothschild, L., & Chelminski, I. (2005). The prevalence of DSM-IV personality disorders in psychiatric outpatients. *American Journal of Psychiatry, 162,* 1911–1918.

Zoccolillo, M., Pickles, A., Quinton, D., & Rutter, M. (1992). The outcome of childhood conduct disorder: Implications for defining adult personality disorder and conduct disorder. *Psychological Medicine, 22,* 971–986.

5a   Three Unresolved Conceptual Issues in Personality Disorders: Commentary on Controversies in the Classification and Diagnosis of Personality Disorders

SCOTT O. LILIENFELD

> For in psychology there are experimental methods and conceptual confusion. The existence of the experimental method makes us think we have the means of solving the problems that trouble us; though problem and method pass one another by.
>
> (Wittgenstein, 1958, p. 232)

Philosopher Ludwig Wittgenstein's remark reminds us that in psychology and allied fields, methodological sophistication cannot substitute for a lack of conceptual clarity. At the risk of painting with an overly broad brush, one might contend with considerable justification that, with a handful of noteworthy exceptions, the field of personality disorders (PDs) has been marked by growing technological sophistication in the absence of concomitant increases in conceptual depth. Even a casual inspection of recent issues of psychology and psychiatry journals reveals a growing number of articles applying rigorous multivariate methods to ascertain the latent structure of PD measures, adopting multilevel modeling to analyze ecological momentary assessment data among individuals with PDs, and using advanced functional brain imaging techniques to examine the neural correlates of personality pathology. I do not intend this statement to be read as a criticism; indeed, as a co-author, I have contributed to several such articles myself (e.g., Rilling et al., 2007).

Still, I worry that the impressive methodological advances in many domains of psychology and psychiatry largely obscure the fact that when it comes to PDs, we are still very much at sea with respect to a plethora of fundamental conceptual questions (Clark, 2007; Lilienfeld & Latzman, 2018). I am reminded of a peer reviewer of an early paper who accused me and my co-authors of "applying Cadillac methods to Chevrolet data" (the reviewer was right, by the way). Similarly, one may legitimately wonder whether many of us in the PD field are guilty of applying high-tech methods to crude diagnostic categories that map poorly onto psychological reality. In fairness, this broader problem surely extends to the field of psychopathology writ large. Nowadays, scholars tend to be rewarded for publishing high-tech studies in top-tier journals and securing large federal research-related grants to conduct these studies, not for authoring incisive theoretical analyses.

As Paris' (this volume) scholarly and well-reasoned chapter reminds us, the field of PDs remains riven by a host of controversies, some primarily theoretical and others primarily methodological. I find myself in agreement with many of Paris' conclusions. For example, I concur with him that some PD categories, such as borderline and antisocial PDs, bear significant clinical implications despite notable shortcomings in their construct validity; I also concur that our rudimentary understanding of the etiology of most or all PDs is a formidable impediment to resolving quandaries in their classification. I also agree that most or all DSM and ICD PDs, like other mental disorders, are marked by unclear boundaries, but that such fuzziness does not by itself vitiate their validity or clinical utility. Although Paris refers to problems of "misdiagnosis" with respect to borderline PD and other PDs, an alternative possibility is that these conditions do not reflect essentialist entities in nature that are detectable with high levels of measurement accuracy. Instead, most or all PDs may be fuzzy densifications or configurations of dimensions in multivariate space, with the boundaries of these patterns being partly a matter of theoretical preference (Hopwood, 2018).

Inspired by Paris' review, I briefly address three largely unresolved conceptual questions in the PD domain that I believe merit considerably more attention than they have received. The issues echo many of those raised by Paris, but go beyond them in several respects.

PERSONALITY TRAITS VERSUS PERSONALITY DISORDERS

Early in his chapter, Paris cuts to the heart of the matter by posing what may be the most vexing question in the PD literature: "Is there any real difference, other than levels of functioning, between personality traits and PD?" (p. 103 in the previous chapter). As he observes, the question remains largely unsettled despite assertions to the contrary. Certainly, burgeoning data demonstrate that omnibus measures of general personality, such as those of the higher-order and lower-order dimensions of the five-factor model (FFM), account for hefty chunks of variance in DSM and ICD PDs (Costa & Widiger, 2013; Ofrat, Krueger, & Clark, 2018). Still, such findings, robust and well-replicated as they are, do not address a fundamental question: What is a PD? Although researchers have demonstrated that they can account for much of the variance in dimensional PD indices using FFM measures, they have generally shown scant interest in the puzzling question of why only certain combinations of FFM traits, but not others, are tied to personality pathology. In many respects, the reasoning here has been asymmetrical: Investigators have demonstrated that they can largely account for PDs in terms of FFM trait patterns, but they have not explained why only a subset of FFM trait patterns are relevant to PDs.

One intriguing possibility, which merits further investigation, is that only certain patterns of FFM traits are tied to personality pathology because these patterns, but not most others, are linked to interpersonal dysfunction. This hypothesis is broadly consistent with findings that antagonism (low agreeableness), which is an inherently interpersonal dimension, courses through most or virtually all DSM PDs (Saulsman & Page, 2004). This hypothesis also dovetails with the possibility that at least some DSM PDs partly reflect "folk concepts" of interpersonal dysfunction, or readily recognized configurations of personality traits that are interpersonally relevant to us because we find them to be aversive or otherwise challenging (see also Lilienfeld & Latzman, 2018; Tellegen, 1993). For example, the folk concept of psychopathic personality (psychopathy) and, to a lesser extent, the overlapping operationalization of antisocial PD in the DSM, may partly mirror the folk concepts of the confidence artist, wolf in sheep's clothing, and two-faced person, stemming from the distinctive and paradoxical admixture of traits (poise, self-confidence, and superficial charm, on the one hand, and callousness, guiltlessness, and interpersonal detachment, on the other) observed in these conditions (Lilienfeld, Watts, Smith, & Latzman, 2018). If the conception of PDs as reflections of folk concepts has merit, it would suggest that investigators should more actively pursue the possibility of multiplicative (interactive) rather than purely additive relations among PD features, as certain patterns of personality pathology may reflect interpersonally confusing configurations of personality traits that are themselves only weakly or even negatively correlated (Grove & Tellegen, 1991; Lilienfeld, 2013).

BASIC TENDENCIES VERSUS CHARACTERISTIC ADAPTATIONS

Although not addressed explicitly by Paris, another reason to doubt the purported synonymy between personality traits and PDs is that many PDs appear to be complex admixtures of *basic tendencies* and *characteristic adaptations*. Admittedly, the distinction between these two concepts is probably one of degree rather than of kind, but it is still useful for theoretical and pragmatic purposes. Basic tendencies are underlying personality traits, whereas characteristic adaptations are the behavioral manifestations of these traits, reflecting people's typical ways of adapting to their own dispositions (DeYoung, 2015; McCrae & Costa, 1995). This distinction is consistent with the longstanding observation that comparable levels of the same personality traits can be expressed in a variety of short-term behaviors and long-term lifestyle choices that differ in their adaptivity versus maladaptivity. For example, levels of sensation seeking are substantially elevated among both firefighters and incarcerated criminals, raising the possibility that this trait can be expressed alternatively in prosocial outcomes, antisocial outcomes, or both, depending on still unidentified moderating variables (Harkness & Lilienfeld, 1997).

Consider the DSM-5 criteria (American Psychiatric Association, 2013) for antisocial PD. A few of these criteria, such as impulsivity, appear to refer primarily to basic tendencies, whereas most others, such as reckless disregard for others' safety and financial/work irresponsibility, appear to refer primarily to characteristic adaptations. For example, in some individuals, impulsivity can be manifested in antisocial behaviors, such as recklessness, whereas in others it can be manifested in prosocial and perhaps even heroic actions (e.g., Neria, Solomon, Ginzburg, & Dekel, 2000; Patton, Smith, & Lilienfeld, 2018). As a consequence, it is *prima facie* implausible that general personality traits alone will ever map entirely onto the PD criterion space. Personality traits can be expressed in a myriad of potential behavioral phenotypes as a function of other (presumably interacting) variables, and only a subset of these phenotypes is relevant to personality pathology. This conceptual problem, which has not received the attention it warrants, dovetails with Paris' point that "it remains unclear as to whether trait dimensions can account for the prominent symptoms seen in some PDs, especially the borderline category" (p. 103 in the previous chapter).

This conceptual framework is also broadly consistent with findings that across the DSM PDs, diagnostic criteria that are more trait-like tend to be more stable over time than criteria that are more behavioral. For example, in borderline PD, affective instability – ostensibly a proxy for the personality trait of neuroticism – tends to be more temporally consistent than self-harming behavior (McGlashan et al., 2005). The former feature is more likely to reflect a basic tendency, whereas the latter is more likely to reflect a maladaptive characteristic adaptation to this tendency.

NETWORK MODELS

An assumption underpinning most models of PDs is that these conditions are *reflective* constructs, meaning that they lie causally downstream of latent variables, such as personality traits (Coltman, Devinney, Midgley, & Venaik, 2008). Nevertheless, recent theoretical and empirical research not addressed by Paris raises the intriguing possibility that certain mental disorders may be better accommodated by *network models*. According to these models, mental disorders are not caused by underlying variables; instead, these disorders can be viewed as complex networks comprising features that exert bi-directional influences on one another (Borsboom & Cramer, 2013). For example, in major depression, lack of sleep may contribute to concentration and memory disturbance; in panic disorder, shortness of breath may contribute to paresthesias (numbness or tingling in the extremities). Such models are a key future avenue for research on the etiology of PDs – an overarching direction highlighted by Paris in his concluding comments.

It is implausible that network models can account entirely for the features of all PDs, as such a view would imply, for example, that the latent trait of neuroticism plays no causal role whatsoever in avoidant, borderline, or dependent PDs. Such an extreme position harkens back to radical behaviorism, which denies any causal role for personality traits (Skinner, 1974). This view is also difficult to reconcile with behavior genetic findings demonstrating that neuroticism shares substantial amounts of genetic variance with borderline PD (Kendler, Myers, & Reichborn-Kjennerud, 2011), suggesting that that this condition is caused by more than the bi-directional relations among its features.

At the same time, it is plausible, if not likely, that network models will help to account for some of the phenomenology of some PDs. For example, in the case of avoidant PD, chronic feelings of social ineptitude seem likely to contribute to fear of intimate social contacts; in the case of paranoid PD, the tendency to read hidden malignant meanings into ambiguous remarks seems likely to contribute to reluctance to confide in others (see also Preszler, Marcus, Edens, & McDermott, 2018 and Verschuere et al., 2018 for the application of network models to psychopathy). In this this respect, hybrid models, which posit that latent variables predispose to certain core features of psychological disorders, but that these features in turn often influence each other bi-directionally (Fried & Cramer, 2017), would seem to be well worth pursuing.

CONCLUDING THOUGHTS

As Paris notes, continued progress in the PD field hinges at least partly on resolution of ongoing conceptual controversies, some of which can be informed by data. In this respect, it would behoove those of us in this discipline to spend more time thinking about deeper conceptual questions and less time thinking about applied questions, such as the optimal factor structure of, or diagnostic criteria for, DSM or ICD PDs (Grove & Tellegen, 1991). At the very least, we should bear in mind Wittgenstein's maxim that

sophisticated research methods, enormously useful as they are, will not by themselves heal all our woes.

REFERENCES

American Psychiatric Association. (2013). *Diagnostic and Statistical Manual of Mental Disorders* (5th ed.). Arlington, VA: American Psychiatric Publishing.

Borsboom, D., & Cramer, A. O. (2013). Network analysis: An integrative approach to the structure of psychopathology. *Annual Review of Clinical Psychology, 9*, 91–121.

Clark, L. A. (2007). Assessment and diagnosis of personality disorder: Perennial issues and an emerging reconceptualization. *Annual Review of Psychology, 58*, 227–257.

Coltman, T., Devinney, T. M., Midgley, D. F., & Venaik, S. (2008). Formative versus reflective measurement models: Two applications of formative measurement. *Journal of Business Research, 61*, 1250–1262.

Costa, P. T., & Widiger, T. A. (Eds.) (2013). *Personality Disorders and the Five Factor Model of Personality* (3rd ed.). Washington, DC: American Psychological Association.

DeYoung, C. G. (2015). Cybernetic big five theory. *Journal of Research in Personality, 56*, 33–58.

Fried, E. I., & Cramer, A. O. (2017). Moving forward: Challenges and directions for psychopathological network theory and methodology. *Perspectives on Psychological Science, 12*, 999–1020.

Grove, W. M., & Tellegen, A. (1991). Problems in the classification of personality disorders. *Journal of Personality Disorders, 5*, 31–41.

Harkness, A. R., & Lilienfeld, S. O. (1997). Individual differences science for treatment planning: Personality traits. *Psychological Assessment, 9*, 349–360.

Hopwood, C. J. (2018). *Interpersonal dynamics in personality and personality disorders. European Journal of Personality, 32*, 499–524.

Kendler, K. S., Myers, J., & Reichborn-Kjennerud, T. (2011). Borderline personality disorder traits and their relationship with dimensions of normative personality: A web-based cohort and twin study. *Acta Psychiatrica Scandinavica, 123*, 349–359.

Lilienfeld, S. O. (2013). Is psychopathy a syndrome? Commentary on Marcus, Fulton, and Edens. *Personality Disorders: Theory, Research, and Treatment, 4*, 85–86.

Lilienfeld, S. O., & Latzman, R. D. (2018). Personality disorders: Current scientific status and ongoing controversies. In J. N. Butcher & J. M. Hooley (Eds.), *Psychopathology: Understanding, Assessing, and Treating Adult Mental Disorders* (pp. 557–606). Washington, DC: American Psychological Association.

Lilienfeld, S. O., Watts, A. L., Smith, S. F., & Latzman, R. D. (2018). Boldness: Conceptual and methodological issues. In C. J. Patrick (Ed.), *Handbook of Psychopathy* (2nd ed., pp. 165–188). New York: Guilford Press.

McCrae, R. R., & Costa, P. T., Jr. (1995). Trait explanations in personality psychology. *European Journal of Personality, 9*, 231–252.

McGlashan, T. H., Grilo, C. M., Sanislow, C. A., Ralevski, E., Morey, L. C., Gunderson, J. G., ... & Stout, R. L. (2005). Two-year prevalence and stability of individual DSM-IV criteria for schizotypal, borderline, avoidant, and obsessive-compulsive personality disorders: Toward a hybrid model of axis II disorders. *American Journal of Psychiatry, 162*, 883–889.

Neria, Y., Solomon, Z., Ginzburg, K., & Dekel, R. (2000). Sensation seeking, wartime performance, and long-term adjustment among Israeli war veterans. *Personality and Individual Differences, 29*, 921–932.

Ofrat, S., Krueger, R. F., & Clark, L. A. (2018). Dimensional approaches to classification. In W. J. Livesley (Ed.), *Handbook of Personality Disorders* (2nd ed., pp. 72–87). New York: Guilford Press.

Patton, C. L., Smith, S. F., & Lilienfeld, S. O. (2018). Psychopathy and heroism in first responders: Traits cut from the same cloth? *Personality Disorders: Theory, Research, and Treatment, 9*, 354–368.

Preszler, J., Marcus, D. K., Edens, J. F., & McDermott, B. E. (2018). Network analysis of psychopathy in forensic patients. *Journal of Abnormal Psychology, 127*, 171–182.

Rilling, J. K., Glenn, A. L., Jairam, M. R., Pagnoni, G., Goldsmith, D. R., Elfenbein, H. A., & Lilienfeld, S. O. (2007). Neural correlates of social cooperation and non-cooperation as a function of psychopathy. *Biological Psychiatry, 61*, 1260–1271.

Saulsman, L. M., & Page, A. C. (2004). The five-factor model and personality disorder empirical literature: A meta-analytic review. *Clinical Psychology Review, 23*, 1055–1085.

Skinner, B. F. (1974). *About Behaviorism*. New York: Vintage.

Tellegen, A. (1993). Folk concepts and psychological concepts of personality and personality disorder. *Psychological Inquiry, 4*, 122–130.

Verschuere, B., van Ghesel Grothe, S., Waldorp, L., Watts, A. L., Lilienfeld, S. O., Edens, J. F., ... Noordhof, A. (2018). What features of psychopathy might be central? A network analysis of the Psychopathy Checklist-Revised (PCL-R) in three large samples. *Journal of Abnormal Psychology, 127*, 51–65.

Wittgenstein, L. (1958). *Philosophical Investigations* (3rd ed., trans. G. E. M. Anscombe). Englewood Cliffs, NJ: Prentice Hall.

5b Classification of Complex Disorders Is a Challenge Solved by Simplicity: Commentary on Controversies in the Classification and Diagnosis of Personality Disorders

PETER TYRER

This erudite and well-informed chapter by Joel Paris is marred only by the absence of answers to the difficult questions posed. What is very clear from all the debate in the last 20 years about personality disorder is that mixed, or hybrid, solutions are not viable. What is described as hybrid vigor by geneticists becomes hybrid failure in classification. So, firm responses are needed, and good responses are those that provide answers too. As an introduction to this commentary, I ask four questions:

1. Who is a classification for?
2. Should a classification in psychiatry be based on clinical utility or science?
3. Is one of the main purposes of a good classification to help in making clinical decisions?
4. Is the long-running argument about categorical and dimensional classification of personality disorder a dead issue?

WHO IS A CLASSIFICATION FOR?

This question can be answered quite easily. A classification is for the people who are expected to use it. A good classification is used frequently and, if really successful, universally. None of the classifications of personality disorder discussed by Joel Paris have been embraced with enthusiasm by health professionals. Paris highlights the great use of PD-NOS as a diagnosis in clinical practice; the very fact that no formal diagnosis is being made, as well as the fact that the diagnosis has no coherent structure (Verheul, Bartak, & Widiger, 2007), illustrates the complete poverty of the categorical classification as it stands.

Most people who debate the merits and demerits of the classification system are those involved in the tertiary management of people with personality disorder or psychologists interested in the whole range of personality variation. However, many more should have an interest in this issue, but are turned off by the complexity and absurdity of the many arguments for and against the different systems that ping about interminably on the personality pinball machine. This is a crying shame; every general

practitioner and physician across the world should know how to diagnose personality disorder. One can go further. A condition that affects 10 percent of the whole adult population needs to be appreciated by all health professionals, not just by a select few who spend their lives seeing a very small proportion of the total sufferers.

SHOULD A CLASSIFICATION IN PSYCHIATRY BE BASED ON CLINICAL UTILITY OR SCIENCE?

The pat answer to this question is that science should always win. However, we know in psychiatry that we are highly vulnerable to criticism that our diagnoses are suspect, as we have so few independent biological markers. This is where clinical utility takes over. We may not know exactly how pathological depression manifests itself in the human brain, but clinicians have a clear idea when it is present and when it appears to be pathological.

Those who support the categorical classification of personality disorder, and this includes Joel Paris in respect to borderline and antisocial personality disorder (although not the others), maintain that something important is lost by removing existing clinical characteristics and replacing them with dimensions. This is understandable when many years have been spent developing treatments for borderline personality disorder in particular, and practitioners fear that something important will be lost if these descriptions are abandoned.

But science has to intrude. It is a sad fact that there is no independent evidence worthy of scientific scrutiny that supports the existence of any of the personality disorders described in DSM-IV or DSM-5. Time after time, they have been shown to be wanting when subjected to independent scrutiny. The dimensional system, by comparison, comes out extremely well in scientific terms (Widiger, 2007). Personality dysfunction can be seen on a continuum with no clear defining points, and the five factor model of normal personality variation can extend into the pathological spectrum without any difficulty (Widiger, Livesley, & Clark, 2009).

IS ONE OF THE MAIN PURPOSES OF A GOOD CLINICAL CLASSIFICATION TO HELP IN MAKING CLINICAL DECISIONS?

It is one of the curious fictions that a psychiatric classification should be considered independently of treatments. This is understandable at one level, as we do not want to see conditions such as "antipsychotic deprivation syndrome" or "danger in the community disorder" being adopted in the psychiatric lexicon.

However, this does not mean that clinical decisions should be divorced from the classification debate. One of the strong points made in favor of keeping borderline personality disorder is the large amount of clinical research and treatment studies that give hope and purpose to clinicians, and this is rightly stressed by Paris. It is also one of the reasons why there was so much concern about losing the diagnosis in ICD-11 (Herpertz et al., 2017).

IS THE LONG-RUNNING ARGUMENT ABOUT CATEGORICAL AND DIMENSIONAL CLASSIFICATION OF PERSONALITY DISORDER A DEAD ISSUE?

The answer to this question is a clear "no" from a quick glance through the rest of this book. The debate remains in full force, but the trends are becoming apparent. The alternative DSM-5 model for personality disorders described by Joel Paris is rapidly becoming the official DSM-5 version because it has been convincingly and carefully developed by Robert Krueger and his colleagues with useful complementary material to aid their dimensional system (Krueger, Derringer, Markon, Watson, & Skodol, 2012). The one categorical diagnosis that has refused to lie down and die is borderline personality disorder.

ADVANTAGES OF THE ICD-11 CLASSIFICATION OF PERSONALITY DISORDER

The World Health Organization published the ICD-11 classification of personality disorder on June 18, 2018 (WHO, 2018). The fundamental elements of the previous version of the classification were preserved (Tyrer et al., 2011; Tyrer, Reed, & Crawford, 2015) and, although there was concern about the radical nature of the reclassification, there was virtually no published criticism until 2017 when important voices were raised by the personality disorder community (Herpertz et al., 2017). These in turn raised a counter-punch from those who support a dimensional system (Hopwood et al., 2018). However, despite the apparent complexity of the arguments, the pugilists were really fighting over one issue: the fate of borderline personality disorder. As Joel Paris has suggested, if the other personality disorder diagnoses described in DSM-III – histrionic, schizoid, schizotypal, avoidant, dependent, narcissistic, and obsessive-compulsive – all became dimensional overnight, few would object. But borderline and, to a lesser extent, antisocial personality disorder are different.

They had a body of adherence and support backed up by other bodies, such as the insurance companies, who liked the clear descriptions of the disorders and their diagnostic criteria.

The ICD-11 classification of personality disorders attempts to give helpful answers to all the questions at the beginning of this chapter. First of all, it is a classification for the majority of health professionals. Many years ago, I became an honorary member of the Central Africa Witchdoctors Association when leading a student expedition to find new pharmacological agents from medicinal plants. My fellow witchdoctors, or n'angas, were familiar with different personalities when carrying out their treatment rituals, and, in particular, knew the relationships people had with other village members. They, I am sure, would have been able to place each of their patients at an appropriate place on the severity scale of personality impairment and adjust their treatment accordingly. This is because the fundamental component of personality status, interpersonal social dysfunction, is one of the easiest to identify. It is possible for all practitioners to stop at the first level of personality assessment. For some patients with very severe personality disorder, it may be difficult for a practitioner to make an accurate assessment of domain traits in an ordinary community setting, but still possible to determine enough about severity to decide that corrective action is needed.

The ICD-11 classification also allows for much better assessment of the effects of treatment. The current dichotomous classification does not allow for variation in personality function to be reflected over time. It is well known that personality function fluctuates, both spontaneously (Clark, 2007) and in response to treatment, and the current classification makes no allowance for this. For disorders where complex treatments are recommended (Department of Health, 2009), it is also important to specify the severity of the personality disorder and probably forgo long-term treatments if the disorder is only mild in severity.

Finally, the place of borderline personality disorder is, at least temporarily, assured. There are some who would prefer all categories to be excluded in what is otherwise a dimensional system, but the arguments for inclusion of a "borderline pattern descriptor" have been strong and many will be pleased to recognize familiar words in this pattern below, now accepted in ICD-11:

The Borderline pattern descriptor may be applied to individuals whose pattern of personality disturbance is characterized by a pervasive pattern of instability of interpersonal relationships, self-image, and affects, and marked impulsivity, as indicated by many of the following: Frantic efforts to avoid real or imagined abandonment; A pattern of unstable and intense interpersonal relationships; Identity disturbance, manifested in markedly and persistently unstable self-image or sense of self; A tendency to act rashly in states of high negative affect, leading to potentially self-damaging behaviours; Recurrent episodes of self-harm; Emotional instability due to marked reactivity of mood; Chronic feelings of emptiness; Inappropriate intense anger or difficulty controlling anger; Transient dissociative symptoms or psychotic-like features in situations of high affective arousal. (World Health Organization, 2018)

However, if the dimensional view of personality classification becomes the norm, the borderline pattern may merge imperceptibly into the general structure of personality disorder, provided that clinicians can embrace its positive attributes. This is not yet certain (Tyrer, 2018).

A few years ago, I was in Long Island in a meeting concentrating almost entirely on borderline personality disorder. On the last day of the meeting, James D. Watson, Nobel prize winner for his work on eliciting the structure of DNA, commented to me after the meeting closed, "Why all this obsession with borderline personality disorder? What about the others? You are not going to get the answer to personality disorder just by working on borderline." I heartily concur.

REFERENCES

Clark, L. A. (2007). Assessment and diagnosis of personality disorder: Perennial issues and an emerging reconceptualization. *Annual Review of Psychology, 58*, 227–257.

Department of Health. (2009). *Borderline Personality Disorder: Recognition and Management. NICE Clinical Guideline [CG78]*. London: Department of Health.

Herpertz, S. C., Huprich, S. K., Bohus, M., Chanen, A., Goodman, M., Mehlum, L., ... Sharp, C. (2017). The challenge of transforming the diagnostic system of personality disorders. *Journal of Personality Disorders, 31*, 577–589.

Hopwood, C. J., Kotov, R., Krueger, R. F., Watson, D., Widiger, T. A., Althoff, R. R. ... Zimmermann, J. (2018). The time has come for dimensional personality disorder diagnosis. *Personality and Mental Health, 12*, 82–86.

Krueger, R. F., Derringer, J., Markon, K. E., Watson, D., & Skodol, A. E. (2012). Initial construction of a maladaptive personality trait model and inventory for DSM-5. *Psychological Medicine, 42*, 1879–1890.

Tyrer, P. (2018). Dimensions fit the data, but can the clinicians fit the dimensions? *World Psychiatry, 7*, 295–296.

Tyrer, P., Crawford, M., Mulder, R., Blashfield, R., Farnam, A., Fossati, A., ... Reed, G. M. (2011). The rationale for the reclassification of personality disorder in the 11th revision of the International Classification of Diseases (ICD-11). *Personality and Mental Health, 5*, 246–259.

Tyrer, P., Reed, G. M., & Crawford, M. J. (2015). Classification, assessment, prevalence and effect of personality disorder. *Lancet, 385*, 717–726.

Verheul, R., Bartak, A., & Widiger, T. (2007). Prevalence and construct validity of Personality Disorder Not Otherwise Specified (PDNOS). *Journal of Personality Disorders, 21*, 359–370.

Widiger, T. A. (2007). Dimensional models of personality disorder. *World Psychiatry, 6*, 79–83.

Widiger, T. A., Livesley, W. J., & Clark, L. A. (2009). An integrative dimensional classification of personality disorder. *Psychological Assessment, 21*, 243–255.

World Health Organization. (2018). *International Classification of Diseases* (11th revision, ICD-11). Geneva: World Health Organization. www.who.int/classifications/icd/

5c Final Thoughts: Author Rejoinder to Commentaries on Controversies in the Classification and Diagnosis of Personality Disorders

JOEL PARIS

I agree with Peter Tyrer that in classification systems, science should trump clinical utility. I am just not sure how solid the science is behind the ICD-11 system. The research literature remains thin, although it is sure to grow now that the revised system has been published. But DSM-5 Section III has, at this point, a larger literature, and its advocates are just as certain that their system is scientific. It may be more accurate to say that both of these systems are provisional, and that it will take many decades of research to improve on them.

I am pleased that, as announced in June 2018, ICD-11 will allow clinicians to diagnose borderline personality disorder as a "pattern" along with five trait domain descriptors. The views of a number of researchers, reflected in a paper by Herpertz et al. (2017), seem to have influenced the final outcome, allowing for this compromise with a strictly dimensional approach. However, I have some concerns about the reliability of the ICD-11 system in practice. Unlike DSM-5 Section III (American Psychiatric Association, 2013), the trait domains and how to rate these traits in diagnostic evaluations are not spelled out in detail.

I have long been an advocate for the construct of borderline personality disorder, which, as a large body of evidence shows (there are thousands of research papers), is as valid as schizophrenia, bipolarity, or depression. Of course, these disorders, even though they are central to psychiatry, set a low bar! In a field trial conducted by the developers of DSM-5, borderline personality disorder had a much higher reliability than major depression (Regier et al., 2013).

For now, my view is that whatever the problems are with the borderline category, we need to retain it, at least until there is something clearly better. And it is compatible with DSM-5 Section III, even if the pathway to making the diagnosis is more complex. I have my doubts about the idea that the diagnosis of borderline personality disorder will eventually drop off as people realize the advantages of the ICD-11 system. Finally, whatever his expertise is on the genome, I suspect that if James Watson had spent a few evenings in an emergency room observing the patients who came in, he would understand why many researchers are "obsessed" with borderline personality.

Scott Lilienfeld has cogently summarized some of crucial unanswered questions about personality and personality disorders. I would add another one. We just do not know enough about mind or brain to understand complex forms of psychopathology that affect emotion, thought, and behavior. This is an understandable problem, given that evolution has shaped a brain with at least 80 billion interacting neuronal components (one can double that if the glia are considered). I am not suggesting, as in the Research Domain Criteria (Cuthbert & Insel, 2013), that solving the puzzle depends largely on the connectivity of neuronal networks. Even if we understood brain wiring, we would still be a long way from explaining mental activity, not to speak of consciousness. Many decades of research lie ahead of us.

Dr. Lilienfeld may have misunderstood me on one point – the problem of misdiagnosis. I was not concerned about separating personality trait profiles, which do overlap greatly. I was referring to the treatment of patients with borderline personality disorder wherein the focus is on abnormal mood – either depression or mania (Paris, 2012). This is where misclassification, and missing personality disorders entirely, is not just an issue for professors, but hurts patients by giving them a treatment they don't need while denying them therapy that they do need.

REFERENCES

American Psychiatric Association. (2013). *Diagnostic and Statistical Manual of Mental Disorders* (5th ed.). Arlington, VA: American Psychiatric Publishing.

Cuthbert, B. N., & Insel, T. R. (2013). Toward the future of psychiatric diagnosis: The seven pillars of RDoC. *BMC Medicine, 11*, 126.

Herpertz, S. C., Huprich, S. K., Bohus, M., Chanen, A., Goodman, M., Mehlum, L., ... Sharp, C. (2017). The challenge of transforming the diagnostic system of personality disorders. *Journal of Personality Disorders, 31*, 577–589.

Paris, J. (2012). *The Bipolar Spectrum: Diagnosis or Fad?* New York: Routledge.

Regier, D. A., Narrow, W. E., Clarke, D., Kraemer, H. C., Kuramoto, S. J., Kuhl, E. A., & Kupfer, D. J. (2013). DSM-5 field trials in the United States and Canada, Part II: Test-retest reliability of selected categorical diagnoses. *American Journal of Psychiatry, 170*, 159–170.

6 Categorical Models of Personality Disorders

IGOR WEINBERG

Categorical models of personality disorders (PDs) have slowly fallen out of favor in the last decade. The burgeoning literature on the dimensional approaches to personality brought a new area and new enthusiasm in research on personality pathology, and in doing so it also raised questions about the viability of the categorical model. In fact, a survey of PD experts showed that 74 percent indicated that the categorical approach should be replaced, 87 percent stated that personality pathology is dimensional in nature, and 70 percent supported a mixed categorical–dimensional approach (Bernstein, Iscan, Maser, & Board of Directors of the Association for Research of Personality Disorders, 2007).

The ever increasing number of publications that focus on dimensional models of personality disorders could lead one to conclude that the categorical models are already a thing of the past. Or some might think that these models have only limited utility and should be reserved for the sidebars and historical sections of our professional textbooks. At least currently, categorical models remain the cornerstone of our current diagnostic approach, understanding, research, and treatment of personality pathology (and all psychiatric pathology for that matter) against which other – alternative – models are often held up for testing and validation. With this in mind, the present chapter provides a general overview of the categorical models of personality pathology focusing on historical developments in the conceptualizations underlying our understanding of PDs, changes in the categorical conceptualization of PDs in the DSM, examination of the strengths of the categorical model (examples of the disorder-specific constructs, documentation of the functional impairment, examination of the construct and predictive validity, as well as of clinical utility), as well as critical examination of the limitations of the model. The chapter concludes with general discussion of future directions.

HISTORY OF THE CONCEPT

Categorical models of personality have a long and varied history. The first known descriptions of character or character type go back to ancient Greece. Hippocrates left us what seems to be the first account of four character types – the choleric, melancholic, sanguine, and phlegmatic. Those corresponded to excesses of four bodily humors: yellow bile, black bile, blood, and phlegm. Hippocrates postulated that imbalances of those four humors constitute the basis for any disorder, including personality types. These humors were bodily analogs of four basic components – earth, water, fire, and air. Those were proposed by the philosopher Empedocles as the basis for understanding the universe and natural phenomena. These four basic categories dominated early conceptualizations of personality, despite efforts to promote other approaches such as Aristotle's suggestion that a person's character could be judged based on their facial characteristics, leading to the term physiognomy.

Following the approach through the nineteenth century of viewing character, including normal character types, in terms of combinations of some basic elements including emotionality, activity, energy level, and energy direction, the twentieth century saw the emergence of temperament and the application of this concept to psychiatric patients (e.g., Hirt, 1902). Despite differences in the approaches, temperament-based descriptions followed the same notion of character being a combination of some basic elements. Attracting the interest of psychiatrists, character pathology began to be featured in clinical descriptions. This resulted in a number of now classical publications, such as Kraepelin (1919) and Schneider (1923) which describe different pathological character presentations and Kretchmer (1925) which related character to a person's physical build.

Important advances in the twentieth-century conceptualization of personality can be attributed to Freud who set the stage for many early psychoanalysts to immerse themselves in study of various characters that were defined by stages of psychosexual development. These descriptions creatively used psychoanalytic thinking and clinical observations to account for presentations and symptoms of patients. The concept of character was first related to the characteristic stage of psychosexual development

(Abraham, 1927; Ferenczi, 1938; Freud, 1908). Later, it was related to specific defense mechanisms (Rappaport, 1961; Reich, 1933), specific solutions to internal conflicts (Horney, 1937) – and with advent of object relation theory – specific ways the person experienced self and others (Fairbairn, 1952; Guntrip, 1968; Klein, 1948; Winnicott, 1965).

Later analytic authors incorporated developments in psychoanalysis and psychiatry, and came forth with further diagnostic classifications and subsequent theories and treatments for personality disorders (Gunderson, 1984; Kernberg, 1975; Kohut, 1971; Stone, 1980). Cognitive behavior theories expanded their interest to include personality pathology, resulting in competing and creative formulations (Beck, Freeman, Davis, & Associates, 2006; Young, Klosko, & Weishaar, 1993). Introduction of the biological model to psychiatry led to original formulations of personality in terms of specific biochemical mechanisms (Cloninger, Svrakic, & Przybeck, 1993, Siever & Davis, 1991), while theorists interested in expanding personality theory into understanding psychopathology proposed alternative, dimensional models (Costa & McCrae, 1985; Costa & Widiger, 1993). This rich history resulted in a voluminous literature on different personality types and different types of personality pathology.

It was in this intellectual climate of categorical classification that DSM was developed. Inheriting its conceptual basis from the categorical literature, earlier versions of DSM described disorders in terms of distinct categories, not dimensions. It was not until DSM-5 that the dimensional focus was added as an alternative approach.

CATEGORICAL APPROACH IN DSM

In DSM, personality disorders are classified as enduring conditions. They were distinguished from episodic disorders (that ultimately found their place on Axis I) in terms of earlier age of onset, persistence, and resistance to treatment. DSM defined personality disorders in terms of polythetic sets of criteria. Each disorder has a cutoff score of number of criteria necessary to meet the classification for the disorder. Such a definition has a pragmatic role in identifying appropriate treatment, framing appropriate treatment foci and hierarchy of treatment targets, as well as facilitating communication.

DSM underwent a number of significant revisions, though preserving the essential spirit of categorical classification. DSM-I was published in 1952, specifying three categories of personality disorders: (i) personality pattern disturbance, which included inadequate, paranoid, cyclothymic, and schizoid personality disorders; (ii) personality trait disturbance, which included emotionally unstable, passive-aggressive dependent or aggressive types, and compulsive personality disorders; and (iii) sociopathic personality disturbance, which included antisocial

dissocial types. These conditions were considered relatively stable and refractory to treatment.

Revision of the ICD system led to a second edition of DSM in 1968 that was less theory-based and more empirically grounded. DSM-II held many similarities with DSM-I in its presentation of the personality disorders, with notable revisions. While inadequate, paranoid, cyclothymic, and schizoid personalities, as well as antisocial sociopathic disturbance remained largely unchanged, emotionally unstable personality was reformulated as hysterical and passive-aggressive personality took the place of passive-aggressive personality, aggressive type. Additionally, compulsive personality was reformulated as obsessive-compulsive personality, and explosive and asthenic personality categories were added.

Further emphasis on reliability and the empirical basis of the diagnosis that evolved in 1970s contributed to the third edition of DSM, published in 1980. Of note, Axis II was created for personality disorders to designate persistent conditions with an early onset. Beginning with the perspective that personality disorders were psychosocial in nature, DSM-III heralded subdivision of the personality disorders into three clusters: (i) Cluster A (odd) including schizotypal (StPD), schizoid (SPD), and paranoid (PPD) personality disorders; (ii) Cluster B (dramatic) including histrionic (HPD), antisocial (ASPD), borderline (BPD), and narcissistic (NPD) personality disorders; and (iii) Cluster C (anxious) including compulsive, avoidant (AvPD), dependent (DPD), and passive-aggressive personality disorders. Within Cluster A, schizoid personality was divided into schizotypal, schizoid, and avoidant personality disorders, with the latter shifting to Cluster C. Within Cluster B, hysterical personality was reformulated as histrionic personality. Within Cluster C dependent personality was added to the list and asthenic personality was omitted. Cyclothymic personality and explosive personality were shifted to Axis I as cyclothymic disorder and intermittent explosive disorder, respectively.

Published in 1994, DSM-IV was based on an extensive set of literature reviews, data analyses, field trials, and feedback from the clinicians and researchers in the field. It preserved the general categorization of DSM-III, with an exception of the omission of the passive-aggressive personality disorder and renaming compulsive personality disorder as obsessive-compulsive personality disorder (OCPD). DSM-5 was published in 2013 after further extensive literature review, data analyses, field trials, and feedback from the clinicians and researchers in the field. DSM-5 also marked the introduction of the alternative trait and dimensional models that have the potential to ultimately supplement the categorical model. Initially, the DSM-5 working group on personality disorders intended to replace the categorical model with the dimensional one. Initially, the dimensional model was proposed by the working group as a conceptually attractive solution for the challenges the categorical model posed (see below). However, this proposal was criticized because it had not accumulated the same level of evidence as the categorical model. A complete transition to the dimensional model would have severed the ties with decades of research and clinical tradition without a comparable empirical basis. Consequently, the dimensional model was included as an alternative conceptualization of personality disorders that is worth further research, not as a primary diagnostic model (for a review of the controversy see Chapter 5). It is to the examination of the validity of the categorical model that we will now turn.

Disorder-Specific Concepts

One of the advantages of the categorical concept is the richness of descriptions and understanding of the individual personality disorders. Coming from a long tradition of conducting therapy with these patients, these descriptions offer empathic and experience-near accounts of the subjective experiences of the patients. Such descriptions not only enrich and broaden our understanding of the disorder, but also create language that helps empathically name experiences for the individual patient.

Stated in the simplest terms, categorical descriptions of the personality disorders create disorder-specific language to label various experiences. This approach also creates a separate semantic network that helps understand the disorder and the patient who suffers from it. In such a way these disorder-specific descriptions and concepts are the *first step* in bridging the gap between the nomothetic understanding of the disorder and the ideographic formulation of the individual patient. However, applying a more generic language borrowed from other domains, including personality research or other personality disorders runs the risk of misrepresenting (misunderstanding) these disorders. In other words, a more generic language runs the risk of obfuscating what is unique and specific about the individual personality disorders and forcing outside concepts on them and the individual patients. This point can be illustrated with a few examples of such concepts and how they apply to different disorders.

Dependence

A large number of studies have focused on understanding the concept of dependence (Bornstein, 1993). Dependence appears in a number of personality disorders, though its meaning differs in each case. In patients with DPD, over-reliance on others and the reported need for others' support and assistance is related to low self-efficacy beliefs. Dependence for patients with BPD is related to fear of abandonment and intolerance of aloneness. Dependence, paradoxically, appears in NPD patients on context of idealization of significant others. In these patients dependence is connected to the need to rely on the idealized others, who are experienced as major sources of self-esteem. Therefore, in these patients, dependence is fueled by a specific way of regulating self-esteem.

These formulations demonstrate the discontinuity of the concept of dependence across various personality disorders, and also highlight the diagnostic and therapeutic significance of such discontinuity. From the diagnostic perspective, identifying these dynamics would prompt the clinician to make a careful assessment of the relevant disorder. From the treatment perspective, the therapist will intervene differently to address these patterns of dependence.

With a DPD patient, the therapist will frame therapy in the context of increasing self-reliance, problem-solving ability, and self-efficacy beliefs, while being vigilant regarding the risk of stepping into a more authoritarian role and solving the problems on the patient's behalf. With a BPD patient, the therapist will need to help the patient identify patterns of avoidance of experiences of abandonment and help develop more efficient strategies to tolerate aloneness and connect with others. With NPD patients, the task of the therapist is helping the patient identify the role of reliance on others in regulating self-esteem and develop alternatives for self-esteem regulation.

Interpersonal Distancing

Distancing appears in a number of disorders, and, similar to the concept of dependence, has a different significance in different disorders. In AvPD, distancing stems from fear of judgment by others and it appears in the context of negative self-perception and a positive perception of others. In SPD, distancing appears in the context of disinterest in connection with others and lack of investment in real relationships with others. In NPD, distancing is usually connected with devaluation of others and the desire to preserve self-sufficiency; therefore – counter-dependence. In PPD, distancing is related to a suspicious stance about others. In PPD others are typically seen as negative and as having malicious intentions, while the self is seen in a more positive light.

Differences associated with dependence indicate differential treatment approaches to these patients and would suggest different prognoses for the symptoms of "distancing." For instance, in AvPD, the therapist could intervene by encouraging exposure-style interventions and engaging the patient in confronting and testing negative expectations of others. With SPD, distancing will require a much longer treatment process that would involve helping the patient become aware of the need for others and create coping skills to make up for the difficulty connecting with others. In NPD patients the therapist will likely target distancing by identifying different ways in which the patient accomplishes that as well as exploring the function of it; encouraging the patient to develop curiosity about what he or she is avoiding is yet another possible intervention. In PPD patients, the therapist is likely to take a stance of promoting trust and understanding as preconditions for any therapeutic process and in this way will start helping with distancing. With this in mind, prognosis is likely to be better for AvPD patients, intermediate for NPD patients, and poor for SPD and PPD patients.

Complexities of Individual Disorders

Some concepts were specifically developed for individual personality disorders and are more likely to lose their specificity and explanatory power within other diagnostic approaches. For example, Ronningstam (2011) lists a long line of concepts central to the understanding of NPD that get lost in other models, but retain their meaning as long as NPD is recognized as a separate disorder. These concepts bridge the gap between the phenomenological, observable aspects of NPD and the subjective and functional aspect of it.

Ronningstam (2011, p. 253) proposes the following reformulation of the construct of narcissism: "enhanced or unrealistic, either overtly interpersonally or behaviorally expressed or internally hidden, sense of superiority and exaggeration of own achievement and capability vulnerability and vulnerable self-esteem with self-criticism and inferiority, and intense reactions to threat, criticism, or defeats; and self-preoccupation with self-enhancement and self-serving interpersonal behavior." Such reformulation is clinically meaningful and humanizing in terms of understanding the individual patient with NPD. It also meaningfully helps facilitate the dialogue with the patient about the disorder and provides guidelines for intervention. Importantly, this formulation also explains the fluidity of the clinical presentation of some NPD patients who, at times, acquire a chameleon-like capacity to blend in and present without any symptoms, despite having the most severe forms of the disorder. While the trait approach might be able to capture some of the aspects of NPD, it misses important sectors of the pathology, including functional significance of behaviors, subjective experiences of the patients, or radically different aspects of the pathology that are simply not represented in the trait models for theoretical reasons.

On the other hand, description of NPD simply in terms of manipulativeness and callousness will misrepresent the NPD patient as too similar to patients with ASPD. Even though many NPD patients have comorbid ASPD (Gunderson & Ronningstam, 2001), their antisocial behaviors are typically guided by self-regulatory function, rather than calculated agenda to accomplish an incentivized goal. In this way application of global traits misrepresents what is specific about the disorder.

Schizoid personality disorder is yet another disorder that can be easily misrepresented if it is reduced to global traits. Many authors describe a seemingly contradictory conglomerate of traits that many SPD patients have that could be confusing at first glance, but perfectly understandable if some of them are understood as serving a self-protective function. For instance, Livesley and colleagues (Livesley, West, & Tanney, 1986) describe presence of active and passive social avoidance, the inner hypersensitivity and the callous persona as well as hypervigilant and absent-minded attitudes. Such schism in terms of various aspects of functioning and experiencing is self-protective and reflects not only facets of functioning, but also aspects of subjective experience.

The concept of the False Self (Winnicott, 1965) was described to characterize a particular aspect of functioning of people with SPD – an overly compliant persona that is detached from the core sense of self and that is protecting the person from the inner experiences of falling into pieces, being disconnected from one's body and experience of disorientation (Winnicott, 1965). This is a complicated construct, but accurately describes subjective and very private experiences of patients with SPD. While many descriptions might capture the interpersonal distancing, it can be argued that only the categorical model has the conceptual power to uniquely associate these experiences of fragmentation and of the False Self to SPD.

Clinical descriptions of PPD present similar complexity. Akhtar (1992, p. 156) summarizes that this disorder has a "contradictory presence of (1) profound mistrust with naive gullibility, (2) arrogant demandingness with hidden inferiority, (3) emotional coldness with marked sensitivity, (4) superficial asexuality with vulnerability to erotomania, (5) moralistic stance with potential corrupt attitudes, (6) acutely vigilant attention with inability to use the whole picture." Such complexity requires seeing the person beyond their individual behaviors and understanding the essence of the person's functioning. This is a complicated matter because it requires the clinician to see the big picture and not necessarily get lost in individual features. Similarly, it requires *understanding* of the person, integrating and not simply compiling phenomenological features.

These examples emphasize the need for distinguishing the diagnostic aspects of the disorder from the aspect of understanding of the individual patient. Symptoms of the disorder represent nomothetic dimensions of the psychopathology and they were designed to identify significant personality disorders. Understanding of the individual patient, while relying on these signs and symptoms is different as it attempts to integrate *all characteristics* of the person to come up with a comprehensive and meaningful understanding of him or her. Diagnosing a specific personality disorder helps in the process of accomplishing such understanding. However, the diagnostic sets designed to *diagnose* each disorder do not aspire to represent an essential *understanding* of each individual patient. While diagnosis does not equal understanding of the patient with the disorder, it is an essential first step to such understanding. Meaningfully formulated understanding, communicated to the patient, paves the way toward alliance building. Finally, clinical concepts associated with each disorder create a conceptual map that guides the clinician through the process of developing understanding of the individual patient. This helps to bridge the gap between the nomothetic and the ideographic and translate generic characteristics of the disorder into personally meaningful concepts.

The difference between meaningful understanding and statistical prediction was emphasized by Holt (1970, p. 347) who warned that "the logic of statistical prediction does need require understanding of the behavior in question ... The statistician's interest ceases once he has found the most efficient and stable formula that combines scores for prediction. On the other hand understanding is concerned with questions regarding 'how things work'."

Taking these points together, the importance of seeing the person behind clinical descriptions is hard to overestimate. Such understanding helps with alliance building and treatment interventions, and it also contributes to clinical prediction (Holt, 1970). Statistical prediction is seeking individual variables that have the statistical power to predict an important outcome. Clinical prediction, on the other hand, relies on understanding how the person functions, experiences self, others and the world, or responds to significant stimuli such as stress or relationships to anticipate important outcomes. An example of this dichotomy relates to the prediction of suicide. Pokorny (1983) failed to predict suicide in a prospective study that relied on statistical prediction, using numerous predictors. On the other hand, Edwin Shneidman, a prominent suicide expert, blindly reviewed clinical material in the prospective study of gifted women conducted by Lewis Terman and successfully identified all completed suicides using clinical judgment – his understanding of women participants of the study (Orbach, personal communication, March 7, 2002).

Functional Impairment and the Categorical Model

Functional impairment is one of the cornerstones of psychopathology in DSM and it is one of the critical components of personality disorders. Functional impairment refers to difficulty performing tasks and roles in such areas as social or interpersonal, school or work, recreational or leisure, self-care, communication and mobility (Skodol, 2018).

The critical role of functional impairment as an important component of the diagnosis of personality disorders is highlighted by the study by Trull and colleagues (Trull, Jahng, Tomko, Wood, & Sher, 2010). Trull and his colleagues used data from the National Epidemiologic Survey on Alcohol and Related Conditions (NESARC) study (Grant, Moore, Shepard, & Kaplan, 2003) that assessed the prevalence of psychiatric disorders. The original NESARC study used only descriptive phenomenology – symptoms – to meet the criteria for personality disorders. Trull and his colleagues re-analyzed prevalence data from the NESARC and introduced a further requirement for personality disorder – functional impairment and/or distress. Table 6.1 shows prevalence of each personality disorder reported by the NESARC study and the prevalence reported by Trull and his colleagues (Trull et al., 2010).

Table 6.1 Prevalence of personality disorders in NESARC: the role of functional impairment and distress

Personality disorder	NESARC results	Trull et al. (2010) results
Schizotypal PD	3.9%	0.6%
Schizoid PD	3.1%	0.6%
Paranoid PD	4.4%	1.9%
Histrionic PD	1.8%	0.3%
Antisocial PD	3.8%	3.8%
Borderline PD	5.9%	2.7%
Narcissistic PD	6.2%	1.0%
Obsessive-compulsive PD	7.9%	1.9%
Dependent PD	0.5%	0.3%
Avoidant PD	2.4%	1.2%

Studies uniformly document that PDs are associated with impairments in one or more areas of functioning. The Collaborative Longitudinal Personality Disorders Study (CLPS) reported that, compared to MDD, StPD and BPD were associated with a more than three-fold decreased chance of having only a high school education, and being less frequently employed; compared to MDD and OCPD, StPD and BPD were associated with lower vocational, social, and leisure functioning. Patients with AvPD fell between these two groups. After controlling for Axis I pathology and demographics, these results remained significant (Skodol et al., 2002).

The NESARC study reported that in Wave 1 PDs were associated with one of the following marital statuses: being divorced, separated, widowed, or never married. AvPD, DPD, SPD, PPD, and ASPD were associated with social impairment, even after controlling for age and Axis I pathology. Interestingly, there was no consistent relationship between OCPD and impairment. HPD was not associated with any impairment. In Wave 2, BPD correlated with unmarried status, lower income, and lower education level, after controlling for demographics and other psychiatric disorders. NPD was associated with not being married and with emotional role impairment; men but not women with NPD had global impairment. StPD was associated with unmarried status and global impairment (Grant et al., 2004, 2008; Penner-Goeke et al., 2015; Pulay et al., 2009; Stinson et al., 2008).

Results from the Children in the Community Study (CICS) indicated that all PDs were associated with social impairment and lower academic achievement after controlling for Axis I disorders. All PDs, and especially Cluster B PD, had poor quality of life at age 33 (Chen, Cohen, Crawford, Kasen, & Johnson, 2006; Crawford et al., 2008; Johnson et al., 2005).

Table 6.2 Requirements to validate psychiatric disorders

Requirement	Explanation
Clinical description	There is a set of clinical descriptors characteristic of the disorder
Laboratory studies	There are psychological, anatomical, chemical, biological, radiological etc. tests that are associated with the presence of the disorder
Delimitation from other disorders	There are criteria that differentiate the described disorder from other disorders
Follow-up studies	Follow-up studies demonstrate similarity of the longitudinal course of the disorder
Family studies	Family studies demonstrate familiality of the disorder – increased likelihood of "running in the family"

The National Comorbidity Survey Replication reported that all PDs had impairments in the following domains: basic role functioning, instrumental role functioning, and social role. However, after controlling for Axis I disorders, most of these associations became not significant, except the association between Cluster B PD and social role functioning as well as between any PD and impairment in productive role functioning, social role functioning, and instrumental role functioning (Lenzenweger, Lane, Loranger, & Kessler, 2007).

The longitudinal course of impairment in personality disorders was examined in three studies. In the CLPS, functional impairment remained mostly stable, with the exception of improvement in social functioning. Even after remission of BPD symptoms (85 percent), only 20 percent displayed also functional remission; others continued to display significant functional impairment (Gunderson et al. 2011; Skodol et al., 2005). The McLean Study of Adult Development (MSAD) reported that among BPD patients, functioning improved so that the proportion of patients with good functioning increased from 26 percent at the baseline to 56 percent six years later. At ten-year follow-up, BPD patients had trouble gaining better functioning or regaining better functioning if they lost it at some point. Vocational impairment was the most persistent (Zanarini, Frankenburg, Hennen, Reich, & Silk, 2005; Zanarini, Frankenburg, Reich, & Fitzmaurice, 2010). In the CICS, PD persistence was associated with persistence of the functional impairment; even when the PD remitted, a mild functional impairment still persisted (Skodol, Johnson, Cohen, Sneed, & Crawford, 2007).

Taken together these studies validate the association of personality disorders and functional impairment – one of the central characteristics of the disorder. One possibility is that psychological symptoms of personality disorders, including problems with emotional regulation, relationship with others, impulsivity or cognition impair one's ability to function. Another possibility is that functional impairment is yet another manifestation of personality disorders, not exclusively mediated by symptoms. Persistence of impairment despite improvement in symptoms supports the latter hypothesis. This suggests that treatments need to target functional impairment in personality disorders. This opens an avenue to the development of new treatments that help patients address various impairments in their functioning, in addition to their symptoms (for a similar suggestion, see Links, 1993).

Construct Validity of the Personality Disorders

The categorical model of personality disorders has the advantage of relying on the categorical conceptualization of other – syndromal – psychiatric disorders. Robins and Guze (1970) defined five requirements to establish construct validity of psychiatric disorders. Table 6.2 describes these requirements.

These research criteria have been the cornerstone of establishing the construct validity of any psychiatric disorders (Aboraya, France, Young, Curci, & Lepage, 2005). Thus, one of the strengths of the categorical model is the possibility of subjecting each personality disorder to such testing of construct validity using criteria spelled out by Robins and Guze (1970).

Tables 6.3–6.5 summarize empirical evidence relevant to construct validity of each personality disorder. Such PDs as schizotypal, antisocial, and borderline have the strongest level of evidence, while such PDs as schizoid, paranoid, histrionic, and dependent PD have the weakest level of evidence, partially because of the paucity of research, inadequate reliability of the diagnostic set, or use of non-clinical samples. In addition to improving methodology in these domains, future translational research needs to operationalize disorder-specific constructs and measure them in relevant disorders. Not only will such studies increase the concept validity of the disorders, but also, by testing experience-near constructs, they will inform clinical work.

Predictive Utility of Categorical Models

Predictive validity of categorical models was compared to dimensional models. Overall, initial studies show that

Table 6.3 General validity of Cluster A personality disorders

	Schizotypal PD	Schizoid PD	Paranoid PD
Clinical description	Excellent inter-rater and fair test/retest reliability of the diagnostic set (Zanarini et al., 2000)	Only fair reliability of the diagnostic set (Zanarini et al., 2000)	Good reliability of the diagnostic set (Zanarini et al., 2000)
Laboratory studies	Disturbances in: prepulse inhibition (Abel et al., 2004), eye tracking (Siever et al., 1989), P300 (Trestman et al., 1996), P50 suppression (Croft et al., 2001), catechol-o-methyltransferase gene (Minzenberg et al., 2006), proline dehydrogenase gene (Stefanis et al., 2007)	Not reported	Paranoid ideation was related to: limited hearing (Zimbardo et al., 1981), external attribution of failure (Bodner & Mikulincer, 1998)
Delimitation from other disorders	Clear differentiation from schizophrenia, schizoid or borderline PD (Chemerinski et al., 2013)	Clear differentiation from avoidant PD	Clear differentiation from other disorders
Follow-up studies	Slow improvement, though 17% develop schizophrenia (McGlashan et al., 2005; Fenton & McGlashan, 1989)	Stability of symptoms (Chanen et al., 2004)	Axis I comorbidity predicts worse outcome in PPD (Hong et al., 2005)
Family studies	Familiality was demonstrated (Siever et al., 1996)	Some (0.29) heritability (Torgersen et al., 2000)	Familiality was demonstrated (Triebwasser et al., 2013)
Conclusion	+++; StPD bears similarity to schizophrenia spectrum disorder – spectrum disorder	+	+

Note: 0: no evidence, +: modest evidence, ++: moderate evidence, +++: strong evidence

dimensional scores of personality outperform the categorical scores in predicting important clinical variables, including functional impairment. For example, incremental *concurrent validity* of the DSM-5 PD system was contrasted with the DSM-IV PD system in a recent cross-sectional study (Skodol, Bender, Gunderson, & Oldham, 2014). The predicted variables were psychosocial functioning, risk of self-harm, violence, criminal behaviors, optimal level of treatment intensity and prognosis. Compared to DSM-IV, DSM-5 showed stronger correlations with the predictors in 11 out of 12 comparisons. However, the level of personality functioning and total level of risk had a stronger association with DSM-IV, than DSM-5. The partial multiple correlations of controlling for the competitive version of DSM showed that DSM-5 was a stronger predictor of all assessed areas.

There also is evidence that points to predictive validity of categorical descriptions. Using data from the CLPS, Morey et al. compared *predictive utility* of the categorical model to that of the Five-Factor Model of Personality (FFM) and Schedule for Non-adaptive and Adaptive Personality (SNAP). These comparisons were tested for baseline functions and years 2 and 4 of the follow-up (Morey et al., 2007) and for years 6, 8, and 10 of the follow-up (Morey et al., 2012). Predictors were psychosocial functioning, work and social functioning, number of

concurrent Axis I diagnosis, number of medications, and depression scores. First, the results consistently demonstrated that dimensional scores outperformed categorical diagnoses of the personality disorders in predicting important areas of outcome. Second, an interesting pattern emerged when categorical diagnoses were transformed into dimensional scores through criteria counting. Results showed that the dimensionalized scores of the categorical PD diagnoses outperformed FFM in terms of prediction of longer term outcome. These findings suggest that categorical diagnoses capture more enduring aspects of the disorder.

Taken together, these results suggest that both categorical and dimensional models have merit and *predict different areas of functioning, including functional impairment.* Along with many other similar reports, these findings paved the way for adding the dimensional approach to personality disorders. Overall, the hybrid model that incorporates both the categorical and dimensional approaches has the strongest predictive validity.

Clinical Utility of a Categorical Model of Personality Disorders

Clinical utility is a pragmatic construct pertaining to the efficiency of use of the clinical diagnosis for six main

Table 6.4 General validity of Cluster B personality disorders

	Antisocial PD	Narcissistic PD	Borderline PD	Histrionic PD
Clinical description	Excellent reliability of the diagnostic set (Zanarini et al., 2000)	Good relability of the diagnostic set (Zanarini et al., 2000)	Good to excellent reliability of the diagnostic set (Zanarini et al., 2000)	Fair to good reliability of the diagnostic set (Zanarini et al., 2000)
Laboratory studies	Specific alleles of 5-HTT and MAO genes (Ficks & Waldman, 2014), abnormalities in prefrontal; cortex (Yang & Raine, 2009), reduced low frequency fluctuations in EEG (Liu et al., 2014)	Emotional empathy deficits (Baskin-Sommers et al., 2014), gray matter abnormalities in the right hemisphere (Schulze et al., 2013)	Abnormalities in amygdala (Ma et al., 2016), prefrontal cortex (Ma et al., 2016), polymorphisms of genes related to HPA axis (Martín-Blanco et al., 2015), decreased level of oxytocin (Bertsch et al., 2013)	Not reported
Delimitation from other disorders	Clear differentiation from other disorders	Clear differentiation from other disorders	Clear differentiation from other disorders (Gunderson et al., 2017)	Clear differentiation from other disorders
Follow-up studies	Relatively stable, with a slow and modest improvement being possible (Black 2015)	Gradual and slow improvement (Plakun, 1990; Ronningstam et al., 1995)	Gradual improvement in symptoms, less in functioning (Gunderson et al., 2011)	Gradual and slow improvement (Nestadt et al., 2010)
Family studies	Some heritability (Ma et al., 2016)	High heritability (0.71; Torgersen et al., 2012)	High heritability (0.70; Torgersen et al., 2000)	Not reported
Conclusion	+++	++	+++	+

Note: 0: no evidence, +: modest evidence, ++: moderate evidence, +++: strong evidence

Table 6.5 General validity of Cluster C personality disorders

	Dependent PD	Avoidant PD	Obsessive-compulsive PD
Clinical description	Fair to excellent reliability of the diagnostic set (Zanarini et al., 2000)	Good reliability of the diagnostic set (Zanarini et al., 2000)	Good reliability of the diagnostic set (Zanarini et al., 2000)
Laboratory studies	Correlates are anxiety, insecurity, fear of negative evaluations, loneliness (Bornstein et al., 2005)	Abnormalities in amygdala, prefrontal cortex and in connectivity between amygdala and insula (Koenigsberg et al., 2014)	Inconsistent findings (Diedrich & Voderholzer, 2015)
Delimitation from other disorders	Clear differentiation from other studies	Clear differentiation from other disorders	Clear differentiation from other disorders
Follow-up studies	No studies that documented outcome	Gradual improvement (Weinbrecht et al., 2013)	Gradual improvement (McGlashan et al., 2005)
Family studies	Some heritability (0.30; Torgersen et al., 2000)	Substantial heritability (0.64; Gjerde et al., 2012)	High heritability (0.78; Torgersen et al., 2000)
Conclusion	+	++	++

Note: 0: no evidence, +: modest evidence, ++: moderate evidence, +++: strong evidence purposes: (i) communication with the patient, (ii) communication with other professionals, (iii) comprehensiveness, (iv) descriptiveness, (v) ease of use, and (vi) utility for treatment planning (First et al., 2004; Morey, Skodol, & Oldham, 2014).

Communication with the Patient

Communication of personality diagnosis, tested for BPD patients (Rubovzki, Gunderson, & Weinberg, 2006), coupled with psychoeducation for the disorder (Zanarini & Frankenburg, 2008) help with destigmatization, relief from shame, and provision of hope. Effective personality disorder descriptions empathically convey various aspects of the person's functioning and explain his or her suffering and difficulties in meaningful ways. In doing so, they contribute to increased treatment alliance and treatment engagement.

Communication with Other Professionals

Effective communication with other professionals relies on simplicity, accuracy, and clarity of the communicated information. In other words, clinicians using categorical diagnoses uniformly understand what they denote and communicate. Use of categorical diagnoses allows quick and efficient documentation and communication of information related to typical clinical presentation and course as well as possible associated comorbidities and risks. For example, the diagnosis of borderline personality disorder captures patterns of emotional, behavioral, and interpersonal instability, possible risk of suicidal and other high risk behaviors, as well as the need to assess likely comorbid conditions – mood disorder, PTSD, and substance use disorders. Clinicians are likely to anticipate reactive and impulsive presentation and adjust their clinical style in service of more efficient clinical encounter. Similarly, the diagnosis of PPD will communicate to the clinician that the patient is likely to be suspicious, sensitive to injustice, and might hold grudges. Therefore, the clinician will be more likely to take a more patient and less confrontational approach.

Comprehensiveness

This aspect of utility pertains to the extent to which the disorder comprehensively describes all important personality problems of the individual. This includes domains of symptoms, but also possible areas of functional impairment – vocational, social, intimacy, leisure, self-care, etc.

Descriptiveness

Descriptiveness refers to the extent to which the disorder describes the individual's global personality. That includes adaptive and maladaptive aspects, strengths and weaknesses, motivations and goals. Descriptiveness also captures features that represent core characteristics of the person that represent who he or she is.

Ease of Use

This has to do with ease of applying diagnostic concepts to the individual. In other words, it refers to the extent to which symptoms of the disorder can be easily deduced from the assessment. Difficulty of use, for example, would require a great deal of inference. Ease of use would rely on very little or no inference.

Treatment Planning Utility

A categorical approach to diagnosis also helps with treatment planning, especially if published and even evidence-based treatments are available for the disorder. Disorder-specific treatments, treatment recommendations, and treatment principles were published for some personality disorders. For example, the diagnosis of BPD is likely to lead to recommendations of evidence-based treatments such as DBT, MBT, GPM, or TFP (for a review, see Gunderson, Weinberg, & Choi-Kain, 2013). For ASPD clinicians are likely to incorporate contingency management as an evidence-based approach (Salekin, 2002). For such conditions as NPD, where no evidence-based treatments are available, the available literature on its treatment relies mostly on clinical expert opinion. Thus, for NPD, the writings of Kernberg (1975), Kohut (1971), Ronningstam (2013), or Young et al. (1993) can inform the treatment. Beck's group published a CBT manual for personality disorder-specific treatment approaches (Beck et al., 2006), while Young developed disorder-specific treatments for BPD and NPD (Young et al., 1993). Principles for personality disorders treatments were published for Cluster A PDs (Williams, 2010), BPD (Gunderson et al., 2013), NPD (Ronningstam, 2013), HPD (Horowitz & Lerner, 2010), ASPD (Meloy & Yakeley, 2010), and Cluster C PDs (Stone, 2013; Svartberg & McCullough, 2010). In other words, the clinical utility of categorical diagnoses relies on many decades of clinical and empirical work on development, testing, validating, and dissemination of disorder-specific treatments. The unique value of categorical models stems from their ability to suggest disorder-specific treatments with demonstrated effectiveness.

The usefulness of the categorical approach was tested in a number of empirical studies with some mixed results. Morey et al. (2014) compared the clinical utility of categorical vs. alternative – dimensional trait – models of personality disorders in DSM-5 in a sample of 337 mental health clinicians. Clinicians evaluated the clinical utility of each model (categorical vs. dimensional) with respect to communication with patients and with other professionals, comprehensiveness, descriptiveness, ease of use, and utility for treatment planning. The categorical model was seen as more useful in terms of communication with other clinicians. In every other respect the alternative – dimensional – model was perceived as more useful. Crego and colleagues (Crego, Sleep, & Widiger 2016) assessed clinical utility of traits in capturing personality disorders.

Traits were taken from the Five-Factor Model as well as each iteration of the trait set development for DSM-5 (37 item set and 25 item set). Participants were psychologists surveyed through section 42. Clinicians regarded the final, 25 version of traits assigned to the following disorders less acceptable than the 37 trait version assignment: AvPD, NPD, OCPD, and SPD. Clinicians thought that FFM assignments were more acceptable than the final 25-item version assignments to the following PDs: AvPD, NPD, OCPD, DPD, and HPD. The authors concluded that there are "potentially important limitations with respect to the dimensional trait descriptions of respective PDs."

These studies reported *perceived* utility, rather than the utility of the *actual clinical use* of these different approaches and tests of the *predictive utility* of them. While predictive utility of the categorical diagnoses will be reviewed below, the testing of the relative utility of different approaches in actual clinical use – more valid than the test of the perceived utility – is waiting for further empirical investigations.

Limitations of the Categorical Model

Over time, the categorical model has accrued a number of criticisms (Morey, Benson, Busch, & Skodol, 2015; Widiger & Mullins-Sweatt, 2005). The four most commonly mentioned criticisms are (i) excessive diagnostic co-occurrence, (ii) phenomenological heterogeneity within the same diagnostic category, (iii) arbitrary diagnostic boundaries, and (iv) inadequate coverage.

Excessive Diagnostic Co-Occurrence

Comorbidity is a natural by-product of applying fixed diagnostic categories on the human complexity. In other words, the categorical diagnostic system anticipates comorbidity – co-occurrence of a number of disorders in the same individual. In fact, disorders are not distributed randomly as one disorder increases the likelihood of having yet another, and having two disorders increases the likelihood of having additional comorbid disorders, and so on (Kessler et al., 1994).

To ascertain true comorbidity, categorical diagnostic systems establish guidelines to rule out differential diagnoses. The process of ruling out the differential diagnoses reduces the number of overall diagnoses and, when conducted properly, establishes accurate diagnoses for the person.

While it is expected that a person might be diagnosed with more than one personality disorder, a number of research findings point out that the number of comorbid personality disorders seems high (Bornstein, 1998; Lilienfield, Waldman, & Israel, 1994; Oldham et al., 1992; Widiger & Sanderson, 1995). In other words, a sizable proportion of patients are being diagnosed with a large number of comorbid disorders. This could mean that the disorders themselves are not adequately capturing the complexity of the individual patients, thus raising a question of their construct validity.

This approach to the challenge of excessive diagnostic co-occurrence involves establishing hierarchical rules (Gunderson, 1992) that would guide the clinician to establish primacy of the personality disorders that are clinically most relevant. Such an approach is likely to make the actual diagnosis more clear and more useful for the purposes of understanding the patient and treatment planning. However, such an approach would not eliminate the actual number of the disorders. It will simply organize them in a more comprehensive picture.

From the standpoint of the categorical diagnostic picture, these findings can be interpreted as a sobering reminder that humans are complicated and so are their disorders. Our attempts to fit different individuals into pre-fixed categories will not account for their inherent complexity. Yet another aspect has to do with the purposes of diagnostic practice. Diagnoses cannot convey the full complexity of human nature and of the individual patient's subjectivity and uniqueness. This would be the purpose of a detailed clinical report or formulation in which the person's unique patterns can be described and spelled out. The purpose of the diagnostic process is to identify those patterns that are consistent, maladaptive, and causing substantial dysfunction and distress. Teasing apart which patterns are causing the dysfunction and distress is likely to take time and so the number of diagnosed disorders will likely diminish as the clinician gets to know the patient and follows him or her over a period of time.

Phenomenological Heterogeneity within the Same Diagnostic Category

The polythetic diagnostic approach taken by the categorical approach suggests that the patient can meet only a fraction of criteria out of the full list of criteria for the disorder. While clinically, such an approach allows for flexibility and accounts for variability of the clinical presentation, it also leads to yet another challenge – substantial heterogeneity in the possible clinical presentations. In fact, statistically speaking the multiplicity of clinical presentation for each personality disorder will be in the hundreds! Such an approach also allows two different patients to not share even one symptom. For instance, in order for a person to meet criteria for OCPD, he or she is required to meet four out of eight criteria, thus allowing for a possibility of two different patients meeting criteria for OCPD without sharing even a single common criterion. Similarly, it is theoretically possible for a patient to meet criteria for BPD without having the prototypical behaviors of affective instability, self-harm/suicidality, and unstable relationships.

One way to address the challenge of the heterogeneity of the clinical presentation is to identify necessary criteria for each disorder. For example, the Diagnostic Interview for Borderline Personality Disorder (Zanarini, Frankenburg, & Vujanovic, 2002) currently used for research purposes only requires the diagnostician-interview to ascertain presence of pathology in four sectors of BPD functioning: affective, behavioral, interpersonal, and cognitive. If a patient meets criteria for less than four sectors of pathology, the BPD diagnosis is not made. Such an approach increases internal consistency, but leaves a large number of patients that are diagnosed with BPD traits or PDNOS (not otherwise specified).

It is also the case that from the clinical perspective not all "types" of clinical presentation of a certain personality disorder that are possible theoretically, actually exist in clinical practice. Individual symptoms do not have an equal base rate and their probability of co-occurrence is contingent on each other. This fact reduces the number of these theoretically possible "types" that are plausibly in existence.

Finally, it is also important to make a distinction between signs and symptoms used to diagnose a condition and actual characteristics of individual patients. In medicine there are plenty of conditions that have a wide range of clinical presentations. However, the numerous presentations do not suggest differences in the actual disorder or differences in the intervention. Probably, the most well-known example is the clinical presentation of heart attacks. Symptoms of heart attacks can vary greatly from person to person and they differ significantly between men and women. Some individuals present with a prototypical picture of chest pain, profuse perspiration, and difficulty breathing, while others will complain only about shoulder or jaw pain. Still others – and many women belong to this category – present without significant symptoms. It is only men who have the "prototypical" clinical presentation, though the treatment for heart attacks will be the same irrespective of variations in clinical presentation. Many chronic conditions in medicine, such as diabetes, hypertension, fibromyalgia, or arthritis present differently from person to person. However, the clinical differences do not suggest a difference in the actual disorder or its treatment. With this in mind, can we hold personality disorder – yet another enduring condition – to the standard of phenomenological heterogeneity? In fact, diagnostic sets were designed to identify the disorder, not to convey everything we know about it. Thus heterogeneity is not posing a threat to conceptual integrity, but invites us to understand the disorder beyond its phenomenological presentation. In fact, in the example of the heart attack, the clinician will administer full treatment for the disorder, regardless of the variations in the clinical presentation and will be targeting the cause, not just the symptoms.

Arbitrary Diagnostic Boundaries

This challenge posed by a critique focused on arbitrary clinical boundaries has to do with two issues. First, the use of polythetic criteria requires a clinician to ascertain the presence of a certain number of criteria to establish a clinical diagnosis. However, the rationale for the cutoff or the number of required criteria, is not empirically established for most personality disorders, though it is suggested for practical use. The notable exceptions are guidelines for thresholds for BPD and StPD in DSM-III, which had an empirical rationale behind them (Spitzer, Endicott, & Gibbons, 1979). For BPD, a threshold of 5 out of 8 criteria was identified based on discrimination between clinically identified BPD patients (n = 234) from the non-BPD patients (n = 808). For StPD, a threshold of 4 out of 8 was identified based on discrimination between patients with the clinical diagnosis of "borderline schizophrenia" (n = 222) from controls (Spitzer et al., 1979). However, despite the revisions in the diagnostic criteria for the subsequent DSM edition, these thresholds remained the same.

The issue of the diagnostic threshold is further complicated by the taxonometric studies that showed that for all but StPD, PD symptoms have a continuous distribution (Edens, Marcus, & Morey, 2009; Edens, Marcus, & Ruiz, 2008; Everett & Linscott, 2015; Rothschild, Cleland, Haslam, & Zimmerman, 2003), thus defying the assumption of the discontinuity from the norm.

The lack of empirical basis for diagnostic thresholds is a common, yet at the same time, certainly an unfortunate occurrence in current diagnostic practice. Heterogeneity of the phenomenological presentation as well as debates as to what constitutes the disorder as opposed to the variability of personality traits complicate testing of this important question. Other features, related to core aspects of the disorder (such as false self or the concept of dependence on others because of the need for admiration) might be difficult to capture empirically, but are more likely to follow a more discontinuous distribution among disorders.

Morey and Skodol (2013) suggested a strategy well suited to diagnostic threshold for the dimensional approach that is similar to one used for the Diagnostic Interview for Borderline Personality Disorder (Zanarini et al., 2002). Accordingly, they identify in what areas the individual is impaired across identity, self-direction, empathy, and intimacy. They suggest requiring a certain number of areas of impairment for the person to meet criteria for a given disorder (e.g., the person must meet criteria for impairment in two out of four areas). They reported that such models have a high degree of sensitivity and specificity (Morey & Skodol, 2013), thus validating an approach to determining thresholds. This approach could be extended to the categorical model by requiring that the person meets criteria from a certain number of domains. For instance, BPD was divided into three sectors or factors – emotional dysregulation, interpersonal dysregulation, and behavioral dysregulation (Sanislow et al., 2002). Thus, it could be required that only those patients that have symptoms in all three sectors meet criteria for BPD. This would require factor division of all PDs. This approach has never been tested, but it has the potential to respond to the criticism of the diagnostic thresholds of PDs.

Inadequate Coverage

Inadequate coverage reflects the fact that there is a substantial number of individuals who meet general criteria for personality disorder, but not criteria for any one of the existing categories of individual personality disorders. In other words, currently described categorical personality diagnoses do not "explain" clinical presentations of a substantially large number of individuals.

Such clinical presentations are assigned the label of not otherwise specified (NOS), which, according to some researchers, is more prevalent than any other individual personality disorder and even any diagnostic category in DSM (Widiger & Mullins-Sweatt, 2005). For instance, a survey of practicing clinicians showed that 60.6 percent of the cases in their practices did not meet criteria for any specific personality disorder, despite meeting the general criteria for personality disorder (Westen & Arkowitz-Westen, 1998). Studies that diagnosed PD directly in the clinical samples reported a lower prevalence. For example, Wilberg and colleagues (Wilberg, Hummelen, Pedersen, & Karterud, 2008) reported that in their sample of patients with any personality disorders, 22 percent met criteria for PDNOS. This could suggest that the actual prevalence of the PDNOS is affected by the accuracy and the systematic nature of the diagnosis of personality disorders. This hypothesis has been confirmed by the finding that in structured interview studies PDNOS is the third most frequently used personality disorder diagnosis, whereas in non-structured interview studies, PDNOS is often the single most frequently used diagnosis (Verheul & Widiger, 2004). In their meta-analysis of 51 studies the absolute prevalence of PDNOS was between 8 and 13 percent (Verheul & Widiger, 2004), though when the absolute prevalence was corrected for the prevalence of all other personality disorders, these figures increased to 21–49 percent (Verheul & Widiger, 2004).

Possible solutions to the challenge of inadequate coverage depend on what we know about the category itself. Unfortunately, beyond reports of prevalence, little has been published regarding the actual composition of this category. While definition of the PDNOS category in terms of general PD criteria leads to higher prevalence, inclusions of the patients that are meeting subthreshold criteria for at least two PDs or having at least ten PD criteria result in lower prevalence rate and include a patient population with higher levels of distress and lower functioning (Wilberg et al., 2008).

When certain PDNOS patients meet subthreshold criteria for two or more PD, these patients can be better understood and treated in the context of existing knowledge of this combination of personality disorders. For patients that meet a wide variety of symptoms without meeting subthreshold criteria for any specific disorders a dimensional approach could be more appropriate (Widiger & Mullins-Sweatt, 2005). It has the power of describing the specific, unique, and atypical clinical presentation of the patients in this category.

DISCUSSION

Categorical models of personality disorders have a long history. These models were influenced by more general philosophical trends of reducing personality to basic components. In this way they antedated the dimensional models of today. However, categorical models were fertile ground for deepening our understanding of individual patients and translating ideographic knowledge into generalized clinical categories. The personality disorders were defined to identify and treat these conditions because of their clinical significance in understanding the patients, explaining atypical clinical presentation and the course of other disorders as well as accounting for risks of suicide, violence, and functional impairment.

Validation of these disorders has made visible progress and supported validity of some of the disorders. Validation of others requires further empirical effort. Studies have validated the relationship between personality disorders and functional impairment, which seems to persist even when the symptoms of the personality disorders remit. The clinical utility of the categorical model has received mixed support, though it has a strong contribution to treatment selection, since most evidence-based treatments are validated in the context of the categorical model. An additional value of the categorical model is its focus on description of separate disorders with specific experiences and processes associated with each one of the disorders. This approach promotes understanding of the individual patient and the use of the initial diagnosis as a starting point to promote further collaboration and alliance building.

Recently, dimensional models are being increasingly suggested as alternatives and in some cases as full replacement for the categorical models. Research demonstrates the value of the dimensional models, although the best prediction is usually provided by a hybrid model that combines categorical and dimensional models. Two models seem to predict somewhat different aspects of the personality disorders and of the functioning. The dimensional model could supplement the categorical model, especially in atypical cases or to characterize PD NOS cases. Moving forward, more research is needed to support further adaptation of the categorical model and to better understand its role in the classification and treatment of personality disorders.

REFERENCES

Abel, K., Jolley, S., Hemsley, D., & Geyer, M. (2004). The influence of schizotypy traits on prepulse inhibition in young healthy controls. *Journal of Psychopharmacology, 18*, 181–188.

Aboraya, A., France, C., Young, J., Curci, K., & Lepage, J. (2005). The validity of the psychiatric diagnosis revisited. *Psychiatry, 2*, 48–55.

Abraham, K. (1927). *Selected Papers of Karl Abraham*. London: Hogarth Press.

Akhtar, S. (1992). *Broken Structures: Severe Personality Disorders and Their Treatment*. New York: Aronson.

Baskin-Sommers, A., Kruzermark, E., & Ronningstam, E. F. (2014). Empathy in narcissistic personality disorder: From clinical and empirical perspectives. *Personality Disorders, 5*, 323–333.

Beck, A. T., Freeman, A., Davis, D. D., & Associates (2006). *Cognitive Therapy of Personality Disorders* (2nd ed.). New York: Guilford Press.

Bernstein, D. P., Iscan, C., Maser, J., & Board of Directors of the Association for Research of Personality Disorders, International Society for Study of Personality Disorders (2007). Opinions of personality disorder experts regarding the DSM-IV personality disorders classification system. *Journal of Personality Disorders, 21*, 536–551.

Bertsch, K., Schmidingerm, I., Neuman, I. D., & Herpertz, S. C. (2013). Reduced plasma cortisol levels in female patients with borderline personality disorder. *Hormones and Behavior, 63*, 424–429.

Black, D. W. (2015). The natural history of antisocial personality disorder. *Canadian Journal of Psychiatry, 60*, 309–314.

Bodner, E., & Mikulincer, M. (1998). Learned helplessness and occurrence of depressive-like and paranoid-like responses: The role of attentional focus. *Journal of Personality and Social Psychology, 74*, 1019–1023.

Bornstein, R. F. (1993). *The Dependent Personality*. New York: Guilford Press.

Bornstein, R. F. (1998). Reconceptualizing personality disorder diagnosis in the DSM-V: The discriminant validity challenge. *Clinical Psychology, 5*, 333–343.

Bornstein, R. F., Ng, H. M., Gallagher, H. R., Kloss, D. M., & Regier, N. G. (2005). Contrasting effects of self-schema priming on lexical decisions and interpersonal Stroop task performance: Evidence for a cognitive/interactionist model of interpersonal dependency. *Journal of Personality, 73*, 731–761.

Chanen, A. M., Jackson, H. J., McGorry, P. D., Allot, K. A., Clarkson, V., & Yuen, H. P. (2004). Two-year stability of personality disorders in older adolescent outpatients. *Journal of Personality Disorders, 18*, 526–541.

Chemerinski, E., Triebwasser, J., Roussos, P., & Siever, L. J. (2013). Schizotypal personality disorder. *Journal of Personality Disorders, 27*, 652–679.

Chen, H., Cohen, P., Crawford, T. N., Kasen, S., & Johnson, J. G. (2006). Relative impact of young adult personality disorders on subsequent quality of life: Findings of a community-based longitudinal study. *Journal of Personality Disorders, 20*, 510–523.

Cloninger, C. R., Svrakic, D. M., & Przybeck, T. R. (1993). A psychobiological model of temperament and character. *Archives of General Psychiatry, 50*, 975–990.

Costa, P. T., & McCrae, R. R. (1985). *The NEO Personality Inventory Manual*. Odessa, FL: Psychological Assessment Resources.

Costa, P. T., & Widiger, T. (Eds.) (1993). *Personality Disorders and the Five-Factor Model of Personality*. Washington, DC: American Psychological Association.

Crawford, T. N., Cohen, P., First, M. B., Skodol, A. E., Johnson, J. G., & Kasen, S. (2008). Comorbid Axis I and Axis II disorders in early adolescence: Outcomes 20 years later. *Archives of General Psychiatry, 65*, 641–648.

Crego, C., Sleep, C. E., & Widiger, T. A. (2016). Clinicians' judgments of the clinical utility of personality disorder trait descriptions. *Journal of Nervous and Mental Disease, 204*, 49–56.

Croft, R., Lee, A., Bertolot, J., & Gruzelier, J. (2001). Association of P50 suppression and desensitization with perceptual and cognitive features of "unreality" in schizotypy. *Biological Psychiatry, 50*, 441–446.

Diedrich, A., & Voderholzer, U. (2015). Obsessive-compulsive personality disorder: A current review. *Current Psychiatry Reports, 17*, 1–10.

Edens, J. F., Marcus, D. K., & Morey, L. C. (2009). Paranoid personality has a dimensional latent structure: Taxometric analyses of community and clinical samples. *Journal of Abnormal Psychology, 118*, 545–553.

Edens, J. F., Marcus, D. K., & Ruiz, M. A. (2008). Taxometric analyses of borderline personality features in a large-scale male and female offender sample. *Journal of Abnormal Psychology, 117*, 705–711.

Everett, K. V., & Linscott, R. J. (2015). Dimensionality vs. taxonicity of schizotypy: Some new data and challenges ahead. *Schizophrenia Bulletin, 41*(Suppl. 2), S465–S474.

Fairbairn, W. R. D. (1952). *Psychoanalytic Studies of Personality*. London: Tavistock.

Fenton, W., & McGlashan, T. (1989). Risk of schizophrenia in character disorder patients. *American Journal of Psychiatry, 146*, 1280–1284.

Ferenczi, S. (1938). *Thalassa: A Theory of Genitality*. New York: Norton.

Ficks, C. A., & Waldman, I. D. (2014). Candidate genes for aggression and antisocial behavior: A meta-analysis of association studies of the 5HTTLPR and MAOA-uVNTR. *Behavioral Genetics, 44*, 427–444.

First, M. B., Pincus, H. A., Levine, J. B., Williams, J. B. W., Ustun, B., & Peele, R. (2004). Clinical utility as a criterion for revisiting psychiatric diagnoses. *American Journal of Psychiatry, 161*, 946–954.

Freud, S. (1908). Character and anal erotism. In *Collected Papers* (*Vol. 2*). London: Hogarth Press.

Gjerde, L. C., Czajkowski, N., Røysamb, E., Ørstavik, R. E., Knudsen, G. P., Østby, K., ... Reichborn-Kjennerud, T. (2012). The heritability of avoidant and dependent personality disorder assessed by personal interview and questionnaire. *Acta Psychiatrica Scandinavica, 126*, 448–457.

Grant, B. F., Chou, S. P., Goldstein, R. B., Huang, B., Stinson, F. S., Saha, T. D., ... Ruan, W. J. (2008). Prevalence, correlates, disability, and comorbidity of DSM-IV borderline personality disorder: Results from the wave 2 National Epidemiologic Survey of Alcohol and Related Conditions. *Journal of Clinical Psychiatry, 69*, 533–545.

Grant, B. F., Hasin, D. S., Stinson, F. S., Dawson, D. A., Chou, S. P., Ruan, W. J., & Pickering, R. P. (2004). Prevalence, correlates, and disability of personality disorders in the United States: Results from the National Epidemiologic Survey of Alcohol and Related Disorders. *Journal of Clinical Psychiatry, 65*, 948–958.

Grant, B. F., Moore, T. C., Shepard, J., & Kaplan, K. (2003). *Source and Accuracy Statement: Wave 1 National Epidemiological Survey on Alcohol and Related Conditions (NESARC)*. Bethesda, MD: National Institute on Alcohol Abuse and Alcoholism.

Gunderson, J. G. (1984). *Borderline Personality Disorder*. Washington, DC: American Psychiatric Press.

Gunderson, J. G. (1992). Diagnostic controversies. In A. Tasman & M. B. Riba (Eds.), *American Psychiatric Press Review of Psychiatry* (Vol. 11, pp. 9–24). Washington, DC: American Psychiatric Press.

Gunderson, J. G., Herpertz, S., Skodol, A. E., Torgersen, S., & Zanarini, M. C. (2017). Borderline personality disorder. *Nature Reviews Disease Primers, 4*, 1–20.

Gunderson, J. G., & Ronningstam, E. F. (2001). Differentiating antisocial and narcissistic personality disorder. *Journal of Personality Disorders, 15*, 103–109.

Gunderson, J. G., Stout, R. L., McGlashan, T. H., Shea, M. T., Morey, L. C., Grilo, C. M., ... Skodol, A. E. (2011). Ten-year course of borderline personality disorder: Psychopathology and function from the Collaborative Longitudinal Personality Disorders Study. *Archives of General Psychiatry, 68*, 827–837.

Gunderson, J. G., Weinberg, I., & Choi-Kain, L. (2013). Borderline personality disorder. In G. O. Gabbard (Ed.), *Gabbard's Treatments of Psychiatric Disorders* (DSM-5 ed.). Washington, DC: American Psychiatric Publishing.

Guntrip, H. (1968). *Schizoid Phenomena, Object Relations, and the Self*. London: Karnac.

Hirt, E. (1902). *Die temperamente*. Leipzig: Barth.

Holt, R. R. (1970). Yet another look at clinical and statistical prediction: Or, is clinical psychology worthwhile? *American Psychologist, 25*, 337–349.

Hong, J. P., Samuels, J., Bienvenu, O. J., Hsu, F. C., Eaton, W. W., & Costa, P. T., Jr. (2005). The longitudinal relationship between personality disorder dimensions and global functioning in a community-residing population. *Psychological Medicine, 35*, 891–895.

Horney, K. (1937). *The Neurotic Personality of Our Time*. New York: Norton.

Horwitz, M. J. & Lerner, U. (2010). Treatment of histrionic personality disorder. In J. F. Clarkin, P. Fonagy, & G. Gabbard (Eds.), *Psychodynamic Psychotherapy for Personality Disorders* (pp. 289–310). Washington, DC: American Psychiatric Publishing.

Johnson, J. G., First, M. B., Cohen, P., Skodol, A. E., Kasen, S., & Brook, J. S. (2005). Adverse outcomes associated with personality disorders not otherwise specified in a community sample. *American Journal of Psychiatry, 162*, 1926–1932.

Kernberg, O. F. (1975). *Borderline Conditions and Pathological Narcissism*. New York: Jason Aronson.

Kessler, R. C., McGonagle, K. A., Zhao, S., Nelson, C. B., Hughes, M., Eshleman, S., ... Kendler, K. S. (1994). Lifetime and 12-month prevalence of DSM-III-R psychiatric disorders in the United States: Results from the National Comorbidity Survey. *Archives of General Psychiatry, 51*, 8–19.

Klein, M. H. (1948). *Contributions to Psychoanalysis, 1921–1945*. London: Hogarth Press.

Koenigsberg, H. W., Denny, B. T., Fan, J., Liu, X., Guerreri, S., Mayson, S. J., ... Siever, L. J. (2014). The neural correlates of anomalous habituation to negative emotional pictures in borderline and avoidant personality disorder patients. *American Journal of Psychiatry, 171*, 82–90.

Kohut, H. (1971). *The Analysis of the Self*. New York: International Universities Press.

Kraepelin, E. (1919). *Dementia Praecox and Paraphrenia*. Edinburgh: Livingstone.

Kretchmer, E. (1925). *Korperbau und character*. Berlin: Springer Verlag.

Lenzenweger, M. F., Lane, M. C., Loranger, A. W., & Kessler, R. C. (2007). DSM-IV personality disorders in the National Comorbidity Survey Replication. *British Journal of Psychiatry, 62*, 533–564.

Lilienfield, S. O., Waldman, I. D., & Israel, A. C. (1994). A critical examination of the issue of the term "comorbidity" in psychopathology research. *Clinical Psychology, 1*, 71–83.

Links, P. S. (1993). Psychiatric rehabilitation model for borderline personality disorder. *Canadian Journal of Psychiatry, 38*(Suppl. 1), S35–S38.

Liu, H., Liao, J., Jiang, W., & Wang, W. (2014). Changes in low-frequency fluctuations in patients with antisocial personality disorder revealed by resting-state functional MRI. *PLoS ONE, 9*, e89790.

Livesley, W. J., West, M., & Tanney, A. (1986). Historical comment on DSM-III schizoid and avoidant personality disorders. *American Journal of Psychiatry, 142*, 1344–1346.

Ma, G., Fan, H., Shen, C., & Wang, W. (2016). Genetic and neuroimaging features of personality disorders: State of the art. *Neuroscience Bulletin, 32*, 286–306.

Martín-Blanco, A., Ferrer, M., Soler, J., Arranz, M. J., Vega, D., Calvo, N., ... Pascual, J. C. (2015). The role of hypothalamus-pituitary-adrenal genes and childhood trauma in borderline personality disorder. *European Archives of Psychiatry and Clinical Neuroscience, 266*, 307–316.

McGlashan, T. H., Grilo, C. M., Sanislow, C. A., Ralevski, E., Morey, L. C., Gunderson, J. G., ... Pagano, M. (2005). Two-year prevalence and stability of individual DSM-IV criteria for schizotypal, borderline, avoidant, and obsessive-compulsive personality disorders: Toward a hybrid model of Axis II disorders. *American Journal of Psychiatry, 162*, 883–889.

Meloy, J. R., & Yakeley, J. (2010). Psychodynamic treatment of antisocial personality disorder. In J. F. Clarkin, P. Fonagy, & G. Gabbard (Eds.), *Psychodynamic Psychotherapy for Personality Disorders* (pp. 311–336). Washington, DC: American Psychiatric Publishing.

Minzenberg, M., Xu, K., & Mitrolopou, V. (2006). Catechol-O-methyltransferase Val158Met genotype variation is associated with prefrontal-dependent task performance in schizotypal personality disorder patients and comparison groups. *Psychiatric Genetics, 16*, 117–124.

Morey, L. C., Benson, K. T., Busch, A. J., & Skodol, A. E. (2015). Personality disorders in DSM-5: Emerging research on the alternative model. *Current Psychiatric Reports, 17*, 1–9.

Morey, L. C., Hopwood, C. J., Gunderson, J. G., Shea M. T., Skodol, A. E., Grilo, C. M., ... McGlashan, T. H. (2007). A comparison of personality disorder models. *Psychological Medicine, 37*, 983–994.

Morey, L. C., Hopwood, C. J., Markowitz, J. C., Gunderson, J. G., Grilo, C. M., McGlashan, T. H., ... Skodol, A. E. (2012). Comparisons of alternative models of personality disorders, II: 6-, 8-, and 10-year follow-up. *Psychological Medicine, 42*, 1705–1713.

Morey, L. C., & Skodol, A. E. (2013). Convergence between DSM-IV-TR and DSM-V diagnostic models for personality disorders: Evaluation of strategies for establishing diagnostic thresholds. *Journal of Psychiatric Practice, 19*, 179–193.

Morey, L. C., Skodol, A. E., & Oldham, J. M. (2014). Clinician judgment of clinical utility: A comparison of DSM-IV-TR personality disorders and the alternative model for DSM-V personality disorders. *Journal of Abnormal Psychology*, *123*, 398–405.

Nestadt, G., Samuels, J. F., Bienvenu, O. J., Reti I. M., Costa, P., Eaton, W. W., & Bandeen-Roche, K. (2010). The stability of the DSM personality disorders over ten to eighteen years. *Journal of Psychiatric Research*, *44*, 1–7.

Oldham, J. M., Skodol, A. E., Kellman, H. D., Hyler, S. E., Rosnick, L., & Davies, M. (1992). Diagnosis of DSM-III-R personality disorders by two structured interviews: Patterns of comorbidity. *American Journal of Psychiatry*, *149*, 213–220.

Penner-Goeke, K., Henrikson, C. A., Chateau, D., Latimer, E., Sareen, J., & Katz, L. Y. (2015). Reduction in quality of life associated with common mental disorders: Results from a national representative sample. *Journal of Clinical Psychiatry*, *76*, 1506–1512.

Plakun, E. M. (1990). Narcissistic personality disorder: A validity study and comparison to borderline personality disorder. *Psychiatric Clinics of North America*, *12*, 603–620.

Pokorny, A. D. (1983). Prediction of suicide in psychiatric patients: *Report of a prospective study*. Archives of General Psychiatry, *40*, 249–257.

Pulay, A. J., Stinson, F. S., Dawson, D. A., Goldstein, R. B., Chou, S. P., Huang, B., ... Grant, B. F. (2009). Prevalence, correlates, disability, and comorbidity of DSM-IV schizotypal personality disorder: Results from the wave 2 National Epidemiologic Survey of Alcohol and Related Conditions. *Primary Care Companion to the Journal of Clinical Psychiatry*, *11*, 53–67.

Rappaport, D. (1961). *The Collected Papers of David Rappaport*. New York: Basic Books.

Reich, W. (1933). *Character Analysis*. New York: Farrar & Rinehart.

Robins, E., & Guze, S. B. (1970). Establishment of diagnostic validity in psychiatric illness: Its application to schizophrenia. *American Journal of Psychiatry*, *126*, 983–987.

Ronningstam, E. (2011). Narcissistic personality disorder in DSM-V: In support of retaining a significant diagnosis. *Journal of Personality Disorders*, *25*, 248–259.

Ronningstam, E. F. (2013). The update on narcissistic personality disorder. *Current Opinion in Psychiatry*, *26*, 102–106.

Ronningstam, E. F., Gunderson, J. G., & Lyons, M. (1995). Changes in pathological narcissism. *American Journal of Psychiatry*, *152*, 253–257.

Rothschild, L., Cleland, C., Haslam, N., & Zimmerman, M. (2003). A taxometric study of borderline personality disorder. *Journal of Abnormal Psychology*, *112*, 657–666.

Rubovzki, G., Gunderson, J. G., & Weinberg, I. (2006). *Patients' acceptance and emotional reactions to disclosure of borderline personality disorder diagnosis*. Paper presented at the APA Conference, Toronto, Canada.

Salekin, R. T. (2002). Psychopathy and therapeutic pessimism: Clinical lore or clinical reality? *Clinical Psychology Review*, *22*, 79–112.

Sanislow, C. A., Grilo, C. M., Morey, L. C., Bender, D. S., Skodol, A. E., Gunderson, J. G., ... McGlashan, T. H. (2002). Confirmatory factor analysis of DSM-IV criteria for borderline personality disorder: Findings from the collaborative longitudinal personality disorders study. *American Journal of Psychiatry*, *159*, 284–290.

Schneider, K. (1923). *Psychopathic Personalities* (9th ed.). London: Cassell.

Schulze, L., Dziobek, I., Vater, A., Heekeren, H. R., Bajbouj, M., Renneberg, B., ... Roepke, S. (2013). Grey matter abnormalities in patients with narcissistic personality disorder. *Journal of Psychiatric Research*, *47*, 1363–1369.

Siever, L., Amin, F., Coccaro, E., Trestman, R. Silverman, J., & Hovath, T. (1996). Schizotypal personality disorder. In T. Widiger, A. Frances, & H. Pincus (Eds.). *DSM-IV Sourcebook* (*vol. 2*, pp. 685–701). Washington, DC: American Psychiatric Association.

Siever, L. J., Coursey, R. D., Alterman, I. S., Zahn, T., Brody, L., Bernad, P., ... Murphy, D. L. (1989). Clinical, psychophysiological, and neurological characteristics of volunteers with impaired smooth pursuit eye movements. *Biological Psychiatry*, *26*, 35–51.

Siever, L. J., & Davis, K. L. (1991). A psychobiological perspective on the personality disorders. *American Journal of Psychiatry*, *148*, 1647–1658.,

Skodol, A. E. (2018). Impact of personality pathology on psychosocial functioning. *Current Opinion in Psychology*, *21*, 33–38.

Skodol, A. E., Bender, D. S., Gunderson, J. G., & Oldham, J. M. (2014). Personality disorders. In R. E. Hales, S. C. Yudofsky, & L. Roberts (Eds.), *American Psychiatric Publishing Textbook of Psychiatry* (6th ed., pp. 851–894). Washington, DC: American Psychiatric Publishing.

Skodol, A. E., Gunderson, J. G., McGlashan, T. H., Dyck, I. R., Stout, R. L., Bender, D. S., ... Oldham, J. M. (2002). Functional impairment in patients with schizotypal, borderline, avoidant, or obsessive-compulsive personality disorder. *American Journal of Psychiatry*, *159*, 276–283.

Skodol, A. E., Johnson, J. G., Cohen, P., Sneed, J. R., & Crawford, T. N. (2007). Personality disorder and impaired functioning from adolescence to adulthood. *British Journal of Psychiatry*, *190*, 415–420.

Skodol, A. E., Oldham, J. E., Bender, D. S, Dyck, I. R., Stout, R. L., Morey, L. C., ... Gunderson, J. G. (2005). Dimensional representations of DSM-IV personality disorders: Relationship to functional impairment. *American Journal of Psychiatry*, *162*, 1919–1925.

Spitzer, R. L., Endicott, J., & Gibbons, M. (1979). Crossing the border into the borderline personality and borderline schizophrenia: T*he development of criteria*. Archives of General Psychiatry, *36*, 17–24.

Stefanis, N. C., Trikalinos, T. A., Avramopoulos, D., Smyrnis, N., Evdokimidis, I., Ntzani, E. E., ... Stefanis, C. N. (2007). Impact of schizophrenia candidate genes on schizotypy and cognitive endophenotypes at the population level. *Biological Psychiatry*, *62*, 784–792.

Stinson, F. S., Dawson, D. A., Goldstein, R. B., Chou, S. P., Huang, B., Smith, S. M., ... Grant, B. F. (2008). Prevalence, correlates, disability, and comorbidity of DSM-IV narcissistic personality disorder: Results from the Wave 2 National Epidemiologic Survey on Alcohol and Related Conditions. *Journal of Clinical Psychiatry*, *69*, 1033–1045.

Stone, M. (1980). *The Borderline Syndromes*. New York: McGraw-Hill.

Stone, M. H. (2013). Paranoid, schizotypal, and schizoid personality disorders. In G. O. Gabbard (Ed.), *Gabbard's Treatments of Psychiatric Disorders* (DSM-5 ed.). Washington, DC: American Psychiatric Publishing.

Svartberg, M., & McCullough, L. (2010). Cluster C personality disorders: Prevalence, phenomenology, treatment effects, and principles of treatment. In J. F. Clarkin, P. Fonagy, & G. Gabbard (Eds.), *Psychodynamic Psychotherapy for Personality Disorders* (pp. 337–368). Washington, DC: American Psychiatric Publishing.

Torgersen, S., Lygren, S., Oien, P. A., Skre, I., Onstad, S., Edvardsen, J., ... Kringlen, E. (2000). A twin study of personality disorders. *Comprehensive Psychiatry, 41*, 416–425.

Torgersen, S., Myers, J., Reichborn-Kjennerud, T., Roysamb, E., Kubarych, T. S., & Kendler, K. S. (2012). The heritability of Cluster B personality disorder assessed both by personal interview and questionnaire. *Journal of Personality Disorders, 26*, 848–866.

Trestman, R. L., Horvath, T., Kalus, O., Peterson, A. E., Coccaro, E., Mitropoulou, V., ... Siever, L. J. (1996). Event-related potentials in schizotypal personality disorder. *Journal of Neuropsychiatry and Clinical Neuroscience, 8*, 33–40.

Triebwasser, J., Chemerinski, E., Roussos, P., & Siever, L.J. (2013). Paranoid personality disorder. *Journal of Personality Disorders, 27*, 795–805.

Trull, T. J., Jahng, S., Tomko, R. L., Wood, P. K. & Sher, K. J. (2010). Revised NESARC personality disorder diagnoses: Gender, prevalence, and comorbidity with substance use disorders. *Journal of Personality Disorders, 24*, 412–426.

Verheul, R., & Widiger, T. A. (2004). A meta-analysis of the prevalence and usage of the personality disorder not otherwise specified (PDNOS) diagnosis. *Journal of Personality Disorders, 18*, 309–319.

Weinbrecht, A., Schulze, L., Boetther, J., & Renneberg, B. (2013). Avoidant personality disorder. *Current Psychiatric Reports, 18*, 1–8.

Westen, D., & Arkowitz-Westen, L. (1998). Limitations of Axis II in diagnosing personality pathology in clinical practice. *American Journal of Psychiatry, 155*, 1767–1771.

Widiger, T. A., & Mullins-Sweatt, S. N. (2005). Categorical and dimensional models of personality disorders. In J. M. Oldham, A. E. Skodol, & D. S. Bender (Eds.), *The American Psychiatric Publishing* Textbook of Personality Disorders (pp. 35–53) Washington, DC: American Psychiatric Publishing.

Widiger, T. A., & Sanderson, C. J. (1995). Towards a dimensional model of personality disorders in DSM-IV and DSM-V. In W. J.

Livesley (Ed.), *The DSM-IV Personality Disorders* (pp. 380–394). New York: Guilford Press.

Wilberg, T., Hummelen, B., Pedersen, G., & Karterud, S. (2008). A study of patients with personality disorder not otherwise specified. *Comprehensive Psychiatry, 49*, 460–468.

Williams, P. (2010). Psychotherapeutic treatment of Cluster A personality disorders. In J. F. Clarkin, P. Fonagy, & G. Gabbard (Eds.), *Psychodynamic Psychotherapy for Personality Disorders* (pp. 165–186). Washington, DC: American Psychiatric Publishing.

Winnicott, D. W. (1965). *The Maturational Process and the Facilitating Environment*. New York: International Universities Press.

Yang, Y., & Raine, A. (2009). Prefrontal structural and functional brain imaging findings in antisocial, violent, and psychopathic individuals: A meta-analysis. *Psychiatric Research, 17*, 81–88.

Young, J. E., Klosko, J. S., & Weishaar, M. E. (1993). *Schema Therapy: A Practitioner's Guide*. New York: Guilford Press.

Zanarini, M. C., & Frankenburg, F. R. (2008). A preliminary, randomized trial of psychoeducation for women with borderline personality disorder. *Journal of Personality Disorders, 22*, 284–290.

Zanarini, M. C., Frankenburg, F. R., Hennen, J. J., Reich, D. B., & Silk, K. R. (2005). Psychosocial functioning of borderline patients and Axis II comparison subjects followed prospectively for six years. *Journal of Personality Disorders, 19*, 19–29.

Zanarini, M. C., Frankenburg, F. R., Reich, D. B., & Fitzmaurice, G. (2010). The 10-year course of psychosocial functioning among patients with borderline personality disorder and Axis II comparison subjects. *Acta Psychiatrica Scandinavica, 122*, 103–109.

Zanarini, M. C., Frankenburg, F. R., & Vujanovic, A. A. (2002). Inter-rater and test-retest reliability of the diagnostic interview for borderlines. *Journal of Personality Disorders, 16*, 270–276.

Zanarini, M. C., Skodol, A. E., Bender, D. S., Dolan, R., Sanislow, C. A., Schaefer, E., ... Gunderson, J. G. (2000). The Collaborative Longitudinal Personality Disorders Study: Reliability of Axis I and II diagnoses. *Journal of Personality Disorders, 14*, 291–299.

Zimbardo, P. G., Andersen, S. M., & Kabat, L. G. (1981). Induced hearing deficit generates experimental paranoia. *Science, 212*, 1529–1531.

6a Good Taxonomy Can Address Classification Challenges in Personality Pathology by Providing Informative Priors That Balance Information Compression and Fidelity: Commentary on Categorical Models of Personality Disorders

NATHAN T. HALL, ALISON M. SCHREIBER, AND MICHAEL N. HALLQUIST

INTRODUCTION

Weinberg documents the history of categorical models of personality disorders (PDs) and presents a model based largely on the *Diagnostic and Statistical Manual of Mental Disorders* (DSM; American Psychiatric Association, 2013). He further argues that this model has notable benefits including the utility of disorder-specific concepts, which may aid in case conceptualization and treatment. The author reviews ubiquitous criticisms of the DSM model such as excessive comorbidity (Widiger & Trull, 2007) that have fueled support for dimensional and hybrid accounts of personality pathology. Indeed, despite the remarkable complexity of psychopathology, there is also structure in the patterns of symptom expression[1] both within an individual and at the population level (Krueger et al., 2018). Building on this overview, we focus specifically on how taxonomic science can help clinicians and scientists navigate the often overwhelming complexity of conceptualizing key features of an individual.

With the recent proliferation of taxonomies of psychopathology – DSM-5 Section II versus III, HiTOP (Kotov et al., 2017), RDoC (Insel et al., 2010), and other dimensional models such as the SNAP (Simms & Clark, 2006) – we believe that now is an important time to reflect on the goals of classification (cf. Blashfield & Draguns, 1976). We propose that any good[2] taxonomy of personality pathology compresses clinical data in order to balance representational simplicity and information fidelity. To explicate this point, we draw an analogy to digital photography, which faces a similar tradeoff between file size and image fidelity.

We note that one challenge to any taxonomy is the risk of reifying the underlying distinctions it makes (Hyman, 2010). In this regard, the DSM's categorical model assumes that diagnoses are "natural kinds" despite empirical evidence that distinctions among PDs are often blurry (Widiger & Trull, 2007). Crucially, the problem of reification can lead to a "taxonomy by authority" that puts up epistemic blinders that likely impede scientific progress (Markon, 2013). Thus, we suggest treating taxonomic constructs as *open concepts* (Zachar, Turkheimer, & Shaffner, in press) that are modifiable in light of new information.

HOW ARE CLINICAL PSYCHOLOGISTS LIKE DIGITAL PHOTOGRAPHERS?

To set the stage for conceptualizing taxonomies of personality pathology, meet Addison, a digital photographer who was recently hired to produce a web exposé on bunnies for a pet website. Addison just finished a photoshoot and has selected 60 of the best bunny pictures. The challenge is that the design manager insists that each picture should be no more than 200 kilobytes so that the web page loads faster and does not tax server bandwidth. Addison's original files are 30 megabytes each and contain rich visual detail, but they are 150 times larger than the acceptable size. To strike a balance between file size and image quality, she applies a "lossy" JPEG compression algorithm. In lossy compression, the information in an image file is compressed into fewer bits by searching for statistical dependencies and removing details that do not unduly harm the fidelity of the picture. For example, subtle changes in hue from one pixel to the next could be collapsed into the same hue. By applying more severe compression, Addison can achieve smaller file sizes, but at the expense of image quality. For a visual depiction of such compression effects, see https://michaelhallquist.github .io/PD_information_compression_fidelity/datacompression_ rabbit_color_web.jpg. The link to the extended version can be found here: https://michaelhallquist.github.io/ PD_information_compression_fidelity/

Next, meet Devon, a first-year graduate student in clinical psychology conducting his first intake assessment. The client presents with a wide array of problems including binge drinking, explosive arguments with romantic

---

[1] We note that there remains an active debate about whether symptoms or underlying mechanisms (biological, cognitive, genetic, etc.) should be the primary focus of taxonomic efforts. The central thesis of this commentary is agnostic on this point, but it is likely that both symptoms and mechanisms will be important to moving forward.

[2] We use the term "good" throughout the commentary to signify positive attributes of a taxonomic system, while acknowledging that any taxonomy provides an imperfect roadmap where information is necessarily lost.

partners, suicidality, frequent self-injury, and intermittent feelings of sadness and anxiety. The client also behaves flirtatiously toward Devon and says that she likes to flirt with people, but that this has led to unwanted sexual attention and even assault. Needless to say, Devon feels overwhelmed by the volume and complexity of clinical information and is now faced with writing an intake report to guide treatment planning. Like Addison, Devon is faced with the problem of how to capture the richness of the client's experience while compressing the complexity into a simpler case formulation such as a diagnosis or personality profile. We propose that a good taxonomy can aid in this endeavor, but that without such guidance, Devon's confusion is not due to ineptitude but to natural limitations in the representational capacity of all humans. The crux of classification problems in personality pathology is, which "compression algorithm" will capture the most clinical information while not overwhelming Devon with details that could lead to suboptimal decisions influenced by cognitive heuristics?

INFORMATION OVERLOAD AND THE NEED TO COMPRESS

When provided with a large quantity of information, humans can suffer from information overload, often performing worse than simple "actuarial" decision rules (Dawes, Faust, & Meehl, 1989). Instead, decisions are often better when clinicians rely on a few highly important pieces of information (Faust, 2012). In the face of uncertainty and complexity, humans use a number of mental heuristics that simplify decision-making, which can lead to biased or idiosyncratic decisions (Tversky & Kahneman, 1974). In fact, in a complex value-based decision-making task, we found that individuals who selectively maintained a few high-value options while forgetting low-value alternatives exhibited better task performance (Hallquist & Dombrovski, 2019). In the case of psychiatric taxonomy, basic work on the limits of human representational capacity (Ma, Husain, & Bays, 2014) suggests that a good taxonomy should prune away or deemphasize peripheral information while retaining the most informative features. Thus, we propose that *information compression* and *information fidelity* are two axiomatic[3] principles of any good taxonomy.

The principle of information compression is that a taxonomy should leverage the regularities in psychopathology features to emphasize dominant sources of covariation. Compression schemes may be hierarchical, as in the case of dimensional models of normal and abnormal personality, where broad distinctions such as internalizing and externalizing can be subdivided into finer

features. Although compression is an important conceptual principle, it also has formal ties to multivariate approaches such as factor analysis and cluster analysis. In factor models, a large correlation matrix is thought to reflect a smaller number of latent dimensions that explain most of the covariation. In this way, if correlations among 80 features of psychopathology can be captured by eight latent factors, we have compressed the data tenfold, substantially simplifying the problem.

The principle of information fidelity is that a taxonomy should maintain essential features that reasonably approximate the structure of an individual or the population. Conceptually, if a taxonomy has high information fidelity, measuring a patient in terms of its features alone, one should be able to infer more detailed aspects of the clinical presentation. For example, if a patient's medical chart contains the diagnoses of borderline personality disorder (BPD) and generalized anxiety disorder, could a clinician use this information to predict the patient's level of antagonism? Returning to factor analysis, if the compression scheme has high information fidelity, we could back-project from scores on the eight factors to estimated responses on all 80 features with reasonable accuracy. Although we necessarily sacrifice detail when we compress the features of psychopathology, a scheme with high information fidelity can still approximate these details.

We believe that attending to the dialectical relationship between information compression and information fidelity (akin to the fit-parsimony tradeoff in statistics) opens a productive space for professionals to consider which taxonomy ("compression algorithm") accomplishes the most with the fewest features. Importantly, the appropriate level of compression may depend on the scientific or clinical question and the evidence of incremental utility for using a less compressed (i.e., more detailed) over a more compressed (i.e., less detailed) representation.

JUDGING TAXONOMIES OF PERSONALITY PATHOLOGY: HOW DO WE MOVE FORWARD?

When choosing among psychiatric taxonomies, we are often faced with the challenging problem of comparing systems that are qualitatively different. For example, the DSM-5's Section II model of PDs compresses 79 symptoms into 10 clinical syndromes, which can be thought of as binary variables, whereas the SNAP compresses 375 items into 12 trait and 3 temperament dimensions. In Devon's case, applying these taxonomies may give rather different clinical impressions.

Using the DSM-5 Section II categorical model, Devon would rate the presence of 79 symptoms and identify whether any sum of symptoms exceeds the stated diagnostic threshold for each PD diagnosis. This approach would likely lead to a diagnosis of BPD, given the presence of unstable relationships, labile affect, and chronic suicidality. Furthermore, the BPD diagnosis would greatly

---

[3] We do not use the terms "axiom" or "axiomatic" in their strict mathematical sense. Instead, we use them to emphasize necessary conditions of a good taxonomy, which we hope can help adjudicate among alternative models.

compress the clinical complexities, framing the patient's presentation in terms of "borderlinearity."[4] As Weinberg notes, diagnostic prototypes can promote further thinking about more specific distinctions among individuals with the same diagnosis, such as the importance of interpersonal hypersensitivity in BPD. Measured by the SNAP, flirtatious behavior would be represented as heightened exhibitionism, whereas the rest of patient's presentation would be described by mistrust, aggression, self-harm, and disinhibition.

Even though this example is intentionally simplified for illustration (i.e., the problems listed in the example are already compressed), the point is that the features that enter into case conceptualization and scientific thinking vary across taxonomies. This highlights the tension between a taxonomy that is reasonably comprehensive (less compressed) and one that is simple, potentially at the expense of explanatory power. Dimensional models of personality disorders have grown up in the tradition of personality psychology, which seeks to describe a wide array of individual differences. This is an admirable approach, but there are also considerable cognitive challenges to interpreting multidimensional trait profiles. For example, the Personality Inventory for DSM-5 (PID-5; Krueger, Derringer, Markon, Watson, & Skodol, 2012) contains five domains and 25 facets, representing a rich, but potentially complex, system for describing personality pathology. By contrast, the categorical diagnosis approach of DSM-5 Section II is probably too simplistic and narrow.

How, then, can we find the "Goldilocks" just-right balance between information compression and fidelity? Part of the answer depends on a judgment of quality, which is difficult to define and open to debate. For Devon's patient, would expanding the feature space beyond "borderlinearity" alone help to mitigate overcompression? Conversely, could the profile from the SNAP be further compressed – for example, by only focusing on extreme elevations such as mistrustfulness and self-harm – to make the complex trait profile more clinically actionable? Regardless, the compression inherent to any taxonomy should preserve the clinical picture, rather than yielding an erroneous or scrambled representation that obscures structure.

An incremental taxonomic science should also pursue an empirical path that compares the quantitative alignment of alternative models to psychopathology data. Using variants of latent variable models, personality pathology researchers can compare the relative evidence for categorical, dimensional, and hybrid taxonomies using information-theoretic fit indices (Markon & Krueger, 2006). These criteria formalize the intuition that more complex models necessarily fit better, but at the expense of parsimony – echoing the tensions between fidelity and compression articulated above. Importantly,

quantitatively comparing taxonomic model evidence depends on the features (i.e., variables) to be compressed being identical between models. That is, to meaningfully compare classification systems, the inputs need to be the same even if the representations differ (e.g., 5 traits versus 10 categories).

In addition, to overcome debatable distinctions about quality, one clear target for advancing taxonomies of personality pathology is to compare their clinical and predictive utility. A taxonomy that provides effective compression may reduce information overload, mitigating the impact of cognitive heuristics and freeing up cognitive resources to make more nuanced judgments. For example, can Devon conceptualize the client's binge drinking, argumentativeness, and suicidality as reflecting a core problem with disinhibition? If so, this could inform treatment strategies that address the shared liability. Furthermore, such a simplification could provide Devon mental space to think about how high SNAP exhibitionism may support a cycle in which romantic infidelity, in conjunction with disinhibition, leads to explosive arguments.

Stepping out to the nomothetic level, studies of predictive utility can also advance taxonomic science. If we can agree on a set of clinical and psychological outcomes that are important to predict (e.g., suicidality), then we can determine which signals are useful to retain and which can be safely compressed. For example, Eaton and colleagues (2013) found that internalizing pathology (a broad latent dimension) outperformed any DSM PD in predicting future internalizing pathology, suicide attempts, and other health-related outcomes.

THE GOAL OF TAXONOMY IS TO PROVIDE INFORMATIVE PRIORS

We propose that a good taxonomy should arm Devon with critical prior information. This is an idea borrowed from Bayesian decision theory, in which decision-makers bring prior information to bear on current decisions, thus potentially reducing uncertainty and focusing attention on key variables. Priors in psychiatric description should provide an empirically based roadmap to make predictions when faced with uncertain information, rather than promoting reification or encouraging overreliance on clinical experience.

In treatment settings, clinicians often operate with noisy information such as brief psychiatric interviews. We propose that a good taxonomy should provide prior information about what features are important to focus on when working with limited data. Indeed, personality pathology is often overlooked in clinical assessments because key features are not systematically assessed or emphasized (e.g., Ruggero, Zimmerman, Chelminski, & Young, 2010). Furthermore, population norms for personality pathology assessments can provide crucial information about the rarity of a trait elevation in a given patient. Such norms would help Devon to incorporate base rates into

---

[4] An evocative phrase borrowed from Aidan G. C. Wright.

clinical judgment, a classic example of how prior information can lead to more accurate decisions (Meehl & Rosen, 1955). Importantly, priors necessarily bias predictions, but taxonomic science should strive to provide priors that bias clinicians toward good decisions (Hertwig & Grüne-Yanoff, 2017).

By emphasizing information compression and information fidelity as two "axiomatic" principles of a good taxonomy, we hope to promote further discussion among advocates of different models of personality pathology. If disparate taxonomies can be judged on similar criteria and compared using quantitative methods that address the parsimony-fit tradeoff, this will motivate incremental progress in the classification of personality pathology. Ultimately, a taxonomy that provides empirically supported informative priors can maximize the system's utility in both clinical science and practice.

REFERENCES

American Psychiatric Association. (2013). *Diagnostic and Statistical Manual of Mental Disorders* (5th ed.). Arlington, VA: American Psychiatric Publishing.

Blashfield, R. K., & Draguns, J. G. (1976). Toward a taxonomy of psychopathology: The purpose of psychiatric classification. *British Journal of Psychiatry*, *129*(6), 574–583.

Dawes, R. M., Faust, D., & Meehl, P. E. (1989). Clinical versus actuarial judgment. *Science*, *243*(4899), 1668–1674.

Eaton, N. R., Krueger, R. F., Keyes, K. M., Wall, M., Hasin, D. S., Markon, K. E., . . . Grant, B. F. (2013). The structure and predictive validity of the internalizing disorders. *Journal of Abnormal Psychology*, *122*(1), 86–92.

Faust, D. (2012). Decision research can increase the accuracy of clinical judgment and thereby improve patient care. In S. O. Lilienfeld & W. T. O'Donohue (Eds.), *The Great Ideas of Clinical Science* (pp. 49–76). New York: Routledge.

Hallquist, M. N., & Dombrovski, A. Y. (2019). Selective maintenance of value information helps resolve the exploration/exploitation dilemma. *Cognition*, *183*, 226–243.

Hertwig, R., & Grüne-Yanoff, T. (2017). Nudging and boosting: Steering or empowering good decisions. *Perspectives on Psychological Science*, *12*(6), 973–986.

Hyman, S. E. (2010). The diagnosis of mental disorders: The problem of reification. *Annual Review of Clinical Psychology*, *6*, 155–179.

Insel, T., Cuthbert, B., Garvey, M., Heinssen, R., Pine, D. S., Quinn, K., . . . Wang, P. (2010). Research Domain Criteria (RDoC): Toward a new classification framework for research on mental disorders. *American Journal of Psychiatry*, *167*(7), 748–751.

Kotov, R., Krueger, R. F., Watson, D., Achenbach, T. M., Althoff, R. R., Bagby, R. M., . . . Zimmerman, M. (2017). The Hierarchical Taxonomy of Psychopathology (HiTOP): A dimensional alternative to traditional nosologies. *Journal of Abnormal Psychology*, *126*(4), 454–477.

Krueger, R. F., Derringer, J., Markon, K. E., Watson, D., & Skodol, A. E. (2012). Initial construction of a maladaptive personality trait model and inventory for DSM-5. *Psychological Medicine*, *42*(9), 1879–1890.

Krueger, R. F., Kotov, R., Watson, D., Forbes, M. K., Eaton, N. R., Ruggero, C. J., . . . Zimmermann, J. (2018). Progress in achieving quantitative classification of psychopathology. *World Psychiatry*, *17*(3), 282–293.

Ma, W. J., Husain, M., & Bays, P. M. (2014). Changing concepts of working memory. *Nature Neuroscience*, *17*(3), 347–356.

Markon, K. E. (2013). Epistemological pluralism and scientific development: An argument against authoritative nosologies. *Journal of Personality Disorders*, *27*(5), 554–579.

Markon, K. E., & Krueger, R. F. (2006). Information-theoretic latent distribution modeling: Distinguishing discrete and continuous latent variable models. *Psychological Methods*, *11*(3), 228–243.

Meehl, P. E., & Rosen, A. (1955). Antecedent probability and the efficiency of psychometric signs, patterns, or cutting scores. *Psychological Bulletin*, *52*(3), 194–216.

Ruggero, C. J., Zimmerman, M., Chelminski, I., & Young, D. (2010). Borderline personality disorder and the misdiagnosis of bipolar disorder. *Journal of Psychiatric Research*, *44*(6), 405–408.

Simms, L. J., & Clark, L. A. (2006). The Schedule for Nonadaptive and Adaptive Personality (SNAP): A dimensional measure of traits relevant to personality and personality pathology. In S. Strack (Ed.), *Differentiating Normal and Abnormal Personality* (2nd ed., pp. 431–450). New York: Springer.

Tversky, A., & Kahneman, D. (1974). Judgment under uncertainty: Heuristics and biases. *Science*, *185*(4157), 1124–1131.

Widiger, T. A., & Trull, T. J. (2007). Plate tectonics in the classification of personality disorder: Shifting to a dimensional model. *American Psychologist*, *62*(2), 71–83.

Zachar, P., Turkheimer, E., & Shaffner, K. (in press). Defining and redefining phenotypes: Operational definitions as open concepts. In A. G. C. Wright & M. N. Hallquist (Eds.), *Handbook of Research Methods in Clinical Psychology*. Cambridge University Press.

6b A Hierarchical, Dimensional Approach Can Advance Personality Disorder Research: Commentary on Categorical Models of Personality Disorders

CHRISTOPHER C. CONWAY

The categorical model of personality disorder (PD) diagnosis, despite its familiarity, may not be the optimal way to represent personality pathology. Weinberg (this volume) enumerates its principal defects: rampant comorbidity, within-diagnosis heterogeneity, poor coverage of personality problems encountered in the clinic, and arbitrary boundaries between disorders and between disorder and wellness.

For many researchers, these problems signal a pressing need to develop evidence-based rubrics that can supplement, and eventually supplant, DSM and ICD as alternate routes to research, assessment, and treatment of PD (e.g., Hopwood et al., 2018). One dimensional system is now gaining traction in the research literature as a viable alternative to the categorical approach: the Hierarchical Taxonomy of Psychopathology (HiTOP; Kotov et al., 2017). In this chapter, I will present evidence that supports HiTOP as a PD research framework.

SKETCHING THE HiTOP MODEL

HiTOP is based on quantitative modeling of the co-occurrence of signs and symptoms of mental illness. This research tradition dates back to factor analytic studies of youth psychopathology symptoms. Achenbach (1966) and others showed that anxiety, depressive, and somatic complaints clustered together to form an internalizing spectrum, whereas disruptive and inattentive behaviors cohered around an externalizing spectrum. Decades later, Krueger and coworkers (e.g., Krueger, Caspi, Moffitt, & Silva, 1998) followed this same quantitative strategy to uncover latent internalizing and externalizing dimensions accounting for diagnostic comorbidity in adult samples.

These latent dimensions subsequently replicated across diverse demographic groups, developmental stages, and regions of the world. Antisocial and borderline PD features often were involved in these modeling efforts, but clinical disorder symptoms predominated in the early stages. More recently, this sort of quantitative modeling research routinely has incorporated a wider array of mental health problems, including the full complement of PD conditions (e.g., Markon, 2010).

The dimensions emerging from these structural models coalesced into the HiTOP framework depicted in Figure 6.b.1. One key property is that the model is hierarchically oriented. Thus, PD can be conceptualized and assessed at various levels of abstraction, depending on the research objective. At the apex, a general factor of psychopathology is presumed to cut across all expressions of mental illness. At the spectrum level, the familiar internalizing and externalizing dimensions are joined by somatoform, thought disorder (reflecting liability to schizoid, schizotypal, and paranoid PDs), and detachment (reflecting avoidant, dependent, histrionic [inversely], and schizoid PDs). At a lower level still, spectra divide into subfactors, such as antisocial behavior, which is a marker of antisocial PD. The DSM PD entities are located at the syndrome level, which, in turn, subsumes symptom components and maladaptive traits at the most granular level of the hierarchy.

The superspectrum, spectrum, and subfactor levels account for the comorbidity commonly observed across PDs. For instance, the well-known overlap of borderline PD with depressive and trauma-related disorders is explained by shared dependence on the distress subfactor (Figure 6.b.1). Meanwhile, the comorbidity between borderline and other Cluster B PDs is reflected in a common placement in the antagonistic externalizing spectrum. In latent variable modeling terms, borderline PD *cross-loads on* (or is saturated by) both internalizing and externalizing dimensions (e.g., Eaton et al., 2011). The heterogeneous expression of borderline PD is captured by various maladaptive traits represented at the base of the hierarchy. The borderline-relevant traits are scattered across several spectra (e.g., identity problems and affective lability under internalizing; impatient urgency and aggression under disinhibited externalizing). In sum, the HiTOP model allows researchers to conceptualize borderline and other PDs in terms of basic units (e.g., maladaptive traits and symptom components); broader, cross-cutting liabilities (e.g., internalizing and antagonistic externalizing spectra); or both.

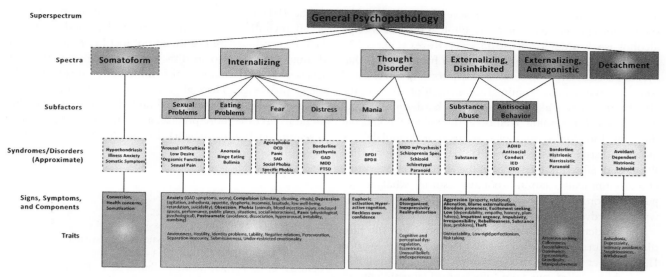

Figure 6.b.1 Hierarchical Taxonomy of Psychopathology (HiTOP) consortium working model. Constructs higher in the figure are broader and more general, whereas constructs lower in the figure are narrower and more specific. Dashed lines denote provisional elements requiring further study. At the lowest level of the hierarchy (i.e., traits and symptom components), for heuristic purposes, conceptually related signs and symptoms (e.g., Phobia) are indicated in bold, with specific manifestations indicated in parentheses. Abbreviations–ADHD: attention-deficit/hyperactivity disorder; GAD: generalized anxiety disorder; IED: intermittent explosive disorder; MDD: major depressive disorder; OCD: obsessive-compulsive disorder; ODD: oppositional defiant disorder; SAD: separation anxiety disorder; PD: personality disorder; PTSD: posttraumatic stress disorder.

HiTOP AS A RESEARCH FRAMEWORK FOR PERSONALITY PROBLEMS

For most PD researchers, HiTOP is a new and potentially foreign taxonomy of personality problems. This unfamiliarity *could* render it inaccessible to most mental health professionals, unless investigators are able to clearly show its practical utility. And I argue that HiTOP does indeed confer benefits, relative to DSM, that extend beyond its quantitative, empirical approach to nosology. Specifically, the dimensions composing HiTOP are useful research targets (Conway et al., 2019). They can illuminate the precise pathways that connect personality problems with putative causes and consequences. They can also make PD research more efficient.

To illustrate obstacles (to utility and efficiency) the categorical system creates for researchers, let's take the case of borderline PD. Borderline PD generally has poor *discriminant validity*. While it is related to plenty of negative outcomes (e.g., hospitalization, romantic dysfunction), so are many other PDs. This observation is problematic because borderline PD rarely presents in isolation, and instead often co-occurs with other PDs including antisocial and schizotypal PDs.

Researchers are therefore faced with the dilemma of trying to disentangle the putative effects of borderline versus other PDs to uncover its unique causes and correlates. One solution is to recruit a "pure" sample of patients with only a borderline diagnosis, but this decision implies collecting an extremely unrepresentative sample, given the laundry list of conditions typically accompanying

borderline in clinically referred samples. Another approach is to collect a representative sample of people with borderline PD who have comorbid diagnoses. The collection of representative data has its merits. At the same time, this strategy also is limited by the fact that statistical associations between borderline PD and outcomes potentially are confounded by co-occurring conditions and thereby undercuts inferences about the unique role of borderline PD. This state of affairs has led, in my view, to borderline PD failing several of Robins and Guze's (1970) standards for disorder validation. That is, there are no laboratory tests (or other criteria) that reliably distinguish borderline from all other PDs and clinical disorders. While Weinberg's (this volume) Table 6.4 summarizes some abnormalities observed in borderline PD (e.g., amygdala hyperreactivity, hypothalamic-pituitary-adrenal axis dysfunction), these characteristics are not specific (i.e., pathognomonic) to that condition. This is the trend for the full gamut of PD entities.

Research based on the HiTOP framework bypasses this dilemma. There is no expectation that syndromes have specific connections with psychopathology causes, correlates, or treatments. In fact, the bulk of the evidence to date suggests that the most potent presumed causes of PD (e.g., child maltreatment, molecular genetic risks) operate at higher-order levels (e.g., superspectrum, spectrum; cf. Conway et al., 2019). For instance, in the National Epidemiological Study of Alcohol and Related Conditions, child abuse was not related directly to antisocial PD, but rather to an overarching externalizing spectrum theorized to represent the commonality of several PDs (e.g., antisocial, borderline, histrionic) and clinical disorders (e.g., alcohol use disorder, drug use disorder; Keyes et al., 2012).

Another way to describe this research framework is that the supposed connection between a syndrome of interest and some covariate can be examined across multiple levels of the HiTOP hierarchy. Take the example of borderline PD and psychosocial functioning. Weinberg (this volume) points out that role functioning in social, occupational, and leisure arenas is disrupted across many PDs, but possibly borderline PD most of all. With the benefit of the HiTOP lens, researchers can empirically examine – not just assume – what part (or parts) of borderline PD account for this close relationship with social dysfunction (cf. Hopwood et al., 2011).

The borderline syndrome itself, comprised of the nine diagnostic criteria codified in DSM-IV and DSM-5 Section II, may be at the heart of functioning deficits. Alternately, social dysfunction may be a fully transdiagnostic characteristic, in which case its strongest connection would be with the general factor of psychopathology. Incidentally, borderline patients have been found to have especially high standing on this general factor (Sharp et al., 2015). Another possibility is that social dysfunction is best explained at the spectrum level, perhaps by variation in disinhibited externalizing. Finally, symptom components or maladaptive traits could be the most potent predictors of dysfunction. Most clinicians would attest that traits like risk-taking, hostility, and withdrawal often contribute to diminished performance in work and social spheres. This research process, which acknowledges the hierarchical organization of personality problems, can more precisely identify the etiological and clinical pathways to disorder, impairment, and treatment response.

SUMMARY AND CONCLUSION

The categorical model of PD diagnosis continues to guide most clinical and research training worldwide. Weinberg (this volume) illustrates that categorical PDs are the basis for most research activity – contributing to the appearance of strong validity – and can be useful summary constructs in clinical communication. Yet a voluminous research literature over the past 50 years has shed light on undeniable problems with this approach for PD research, assessment, and treatment across mental health disciplines. An international consortium of mental health professionals has assembled to study the HiTOP as an evidence-based alternative to the DSM and ICD rubrics (for more detail, see Kotov et al., 2017; Krueger et al., 2018).

I underlined here that HiTOP potentially has value not just for PD nosology, but also for PD research. There are clear motivations for a new perspective on PD research. Few diagnostic categories are routinely studied, discriminant validity evidence is scarce, and categories are so heterogeneous that the exact mechanisms linking PDs to their causes and consequences are difficult to establish.

The HiTOP system offers an alternate approach that could revitalize PD research. Under this model, mental health correlates are examined not just in relation to syndromal PD, but also to dimensions at higher and lower levels of breadth in an empirical hierarchy of psychopathology processes. Through this sort of reformulation of research questions, etiological and clinical models of PD stand to become more precise, accurate, and efficient, but research on this framework in the PD literature is just beginning.

REFERENCES

Achenbach, T. M. (1966). The classification of children's psychiatric symptoms: A factor-analytic study. *Psychological Monographs: General and Applied, 80*, 1–37.

Conway, C. C., Forbes, M. K., Forbush, K. T., Fried, E. I., Hallquist, M. N., Kotov, R., ... Eaton, N. R. (2019). A hierarchical taxonomy of psychopathology can transform mental health research. *Perspectives on Psychological Science, 14*, 419–436.

Eaton, N. R., Krueger, R. F., Keyes, K. M., Skodol, A. E., Markon, K. E., Grant, B. F., & Hasin, D. S. (2011). Borderline personality disorder co-morbidity: Relationship to the internalizing–externalizing structure of common mental disorders. *Psychological Medicine, 41*, 1041–1050.

Hopwood, C. J., Kotov, R., Krueger, R. F., Watson, D., Widiger, T. A., Althoff, R. R., ... Bornovalova, M. A. (2018). The time has come for dimensional personality disorder diagnosis. *Personality and Mental Health, 12*, 82–86.

Hopwood, C. J., Malone, J. C., Ansell, E. B., Sanislow, C. A., Grilo, C. M., McGlashan, T. H., ... Gunderson, J. G. (2011). Personality assessment in DSM-5: Empirical support for rating severity, style, and traits. *Journal of Personality Disorders, 25*, 305–320.

Keyes, K. M., Eaton, N. R., Krueger, R. F., McLaughlin, K. A., Wall, M. M., Grant, B. F., & Hasin, D. S. (2012). Childhood maltreatment and the structure of common psychiatric disorders. *British Journal of Psychiatry, 200*, 107–115.

Kotov, R., Krueger, R. F., Watson, D., Achenbach, T. M., Althoff, R. R., Bagby, R. M., ... Zimmerman, M. (2017). The Hierarchical Taxonomy of Psychopathology (HiTOP): A dimensional alternative to traditional nosologies. *Journal of Abnormal Psychology, 126*, 454–477.

Krueger, R. F., Caspi, A., Moffitt, T. E., & Silva, P. A. (1998). The structure and stability of common mental disorders (DSM-III-R): A longitudinal-epidemiological study. *Journal of Abnormal Psychology, 107*, 216–227.

Krueger, R. F., Kotov, R., Watson, D., Forbes, M. K., Eaton, N. R., Ruggero, C. J., ... Zimmermann, J. (2018). Progress in achieving quantitative classification of psychopathology. *World Psychiatry, 17*, 282–293.

Markon, K. E. (2010). Modeling psychopathology structure: A symptom-level analysis of Axis I and II disorders. *Psychological Medicine, 40*, 273–288.

Robins, E., & Guze, S. B. (1970). Establishment of diagnostic validity in psychiatric illness: Its application to schizophrenia. *American Journal of Psychiatry, 126*, 983–987.

Sharp, C., Wright, A. G., Fowler, J. C., Frueh, B. C., Allen, J. G., Oldham, J., & Clark, L. A. (2015). The structure of personality pathology: Both general ('g') and specific ('s') factors? *Journal of Abnormal Psychology, 124*, 387–398.

6c

The Search for Clinically Meaningful Dimensions Requires a Clinical Theory: Author Rejoinder to Commentaries on Categorical Models of Personality Disorders

IGOR WEINBERG

First, I would like to thank Conway (this volume) and Hallquist and colleagues (this volume) for their thoughtful commentaries. Hallquist and colleagues introduce two principles – the principle of information compression and the principle of information fidelity. The balance between the principles creates a "space" that optimally conceptualizes the psychopathological phenomena, such as personality pathology. Such conceptualization has a pragmatic nature of informing clinical thinking and intervention.

Conway introduces a comprehensive model – an alternative to the categorical one – that arguably better aligns with the dimensional nature of markers of pathology and with putative risk factors. The model incorporates five dimensions: internalizing, externalizing, somatoform, thought disorder, and detachment. The argument for the dimensionality of markers associated with personality disorders (lack of pathognomonic signs) is by no means unique to personality disorders. No condition in psychiatry is associated with such markers either. The search for "X-ray" tests for psychiatric disorder still continues and is a valuable avenue of study, but no objective pathognomonic signs have been identified yet. Similarly, putative etiological risk factors related to personality disorders are not specific and many people with such factors do not go on to develop personality disorders. This is not unlike other conditions in psychiatry. Many people experience traumatic events, but only a minority goes on to develop posttraumatic stress disorder. Loss is a tragic and ubiquitous part of human existence, but only some people develop a major depressive episode in response to it. In medicine, many people suffer from hypertension, but only a fraction of them suffers a heart attack. This fact, however, never questions the validity of the heart attack as a medical diagnosis.

The appeal of the dimensional model is in its capacity to represent or cover all aspects of the personality pathology. This is consistent with the principle of information fidelity, described by Hallquist and colleagues (this volume). The richness of data introduces the possibility of mathematic modeling and identification of implicit dimensions that lend themselves to concise theoretical model of pathology. Such models have statistical strength and the capacity to explain variability of the psychopathology. In fact, compared to the binary nature of categorical diagnoses, dimensional data are a better statistical predictor. This fact, at least in part, explains why dimensional models sometimes outperform the categorical models on some dimensions of prediction. However, the appeal of abstract dimensions has to be considered against the loss of data resulting from transformation of data and blurring the boundaries between clinically distinct phenomena that statistically load on the same dimension.

From a categorical perspective, the transformation required in a dimensional perspective moves description away from the clinical complexity and the experience-near phenomena into the realm of abstract, theoretical constructs. Statistical techniques that unify variables into one dimension are based on the assumption that variables that correlate with each other are conceptually related. In such a way conceptually unrelated phenomena that correlate with each other might load on the same dimension, creating an illusion of common factors. For instance, distancing is common to schizoid, avoidant, and narcissistic personality disorders. However, the nature of distancing in each disorder is different. Statistically speaking, this invites identification of moderating variables.

Both approaches have their strengths and weaknesses. As reviewed earlier in the chapter, both models have their utility in predicting slightly different aspects of functioning (Morey et al., 2007, 2012). The heated debate as to which of the models has the greatest advantages reminds one of the rift between the Ptolemaic model (Earth-centric system) of the solar system and the model proposed by Copernicus (Solar-centric system). As the history of the personality disorders shows, early categorical models implicitly used dimensions, suggesting that there is a room for a creative integration. In other words, personality disorder models are somewhat akin to the definition of light in physics, which behaves as both particle and wave. Initially, Newton published his famous treatise on optics describing light as particles (Newton, 1988). Even though he cited numerous and quite convincing experiments to support his theory, it was later replaced by a combined one.

Considering the strengths of both, categorical models are more sensitive to unique and specific characteristics of the disorder, while the dimensional models typically are concerned with identification of dimensions that are common to a number of disorders. One way to combine these models is to define dimensions clinically and conceptually, as opposed to statistically. The challenge is to identify dimensions that are close to the clinical experience. For example, the currently proposed alternative model with dimensions of interpersonal relations and self-definition is one such definition. Categorical disorders can be conceptualized in terms of interaction between these universal dimensions and disorder-specific moderators. For example, dependence on others is related to a sense of helplessness and the self-image of being a helpless child in people with dependent personality disorder, the need for self-validation from admiring others in narcissistic personality disorder, and fear of abandonment in patients with borderline personality disorder.

Another challenge is to account for the presence of seemingly contradictory traits that constitute part and parcel of personality disorders. Patients with narcissistic personality disorder present with both grandiose and inferior self-image and some patients with schizoid personality disorder present with aloofness and secret longing for connection. Therefore, rather than thinking in terms of dimensions that connect polar opposites (e.g., superior/inferior, connected/disconnected, dependent/independent), it is important to conceptualize those as orthogonal dimensions. With such conceptualizing, categorical disorders can be organized around these dimensions, moderated by disorder-specific variables. A personality disorder not otherwise specified (NOS) can "fill in the space" around them. Not surprisingly, PDs NOS can be more meaningfully understood in terms of their dimensional representation (Widiger & Mullins-Sweatt, 2005).

The search for clinically meaningful dimensions requires a clinical theory. Statistical analyses are not able to give meaning to clinical phenomena. They can only organize data in a systematic way. One such example of theory is description of personality pathology using the object relation model (Caligor, Kernberg, Clarkin, & Yeomans, 2018). Such an approach incorporates dimensional and categorical models and it incorporates meaningful clinically derived dimensions. This is a promising example, demonstrating the importance of integration of clinical observation with a theory of personality. One can only hope that further efforts will be made to propose similar integrations that conceptualize personality disorders in a meaningful way that is close to the clinical experience of patients and clinicians.

REFERENCES

Caligor, E., Kernberg, O. F., Clarkin, J. F., & Yeomans, F. E. (2018). *Psychodynamic Therapy for Personality Pathology: Treating Self and Interpersonal Functioning*. Washington, DC: American Psychiatric Publishing.

Morey, L. C., Hopwood, C. J., Gunderson, J. G., Shea M. T., Skodol, A. E., Grilo, C. M., ... McGlashan, T. H. (2007). A comparison of personality disorder models. *Psychological Medicine*, 37, 983–994.

Morey, L. C., Hopwood, C. J., Markowitz, J. C., Gunderson, J. G., Grilo, C. M., McGlashan, T. H., ... Skodol, A. E. (2012). Comparisons of alternative models of personality disorders, II: 6-, 8-, and 10-year follow-up. *Psychological Medicine*, 42, 1705–1713.

Newton, I. (1988). *Opticks: or, a treatise of the reflexions, refractions, inflexions and colours of light. Also two treatises of the species and magnitude of curvilinear figures. Commentary by Nicholas Humez* (Octavo ed.). Palo Alto, CA: Octavo. (*Opticks* was originally published in 1704.)

Widiger, T. A., & Mullins-Sweatt, S. N. (2005). Categorical and dimensional models of personality disorders. In J. M. Oldham, A. E. Skodol, & D. S. Bender (Eds.), *The American Psychiatric Publishing Textbook of Personality Disorders* (pp. 35–53) Washington, DC: American Psychiatric Publishing.

7 The Five-Factor Model of Personality Disorders

JOSHUA D. MILLER AND THOMAS A. WIDIGER

Trait-based, dimensional approaches to personality disorders (PDs) have finally entered mainstream psychiatric nosology with their inclusion in Section III of the fifth edition of the *Diagnostic and Statistical Manual of Mental Disorders* (DSM-5; APA, 2013) and the upcoming release of ICD-11. The adoption of such approaches did not proceed smoothly or swiftly, however, as such models have been offered as empirically grounded approaches for well over 20 years (e.g., Costa & McCrae, 1992a; Frances, 1993; Livesley, Jackson, & Schroeder, 1992; Widiger & Trull, 1992). The DSM-5 Section III model, which assesses personality pathology via a combination of signs of personality dysfunction (Criterion A) and personality disorder traits (Criterion B), was included as an emerging model in Section III, in part, due to concerns with its empirical grounding. Although this model's empirical grounding could have been better articulated and defended (Miller & Lynam, 2013), it is possible that inclusion in Section III was the best outcome available (Widiger, 2013), given its chilly reception by scholars and clinicians wed to more traditional personality disorder constructs and diagnostic approaches (e.g., Gunderson, 2010, 2013).

Substantial portions of this new diagnostic model of personality disorders – the use of pathological traits with clear ties to general or "normal" personality traits and the recreation of traditional PDs via a summation of traits – have ties to several empirical traditions, perhaps most notably work on the Five-Factor Model of PD (Widiger & Costa, 2012). In this chapter, we review the robust literature on the Five-Factor Model of PD and demonstrate its "power" with regard to efficiency, parsimony, validity, and utility. Importantly, throughout this chapter we take steps to demonstrate why this literature is so relevant and foundational to the changes being made to the major psychiatric taxonomies with regard to the conceptualization, assessment, and diagnosis of personality disorders and why a failure to adequately attend to it in the lead-up to the DSM-5 left the door open for substantial criticisms regarding the validity of the Section III diagnostic model of PD.

THE FIVE-FACTOR MODEL OF PERSONALITY: AN INTRODUCTION

The Five-Factor Model (FFM) is the predominant model of personality structure (John, Naumann, & Soto, 2008). It has its roots in the "lexical" tradition: what is of most importance, interest, or meaning to persons will be naturally encoded within the language. The most important domains of personality are those with the greatest number of terms to describe and differentiate their various manifestations and nuances, and the structure of personality is provided by the empirical relationship among these trait terms (Goldberg, 1993). Lexical research in the English language, and all other languages examined, have converged well onto the Big Five or FFM.

The FFM includes the domains of neuroticism (or negative affectivity), extraversion (versus introversion), openness (or unconventionality), agreeableness (versus antagonism), and conscientiousness (or constraint). Each broad domain can be broken down into more specific components. For example, the domain of agreeableness versus antagonism includes compassion vs. callousness, morality vs. immorality, modesty vs. arrogance, affability vs. combativeness, and trust vs. distrust (Crowe, Lynam, & Miller, 2018). Each domain includes both adaptive and maladaptive personality traits (Widiger, Gore, Crego, Rojas, & Oltmanns, 2017). Consider again the domain of agreeableness versus antagonism. Most of the traits of agreeableness are adaptive (e.g., trusting, honest, generous, cooperative, and humble) but there are also maladaptive variants of these traits (e.g., gullible, guileless, selflessly sacrificial, subservient, and self-denigrating, respectively). Most of the traits of antagonism are maladaptive (e.g., cynical-suspicious, manipulative, boastful, and callous) but there are also adaptive variants of these traits (e.g., cautious-skeptical, savvy, confident, and tough-minded).

One of the compelling attributes of the FFM is its robustness, which is a natural consequence of accounting for virtually every trait term within the language as a result of its developmental ties to the lexical hypothesis. Other dimensional models of general personality are well understood in terms of the domains and facets of the FFM (O'Connor, 2017). For example, Neuroticism and Extraversion within Eysenck's PEN model (Eysenck & Eysenck, 1970) can be considered isomorphic with Extraversion and Neuroticism from the FFM, whereas Eysenck's Psychoticism dimension can be considered a blend of FFM Antagonism and low Conscientiousness (Costa & McCrae, 1995).

The FFM has amassed a considerable body of empirical support, including childhood antecedents (Mervielde, De Clercq, De Fruyt, & Van Leeuwen, 2005), multivariate behavior genetics with respect to its structure (Jarnecke & South, 2017), temporal stability across the lifespan (Roberts & DelVecchio, 2000), and cross-cultural replication (Allik & Realo, 2017). The FFM is associated with a wide array of important life outcomes, both positive and negative, including diverse forms of psychopathology (Bagby, Uliaszek, Gralnick, & Al-Dajani, 2017), mortality, divorce, and occupational attainment (Roberts, Kuncel, Shiner, Caspi, & Goldberg, 2007), as well as subjective well-being, social acceptance, criminality, and interpersonal conflict (Ozer & Benet-Martinez, 2006).

DESCRIBING PDS AS CONFIGURATIONS OF *GENERAL* TRAITS: EXPERT RATINGS

Explicit descriptions of PDs as general trait configurations from the perspective of the FFM can be traced back, in part, to translations of DSM-III-R (APA, 1987) and IV (APA, 1994) PDs into the language of the FFM by Widiger and colleagues (Widiger, Trull, Clarkin, Sanderson, & Costa, 1994). These experts in PD rated the 30 facets of the FFM on their degree of relevance (low or high levels) to each DSM PD based on the DSM symptoms and text-based descriptions, as well as the empirical literature on each. For instance, antisocial PD was described by the following set of FFM facets: angry hostility (high), excitement seeking (high), straightforwardness (low), altruism (low), compliance (low), tendermindedness (low), dutifulness (low), self-discipline (low), and deliberation (low). Widiger and Lynam (1998) used the same approach to describe psychopathic PD, as assessed by Hare's Psychopathy Checklist–Revised (Hare, 2003), and, like with antisocial PD described above, showed that facets/traits from the domains of agreeableness and conscientiousness were most critical, with more complex (i.e., highs and lows) relations for traits from the domains of neuroticism and extraversion.

Since this initial work, there have been more comprehensive studies in which a greater number of ratings were collected, some of which used academicians and others used practicing clinicians as raters. For instance, expert raters (i.e., individuals who have published a study or more on the PD they were asked to rate) were asked to describe individuals considered prototypical of

psychopathy (Miller, Lynam, Widiger, & Leukefeld, 2001) and the 10 DSM-IV PDs (Lynam and Widiger, 2001) using the 30 facets of the FFM. Unlike the initial studies where a more dichotomous rating approach was used, here raters were asked to describe a prototypical case of each disorder using a 1 (prototypical case would be extremely low on given facet) to 5 scale (prototypical case would be extremely high on given facet).

Across the 11 PDs (psychopathy and 10 DSM-IV PDs), data were collected from an average of 17 experts; these raters proved to be relatively reliable and consistent with the initial Widiger et al. (1994) ratings. Given the reasonable agreement among raters, these ratings were then averaged to create an FFM prototype for each PD construct. As an example, the expert-rated FFM prototype for narcissistic personality disorder was characterized by elevations (i.e., mean expert ratings of a 4 or higher) on angry hostility, assertiveness, and excitement seeking, as well as low scores (i.e., mean expert ratings of 2 or lower) on all six facets of agreeableness (e.g., modesty, straightforwardness), dutifulness, self-discipline, deliberation, warmth, anxiety, depression, self-consciousness, and vulnerability. The academician ratings for psychopathy and the DSM-IV PDs can be found in Table 7.1. A second set of FFM PD prototypes were developed using the same approach except employing clinicians and a larger number of raters (mean of 31; Samuel & Widiger, 2004). As with the academician ratings, the clinical ratings manifested good inter-rater agreement for all the PDs (see Table 7.1).

FFM PD Meta-Analyses

Following the development of expert ratings for these 11 PDs, several meta-analyses were published that examined the FFM trait correlates of the DSM PDs (Samuel & Widiger, 2008; Saulsman & Page, 2004) and psychopathy (Decuyper, De Pauw, De Fruyt, De Bolle, & De Clercq., 2009; O'Boyle, Forsyth, Banks, Story, & White, 2015). Using data from 18 samples (n = 3207), Samuel and Widiger (2008) documented the facet level FFM relations with DSM PDs. For instance, borderline PD was characterized by significant positive correlations with all six neuroticism facets (e.g., depressiveness, angry hostility) and negative correlations with traits from agreeableness (e.g., trust, compliance), conscientiousness (e.g., competence, self-discipline), and extraversion (e.g., positive emotions). Similarly, Decuyper et al. compiled data from 26 independent samples (n = 6913) to present the meta-analytic correlations between the 30 FFM traits and psychopathy scores. Psychopathy was most consistently negatively correlated with facets from agreeableness (e.g., straightforwardness, compliance) and conscientiousness (e.g., deliberation, dutifulness), and manifested both positive and negative correlations with neuroticism (*positive*: angry hostility, impulsiveness; *negative*: anxiety) and extraversion (*positive*: excitement seeking; *negative*: warmth). See Table 7.1 for the meta-analytically derived FFM profiles for psychopathy and DSM PDs.

In general, the academic and clinician FFM PD profiles were highly correlated with one another (*range*: .90–.95; *mean r* = .94) and converged with the meta-analytic profiles (academic ratings: *mean r* = .80; clinician ratings: *mean r* = .80), documenting the robustness of the FFM profiles. Dependent PD was the only case with substantive divergence between expected (i.e., expert) and obtained profiles such that both sets of expert ratings characterized individuals with dependent PD using high levels of agreeableness (e.g., trust, compliance, modesty) whereas the empirical data do not support this relation (see Miller & Lynam, 2008 and Lowe, Edmundson, & Widiger, 2009 for a discussion of these issues). Instead, lower levels of conscientiousness (paired with high neuroticism) may better characterize this PD from the perspective of the FFM.

Prototype Matching for FFM PDs

The previous findings demonstrated that traits can be used to reliably and robustly describe PDs within approaches and across them. We next examined whether personality traits scores on measures of the FFM could be used to assess PDs. In this vein, two scoring techniques were developed utilizing the expert ratings described above. The first strategy was a prototype matching approach in which an individual's scores on a faceted measure of the FFM was quantitatively compared to one or more of the FFM PD prototypes using a double entry-q intraclass correlation (r_{ICC}), which quantifies the absolute similarity of the two set of traits (e.g., individual A's scores on the 30 FFM facets vs. the FFM PD prototype).

Another means of scoring an individual's FFM data with regard to the FFM PD prototypes is the additive count procedure (Miller, Bagby, Pilkonis, Reynolds, & Lynam, 2005). In this far simpler approach, an individual's FFM PD scores are calculated by summing scores on only the FFM facets considered particularly relevant for the PDs of interest. The cutoffs typically used to determine a facet's relevance are scores of 4 or higher or 2 or lower; facets that are deemed relevant at low levels (e.g., deliberation for antisocial PD) are reversed scored before being summed. The two scoring approaches for the FFM PDs yield scores that are highly correlated with one another (median *r* for DSM-IV PDs across two samples: .91; Miller et al., 2005). Given the similarity of the resultant scores, the count approach is preferred primarily because the scores are easier to calculate.

Validity of the FFM PD Scores: Convergent Validity

Several studies have examined the correlations between the FFM PD similarity scores and/or counts and DSM-IV PD symptom counts using self-report data. Miller (2019)

conducted a meta-analytic review of the convergent validity correlations across these studies (k range: 11 [psychopathy] to 20 [borderline]; N range: 3094 [Cluster A PDs] to 4394 [borderline]). The studies included in the review scored the FFM data based on self-reported data from the NEO PI-R, interview data from the Structured Interview for the Five Factor Model (SIFFM; Trull & Widiger, 1997), and clinician ratings from the Five Factor Model Scoring Sheet (FFMSS; Few et al., 2010). The official DSM PD symptoms were assessed using interviews, expert consensus ratings, and self-report measures. The unweighted mean correlations ranged from .17 (Obsessive-Compulsive PD [OCPD]) to .60 (avoidant PD) with a median of .46. The largest convergent validity correlations for the FFM PDs were for avoidant, borderline, and psychopathy, whereas the smallest convergent validity effect sizes were found for OCPD, schizotypal, and histrionic PDs. In general, OCPD and histrionic demonstrate substantial heterogeneity in effect sizes with regard to their trait correlates (Samuel and Widiger, 2008), which likely affects their convergent correlations when scored using an FFM PD approach. Overall, however, the convergent validity correlations for the FFM PDs are relatively strong when considering that they are similar in size to those found when comparing two explicit measures of DSM PDs with one another (Miller, Few, & Widiger, 2012), are derived from studies that utilize a wide array of methodologies to assess the FFM facets and the PDs, and most of the FFM scores were derived from instruments that were not written to assess pathological variants of these traits.

Discriminant Validity/Comorbidity

Several studies have examined the convergent *and* discriminant validity of the FFM PD prototypes. In most cases, the FFM PD scores manifest their strongest correlations with the convergent DSM-IV PD (e.g., FFM antisocial and DSM-IV antisocial) and in cases where this is not true, the FFM PD score is typically slightly more correlated with another PD from the same cluster (e.g., FFM dependent and DSM avoidant) or another PD known to be comorbid with the target PD (e.g., schizoid and avoidant; e.g., Zimmerman, Rothschild, & Chelminski, 2005). Of course, finding strong discriminant validity for the FFM PDs scores is difficult as the DSM PDs themselves are notoriously deficient in this domain. One benefit of a trait-based approach to PDs, in fact, is that the co-occurrence found among DSM PDs can be modeled by the degree to which they share underlying FFM traits (i.e., Lynam & Widiger, 2001).

Criterion Validity: Convergence of Empirical Networks

Another, perhaps more important, way of testing the validity of the FFM PD scores is to examine the degree to

Table 7.1 FFM PD prototypes

	Psychopathy		Paranoid			Schizoid			Schizotypal			Antisocial		
	AR	MA	AR	CR	MA	AR	CR	MA	AR	CR	MA	AR	CR	MA
Neuroticism														
Anxiety	1.47	-.15	3.60	4.25	.27	2.23	3.06	.13	4.25	3.85	.27	1.82	2.00	.00
Angry Hostility	3.87	.29	4.00	4.39	.41	2.54	2.84	.19	3.08	3.42	.29	4.14	3.93	.27
Depression	1.40	.05	3.30	3.64	.35	3.15	3.42	.28	3.58	3.62	.39	2.45	2.70	.12
Self-consciousness	1.07	-.09	3.30	2.94	.29	3.31	3.37	.23	4.00	3.69	.32	1.36	1.63	.02
Impulsiveness	4.53	.24	2.90	3.17	.15	2.08	2.03	.00	3.17	3.16	.17	4.73	4.22	.27
Vulnerability	1.47	.00	3.60	3.36	.22	3.31	2.97	.14	3.75	3.96	.25	2.27	2.07	.04
Extraversion														
Warmth	1.73	-.20	1.30	1.61	-.28	1.08	1.19	-.42	1.58	1.58	-.28	2.14	2.00	-.13
Gregariousness	3.67	.03	1.70	1.89	-.20	1.00	1.06	-.48	1.58	1.62	-.25	3.32	3.48	.02
Assertiveness	4.47	.16	2.90	3.25	-.08	1.54	1.90	-.22	2.17	2.04	-.13	4.23	4.07	.06
Activity	3.67	.07	2.90	3.19	-.08	1.92	2.00	-.25	2.25	2.23	-.13	4.00	4.00	.02
Excitement Seek	4.73	.31	2.20	2.42	-.01	1.38	1.71	-.21	2.17	2.12	-.04	4.64	4.30	.25
Positive Emotions	2.53	-.10	2.20	2.08	-.27	1.23	1.55	-.38	1.92	1.65	-.26	2.86	3.52	-.09
Openness														
Fantasy	3.07	.05	2.90	3.14	.00	3.23	2.81	-.05	3.83	4.00	.14	2.82	3.48	.10
Aesthetics	2.33	-.01	2.20	2.54	-.05	2.77	2.42	-.06	3.17	3.31	.07	2.36	2.78	.00
Feelings	1.80	-.10	2.40	2.46	-.02	1.31	1.52	-.17	2.17	2.31	.03	2.27	2.41	-.02
Actions	4.27	.09	2.00	2.37	-.10	1.62	2.13	-.13	2.42	2.81	-.06	4.23	4.07	.10
Ideas	3.53	.03	3.50	3.29	-.03	3.38	3.45	.00	4.33	4.38	.09	2.91	3.26	.04
Values	2.87	.00	1.90	1.69	-.05	2.31	2.42	-.05	2.42	2.81	.01	3.00	3.48	.08

Agreeableness

Trust	1.73	*-.34*	1.00	1.19	*-.45*	2.38	1.68	*-.28*	2.08	2.04	*-.31*	1.45	1.70	*-.22*
Straightforwardness	1.13	*-.61*	2.00	1.89	*-.24*	2.77	2.42	*-.09*	3.00	2.46	*-.16*	1.41	1.41	*-.37*
Altruism	1.33	*-.41*	1.90	1.86	*-.21*	2.38	2.29	*-.19*	2.75	2.50	*-.15*	1.41	1.41	*-.24*
Compliance	1.33	*-.48*	1.40	1.92	*-.27*	3.00	2.77	*-.08*	2.50	2.65	*-.13*	1.77	1.81	*-.32*
Modesty	1.00	*-.31*	2.40	2.53	*-.06*	3.31	3.48	*.08*	3.08	3.27	*.05*	1.68	1.70	*-.17*
Tendermindedness	1.27	*-.31*	1.80	2.14	*-.18*	2.38	2.58	*-.11*	3.00	2.88	*-.05*	1.27	1.52	*-.19*
Conscientiousness														
Competence	**4.20**	*-.17*	3.30	3.53	*-.13*	2.85	3.00	*-.13*	2.33	2.85	*-.18*	2.09	2.52	*-.21*
Order	2.60	*-.17*	3.70	3.56	*.00*	3.08	3.19	*-.02*	2.00	2.58	*-.06*	2.41	2.74	*-.18*
Dutifulness	1.20	*-.32*	3.40	3.39	*-.10*	3.00	3.16	*-.08*	2.50	2.77	*-.10*	1.41	1.52	*-.29*
Achievement Strive.	3.07	*-.11*	3.00	3.08	*-.07*	2.38	2.68	*-.13*	2.25	2.35	*-.13*	2.09	2.33	*-.19*
Self-discipline	1.87	*-.22*	3.50	3.19	*-.14*	3.15	3.10	*-.12*	2.67	2.77	*-.18*	1.81	1.85	*-.25*
Deliberation	1.60	*-.38*	3.80	3.56	*-.09*	3.23	3.71	*-.02*	2.67	3.73	*-.10*	1.64	1.96	*-.38*
Profile rs: AR-CR			.95*			.91*			.91*			.97*		
AR-MA/CR-MA	.77*		.71*	.75*		.73*	.81*		.80*	.79*		.80*	.79*	

AR = Academician Ratings (Lynam & Widiger, 2001; Miller et al., 2001); CR = Clinician Ratings (Samuel & Widiger, 2004); MA = Meta-analytically derived *rs* (Decuyper et al., 2009; Samuel & Widiger, 2008). Expert rated items rated 2 or lower are underlined; items rated 4 or higher are bolded. Correlations ≥ .20 are italicized. *$p \leq .01$. OCPD = Obsessive-Compulsive PD.

Table 7.1 (cont.)

	Borderline			Histrionic			Narcissistic			Avoidant			Dependent			OCPD		
	AR	CR	MA	AR	CR	MA	AR	CR	MA	AR	CR	MA	AR	CR	MA	AR	CR	MA
Neuroticism																		
Anxiety	4.04	4.25	.38	3.42	4.07	.00	2.33	2.71	.02	4.76	4.34	.41	4.32	4.46	.39	4.00	4.49	.16
Angry Hostility	4.75	4.56	.48	3.42	3.55	.08	4.08	3.90	.23	2.81	2.90	.29	2.42	2.95	.18	3.00	3.24	.10
Depression	4.17	4.03	.50	2.68	3.27	-.06	2.42	2.75	.03	3.95	3.72	.53	3.63	4.03	.41	3.18	3.76	.09
Self-consciousness	3.17	2.94	.35	2.00	2.45	-.11	1.50	1.67	-.03	4.67	4.45	.56	4.16	4.42	.42	3.29	3.86	.13
Impulsiveness	4.79	4.38	.34	4.32	4.16	.17	3.17	3.57	.14	1.62	2.14	.14	2.32	2.49	.17	1.53	2.18	-.07
Vulnerability	4.17	4.03	.39	3.95	3.90	.01	2.92	2.76	-.01	4.52	3.90	.40	4.32	4.64	.43	3.12	3.49	.03
Extraversion																		
Warmth	3.21	2.69	-.20	3.89	3.50	.26	1.42	2.05	-.07	2.33	2.45	-.35	3.84	3.49	-.03	2.06	2.24	-.07
Gregariousness	2.92	3.28	-.12	4.74	4.32	.35	3.83	3.95	.04	1.29	1.45	-.42	3.26	2.54	-.03	2.18	2.40	-.16
Assertiveness	3.17	3.69	-.09	3.84	3.39	.27	4.67	4.00	.19	1.19	1.52	-.39	1.32	1.46	-.21	3.00	3.03	-.01
Activity	3.29	3.56	-.10	4.16	3.94	.25	3.67	4.14	.09	2.05	2.07	-.29	2.26	2.00	-.12	3.35	3.31	.03
Excitement Seek	3.88	4.06	.06	4.47	4.13	.27	4.17	4.10	.16	1.24	1.55	-.23	2.26	1.69	-.06	1.59	1.88	-.12
Positive Emotions	2.63	3.16	-.26	4.16	3.80	.23	3.33	3.52	-.02	1.67	1.79	-.39	2.53	2.03	-.15	2.41	2.29	-.09
Openness																		
Fantasy	3.29	4.00	.13	4.37	4.13	.16	3.75	3.82	.11	3.14	3.07	.00	3.05	2.95	.05	2.06	2.52	-.09
Aesthetics	2.96	3.19	.05	3.53	3.60	.10	3.25	3.32	.04	3.05	2.69	-.03	2.89	2.58	.01	2.59	2.56	.01
Feelings	4.00	3.84	.09	4.16	4.13	.18	1.92	2.68	.05	3.43	3.07	-.04	3.74	3.45	.05	1.82	2.22	.01
Actions	4.00	3.78	-.03	4.21	3.70	.12	4.08	3.36	.04	2.00	1.83	-.20	2.21	1.79	-.13	1.53	1.76	-.12
Ideas	3.21	3.69	-.01	3.11	3.30	.04	2.92	3.09	.07	3.19	2.69	-.05	2.84	2.26	-.12	1.76	2.48	.03
Values	2.88	3.00	.05	3.63	3.50	.04	2.67	2.68	-.01	2.57	2.34	-.05	2.89	2.05	-.04	1.76	1.82	-.09

Agreeableness

Trust	2.21	1.69	-.29	4.00	3.39	.05	1.42	1.86	-.20	2.24	2.39	-.29	4.26	3.95	-.07	2.65	2.20	-.08
Straightforwardness	2.08	1.94	-.21	2.32	2.29	-.10	1.83	1.91	-.37	2.90	2.82	-.06	3.11	2.90	.00	3.47	3.06	.04
Altruism	2.46	2.31	-.18	2.21	2.52	.02	1.00	1.73	-.20	2.90	2.93	-.12	3.95	3.85	.03	2.76	2.63	.04
Compliance	2.00	1.81	-.27	2.53	2.90	-.12	1.58	1.77	-.26	3.52	3.21	-.02	4.68	4.50	.10	3.18	2.82	.01
Modesty	2.83	2.56	.03	2.32	2.20	-.16	1.08	1.23	-.37	4.33	3.68	.20	4.26	4.23	.16	3.06	3.17	.02
Tendermindedness	2.79	2.47	-.09	3.05	3.00	.02	1.50	1.77	-.17	3.43	3.43	-.02	3.89	3.79	.09	2.82	2.76	.00
Conscientiousness																		
Competence	2.71	2.78	-.29	2.37	2.68	-.01	3.25	3.00	.01	3.05	3.45	-.23	2.58	3.28	-.25	4.53	4.41	.19
Order	2.38	2.31	-.10	2.10	2.30	-.05	2.92	3.00	-.03	3.43	3.48	-.03	2.89	3.21	-.06	4.76	4.59	.25
Dutifulness	2.29	2.22	-.22	2.10	2.32	-.08	2.42	2.50	-.10	3.29	3.45	-.09	3.79	3.79	-.08	4.76	4.20	.25
Achievement Strive.	2.50	2.72	-.19	2.68	2.60	.04	3.92	3.18	.02	2.67	2.90	-.19	2.47	2.97	-.16	4.29	4.03	.25
Self-discipline	2.33	2.34	-.29	1.79	2.13	-.04	2.08	2.23	-.09	3.05	3.07	-.22	2.84	3.31	-.23	4.53	4.06	.21
Deliberation	1.88	2.09	-.27	1.74	1.94	-.16	2.25	2.45	-.13	3.43	3.62	-.01	3.00	3.36	-.06	4.59	4.37	.24
Profile rs: AR-CR	.93*			.95*			.95*			.96*			.90*			.94*		
AR-MA/CR-MA	.84*	.77*		.86*	.79*		.81*	.87*		.78*	.76*		.60*	.63*		.91*	.92*	

which they can recreate the nomological networks associated with specific DSM-IV PDs. For example, one can compare the empirical profiles generated by the FFM PD scores with those generated by DSM-IV PD scores. For instance, Miller and colleagues (Miller, Reynolds, & Pilkonis, 2004; Miller et al., 2010) compared the empirical trait profile derived from FFM and DSM PD scores on the 15 traits from Clark's (1993) Schedule for Nonadaptive and Adaptive Personality (SNAP) and found substantial absolute similarity (mean r_{ICC} = .73), suggesting both approaches are capturing the same underlying trait constructs. One can use a similar quantitative approach to compare the two sets of scoring using non-trait based correlates as well. Such an approach has been used to examine the similarity of FFM and DSM-based conceptualizations of borderline PD, which is a particularly important test given that some experts have posited that such trait-based approaches are likely insufficient for the assessment of this important construct (e.g., Gunderson, 2010, 2013). Both, Trull, Widiger, Lynam, and Costa (2003) and Miller and colleagues (Miller, Morse, Nolf, Stepp, & Pilkonis, 2012) demonstrated that FFM borderline PD scores yielded empirical profiles with a number of relevant constructs such as developmental history (e.g., child abuse; parental psychopathology), emotional experiences, pathological personality traits, and functioning, that were very similar to the relations modeled using official DSM borderline scores (i.e., combining data from these two studies: r_{ICC} = .87; see Table 7.2). The substantial absolute similarity in relations evinced from FFM and DSM PD scores is all the more noteworthy when considering that the FFM PDs are typically assessed with instruments that have no conceptual ties to the DSM and do not explicitly assess functional impairment. Similar studies offering support for the FFM PD perspective have been conducted for psychopathy (Derefinko & Lynam, 2007; Miller & Lynam, 2003; Miller et al., 2001) and antisocial PD (Gudonis, Miller, Miller, & Lynam, 2008).

Sex Differences

A useful trait-based model should be able to explain key questions in the field, especially if it is to claim to be a more parsimonious approach. This is true for issues related to comorbidity (Lynam & Widiger, 2001), as noted previously. Another area in which a trait-based approach might prove useful is in explaining commonly found sex differences among the DSM personality disorders, which has been plagued with questions as to whether such differences reflect issues of bias (in terms of criteria included in the DSM or how clinicians differentially apply the official criteria) or genuine differences. Lynam and Widiger (2007) examined whether sex differences for DSM PDs could be accounted for by sex differences on the FFM traits that underlie PDs by correlating sex differences for

each FFM PD based on what is known about sex differences in the facets of the FFM with the actual sex differences (ds) found for the DSM PDs compiled via a meta-analytic review. The two sets of data were substantially related (r = .72), indicating that sex differences in DSM PDs may be due, in part, to differences on the general personality traits that comprise each PD. That is, PDs for which low agreeableness is a central component (e.g., antisocial and narcissistic PDs), men will score higher; PDs in which high neuroticism is a key aspects (e.g., borderline and dependent), women will tend to score higher.

Clinical Utility

There are many ways to examine the clinical utility of different approaches to the conceptualization, assessment, and diagnosis of PDs. One common approach (referred to often as a consumer preference approach) is to present clinicians the different models and inquire about their preferences (e.g., DSM vs. FFM-based models). A second approach that speaks more to actual, performance-based utility is to compare models as to their capabilities to provide important, clinically relevant information (e.g., treatment utilization or compliance). Several consumer preference types of surveys have been conducted in which DSM and FFM based conceptualizations are compared (e.g., Rottman, Ahn, Sanislow, & Kim, 2009; Samuel & Widiger, 2006; Spitzer, First, Shedler, Westen, & Skodol, 2008; Sprock, 2003). When comparable methods are used, however, the FFM fares as well or better than the DSM-based approach in terms of preferences (Mullins-Sweatt & Lengel, 2012).

The second and arguably better approach to clinical utility is to compare how well different approaches do in providing clinically relevant information. For example, Miller et al. (2010) examined the relations between the FFM PD prototypes, as measured by a brief clinician rating form, and several indices of impairment and found that the FFM PD counts were significantly related to overall impairment, occupational impairment, social impairment, and distress caused to others; more importantly, the FFM PD counts consistently accounted for greater unique variance in the impairment scores than did DSM-IV PD symptoms. Studies of FFM approaches to borderline PD have demonstrated substantial relations with self-harm behavior and multiple ratings of impairment (Miller et al., 2012; Trull et al., 2003). Similarly, FFM antisocial and borderline PD scores predicted externalizing behaviors across several years (Stepp & Trull, 2007). In fact, data suggest that personality variables are excellent targets of clinical interventions (Presnall, 2012) given (a) that they change with intervention (Roberts et al., 2017) and (b) that changes in PD traits portend change in DSM PD symptoms (e.g., Warner et al., 2004; Wright, Hopwood, & Zanarini, 2015).

Table 7.2 Nomological network of DSM-IV and FFM BPD scores in two samples

	Borderline PD	
	FFM BPD	DSM-IV BPD
	r	r
Childhood Abuse		
Sexual [T]	.19	.21
Physical [T]	.20	.20
Parental Psychopathology		
Bio. Parent – any disorder [T]	.26	.20
Bio. Father substance use disorder [T]	.23	.14
Bio. Father mood disorder [T]	.09	.10
Bio. Mother substance use disorder [T]	.05	.06
Bio. Mother mood disorder [T]	.21	.19
Psychological Distress		
Depression [M]	.56	.58
Anxiety [M]	.58	.59
Distress [M]	.65	.54
Affect		
Negative [M]	.56	.41
Positive [M]	−.44	−.29
Attachment Style		
Anxiety [M]	.60	.48
Avoidance [M]	.29	.30
Informant-report PDs		
Paranoid [M]	.40	.46
Schizoid [M]	.23	.27
Schizotypal [M]	.45	.46
Antisocial [M]	.43	.54
Borderline [M]	.53	.53
Histrionic [M]	.36	.50
Narcissistic [M]	.28	.36
Avoidant [M]	.48	.33
Dependent [M]	.36	.41
Obsessive-Compulsive [M]	.19	.22

	Borderline PD	
Self-harm		
No intent to die [M]	.39	.45
Intent to die [M]	.36	.56
Aggression – perpetration		
Aggression [M]	.33	.38
Assault [M]	.20	.35
Aggression – victimization		
Aggression [M]	.27	.31
Assault [M]	.21	.23
Interpersonal Functioning		
Interpersonal sensitivity [M]	.73	.55
Interpersonal ambivalence [M]	.55	.38
Aggression [M]	.59	.47
Need for approval [M]	.59	.46
Lack of sociability [M]	.56	.44
Functioning		
Distress [M]	.64	.62
Romantic [M]	.39	.44
Parental [M]	.44	.58
Occupational [M]	.46	.54
Social [M]	.45	.54
Distress on others [M]	.59	.76
Interpersonal [T]	.53	.39
Global dysfunction [T]	.52	.39
Profile Similarity (r_{ICC})	.87*	

Note. [T] = data from Trull et al. (2003); [M] = data from Miller et al. (2012)
BPD = Borderline PD.

FFM PD Scales

It is a strong testament to the validity of understanding the DSM personality disorders from the perspective of the FFM that one can use an existing measure of the FFM, such as the NEO PI-R (Costa & McCrae, 1992b) to provide an assessment of a PD that is just as valid as any existing, direct measure of that PD (Miller et al., 2012). However, there have now been developed a number of self-report measures of respective PDs from the perspective of the FFM, thereby bridging the gap between normal-range and disordered personality (Bagby & Widiger, 2018; Widiger, Lynam, Miller, & Oltmanns, 2012). Eight FFM PD inventories have been developed, including (but not limited to) the Elemental Psychopathy Assessment (EPA; Lynam et al., 2011), the Five Factor Borderline Inventory (FFBI; Mullins-Sweatt et al., 2012), the Five Factor Obsessive-Compulsive Inventory (FFOCI; Samuel, Riddell, Lynam, Miller, & Widiger, 2012), and the Five Factor Narcissism Inventory (FFNI; Glover, Miller, Lynam, Crego, & Widiger, 2012). Each was constructed by first identifying which facets of the FFM appeared to be most relevant for each respective personality disorder. The facet selections were based on researchers' FFM descriptions of each PD (i.e., Lynam & Widiger, 2001), clinicians' descriptions (i.e., Samuel & Widiger, 2004), and FFM-PD research (e.g., Samuel & Widiger, 2008). Scales were then constructed to assess the maladaptive variants of each facet that were specific to each personality disorder, yielding scales at both poles of all five domains of the FFM (Widiger et al., 2012).

The FFM PD scales have been validated in part by demonstrating convergence with alternative measures of the respective personality disorder (e.g., Lynam et al., 2011; Samuel, Lynam, Widiger, & Ball, 2012). Each of the scales have also been shown to have incremental validity over a respective NEO PI-R facet scale in accounting for variance within a respective personality disorder (e.g., Glover et al., 2012; Lynam et al., 2011; Mullins-Sweatt et al., 2012). Demonstrating that a maladaptive personality trait scale has incremental validity over a normal personality trait scale in accounting for variance in a measure of personality disorders is not though a particularly striking finding. However, the FFM PD inventories have also demonstrated incremental validity over the more traditional and established measures of the respective personality disorders (e.g., Glover et al., 2012; Mullins-Sweatt et al., 2012; Samuel, Riddell, et al., 2012), due in part to the fact that these self-report measures include quite a number of subscales assessing the more specific components of each heterogeneous PD syndrome.

Perhaps most importantly, the FFM PD scales have also demonstrated strong convergent and discriminant validity with respect to the domains of the FFM. FFM PD scales have even demonstrated convergent and discriminant validity with respect to individual facet scales. It should be noted though that facet-level predictions have not even been attempted for other comparable maladaptive trait scales, such as the Personality Inventory for DSM-5 (PID-5; Krueger, Derringer, Markon, Watson, & Skodol, 2012) and the Computerized Adaptive Test-Personality Disorder-Static Form (CAT-PD-SF; Simms et al., 2011).

CHARACTERIZATION OF PDS AS COLLECTIONS OF *PATHOLOGICAL* TRAITS: DSM-5 SECTION III

As noted earlier, the recognition of the role of traits in the conceptualization, assessment, and diagnosis of PDs took a major leap forward in DSM-5, as traits now play a

fundamental role in the assessment of DSM-5 PDs in Section III of the manual. In what follows, the new alternative model of PD (AMPD) is reviewed, along with initial empirical evidence as to its performance.

Connection to the FFM

The DSM-5 AMPD involves two major components, an evaluation/consideration of the presence of personality dysfunction in two domains (self and interpersonal), as well as documentation of the presence of pathological personality traits. These pathological traits can then be used in place of the previous criteria lists to diagnose six of the ten DSM-IV PDs (schizotypal, antisocial, borderline, narcissistic, avoidant, OCPD) or to generate PD-Trait Specified diagnoses for cases where an individual manifests significant personality dysfunction paired with one or more trait elevations. Although the DSM-5 trait model and its description changed over the course of time (see Widiger, 2013 for a review), the final model comprises five broader domains (i.e., negative affectivity, detachment, antagonism, disinhibition, and psychoticism) and 25 more specific facets (e.g., anxiousness, withdrawal, grandiosity, irresponsibility, unusual beliefs and experiences). The domains of the DSM-5 trait model are explicitly linked to the FFM as they are described as "maladaptive variants of the extensively validated and replicated model of personality known as the 'Big Five,' or Five-Factor Model of personality (FFM)" (APA, 2013, p. 773), although this was not initially the case (Miller & Lynam, 2013).

The DSM-5 trait model is typically assessed using the Personality Inventory for DSM-5 (Krueger et al., 2012; see Maples et al., 2015 for a briefer, faceted version as well). Miller (2019) examined the convergence between the DSM-5 and FFM domains across seven studies ($n = 2471$); convergent correlations ranged from .20 (psychoticism – openness) to .71 (negative affectivity – neuroticism) with a mean correlation of .56. Despite differences in how these models were assessed across these studies, with regard to FFM-based instruments (e.g., NEO PI-R; Five Factor Model Rating Form) and raters (self; clinical ratings), the effect sizes did not vary dramatically except in the case of openness. For this domain, the convergent correlations ranged from −.18 to .46. Not surprisingly, there continues to be an ongoing debate as to the nature of the relations between these dimensions (e.g., Chmielewski, Bagby, Markon, Ring, & Ryder, 2014; Edmundson, Lynam, Miller, Gore, & Widiger, 2011).

Expert Ratings of the DSM-5 Section III Traits Associated with DSM-IV/5 PDs

The DSM-5 Personality and Personality Disorder (P & PD) Work Group specified the manner in which the AMPD traits would be used to diagnose the DSM-IV PDs (see Table 7.3). For instance, the DSM-5 AMPD approach states that antisocial PD is diagnosed using the following

Table 7.3 Academician and DSM-5 Ratings of PDs using the DSM-5 trait model

	SCT		APD		BPD		NPD		AVD		OCPD	
	AR	D5	AR	D5	AR	D5	AR	D5	AR	D5	AR	D5
Submissiveness	0.43		0.09		1.43		0.14		**2.07**		0.54	
Depressivity	0.59		0.35		1.85	x	0.55		1.67		0.95	
Separation insecurity	0.43		0.09		**2.69**	x	0.62		1.07		0.54	
Anxiousness	1.64		0.23		1.93	x	0.83		**2.43**	x	1.62	
Emotional lability	0.64		1.36		**2.79**	x	1.28		0.43		0.33	
Suspiciousness	**2.50**	x	1.57		1.32		1.45		0.79		0.38	
Perseveration	0.62		0.14		0.45		0.38		0.29		**2.46**	x
Restricted affectivity	1.93	x	1.62		0.29		0.86		1.21		1.46	x
Withdrawal	**2.50**	x	0.93		0.39		0.36		1.79	x	0.93	
Intimacy avoidance	**2.29**		1.10		0.67		1.14		1.79	x	0.92	x
Anhedonia	1.79		0.48		0.57		0.41		1.36	x	0.85	
Manipulativeness	0.29		**2.95**	x	0.95		**2.38**		0.07		0.85	
Deceitfulness	0.29		**2.67**	x	0.69		1.59		0.07		0.31	
Hostility	0.54		**2.50**	x	1.42	x	1.69		0.07		0.96	
Callousness	0.47		**2.84**	x	1.24		**2.07**		0.00		0.79	
Attention seeking	0.36		1.43		1.10		1.83	x	0.00		0.23	
Grandiosity	0.50		**2.57**		0.55		**3.00**	x	0.36		1.00	
Irresponsibility	0.79		**2.76**	x	1.12		0.86		0.00		0.15	
Impulsivity	0.71		**2.62**	x	**2.48**	x	0.93		0.07		0.31	
Distractibility	1.36		1.38		1.12		0.17		0.50		0.46	
Risk taking	1.50		**2.85**	x	**2.23**	x	1.85		0.50		0.62	
Rigid Perfectionism	0.74		0.19		0.52		0.83		0.55		**3.00**	x
Eccentricity	**2.79**	x	0.24		0.96		0.18		0.04		0.31	
Cognitive/perceptual dysregulation	**2.00**	x	0.05		1.70		0.07		0.07		0.23	
Unusual beliefs/experiences	**2.90**	x	0.17		0.56		0.14		0.04		0.23	
Profile rs	0.79*		0.73*		0.82*		0.53*		0.68*		0.73*	

Note: AR = Academician Ratings (compiled from Samuel, Lynam, et al., 2012); D5 = DSM-5 Trait assignments; SCT = Schizotypal; APD = Antisocial Personality Disorder; BPD = Borderline; NPD = Narcissistic; AVD = Avoidant; OCPD = Obsessive-Compulsive Data compiled from Samuel, Lynam, et al., 2012. Ratings of 2 or higher are bolded. Profile correlations calculated by replacing "xs" with 1 for the DSM-5 ratings (and traits without an "x" were given a 0).

traits (in addition to evidence of both self and interpersonal dysfunction): manipulativeness, callousness, deceitfulness, hostility, risk taking, impulsivity, and irresponsibility. In addition to the ratings provided by the DSM-5 P & PD Work Group, independent expert ratings of the relevance of DSM-5 traits to each DSM-IV PD were collected by Samuel, Lynam, Widiger, and Ball (2012). These ratings were collected by asking individuals who had published on the PD for which they provided ratings to rate the relevance of all AMPD traits in relation to a specific PD using a 0 (not at all or very little) to 3

(extremely descriptive) metric.[1] See Table 7.3 for these expert ratings. In general, the DSM-5 P & PD Work Group trait assignments were correlated (traits included in the DSM-5 count were given a "1," those not included in a given PD diagnosis were given a "0") with these expert ratings with correlations ranging from .51 (paranoid) to .91 (schizoid) with a median of .73. A comparison of these

[1] These ratings were conducted on the original 37 traits put forth by the DSM-5 P & PD Work Group but can be translated to the official 25-trait model following Krueger et al. (2012).

two sets of ratings demonstrates where the two diverge. For instance, the DSM-5 P & PD Work Group chose only two traits for the diagnosis of narcissistic PD – grandiosity and attention seeking – whereas the Samuel et al. experts rated grandiosity (3.00), manipulativeness (2.38), and callousness (2.07) as being most prototypical of this disorder (attention seeking, which the DSM-5 P & PD Work Group included, was given only a rating of 1.83 by the Samuel et al.). Decisions as to which traits to include in which PD may have overemphasized concerns with discriminant validity at the cost of overall construct validity. Similarly, the experts included in Samuel, Lynam, et al. (2012) chose submissiveness as being relevant to avoidant PD, which was not included by the DSM-5 P & PD Work Group; conversely, the AMPD includes the traits of withdrawal, intimacy avoidance, and anhedonia, which the experts did not feel were as relevant.

Validity of the DSM-5 Trait PD Counts: Convergent Validity

Several studies have examined the correlations between the traditional DSM-5 Section II PD counts and the AMPD scores (e.g., Anderson, Snider, Sellbom, Krueger, & Hopwood, 2014; Hopwood, Thomas, Markon, Wright, & Krueger, 2012; Miller, Few, Lynam, & MacKillop, 2015; Samuel, Hopwood, Krueger, Thomas, & Ruggero, 2013). Although there are a variety of ways one might calculate counts (see Samuel et al., 2013 for a review), the procedure that is used most commonly and is consistent with the one used in the FFM literature simply sums scores for each relevant facet. Averaged across these four studies, the convergent validity correlations for the Section III PD counts and the Section II PD scores range from .39 (obsessive-compulsive) to .71 (borderline) with a median of .60 (see Table 7.4). The size of these correlations were relatively similar across the samples despite differences in sample composition (e.g., Miller et al., 2015: community participants in mental health treatment; Anderson et al., 2014; Hopwood et al., 2012; Samuel et al., 2013: undergraduates) and assessment of the Section II and III PDs (Miller et al., 2015: clinical ratings; Anderson et al., 2014; Hopwood et al., 2012; Samuel et al., 2013: self-reports). It is also noteworthy that the average convergent correlations manifested by the Section III PD counts and Section II PD scores were significantly correlated ($r = .72$) with the number of traits used to assess each PD in the Section III approach (range: 2 [narcissistic] to 7 [antisocial; borderline]), suggesting that greater convergence may be attainable for several PDs if additional traits are added to the Section III DSM-5 PDs.

Discriminant Validity/Comorbidity

Miller and colleagues (2015) examined the discriminant validity of the DSM-5 PD counts and found that for seven of the ten PDs they manifested their largest correlation (or tied for the largest) with the corresponding DSM-5 Section II PD. For two of the remaining three (paranoid and narcissistic) they manifested slightly higher correlations with PDs from the same cluster (schizotypal and histrionic, respectively). Much like the findings reported previously for the FFM PDs, one would expect that the DSM-5 Section III PD counts would also recreate the comorbidity found among the Section II PDs; Miller et al. (2015) found that this was the case as the patterns of relations among the two sets of PD scores were significantly correlated with one another ($r = .78$) and that the comorbidity among the DSM-5 Section III PD counts was significantly associated with the number of traits shared among the PDs ($r = .76$).

Criterion Validity: Convergence of Empirical Networks

Miller et al. (2015) also examined whether the DSM-5 Section II and III PDs manifested similar empirical networks with relation to the 30 general traits from the FFM. To do this, the two sets of DSM-5 PD scores were first correlated with the 30 facets of the FFM and the absolute similarities between the two sets of correlations were tested. The intraclass correlations among these FFM trait profiles for the ten PDs ranged from .59 (obsessive-compulsive) to .98 (borderline) with a mean of .90. While most demonstrated nearly perfectly correlated trait profiles, more moderate overlap was found for the trait correlates of the Section II and III OCPD scores. Here the correlations differed primarily in relation to facets from extraversion with the AMPD OCPD scores manifesting substantially larger negative correlations with traits such as gregariousness, warmth, and positive emotions. It is worth nothing that the original DSM-5 trait based diagnosis of OCPD involved only two facets: perseveration and rigid perfectionism. However, this diagnosis was revised prior to inclusion in the DSM-5 and two other traits were added: restricted affectivity and intimacy avoidance. Miller et al. (2015) demonstrated that removal of these two "new" traits from the Section III OCPD count resulted in an increased convergent correlation with the Section II OCPD scores ($r = .56$ for two traits vs. .43 for all four traits) and better convergence with the FFM profile generated by the DSM-5 Section II OCPD scores (two traits: $r_{ICC} = .78$; four traits: $r_{ICC} = .59$). This does not speak to whether these traits belong in the AMPD or not, but simply demonstrates that their inclusion is responsible, in part, for the lower convergence with the traditional, DSM-5 Section II OCPD construct.

Sex Differences

Mirroring the findings for the FFM, it is possible that the sex differences found for DSM PDs might be explained by

Table 7.4 Convergent correlations among DSM-5 PD trait counts and Section II DSM-5 PDs

DSM PD Counts	Anderson et al., 2014 (N = 397)	Hopwood et al., 2012 (N = 808)	Miller et al., 2015 (N = 109)	Samuel et al., 2013 (N = 1025)	*Mean r*
Schizotypal	.50	.70	.56	.71	.63
Antisocial	.54	.68	.81	.61	.67
Borderline	.62	.70	.81	.66	.71
Narcissistic	.45	.60	.53	.58	.54
Avoidant	.50	.57	.55	.60	.56
OCPD	.03	.56	.43	.49	.39

Note: OCPD = Obsessive-Compulsive PD. Anderson et al. (2014) and Hopwood et al. (2012) did not present these exact analyses but were communicated via personal communication (December 6 and 18, 2017, respectively).

differences on the AMPD pathological traits. Based on the gender differences found for the DSM-5 traits in the Few et al. (2013) study, men had higher scores on risk taking, restricted affect, and eccentricity, whereas women had higher scores for traits such as emotional lability and depressivity. Similar to the Lynam and Widiger (2007) finding using FFM traits, sex differences on the DSM-5 Section III PD trait counts were significantly correlated with the sex differences reported for the DSM PDs on the basis of Lynam and Widiger's meta-analytic review ($r = .64$). As with the FFM data, it seems that sex differences in PDs may be due, at least in part, to differences in pathological personality traits that comprise these disorders.

Clinical Utility

As with the FFM, there are now results that speak to the clinical utility of the DSM-5 Section III approach from the perspective of clinicians' preferences, as well as data that examine these models in relation to clinically relevant outcomes. Morey, Skodol, and Oldham (2014) compared clinicians' preference for the DSM-5 Section II and III PD models and found that for five of six outcomes (e.g., ease of use; communicating with patients; communicating with professionals; useful for formulating intervention plans), the DSM-5 Section III trait model was seen as having greater clinical utility than the DSM-5 Section II PD approach.

With regard to a focus on clinically relevant correlates and outcomes, Few and colleagues (2013) demonstrated that the DSM-5 Section III traits were substantially correlated with interview-based ratings of personality impairment including impairments in identity (*mean r* = .48), self-directness (*mean r* = .46), empathy (*mean r* = .44), and intimacy (*mean r* = .50). The DSM-5 Section III traits were also significantly correlated with DSM-5 Section II PDs, as well as symptoms of anxiety, depression, and overall distress. With regard to incremental validity, the DSM-5 traits provided twice the incremental validity in the

impairment variables above and beyond the variance accounted for by the DSM-5 Section II PDs (mean ΔR^2 = .11) as compared to that provided by the DSM-5 Section II PDs above the Section III trait domains (mean ΔR^2 = .06). With regard to symptoms of depression and anxiety, as well as general distress, the DSM-5 traits again accounted for additional variance over the Section II PDs (mean ΔR^2 = .08), although the PDs accounted for additional variance as well (mean ΔR^2 = .08).[2]

CONCLUSIONS

The inclusion of a trait-model in the DSM-5 represented an important advance towards an empirically based, valid, and clinically useful approach to research and treatment of personality pathology. There is a robust literature on the validity and utility of general trait models, much of which generalizes to the DSM-5 pathological trait model. We believe the existing empirical base could have been used to provide a stronger foundation for the DSM-5 PD proposal (Miller & Lynam, 2013) as much of this pertinent literature was ignored in publications originally put out by the DSM-5 P & PD Work Group (Blashfield & Reynolds, 2012; Lilienfeld, Watts, & Smith, 2012). The best chance that the DSM-5 AMPD, or a similar trait-based model, has of eventually becoming the sole or primary diagnostic approach used in the future iterations of the DSM is to combine the existing literature on the FFM (and other trait models) approaches to PDs with the rapidly growing research on the DSM-5 pathological trait model. The integration of the extant empirical literature on trait models of PDs with the burgeoning research on the AMPD would go far in rebutting claims that the DSM-5 Section III PD

---

[2] It is worth noting that the trait component of the AMPD generally accounts for substantially more unique variance in Section II PDs than does the impairment component (Criterion A), raising some questions about the necessity and utility of Criterion A (see Miller, Sleep, & Lynam, 2018 for a review).

model, as least the trait portion, represents a brand new and untested model. Another important task will be to work towards building consensus within the field, a Herculean task, given the substantial criticisms that have been levied against various aspects of the DSM-5 Section II PD approach (Gunderson, 2010, 2013; Livesley, 2012; Shedler et al., 2010). Moving forward, it will be important that objective considerations of the existing data drive decisions as to how PDs are conceptualized, assessed, and diagnosed in the official diagnostic nosology.

REFERENCES

Allik, J., & Realo, A. (2017). Universal and specific in the five factor model. In T. A. Widiger (Ed.), *The Oxford Handbook of the Five Factor Model* (pp. 173–190). New York: Oxford University Press.

American Psychiatric Association. (1987). *Diagnostic and Statistical Manual of Mental Disorders* (revised 3rd ed.). Washington, DC: American Psychiatric Association.

American Psychiatric Association. (1994). *Diagnostic and Statistical Manual of Mental Disorders* (4th ed.). Washington, DC: American Psychiatric Association.

American Psychiatric Association. (2013). *Diagnostic and Statistical Manual of Mental Disorders* (5th ed.). Arlington, VA: American Psychiatric Publishing.

Anderson, J., Snider, S., Sellbom, M., Krueger, R., & Hopwood, C. (2014). A comparison of the DSM-5 Section II and Section III personality disorder structures. *Psychiatry Research, 216*, 363–372.

Bagby, R. M., Uliaszek, A. A., Gralnick, T. M., & Al-Dajani, N. (2017). Axis I disorders. In T. A. Widiger (Ed.), *The Oxford Handbook of the Five Factor Model* (pp. 479–506). New York: Oxford University Press.

Bagby, R. M., & Widiger, T. A. (2018). Five factor model personality disorder scales: An introduction to a special section on assessment of maladaptive variants of the five factor model. *Psychological Assessment, 30*, 1–9.

Blashfield, R. K., & Reynolds, S. M. (2012). An invisible college view of the DSM-5 personality disorder classification. *Journal of Personality Disorders, 26*, 821–829.

Chmielewski, M., Bagby, R. M., Markon, K., Ring, A. J., & Ryder, A. G. (2014). Openness to experience, intellect, schizotypal personality disorder, and psychoticism: Resolving the controversy. *Journal of Personality Disorders, 28*, 483–499.

Clark, L. A. (1993). *Manual for the Schedule for Nonadaptive and Adaptive Personality (SNAP)*. Minneapolis, MN: University of Minnesota Press.

Costa, P. T., & McCrae, R. R. (1992a). The five-factor model of personality and its relevance to personality disorders. *Journal of Personality Disorders, 6*, 343–359.

Costa, P. T., & McCrae, R. R. (1992b). *Revised NEO Personality Inventory (NEO-PI-R) and NEO Five-Factor Inventory (NEO-FFI) Professional Manual*. Odessa, FL: Psychological Assessment Resources.

Costa, P. T., & McCrae, R. R. (1995). Primary traits of Eysenck's P-E-N model: Three- and five-factor solutions. *Journal of Personality and Social Psychology, 69*, 308–317.

Crowe, M. L., Lynam, D. R., & Miller, J. D. (2018). Uncovering the structure of agreeableness from self-report measures. *Journal of Personality, 86*, 771–787.

Decuyper, M., De Pauw, S., De Fruyt, F., De Bolle, M., & De Clercq, B. J. (2009). A meta-analysis of psychopathy-, antisocial PD- and FFM associations. *European Journal of Personality, 23*, 531–565.

Derefinko, K. J., & Lynam, D. R. (2007). Using the FFM to conceptualize psychopathy: A test using a drug abusing sample. *Journal of Personality Disorders, 21*, 638–656.

Edmundson, M., Lynam, D. R., Miller, J. D., Gore, W. L., & Widiger, T. A. (2011). A five-factor measure of schizotypal personality traits. *Assessment, 18*, 321–334.

Eysenck, S. G., & Eysenck, H. J. (1970). Crime and personality: An empirical study of the three-factor theory. *British Journal of Criminology, 10*, 225–239.

Few, L. R., Miller, J. D., Morse, J. Q., Yaggi, K. E., Reynolds, S. K., & Pilkonis, P. A. (2010). Examining the reliability and validity of clinician ratings on the Five-Factor Model score sheet. *Assessment, 17*, 440–453.

Few, L. R., Miller, J. D., Rothbaum, A., Meller, S., Maples, J., Terry, D., … MacKillop, J. (2013). Examination of the Section III DSM-5 diagnostic system for personality disorders in an outpatient clinical sample. *Journal of Abnormal Psychology, 22*, 1057–1069.

Frances, A. (1993). Dimensional diagnosis of personality: Not whether, but when and which. *Psychological Inquiry, 4*, 110–111.

Glover, N., Miller, J. D., Lynam, D. R., Crego, C., & Widiger, T. A. (2012). The Five-Factor Narcissism Inventory: A five-factor measure of narcissistic personality traits. *Journal of Personality Assessment, 94*, 500–512.

Goldberg, L. R. (1993). The structure of phenotypic personality traits. *American Psychologist, 48*, 26–34.

Gudonis, L. C., Miller, D. J., Miller, J. D., & Lynam, D. R. (2008). Conceptualizing personality disorders from a general model of personality functioning: Antisocial personality disorder and the five-factor model. *Personality and Mental Health, 2*, 249–264.

Gunderson, J. G. (2010). Revising the borderline diagnosis for DSM-V: An alternative proposal. *Journal of Personality Disorders, 24*, 694–708.

Gunderson, J. G. (2013). Seeking clarity for future revisions of the personality disorders in DSM-5. *Personality Disorders: Theory, Research, and Treatment, 4*, 368–376.

Hare, R. D. (2003). *The Psychopathy Checklist–Revised*. Multi-Health Systems, Toronto, Ontario, Canada.

Hopwood, C. J., Thomas, K. M., Markon, K. E., Wright, A. G., & Krueger, R. F. (2012). DSM-5 personality traits and DSM-IV personality disorders. *Journal of Abnormal Psychology, 121*, 424–432.

Jarnecke, A. M., & South, S. C. (2017). Behavior and molecular genetics of the five-factor model. In T. A. Widiger (Ed.), *The Oxford Handbook of the Five Factor Model* (pp. 301–318). New York: Oxford University Press.

John, O. P., Naumann, L. P., & Soto, C. J. (2008). Paradigm shift to the integrative Big Five trait taxonomy: History, measurement, and conceptual issues. In O. P. John, R. R. Robins, & L. A. Pervin (Eds.), *Handbook of Personality: Theory and Research* (3rd. ed., pp. 114–158). New York: Guilford Press.

Krueger, R. F., Derringer, J., Markon, K., Watson, D., & Skodol, A. (2012). Initial construction of a maladaptive personality trait model and inventory for DSM-5. *Psychological Medicine, 42*, 1879–1890.

Lilienfeld, S. O., Watts, A. L., & Smith, S. F. (2012). The DSM revision as a social psychological process: A commentary on Blashfield and Reynolds. *Journal of Personality Disorders, 26*, 830–834.

Livesley, J. (2012). Tradition versus empiricism in the current DSM-5 proposal for revising the classification of personality disorders. *Criminal Behaviour and Mental Health*, 22, 81–90.

Livesley, W. J., Jackson, D. N., & Schroeder, M. L. (1992). Factorial structure of traits delineating personality disorders in clinical and general population samples. *Journal of Abnormal Psychology*, 101, 432–440.

Lowe, J. R., Edmundson, M., & Widiger, T. A. (2009). Assessment of dependency, agreeableness, and their relationship. *Psychological Assessment*, 21, 543–553.

Lynam, D. R., Gaughan, E. T., Miller, J. D., Miller, D. J., Mullins-Sweatt, S., & Widiger, T. A. (2011). Assessing the basic traits associated with psychopathy: Development and validation of the Elemental Psychopathy Assessment. *Psychological Assessment*, 23, 108–124.

Lynam, D. R., & Widiger, T. A. (2001). Using the five-factor model to represent the DSM-IV personality disorders: An expert consensus approach. *Journal of Abnormal Psychology*, 110, 401–412.

Lynam, D. R., & Widiger, T. A. (2007). Using a general model of personality to understand sex differences in the personality disorders. *Journal of Personality Disorders*, 21, 583–602.

Maples, J. L., Carter, N. T., Few, L. R., Crego, C., Gore, W. L., Samuel, D. B., . . . Miller, J. D. (2015). Testing whether the DSM-5 personality disorder trait model can be measured with a reduced set of items: An item response theory investigation of the Personality Inventory for DSM-5. *Psychological Assessment*, 27, 1195–1210.

Mervielde, I., De Clercq, B., De Fruyt, F., & Van Leeuwen, K. (2005). Temperament, personality, and developmental psychopathology as childhood antecedents of personality disorders. *Journal of Personality Disorders*, 19, 171–201.

Miller, J. D. (2019). Personality disorders as collections of traits. In D. B. Samuel & D. L. Lynam (Eds.), *Using Basic Personality Research to Inform Personality Pathology* (pp. 40–69). New York: Oxford University Press.

Miller, J. D., Bagby, R. M., Pilkonis, P. A., Reynolds, S. K., & Lynam, D. R. (2005). A simplified technique for scoring the DSM-IV personality disorders with the five-factor model. *Assessment*, 12, 404–415.

Miller, J. D., Few, L. R., Lynam, D. R., & MacKillop, J. (2015). Pathological personality traits can capture DSM-IV personality disorder types. *Personality Disorders: Theory, Research, and Treatment*, 6, 32–40.

Miller, J. D., Few, L. R., & Widiger, T. A. (2012). Assessment of personality disorders and related traits: Bridging DSM-IV-TR and DSM-5. In T. A. Widiger (Ed.), *The Oxford Handbook of Personality Disorders* (pp. 108–140). New York: Oxford University Press.

Miller, J. D., & Lynam, D. R. (2003). Psychopathy and the five factor model of personality: A replication and extension. *Journal of Personality Assessment*, 81, 168–178.

Miller, J. D., & Lynam, D. R. (2008). Dependent personality disorder: Comparing an expert generated and empirically derived five-factor model personality disorder count. *Assessment*, 15, 4–15.

Miller, J. D., & Lynam, D. R. (2013). Missed opportunities in the DSM-5 section III personality disorder model. *Personality Disorders: Theory, Research, and Treatment*, 4, 365–366.

Miller, J., Lynam, D., Widiger, T., & Leukefeld, C. (2001). Personality disorders as extreme variants of common personality dimensions: Can the five factor model adequately represent psychopathy? *Journal of Personality*, 69, 253–276.

Miller, J. D., Maples, J., Pryor, L. R., Morse, J. Q., Yaggi, K., & Pilkonis, P. A. (2010). Using clinician-rated five-factor model data to score the DSM-IV personality disorders. *Journal of Personality Assessment*, 92, 296–305.

Miller, J. D., Morse, J. Q., Nolf, K., Stepp, S. D., & Pilkonis, P. A. (2012). Can DSM-IV borderline personality disorder be diagnosed via dimensional personality traits? Implications for the DSM-5 personality disorder proposal. *Journal of Abnormal Psychology*, 121, 944–950.

Miller, J. D., Reynolds, S. K., & Pilkonis, P. A. (2004). The validity of the five-factor model prototypes for personality disorders in two clinical samples. *Psychological Assessment*, 16, 310–322.

Miller, J. D., Sleep, C. E., & Lynam, D. R. (2018). DSM-5 alternative model of personality disorder: Testing the trait perspective captured in criterion B. *Current Opinion in Psychology*, 21, 50–54.

Morey, L. C., Skodol, A. E., & Oldham, J. M. (2014). Clinician judgments of clinical utility: A comparison of DSM-IV-TR personality disorders and the alternative model for DSM-5 personality disorders. *Journal of Abnormal Psychology*, 123, 398–405.

Mullins-Sweatt, S. N., Edmundson, M., Sauer-Zavala, S., Lynam, D. R., Miller, J. D., & Widiger, T. A. (2012). Five-factor measure of borderline personality traits. *Journal of Personality Assessment*, 94, 475–487.

Mullins-Sweatt, S. N., & Lengel, G. J. (2012). Clinical utility of the five-factor model of personality disorder. *Journal of Personality*, 80, 1615–1639.

O'Boyle, E. H., Forsyth, D. R., Banks, G. C., Story, P. A., & White, C. D. (2015). A meta-analytic test of redundancy and relative importance of the dark triad and five-factor model of personality. *Journal of Personality*, 83, 644–664.

O'Connor, B. P. (2017). Robustness. In T. A. Widiger (Ed.), *The Oxford Handbook of the Five Factor Model* (pp. 151–172). New York: Oxford University Press.

Ozer, D. J., & Benet-Martinez, V. (2006). Personality and the prediction of consequential outcomes. *Annual Review of Psychology*, 57, 401–421.

Presnall, J. R. (2012). Disorders of personality: Clinical treatment from a five-factor perspective. In T. A. Widiger & P. T Costa (Eds.), *Personality Disorders and the Five-Factor Model of Personality* (3rd ed., pp. 409–432). Washington, DC: APA.

Roberts, B. W., & DelVecchio, W. F. (2000). The rank-order consistency of personality traits from childhood to old age: A quantitative review of longitudinal studies. *Psychological Bulletin*, 126, 3–25.

Roberts, B. W., Kuncel, N. R., Shiner, R., Caspi, A., & Goldberg, L. R. (2007). The power of personality: The comparative validity of personality traits, socioeconomic status, and cognitive ability for predicting important life outcomes. *Perspectives on Psychological Science*, 2, 313–345.

Roberts, B. W., Luo, J., Briley, D. A., Chow, P. I., Su, R., & Hill, P. L. (2017). A systematic review of personality trait change through intervention. *Psychological Bulletin*, 143, 117–141.

Rottman, B., Ahn, W. K., Sanislow, C., & Kim, N. (2009). Can clinicians recognize DSM-IV personality disorders from five-factor model descriptions of patient cases? *American Journal of Psychiatry*, 166, 427–433.

Samuel, D. B., Hopwood, C. J., Krueger, R. F., Thomas, K. M., & Ruggero, C. J. (2013). Comparing methods for scoring personality disorder types using maladaptive traits in DSM-5. *Assessment*, 20, 353–361.

Samuel, D. B., Lynam, D. R., Widiger, T. A., & Ball, S. A. (2012). An expert consensus approach to relating the proposed DSM-5 types and traits. *Personality Disorders: Theory, Research, and Treatment*, 3, 1–16.

Samuel, D. B., Riddell, A. D. B., Lynam, D. R., Miller, J. D., & Widiger, T. A. (2012). A five-factor measure of obsessive-compulsive personality traits. *Journal of Personality Assessment*, 94, 456–465.

Samuel, D. B., & Widiger, T. A. (2004). Clinicians' personality descriptions of prototypic personality disorders. *Journal of Personality Disorders*, 18, 286–308.

Samuel, D. B., & Widiger, T. A. (2006). Clinicians' judgments of clinical utility: A comparison of the DSM-IV and five-factor models. *Journal of Abnormal Psychology*, 115, 298–308.

Samuel, D. B., & Widiger, T. A. (2008). A meta-analytic review of the relationships between the five-factor model and DSM-IV-TR personality disorders: A facet level analysis. *Clinical Psychology Review*, 28, 1326–1342.

Saulsman, L. M., & Page, A. C. (2004). The five-factor model and personality disorder empirical literature: A meta-analytic review. *Clinical Psychology Review*, 23, 1055–1085.

Shedler, J., Beck, A., Fonagy, P., Gabbard, G. O., Gunderson, J., Kernberg, O., ... Westen, D. (2010). Personality disorders in DSM-5. *American Journal of Psychiatry*, 167, 1026–1028.

Simms, L. J., Goldberg, L. R., Roberts, J. E., Watson, D., Welte, J., & Rotterman, J. H. (2011). Computerized adaptive assessment of personality disorder: Introducing the CAT-PD project. *Journal of Personality Assessment*, 93, 380–389.

Spitzer, R. L., First, M. B., Shedler, J., Westen, D., & Skodol, A. E. (2008). Clinical utility of five dimensional systems for personality diagnosis: A "consumer preference" study. *Journal of Nervous and Mental Disease*, 196, 356–374.

Sprock, J. (2003). Dimensional versus categorical classification of prototypic and nonprototypic cases of personality disorder. *Journal of Clinical Psychology*, 59, 991–1014.

Stepp, S., & Trull, T. J. (2007). Predictive validity of the five-factor model prototype scores for antisocial and borderline personality disorders. *Personality and Mental Health*, 1, 27–39.

Trull, T. J., & Widiger, T. A. (1997). *Structured Interview for the Five-Factor Model of Personality (SIFFM): Professional Manual*. Odessa, FL: Psychological Assessment Resources.

Trull, T. J., Widiger, T. A, Lynam, D. R., & Costa, P. T. (2003). Borderline personality disorder from the perspective of general

personality functioning. *Journal of Abnormal Psychology*, 112, 193–202.

Warner, M. B., Morey, L. C., Finch, J. F., Gunderson, J. G., Skodol, A. E., Sanislow, C. A., ... Grilo, C. M. (2004). The longitudinal relationship of personality traits and disorders. *Journal of Abnormal Psychology*, 113, 217–227.

Widiger, T. A. (2013). A postmortem and future look at the personality disorders in DSM-5. *Personality Disorders: Theory, Research, and Treatment*, 4, 382–387.

Widiger, T. A., & Costa, P. T. (Eds.) (2012). *Personality Disorders and the Five-Factor Model of Personality* (3rd ed.). Washington, DC: APA.

Widiger, T. A., Gore, W. L, Crego, C., Rojas, S. L., & Oltmanns, J. R. (2017). Five factor model and personality disorder. In T. A. Widiger (Ed.), *The Oxford Handbook of the Five Factor Model* (pp. 449–478). New York: Oxford University Press.

Widiger, T. A., & Lynam, D. R. (1998). Psychopathy and the five-factor model of personality. In T. Millon & E. Simonsen (Eds.), *Psychopathy: Antisocial, Criminal, and Violent Behavior* (pp. 171–187). New York, NY: Guilford Press.

Widiger, T. A., Lynam, D. R., Miller, J. D., & Oltmanns, T. F. (2012). Measures to assess maladaptive variants of the five factor model. *Journal of Personality Assessment*, 94, 450–455.

Widiger, T. A., & Trull, T. J. (1992). Personality and psychopathology: An application of the five-factor model. *Journal of Personality*, 60, 363–393.

Widiger, T. A., Trull, T. J., Clarkin, J. F., Sanderson, C. J., & Costa, P. T. (1994). A description of the DSM-III-R and DSM-IV personality disorders with the five-factor model of personality. In P. T. Costa, Jr. & T. A. Widiger (Eds.), *Personality Disorders and the Five-Factor Model of Personality* (pp. 41–56). Washington, DC: APA.

Wright, A. G., Hopwood, C. J., & Zanarini, M. C. (2015). Associations between changes in normal personality traits and borderline personality disorder symptoms over 16 years. *Personality Disorders: Theory, Research, and Treatment*, 6, 1–11.

Zimmerman, M., Rothschild, L., & Chelminski, I. (2005). The prevalence of DSM-IV personality disorders in psychiatric outpatients. *American Journal of Psychiatry*, 162, 1911–1919.

7a Personality Disorders are Disorders of Personality: Commentary on the Five-Factor Model of Personality Disorders

FILIP DE FRUYT AND BARBARA DE CLERCQ

Miller and Widiger (this volume) provide a comprehensive and up-to-date review of the current status of trait-based models to describe personality disorders, with a particular emphasis on the Five-Factor Model (FFM) of personality. Their summary makes clear that considerable progress has been made for a trait-based description of personality disorders, although the *Diagnostic and Statistical Manual of Mental Disorders* in its current edition (DSM-5; American Psychiatric Association, 2013) still only proposes the ten categorical personality disorders in its official section. The trait-based DSM-5 alternative model has been put in the waiting-room (Section III), as a model requiring additional research and guidelines for practical implementation, reflecting the long way to go before trait-based models will be formally accepted in established diagnostic taxonomies and – related to this – be routinely used in professional diagnostic practice.

Besides pointing to the potential and benefits of a trait-based description of personality disorders, Miller and Widiger (this volume) underscore that, by adopting the trait perspective, considerable knowledge from the field of general personality was infused in the field of personality disorders, which was previously kept distinct from the clinical field. Indeed, increasing empirical evidence points to the biological (Riccelli, Toschi, Nigro, Terracciano, & Passamonti, 2017) and genetic (Vukasovic & Bratko, 2015) underpinnings of general traits, how they naturally develop across the life course (Roberts, Walton, & Viechtbauer, 2006; Soto, John, Gosling, & Potter, 2011), and whether traits can be the subject of intentional change (Allan, Leeson, De Fruyt, & Martin, 2018; Hudson & Fraley, 2015; Roberts et al., 2017). Likewise, the relatively new trend to also investigate more fluctuating and state-like within-individual differences (Hofmans, De Clercq, Kuppens, Verbeke, & Widiger, 2019; Jayawickreme, Zachry, & Fleeson, 2019) beyond the traditional perspective on between-individual differences, has shown its potential for research on personality disorder symptoms (e.g., in borderline personality disorder pathology; Wright, Hopwood, & Simms, 2015). Finally, also the consequential outcomes of traits have been described well during the past years both in adulthood (Skodol, 2018) and at younger ages (De Fruyt, De Clercq, & De Bolle, 2017), increasing our knowledge on the daily and potential long-term impact of traits on the development and course of personality pathology.

Moreover, the field of mental disorders, including personality disorders and their symptoms, further benefited from a more integrative consideration of its phenotypic manifestations, by research examining the underlying structural properties in association with personality traits. Such approaches may better account for the arbitrary boundaries between what is considered adaptive or maladaptive, the observed comorbidities among different disorders and their symptoms (e.g., substance abuse and borderline personality disorder), heterogeneity within particular diagnoses, and instability of diagnoses due to fluctuating symptoms (Kotov, Krueger, & Watson, 2018; Kotov et al., 2017). Research initiatives like the Hierarchical Taxonomy of Psychopathology (HiTOP; Kotov et al., 2018) or Caspi and colleagues' work on the general P-(sychopathology) factor (Caspi et al., 2014) are promising avenues to redesign our thinking on the structure of psychopathology and its relationship with personality (Widiger et al., 2019). Together, these new directions also contribute to a more holistic consideration of the individual patient, integrating findings from various research disciplines into clinical practice.

PERSONALITY PATHOLOGY: DISENTANGLING DESCRIPTION FROM DYSFUNCTION

Personality disorders are disorders of personality traits. This statement is a fundamental assumption of the dimensional perspective on personality disorders, implying that personality disorders share variance with nearly all general personality descriptive models. This will certainly be the case with the FFM (Widiger, Trull, Clarkin, Sanderson, & Costa, 2002), considered to be a comprehensive model of personality description, for which empirical overlap has been hypothesized already decades ago, generating a successful stream of research describing DSM-based personality disorders in terms of (facets of) the FFM (Bastiaansen, Rossi, & De Fruyt, 2013; Samuel & Widiger, 2008). Widiger, with various collaborators (for an overview, see: Crego, Oltmanns, & Widiger, 2018), took this approach a step further, describing several personality disorders in terms of specific configurations of maladaptive traits. These various sources of evidence have in common, however, that they still treat the DSM-based personality disorders as the prime targets to assess, although there is abundant evidence that the categorical conceptualization of personality disorders is fundamentally flawed (Widiger, 2000; Widiger, Livesley, & Clark, 2009). In this respect, one could argue that it may be better to talk about personality pathology, instead of referring to personality disorders, because the disorder concept is too strongly bound to the questionable categorical DSM-tradition. In the comment of this chapter, we therefore prefer to talk about the assessment of personality pathology, because the comment exceeds the focus on the familiar personality disorder constructs, and also includes for instance the personality disorder trait-specifier.

Personality pathology is a multi-layer condition, including the traits around which the pathology develops, but also encompassing an aspect of dysfunction, arising from an interaction between a trait vulnerability and a relevant context. This interactional viewpoint on the development of psychopathology, including personality disorders, forms a cornerstone of psychological science and points to the importance of including context in evaluating the level of functioning of the individual. In our developmental model on personality pathology (De Fruyt & De Clercq, 2014), we have consistently argued that a clinical diagnosis of personality pathology requires a separate evaluation of the functioning of the young individual, i.e., whether her/his standing on personality traits is associated with an impaired functioning in three significant contexts: (a) functioning within the family, (b) interaction with peers and friends, and (c) functioning at school. These contexts not only represent relevant sources of cues that may trigger maladaptive traits at a certain age, but also create an important avenue for evaluating the consistency of maladaptation across situations, which is useful for clinical decision-making in terms of the trait-based nature of the symptoms (De Clercq, 2018). This model is directly applicable to adulthood by orienting the evaluation of functioning towards (a) family and intimate relationships, (b) interpersonal relationships, and (c) functioning at work. This conceptual model is to some extent also in line with the alternative model of personality disorders in DSM-5 (American Psychiatric Association, 2013), although the prerequisite of dysfunction (Criterion A) before moving on to the trait description (Criterion B) may be inconsistent with the idea that it is the traits that form the heart of personality pathology, with the dysfunction resulting from a person's trait vulnerabilities in their encounter with environmental challenges.

PERSONALITY PATHOLOGY: COVERAGE

Besides a consideration of the evaluation of dysfunction, diagnostic task forces for DSM or other mental disorder classification systems will also have to (re)define the content of the field they ultimately want to cover. For example, DSM-5 Section III attempts to considerably redefine the content field of personality disorders, providing only trait configurations for six of the previous ten personality disorders. In addition, one can also make trait-specified diagnoses (Personality Disorder – Trait-Specified) when criteria for individual personality disorders are not fully met, and the individual has an extreme standing on some of the DSM-5 traits and shows significant dysfunction. The trait-specified diagnoses have the potential to go beyond the traditional categorical personality disorder concepts, to accommodate the large number of diagnoses of Personality Disorders Not Otherwise Specified (PDNOS) in DSM-IV (American Psychiatric Association, 2000). The field hence needs to think carefully about the content domain it wants to represent. Such decisions may be most fruitful when based on our improved knowledge on the structure of psychopathology in general, taking findings from HiTOP or the general P-factor research into account, but also findings on the development of personality and maladaptive traits in particular.

CHALLENGES

A crucial question for this field is how to go from here and move the trait-based approach (with or without amendments) from Section III to DSM's Section II. Although there was strong dissatisfaction with the categorical personality disorders, its replacement by a particular trait system, i.e., the DSM-5 trait set (Krueger, Derringer, Markon, Watson, & Skodol, 2012), turned out to be complex and demanding. On top of a particular trait set (Criterion B) also a Criterion A was proposed, that involves a separate assessment of the individual's functioning of the Self (identity and self-direction) and Interpersonal (empathy and intimacy) areas. Although there seems to be more consensus on the usefulness of the DSM-5 trait set, there are divergent opinions on whether we still need to retain (some) personality disorder concepts and propose trait configurations that maximally account for variance in these (Herpertz et al., 2017; Hopwood et al., 2018). In addition, there is discussion on the utility and necessity of Criterion A, and especially the way this criterion is operationalized. Bastiaansen and colleagues (Bastiaansen, De Fruyt, Rossi, Schotte, & Hofmans, 2013; Bastiaansen et al., 2016), for example, examined this two-fold diagnosis of personality disorder, operationalizing personality dysfunction using the Severity Index of Personality Problems (SIPP; Verheul et al., 2008) and using the NEO-PI-R (Costa & McCrae, 1992) or the DAPP-BQ (Livesley & Jackson, 2009) to assess general or maladaptive traits respectively. They (Bastiaansen, De Fruyt, et al., 2013; Bastiaansen et al., 2016) concluded that both criteria overlapped substantially though had some added value to explain traditional personality disorder concepts.

In sum, it is likely that a successful transition to trait-based systems to describe personality pathology will have to rely on the available empirical evidence regarding the taxonomic representation of (personality) pathology and its suitability and utility in clinical practice. We hope that this transition process can be conducted in an open dialogue with all stakeholders where participants to the debate are willing to learn from each other, adapt opinions or even reconsider positions so trait-based assessment becomes a reality in clinical assessment.

REFERENCES

Allan, J., Leeson, P., De Fruyt, F., & Martin, S. (2018). Application of a 10 week coaching program designed to facilitate volitional personality change: Overall effects on personality and the impact of targeting. *International Journal of Evidence Based Coaching & Mentoring*, 16(1), 80–94.

American Psychiatric Association. (2000). *Diagnostic and Statistical Manual of Mental Disorders* (4th ed., Text Revision). Washington, DC: American Psychiatric Association.

American Psychiatric Association. (2013). *Diagnostic and Statistical Manual of Mental Disorders* (5th ed.). Arlington, VA: American Psychiatric Publishing.

Bastiaansen, L., De Fruyt, F., Rossi, G., Schotte, C., & Hofmans, J. (2013). Personality disorder dysfunction versus traits: Structural and conceptual issues. *Personality Disorders: Theory Research and Treatment*, 4(4), 293–303.

Bastiaansen, L., Hopwood, C. J., Van den Broeck, J., Rossi, G., Schotte, C., & De Fruyt, F. (2016). The twofold diagnosis of personality disorder: How do personality dysfunction and pathological traits increment each other at successive levels of the trait hierarchy? *Personality Disorders: Theory Research and Treatment*, 7(3), 280–292.

Bastiaansen, L., Rossi, G., & De Fruyt, F. (2013). Comparing five sets of Five-Factor Model personality disorder counts in a heterogeneous sample of psychiatric patients. *European Journal of Personality*, 27(4), 377–388.

Caspi, A., Houts, R. M., Belsky, D. W., Goldman-Mellor, S. J., Harrington, H., Israel, S., ... Moffitt, T. E. (2014). The p factor: One general psychopathology factor in the structure of psychiatric disorders. *Clinical Psychological Science*, 2(2), 119–137.

Costa, P. T., & McCrae, R. R. (1992). *Revised NEO Personality Inventory and Five-Factor Inventory Professional Manual*. Odessa, FL: Psychological Assessment Resources.

Crego, C., Oltmanns, J. R., & Widiger, T. A. (2018). FFMPD scales: Comparisons with the FFM, PID-5, and CAT-PD-SF. *Psychological Assessment*, 30(1), 62–73.

De Clercq, B. (2018). Integrating developmental aspects in current thinking about personality pathology. *Current Opinion in Psychology*, 21, 69–73.

De Fruyt, F., & De Clercq, B. (2014). Antecedents of personality disorder in childhood and adolescence: Toward an integrative developmental model. *Annual Review of Clinical Psychology*, 10, 449–476.

De Fruyt, F., De Clercq, B., & De Bolle, M. (2017). The Five Factor Model of personality and consequential outcomes in childhood and adolescence. In T. A. Widiger (Ed.), *The Oxford Handbook of the Five Factor Model* (pp. 507–520). New York: Oxford University Press.

Herpertz, S. C., Huprich, S. K., Bohus, M., Chanen, A., Goodman, M., Mehlum, L., ... Sharp, C. (2017). The challenge of transforming the diagnostic system of personality disorders. *Journal of Personality Disorders*, 31(5), 577–589.

Hofmans, J., De Clercq, B., Kuppens, P., Verbeke, L., & Widiger, T. A. (2019). Testing the structure and process of personality using ambulatory assessment data: An overview of within-person and person-specific techniques. *Psychological Assessment*, 31(4), 432–443.

Hopwood, C. J., Kotov, R., Krueger, R. F., Watson, D., Widiger, T. A., Althoff, R. R., ... Zimmermann, J. (2018). The time has come for dimensional personality disorder diagnosis. *Personality and Mental Health*, 12(1), 82–86.

Hudson, N. W., & Fraley, R. C. (2015). Volitional personality trait change: Can people choose to change their personality traits? *Journal of Personality and Social Psychology*, 109(3), 490–507.

Jayawickreme, E., Zachry, C. E., & Fleeson, W. (2019). Whole trait theory: An integrative approach to examining personality structure and process. *Personality and Individual Differences*, 136, 2–11.

Kotov, R., Krueger, R. F., & Watson, D. (2018). A paradigm shift in psychiatric classification: The Hierarchical Taxonomy of Psychopathology (HiTOP). *World Psychiatry*, 17(1), 24–25.

Kotov, R., Krueger, R. F., Watson, D., Achenbach, T. M., Althoff, R. R., Bagby, R. M., ... Zimmerman, M. (2017). The Hierarchical Taxonomy of Psychopathology (HiTOP): A dimensional alternative to traditional nosologies. *Journal of Abnormal Psychology*, 126(4), 454–477.

Krueger, R. F., Derringer, J., Markon, K., Watson, D., & Skodol, A. (2012). Initial construction of a maladaptive personality trait model and inventory for DSM-5. *Psychological Medicine*, 42, 1879–1890.

Livesley, W. J., & Jackson, D. N. (2009). *Manual for the Dimensional Assessment of Personality Pathology – Basic Questionnaire*. Port Huron, MI: Sigma Press.

Riccelli, R., Toschi, N., Nigro, S., Terracciano, A., & Passamonti, L. (2017). Surface-based morphometry reveals the neuroanatomical basis of the five-factor model of personality. *Social Cognitive and Affective Neuroscience*, 12(4), 671–684.

Roberts, B. W., Luo, J., Briley, D. A., Chow, P. I., Su, R., & Hill, P. L. (2017). A systematic review of personality trait change through intervention. *Psychological Bulletin*, 143(2), 117–122.

Roberts, B. W., Walton, K. E., & Viechtbauer, W. (2006). Patterns of mean-level change in personality traits across the life course: A meta-analysis of longitudinal studies. *Psychological Bulletin*, 132(1), 1–25.

Samuel, D. B., & Widiger, T. A. (2008). A meta-analytic review of the relationships between the five-factor model and DSM-IV-TR personality disorders: A facet level analysis. *Clinical Psychology Review*, 28, 1326–1342.

Skodol, A. (2018). Impact of personality pathology on psychosocial functioning. *Current Opinion in Psychology*, 21, 33–38.

Soto, C. J., John, O. P., Gosling, S. D., & Potter, J. (2011). Age differences in personality traits from 10 to 65: Big Five domains and facets in a large cross-sectional sample. *Journal of Personality and Social Psychology*, 100(2), 330–348.

Verheul, R., Andrea, H., Berghout, C. C., Dolan, C., Busschbach, J. J. V., Van der Kroft, P. J. A., ... Fonagy, P. (2008). Severity indices of personality problems (SIPP-118): Development, factor structure, reliability, and validity. *Psychological Assessment*, *20*(1), 23–34.

Vukasovic, T., & Bratko, D. (2015). Heritability of personality: A meta-analysis of behavior genetic studies. *Psychological Bulletin*, *141*(4), 769–785.

Widiger, T. A. (2000). Personality disorders in the 21st century. *Journal of Personality Disorders*, *14*(1), 3–16.

Widiger, T. A., Livesley, W. J., & Clark, L. A. (2009). An integrative dimensional classification of personality disorder. *Psychological Assessment*, *21*(3), 243–255.

Widiger, T. A., Sellbom, M., Chmielewski, M., Clark, L. A., DeYoung, C. G., Kotov, R., ... Wright, A. G. C. (2019). Personality in a hierarchical model of psychopathology. *Clinical Psychological Science*, *7*(1), 77–92.

Widiger, T. A., Trull, T. J., Clarkin, J. F., Sanderson, C., & Costa, P. T. (2002). A description of the DSM-IV personality disorders with the five-factor model of personality. In P. T. Costa & T. A. Widiger (Eds.), *Personality Disorders and the Five-Factor Model of Personality* (2nd ed., pp. 89–99). Washington, DC: American Psychological Association.

Wright, A. G. C., Hopwood, C. J., & Simms, L. J. (2015). Daily interpersonal and affective dynamics in personality disorder. *Journal of Personality Disorders*, *29*(4), 503–525.

7b Assessment and Operationalization of Personality Disorders from a Five-Factor Model Perspective: Commentary on the Five-Factor Model of Personality Disorders

MARTIN SELLBOM

Miller and Widiger (this volume) have provided an impressive analysis of the conceptualization and diagnostic operationalization of personality disorders (PDs) from two similar but distinct five-factor models of personality: the Five-Factor Model of personality (FFM) and the alternative DSM-5 model for personality disorders (AMPD; American Psychiatric Association [APA], 2013) trait model (Criterion B in the DSM-5 Section III). They make a persuasive argument that the field of PD is ready to adopt a trait model for formal diagnostic operationalization in light of the extensive evidence for both construct validity and clinical utility.

I do not take any significant issue with Miller and Widiger's scholarly analysis and I agree with their general perspective and contention that the field of PD diagnosis is ready for a well-established trait model. Although I am not fully convinced that the FFM or the AMPD trait models must represent the actual trait operationalizations for PD diagnosis, I will not argue against their use here. Rather, in this commentary, I will discuss a few issues of importance as the field moves forward in this regard, most of which center on clinical application.

WHAT LEVEL OF ABSTRACTION IS NECESSARY?

The FFM and AMPD trait models are viewed as five-factor models owing to their higher order structures representing five broad domains. However, most of the research and data presented in Miller and Widiger (this volume) are not really focused on that level of abstraction. In a way, these can be considered 30 factor or 25 factor models, respectively, given that each of the PDs are considered within this level of abstraction. Although it is clear that a five-factor level of abstraction of personality and personality psychopathology has garnered impressive evidence as a higher order structure (e.g., Markon, Krueger, & Watson, 2005), the evidence is less clear at the facet level. Krueger and colleagues (Krueger, Derringer, Markon, Watson, & Skodol, 2012), for instance, started with 37 facet traits and eventually decided on 25 through a number of iterative factor analyses. Costa and McCrae (1992) decided on six

rational facets underlying each revised NEO Personality Inventory (NEO PI-R) domain. Other extensive efforts to capture abnormal-range personality from a dimensional trait perspective with promising validity have yielded 15 (Schedule for Nonadaptive and Adaptive Personality, 2nd ed. [SNAP-2]; Clark, Simms, Wu, & Casillas, 2007), 18 (Dimensional Assessment of Personality Pathology – Basic Questionnaire [DAPP-BQ]; Livesley & Jackson, 2009), and 33 (Computer Adaptive Test for Personality Disorders [CAT-PD]; Simms et al., 2011) facets.

Psychometric properties of measurement aside, these various models are not distinct per se and can be identified in one another (e.g., Markon et al., 2005). Although some experts would likely argue that the selected trait model does not matter as long as they have sufficient validity and utility in capturing PDs, it would behoove the field to arrive at some degree of consensus about a level of abstraction optimal for PD. Also, the smaller the set of trait facets necessary to capture PD variance, the easier and less labor-intensive the process will become. As the field moves away from its attempt to retrofit fallacious DSM-IV/DSM-5 PD categories, for which facets are clearly needed for optimal distinction, perhaps description of personality even at the domain level might suffice? This is an empirical question that is still unanswered but, in my opinion, would serve to advance the field.

ARE TRAIT MODELS READY FOR USE IN CLINICAL ASSESSMENT?

There are a number of issues that need to be resolved before trait models can be fully implemented in clinical practice for diagnostic purposes. I highlight only a few pertinent ones here.

What Constitutes the Presence of a Maladaptive Trait?

DSM-5 Section III calls for the presence of maladaptive traits (for Criterion B) in the diagnosis of personality disorder in the AMPD. They describe these traits as dimensional entities but provide for no clarity as to how presence of such traits would be indicated. In general, while extreme levels of traits are necessary for the maladaptive range, I do not believe the field has arrived at a consensus on how such elevations or extremities would be determined (Al-Dajani, Gralnick, & Bagby, 2016; Samuel, Hopwood, Krueger, Thomas, & Ruggero, 2013). In the assessment of Intellectual Disability (ID), for instance, the presence of extremely low intelligence coupled with associated impairment in functioning is required. And indeed, for ID, there is clear operational guidance in terms of what is considered extremely low intelligence (typically two standard deviations below the mean, but these thresholds have loosened somewhat [APA, 2013]). Of course, the same principles can (and, in my opinion, should) be applied to personality disorder diagnosis as well, but unlike for ID, the optimal threshold for maladaptivity still needs to be determined. Many common personality assessment instruments (e.g., Minnesota Multiphasic Personality Inventory – 2 – Restructured Form [MMPI-2-RF; Ben-Porath & Tellegen, 2008], Personality Assessment Inventory [PAI; Morey, 2007]) use standardized scores of 1.5 to 2 SDs above a normative mean to indicate a clinical elevation, but these levels have rarely been directly examined for diagnostic decision-making. Clinical judgment is an alternative (i.e., a clinician decides on whether certain maladaptive traits are present, which is how PD diagnosis is typically currently assigned), but it is imprecise. Such judgment alone would also be viewed as unacceptable in ID assessment, so why should psychopathology assessment broadly be held to a lower standard? After all, dimensional trait models are tailored for a more quantitative approach.

Is There an Assessment Device Already Available?

There is one five-factor assessment device currently available for measuring the FFM that meets most agreed upon *Standards for Educational and Psychological Testing* (see American Psychological Association, American Educational Research Association, & National Council on Measurement in Education [APA/AERA/NCME], 2014): the NEO PI-3 (Costa & McCrae, 2010).[1] However, Miller and Widiger have seemingly moved away from the NEO instruments as acceptable for this purpose, as their scale scores do not have a sufficiently maladaptive range. Instead, Miller, Widiger, Lynam and their colleagues have developed eight promising FFM tools for the majority of PDs that do have a greater range of maladaptivity (see

Miller & Widiger's [this volume] review). In my view, these instruments do indeed have promising psychometric properties, but far more work is necessary across a range of settings before they can be applied clinically. Furthermore, the AMPD trait model is directly associated with the Personality Inventory of DSM-5 (PID-5; Krueger et al., 2012) – a self-report inventory which has amassed an extensive research base (e.g., Al-Dajani et al., 2016).[2] Even so, the PID-5 is also not a current alternative for clinical practice, because it does not meet current standards for psychological testing (APA/AERA/NCME, 2014). More specifically, it lacks a sufficient normative sample, has no test manual guiding its use, and does not have formal measures of response bias (see Al-Dajani et al., 2016, for a detailed review), though the latter situation is currently being rectified (see later section). Any viable clinical alternative should meet these recommendations prior to formal clinical use.

Need for test manuals. The Standards for Educational and Psychological Testing (APA/AERA/NCME, 2014) state that psychological tests should have a manual that provides clear instructions and articulated rationale for test administration, scoring, and interpretation. Such manuals are not currently available for most five-factor PD instruments that assess dimensional personality traits, but are needed for widespread clinical application. For instance, one of the factors that are evaluated in court expert testimony is whether techniques upon which experts rely to inform their opinions have formal guides for their administration and use (*Daubert v. Merrell Dow Pharmaceuticals, Inc.*, 1993).

Normative referencing. Dimensional constructs lend themselves well to normative referencing, but the field needs to determine the most appropriate reference group (usually a representative community sample) to which a test taker's scores should be compared. Most common clinical personality inventories (e.g., MMPI-2-RF, PAI) and standard intelligence tests rely on normative referencing, which allows for the calculation of standardized scores. The FFM-PD measures and PID-5, for instance, do not have formal normative samples. It will therefore behoove dimensional PD assessment researchers to either select instruments with a large representative normative sample or generate such samples for existing or new measures before a psychometric approach to determining maladaptivity in traits can be achieved. If other types of norming are to be preferred (e.g., criterion-based referencing), then such need to be articulated as well, along with sound empirical justification.

Measures of non-credible responding. Self-report inventories are susceptible to response bias, which can have tremendous effects on both the observed scores and

---

[1] In this section, I emphasize instruments developed for the five-factor models Miller and Widiger discussed. There are other dimensional trait measures with a lower order structure (e.g., DAPP-BQ and SNAP-2) that are likely further along with respect to meeting the criteria I highlight, but might not be optimal for other reasons (e.g., Krueger & Markon, 2014).

[2] There is also a structured clinical interview available for the AMPD (First, Skodol, Bender, & Oldham, 2014), but I cannot find a single study in which it has been used, and therefore do not view it as a viable alternative at this time.

their psychometric validity if left unmeasured (e.g., Dhillon, Bagby, Kushner, & Burchett, 2017). Response bias is particularly common in forensic settings (e.g., Ardoff, Denney, & Houston, 2007) and it is probably not a preposterous suggestion that individuals with personality pathology might be apt to mischaracterize themselves either intentionally or unintentionally (e.g., poor insight). The most common clinical assessment inventories (e.g., MMPI-2-RF, PAI) have established validity scales to assess for non-credible responding, with a range of validation studies to support their use.

Some efforts to assess response bias are underway. Some FFM-PD measures (e.g., Elemental Psychopathy Assessment; Lynam et al., 2011) have validity scales. The PID-5 does not have formal validity scales, though experimental versions have been published that assess both inconsistent responding (Keeley, Webb, Peterson, Roussin, & Flanagan, 2016) and over-reporting (Sellbom, Dhillon, & Bagby, 2018) with promising utility. I am encouraged that some PD assessment scholars consider this an important issue, but any validity scales for newer measures need to be extensively validated before widespread use. The MMPI-2-RF Validity Scales, for instance, have over 70 studies supporting their use in a variety of contexts (e.g., Sellbom, 2019).

Superiority over existing clinical measures. Finally, although multi-scale clinical assessment instruments like the MMPI-2-RF and PAI are not directly designed to measure the trait facets as articulated in contemporary models, such as the FFM or AMPD, they nevertheless capture the relevant variance (e.g., Anderson et al., 2015). The MMPI-2-RF, in particular, has the Personality Psychopathology Five (PSY-5) scales, which are both conceptual and empirical cognates of the PID-5 domain scales (Anderson et al., 2013, 2015). Given how well-established such instruments are in clinical practice, and that they meet the recommendations for standard psychological tests (APA/AERA/NCME, 2014), it is important that newer measures for clinical use also demonstrate some superiority over these well-known alternatives in the assessment of PD diagnosis (Al-Dajani et al., 2016). Furthermore, other measures such as the DAPP-BQ and the SNAP-2, which might not have garnered the same clinical attention as the MMPI-2-RF and PAI, still assess established dimensional trait models, are further developed in terms of Standards for Educational and Psychological Testing (APA/AERA/NCME, 2014) guidelines (especially DAPP-BQ), and should therefore also at least be considered as viable alternatives (but see Krueger & Markon [2014] for why these trait model measures might not be sufficient conceptually).

CONCLUSIONS

Miller and Widiger (this volume) have authored a very illuminating and persuasive chapter with impressive evidence to support their main argument for considering five-factor models in PD diagnosis. I agree with them that this direction is important for the field. But, as I articulated, there remain important areas of scientific inquiry and applied assessment developments before we can fully realize these models' clinical use. I believe that such scholarship is in progress and I look forward to the field's development in this regard.

REFERENCES

Al-Dajani, N., Gralnick, T. M., & Bagby, R. M. (2016). A psychometric review of the Personality Inventory for DSM–5 (PID–5): Current status and future directions. *Journal of Personality Assessment*, 98, 62–81.

American Educational Research Association, American Psychological Association, & National Council on Measurement in Education. (2014). *Standards for Educational and Psychological Testing*. Washington, DC: American Educational Research Association.

American Psychiatric Association. (2013). *Diagnostic and Statistical Manual of Mental Disorders* (5th ed.). Arlington, VA: American Psychiatric Publishing.

Anderson, J. L., Sellbom, M., Ayearst, L., Quilty, L. C., Chmielewski, M., & Bagby, R. M. (2015). Associations between DSM-5 Section III personality traits and the Minnesota Multiphasic Personality Inventory-2-Restructured Form (MMPI-2-RF) scales in a psychiatric patient sample. *Psychological Assessment*, 27, 801–815.

Anderson, J. L., Sellbom, M., Bagby, R. M., Quilty, L. C., Veltri, C. O. C., Markon, K. E., & Krueger, R. F. (2013). On the convergence between PSY-5 domains and PID-5 domains and facets: Implications for assessment of DSM-5 personality traits. *Assessment*, 20, 286–294.

Ardoff, B. R., Denney, R. L., & Houston, C. M. (2007). Base rates of negative response bias and malingered neurocognitive dysfunction among criminal defendants referred for neuropsychological evaluation. *Clinical Neuropsychologist*, 21, 899–916.

Ben-Porath, Y., & Tellegen, A. (2008/2011). *Minnesota Multiphasic Personality Inventory-2 Restructured Form: Manual for Administration, Scoring, and Interpretation*. Minneapolis: University of Minnesota Press.

Clark, L. A., Simms, L. J., Wu, K. D., & Casillas, A. (2007). *Manual for the Schedule for Nonadaptive and Adaptive Personality–2nd Edition (SNAP-2)*. South Bend, IN: Author.

Costa, P. T., Jr., & McCrae, R. R. (1992). *Revised NEO Personality Inventory (NEO PI-R) and NEO Five-Factor Inventory (NEO-FFI) Professional Manual*. Odessa, FL: Psychological Assessment Resources.

Costa, P. T., Jr., & McCrae, R. R. (2010). *NEO Personality Inventory-3 (NEO PI-3) and NEO Five-Factor Inventory-3 (NEO-FFI-3) Professional Manual*. Odessa, FL: Psychological Assessment Resources.

Daubert v. Merrell Dow Pharmaceuticals, *Inc.*, 509 U.S. 579, 113 S. Ct. 2786, 125 L. Ed. 2d *469* (1993).

Dhillon, S., Bagby, R. M., Kushner, S. C., & Burchett, D. (2017). The impact of underreporting and overreporting on the validity of the Personality Inventory for DSM-5 (PID-5): A simulation analog design investigation. *Psychological Assessment*, 29, 473.

First, M. B., Skodol, A. E., Bender, D. S., & Oldham, J. M. (2014). *Structured Clinical Interview for the DSM-5 Alternative Model for*

Personality Disorders (SCID–AMPD). New York: New York State Psychiatric Institute.

Keeley, J. W., Webb, C., Peterson, D., Roussin, L., & Flanagan, E. H. (2016). Development of a response inconsistency scale for the Personality Inventory for DSM–5. *Journal of Personality Assessment, 98*, 351–359.

Krueger, R. F., Derringer, J., Markon, K. E., Watson, D., & Skodol, A. V. (2012). Initial construction of a maladaptive personality trait model and inventory for DSM-5. *Psychological Medicine, 42*, 1879–1890.

Krueger, R. F., & Markon, K. E. (2014). The role of the DSM-5 personality trait model in moving toward a quantitative and empirically based approach to classifying personality and psychopathology. *Annual Review of Clinical Psychology, 10*, 477–501.

Livesley, W. J., & Jackson, D. N. (2009). *DAPP–BQ: Dimensional Assessment of Personality Pathology–Basic Questionnaire*. Port Huron, MI: Sigma Press.

Lynam, D. R., Gaughan, E. T., Miller, J. D., Miller, D. J., Mullins-Sweatt, S., & Widiger, T. A. (2011). Assessing the basic traits associated with psychopathy: Development and validation of the Elemental Psychopathy Assessment. *Psychological Assessment, 23*, 108–124.

Markon, K. E., Krueger, R. F., & Watson, D. (2005). Delineating the structure of normal and abnormal personality: An integrative hierarchical approach. *Journal of Personality and Social Psychology, 88*, 139–157.

Morey, L. C. (2007). *Personality Assessment Inventory Professional Manual* (2nd ed.). Odessa, FL: Psychological Assessment Resources.

Samuel, D. B., Hopwood, C. J., Krueger, R. F., Thomas, K. M., & Ruggero, C. J. (2013). Comparing methods for scoring personality disorder types using maladaptive traits in DSM-5. *Assessment, 20*, 353–361.

Sellbom, M. (2019). The MMPI-2 Restructured Form (MMPI-2-RF): Assessment of personality and psychopathology in the 21st century. *Annual Review of Clinical Psychology, 15*, 149–177.

Sellbom, M., Dhillon, S., & Bagby, R. M. (2018). Development and validation of an Overreporting Scale for the Personality Inventory for DSM-5 (PID-5). *Psychological Assessment, 30*(5), 582–593.

Simms, L. J., Goldberg, L. R., Roberts, J. E., Watson, D., Welte, J., & Rotterman, J. H. (2011). Computerized adaptive assessment of personality disorder: Introducing the CAT-PD project. *Journal of Personality Assessment, 93*, 380–389.

7c Challenges but Optimism Regarding the Adoption of Trait Models of Personality Disorders: Author Rejoinder to Commentaries on the Five-Factor Model of Personality Disorders

JOSHUA D. MILLER AND THOMAS A. WIDIGER

We appreciate the thoughtful commentaries provided by De Fruyt and De Clercq (this volume) as well as Sellbom (this volume) on our chapter on trait models of personality disorder (PD). We use this rejoinder to address a few of the comments articulated in the two commentaries, starting with De Fruyt and De Clercq's.

DRS. DE FRUYT AND DE CLERCQ

De Fruyt and De Clercq are quite supportive of the overall trait model approach albeit they appear to be more pessimistic about the ease and amount of time before trait-based models of PDs are instantiated in diagnostic taxonomies in a more central and singular manner. For instance, they state that there is a "long way to go before trait-based models will be formally accepted in established diagnostic taxonomies." However, it now appears that the World Health Organization will approve in 2019 for ICD-11 a five-domain trait model that will replace (with one exception) the diagnostic PD categories (Reed et al., 2019). This trait model overlaps substantially with the alternative model of PD (AMPD) included in DSM-5 and will consist of negative affectivity, detachment, disinhibition, dissocial, and anankastic, along with a borderline pattern specifier; diagnoses will also include a single severity dimension ranging from mild to severe personality disorder. We believe clinicians will adapt and adopt these new models with relative ease given their relatively straightforward application and their prior judgments of the substantial clinical utility of trait models (e.g., see Widiger, 2019, for a review).

We largely agree with De Fruyt and De Clercq's suggestions regarding the measurement of impairment, particularly the notion that its assessment should follow rather than precede the assessment of personality disorder traits and their call for a more explicit focus on concrete domains of functioning (e.g., love and work; see also Pilkonis, Hallquist, Morse, & Stepp, 2011). There is even a degree of specificity of the five-factor model personality domains with regard to the impairment identified by De Fruyt and De Clercq, with the domains of antagonism and introversion concerning interpersonal impairments, low conscientiousness concerning work and school, and neuroticism concerning level of distress (Mullins-Sweatt & Widiger, 2010). We note, however, that it is remarkably difficult to separate the assessment of personality traits, especially personality disorder traits, from impairment given that the vast majority of traits inherently include information with respect to impairment (e.g., Miller, Sleep, & Lynam, 2018; Sleep, Lynam, Widiger, Crowe, & Miller, 2019). That is, elevations on trait domains such as negative affectivity, antagonism, or disinhibition already provide information about impairment.

DR. SELLBOM

Sellbom's commentary focuses on additional challenges to the adoption of these models including which level of the trait hierarchy should be used, broader domains or narrower facets. It is noteworthy that the DSM-5 and ICD-11 are at odds in this respect such that the ICD-11 model operates only at the domain level, whereas the DSM-5 AMPD focuses on 25 narrower traits that covary in such a way as to yield five higher order factors. Sellbom raises the important point that more work is needed to determine the optimal level of abstraction needed that balances coverage and parsimony. Although facet level descriptions are more complex than domain level descriptions, we expect that clinicians will embrace the more nuanced description that facets allow for once the clinicians become more adept with the application of the five domains

Sellbom noted a number of other issues in adopting these models, including the lack of formal test manuals, normative data, and measures of non-credible responding for many but not all existing PD trait measures. Sellbom comes at these issues, in part, from the perspective of a scholar working primarily on issues related to the Minnesota Multiphasic Personality Inventory (MMPI), in which these criteria have long been met. For instance, Sellbom notes that the MMPI-2 Restructured Form uses "standard-ized scores of 1.5 to 2 SDs above a normative mean to indicate a clinical elevation." We agree that normative data are informative, but are worried about the notion of identifying "clinical" elevations simply on the degree of elevation, as if all forms of psychopathology have an equal prevalence rate. Cut scores on maladaptive trait scales should be based (in part) on the degree of social and/or occupational impairment, which is the case for DSM-5 Section III and ICD-11. We agree normative data would be helpful but believe that a field-wide discussion of the type of normative data needed is necessary, as well as the solicitation of funds necessary to collect samples of this nature. Such funding will be necessary given the costs of such endeavors. The American Psychiatric Association might well be able to fund such work given that it owns the copyright to the most commonly used measure of the DSM-5 AMPD. Of course, it should perhaps be noted that the profits from the clinical and research applications of the MMPI help to fund its validation and construction of supportive material, whereas the DSM-5 AMPD is assessed by freely available measures. Finally, we agree with Sellbom that the creation of scales to measure non-credible responding (e.g., incon-sistent responding; over- and under-reporting) will be important, particularly if these scales are to be used in high stake settings. Such scales have been created for the family of FFM PD scales discussed in our chapter but these scales require further validation as do the newer post-hoc scales being created for the measures aligned with the DSM-5 AMPD.

CONCLUSIONS

In conclusion, while some challenges to the adoption of trait-based models of PD remain, including those highlighted by Drs. De Fruyt, De Clercq, and Sellbom, we are optimistic that they are surmountable given the immense motivation within the field to move to a more empirically valid and useful model of personality dis-orders. The instantiation of such models in both the DSM-5 and the soon to be released ICD-11 suggest that such long anticipated change is finally here (e.g., Frances, 1993).

REFERENCES

Frances, A. (1993). Dimensional diagnosis of personality: Not whether, but when and which. *Psychological Inquiry, 4*, 110–111.

Miller, J. D., Sleep, C. E., & Lynam, D. R. (2018). DSM-5 alterna-tive model of personality disorder: Testing the trait perspective captured in criterion B. *Current Opinion in Psychology, 21*, 50–54.

Mullins-Sweatt, S. N., & Widiger, T. A. (2010). Personality-related problems in living: An empirical approach. *Personality Disorders: Theory, Research, and Treatment, 1*, 230–238.

Pilkonis, P. A., Hallquist, M. N., Morse, J. Q., & Stepp, S. D. (2011). Striking the (im)proper balance between scientific advances and clinical utility: Commentary on the DSM-5 pro-posal for personality disorders. *Personality Disorders: Theory, Research, and Treatment, 2*, 68–82.

Reed, G. M., First, M. B., Kogan, C. S., Hyman, S. E., Gureje, O., Gaebel, W., ... Saxena, S. (2019). Innovations and changes in the ICD-11 classification of mental, behavioural and neurode-velopmental disorders. *World Psychiatry, 18*, 3–19.

Sleep, C. E., Lynam, D. R., Widiger, T. A., Crowe, M., & Miller, J. D. (2019). An evaluation of DSM-5 Section III Personality Dis-order Criterion A (Impairment) in accounting for psychopath-ology. *Psychological Assessment, 31*(10), 1181–1191

Widiger, T. A. (2019). Considering the research: Commentary on "The trait-type dialectic: construct validity, clinical utility, and the diagnostic process." *Personality Disorders: Theory, Research, and Treatment, 10*, 215–219.

8 Interpersonal Models of Personality Pathology

MICHAEL J. ROCHE AND EMILY B. ANSELL

A central feature of personality disorders is the interpersonal impairment and relationship difficulties with which individuals with these diagnoses often struggle (APA, 2013). As such, interpersonal theory can provide an organizing structure for describing personality pathology. The present chapter reviews contemporary assumptions of interpersonal theory, proposes additional context-driven factors that underlie the assumptions of interpersonal theory, describes the interpersonal circle model, and then examines how static and temporally-dynamic interpersonal data can inform description and treatment approaches for patients with personality disorder diagnoses.

The interpersonal tradition starts with the seminal work of Harry Stack Sullivan (1953a, 1953b, 1954, 1956, 1962, 1964), a psychiatrist who, through his work with patients with schizophrenia, developed a theoretical model that emphasizes the importance of social relationships in the management of psychiatric symptoms (Hooley, 2010). Sullivan defined personality as "the relatively enduring pattern of recurrent interpersonal situations which characterize a human life" (Sullivan, 1953b, pp. 110–111). Subsequent work operationalized his ideas into a model of interpersonal phenomena organized around two interpersonal dimensions, termed the interpersonal circumplex (LaForge, 2004; Leary, 1957). Whereas an overview of the history of interpersonal theory is available elsewhere (e.g., Pincus, 1994; Strack & Horowitz, 2011; Wiggins, 1996), the current chapter focuses on recent theoretical and empirical advances to interpersonal theory (e.g., Pincus, Lukowitsky, & Wright, 2010).

THE INTERPERSONAL PARADIGM

Decades of interpersonal theorizing and model development have been incorporated into what some describe as an interpersonal paradigm (Wiggins, 2003) or meta-theory (Pincus & Ansell, 2013) for clinical psychological science. Indeed, the interpersonal paradigm articulates both static and temporally-dynamic psychological processes that can

be integrated with other existing theories, including attachment (Bartholomew & Horowitz, 1991; Benjamin, 1993; Florsheim & McArthur, 2009), psychodynamic (Lukowitsky & Pincus, 2011; Luyten & Blatt, 2011), social-cognitive (Locke & Sadler, 2007; Safran, 1990a, 1990b), evolutionary (Fournier, Zuroff, & Moskowitz, 2007; Zuroff, Moskowitz, & Côté, 1999), and neurobiological (Depue, 2006; Moskowitz, Zuroff, aan het Rot, & Young, 2011) theories. The interpersonal paradigm has also been applied to the study of psychological assessment (Hopwood et al., 2016; Pincus, 2010; Pincus et al., 2014), psychopathology (Horowitz, 2004; Pincus & Wright, 2011), health (Smith & Cundiff, 2011), and psychotherapy (Anchin & Pincus, 2010; Benjamin, 2003; Cain & Pincus, 2016; Pincus & Cain, 2008). The present chapter focuses on how interpersonal theory, and more specifically the interpersonal paradigm, can inform the description and treatment of personality disorders.

CONTEMPORARY INTEGRATIVE INTERPERSONAL THEORY

Contemporary Integrative Interpersonal Theory (CIIT; Pincus, 2005; Pincus & Ansell, 2013) proposes four assumptions that guide the framework of the interpersonal paradigm. The first is that the propaedeutic expressions of personality (and its disorder) are interpersonal in nature. Indeed, most trait models of personality include dimensions that capture interpersonal style (e.g., extraversion, agreeableness; McCrae & Costa, 1989). The alternative model of personality disorders in the DSM-5 also emphasizes interpersonal dysfunction in the definition of core deficits in personality functioning (APA, 2013).

The second assumption is that two bipolar dimensions labeled agency and communion can efficiently organize the description of interpersonal phenomena. These terms serve as meta-constructs for interpersonal theory, as they can be applied to describe several units of analysis such as interpersonal motivations, perceptions/behaviors, strengths, and problems (Bakan, 1966; Wiggins, 1991).

Agency can be defined as the condition of differentiation (vs. enmeshment), with more specific descriptions for motivations (to control vs. to give control), perceptions/behaviors (dominance vs. submissiveness), strengths (to lead vs. to cooperate), and problems (domineering vs. nonassertive). Communion can be defined as the condition of affiliation and connectedness with others (vs. isolation), and can similarly be described more specifically for motivations (to affiliate vs. to separate), perceptions/behaviors (friendly vs. unfriendly), strengths (to connect vs. to separate for personal space), and problems (overly nurturant vs. cold).

The third assumption recognizes that interpersonal phenomena (including themes of agency and communion) can describe observable social exchanges, as well as "imagined" social exchanges that exist inside the mind via mental representations of self and others (e.g., Benjamin, 2003; Lukowitsky & Pincus, 2011). These mental representations are formed through the combination of past experiences (e.g., memories of past relationships, distorted memories from the past), present information, and future expectations (e.g., dreams/fantasies about current relationships, (in)accurate expectations about future social exchanges and relationships). As such, personality dysfunction can occur if individuals are so strongly guided by experiences that they discount present evidence and information, have unrealistic expectations about future relationships, or simply fail to perceive an interaction partner's behavior (or interpersonal intentions) accurately. These distortions may lead to characteristic ways patients see themselves and other people.

The fourth assumption is that there is a normative pattern to how interpersonal exchanges unfold over time. Generally, perceiving an interaction partner as dominant pulls for submission, and vice versa. If both people remain dominant, it is difficult to agree on a decision, and if both remain submissive, no decision can ever be made. This is referred to as agentic complementarity. Along the dimension of communion, there is an expectation that interaction partners will match each other on level of communion. If one person is more communal, she or he may be perceived as intrusive or overly invested in the relationship. If one person is less communal, that individual may be perceived as cold, uncaring, and disconnected from the other person. The research support for complementarity (Carson, 1969) will be reviewed later in the chapter.

A fifth, not previously articulated assumption within CIIT, is that context matters to the expression of these social exchanges, particularly when identifying pathological interpersonal patterns. Although normative, complementary social exchanges may predominate our interpersonal world, specific contexts may evoke non-normative patterns that reflect the characteristic interpersonal problems associated with a given personality disorder. There may be homogeneous non-normative responses that characterize a personality disorder (e.g.,

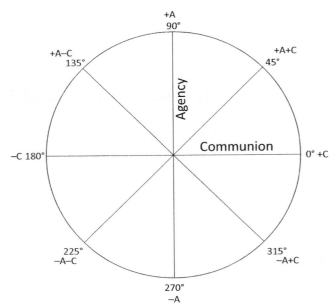

Figure 8.1 The interpersonal circle.

responses to dominance in narcissistic personality disorder) or heterogeneous non-normative responses that help explain diversity of interpersonal behavior within a disorder (e.g., borderline personality disorder). These context-driven expressions may best be assessed by temporally-dynamic methods, both at idiographic and nomothetic levels.

In summary, interpersonal phenomena are crucial to understanding the pathology in personality disorder. The dimensions of agency and communion can bring an organizing structure to describing interpersonal exchanges, both real and imagined. Additionally, there are normative patterns to how agency and communion are exchanged within social interactions, and chronic departures from those normative patterns are indicative of psychopathology. In the next sections, we review how agency and communion can be operationalized, and then present research using static and temporally-dynamic methods to capture interpersonal dysfunction in personality disorders.

THE INTERPERSONAL CIRCLE

Agency and communion can be organized conceptually and empirically as axes of an interpersonal circle (IPC; see Figure 8.1), where agency is denoted along the Y-axis and communion along the X-axis. The space between these axes represents combinations of agency and communion. IPC self-report measures typically contain 32 or 64 items that organize into eight scales (termed octants). By convention, the communion scale is set at 0°, and the other scales are separated by 45°, moving counterclockwise: +C (0°), +A+C (45°), +A (90°), +A–C (135°), –C (180°), –A–C (225°), –A (270°), and –A+C (315°).

The eight scales correlate in a circular pattern, where scales conceptually opposite (e.g., –A and +A) will have a strong negative correlation, scales conceptually independent (e.g., +A and +C) will have a near zero correlation, and scales conceptually closer (e.g., +A and +A+C) will have a positive correlation. The circular properties of the eight scales can be tested through various methods (e.g., RANDALL; Tracey, 1997; CIRCUM; Browne, 1992). Numerous studies have demonstrated several interpersonal measures conform to these circumplex properties (e.g., Acton & Revelle, 2002; Alden, Wiggins, & Pincus, 1990; Wilson, Revelle, Stroud, & Durbin, 2013).

Although researchers can examine these eight scales separately, the unique circular structure among the interpersonal scales allow for a more sophisticated approach. The structural summary method (SSM; Gurtman, 1994; Gurtman & Pincus, 2003) was developed to calculate four parameters with substantive interpretation: elevation, prototypicality, amplitude, and angular displacement. Elevation is calculated by averaging the eight scales together, and is simply interpreted as the average scale score (akin to a factor score being the average of the facets). Prototypicality (also termed R^2) examines how well the interpersonal profile conforms to a circular structure (e.g., a sinusoidal curve), a necessary step before interpreting the other parameters. An R^2 above .8 indicates a good fit to circular structure, and R^2 above .7 indicates acceptable fit (Zimmerman & Wright, 2017). The amplitude measures how differentiated or distinct the interpersonal profile is. For instance, how much do octant scales differ from the elevation score? If there is minimal differentiation, then the elevation score is the most efficient score to describe an individual's profile. In contrast, if the amplitude is .15 or higher, it indicates that some octant scales are higher than others and warrants exploration into which scales are particularly high. This could be done by looking at octant scale values, but the more precise way is to examine the angular displacement, which calculates the angle of the circle where the score peaks (across a 0° to 360° continuum described earlier). Thus, the angular displacement score is only meaningful if the interpersonal profile is circular and differentiated. A thorough review of circular statistics and calculations can be found in Wright, Pincus, Conroy, and Hilsenroth (2009).

Interpersonal Assessment Instruments

Whereas the eight octants and circular structure are similar across interpersonal circle (IPC) measures, different interpersonal measures can capture different interpersonal phenomena. For instance, the inventory of interpersonal problems circumplex (IIP-C; Alden et al., 1990) is a commonly used IPC self-report measure that captures behaviors that individuals do too much or too little, but that still conform to themes of agency (e.g., I am too aggressive towards other people) and communion (e.g.,

It's hard for me to introduce myself to new people). Here, the elevation represents a general factor of interpersonal distress, whereas the angular displacement represents the most characteristic theme of their distress. In contrast, the interpersonal adjective scale (IAS-R; Wiggins, Trapnell, & Phillips, 1988) is captured through a list of adjectives, where the elevation is thought to represent a response style that is not often of substantive interest. Other interpersonal measures exist to capture a person's values or motivations, goals, traits, efficacies, strengths, impact messages, and sensitivity towards other's behaviors (see Locke, 2011 for a more extensive review of IPC measures). Whereas each measure captures a different element of interpersonal phenomena, the structure around agentic and communal themes is similar, allowing for easy interpretation across instruments.

PERSONALITY DISORDER RESEARCH USING STATIC IPC INSTRUMENTS

At the broadest level, the IPC can serve as a conceptual map to organize constructs such as personality disorders. For instance, researchers can collect an IPC measure along with a measure of personality disorder. Then, researchers can correlate the personality disorder with each of the IPC octants, apply SSM calculations to those correlations, and examine how the personality disorder relates to the IPC in terms of elevation, angular displacement, differentiation, and prototypicality. Interpersonal models are especially appealing to the study of personality disorders because all are characterized by interpersonal dysfunction, and yet each specific personality disorder contains its own specific style of pathology. The elevation parameter can capture this central theme of interpersonal dysfunction, whereas angular displacement scores can capture the individual interpersonal styles characteristic of specific personality disorders.

Several researchers have examined the relationships between interpersonal style and personality disorders over the last several decades. Recently, this research was efficiently summarized in a meta-analysis containing 127 published and unpublished studies between the years of 1994–2013 (Wilson, Stroud, & Durbin, 2017). These researchers reported the correlations between interpersonal octant scales and personality disorders, and then examined the pattern of correlations using the SSM (several different interpersonal measures and personality disorder measures were used). They found that all but two personality disorders (dependent personality disorder, obsessive-compulsive personality disorder) exhibited a prototypical pattern ($R^2 > 0.8$), with adequate differentiation (amplitude > 0.15). Elevation was moderate across the personality disorders (0.17–0.39), indicating that each personality disorder shares a core of interpersonal dysfunction. Though, some personality disorders evidenced a weaker elevation (schizoid, antisocial), which may reflect the egosyntonic nature of

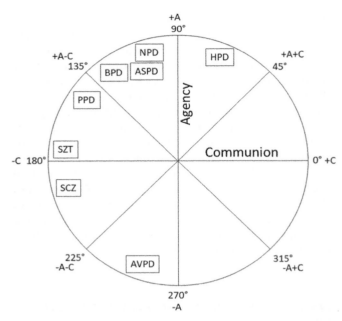

Figure 8.2 Interpersonal themes of personality disorder (PD) Note: Findings summarized from Wilson et al. (2017). Angular displacements are approximate. NPD = Narcissistic PD. ASPD = Antisocial PD. BPD = Borderline PD. PPD = Paranoid PD. SZT = Schizotypal PD. SCZ = Schizoid PD. AVPD = Avoidant PD HPD = Histrionic PD.

their interpersonal difficulties. Personality disorders also reflected distinct interpersonal themes (see Figure 8.2). Histrionic personality disorder was reflected in friendly-dominance, whereas narcissistic, antisocial, borderline, and paranoid personality disorders had themes of dominance or unfriendly-dominance. Schizotypal and schizoid personality disorders reflected themes of coldness/unfriendliness, whereas avoidant personality disorder contained themes of submissiveness. Though dependent personality disorder did not have adequate structural summary parameters to confidently interpret the interpersonal theme in this study, other studies have found dependent personality disorder to reside in the friendly-submissive area of the circle (Pincus & Wiggins, 1990), which was also the area indicated in the meta-analysis.

The researchers further noted that the correlations between personality disorders and dominant/cold themes were stronger in samples that were predominantly female and non-clinical, and in studies using non self-report methods to assess for personality disorders. In contrast, submissive/warm themes were more strongly related to personality disorders in samples that were predominantly male and clinical, and in studies that used self-report methods to assess for personality disorders. In total, this research suggests that the interpersonal model does a good job of capturing the convergent (interpersonal problems) and discriminant (themes of interpersonal problems) qualities of personality disorders.

The interpersonal circle can also be used to evaluate new models of personality disorder. For instance, the

Alternative Model for Personality Disorders (AMPD; APA, 2013; Pincus & Roche, 2019) proposes a severity dimension to describe personality impairment, which includes themes of self and other dysfunction. Dowgwillo, Roche, and Pincus (2018) found that this severity dimension was associated with elevation in interpersonal distress as measured by the inventory of interpersonal problems short circumplex (IIP-SC; Soldz, Budman, Demby, & Merry, 1995). Thus, diagnostic personality models and interpersonal models overlap in their conceptualizations of core interpersonal dysfunction.

The AMPD also includes five pathological personality traits that are meant to capture stylistic differences in how personality disorders are expressed. In a sample of several thousand students, researchers found that the several pathological personality traits exhibited adequate prototypicality and differentiation, suggesting that they capture interpersonal themes of personality dysfunction (Wright et al., 2012). Specifically, dominant problems characterized the antagonism trait, unfriendly-dominant problems characterized the disinhibition and psychoticism traits, unfriendly-submissiveness problems characterized the detachment trait, and overly-friendly problems characterized the negative affectivity trait. Another study of several hundred psychiatric patients found similar results (Williams & Simms, 2016).

Using a more advanced method to contrast interpersonal themes with confidence intervals (Zimmermann & Wright, 2017), researchers examined the associations between the inventory of interpersonal problems circumplex (IIP-C; Alden et al., 1990) and both pathological traits and categorical personality disorders in a large patient sample. This research largely replicated the previously noted meta-analysis findings regarding the elevation and angular displacement of personality disorders and pathological traits. Thus, the IPC provides support for the AMPD model, in that interpersonal distress is significantly associated with the severity measure of AMPD and the pathological traits organize around the circle in theoretically expected ways (antagonism corresponds to dominance problems, detachment corresponds to unfriendly-submissive problems, etc.).

Interpersonal Pathoplasticity

Pathoplasticity research examines the influence personality has on the course of mental health disorders (Boroughs & O'Cleirigh, 2015). Interpersonal pathoplasticity (Pincus & Wright, 2011) recognizes that not everyone with a disorder shares the same interpersonal style, and that different interpersonal styles can suggest different treatment outcomes and experiences. Using a form of cluster analysis, researchers have identified subgroups of patients within a disorder that have different interpersonal styles (e.g., angular displacement) and found that these subgroups are differentially associated with several important factors, such as symptoms and treatment outcomes. These effects have been demonstrated in social phobia (Cain, Pincus, & Grosse Holtforth, 2010; Kachin, Newman, & Pincus, 2001), generalized anxiety disorder (Newman, Jacobson, Erickson, & Fisher, 2017; Przeworski et al., 2011; Salzer et al., 2008; Salzer, Pincus, Winkelbach, Leichsenring, & Leibing, 2011), panic disorder (Zilcha-Mano et al., 2015), depression (Cain et al., 2012; Dawood, Thomas, Wright, & Hopwood, 2013; Simon, Cain, Samstag, Meehan, & Muran, 2015), posttraumatic stress disorder (Thomas, Hopwood, Donnellan, et al., 2014), and eating pathology (Ambwani & Hopwood, 2009; Hopwood, Clarke, & Perez, 2007).

Interpersonal pathoplasticity also extends to personality disorders. Although the previously reviewed meta-analysis suggested that most personality disorders conform to a characteristic interpersonal theme, several studies have found a more nuanced picture. In a sample of avoidant personality disorder patients, friendly-submissive and unfriendly-submissive subtypes exhibited differential responses to interventions emphasizing habituation and intimacy training, respectively (Alden & Capreol, 1993). Leichsenring, Kunst, and Hoyer (2003) found a dominant subtype and friendly subtype in borderline personality disorder patients, where the dominant subtype reported primitive defenses and object relations and the friendly subtype reported identity diffusion. Wright and colleagues (2013) found several subtypes of borderline personality disorder, with certain subtypes endorsing more anger, self-harm, identity disturbance, and emptiness compared to the others. Other researchers have found that the unfriendly-submissive subtype of borderline personality disorder can be associated with a lower therapeutic alliance (Salzer et al., 2013). These studies demonstrate that interpersonal style can be associated with different themes of borderline personality pathology and that this heterogeneity is meaningful when planning for, and conducting, treatment.

Taken together, the value of IPC models for personality disorder description and treatment is in enhancing, integrating, and synthesizing theory with assessment and treatment. Research can articulate similarities (elevation) and distinctions (angular displacement) in personality disorder diagnoses for DSM-IV/5 descriptions, as well as provide support for the alternative model. The observed heterogeneity in pathoplasticity research may be descriptive of the interpersonal situations that characterize the expression of problems. Drilling deeper into groups of patients with a diagnosis can reveal how interpersonal style influences symptom expression, therapeutic alliance, and the success of interventions across several diagnoses, including personality disorder diagnoses. These findings support the potential meaning in idiographic approaches to interpersonal assessment. Indeed, there is even greater nuance available when considering IPC models applied to an individual patient.

IPC Profile at the Individual Level

For a personality disorder patient, an IPC profile (e.g., IIP-C) can describe how much interpersonal distress they are experiencing (elevation), as well as the central theme of that distress (angular displacement) and whether their descriptions of interpersonal problems are conventional or non-prototypical (R^2). Another extension of this is to collect collateral reports of an individual's interpersonal problems and examine discrepancies. This occurred for Madeline G, a well-known case study in Jerry Wiggins' *Paradigms of Personality Assessment* book (Wiggins, 2003). Madeline reported her interpersonal problems and her partner gave ratings of her problems as well. Not only were the scores discrepant on the overall problems Madeline G experienced (e.g., elevation), but Madeline described the theme of her problems as friendly-dominant, whereas her partner saw her problems as unfriendly-dominant.

Another application to the individual level is to use multiple interpersonal assessment instruments and examine across-instrument discrepancies. For instance, if a patient's interpersonal values (elevation) are higher than their interpersonal strengths (elevation), then they may feel ineffective interpersonally. Or, a patient may have the value of being dominant and friendly, but only the strength of being dominant and unfriendly, leading to a specific interpersonal deficit to target in treatment. Moreover, an individual may report a clear theme to their problems (R^2), but be puzzled about their strengths, leading to a non-prototypical profile (R^2). A case example of such an approach is available in Dawood and Pincus (2016), along with more specific recommendations for how to interpret across multiple interpersonal measures.

PERSONALITY DISORDER RESEARCH USING TEMPORALLY-DYNAMIC IPC INSTRUMENTS

Recall that the fourth assumption of CIIT is that there is a normative pattern for how interpersonal exchanges unfold over time. This pattern, referred to as complementarity in the interpersonal literature, can be described using the dimensions of agency and communion. Specifically, a normative pattern of reciprocity or "oppositeness" is expected along the dimension of agency, where perceiving another person as dominant invites one to respond with submissiveness (and vice versa). A pattern of correspondence or "sameness" is expected along the dimension of communion, such that perceiving another person as friendly invites one to respond with friendliness (and vice versa).

One method to assess for context and complementarity is the Continuous Assessment of Interpersonal Dynamics (CAID; Sadler, Ethier, Gunn, Duong, & Woody, 2009) approach. Participants arrive at a laboratory and complete a discussion task with another person, and their behavior is coded using a joystick apparatus that captures second-to-second ratings of agency and communion. The discussion task can be with a stranger or person the participant knows, and the topic of the discussion can be unstructured or predetermined (discuss a conflict, recall a pleasant time, etc.). Multiple coders are used to obtain reliability. Although there are sophisticated techniques for modeling this type of data (e.g., Sadler et al., 2009; Thomas, Hopwood, Woody, Ethier, & Sadler, 2014), these results tend to correspond with a basic correlation that is easier to implement and interpret. Similarly, whereas lagged effects may be of interest, research has demonstrated that complementarity was strongest in unlagged data (Sadler et al., 2009). Simply put, in general, people tend to respond rapidly and normatively in interpersonal situations.

The results of several studies confirm that interpersonal complementarity is observed in the second-to-second interactions captured in laboratory settings. Sadler and colleagues (2009) asked 50 dyads to complete a collaborative task, finding evidence for both communal and agentic complementarity. Complementarity was also found in a group of female dyads, with higher communal complementarity being associated with completing tasks more efficiently (Markey, Lowmaster, & Eichler, 2010). Similarly, complementarity on communion and agency was found among mothers and their children, though that complementarity was influenced by gene–environment correlational processes (Klahr, Thomas, Hopwood, Klump, & Burt, 2013). In a study of in-session therapeutic alliance and interpersonal behavior (Altenstein, Krieger, & Grosse Holtforth, 2013), the authors again found evidence for complementarity on communion and agency. They further found that emotional activation was positively associated with decreased complementarity in session for communion and agency, supporting the importance of affect in driving non-normative interpersonal exchanges.

Although we are unaware of any study directly examining the associations among personality disorders and complementarity using this method, other research suggests that attention deficit hyperactivity disorder symptoms can influence complementarity in mother–child exchanges (Nilsen, Lizdek, & Ethier, 2015) and depression symptoms can influence complementarity in married couples (Lizdek, Woody, Sadler, & Rehman, 2016). Given recent conceptualizations that personality pathology relates broadly to meta-constructs of psychopathology (Kotov et al., 2017), these associations fit with interpersonal theory. Although the majority of these studies look mainly at complementarity, there is increasing interest in identifying contexts within and outside laboratory settings that can influence these processes (affect, type of conflict/collaboration task chosen, etc.).

CONTEXT MATTERS: EXAMINING A FIFTH INTERPERSONAL ASSUMPTION OF CIIT

Despite the ubiquitous nature of complementarity, deviations from normative interpersonal patterns happen throughout daily life and across individuals. Non-complementary behavior may even at times be adaptive. For instance, when a boss makes an unfriendly/hostile comment, it is ultimately unwise to complement that behavior with an unfriendly/hostile response. An individual who is hostile (e.g., low communion) may pull for her or his romantic partner to reciprocate that hostility/disconnection. Yet, if the partner explores her or his inner feelings (fondness) and wishes (to maintain the relationship, communion), it may lead to a non-complementary response (meeting hostility with engagement and understanding) in service of preserving the relationship. As therapists, we may wish to challenge the predominant interpersonal exchange with our patients by engaging specifically in a non-complementary pattern. By doing this, we may effectively "move" our patients into new or uncomfortable interpersonal spaces that will prove beneficial for their growth. Taken together, it is clear that complementarity in daily life is influenced by myriad other contextual factors (e.g., the interaction partner, current affect, interpersonal motives).

Our proposed fifth assumption synthesizes personality disorder models with the existing CIIT theory to further articulate what has always been an underlying assumption within CIIT – context-driven, systematic, non-normative interpersonal exchanges disrupt the interpersonal situation in a manner that is characteristic of personality pathology. Interpersonal complementarity is one normative pattern, but other normative patterns (how affect drives behavior, how motives and behaviors connect, etc.) are also relevant for a full understanding of the interpersonal situation. As noted before, interpersonal exchanges associated with personality pathology include those that chronically deviate from the expected normative patterns, or when a given context leads to a rigidly applied non-normative pattern.

These complex processes can be best assessed using temporally-dynamic approaches to better inform assessment and treatment of personality pathology. This method can capture discrepancies that are (a) nomothetic and common across all individuals with a specific personality pathology, or (b) idiographic.

The specific contexts that drive the non-normative behavior may include: (a) the specific interactant (e.g., significant other, parent); (b) the interpersonal behavior in a given exchange (e.g., dominant behavior); (c) the perception of interpersonal behavior in the other (e.g., hostile or low communion behaviors in the other); (d) the motives one has in a situation (e.g., to maintain or dissolve a relationship); or (e) the affect associated with a given exchange (e.g., negative or positive affect). These contexts have long been understood as fundamental to describing and understanding the interpersonal situation in CIIT and have been recently articulated in models of CIIT (Figure 8.3, see Pincus, Hopwood, & Wright, 2017). The benefit in adding this as a separate assumption is to better articulate, define, and test the theoretical basis

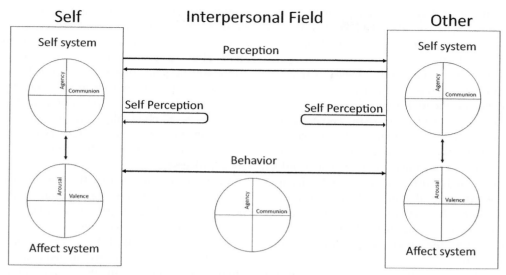

Figure 8.3 The expanded interpersonal situation model.

underlying ongoing efforts (described below) to understand which temporally-dynamic, non-normative responses within specific contexts underlie the interpersonal exchanges that characterize personality pathology. By articulating the how, when, and for whom these non-normative responses occur, we can inform novel treatment approaches that incorporate these data in increasingly personalized ways. Recent advances have moved the assessment of these non-normative interpersonal processes forward in increasingly relevant and informative ways.

One approach to examining complementarity along with the other context-driven processes is to employ intensive repeated measurements (IRM) in daily life. IRM designs typically ask participants to record information about social exchanges just after they end (e.g., six reports of social interactions per day) across several days. Interpersonally focused IRM designs will typically ask participants to record their own agency and communion as well as their interaction partner's agency and communion.

Several studies using this approach support the normative pattern for complementarity on communion, with mixed support for complementarity on agency. In a 20-day IRM study of community members, participants rated perceptions of their own behavior and the behavior of their interaction partner in social situations occurring in their daily life. As expected, complementarity on the dimension of communion (e.g., meeting friendliness with friendliness) and agency (e.g., meeting dominance with submission) were confirmed (Fournier, Moskowitz, & Zuroff, 2008). In a similar design of community members, Moskowitz and colleagues (Moskowitz, Ringo Ho, & Turcotte-Tremblay, 2007) found support for communal complementarity. Agentic complementarity was only found in work settings, and the effect was strengthened if the participant was in the higher-status work role (e.g., the boss). This finding supports the relevance of normative

interpersonal processes in daily life, with more evidence for communal complementarity.

A few studies have examined how personality dysfunction moderates or mediates complementarity within IRM research designs. In a seven-day IRM study using a student sample, narcissism disrupted agentic complementarity, such that higher narcissism was related to increased dominant behavior when perceiving the other as dominant and friendly (Roche, Pincus, Conroy, Hyde, & Ram, 2013). Wright and colleagues (2017) expanded this research into a clinical sample of psychiatric outpatients, completing a 21-day IRM study of affect, interpersonal perceptions, and behavior. The authors also evaluated the role of narcissism in these relations when controlling for other personality disorder symptoms. First, they found that personality disorder symptoms in general were associated with reporting higher negative affectivity, perceiving others as unfriendly, and behaving with submissiveness and unfriendliness. Narcissism, in contrast, was associated with behaving with more dominance. Examining complementarity across the sample, there was evidence for communal but not agentic complementarity. A unique pattern emerged such that perceiving dominance was associated with responding in an unfriendly manner, and this effect was mediated by negative affect. Narcissism moderated (strengthened) these patterns when controlling for other personality disorder symptoms..

Sadikaj and colleagues (Sadikaj, Moskowitz, Russell, Zuroff, & Paris, 2013) examined the role of interpersonal perceptions, affect, and interpersonal behavior in a sample of community adults and patients with borderline personality disorder who reported on their social interactions over 20 days. Individuals with borderline personality disorder were more likely to respond to perceptions of less communion (quarrelsomeness) with increased negative affect and increased quarrelsomeness (complementarity). This pattern was extended by partners who complement the negative affect and quarrelsomeness with even less communal behavior. This, in turn, led to more negative affect and less communion in the patient, which potentiated the cycle further.

The two examples described above speak to the relevance of non-normative interpersonal patterns that are context-driven and specific to different forms of personality pathology. In the case of narcissism, perceptions of dominance led to negative affect, which led to increasingly hostile interpersonal behaviors, whereas in borderline personality, perceptions of hostility led to negative affect, which led to increasingly hostile interpersonal behaviors. In both cases, the experienced affect and the interpersonal behavior are the same. Importantly, the context (perceptions of others' behavior) distinguishes the type of personality pathology and the underlying non-normative interpersonal pattern.

Interpersonal studies using IRM designs have been conducted to examine normative patterns of interpersonal perception and affect, generally finding that perceiving lower communion (unfriendly or hostility) is associated with negative affect (Cain, Meehan, Roche, Clarkin, & De Panfilis, 2019). However, personality pathology tends to enhance or alter these associations. For example, dependency moderated this relation, such that perceiving others as submissive and unfriendly was associated with increased negative affect in a sample of student participants (Wang et al., 2014). Similarly, in a community sample, negative affect was associated with lower communal perceptions, and this relation was stronger for those with anxious attachment and weaker for those with avoidant attachment (Sadikaj, Moskowitz, & Zuroff, in press). In a study comparing borderline personality disorder patients with community controls, the borderline personality disorder group had a weaker association between perceiving higher communion and positive affect, but a stronger association between perceiving low communion and negative affect (Sadikaj, Russell, Moskowitz, & Paris, 2010).

Personality pathology also impacts how agentic and communal perceptions are experienced in daily life. In a student sample, perceiving friendliness was positively associated with perceiving dominance, and this relation was strengthened for individuals higher in dependency but weakened for individuals higher in narcissism (Roche, Pincus, Hyde, Conroy, & Ram, 2013). This suggests that the strengthening or decoupling of normative perceptions may drive problematic interpersonal processes in different types of personality pathology.

Taken together, the emerging research using IRM designs suggests that the interpersonal patterns that occur in a person's daily life are influenced in systematic ways by the presence of personality pathology. Findings from studies using these methods are already proving fruitful in articulating the differential processes underlying different forms of personality pathology. Individuals with borderline personality disorder are more sensitive to low

communion, which, in turn, affects their affect and behavioral processes. In contrast, perceptions of agency are disruptive to individuals with narcissism, influencing their affect and behavior. Perceptions of unfriendly-submissiveness are unsettling to individuals with higher dependency, presumably because it thwarts their need for others to be in control and willing to help them. This emerging research highlights the importance of a broader definition of non-normative interpersonal interactions and a broader understanding of how affect influences interpersonal processes.

An expanded model of CIIT has been proposed that incorporates affect and motives along with interpersonal perceptions and behaviors to describe the interpersonal situation (Figure 8.3, see Pincus et al., 2017). It includes a self-system organized by interpersonal motives and affect. Here, affect is also articulated in a two-dimensional circular structure, with the X-axis capturing valence ranging from pleasant to unpleasant, and the Y-axis capturing arousal ranging from alert to fatigued. This same system is also captured for the perceived other. It further includes a section for interpersonal behavior of self and other (organized on agency and communion) as well as perceptions and self-perceptions (how I view my interpersonal qualities, affect, etc.).

This dynamic model captures the contexts of personality dysfunction, and highlights the role of the fifth assumption within CIIT models in articulating these complex processes. For instance, conflicts among motives (e.g., identity integration) or intense emotions are located within the self-system. Engaging in non-complementarity in interpersonal behavior is described as field dysregulation, as the behaviors exist outside of the self. Finally, dysfunction can result by distorting the views of self (e.g., misperceiving one's own motives of agency and/or communion), the views of others (e.g., perceiving them as focused on agency when they in fact are not), or engaging in interpersonal behaviors that are inconsistent with one's interpersonal motivations.

TEMPORALLY-DYNAMIC IPC AT THE INDIVIDUAL LEVEL

Although the majority of research has examined group level differences, theory supports the potential for an idiographic approach that informs personalized treatment. At least one research study has employed an IRM design to articulate the interpersonal and emotional exchanges occurring in daily life at an individual level (Roche, Pincus, Rebar, Conroy, & Ram, 2014). In this study, both husband and wife reported on approximately 130 social interactions, including information about their agentic and communal behavior, their anger and self-esteem, and their perception of the other's agency and communion. Of the 130 social interactions reported, 85 of them were social interactions where both husband and wife reported on their spouse during the same social exchange, permitting an examination of discrepancy across reports.

From the vantage point of the husband, his field regulation was mostly normative, as he engaged in both agentic and communal complementarity in his social interactions experienced in daily life. However, he would only engage in agentic complementarity when he was in the dominant position relative to his interaction partner (e.g., he is dominant, they are submissive). Engaging in less agentic complementarity was associated with the husband experiencing lower self-esteem, indicating a self-system dysregulation. In other words, he could only feel good about himself when he was dominant and others were submissive.

Regarding his perception accuracy and possible interpersonal distortion, he tended to perceive most people as both dominant and friendly, but perceived his wife consistently as dominant and unfriendly. This demonstrates that his perceptions were not uniformly biased and identifies a specific context for non-normative processes. His wife did not report her own dominant behaviors as being unfriendly, and the couple appeared to agree on her level of agency but not her level of communion (reminiscent of the Madeline G case). As with the Madeline G case, it is not known whether husband or wife is correct in their perceptions, but it does demonstrate how a discrepancy or context can be identified and then targeted for treatment.

INTERPERSONAL MODELS AND PERSONALITY DISORDER TREATMENT

Interpersonal models (both static and temporally-dynamic) have conceptual nuances that can enhance personality disorder treatment. A baseline assessment of interpersonal problems may be able to identify which types of treatment approaches will be more (or less) successful. IPC measures can also serve as an outcome measure for treatment, to monitor overall distress (elevation), clarity of problems (R^2), and themes of problems (angular displacement). In the session, therapist and patient behaviors can be coded for interpersonal complementarity, identifying treatment ruptures (e.g., therapist talking over patient leading to patient disengagement) or areas for therapist growth (e.g., remaining interpersonally neutral during patient hostile projections). Several studies have recently demonstrated how IPC instruments (cross-sectional, CAID, and IRM methods) can empirically guide treatment planning and patient care, and provide a digestible system for training new clinicians (Blais & Hopwood, 2017; Hopwood et al., 2016; Levendosky & Hopwood, 2017).

Psychodynamic

Interpersonal models can be conceptually incorporated into psychodynamic treatments of personality disorder.

Transference focused psychotherapy is an empirically supported treatment for personality disorders (Clarkin, Yeomans, & Kernberg, 2006) based on the assumption that patients form self and other object relations that link with affective experiences. Over time, these self–other relationship patterns form into object relational dyads that individuals use to understand their world. Personality dysfunction occurs when these dyads are used as templates to relate to others, rather than responding to the actual behaviors/intentions of the other person. Thus, the goal is to understand a patient's typical dyadic conceptualizations and gain insight into how these dyads influence affect and result in maladaptive behaviors and relationship functioning. The IPC models can primarily add to this approach by offering a conceptual map to describe dyads. The dimensions of agency and communion can efficiently describe and organize most dyads, leading to a simpler conceptual framework for both therapist and patient to utilize. Furthermore, the principles of CIIT suggest particular ways in which self and other relate, which can further clarify how the patient is responding to others in a maladaptive fashion.

Interpersonal psychotherapy principles have been articulated that are quite consistent with psychodynamic processing of the therapist–patient relationship (Anchin & Pincus, 2010). This approach recognizes that the therapeutic relationship is fundamentally an interpersonal relationship, with opportunities for patients to develop new social patterns via social learning from therapist–patient exchanges and explicit dialogue about those exchanges. Patients with personality disorders may have difficulty forming an early alliance given their rigid interpersonal style, negative concerns about the therapist, and/or skill at transforming social exchanges into the very relational dysfunctions they purport to disdain and encounter all too often in their daily lives. The therapist's role is to identify these maladaptive patterns so that they are not remade within the therapeutic relationship.

Generally, within psychodynamic treatments, therapists search their own feelings, action-tendencies, and fantasies to understand what the patient is evoking in them (e.g., impact message, counter-transference, see Kiesler, 1982), and then decide on the most therapeutic response. This will often include facilitating a healthy exchange of dominance within the therapy session, along with some closeness/distance pulls on communion (without occupying the extremes of those pulls, i.e., total enmeshment vs. rejection). Therapists will also connect interpersonal patterns in therapy to similar patterns recalled in the patient's daily life, highlighting both the costs of maintaining such patterns and the functions that they serve (see Benjamin, 2003).

Consistent with CIIT assumptions and the empirical findings presented earlier, different personality disorders may pull for different maladaptive exchanges in line with their pathology. The patient with narcissistic or obsessive-compulsive personality disorder may provoke unhelpful bids for dominance that prevent learning new information, or prioritize agency at the expense of communion (e.g., Campbell, Brunell, & Finkel, 2006). The therapist is tasked with monitoring these non-normative exchanges and refraining from responding in a complementary pattern in order to facilitate the patient's acceptance of a relationship with mutual parties contributing and awareness of the merit in attending to communion motives and perceptions. The patient with borderline or histrionic personality disorder may promote non-normative patterns via an intense communal complementarity response in therapy. This will lead to a chaotically deep enmeshment, sudden withdrawal as a more normative process is sought, or both. The therapist will be pulled to engage in these non-normative processes of alternating extremes, but can help shape more normative processes instead by providing consistent and appropriate communal complementarity which will help the patient begin to regulate these disconnections more effectively. This may include educating the patient about varying degrees of communal connection (e.g., what distinguishes a rejection from a small disconnection), and helping the patient form an identity that is understood as unique from how others perceive her or him (i.e., a robust self-system that can maintain a positive and accurate self-image even when others perceive the patient negatively).

Patients with paranoid personality disorder may expect therapists to deceive them, and yet their hostility may provoke vacillations in normative interpersonal exchanges as the therapist tries to elicit more affiliative interpersonal responses. This may result in comments from therapists that are indeed less genuine and thus fit into their narrative of anticipated deception. Instead, therapists can be cautious to not provide an overly-communal (non-complementary) presentation, and avoid mutual disengagement (complementary unfriendly-submissiveness) by instilling a neutral curiosity towards the patient's concerns. This specific non-complementary process will facilitate alliance within a non-normative interpersonal dynamic. Patients with avoidant and dependent personality disorder may pull for the therapist to be dominant in a way that is ultimately not therapeutic. The therapist will need to seek out ways to engage the patient in his/her own goals and insights.

So, although personality disorder patients share a theme of interpersonal dysfunction, it is clear that the specifics of non-normative patterns are specific to groups and individuals. Thus, therapist actions to facilitate change can be quite complex and driven in part by the flavor of personality pathology present in the room. Interpersonal models provide a basic framework from which to understand these relationship pulls and enactments and enhance normative social exchanges both within and outside the therapeutic relationship.

Cognitive Behavioral

Dialectical behavior therapy (DBT; Linehan, 1993, 2015) is an empirically supported cognitive-behavioral treatment designed to treat patients with suicidality, emotion dysregulation, and borderline personality disorder. It emphasizes both acceptance and change based principles through a combination of group skills training/psychoeducation, individual therapy, and other additional components (e.g., phone coaching, weekly consultation team for therapists). The interpersonal effectiveness skills module of DBT, in particular, can be enhanced by considering interpersonal models. Interpersonal effectiveness comprises effectiveness in three different areas that patients are taught to consider when approaching any interpersonal interaction: namely, their objectives, relationship, and self-respect goals. Each of these sets of goals has a specific set of skills that are described through various acronyms.

The objectives domain of interpersonal effectiveness helps patients ask for what they need (motive) or refuse an unreasonable request. In other words, it is a formula for enacting a dominant social exchange. The formula for doing this follows the acronym DEAR MAN, with the first word describing what to do and the second word describing how to do it. DEAR represents the steps of **d**escribing (facts), **e**xpressing (emotions, opinions), **a**sserting (specific requests), and **r**einforcing (explaining consequences). Interpersonal problems may arise when patients start with the assert without building the context for their assertion (e.g., what are the facts that make this request understandable?). Patients also may have difficulty distinguishing a describe statement (e.g., my husband turns on the TV while I am speaking to him) from an express statement (i.e., this makes me feel underappreciated). Finally, patients often fail to include the reinforce statement, make the reinforce ineffective (e.g., I will leave you if you watch the TV when I am speaking), or forget that reinforcement can be positive (e.g., If you turn off the TV in the future it will really mean a lot to me). The acronym MAN ensures that the patient executes the DEAR statement in a **m**indful way (of one's objectives), **a**ppearing confident (e.g., using a confident tone to promote agentic reciprocity), and being willing to **n**egotiate (e.g., being flexible to alternative solutions, taking a short-term submissive position in service of the overall objective being met).

Thus, the DEAR MAN structure provides the patient with specific instructions on how to enact an agentic request, and provides the clinician with specifics to diagnose where agentic complementarity breaks down. In other words, if both parties in the interpersonal exchange are dominant, the DEAR MAN can help the therapist diagnose aspects of the conversation that may have led to that anti-complementary exchange (e.g., neither party described the facts, one party used reinforcements that amplified the conflict, one party refused to negotiate). When both parties are submissive, the therapist might similarly be able to diagnose the source of the disconnection (e.g., neither party was willing to assert, hoping that their expression of feelings would communicate their unspoken needs).

Goals within self-respect effectiveness focus on building and promoting self-respect by interacting in a way that makes the patient feel competent and balanced in her or his integration of thoughts and emotions (i.e., wise mind). The acronym FAST suggests that the patient be fair (to themselves and others), not apologize, stick to their values, and be truthful. The fair skill guards against unmitigated agency (i.e., pursuing goals with too much dominance), yet also suggests that submissive behaviors enacted at one's own expense (e.g., over-apologizing, abandoning values) are not an effective way of managing a motivation to be agentic. Here, agentic complementarity adds coherence to what previously appeared to be four disconnected skills (FAST).

Relationship effectiveness goals focus on acting in ways that elicit a positive response from others (e.g., liking, respect) and that balance short- and long-term relationship goals. Importantly, these skills can be used even, and especially, in times of conflict. The acronym GIVE represents the skills of being gentle (courteous, avoiding attacks), interested (acting interested in the other's perspective), validating (acknowledging the other's feelings), and acting in an easy manner (smiling, being friendly). Essentially, the GIVE skills are specific ways to increase communion during conflict, and a reminder that communion is an important part of any agentic exchange. In other words, agency and communion are orthogonal, and one can ask for something (higher agency) in a nice way (higher communion). Relatedly, being nice is not the same thing as being weak, nor is being mean necessary to being assertive.

Interpersonal theory adds an important organizing structure to the interpersonal effectiveness skills in DBT. In particular, interpersonal effectiveness skills are sometimes organized around an exchange where the patient needs to be dominant and is hoping for submissive reciprocity in the exchange. The method explicitly articulates how adding a dose of communion to the request is useful in meeting the goals of the exchange. Although not explicit in the DBT theory, providing patients with this simplified two-dimensional structure (agency and communion) may facilitate patients' engagement, comprehension, monitoring, and implementation in the initial stages. It may also help patients report back and describe specific interpersonal situations that drive affective or behavioral dysregulation.

CONCLUSION

Diagnostic descriptions of personality disorders and pathology emphasize relationship dysfunction that is relatively pervasive across time and contexts. Interpersonal models have the ability to describe this dysfunction in both static and temporally-dynamic forms, giving greater clarity to the description and treatment of personality disorders. In particular, psychological research has emphasized how interpersonal models can capture both the severity and theme of interpersonal dysfunction, how particular non-normative interpersonal situations may characterize specific forms of personality pathology, and how interpersonal dysfunction can alternatively impact therapeutic alliance and inform personalized and successful treatment techniques. Temporally-dynamic research studies across at least two timescales support the normative patterns of interpersonal complementarity. Moreover, deviations from complementarity do not entirely capture the non-normative interpersonal exchanges that characterize personality pathology. Understanding the contexts of non-normative social exchanges can enhance one's understanding of specific patterns underlying personality pathology, inform the expected therapeutic exchanges, and identify the key relationship patterns existing in the patient's daily life. The interpersonal paradigm is pan-theoretical, having broad applications to many theories of psychopathology and treatment; the integration with two approaches to treatment was explicated in the previous pages. In totality, we see the research and clinical potential in tethering the study of personality disorders to interpersonal models in order to better articulate, assess, and treat the non-normative interpersonal patterns that lead to dysfunction in the everyday lives of individuals who struggle with these disorders.

REFERENCES

Acton, G. S., & Revelle, W. (2002). Interpersonal personality measures show circumplex structure based on new psychometric criteria. *Journal of Personality Assessment, 79*, 446–471.

Alden, L. E., & Capreol, M. J. (1993). Avoidant personality disorder: Interpersonal problems as predictors of treatment response. *Behavior Therapy, 24*, 357–376.

Alden, L. E., Wiggins, J. S., & Pincus, A. L. (1990). Construction of circumplex scales for the Inventory of Interpersonal Problems. *Journal of Personality Assessment, 55*, 521–536.

Altenstein, D., Krieger, T., & Grosse Holtforth, M.G. (2013). Interpersonal microprocesses predict cognitive-emotional processing and the therapeutic alliance in psychotherapy for depression. *Journal of Counseling Psychology, 60*, 445–452.

Ambwani, S., & Hopwood, C. J. (2009). The utility of considering interpersonal problems in the assessment of bulimic features. *Eating Behaviors, 10*, 247–253.

American Psychiatric Association. (2013). *Diagnostic and Statistical Manual of Mental Disorders* (5th ed.). Arlington, VA: American Psychiatric Publishing.

Anchin, J. C., & Pincus, A. L. (2010). Evidence-based interpersonal psychotherapy with personality disorders: Theory, components, and strategies. In J. J. Magnavita (Ed.), *Evidence-Based Treatment of Personality Dysfunction: Principles, Methods, and Processes* (pp. 113–166). Washington, DC: American Psychological Association.

Bakan, D. (1966). *The Duality of Human Existence: Isolation and Communion in Western Man*. Boston: Beacon Press.

Bartholomew, K., & Horowitz, L. M. (1991). Attachment styles among young adults: A test of a four-category model. *Journal of Personality and Social Psychology, 61*, 226–244.

Benjamin, L. S. (1993). Every psychopathology is a gift of love. *Psychotherapy Research*, *3*, 1–24.

Benjamin, L. S. (2003). *Interpersonal Reconstructive Therapy: Promoting Change in Nonresponders*. New York: Guilford Press.

Blais, M. A., & Hopwood, C. J. (2017). Model-based approaches for teaching and practicing personality assessment. *Journal of Personality Assessment*, *99*, 136–145.

Boroughs, M. S., & O'Cleirigh, C (2015). Pathoplasticity. In *The Encyclopedia of Clinical Psychology*. Chichester: John Wiley. https://doi.org/10.1002/9781118625392.wbecp296.

Browne, M. W. (1992). Circumplex models for correlation matrices. *Psychometrika*, *57*, 469–497.

Cain, N. M., Ansell, E. B., Wright, A. G. C., Hopwood, C. J., Thomas, K. M., Pinto, A., . . . Grilo, C. M. (2012). Interpersonal pathoplasticity in the course of major depression. *Journal of Consulting and Clinical Psychology*, *80*, 78–86.

Cain, N. M., Meehan, K. B., Roche, M. J., Clarkin, J. F., & De Panfilis, C. (2019). Effortful control and interpersonal behavior in daily life. *Journal of Personality Assessment*, *101*, 315–325.

Cain, N. M. & Pincus, A. L. (2016). Treating maladaptive interpersonal signatures. In W. J. Livesley, G. S. Dimaggio, & J. F. Clarkin (Eds.), *Integrated Treatment of Personality Disorder: A Modular Approach* (pp. 305–324). New York: Guilford Press.

Cain, N. M., Pincus, A. L., & Grosse Holtforth, M. (2010). Interpersonal subtypes in social phobia: Diagnostic and treatment implications. *Journal of Personality Assessment*, *92*, 514–527.

Campbell, W. K., Brunell, A. B., & Finkel, E. J. (2006). Narcissism, interpersonal self-regulation, and romantic relationships: An agency model approach. In K. D. Vohs & E. J. Finkel (Eds.), *Self and Relationships: Connecting Intrapersonal and Interpersonal Processes* (pp. 57–83). New York: Guilford Press.

Carson, R. C. (1969). *Interaction Concepts of Personality*. Chicago: Aldine.

Clarkin, J. F., Yeomans, F. E., & Kernberg, O. F. (2006). *Psychotherapy of Borderline Personality: Focusing on Object Relations*. Arlington, VA: American Psychiatric Publishing.

Dawood, S., & Pincus, A. L. (2016). Multi-surface interpersonal assessment in a cognitive-behavioral therapy context. *Journal of Personality Assessment*, *98*, 449–460.

Dawood, S., Thomas, K. M., Wright, A. G. C., & Hopwood, C. J. (2013). Heterogeneity of interpersonal problems among depressed young adults: Associations with substance abuse and pathological personality traits. *Journal of Personality Assessment*, *95*, 513–522.

Depue, R. A. (2006). Interpersonal behavior and the structure of personality: Neurobehavioral foundation of agentic extraversion and affiliation. In T. Canli (Ed.), *Biology of Personality and Individual Differences* (pp. 60–92). New York: Guilford Press.

Dowgwillo, E. A., Roche, M. J., & Pincus, A. L. (2018). Examining the interpersonal nature of Criterion A of the DSM-5 Section III Alternative Model for Personality Disorders using bootstrapped circular confidence intervals. *Journal of Personality Assessment*, *100*, 581–592.

Florsheim, P., & McArthur, L. (2009). An interpersonal approach to attachment and change. In J. H. Obegi & E. Berent (Eds.), *Attachment Theory and Research in Clinical Work with Adults* (pp. 379–409). New York: Guilford Press.

Fournier, M. A., Moskowitz, D. S., & Zuroff, D. C. (2008). Integrating dispositions, signatures, and the interpersonal domain. *Journal of Personality and Social Psychology*, *94*, 531–545.

Fournier, M. A., Zuroff, D. C., & Moskowitz, D. S. (2007). The social competition theory of depression: Gaining from an evolutionary approach to losing. *Journal of Social and Clinical Psychology*, *26*, 786–790.

Gurtman, M. B. (1994). The circumplex as a tool for studying normal and abnormal personality: A methodological primer. In S. Strack & M. Lorr (Eds.), *Differentiating Normal and Abnormal Personality* (pp. 243–263). New York: Springer.

Gurtman, M. B., & Pincus, A. L. (2003). The circumplex model: Methods and research applications. In J. A. Schnika & W. F. Velicer (Eds.), *Comprehensive Handbook of Psychology, Volume 2: Research Methods in Psychology* (pp. 407–428). Hoboken, NJ: John Wiley & Sons.

Hooley, J. M. (2010). Social factors in schizophrenia. *Current Directions in Psychological Science*, *19*, 238–242.

Hopwood, C. J., Clarke, A. N., & Perez, M. (2007). Pathoplasticity of bulimic features and interpersonal problems. *International Journal of Eating Disorders*, *40*, 652–658.

Hopwood, C. J., Thomas, K. M., Luo, X., Bernard, N., Lin, Y., & Levendosky, A. A. (2016). Implementing dynamic assessments in psychotherapy. *Assessment*, *23*, 507–517.

Horowitz, L. M. (2004). *Interpersonal Foundations of Psychopathology*. Washington, DC: American Psychological Association.

Kachin, K. E., Newman, M. G., & Pincus, A. L. (2001). An interpersonal problem approach to the division of social phobia subtypes. *Behavior Therapy*, *32*, 479–501.

Kiesler, D. J. (1982). Confronting the client–therapist relationship in psychotherapy. In J. C. Anchin & D. J. Kiesler (Eds.), *Handbook of Interpersonal Psychotherapy* (pp. 274–295). New York: Pergamon.

Klahr, A. M., Thomas, K. M., Hopwood, C. J., Klump, K. L., & Burt, S. A. (2013). Evocative gene–environment correlation in the mother–child relationship: A twin study of interpersonal processes. *Development and Psychopathology*, *25*, 105–118.

Kotov, R., Krueger, R. F., Watson, D., Achenbach, T. M., Althoff, R. R., Bagby, R. M., . . . & Eaton, N. R. (2017). The Hierarchical Taxonomy of Psychopathology (HiTOP): A dimensional alternative to traditional nosologies. *Journal of Abnormal Psychology*, *126*, 454–477.

LaForge, R. (2004). The early development of the interpersonal system of personality (ISP). *Multivariate Behavioral Research*, *39*, 359–378.

Leary, T. (1957). *Interpersonal Diagnosis of Personality*. New York: Ronald Press.

Leichsenring, F., Kunst, H., & Hoyer, J. (2003). Borderline personality organization in violent offenders: Correlations of identity diffusion and primitive defense mechanisms with antisocial features, neuroticism, and interpersonal problems. *Bulletin of the Menninger Clinic*, *67*, 314–327.

Levendosky, A. A., & Hopwood, C. J. (2017). A clinical science approach to training first year clinicians to navigate therapeutic relationships. *Journal of Psychotherapy Integration*, *27*, 153–171.

Linehan, M. (1993). *Cognitive-Behavioral Treatment of Borderline Personality Disorder*. New York: Guilford Press.

Linehan, M. M. (2015). *DBT Skills Training Manual* (2nd ed.). New York: Guilford Press.

Lizdek, I., Woody, E., Sadler, P., & Rehman, U. S. (2016). How do depressive symptoms in husbands and wives relate to the interpersonal dynamics of marital interactions? *Journal of Counseling Psychology*, *63*, 721–735.

Locke, K. D. (2011). Circumplex measures of interpersonal constructs. In L. M. Horowitz & S. Strack (Eds.), *Handbook of*

Interpersonal Psychology: Theory, Research, Assessment, and Therapeutic Interventions (pp. 313–324). Hoboken, NJ: John Wiley.

Locke, K. D., & Sadler, P. (2007). Self-efficacy, values, and complementarity in dyadic interactions: Integrating interpersonal and social-cognitive theory. *Personality and Social Psychology Bulletin, 33*, 94–109.

Lukowitsky, M. R., & Pincus, A. L. (2011). The pantheoretical nature of mental representations and their ability to predict interpersonal adjustment in a nonclinical sample. *Psychoanalytic Psychology, 28*, 48–74.

Luyten, P., & Blatt, S. J. (2011). Integrating theory-driven and empirically-derived models of personality development and psychopathology: A proposal for DSM V. *Clinical Psychology Review, 31*, 52–68.

Markey, P., Lowmaster, S., & Eichler, W. (2010). A real-time assessment of interpersonal complementarity. *Personal Relationships, 1*, 13–25.

McCrae, R. R., & Costa, P. T. (1989). The structure of interpersonal traits: Wiggins's circumplex and the five-factor model. *Journal of Personality and Social Psychology, 56*, 586–595.

Moskowitz, D. S., Ringo Ho, M.-H., & Turcotte-Tremblay, A. (2007). Contextual influences on interpersonal complementarity. *Personality and Social Psychology Bulletin, 33*, 1051–1063.

Moskowitz, D. S., Zuroff, D. C., aan het Rot, M., & Young, S. N. (2011). Tryptophan and interpersonal spin. *Journal of Research in Personality, 45*, 692–696.

Newman, M. G., Jacobson, N. C., Erickson, T. M., & Fisher, A. J. (2017). Interpersonal problems predict differential response to cognitive versus behavioral treatment in a randomized controlled trial. *Behavior Therapy, 48*, 56–68.

Nilsen, E. S., Lizdek, I., & Ethier, N. (2015). Mother–child interpersonal dynamics: The influence of maternal and child ADHD symptoms. *Journal of Experimental Psychopathology, 6*, 313–329.

Pincus, A. L. (1994). The interpersonal circumplex and the interpersonal theory: Perspectives on personality and its pathology. In S. Strack & M. Lorr (Eds.), *Differentiating Normal and Abnormal Personality* (pp. 114–136). New York: Springer.

Pincus, A. L. (2005). A contemporary integrative interpersonal theory of personality disorders. In J. Clarkin & M. Lenzenweger (Eds.), *Major Theories of Personality Disorder* (2nd ed., pp. 282–331). New York: Guilford Press.

Pincus, A. L. (2010). Interpersonal theory of personality. In I. B. Weiner & W. E. Craighead (Eds.), *The Corsini Encyclopedia of Psychology* (4th ed., pp. 1213–1215). Hoboken, NJ: John Wiley.

Pincus, A. L., & Ansell, E. B. (2013). Interpersonal theory of personality. In J. Suls & H. Tennen (Eds.), *Handbook of Psychology, Volume 5: Personality and Social Psychology* (2nd ed., pp. 141–159). Hoboken, NJ: John Wiley.

Pincus, A. L., & Cain, N. M. (2008). Interpersonal psychotherapy. In D. C. S. Richard & S. K. Huprich (Eds.), *Clinical Psychology: Assessment, Treatment, & Research* (pp. 213–245). New York: Academic Press.

Pincus, A. L., Hopwood, C. J., & Wright, A. G. C. (2017). The interpersonal situation: An integrative framework for the study of personality, psychopathology, and psychotherapy. In D. Funder, J. F. Rauthmann, & R. Sherman (Eds.), *The Oxford Handbook of Psychological Situations*. New York: Oxford University Press.

Pincus, A. L., Lukowitsky, M. R., & Wright, A. G. C. (2010). The interpersonal nexus of personality and psychopathology. In T.

Millon, R. F. Krueger, & E. Simonsen (Eds.), *Contemporary Directions in Psychopathology: Scientific Foundations of the DSM-5 and ICD-11* (pp. 523–552). New York: Guilford Press.

Pincus, A. L., & Roche, M. J. (2019). Paradigms of personality assessment and level of personality functioning in Criterion A of the AMPD. In C. J. Hopwood, A. L. Mulay, & M. Waugh (Eds.), *The DSM-5 Alternative Model for Personality Disorders: Integrating Multiple Paradigms of Personality Assessment* (pp. 48–59). Abingdon: Routledge.

Pincus, A. L., Sadler, P., Woody, E., Roche, M. J., Thomas, K. M., & Wright, A. G. C. (2014). Assessing interpersonal dynamics. In C. J. Hopwood & R. F. Bornstein (Eds.), *Multimethod Clinical Assessment* (pp. 51–91). New York: Guilford Press.

Pincus, A. L., & Wiggins, J. S. (1990). Interpersonal problems and conceptions of personality disorders. *Journal of Personality Disorders, 4*, 342–352.

Pincus, A. L., & Wright, A. G. C. (2011). Interpersonal diagnosis of psychopathology. In L. M. Horowitz & S. Strack (Eds.), *Handbook of Interpersonal Psychology: Theory, Research, Assessment, and Therapeutic Interventions* (pp. 359–381). Hoboken, NJ: John Wiley.

Przeworski, A., Newman, M. G., Pincus, A. L., Kasoff, M. B., Yamasaki, A. S., Castonguay, L. G., & Berlin, K. S. (2011). Interpersonal pathoplasticity in individuals with generalized anxiety disorder. *Journal of Abnormal Psychology, 120*, 286–298.

Roche, M. J., Pincus, A. L., Conroy, D. E., Hyde, A. L., & Ram, N. (2013). Pathological narcissism and interpersonal behavior in daily life. *Personality Disorders: Theory, Research, and Treatment, 4*, 315–323.

Roche, M. J., Pincus, A. L., Hyde, A. L., Conroy, D. E., & Ram, N. (2013). Within-person covariation of agentic and communal perceptions: Implications for interpersonal theory and assessment. *Journal of Research in Personality, 47*, 445–452.

Roche, M. J., Pincus, A. L., Rebar, A. L., Conroy, D. E., & Ram, N. (2014). Enriching psychological assessment using a person-specific analysis of interpersonal processes in daily life. *Assessment, 21*, 515–528.

Sadikaj, G., Moskowitz, D. S., Russell, J. J., Zuroff, D. C., & Paris, J. (2013). Quarrelsome behavior in borderline personality disorder: Influence of behavioral and affective reactivity to perceptions of others. *Journal of Abnormal Psychology, 122*, 195–207.

Sadikaj, G., Moskowitz, D. S., & Zuroff, D. C. (in press). What's interpersonal in interpersonal perception? The role of target's attachment in the accuracy of perception. *Journal of Personality*.

Sadikaj, G., Russell, J. J., Moskowitz, D. S., & Paris, J. (2010). Affect dysregulation in individuals with borderline personality disorder: Persistence and interpersonal triggers. *Journal of Personality Assessment, 92*, 490–500.

Sadler, P., Ethier, N., Gunn, G. R., Duong, D., & Woody, E. (2009). Are we on the same wavelength? Interpersonal complementarity as shared cyclical patterns during interactions. *Journal of Personality and Social Psychology, 97*, 1005–1020.

Safran, J. D. (1990a). Towards a refinement in cognitive therapy in light of interpersonal theory: I. Theory. *Clinical Psychology Review, 10*, 87–105.

Safran, J. D. (1990b). Towards a refinement of cognitive therapy in light of interpersonal theory: II. Practice. *Clinical Psychology Review, 10*, 107–121.

Salzer, S., Pincus, A. L., Hoyer, J., Kreische, R., Leichsenring, F., & Leibling, E. (2008). Interpersonal subtypes within generalized anxiety disorder. *Journal of Personality Assessment, 90*, 292–299.

Salzer, S., Pincus, A. L., Winkelbach, C., Leichsenring, F., & Leibing, E. (2011). Interpersonal subtypes and change of interpersonal problems in the treatment of patients with generalized anxiety disorder: A pilot study. *Psychotherapy: Theory, Research, Practice, & Training, 48*, 304–310.

Salzer, S., Streeck, U., Jaeger, U., Masuhr, O., Warwas, J., Leichsenring, F., ... Leibing, E. (2013). Patterns of interpersonal problems in borderline personality disorder. *Journal of Nervous and Mental Disease, 201*, 94–98.

Simon, S., Cain, N. M., Samstag, L. W., Meehan, K. B., & Muran, J. C. (2015). Assessing interpersonal subtypes in depression. *Journal of Personality Assessment, 97*, 364–373.

Smith, T. W., & Cundiff, J. M. (2011). An interpersonal perspective on risk for coronary heart disease. In L. M. Horowitz & S. Strack (Eds.), *Handbook of Interpersonal Psychology: Theory, Research, Assessment, and Therapeutic Interventions* (pp. 471–490). Hoboken, NJ: John Wiley.

Soldz, S., Budman, S., Demby, A., & Merry, J. (1995). A short form of the inventory of interpersonal problems circumplex scales. *Assessment, 2*, 53–63.

Strack, S., & Horowitz, L. M. (2011). Introduction. In L. M. Horowitz & S. Strack (Eds.), *Handbook of Interpersonal Psychology: Theory, Research, Assessment, and Therapeutic Interventions* (pp. 1–13). Hoboken, NJ: John Wiley.

Sullivan, H. S. (1953a). *Conceptions of Modern Psychiatry*. New York: W. W. Norton.

Sullivan, H. S. (1953b). *The Interpersonal Theory of Psychiatry*. New York: W. W. Norton.

Sullivan, H. S. (1954). *The Psychiatric Interview*. New York: W. W. Norton.

Sullivan, H. S. (1956). *Clinical Studies in Psychiatry*. New York: W. W. Norton.

Sullivan, H. S. (1962). *Schizophrenia as a Human Process*. New York: W. W. Norton.

Sullivan, H. S. (1964). *The Fusion of Psychiatry and Social Science*. New York: W. W. Norton.

Thomas, K. M., Hopwood, C. J., Donnellan, M. B., Wright, A. G., Sanislow, C. A., McDevitt-Murphy, M. E., ... Morey, L. C. (2014). Personality heterogeneity in PTSD: Distinct temperament and interpersonal typologies. *Psychological Assessment, 26*, 23–34.

Thomas, K. M., Hopwood, C. J., Woody, E., Ethier, N., & Sadler, P. (2014). Interpersonal processes in psychotherapy: A reanalysis of the Gloria Films. *Journal of Counseling Psychology, 61*, 1–14.

Tracey, T. J. (1997). RANDALL: A Microsoft FORTRAN program for a randomization test of hypothesized order relations. *Educational and Psychological Measurement, 57*, 164–168.

Wang, S., Roche, M. J., Pincus, A. L., Conroy, D. E., Rebar, A. L., & Ram, N. (2014). Interpersonal dependency and emotion in everyday life. *Journal of Research in Personality, 53*, 5–12.

Wiggins, J. S. (1991). Agency and communion as conceptual coordinates for the understanding and measurement of interpersonal behavior. In D. Cicchetti & W. M. Grove (Eds.), *Thinking Clearly about Psychology: Essays in Honor of Paul E. Meehl, Volume 2: Personality and Psychopathology* (pp. 89–113). Minneapolis, MN: University of Minnesota Press.

Wiggins, J. S. (1996). An informal history of the interpersonal circumplex tradition. *Journal of Personality Assessment, 66*, 217–233.

Wiggins, J. S. (2003). *Paradigms of Personality Assessment*. New York: Guilford Press.

Wiggins, J. S., Trapnell, P., & Phillips, N. (1988). Psychometric and geometric characteristics of the revised interpersonal adjective scales (IAS-R). *Multivariate Behavioral Research, 23*, 517–530.

Williams, T. F., & Simms, L. J. (2016). Personality disorder models and their coverage of interpersonal problems. *Personality Disorders: Theory, Research, and Treatment, 7*, 15–27.

Wilson, S., Revelle, W., Stroud, C. B., & Durbin, C. E. (2013). A confirmatory bifactor analysis of the Inventory of Interpersonal Problems: Circumplex and associations of interpersonal traits across multiple relationship contexts and measures. *Psychological Assessment, 25*, 353–365.

Wilson, S., Stroud, C. B., & Durbin, C. E. (2017). Interpersonal dysfunction in personality disorders: A meta-analytic review. *Psychological Bulletin, 143*, 677–734.

Wright, A. G. C., Hallquist, M. N., Morse, J. Q., Scott, L. N., Stepp, S. D., Nolf, K. A., & Pilkonis, P. A. (2013). Clarifying interpersonal heterogeneity in borderline personality disorder using latent mixture modeling. *Journal of Personality Disorder, 27*, 125–143.

Wright, A. G. C., Pincus, A. L., Conroy, D. E., & Hilsenroth, M. J. (2009). Integrating methods to optimize circumplex description and comparison of groups. *Journal of Personality Assessment, 91*, 311–322.

Wright, A. G., Pincus, A. L., Hopwood, C. J., Thomas, K. M., Markon, K. E., & Krueger, R. F. (2012). An interpersonal analysis of pathological personality traits in DSM-5. *Assessment, 19*, 263–275.

Wright, A. G., Stepp, S. D., Scott, L., Hallquist, M., Beeney, J. E., Lazarus, S. A., & Pilkonis, P. A. (2017). The effect of pathological narcissism on interpersonal and affective processes in social interactions. *Journal of Abnormal Psychology, 126*, 898–910.

Zilcha-Mano, S., McCarthy, K. S., Dinger, U., Chambless, D. L., Milrod, B. L., Kunik, L., & Barber, J. P. (2015). Are there subtypes of panic disorder? An interpersonal perspective. *Journal of Consulting and Clinical Psychology, 83*, 938–950.

Zimmermann, J., & Wright, A. G. (2017). Beyond description in interpersonal construct validation: Methodological advances in the circumplex structural summary approach. *Assessment, 24*, 3–23.

Zuroff, D. C., Moskowitz, D. S., & Côté, S. (1999). Dependency, self-criticism, interpersonal behavior, and affect: Evolutionary perspectives. *British Journal of Clinical Psychology, 38*, 231–250.

8a Interpersonal Nuance in Context: Commentary on Interpersonal Models of Personality Pathology

C. EMILY DURBIN

Roche and Ansell (this volume) offer a model that integrates the basic descriptive literature on interpersonal behavior in personality disorders (PDs) with literature on interpersonal psychotherapy (CIIT) for patients with personality pathology. Their argument for the utility of this model includes the following key claims: (1) all interpersonal behavior can be captured by its space on the dimensions of agency and communion, and individual PDs are characterized by tendencies to occupy specific areas in these spaces; (2) the types of problems in interpersonal interactions typical of persons with personality pathology cannot be understood solely as emerging from problems with one interpersonal process (complementarity), but from the specificity of the region of interpersonal space occupied by these persons' behaviors and the impairments this can create; and (3) knowing the specifics of the patterns of problematic interpersonal behavior and the nuances of how these behaviors emerge in response to behaviors from interaction partners can help therapists design strategies for treating personality pathology.

In this commentary, I offer some thoughts about these pieces of their argument and some suggestions for reconsideration and further exploration. The richness and breadth of the literature on individual differences in interpersonal styles provides an elegant model for organizing a large body of evidence regarding persistent patterns of interpersonal behavior and their implications for psychological functioning and adjustment. The simplicity of these models and their intuitive application to understanding therapist–patient interactions are appealing. In their chapter, Roche and Ansell aim to add specificity and nuance to this model in an attempt to concretize how the model can inform therapeutic practice with those who present with personality pathology. This is a worthy goal, both because specific recommendations are more readily translatable and lend themselves to empirical test of their efficacy and also because the therapeutic context provides an interesting one in which predictions made by an interpersonal model of personality functioning can be tested. My impression is that, in attempting to consider more fine-grained processes, some of the practical utility of

these models' simplicity is obscured. Focusing on fleshing out the nuances of distinct interpersonal styles in different PDs may be less productive than other strategies for building a therapeutic model, such as identifying common mechanisms as a basis for intervention strategies or elucidating distinctions between the varying challenges patients face across relationships of disparate kinds.

INTERPERSONAL STYLES DON'T NEED TO BE UNIQUE TO PARTICULAR PD CATEGORIES TO BE INFORMATIVE FOR TREATMENT

The authors argue that the utility of the interpersonal model for informing treatment of personality pathology lies in both the ubiquity of interpersonal problems in PDs and in the specificity with which each PD manifests particular problematic interpersonal styles. For example, they state that "Interpersonal models are especially appealing to the study of personality disorders because all are characterized by interpersonal dysfunction, and yet each specific personality disorder contains its own specific style of pathology" (p. 173 in the previous chapter by Roche). Much of their argument about the utility of these models for informing treatment matching and selecting treatment targets and techniques rests on this claim of specificity. I am not convinced that the empirical literature outlining the kinds of nuance that Roche and Ansell emphasize is sufficiently developed to support these kinds of distinctions, and wonder if more effort in other directions could provide some of the detail and specificity they are seeking to provide. Moreover, given high rates of comorbidity across PDs (and between PDs and other psychopathology) and evidence that their covariance is partially attributable to common personality trait factors (Kotov et al., 2011; Krueger & Markon, 2014), arguments built on a high degree of uniqueness across PDs are facing stiff headwinds. Evidence that correlates of different PDs – such as their characteristic interpersonal styles (rather than their diagnostic criteria) – have discriminant validity and treatment utility would be an important contribution to the literature, but the evidence to date in support of this premise seems underdeveloped.

In a comprehensive meta-analysis cited by Roche and Ansell, we (Wilson, Stroud, & Durbin, 2017) found that the individual PDs included in DSM-IV and DSM-5 showed discriminant validity in their profile of exhibited interpersonal problems. This discriminant validity took the form of somewhat distinctive profiles of elevation across the eight interpersonal styles that populate the interpersonal circumplex, such that the peak scale elevation and rank ordering of elevations varied across the different PDs (with the exception of obsessive-compulsive and dependent PDs, which were less distinctive). This lends support for Roche and Ansell's argument that there are predictable variations in how interpersonal problems manifest across persons with personality pathology that could form the basis for developing targeted techniques for behavior change with these populations. However, it is always worth considering what is gained by adopting a more granular conceptual model in terms of how the model performs when it is used for applied purposes. How many different techniques for different kinds of interpersonal presentations are warranted, and what is the magnitude of uniqueness needed to support the development of new techniques? The fact that there are identifiable differences in profiles across PDs is not itself evidence that the specific information that distinguishes them is in fact the most productive way to conceptualize either the causes of these problems or how they may be most effectively treated. There is likely a limit to the degree to which treatment developers (and ultimately clinicians) will be able to articulate, validate, and employ strategies to address patterns of uniqueness defined by profiles across the eight octants of the circumplex.

If you look at the results of our meta-analysis with a viewpoint that is less granular, many PDs that share symptom features and conceptual space tended to occupy similar quadrants of the interpersonal circumplex, indicating that they could also be thought of as variations within a broader theme of problematic interpersonal behavior. There may be some utility to considering the ways in which different PDs share common interpersonal problems, as these may indicate core challenges that could be addressed in a treatment program for many different PDs that commonly co-occur. In our meta-analysis, the one interpersonal style/octant that was elevated in common across all PDs was vindictiveness. This quadrant includes elements of suspicion, distrust, stewing over hurts and slights, punishing or hurting others to redeem the self, using competition as a means of defeating others, and being self-serving to the detriment of acknowledging the needs and promoting the well-being of others. What are the specific treatment recommendations for addressing this negatively affectively laden style with prominent cognitive distortions and ruminations about self–other relations? I would be interested to hear how the CIIT approach would be used to enact behavior change on this

style common across PDs. Would targeting this style common across PDs, which seems likely to be a barrier to openness to a therapeutic relationship, be an effective strategy for initiating interpersonal change?

IMPORTANT SPECIFICITY MAY RESIDE IN RELATIONSHIP CONTEXT, INSTEAD OF (OR IN ADDITION TO) THE INTERPERSONAL PROFILE

Roche and Ansell focus on the nuances of distinct patterns of interpersonal problems that characterize the person with personality pathology, foregrounding the trait-like elements of interpersonal behavior and localizing the target of treatment within the person's characteristic mode of relating to other people. In the background, however, lies a critical element that is probably very important for understanding and helping those with personality pathology improve their social adjustment, namely relationship contexts. Patients may come to treatment with a longstanding pattern of problematic ways of behaving in multiple relationships (a "forest" that the clinician is likely more skilled at discerning from the patient's history and presenting problems than is the patient). However, people also come to treatment with highly contextualized relationship problems: they worry they chose the wrong marital partner, they are estranged from a sibling, they have struggled to maintain adult friendships after leaving college, etc. Problematic interpersonal styles influence their lives by playing out in the context of these important relationships and self-defining relationship struggles. The particularities of these relationship problems have personal meaning and implications that extend beyond their representation as exemplars of the person's characteristic stylistic problems. People are motivated to change longstanding beliefs about other people and to explore uncomfortable and new interpersonal spaces because doing so may help to resolve the issues in these very relationships.

In our meta-analysis, we found evidence that PDs are associated with functioning in key adult interpersonal domains (family, peer, parent–child, and romantic partner relationships), as one would expect for patterns thought to have a broad impact on interpersonal functioning in general. More tellingly, though, we showed that these different relationship contexts are not equivalent; the degree to which different PDs were associated with problems in functioning varied across the different relationships domains. For example, among all the PDs, only borderline PD showed significant impairment in the romantic relationship domain. It seems critical that any therapeutic approach aiming to change characteristic interpersonal styles not treat them as fungible across relationship contexts. Rather, interventions should seek to understand how people's behavior in a particular relationship context contributes to the quality of that relationship and how the way in which someone interacts with another person is tied to both the meaning of that relationship and the individual's broader life goals.

Different relationships obviously afford different kinds of interpersonal behavior, with some relationships constraining what behaviors will be viewed as normative or adaptive, and other relationships allowing a wider variety of behaviors. For example, successful parenting takes a different kind of give-and-take than a successful romantic relationship. Conveying warmth and nurturance means different things when done in the context of a friendship than one's family of origin. Most people are simultaneously managing being in many different kinds of relationships at once. The variability across them could pose differential challenges for people whose characteristic interpersonal styles are dysfunctional or rigid. It is important to consider that people with personality dysfunction may struggle differentially across relationship domains – some relationships may be intact while others are severely damaged or nonexistent. Understanding this will help us to consider how relationship roles interact with styles to determine the quality of and satisfaction with relationships, as well as to identify ways to generalize patients' existing strengths in one context (e.g., their ability to be assertive in one relationship domain) to additional relational contexts. It is also important to consider that the patient–therapist relationship has its own structure and role guidelines that influence the behaviors typically expressed within this relationship, as well as the ways in which interventions focused on this relationship do or do not readily translate to new behaviors in relationship contexts that are structurally different from the patient–therapist relationship.

WHAT IS THE GOAL OF THERAPY INFORMED BY INTERPERSONAL STYLES? CHANGES IN RELATIONSHIP QUALITY/SATISFACTION, "NORMALIZATION" OF INTERPERSONAL STYLES, OR SOMETHING ELSE?

Roche and Ansell describe CIIT as building upon an understanding of a "normative pattern for how interpersonal exchanges unfold over time" (p. 175 in the previous chapter), particularly the principle of complementarity, and refer specifically to a treatment technique that aims at "facilitating a healthy exchange of dominance within the therapy session, along with some closeness/distance pulls on communion (without occupying the extremes of those pulls, i.e., total enmeshment vs. rejection)" (p. 179 in the previous chapter). For all their interest in specificity, this leaves some lacking in terms of offering a working definition of what amounts to a "healthy exchange of dominance." Further, it seems there are many opportunities for empirical work to help validate such working definitions and to test whether the predictions Roche and Ansell make about how one interaction partner can move another into a new interpersonal space

hold. At a broader level, it would be important to know what this model defines as a positive treatment outcome, how change in interpersonal styles would be assessed, and what types of validation would provide support for this model as a conceptual framework for both interpersonal behavior change and improving mental health outcomes.

A potentially fruitful area of exploration would be to examine how the patterns of interpersonal behavior observed in interaction dyads can be used to understand the particular mechanics of how those with interpersonal problems are behaving in interactions and how that behavior is being received. As Roche and Ansell note, not all interpersonal behavior is complementary and non-complementary behavior can be adaptive. So, what defines a problematic interpersonal style without reference to external criteria by which a behavior is deemed "adaptive"? If someone is experiencing few problems in their key relationships, should a therapist address their interpersonal style? If someone is struggling with an important relationship but is unremarkable in their interpersonal style, what is the recommended treatment approach?

SUMMARY

The model described by Roche and Ansell has the potential to inform new questions about how interpersonal models can be deployed to address the relationship problems common to people with personality dysfunction. Whereas they focus in particular on the distinctions across different interpersonal styles and the properties of how these styles contribute to patterns of interactions across people, the model could benefit from (1) considering areas of commonality in addition to differences across both PDs and styles; (2) placing these considerations within the broader context of relationship context and roles; and (3) mapping out an agenda for delineating what constitute normative interpersonal processes, how to measure them, and how to identify techniques that address patterns that are non-normative.

REFERENCES

Kotov, R., Ruggero, C. J., Krueger, R. F., Watson, D., Yuan, Q., & Zimmerman, M. (2011). New dimensions in the quantitative classification of mental illness. *Archives of General Psychiatry*, *68*, 1003–1011.

Krueger, R. F., & Markon, K. E. (2014). The role of the DSM-5 personality trait model in moving toward a quantitative and empirically based approach to classifying personality and psychopathology. *Annual Review of Clinical Psychology*, *10*, 477–501.

Wilson, S., Stroud, C. B., & Durbin, C. E. (2017). Interpersonal dysfunction in personality disorders: A meta-analytic review. *Psychological Bulletin*, *143*(7), 677–734.

8b Contextual Dynamics in the Interpersonal Theory of Personality and Personality Disorder: Commentary on Interpersonal Models of Personality Pathology

CHRISTOPHER J. HOPWOOD

Roche and Ansell (this volume) deliver the latest in a series of papers and chapters that outline Contemporary Integrative Interpersonal Theory (CIIT). They review a number of approaches to and findings from interpersonal research, in the context of the theory's assumptions as originally proposed by their mentor, Aaron Pincus. As a person who follows this empirical literature closely, their addition of a fifth assumption was the most interesting part of the chapter to me, so I will focus my comments on that.

First, a word about the theory more generally. Like some of its iconoclastic forebears (e.g., Harry Stack Sullivan & Timothy Leary), the interpersonal perspective tends to be misunderstood. One reason may be that, somewhat unlike proponents of other theories, interpersonal theorists and researchers characteristically prioritize synthesis over superiority (see Wiggins, 1991). The focus tends to be more on connection than distinction, and it doesn't have a particular brand of therapy or a preferred instrument. Perhaps in part for these reasons, CIIT has never been in a position to win a popularity contest outright; it sort of hangs around, and people aren't always sure what to make of it.

This is where the assumptions come in handy. Following Sullivan, Pincus' first assumption established a clear boundary in relation to other models by declaring CIIT a theory about how people relate to one another in a world that favors theories about what people are like. But the other assumptions are more agnate. His delineation of the meta-traits agency and communion as its fundamental dimensions in the second assumption is a nod toward potential integration, insofar as most theories about personality and psychopathology that try to identify meta-dimensions end up somewhere close to agency and communion (e.g., Bakan, 1966; Beck, Epstein, & Harrison, 1983; Blatt, 2008; DeYoung, 2006; Digman, 1997; Michaelson & Aaland, 1976; Ryan & Deci, 2000).

Integrative possibilities are also enabled by the third assumption, which clarifies that interpersonal relations include both actual relationships and relationships within the mind. This is a core feature of psychodynamic and social-cognitive models of personality and disorder;

however, it puzzles some trait advocates, who have argued that (1) someone could have personality disorder on a desert island (with nobody around) and, thus, personality disorder is not "interpersonal," or (2) traits like conscientiousness or neuroticism are important for understanding personality disorder even though they are "not interpersonal." What matters, from an interpersonal perspective, is the functional relationship between self and objects, the latter which may or may not be other people. If you believe the person on the island is conscientious or neurotic about *something* (even a coconut or a soccer ball), and the disorder has to do with how that relationship is somehow dysregulated, you are expressing the interpersonal point of view. In some sense, this point is so mundane it is difficult to dispute, and it makes interpersonal and trait perspectives readily commensurable (Ansell & Pincus, 2004; Wiggins & Trapnell, 1996).

The fourth assumption's focus on process fastens interpersonal theory to the increasing popularity of temporally-dynamic research, an issue that gets significant play by Roche and Ansell. Research on within-person dynamic processes is perhaps the most exciting area of work on personality disorders at the moment. Studies like those that were reviewed in this chapter have significant potential to argument the clinical utility of existing models focused on the structure of personality variables in cross-sectional, between-person data.

To be sure, there are issues with some of the assumptions stated by Pincus. Roche and Ansell mention recent work elaborating the interpersonal situation model to account for motives, affects, behaviors, and perceptions, which requires more dimensions (or at least an embellishment of the meta-dimensions) than agency and communion *per se*. They could also have mentioned recent studies that suggest that greater levels of dominance complementarity are actually maladaptive, which adds some nuance to the fourth assumption (Dermody, Thomas, Hopwood, Durbin, & Wright, 2017; Hopwood et al., in press).

Roche and Ansell boldly aim to address these issues and expand the theoretical boundaries more generally via a fifth assumption that centers attention on contextual dynamics. In some ways, this new assumption is not as new as it may seem. Context is a core feature of interpersonal theory (by definition), and interpersonal researchers have been at the forefront of research on contextual factors and temporal dynamics, as illustrated by Roche and Ansell's abridged review. Thus, this assumption both builds on the edifice of CIIT and links nicely to major current trends in the field.

However, there are at least three difficulties with their fifth assumption. Overcoming these challenges could strengthen an already robust model of personality disorder. First, more could be done to incorporate other perspectives on context, such as recent research developing situation taxonomies (Rauthmann et al., 2014), in keeping with the integrative backdrop of CIIT. Second, many of the studies reviewed by Roche and Ansell used cross-sectional measures to define personality disorder, creating a kind of tension with their underlying point about the importance of context and process that goes unaddressed. The recent emphasis in interpersonal theory has been to conceptualize personality disorder as a dynamic signature rather than a list of static characteristics (e.g., Cain & Pincus, 2016; Hopwood, 2018; Hopwood, Zimmermann, Pincus, & Krueger, 2015; Pincus & Hopwood, 2012). Interpersonal researchers should lead the field toward dynamic interpersonal definitions of disorder, just as they have led the field toward dynamic models of assessment and research. Making this point explicit would have added more punch to the fifth assumption than a review of studies organized around DSM-like definitions.

Third, unlike assumptions 1–4 that are logically discrete, assumption 5 folds in on some of the previous assumptions. For instance, context is also addressed in assumption 3, and dynamics are embedded in assumption 4. Capturing the kinds of dynamics referenced by assumption 5 may require elaborating upon the agency and communion meta-traits specified in assumption 2, as is done in the interpersonal situation model. In some ways, assumption 5 corrects potential limitations of these assumptions. However, these commonalities incorporate some level of overlap and redundancy in the overall system, and borders between assumptions are less clear. The implication is that an assumption that explicitly addresses temporally dynamic contextual factors may necessitate reworking assumptions 2–4 somewhat, so that each can offer a discrete, non-redundant piece of information.

Overall, the key contributions of Roche and Ansell's excellent chapter were highlighting how interpersonal theory continues to lead the way in conceptualizing contextual dynamics and pushing it toward an even more nuanced model of personality and personality disorder. With the outdated model – in which defunct categories are treated by acronymed therapies whose differences are empirically dubious – dying, we seem to be entering a new age for personality disorder research and practice. One hopes this will be a more flexible epoch, in which the

boundaries between personality, personality disorders, and other problems in living will be permeable, where rigid ideas are more readily sublated, and where treatments are designed to help people rather than to treat diagnostic categories. This is a world in which contextual dynamics will matter, and where CIIT will feel at home.

REFERENCES

Ansell, E. B., & Pincus, A. L. (2004). Interpersonal perceptions of the five-factor model of personality: An examination using the structural summary method for circumplex data. *Multivariate Behavioral Research*, 39(2), 167–201.

Bakan, D. (1966). *The Duality of Human Existence: An Essay on Psychology and Religion*. Oxford: Rand McNally.

Beck, A. T., Epstein, N., & Harrison, R. (1983). Cognitions, attitudes and personality dimensions in depression. *British Journal of Cognitive Psychotherapy*, 1(1), 1–16.

Blatt, S. J. (2008). *Polarities of Experience: Relatedness and Self-Definition in Personality Development, Psychopathology, and the Therapeutic Process*. Washington, DC: American Psychological Association.

Cain, N. M. & Pincus, A. L. (2016). Treating maladaptive interpersonal signatures. In W. J. Livesley, G. S. Dimaggio, & J. F. Clarkin (Eds.), *Integrated Treatment of Personality Disorder: A Modular Approach* (pp. 305–324). New York: Guilford Press.

Dermody, S. S., Thomas, K. M., Hopwood, C. J., Durbin, C. E., & Wright, A. G. (2017). Modeling the complexity of dynamic, momentary interpersonal behavior: Applying the time-varying effect model to test predictions from interpersonal theory. *Journal of Research in Personality*, 68, 54–62.

DeYoung, C. G. (2006). Higher-order factors of the Big Five in a multi-informant sample. *Journal of Personality and Social Psychology*, 91(6), 1138–1151.

Digman, J. M. (1997). Higher-order factors of the Big Five. *Journal of Personality and Social Psychology*, 73, 1246–1256.

Hopwood, C. J. (2018). Interpersonal dynamics in personality and personality disorder. *European Journal of Personality*, 32(5), 499–524.

Hopwood, C. J., Harrison, A. L., Amole, M., Girard, J. M., Wright, A. G., & Thomas, K. M., . . . Kashy, D. A. (in press). Properties of the Continuous Assessment of Interpersonal Dynamics across sex, level of familiarity, and interpersonal conflict. *Assessment*. Online First. https://doi.org/10.1177/1073191118798916

Hopwood, C. J., Zimmermann, J., Pincus, A. L., & Krueger, R. F. (2015). Connecting personality structure and dynamics: Towards a more evidence-based and clinically useful diagnostic scheme. *Journal of Personality Disorders*, 29(4), 431–448.

Michaelson, E. J., & Aaland, L. M. (1976). Masculinity, femininity, and androgyny. *Ethos*, 4(2), 251–270.

Pincus, A. L., & Hopwood, C. J. (2012). A contemporary interpersonal model of personality pathology and personality disorder. In T.A. Widiger (Ed.), *The Oxford Handbook of Personality Disorders* (pp. 372–398). New York: Oxford University Press.

Rauthmann, J. F., Gallardo-Pujol, D., Guillaume, E. M., Todd, E., Nave, C. S., Sherman, R. A., . . . Funder, D. C. (2014). The Situational Eight DIAMONDS: A taxonomy of major dimensions of situation characteristics. *Journal of Personality and Social Psychology*, 107(4), 677–718.

Ryan, R. M., & Deci, E. L. (2000). Self-determination theory and the facilitation of intrinsic motivation, social development, and well-being. *American Psychologist*, 55(1), 68–78.

Wiggins, J. S. (1991). Agency and communion as conceptual coordinates for the understanding and measurement of interpersonal behavior. In D. Cicchetti & W. M. Grove (Eds.), *Thinking Clearly about Psychology: Essays in Honor of Paul E. Meehl, Volume 2: Personality and Psychopathology* (pp. 89–113). Minneapolis, MN: University of Minnesota Press.

Wiggins, J. S., & Trapnell, P. D. (1996). A dyadic-interactional perspective on the five-factor model. In J. S. Wiggins (Ed.), *The Five-Factor Model of Personality: Theoretical Perspectives* (pp. 88–162). New York: Guilford Press.

8c   Expanding on Interpersonal Models of Personality Pathology: Author Rejoinder to Commentaries on Interpersonal Models of Personality Pathology

MICHAEL J. ROCHE AND EMILY B. ANSELL

First, we wish to thank Drs. Durbin and Hopwood for their insightful remarks on our chapter. We will begin by addressing the questions posed by Dr. Durbin, primarily the concern around using specific interpersonal styles to inform treatment approaches. Specifically, she notes that it is important to consider the role of relationship context, and challenged us to be more specific around the goal of therapy informed by interpersonal styles.

Although we do feel interpersonal styles can inform treatment targets (as described in our chapter), we agree that it should not be the only consideration. Another limitation she noted was the diagnostic overlap of PDs, making it difficult to advance an approach where PD and interpersonal style link to specific interventions. Although we agree this is a concern, both could be merged to enhance treatment. For example, the interpersonal theme (e.g., vindictiveness) could guide the initial treatment target (e.g., to decrease vindictive intensity and create flexibility so that other interpersonal styles are possible), whereas the personality disorder(s) may further inform the motivations underlying that behavior (e.g., paranoid defensiveness, narcissistic entitlement).

Depending on the case conceptualization, the treatment targets could be pursued in myriad ways, drawing from cognitive-behavioral (e.g., psychoeducation about interpersonal rigidity, addressing hostile attribution biases, behavioral rehearsal and exposure to social interactions) or psychodynamic (exploring the function of vindictiveness in past and current relationships, identifying the style as a defense against a more vulnerable interpersonal style toward others, etc.) approaches. Hopwood (2018) recently published a paper linking pathological personality traits from the DSM-5 alternative model for personality disorders to associated treatment techniques. As such, interpersonal traits like antagonism (dominance and unfriendliness) and detachment (submissiveness and unfriendliness) were explicitly linked to possible interventions.

Dr. Durbin also aptly noted that patients with personality disorders are often distressed about specific relationships in their lives. This fits with the fifth assumption's premise that context-driven demands for specific relationships may drive normative or non-normative patterns. For some patients we've seen, the theme is strikingly similar across all relationships (e.g., the individual with narcissistic personality pathology who treats coworkers, family, and friends as an opportunity to communicate superiority); in those cases, the interpersonal style of dominance is clear and informs a specific treatment target (e.g., decrease intensity of dominance, increase flexibility toward interpersonal behaviors other than dominance). Other, less severe cases will present as a more nuanced picture where only certain relationship contexts are relevant for the personality dysfunction. We noted this specifically in our chapter with a person-specific application that described a patient who had a specific relational difficulty with his wife (but not others). Here, we can see the utility of considering unique relationships as both we and Dr. Durbin are advocating for.

Dr. Hopwood correctly noted that our chapter defined personality disorder as a static construct. Our approach is consistent with the DSM-5 definition, which assumes personality dysfunction is relatively stable over time and circumstances. We recognize and agree with Dr. Hopwood that the field is in flux regarding this definition, and that evidence is already accumulating that dynamic processes underlie personality pathology. Our view is that a personality disorder is best characterized through *both* between-person (static) distinctions (e.g., *who* has a higher level of personality dysfunction) and within-person (temporally dynamic) contrasts (e.g., *when* does that individual evince greater difficulty). As we noted earlier, the interpersonal model can identify the "who" through static self-report measures that capture profile elevation and style, which sometimes can be used to formulate treatment goals (around intensity and flexibility). The interpersonal model increasingly also recognizes methods to identify "when" and "in what context," which we would describe as *additionally* informative.

Dr. Hopwood also suggested further refinement for the fifth assumption, noting that elements of this assumption could be captured in previous assumptions. For instance, he suggested that our addition of "context" could be folded into assumption 2, noting that agency and communion may vary in relation to additional important constructs (e.g., emotions, motives, perceptions of contexts) needed to comprehensively describe the interpersonal situation. Those additional constructs can be a part of the real or imagined exchange (assumption 3), and can be described in normative patterns (assumption 4). As both we and Hopwood have noted, context is nothing new to interpersonal theory, but the theory and research around the interpersonal constructs of agency and communion are better articulated than those related to these other components. For instance, the term complementarity governs how exchanges of agency should unfold, but what about interpersonal exchanges of emotions (e.g., to match the valence and arousal of one's interaction partner) or the link between acting dominant and one's own emotions? Our efforts were aimed at updating these assumptions to be in line with recent research that often includes more context-related nuance than was specifically articulated in those assumptions. By adding a fifth assumption, we hope that clinicians and researchers alike will take particular notice of the importance of context and dynamic processes throughout their work.

In summary, both Drs. Durbin and Hopwood provided important insights into how our description of interpersonal theory can be better articulated. We look forward to further refinement of this model so that conceptualization and treatment of personality disorders can be enhanced.

REFERENCES

Hopwood, C. J. (2018). A framework for treating DSM-5 alternative model for personality disorder features. *Personality and Mental Health, 12*(2), 107–125.

PART III INDIVIDUAL DISORDERS AND CLUSTERS

9 Cluster A Personality Disorders

JOHN G. KERNS

People with Cluster A personality disorders are often characterized as odd and eccentric (American Psychiatric Association, 2013). There are three Cluster A disorders in the DSM-5: schizotypal personality disorder (PD), schizoid PD, and paranoid PD. Research on schizoid and paranoid PD is rare and some researchers argued that these disorders should be dropped from DSM-5 (e.g., Triebwasser, Chemerinski, Roussos, & Siever, 2012, 2013). By far most of the research on Cluster A disorders involves research on schizotypal PD. There are at least two different but potentially complementary views of schizotypal PD. One view is that it is a schizophrenia-spectrum disorder, meaning a disorder less severe than schizophrenia but genetically related to it (Siever & Davis, 2004). A second view is that it reflects variation of normal personality traits (Widiger, Crego, Rojas, & Oltmanns, 2018).

CLUSTER A DISORDERS AND THE SCHIZOPHRENIA-SPECTRUM

Again, one conceptualization of schizotypal PD is that it reflects a schizophrenia-spectrum disorder. Schizotypal, meaning "like schizophrenia," PD was first introduced in DSM-III and it arose out of the concept of borderline schizophrenia or stable characteristics thought to be genetically related to schizophrenia (Spitzer, Endicott, & Gibbon, 1979). If schizotypal PD was genetically related to schizophrenia, then it would be expected that relatives of people with schizophrenia would be more likely to have schizotypal PD. This hypothesis has been strongly supported in previous research (Kendler & Walsh, 1995). For instance, Kendler and colleagues (Kendler, McGuire, Gruenberg, & Walsh, 1995) reported that rates of schizotypal PD were higher in relatives of people with schizophrenia than in either relatives of controls or in relatives of people with mood disorders. Further, among Cluster A disorders, there is stronger evidence that schizotypal PD is familially related to schizophrenia than there is for the other Cluster A disorders; and with stronger evidence that paranoid PD is familially related to schizophrenia

than schizoid PD (Kendler et al., 2006). There is also some research finding that avoidant PD is familially related to schizophrenia (Triebwasser et al., 2012).

If schizotypal PD was genetically related to schizophrenia, then it would also be expected that relatives of people with schizotypal PD would be more likely to have schizophrenia. Consistent with this, Kendler and Walsh (1995) found that for probands with schizophrenia, also having a parent with schizotypal PD increased risk for schizophrenia in the proband's siblings, but parental schizotypal PD did not increase sibling risk for mood or anxiety disorders. However, finding elevated rates of schizophrenia in relatives of people with schizotypal PD has not been consistently reported (Siever & Davis, 2004), possibly due to the small numbers of probands with schizotypal PD in these studies (Kendler & Walsh, 1995).

If schizotypal PD was genetically related to schizophrenia, then it might also be expected that schizotypal PD might often be a precursor to developing schizophrenia. Consistent with this, there is evidence that about 20–50 percent of people with schizotypal PD go on to develop schizophrenia. For instance, recently in a nationwide Danish registry study it was reported that risk of 20-year schizophrenia diagnosis in those initially diagnosed with ICD-10 schizotypal disorder was 33 percent (Hjorthøj, Albert, & Nordentoft, 2018). Hence, this suggests that an incident diagnosis of schizotypal PD may be more predictive of future onset of schizophrenia than having two parents with schizophrenia (Gottesman, Laursen, Bertelsen, & Mortensen, 2010). Therefore, there is strong evidence that schizotypal PD is a schizophrenia-spectrum disorder, with schizotypal PD indicating a markedly increased risk for schizophrenia.

Schizotypal PD (SPD) and Schizotypy

The term schizotypy is often used interchangeably with the term schizotypal (Raine, 2006), but there are distinctions between schizotypy and schizotypal PD (Lenzenweger, 2018). Schizotypy has been defined as a latent personality organization reflecting liability for schizophrenia (Lenzenweger, 2018). There has been an extensive amount of research on schizotypy, with a decent amount of schizotypy research involving the use of questionnaires to assess schizotypy. On average, people with extremely elevated questionnaire measured schizotypy are rated as having more interview measured schizotypal/Cluster A symptoms than people with average or lower schizotypy (Kwapil, Gross, Silvia, & Barrantes-Vidal, 2013). However, most people with markedly elevated questionnaire measured schizotypy would not meet criteria for schizotypal PD (Chapman, Chapman, Kwapil, Eckblad, & Zinser, 1994).

SPD and Relation to Schizophrenia Premorbid and Prodromal Phases

As a schizophrenia-spectrum disorder, one can view schizotypal PD as possibly reflecting the premorbid phase of schizophrenia, the prodromal phase of schizophrenia, or both (Raine, 2006). The years before developing schizophrenia are often divided into premorbid and prodromal phases (Tandon, Nasrallah, & Keshavan, 2009). The premorbid phase is from birth until the onset of the prodromal phase (e.g., in one person, from birth until let's say age 20). The premorbid phase is often associated with enduring deficits (e.g., poorer cognition and social problems). Hence, one can imagine someone first meeting criteria for schizotypal PD in the premorbid phase, with schizotypal PD reflecting enduring deficits developing in childhood and adolescence. Consistent with this, Esterberg and colleagues (Esterberg, Ousley, Cubells, & Walker, 2013) found that adolescents with schizotypal PD were rated by their parents as more socially impaired and with more repetitive interests and behaviors beginning in childhood. These deficits were even more pronounced than in people with 22q11 deletion syndrome who also have markedly elevated schizophrenia risk.

The prodromal phase (e.g., in one person, let's say from age 20 until age 22) reflects an increase of symptoms and functional disability, sometimes ending in the onset of schizophrenia (Tandon et al., 2009). In most people with schizophrenia, this putative prodromal phase appears to last for more than a year, with the median prodromal phase being more than two years in length. In addition, there is evidence that people can recover from a prodromal phase and become less symptomatic, perhaps to never develop schizophrenia. Hence, someone could also potentially first meet criteria for schizotypal PD in the prodromal phase. Consistent with this, in the NAPLS study attempting to identify people in the prodromal phase at imminent risk for psychotic disorder onset, over 30 percent of the sample was diagnosed with schizotypal PD (Esterberg, Goulding, & Walker, 2010). Further, Esterberg et al. (2013) reported increased positive attenuated psychotic symptoms, thought to be of prodromal intensity,

in adolescents with schizotypal PD compared to both a control group and to people with 22q11 deletion syndrome. Given that some people recover from the prodromal phase, this suggests that some temporal instability in schizotypal PD might reflect recovery from the prodromal phase. Importantly, the period of greatest risk for schizophrenia ends in middle adulthood (Tandon et al., 2009). Hence, after that time, it would be expected that few people with schizotypal PD would develop schizophrenia. Consistent with this, in the recent Danish registry study, rate of conversion from schizotypal disorder to schizophrenia decreased through the follow-up period, with conversion rate being 11.7 percent by year 1, 16.3 percent by year 2, and again being 33 percent by year 20 (Hjorthøj et al., 2018). Hence, for people with schizotypal PD who do not develop schizophrenia, it is thought that some protective factors could be present that prevent the onset of schizophrenia (Chemerinski, Triebwasser, Roussos, & Siever, 2013).

SPD Heterogeneity

It has long been argued that a key feature of schizophrenia is its heterogeneity, with any two people with schizophrenia potentially varying widely in types of symptoms, cognitive functioning, and outcome (Tandon et al., 2009). Schizophrenia is thought to involve multiple symptom factors, with at least three commonly identified: positive (e.g., delusions and hallucinations), disorganized (disorganized speech and behavior, inappropriate affect), and negative (decreased verbal and emotional expression; and decreased motivation and pleasure and increased social withdrawal). Given the conceptualization of schizotypal PD as a schizophrenia-spectrum disorder, then it would be expected that schizotypal PD would be similarly very heterogeneous. In fact, it might be argued that schizotypal PD could even be more heterogeneous than schizophrenia, as it has been argued that some people might meet criteria for schizotypal PD without actually having increased genetic risk for schizophrenia, labeled pseudoschizotypy by Raine (2006).

Schizotypal PD does appear to reflect a multidimensional array of symptoms and deficits. This includes symptoms that appear at least somewhat similar to the positive symptoms of schizophrenia, specifically ideas of reference, odd beliefs/magical thinking, unusual perceptual experiences, and paranoia (American Psychiatric Association, 2013). Schizotypal PD also includes excessive social anxiety that appears at least somewhat related to paranoia (i.e., does not abate and reflects paranoid fears), although this has also often been viewed as a negative, or interpersonal, symptom. Schizotypal PD also includes three symptoms that appear most similar to the disorganized symptoms of schizophrenia, specifically odd thinking and speech, odd/eccentric behavior, and inappropriate affect. Schizotypal PD also includes at least two symptoms that appear perhaps most similar to the negative symptoms of schizophrenia, specifically lack of close friends and constricted affect. However, Rosell and colleagues (Rosell, Futterman, McMaster, & Siever, 2014) noted that interview (rather than self-report) measures of constricted affect are more likely to load with disorganized schizotypal symptoms.

Research on schizotypal symptoms has often found a three-factor structure that appears roughly similar to the three-factor symptom structure of schizophrenia. For instance, in a factor analysis of the nine schizotypal symptoms rated using semi-structured interviews, Bergman and colleagues (Bergman, Silverman, Harvey, Smith, & Siever, 2000) found three factors: cognitive/perceptual (i.e., positive), disorganization, and interpersonal (i.e., negative). For the commonly used schizotypal personality questionnaire (SPQ; Raine, 1991), Fonseca-Pedrero et al. (2018) examined the factor structure across 12 countries (n = 27,001) using confirmatory factor analysis. They found support for previously examined three- or four-factor models: a three-factor model with paranoia loading on both the positive/cognitive perceptual and negative/interpersonal factors and with excessive social anxiety loading on the negative/interpersonal factor; and a four-factor model with a separate suspiciousness factor comprised of ideas of references, paranoia, and excessive social anxiety, with both paranoia and excessive social anxiety cross-loading on the negative/interpersonal factor. However, some research has observed more complex schizotypal factor structures. For instance, in an SPQ item-level factor analysis, Chmielewski and Watson (2008) found at least five factors: unusual beliefs and experiences, mistrust, eccentricity/oddity (i.e., disorganized), social anhedonia, and social anxiety. Further, Kendler et al. (1995; n = 1272) found six different factors using the Structured Interview for Schizotypy that includes 20 signs and symptoms. All six factors were more common in the first-degree relatives of people with schizophrenia, which were labeled positive schizotypy, suspicious behavior, odd speech, negative schizotypy (e.g., poor rapport, aloofness), social dysfunction (i.e., amotivation and poor occupational functioning), and avoidant symptoms (including social isolation and social anxiety).

SPD Negative Symptom Coverage

From the perspective of schizophrenia, one could question how well DSM-5 schizotypal PD criteria reflect symptoms that are like the negative symptoms of schizophrenia. Negative-like symptoms have often been most emphasized in descriptions of the relatives of people with schizophrenia (Raine, 2006). Further, negative symptoms were also argued to be neglected in the DSM-III diagnostic criteria of schizophrenia, which could potentially account for their relative neglect in the diagnostic criteria of schizotypal PD, which have not changed much since DSM-III. At the same time, in the schizophrenia literature there has been a continued refinement in the conceptualization and assessment of negative symptoms (e.g., Kring, Gur, Blanchard, Horan, & Reise, 2013). Hence, it could be argued that the negative symptoms of schizotypal PD (again, often labeled interpersonal symptoms) do not reflect the broad range of the negative symptoms of schizophrenia.

Negative symptoms in schizophrenia appear to fall into at least two dimensions (Kring et al., 2013). One negative symptom dimension involves decreased expression, specifically decreased amount of speech, or alogia, and blunted affect. Poverty of speech has been found to predict risk of schizophrenia-spectrum disorders when assessed in mid-childhood (Gooding, Ott, Roberts, & Erlenmeyer-Kimling, 2013). However, decreased amount of speech does not appear among schizotypal criteria. The schizotypal criterion of constricted affect does have some similarity to the schizophrenia negative symptom blunted affect. In schizophrenia, blunted affect has been consistently found to reflect a deficit in emotional expression but not in experience. For instance, decreased emotional facial expressions have been consistently found in schizophrenia in response to standardized stimuli such as film clips (e.g., Mote, Stuart, & Kring, 2014). In contrast, in schizotypal PD there is emphasis on restricted affective expression as being disruptive in interpersonal contexts rather than it reflecting a more primary deficit in emotional expression. Hence, DSM-5 schizotypal PD does not appear to reflect negative symptoms of decreased verbal expression and may not clearly reflect decreased emotional expression.

Although at least somewhat absent in DSM-5, there is some evidence that suggests that people with schizotypal PD, or people with elevated Cluster A symptomatology more broadly, do exhibit decreased verbal and emotional expression. This includes decreased emotion in speech, increased pauses in speech (Dickey et al., 2012), and decreased communicative gestures during speech, which could reflect a similar type of expressive deficit (Mittal et al., 2006). Kosson and colleagues (Kosson et al., 2008) developed the Interpersonal Measure of Schizoid Personality Disorder (IM-SZ) to make behavioral ratings thought to capture signs of schizoid PD, with these ratings strongly correlated with interview-rated schizoid PD symptoms and moderately correlated with schizotypal PD symptoms. Many of the IM-SZ items, especially those with the highest item-total correlations, reflect decreased verbal and emotional expression. Other research on decreased verbal and emotional expression in the schizophrenia-spectrum has focused on social anhedonia. Social anhedonia is associated with Cluster A symptoms, predicts increased risk for schizophrenia-spectrum PDs, and has been associated with increased Cluster A disorders in biological parents (specifically being found in fathers; Cohen, Emmerson, Mann, Forbes, & Blanchard, 2010). Social anhedonia is associated with increased IM-SZ scores, especially items reflecting decreased verbal and emotional expression (Collins, Blanchard, & Biondo, 2005), and with fewer positive facial expressions to positive and neutral film clips (Leung, Couture, Blanchard, Lin, & Llerena, 2010). Hence, overall there is evidence suggesting that people with schizotypal PD or with elevated Cluster A symptoms do exhibit decreased verbal and facial expression. However, it is interesting that the one instance where this was not found was in a study where people with social anhedonia did not display decreased facial expressions specifically in a social interaction task (Llerena, Park, Couture, & Blanchard, 2012), whereas again DSM-5 criteria emphasize rating constricted affect specifically in interpersonal contexts (although people with social anhedonia in Llerena et al. were rated as less socially skilled and affiliative during the task). Overall, decreased verbal and emotional expression seems to reflect schizophrenia-spectrum conditions and could potentially be further emphasized either in schizotypal PD or in attempts to more directly assess risk for schizophrenia (Kendler, Lieberman, & Walsh, 1989).

In addition to decreased verbal and emotional expression, a second schizophrenia negative symptom dimension involves decreased motivation and pleasure and increased social withdrawal. The schizotypal criterion of no close friends appears similar to social withdrawal in schizophrenia. However, a broader focus on decreased motivation, goal-directed activity, and pleasure is missing from the schizotypal PD criteria. Hence, here again, schizotypal PD appears limited in attempting to capture negative symptoms that might be related to schizophrenia.

Schizoid PD and Negative Symptoms of Schizophrenia

In contrast to schizotypal PD, diagnostic criteria for schizoid PD appear to more strongly capture some of the decreased motivation and pleasure and increased social withdrawal symptoms of schizophrenia. This includes lack of social interaction (i.e., lacking close friends; preference for solitary tasks) as well as decreased social motivation (i.e., not desiring close relationships) and decreased social and other types of pleasure (i.e., enjoys few activities; little interest in sexual experiences with another person). Schizoid PD also includes flattened affectivity (and indifference to praise and criticism). However, schizoid PD criteria do not include decreased verbal expression. Further, they do not explicitly involve a broader decrease in motivation and lack of goal-directed activity as is found in schizophrenia (Gard et al., 2014). Another issue for schizoid PD is how well these decreased motivation and pleasure symptoms are assessed. In schizophrenia research, recent negative symptom assessments have been developed to more accurately assess these symptoms (Kring et al., 2013), including using ecological momentary and behavioral task assessment (Gard et al., 2014; Moran, Culbreth, & Barch, 2017). An issue for future research might be whether more valid assessment of these decreased motivation and pleasure symptoms, perhaps

specifically in the context of schizoid PD, would increase their sensitivity to detecting genetic risk for schizophrenia, with again schizoid PD being the Cluster A PD least clearly associated with schizophrenia liability. In addition, given that recent research on negative symptoms in schizophrenia has made progress in clarifying potential mechanisms (Strauss & Cohen, 2017), this suggests that research on Cluster A disorders would benefit from testing similar negative symptom mechanisms.

Paranoid PD Symptoms and Factor Structure

Although paranoid PD has rarely been studied, it is thought to be fairly common in clinical and general population samples (Triebwasser et al., 2013). Paranoid PD appears to reflect delusion-like persecutory beliefs. In schizophrenia, the most common type of delusion is persecutory (e.g., thinking others are out to harm them; Appelbaum, Robbins, & Roth, 1999). Paranoid PD symptoms bear some similarity to this type of delusion. There is also evidence suggesting that paranoid PD might be closely related to delusional disorder (Triebwasser et al., 2013).

In a large interview study ($n = 903$ with PDs; $n = 114$ with paranoid PD), Falkum and colleagues (Falkum, Pedersen, & Karterud, 2009) found that a two-factor symptom structure for DSM-IV paranoid PD fit better than a one-factor structure using confirmatory factor analysis. One factor was labeled suspiciousness, including doubts about loyalty of friends, suspecting harm from others, reading hidden meanings, and reluctance to confide. The second factor was labeled hostility and included reacting angrily to perceived attacks, persistently bearing grudges, and recurrent suspicions about partner. However, the item recurrent suspicions about partner had the lowest factor loading of any item and it also had the lowest item-total correlation when analyzing all paranoid PD symptoms.

CLUSTER A DISORDERS AND RELATION TO NORMAL PERSONALITY

Again, in addition to being a schizophrenia-spectrum disorder, a potentially complementary view of schizotypal PD conceptualizes it as an extreme manifestation of normal personality traits (Widiger et al., 2018). This is also consistent with attempts to view all mental disorders, including psychotic disorders, as variations on traits that occur in the general population (Forbes et al., 2017). Alternatively, one could imagine that both schizophrenia and schizotypal PD reflect some disorder-specific risk that is not shared with the general population. This also seems to echo debates about whether liability for schizophrenia is dimensional in the general population or whether it is taxonic (Lenzenweger, 1999; Linscott, Morton, & GROUP, 2018).

Research from the perspective that schizotypal PD reflects variation of normal personality traits has found that schizotypal PD and other Cluster A disorders have some moderate to large associations with normal personality traits. For instance, in a meta-analysis, Samuel and Widiger (2008) reported that among Five-Factor Model traits schizotypal PD was most associated with increased neuroticism, $r = .38$, followed by decreased extraversion, $r = -.28$. In a recent large interview study that involved joint analyses of clinical and personality disorders (Forbes et al., 2017), schizotypal PD had a single large loading (.77) on detachment (i.e., low extraversion). Schizotypal PD also had a smaller loading (.32) on a core thought disorder factor (highest loadings on this factor for mania and psychosis). Research on specific schizotypal symptom dimensions has found that the negative symptoms tend to be most associated with decreased extraversion (Cicero & Kerns, 2010). Further, disorganized schizotypal symptoms have been most associated with increased neuroticism as well as decreased conscientiousness. However, much of this research has involved self-report measures and it is not clear whether research using observational ratings of disorganized symptoms would find similar results (see below). In contrast, Samuel and Widiger (2008) found that schizotypal PD was not strongly associated with openness to experience, $r = .09$. However, it is still debated whether and how schizotypal PD might be associated with openness to experience.

In a recent study, Czajkowski et al. (2018) examined how much PD genetic variance was shared with Big Five traits. They found that only 47.3 percent of schizotypal PD variance was shared with Big Five traits, suggesting a sizable amount of disorder-specific variance not shared with normal personality. However, other research has assessed normal personality (or maladaptive extremes of the Five-Factor Model) using the Personality Inventory for DSM-5 (PID-5), which includes the construct psychoticism as a dimension of normal personality. Using the PID-5, Reichborn-Kjennerud et al. (2017) found that 100 percent of the genetic variance for schizotypal PD was shared with normal personality. Further, this study found genetic correlations between schizotypal PD and psychoticism $\geq .80$. Hence, it appears that how normal personality is conceptualized and whether it includes openness to experience or psychoticism can have large consequences for how well schizotypal PD appears to be related to normal personality (more on openness below).

In their meta-analytic review, Samuel and Widiger (2008) also found that both schizoid and paranoid PD were associated with extraversion and neuroticism, although they varied in the strength of these associations. Specifically, schizoid PD was most associated with decreased extraversion, $r = -.46$, and also associated with increased neuroticism, $r = .22$. In a recent study, Forbes et al. (2017) found that schizoid PD loaded .85 on a detachment factor. For paranoid PD, Samuel and Widiger found it was associated with increased neuroticism, $r = .40$ and decreased extraversion, $r = -.21$. Further, paranoid PD was also negatively associated with agreeableness, $r = -.34$. Forbes et al. (2017) found that paranoid PD had its highest loadings on antagonism (.42) and detachment (.41). Recently, Czajkowski et al. (2018) reported that paranoid PD shared much more genetic variance with Big Five traits (79.4 percent) than schizotypal PD (47.3 percent). There was also evidence in this study that schizoid PD might share even more genetic variance with Big Five traits than paranoid PD. Hence, there is some evidence that schizoid and paranoid PD are, if anything, perhaps more strongly related to maladaptive levels of normal personality traits than is schizotypal PD.

PREVALENCE OF CLUSTER A DISORDERS

The prevalence of Cluster A disorders is still at least somewhat unclear. There has been an impression that Cluster A disorders are rare (Triebwasser et al., 2012). Research on the prevalence of Cluster A disorders in representative community samples has produced some conflicting results. Discrepant results might be due to the use of different assessment instruments, including whether there is reliance on structured versus semi-structured interviews, or differences in sampling methods, or other reasons (Quirk et al., 2016). Across five studies, the average Cluster A prevalence is 4.0 percent, ranging from 1.6 percent to 7.1 percent (reviewed in Quirk et al., 2016). Average rate for schizotypal PD across four studies is 1.29 percent, ranging from 0.06 percent to 3.9 percent. In the National Comorbidity Survey Replication (NCS-R; Lenzenweger, Lane, Loranger, & Kessler, 2007), rate of schizotypal PD was not directly measured, but it was estimated at 3.3 percent, although the authors note that this is expected to be at least a slight overestimate. For schizoid PD across four studies the average is 1.55 percent, ranging from 0.6 percent to 3.1 percent; and for paranoid PD, across four studies the average is 2.35 percent, ranging from 0.7 percent to 4.4 percent. Estimated rates of schizoid PD and paranoid PD in the NCS-R were 4.9 percent and 2.3 percent (again, at least slight overestimates; Lenzenweger et al., 2007). Overall, there is some evidence that prevalence of Cluster A disorders might be higher than often assumed, although again the variability in results across studies also makes this conclusion somewhat tentative.

Socio-demographic correlates of Cluster A disorders have also been found to vary across studies. It is often assumed that the rates of these disorders are higher in males. Consistent with this, in a cross-national study, Huang et al. (2009) reported that the odds ratio for males (relative to females) for Cluster A PDs was 5.0 (with younger age and lower education also associated with Cluster A PDs). In contrast, in the NCS-R, prevalence of Cluster A disorders did not vary by sex or by any other socio-demographic variable (Lenzenweger et al., 2007).

Overall, if anything rates might be higher in males, but whether and the extent to which this is true is still unclear.

Another area where these studies have produced some conflicting results concerns relationships with other personality disorders. For instance, in the NCS-R, among Cluster A disorders, schizotypal and schizoid were most highly correlated (tetrachoric correlation = .96), whereas schizotypal and paranoid PD were more modestly associated. Instead, paranoid PD was more highly correlated with Cluster B disorders than with schizotypal PD. In contrast, schizotypal PD was not strongly correlated with Cluster B disorders (tetrachoric correlation = .27), including with borderline PD (tetrachoric correlation = .34). Using NESARC data, Lentz and colleagues (Lentz, Robinson, & Bolton, 2010) also reported that schizotypal and paranoid PD were not strongly (in fact, not significantly) associated. However, Lentz et al. also reported that schizotypal PD was more strongly associated with borderline and narcissistic PDs than with schizoid PD. Again, this seems to suggest marked differences in what some of these interview instruments are assessing.

The NCS-R also reported some other important results for Cluster A disorders. It was found that 41 percent of people with Cluster A disorders had a comorbid Axis I disorder in the past year, with 25 percent of people with Cluster A disorders seeking treatment in the past year (Lenzenweger et al., 2007). These rates were much lower than the rates in Cluster B disorders. This seems to confirm the impression that these Cluster A disorders are less likely to be seen in clinical settings relative to Cluster B PDs. This also suggests that which people with Cluster A disorders are seen in clinical contexts could have an effect on perceptions of these disorders.

SPD AND COGNITIVE AND NEURAL DEFICITS

A prominent characteristic of schizophrenia is cognitive deficits, with these deficits being fairly generalized across domains and with these deficits related to poorer real-world functioning (Tandon et al., 2009). This suggests that as a schizophrenia-spectrum disorder schizotypal PD should also be related to poorer cognition. As expected, evidence for poorer cognition in schizotypal PD has been found in a large number of studies (Raine, 2006). As in schizophrenia, there is evidence that cognitive deficits in schizotypal PD are fairly general and found across a range of cognitive domains, although perhaps the most examined cognitive domains have been cognitive control, working memory, and processing speed. For instance, McClure and colleagues (McClure, Harvey, Bowie, Iacoviello, & Siever, 2013) found that people with schizotypal PD (n = 46) were impaired on a broad cognitive battery compared both to healthy controls (n = 55), d = .96, and to people with avoidant PD (n = 38), d = .70. Hazlett et al. (2014) found that people with schizotypal PD (n = 51) were impaired on a verbal memory and learning task, d = .57,

compared to healthy controls. Dickey et al. (2010) found impairments in verbal fluency tasks ranging from small (d = .37) to medium (d = .52) in effect size in people with schizotypal PD (ns > 120) versus healthy controls (ns > 130). As one final example, McClure and colleagues (McClure, Flory, Barch, Harvey, & Siever, 2008) found that people with schizotypal PD (n = 63) were impaired on the AX-CPT task, d = .92, compared to healthy controls (n = 42). Overall, evidence of broad cognitive deficits in schizotypal PD appears to be well-established, although some examples of potentially intact functioning in some domains have also been observed (Maróthi & Kéri, 2018). There has also been some evidence that it might be possible to improve cognition in schizotypal PD pharmacologically (Rosell et al., 2014).

As might be expected given that schizotypal PD presumably reflects a less severe disorder than schizophrenia, cognitive deficits in schizotypal PD do not appear to be as severe as in schizophrenia (Chemerinski, Triebwasser, et al., 2013; Rosell et al., 2014). Hence, it is possible that one reason why people with schizotypal PD do not develop schizophrenia is that they have less severe cognitive deficits than in schizophrenia. Note that finding less severe cognitive deficits in people with schizotypal PD is also consistent with research on people considered at clinical high risk for psychosis (i.e., prodromal phase) which has also found that these individuals exhibit broad cognitive deficits that are not as severe as found in schizophrenia (e.g., across broad range of cognitive tasks, median effect size d = .49; Seidman et al., 2016). Furthermore, there is also evidence of cognitive deficits being associated with schizotypy. Moreover, given that the vast majority of the people in these studies who have elevated schizotypy would not be expected to meet criteria for schizotypal PD, then it might be expected that cognitive deficits in people with elevated schizotypy would be smaller than in people with schizotypal PD. This appears to be the case (Chun, Minor, & Cohen, 2013), with a recent meta-analysis reporting that effect sizes for associations between schizotypy and most cognitive domains were small (Siddi, Petretto, & Preti, 2017).

Given broad cognitive deficits in both schizophrenia and schizotypal PD, one might expect evidence of fairly broad neural deficits as well. For instance, in schizophrenia there is evidence of widespread decreased gray matter throughout the cortex (Ivleva et al., 2013). Consistent with this, there is also some evidence of widespread decreased gray matter in schizotypal PD (Asami et al., 2013). For instance, in a study of women with schizotypal PD (n = 31), Koo and colleagues (Koo, Dickey, et al., 2006) reported overall decreased cortical gray matter compared to healthy control women (n = 29), with deficits found across temporal, frontal, and parietal regions. Similarly, in a study of men with schizotypal PD (n = 54), Asami et al. (2013) also found globally decreased cortical gray matter compared to healthy control men (n = 54), with decreased gray matter specifically found across a broad range of cortical regions. Hence, as in schizophrenia, neural deficits in schizotypal PD also appear to be potentially broad. One brain area that has been investigated perhaps the most in schizotypal PD is the superior temporal lobe, with frequent evidence of decreased gray matter in the temporal lobe (Rosell et al., 2014), although again deficits do not appear restricted only to this region. There is also evidence of decreased white matter integrity in schizotypal PD. For instance, Lener et al. (2015) reported that fractional anisotropy (thought to reflect white matter integrity) values were intermediate in schizotypal PD (n = 49) relative to people with schizophrenia (n = 22) and healthy controls (n = 55). There are also isolated neural results that could be potentially very important if further established. This includes evidence of preserved volume in one part of the frontal lobe (BA 10; Rosell et al., 2014), decreased caudate volume (Koo, Levitt, et al., 2006), increased putamen volume (Chemerinski, Byne, et al., 2013), and decreased white matter integrity in the genu of the corpus callosum (Lener et al., 2015; Zhang et al., 2017).

A number of studies have found that people with schizotypal PD also exhibit a number of psychophysiological deficits that are also observed in schizophrenia (Chemerinski, Triebwasser, et al., 2013). This includes reduced prepulse inhibition and impaired P50 suppression. It also includes eye tracking impairment as well as reduced P300 amplitude. As in schizophrenia, there is also some evidence suggesting that decreased ventral striatal dopamine (Thompson et al., 2014) and decreased cortical dopamine (Siever & Davis, 2004) might be associated with cognitive deficits and negative symptoms in schizotypal PD (Rosell et al., 2015; more on *increased* dorsal striatum dopamine below). In addition, based on schizophrenia research, there are a number of other potential neurobiological mechanisms that might be relevant for schizotypal PD (e.g., neurotransmitters GABA and glutamate).

CLUSTER A PDS AND FUNCTIONAL IMPAIRMENT

In schizophrenia, two predictors of functional impairment are negative symptoms, especially symptoms of decreased motivation and pleasure (Kring et al., 2013), and cognitive deficits (Tandon et al., 2009). Hence, given elevated negative symptoms and cognitive deficits in schizotypal PD, it would be expected that schizotypal PD would also be associated with evidence of functional impairment. McGurk et al. (2013) examined vocational functioning in people with schizotypal PD (n = 38), paranoid PD (n = 17), both PDs (n = 37), or controls (n = 82). They found that people with these Cluster A PDs were less likely to be currently working. For those who were working, they were less likely to have jobs involving cognitive complexity. Both lack of work and lack of work complexity were associated with poor cognition. For people with schizotypal PD, they were less likely to have a job with much social contact. For people with paranoid PD, they were less likely

to have a history of work. Hence, as expected, these disorders do appear to be associated with evidence of functional impairment, with some evidence that this is related to cognitive deficits and perhaps to interpersonal deficits.

Other research has also reported functional impairment in schizotypal PD samples, with evidence that this disorder is one of the most functionally impairing of PDs (Chemerinski, Triebwasser, et al., 2013b). Generally consistent with McGurk et al. (2013), Dickey et al. (2005) reported that people with schizotypal PD (n = 104) were more likely to have a period of time unable to work than healthy controls (n = 110). McClure et al. (2013) found that people with schizotypal PD (n = 46; average age = 38) were less likely be living independently (44 percent) than healthy controls (n = 55; 72 percent). In a recent study with adolescents, Verbeke and colleagues (Verbeke, De Clercq, Van der Heijden, Hutsebaut, & van Aken, 2017) found that different schizotypal symptom dimensions were related to impaired interpersonal functioning. Finally, in the NCS-R study, Lenzenweger et al. (2007) found that Cluster A disorders were associated with both instrumental role functioning disability and cognitive disability. However, Cluster A disorders were no longer associated with disability after statistically adjusting for Axis I disorders. Hence, it is still unclear how much disability in Cluster A disorders is not due to other comorbid disorders.

Schizotypal PD has also been associated with substance use disorders (Hjorthøj et al., 2018). In a twin study, Gillespie et al. (2018) reported that although schizotypal PD symptoms were associated with cannabis use and cannabis use disorder, when statistically adjusting for other PD symptoms this was no longer the case. However, in a Danish registry study, Toftdahl and colleagues (Toftdahl, Nordentoft, & Hjorthøj, 2016) found that 35 percent of people with ICD-10 schizotypal disorder had a substance use disorder, with the most common being alcohol (25 percent) and cannabis (11.6 percent). Rates of cannabis use disorders in schizotypal disorder were more than double the rate for all disorders other than schizophrenia (with all PDs examined as a single category). Further, cannabis use disorder and substance abuse more broadly has been found to predict conversion from schizotypal disorder to schizophrenia (Hjorthøj et al., 2018). For other Cluster A disorders, Gillespie et al. (2018) found that paranoid PD symptoms were associated with cannabis use regardless of statistically adjusting for other PD symptoms. Interestingly, schizoid PD was one of the few PDs where its symptoms were not associated with increased cannabis use, with schizoid PD symptoms significantly negatively associated with cannabis when statistically adjusting for other PD symptoms.

SPD POSITIVE SYMPTOMS AND SZ GENETIC RISK

Another potential issue with the diagnostic criteria of schizotypal PD that has been raised is that they are heavily weighted towards the symptoms that are more like the positive symptoms of schizophrenia. Raine (2006) argued that this is in contrast to the descriptions of negative symptoms that tend to predominate historic descriptions of relatives of people with schizophrenia. Similarly, Kendler et al. (1995) argued that especially negative schizotypy, social dysfunction, and odd speech strongly identify relatives of people with schizophrenia, with, in contrast, positive schizotypy, suspicious behavior, and avoidant symptoms more weakly related to familial risk. Hence, there are some concerns about whether positive schizotypal symptoms are overly weighted in the schizotypal PD diagnostic criteria and even whether positive schizotypal symptoms are strongly related to genetic risk for schizophrenia (Raine, 2006).

For instance, in a review of studies of relatives of people with schizophrenia, Tarbox and Pogue-Geile (2011) found that there was only a small effect size increase ($d = .37$) in positive schizotypal symptoms among first-degree relatives, found in both questionnaire and interview studies. If anything, this small effect size increase might be an overestimate, as these authors also noted some potentially relevant negative evidence from questionnaire schizotypy studies that they did not include in the overall effect size estimate. Further, a more recent study by Tarbox and colleagues found if anything a negative association between positive schizotypal symptoms and genetic risk (Tarbox, Almasy, Gur, Nimgaonkar, & Pogue-Geile, 2012). Moreover, overall positive schizotypal symptoms have not been found to differentiate those with a first-degree relative with schizophrenia versus those with a first-degree relative with mood disorders (Tarbox & Pogue-Geile, 2011). One possible suggested explanation for these results is that relatives of people with schizophrenia might have a tendency to underreport psychotic-like symptoms. Although possible, other evidence does not clearly support a general underreporting of symptoms (e.g., MMPI K-scale scores; Tarbox et al., 2012). At the same time, people with schizophrenia themselves may not report a very high level of positive schizotypy (Horan, Reise, Subotnik, Ventura, & Nuechterlein, 2008), with these positive schizotypy measures being highly correlated with positive schizotypal symptoms. Further, positive schizotypy has been found to be very strongly related to, and perhaps even indistinguishable from, dissociation (Cicero & Kerns, 2010). And similar to positive schizotypy, people with schizophrenia are not markedly elevated on dissociation (Lyssenko et al., 2018). However, perhaps people with schizophrenia are not markedly elevated on positive schizotypy measures that are highly correlated with positive schizotypal symptoms because of antipsychotic medication and illness chronicity. But on the whole, previous evidence does raise questions about whether positive schizotypal symptoms are highly prevalent in schizophrenia and whether they are strongly related to genetic risk for schizophrenia.

Other evidence suggesting that positive schizotypal symptoms may not strongly reflect genetic risk for schizophrenia comes from research on schizophrenia polygenic risk scores (SPRS). These scores reflect genetic loci each at least weakly statistically associated with schizophrenia in genome-wide association studies and that collectively have a sizable relation to schizophrenia genetic risk (e.g., highest 10 percent with odds ratio for SZ between 7.8 and 20.3 relative to the lowest 10 percent; Schizophrenia Working Group of the Psychiatric Genomics Consortium, 2014). SPRS have been associated with a number of other variables, including being strongly related to risk for bipolar disorder, as well as increased nicotine use, symptoms and family history of depression and anxiety, increased neuroticism, family history of drug and alcohol use disorders, and increased interpersonal trauma (Docherty et al., 2018; Duncan et al., 2018). However, despite these other associations, as of yet, no study has reported that self-reported positive schizotypal symptoms, or self-reported psychotic-like experiences more broadly, are positively associated with SPRS (Ronald & Pain, 2018). In fact, one recent study in a high stress (recent conscript) sample reported that positive schizotypal symptoms were significantly negatively associated with SPRS (Hatzimanolis et al., 2018). Another study only found a significant positive association between SPRS with hallucinations and paranoia after removing people with scores of zero on the hallucinations and paranoia measures (Pain et al., 2018). This study also reported a negative association between self-reported hallucinations and paranoia with bipolar polygenic risk score, which is surprising given a strong positive correlation between schizophrenia and bipolar polygenic risk scores (Lo et al., 2017). Overall, this potentially absent association between positive schizotypal symptoms and SPRS seems consistent with Raine's concept of pseudoschizotypy, meaning some people with positive schizotypal symptoms are not at increased genetic risk for schizophrenia.

One factor in research on whether positive schizotypal symptoms reflect genetic risk for schizophrenia might be the mode of assessment. Again, self-report studies have not found a significant positive association with SPRS. However, one study that used a semi-structured interview measure of positive schizotypal symptoms (the Structured Interview for Schizotypy) did report a significant positive association with SPRS (van Os et al., 2017). In addition, two other related studies (Jones et al., 2016; Zammit et al., 2014) using semi-structured interviews found near significant positive associations between SPRS and psychotic-like symptoms that presumably would be highly correlated with measures of positive schizotypal symptoms. This suggests that perhaps semi-structured interview measures of positive schizotypal symptoms might be more associated with SPRS than self-report studies. This is also consistent with other evidence indicating the difficulty of measuring psychotic-like symptomatology with questionnaire or fully structured interview (Kendler, Gallagher, Abelson, & Kessler, 1996).

Also relevant for interpreting the general lack of significant associations between SPRS and positive schizotypal symptoms is that associations have also been inconsistent with measures of negative schizotypal symptoms. Again, relatives of people with schizophrenia do exhibit increased negative schizotypal symptoms (Kendler et al., 1995). For instance, in their review, Tarbox and Pogue-Geile (2011) reported that the effect size increase in negative symptoms in first-degree relatives was $d = .67$ across studies, $d = .74$ in interview studies, and $d = .46$ in questionnaire studies, with this also increased compared to first-degree relatives of people with affective disorder. However, five self-report studies did not find a significant positive association between SPRS and negative schizotypal symptoms (Ronald & Pain, 2018). In contrast, three studies, one interview-based, have found that negative schizotypal symptoms are positively associated with SPRS. Hence, there is seemingly more evidence that negative schizotypal symptoms are associated with polygenic risk scores than positive schizotypal scores, but neither appears to be clearly and strongly related thus far.

In addition to whether schizotypal symptoms have been assessed using semi-structured interviews or not, there might be other methodological issues with these polygenic risk studies. It has been suggested that these studies might be affected by collider bias, with people with both high genetic risk and increased schizotypal symptoms being less likely to participate, thereby decreasing what might otherwise be a stronger positive association between schizophrenia genetic risk and schizotypal symptoms (Munafò, Tilling, Taylor, Evans, & Davey Smith, 2018). Further, Ronald and Pain (2018) argued that studies with larger sample sizes and that used more recently developed polygenic risk scores (i.e., based on PGC2) might be more likely to report significant associations. Hence, perhaps these methodological factors could account for the weak to inconsistent evidence associating schizophrenia polygenic risk scores and schizotypal symptoms.

SPD DISORGANIZED SYMPTOMS: OBSERVATIONAL RATING VERSUS SELF-REPORT

As previously noted, there is some evidence that interview measures of schizotypal symptoms might be more strongly related to schizophrenia genetic risk than self-report measures. This might be particularly relevant for assessing disorganized schizotypal symptoms. In particular, there is evidence that only observational ratings of disorganized schizotypal symptoms are clearly related to familial risk of schizophrenia. Kendler et al. (1995) found that disorganized schizotypal symptoms measured observationally were the schizotypal symptom most associated with having a first-degree relative with schizophrenia (effect size $d = .96$; Tarbox & Pogue-Geile, 2011). There is also a long line of research on disorganized speech (i.e., thought disorder; communication deviance) consistently finding increased

disorganized speech in the relatives of people with schizophrenia (Gooding et al., 2012). This is also consistent with some evidence that disorganization symptoms in people with schizophrenia also might be the schizophrenia symptom factor most associated with increased familial risk (Rietkerk et al., 2008). In contrast, using self-report measures of disorganization, there is at best a small increase of disorganization in first-degree relatives of people with schizophrenia (across five studies, effect size $d = .22$; Tarbox & Pogue-Geile, 2011). Hence, observational ratings of disorganization appear to be much more strongly related to familial risk than self-reported disorganization.

Importantly, disorganized speech in schizophrenia has been consistently associated with poor cognitive control (Becker, Cicero, Cowan, & Kerns, 2012). Further, cognitive control deficits are associated with impaired self-monitoring. Hence, given cognitive control deficits in schizophrenia and in schizotypal PD (McClure et al., 2008), people with schizophrenia-spectrum disorders may be poor at monitoring and identifying their own disorganization. Consistent with this, people with schizophrenia have not been found to give valid self-reports of their own cognitive deficits (Medalia, Thysen, & Freilich, 2008) or of their level of disorganization (Becker et al., 2012). At the same time, although objectively rated disorganization is associated with cognitive deficits in schizophrenia, it is still unclear whether and how strongly self-reported disorganized schizotypal symptoms is associated with cognitive deficits (e.g., Kane et al., 2016). Hence, it is not clear to what extent observed versus self-reported disorganized schizotypal symptoms are measuring the same construct. This is consistent with concerns raised by Kendler et al. (1995) and by Rosell et al. (2014) that interview and observational schizotypal measures are more valid than self-report measures.

SPD AND STRIATAL DOPAMINE

Psychotic disorders are strongly associated with increased striatal dopamine, especially in the dorsal striatum, with dopamine thought to be specifically related to psychotic symptoms in this disorder (i.e., positive and to some extent disorganized symptoms; Howes, McCutcheon, Owen, & Murray, 2017). Hence, it might then be expected that schizotypal PD, perhaps especially the positive schizotypal symptoms, would be associated with increased striatal dopamine. Consistent with increased striatal dopamine in schizotypal PD, two studies have found increased dopamine metabolites in schizotypal PD, with this correlated with their level of positive schizotypal symptoms (Siever & Davis, 2004). Moreover, at least one study has examined dopamine levels specifically in the striatum in schizotypal PD, finding that schizotypal PD is associated with increased dysregulated release of striatal dopamine (Abi-Dargham et al., 2004). At the same time, this increase in striatal dopamine in schizotypal PD was not as elevated as typically found in psychotic disorders. However, in psychotic disorders, dopamine is especially increased while in an acute psychotic phase (Laruelle, Abi-Dargham, Gil, Kegeles, & Innis, 1999). Further, fluctuations in the intensity of sub-psychotic, or attenuated, symptoms are thought to also occur in schizotypal PD (Stone, 1985). However, it is not clear whether people with schizotypal PD in the study by Abi-Dargham and colleagues were all in a commensurate acute phase. Hence, on the whole, perhaps the results of Abi-Dargham et al. do seem consistent with the idea that people with schizotypal PD can experience marked elevations in dorsal striatal dopamine. It is also possible that one protective factor that prevents some people with schizotypal PD from developing schizophrenia is that their levels of striatal dopamine do not get as dysregulated as in schizophrenia (Chemerinski, Triebwasser, et al., 2013). Hence, on the whole, there is evidence of increased striatal dopamine in schizotypal PD, but there is certainly a need for further research on this.

The fact that dopamine levels are thought to episodically fluctuate in psychotic disorders seemingly correlated with episodic changes in psychotic symptoms also might have implications for understanding positive schizotypal symptoms. As noted by Spitzer et al. (1979), original schizotypal PD diagnostic criteria were selected to be stable and not to episodically fluctuate. However, this does raise some conceptual issues about the nature of positive schizotypal symptoms. If these symptoms are stable, then this makes it less clear whether they are caused by the same mechanism(s) that cause psychotic symptoms in schizophrenia that tend to be very episodic (Appelbaum et al., 1999). The possibility that positive schizotypal symptoms may reflect different mechanisms than those that cause psychotic symptoms in schizophrenia might also be consistent with earlier reviewed evidence questioning how strongly these symptoms are related to schizophrenia familial risk and be consistent with Raine's concept of pseudoschizotypy.

However, although psychotic symptoms do fluctuate episodically in psychotic disorder, they can also often remain in a residual form in the chronic phase, even in the face of antipsychotic medication (Appelbaum et al., 1999). This suggests that in some people positive schizotypal symptoms might also reflect in part a residual form of perhaps an attenuated psychotic symptom that arose in a period of increased striatal dopamine. Therefore, speculatively, there might be at least two different forms of positive schizotypal symptoms. One form might be related in part to increased striatal dopamine that might episodically fluctuate in intensity, and perhaps at times reflects a residual attenuated psychotic symptom. A second form might be unrelated to increased striatal dopamine and might be less likely to be familially related to schizophrenia (Raine, 2006). Potentially generally consistent with this is the evidence from Chapman et al. (1994) who found that only people with extremely elevated positive schizotypy with interview evidence of attenuated psychotic symptoms had increased risk for psychotic disorder. In contrast, people with elevated positive schizotypy but without a history of attenuated psychotic symptoms, and potentially without increased striatal dopamine, did not have increased risk of psychotic disorder.

SPD AND COGNITIVE BIASES

Another factor related to persistence and severity of psychotic symptoms in schizophrenia is cognitive biases (Moritz et al., 2014). For instance, there is a long line of evidence finding that delusions in psychotic disorders are related to a jumping to conclusions bias whereby people make confident decisions on the basis of limited evidence. This bias also does not appear related to striatal dopamine (So, Peters, Swendsen, Garety, & Kapur, 2014). Hence, one reason why someone might adopt a delusional belief when in a high dopamine state, or why someone might maintain a delusion when in a low dopamine state, is due to cognitive biases that result in faulty inferences. Importantly, although the jumping to conclusions bias is more common in psychotic disorder, it is also present in a sizable minority of people without psychotic disorder (Ross, McKay, Coltheart, & Langdon, 2015). In fact, there is evidence that cognitive biases like this and a tendency to make faulty inferences can be quite common (Risen, 2016). Other research suggests that cognitive biases might also play a role in positive schizotypal symptoms. For instance, psychotic-like beliefs, which are correlated with positive schizotypal symptoms, have also been associated with a jumping to conclusions bias, although it should be noted that the average effect size might be small (Ross et al., 2015).

Consistent with an association between cognitive biases and positive schizotypal symptoms, research on magical and superstitious thinking in the general population also supports a role for cognitive biases. In particular, Risen (2016) has argued that magical thinking often arises from cognitive biases due to increased influence of intuitive and implicit cognitive processes, such as a reliance on heuristics. Moreover, magical thinking is also thought to reflect an inability or unwillingness for people to use controlled and effortful cognition in order to override the often flawed conclusions that arise from the use of heuristics. This suggests the possibility that in people with schizotypal PD that they also might entertain and adopt odd and magical beliefs because they are overly reliant on biased cognitive heuristics and are unable or unwilling to override these conclusions. Hence, in addition to positive schizotypal symptoms reflecting increased striatal dopamine, it is possible that these symptoms can also reflect, or perhaps in some people perhaps only reflect, an overreliance on biased heuristic processing.

SPD AND TRAUMA

In addition to research on whether schizotypal symptoms are related to familial risk for schizophrenia, many studies have examined whether they are also related to experiences of trauma. There is now a wealth of evidence that schizotypal symptoms are fairly strongly associated with childhood abuse and trauma. For instance, in a recent review, Velikonja and colleagues (Velikonja, Fisher, Mason, & Johnson, 2015) found that odds ratios for overall trauma and schizotypal symptoms across 25 studies ranged from 2.01 to 4.15, with all studies supporting the association. This association was especially strong for positive schizotypal symptoms. However, associations with trauma have been reported for other schizotypal dimensions too, making it difficult to conclude whether the association is particularly specific to positive schizotypal symptoms. Similarly, associations with types of trauma are also broad and it is not clear whether associations are particularly specific to a certain type of trauma.

The association between trauma and schizotypal symptoms, especially positive schizotypal symptoms, is also consistent with other research on psychosis. For instance, self-reported psychotic-like symptoms have been consistently associated with stress and trauma (Kelleher et al., 2013). In addition, again the most established neurobiological correlate of psychosis is increased striatal dopamine. Both animal and human research supports an influence of stress on striatal dopamine, including in people with schizophrenia and in people at clinical high risk for psychosis (Howes et al., 2017). Further, there is also evidence that stress and trauma are associated with increased risk for psychotic disorders, with a host of psychosocial adversity variables associated with increased rate of psychotic disorder. At the same time, there is also evidence that genetic risk for schizophrenia is itself associated with increased risk of experiencing interpersonal trauma (Docherty et al., 2018). Hence, the association between stress and trauma with positive schizotypal symptoms seems consistent with other research on psychosis.

Among psychotic symptoms, perhaps the one symptom most clearly associated with trauma is hallucinations. This has even been found in people who experience hallucinations without a clinical need for care (Longden, Madill, & Waterman, 2012). Further, in people with PTSD without a psychotic disorder diagnosis the occurrence of hallucinations has also been found to be relatively common (Waters, Blom, Jardri, Hugdahl, & Sommer, 2018). This suggests that trauma might be especially associated with unusual perceptual experiences in schizotypal PD. There is also research on the experimental inducement of anomalous experiences in the general population that suggests that our normal perceptual and bodily experience might be constructed from the integration of multiple streams of information (Lenggenhager, Tadi, Metzinger, & Blanke, 2007). When this normal integration is disrupted, it appears surprisingly easy to induce perceptual and bodily distortions (Botvinick & Cohen, 1998). Speculatively, it might be that the experience of trauma induces a less integrated, dissociative processing style which then increases the chance of experiencing future

perceptual distortions. At least generally consistent with this, dissociation as a construct is thought to reflect disruption in integrated processing (Lyssenko et al., 2018). Further, both dissociation and trauma have been strongly associated with hallucinations in people with psychotic disorder (Longden et al., 2012). Moreover, dissociation is also strongly associated with positive schizotypy (Cicero & Kerns, 2010). Hence, a potential issue for future research might be to further examine integration of perceptual and bodily experiences and their relation to unusual perceptual experiences in schizotypal PD.

POSITIVE SCHIZOTYPAL SYMPTOMS AND OPENNESS TO EXPERIENCE

As noted earlier, an important question about the nature of schizotypal symptoms, perhaps especially positive and to some extent disorganized schizotypal symptoms, is whether these symptoms are related to increased openness to experience (Widiger et al., 2018). In general, correlations between self-reported positive schizotypal symptoms and broad measures of openness to experience tend to be only weakly to moderately associated (Widiger et al., 2018). A number of different explanations have been proposed to account for why this association is not stronger. One is that openness and positive schizotypal symptoms (or psychoticism; Reichborn-Kjennerud et al., 2017) are distinct, with psychoticism forming a sixth personality factor (Crego & Widiger, 2017; Watson, Clark, & Chmielewski, 2008). Another explanation is that some openness measures may not effectively assess the maladaptive high end of the trait, which might truncate associations with positive schizotypal symptoms (Haigler & Widiger, 2001).

It has also been suggested that positive schizotypal symptoms are only associated with just one or more particular sub-facets of openness (Crego & Widiger, 2017; Sutin, 2017). For instance, some facets of openness reflect adventurousness and liberal values. It is possible that these facets may not be strongly related to positive schizotypal symptoms (DeYoung, Grazioplene, & Peterson, 2012). In contrast, openness facets reflecting imagination and fantasy appear to be more strongly related to positive schizotypal symptoms (Moorman & Samuel, 2018). Further, some conceptualizations of openness or of related constructs include facets such as unconventionality or oddity/eccentricity and these facets might have higher associations with positive schizotypal symptoms (Crego & Widiger, 2017).

A related possibility is that the broader construct of openness reflects both openness and intellect (DeYoung et al., 2012). However, positive schizotypal PD might reflect elevation on only openness and might be associated with decreased intellect (Chmielewski, Bagby, Markon, Ring, & Ryder, 2014; DeYoung, Carey, Krueger, & Ross, 2016). An association with decreased intellect also seems consistent with evidence that schizotypal PD does involve cognitive deficits. And it also seems consistent with the general explanation for magical thinking offered by Risen (2016) that this reflects being high on intuitive and implicit cognition (possibly reflected by increased openness) while being unwilling or unable to use systematic and effortful cognition (possibly reflected by decreased intellect) to counteract the illogical conclusions made by intuitive cognition. Furthermore, openness has been associated with better implicit learning (Kaufman et al., 2010), potentially consistent with an increased reliance on intuitive cognition in people high on openness. However, on the whole, it does not appear that whether and how positive schizotypal symptoms are associated with openness to experience has been resolved. Some tentative conclusions are that positive schizotypal symptoms are not strongly correlated with broad measures of openness, but that some positive schizotypal symptoms are more strongly correlated with particular facets of openness.

Although possible relations between positive schizotypal symptoms and openness are still unclear, there is other converging evidence that does support a relationship between these two constructs. First, openness is associated with some measures of creativity (Sutin, 2017). Further, positive schizotypal symptoms are also associated with measures of creativity, although effect sizes are small in magnitude (Baas, Nijstad, Boot, & De Dreu, 2016). There is also evidence that people who pursue artistic education have an increased risk of schizophrenia (MacCabe et al., 2018). In addition, first-degree relatives of people with schizophrenia might have increased creativity (Kyaga et al., 2011). In particular, first-degree relatives of people with schizophrenia have been found to be more likely to pursue occupations that involve artistic creativity (although perhaps another interpretation of this association is being more likely to pursue less social professions; McGurk et al., 2013). Hence, there is some evidence consistent with links between openness, schizotypal PD, and schizophrenia.

Further, like positive schizotypal symptoms, openness is also associated with increased childhood trauma and abuse; this is specifically true for openness measured in adults but not when measured in children (Sutin, 2017). Moreover, both schizotypal PD and openness have been associated with increased use of cannabis. Schizotypal PD includes odd and eccentric appearance whereas openness is associated with a more distinctive and more messy appearance. In addition, there are theoretical and empirical links between both positive schizotypal symptoms and openness with increased striatal dopamine (Allen & DeYoung, 2017).

And perhaps most importantly, increased openness has been associated with increased genetic risk for schizophrenia based on polygenic risk scores. For instance, Lo et al. (2017) found relations between openness with both schizophrenia and bipolar disorder, with an openness–schizophrenia genetic correlation of .36. In a follow-up

study, Smeland et al. (2017) found six genetic loci that overlap between schizophrenia and openness. Finally, Duncan et al. (2018) reported that the genetic correlation between schizophrenia and openness was .21. Hence, it appears that people with increased genetic risk for schizophrenia also tend to score more highly on measures of openness. There is also evidence that increased schizophrenia polygenic risk score, even in people without a family history of schizophrenia, is associated with increased creativity and creative success (Power et al., 2015), again suggesting a genetic association between openness and schizophrenia.

It should be noted that people with schizophrenia actually report *decreased* openness (Ohi et al., 2016). Perhaps this decrease in openness could reflect the chronic use of antipsychotic medications that block striatal dopamine. It could also reflect pervasive cognitive deficits in schizophrenia that decrease the intellect component of openness. There is also recent evidence suggesting that the cognitive deficits of schizophrenia appear to be strongly related to non-familial risk factors (Kendler, Ohlsson, Mezuk, Sundquist, & Sundquist, 2016). Hence, it is possible that schizophrenia is genetically associated with increased openness yet this relation is somewhat obscured by non-familial cognitive deficits. However, another potential issue with the genetic association between openness and schizophrenia could be possible collider bias (Munafò et al., 2018). For instance, if people with increased genetic risk for schizophrenia are less likely to participate in research and people with increased openness are more likely to participate in research, then this could result in a spuriously more positive polygenic association between openness and schizophrenia (because people with both high schizophrenia genetic risk and low openness would be less likely to be in research samples). On the whole, there are intriguing empirical connections between openness with both schizotypal PD and schizophrenia. However, whether and how these constructs are related is still unresolved.

SPD TREATMENT

There are few high quality treatment studies of schizotypal PD. For instance, there have been no RCTs for psychotherapy of schizotypal PD (Dixon-Gordon, Turner, & Chapman, 2011). In a non-experimental study, Bartak et al. (2011) did report some evidence that people with Cluster A personality disorders (n = 57, most with paranoid PD) benefited from psychotherapy. Rosell et al. (2014) noted that a still recommended source for information on psychotherapy on schizotypal PD is the paper by Stone (1985).

There have been some pharmacotherapy studies that have examined the use of antipsychotic medication in people with schizotypal PD or with schizotypal symptoms (Raine, 2006). In recent reviews of antipsychotic medication in schizotypal

PD, it has been noted that few studies meet standards for high quality, with recommendations that this evidence should be viewed with caution and that no firm clinical recommendations can be made (Jakobsen et al., 2017; Koch et al., 2016). Rosell et al. (2014) also suggested caution because positive schizotypal symptoms may not be the most disturbing or problematic symptoms for people with schizotypal PD. Given the high proportion of people with schizotypal PD who develop schizophrenia, treatment recommendations for people at clinical high risk for schizophrenia might also be relevant.

Rosell et al. (2014) suggested that stimulants might be useful for cognitive deficits in schizotypal PD, although that they need to be closely monitored given risk for psychosis. In contrast, research on antidepressant medication in schizotypal PD has generally not found evidence that supports its efficacy (Chemerinski, Triebwasser, et al., 2013). A source now or in the future for schizotypal PD treatment might be research attempting to treat cognitive deficits (e.g., Bowie, McGurk, Mausbach, Patterson, & Harvey, 2012) and negative symptoms (Grant, Huh, Perivoliotis, Stolar, & Beck, 2012) in schizophrenia. In addition, metacognitive training for positive schizotypal symptoms might also prove useful (Moritz et al., 2014).

CONCLUSIONS

There is strong evidence that schizotypal PD is a schizophrenia-spectrum disorder and an initial diagnosis of schizotypal PD is a strong predictor of future onset of schizophrenia. Despite this evidence, there are questions about whether schizotypal PD or the other Cluster A disorders as currently diagnosed best reflect traits indicating risk for schizophrenia. Further, it is still not empirically resolved to what extent positive schizotypal symptoms reflect genetic risk for schizophrenia. There is strong evidence that schizotypal PD is related to psychological trauma. At the same time, there is evidence that some schizotypal symptoms do appear to reflect variation on normal personality traits, but it is still unresolved whether and how schizotypal symptoms reflect high levels of openness to experience. Cluster A disorders appear to be more common than often assumed and have been associated with poor functioning, but there is a lack of treatment research on these disorders.

REFERENCES

Abi-Dargham, A., Kegeles, L. S., Zea-Ponce, Y., Mawlawi, O., Martinez, D. Mitropoulou, V., ... Siever, L. J. (2004). Striatal amphetamine-induced dopamine release in patients with schizotypal personality disorder studied with single photon emission computed tomography and [123I]iodobenzamide. *Biological Psychiatry, 55,* 1001–1006.

Allen, T. A., & DeYoung, C. G. (2017). Personality neuroscience and the Five Factor Model. In T. A. Widiger (Ed.), *The Oxford Handbook of the Five Factor Model* (pp. 319–349). New York: Oxford University Press.

American Psychiatric Association. (2013). *Diagnostic and Statistical Manual of Mental Disorders* (5th ed.). Arlington, VA: American Psychiatric Publishing.

Appelbaum, P. S., Robbins, P. C., & Roth, L. H. (1999). Dimensional approach to delusions: Comparison across types and diagnoses. *American Journal of Psychiatry, 156,* 1938–1943.

Asami, T., Whitford, T. J., Bouix, S., Dickey, C. C., Niznikiewicz, M., Shenton, M. E., ... McCarley, R. W. (2013). Globally and locally reduced MRI gray matter volumes in neuroleptic-naive men with schizotypal personality disorder: Association with negative symptoms. *JAMA Psychiatry, 70,* 361–372.

Baas, M., Nijstad, B. A., Boot, N. C., & De Dreu, C. K. W. (2016). Mad genius revisited: Vulnerability to psychopathology, biobehavioral approach-avoidance, and creativity. *Psychological Bulletin, 142,* 668–692.

Bartak, A., Andrea, H., Spreeuwenberg, M. D., Thunnissen, M., Ziegler, U. M., Dekker, J., ... Emmelkamp, P. M. (2011). Patients with Cluster A personality disorders in psychotherapy: An effectiveness study. *Psychotherapy and Psychosomatics, 80,* 88–99.

Becker, T. M., Cicero, D. C., Cowan, N., & Kerns, J. G. (2012). Cognitive control components and speech symptoms in people with schizophrenia. *Psychiatry Research, 196,* 20–26

Bergman, A. J., Silverman, J. M., Harvey, P. D., Smith, C. J., & Siever, L. J. (2000). Schizotypal symptoms in the relatives of schizophrenia patients: An empirical analysis of the factor structure. *Schizophrenia Bulletin, 26,* 577–586.

Botvinick, M., & Cohen, J. (1998). Rubber hands 'feel' touch that eyes see. *Nature, 391,* 756.

Bowie, C. R., McGurk, S. R., Mausbach, B., Patterson, T. L., & Harvey, P. D. (2012). Combined cognitive remediation and functional skills training for schizophrenia: Effects on cognition, functional competence, and real-world behavior. *American Journal of Psychiatry, 169,* 710–718.

Chapman, L. J., Chapman, J. P., Kwapil, T. R., Eckblad, M., & Zinser, M. C. (1994). Putatively psychosis-prone subjects 10 years later. *Journal of Abnormal Psychology, 103,* 171–183.

Chemerinski, E., Byne, W., Kolaitis, J. C., Glanton, C. F., Canfield, E. L., Newmark, R. E., ... Hazlett, E. A. (2013). Larger putamen size in antipsychotic-naïve individuals with schizotypal personality disorder. *Schizophrenia Research, 143,* 158–164.

Chemerinski, E., Triebwasser, J., Roussos, P., & Siever, L. J. (2013). Schizotypal personality disorder. *Journal of Personality Disorders, 27,* 652–679.

Chmielewski, M., Bagby, R. M., Markon, K., Ring, A. J., & Ryder, A.G. (2014). Openness to experience, intellect, schizotypal personality disorder, and psychoticism: Resolving the controversy. *Journal of Personality Disorders, 28,* 483–489.

Chmielewski, M., & Watson, D. (2008). The heterogeneous structure of schizotypal personality disorder: Item-level factors of the Schizotypal Personality Questionnaire and their associations with obsessive-compulsive disorder symptoms, dissociative tendencies, and normal personality. *Journal of Abnormal Psychology, 117,* 364–376.

Chun, C. A., Minor, K. S., & Cohen, A. S. (2013). Neurocognition in psychometrically defined college schizotypy samples: We are not measuring the "right stuff." *Journal of the International Neuropsychological Society, 19,* 324–337.

Cicero, D. C., & Kerns, J. G. (2010). Can disorganized and positive schizotypy be discriminated from dissociation? *Journal of Personality, 78,* 1239–1270.

Cohen, A. S., Emmerson, L. C., Mann, M. C., Forbes, C. B., & Blanchard, J. J. (2010). Schizotypal, schizoid and paranoid characteristics in the biological parents of social anhedonics. *Psychiatry Research, 178,* 79–83.

Collins, L. M., Blanchard, J. J., & Biondo, K. M. (2005). Behavioral signs of schizoidia and schizotypy in social anhedonics. *Schizophrenia Research, 78,* 309–322.

Crego, C., & Widiger, T. A. (2017). The conceptualization and assessment of schizotypal traits: A comparison of the FFSI and PID-5. *Journal of Personality Disorders, 31,* 606–623.

Czajkowski, N., Aggen, S. H., Krueger, R., F., Kendler, K. S., Neale, M. C., Knudsen, G. P., ... Reichborn-Kjennerud, T. (2018). A twin study of normative personality and DSM-IV personality disorder criterion counts: Evidence for separate genetic influences. *American Journal of Psychiatry, 175,* 649–656.

DeYoung, C. G., Carey, B. E., Krueger, R. F., & Ross, S. R. (2016). Ten aspects of the Big Five in the Personality Inventory for DSM-5. *Personality Disorders, 7,* 113–123.

DeYoung, C. G., Grazioplene, R. G., & Peterson, J. B. (2012). From madness to genius: The Openness/Intellect trait domain as a paradoxical simplex. *Journal of Research in Personality, 46,* 63–78.

Dickey, C. C., McCarley, R. W., Niznikiewicz, M. A., Voglmaier, M. M., Seidman, L. J., Kim, S., & Shenton, M. E. (2005). Clinical, cognitive, and social characteristics of a sample of neuroleptic-naive persons with schizotypal personality disorder. *Schizophrenia Research, 78,* 297–308.

Dickey, C. C., Morocz, I. A., Minney, D., Niznikiewicz, M. A., Voglmaier, M. M., Panych, L. P., ... McCarley, R. W. (2010). Factors in sensory processing of prosody in schizotypal personality disorder: An fMRI experiment. *Schizophrenia Research, 121,* 75–89.

Dickey, C. C., Vu, M. A., Voglmaier, M. M., Niznikiewicz, M. A., McCarley, R. W. & Panych, L. P. (2012). Prosodic abnormalities in schizotypal personality disorder. *Schizophrenia Research, 142,* 20–30.

Dixon-Gordon, K. L., Turner, B. J., & Chapman, A. L. (2011). Psychotherapy for personality disorders. *International Review of Psychiatry, 23,* 282–302.

Docherty, A. R., Moscati, A., Dick, D., Savage, J. E., Salvatore, J. E., Cooke, M., ... Kendler, K. S. (2018). Polygenic prediction of the phenome, across ancestry, in emerging adulthood. *Psychological Medicine, 48,* 1814–1823.

Duncan, L. E., Shen, H., Ballon, J. S., Hardy, K. V., Noordsy, D. L., & Levinson, D. F. (2018). Genetic correlation profile of schizophrenia mirrors epidemiological results and suggests link between polygenic and rare variant (22q11.2) cases of schizophrenia. *Schizophrenia Bulletin, 44,* 1350–1361.

Esterberg, M. L., Goulding, S. M., & Walker, E. F. (2010). A personality disorders: Schizotypal, schizoid and paranoid personality disorders in childhood and adolescence. *Journal of Psychopathology and Behavioral Assessment, 32,* 515–528.

Esterberg, M. L., Ousley, O. Y., Cubells, J. F., & Walker, E. F. (2013). Prodromal and autistic symptoms in schizotypal personality disorder and 22q11.2 deletion syndrome. *Journal of Abnormal Psychology, 122,* 238–249.

Falkum, E., Pedersen, G., & Karterud, S. (2009). Diagnostic and Statistical Manual of Mental Disorders, Fourth Edition, paranoid personality disorder diagnosis: A unitary or a two-dimensional construct? *Comprehensive Psychiatry, 50,* 533–541.

Fonseca-Pedrero, E., Debbané, M., Ortuno-Sierra, J., Chan, R. C. K., Cicero, D. C., Zhang, L. C., ... Jablensky, A. (2018). The structure of schizotypal personality traits: A cross-national study. *Psychological Medicine, 48,* 451–462.

Forbes, M. K., Kotov, R., Ruggero, C. J., Watson, D., Zimmerman, M., & Krueger, R. F. (2017). Delineating the joint hierarchical structure of clinical and personality disorders in an outpatient psychiatric sample. *Comprehensive Psychiatry, 79,* 19–30.

Gard, D. E., Sanchez, A. H., Cooper, K., Fisher, M., Garrett, C., & Vinogradov, S. (2014). Do people with schizophrenia have difficulty anticipating pleasure, engaging in effortful behavior, or both? *Journal of Abnormal Psychology, 123,* 771–782.

Gillespie, N. A., Aggen, S. H., Neale, M. C., Knudsen, G. P., Krueger, R. F., South, S. C., ... Reichborn-Kjennerud, T. (2018). Associations between personality disorders and cannabis use and cannabis use disorder: A population-based twin study. *Addiction, 113,* 1488–1498.

Gooding, D. C., Coleman, M. J., Roberts, S. A., Shenton, M. E., Levy, D. L., & Erlenmeyer-Kimling, L. (2012). Thought disorder in offspring of schizophrenic parents: Findings from the New York High-Risk Project. *Schizophrenia Bulletin, 38,* 263–271.

Gooding, D. C., Ott, S. L., Roberts, S. A., & Erlenmeyer-Kimling, L. (2013). Thought disorder in mid-childhood as a predictor of adulthood diagnostic outcome: Findings from the New York High-Risk Project. *Psychological Medicine, 43,* 1003–1012.

Gottesman, I. I., Laursen, T. M., Bertelsen, A., & Mortensen, P. B. (2010). Severe mental disorders in offspring with 2 psychiatrically ill parents. *Archives of General Psychiatry, 67,* 252–257.

Grant, P. M., Huh, G. A., Perivoliotis, D., Stolar, N. M., & Beck, A. T. (2012). Randomized trial to evaluate the efficacy of cognitive therapy for low-functioning patients with schizophrenia. *Archives of General Psychiatry, 69,* 121–127.

Haigler, E. D., & Widiger, T. A. (2001). Experimental manipulation of NEO PI-R items. *Journal of Personality Assessment, 77,* 339–358.

Hatzimanolis, A., Avramopoulos, D., Arking, D. E., Moes, A., Bhatnagar, P., Lencz, T., ... Stefanis, N. C. (2018). Stress-dependent association between polygenic risk for schizophrenia and schizotypal traits in young army recruits. *Schizophrenia Bulletin, 44,* 338–347.

Hazlett, E. A., Lamade, R. V., Graff, F. S., McClure, M. M., Kolaitis, J. C., Goldstein, K. E., ... Moshier E. (2014). Visual-spatial working memory performance and temporal gray matter volume predict schizotypal personality disorder group membership. *Schizophrenia Research, 152,* 350–357.

Hjorthøj, C., Albert, N., & Nordentoft, M. (2018). Association of substance use disorders with conversion from schizotypal disorder to schizophrenia. *JAMA Psychiatry, 75,* 733–739.

Horan, W. P., Reise, S. P., Subotnik, K. L., Ventura, J., & Nuechterlein, K. H. (2008). The validity of Psychosis Proneness Scales as vulnerability indicators in recent-onset schizophrenia patients. *Schizophrenia Research, 100,* 224–236.

Howes, O. D., McCutcheon, R., Owen, M. J., & Murray, R. M. (2017). The role of genes, stress, and dopamine in the development of schizophrenia. *Biological Psychiatry, 81,* 9–20.

Huang, Y., Kotov, R., de Girolamo, G., Preti, A., Angermeyer, M., Benjet, C., ... Kessler, R. C. (2009). DSM-IV personality disorders in the WHO World Mental Health Surveys. *British Journal of Psychiatry, 195,* 46–53.

Ivleva, E. I., Bidesi, A. S., Keshavan, M. S., Pearlson, G. D., Meda, S. A., Dodig, D., ... Tamminga, C. A. (2013). Gray matter volume as an intermediate phenotype for psychosis:

Bipolar-Schizophrenia Network on Intermediate Phenotypes (B-SNIP). *American Journal of Psychiatry, 170*, 1285–1296.

Jakobsen, K. D., Skyum, E., Hashemi, N., Schjerning, O., Fink-Jensen, A., & Nielsen, J. (2017). Antipsychotic treatment of schizotypy and schizotypal personality disorder: A systematic review. *Journal of Psychopharmacology, 31*, 397–405.

Jones, H. J., Stergiakouli, E., Tansey, K. E., Hubbard, L., Heron, J., Cannon, M., ... Zammit, S. (2016). Phenotypic manifestation of genetic risk for schizophrenia during adolescence in the general population. *JAMA Psychiatry, 73*, 221–228.

Kane, M. J., Meier, M. E., Smeekens, B. A., Gross, G. M., Chun, C. A., Silvia, P. J., & Kwapil, T. R. (2016). Individual differences in the executive control of attention, memory, and thought, and their associations with schizotypy. *Journal of Experimental Psychology: General, 145*, 1017–1048.

Kaufman, S. B., DeYoung, C. G., Gray, J. R., Jiménez, L., Brown, J., & Mackintosh, N. (2010). Implicit learning as an ability. *Cognition, 116*, 321–340.

Kelleher, I., Keeley, H., Corcoran, P., Ramsay, H., Wasserman, C., Carli, V., ... Cannon, M. (2013). Childhood trauma and psychosis in a prospective cohort study: Cause, effect, and directionality. *American Journal of Psychiatry, 170*, 734–741.

Kendler, K. S., Czajkowski, N., Tambs, K., Torgersen, S., Aggen, S. H., Neale, M. C., & Reichborn-Kjennerud, T. (2006) Dimensional representations of DSM-IV Cluster A personality disorders in a population-based sample of Norwegian twins: A multivariate study. *Psychological Medicine, 36*, 1583–1591.

Kendler, K. S., Gallagher, T. J., Abelson, J. M., & Kessler, R. C. (1996). Lifetime prevalence, demographic risk factors, and diagnostic validity of nonaffective psychosis as assessed in a US community sample: *The National Comorbidity Survey. Archives of General Psychiatry, 53*, 1022–1031.

Kendler, K. S., Lieberman, J. A., & Walsh, D. (1989). The Structured Interview for Schizotypy (SIS): A preliminary report. *Schizophrenia Bulletin, 15*, 559–571.

Kendler, K. S., McGuire, M., Gruenberg, A. M., & Walsh, D. (1995) Schizotypal symptoms and signs in the Roscommon Family Study: Their factor structure and familial relationship with psychotic and affective disorders. *Archives of General Psychiatry, 52*, 296–303.

Kendler, K. S., Ohlsson, H., Mezuk, B., Sundquist, J. O., & Sundquist, K. (2016). Observed cognitive performance and deviation from familial cognitive aptitude at age 16 years and ages 18 to 20 years and risk for schizophrenia and bipolar illness in a Swedish national sample. *JAMA Psychiatry, 73*, 465–471.

Kendler, K. S., & Walsh, D. (1995). Schizotypal personality disorder in parents and the risk for schizophrenia in siblings. *Schizophrenia Bulletin, 21*, 47–52.

Koch, J., Modesitt, T., Palmer, M., Ward, S., Martin, B., Wyatt, R., & Thomas, C. (2016). Review of pharmacologic treatment in Cluster A personality disorders. *Mental Health Clinician, 6*, 75–81.

Koo, M. S., Dickey, C. C., Park, H.-J., Kubicki, M., Young Ji, N., Bouix, S., ... McCarley R. W. (2006). Smaller neocortical gray matter and larger sulcal cerebrospinal fluid volumes in neuroleptic-naive women with schizotypal personality disorder. *Archives of General Psychiatry, 63*, 1090–1100.

Koo, M. S., Levitt, J. J., McCarley, R. W., Seidman, L. J., Dickey, C. C., Niznikiewicz, M. A., ... Shenton, M. E. (2006). Reduction of caudate nucleus volumes in neuroleptic-naïve female subjects with schizotypal personality disorder. *Biological Psychiatry, 60*, 40–48.

Kosson, D. S., Blackburn, R., Byrnes, K. A., Park, S., Logan, C., & Donnelly, J. P. (2008). Assessing interpersonal aspects of schizoid personality disorder: Preliminary validation studies. *Journal of Personality Assessment, 90*, 185–196.

Kring, A. M., Gur, R. E., Blanchard, J. J., Horan, W. P., & Reise, S. P. (2013). The Clinical Assessment Interview for Negative Symptoms (CAINS): Final development and validation. *American Journal of Psychiatry, 170*, 165–172.

Kwapil, T. R., Gross, G. M., Silvia, P. J., & Barrantes-Vidal, N. (2013). Prediction of psychopathology and functional impairment by positive and negative schizotypy in the Chapmans' ten-year longitudinal study. *Journal of Abnormal Psychology, 122*, 807–815.

Kyaga, S., Lichtenstein, P., Boman, N., Hultman, C., Långström, N., & Landén, M. (2011). Creativity and mental disorder: Family study of 300,000 people with severe mental disorder. *British Journal of Psychiatry, 199*, 373–379.

Laruelle, M., Abi-Dargham, A., Gil, R., Kegeles, L., & Innis, R. (1999). Increased dopamine transmission in schizophrenia: Relationship to illness phases. *Biological Psychiatry, 46*, 56–72.

Lener, M. S., Wong, E., Tang, C. Y., Byne, W., Goldstein, K. E., Blair, N. J., ... Hazlett, E. A. (2015). White matter abnormalities in schizophrenia and schizotypal personality disorder. *Schizophrenia Bulletin, 41*, 300–310.

Lenggenhager, B., Tadi, T., Metzinger, T., & Blanke, O. (2007). Video ergo sum: Manipulating bodily self-consciousness. *Science, 317*, 1096–1099.

Lentz, V., Robinson, J., & Bolton, J. M. (2010). Childhood adversity, mental disorder comorbidity, and suicidal behavior in schizotypal personality disorder. *Journal of Nervous and Mental Disease, 198*, 795–801.

Lenzenweger, M. F. (1999). Deeper into the schizotypy taxon: On the robust nature of maximum covariance analysis. *Journal of Abnormal Psychology, 108*, 182–187.

Lenzenweger, M. F. (2018). Schizotypy, schizotypic psychopathology and schizophrenia. *World Psychiatry, 17*, 25–26.

Lenzenweger, M. F., Lane, M. C., Loranger, A. W., & Kessler, R. C. (2007). DSM-IV personality disorders in the National Comorbidity Survey Replication. *Biological Psychiatry, 62*, 553–564.

Leung, W. M., Couture, S. M., Blanchard, J. J., Lin, S., & Llerena, K. (2010). Is social anhedonia related to emotional responsivity and expressivity? A laboratory study in women. *Schizophrenia Research, 124*, 66–73.

Linscott, R. J., Morton, S. E., & GROUP (Genetic Risk and Outcome of Psychosis) Investigators (2018). The latent taxonicity of schizotypy in biological siblings of probands with schizophrenia. *Schizophrenia Bulletin, 44*, 922–932.

Llerena, K., Park, S. G., Couture, S. M., & Blanchard, J. J. (2012). Social anhedonia and affiliation: Examining behavior and subjective reactions within a social interaction. *Psychiatry Research, 200*, 679–686.

Lo, M., Hinds, D. A., Tung, J. Y., Franz, C., Fan, C.-C., Wang, Y., ... Chen, C. H. (2017). Genome-wide analyses for personality traits identify six genomic loci and show correlations with psychiatric disorders. *Nature Genetics, 49*, 152–156.

Longden, E., Madill, A., & Waterman, M. G. (2012). Dissociation, trauma, and the role of lived experience: Toward a new conceptualization of voice hearing. *Psychological Bulletin, 138*, 28–76.

Lyssenko, L., Schmahl, C., Bockhacker, L., Vonderlin, R., Bohus, M., & Kleindienst, N. (2018). Dissociation in psychiatric disorders: A meta-analysis of studies using the dissociative experiences scale. *American Journal of Psychiatry, 175*, 37–46.

MacCabe, J. H., Sariaslan, A., Almqvist, C., Lichtenstein, P., Larsson, H., & Kyaga, S. (2018). Artistic creativity and risk for schizophrenia, bipolar disorder and unipolar depression: A Swedish population-based case-control study and sib-pair analysis. *British Journal of Psychiatry, 212*, 370–376.

Maróthi, R., & Kéri, S. (2018). Enhanced mental imagery and intact perceptual organization in schizotypal personality disorder. *Psychiatry Research, 259*, 433–438.

McClure, M. M., Flory, J. D., Barch, D. M., Harvey, P. D., & Siever, L. J. (2008). Context processing in schizotypal personality disorder: Evidence of specificity of impairment to the schizophrenia spectrum. *Journal of Abnormal Psychology, 117*, 342–354.

McClure, M. M., Harvey, P. D., Bowie, C. R., Iacoviello, B., & Siever, L. J. (2013). Functional outcomes, functional capacity, and cognitive impairment in schizotypal personality disorder. *Schizophrenia Research, 144*, 146–150.

McGurk, S. R., Mueser, K. T., Mischel, R., Adams, R., Harvey, P. D., McClure, M. M., ... Siever, L. J. (2013). Vocational functioning in schizotypal and paranoid personality disorders. *Psychiatry Research, 210*, 498–504.

Medalia, A., Thysen, J., & Freilich, B. (2008). Do people with schizophrenia who have objective cognitive impairment identify cognitive deficits on a self report measure? *Schizophrenia Research, 105*, 156–164.

Mittal, V. A., Tessner, K. D., McMillan, A. L., Delawalla, Z., Trotman, H. D., & Walker, E. F. (2006). Gesture behavior in unmedicated schizotypal adolescents. *Journal of Abnormal Psychology, 115*, 351–358.

Moorman, E. L., & Samuel, D. B. (2018). Representing schizotypal thinking with dimensional traits: A case for the Five Factor Schizotypal Inventory. *Psychological Assessment, 30*, 19–30.

Moran, E. K., Culbreth, A. J., & Barch, D. M. (2017). Ecological momentary assessment of negative symptoms in schizophrenia: Relationships to effort-based decision making and reinforcement learning. *Journal of Abnormal Psychology, 126*, 96–105.

Moritz, S., Veckenstedt, R., Andreou, C., Bohn, F., Hottenrott, B., Leighton, L., ... Roesch-Ely, D. (2014). Sustained and "sleeper" effects of group metacognitive training for schizophrenia: A randomized clinical trial. *JAMA Psychiatry, 71*, 1103–1011.

Mote, J., Stuart, B. K., & Kring, A. M. (2014). Diminished emotion expressivity but not experience in men and women with schizophrenia. *Journal of Abnormal Psychology, 123*, 796–801.

Munafò, M. R., Tilling, K., Taylor, A. E., Evans, D. M., & Davey Smith, G. (2018). Collider scope: When selection bias can substantially influence observed associations. *International Journal of Epidemiology, 47*, 226–235.

Ohi, K., Shimada, T., Nitta, Y., Kihara, H., Okubo, H., Uehara, T., & Kawasaki, Y. (2016). The Five-Factor Model personality traits in schizophrenia: A meta-analysis. *Psychiatry Research, 240*, 34–41.

Pain, O., Dudbridge, F., Cardno, A. G., Freeman, D., Lu, Y., Lundstrom, S., ... Ronald, A. (2018). Genome-wide analysis of adolescent psychotic-like experiences shows genetic overlap with psychiatric disorders. *American Journal of Medical Genetics, Part B: Neuropsychiatric Genetics, 177*, 416–425.

Power, R. A., Steinberg, S., Rietveld, C. A., Abdellaoui, A., Nivard, M. M., Johannesson, M., ... Stefansson, K. (2015). Polygenic risk scores for schizophrenia and bipolar disorder predict creativity. *Nature Neuroscience, 18*, 953–955.

Quirk, S. E., Berk, M., Chanen, A. M., Koivumaa-Honkanen, H., Brennan-Olsen, S. L., Pasco, J. A., & Williams, L. J. (2016). Population prevalence of personality disorder and associations with physical health comorbidities and health care service utilization: A review. *Personality Disorders, 7*, 136–146.

Raine, A. (1991). The SPQ: A scale for the assessment of schizotypal personality based on DSM-III-R criteria. *Schizophrenia Bulletin, 17*, 555–564.

Raine, A. (2006). Schizotypal personality: Neurodevelopmental and psychosocial trajectories. *Annual Review of Clinical Psychology, 2*, 291–326.

Reichborn-Kjennerud, T., Krueger, R. F., Ystrom, E., Torvik, F. A., Rosenström, T. H., Aggen, S. H., ... Czajkowski, N. O. (2017). Do DSM-5 Section II personality disorders and Section III personality trait domains reflect the same genetic and environmental risk factors? *Psychological Medicine, 47*, 2205–2215.

Rietkerk, T., Boks, M. P., Sommer, I. E., Liddle, P. F., Ophoff, R. A., & Kahn, R. S. (2008). The genetics of symptom dimensions of schizophrenia: Review and meta-analysis. *Schizophrenia Research, 102*, 197–205.

Risen, J. L. (2016). Believing what we do not believe: Acquiescence to superstitious beliefs and other powerful intuitions. *Psychological Review, 123*, 182–207.

Ronald, A., & Pain, O. (2018). A systematic review of genome-wide research on psychotic experiences and negative symptom traits: New revelations and implications for psychiatry. *Human Molecular Genetics, 27*(R2), R136–R152.

Rosell, D. R., Futterman, S. E., McMaster, A., & Siever, L. J. (2014). Schizotypal personality disorder: A current review. *Current Psychiatry Reports, 16*, 452.

Rosell, D. R., Zaluda, L. C., McClure, M. M., Perez-Rodriguez, M. M., Sloan Strike, K., Barch, D. M., ... Siever, L. J. (2015). Effects of the D1 dopamine receptor agonist dihydrexidine (DAR-0100A) on working memory in schizotypal personality disorder. *Neuropsychopharmacology, 40*, 446–453.

Ross, R. M., McKay, R., Coltheart, M., & Langdon, R. (2015). Jumping to conclusions about the beads task? A meta-analysis of delusional ideation and data-gathering. *Schizophrenia Bulletin, 41*, 1183–1191.

Samuel, D. B., & Widiger, T. A. (2008). A meta-analytic review of the relationships between the five-factor model and DSM-IV-TR personality disorders: A facet level analysis. *Clinical Psychology Review, 28*, 1326–1342.

Schizophrenia Working Group of the Psychiatric Genomics Consortium. (2014). Biological insights from 108 schizophrenia-associated genetic loci. *Nature, 511*, 421–427.

Seidman, L. J., Shapiro, D. I., Woodberry, K. A., Ronzio, A., Cornblatt, B. A., Addington, J., ... Woods, S. W. (2016). Association of neurocognition with transition to psychosis: Baseline functioning in the second phase of the North American prodrome longitudinal study. *JAMA Psychiatry, 73*, 1239–1248.

Siddi, S., Petretto, D. R., & Preti, A. (2017). Neuropsychological correlates of schizotypy: A systematic review and meta-analysis of cross-sectional studies. *Cognitive Neuropsychiatry, 22*, 186–212.

Siever, L. J., & Davis, K. L. (2004). The pathophysiology of schizophrenia disorders: Perspectives from the spectrum. *American Journal of Psychiatry, 161*, 398–413.

Smeland, O. B., Wang, Y., Lo, M.-T., Li, W., Frei, O., Witoelar, A., ... Andreassen, O. A. (2017). Identification of genetic loci shared between schizophrenia and the Big Five personality traits. *Scientific Reports, 7*, 2222.

So, S. H., Peters, E. R., Swendsen, J., Garety, P. A., & Kapur, S. (2014). Changes in delusions in the early phase of antipsychotic treatment: An experience sampling study. *Psychiatry Research, 215*, 568–573.

Spitzer, R. L., Endicott, J., & Gibbon, M. (1979). Crossing the border into borderline personality and borderline schizophrenia: *The development of criteria.* Archives of General Psychiatry, *36*, 17–24.

Stone, M. (1985). Schizotypal personality: Psychotherapeutic aspects. *Schizophrenia Bulletin, 11*, 576–589.

Strauss, G. P., & Cohen, A. S. (2017). A transdiagnostic review of negative symptom phenomenology and etiology. *Schizophrenia Bulletin, 43*, 712–719.

Sutin, A. R. (2017). Openness. In T. A. Widiger (Ed.), *The Oxford Handbook of the Five Factor Model* (pp. 83–104). New York: Oxford University Press.

Tandon, R., Nasrallah, H. A., & Keshavan, M. S. (2009). Schizophrenia, "just the facts" 4. Clinical features and conceptualization. *Schizophrenia Research, 110*, 1–23.

Tarbox, S. I., Almasy, L., Gur, R. E., Nimgaonkar, V. L., & Pogue-Geile, M. F. (2012). The nature of schizotypy among multigenerational multiplex schizophrenia families. *Journal of Abnormal Psychology, 121*, 396–406.

Tarbox, S. I., & Pogue-Geile, M. F. (2011). A multivariate perspective on schizotypy and familial association with schizophrenia: A review. *Clinical Psychology Review, 31*, 1169–1182.

Thompson, J. L., Rosell, D. R., Slifstein, M., Girgis, R. R., Xu, X., Ehrlich, Y., . . . Siever, L. J. (2014). Prefrontal dopamine D1 receptors and working memory in schizotypal personality disorder: A PET study with [11C]NNC112. *Psychopharmacology, 231*, 4231–4240.

Toftdahl, N. G., Nordentoft, M., & Hjorthøj, C. (2016). Prevalence of substance use disorders in psychiatric patients: A nationwide Danish population-based study. *Social Psychiatry and Psychiatric Epidemiology, 51*, 129–140.

Triebwasser, J., Chemerinski, E., Roussos, P., & Siever, L. J. (2012). Schizoid personality disorder. *Journal of Personality Disorders, 26*, 919–926.

Triebwasser, J., Chemerinski, E., Roussos, P., & Siever, L. J. (2013). Paranoid personality disorder. *Journal of Personality Disorders, 27*, 795–805.

van Os, J., van der Steen, Y., Islam, M. A., Gülöksüz, S., Rutten, B. P., Simons, C. J., & GROUP Investigators (2017). Evidence that polygenic risk for psychotic disorder is expressed in the domain of neurodevelopment, emotion regulation and attribution of salience. *Psychological Medicine, 47*, 2421–2437.

Velikonja, T., Fisher, H. L., Mason, O., & Johnson, S. (2015). Childhood trauma and schizotypy: A systematic literature review. *Psychological Medicine, 45*, 947–963.

Verbeke, L., De Clercq, B., Van der Heijden, P., Hutsebaut, J., & van Aken, M. A. (2017). The relevance of schizotypal traits for understanding interpersonal functioning in adolescents with psychiatric problems. *Personality Disorders, 8*, 54–63.

Waters, F., Blom, J. D., Jardri, R., Hugdahl, K., & Sommer, I. E. C. (2018). Auditory hallucinations, not necessarily a hallmark of psychotic disorder. *Psychological Medicine, 48*, 529–536.

Watson, D., Clark, L. A., & Chmielewski, M. (2008). Structures of personality and their relevance to psychopathology: II. *Further articulation of a comprehensive unified trait structure.* Journal of Personality, *76*, 1545–1586.

Widiger, T. A., Crego, C., Rojas, S. L., & Oltmanns, J. R. (2018). Basic personality model. *Current Opinion in Psychology, 21*, 18–22.

Zammit, S., Hamshere, M., Dwyer, S., Georgiva, L., Timpson, N., Moskvina, V., . . . O'Donovan, M. C. (2014) A population-based study of genetic variation and psychotic experiences in adolescents. *Schizophrenia Bulletin, 40*, 1254–1262.

Zhang, T., Wang, D., Zhang, Q., Wu, J., Lv, J., & Shi, L. (2017). Supervoxel-based statistical analysis of diffusion tensor imaging in schizotypal personality disorder. *NeuroImage, 163*, 368–378.

9a Conceptual and Methodological Reflections on Schizotypy, Schizotypic Psychopathology, Cluster A Disorders, and Schizophrenia: Commentary on Cluster A Personality Disorders

MARK F. LENZENWEGER

The overview of Cluster A personality disorders, focused primarily on schizotypal personality disorder (SPD), by Kerns (this volume) is rich and robust. It provides an excellent survey of the wave tops from multiple research literatures bearing upon the SPD condition/construct, which is reflective of the American Psychiatric Association's DSM-system definition of the condition from DSM-III through DSM-5. There is much to like about this review and it presents an opportunity to reflect on conceptual and methodological issues related to the schizotypy construct, schizotypic psychopathology, schizotypal personality disorder, and schizophrenia. I offer these reflections in the spirit of advancing the discourse in this area as well as to provide historical and empirical context. My reflections are offered in no particular order and I seek to be succinct.

BRIEF BACKGROUND AND ORIENTING COMMENTS

It is important to explicate several relevant distinctions regarding the meaning of the term *schizotypic*. The terms *schizotypal* PD and *paranoid* PD (PPD) denote the personality disorders as defined by the DSM nomenclature. SPD and PPD are defined by sets of *atheoretical* descriptors (signs and symptoms) that serve as diagnostic criteria; DSM systems (from 1980 [DSM-III] to the present [DSM-5]) eschew any relationship to an explanatory framework or theory for these disorders. Moreover, given their relatively high degree of comorbidity, shared phenomenological features, and empirical relationship to clinical schizophrenia, SPD and PPD are often referred to as the "schizophrenia-related personality disorders" (SRPDs) and are viewed as falling within the realm of "schizophrenia spectrum disorders." In contrast to the term SRPD, *schizotypic* can be used to describe a range of signs and symptoms that are the phenotypic manifestation of *schizotypy*, or a latent personality organization that derives from a liability for schizophrenia. The term *schizotypic* can also serve as a generic shorthand descriptor of attenuated "schizophrenia-like" phenomenology that is

fundamentally nonpsychotic. The schizotypic – schizophrenia phenomenological similarities are compelling, for example, perceptual aberrations ≈ hallucinations; suspiciousness/paranoid ≈ delusions; odd speech ≈ thought disorder; odd behavior ≈ bizarre behavior; social isolation ≈ asociality/withdrawal; blunted emotions ≈ flattened affect; peculiar ideas ≈ bizarre beliefs; and diminished pleasure ≈ anhedonia. SPD and PPD can readily be conceived of as manifestations of schizotypy as well, but they are not isomorphic with the schizotypy construct (Figure 9.a.1). *Schizotypic psychopathology* serves as a generic term for this broader class of schizophrenia-related mental disturbance. A *schizotype* is a person displaying evidence of schizotypic psychopathology. DSM-defined schizoid personality disorder is not always considered an SRPD (albeit a Cluster A condition) in light of available evidence.

SPD and schizotypy represent rich and complex constructs. However, *schizotypy and SPD are not fungible concepts*, although the terms have been used interchangeably by some and this has unfortunately introduced some lack of conceptual clarity in the theoretical and empirical literature. Schizotypy implies a theoretical model that has considerable utility as an organizing framework for the study of schizophrenia (see Meehl, 1962, 1990; see also Lenzenweger, 2006, 2010), schizophrenia-related psychopathology (e.g., delusional disorder, psychosis-NOS, schizotypal and paranoid personality disorder), and putative schizophrenia endophenotypes, a view I have advocated for over 30 years (Lenzenweger, 1994, 1998, 2006, 2010, 2015, 2018; Lenzenweger & Loranger, 1989). The leverage provided by the schizotypy model, especially as advocated by Meehl (1962, 1990; Figure 9.a.1), for understanding schizophrenia and its pathogenesis has been shown to be appreciable and Kerns rightly promotes this substantive thrust implicitly. Moreover, the schizotypy model and associated empirical research have helped to adjust the phenotypic boundaries of schizophrenia phenotype in the DSM-5 (e.g., schizotypal pathology is now included with schizophrenia). Illuminating the nature of schizotypy may aid in unraveling the current puzzle of the very low

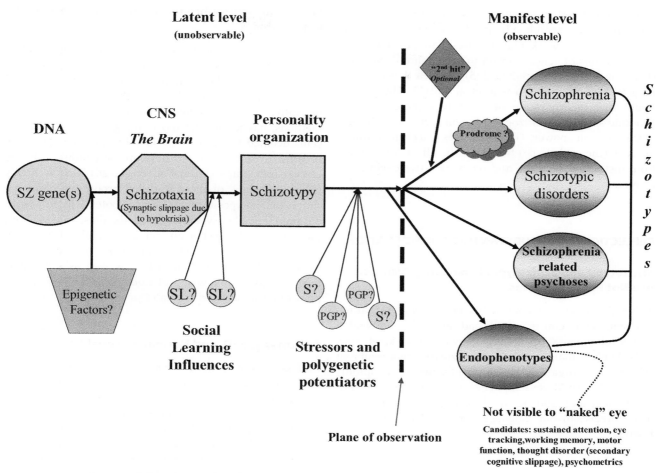

Figure 9.a.1 Developmental model relating the genetic diathesis for schizophrenia, schizotaxia, and schizotypy and implied levels of analysis (inspired by Meehl 1962, 1990, with modifications by Lenzenweger, 2010). Those factors to the left of the vertical broken line (i.e., plane of observation) are "latent" and therefore unobservable with the unaided naked eye, whereas those factors to the right of the plane of observation are manifest (or observable). A DNA based liability – primary synaptic slippage (embodied in Meehl's hypothetical process denoted "hypokrisia") – creates impaired CNS based neural circuitry (schizotaxia) that eventuates in a personality organization (schizotypy) that harbors the liability for schizophrenia. Meehl (1962, 1990) viewed the genetically-determined liability to be entirely taxonic in nature (i.e., present or absent). However, this liability could also be determined by a confluence of genetic factors, probably many in number and of small effect, that have summed to pass a critical *threshold* (perhaps as many as 108 loci contribute to this liability: Schizophrenia Working Group of the Psychiatrics Genomics Consortium, 2014). The "synaptic slippage" in this model is consistent with modern-day concepts as diminished synaptic connectivity, abnormal connectivity, cognitive dysmetria, and so on. Social learning (SL) schedules interact with schizotaxia to yield to yield schizotypy. Psychosocial stressors (S) and polygenic potentiators (PGP) interact with schizotypy to yield manifest outcomes across a range of clinical compensation. Various possible manifest developmental outcomes include schizophrenia (which may involve an *optional* "second hit," e.g., *in utero* exposure to maternal influenza), schizotypic psychopathology (e.g., schizotypal and/ or paranoid personality disorders), or schizophrenia-related psychoses (e.g., delusional disorder). So-called "prodromal features" (withdrawal, reduced ideational richness, disorganized communication) may precede the onset of some (but *not* all) cases of schizophrenia. Endophenotypes (e.g., sustained attention deficits, eye tracking dysfunction, working memory impairments, motor dysfunction, thought disorder (secondary cognitive slippage), and/or psychometric deviance (PAS); see Gottesman & Gould, 2003), which are invisible to the unaided, "naked" eye (but detectable with appropriate technologies), are found below the plane of observation. Epigenetic factors refer to non-mutational phenomena, such as DNA methylation and histone acetylation (modification), that alter the expression of the schizophrenia gene (or genes). For example, there is the possibility that a hypermethylation process may serve to downregulate genes of relevance to schizophrenia. All individuals represented across this range of manifest outcomes are considered "schizotypes," which does not necessarily imply an ICD or DSM diagnosis. Finally, if there are genetically distinct variants of schizophrenia (Arnedo et al., 2014), then each variant could follow a distinct developmental pathway comparable to that shown here but with different causal factors playing different roles across the variants. © 2010, 2015 M. F. Lenzenweger, and used with permission

conversion to schizophrenia rates seen in "prodromal" schizophrenia research. Finally, I have argued that the schizotypy framework may be useful in understanding *configurations* of genes relevant to schizophrenia variants (Lenzenweger, 2010, pp. 234–235), an idea that is beginning to gain traction (Arnedo et al., 2015). There is no doubt that incorporation of schizotypy indicators into genomic studies of schizophrenia will increase their statistical resolving power. The advantages of a cleaner unit of analysis (the schizotype) free from the effects of medication, institutionalization, and neurocognitive decline are axiomatic.

REFLECTIONS AND SUBSTANTIVE CONSIDERATIONS

Schizotypy and Schizotypal Personality Disorder Are Not Fungible Terms

Although mentioned above, this point bears repeating. The schizotypy construct is broad and richly embedded in a developmental psychopathology framework, whereas SPD (likely a manifestation of schizotypy) represents an atheoretically organized collection of signs and symptoms as per the DSM system. The two concepts are not interchangeable and Kerns has encouraged the field to be precise in our language here, a view with which I agree.

Multidimensionality and Schizotypic Indicators

There has been a flood of reports in recent years that speak to the "multidimensionality" of schizotypic indicators. My dear friend, now late, Professor Irving Gottesman once quipped to me, "multidimensionality is simply a term that means complexity we do not understand." That schizotypic indicators exist in some variety (the "multi" part) has been known since the time of Kraepelin and Bleuler and was emphasized by Meehl and others. The "dimensionality" part of the expression is trickier. What this typically means is that the multivariate statistical procedure factor analysis provided some evidence for more than one factor or component underlying the observed covariation in an indicator data set (symptoms or psychometric values). One must, however, be alert to the fact that factor analytic procedures by their very nature *always* find dimensions – that is all that they can do. Whether or not the resolved components have a genuinely quantitative (dimensional) nature at a *latent* level is an entirely different scientific question and calls for other analytic procedures that can answer it (see Lenzenweger, 2010 for extended discussion). There is complexity to schizotypal signs and symptoms for sure, that such complexity can be reduced to a smaller number of factors is true, but, in my view, the interesting questions emerge at the latent structure level.

Prodromal Schizophrenia and the Low Conversion Rate Problem

Professor Kerns draws important attention to the very low conversion rate to psychosis seen in the various prodromal schizophrenia studies. The prodromal (sometimes called "clinical high-risk" or "ultra high-risk") approach, a derivative of earlier genetic and psychometric high-risk methods, has found that most young people (60–70 percent) deemed to be *en route* to schizophrenia (or, more broadly, psychosis) do *not* develop the condition during critical follow-ups (Fusar-Poli et al., 2013). It is highly likely that many of these so-called prodromal cases are simply schizotypes that will remain potentially impaired, but not clinically psychotic, across the lifespan. However, they may validly harbor an increased liability for schizophrenia (see Figure 9.a.1). I would argue that researchers interested in Cluster A disorders as well as schizotypy begin to probe this group of non-converters among the prodromal samples with greater precision.

Schizotypy, SPD, and Normal Personality

Professor Kerns writes "One view is that it is a schizophrenia-spectrum disorder, meaning a disorder less severe than schizophrenia but genetically related to it ... A second view is that it reflects variation of normal personality traits" (p. 199 in the previous chapter). Sando Rado, Paul E. Meehl, myself, and others have long viewed schizotypy and schizotypic psychopathology as intimately connected to the illness we know as schizophrenia (see Lenzenweger, 1998, 2010, 2018). There is an alternative view, properly attributed to Claridge (1997) and colleagues, which views schizotypy as a "collection of *psychotic traits* [that] *constitute an essentially healthy dimension of personality*, which in adaptive form contributes to psychological variations as creativity, non-threatening hallucinations, and rewarding spiritual and mystical beliefs and experiences" (Rawlings, Williams, Haslam, & Claridge, 2008, p. 1670, italics added). This is known as the benign schizotypy model wherein schizotypy is viewed as a normal range *personality* trait varying by degree along a continuum and can even yield what is termed "healthy psychosis" (see Lenzenweger, 2015).

Most psychopathologists subscribe to a model that views schizophrenia as an illness and schizotypic conditions as falling within a spectrum of phenotypic outcomes derivative of an underlying liability for schizophrenia. Can we meaningfully relate schizotypic features to measures of normal personality? Of course, one can do so. The meaning of such associations, however, is an entirely different matter. We must always bear in mind that *correlation does not imply continuity*. Thus, while one can find correlations between indicators of schizotypy or SPD and measures of normal personality, it does *not* follow that one is the continuous extension of the other. *Gedankenexperiment*: I would imagine that schizophrenia symptoms correlate with neuroticism and openness to experience, but would we conclude that schizophrenia is an extreme expression of neuroticism or openness? The complexities of fitting schizotypic personality features, as expressive of schizophrenia liability, into frameworks seeking to model normal personality has always seemed challenging to me (Lenzenweger & Depue, 2016).

Parsimony in Language

Professor Kerns superbly shows an acute awareness of different methods of assessment for SPD and schizotypy. Others in the field, however, have conflated *method* of assessment with the nature of the construct under consideration (e.g., SPD or schizotypy measures). I see no conceptual gain in introducing idiosyncratic concepts such as "psychometric schizotypy" or "self-report schizotypy" as one has seen in recent years. If a measurement device is construct valid for the intended construct, how does the method of assessment being included in the name of the construct advance substantive discourse? We do not speak of "structured-clinical interview depression," "self-report panic disorder," or "observer-rated borderline personality disorder."

Hedonic Capacity in Schizotypy, SPD, and Schizophrenia

Space limitations preclude a careful dissection of this issue; however, I believe hedonic capacity in relation to SPD (thinking narrowly) or schizotypy (thinking more broadly) is ripe for substantive and empirical development. It may well be that the diminished hedonic capacity we see in schizotypes may be reflective of the aversive impact that the harbored schizophrenia liability exerts on the psychosocial development and experience of schizotypic persons. This suggests the interesting possibility that the diminished hedonic capacity (sometimes referred to as "anhedonia") is more of a psychological effect or artifact than otherwise. The work of Strauss and colleagues is relevant here (Strauss & Cohen, 2018).

GENETIC INFLUENCES ON SPD FEATURES

The most influential early evidence that established a link between schizotypic phenomenology and clinical schizophrenia came from the Danish Adoption Study of Schizophrenia (Kety, Rosenthal, Wender, & Schulsinger, 1968). Using a definition of "borderline schizophrenia" heavily influenced by the clinical tradition, Kety et al. (1968) found elevated rates of borderline or latent schizophrenia in the biological relatives of adoptees with schizophrenia (replicated in Kety et al., 1994). These early adoption-study results provided compelling evidence for a genetically transmitted component underlying manifest schizophrenia and the less severe schizophrenia-like disorders.

The hypothesized continuity between the schizophrenia and schizotypic conditions was thus not merely phenomenological, but also genetically influenced.

Clearly, this focus on the genetic bridge to schizophrenia has been sustained through a rich descriptive tradition and supported by findings indicating that schizotypic pathology is related genetically to schizophrenia *per se* (see Kendler, 2015, for review). Indeed, recent evidence, in the form of genome-wide association studies (GWAS) for loci relevant to schizophrenia and schizotypic psychopathology dimensions, confirms shared genetic substrates for the two forms of psychopathology (Bigdeli et al., 2014; Fanous et al., 2007).

The genes/symptoms puzzle is a fascinating one and Kerns directs us to it effectively. Consider also that empirical data have shown, in twin studies, that genetic influences for schizophrenia are clearly connected to negative schizophrenia symptoms, perhaps less so for the positive symptoms (Dworkin & Lenzenweger, 1984). That said the clinical schizophrenia diagnostic phenotype, which features positive symptoms quite prominently with a far more diminished role for negative symptoms, is clearly highly heritable. Perceptual aberrations (a positive schizotypic feature) predict elevated morbid risk for treated schizophrenia in the biological first-degree relatives of non-psychotic individuals (Lenzenweger & Loranger, 1989) and perceptual aberrations are associated with variation in genetic loci of interesting in schizophrenia (e.g., catechol-O-methyltransferase (COMT); neuregulin-1) (see Lenzenweger, 2018). Thus, the positive/negative distinction in both schizophrenia and in schizotypic conditions (including SPD) will need to be probed more deeply to extract all available meaning, an area where newer molecular genetic tools will be helpful. Finally, in this context it is worth considering the proposed notion of "pseudoschizotypy" (a putative false schizotype due to absence of a genetic liability for schizophrenia), a concept that is interesting but difficult to assess absent a gold standard criterion of validity against which to evaluate presumed schizotypy cases. How might we proceed on this notion? How can it be made empirically useful?

SUMMARY

The utility of studying non-psychotic phenotypic variants of schizophrenia liability continues to represent an important vector in schizophrenia research. The viability and utility of the SPD phenotype is unquestionable; an expanded view of schizotypy (beyond simply SPD) will likely lend greater power and precision to further study of the nature of schizophrenia spectrum going forward.

REFERENCES

Arnedo, J., Svrakic, D., del Val, C., Romero-Zaliz, R., Hernandez-Cuervo, H., Molecular Genetics of Schizophrenia Consortium, . . .

Zwir, I.(2015). Uncovering the hidden risk architecture of the schizophrenias: Confirmation in three independent genome-wide association studies. *American Journal of Psychiatry, 172,* 139–153.

Bigdeli, T. B., Bacanu, S. A., Webb, B. T., Walsh, D., O'Neill, F. A., Fanous , A. H., . . . Kendler, K. S. (2014). Molecular validation of the schizophrenia spectrum. *Schizophrenia Bulletin, 40,* 60–65.

Claridge, G. (Ed.) (1997). *Schizotypy: Implications for Illness and Health.* New York: Oxford University Press.

Dworkin, R. H., & Lenzenweger, M. F. (1984). Symptoms and the genetics of schizophrenia: Implications for diagnosis. *American Journal of Psychiatry, 141,* 1541–1546.

Fanous, A. H., Neale, M. C., Gardner, C. O., Webb, B. T., Straub, R. E., O'Neill, F. A., . . . Kendler, K. S. (2007). Significant correlation in linkage signals from genome-wide scans of schizophrenia and schizotypy. *Molecular Psychiatry, 12,* 958–965.

Fusar-Poli, P., Borgwardt, S., Bechdolf, A., Addington, J., Riecher-Rössler, A., Schultze-Lutter, F., . . . Yung, A. (2013). The psychosis high-risk state: A comprehensive state-of-the-art review. *JAMA Psychiatry, 70,* 107–120.

Gottesman, I. I., & Gould, T. D. (2003). The endophenotype concept in psychiatry: Etymology and strategic intentions. *American Journal of Psychiatry, 160,* 636–645.

Kendler, K. S. (2015). A joint history of the nature of genetic variation and the nature of schizophrenia. *Molecular Psychiatry, 20,* 77–83.

Kety, S. S., Rosenthal, D., Wender, P. H., & Schulsinger, F. (1968). The types and prevalence of mental illness in the biological and adoptive families of adopted schizophrenics. *Journal of Psychiatric Research, 6,* 345–362.

Kety, S. S., Wender, P. H., Jacobsen, B., Ingraham, L. J., Jansson, L., Faber, B., & Kinney, D. K. (1994). Mental illness in the biological and adoptive relatives of schizophrenic adoptees: Replication of the Copenhagen Study in the rest of Denmark. *Archives of General Psychiatry, 51,* 442–455.

Lenzenweger, M. F. (1994). The psychometric high-risk paradigm, perceptual aberrations, and schizotypy: An update. *Schizophrenia Bulletin, 20,* 121–135.

Lenzenweger, M. F. (1998). Schizotypy and schizotypic psychopathology: Mapping an alternative expression of schizophrenia liability. In M. F. Lenzenweger & R. H. Dworkin (Eds.), *Origins and Development of Schizophrenia: Advances in Experimental Psychopathology* (pp. 93–121). Washington, DC: American Psychological Association.

Lenzenweger, M. F. (2006). Schizotypy: An organizing framework for schizophrenia research. *Current Directions in Psychological Science, 15,* 162–166.

Lenzenweger, M. F. (2010). *Schizotypy and Schizophrenia: The View from Experimental Psychopathology.* New York: Guilford Press.

Lenzenweger, M. F. (2015). Schizotypic psychopathology: Theory, evidence, and future directions. In P. H. Blaney, T. Millon, & R. Krueger (Eds.), *Oxford Textbook of Psychopathology* (3rd ed., pp. 729–767). New York: Oxford University Press.

Lenzenweger, M. F. (2018). Schizotypy, schizotypic psychopathology, and schizophrenia: Understanding the nature, basis, and manifestation of the schizophrenia spectrum. In J. Butcher, J. M. Hooley, & P. Kendall (Eds.), *American Psychological Association Handbook of Psychopathology* (pp. 343–373). Washington, DC: APA.

Lenzenweger, M. F., & Depue, R.A. (2016). Toward a developmental psychopathology of personality disturbance: A neurobehavioral dimensional model incorporating genetic, environmental, and epigenetic factors. In D. Cicchetti (Ed.), *Developmental Psychopathology, Volume 3: Maladaptation and Psychopathology* (3rd ed., pp. 1079–1110). New York: Wiley.

Lenzenweger, M. F., & Loranger, A. W. (1989). Detection of familial schizophrenia using a psychometric measure of schizotypy. *Archives of General Psychiatry, 46,* 902–907.

Meehl, P. E. (1962). Schizotaxia, schizotypy, schizophrenia. *American Psychologist, 17,* 827–838.

Meehl, P. E. (1990). Toward an integrated theory of schizotaxia, schizotypy, and schizophrenia. *Journal of Personality Disorders, 4,* 1–99.

Rawlings, D., Williams, B., Haslam, N., & Claridge, G. (2008). Taxometric analysis supports a dimensional latent structure for schizotypy. *Personality and Individual Differences, 44,* 1640–1651.

Schizophrenia Working Group of the Psychiatric Genomics Consortium. (2014). Biological insights from 108 schizophrenia-associated genetic loci. *Nature, 511,* 421–427.

Strauss, G. P., & Cohen, A. S. (2018). The schizophrenia spectrum anhedonia paradox. *World Psychiatry, 17,* 221–222.

9b Improved Operationalization and Measurement Are Central to the Future of Cluster A Personality Disorders: Commentary on Cluster A Personality Disorders

THANH LE AND ALEX S. COHEN

The chapter by Kerns (this volume) on "Cluster A" disorders provides an authoritative and thoughtful discussion of schizoid, paranoid, and schizotypal personality disorders as operationalized in the Diagnostic and Statistical Manual – 5th edition (DSM-5; American Psychiatric Association [APA], 2013) and among many researchers. From this chapter, it is clear that these diagnoses offer value to clinical, scientific, and consumer communities.

First, these disorders provide a valuable clinical tool for demarcating a particular type of functional deficit and distress and help identify appropriate evidence-based pharmacological and psychosocial treatments to address them. Second, they provide important prognostic information regarding social, cognitive, and vocational functioning and co-occurring psychopathology (e.g., substance use, depression, anxiety). Finally, they provide a tool for understanding clinical and individual differences associated with the development of other psychosis and schizophrenia-spectrum disorders; collectively one of the most economically costly and devastating illnesses known to humankind (Barbato, 1998).

It is also clear that DSM-5 Cluster A disorders suffer from issues as a scientific construct; issues which dovetail criticisms levied against DSM-5 disorders more broadly (Cuthbert & Insel, 2013; Krueger et al., 2018). For example, there are no diagnostic criteria unique to Cluster A disorders that aren't common to other disorders (Strauss & Cohen, 2017). Moreover, Cluster A disorders each allow for dramatically heterogeneous phenotypes (Bollini & Walker, 2007). Of particular note, schizotypal personality disorder encompasses nine symptoms reflecting abnormalities in a broad array of behavioral, social, language, perceptual, meta-cognitive, and affective systems; of which only five symptoms are required for diagnosis (thus allowing for many different combinations of symptoms to meet criteria). From a neurodevelopmental perspective, it is not clear that Cluster A disorders are categorically distinct from each other (Chun, Barrantes-Vidal, Sheinbaum, & Kwapil, 2017) or from schizophrenia-spectrum pathology broadly defined (Insel, 2010). Finally, diagnostic reliability via clinical interviews

and patient self-report is far from optimal (Chmielewski, Clark, Bagby, & Watson, 2015).

Given these limitations, it should be no surprise that cures for them do not exist, treatment is palliative at best, and no "necessary and sufficient" genetic, epigenetic, neurobiological, or functional mechanisms underlying them have been identified (Cohen, Chan & Debbané, 2018; Kirchner, Roeh, Nolden, & Hasan, 2018). In this commentary, we posit that the imprecision of DSM-5 Cluster A diagnoses constrains our ability to meaningfully measure, treat, and understand individual patients, at least, at a level expected by consumers and clinicians and comparable to that seen in many biomedical and bioengineering fields (Cohen, 2019). To address this, we consider how diagnosis and measurement of Cluster A disorders could conceivably change in the future. In doing so, we address (a) the viability of alternative diagnostic systems for operationalizing and measuring Cluster A disorders, (b) the utility of operationalizing Cluster A disorders within a broader spectrum of schizophrenia-related disorders and conditions, and (c) the viability of objectifying Cluster A disorders using various genotyping and phenotyping technologies.

VIABILITY OF ALTERNATIVE SYSTEMS FOR OPERATIONALIZING AND MEASURING CLUSTER A DISORDERS

Alternative systems for operationalizing and measuring personality disorders, mental disorders, and their underlying psychological/physiological strata have been gaining traction in recent years, including: the DSM-5 alternative personality disorder (i.e., Section III of DSM 5 – "emerging measures and models," APA, 2013), the Five-Factor Model (FFM; McCrae & John, 1992), the Research Domain Criteria (RDoC; Insel et al., 2010), and the Hierarchical Taxonomy of Psychopathology (HiTOP; Krueger et al., 2018) systems. These systems are potentially advantageous for clinical and research applications in that they are each associated with established assessments, hence potentially improving their "inter-rater" reliability. Moreover, they are each embedded within a hierarchy of other mental illness traits and symptoms, thus providing a framework for understanding and documenting phenotypic heterogeneity within Cluster A disorders and with co-occurring disorders. Finally, scientific literatures associated with these alternate systems are quite large, at least in regards to some of their domains. This helps provide clues to their underlying pathophysiological causes and mechanisms. Although these systems can hypothetically accommodate Cluster A disorders, none can yet satisfactorily explain all of their traits. For example, the DSM-5 alternative personality disorder section provides a theoretically-driven classification system that includes five personality domains: negative affect, detachment, psychoticism, antagonism, and disinhibition that roughly correspond to traditional FFM domains. This system can accommodate much of the phenotypic heterogeneity of Cluster A disorders, with suspiciousness, social anxiety, diminished social drive, odd speech/behavior, and other traits being reflected in varying and mutually exclusive levels of neuroticism, extraversion, openness to experience, agreeableness, and conscientiousness. However, both the DSM-5 alternative personality (i.e., psychoticism) and the FFM (i.e., openness to experience) struggle to meaningfully capture core positive schizotypal traits. As noted by Kerns (this volume), psychoticism has been proposed to be a component of openness to experience, though this is far from universally accepted (Chmielewski, Bagby, Markon, Ring, & Ryder, 2014). Similar struggles in integrating positive schizophrenia symptoms into both HiTOP and RDoC have been noted (Ford et al., 2014; Weinberger, Glick, & Klein, 2015; Wittchen & Beesdo-Baum, 2018). While proposed alternate systems offer some benefits for understanding Cluster A disorders, they cannot yet accommodate the full spectrum of Cluster A disorder traits.

UTILITY OF OPERATIONALIZING CLUSTER A DISORDERS WITHIN A SCHIZOPHRENIA-SPECTRUM

Alternatively, Cluster A disorders can be operationalized as components within a broader "schizophrenia-spectrum" (Kerns, this volume). Conceptual (Bollini & Walker, 2007) and empirical (Kendler, Neale, & Walsh, 1995) links between Cluster A disorders and schizophrenia are well established, and there is a general consensus that both reflect "schizotypal" traits (Lenzenweger, 2006). Within the schizophrenia research space, there is considerable effort worldwide to identify genetic and objective markers of this risk, and to use these markers in nomothetic risk rubrics for providing individual-level prognostic information. Moreover, the positive, negative, and disorganized traits associated with Cluster A disorders are conceptually and pathophysiologically related to the positive, negative, and disorganized symptoms of schizophrenia (Lenzenweger, 2006). Hence, efforts to understand and treat individual traits/symptoms within the broader schizophrenia-spectrum can hold importance for Cluster A disorders. That being said, our understanding of the mechanisms (e.g., genetic, psychosocial) underlying the diverse phenotypic expression in schizophrenia is poor, and treatments are palliative at best. While integrating Cluster A disorders within a schizophrenia-spectrum helps create continuity between them, there are likely few obvious treatment or assessment applications for schizophrenia that have not been already considered for Cluster A disorders (e.g., Kirchner et al., 2018; Kerns, this volume).

DEFINING AND MEASURING CLUSTER A DISORDERS USING OBJECTIVE TECHNOLOGIES

The rise of "digital phenotyping" offers enticing opportunities for re-operationalizing Cluster A disorders. Digital phenotyping refers to the use of various objective biobehavioral technologies (e.g., electrophysiology, language analysis, geolocation) to quantify aspects of psychopathology (Insel, 2017; Wright & Simms, 2016). Psychological constructs that map onto Cluster A traits, such as social drive/behavior, speech coherence, emotional expression, and emotional and perceptual experience, can be quantified using a host of subjective and objective recording technologies. The near omnipresent availability of natural behavior tracked with audio, video, and mobile devices provides unprecedented volumes of data that are "high resolution" with respect to temporal (i.e., changes over time) and spatial (i.e., changes in reaction to environmental events) characteristics (see Cohen, 2019 for elaboration of this point). Importantly, these data are scalable, such that they can be aggregated over user-defined time and space. For example, an individual's speech can be compared to existing corpuses to quantify level of "coherence," emotional intensity, and aloofness. It can then be evaluated as a function of setting (e.g., work), type of social interaction (e.g., familial, professional), circadian rhythm, and other epochs of interest.

Digital phenotyping is an increasingly important component of the RDoC effort (Torous, Onnela, & Keshavan, 2017), and can complement the other "alternate" diagnostic systems discussed above. However, operationally defining Cluster A disorders based on high resolution, objective data represents a huge challenge. In large part, this is because the dynamics of Cluster A traits are poorly understood. It is well established that Cluster A traits tend to be fairly stable across family pedigrees (Kendler, McGuire, Gruenberg, & Walsh, 1995) and, within probands, are static over time using self-report questionnaires and interview ratings. However, individuals show incredible variability in phenotypes and corollary functional deficits over their lifespan. Even patients with severely debilitating psychosis recruited from inpatient settings show remitted symptoms, occupational and academic successes, and improved quality of life over large temporal epochs (e.g., Harrow, Jobe, & Faull, 2012). Over brief temporal epochs and across varied contexts, traits and symptoms associated with suspiciousness, delusional content, confusing language, anhedonia and so on, all vary considerably (Ben-Zeev, Ellington, Swendsen, & Granholm, 2011; Chun et al., 2017; Swendsen, Ben-Zeev, & Granholm, 2011). Individuals who are eccentric, aloof, or suspicious in one moment may be very different another moment in a different context.

To complicate matters further, the behaviors underlying Cluster A traits are highly variant over culture, gender, age, socioeconomic status, and cognitive ability (e.g., Fonseca-Pedrero et al., 2018). Hence, defining pathology based solely on "high resolution" data, as is done in many biomedical fields (e.g., diabetes, hypertension), is unfeasible for Cluster A disorders at the present time.

SUMMARY

In sum, there is a pressing need for a more "precise" operationalization of Cluster A disorders. Ideally, this operationalization could account for their phenotypic heterogeneity, provide objective "necessary and sufficient" markers of risk and illness severity, and facilitate individualized assessment/monitoring, treatment and even prevention and cures. Substantial scientific resources are being devoted to develop alternate systems for operationalizing psychopathology, though these systems are inadequate for explaining Cluster A disorders at the present time. To help advance these efforts with respect to schizophrenia-spectrum pathology, the newly-formed International Consortium on Schizotypy Research (ICSR; Cohen et al., 2018; Docherty et al., 2018) is focused on information, technology, and data sharing within an international network of multidisciplinary collaborators. It is hoped that this effort, and efforts like it, can yield large translational data sets from culturally-diverse individuals to provide better resolution for understanding, redefining, and objectifying Cluster A disorders. For the time being, however, DSM-5 offers the most accepted operational definition for Cluster A disorders, and a combination of clinical interviews and self-reports are the most accepted methods of assessing them.

REFERENCES

American Psychiatric Association. (2013). *Diagnostic and Statistical Manual of Mental Disorders* (5th ed.). Arlington, VA: American Psychiatric Publishing.

Barbato, A. (1998). *Schizophrenia and Public Health*. World Health Organization: Division of Mental Health and Prevention of Substance Abuse.

Ben-Zeev, D., Ellington, K., Swendsen, J., & Granholm, E. (2011). Examining a cognitive model of persecutory ideation in the daily life of people with schizophrenia: A computerized experience sampling study. *Schizophrenia Bulletin, 37*(6), 1248–1256.

Bollini, A. M., & Walker, E. F. (2007). Schizotypal personality disorder. In W. O'Donohue, K. A. Fowler, & S. O. Lilienfeld (Eds.), *Personality Disorders: Toward the DSM-V* (pp. 81–108). Thousand Oaks, CA: Sage Publications.

Chmielewski, M., Bagby, R. M., Markon, K., Ring, A. J., & Ryder, A.G. (2014). Openness to experience, intellect, schizotypal personality disorder, and psychoticism: Resolving the controversy. *Journal of Personality Disorders, 28*, 483–489.

Chmielewski, M., Clark, L. A., Bagby, R. M., & Watson, D. (2015). Method matters: Understanding diagnostic reliability in DSM-IV and DSM-5. *Journal of Abnormal Psychology, 124*(3), 764–769.

Chun, C. A., Barrantes-Vidal, N., Sheinbaum, T., & Kwapil, T. R. (2017). Expression of schizophrenia-spectrum personality traits in daily life. *Personality Disorders: Theory, Research, and Treatment, 8*(1), 64–74.

Cohen, A. S. (2019). Advancing ambulatory biobehavioral technologies beyond "proof of concept": Introduction to the special section. *Psychological Assessment, 31*(3), 277–284.

Cohen, A. S., Chan, R. C., & Debbané, M. (2018). Crossing boundaries in schizotypy research: An introduction to the special supplement. *Schizophrenia Bulletin, 44*(Suppl. 2), S457–S459.

Cuthbert, B. N., & Insel, T. R. (2013). Toward the future of psychiatric diagnosis: The seven pillars of RDoC. *BMC Medicine, 11*, 126.

Docherty, A. R., Fonseca-Pedrero, E., Debbané, M., Chan, R. C. K., Linscott, R. J., Jonas, K. G., ... Cohen, A. S. (2018). Enhancing psychosis-spectrum nosology through an international data sharing initiative. *Schizophrenia Bulletin, 44*(Suppl. 2), S460–S467.

Fonseca-Pedrero, E., Chan, R. C. K., Debbané, M., Cicero, D., Zhang, L. C., Brenner, C., ... Ortuño-Sierra, J. (2018). Comparisons of schizotypal traits across 12 countries: Results from the International Consortium for Schizotypy Research. *Schizophrenia Research, 199*, 128–134.

Ford, J. M., Morris, S. E., Hoffman, R. E., Sommer, I., Waters, F., McCarthy-Jones, S., ... Cuthbert, B. N. (2014). Studying hallucinations within the NIMH RDoC framework. *Schizophrenia Bulletin, 40*(Suppl. 4), S295–S304.

Harrow, M., Jobe, T. H., & Faull, R. N. (2012). Do all schizophrenia patients need antipsychotic treatment continuously throughout their lifetime? A 20-year longitudinal study. *Psychological Medicine, 42*(10), 2145–2155.

Insel, T. R. (2010). Rethinking schizophrenia. *Nature, 468*(7321), 187–193.

Insel, T. R. (2017). Digital phenotyping: Technology for a new science of behavior. *JAMA: Journal of the American Medical Association, 318*(13), 1215–1216.

Insel, T., Cuthbert, B., Garvey, M., Heinssen, R., Pine, D. S., Quinn, K., ... Wang, P. (2010). Research Domain Criteria (RDoC): Toward a new classification framework for research on mental disorders. *American Journal of Psychiatry, 167*(7), 748–751.

Kendler, K. S., McGuire, M., Gruenberg, A. M., & Walsh, D. (1995) Schizotypal symptoms and signs in the Roscommon Family Study: Their factor structure and familial relationship with psychotic and affective disorders. *Archives of General Psychiatry, 52*, 296–303.

Kendler, K. S., Neale, M. C., & Walsh, D. (1995). Evaluating the spectrum concept of schizophrenia in the Roscommon Family Study. *American Journal of Psychiatry, 152*(5), 749–754.

Kirchner, S. K., Roeh, A., Nolden, J., & Hasan, A. (2018). Diagnosis and treatment of schizotypal personality disorder: Evidence from a systematic review. *NPJ Schizophrenia, 4*(1), 20.

Krueger, R. F., Kotov, R., Watson, D., Forbes, M. K., Eaton, N. R., Ruggero, C. J., ... Zimmermann, J. (2018). Progress in achieving quantitative classification of psychopathology. *World Psychiatry*, *17*, 282–293.

Lenzenweger, M. F. (2006). Schizotaxia, schizotypy, and schizophrenia: Paul E. Meehl's blueprint for the experimental psychopathology and genetics of schizophrenia. *Journal of Abnormal Psychology*, *115*(2), 195–200.

McCrae, R. R., & John, O. P. (1992). An introduction to the five-factor model and its applications. *Journal of Personality*, *60*(2), 175–215.

Strauss, G. P., & Cohen, A. S. (2017). A transdiagnostic review of negative symptom phenomenology and etiology. *Schizophrenia Bulletin*, *43*, 712–719.

Swendsen, J., Ben-Zeev, D., & Granholm, E. (2011). Real-time electronic ambulatory monitoring of substance use and symptom expression in schizophrenia. *American Journal of Psychiatry*, *168*(2), 202–209.

Torous, J., Onnela, J. P., & Keshavan, M. (2017). New dimensions and new tools to realize the potential of RDoC: Digital phenotyping via smartphones and connected devices. *Translational Psychiatry*, *7*, e1053.

Weinberger, D. R., Glick, I. D., & Klein, D. F. (2015). Whither research domain criteria (RDoC)? The good, the bad, and the ugly. *JAMA Psychiatry*, *72*(12), 1161–1162.

Wittchen, H.-U., & Beesdo-Baum, K. (2018). "Throwing out the baby with the bathwater"? Conceptual and methodological limitations of the HiTOP approach. *World Psychiatry: Official Journal of the World Psychiatric Association (WPA)*, *17*(3), 298–299.

Wright, A. G. C., & Simms, L. J. (2016). Stability and fluctuation of personality disorder features in daily life. *Journal of Abnormal Psychology*, *125*(5), 641–656.

9c

Cluster A Heterogeneity: Author Rejoinder to Commentaries on Cluster A Personality Disorders

JOHN G. KERNS

I greatly value the comments by Lenzenweger (this volume) and by Le and Cohen (this volume), and I think they add important complementary perspectives to understanding and conceptualizing Cluster A disorders. Professor Lenzenweger discusses Cluster A disorders in the context of previous theory and research on schizotypy and schizophrenia, for instance discussing how schizotypy is a distinct construct from schizotypal personality disorder. Le and Professor Cohen focus on situating Cluster A symptomatology in the context of efforts to move beyond traditional DSM categorical personality disorders as well as efforts to develop alternative assessment methods. I think these are both valuable complementary perspectives to my chapter that was focused primarily on research specifically on DSM Cluster A personality disorder categories. I have some additional comments to offer here in the hope this might further help us understand the nature of Cluster A disorders and symptomatology.

One point made by Professor Lenzenweger with which I strongly agree is that we should not be wedded to a particular methodology to study or conceptualize schizophrenia-spectrum conditions (e.g., his discussion of "psychometric schizotypy"). And as noted by Le and Cohen, new assessment techniques have great potential to help us assess and understand Cluster A disorders. A possibly related tangential comment is that researchers probably should not be constrained by DSM Cluster A disorders in assessing conditions reflective of schizophrenia risk. For instance, negative symptoms in people without schizophrenia do appear to reflect schizophrenia risk, yet the Cluster A disorder that on its surface is thought to be most directly reflective of schizophrenia negative symptoms, schizoid PD, is not strongly related to schizophrenia.

It is interesting to note that schizoid PD is the one Cluster A disorder that has been present in all versions of the DSM. However, given limited research on it, some have argued it should be removed from the DSM (e.g., Triebwasser, Chemerinski, Roussos, & Siever, 2012), further suggesting weaknesses in how well Cluster

A disorders capture negative symptoms. Hence research on negative symptoms that potentially indicate increased risk for schizophrenia-spectrum conditions might need to also consider alternative conceptualizations of schizophrenia-spectrum disorders. For instance, Kwapil (1998) found that increased social anhedonia predicts increased risk for Cluster A personality disorders. But given problems with schizoid PD, one wonders if this could be underestimating to what extent social anhedonia predicts clinically relevant schizophrenia-spectrum conditions.

One issue discussed by both of the commentaries is whether Cluster A symptomatology relates to variation in normal personality traits. In this regard, a recent study examined relations between schizophrenia symptoms, schizotypy, and five normal personality traits, with psychoticism, but not openness, included as one of the five normal personality traits (Cicero, Jonas, Li, Perlman, & Kotov, in press). This study of people with psychotic disorders ($n = 288$) and people without psychosis ($n = 257$) found that best fitting models included both schizophrenia symptoms and schizotypy on the same factors as normal personality traits. Hence, this provides evidence that not only schizotypy but also schizophrenia symptoms are meaningfully related to normal personality. As noted by Professor Lenzenweger, this in some ways is not a surprising result. Further, this result could be interpreted in multiple ways. At the same time, it is somewhat interesting that models that included separate schizophrenia symptom factors exhibited poorer fit.

Maybe one perspective that could be useful in viewing this research is the idea that Cluster A disorders and schizophrenia, like most forms of psychopathology, might be highly heterogeneous. For instance, one factor in schizophrenia negative symptomatology might be low extraversion. Research focused on testing a low extraversion–negative symptoms link might be a productive line of research. As noted by Le and Cohen, one advantage of such a line of research is that it would benefit from the wealth of existing research on extraversion. But ultimately it would be very surprising to me if a low extraversion explanation would suffice to understand negative symptoms. However, by accounting for the influence of extraversion, and by illustrating aspects of negative symptoms not accounted for extraversion, this research then might help more clearly reveal other non-extraversion negative symptom mechanisms. And again, given heterogeneity, we might expect that any explanation (e.g., negative symptoms reflect low extraversion) to be only a partial explanation.

As noted by Le and Cohen, an RDoC approach might be very valuable in disentangling relations between Cluster A disorders, psychotic disorders, and normal personality. As an example, some positive Cluster A symptoms might lack certain mechanisms critical for schizophrenia (e.g., speculatively, perhaps lacking striatal dopamine dysregulation). However, perhaps these positive Cluster A symptoms might still share some mechanisms in common with schizophrenia. For instance, magical thinking in the general population has been related to cognitive biases (Risen, 2016). One could imagine that these biases on their own might not be sufficient to cause psychotic disorder. On the other hand, cognitive biases have been found to moderate delusion severity in psychotic disorder (Dudley, Taylor, Wickham, & Hutton, 2016). Hence, cognitive biases that contribute to magical thinking in people

without psychotic disorder might also be deleterious in people with psychotic disorder. Therefore, an RDoC focus on mechanisms might be very valuable in helping to reveal similarities and differences between Cluster A disorders, psychotic disorders, and normal personality.

REFERENCES

Cicero, D. C., Jonas, K. G., Li, K., Perlman, G., & Kotov, R. (in press). Common taxonomy of traits and symptoms: Linking schizophrenia symptoms, schizotypy, and normal personality. *Schizophrenia Bulletin*.

Dudley, R., Taylor, P., Wickham, S., & Hutton P. (2016). Psychosis, delusions and the "jumping to conclusions" reasoning bias: A systematic review and meta-analysis. *Schizophrenia Bulletin*, 42, 652–665.

Kwapil, T. R. (1998). Social anhedonia as a predictor of the development of schizophrenia-spectrum disorders. *Journal of Abnormal Psychology*, 107, 558–565.

Risen, J. L. (2016). Believing what we do not believe: Acquiescence to superstitious beliefs and other powerful intuitions. *Psychological Review*, *123*, 182–207.

Triebwasser, J., Chemerinski, E., Roussos, P., & Siever, L. J. (2012). Schizoid personality disorder. *Journal of Personality Disorders*, *26*, 919–926.

10 Borderline Personality Disorder

ALEXANDER L. CHAPMAN, NORA H. HOPE, AND BRIANNA J. TURNER

INTRODUCTION

Characterized by a combination of interpersonal, emotional, behavioral, and cognitive instability, BPD is a serious, fascinating, and often misunderstood condition. I (ALC) first encountered patients with BPD when I was an undergraduate working part-time at a transitional, residential crisis center. Patients lived at this center for a few days to a couple of weeks to have their risk monitored and ease the transition home following suicide-related hospitalizations. I knew next to nothing about BPD, aside from what I had gleaned from my abnormal psychology course. I admittedly had the stereotyped image of a distraught, unstable, out of control young woman in a hospital gown with long and unkempt hair, suffering after a breakup and resorting to self-cutting and pills to cope with her pain. I also had the sense that people with BPD were unpredictable, extremely sensitive, and could blow up or do something drastic at the drop of a hat.

In my work at this and other mental health centers, I learned that those with BPD are among the most misunderstood and stigmatized individuals in the mental health community. When patients presented interpersonal challenges, clinicians often labeled them "Axis II," or said they had "characterological" issues; these terms often were euphemisms for BPD. Indeed, people with BPD often suffer intense relationship turmoil and rejection even from the treatment providers charged with their care (clinicians often are reluctant to diagnose or treat BPD). Further compounding these problems is the abundance of misinformation about the disorder, such as the myths that people with BPD cannot recover, are untreatable, or are manipulative and at high risk of violence (Chapman & Gratz, 2007). Some, but fortunately not all, of the clinicians I encountered spoke as if people with BPD were an entirely different kind of human being: oversensitive,

unable to have normal relationships, unlikely to benefit from treatment, and uniformly difficult to work with.

The BPD patients I met, although often distraught, did not seem like members of a different species. They seemed sensitive, overwhelmed with their emotions, and sometimes confused and frustrated that their lives were fraught with such conflict and crisis. I probably would have felt and acted the same way if I were in their shoes. Moreover, they wanted their lives to change, often felt guilty and ashamed of their behavior, and had many strengths, chief among these being passion, sensitivity, and empathy. It was not until I was a young graduate student (and still knew next to nothing) that I had the opportunity to work in therapy with someone with BPD. I realized then that if I could help this person, there was hope for people with BPD. I refocused my interests and have continued to study (and treat) people suffering from BPD throughout my career, bringing several others along for the ride (including the co-authors of this chapter).

Within this chapter, we provide an overview of theory and research on and treatment of BPD. Research on BPD has consistently outpaced that of many other personality disorders over the past several years, with a quick PsychInfo search (conducted on February 15, 2018) for articles with "borderline personality disorder" in their titles revealing 327 publications (276 journal articles, 30 books, 21 dissertations) in 2015, 268 (248 journal articles, 5 books, 15 dissertations) in 2016, and 269 (246 journal articles, 9 books, 12 dissertations, 2 electronic collections) in 2017. Given the abundance of research on BPD since it first appeared in the *Diagnostic and Statistical Manual for Mental Disorders, 3rd Edition* (DSM-III; American Psychiatric Association, 1980), it would be impossible to cover BPD adequately in a single chapter. As such, we have selected some areas to focus on and others to largely neglect. Of note, our theoretical perspective is that BPD arises from a complex transaction of biological, social, and environmental forces resulting in core dysfunctions in the emotion regulation system (Chapman, 2009; Crowell, Beauchaine, & Linehan, 2009; Linehan, 1993a). Our aim is to provide an overview of BPD that is broad enough

A Michael Smith Foundation for Health Research Career Investigator to the first author supported the writing of this chapter. Author Email: alchapma@sfu.ca.

to provide a reasonable snapshot of the field and focused enough to provide cohesiveness, depth, and logical future directions for research and treatment on this fascinating disorder.

THE PREVALENCE AND IMPACT OF BORDERLINE PERSONALITY DISORDER

A serious, severe, and complex disorder, BPD is associated with inordinate suffering and impact on health and mental health systems. Representative epidemiological surveys show that BPD affects about 1.4–5.9 percent of people in the general population (Grant et al., 2008; Lenzenweger, Lane, Loranger, & Kessler, 2007). In clinical settings, however, BPD is estimated to affect 15–25 percent of psychiatric outpatients and up to 30–50 percent of inpatients (Gunderson, 2001; Lieb, Zanarini, Schmahl, Linehan, & Bohus, 2004; Sar, Akyuz, Kugu, Ozturk, & Ertem-Vehid, 2006; Skodol et al., 2002). This discrepancy between community and clinical prevalence underscores the high rates of healthcare utilization in this population. Reflecting the complexity and profound suffering accompanying BPD, 70–80 percent of people with this disorder have a history of nonsuicidal self-injury and/or suicide attempts, and approximately 10 percent die by suicide (Black, Blum, Pfohl, & Hale, 2004; Gunderson, 2001; Paris & Zweig-Frank, 2001; Skodol et al., 2002). BPD is associated with frequent utilization of emergency, inpatient, outpatient psychiatric, and primary care services (Ansell, Sanislow, McGlashan, & Grilo, 2007; Bateman & Fonagy, 2003; Bender et al., 2006; Jackson & Burgess, 2004; Sansone, Farukhi, & Wiederman, 2011; Zanarini, Frankenburg, Hennen, & Silk, 2004). Accordingly, average yearly costs for inpatient and outpatient treatment range from $12,000 to $30,000 (USD) per patient (Comtois, Elwood, Holdcraft, Smith, & Simpson, 2007; Linehan & Heard, 1999). Further, estimates from research in Canada suggest that BPD is as burdensome as diabetes and rheumatic disease combined, costing approximately $20,000 to $50,000 (CDN) per quality of life year to treat (Van Busschbach, 2012).

BPD also is associated with considerable and persistent functional impairment. Although disorders such as schizophrenia and severe mood disorders often appear more strongly associated with disability and functional impairments, evidence suggests that similar impairments in social and occupational functioning occur among those with BPD, often reaching a level requiring public assistance, such as psychiatric disability support (Bateman & Fonagy, 2003, 2008; Grant et al., 2008; Jørgensen et al., 2009; Koons et al., 2006; Soloff & Chiappetta, 2017). In one study comparing patients with BPD to those with other personality disorders, those with BPD were approximately three times more likely to receive social security disability income benefits (Zanarini, Jacoby, Frankenburg, Reich, & Fitzmaurice, 2009). Although improvements are apparent over time, particularly among BPD patients who experience a remission in their diagnostic status (Zanarini, Frankenburg, Hennen, Reich, & Silk, 2005), psychosocial functioning can remain lower than optimal for several years, with one study finding that 51.2 percent of BPD patients remained at the level of poor psychosocial functioning over an eight-year follow-up period (Soloff & Chiappetta, 2017). Further, five years following mentalization-based treatment (MBT; Bateman & Fonagy, 2006), 54 percent of patients remained below a score of 60 on the General Assessment of Functioning (GAF) scale (Bateman & Fonagy, 2008). In our clinical experience, emotion dysregulation, intense interpersonal sensitivity, anxiety, negative beliefs about themselves, and co-occurring mood disorders often hamper functioning in school and occupational settings. Patients often describe intense frustration and sadness, knowing they have considerable potential but constantly hitting emotional and interpersonal roadblocks in their pursuit of important goals. Although good to outstanding functioning sometimes occurs in one or more areas of life (sometimes referred to as "apparent competence"; Linehan, 1993a), the impact of BPD on social and occupational functioning deserves considerable attention. Indeed, the development of educational initiatives and family-oriented programs (e.g., www.tara4bpd.org; www.borderlinepersonalitydisorder.org), and the publication of books to help loved ones navigate relationships with those with BPD (e.g., Manning, 2011), further underscore the important impact of this disorder on social functioning with family and loved ones.

A BRIEF HISTORY OF BORDERLINE PERSONALITY DISORDER

In this section, we will briefly review the evolution of the construct and diagnosis of BPD, including current areas of active research and controversy. Descriptions of a syndrome marked by extreme interpersonal sensitivity, difficulty managing intense emotions, and impulsive, self-defeating, or aggressive behaviors date back hundreds of years (see Friedel, 2004; Millon, Grossman, & Meagher, 2004). Something resembling the construct of BPD was first described in the psychiatric nomenclature in 1938 (Stern, 1938). This modern name has its roots in psychoanalytic formulations of BPD as a syndrome on the *borderline* between psychotic and neurotic illness (Stern, 1938; Knight, 1953), given prominent mood disturbances combined with the loose associations and quasi-psychotic symptoms that sometimes emerged in unstructured situations. Features described by Stern (1938) that overlap with contemporary conceptualizations of BPD include hypersensitivity and interpersonal hypervigilance, difficulty coping under stressful conditions, idealization of others (including the treatment provider), feelings of inferiority, and difficulty effectively navigating treatment (and other) relationships (marked by dependency, hypersensitivity, etc.).

Although recent taxonomies no longer classify psychiatric illnesses along psychotic-neurotic dimensions, we still owe much to early formulations and case descriptions of BPD. For instance, early formulations correctly observed that BPD typically involves instability across affective, cognitive, and behavioral systems (Kernberg, 1967). Additionally, many early case histories noted that early childhood adversity, difficulty accurately perceiving and integrating contradictory thoughts and feelings, and predispositions toward intense emotional experiences figure prominently in the pathogenesis of this disorder (Kernberg, 1967; Masterson, 1972). Early conceptualizations also posited that different aspects of BPD might respond differently to treatment given its position between the more easily and successfully treated neurotic illnesses and the more chronic and persistent psychotic illnesses (Kernberg, 1967). Consistent with this hypothesis, we now know that some components of BPD respond very well to treatment, whereas others are more persistent (Zanarini, Frankenburg, Reich, & Fitzmaurice, 2010, 2012). Finally, the notion that BPD is optimally addressed through longer-term psychotherapy, rather than other forms of psychiatric intervention, has persisted (Kernberg, 1968; Masterson, 1972).

Following Kernberg's pioneering theories in the 1960s (Kernberg, 1967, 1968), advances in defining BPD proceeded rapidly, sparked by increasing empirical research. Core features of BPD were defined in the late 1960s (Grinker, Werble, & Drye, 1968; Kernberg, 1967), interview criteria to assess these features were developed in 1975 (Gunderson & Singer, 1975), and by 1978, these observations had coalesced into a set of seven symptoms that could distinguish people with BPD from those with other psychiatric illnesses (Gunderson & Kolb, 1978). Soon after, BPD was officially recognized as a distinct diagnosis in the third edition of the *Diagnostic and Statistical Manual of Mental Disorders* (DSM; APA, 1980). Since this time, our knowledge of the prevalence, impact, course, and effective treatment of this disorder has grown considerably (Gunderson, 2009). We have quickly learned that BPD could be reliably and validly diagnosed using structured criteria (Hurt, Hyler, Frances, Clarkin, & Brent, 1989), clearly differentiated from other psychiatric syndromes (Gunderson & Phillips, 1991; Loranger, Oldham, & Tulis, 1982; Pope, Jonas, Hudson, Cohen, & Gunderson, 1983), and successfully treated using structured psychotherapies (Bateman & Fonagy, 1999; Linehan, Armstrong, Suarez, Allmon, & Heard, 1991; Silk et al., 1994). Yet, as research and practice continue to advance the frontiers of our knowledge, new controversies and challenges emerge. Below, we review the current state of knowledge regarding the definition and diagnosis of BPD, and some emerging areas of debate.

CURRENT CRITERIA AND CONCEPTUALIZATIONS OF BORDERLINE PERSONALITY DISORDER

BPD is recognized as a discrete diagnosis in the fifth edition of the *Diagnostic and Statistical Manual of Mental Disorders* (DSM-5; APA, 2013). In the tenth edition of the *International Classification of Diseases* (ICD-10; World Health Organization [WHO], 2016), symptoms of BPD are described under the label emotionally unstable personality disorder. According to these classification systems, core symptoms of BPD include disturbances in emotion (i.e., inappropriate and intense anger; marked reactivity of mood resulting in mood instability), cognition (i.e., persistently unstable self-image; chronic feelings of emptiness; stress-related paranoid ideation or dissociation), interpersonal relationships (i.e., frantic or excessive efforts to avoid real or perceived abandonment; persistent patterns of intense and unstable relationships), and behavior (i.e., impulsive and potentially self-damaging behavior; recurrent suicidal or self-harm behavior). The DSM requires a minimum of five of nine criteria to be met for a diagnosis of BPD. The ICD requires three of five criteria describing persistent impulsivity and at least two of six criteria describing symptoms unique to BPD. The upcoming eleventh revision of the ICD proposes to include a mild, moderate, or severe personality disorder category with a borderline pattern specifier to recognize symptoms of BPD (WHO, 2018).

Although clinicians often experience BPD patients as distinctly different from people with other mental health problems (depression, anxiety disorders, etc.), BPD has been difficult to delineate. A seemingly heterogeneous assortment of symptoms together with heterogeneity among individuals meeting diagnostic thresholds presents challenges. Following DSM-5 criteria, there are 256 potential combinations of five of nine features, and, theoretically, many different clinical presentations that fall within the BPD category. Some evidence from factor analytic studies of DSM criteria has similarly suggested that BPD may be a multidimensional construct (Sanislow, Grilo, & McGlashan, 2000; Sanislow et al., 2002). Providing a single diagnostic label to a multidimensional syndrome potentially consisting of many different "types" of people with BPD may lead clinicians to assume that people with the BPD label are more similar than they actually are. People with BPD often do not fit neatly into other diagnostic categories, in part because of their episodic and varied symptoms that seem to encompass several other psychiatric problems and make it difficult to discern characteristics that are unique to BPD or secondary to other disorders. Indeed, with BPD, comorbidity is the norm, with BPD patients often meeting criteria for a host of co-occurring disorders, such as depression, anxiety disorders, eating disorders, substance use disorders, other personality disorders, and so forth (Grant et al., 2008; Lieb et al., 2004; Sar et al., 2006; Zanarini et al., 2004). Whereas the conceptualization of BPD on the border of psychosis and neurosis has been debunked and the name "borderline" remains anachronistic, the construct and presentation of BPD continue to present challenges to researchers and clinicians alike.

Table 10.1 Correspondence between DSM-5 and ICD-10 diagnostic criteria for BPD

DSM-5	ICD-10
Frantic efforts to avoid real or imagined abandonment	… excessive efforts to avoid abandonment
A pattern of intense and unstable interpersonal relationships characterized by alternating between extremes of idealization and devaluation	A liability to become involved in intense and unstable relationships …
Identity disturbance: Markedly and persistently unstable self-image or sense of self	… the patient's own self-image, aims, and internal preferences (including sexual) are often unclear or disturbed.
Impulsivity in at least two areas that are potentially self-damaging	… marked tendency to act impulsively without consideration of the consequences … (general criterion: emotionally unstable personality disorder).
Recurrent suicidal behavior, gestures, or threats, or self-mutilating behavior	… series of suicidal threats or act of self-harm …
Affective instability due to a marked reactivity of mood	… characteristics of emotional instability
Chronic feelings of emptiness	… chronic feelings of emptiness.
Inappropriate, intense anger or difficulty controlling anger	… outbursts of intense anger may often lead to violence or "behavioral explosions" … (general criterion: emotionally unstable personality disorder).
Transient, stress-related paranoid ideation or severe dissociative symptoms	

A couple of key advancements have begun to address these challenges. One advance has been the use of empirical and theoretical means to delineate core features of the disorder. For instance, factor analytic techniques show that criteria can be reduced to three latent features: *disturbed relatedness* consisting of identity problems, chronic emptiness, and interpersonal difficulties; *affective dysregulation* consisting of mood instability, inappropriate anger, and efforts to avoid abandonment; and *behavioral dysregulation* consisting of self-harm and impulsivity (Clarkin, Hull, & Hurt, 1993; Sanislow et al., 2000). Alternatively, evidence from genetic and neurobiological research has suggested two core biological predispositions underlying BPD: *affective dysregulation* and *behavioral dyscontrol* (Siever, Torgersen, Gunderson, Livesley, & Kendler, 2002). Still others have attempted to identify features that most clearly differentiate BPD from other syndromes, highlighting *pervasive difficulties in emotion regulation* (Glenn & Klonsky, 2009), *impulsivity* (Links, Heslegrave, & van Reekum, 1999; McCloskey et al., 2009), and *interpersonal hypersensitivity* (Gunderson, 2007) as candidate phenotypes or essential features of BPD. Nonetheless, consensus on the core, unique features of BPD remains elusive (Trull, Distel, & Carpenter, 2011). Further complicating this issue is the possibility that what appear to be core features of BPD are secondary to other, co-occurring disorders. For example, some research exploring impulsivity as a core

feature of BPD has suggested that the co-occurrence of ADHD among individuals with BPD may largely account for the elevated impulsivity seen in this disorder, particularly when measured with laboratory impulsivity paradigms (Sebastian et al., 2013).

A second potential advance has been a renewed interest in dimensional models of personality pathology (Trull et al., 2011). The DSM-5 (APA, 2013) provides a framework for an alternative, dimensional model of BPD in Section III, which requires at least four of seven maladaptive traits, a minimum of mild interpersonal or personal impairment resulting from these traits, stable expression of traits across time and situation, and cultural incongruence of the traits compared to a person's dominant culture. Dimensional systems, incorporating decades of personality science, may be more stable and valid than syndrome-based systems (Morey et al., 2003; Samuel et al., 2013) but can become complex and cumbersome for clinicians in everyday practice (Rottman, Ahn, Sanislow, & Kim, 2009; Rottman, Kim, Ahn, & Sanislow, 2011; Trull et al., 2011). Clinicians practicing within this type of system must grapple with many different traits and characteristics, synthesize them in a meaningful and valid manner, and use them to guide assessment and treatment. Some authors have suggested that further improvements to make these dimensional frameworks more user friendly could include reducing the number of criteria, weighting criteria to reflect their centrality or importance, and developing more objective markers for diagnosis (Trull et al., 2011).

As it stands now, both the DSM-5 and the proposed eleventh edition of the ICD include both categorical and dimensional frameworks for diagnosing BPD. The next several years will be important in gauging their adoption in research and clinical settings.

In addition to issues related to the relative utility and validity of dimensional versus categorical diagnostic frameworks, a number of other controversies surround the conceptualization of BPD. First, given the high prevalence of childhood abuse and interpersonal trauma among people with BPD, debate has reemerged regarding whether BPD would be better conceptualized as a form of posttraumatic stress disorder, with vigorous arguments on both sides (see, for example, Cloitre, Garvert, Weiss, Carlson, & Bryant, 2014; Ford & Courtois, 2014; Trippany, Helm, & Simpson, 2006; van der Kolk, Pelcovitz, Roth & Mandel, 1996). Past abuse or trauma, however, is neither a necessary nor sufficient precondition for a BPD diagnosis (Zanarini, Williams, Lewis, & Reich, 1997). Further, given evidence (discussed below) that BPD is likely multiply determined through a complex transaction of environmental and individual (e.g., biological, genetic, temperament, behavioral) factors, it is perhaps most accurate to conclude that there are multiple pathways to the development of BPD, with trauma and related symptoms being important factors for *some* people with this diagnosis (Chapman & Gratz, 2007).

Second, although the most recent edition of the DSM eliminates the multiaxial system, there has been some debate as to whether BPD is more similar to the emotional disorders that were formerly recognized on Axis I than the personality disorders that were recognized on Axis II. On the one hand, BPD's severity, unstable course, and positive response to treatment support its conceptualization alongside major emotional disorders, and this repositioning could provide much needed support for the value of providing reimbursement of psychotherapeutic services (Gunderson, 2009). On the other hand, placing BPD alongside other emotional disorders could increase the likelihood that this disorder would be overlooked during clinical assessment (Gunderson, 2010).

Third, there is some controversy regarding whether BPD should be diagnosed in adolescence (Kaess, Brunner, & Chanen, 2014; Larrivée, 2013). Initial arguments against earlier diagnosis held that many symptoms of BPD are developmentally normative in adolescence (e.g., unstable mood, intense relationships, and unstable sense of self), that personality may not be sufficiently stable to merit such a diagnosis, and that, given the unfortunate but persistent stigma that often accompanies this diagnosis, labeling adolescents with BPD may result in unintended harm. Emerging evidence, however, suggests that BPD can be reliably and validly differentiated from normal personality in adolescence and that these symptoms are stable from adolescence through later developmental stages, supporting the utility of earlier diagnosis (Chanen et al., 2004; Chanen, Jovev, McCutcheon, Jackson, & McGorry, 2008; Kaess et al., 2014; Miller, Muehlenkamp, & Jacobson, 2008; Winograd, Cohen, & Chen, 2008). Moreover, several authors have noted that diagnosis in adolescence would facilitate earlier intervention, and that adolescents with borderline personality pathology show favorable outcomes with psychotherapy (Miller et al., 2008). As a result of this emerging evidence, diagnosis of BPD in adolescence is permitted according to guidelines in Section III of the DSM-5 (APA, 2013) and the eleventh edition of the ICD (Tyrer, Crawford, Mulder, & the ICD-11 Working Group for the Revision of Classification of Personality Disorders, 2011; WHO, 2018). Whether this diagnostic category will be regularly applied to younger patients remains to be seen.

COURSE AND RECOVERY FROM BPD

Although the symptoms associated with BPD can be debilitating and life-threatening, longitudinal research paints a relatively optimistic picture of the trajectory of the disorder. Looking at the prevalence of BPD across the lifespan, diagnosis of BPD peaks in young adulthood, and the prevalence decreases in middle age and beyond (Grant et al., 2008).[1] Contrary to the historical notion that BPD was chronic and not responsive to treatment, longitudinal studies have found that most individuals remit from the disorder with age. In an ongoing longitudinal study spanning 16 years, 78 percent of patients with BPD at the start of the study had achieved eight years of remission, while 99 percent had achieved two years of remission at some point during follow-up (Zanarini et al., 2012). Another study reassessed patients diagnosed with BPD after 27 years and found that 92 percent of the living patients who were reassessed no longer met diagnostic criteria for BPD (Paris & Zweig-Frank, 2001).

Research has also revealed that certain BPD symptoms are more likely to remit over time than others, supporting the notion that extreme behaviors may "burn-out" over the lifespan (as suggested by Stone, 1993). In a cohort study of BPD patients, Stepp and Pilkonis (2008) found significant differences in impulsivity and suicidality as a function of age, with both the over 30 and over 40 cohorts reporting significantly less impulsivity and suicidality than the younger cohorts. In contrast, emotional distress did not differ across the cohorts.

An important aim of research in this area is the early identification of youth at risk for developing BPD, as less is known about the trajectory of those at risk for this disorder (who do not yet met criteria for BPD) and early intervention may mitigate core symptoms of impulsivity and affective instability. Investigating the relationship between childhood psychopathology and later

[1] In a nationally representative sample of American adults (n = 34,653), the prevalence of BPD for ages 20–29 was 9.3%, while it was 5.5% for ages 45–64 (Grant et al., 2008).

development of BPD in a large longitudinal cohort study (The Pittsburgh Girls Study; $n = 1233$), Stepp and colleagues (Stepp, Burke, Hipwell, & Loeber, 2012) found a correspondence between childhood symptoms of attention deficit hyperactivity disorder (ADHD) and oppositional defiant disorder (ODD), both of which are associated with poor impulse control and self-regulation, and symptoms of BPD in adolescence. Additionally, the Children in the Community (CIC) study, which followed 800 children in diverse socioeconomic areas of New York over 20 years, offers a unique glimpse into the early life of individuals who experience symptoms of BPD in adolescence versus those who do not (e.g., greater instances of childhood sexual abuse predicted BPD symptoms but not other PDs), as well as the correspondence between BPD symptoms in adolescence and adulthood (Cohen, Crawford, Johnson, & Kasen, 2005). Regarding the trajectory of BPD symptoms from adolescence to adulthood, BPD symptoms in early adolescence in the CIC (mean age = 14) were associated with BPD symptoms in early adulthood (mean age = 33), as well as lower academic and occupational attainment and greater psychosocial impairment (e.g., lower global assessment of functioning; lower role function), although age-related declines in symptoms were found (Winograd et al., 2008). Nonetheless, the CIC did not include any genetic, physiological, or neurobiological markers related to emotion dysregulation (Chapman, 2019a) or impulsivity, and future research should incorporate such markers in order to identify key person × environment transactions associated with the development and course of BPD. Finally, emerging research on evidence-based practice for children and adolescents with BPD and related problems has underscored the potential effectiveness of early intervention (Chanen & McCutcheon, 2013; Mehlum et al., 2014; Perepletchikova et al., 2017).

Together, findings thus far suggest that reliable early markers for BPD exist and predict future functioning, and that treatment of adolescents with BPD features and related behavioral problems (suicidality, self-harm) is promising. Future directions in this area should include multi-method longitudinal research, replication of treatment studies, and examination of preventative interventions.

ETIOLOGICAL FACTORS

Since BPD was first conceptualized, theorists, researchers, and clinicians have speculated on the origins of the disorder (e.g., Kernberg, 1975). Nonetheless, rigorous empirical investigations of the etiology of BPD have been scarce. The past few decades have marked significant advancement in scientific understanding of BPD, and many methods have been employed for identifying developmental factors that increase later risk for BPD or distinguish individuals with BPD from individuals with other

psychiatric disorders or healthy controls. Longitudinal studies have helped to identify socio-developmental factors that predict later development of BPD, whereas translational experimental studies have helped identify neurobiological, emotional, interpersonal, and behavioral processes distinguishing those with BPD from other groups. In the brief review below, we focus primarily on longitudinal and translational research to circumvent some of the key limitations of cross-sectional, self-report data. We approach this research from a biopsychosocial framework, similar to Linehan's (1993a; see also Crowell et al., 2009) biosocial theory of BPD and the models proposed by Zanarini and colleagues (Zanarini & Frankenburg, 1997; Zanarini et al., 2005), whereby BPD results from a transaction of core vulnerabilities in biology and temperament and socio-developmental factors, such as invalidating or adverse environments.

Genetic Factors

Genetic studies can help guide research and intervention by identifying candidate genes that are associated with BPD diagnosis, whereas twin and adoption studies allow for estimation of the heritability of BPD (e.g., the proportion of variability in BPD accounted for by genetic factors). Findings indicating that first-degree relatives of individuals with BPD are several times more likely to have BPD than the general population (Baron, Gruen, Asnis, & Lord, 1985; Links, Steiner, & Huxley, 1988; Zanarini, Gunderson, Marino, Schwartz, & Frankenburg, 1988) suggest that BPD may be heritable to some degree. Stronger evidence has emerged from twin studies suggesting a moderately high heritability of BPD. Torgersen et al. (2000) assessed 221 twin pairs for personality disorders using a reliable diagnostic interview and found a heritability of .69 for BPD, although the small sample size limits interpretability of these results and may overestimate heritability. In a large-scale study on over 5000 twins across three countries (The Netherlands, Belgium, and Australia), similar heritability estimates of .42 for BPD features were found in all three countries using a self-report measure of BPD features (Distel et al., 2008). More twin studies with multiple assessment methods and larger samples are needed to clarify the precise heritability of BPD.

Although no specific genes have been found to reliably predict BPD (or to differentiate vulnerability to BPD from vulnerability to other psychopathology), candidate genes have been identified that may confer risk. A focus of genetic research to date has been on genes involved in serotonin transport (e.g., 5-HTT), uptake (e.g., serotonin 1B receptor gene), and synthesis (e.g., tryptophan hydroxolase-1 gene); however, a recent systematic review and meta-analysis concluded that there was no reliable association of these genes with BPD (Amad, Ramoz, Thoma, Jardri, & Gorwood, 2014). Amad et al. (2014) have suggested that inconsistent results for candidate genes may support a "plasticity" theory in which genes confer vulnerability to *environmental risk factors* rather than directly to BPD itself. This hypothesis of an indirect genetic effect is congruent with transactional biosocial models (Crowell et al., 2009; Linehan, 1993a), which propose that biological vulnerabilities may contribute to and exacerbate environmental vulnerabilities (e.g., a child with a genetic vulnerability may experience more negative life events during development, contributing to development of emotion dysregulation) and vice versa. Combined longitudinal and genetic studies following youth over time are called for to fully test this plasticity hypothesis.

Adverse Environments

Numerous studies have found an association between BPD and negative early experiences. Zanarini et al. (2002) found that 62 percent of individuals with BPD in an inpatient sample reported childhood sexual abuse, and that level of abuse was correlated with BPD symptom severity. Compared to patients with other personality disorders, individuals with BPD report more experience of trauma, including greater frequency of childhood sexual abuse (Paris, Zweig-Frank, & Guzder, 1994; Yen et al., 2002) and physical abuse (Paris et al., 1994), and younger age of exposure to trauma (Yen et al., 2002). Corroborating self-report studies, Westen and colleagues (Westen, Ludolph, Misle, Ruffins, & Block, 1990) found documented childhood sexual abuse in the medical charts of over 50 percent of adolescents living with BPD in an inpatient sample. Nonetheless, as mentioned earlier, childhood trauma (including childhood sexual abuse) is not sufficient to explain the development of BPD. Further, most individuals who experience childhood sexual abuse do not go on to develop diagnosable personality disorders (Paris, 1998; Zanarini et al., 1997).

Experts have pointed out that childhood abuse does not usually occur in isolation, and is typically part of a pattern of family dysfunction (Zanarini et al., 1997). As suggested by genetic studies reviewed above, negative life events may also be intertwined with genetic vulnerability to BPD. An investigation by Distel at al. (2011) on a large sample of twins and siblings found that the impact of negative life events (including breakup, violent assault, sexual assault) on BPD features was moderated by genetic vulnerability, except for the impact of sexual assault. Sexual assault conferred increased risk for BPD features regardless of genetic predisposition. This finding suggests a unique impact of sexual trauma that cannot be explained by genetic predisposition, although replication studies with diagnostic assessment of BPD are warranted. Moreover, exposure to negative events was found to moderate heritability estimates for BPD, which were lower among those exposed to negative life events than for those who had not been exposed to such events. These findings suggest different pathways to the development of BPD, with adverse

environments and trauma playing a larger role for some individuals than others, as well as the importance of person × environment transactions in the development of BPD.

Further reflecting the complex interplay of environmental and individual factors is research suggesting that parental psychopathology may play a role in the development of BPD. Parents of children with BPD are more likely to have BPD, other personality disorders (e.g., antisocial personality disorder), and substance use disorders (see Helgeland and Torgersen, 2004 for review). Likewise, in a systematic review of studies examining psychopathology in relatives of individuals with BPD, White and colleagues (White, Gunderson, Zanarini, & Hudson, 2003) found the greatest evidence for a relationship between BPD and both familial BPD and familial impulse control disorders (e.g., substance use disorders and antisocial personality disorder), whereas the link between BPD and familial schizophrenia was not supported and the link between BPD and familial depression was tenuous. White et al. also noted that studies that relied on indirect assessment of familial history of psychopathology tended to over-inflate effects, whereas studies with more rigorous methodologies (e.g., direct assessment of family members using reliable diagnostic interviews) yielded more conservative estimates. Finally, in a study of the etiological factors associated with BPD in a large nonclinical sample, the contribution of parental psychopathology to BPD features was not better explained by abuse in childhood (Trull, 2001). Family history of psychopathology likely confers both environmental and biological risks to the development of BPD. Genetic, twin, or adoption studies, however, are necessary to disentangle the pathways underlying the intergenerational transmission of BPD.

Neurobiological Factors

Advances in neuroimaging have allowed for the identification of neurobiological characteristics of individuals with BPD, compared with other groups (often, healthy controls, and less often, psychiatric controls). Some studies have found reduced hippocampal and amygdala volume (Schmahl, Vermetten, Elzinga & Bremner 2003; van Elst et al., 2003) among BPD patients compared with healthy controls. Functional MRI studies have found that individuals with BPD have greater amygdala activation when confronted with emotional stimuli compared to controls (Donegan et al., 2003; Goodman et al., 2014; Herpertz et al., 2001; Minzenberg, Fan, New, Tang, & Siever, 2007; Silvers et al., 2016), leading to speculation that overactivity of the amygdala underlies emotion dysregulation (Krause-Utz, Winter, Niedtfeld, & Schmahl, 2014). Multiple methodologies have found evidence of additional fronto-limbic dysfunction in BPD, with PET imaging showing decreased frontal metabolism of glucose (Schmahl, Vermetten, Elzinga, & Bremner, 2004) and fMRI showing aberrant activation of the anterior cingulate, superior temporal sulcus, and superior front gyrus compared to controls in response to a task requiring cognitive control in response to emotional pictures (Koenigsberg et al., 2009). Taken together, the findings broadly suggest poor frontal regulation of the limbic system in BPD (Baczkowski et al., 2017; Schulz, Schmahl, & Niedtfeld, 2016). These findings converge with behavioral and self-report research showing (a) heightened negative emotional reactivity among people with BPD (Rosenthal et al., 2008), particularly in certain contexts (e.g., social rejection; Chapman, Dixon-Gordon, Walters, & Butler, 2015; Chapman, Walters, & Gordon, 2014) and (b) difficulty inhibiting impulsive behavior in negative emotional contexts among individuals with BPD pathology (Chapman, Dixon-Gordon, Layden & Walters, 2010; Sebastian et al., 2013).

Nonetheless, there are some key limitations of the extant research on putative neurobiological factors contributing to BPD. First, much of the research has compared BPD patients to healthy, non-psychiatric controls, making it difficult to discern whether functional or anatomical characteristics are unique to BPD or attributable to co-occurring disorders or psychopathology in general. Reduced amygdala and hippocampal volumes, for example, are not specific to BPD and may be better accounted for by co-occurring PTSD (see Leichsenring, Leibing, Kruse, New, & Leweke, 2011). More research distinguishing BPD from other psychiatric groups is needed. Second, neuroanatomical differences demonstrated in cross-sectional studies do not necessarily represent etiological factors. Brain, behavior, and the environment all transact, and differences in brain function or anatomy could be associated with adverse environmental events or prolonged engagement in particular behaviors (e.g., self-injury, drug or alcohol use), among others. Additional longitudinal investigations involving neuroimaging and appropriate controls (e.g., both healthy controls and psychiatric controls) are necessary to determine the association between neurobiological factors and emergence of BPD over time.

EVIDENCE-BASED TREATMENT

Beyond the aforementioned challenges defining BPD and pinpointing the precise etiology of this disorder, clinicians often experience challenges in the treatment of people with BPD, and for good reasons. The combination of suicide risk, severe and out of control behaviors, rapidly shifting emotional states, impulsivity, and interpersonal relations characterized by idealization and devaluation of others (sometimes including the therapist) can make treatment a complex and challenging endeavor. Persons with BPD often show slow, inconsistent, and episodic progress in treatment (Linehan, 1993a). In our experience, people with BPD often want help but have hit many roadblocks in previous treatment. The notion that BPD patients have a

difficult time finding the right therapeutic fit is underscored by data suggesting that the vast majority of such patients (97 percent) will receive outpatient treatment from an average of 6.1 therapists (Perry, Herman, Van Der Kolk, & Hoke, 1990; Skodol, Buckley, & Charles, 1983). Perhaps not surprisingly, when I (ALC) first began giving clinical workshops and asked how many people in the audience looked forward to treating their BPD patients, few courageous hands went up. Fortunately, over the past few decades, advances in our understanding of BPD, research on recovery from BPD, and studies showing that BPD can be effectively treated have increased clinicians' enthusiasm to help this often disenfranchised group. I see more and more hands go up when I ask clinicians that fateful question. That said, research and public awareness campaigns targeting stigma around BPD lag well behind other disorders, such as bipolar disorder (Ellison, Mason, & Scior, 2013).

Dialectical behavior therapy (DBT), mentalization-based treatment (MBT), and transference-focused psychotherapy (TFP) have been described as "the big three" of evidence-based, specialized psychotherapeutic treatments for BPD (Gunderson, 2016). Chambless and Hollon (1998) established guidelines for deeming a specific therapy to be empirically supported, defining *efficacious* therapies as those that demonstrated superiority to no treatment in at least two randomized controlled trials and by at least two independent research teams (minimizing allegiance effects). In this section, we only consider psychotherapeutic interventions with at least two RCTs supporting the therapy in question above treatment-as-usual or against another evidence-based treatment.

Comprehensive Treatments

Dialectical Behavior Therapy
Stemming from Dr. Marsha Linehan's attempts to develop and enhance treatment for highly suicidal individuals, DBT (Linehan, 1993a) has evolved into a comprehensive cognitive-behavioral approach addressing BPD and several other clinical problems. DBT is based on the biosocial theory (Crowell et al., 2009; Linehan, 1993a) that BPD results from the transaction of an invalidating rearing environment and a biological emotional vulnerability. Emotional vulnerability consists of proneness to a low threshold for emotional arousal, intense emotional reactions, and slow return to emotional baseline (often referred to as delayed recovery). The invalidating environment consists of the following characteristics: (a) indiscriminate rejection of the child's communication of thoughts and emotions, (b) intermittent reinforcement of emotional escalation, and (c) oversimplification of the ease of coping and problem solving. The biosocial theory holds that, in a developmental context, emotional vulnerability transacts with the invalidating environment, such that both factors exacerbate each other. Intense emotion

Table 10.2 DBT modes and functions

Mode	Function
Individual Therapy	Improve motivation, generalize treatment gains, solve life problems, build a life worth living
Group Skills Training	Increase capabilities (mindfulness, distress tolerance, interpersonal effectiveness, emotion regulation, self-management/regulation)
Telephone Consultation	Generalize new behaviors to relevant situations
Consultation Team	Maintain and improve therapist motivation and capability

Source: Chapman & Hope (in press).

vulnerability, especially when expressed through emotional outbursts or tantrums, can occasion invalidating parenting, particularly among parents bereft of the skills to cope with and parent an emotional child. Invalidation can amplify emotionality and does not teach the child to understand, trust, or regulate her or his emotional responses. Within this framework, persons with BPD have core skill deficits in emotion regulation, and many of the behavioral problems seen in this disorder are thought to occur in response to emotion dysregulation or function to regulate emotions (e.g., nonsuicidal self-injury; Brown, Comtois, & Linehan, 2002) (Linehan, 1993a).

DBT addresses five key functions of treatment within four primary modes of treatment. The key functions include: (a) increasing client motivation to change, (b) structuring the environment (the treatment and natural environment), (c) improving client capabilities, (d) generalizing skills and capabilities to relevant environments, and (e) maintaining and improving therapist motivation and skills. The four components of DBT include weekly individual therapy, telephone consultation (availability of the therapist between sessions for skills coaching; see Chapman, 2019b, for a book on this mode of DBT), weekly group skills training, and a therapist consultation team meeting. See Table 10.2 for a description of how these modes and functions fit together.

DBT is dialectical in that the treatment involves the balancing and synthesis of acceptance and change-oriented therapeutic styles, interventions, and skills. In developing DBT, Linehan discovered that the predominantly change-oriented approach to CBT was upsetting to clients who received the message that they simply needed to change their thinking and behavior to conquer longstanding, complex suffering. As a result, Linehan began to incorporate acceptance-oriented strategies stemming from both client-centered approaches and Zen practice. DBT, therefore, balances a problem solving and skills-training oriented treatment with validation and acceptance of clients, and teaches clients how to accept themselves. The DBT skills, similarly, involve a balance of change-oriented (interpersonal effectiveness, emotion regulation) and acceptance-oriented (reality acceptance skills, mindfulness) skills (Linehan, 1993b, 2014).

In the decades since the first RCT comparing DBT to treatment as usual (TAU) for the reduction of parasuicidal behavior (i.e., suicide attempts and self-injury; Linehan et al., 1991) among BPD patients, evidence has supported DBT as a well-established treatment. More than 20 published RCTs have examined standard DBT (all modes and functions as described above), and others have examined components of DBT, such as DBT skills training (nearly 20 studies). In addition, numerous open and uncontrolled trials and effectiveness and other studies have examined standard DBT, DBT-informed adaptations, or components of DBT (such as DBT skills training) for a variety of other clinical problem areas and in many settings (e.g., correctional, inpatient, outpatient, community, university). Overall, the findings have supported the efficacy of standard DBT for BPD and related problems, and suggest promise for DBT skills training for BPD, emotion regulation problems, depression, anxiety, and disordered eating (bingeing and purging), among other difficulties (see Neacsiu, Eberle, Kramer, Wiesmann, & Linehan, 2014, for a recent review, and McMain, Guimond, Barnhart, Habinski, & Streiner, 2017, for a recent study examining DBT skills group alone for suicidal patients with BPD). In a systematic Cochrane review, Stoffers et al. (2012) found moderate to large effects supporting DBT over TAU for reducing inappropriate anger and parasuicidal behavior (including suicide attempts and nonsuicidal self-injury) and improving psychiatric symptoms (Stoffers et al., 2012). DBT has been widely disseminated and recognized as an efficacious treatment for BPD, with both the Australian National Health and Medical Resource Council and the United Kingdom's National Collaborating Centre for Mental Health concluding that DBT has the most evidence among current treatments for BPD (NHMRC, 2012; NICE, 2009). Until relatively recently, it was difficult to find a psychosocial treatment other than DBT that had been subject to carefully designed randomized trials. The field of promising treatments for BPD, however, has expanded to include other treatments described below.

Mentalization-Based Treatment

Developed by two experts with a psychoanalytic orientation, Anthony Bateman and Peter Fonagy, MBT is based on the theory that BPD results from impairments in early attachment relationships leading to poor *mentalization*, the ability to understand the internal states (e.g., thoughts, emotions) of oneself and others (Bateman & Fonagy, 1999). As such, a major focus of MBT is on monitoring mentalization and attachment in the therapeutic relationship and improving mentalization through patient–therapist interactions. For example, in individual therapy, the therapist expresses her or his own states of mind and their relation to the patient's behaviors, invites patients to verbalize their own states of mind, and collaboratively addresses misunderstandings with patients ("understand misunderstanding"; Fonagy et al., 2014, p. 319). The MBT therapist retains a stance of curious inquiry into the patient's thoughts, emotions, and interpretations and their relations to the therapist's internal states.

MBT has been developed for delivery in both partial-hospitalization and outpatient settings. In the initial development of MBT, treatment was delivered in the context of routine psychiatric care for patients with BPD in a partial hospital program with one MBT group and individual therapy session per week. In outpatient MBT, patients typically meet with their individual therapist for one session of individual therapy and one session of group therapy per week.

To date, findings of the four existing RCTs on MBT have shown positive outcomes. One RCT examined the efficacy of MBT in the partial hospitalization program compared to TAU, finding that 18 months of MBT led to significantly greater improvement in BPD symptoms, fewer suicide attempts, greater psychosocial functioning, and more stable employment compared to TAU (Bateman & Fonagy, 1999, 2001). Upon follow-up five years later, the MBT group continued to maintain gains, evidencing fewer suicide attempts, lower use of psychiatric services, and higher rates of remission from BPD, compared to the TAU participants (Bateman & Fonagy, 2008). In the first RCT of outpatient MBT, results revealed that this treatment outperformed structured clinical management in several domains (Bateman & Fonagy, 2009). Patients assigned to outpatient MBT experienced greater reductions in suicide attempts and hospitalization after 12 months compared to patients in structured clinical management. Jørgensen et al. (2013) conducted the first independent investigation of the efficacy of MBT, comparing two years of more intensive outpatient MBT to two years of less intensive biweekly supportive group therapy. They found that MBT resulted in superior outcomes in therapist-rated global functioning, whereas both treatments resulted in comparable improvements in depression, social functioning, and BPD symptom severity (number of diagnostic criteria met in SCID-II assessment). Lastly, one RCT has examined MBT for adolescents with comorbid depression and self-harm (Rossouw & Fonagy, 2012). Whereas this study was not conducted on a sample selected for BPD diagnosis or features, emergent BPD symptoms were assessed in the study. Rossouw and Fonagy found that 12 months of MBT, adapted for adolescents, outperformed TAU in reducing the primary outcomes of self-harm and depression, and that improved mentalization, changes in attachment style (less avoidance), and reduced emergent BPD symptoms accounted for these group differences in outcomes.

Transference-Focused Psychotherapy

Rooted in Kernberg's theory of the borderline personality organization (Kernberg, 1967), TFP is a psychoanalytically oriented therapy for BPD. TFP posits that the primitive defense mechanisms engaged in by the individual with BPD, such as splitting (e.g., rigidly categorizing others into "good" and "bad"), cause substantial impairment in relationships, identity, and self-regulation. TFP aims to correct both interpersonal dysfunction and the emotional reactivity that follows by exploring dynamics in the therapeutic relationship (Choi-Kain, Finch, Masland, Jenkins, & Unruh, 2017). For example, in individual therapy, the therapist addresses defense mechanisms by analyzing transference in the therapeutic relationship. TFP typically involves two weekly individual therapy sessions for three years. As such, this is the longest and most time-intensive of the "big three" treatments for BPD.

Three RCTs have been conducted on TFP to date, and two have supported the efficacy of TFP. Clarkin and colleagues (Clarkin, Levy, Lenzenweger, & Kernberg, 2007) evaluated one year of TFP, DBT, or supportive psychotherapy for patients with BPD in an RCT with three active treatment conditions. They found that both TFP and DBT outperformed supportive psychotherapy in reducing suicidality, and that TFP resulted in greater improvements in anger than DBT or supportive psychotherapy. A second RCT was conducted by an independent research team on schema-focused therapy (SFT) versus TFP in the treatment of BPD and found both to reduce symptoms of BPD and general psychopathology, with SFT outperforming TFP on all outcome measures (Giesen-Bloo et al., 2006). Most recently, Doering et al. (2010) evaluated one year of TFP versus an enhanced TAU condition of treatment by community experts. TFP resulted in greater reductions in symptoms of BPD, fewer suicide attempts, less hospitalization, and greater psychosocial functioning than TAU, whereas improvements in depression and anxiety occurred in both conditions but did not significantly differ between conditions. There was no significant change in self-harm in either condition. Reviewing this accumulated empirical evidence from these three RCTs, TFP seems to be a possibly efficacious treatment for certain clinical problem areas among BPD patients, although more well-controlled efficacy studies with consistent findings are needed before concluding that TFP has robust empirical support. As of the writing of this chapter, additional RCTs have been published on TFP since the latest Cochrane review of treatments for BPD (Stoffers et al., 2012).

Non-Comprehensive or Ancillary Approaches

Systems Training for Emotional Predictability and Problem Solving (STEPPS)

STEPPS is a short-term group treatment for BPD designed to serve as an adjunct to a patient's TAU (Blum et al., 2008). Patients attend a weekly, seminar-style, group session where they are provided psychoeducation about BPD, emotion management skills training, and behavioral skills training (e.g., goal setting; building healthy habits around eating, sleep and exercise; stopping self-harm) based on cognitive behavioral principles. Additionally, the treatment is considered "systems-based" in that participants are encouraged to share their new skills with other people in their lives to help build support, and a one-time group psychoeducation session is offered to participants' family members and friends.

Evidence for STEPPS. The first RCT, conducted by the treatment developers, found that STEPPS plus TAU resulted in greater reductions in BPD symptoms, impulsivity, and negative affectivity than TAU alone, although patients in the STEPPS condition had a higher drop-out rate (31 percent versus 14 percent; Blum et al., 2008). There were no differences in self-harm or suicide attempts between the two conditions. In a second RCT, STEPPS plus a complementary individual therapy (based on STEPPS principles, and offered every two weeks) was compared to TAU (Bos, van Wel, Appelo, & Verbraak, 2010). STEPPS recipients demonstrated greater reductions in general psychiatric symptoms and BPD symptoms, and gains were maintained at six-month follow-up. As with the first RCT, no differences were observed in terms of engagement in impulsive or self-damaging behaviors. Although initial evidence for STEPPS is promising, it is still unknown whether STEPPS is efficacious as a stand-alone treatment. As a brief intervention, STEPPS seems to be a beneficial adjunct to TAU and may serve patients and healthcare providers well when specialized comprehensive treatments for BPD are unavailable. Nonetheless, it will be important for future RCTs to compare STEPPS to enhanced TAU (e.g., treatment by community experts) or to treatments that have been established to be superior to TAU, such as DBT or MBT.

Emotion Regulation Group Therapy

Emotion regulation group therapy (ERGT) (Gratz & Gunderson, 2006; Gratz, Tull, & Levy, 2014) is another short-term group therapy designed as an adjunct to TAU for BPD. The focus of ERGT is on the treatment of self-harm within BPD by targeting the proposed underlying mechanism of emotion dysregulation. In ERGT, patients with repeated self-harm and BPD attend a weekly group for 14 weeks focused on teaching skills related to emotion regulation and acceptance, emphasizing *acceptance* of emotions and *control* of behaviors (Gratz & Gunderson, 2006; Gratz et al., 2014).

Two RCTs (Gratz & Gunderson, 2006; Gratz et al., 2014) and two open trials (Gratz & Tull, 2011; Sahlin et al., 2017) have evaluated the efficacy/utility of ERGT as an adjunct to TAU for BPD. Initial results have supported the possible efficacy of this brief intervention, with ERGT plus TAU reducing self-harm, emotion dysregulation, and BPD symptoms more than TAU alone in all four trials (Gratz & Gunderson; 2006; Gratz & Tull, 2011; Gratz et al., 2014;

Sahlin et al., 2017). Further, upon follow-up nine months after treatment in the largest RCT, participants in the ERGT condition experienced significant post-treatment improvements in self-harm, emotion dysregulation, BPD symptoms, and quality of life compared to TAU, indicating that benefits of attending ERGT may continue to materialize even after patients end group (Gratz et al., 2014). Aside from DBT, ERGT has been identified as the only other psychotherapy with two or more controlled trials examining efficacy for reducing deliberate self-harm (see Turner, Austin & Chapman, 2014 for systematic review of psychotherapy for self-harm). Nonetheless, all controlled trials to date have been conducted by the treatment developer, and independent evaluation of the efficacy of ERGT is needed in order to define ERGT as efficacious.

Generalist Approaches

Following the emergence of evidence-based, specialized psychotherapeutic treatments for BPD, generalist approaches are gaining momentum. Accumulating evidence suggests that these approaches may offer sufficient treatment for core symptoms of BPD with the benefit of requiring less intensive training of clinicians for treatment delivery. Choi-Kain and colleagues (2017) classified the latest "wave" of efficacy studies on psychotherapeutic treatments for BPD as that of specialist therapies (e.g., DBT; MBT; TFP) vs. generalist approaches, such as general psychiatric management (Gunderson, 2014), and identified three RCTs (Bateman & Fonagy, 2009; Jørgensen et al., 2013; McMain et al., 2009) that fit into this wave. Based on these three RCTs, the authors concluded that "these enhanced, structured, and well-informed generalist treatment approaches performed as well in most ways to their already established specialized counterparts" (Choi-Kain et al., 2017, p. 22). Both Gunderson (2016) and Choi-Kain et al. (2017) posit that well-structured generalist approaches may fill the pressing need for less-intensive, more cost-effective treatment when specialized manualized treatments, such as DBT, are unavailable.

Medications

Although there are no "anti-BPD" medications approved for use by the US Food and Drug Administration or any other national authority, there is some evidence for a role of pharmacology in the treatment of specific symptoms. The most comprehensive review of high quality evidence for pharmacological intervention is presented in a Cochrane review (Lieb, Völlm, Rücker, Timmer, & Stoffers, 2010) including 27 RCTs from 1979–2008. On one hand, certain medications were found to be somewhat effective at treating specific symptoms of BPD, including the first-generation antipsychotic medications of haloperidol (for anger) and flupentixol (for suicidal behavior), second-generation antipsychotic medications of aripiprazole (for anger, psychotic symptoms, impulsivity, depression, and anxiety) and olanzapine (for anger, psychotic symptoms, anxiety), the mood stabilizers valproate, divalproex sodium, and topiramate (for interpersonal problems, anger, and impulsivity), and supplementary omega-3 fatty acids (for suicidality and depression[2]). On the other hand, there is little support for the use of antidepressants in treating symptoms of depression or affective instability among patients with BPD. No significant effects were found for the use of SSRI antidepressants compared to placebo, and only one significant effect was found for other antidepressants (the tricyclic amitriptyline; see Lieb et al., 2010). The authors noted that the overall quality of evidence for pharmacological treatment of BPD is low, due to few RCTs and small sample sizes. Additionally, actively suicidal clients were excluded from most RCTs, eliminating a sizable subset of the BPD patient population and resulting in uncertainty as to the helpfulness of medications for suicidal patients with BPD.

Descriptive research on the common medication prescription practices of physicians for patients with BPD paints a different picture that deviates from the empirical evidence on their efficacy. Despite the lack of evidence for SSRIs on symptoms of BPD in clinical trials, SSRIs are widely prescribed to patients with BPD (Baken-Glenn, Steels, & Evans, 2010; Knappich, Hörz-Sagstetter, Schwerthöffer, Leucht, & Rentrop, 2014; Zanarini, Frankenburg, Khera, & Bleichmar, 2001). Additionally, patients with BPD may be at particular risk of poly-pharmacy (Tyrer & Bateman, 2004), given the presence of multiple symptom domains and common co-occurrence of BPD with other disorders. An update to the Cochrane review by two of the original authors, Stoffers and Lieb, concluded that the current evidence is "unsatisfying" and suggested that the way patients with BPD tend to be treated with medication in community and hospital settings does not reflect the limited evidence base (Stoffers & Lieb, 2015). In addition, Paris (2002) has warned of physicians responding to limited effectiveness of any one medication for BPD by over-prescribing with multiple medications. This warning is particularly important given evidence that BPD patients were found to have substantially higher rates of prescribed opioid medications than a clinical comparison group of patients with other personality disorders (Frankenburg, Fitzmaurice, & Zanarini, 2014).

Common Ground among Evidence-Based Psychosocial Approaches

Despite differing theoretical foundations (object relations, psychodynamic, psychoanalytic, behavioral, etc.),

psychosocial treatments with empirical support for BPD have some common elements, including an emphasis on the therapeutic relationship, emotion regulation and self-control, and interpersonal processes. Treatments vary in their degree of emphasis on these variables, with DBT most strongly emphasizing emotion and self-regulation, and MBT and TFP emphasizing interpersonal processes and the therapy relationship as a vehicle for change. In DBT, the therapy relationship is considered necessary but not sufficient, although the therapist ideally takes the opportunity to use interpersonal transactions in the therapy room to help the client develop skills to navigate interpersonal contexts in daily life. In addition, each of the treatments discussed here emphasizes the effectiveness of a fairly structured approach, consistent with the notion that therapeutic structure has a regulating effect and provides a "contained" context in which BPD patients can engage in the therapeutic process (whether that process involves increasing or decreasing specific behaviors, as in DBT, or processing interactions between the therapist and client, as in MBT and TFP).

Commonalities across empirically supported treatments for BPD suggest the possibility of transtheoretical processes of change that could be used in routine clinical practice. In other areas, treatment developers have distilled commonalities in discrete treatment manuals into broader, flexible approaches, such as the emerging transdiagnostic protocol to emotional disorders (Barlow, Allen, & Choate, 2004) and the transdiagnostic approach for eating disorders (Fairburn, Cooper, & Shafran, 2003). It is fortunate that the growing treatment literature suggests that BPD can be treated successfully; however, practitioners who provide specific, manualized treatments often are hard to find, even in large, urban areas. Further, as described above, there is some evidence that more general approaches to BPD treatment, based on common principles rather than specific techniques, such as general psychiatric management (McMain & Pos, 2007), have promise and may ease dissemination and implementation.

Predictors of Outcome and Mechanisms of Change

For the refinement of treatments for BPD to proceed efficiently, more research is needed to identify predictors of treatment outcome and mechanisms of change. The key questions here are: (1) How do treatments for BPD result in positive outcomes (mechanisms of change)? (2) For whom do treatments for BPD result in positive outcomes, and relatedly, for which groups of BPD patients do we need to modify or refine treatment? If key mechanisms of change were identified, treatment elements targeting these mechanisms could be emphasized to provide a more efficient and easily disseminated intervention. If we knew the patients for whom specific treatments were more or less likely to work, it would be easier to determine key research and treatment priorities targeting subgroups of patients who do not respond to existing treatments.

---

[2] Two small studies ($n = 49$ and $n = 27$) included in the Cochrane review have suggested efficacy for dietary supplements of omega-3 fatty acids reducing suicidality (study 1 only) and depressive symptoms.

In terms of predictors of outcome for BPD, a review by Barnicott and colleagues (Barnicot, Katskou, Bhatti, Fearns, & Priebe, 2012) found some evidence that greater pre-treatment BPD severity predicted greater change in BPD symptoms (but only inconsistently change in diagnostic status) over the course of treatment, and that patients with a history of self-injury pre-treatment showed greater improvements in self-injury. Further, some studies showed evidence that therapeutic alliance positively predicted outcome.

In terms of mechanisms of change, one review of 14 studies addressing mechanisms in DBT or CBT found the most consistent evidence for the use of skills (Rudge, Feigenbaum, & Fonagy, 2017). From a DBT framework (and to some extent, a CBT framework), one key aim is for patients with BPD to increase their behavioral capabilities (skills) in key areas. In one study examining DBT skills use as a potential mechanism of change, Neacsiu and colleagues (Neacsiu, Rizvi, & Linehan, 2010) found that DBT skills use mediated decreases in suicide attempts and depression and increases in control of anger, and partially mediated decreases in self-injury. Other studies have examined a variety of potential mechanisms falling broadly under the category of skills, such as mindfulness (O'Toole, Diddy, & Kent, 2012; Perroud, Uher, Dieben, Nicastro, & Huguelet, 2010), negative/compensatory thinking patterns (Gibbons et al., 2010), and DBT skills use (Barnicot et al., 2012; Stepp, Epler, Jahng, & Trull, 2008).

Other studies have examined whether treatments change putative neurocognitive and neurobiological mechanisms associated with BPD. Thomsen and colleagues (Thomsen, Ruocco, Uliaszek, Mathiesen, & Simonsen, 2017) examined changes in neurocognitive functioning following six months of MBT among 18 women with BPD, compared with changes observed among non-psychiatric controls during a similar period (with no treatment). The study examined a range of neurocognitive measures and found that both patients and controls showed improvement on some of these measures, such as processing speed and perceptual reasoning. Results, however, revealed a significant interaction for only sustained attention, such that whereas patients began with lower performance than controls, these differences were non-significant at post-treatment. Another line of research has examined whether DBT changes the neurobiological fronto-limbic dysfunction often observed in some of the studies reviewed previously. Goodman et al. (2014), for example, compared changes in amygdala activation to pleasant, unpleasant, or neutral images among patients receiving 12 months of standard DBT versus healthy controls not receiving treatment. Findings suggested that the patients with BPD displayed significant reductions in both amygdala activity and self-reported emotion regulation difficulties (assessed via the Difficulties in Emotion Regulation Scale [DERS]; Gratz & Roemer, 2004), and that reductions in amygdala activity were associated with reductions in DERS scores. The findings of this and other studies (Schmitt, Winter, Niedtfeld, Herpertz, & Schmahl, 2016) suggest that DBT may have promise in reducing amygdala hyperactivity, increasing prefrontal connectivity to the amygdala, and increasing activity in prefrontal areas associated broadly with executive functioning and behavioral control (e.g., dorsolateral prefrontal cortex).

CONCLUSIONS AND FUTURE DIRECTIONS

A severe, complex, and often stigmatized disorder, BPD has mystified clinicians and researchers alike. Developments over the past three to four decades have helped to shape and define the conceptualization of BPD, clarify potential causes and contributing factors, and highlight effective treatments. We know that (a) BPD characterized by impulsivity, emotional dysregulation, and interpersonal dysfunction, (b) the course of BPD is much more variable and positive than previously thought, and (c) psychosocial treatments work for BPD. For the field to move forward, several important future directions include: (a) research examining the validity and acceptability of alternative (e.g., dimensional, trait-based) conceptualizations of BPD, (b) increased longitudinal and translational research highlighting the dynamic interplay of factors conferring risk for BPD, and (c) treatment research highlighting predictors of outcome, the characteristics of treatment responders and non-responders, and potential mechanisms of change that could inform the development of streamlined, targeted, and efficient treatments. In addition, although we believe that inroads have been made in reducing the stigma associated with BPD and countering common myths about this disorder, there is the need to devote more resources to public education on BPD and efforts to reduce stigma. Finally, although treatment works for many people with BPD, it is still very hard for patients to find evidence-based treatment. More work is needed to increase access to treatment for this group of patients, who, in many cases, wish to overcome suffering, improve their lives and relationships, and make meaningful contributions to others' lives.

REFERENCES

Amad, A., Ramoz, N., Thomas, P., Jardri, R., & Gorwood, P. (2014). Genetics of borderline personality disorder: Systematic review and proposal of an integrative model. *Neuroscience & Biobehavioral Reviews, 40*, 6–19.

American Psychiatric Association. (1980). *Diagnostic and Statistical Manual of Mental Disorders* (3rd ed.). Washington, DC: American Psychiatric Association.

American Psychiatric Association. (2013). Diagnostic *and Statistical Manual of Mental Disorders* (5th ed.). Arlington, VA: American Psychiatric Publishing.

Ansell, E. B., Sanislow, C. A., McGlashan, T. H., & Grilo, C. M. (2007). Psychosocial impairment and treatment utilization by patients with borderline personality disorder, other personality disorders, mood and anxiety disorders, and a healthy comparison group. *Comprehensive Psychiatry, 48*, 329–336.

Baczkowski, B. M., van Zutphen, L., Siep, N., Jacob, G. A., Domes, G., Maier, S., . . . Arntz, A. (2017). Deficient amygdala–prefrontal intrinsic connectivity after effortful emotion regulation in borderline personality disorder. *European Archives of Psychiatry and Clinical Neuroscience, 267*, 551–565.

Baker-Glenn, E., Steels, M., & Evans, C. (2010). Use of psychotropic medication among psychiatric out-patients with personality disorder. *The Psychiatrist, 34*(3), 83–86.

Barlow, D. H., Allen, L. B., & Choate, M. L. (2004). Toward a unified treatment for emotional disorders. *Behavior Therapy, 35*(2), 205–230.

Barnicot, K., Katskou, C., Bhatti, N., Fearns, N., & Priebe, S. (2012). Factors predicting the outcome of psychotherapy for borderline personality disorder: A systematic review. *Clinical Psychology Review, 32*(5), 400–412.

Baron, M., Gruen, R., Asnis, L., & Lord, S. (1985). Familial transmission of schizotypal and borderline personality disorders. *American Journal of Psychiatry, 142*(8), 927–934.

Bateman, A., & Fonagy, P. (1999). Effectiveness of partial hospitalization in the treatment of borderline personality disorder: A randomized controlled trial. *American Journal of Psychiatry, 156*(10), 1563–1569.

Bateman, A., & Fonagy, P. (2001). Treatment of borderline personality disorder with psychoanalytically oriented partial hospitalization: An 18-month follow-up. *American Journal of Psychiatry, 158*(1), 36–42.

Bateman, A., & Fonagy, P. (2003). Health service utilization costs for borderline personality disorder patients treated with psychoanalytically oriented partial hospitalization versus general psychiatric care. *American Journal of Psychiatry, 160*(1), 169–171.

Bateman, A., & Fonagy, P. (2006). *Mentalization-Based Treatment for Borderline Personality Disorder: A Practical Guide.* New York: Oxford University Press.

Bateman, A., & Fonagy, P. (2008). Eight-year follow-up of patients treated for borderline personality disorder: Mentalization-based treatment versus treatment as usual. *American Journal of Psychiatry, 165*(5), 631–638.

Bateman, A., & Fonagy, P. (2009). Randomized controlled trial of outpatient mentalization-based treatment versus structured clinical management for borderline personality disorder. *American Journal of Psychiatry, 166*(12), 1355–1364.

Bender, D. S., Skodol, A. E., Pagano, M. E., Dyck, I. R., Grilo, C. M., Shea, M. T., . . . Gunderson, J. G. (2006). Prospective assessment of treatment use by patients with personality disorders. *Psychiatric Services, 57*, 254–257.

Black, D. W., Blum, N., Pfohl, B., & Hale, N. (2004). Suicidal behavior in borderline personality disorder: Prevalence, risk factors, prediction, and prevention. *Journal of Personality Disorders, 18*, 226–239.

Blum, N., St. John, D., Pfohl, B., Stuart, S., McCormick, B., Allen, J., . . . Black, D. W. (2008). Systems Training for Emotional Predictability and Problem Solving (STEPPS) for outpatients with borderline personality disorder: A randomized controlled trial and 1-year follow-up. *American Journal of Psychiatry, 165*, 468–478.

Bos, E. H., van Wel, E. B., Appelo, M. T., & Verbraak, M. J. (2010). A randomized controlled trial of a Dutch version of systems training for emotional predictability and problem solving for borderline personality disorder. *Journal of Nervous and Mental Disease, 198*(4), 299–304.

Brown, M. Z., Comtois, K. A., & Linehan, M. M. (2002). Reasons for suicide attempts and non-suicidal self-injury in women with borderline personality disorder. *Journal of Abnormal Psychology, 111*, 198–202.

Chambless, D. L., & Hollon, S. D. (1998). Defining empirically supported therapies. *Journal of Consulting and Clinical Psychology, 66*, 7–18.

Chanen, A. M., Jackson, H. J., McGorry, P. D., Allot, K. A., Clarkson, V., & Yuen, H. P. (2004). Two-year stability of personality disorder in older adolescent outpatients. *Journal of Personality Disorders, 18*, 526–541.

Chanen, A. M., Jovev, M., McCutcheon, L. K., Jackson, H. J., & McGorry, P. D. (2008). Borderline personality disorder in young people and the prospects for prevention and early intervention. *Current Psychiatry Reviews, 4*, 48–57.

Chanen, A. M., & McCutcheon, L. (2013). Prevention and early intervention for borderline personality disorder: Current status and recent evidence. *British Journal of Psychiatry, 202*, 24–29.

Chapman, A. L. (2009). Borderline personality disorder. In J. S. Abramowitz, D. McKay, & S. Taylor (Eds.), *The Expanded Scope of Cognitive-Behavior Therapy: Lessons Learned from Refractory Cases* (pp. 347–367). Washington, DC: American Psychological Association.

Chapman, A. L. (2019a). Borderline personality disorder and emotion dysregulation. *Development and Psychopathology, 31*, 1143–1156.

Chapman, A. L. (2019b). *Phone Coaching in Dialectical Behavior Therapy.* New York: Guilford Press.

Chapman, A. L., Dixon-Gordon, K. L., Layden, B. K., & Walters, K. N. (2010). Borderline personality features moderate the effect of a fear induction on impulsivity. *Personality Disorders: Theory, Research, and Treatment, 1*, 139–152.

Chapman, A. L., Dixon-Gordon, K. L., Walters, K. N., & Butler, S. M. (2015). Emotional reactivity to social rejection versus a frustration induction among persons with borderline personality features. *Personality Disorders: Theory, Research, and Treatment, 6*, 88–96.

Chapman, A. L., & Gratz, K. L. (2007). *The Borderline Personality Disorder Survival Guide: Everything You Need to Know About Living with BPD.* Oakland, CA: New Harbinger Publications.

Chapman, A. L., & Hope, N. H. (in press). Dialectical behaviour therapy and treatment of emotion dysregulation. In T. Beauchaine & S. Crowell (Eds.), *The Oxford Handbook of Emotion Dysregulation.*

Chapman, A. L., Walters, K. N., & Gordon, K. L. (2014). Emotional reactivity to social rejection and negative evaluation among persons with borderline personality features. *Journal of Personality Disorders, 28*, 720–733.

Choi-Kain, L. W., Finch, E. F., Masland, S. R., Jenkins, J. A., & Unruh, B. T. (2017). What works in the treatment of borderline personality disorder. *Current Behavioral Neuroscience Reports, 4*, 21–30.

Clarkin, J. F., Hull, J. W., & Hurt, S. W. (1993). Factor structure of borderline personality disorder criteria. *Journal of Personality Disorders, 7*(2), 137–143.

Clarkin, J. F., Levy, K. N., Lenzenweger, M. F., & Kernberg, O. F. (2007). Evaluating three treatments for borderline personality disorder: A multiwave study. *American Journal of Psychiatry, 164*, 922–928.

Cloitre, M., Garvert, D. W., Weiss, B., Carlson, E. B., & Bryant, R. A. (2014). Distinguishing PTSD, complex PTSD, and borderline personality disorder: A latent class analysis. *European Journal of Psychotraumatology*, 5, 10.

Cohen, P., Crawford, T. N., Johnson, J. G., & Kasen, S. (2005). The Children in the Community study of developmental course of personality disorder. *Journal of Personality Disorders*, 19, 466–486.

Comtois, K. A., Elwood, L., Holdcraft, L. C., Smith, W. R., & Simpson, T. L. (2007). Effectiveness of dialectical behavior therapy in a community mental health center. *Cognitive and Behavioral Practice*, 14, 406–414.

Crowell, S. E., Beauchaine, T. P., & Linehan, M. M. (2009). A biosocial developmental model of borderline personality: Elaborating and extending Linehan's theory. *Psychological Bulletin*, 135(3), 495–510.

Distel, M. A., Middeldorp, C. M., Trull, T. J., Derom, C. A., Willemsen, G., & Boomsma, D. I. (2011). Life events and borderline personality features: The influence of gene–environment interaction and gene–environment correlation. *Psychological Medicine*, 41(4), 849–860.

Distel, M. A., Trull, T. J., Derom, C. A., Thiery, E. W., Grimmer, M. A., Martin, N. G., ... Boomsma, D. I. (2008). Heritability of borderline personality disorder features is similar across three countries. *Psychological Medicine*, 38(9), 1219–1229.

Doering, S., Hörz, S., Rentrop, M., Fischer-Kern, M., Schuster, P., Benecke, C., ... Buchheim, P. (2010). Transference-focused psychotherapy v. treatment by community psychotherapists for borderline personality disorder: Randomised controlled trial. *British Journal of Psychiatry*, 196(5), 389–395.

Donegan, N. H., Sanislow, C. A., Blumberg, H. P., Fulbright, R. K., Lacadie, C., Skudlarski, P., ... Wexler, B. E. (2003). Amygdala hyperreactivity in borderline personality disorder: Implications for emotional dysregulation. *Biological Psychiatry*, 54, 1284–1293.

Ellison, N., Mason, O., & Scior, K. (2013). Bipolar disorder and stigma: A systematic review of the literature. *Journal of Affective Disorders*, 151(3), 805–820.

Fairburn, C. G., Cooper, Z., & Shafran, R. (2003). Cognitive behaviour therapy for eating disorders: A "transdiagnostic" theory and treatment. *Behavior Research and Therapy*, 41, 509–528.

Fonagy, P., Rossouw, T., Sharp, C., Bateman, A., Allison, L., & Farrar, C. (2014). Mentalization-based treatment for adolescents with borderline traits. In C. Sharp & J. Tackett (Eds.), *Handbook of Borderline Personality Disorder in Children and Adolescents* (pp. 313–332). New York: Springer.

Ford, J. D., & Courtois, C. A. (2014). Complex PTSD, affect dysregulation, and borderline personality disorder. *Borderline Personality Disorder and Emotion Dysregulation*, 1(9).

Frankenburg, F. R., Fitzmaurice, G. M., & Zanarini, M. C. (2014). The use of prescription opioid medication by patients with borderline personality disorder and axis II comparison subjects: A 10-year follow-up study. *Journal of Clinical Psychiatry*, 75(4), 357–361.

Friedel, R. O. (2004). *Borderline Personality Disorder Demystified*. New York: Marlowe & Company.

Gibbons, M. B. C., Crits-Christophe, P., Barber, J. P., Stirman, S. W., Gallop, R., Goldstein, L. A., ... Ring-Kurtz, S. (2010). Unique and common mechanisms of change across cognitive and dynamic psychotherapies. *Journal of Consulting and Clinical Psychology*, 77, 801–813.

Giesen-Bloo, J., Van Dyck, R., Spinhoven, P., Van Tilburg, W., Dirksen, C., Van Asselt, T., ... Arntz, A. (2006). Outpatient psychotherapy for borderline personality disorder: Randomized trial of schema-focused therapy vs transference-focused psychotherapy. *Archives of General Psychiatry*, 63, 649–658.

Glenn, C. R., & Klonsky, E. D. (2009) Emotion dysregulation as a core feature of borderline personality disorder. *Journal of Personality Disorders*, 23, 20–28.

Goodman, M., Carpenter, D., Tang, C. Y., Goldstein, K. E., Avedon, J., Fernandez, N., ... Hazlett, E. A. (2014). Dialectical behavior therapy alters emotion regulation and amygdala activity in patients with borderline personality disorder. *Journal of Psychiatric Research*, 57, 108–116.

Grant, B. F., Chou, S. P., Goldstein, R. B., Huang, B., Stinson, F. S., Saha, T. D., ... Ruan, W. J. (2008). Prevalence, correlates, disability, and comorbidity of DSM-IV borderline personality disorder: Results from the Wave 2 National Epidemiologic Survey on Alcohol and Related Conditions. *Journal of Clinical Psychiatry*, 69(4), 533–545.

Gratz, K. L., & Gunderson, J. G. (2006). Preliminary data on an acceptance-based emotion regulation group intervention for deliberate self-harm among women with borderline personality disorder. *Behavior Therapy*, 37(1), 25–35.

Gratz, K. L., & Roemer, L. (2004). Multidimensional assessment of emotion regulation and dysregulation: Development, factor structure, and initial validation of the difficulties in emotion regulation scale. *Journal of Psychopathology and Behavioral Assessment*, 26(1), 41–54.

Gratz, K. L., & Tull, M. T. (2011). Extending research on the utility of an adjunctive emotion regulation group therapy for deliberate self-harm among women with borderline personality pathology. *Personality Disorders: Theory, Research, and Treatment*, 2 (4), 316–326.

Gratz, K. L., Tull, M. T., & Levy, R. (2014). Randomized controlled trial and uncontrolled 9-month follow-up of an adjunctive emotion regulation group therapy for deliberate self-harm among women with borderline personality disorder. *Psychological Medicine*, 44(10), 2099–2112.

Grinker, R., Werble, B., & Drye, R. (1968). *The Borderline Syndrome*. New York: Basic Books.

Gunderson, J. G. (2001). *Borderline Personality Disorder: A Clinical Guide*. Washington, DC: American Psychiatric Publishing.

Gunderson J. G. (2007). Disturbed relationships as a phenotype for borderline personality disorder (commentary). *American Journal of Psychiatry*, 164, 1637–1640.

Gunderson, J. G. (2009). Borderline personality disorder: Ontogeny of a diagnosis. *American Journal of Psychiatry*, 166, 530–539.

Gunderson, J. G. (2010). Revising the borderline diagnosis for DSM-V: An alternative proposal. *Journal of Personality Disorders*, 24(6), 694–708.

Gunderson, J. G. (2014). *Handbook of Good Psychiatric Management for Borderline Personality Disorder*. Washington, DC: American Psychiatric Publishing.

Gunderson, J. G. (2016). The emergence of a generalist model to meet public health needs for patients with borderline personality disorder. *American Journal of Psychiatry*, 173, 452–458.

Gunderson, J. G., & Kolb, J. E. (1978). Discriminating features of borderline patients. *American Journal of Psychiatry*, 135, 792–796.

Gunderson, J. G., & Phillips, K. A. (1991). A current view of the interface between borderline personality disorder and depression. *American Journal of Psychiatry*, 148, 967–975.

Gunderson, J. G., & Singer, M. T. (1975). Defining borderline patients: An overview. *American Journal of Psychiatry, 132,* 1–10.

Helgeland, M. I., & Torgersen, S. (2004). Developmental antecedents of borderline personality disorder. *Comprehensive Psychiatry, 45,* 138–147.

Herpertz, S. C., Dietrich, T. M., Wenning, B., Krings, T., Erberich, S. G., Willmes, K., ... Sass, H. (2001). Evidence of abnormal amygdala functioning in borderline personality disorder: A functional MRI study. *Biological Psychiatry, 50,* 292–298.

Hurt, S. W., Hyler, S. E., Frances, A., Clarkin, J. F., & Brent, R. (1989). Assessing borderline personality disorder with self-report, clinical interview, or semistructured interview. *American Journal of Psychiatry, 141,* 1228–1231.

Jackson, H. J., & Burgess P. M. (2004). Personality disorders in the community: results from the Australian National Survey of Mental Health and Well-being Part III. Relationships between specific type of personality disorder, Axis I mental disorders and physical conditions with disability and health consultations. *Social Psychiatry & Psychiatric Epidemiology, 39,* 765–776.

Jørgensen, C. R., Freund, C., Bøye, R., Jordet, H., Andersen, D., & Kjølbye, M. (2013). Outcome of mentalization-based and supportive psychotherapy in patients with borderline personality disorder: A randomized trial. *Acta Psychiatrica Scandinavica, 127,* 305–317.

Jørgensen, C. R., Kjølbye, M., Freund, C., Bøye, R., Jordet, H., & Andersen, D. (2009). Level of functioning in patients with borderline personality disorder: The Risskov-I study. *Nordic Psychology, 61,* 42–60.

Kaess, M., Brunner, R., & Chanen, A. (2014). Borderline personality disorder in adolescence. *Pediatrics, 134*(4), 782–793.

Kernberg, O. F. (1967). Borderline personality organization. *Journal of the American Psychoanalytic Association, 15*(3), 641–685.

Kernberg, O. F. (1968). The treatment of patients with borderline personality organization. *International Journal of Psychoanalysis, 49,* 600–619.

Kernberg, O. F. (1975). *Borderline Conditions and Pathological Narcissism.* New York: Jason Aronson.

Knappich, M., Hörz-Sagstetter, S., Schwerthöffer, D., Leucht, S., & Rentrop, M. (2014). Pharmacotherapy in the treatment of patients with borderline personality disorder: Results of a survey among psychiatrists in private practices. *International Clinical Psychopharmacology, 29*(4), 224–228.

Knight, R. P. (1953). Borderline states. *Bulletin of the Menninger Clinic, 17*(1), 1–12.

Koenigsberg, H. W., Fan, J., Ochsner, K. N., Liu, X., Guise, K. G., Pizzarello, S., ... New, A. (2009). Neural correlates of the use of psychological distancing to regulate responses to negative social cues: A study of patients with borderline personality disorder. *Biological Psychiatry, 66*(9), 854–863.

Koons, C. R., Chapman, A. L., Betts, B. B., O'Rourke, B., Morse, N., & Robins, C. J. (2006). Dialectical behavior therapy adapted for the vocational rehabilitation of significantly disabled mentally ill adults. *Cognitive and Behavioral Practice, 13,* 146–156.

Krause-Utz, A., Winter, D., Niedtfeld, I., & Schmahl, C. (2014). The latest neuroimaging findings in borderline personality disorder. *Current Psychiatry Reports, 16*(3), 438–450.

Larrivée, M.-P. (2013). Borderline personality disorder in adolescents: the He-who-must-not-be-named of psychiatry. *Dialogues in Clinical Neuroscience, 15*(2), 171–179.

Leichsenring, F., Leibing, E., Kruse, J., New, A. S., & Leweke, F. (2011). Borderline personality disorder. *The Lancet, 377,* 74–84.

Lenzenweger, M. F., Lane, M. C., Loranger, A. W., & Kessler, R. C. (2007). DSM-IV personality disorders in the National Comorbidity Survey replication. *Biological Psychiatry, 62,* 553–564.

Lieb, K., Völlm, B., Rücker, G., Timmer, A., & Stoffers, J. M. (2010). Pharmacotherapy for borderline personality disorder: Cochrane systematic review of randomised trials. *British Journal of Psychiatry, 196*(1), 4–12.

Lieb, K., Zanarini, M. C., Schmahl, C., Linehan, M. M., & Bohus (2004). Borderline personality disorder. *Lancet, 364,* 453–461.

Linehan, M. M. (1993a). *Cognitive-Behavioral Treatment of Borderline Personality Disorder.* New York: Guilford Press.

Linehan, M. M. (1993b). *Skills Training Manual for Treating Borderline Personality Disorder.* New York: Guilford Press.

Linehan, M. M. (2014). *DBT Skills Training Manual.* New York: Guilford Press.

Linehan, M. M., Armstrong, H. E., Suarez, A., Allmon, D., & Heard, H. (1991). Cognitive behavioral treatment of chronically parasuicidal borderline patients. *Archives of General Psychiatry, 48,* 1060–1064.

Linehan, M. M., & Heard, H. L. (1999). Borderline personality disorder: Costs, course, and treatment outcomes. In N. Miller & K. Magruder (Eds.) *The Cost-Effectiveness of Psychotherapy: A Guide for Practitioners, Researchers and Policy Makers* (pp. 291–305). New York: Oxford University Press.

Links, P.S., Heslegrave, R., & van Reekum, R. (1999). Impulsivity: Core aspect of borderline personality disorder. *Journal of Personality Disorders, 12,* 1–9.

Links, P. S., Steiner, M., & Huxley, G. (1988). The occurrence of borderline personality disorder in the families of borderline patients. *Journal of Personality Disorders, 2*(1), 14–20.

Loranger, A. W., Oldham, J. M., & Tulis, E. H. (1982). Familial transmission of DSM-III borderline personality disorder. *Archives of General Psychiatry, 39*(7), 795–799.

Manning, S. (2011). *Loving Someone with Borderline Personality Disorder.* New York: Guilford Press.

Masterson, J. (1972). *Treatment of the Borderline Adolescent: A Developmental Approach.* New York: John Wiley & Sons.

McCloskey, M. S., New, A. S., Siever, L. J., Goodman, M., Koenigsberg, H. W., Flory, J. D., & Coccaro, E. F. (2009). Evaluation of behavioral impulsivity and aggression tasks as endophenotypes for borderline personality disorder. *Journal of Psychiatric Research, 43*(12), 1036–1048.

McMain, S. F., Guimond, T., Barnhart, R., Habinski, L., & Streiner, D. L. (2017). A randomized trial of brief dialectical behaviour therapy skills training in suicidal patients suffering from borderline disorder. *Acta Psychiatrica Scandinavica, 135,* 138–148.

McMain, S. F., Links, P. S., Gnam, W. H., Guimond, T., Cardish, R. J., Korman, L., & Streiner, D. L. (2009). A randomized trial of dialectical behavior therapy versus general psychiatric management for borderline personality disorder. *American Journal of Psychiatry, 166,* 1365–1374.

McMain, S., & Pos, A. E. (2007). Advances in psychotherapy of personality disorders: A research update. *Current Psychiatry Reports, 9*(1), 46–52.

Mehlum, L., Tørmoen, A. J., Ramberg, M., Haga, E., Diep, L. M., Laberg, S., ... Grøholt, B. (2014). Dialectical behavior therapy for adolescents with repeated suicidal and self-harming behavior: A randomized trial. *Journal of the American Academy of Child & Adolescent Psychiatry, 53,* 1082–1091.

Miller, A. L., Muehlenkamp, J. J., & Jacobson, C. M. (2008). Fact or fiction: Diagnosing borderline personality disorder in adolescents. *Clinical Psychology Review, 28*(6), 969–981.

Millon, T., Grossman, S., & Meagher, S. E. (2004). *Masters of the Mind: Exploring the Story of Mental Illness from Ancient Times to the New Millennium*. New York: John Wiley & Sons.

Minzenberg, M. J., Fan, J., New, A. S., Tang, C. Y., & Siever, L. J. (2007). Fronto-limbic dysfunction in response to facial emotion in borderline personality disorder: An event-related fMRI study. *Psychiatry Research: Neuroimaging, 155*(3), 231–243.

Morey, L. C., Warner, M. B., Shea, M. T., Gunderson, J. G., Sanislow, C. A., Grilo, C., … McGlashan, T. H. (2003). The representation of four personality disorders by the schedule for nonadaptive and adaptive personality dimensional model of personality. *Psychological Assessment, 15*(3), 326–332.

National Collaborating Centre for Mental Health (NICE). (2009). *Borderline Personality Disorder: Treatment and Management*. London: The British Psychological Society and The Royal College of Psychiatrists.

National Health and Medical Research Council (NHMRC). (2012). *Clinical Practice Guideline for the Management of Borderline Personality Disorder*. Melbourne: National Health and Medical Research Council.

Neacsiu, A. D., Eberle, J. W., Kramer, R., Wiesmann, T., & Linehan, M. M. (2014). Dialectical behavior therapy skills for transdiagnostic emotion dysregulation: A pilot randomized controlled trial. *Behaviour Research and Therapy, 59*, 40–51.

Neacsiu, A. D., Rizvi, S. L., & Linehan, M. M. (2010). Dialectical behavior therapy skills use as a mediator and outcome of treatment for borderline personality disorder. *Behaviour Research and Therapy, 48*(9), 832–839.

O'Toole, S. K., Diddy, E., & Kent, M. (2011). Mindfulness and emotional well-being in women with borderline personality disorder. *Mindfulness, 3*, 117–123.

Paris, J. (1998). Does childhood trauma cause personality disorders in adults? *Canadian Journal of Psychiatry, 43*(2), 148–153.

Paris, J. (2002). Commentary on the American Psychiatric Association guidelines for the treatment of borderline personality disorder: Evidence-based psychiatry and the quality of evidence. *Journal of Personality Disorders, 16*(2), 130–134.

Paris, J., & Zweig-Frank, H. (2001). A 27-year follow-up of patients with borderline personality disorder. *Comprehensive Psychiatry, 42*(6), 482–487.

Paris, J., Zweig-Frank, H., & Guzder, J. (1994). Psychological risk factors for borderline personality disorder in female patients. *Comprehensive Psychiatry, 35*(4), 301–305.

Perepletchikova, F., Nathanson, D., Axelrod, S. R., Merrill, C., Walker, A., Grossman, M., … Walkup, J. (2017). Randomized clinical trial of dialectical behavior therapy for preadolescent children with disruptive mood dysregulation disorder: Feasibility and outcomes. *Journal of the American Academy of Child & Adolescent Psychiatry, 56*, 832–840.

Perroud, N., Uher, R., Dieben, K., Nicastro, R., & Huguelet, P. (2010). Predictors of response and drop-out during intensive dialectical behavior therapy. *Journal of Personality Disorders, 24*(5), 634–650.

Perry, J. C., Herman, J. L., Van Der Kolk, B. A., & Hoke, L. A. (1990). Psychotherapy and psychological trauma in borderline personality disorder. *Psychiatric Annals, 20*(1), 33–43.

Pope, H. G., Jonas, J. M., Hudson, J. I., Cohen, B. M., & Gunderson, J. G. (1983). The validity of DSM-III borderline personality disorder: A phenomenologic, family history, treatment response, and long-term followup study. *Archives of General Psychiatry, 40*, 23–30.

Rosenthal, M. Z., Gratz, K. L., Kosson, D. S., Cheavens, J. S., Lejuez, C. W., & Lynch, T. R. (2008). Borderline personality disorder and emotional responding: A review of the research literature. *Clinical Psychology Review, 28*, 75–91.

Rossouw, T. I., & Fonagy, P. (2012). Mentalization-based treatment for self-harm in adolescents: A randomized controlled trial. *Journal of the American Academy of Child & Adolescent Psychiatry, 51*, 1304–1313.

Rottman, B. M., Ahn, W. K., Sanislow, C. A., & Kim, N. S. (2009). Can clinicians recognize DSM-IV personality disorders from five-factor model descriptions of patient cases? *American Journal of Psychiatry, 166*(4), 427–433.

Rottman, B. M., Kim, N. S., Ahn, W. K., & Sanislow, C. A. (2011). Can personality disorder experts recognize DSM-IV personality disorders from five-factor model descriptions of patient cases? *Journal of Clinical Psychiatry, 72*(5), 630–639.

Rudge, S., Feigenbaum, J. D., & Fonagy, P. (2017). Mechanisms of change in dialectical behaviour therapy and cognitive behaviour therapy for borderline personality disorder: A critical review of the literature. *Journal of Mental Health.* doi:10.1080/09638237.2017.1322185

Sahlin, H., Bjureberg, J., Gratz, K. L., Tull, M. T., Hedman, E., Bjärehed, J., … Hellner, C. (2017). Emotion regulation group therapy for deliberate self-harm: A multi-site evaluation in routine care using an uncontrolled open trial design. *BMJ Open, 7*, e016220. doi:10.1136/bmjopen-2017-016220

Samuel, D. B., Sanislow, C. A., Hopwood, C. J., Shea, M. T., Skodol, A. E., Morey, L. C., … Grilo, C. M. (2013). Convergent and incremental predictive validity of clinician, self-report, and structured interview diagnoses for personality disorders over 5 years. *Journal of Consulting and Clinical Psychology, 81*(4), 650–659.

Sanislow, C. A., Grilo, C. M., & McGlashan, T. H. (2000). Factor analysis of the DSM-III-R borderline personality disorder criteria in psychiatric inpatients. *American Journal of Psychiatry, 157*, 1629–1633.

Sanislow, C. A., Grilo, C. M., Morey, L. C., Bender, D. S., Skodol, A. E., Gunderson, J. G., … McGlashan, T. H. (2002). Confirmatory factor analysis of DSM-IV criteria for borderline personality disorder: Findings from the collaborative longitudinal personality disorders study. *American Journal of Psychiatry, 159*(2), 284–290.

Sansone, R. A., Farukhi, S., & Wiederman, M. W. (2011). Utilization of primary care physicians in borderline personality. *General Hospital Psychiatry, 33*(4), 343–346.

Sar, V., Akyuz, G., Kugu, N., Ozturk, E., & Ertem-Vehid, H. (2006). Axis I dissociative disorder comorbidity in borderline personality disorder and reports of childhood trauma. *Journal of Clinical Psychiatry, 67*, 1583–1590.

Schmahl, C. G., Vermetten, E., Elzinga, B. M., & Bremner, J. D. (2003). Magnetic resonance imaging of hippocampal and amygdala volume in women with childhood abuse and borderline personality disorder. *Psychiatry Research: Neuroimaging, 122*(3), 193–198.

Schmahl, C. G., Vermetten, E., Elzinga, B. M., & Bremner, J. D. (2004). A positron emission tomography study of memories of childhood abuse in borderline personality disorder. *Biological Psychiatry, 55*(7), 759–765.

Schmitt, R., Winter, D., Niedtfeld, I., Herpertz, S. C., & Schmahl, C. (2016). Effects of psychotherapy on neuronal correlates of reappraisal in female patients with borderline personality disorder. *Biological Psychiatry: Cognitive Neuroscience and Neuroimaging, 1*, 548–557.

Schulze, L., Schmahl, C., & Niedtfeld, I. (2016). Neural correlates of disturbed emotion processing in borderline personality disorder: A multimodal meta-analysis. *Biological Psychiatry, 79*, 97–106.

Sebastian, A., Pohl, M. F., Klöppel, S., Feige, B., Lange, T., Stahl, C., ... Tüscher, O. (2013). Disentangling common and specific neural subprocesses of response inhibition. *NeuroImage, 24*, 601–615.

Siever, L. J., Torgersen, S., Gunderson, J. G., Livesley, W. J., & Kendler, K. S. (2002). The borderline diagnosis III: Identifying endophenotypes for genetic studies. *Biological Psychiatry, 51*(12), 964–968.

Silk, K. R., Eisner, W., Allport, C., Demars, C., Miller, C., Justice, R. W., & Lewis, M. (1994). Focused time-limited inpatient treatment of borderline personality disorder. *Journal of Personality Disorders, 8*, 268–278.

Silvers, J. A., Hubbard, A. D., Biggs, E., Shu, J., Fertuck, E., Chaudhury, S., ... Brodsky, B. S. (2016). Affective lability and difficulties with regulation are differentially associated with amygdala and prefrontal response in women with borderline personality disorder. *Psychiatry Research: Neuroimaging, 254*, 74–82.

Skodol, A. E., Buckley, P., & Charles, E. (1983). Is there a characteristic pattern to the treatment history of clinic outpatients with borderline personality? *Journal of Nervous and Mental Disease, 171*, 405–410.

Skodol, A. E., Siever, L. J., Livesley, W. J., Gunderson, J. G., Pfohl, B., & Widiger T. A. (2002). The borderline diagnosis II: Biology, genetics and clinical course. *Society of Biological Psychiatry, 51*, 951–963.

Soloff, P. H., & Chiappetta, L. (2017). Suicidal behavior and psychosocial outcome in borderline personality disorder at 8-year follow-up. *Journal of Personality Disorders, 31*(6), 774–789.

Stepp, S. D., Burke, J. D., Hipwell, A. E., & Loeber, R. (2012). Trajectories of attention deficit hyperactivity disorder and oppositional defiant disorder symptoms as precursors of borderline personality disorder symptoms in adolescent girls. *Journal of Abnormal Child Psychology, 40*(1), 7–20.

Stepp, S. D., Epler, A. J., Jahng, S., & Trull, T. J. (2008). The effect of dialectical behavior therapy skills use on borderline personality disorder features. *Journal of Personality Disorders, 22*(6), 549–563.

Stepp, S. D., & Pilkonis, P. A. (2008). Age-related differences in individual DSM criteria for borderline personality disorder. *Journal of Personality Disorders, 22*(4), 427–432.

Stern, A. (1938) Psychoanalytic investigation of and therapy in the borderline group of neuroses. *The Psychoanalytic Quarterly, 7*, 467–489.

Stoffers, J. M., & Lieb, K. (2015). Pharmacotherapy for borderline personality disorder: Current evidence and recent trends. *Current Psychiatry Reports, 17*(534) 1–11.

Stoffers, J. M., Voellm, B. A., Rücker, G., Timmer, A., Huband, N., & Lieb, K. (2012). Psychological therapies for people with borderline personality disorder. *The Cochrane Library.* doi: 10.1002/14651858.CD005652.pub2

Stone, M. H. (1993). Long-term outcome in personality disorders. *British Journal of Psychiatry, 162*(3), 299–313.

Thomsen, M. S., Ruocco, A. C., Uliaszek, A. A., Mathiesen, B. B., & Simonsen, E. (2017). Changes in neurocognitive functioning after 6 months of mentalization-based treatment for borderline personality disorder. *Journal of Personality Disorders, 31*(3), 306–324.

Torgersen, S., Lygren, S., Øien, P. A., Skre, I., Onstad, S., Edvardsen, J., ... Kringlen, E. (2000). A twin study of personality disorders. *Comprehensive Psychiatry, 41*(6), 416–425.

Trippany, R. L., Helm, H. M., & Simpson, L. (2006). Trauma reenactment: Rethinking borderline personality disorder when diagnosing sexual abuse survivors. *Journal of Mental Health Counseling, 28*(2), 95–110.

Trull, T. J. (2001). Structural relations between borderline personality disorder features and putative etiological correlates. *Journal of Abnormal Psychology, 110*(3), 471–481.

Trull, T. J., Distel, M. A., & Carpenter, R. W. (2011). DSM-5 borderline personality disorder: At the border between a dimensional and a categorical view. *Current Psychiatry Reports, 13*(1), 43–49.

Turner, B. J., Austin, S. B., & Chapman, A. L. (2014). Treating nonsuicidal self-injury: A systematic review of psychological and pharmacological interventions. *Canadian Journal of Psychiatry, 59*, 576–585.

Tyrer, P., & Bateman, A. W. (2004). Drug treatment for personality disorders. *Advances in Psychiatric Treatment, 10*(5), 389–398.

Tyrer, P., Crawford, M., Mulder, R., & the ICD-11 Working Group for the Revision of Classification of Personality Disorders (2011). Reclassifying personality disorders. *Lancet, 377*, 1814–1815.

Van Busschbach, J (2012). Health economics and borderline personality disorders: Methods, arguments and perspectives. Paper presented at The 2nd International congress on Borderline Personality Disorder and Allied Disorders, Amsterdam, Netherlands.

van der Kolk, B. A., Pelcovitz, D., Roth, S., & Mandel, F. S. (1996). Dissociation, somatization, and affect dysregulation: The complexity of adaption to trauma. *American Journal of Psychiatry, 153*, 83–93.

van Elst, L. T., Hesslinger, B., Thiel, T., Geiger, E., Haegele, K., Lemieux, L., ... Ebert, D. (2003). Frontolimbic brain abnormalities in patients with borderline personality disorder: A volumetric magnetic resonance imaging study. *Biological Psychiatry, 54*(2), 163–171.

Westen, D., Ludolph, P., Misle, B., Ruffins, S., & Block, J. (1990). Physical and sexual abuse in adolescent girls with borderline personality disorder. *American Journal of Orthopsychiatry, 60*(1), 55–66.

White, C. N., Gunderson, J. G., Zanarini, M. C., & Hudson, J. I. (2003). Family studies of borderline personality disorder: A review. *Harvard Review of Psychiatry, 11*(1), 8–19.

Winograd, G., Cohen, P., & Chen, H. (2008). Adolescent borderline symptoms in the community: Prognosis for functioning over 20 years. *Journal of Child Psychology & Psychiatry, 49*, 933–941.

World Health Organization [WHO]. (2016). *International Statistical Classification of Diseases and Related Health Problems* (10th rev.). Geneva: WHO Press.

World Health Organization [WHO]. (2018). *International Statistical Classification of Diseases and Related Health Problems* (11th rev.). Geneva: WHO Press.

Yen, S., Shea, M. T., Battle, C. L., Johnson, D. M., Zlotnick, C., Dolan-Sewell, R., ... Zanarini, M. C. (2002). Traumatic exposure and posttraumatic stress disorder in borderline, schizotypal, avoidant, and obsessive-compulsive personality disorders: Findings from the Collaborative Longitudinal Personality Disorders study. *Journal of Nervous and Mental Disease, 190*(8), 510–518.

Zanarini, M. C., & Frankenburg, F. R. (1997). Pathways to the development of borderline personality disorder. *Journal of Personality Disorders, 11*, 93–104.

Zanarini, M. C., Frankenburg, F. R., Hennen, J., Reich, D. B., & Silk, K. R. (2005). The McLean Study of Adult Development (MSAD): Overview and implications of the first six years of prospective follow-up. *Journal of Personality Disorders, 19*(5), 505–523.

Zanarini, M. C., Frankenburg, F. R., Hennen, J., & Silk, K. R. (2004). Mental health service utilization by borderline personality disorder patients and Axis II comparison subjects followed prospectively for 6 years. *Journal of Clinical Psychiatry, 65*, 28–36.

Zanarini, M. C., Frankenburg, F. R., Khera, G. S., & Bleichmar, J. (2001). Treatment histories of borderline inpatients. *Comprehensive Psychiatry, 42*(2), 144–150.

Zanarini, M. C., Frankenburg, F. R., Reich, D. B., & Fitzmuarice, G. (2010). Time to attainment of recovery from borderline personality disorder and stability of recovery: A 10-year prospective follow-up study. *American Journal of Psychiatry, 167*(6), 663–667.

Zanarini, M. C., Frankenburg, F. R., Reich, D. B., & Fitzmuarice, G. (2012). Attainment and stability of sustained symptomatic remission and recovery among patients with borderline personality disorder and Axis II comparison subjects: A 16-year prospective follow-up study. *American Journal of Psychiatry, 169*(5), 476–483.

Zanarini, M. C., Gunderson, J. G., Marino, M. F., Schwartz, E. O., & Frankenburg, F. R. (1988). DSM-III disorders in the families of borderline outpatients. *Journal of Personality Disorders, 2*(4), 292–302.

Zanarini, M. C., Jacoby, R. J., Frankenburg, F. R., Reich, D. B., & Fitzmaurice, G. (2009). The 10-year course of social security disability income reported by patients with borderline personality disorder and axis II comparison subjects. *Journal of Personality Disorders, 23*(4), 346–356.

Zanarini, M. C., Williams, A. A., Lewis, R. E., & Reich, R. B. (1997). Reported pathological childhood experiences associated with the development of borderline personality disorder. *American Journal of Psychiatry, 154*(8), 1101–1106.

Zanarini, M. C., Yong, L., Frankenburg, F. R., Hennen, J., Reich, D. B., Marino, M. F., & Vujanovic, A. A. (2002). Severity of reported childhood sexual abuse and its relationship to severity of borderline psychopathology and psychosocial impairment among borderline inpatients. *Journal of Nervous and Mental Disease, 190*(6), 381–387.

10a Further Reflections on Assessment, Etiology, and Treatment: Commentary on Borderline Personality Disorder

LORI N. SCOTT AND PAUL A. PILKONIS

We appreciate the cogent chapter on borderline personality disorder (BPD) provided by Chapman, Hope, and Turner (this volume). Our goal in this commentary is to provide additional emphasis and recommendations relevant to three themes – assessment, etiology, and treatment – that we hope can guide further research and innovation in these areas.

ASSESSMENT OF BPD

Debates have emerged in recent years about how best to define and diagnose BPD, as well as personality disorders (PDs) in general. The most controversial issue has been whether to abandon the traditional categorical system of the DSM in favor of dimensional trait models. A related issue is whether BPD should be conceptualized as a multidimensional or unidimensional construct. As reviewed by Chapman et al., some factor analytic studies (Clarkin, Hull, & Hurt, 1993; Sanislow, Grilo, & McGlashan, 2000) identified three factors underlying the BPD criteria (i.e., affective dysregulation, behavioral dysregulation, and disturbed relatedness). Though these findings have been interpreted as evidence of multidimensionality, the high correlations between these factors (above .90) are more suggestive of a higher-order unidimensional construct than multiple independent domains. Accordingly, findings from several other studies (e.g., Clifton & Pilkonis, 2007; Feske, Kirisci, Tarter, & Pilkonis, 2007) demonstrated that a single-factor solution is the most psychometrically sound when compared to multidimensional structures, supporting the unidimensionality of BPD for measurement purposes. These findings suggest that the DSM criteria for BPD (despite their apparent diversity) form a single coherent construct, for which BPD severity can be assessed along a dimensional continuum.

However, Feske and colleagues (2007) found that the DSM criteria functioned best for the assessment of BPD at moderate to severe levels of symptom severity. Given evidence for significant functional impairment among people with subthreshold BPD symptoms (e.g., Trull,

Useda, Conforti, & Doan, 1997), there is a need to develop criteria and measures by which to identify individuals with lower levels of symptoms (including prodromal symptoms) who could benefit from BPD-relevant interventions to prevent full development of the acute disorder. Evidence indicates that the presence of three or more BPD criteria has clinical significance in terms of functional outcomes (Clifton & Pilkonis, 2007). Studies with college student samples have identified a score of 38 or higher (T > 70) on the Personality Assessment Inventory – Borderline Features Scale (Morey, 1991) as a clinically meaningful threshold for BPD (Trull et al., 1997). These thresholds, however, rely on a conceptualization of BPD consistent with the DSM criteria. Clinically validated thresholds for dimensional trait measures of BPD (and PDs in general) are missing, limiting the clinical utility of a dimensional framework for assessment and diagnosis. If alternative models of PDs are to gain traction in clinical settings, measures capturing the full range of PD severity need to be developed, along with clinically valid cutoffs and corresponding recommendations for clinical care at various levels of severity and stages of the development of a disorder.

ETIOLOGY OF BPD

Though diagnosis of BPD in children and adolescents has been controversial, considerable evidence has now accumulated to challenge the view that BPD cannot be diagnosed until adulthood (Winsper et al., 2016). In addition, much has been learned from longitudinal studies about risk factors for the development of BPD in childhood and adolescence (Stepp, Lazarus, & Byrd, 2016). Some of the most consistently identified early risk factors for BPD include low socioeconomic status, stressful life events, early adversity, maternal psychopathology, maladaptive parenting, maltreatment, and child temperamental characteristics (for a review, see Stepp et al., 2016). Unfortunately, however, there is a lack of specificity of identified risk markers for BPD, as all the identified factors are known risk factors for multiple types of psychopathology. Further, few studies have been able to identify predictors of *onset* of the disorder, which is important for achieving our goal of preventing BPD.

As noted in the target chapter, much of what is known about risk for BPD in children and adolescents has come from community-based longitudinal studies, such as the Pittsburgh Girls Study (PGS; for details, see Keenan et al., 2010). Findings from several analyses from the PGS support the stability and validity of BPD features in childhood and adolescence (Stepp & Lazarus, 2017; Stepp, Pilkonis, Hipwell, Loeber, & Stouthamer-Loeber, 2010). Analyses from the PGS have also elucidated how childhood temperament, environmental, and parenting factors interact (Scott, Zalewski, Beeney, Jones, & Stepp, 2017; Stepp, Scott, Jones, Whalen, & Hipwell, 2015) and transact (e.g., Stepp et al., 2014) to shape the course of BPD symptoms in adolescence. These results highlight the importance of longitudinal research during critical developmental periods to further assess the *transactional* nature of both static and dynamic child and environmental factors, especially in the parent–child context, as these are likely to be important targets in both individual and family-based interventions for emergent BPD in youth.

FUTURE DIRECTIONS IN TREATMENT DEVELOPMENT

Need for Psychosocial Rehabilitation

Despite increased optimism about the remission of BPD (defined as no longer meeting full diagnostic criteria for the disorder), many patients who remit in categorical terms remain functionally impaired. In one longitudinal study of BPD patients at 10-year follow-up (Soloff & Chiappetta, 2018), 44 percent still suffered from poor overall psychosocial, vocational, and economic functioning even though most participants showed significant decreases in BPD symptoms and substance abuse. Similarly, despite the high rate of remission in the McLean Study of Adult Development, 40 percent of patients demonstrated poor psychosocial functioning (defined as a Global Assessment of Functioning (GAF) score < 61) at 16- and 20-year follow-ups (Zanarini, Frankenburg, Reich, & Fitzmaurice, 2012; Zanarini, Temes, Frankenburg, Reich, & Fitzmaurice, 2018). We agree with others (e.g., Links, 1993; Zanarini et al., 2012, 2018) who have proposed a psychosocial rehabilitation model of treatment for BPD patients, regardless of any specific theoretical approach. Evidence from longitudinal studies supports the need to target improved social integration, engagement, and effectiveness in major social roles (i.e., work and love).

Improving Interpersonal Relatedness

Chapman and colleagues discuss emotion dysregulation as the central difficulty in BPD and the driving force behind other BPD symptoms (e.g., interpersonal conflict, self-harm, dissociation). We would argue that there is a more reciprocal relationship between emotion dysregulation and the challenging interpersonal behaviors seen in those with BPD, and that this relationship can be understood through the lens of attachment theory (Bowlby, 1969), which is fundamentally about emotion regulation within interpersonal contexts. One implication of this is that improving interpersonal relatedness, especially with important attachment figures, may be as valuable a target for treatments of BPD as enhancing intrapersonal capacities for emotion regulation.

A sense of felt attachment security serves a number of important self-regulatory functions, including the ability to regulate emotional experiences through constructive strategies (e.g., reappraisal, self-soothing, problem-solving) and to effectively seek and obtain support from others in times of distress (Shaver & Mikulincer, 2007). Both clinical and empirical observations (for a review, see Gunderson & Lyons-Ruth, 2008) suggest that persons with BPD lack a sense of felt security and are prone to a *hyperactivation* of the attachment system in the context of emotional distress or perceived threat of abandonment, resulting in hypervigilance to the availability of attachment figures, intensification and exaggeration of negative affect, and other maladaptive behaviors that exacerbate distress (e.g., impulsive self-destructive behaviors and frantic attempts to avoid abandonment). Hence, many of the interpersonal and mood-dependent behaviors of persons with BPD can be understood as ineffective attempts to seek support and soothing from important others and to modulate emotional distress through interpersonal relatedness.

Our previous work suggests that these behaviors are most pronounced in romantic relationships, which form the basis for most attachment bonds in adulthood (Hill et al., 2008, 2011). We have also demonstrated that, in BPD, a hyperactivated, anxious attachment to the romantic partner is displayed as both intense emotional reactivity (especially in terms of anger and hostility) in response to perceived rejection and attenuated positive emotions in response to acceptance from romantic partners (Lazarus et al., 2018). These findings, combined with evidence for the importance of positive relationships in predicting the longitudinal course of BPD symptoms (Links & Heslegrave, 2000; Pagano et al., 2004), suggest that enhancing patients' ability for positive relatedness and modulation of emotions through transactions with attachment figures (including couples-based interventions) may lead to improved emotion regulation and a better chance for sustained recovery through the buffering effects of secure attachment.

Developing Personalized Interventions

Though evidence-based treatments for BPD now exist, their effects are modest, variable (including high rates of dropout; Levy, 2008), and unstable over follow-up (Cristea et al., 2017). One limitation to clinical trials is their focus on group differences in response to treatment, which have limited utility for conceptualizing and treating an individual patient. Such variable-centered approaches cannot address person-centered dynamic processes and heterogeneity in these processes. This limitation has impeded progress in understanding mechanisms of change and resulted in the use of one-size-fits-all treatment packages for patients who are heterogeneous. In this current era of evolving precision medicine, we must embrace methods that have greater sensitivity to the dynamic nature of both symptoms and therapeutic change processes and that examine change at both the group and person levels.

Of primary interest to most clinicians is how to predict *when* or *under what conditions* any specific individual may experience *an increase* in a specific symptom, or how a specific intervention or changes in a supposed mechanism may relate to change in a symptom *within the same individual* (Hoffart & Johnson, 2017). Such dynamic processes can now be captured more easily with available technologies. With mobile devices, patients can report on their moods, behaviors, and other experiences in real time. Continuous background data (e.g., ambient noise, sleep quality, social interactions, physical activity) can also be collected by mobile and wearable devices. Given such advances, clinicians should be encouraged to consider ambulatory assessment of patients and applications that promote the translation of real-time data into individually tailored adaptive interventions. Researchers should also be encouraged to embrace novel statistical methods for understanding heterogeneity in idiographic dynamic processes and developing person-specific models, e.g., group iterative multiple model estimation (Beltz, Wright, Sprague, & Molenaar, 2016) and machine learning (Patrick & Hajcak, 2016). Such work can lead to the development of personalized approaches to case conceptualization and intervention for BPD, ultimately providing hope for recovery to more patients and their loved ones.

REFERENCES

Beltz, A. M., Wright, A. G. C., Sprague, B. N., & Molenaar, P. C. M. (2016). Bridging the nomothetic and idiographic approaches to the analysis of clinical data. *Assessment*, 23(4), 447–458.

Bowlby, J. (1969). *Attachment and Loss, Volume 1: Attachment*. New York: Basic Books.

Clarkin, J. F., Hull, J. W., & Hurt, S. W. (1993). Factor structure of borderline personality disorder criteria. *Journal of Personality Disorders*, 7(2), 137–143.

Clifton, A., & Pilkonis, P. A. (2007). Evidence for a single latent class of Diagnostic and Statistical Manual of Mental Disorders borderline personality pathology. *Comprehensive Psychiatry*, 48(1), 70–78.

Cristea, I. A., Gentili, C., Cotet, C. D., Palomba, D., Barbui, C., & Cuijpers, P. (2017). Efficacy of psychotherapies for borderline personality disorder: A systematic review and meta-analysis. *JAMA Psychiatry*, 74(4), 319–328.

Feske, U., Kirisci, L., Tarter, R. E., & Pilkonis, P. A. (2007). An application of item response theory to the DSM-III-R criteria for borderline personality disorder. *Journal of Personality Disorders*, 21(4), 418–433.

Gunderson, J. G., & Lyons-Ruth, K. (2008). BPD's interpersonal hypersensitivity phenotype: A gene-environment-developmental model. *Journal of Personality Disorders*, 22(1), 22–41.

Hill, J., Pilkonis, P., Morse, J., Feske, U., Reynolds, S., Hope, H., . . . Broyden, N. (2008). Social domain dysfunction and disorganization in borderline personality disorder. *Psychological Medicine*, 38(1), 135–146.

Hill, J., Stepp, S. D., Wan, M. W., Hope, H., Morse, J. Q., Steele, M., . . . Pilkonis, P. A. (2011). Attachment, borderline personality, and romantic relationship dysfunction. *Journal of Personality Disorders*, 25(6), 789–805.

Hoffart, A., & Johnson, S. U. (2017). Psychodynamic and cognitive-behavioral therapies are more different than you think: Conceptualizations of mental problems and consequences for studying mechanisms of change. *Clinical Psychological Science*, 5(6), 1070–1086.

Keenan, K., Hipwell, A., Chung, T., Stepp, S., Stouthamer-Loeber, M., Loeber, R., & McTigue, K. (2010). The Pittsburgh Girls Study: Overview and initial findings. *Journal of Clinical Child and Adolescent Psychology*, 39(4), 506–521.

Lazarus, S. A., Scott, L. N., Beeney, J. E., Wright, A. G., Stepp, S. D., & Pilkonis, P. A. (2018). Borderline personality disorder symptoms and affective responding to perceptions of rejection and acceptance from romantic versus nonromantic partners. *Personality Disorders: Theory, Research, and Treatment*, 9(3), 197–206.

Levy, K. N. (2008). Psychotherapies and lasting change. *American Journal of Psychiatry*, 165(5), 556–559.

Links, P. S. (1993). Psychiatric rehabilitation model for borderline personality disorder. *Canadian Journal of Psychiatry*, 38(Suppl. 1), 35–38.

Links, P. S., & Heslegrave, R. J. (2000). Prospective studies of outcome: Understanding mechanisms of change in patients with borderline personality disorder. *Psychiatric Clinics of North America*, 23(1), 137–150.

Morey, L. C. (1991). *Personality Assessment Inventory: Professional Manual*. Odessa, FL: Psychological Assessment Resources.

Pagano, M. E., Skodol, A. E., Stout, R. L., Shea, M. T., Yen, S., Grilo, C. M., . . . Gunderson, J. G. (2004). Stressful life events as predictors of functioning: Findings from the collaborative longitudinal personality disorders study. *Acta Psychiatrica Scandinavica*, 110(6), 421–429.

Patrick, C. J., & Hajcak, G. (2016). RDoC: Translating promise into progress. *Psychophysiology*, 53(3), 415–424.

Sanislow, C. A., Grilo, C. M., & McGlashan, T. H. (2000). Factor analysis of the DSM-III-R borderline personality disorder criteria in psychiatric inpatients. *American Journal of Psychiatry*, 157(10), 1629–1633.

Scott, L. N., Zalewski, M., Beeney, J. E., Jones, N. P., & Stepp, S. D. (2017). Pupillary and affective responses to maternal feedback and the development of borderline personality disorder symptoms. *Developmental Psychopathology*, 29(3), 1089–1104.

Shaver, P. R., & Mikulincer, M. (2007). Adult attachment strategies and the regulation of emotion. In J. J. Gross (Ed.), *Handbook of Emotion Regulation* (pp. 446–465). New York: Guilford Press.

Soloff, P. H., & Chiappetta, L. (2018). Ten-year outcome of suicidal behavior in borderline personality disorder. *Journal of Personality Disorders, 33*(1), 1–19.

Stepp, S. D., & Lazarus, S. A. (2017). Identifying a borderline personality disorder prodrome: Implications for community screening. *Personality and Mental Health, 11*(3), 195–205.

Stepp, S. D., Lazarus, S. A., & Byrd, A. L. (2016). A systematic review of risk factors prospectively associated with borderline personality disorder: Taking stock and moving forward. *Personality Disorders: Theory, Research, and Treatment, 7*(4), 316–323.

Stepp, S. D., Pilkonis, P. A., Hipwell, A. E., Loeber, R., & Stouthamer-Loeber, M. (2010). Stability of borderline personality disorder features in girls. *Journal of Personality Disorders, 24*(4), 460–472.

Stepp, S. D., Scott, L. N., Jones, N. P., Whalen, D. J., & Hipwell, A. E. (2015). Negative emotional reactivity as a marker of vulnerability in the development of borderline personality disorder symptoms. *Development and Psychopathology, 28*(1), 213–224.

Stepp, S. D., Whalen, D. J., Scott, L. N., Zalewski, M., Loeber, R., & Hipwell, A. E. (2014). Reciprocal effects of parenting and borderline personality disorder symptoms in adolescent girls. *Development and Psychopathology, 26*(2), 361–378.

Trull, T. J., Useda, J. D., Conforti, K., & Doan, B. T. (1997). Borderline personality disorder features in nonclinical young adults: 2. Two-year outcome. *Journal of Abnormal Psychology, 106*(2), 307–314.

Winsper, C., Lereya, S. T., Marwaha, S., Thompson, A., Eyden, J., & Singh, S. P. (2016). The aetiological and psychopathological validity of borderline personality disorder in youth: A systematic review and meta-analysis. *Clinical Psychology Review, 44*, 13–24.

Zanarini, M. C., Frankenburg, F. R., Reich, D. B., & Fitzmaurice, G. (2012). Attainment and stability of sustained symptomatic remission and recovery among patients with borderline personality disorder and Axis II comparison subjects: A 16-year prospective follow-up study. *American Journal of Psychiatry, 169* (5), 476–483.

Zanarini, M. C., Temes, C. M., Frankenburg, F. R., Reich, D. B., & Fitzmaurice, G. M. (2018). Description and prediction of time-to-attainment of excellent recovery for borderline patients followed prospectively for 20 years. *Psychiatry Research, 262*, 40–45.

10b Integrating Neuroscience and Psychotherapy: Commentary on Borderline Personality Disorder

INGA NIEDTFELD, CHRISTIAN PARET, AND CHRISTIAN SCHMAHL

The chapter by Chapman and colleagues (this volume) gives an excellent overview of the current state of knowledge on all aspects of borderline personality disorder (BPD). We would like to take the opportunity to extend the scope of the chapter by adding our view regarding a particularly important issue, namely the interaction between neuroscientific and psychotherapy research. We are convinced that integration of both research methodologies (which have traditionally been separated), may significantly help to improve the basic understanding of mechanisms behind the disorder as well as the treatment of BPD.

As mentioned in this chapter, emotion dysregulation is one of the core features of BPD and the main target of dialectical behavior therapy (DBT). Neuroimaging studies investigating alterations after treatment found normalization of limbic hyper-reactivity (Goodman et al., 2014; Niedtfeld et al., 2017; Schmitt, Winter, Niedtfeld, Schmahl, & Herpertz, 2016; Schnell & Herpertz, 2007; Winter et al., 2017). After successful therapy, patients exhibited changes in brain activity, pointing to reduced hypersensitivity of limbic brain regions and increased prefrontal brain activity during emotional challenge. An early study investigated six BPD patients before and after a 12-week residential DBT treatment. In response to negative pictures, patients showed reduced activity of insula and ACC after successful psychotherapy (Schnell & Herpertz, 2007). Investigating habituation processes, negative pictures were repeatedly presented to patients before and after standard DBT. The amygdala was activated to a lesser extent after 12 months of DBT, pointing to improved habituation (Goodman et al., 2014). A recent study observed reduced neural activity in eight patients with BPD in brain areas supporting emotion processing and theory of mind after brief psychiatric treatment of ten sessions (Kramer et al., 2018). Notably, these studies did not include a control group of patients without DBT, and so they cannot differentiate between DBT-specific effects and unspecific therapy, or time, effects.

Three studies were conducted in a large project investigating different emotion regulation strategies (reappraisal, distraction, and pain) before and after a 12-week residential DBT treatment (Niedtfeld et al., 2017; Schmitt et al., 2016; Winter et al., 2017), as compared to treatment as usual and HC subjects. When engaging in reappraisal of negative pictures, those with BPD showed decreased anterior insula and dorsal anterior cingulate cortex (ACC) activity during and after DBT. Therapy responders also showed reduced activation in amygdala, ACC, orbitofrontal, and DLPFC, together with increased limbic-prefrontal coupling (Schmitt et al., 2016). In the second study, DBT treatment responders also showed reduced ACC activity when viewing negative (as compared to neutral) pictures. During cognitive distraction from negative pictures, decreased activity in the right inferior parietal lobe was found in BPD patients after DBT (Winter et al., 2017). The third study examined the effect of pain on emotional reactions and found that pain-mediated affect regulation (i.e., amygdala deactivation in response to painful stimulation, a mechanism assumed to underlie non-suicidal self-injury) was reduced after DBT treatment (Niedtfeld et al., 2017).

Taken together, there is strong evidence for limbic hyper-reactivity in BPD, leading to intense and long-lasting emotional reactions. Additionally, down-regulation of emotional arousal appears to be deficient in BPD, as demonstrated by decreased recruitment of prefrontal regulation networks. These two aspects might result in affective instability in BPD. However, it is important to note that most of these effects might be not specific to BPD patients. A study in healthy subjects with childhood maltreatment demonstrated functional alterations that were strikingly similar to the findings described here for BPD (Dannlowski et al., 2012). It is possible that adverse childhood experiences lead to alterations in limbic brain regions, which in turn increase the risk for the development of psychiatric disorders in general (Gilbert et al., 2009). With regard to BPD, it has been argued that the co-occurrence of adverse childhood experiences and dysfunctional emotion regulation, together with increased impulsivity and interpersonal problems, might be more specific for the development of BPD (Crowell, Beauchaine, & Linehan, 2009).

Another example supporting an integrated neuroscientific-psychotherapeutic as well as mechanism-based approach for understanding BPD is real-time fMRI neurofeedback (rtfMRI-NF). RtfMRI-NF has recently become a focus of clinical psychiatry and psychotherapy research (deCharms et al., 2005; Linden, 2014; Linden et al., 2012; Ruiz, Birbaumer, & Sitaram, 2013; Ruiz, Lee, et al., 2013; Young et al., 2014; Zilverstand, Sorger, Sarkheil, & Goebel, 2014), with pioneering studies providing initial evidence that it might play a promising role in future therapies for chronic pain, and mental disorders such as depression, schizophrenia, and phobias. Several studies conducted in healthy participants have demonstrated improvement in control over key areas of emotional responding, such as the amygdala or the insula (Brühl et al., 2014; Caria, Sitaram, Veit, Begliomini, & Birbaumer, 2010; Hamilton, Glover, Hsu, Johnson, & Gotlib, 2011; Johnston, Boehm, Healy, Goebel, & Linden, 2010; Lawrence et al., 2013; Paret et al., 2014; Scheinost et al., 2013; Sulzer et al., 2013; Veit et al., 2012; Zotev et al., 2011). This literature supports the feasibility of using neurofeedback to target brain regions of the affective system, such as the amygdala, as an alternative or at least an add-on to psychotherapy for mental disorders that are associated with emotion dysregulation.

Extending this important body of work on real-time fMRI NF, our research team has conducted three studies to test the feasibility of this approach in BPD. First, we investigated whether participants would be able to down-regulate their amygdala response to aversive pictures when they were provided with continuous feedback from this region. The first study was conducted in healthy persons (Paret et al., 2014). Thirty-two female participants completed one session of training that comprised four runs, with each run presenting aversive pictures under three different conditions. In the REGULATE condition, participants were provided with continuous visual feedback on brain activation via a thermometer display, and were instructed to use this feedback to try to consciously down-regulate the thermometer. One-half of the participants received feedback on activation in the amygdala, while the other half received it from a control region located in the basal ganglia. In the VIEW condition, they were instructed to respond naturally to the aversive pictures; i.e., to not make any attempt to regulate the thermometer. In the fourth run, they were given the same instructions about down-regulation that they had been given in the REGULATE condition, but this time they did not receive feedback on brain activation, in order to assess the transfer of the regulation training. RtfMRI-NF was associated with successful down-regulation of the amygdala response in both groups. During transfer, we found evidence for a differential influence of Group on brain self-regulation and of down-regulation of the right amygdala response in the experimental group.

In a second study (Paret, Kluetsch, et al., 2016), we applied the same protocol to eight BPD patients to investigate if down-regulation of amygdala activation could be achieved in this population as well. Participants underwent four training sessions over two weeks. We found a reduced amygdala response in the REGULATE condition as contrasted with the VIEW condition, with reduction already seen in the first session. BPD patients also demonstrated an increase of amygdala-prefrontal connectivity over the course of training, a pattern which was also observed in healthy subjects during one session of rtfMRI-NF (Paret, Ruf, et al., 2016).

Finally, in a recently completed study (Zaehringer et al., 2019), we were interested in which aspects of emotion dysregulation would be amenable to change with NF. Twenty-five female BPD patients (mean age = 33.36, SD = 10.65) participated in three rtfmri-NF sessions and were tested again six weeks later. Patients were on constant medication or outpatient treatment throughout the study period. Emotion regulation was assessed on physiological, behavioral, and self-report levels. Results show significant down-regulation of amygdala activation. After training, patients indicated less aversive arousal and negative emotions, as well as lower hour-to-hour variability in these measures. BPD symptoms decreased in results from the Zanarini Scale for BPD. In the psychophysiology lab, patients improved emotion regulation skills after training, indicated by decreased startle response to negative pictures. However, repeated measures analysis of variance showed that this effect did not persist until the follow-up test. Taken together, this one-arm clinical study revealed significant improvement in emotion regulation and reductions in affective instability in daily life after fMRI-NF in BPD. The treatment affected emotion processing on several systems levels, including psychophysiology, behavior, and subjective experience. In order to control for psychosocial effects, future studies need to compare the treatment with a control group.

The examples depicted here may help to illustrate how state-of-the art neuroscientific methodology and psychotherapy work hand in hand to understand mechanisms of change in BPD treatment as well as develop innovative, yet experimental therapy approaches. This integrated approach not only broadens our view on this complex disorder but also gives hope to a better understanding and treatment of disturbed emotion regulation in and beyond BPD.

REFERENCES

Brühl, A. B., Scherpiet, S., Sulzer, J., Stampfli, P., Seifritz, E., & Herwig, U. (2014). Real-time neurofeedback using functional MRI could improve down-regulation of amygdala activity during emotional stimulation: A proof-of-concept study. *Brain Topography, 27*(1), 138–148.

Caria, A., Sitaram, R., Veit, R., Begliomini, C., & Birbaumer, N. (2010). Volitional control of anterior insula activity modulates the response to aversive stimuli: A real-time functional magnetic resonance imaging study. *Biological Psychiatry, 68*(5), 425–432.

Crowell, S. E., Beauchaine, T. P., & Linehan, M. M. (2009). A biosocial developmental model of borderline personality: Elaborating and extending Linehan's theory. *Psychological Bulletin, 135*(3), 495–510.

Dannlowski, U., Stuhrmann, A., Beutelmann, V., Zwanzger, P., Lenzen, T., Grotegerd, D., . . . Kugel, H. (2012). Limbic scars: Long-term consequences of childhood maltreatment revealed by functional and structural magnetic resonance imaging. *Biological Psychiatry, 71*(4), 286–293.

deCharms, R. C., Maeda, F., Glover, G. H., Ludlow, D., Pauly, J. M., Soneji, D., . . . Mackey, S. C. (2005). Control over brain activation and pain learned by using real-time functional MRI. *Proceedings of the National Academy of Sciences USA, 102*(51), 18626–18631.

Gilbert, R., Widom, C. S., Browne, K., Fergusson, D., Webb, E., & Janson, S. (2009). Burden and consequences of child maltreatment in high-income countries. *Lancet, 373*(9657), 68–81.

Goodman, M., Carpenter, D., Tang, C. Y., Goldstein, K. E., Avedon, J., Fernandez, N., . . . Hazlett, E. A. (2014). Dialectical behavior therapy alters emotion regulation and amygdala activity in patients with borderline personality disorder. *Journal of Psychiatric Research, 57*, 108–116.

Hamilton, J. P., Glover, G. H., Hsu, J. J., Johnson, R. F., & Gotlib, I. H. (2011). Modulation of subgenual anterior cingulate cortex activity with real-time neurofeedback. *Human Brain Mapping, 32*(1), 22–31.

Johnston, S. J., Boehm, S. G., Healy, D., Goebel, R., & Linden, D. E. (2010). Neurofeedback: A promising tool for the self-regulation of emotion networks. *NeuroImage, 49*(1), 1066–1072.

Kramer, U., Kolly, S., Maillard, P., Pascual-Leone, A., Samson, A. C., Schmitt, R., . . . de Roten, Y. (2018). Change in emotional and theory of mind processing in borderline personality disorder: A pilot study. *Journal of Nervous and Mental Disease, 206*(12), 935–943.

Lawrence, E. J., Su, L., Barker, G. J., Medford, N., Dalton, J., Williams, S. C., . . . David, A. S. (2013). Self-regulation of the anterior insula: Reinforcement learning using real-time fMRI neurofeedback. *NeuroImage, 88C*, 113–124.

Linden, D. E. (2014). Neurofeedback and networks of depression. *Dialogues in Clinical Neuroscience, 16*(1), 103–112.

Linden, D. E., Habes, I., Johnston, S. J., Linden, S., Tatineni, R., Subramanian, L., . . . Goebel, R. (2012). Real-time self-regulation of emotion networks in patients with depression. *PLoS ONE, 7*(6), e38115.

Niedtfeld, I., Schmitt, R., Winter, D., Bohus, M., Schmahl, C., & Herpertz, S. C. (2017). Pain-mediated affect regulation is reduced after dialectical behavior therapy in borderline personality disorder: A longitudinal fMRI study. *Social Cognitive and Affective Neuroscience, 12*(5), 739–747.

Paret, C., Kluetsch, R., Ruf, M., Demirakca, T., Hoesterey, S., Ende, G., & Schmahl, C. (2014). Down-regulation of amygdala activation with real-time fMRI neurofeedback in a healthy female sample. *Frontiers in Behavioral Neuroscience, 8*, 299.

Paret, C., Kluetsch, R., Zaehringer, J., Ruf, M., Demirakca, T., Bohus, M., . . . Schmahl, C. (2016). Alterations of amygdala-prefrontal connectivity with real-time fMRI neurofeedback in BPD patients. *Social Cognitive and Affective Neuroscience, 11*(6), 952–960.

Paret, C., Ruf, M., Gerchen, M. F., Kluetsch, R., Demirakca, T., Jungkunz, M., . . . Ende, G. (2016). fMRI neurofeedback of amygdala response to aversive stimuli enhances prefrontal-limbic brain connectivity. *NeuroImage, 125*, 182–188.

Ruiz, S., Birbaumer, N., & Sitaram, R. (2013). Abnormal neural connectivity in schizophrenia and fMRI-brain-computer interface as a potential therapeutic approach. *Frontiers in Psychiatry, 4*, 17.

Ruiz, S., Lee, S., Soekadar, S. R., Caria, A., Veit, R., Kircher, T., . . . Sitaram, R. (2013). Acquired self-control of insula cortex modulates emotion recognition and brain network connectivity in schizophrenia. *Human Brain Mapping, 34*(1), 200–212.

Scheinost, D., Stoica, T., Saksa, J., Papademetris, X., Constable, R. T., Pittenger, C., & Hampson, M. (2013). Orbitofrontal cortex neurofeedback produces lasting changes in contamination anxiety and resting-state connectivity. *Translational Psychiatry, 3*(4), e250.

Schmitt, R., Winter, D., Niedtfeld, I., Schmahl, C., & Herpertz, S. C. (2016). Effects of psychotherapy on neuronal correlates of reappraisal in female patients with borderline personality disorder. *Biological Psychiatry: Cognitive Neuroscience and Neuroimaging.* doi:10.1007/s00406-016-0689-2

Schnell, K., & Herpertz, S. C. (2007). Effects of dialectic-behavioral-therapy on the neural correlates of affective hyperarousal in borderline personality disorder. *Journal of Psychiatric Research, 41*(10), 837–847.

Sulzer, J., Sitaram, R., Blefari, M. L., Kollias, S., Birbaumer, N., Stephan, K. E., . . . Gassert, R. (2013). Neurofeedback-mediated self-regulation of the dopaminergic midbrain. *NeuroImage, 83*, 817–825.

Veit, R., Singh, V., Sitaram, R., Caria, A., Rauss, K., & Birbaumer, N. (2012). Using real-time fMRI to learn voluntary regulation of the anterior insula in the presence of threat-related stimuli. *Social Cognitive and Affective Neuroscience, 7*(6), 623–634.

Winter, D., Niedtfeld, I., Schmitt, R., Bohus, M., Schmahl, C., & Herpertz, S. C. (2017). Neural correlates of distraction in borderline personality disorder before and after dialectical behavior therapy. *European Archives of Psychiatry and Clinical Neuroscience, 267*(1), 51–62.

Young, K. D., Zotev, V., Phillips, R., Misaki, M., Yuan, H., Drevets, W. C., & Bodurka, J. (2014). Real-time fMRI neurofeedback training of amygdala activity in patients with major depressive disorder. *PLoS ONE, 9*(2), e88785.

Zaehringer, J., Ende, G., Santangelo, P., Kleindienst, N., Ruf, M., Bertsch, K., . . . Paret, C. (2019). Improved emotion regulation after neurofeedback: A single-arm trial in patients with borderline personality disorder. Retrieved from psyarxiv.com/wemfq

Zilverstand, A., Sorger, B., Sarkheil, P., & Goebel, R. (2014). Towards therapy in the scanner: Enhancing fear regulation in spider phobia through fMRI neurofeedback. Paper presented at the Human Brain Mapping conference, Hamburg.

Zotev, V., Krueger, F., Phillips, R., Alvarez, R. P., Simmons, W. K., Bellgowan, P., . . . Bodurka, J. (2011). Self-regulation of amygdala activation using real-time FMRI neurofeedback. *PLoS ONE, 6*(9), e24522.

10c The Promise of Applying a Developmental Psychopathology Framework to the Etiology and Treatment of Borderline Personality Disorder: Author Rejoinder to Commentaries on Borderline Personality Disorder

ALEXANDER L. CHAPMAN, NORA H. HOPE, AND BRIANNA J. TURNER

We appreciate the astute commentaries by Scott and Pilkonis (this volume) and Niedtfeld, Paret, and Schmahl (this volume). Scott and Pilkonis address some very important big picture themes regarding the conceptualization, etiology, and treatment of BPD, and Niedtfeld et al. comment on innovative research highlighting the interplay of neuroscience and psychotherapy.

CLARIFYING THE BPD CONSTRUCT AND ETIOLOGICAL PATHWAYS

Scott and Pilkonis suggest the overarching construct of BPD is best conceptualized as unidimensional and assessed on a continuum of severity. To further clarify the BPD construct and its possible etiology, we believe studies should continue to examine the interplay of heritable and environmental influences on BPD. Findings are beginning to illuminate the nature of the BPD construct and the heritable and environmental influences on the development of BPD and its features. Reichborn-Kjennerud et al. (2013), for example, found that BPD features were best accounted for by a model including a moderately heritable latent BPD factor, with heritable and unique environmental factors accounting for 55 percent and 45 percent of this factor, respectively. The subset of interpersonal BPD symptoms had low heritability (2.2 percent), and the heritability of affective instability was 29.3 percent. Findings suggested that unique environmental influences carry most of the weight when it comes to interpersonal symptoms and substantially influence affective instability.

As suggested by both commentaries, an integrative approach to theory and research can be immensely helpful in understanding and helping those with BPD. Studies using a variety of innovative methods have highlighted the nature of the BPD construct as well as neurobiological factors related to problems with emotion dysregulation among adults with BPD. We would further argue that, consistent with a developmental psychopathology approach, continued research is needed to understand the biopsychosocial processes operating at various levels of development to contribute to BPD and its serious behavioral and functional problems.

A DEVELOPMENTAL PSYCHOPATHOLOGY FRAMEWORK FOR UNDERSTANDING BPD

Increasingly, studies over the past several years have examined key precursors, heritable and environmental influences, and symptom patterns of BPD over time. Some contemporary developmental theories of BPD suggest that heritable vulnerabilities manifest heterotypically at various stages of development and transact with environmental risk factors to contribute to the development of BPD (e.g., see Beauchaine, Hinshaw, & Bridge, 2019; Crowell, Kaufman & Beauchaine, 2014).

Crowell et al. (2014; see also Beauchaine, Hinshaw, & Bridge, 2019), for example, have proposed that trait impulsivity (a) is a key heritable influence associated with a heterotypic set of childhood and adolescent behavioral problems (e.g., oppositional defiant disorder, attention-deficit hyperactivity disorder, adolescent mental health problems) and (b) makes children particularly vulnerable to the effects of adverse environments. Further, this model proposes that invalidating rearing environments shape the development of emotion dysregulation. In adolescence, the development of self-injury and other behavioral problems signify worsening emotion dysregulation and have adverse interpersonal and intrapersonal consequences that further contribute to the development of BPD.

Over the past several years, findings have indicated that developmental psychopathology models of BPD have promise and suggest directions for prevention and treatment. These models suggest that (a) we should be able to identify at-risk children and adolescents well before they begin to engage in seriously self-damaging behaviors and (b) key prevention and treatment targets include socialization factors (parenting), emotion dysregulation, and self-injury (as suggested by Beauchaine, Hinshaw, & Bridge, 2019). One randomized clinical trial (RCT) applied DBT to children with disruptive mood dysregulation disorder (DMRD), finding an advantage of DBT over treatment as usual in terms of dropout rates, positive treatment response, and remission from DMRD (Perepletchikova et al., 2017). It remains to be seen whether DBT or other approaches can curtail the later development of nonsuicidal self-injury (NSSI), suicidal behavior, or BPD. Further, findings from two large studies have supported the efficacy of DBT for reducing suicide attempts, self-injury, suicidal ideation, and depression among self-injuring adolescents (e.g., McCauley et al., 2018; Mehlum et al., 2014). It will be important to determine whether treatment or prevention strategies occurring before BPD is crystallized can curb a trajectory toward worsening behavioral problems and eventual BPD.

THE DEVELOPMENT OF NEUROBIOLOGICAL CHARACTERISTICS OF BPD

Niedtfeld et al. summarize findings broadly suggesting poor frontal regulation of the limbic system in BPD. Findings have begun to suggest that the aberrations in brain structure or function observed among adults with BPD may begin to appear, albeit in a narrower fashion, among at-risk adolescents (e.g., Beauchaine, Sauder, Derbidge, & Uyeji, 2019). Researchers have proposed that adolescence is an important period for the development of limbic and prefrontal regions and the stress-response system (Ahmed, Bittencourt-Hewitt, & Sebastian, 2015; Miller & Prinstein, 2019). Abnormalities in the development of these systems can, in turn, contribute to the development of self-injury (Miller & Prinstein, 2019), a key indicator of future BPD. Future research should examine whether psychosocial and other approaches (e.g., neurofeedback) can influence neurobiological development and reduce the risk of broader emotion regulation problems throughout later adolescence and adulthood.

CONCLUSIONS

In conclusion, Scott and Pilkonis (this volume) and Niedtfeld et al. (this volume) have provided insightful contributions to the continuing and sometimes confusing conversation about the nature of BPD. To best understand the nature of BPD and the complex person × environment transactions that contribute to this disorder, we should conceptualize and examine BPD developmentally across the lifespan, using a biopsychosocial framework. We should also continue to develop and examine ways to help at-risk individuals and people with BPD reduce suffering and build lives that are worth living.

REFERENCES

Ahmed, S. P., Bittencourt-Hewitt, A., & Sebastian, C. L. (2015). Neurocognitive bases of emotion regulation development in adolescence. *Developmental Cognitive Neuroscience, 15*, 11–25.

Beauchaine, T. P., Hinshaw, S. P., & Bridge, J. A. (2019). Nonsuicidal self-injury and suicidal behaviors in girls: The case for targeted prevention in preadolescence. *Clinical Psychological Science, 7*, 643–667.

Beauchaine, T. P., Sauder, C. L., Derbidge, C. M., & Uyeji, L. L. (2019). Self-injuring adolescent girls exhibit insular cortex volumetric abnormalities that are similar to those observed in adults with borderline personality disorder. *Development and Psychopathology*. doi:10.1017/S0954579418000822

Crowell, S. E., Kaufman, E. A., & Beauchaine, T. P. (2014). A biosocial model of BPD: Theory and empirical evidence. In C. Sharp & J. L. Tackett (Eds.), *Handbook of Borderline Personality Disorder in Children and Adolescents* (pp. 143–157). New York: Springer.

McCauley, E., Berk, M. S., Asarnow, J. R., Adrian, M., Cohen, J., Korslund, K., ... Linehan, M. M. (2018). Efficacy of dialectical behavior therapy for adolescents at high risk for suicide: A randomized clinical trial. *JAMA Psychiatry, 75*, 777–785.

Mehlum, L., Tørmoen, A. J., Ramberg, M., Haga, E., Diep, L. M., Laberg, S., ... Grøholt, B. (2014). Dialectical behavior therapy for adolescents with repeated suicidal and self-harming behavior: A randomized trial. *Journal of the American Academy of Child & Adolescent Psychiatry, 53*, 1082–1091.

Miller, A. B., & Prinstein, M. J. (2019). Adolescent suicide as a failure of acute stress-response systems. *Annual Review of Clinical Psychology, 15*, 21.1–21.26.

Perepletchikova, F., Nathanson, D., Axelrod, S. R., Merrill, C., Walker, A., Grossman, M., ... Walkup, J. (2017). Randomized clinical trial of dialectical behavior therapy for preadolescent children with disruptive mood dysregulation disorder: Feasibility and outcomes. *Journal of the American Academy of Child & Adolescent Psychiatry, 56*, 832–840.

Reichborn-Kjennerud, T., Ystrom, E., Neale, M. C., Aggen, S. H., Mazzeo, S. E., Knudsen, G. P., ... Kendler, K. S. (2013). Structure of genetic and environmental risk factors for symptoms of DSM-IV borderline personality disorder. *JAMA Psychiatry, 70*, 1206–1214.

11 An Integrative Biobehavioral Trait Perspective on Antisocial Personality Disorder and Psychopathy

SARAH J. BRISLIN AND CHRISTOPHER J. PATRICK

Antisocial personality disorder (ASPD) and psychopathy are related but distinguishable conditions with long histories in the mental health field. Mirroring developments in the broader literatures on personality disorders and general psychopathology, a shift has occurred toward viewing these conditions as continuous-dimensional and multifaceted in nature rather than discrete and unitary. In this chapter, we begin with a description of the history of these diagnoses, focusing on theoretical accounts and methods of assessment. Second we discuss current conceptions of ASPD and psychopathy and how these two diagnostic conditions differ in terms of their symptomatic features and etiologic bases. Next, we describe dimensional approaches to assessing psychopathy and three phenotypic-dispositional constructs that have recently been used as a framework for conceptualizing ASPD and psychopathy. These dispositions, termed boldness, meanness, and disinhibition, are viewed as contributing to distinct symptom configurations recognizable as ASPD and psychopathy, and help to account for how these conditions relate to other forms of psychopathology. In line with recent trends toward conceptualizing and studying clinical problems in biobehavioral terms, we next consider how these three dispositional facets relate to biobehavioral systems/processes. Drawing on what has been learned about these dispositional constructs and their biobehavioral bases, we conclude with suggestions as to steps that can be taken to advance our understanding of ASPD and psychopathy, with a particular focus on multi-method assessments and targeted treatments.

HISTORIC DESCRIPTIONS OF ASPD AND PSYCHOPATHY

Individuals who exhibit impulsive, aggressive, disinhibited behavior without signs of thought disturbance have long been of interest to mental health scholars and practitioners. Whether described as *manie sans delire* ("insanity without delirium") as suggested by Phillippe Pinel (1801), "moral insanity" as proposed by James Prichard (1837), or

"moral weakness" as preferred by Benjamin Rush (1823) – early psychopathology experts grappled with the etiology of this pattern of norm-violating behaviors. While some early experts postulated that this symptom pattern arises from deficits in moral development, J. L. Koch (1841–1908) was the first to use the term *psychopathic*, connoting "in-born" and "biologically-based," which he applied to a broad array of psychiatric conditions. Kraepelin (1915), by contrast, used the label "psychopathic personalities" for a narrower set of characterological (personality-based) conditions that resemble modern conceptions of ASPD and psychopathy.

Conceptions of antisocial behavior and psychopathy remained vague and diffuse into the twentieth century. In 1941, Hervey Cleckley's book *The Mask of Sanity* introduced a much more focused definition for the term "psychopathic," based on his clinical observation and scholarly analysis of many psychiatric inpatient cases. Cleckley characterized psychopathy as a distinct and severe form of psychopathology masked by an appearance of good psychological health. Sixteen symptom criteria broadly covering impulsive and deviant behavior, shallow emotions, and a lack of close relationships – evident in a context of ostensible psychological stability (normal or higher intelligence, social poise, lack of "neurotic" [internalizing] features or thought disorder symptoms) – were proposed as a concrete basis for diagnosing psychopathy. By contrast, other forensic researchers at the time (e.g., McCord & McCord, 1964) emphasized the importance of a predatory affective-interpersonal style and lack of remorse while excluding indications of psychological well-being from their conceptualization. These contrasting views are still evident in alternative conceptualizations of psychopathy in use today.

Differing conceptualizations of psychopathy are also evident in proposed subtyping schemes for this condition. One of the first of these, by Karpman (1941), described a subset of antisocial individuals who exhibited high levels of anxiousness and depressivity along with disinhibitory features of psychopathy such as impulsiveness, rebelliousness, and aggression. He labeled these individuals "secondary psychopaths" and posited that their psychopathic symptomatology arose from adverse early environments. On the other hand, mirroring Cleckley's "masked pathology" conception, Karpman characterized "primary psychopathy" as involving low anxiousness and a lack of emotional sensitivity alongside salient antisocial behavior. Evidence for this distinction was provided by research demonstrating differing responses in laboratory tasks for these two subtypes, with the primary type exhibiting a failure to inhibit punished responses and reduced physiological arousal during anticipation of pain relative to the secondary type (Lykken, 1957). Based on empirical evidence of this and other types reported over the years, Lykken (1995) proposed that primary psychopathy reflects low dispositional fear whereas secondary psychopathy arises from temperamentally-based oversensitivity to reward cues.

The first two editions of the *Diagnostic and Statistical Manual of Mental Disorders* (DSM-I and II; American Psychiatric Association [APA], 1952, 1968) defined ASPD (termed "Antisocial Reaction" in DSM-I and "Antisocial Personality" in DSM-II) in prototypic-descriptive terms that aligned with Cleckley's characterization of psychopathy. In addition to a history of rule- and law-breaking behavior, these early DSM editions included callousness towards others, lack of guilt, and lack of ability to learn from punishment as characteristic features. In an effort to address well-documented deficiencies in the reliability of psychiatric diagnoses made using DSM-I and II, prototype descriptions were replaced with criterion-based diagnoses in DSM-III (APA, 1980), and the criteria for ASPD (labeled as such within this edition) consisted of behavioral symptoms including irresponsible, aggressive, and unlawful conduct, and the presence of behavioral deviancy before age 15.

In the revised third edition (DSM-III-R; APA, 1987), a criterion pertaining to lack of remorse was added, and this criterion was retained in DSM-IV (APA, 1994). The diagnostic criteria for personality disorders in this edition of the DSM were carried over to the main Diagnostic Criteria and Codes portion (Section II) of the current fifth edition (DSM-5; APA, 2013), and thus the criteria for ASPD remain the same as those in DSM-IV.

As with prior editions of the DSM, the definition of ASPD in DSM-5 does not fully capture psychopathy – in particular, providing only partial, inadequate coverage of affective-interpersonal features considered most central to this condition (Hare, 1996; Lynam & Vachon, 2012; Patrick & Drislane, 2015). Consequently, even though the diagnosis of "antisocial personality" was originally included in the DSM system to represent the syndrome of psychopathy, drift occurred across successive editions of this system. As a result, differences between the phenotypic presentations of the two disorders are often muddied by misconceptions about diagnostic differentiation. In the next section, we discuss in more specific detail points of overlap and distinctiveness between the two diagnoses as currently defined.

CURRENT DEFINITIONS OF ASPD AND PSYCHOPATHY

ASPD: DSM-5 Definitions

Section II of DSM-5 (APA, 2013) defines ASPD as a pattern of behavioral deviancy with onset in childhood (before age 15) that persists into adulthood. The child symptom criteria match those for conduct disorder, and the adult criteria include impulsiveness, irresponsibility, irritability or aggression, unlawful behavior, disregard for the safety of self or others, and a lack of remorse. In addition to overlapping with psychopathy, ASPD exhibits systematic comorbidity with other DSM disorders (Black, Gunter, Loveless, Allen, & Sieleni, 2010) – most notably substance use disorders and other impulse control disorders (e.g., attention deficit hyperactivity disorder, nonsubstance addictions, borderline personality). We consider this pattern of comorbidity again at a later point in this chapter, where we discuss evidence indicating that the co-occurrence among these different disorders can be accounted for by a common externalizing factor (Krueger et al., 2002).

The DSM-5 (APA, 2013) contains an alternative dimensional-trait system for personality disorders, in Section III, titled "Emerging Measures and Models." This alternative system represents conditions of these types in terms of pathological personality traits from five domains: Disinhibition, Antagonism, Negative Affect, Detachment, and Psychoticism. ASPD is characterized by high levels of Disinhibition, Antagonism, and Negative Affect, while psychopathy is specified as including additional lower order traits – low anxiousness, low social withdrawal, and high attention seeking. A self-report instrument, the Personality Inventory for DSM-5 (PID-5; Krueger, Derringer, Markon, Watson, & Skodol, 2012), was developed as a means to index the personality traits specified within the Section III trait system.

Psychopathy: Interview- and Questionnaire-Based Measures

Currently, the clinician administered Psychopathy Checklist – Revised (PCL-R; Hare, 2003) is the most commonly used method for assessing psychopathy in correctional and forensic hospital settings. The PCL-R is rated using information obtained from a structured clinical interview and a review of institutional file records, and includes 20 items; each item is rated on a 0–2 scale, resulting in a maximum score of 40. The PCL-R was developed to differentiate offenders judged to be high versus low in resemblance to Cleckley's clinical description of psychopathy, utilizing a global rating system. As such, the PCL-R includes items that index the affective-interpersonal deficits included in Cleckley's description along with items pertaining to criminal behaviors and attitudes. For many years, research studies using the PCL-R focused on subgroups of offender participants classified as psychopathic versus nonpsychopathic based on low and high cutoffs for overall symptom scores (e.g., >30 and <20, respectively).

However, recent research has moved toward use of continuous scores, for symptom subdimensions (factors) as well as for the PCL-R as a whole. The focus on subdimensions derives from structural analyses of the inventory (e.g., Harpur, Hare, & Hakstian, 1989) demonstrating two broad factors underlying its items: Factor 1, encompassing interpersonal-affective features of psychopathy, and Factor 2, reflecting impulsive-antisocial symptoms. Following the delineation of these factors, further analytic work revealed that Factor 1 could be subdivided into distinct Interpersonal and Affective facets (Cooke & Michie, 2001) and that Factor 2 could be subdivided into an impulsive-irresponsible ("Lifestyle") facet and an Antisocial facet (Hare, 2003; Hare & Neumann, 2008).

While intercorrelated, the factors and facets of the PCL-R exhibit diverging relations with assorted criterion variables. Factor 1, for example, is selectively associated with narcissism, instrumental aggression, and low levels of anxiety and depression (Hare, 2003; Hicks & Patrick, 2006). Factor 2, on the other hand, is associated with reactive aggression, substance use problems, and suicidal behavior (Hare, 1991, 2003; Verona, Patrick, & Joiner, 2001). Factor 2 also accounts for most of the overlap between PCL-R psychopathy and ASPD. The PCL-R factors also show divergent relations with physiological criterion measures (e.g., Drislane, Vaidyanathan, & Patrick, 2013; Vaidyanathan, Hall, Patrick, & Bernat, 2011; Venables & Patrick, 2012), as discussed later in this chapter.

In addition to containing factors/facets that show contrasting associations with criterion variables, studies using the classification technique of model-based cluster analysis have identified distinct variants ("subtypes") of high-PCL-R scoring offenders. The first study of this sort, by Hicks, Markon, Patrick, Krueger, and Newman (2004), identified two subtypes of psychopathic criminals on the basis of personality trait profiles: an "emotionally stable" subtype and an "aggressive" subtype. A subsequent study by Skeem, Johansson, Andershed, Kerr, and Louden (2007) that clustered high PCL-R offenders based on psychopathy facet scores and anxiety-scale scores also identified two subgroups, differentiated in particular by low versus high anxiousness, which they termed "primary" and "secondary." A further study by Hicks, Vaidyanathan, and Patrick (2010), focusing on female offenders clustered on the basis of personality trait profiles, reported a similar pair of subtypes, with the secondary (high-anxious) psychopathic group showing greater violent behavior and substance abuse, along with more mental health problems of other types, than the primary (low-anxious) group.

Self-report instruments are also widely used to assess psychopathy. Some of these, such as Paulhus, Neumann, & Hare's (2014) Self-Report Psychopathy Scale (SRP) and

Levenson and colleagues' (Levenson, Kiehl, & Fitzpatrick, 1995) Self-Report Psychopathy (LSRP) measure, were developed to parallel the PCL-R. These instruments, like the PCL-R, contain correlated but distinct subdimensions ("factors" or "facets"). Other self-report inventories exist that were developed separately from the PCL-R. These include the Psychopathic Personality Inventory (PPI; Lilienfeld & Andrews, 1996; Lilienfeld & Widows, 2005), the Elemental Psychopathy Assessment (EPA; Lynam et al., 2011), and the Triarchic Psychopathic Measure (TriPM; Patrick, 2010). Rather than emulating the item content of the PCL-R, these inventories rely more broadly on historic conceptualizations and theoretic perspectives, and approach psychopathy from a trait-based (rather than syndrome-based) perspective. These measures are discussed in detail later in this chapter, as they provide points of intersection for psychopathy with broad models of personality.

As a final point, it should be noted that cluster analytic studies of individuals assessed using self-report measures of psychopathy have also revealed distinct subgroups of high scorers resembling those identified in PCL-R/ offender studies (e.g., Drislane et al., 2015; Falkenbach, Stern & Creevy, 2014). Specifically, such studies have generally revealed a "primary" subtype exhibiting low anxiousness and high social assertiveness along with prominent antisocial deviance, and a "secondary" subtype exhibiting high anxiousness, high negative affectivity, and internalizing disorder symptoms along with alienation, hostility, aggressiveness, and substance problems. Individuals in the secondary group more often report histories of childhood abuse.

DIMENSIONAL APPROACHES TO DIAGNOSIS

In this next section, we discuss advances in the field of general psychopathology – in particular, growing empirical evidence supporting a continuous-dimensional characterization of personality and clinical disorders. Following this, we describe how these advances relate to developments in the study of psychopathy and ASPD.

For some time now, there has been a general consensus that personality pathology is dimensional rather than categorical in nature. For example, researchers in the 1980s examined the distribution of personality disorder symptoms specified in DSM-III-R (APA, 1987) and were unable to find evidence for a clear distinction between individuals diagnosed with and without personality disorders (e.g., Kass, Skodol, Charles, Spitzer, & Williams, 1985; Widiger, Hurt, Frances, Clarkin, & Gilmore, 1984; Zimmerman & Coryell, 1990). In response to these findings, it was suggested that personality pathology should be conceptualized in terms of general trait frameworks such as the Five-Factor Model (FFM; Costa & McCrae, 1992).

Research has produced evidence to suggest that episodic clinical disorders are also better conceptualized as dimensional in nature, rather than discrete. In particular, empirical evidence points to gradations in severity of symptomatology and systematic overlap among different disorders as support for a dimensional conceptualization. For example, based on patterns of comorbidity among adult DSM-III-R disorders, Krueger (1999) proposed that two underlying core psychopathological processes – internalizing (encompassing anxious-misery and fear sub-factors) and externalizing – give rise to common mental disorders. These higher order dimensions of psychopathology have also been found consistently in studies of child psychopathology (Achenbach & Edelbrock, 1978, 1984).

In subsequent work, Krueger and colleagues (Krueger, McGue, & Iacono, 2001) sought to interface internalizing and externalizing factors of psychopathology with normal range personality, as indexed by the Multidimensional Personality Questionnaire (MPQ; Tellegen, 2011). These investigators found internalizing to be associated with high negative emotionality (NEM) and low positive emotionality (PEM), and externalizing to be associated with low constraint (CON) and high NEM. These findings support a view of comorbidity as arising from variations in basic temperament dispositions that contribute to a range of adverse outcomes (Clark, Watson, & Mineka, 1994).

In a move toward implementing the dimensional approach to diagnosis in the formal psychiatric nosology, Section III of DSM-5 – titled "Emerging Measures and Models" – includes a system for characterizing personality pathology in terms of continuous traits, organized within broader dispositional domains. Recently, a more comprehensive dimensional model of psychopathology, encompassing episodic clinical syndromes as well as personality disorders, has been advanced. This model, termed the Hierarchical Taxonomy of Psychopathology (HiTOP; Kotov et al., 2017), characterizes psychopathological syndromes and their affiliated symptoms in a multilevel system that reflects empirically-observed patterns of covariation among them. The levels of the HiTOP model range from specific symptom dimensions at the lowest level to a general psychopathology factor at the highest level – with symptom clusters ("components"), disorders ("syndromes"), and disorder dimensions ("spectra") in between. The model considers higher levels of the psychopathology hierarchy (syndromes, spectra) to be related to broad dimensions of normative personality.

Reflecting these advances in conceptualizing personality disorders, and psychopathological conditions more broadly, a shift has occurred in the study of psychopathy and ASPD toward viewing these disorders as multifaceted and encompassing different configurations of trait-based proclivities. This shift is reflected, for example, in a move toward use of dimensional terminology in published work (e.g., "individuals high in psychopathic traits," in place of "psychopaths"), changes in research design (i.e., away from extreme-group studies toward continuous-score studies), and a broadening of target populations for study (i.e., to include younger and older individuals from the general community, along with institutionalized and clinic-referred samples). Recent studies have shown that both psychopathy and ASPD are represented effectively within the DSM-5 Section III trait system as operationalized by the PID-5 (e.g., Strickland, Drislane, Lucy, Krueger, & Patrick, 2013).

In the next section we describe the triarchic model, a biobehavioral trait framework that can be used to integrate alternative historic conceptions of psychopathy and antisocial behavior as well as facilitate neurobiological investigations. The triarchic model is also compatible with broader dimensional models of psychopathology such as the DSM-5 Section III and HiTOP models.

TRIARCHIC MODEL

The triarchic model of psychopathy (Patrick, Fowles, & Krueger, 2009) posits that three distinct dispositional constructs account for the observable symptoms and correlates of psychopathy: boldness, which encompasses social dominance, venturesomeness, and emotional resilience, and connects with the biobehavioral process of defensive reactivity; meanness, which entails low empathy, callousness, and aggressive manipulation of others, and relates to biobehavioral systems for social caring and connectedness; and disinhibition, which involves deficient planfulness/control, irresponsibility, and emotional dysregulation, and is associated with the biobehavioral process of inhibitory control.

These triarchic model dispositions are represented to varying degrees in pre-existing psychopathy assessment instruments, including those mentioned above (Drislane, Patrick, & Arsal, 2014; Sellbom & Phillips, 2013). In addition, the triarchic model connects to established models of general personality including the FFM (Poy, Segarra, Esteller, López, & Moltó, 2014) and Tellegen's (2011) Multidimensional Personality framework (Brislin, Drislane, Smith, Edens, & Patrick, 2015). The representation of triarchic model constructs within these well-established measures and models provides a link between their nomological networks, allowing for different facets and factors of psychopathy to be interfaced with broader psychopathology domains.

The Triarchic Psychopathy Measure (TriPM; Drislane et al., 2014; Patrick, 2010) was developed as a specific operationalization of the triarchic model constructs. The TriPM is a 58-item self-report inventory that yields scores on boldness, meanness, and disinhibition. While the TriPM was developed specifically to index the triarchic dispositional constructs, it is viewed as just one means for operationalizing these constructs. Consistent with the idea of the triarchic constructs as linked to normative personality traits and represented in different conceptualizations of psychopathy, research has shown that these constructs can be effectively indexed using items from existing psychopathy inventories (Hall et al., 2014;

Drislane et al., 2015) as well as omnibus measures of personality (Brislin et al., 2015; Drislane, Brislin, Jones, & Patrick, 2018).

In the subsections that follow, we describe referents in the literature for each of the triarchic model constructs – disinhibition, meanness, and boldness – and we discuss what we have learned about these dispositional constructs through systematic research focusing on each. In particular, each construct is discussed as it relates to current models of personality, common measurement tools, and correlates across modalities (methods) of measurement. We also consider how different configurations of these dispositional tendencies might give rise to alternative clinical presentations of ASPD and psychopathy. In the final major section following this, we consider how the three triarchic model constructs can help to clarify the nature and bases of psychopathic symptomatology in neurobiological terms.

Disinhibition

A pervasive lack of behavioral restraint is central to all definitions of ASPD and psychopathy. Represented in the disinhibitory-behavioral features of the PCL-R (Factor 2), the Self-Centered Impulsivity factor of the PPI-R, and the DSM criteria for ASPD, impulsive and disinhibited behaviors are a core, common feature of these two disorders. Thomas Achenbach first delineated *externalizing* as a dimension of psychopathology, along with a second major dimension labeled internalizing, in factor analytic work focusing on child mental disorders. He conceptualized externalizing problems as products of conflict directed toward the external world, and internalizing problems as arising from psychological turmoil maintained within (Achenbach, 1966, 1974). These empirically derived constructs mapped onto broad categories of child psychiatric conditions as defined at the time, with externalizing encompassing "undercontrolled" conditions marked by aggression and rule-breaking, and internalizing encompassing "overcontrolled" conditions involving anxiousness, social withdrawal, and depressivity (Achenbach & Edelbrock, 1978). This work was the first to present evidence that psychopathologic conditions that had been defined up to that point as discrete and categorical might share common liabilities, resulting in systematic patterns of comorbidity.

Subsequent to this, Gorenstein and Newman (1980) advanced the idea of a disinhibitory spectrum encompassing ASPD, alcohol use problems, hyperactivity, impulsivity, and psychopathy. Citing findings demonstrating systematic comorbidity among these conditions (i.e., individuals meeting diagnostic criteria for one of these conditions would frequently meet criteria for others), these investigators proposed that these different conditions arise from a shared liability. Viewed in this way, it became important to clarify the nature and etiologic bases of this

liability, as a basis for improving the parsimony of clinical diagnoses and providing a broad-range target for treatment (Krueger, 1999; Krueger, Caspi, Moffitt, & Silva, 1998).

Gorenstein and Newman's (1980) conceptualization set the stage for further research directed at clarifying patterns of comorbidity among mental disorders using advanced statistical modeling methods. Research focusing on patterns of overlap among common adult forms of psychopathology yielded factors compatible with those reported for childhood disorders – namely, an externalizing factor, reflecting covariance between substance use problems and antisocial personality, and an internalizing factor, reflecting the covariation between anxious-fearful and depressive disorders (Kendler, Prescott, Myers, & Neale, 2003; Krueger, 1999; Krueger et al., 1998). Following from this work, Krueger and colleagues (2002) used twin-modeling analyses to demonstrate a strong heritable basis (i.e., ~80 percent of variance attributable to additive genetic influences) to the broad externalizing factor reflecting the variance in common among child and adult symptoms of ASPD, substance use problems, and disinhibitory personality traits. Based on this evidence, these investigators proposed that a common dispositional liability contributes to differing conditions of this sort, with the precise symptomatic expression determined by disorder-specific etiological influences. Research conducted subsequent to this study supports the conclusion that externalizing proneness is highly heritable, and indicates that it operates in a similar way across genders (Hicks et al., 2007; Kendler et al., 2003; Krueger et al., 2002).

The externalizing spectrum was delineated in further detail by Krueger and colleagues (Krueger, Markon, Patrick, Benning, & Kramer, 2007). These investigators mapped out a multifaceted model of this problem domain in the form of a self-report instrument for use in research on disinhibitory psychopathology: the Externalizing Spectrum Inventory (ESI). The ESI quantifies externalizing problems and traits through 23 content scales that load together onto a general *externalizing proneness* factor, with residual variances of certain scales also loading onto separate *callous aggression* and *substance abuse* factors. The general externalizing factor reflects proclivities toward nonplanfulness, impulsiveness, irresponsibility, mistrust, and rule-breaking – consistent with the idea of a broad dispositional liability involving deficient behavioral and emotional control. This externalizing factor demonstrates strong associations with the impulsive-antisocial (Factor 2) dimension of psychopathy, whether assessed by self-report (PPI-R) or clinician rating (PCL-R; Venables & Patrick, 2012; Venables, Hall, & Patrick, 2014), and accounts for much of the overlap between ASPD and psychopathy (Venables et al., 2014; Wall, Wygant, & Sellbom, 2015).

The TriPM Disinhibition scale was developed to index the general factor of the ESI model, and it shows robust associations with Factor 2 of the PCL-R, the Self-Centered

Impulsivity factor of the PPI, and FFM Neuroticism and low Conscientiousness (Patrick & Drislane, 2015; Sellbom & Phillips, 2013; Poy et al., 2014). In addition, recent research has demonstrated that disinhibition as indexed by the TriPM is well represented in the trait-based definition for ASPD in Section III of DSM-5. Specifically, Strickland et al. (2013) reported that TriPM Disinhibition demonstrated appreciable correlations with traits from the Section III domains of Disinhibition, Antagonism, and Detachment, as indexed by the PID-5; as noted earlier, Section III defines ASPD in terms of traits from these domains.

Disinhibition also demonstrates robust and reliable associations with impulse-related conditions apart from ASPD and psychopathy. For example, disinhibition as indexed by the ESI general factor is positively associated with substance use disorders (alcohol, cannabis, other drugs; Nelson, Strickland, Krueger, Arbisi, & Patrick, 2016; Venables & Patrick, 2012). Disinhibition also demonstrates associations with the hyperactive-impulsive symptoms of attention deficit/hyperactivity disorder (Young, Stallings, Corley, Krauter, & Hewitt, 2000; Young et al., 2009), which are theorized to reflect a weakened behavioral inhibition system (Barkley, 1997). In addition, externalizing proneness has been found to be predictive of suicidal behaviors both on its own and in conjunction with high levels of dispositional fear (Venables, Sellbom, et al., 2015). This interactive aspect of personality traits may account for convergence and divergence among correlates of ASPD and psychopathy, as individuals high in psychopathy are characterized by relatively low levels of internalizing problems and suicidal behaviors.

Meanness

Meanness (or callous unemotionality; Frick, Ray, Thornton, & Kahn, 2014) is a core feature of psychopathic personality and is represented, in part, in the DSM-5 definition of ASPD. The affective facet of the PCL-R contains criteria relating to callousness, lack of remorse, and shallow affect, intended to capture the emotional insensitivity and predatory-exploitative tendencies described in historical conceptualizations of psychopathy. ASPD as defined in DSM-5 Section II includes a "lack of remorse" symptom. While this single symptom provides only partial coverage of core affective features of psychopathy (Hare, 2003), it does represent guiltlessness and to some extent callous disregard. Given its limited role in the criterion-based diagnosis of ASPD and the heterogeneous nature of this DSM diagnosis, meanness has largely been studied within the child and adult psychopathy literatures.

Meanness, though not recognized as such, has been represented in adult measures of psychopathy for some time. The PCL-R assesses for this facet of psychopathy through four items that index lack of remorse, shallow affect, deficient empathy, and failure to accept responsibility for one's actions (Hare, 2003). These items covary to form a "deficient affective experience" subdimension (Cooke & Michie, 2001). The self-report based PPI-R (Lilienfeld & Widows, 2005) includes specific representation of meanness in its Coldheartedness subscale, which indexes manipulative disregard for others and lack of emotional sensitivity, as distinct from impulsive and fearless tendencies (Drislane et al., 2014).

Meanness has also been studied from a developmental perspective, by child psychopathy researchers interested in how this dispositional tendency (termed "callous-unemotional traits" in their writings) manifests at a young age and develops over time. Initially, adult measures of psychopathy, most notably the PCL-R, served as referents for developing measures suitable for use with children and adolescents. The interview-based PCL:Youth Version (PCL:YV) assesses meanness based on the same four symptoms included in the adult version, with slight modifications to the scoring criteria to enhance relevancy for adolescent-aged subjects. The informant-rated Antisocial Process Screening Device (APSD; Frick & Hare, 2001), also patterned after the PCL-R, is designed for use with younger individuals (aged 6–13). Self-report measures have also been developed to index callous-unemotional traits in youth. One of these, the Inventory of Callous-Unemotional Traits (ICU; Frick, 2004), was developed to measure the affective (meanness) facet of psychopathy with greater specificity – using the callous-unemotional items of the APSD as a referent. Along with four items taken directly from the APSD, the ICU includes 20 other items intended to provide greater content coverage of the affective features of psychopathy. Another youth-oriented inventory patterned after the PCL-R, the Youth Psychopathic Traits Inventory (YPI; Andershed, Gustafson, Kerr, & Stattin, 2002), assesses psychopathy in terms of three dimensions: callous-unemotional, grandiose-manipulative, and impulsive-irresponsible. These different interview, informant, and self-report based measures are widely used in child and adolescent research; however, they are largely based on adult conceptualizations of psychopathy and since critics have expressed concerns about their structural coherency and validity (Salekin, Andershed, & Clark, 2018), it is likely that new or revised instruments will be proposed in the coming years.

Meanness is also represented in the ESI externalizing model (Krueger et al., 2007). As noted above, residual variances in certain subscales of the ESI – in particular, those indexing empathy (reversed), relational aggression, and destructive aggression – define a distinct Callous-Aggression factor. As a counterpart to the TriPM Disinhibition scale, which measures general externalizing proneness, the Meanness scale of the TriPM was developed to index the ESI Callous-Aggression factor through items from scales that load most strongly onto this factor in the ESI structural model. This scale shows selective associations with other indices of meanness including PPI Coldheartedness and the PCL-R's Affective facet (Patrick

& Drislane, 2015) – as well as with key neurobiological measures (as described in the next major section).

With regard to DSM-5 ASPD, research demonstrates that TriPM Meanness is related most strongly to traits from the DSM-5 Section III domain of Antagonism, and to lesser degree with traits from the Disinhibition and Detachment domains (Strickland et al., 2013). The balanced representation of traits associated with Antagonism and Disinhibition in the Section III definition of ASPD results in a more callousness-infused characterization of this condition than in Section II of the manual.

Apart from ASPD, meanness exhibits associations mainly with other erratic-dramatic (Cluster B) personality disorders in the DSM – in particular, narcissistic personality disorder (Paulhus & Williams, 2002). Meanness shows some relationship as well with substance use problems, but this appears attributable to its overlap with disinhibition (Venables & Patrick, 2012). Meanness is well represented in normal-range personality models, demonstrating a significant negative association with FFM Agreeableness (Poy et al., 2014) and significant positive and negative associations, respectively, with MPQ Aggression and Social Closeness (Brislin et al., 2015).

Boldness

Cleckley (1976) described boldness when he highlighted the "mask" features of psychopathic individuals. Indeed, features that marked these psychiatric patients as unusual and interesting were their charm and social poise, lack of anxiety or internalizing problems, and low suicide risk. Lykken (1957, 1995), Hare (1965), and Fowles (1980) all reported evidence in support of the idea of psychopathy involving low fear and nonanxiousness. Although clearly represented in Cleckley's description of psychopathy (see Crego & Widiger, 2016) and in contemporary measures of this condition (Drislane et al., 2014), boldness does not enter into the DSM diagnosis of ASPD (Venables et al., 2014), and as described below, is largely unrelated to disorders associated with ASPD.

One of the first measures to represent boldness as a distinct facet of psychopathic personality was the PPI (Lilienfeld & Andrews, 1996). Factor analytic work on the structure of the PPI (Benning, Patrick, Hicks, Blonigen, & Krueger, 2003) demonstrated the presence of a Fearless Dominance (PPI-FD) factor – reflecting social assertiveness, immunity to stressful experience, and fearless risk-taking – separate from the PPI's impulsive-antisocial (Self-Centered Impulsivity; Lilienfeld & Widows, 2005) factor. Boldness, operationalized as PPI-FD, appears not to be represented in the Section II conception of DSM-5 ASPD: a meta-analytic study by Miller and Lynam (2012) reported that FD was only weakly correlated with symptoms of ASPD and unassociated or only weakly associated with other externalizing conditions

(e.g., aggression, substance abuse). By contrast, this meta-analytic study reported that FD was associated to a robust negative degree with internalizing psychopathology, consistent with Cleckley's clinical description of psychopathic individuals.

Despite its prominent role in historic conceptualizations and early research on psychopathic personality, the role of boldness has been recently questioned as a component of psychopathy. A particular point of concern has been that that PPI-FD scores are only modestly correlated with scores on Factor 1 of the PCL-R and unassociated with Factor 2 scores (Miller & Lynam, 2012), suggesting weak relevance to this well-established clinical measure of psychopathy. However, when examined on a facet level, PPI-FD has been found to be robustly and consistently associated with the Interpersonal facet of the PCL-R, encompassing glibness/charm, grandiosity, and manipulativeness (Hall et al., 2014; Venables et al., 2014; Wall et al., 2015) – features considered "core" to psychopathy (Harpur, Hare, & Hakstian, 1989). Of note, PPI-FD is assessed in a different modality (self-report) than the PCL-R (clinical interview), a factor known to attenuate convergent relations (Blonigen et al., 2010). Indeed, PPI-FD correlates to a higher degree with various self-report based measures including the SRP, YPI, EPA, and with Miller and colleagues' (Miller, Lynam, Widiger, & Leukefeld, 2001) FFM-based psychopathy prototype (Drislane et al., 2014; Lilienfeld et al., 2016; Poy et al., 2014), though it is not represented in certain others (e.g., LSRP; Drislane et al., 2014). PPI-FD has also been found to differentiate primary and secondary variants of psychopathy in cluster analytic work focusing on high PCL-R scoring offenders (Hicks et al., 2004).

Boldness is one of three major facets of psychopathy identified by the triarchic model (Patrick et al., 2009). The TriPM Boldness scale is one commonly used operationalization of the construct, developed to assess fearless proclivities in the domains of interpersonal behavior, affective experience, and venturesomeness. Within the triarchic model, boldness is characterized as overlapping to a modest degree with meanness and as uncorrelated with disinhibition.

Section III of the DSM-5 includes a psychopathy specifier for the trait-based definition of ASPD. This specifier consists of traits related to low anxiousness and social assertiveness (i.e., lack of social withdrawal and attention seeking). As expected given the traits composing it, this specifier (when operationalized using the PID-5) correlates appreciably with established indicators of boldness including PPI-FD and TriPM Boldness (Anderson, Sellbom, Wygant, Salekin, & Krueger, 2014). Reciprocally, Strickland et al. (2013) reported that TriPM Boldness, when controlling for modest overlap with TriPM Meanness, showed a positive association with the PID-5 trait domain of Antagonism, as well as negative associations with trait domains of Negative Affect and Detachment – demonstrating that boldness as assessed by the TriPM encompasses both maladaptive (i.e., disagreeable) as well as adaptive (i.e., stable/assertive) features.

In line with the idea that boldness operates as a mask of psychological well-being, higher levels of PPI-FD are negatively associated with social phobia and other fear conditions, while correlating positively with grandiose-narcissistic tendencies (Benning, Patrick, & Iacono, 2005). Moderate negative associations between PPI-FD and internalizing disorders symptoms more broadly (i.e., symptoms of mood as well as anxiety disorders) have been consistently found (see Miller & Lynam, 2012, for meta-analytic evidence). Though related weakly if at all to ASPD, PPI-FD shows robust positive and negative associations with two other Cluster B personality disorders-narcissistic and borderline, respectively (Miller & Lynam, 2012).

Boldness also has clear ties to established models of normal range personality, including the FFM (Costa & McCrae, 1992) and Tellegen's three-factor MPQ model (Tellegen & Waller, 2008). Boldness, as defined by PPI-FD, shows moderate-level associations with FFM traits of Extraversion (+) and Neuroticism (–), and a modest positive association with Openness to Experience (Miller & Lynam, 2012). With respect to the MPQ model, PPI-FD is associated with high Social Potency (domain of Positive Emotionality), low stress reactivity (domain of Negative Emotionality), and low harm avoidance (domain of Constraint; Benning et al., 2003). These findings provide support for the perspective that boldness is associated both with psychologically adaptive characteristics and with fearless, risk taking behavior.

CONNECTIONS TO BIOBEHAVIORAL SYSTEMS AND PROCESSES

Trait based models of personality such as the triarchic model provide a framework for linking ASPD and psychopathy to scientific initiatives to incorporate data from neural and behavioral modalities into the assessment and conceptualization of clinical disorders. Initiatives such as the NIMH's Research Domain Criteria (RDoC) system have called for integrating variables from biological and neurophysiological modalities with more standard assessment measures to move the field towards a neurobiologically-informed science of psychopathology. Similarly, the National Institute on Alcohol Abuse and Alcoholism (see Kwako, Momenan, Litten, Koob, & Goldman, 2016) and the National Research Council (2015) are also promoting the use of measures other than self- and other-report. In this final major section, we discuss psychopathy and ASPD in relation to three biobehavioral processes: inhibitory control, empathic sensitivity, and defensive reactivity. These processes connect clearly to the triarchic model phenotypes and provide a basis for linking what we know about psychological aspects of psychopathy and ASPD with neurophysiological and behavioral variables.

Inhibitory Control

Inhibitory control is a biobehavioral process presumed to reflect frontal-brain based differences in the capability to restrain behavior and regulate emotional reactivity (Patrick, Durbin, & Moser, 2012). This biobehavioral process interfaces with the triarchic model construct of disinhibition (i.e., externalizing proneness). Across many studies, individuals high in externalizing demonstrate patterns of dysregulated responding in the context of inhibitory control tasks administered in laboratory settings. For example, Fein, Klein, and Finn (2004) reported that individuals with substance use problems and high levels of externalizing behaviors exhibited a propensity to make risky choices during a simulated gambling task. In another study involving twins, Young and colleagues (2009) administered a set of lab-based tasks (Stroop, stop-signal, antisaccade) that called for participants to override prepotent responses, and used the covariance among performance measures from these tasks to define an "executive function" (EF) factor. Scores on this EF factor were negatively correlated with externalizing proneness, and twin modeling analyses demonstrated that this phenotypic association was attributable largely to shared genetic influences (Young et al., 2009).

Other work has shown that the ability to regulate autonomic nervous system responses (i.e., cardiovascular, electrodermal) is related both to cognitive functioning and externalizing psychopathology. Evidence for a relationship with cognitive functioning comes from work demonstrating facilitative effects of autonomic regulation on memory performance (Clark, Naritoku, Smith, Browning, & Jensen, 1999) and the ability to manage attentional demands (Borenstein & Seuss, 2000). Evidence for a relationship with externalizing proneness comes from studies demonstrating that individuals exhibiting antisocial behavior show reduced baseline levels of autonomic activity but increased autonomic reactivity in response to stress (Lorber, 2004; Ortiz & Raine, 2004). Other studies have reported elevated HR variability in antisocial individuals and interpreted this as evidence for weak vagal-parasympathetic regulation (Ortiz & Raine, 2004). Consistent with results from behavioral performance studies (e.g., Fein et al., 2004; Young et al., 2009), these psychophysiological findings support a link between externalizing proneness and inhibitory control deficits.

Multiple lines of neurophysiological evidence also indicate that externalizing proneness reflects, in part, impairment in anterior brain systems that regulate affect and behavior. In studies using electroencephalographic (EEG) methods to measure electrocortical activity, individuals high in externalizing proneness show reductions in event-related potential (ERP) response during cognitive processing tasks (Patrick et al., 2012). Reduced amplitude of the P3 component of the ERP response to target stimuli in an oddball task paradigm is the best-established brain response indicator of externalizing proneness (Iacono, Carlson, Malone, & McGue, 2002; Patrick et al., 2006). This association between externalizing and P300 has been shown to be attributable mainly to shared genetic influences (Hicks et al., 2007; Yancey, Venables, Hicks, & Patrick, 2013). In addition to blunted P3 response to oddball-target stimuli, blunted P3 in relation to stimuli in other cognitive tasks is also associated with high levels of externalizing (Nelson, Patrick, & Bernat, 2011). In addition to reduced P3 response in different tasks, individuals high in externalizing proneness show reduced amplitude of the error-related negativity (ERN), a negative-going cortical response that follows incorrect responses in a performance task (Dikman & Allen, 2000; Hall, Bernat, & Patrick, 2007), suggesting difficulties in endogenous error-monitoring. Taken together, findings for these ERP measures provide further evidence that externalizing proneness (disinhibition) is related to impairments in cognitive processing and control.

Neuroimaging studies have also produced evidence for differential brain reactivity on the part of externalizing-prone individuals in visual processing paradigms. For example, Foell and colleagues (2015) found that individuals high in trait disinhibition showed increased amygdala reactivity to affective pictures in the context of a pre-cueing task that enabled participants to anticipate picture presentations before their occurrence. The authors' interpretation was that high-disinhibited individuals failed to anticipate the occurrence of pictures, and thereby down-regulate their emotional reactions, in a normal way. Other neuroimaging research has demonstrated abnormal patterns of functional connectivity among particular brain regions in high-externalizing individuals (Abram et al., 2015).

Taken together, findings from these various lines of research suggest that highly disinhibited individuals show impaired processing of or attention to events occurring within an ongoing task, and that this results in reduced recognition of implicit and explicit task contingencies. In turn, this is consistent with Patrick and Bernat's (2009) conceptualization of trait disinhibition as involving a failure to link and integrate ongoing stimulus events and response outcomes with situation-relevant memories related to goals and consequences. These neurocognitive impairments disrupt automatic processes needed to anticipate, reflect upon, and self-regulate emotions and behaviors.

Empathic Sensitivity

Psychopathy is characterized by distinct affective and interpersonal features. A lack of concern for the well-being of others coupled with restricted emotional sensitivity are conceptualized to give rise to aggressive and manipulative behaviors. Consistent with this behavioral presentation, children and adults high in trait callousness demonstrate difficulties in processing emotions, empathizing with others, and altering their behavior when punished. Multiple studies have found that children and adults high in trait callousness are less likely to recognize, react to, or pay attention to affective faces – particularly fearful faces (Brislin et al., 2018; Brislin & Patrick, 2019; Dawel, O'Kearney, McKone, & Palermo, 2012; Marsh et al., 2008). Research studies have also found that callousness is associated with slower modification of behavior following punishment (Blair, 2001).

These differences in reactivity to affective faces and punishment cues are also accompanied by differences in neural responses, in high-callous youth as well as adults. Different studies have reported decreased amygdala reactivity to fearful faces in children high in callous-unemotional traits (Jones, Laurens, Herba, Barker, & Viding, 2009; Marsh et al., 2008; Viding et al., 2012). Consistent with the idea that blunted response to negative emotional cues allows high-callous individuals to act aggressively without an affective appreciation of the harm they cause to others, Lozier and colleagues (Lozier, Cardinale, VanMeter, & Marsh, 2014) found that reduced amygdala reactivity mediated the well-established association between trait callousness and proactive aggression. Recent work in adults using ERP measurement has also determined that reduced responsiveness to fearful face stimuli occurs early in the processing of such stimuli (Brislin et al., 2018; Brislin & Patrick, 2019).

Neurophysiological studies have also found that trait callousness is associated with decreased responsiveness to painful stimulation. Studies using both fMRI and ERP measurement (Cheng, Hung, & Decety, 2012; Lockwood et al., 2013; Marsh et al., 2013; Michalska, Zeffiro, & Decety, 2016; Yoder, Lahey, & Decety, 2016) have revealed evidence for reduced activity and altered connectivity in areas of the brain associated with empathy for pain (i.e., anterior insula, posterior insula, anterior cingulate cortex, amygdala) in individuals with high levels of callousness. Additionally, trait callousness has been found to be associated with heightened pain tolerance (Miller, Rausher, Hyatt, Maples, & Zeichner, 2014; Brislin, Buchman-Schmitt, Joiner, & Patrick, 2016). Further research is needed on how the physical experience of pain and neural empathic response to the pain of others are associated, and in turn, how they relate to trait callousness.

Lastly, studies with younger samples have consistently revealed evidence for differential neural reactivity to punishment in high-callous participants. Typically developing youth and those diagnosed with ADHD show a reduction in ventromedial prefrontal cortex (vmPFC) activity following an unexpected punishment (Finger et al., 2008). By contrast, youth high in both conduct problems and callousness do not demonstrate this reduction in vmPFC activation (Finger et al., 2008). In another study where children were taught that certain stimuli were "good" and others "bad" (because they were either rewarded or unrewarded), children high in callousness demonstrated less reactivity in orbitofrontal cortex (OFC) and caudate regions early in the task, and less OFC responsiveness to reward (Finger et al., 2011). In other work, Cohn et al. (2013) demonstrated that callousness in delinquent boys was negatively associated with anterior cingulate cortex (ACC) activity during fear conditioning. However, more work is needed on punishment responsiveness, as recent studies have suggested that these deficits may not be unique to callousness, but instead may occur in children with conduct problems more broadly (White et al., 2013, 2014). Indeed, the finding of deficits in error monitoring in high-externalizing adults appears consistent with this latter possibility. Further research using dimensional assessments of both callousness and disinhibition and measurement of neural reactivity in different tasks within the same participants will be needed to resolve this issue.

Defensive Reactivity

Psychopathy is also characterized by a weak defensive reactivity system, as evidenced for example by deficient startle potentiation in the presence of threat cues. Research with adult offenders has indicated that variations in defensive reactivity as indexed by startle modulation are most associated with the affective-interpersonal (Factor 1) features of psychopathy (e.g., Patrick, 1994; Vaidyanathan et al., 2011). Other work with non-offender samples has shown that scales that index boldness – the triarchic model construct most uniquely associated with psychopathy Factor 1 (Venables et al., 2014) – are associated with variations in aversive startle potentiation (Benning et al., 2005; Dvorak-Bertsch, Curtin, Rubinstein, & Newman, 2009; Esteller, Poy, & Moltó, 2016; Vaidyanathan, Patrick, & Bernat, 2009). Boldness is also associated with decreased electrodermal activation during anticipation of noxious stimulus events (Dindo & Fowles, 2011).

Defensive reactivity has also been studied through examination of electrocortical response to sudden unexpected noise probes. In this context, P3 amplitude can be viewed as indexing the coordination of cognitive resources to determine if sustained defensive mobilization is needed (Herbert, Kissler, Junghöfer, Peyk, & Rockstroh, 2006). Researchers have found that the affective-interpersonal component (Factor 1) of the PCL-R is associated with a reduced P3 brain response to abrupt noise probes occurring during viewing of picture stimuli (Drislane et al., 2013; Patrick et al., 2012). Similarly, PCL-R Factor 1 has been found to be associated with decreased elaborative response to aversive images, reflected in blunted late positive potential (LPP) response (Venables, Hall, Yancey, & Patrick, 2015). The LPP is a longer-latency, more persistent ERP component that is thought to reflect sustained processing of motivationally salient stimuli. The finding of blunted LPP response to aversive stimuli in individuals high in PCL-R Factor 1 is therefore consistent with the hypothesis that weak defensive reactivity is a distinct substrate for the fearless (bold) clinical presentation of individuals high in psychopathic traits.

In sum, these findings suggest that the defensive reactivity system contributes, through the boldness phenotype, to psychopathic traits. However, the defensive reactivity continuum is not psychopathy specific. While clinical presentations of psychopathy marked by boldness appear to occupy the low pole of this continuum, fear disorders appear to lie at the other end, where increased startle reactivity during negative emotional cueing is characteristic.

FUTURE DIRECTIONS

Psychoneurometric Measurement Models

Recent initiatives have called for a shift toward characterizing psychological disorders in terms of behavioral and neurobiological indicators in concert with traditional report-based measures. As discussed in earlier portions of this chapter, externalizing proneness, trait callousness, and threat sensitivity have correlates in behavior and neurobiology. The psychoneurometric measurement approach (Patrick et al., 2012; Patrick, Iacono, & Venables, 2019; Yancey et al., 2016) was proposed as a framework for conceptualizing and quantifying clinically-relevant attributes across differing modalities (methods) of measurement. This approach relies on the idea that psychological attributes, when conceptualized in neurobehavioral terms, can be quantified using variables from different measurement domains.

Using a psychoneurometric approach, researchers have formulated multi-method measurement models for the constructs of threat sensitivity (Yancey, Venables, & Patrick, 2016), akin to boldness in reverse (Kramer, Patrick, Krueger, & Gasperi, 2012), and inhibitory control (Venables et al., 2018), akin to disinhibition in reverse (Patrick et al., 2012, 2013). In these studies, a latent variable representation of the target attribute was defined using indicators from modalities of self-report and physiology, along with behavioral response in the case of inhibitory control. And in each case, the latent multi-method factor showed substantially more balanced associations with criterion measures from different modalities (methods) of measurement than individual modality indicators or modality factors.

These multi-method measurement models for threat sensitivity (/boldness) and inhibitory control (/disinhibition) can serve as valuable platforms for investigating the role of biobehavioral systems and processes in psychopathy, and clarifying how it relates to and differs from ASPD and other forms of psychopathology. Further work is still needed to investigate interrelations among known indicators of meanness, and biological correlates of empathic sensitivity as described earlier may provide a suitable starting point for this. Along with reshaping clinical assessments to incorporate non-report measures, work of this kind can provide insight into the functional role that neural and behavioral variables identified as indicators play in a given phenotype. Along with advancing our understanding of basic processes underlying differing expressions of psychopathy and ASPD, multi-method assessments of these biobehavioral attributes can serve as important referents for neuropsychologically oriented treatments.

Clinical Implications

ASPD and psychopathy have long been characterized as either highly resistant to treatment or even untreatable. These conditions certainly are challenging for clinicians as their core characteristics are at odds with motivation for change, treatment compliance, and therapeutic rapport (Skeem, Polaschek, Patrick, & Lilienfeld, 2011). Nonetheless, treatments that focus on targeting phenotypic facets of psychopathy as opposed to the disorder as a discrete taxon have shown some promise. For example, Caldwell and colleagues (Caldwell, Skeem, Salekin, & Van Rybrock, 2006) implemented a treatment program with children high in psychopathic traits that focused on reward instead of punishment, targeted self-interest, and taught empathy skills, and found decreased recidivism over a two-year follow-up period. Interventions that are tailored to the specific cognitive and emotional deficits that underlie externalizing proneness, trait callousness, and threat sensitivity may treatments with improved effectiveness.

Treatments targeting behavioral and physiological deficits associated with disinhibition could focus on the use of feedback-based response modification. In line with the idea that disinhibition is a core disposition that contributes to an aggressive, dysregulated clinical presentation, studies by Kahn and colleagues (e.g., Kahn, Ducharme, Travers, & Gonzalez-Heydrich, 2009) have shown that children who participated in a video game intervention, the Regulate and Gain Emotional (RAGE) Control procedure, learned how to focus, respond effectively, and keep their heart rates down other demanding tasks. While this project in its early stages, the utility of this treatment appears promising, as it may be more engaging than a CBT-based therapy for children and adults who are high in disinhibition. Another study by Konicar et al. (2015) provided instruction to high-psychopathic participants in how to regulate their cortical activity through biofeedback training, in a manner designed to enhance cognitive control capacity. These investigators found that improved cognitive control resulting from the biofeedback training was associated with decreased self-reported aggressive and impulsive behaviors, and improvements in both behavioral-inhibition performance and ERN reactivity in a laboratory-based task (Konicar et al., 2015).

To target callousness (meanness), treatments can integrate biofeedback with another targeted component – attentional retraining. Attentional retraining focuses on modifying attentional biases through reward cues. This method has been used primarily in treatment of anxiety disorders, but could theoretically be applied to teach individuals high in callousness to attend to distress cues. As individuals high in this attribute demonstrate poor attention to emotional face cues, attentional retraining could be used to teach these individuals to attend to faces and correctly identify them. A biofeedback component in which high-callous individuals are rewarded for increasing their emotional arousal to negatively valenced images could promote improvements in attending and responding appropriately to emotional cues in others. This approach to treatment is hypothetical at this point, but warrants future examination.

Given evidence for boldness as a dispositional characteristic with relevance to psychopathy, targeted treatments for this phenotypic facet also warrant consideration. When boldness co-occurs with high levels of meanness or disinhibition, it may be useful to focus treatment on enhancing threat sensitivity to more normative levels. For example, attentional retraining could be used in a manner opposite to how it is used to treat anxiety patients – in order to enhance attentiveness toward threatening or aversive stimuli. As with targeted treatments for meanness, research is needed to determine whether attention-oriented therapy can produce change in this psychopathy facet.

REFERENCES

Abram, S. V., Wisner, K. M., Grazioplene, R. G., Krueger, R. F., MacDonald, A. W., & DeYoung, C. G. (2015). Functional coherence of insula networks is associated with externalizing behavior. *Journal of Abnormal Psychology, 124*, 1079–1091.

Achenbach, T. M. (1966). The classification of children's psychiatric symptoms: A factor-analytic study. *Psychological Monographs: General and Applied, 80*(7), 1–37.

Achenbach, T. M. (1974). *Developmental Psychopathology*. Oxford: Ronald Press.

Achenbach, T. M., & Edelbrock, C. S. (1978). The classification of child psychopathology: A review and analysis of empirical efforts. *Psychological Bulletin, 85*, 1275–1301.

Achenbach, T. M., & Edelbrock, C. S. (1984). Psychopathology of childhood. *Annual Review of Psychology, 35*, 227–256.

American Psychiatric Association. (1952). *Diagnostic and Statistical Manual of Mental Disorders*. Washington, DC: American Psychiatric Association.

American Psychiatric Association. (1968). *Diagnostic and Statistical Manual of Mental Disorders* (2nd ed.). Washington, DC: American Psychiatric Association.

American Psychiatric Association. (1980). *Diagnostic and Statistical Manual of Mental Disorders* (3rd ed.). Washington, DC: American Psychiatric Association.

American Psychiatric Association. (1987). *Diagnostic and Statistical Manual of Mental Disorders* (revised 3rd ed.). Washington, DC: American Psychiatric Association.

American Psychiatric Association. (1994). *Diagnostic and Statistical Manual of Mental Disorders* (4th ed.). Washington, DC: American Psychiatric Association.

American Psychiatric Association. (2013). *Diagnostic and Statistical Manual of Mental Disorders* (5th ed.). Arlington, VA: American Psychiatric Publishing.

Andershed, H., Gustafson, S. B., Kerr, M., & Stattin, H. (2002). The usefulness of self-reported psychopathy-like traits in the study of antisocial behaviour among non-referred adolescents. *European Journal of Personality*, *16*(5), 383–402.

Anderson, J. L., Sellbom, M., Wygant, D. B., Salekin, R. T., & Krueger, R. F. (2014). Examining the associations between DSM-5 Section III antisocial personality disorder traits and psychopathy in community and university samples. *Journal of Personality Disorders*, *28*(5), 675–697.

Barkley, R. A. (1997). Behavioral inhibition, sustained attention, and executive functions: Constructing a unifying theory of ADHD. *Psychological Bulletin*, *121*(1), 65–94.

Benning, S. D., Patrick, C. J., Hicks, B. M., Blonigen, D. M., & Krueger, R. F. (2003). Factor structure of the psychopathic personality inventory: Validity and implications for clinical assessment. *Psychological Assessment*, *15*(3), 340–350.

Benning, S. D., Patrick, C. J., & Iacono, W. G. (2005). Psychopathy, startle blink modulation, and electrodermal reactivity in twin men. *Psychophysiology*, *42*(6), 753–762.

Black, D. W., Gunter, T., Loveless, P., Allen, J., & Sieleni, B. (2010). Antisocial personality disorder in incarcerated offenders: Psychiatric comorbidity and quality of life. *Annals of Clinical Psychiatry*, *22*(2), 113–120.

Blair, R. J. R. (2001). Neurocognitive models of aggression, the antisocial personality disorders, and psychopathy. *Journal of Neurology, Neurosurgery & Psychiatry*, *71*, 727–731.

Blonigen, D. M., Patrick, C. J., Douglas, K. S., Poythress, N. G., Skeem, J. L., Lilienfeld, S. O., ... Krueger, R. F. (2010). Multimethod assessment of psychopathy in relation to factors of internalizing and externalizing from the Personality Assessment Inventory: The impact of method variance and suppressor effects. *Psychological Assessment*, *22*(1), 96–107.

Borenstein, M. H., & Seuss, P. E. (2000). Physiological self-regulation and information processing in infancy: Cardiac vagal tone and habituation. *Child Development*, *71*(2), 273–287.

Brislin, S. J., Buchman-Schmitt, J. M., Joiner, T. E., & Patrick, C. J. (2016). "Do unto others"? Distinct psychopathy facets predict reduced perception and tolerance of pain. *Personality Disorders: Theory, Research, and Treatment*, *7*(3), 240–246.

Brislin, S. J., Drislane, L. E., Smith, S. T., Edens, J. F., & Patrick, C. J. (2015). Development and validation of triarchic psychopathy scales from the Multidimensional Personality Questionnaire. *Psychological Assessment*, *27*(3), 838–851.

Brislin, S. J., & Patrick, C. J. (2019). Callousness and affective face processing: Clarifying the neural basis of behavioral-recognition deficits through use of ERPs. *Clinical Psychological Science*. Advance online publication. doi: 10.1177/2167702619856342

Brislin, S. J., Yancey, J. R., Perkins, E. R., Palumbo, I. M., Drislane, L. E., Salekin, R. T., ... Patrick, C. J. (2018). Callousness and affective face processing in adults: Behavioral and brain-potential indicators. *Personality Disorders: Theory, Research, and Treatment*, *9*(2), 122–132.

Caldwell, M., Skeem, J., Salekin, R., & Van Rybrock, G. (2006). Treatment response of adolescent offenders with psychopathy features: A 2-year follow-up. *Criminal Justice and Behavior*, *33*, 571–596.

Cheng, Y., Hung, A. Y., & Decety, J. (2012). Dissociation between affective sharing and emotion understanding in juvenile psychopaths. *Development and Psychopathology*, *24*(2), 623–636.

Clark, K. B., Naritoku, D. K., Smith, D. C., Browning, R. A., & Jensen, R. A. (1999). Enhanced recognition memory following vagus nerve stimulation in human subjects. *Nature Neuroscience*, *2*(1), 94–98.

Clark, L. A., Watson, D., & Mineka, S. (1994). Temperament, personality, and the mood and anxiety disorders. *Journal of Abnormal Psychology*, *103*(1), 103–116.

Cleckley, H. (1976). *The Mask of Sanity* (5th ed.). St. Louis.: Mosby. (Original edition published in 1941)

Cohn, M. D., Popma, A., van den Brink, W., Pape, L. E., Kindt, M., van Domburgh, L., ... Veltman, D. J. (2013). Fear conditioning, persistence of disruptive behavior and psychopathic traits: An fMRI study. *Translational Psychiatry*, *3*(10), e319.

Cooke, D. J., & Michie, C. (2001). Refining the construct of psychopathy: Towards a hierarchical model. *Psychological Assessment*, *13*(2), 171–188.

Costa, P. T., & McCrae, R. R. (1992). *Revised NEO Personality Inventory (NEO-PI-R) and NEO Five-Factor Inventory (NEO-FFI) Professional Manual*. Odessa, FL: Psychological Assessment Resources.

Crego, C., & Widiger, T. A. (2016). Cleckley's psychopaths: Revisited. *Journal of Abnormal Psychology*, *125*(1), 75–87.

Dawel, A., O'Kearney, R., McKone, E., & Palermo, R. (2012). Not just fear and sadness: Meta-analytic evidence of pervasive emotion recognition deficits for facial and vocal expressions in psychopathy. *Neuroscience & Biobehavioral Reviews*, *36*(10), 2288–2304.

Dikman, Z. V., & Allen, J. J. (2000). Error monitoring during reward and avoidance learning in high-and low-socialized individuals. *Psychophysiology*, *37*(1), 43–54.

Dindo, L., & Fowles, D. (2011). Dual temperamental risk factors for psychopathic personality: Evidence from self-report and skin conductance. *Journal of Personality and Social Psychology*, *100*(3), 557–566.

Drislane, L. E., Brislin, S. J., Jones, S., & Patrick, C. J. (2018). Interfacing five-factor model and triarchic conceptualizations of psychopathy. *Psychological Assessment*, *30*(6), 834–840.

Drislane, L. E., Brislin, S. J., Kendler, K. S., Andershed, H., Larsson, H., & Patrick, C. J. (2015). A triarchic model analysis of the Youth Psychopathic Traits Inventory. *Journal of Personality Disorders*, *29*(1), 15–41.

Drislane, L. E., Patrick, C. J., & Arsal, G. (2014). Clarifying the content coverage of differing psychopathy inventories through reference to the triarchic psychopathy measure. *Psychological Assessment*, *26*(2), 350–362.

Drislane, L. E., Vaidyanathan, U., & Patrick, C. J. (2013). Reduced cortical call to arms differentiates psychopathy from antisocial personality disorder. *Psychological Medicine*, *43*, 825–835.

Dvorak-Bertsch, J. D., Curtin, J. J., Rubinstein, T. J., & Newman, J. P. (2009). Psychopathic traits moderate the interaction between cognitive and affective processing. *Psychophysiology*, *46*, 913–921.

Esteller, À., Poy, R., & Moltó, J. (2016). Deficient aversive-potentiated startle and the Triarchic model of psychopathy: The role of boldness. *Biological Psychology*, *117*, 131–140.

Falkenbach, D. M., Stern, S. B., & Creevy, C. (2014). Psychopathy variants: Empirical evidence supporting a subtyping model in a community sample. *Personality Disorders: Theory, Research, and Treatment*, *5*(1), 10–19.

Fein, G., Klein, L., & Finn, P. (2004). Impairment on a simulated gambling task in long-term abstinent alcoholics. *Alcoholism: Clinical and Experimental Research, 28*(10), 1487–1491.

Finger, E. C., Marsh, A. A., Blair, K. S., Reid, M. E., Sims, C., Ng, P., . . . Blair, R. J. R. (2011). Disrupted reinforcement signaling in the orbitofrontal cortex and caudate in youths with conduct disorder or oppositional defiant disorder and a high level of psychopathic traits. *American Journal of Psychiatry, 168*(2), 152–162.

Finger, E. C., Marsh, A. A., Mitchell, D. G., Reid, M. E., Sims, C., Budhani, S., . . . Blair, J. R. (2008). Abnormal ventromedial prefrontal cortex function in children with psychopathic traits during reversal learning. *Archives of General Psychiatry, 65*(5), 586–594.

Foell, J., Brislin, S. J., Strickland, C. M., Seo, D., Sabatinelli, D., & Patrick, C. J. (2015). Externalizing proneness and brain response during pre-cuing and viewing of emotional pictures. *Social Cognitive and Affective Neuroscience, 11*(7), 1102–1110.

Fowles, D. C. (1980). The three arousal model: Implications of Gray's two-factor learning theory for heart rate, electrodermal activity, and psychopathy. *Psychophysiology, 17*(2), 87–104.

Frick, P. J. (2004). The Inventory of Callous-Unemotional Traits. Unpublished rating scale.

Frick, P. J., & Hare, R. D. (2001). *The Antisocial Process Screening Device.* Toronto: Multi-Health Systems.

Frick, P. J., Ray, J. V., Thornton, L. C., & Kahn, R. E. (2014). Can callous-unemotional traits enhance the understanding, diagnosis, and treatment of serious conduct problems in children and adolescents? A comprehensive review. *Psychological Bulletin, 140*(1), 1–57.

Gorenstein, E. E., & Newman, J. P. (1980). Disinhibitory psychopathology: A new perspective and a model for research. *Psychological Review, 87*(3), 301–315.

Hall, J. R., Bernat, E. M., & Patrick, C. J. (2007). Externalizing psychopathology and the error-related negativity. *Psychological Science, 18*(4), 326–333.

Hall, J. R., Drislane, L. E., Murano, M., Patrick, C. J., Lilienfeld, S. O., & Poythress, N. G. (2014). Development and validation of triarchic construct scales from the Psychopathic Personality Inventory. *Psychological Assessment, 26*(2), 447–461.

Hare, R. D. (1965). Temporal gradient of fear arousal in psychopaths. *Journal of Abnormal Psychology, 70*, 442–445.

Hare, R. D. (1996). Psychopathy: A clinical construct whose time has come. *Criminal Justice and Behavior, 23*(1), 25–54.

Hare, R. D. (1991). *The Hare Psychopathy Checklist – Revised.* Toronto: Multi-Health Systems.

Hare, R. D. (2003). *The Hare Psychopathy Checklist – Revised* (2nd ed.). Toronto: Multi-Health Systems.

Hare, R. D., Hart, S. D., & Harpur, T. J. (1991). Psychopathy and the DSM-IV criteria for antisocial personality disorder. *Journal of Abnormal Psychology, 100*(3), 391–398.

Hare, R. D., & Neumann, C. S. (2008). Psychopathy as a clinical and empirical construct. *Annual Review of Clinical Psychology, 4*, 217–246.

Harpur, T. J., Hare, R. D., & Hakstian, A. R. (1989). Two-factor conceptualization of psychopathy: Construct validity and assessment implications. *Psychological Assessment, 1*(1), 6–17.

Herbert, C., Kissler, J., Junghöfer, M., Peyk, P., & Rockstroh, B. (2006). Processing of emotional adjectives: Evidence from startle EMG and ERPs. *Psychophysiology, 43*(2), 197–206.

Hicks, B. M., Bernat, E. M., Malone, S. M., Iacono, W. G., Patrick, C. J., Krueger, R. F., & McGue, M. (2007). Genes mediate the association between P300 amplitude and externalizing psychopathology. *Psychophysiology, 44*(1), 98–105.

Hicks, B. M., Markon, K. E., Patrick, C. J., Krueger, R. F., & Newman, J. P. (2004). Identifying psychopathy subtypes on the basis of personality structure. *Psychological Assessment, 16*, 276–288.

Hicks, B. M., & Patrick, C. J. (2006). Psychopathy and negative emotionality: Analyses of suppressor effects reveal distinct relations with emotional distress, fearfulness, and anger-hostility. *Journal of Abnormal Psychology, 115*(2), 276–287.

Hicks, B. M., Vaidyanathan, U., & Patrick, C. J. (2010). Validating female psychopathy subtypes: Differences in personality, antisocial and violent behavior, substance abuse, trauma, and mental health. *Personality Disorders: Theory, Research, and Treatment, 1*(1), 38–57.

Iacono, W. G., Carlson, S. R., Malone, S. M., & McGue, M. (2002). P3 event-related potential amplitude and risk for disinhibitory disorders in adolescent boys. *Archives of General Psychiatry, 59*, 750–757.

Jones, A. P., Laurens, K. R., Herba, C. M., Barker, G. J., & Viding, E. (2009). Amygdala hypoactivity to fearful faces in boys with conduct problems and callous-unemotional traits. *American Journal of Psychiatry, 166*, 95–102.

Kahn, J., Ducharme, P., Travers, B., & Gonzalez-Heydrich, J. (2009). RAGE control: Regulate and gain emotional control. In R. G. Bushko (Ed.) *Strategy for the Future of Health* (pp. 335–343). Amsterdam: IOS Press.

Karpman, B. (1941). On the need for separating psychopathy into two distinct clinical types: Symptomatic and idiopathic. *Journal of Criminology and Psychopathology, 3*, 112–137.

Kass, F., Skodol, A. E., Charles, E., Spitzer, R. L., & Williams, J. B. (1985). Scaled ratings of DSM-III personality disorders. *American Journal of Psychiatry, 142*(5), 627–630.

Kendler, K. S., Prescott, C. A., Myers, J., & Neale, M. C. (2003). The structure of genetic and environmental risk factors for common psychiatric and substance use disorders in men and women. *Archives of General Psychiatry, 60*, 929–937.

Konicar, L., Veit, R., Eisenbarth, H., Barth, B., Tonin, P., Strehl, U., & Birbaumer, N. (2015). Brain self-regulation in criminal psychopaths. *Scientific Reports, 5*, 9426.

Kotov, R., Krueger, R. F., Watson, D., Achenbach, T. M., Althoff, R. R., Bagby, R. M., . . . Eaton, N. R. (2017). The Hierarchical Taxonomy of Psychopathology (HiTOP): A dimensional alternative to traditional nosologies. *Journal of Abnormal Psychology, 126*(4), 454–477.

Kraepelin, E. (1915). *Psychiatrie: Ein lehrbuch* (8th ed.). Leipzig: Barth.

Kramer, M. D., Patrick, C. J., Krueger, R. F., & Gasperi, M. (2012). Delineating physiologic defensive reactivity in the domain of self-report: Phenotypic and etiologic structure of dispositional fear. *Psychological Medicine, 42*, 1305–1320.

Krueger, R. F. (1999). The structure of common mental disorders. *Archives of General Psychiatry, 56*, 921–926.

Krueger, R. F., Caspi, A., Moffitt, T. E., & Silva, P. A. (1998). The structure and stability of common mental disorders (DSM-III-R): A longitudinal-epidemiological study. *Journal of Abnormal Psychology, 107*(2), 216–227.

Krueger, R. F., Derringer, J., Markon, K. E., Watson, D., & Skodol, A. E. (2012). Initial construction of a maladaptive personality trait model and inventory for DSM-5. *Psychological Medicine, 42*, 1879–1890.

Krueger, R. F., Hicks, B., Patrick, C. J., Carlson, S., Iacono, W. G., & McGue, M. (2002). Etiologic connections among substance dependence, antisocial behavior, and personality: Modeling the externalizing spectrum. *Journal of Abnormal Psychology, 111,* 411–424.

Krueger, R. F., Markon, K. E., Patrick, C. J., Benning, S. D., & Kramer, M. (2007). Linking antisocial behavior, substance use, and personality: An integrative quantitative model of the adult externalizing spectrum. *Journal of Abnormal Psychology, 116,* 645–666.

Krueger, R. F., McGue, M., & Iacono, W. G. (2001). The higher-order structure of common DSM mental disorders: Internalization, externalization, and their connections to personality. *Personality and Individual Differences, 30*(7), 1245–1259.

Kwako, L. E., Momenan, R., Litten, R. Z., Koob, G. F., & Goldman, D. (2016). Addictions neuroclinical assessment: A neuroscience-based framework for addictive disorders. *Biological Psychiatry, 80*(3), 179–189.

Levenson, M. R., Kiehl, K. A., & Fitzpatrick, C. M. (1995). Assessing psychopathic attributes in a noninstitutionalized population. *Journal of Personality and Social Psychology, 68*(1), 151–158.

Lilienfeld, S. O., & Andrews, B. P. (1996). Development and preliminary validation of a self-report measure of psychopathic personality traits in noncriminal populations. *Journal of Personality Assessment, 66,* 488–524.

Lilienfeld, S. O., Smith, S. F., Sauvigné, K. C., Patrick, C. J., Drislane, L. E., Latzman, R. D., & Krueger, R. F. (2016). Is boldness relevant to psychopathic personality? Meta-analytic relations with non-Psychopathy Checklist-based measures of psychopathy. *Psychological Assessment, 28*(10), 1172–1185.

Lilienfeld, S. O., & Widows, M. R. (2005). *Psychopathic Personality Inventory—Revised (PPI-R) Professional Manual.* Odessa, FL: Psychological Assessment Resources.

Lockwood, P. L., Sebastian, C. L., McCrory, E. J., Hyde, Z. H., Gu, X., De Brito, S. A., & Viding, E. (2013). Association of callous traits with reduced neural response to others' pain in children with conduct problems. *Current Biology, 23*(10), 901–905.

Lorber, M. F. (2004). Psychophysiology of aggression, psychopathy, and conduct problems: A meta-analysis. *Psychological Bulletin, 130,* 531–552.

Lozier, L. M., Cardinale, E. M., VanMeter, J. W., & Marsh, A. A. (2014). Mediation of the relationship between callous-unemotional traits and proactive aggression by amygdala response to fear among children with conduct problems. *JAMA Psychiatry, 71*(6), 627–636.

Lykken, D. T. (1957). A study of anxiety in the sociopathic personality. *Journal of Abnormal and Clinical Psychology, 55,* 6–10.

Lykken, D. T. (1995). *The Antisocial Personalities.* Hillsdale, NJ: Lawrence Erlbaum.

Lynam, D. R., Gaughan, E. T., Miller, J. D., Miller, D. J., Mullins-Sweatt, S., & Widiger, T. A. (2011). Assessing the basic traits associated with psychopathy: Development and validation of the Elemental Psychopathy Assessment. *Psychological Assessment, 23,* 108–124.

Lynam, D. R., & Vachon, D. D. (2012). Antisocial personality disorder in DSM-5: Missteps and missed opportunities. *Personality Disorders: Theory, Research, and Treatment, 3*(4), 483–495.

Marsh, A. A., Finger, E. C., Fowler, K. A., Adalio, C. J., Jurkowitz, I. T., Schechter, J. C., … Blair, R. J. R. (2013). Empathic responsiveness in amygdala and anterior cingulate cortex in youths with psychopathic traits. *Journal of Child Psychology and Psychiatry, 54*(8), 900–910.

Marsh, A., Finger, E., Mitchell, D., Reid, M., Sims, C., Kosson, D. S., …Blair, R. J. R. (2008). Reduced amygdala response to

fearful expressions in children and adolescents with callous-unemotional traits and disruptive behavior disorders. *American Journal of Psychiatry, 165,* 712–720.

McCord, W., & McCord, J. (1964). *The Psychopath: An Essay on the Criminal Mind.* Princeton, NJ: Van Nostrand.

Michalska, K. J., Zeffiro, T. A., & Decety, J. (2016). Brain response to viewing others being harmed in children with conduct disorder symptoms. *Journal of Child Psychology and Psychiatry, 57* (4), 510–519.

Miller, J. D., & Lynam, D. R. (2012). An examination of the Psychopathic Personality Inventory's nomological network: A meta-analytic review. *Personality Disorders: Theory, Research, and Practice, 3,* 305–326.

Miller, J. D., Lynam, D. R., Widiger, T., & Leukefeld, C. (2001). Personality disorders as extreme variants of common personality dimensions: Can the five factor model adequately represent psychopathy? *Journal of Personality, 69,* 253–276.

Miller, J. D., Rausher, S., Hyatt, C. S., Maples, J., & Zeichner, A. (2014). Examining the relations among pain tolerance, psychopathic traits, and violent and nonviolent antisocial behavior. *Journal of Abnormal Psychology, 123*(1), 205–213.

National Research Council (2015). *Measuring Human Capabilities: An Agenda for Basic Research on the Assessment of Individual and Group Performance Potential for Military Accession.* Committee on Measuring Human Capabilities, Division of Behavioral and Social Sciences and Education. Washington, DC: National Academy of Sciences.

Nelson, L. D., Patrick, C. J., & Bernat, E. M. (2011). Operationalizing proneness to externalizing psychopathology as a multivariate psychophysiological phenotype. *Psychophysiology, 48,* 64–72.

Nelson, L. D., Strickland, C., Krueger, R. F., Arbisi, P. A., & Patrick, C. J. (2016). Neurobehavioral traits as transdiagnostic predictors of clinical problems. *Assessment, 23*(1), 75–85.

Ortiz, J., & Raine, A. (2004). Heart rate level and antisocial behavior in children and adolescents: A meta-analysis. *Journal of the American Academy of Child and Adolescent Psychiatry, 43,* 154–162.

Patrick, C. J. (1994). Emotion and psychopathy: Startling new insights. *Psychophysiology, 31,* 319–330.

Patrick, C. J. (2010). Operationalizing the Triarchic conceptualization of psychopathy: Preliminary description of brief scales for assessment of boldness, meanness, and disinhibition. Unpublished test manual. Florida State University, Tallahassee, FL.

Patrick, C. J., & Bernat, E. (2009). Neurobiology of psychopathy: A two-process theory. In G. G. Berntson & J. T. Cacioppo (Eds.), *Handbook of Neuroscience for the Behavioral Sciences* (pp. 1110–1131). New York: John Wiley & Sons.

Patrick, C. J., Bernat, E., Malone, S. M., Iacono, W. G., Krueger, R. F., & McGue, M. K. (2006). P300 amplitude as an indicator of externalizing in adolescent males. *Psychophysiology, 43,* 84–92.

Patrick, C. J., & Drislane, L. E. (2015). Triarchic model of psychopathy: Origins, operationalizations, and observed linkages with personality and general psychopathology. *Journal of Personality, 83*(6), 627–643.

Patrick, C. J., Durbin, C. E., & Moser, J. S. (2012). Reconceptualizing antisocial deviance in neurobehavioral terms. *Development and Psychopathology, 24,* 1047–1071.

Patrick, C. J., Fowles, D. C., & Krueger, R. F. (2009). Triarchic conceptualization of psychopathy: Developmental origins of disinhibition, boldness, and meanness. *Development and Psychopathology, 21*, 913–938.

Patrick, C. J., Iacono, W. G., & Venables, N. C. (2019). Incorporating neurophysiological measures into clinical assessments: Fundamental challenges and a strategy for addressing them. *Psychological Assessment.* Advance online publication. doi: 10.1037/pas0000713

Patrick, C. J., Venables, N. C., Yancey, J. R., Hicks, B. M., Nelson, L. D., & Kramer, M. D. (2013). A construct-network approach to bridging diagnostic and physiological domains: Application to assessment of externalizing psychopathology. *Journal of Abnormal Psychology, 122*, 902–916.

Paulhus, D. L., Neumann, C. S., & Hare, R. D. (2014). *Manual for the Self-Report Psychopathy Scale.* Toronto: Multi-Health Systems.

Paulhus, D. L., & Williams, K. M. (2002). The dark triad of personality: Narcissism, Machiavellianism, and psychopathy. *Journal of Research in Personality, 36*(6), 556–563.

Pinel, P. (1962). *A Treatise on Insanity* (trans. D. Davis). New York: Hafner. (Original edition published in 1801)

Poy, R., Segarra, P., Esteller, À., López, R., & Moltó, J. (2014). FFM description of the triarchic conceptualization of psychopathy in men and women. *Psychological Assessment, 26*(1), 69–76.

Prichard, J. C. (1837). *A Treatise on Insanity and other Disorders Affecting the Mind*. Philadelphia, PA: Haswell, Barrington, and Haswell.

Rush, B. (1823). *An Inquiry into the Effects of Ardent Spirits upon the Human Body and Mind: With an account of the Means of Preventing, and of the Remedies for Curing Them* (8th ed.). Boston, MA: James Loring.

Salekin, R. T., Andershed, H., & Clark, A. P. (2018) Psychopathy in children and adolescents: Assessment and critical questions regarding conceptualization. In C. J. Patrick (Ed.), *Handbook of Psychopathy* (2nd ed., pp. 479–508). New York: Guilford Press.

Sellbom, M., & Phillips, T. R. (2013). An examination of the triarchic conceptualization of psychopathy in incarcerated and nonincarcerated samples. *Journal of Abnormal Psychology, 122*(1), 208–214.

Skeem, J. L., Johansson, P., Andershed, H., Kerr, M., & Louden, J. E. (2007). Two subtypes of psychopathic violent offenders that parallel primary and secondary variants. *Journal of Abnormal Psychology, 116*, 395–409.

Skeem, J. L., Polaschek, D. L., Patrick, C. J., & Lilienfeld, S. O. (2011). Psychopathic personality: Bridging the gap between scientific evidence and public policy. *Psychological Science in the Public Interest, 12*(3), 95–162.

Strickland, C. M., Drislane, L. E., Lucy, M., Krueger, R. F., & Patrick, C. J. (2013). Characterizing psychopathy using DSM-5 personality traits. *Assessment, 20*, 327–338.

Tellegen, A. (2011). *Multidimensional Personality Questionnaire.* Minneapolis: University of Minnesota Press.

Tellegen, A., & Waller, N. G. (2008). Exploring personality through test construction: Development of the Multidimensional Personality Questionnaire. In G. J. Boyle, G. Matthews, & D. H. Saklofske (Eds.), *Handbook of Personality Theory and Testing: Personality Measurement and Assessment* (Vol. II, pp. 261–292). London: Sage.

Vaidyanathan, U., Hall, J. R., Patrick, C. J., & Bernat, E. M. (2011). Clarifying the role of defensive reactivity deficits in psychopathy and antisocial personality using startle reflex methodology. *Journal of Abnormal Psychology, 120*, 253–258.

Vaidyanathan, U., Patrick, C. J., & Bernat, E. M. (2009). Startle reflex potentiation during aversive picture viewing as an indicator of trait fear. *Psychophysiology, 46*, 75–85.

Venables, N. C., Foell, J., Yancey, J. R., Kane, M. J., Engle, R. W., & Patrick, C. J. (2018). Quantifying inhibitory control as externalizing proneness: A cross-domain model. *Clinical Psychological Science, 6*(4), 561–580.

Venables, N. C., Hall, J. R., & Patrick, C. J. (2014). Differentiating psychopathy from antisocial personality disorder: A triarchic model perspective. *Psychological Medicine, 44*, 1005–1013.

Venables, N. C., Hall, J. R., Yancey, J. R., & Patrick, C. J. (2015). Factors of psychopathy and electrocortical response to emotional pictures: Further evidence for a two-process theory. *Journal of Abnormal Psychology, 124*(2), 319–328.

Venables, N. C., & Patrick, C. J. (2012). Validity of the Externalizing Spectrum Inventory in a criminal offender sample: Relations with disinhibitory psychopathology, personality, and psychopathic features. *Psychological Assessment, 24*, 88–100.

Venables, N. C., Sellbom, M., Sourander, A., Kendler, K. S., Joiner, T. E., Drislane, L. E., ... Patrick, C. J. (2015). Separate and interactive contributions of weak inhibitory control and threat sensitivity to prediction of suicide risk. *Psychiatry Research, 226*(2), 461–466.

Verona, E., Patrick, C. J., & Joiner, T. E. (2001). Psychopathy, antisocial personality, and suicide risk. *Journal of Abnormal Psychology, 110*(3), 462–470.

Viding, E., Sebastian, C. L., Dadds, M. R., Lockwood, P. L., Cecil, C. A., De Brito, S. A., & McCrory, E. J. (2012). Amygdala response to preattentive masked fear in children with conduct problems: The role of callous-unemotional traits. *American Journal of Psychiatry, 169*(10), 1109–1116.

Wall, T. D., Wygant, D. B., & Sellbom, M. (2015). Boldness explains a key difference between psychopathy and antisocial personality disorder. *Psychiatry, Psychology, and Law, 22*(1), 94–105.

Widiger, T. A., Hurt, S. W., Frances, A., Clarkin, J. F., & Gilmore, M. (1984). Diagnostic efficiency and DSM-III. *Archives of General Psychiatry, 41*(10), 1005–1012.

White, S. F., Brislin, S. J., Sinclair, S., Fowler, K. A., Pope, K., & Blair, R. J. R. (2013). The relationship between large cavum septum pellucidum and antisocial behavior, callous-unemotional traits and psychopathy in adolescents. *Journal of Child Psychology and Psychiatry, 54*(5), 575–581.

White, S. F., Fowler, K. A., Sinclair, S., Schechter, J. C, Majestic, C. M., Pine, D. S, & Blair, R. J. (2014). Disrupted expected value signaling in youth with disruptive behavior disorders to environmental reinforcers. *Journal of American Academy of Child and Adolescent Psychiatry, 53*(5), 579–588.

Yancey, J. R., Venables, N. C., Hicks, B. M., & Patrick, C. J. (2013). Evidence for a heritable brain basis to deviance-promoting deficits in self-control. *Journal of Criminal Justice, 41*, 309–317.

Yancey, J. R., Venables, N. C., & Patrick, C. J. (2016). Psychoneurometric operationalization of threat sensitivity: Relations with clinical symptom and physiological response criteria. *Psychophysiology, 53*(3), 393–405.

Yoder, K. J., Lahey, B. B., & Decety, J. (2016). Callous traits in children with and without conduct problems predict reduced connectivity when viewing harm to others. *Scientific Reports, 6*, 20216.

Young, S. E., Friedman, N. P., Miyake, A., Willcutt, E. G., Corley, R. P., Haberstick, B. C., & Hewitt, J. K. (2009). Behavioral disinhibition: Liability for externalizing spectrum disorders and its genetic and environmental relation to response inhibition across adolescence. *Journal of Abnormal Psychology, 118*, 117–130.

Young, S. E., Stallings, M. C., Corley, R. P., Krauter, K. S., & Hewitt, J. K. (2000). Genetic and environmental influences on behavioral disinhibition. *American Journal of Medical Genetics, 96*(5), 684–695.

Zimmerman, M., & Coryell, W. H. (1990). Diagnosing personality disorders in the community: A comparison of self-report and interview measures. *Archives of General Psychiatry, 47*(6), 527–531.

11a What Do We Talk about When We Talk about Psychopathy? Commentary on an Integrative Biobehavioral Trait Perspective on Antisocial Personality Disorder and Psychopathy

DAVID K. MARCUS AND MADELINE G. NAGEL

Brislin and Patrick's chapter (this volume) on antisocial personality disorder and psychopathy provides a comprehensive and scholarly review of the past and current thinking about these two related, but distinct, conditions. These authors are ideally suited to contribute this chapter because their work developing the triarchic model of psychopathy has been highly influential in shaping the modern conceptualization of psychopathy as a constellation of overlapping, yet distinct traits, as well as generating research in the field. Although the paper that introduced the triarchic model (Patrick, Fowles, & Krueger, 2009) is fewer than 10 years old, according to PsychINFO it has already been cited over 450 times. Our own work on psychopathy has been strongly influenced by this model.

The debate over what components are essential to, or part of psychopathy may have its origins in the differing classic accounts provided by Cleckley (1976), who described psychiatric inpatients who were irresponsible, egocentric, but also charming and socially influential; and the more aggressive and vicious criminal offenders identified as psychopaths by McCord and McCord (1964) and Robbins (1966). However, this question about what constitutes psychopathy remains controversial today (e.g., Hare & Neumann, 2010; Lilienfeld et al., 2012; Miller & Lynam, 2015; Skeem & Cooke, 2010). The power of the triarchic model is that it provides an inclusive framework for organizing the various elements that have been proposed to constitute psychopathy into three dispositional constructs: boldness, meanness, and disinhibition. By erecting a big tent that encompasses all of the primary components that have been implicated in classic and contemporary conceptualizations of the psychopathy, the triarchic model avoids getting pulled into some of the most contentious debates among psychopathy researchers. Paradoxically, the triarchic model's broad formulation may leave the basic question of what is psychopathy unanswered. In this brief commentary we attempt to describe this central challenge to the field.

There are some personality disorders whose various symptoms are essentially expressions of a single trait.

For example, the seven symptoms of paranoid personality disorder are different descriptions or manifestations of suspiciousness, and the seven symptoms of avoidant personality disorder each describe different aspects of excessive sensitivity to social judgment and rejection. Hence, there is no need for a multifaceted model of paranoid or avoidant personality disorder. There may be controversies associated with each of these disorders (e.g., is avoidant personality disorder distinct from social anxiety disorder?), but there is no controversy about what is at the core of these personality disorders. In contrast, despite its long history and status as one of the most studied forms of personality pathology (a PsychINFO search of "psychopathy or psychopath" yields over 9,500 citations), there is little agreement about what (if anything) is at the core of psychopathy and the very definition of psychopathy can differ between researchers.

According to the triarchic model, boldness, meanness, and disinhibition are the three constructs that "account for the observable symptoms and correlates of psychopathy" (Brislin & Patrick, this volume, p. 254 in the previous chapter). This formulation does not, however, stipulate that all three of these constructs must be present for a "diagnosis" of psychopathy. Miller and Lynam (2015) identified this issue as the debate regarding necessity and sufficiency. In a previous paper, Patrick and Drislane (2015, p. 628) suggested that individuals high in disinhibition "would warrant a diagnosis of psychopathy if also high in boldness and/or meanness, which contribute to a more detached (insouciant-persuasive or callous-predatory) expression of disinhibitory tendencies, but not if high on only one of these tendencies." It would follow from this formulation that none of the components of the triarchic model are sufficient for psychopathy, but that disinhibition is necessary. Nevertheless, disinhibition may not be essential to psychopathy, especially to primary psychopathy (Poythress & Hall, 2011). As Karpman (1948, p. 527) wrote over 60 years ago, "the true psychopath is the least impulsive of them all" noting that "the psychopath often coolly and deliberately plans his actions as seen in the case of professional criminals; there is no hot-headedness here at all."

Conversely, it is also questionable whether all individuals who are high in disinhibition and boldness would necessarily be psychopathic (e.g., a fearless, charming, assertive person with ADHD who is scrupulously moral).

In contrast, Miller and Lynam (2015) have asserted that antagonism/disagreeableness, as represented by the meanness component of the triarchic model, is necessary and possibly sufficient for psychopathy. In fact, two recent network analyses of the items from the Psychopathy Checklist – Revised (Hare, 1991) found that meanness items, such as callousness and a lack of remorse, were among the most central items across a variety of forensic samples (Preszler, Marcus, Edens, & McDermott, 2018; Verschuere et al., 2018). It seems unlikely, however, that meanness or disagreeableness is sufficient for psychopathy, because there are other conditions or personality types that are also characterized by disagreeableness or meanness that are distinct from psychopathy. For example, sadism appears to be at least as strongly associated with disagreeableness as psychopathy is (e.g., van Geel, Goemans, Toprak, & Vedder, 2017), but sadism and psychopathy are distinguishable constructs (e.g., Buckels, Jones, & Paulhus, 2013). If meanness were to be sufficient for psychopathy it would have to be a more specific subtype or form of antagonism than general disagreeableness. Furthermore, meanness may not be necessary for psychopathy. Community participants who rated the original Cleckley (1976) case studies on a set of psychopathy-related and general personality traits did not rate most of the cases as especially high in meanness (Crego & Widiger, 2016). Thus many of the patients who informed Cleckley's conceptualization of psychopathy, which influenced most subsequent psychopathy research, including the development of the Psychopathy Checklist scales (Hare, Neumann, & Mokros, 2018) "were not particularly cruel, callous, or physically aggressive" (Crego & Widiger, 2016, p. 86).

Whereas there is reason to question whether disinhibition or meanness are each necessary or sufficient for psychopathy, as noted by Brislin and Patrick, there is controversy regarding whether boldness should even be included as a component of psychopathy. Measures of boldness are at best weakly correlated with other measures of psychopathy. Furthermore, boldness is negatively associated with internalizing pathology and can be adaptive in some situations, leading some (e.g., Miller, Lamkin, Maples-Keller, Sleep, & Lynam, 2018; Miller & Lynam, 2012) to argue that it should not be included as an element of a pathological construct. Brislin and Patrick's chapter made a strong case for the inclusion of boldness, noting that boldness to a greater extent than meanness characterized Cleckley's cases (Crego & Widiger, 2016), and that boldness may be the component of the triarchic model that differentiates psychopathy from antisocial personality disorder (Venables, Hall, & Patrick, 2014; Wall, Wygant, & Sellbom, 2014). In our own research, we found that self-reported boldness was significantly related to

peer reports of academic dishonesty but not to self-reported academic dishonesty among well-acquainted college students (Marcus, Robinson, & Eichenbaum, 2019), suggesting that studies that rely entirely on self-reports may underestimate the association between boldness and antisocial behavior. Thus, despite concerns that boldness is not pathological in and of itself, removing boldness from the psychopathy is likely to diminish the construct, possibly reducing psychopathy simply to antisociality.

Further complicating matters, the three components of the triarchic model do not all hang together. In most studies, boldness is unrelated to or weakly positively correlated with meanness, and boldness is often weakly negatively correlated with disinhibition. If boldness is hardly related to the other two components of the triarchic model and the triarchic model is an accurate representation of psychopathy, then psychopathy is not a syndrome in the traditional sense of the term (Marcus, Fulton, & Edens, 2013). Lilienfeld (2013) proposed that psychopathy may be better understood as an emergent trait. Because an emergent trait arises when two (or more) characteristics co-occur, this proposal suggests that powerful interaction effects should be found when the components of the triarchic model are analyzed (e.g., the interaction of boldness and disinhibition should lead to especially negative outcomes). A few studies have found that the interaction of boldness and disinhibition is associated with negative outcomes such as predatory aggression by forensic psychiatric inpatients (Smith, Edens, & McDermott, 2013) and more positive attitudes toward sexually manipulative tactics by college men (Marcus & Norris, 2014). However, other studies have failed to find this posited interaction between boldness and disinhibition (e.g., Gatner, Douglas, & Hart, 2016; Miller, Maples-Keller, & Lynam, 2016). Some studies have even found interactions between boldness and disinhibition in which high levels of boldness served as a protective factor for individuals high in disinhibition against negative outcomes such as heavy episodic drinking (Sylvers, Landfield, & Lilienfeld, 2011) and maladjustment following risky sexual behavior (Fulton, Marcus, & Zeigler-Hill, 2014).

The three components of the triarchic model all clearly have something to do with psychopathy, but none appear to be necessary or sufficient. Although the idea of psychopathy as a compound trait that emerges from the interaction of various combinations of three components is intriguing and could clarify the definition of psychopathy, the empirical support for this proposition is mixed, at best. Given that the triarchic model posits that the three components of the model are each underpinned by a different biobehavioral system (inhibitory control for disinhibition, empathic sensitivity for meanness, and defensive reactivity for boldness), this model would not necessarily predict strong associations among its three components. If anything, the high correlations between the Triarchic Psychopathy Measure (Patrick, 2010) Disinhibition and Meanness scales raise questions about why these presumably independent dimensions should be so closely related. Ultimately, the value of the triarchic model comes from its ability to generate research that advances the field and it is not responsible for solving a problem that has bedeviled psychopathy scholars going back to pioneers like Cleckely (1976) and Karpman (1948). Still, it would be reassuring to know that psychopathy experts are all talking about the same thing when we talk about psychopathy.

REFERENCES

Buckels, E. E., Jones, D. N., & Paulhus, D. L. (2013). Behavioral confirmation of everyday sadism. *Psychological Science, 24*(11), 2201–2209.

Cleckley, H. (1976). *The Mask of Sanity* (5th ed.). St. Louis.: Mosby. (Original edition published in 1941)

Crego, C., & Widiger, T. A. (2016). Cleckley's psychopaths: Revisited. *Journal of Abnormal Psychology, 125*, 75–87.

Fulton, J. J., Marcus, D. K., & Zeigler-Hill, V. (2014). Psychopathic personality traits predict risky sexual behavior among college-age women. *Journal of Social and Clinical Psychology, 33*, 143–168.

Gatner, D. T., Douglas, K. S., & Hart, S. D. (2016). Examining the incremental and interactive effects of boldness with meanness and disinhibition within the triarchic model of psychopathy. *Personality Disorders: Theory, Research, and Treatment, 3*, 259–268.

Hare, R. D. (1991). *The Hare Psychopathy Checklist – Revised (PCL-R): Technical Manual.* North Tonawanda, NY: Multi-Health Systems.

Hare, R. D., & Neumann, C. S. (2010). The role of antisociality in the psychopathy construct: Comment on Skeem and Cooke (2010). *Psychological Assessment, 22*, 446–454.

Hare, R. D., Neumann, C. S., & Mokros, A. (2018). The PCL-R assessment of psychopathy. In C. J. Patrick (Ed.), *Handbook of Psychopathy* (2nd ed., pp. 39–79). New York: Guilford Press.

Karpman, B. (1948). The myth of the psychopathic personality. *American Journal of Psychiatry, 104*, 523–534.

Lilienfeld, S. O. (2013). Is psychopathy a syndrome? Comment on Marcus, Fulton, and Edens. *Personality Disorders: Theory, Research, and Treatment, 4*, 85–86.

Lilienfeld, S. O., Patrick, C. J., Benning, S. D., Berg, J., Sellbom, M., & Edens, J. F. (2012). The role of fearless dominance in psychopathy: Confusions, controversies, and clarifications. *Personality Disorders: Theory, Research, and Treatment, 3*, 327–340.

Marcus, D. K., Fulton, J. J., & Edens, J. F. (2013). The two-factor model of psychopathic personality: Evidence from the Psychopathic Personality Inventory. *Personality Disorders: Theory, Research, and Treatment, 4*, 67–76.

Marcus, D. K., & Norris, A. L. (2014). A new measure of attitudes toward sexually predatory tactics and its relation to the triarchic model of psychopathy. *Journal of Personality Disorders, 28*, 247–261.

Marcus, D. K., Robinson, S. L., & Eichenbaum, A. E. (2019). Externalizing behavior and psychopathy: A social relations analysis. *Journal of Personality Disorders, 33*, 310–325.

McCord, W., & McCord, J. (1964). *The Psychopath: An Essay on the Criminal Mind.* Princeton, NJ: Van Nostrand.

Miller, J. D., Lamkin, J., Maples-Keller, J., Sleep, C. E., & Lynam, D. R. (2018). A test of the empirical profile and coherence of the DSM-5 psychopathy specifier. *Psychological Assessment, 30*, 870–881.

Miller, J. D., & Lynam, D. R. (2012). An examination of the Psychopathic Personality Inventory's nomological network: A meta-analytic review. *Personality Disorders: Theory, Research, and Practice, 3*, 305–326.

Miller, J. D., & Lynam, D. R. (2015). Psychopathy and personality: Advances and debates. *Journal of Personality, 83*, 585–592.

Miller, J. D., Maples-Keller, J. L., & Lynam, D. R. (2016). An examination of the three components of the Psychopathic Personality Inventory: Profile comparisons and tests of moderation. *Psychological Assessment, 28*, 692–701.

Patrick, C. J. (2010). *Triarchic Psychopathy Measure (TriPM).* PhenX Toolkit Online assessment catalog. Retrieved from www.phenxtoolkit.org/index.php?pageLink=browse.protocoldetails&id=121601

Patrick, C. J., & Drislane, L. E. (2015). Triarchic model of psychopathy: Origins, operationalizations, and observed linkages with personality and general psychopathology. *Journal of Personality, 83*(6), 627–643.

Patrick, C. J., Fowles, D. C., & Krueger, R. F. (2009). Triarchic conceptualization of psychopathy: Developmental origins of disinhibition, boldness, and meanness. *Development and Psychopathology, 21*, 913–938.

Poythress, N. G., & Hall, J. R. (2011). Psychopathy and impulsivity reconsidered. *Aggression and Violent Behavior, 16*, 120–134.

Preszler, J., Marcus, D. K., Edens, J. F., & McDermott, B. E. (2018). Network analysis of psychopathy in forensic inpatients. *Journal of Abnormal Psychology, 127*, 171–182.

Robins, L. N. (1966). *Deviant Children Grown Up.* Baltimore, MD: Williams & Wilkins.

Skeem, J. L., & Cooke, D. J. (2010). Is criminal behavior a central component of psychopathy? Conceptual directions for resolving the debate. *Psychological Assessment, 22*, 433–445.

Smith, S. T., Edens, J. F., & McDermott, B. E. (2013). Fearless dominance and self-centered impulsivity interact to predict predatory aggression among forensic psychiatric inpatients. *International Journal of Forensic Mental Health, 12*, 33–41.

Sylvers, P., Landfield, K. E., & Lilienfeld, S. O. (2011). Heavy episodic drinking in college students: Associations with features of psychopathy and antisocial personality disorder. *Journal of American College Health, 59*, 367–372.

van Geel, M., Goemans, A., Toprak, F., & Vedder, P. (2017). Which personality traits are related to traditional bullying and cyber-bullying? A study with the big five, dark triad and sadism. *Personality and Individual Differences, 106*, 231–235.

Venables, N. C., Hall, J. R., & Patrick, C. J. (2014). Differentiating psychopathy from antisocial personality disorder: A triarchic model perspective. *Psychological Medicine, 44*, 1005–1013.

Verschuere, B., van Ghesel Grothe, S., Waldorp, L., Watts, A. L., Lilienfeld, S. O., Edens, J. F., … Noordhof, A. (2018). What features of psychopathy might be central? A network analysis of the Psychopathy Checklist – Revised (PCL-R) in three large samples. *Journal of Abnormal Psychology, 127*, 51–65.

Wall, T. D., Wygant, D. B., & Sellbom, M. (2014). Boldness explains a key difference between psychopathy and antisocial personality disorder. *Psychiatry, Psychology, and Law, 22*(1), 94–105.

11b Issues of Emphasis in the Triarchic Psychopathy Model: Commentary on an Integrative Biobehavioral Trait Perspective on Antisocial Personality Disorder and Psychopathy

DONALD R. LYNAM

Brislin and Patrick provide an excellent discussion of descriptive work on psychopathy since Cleckley and on the relations between DSM antisocial personality disorder and psychopathy as typically assessed using Hare's PCL. In addition, they provide a very thorough description of the triarchic model of psychopathy (TPM). In this commentary, I highlight a few key tenets of the model that I believe deserve more careful scrutiny and consideration. My main concerns lie with the underlying theoretical and empirical support for the relative emphases placed on each component of the model, with an especial focus on the dominant role played by Boldness and the more limited roles played by antisocial behavior (ASB) and Meanness. Because of limited space, I restrict myself to the concerns regarding points of emphasis.

I will repeatedly reference traits from the Five-Factor Model of personality (FFM) – a model that my colleagues and I use to conceptualize and assess psychopathy. A number of studies have shown a strong correspondence between the TPM components and FFM traits (e.g., Crego & Widiger, 2016; Miller, Lamkin, Maples-Keller, & Lynam, 2016). In recent work, we have shown that the TPM can be understood using the FFM (Hyatt, Crowe, Lynam, & Miller, in press) where Boldness is represented using a combination of FFM Extraversion and reversed FFM Neuroticism (E+/N–), Meanness is represented with reversed FFM Agreeableness (A–), and Disinhibition is represented with reversed FFM Conscientiousness (C–). In fact, these FFM dimensions can largely recreate the empirical relations manifested by the Triarchic Psychopathic Measure (TriPM), suggesting that the latter is embedded within the former.

THE (OVER)IMPORTANCE OF BOLDNESS (AND FEARLESS DOMINANCE)

Newer measures and models of psychopathy, including the TPM and PPI (Lilienfeld & Andrews, 1996), have placed great emphasis the role of Boldness or Fearless Dominance (FD) in psychopathy – claiming to have discovered Cleckley's mask of sanity. While it is true that Cleckley referenced the absence of anxiety and overt psychosis in his descriptions, there is a strong argument to be made that Boldness/FD is too salutatory a construct to take on the prominent role it has been granted. In a meta-analysis of the PPI, Miller and Lynam (2012) found FD to be mostly unrelated to ASB, aggression, and broad externalizing. Results were similar in a recently completed meta-analysis of the TriPM (Sleep, Weiss, Lynam, & Miller, 2019); Boldness was weakly related to ASB, aggression, and broad externalizing. Rather than being related to what has typically driven interest in psychopathy (i.e., ASB), scores on Boldness/FD are most strongly related to positive psychological outcomes. The largest effect sizes observed by Miller and Lynam for FD were the positive ones for positive affect and extraversion and the negative ones for negative affect and internalizing. Results from Sleep et al. for Boldness were virtually identical. Boldness had strong positive correlations with indicators of extraversion and positive emotionality, and strong negative correlations with indicators of negative affect and internalizing psychopathology.

Emotionally stable Extraversion and immunity from internalizing psychopathology are not the outcomes that have driven interest in psychopathy for the last 40 years, nor is Boldness/FD, as is sometimes claimed, Lykken's (1995) fearlessness – that etiologic factor underlying primary psychopathy and accounting for all of its symptoms including serious ASB. The absence of substantial relations between Boldness/FD and ASB and other features of psychopathy, including Meanness and Disinhibition rules Boldness/FD out as an index of Lykken's fearlessness. Neither are these the outcomes that placed psychopathic individuals in the institutions at which Cleckley worked. It is interesting that among all of the potential differential diagnoses for psychopathy that Cleckley described (e.g., psychosis, criminality, alcoholism, and malingering), good adjustment/psychological health was not one of them. However, that is exactly the diagnostic confusion posed by Boldness/FD.

Instead of serving as the core for psychopathy, data suggest that Boldness/FD and its outcomes may be the core of what makes for healthy people and good friends and neighbors. For example, Bleidorn and colleagues (in press) recently developed an expert rated personality index of the healthy personality and provided correlations between their index and 52 other indicators of health and dysfunction, including the TriPM. Boldness was correlated at .48 with this index – the fifth highest of the criteria examined. The only four correlations that were higher were for explicit indices of positive adjustment (rs range from .52 to .60).

In the context of empirical and theoretical arguments that are inconsistent with the approach to Boldness/FD taken in the TPM, several modifications of the role of Boldness/FD in ASB have been offered. Lilienfeld et al (2012) suggested that Boldness/FD might predict ASB when combined with high scores on Meanness or Disinhibition but this hypothesis has received little support (e.g., Gatner, Douglas, & Hart, 2016; Maples et al., 2014; Miller, Maples-Keller, & Lynam, 2016; Vize, Lynam, Lamkin, Miller, & Pardini, 2016). Alternatively, Blonigen (2013) offered that Boldness/FD might be related to ASB at especially high ends of the trait, but this hypothesis has not been supported (Crowe, Lynam, & Miller, 2018; Gatner et al., 2016; Vize et al., 2016). In the end, the existing evidence suggest that Boldness/FD is related to positive psychological health and unrelated to externalizing behaviors, the long-time hallmark of psychopathy.

THE (UNDER)IMPORTANCE OF ANTISOCIAL BEHAVIOR

This new emphasis on Boldness/FD and elevation of psychological health to a cardinal feature has been accompanied by a corresponding de-emphasis on the role of ASB in psychopathy – a serious departure from previous conceptions. The core feature of psychopathy has always been intransigent ASB. Patrick and Brislin correctly note this in their descriptions of *manie sans delirium*, "moral insanity," and "moral weakness," but they underemphasize ASB in modern conceptualizations. They write: "Cleckley characterized psychopathy as a distinct and severe form of psychopathology masked by an appearance of good psychological health." This is misleading, as the psychopathology that Cleckley (1976) observed in all 15 of his cases was serious and chronic antisocial behavior. He explicitly included "inadequately motivated ASB" as a key characteristic, writing that "not only is the psychopath undependable, but also in more active ways he cheats, deserts, annoys, brawls, fails, and lies without any apparent compunction. He will commit theft, forgery, adultery, fraud, and other deeds" (1976, p. 343). Long histories of ASB appear in all 15 of Cleckley's cases (see Lynam & Miller, 2012); without such behavior, there is no psychopathy.

Recalcitrant ASB is the feature that is shared across Karpman's two subtypes – primary and secondary – where Boldness is frequently taken as an indicator of the former. Karpman's (1941) distinction between primary and secondary psychopathy was offered as a means of reducing the heterogeneity in the larger group of patients labeled psychopathic on the basis of their long histories of ASB. He argued that scholars of his day had created a problematically heterogeneous construct by failing to consider the "dynamics" that contribute to the observed traits. Persistent and pervasive ASB was characteristic of both forms of psychopathy, although the underlying causes of these behaviors were different – a lack of conscience and concern for others in the primary variant and frustration/anger due to conscious or unconscious conflicts in the secondary variant.

ASB is central to psychopathy in Lykken's (1995) writings as well. He wrote: "I use psychopath to refer to these people who have puzzled psychiatry for so long, whose ASB appears to result from a defect or aberration within themselves rather than in their rearing" (1995, p. 113). In his taxonomy, Lykken indicated that psychopathy is a genus belonging to the family of antisocial personalities whose members "are characterized by a persisting disposition toward ASB" (1995, p. 21).

THE (UNDER)IMPORTANCE OF MEANNESS (ANTAGONISM)

There is considerable evidence indicating that the cardinal trait for psychopathy beyond ASB in the TPM is meanness – a trait that shares great similarity with the FFM trait of Antagonism. Defined extensionally, the Antagonism–Agreeableness dimension consists of five lower-order traits: callousness, immorality, distrust, combativeness, and arrogance (Crowe et al., 2018). As with ASB, Brislin and Patrick undersell the role of Meanness/Antagonism in historical and contemporary conceptualizations of psychopathy. For example, they suggest that Meanness is present in only one of four facets of the PCL-R (i.e., the affective facet), in only a single criterion within the DSM-5 APD criteria (i.e., lack of remorse), and in only a single subscale of the PPI-R (i.e., "coldheartedness"). In actuality, Antagonism is the most ubiquitous element in trait descriptions of psychopathy, the strongest and most consistent correlate of all measures of psychopathy, and the glue that holds psychopathy inventories together.

From Cleckley (1976) through more current conceptualizations, descriptions of psychopathy are rife with Antagonism-related content. First, any description that includes an explicit representation of ASB (i.e., Cleckley, Karpman, Hare (2003), and DSM-5), is assessing Antagonism as it is the largest and most robust personality correlate of all forms of ASB. In their meta-analytic investigation of the relation between the FFM and antisocial and aggressive behavior, Vize, Collison, Miller, and

Lynam (2019) found the average effect size for Agreeableness (r = −.38) was largest, followed by the effect size for Conscientiousness, the FFM variant of TPM Disinhibition (r = −.22), and then Neuroticism (r = .15). Second, beyond the indirect assessments of Antagonism via ASB, these descriptions are rife with Antagonism-related content: lack of empathy and remorse, lying and manipulation, arrogance and egocentricity, and incapacity to love others. Fully six of Cleckley's 16 criteria, 12 of Hare's 20 PCL-R criteria, and four of the seven DSM-5 APD criteria assess Antagonism. In direct contradiction to what Brislin and Patrick suggested, Antagonism is represented by three subscales within the PPI-R – Coldheartedness, Machiavellian Egocentricity, and Blame Externalization. Within our own Elemental Psychopathy Assessment (Lynam et al., 2011), eight of the 18 subscales assess a higher-factor labeled Interpersonal Antagonism.

Clinical scientists view Antagonism/Meanness as the central aspect of psychopathy. Miller et al. (2016) presented clinical scientists with empirically-derived FFM profiles of the components of the TriPM (plus the total score) and asked them to rate the degree to which such profiles could be expected to manifest symptoms of various forms of psychopathology. For psychopathy, the Meanness profile was seen as most psychopathic with a mean of 3.90 on a scale ranging from 0 to 6 with 3 representing "many symptoms." The profile for the total TPM scale was rated as next most symptomatic (M = 3.09), followed by the profiles for Disinhibition (M = 2.00) and Boldness (M = 1.27).

Antagonism is the strongest personality correlate of psychopathy; Lynam and Miller (2019) examined four meta-analyses of the relations between psychopathy and the FFM. Applying relative weights analyses to these meta-analyses, they found that Antagonism accounts for the majority of the variance in psychopathy, 50–75 percent, accounted for by FFM traits.

Finally, not only does Antagonism unify different operationalizations of psychopathy, it binds subscales within an inventory together. For example, the Childhood Psychopathy Scale (CPS; Lynam, 1997) is an early developmental analog of the PCL-R, with two factors. Antagonism accounts for large portions of the variance in Factor 1 and Factor 2 with Conscientiousness and Neuroticism also contributing to Factor 2 (Lynam et al., 2005). When a measure of Antagonism is partialed out of the two factors, their inter-correlations are significantly reduced; the same pattern has been demonstrated for a number of different inventories including the Youth Psychopathic Traits Inventory, Levenson Self-Report Psychopathy Scale, and the Self-Report Psychopathy Scale-III (Lynam & Miller, 2015).

In my commentary, I have critically evaluated the TPM's overemphasis on Boldness and underemphasis on ASB and Meanness/Antagonism. These specific concerns align well with other critiques that address the idiosyncratic derivation and absence of factor-analytic support for the

three TPM domains (Gatner, Douglas, & Hart, 2018; Neumann, Uzieblo, Crombez, & Hare, 2013; Shou, Sellbom, & Xu, 2017). The most compelling support for the three TPM domains may lie in the similarities they bear to their FFM counterparts (Hyatt, Crowe, Lynam, & Miller, in press). Given that the TPM has become quite widely used – indeed, Sleep et al. (2019) identified 87 studies using the TPM measure or one of eight translations – it is important for the issues raised here and elsewhere to be given further attention as the field considers the most appropriate approach to conceptualize the relevant factors at the heart of psychopathy.

REFERENCES

Bleidorn, W., Hopwood, C. J., Ackerman, R. A., Witt, E. A., Kandler, C., Riemann, R., . . . Donnellan, M. B. (in press). The healthy personality from a basic trait perspective. *Journal of Personality and Social Psychology*.

Blonigen, D. M. (2013). Is fearless dominance relevant to the construct of psychopathy? Reconciling the dual roles of theory and clinical utility. *Personality Disorders: Theory, Research, and Treatment*, 4, 87–88.

Cleckley, H. (1976). *The Mask of Sanity* (5th ed.). St. Louis.: Mosby. (Original edition published in 1941).

Crego, C., & Widiger, T. A. (2016). Cleckley's psychopaths: Revisited. *Journal of Abnormal Psychology*, 125, 75–87.

Crowe, M. L., Lynam, D. R., & Miller, J. D. (2018). Uncovering the structure of agreeableness from self-report measures. *Journal of Personality*, 86, 771–787.

Gatner, D. T., Douglas, K. S., & Hart, S. D. (2016). Examining the incremental and interactive effects of boldness with meanness and disinhibition within the triarchic model of psychopathy. *Personality Disorders: Theory, Research, and Treatment*, 3, 259–268.

Gatner, D. T., Douglas, K. S., & Hart, S. D. (2018). Comparing the lexical similarity of the triarchic model of psychopathy to contemporary models of psychopathy. *Journal of Personality*, 86(4), 577–589

Hare, R. D. (2003). *The Hare Psychopathy Checklist – Revised (PCL-R): Technical Manual* (2nd ed.). Toronto: Multi-Health Systems.

Hyatt, C. S., Crowe, M. L., Lynam, D. R., & Miller, J. D. (in press). Components of the Triarchic Model of Psychopathy and the Five-Factor Model domains share largely overlapping nomological networks. *Assessment*.

Karpman, B. (1941). On the need of separating psychopathy into two distinct clinical types: The symptomatic and the idiopathic. *Journal of Criminology and Psychopathology*, 3, 112–137.

Lilienfeld, S. O., & Andrews, B. P. (1996). Development and preliminary validation of a self-report measure of psychopathic personality traits in noncriminal population. *Journal of Personality Assessment*, 66, 488–524.

Lilienfeld, S. O., Patrick, C. J., Benning, S. D., Berg, J., Sellbom, M., & Edens, J. F. (2012). The role of fearless dominance in psychopathy: Confusions, controversies, and clarifications. *Personality Disorders: Theory, Research, and Treatment*, 3, 327–340.

Lykken, D. T. (1995). *The Antisocial Personalities*. Hillsdale, NJ: Lawrence Erlbaum.

Lynam, D. R. (1997). Pursuing the psychopath: Capturing the fledgling psychopath in a nomological net. *Journal of Abnormal Psychology*, 106, 425–438.

Lynam, D. R., Caspi, A., Moffitt, T. E., Raine, A., Loeber, R., & Stouthamer-Loeber, M. (2005). Adolescent psychopathy and the Big Five: Results from two samples. *Journal of Abnormal Child Psychology, 33,* 431–443.

Lynam, D. R., Gaughan, E. T., Miller, J. D., Miller, D. J., Mullins-Sweatt, S., & Widiger, T. A. (2011). Assessing the basic traits associated with psychopathy: Development and validation of the Elemental Psychopathy Assessment. *Psychological Assessment, 23,* 108–124.

Lynam, D. R., & Miller, J. D. (2012). Fearless dominance and psychopathy: Response to Lilienfeld et al. *Personality Disorders: Theory, Research, and Treatment, 3,* 341–353.

Lynam, D. R., & Miller, J. D. (2015). Psychopathy from a basic trait perspective: The utility of a five-factor model approach. *Journal of Personality, 83,* 611–626.

Lynam, D. R., & Miller, J. D. (2019). On the ubiquity and importance of antagonism. In J. D. Miller & D. R. Lynam (Eds.), *The Handbook of Antagonism: Conceptualizations, Assessment, Consequences, and Treatment of the Low End of Agreeableness* (pp. 1–24). London: Elsevier.

Maples, J., Miller, J. D., Fortune, E., MacKillop, J., Campbell, W. K., Lynam, D. R., . . . Goodie, A. S. (2014). An examination of the correlates of fearless dominance and self-centered impulsivity among high frequency gamblers. *Journal of Personality Disorders, 28,* 379–393.

Miller, J. D., Lamkin, J., Maples-Keller, J. L., & Lynam, D. R. (2016). Viewing the Triarchic Model of Psychopathy through general personality and expert-based lenses. *Personality Disorders: Theory, Research, and Treatment, 7,* 247–258.

Miller, J. D., & Lynam, D. R. (2012). An examination of the Psychopathic Personality Inventory's nomological network: A meta-analytic review. *Personality Disorders: Theory, Research, and Practice, 3,* 305–326.

Miller, J. D., Maples-Keller, J. L., & Lynam, D. R. (2016). An examination of the three components of the Psychopathic Personality Inventory: Profile comparisons and tests of moderation. *Psychological Assessment, 28,* 692–701.

Neumann, C. S., Uzieblo, K., Crombez, G., & Hare, R. D. (2013). Understanding the Psychopathic Personality Inventory (PPI) in terms of unidimensionality, orthogonality, and construct validity of PPI-I and -11. *Personality Disorders: Theory, Research, and Treatment, 4,* 77–79.

Shou, Y., Sellbom, M., & Xu, J. (2017). Psychometric properties of the Triarchic Psychopathy Measure: An item response theory approach. *Personality Disorders: Theory, Research, and Treatment, 9,* 217–227.

Sleep, C. E., Weiss, B., Lynam, D. R., & Miller, J. D. (2019). An examination of the Triarchic Model of psychopathy's nomological network: A meta-analytic review. *Clinical Psychology Review, 71,* 1–26.

Vize, C. E., Collison, K. L., Miller, J. D., & Lynam, D. R. (2019). Using Bayesian methods to update and expand the meta-analytic evidence of the Five-Factor Model's relation to antisocial behavior. *Clinical Psychology Review, 67,* 61–77.

Vize, C. E., Lynam, D. R., Lamkin, J., Miller, J. D., & Pardini, D. (2016). Identifying essential features of juvenile psychopathy in the prediction of later antisocial behavior: Is there an additive, synergistic, or curvilinear role for Fearless Dominance? *Clinical Psychological Science, 4,* 572–590.

11c An Agreeable Response to Questions and Criticisms: Author Rejoinder to Commentaries on an Integrative Biobehavioral Trait Perspective on Antisocial Personality Disorder and Psychopathy

SARAH J. BRISLIN AND CHRISTOPHER J. PATRICK

MYSTERIES STILL TO BE SOLVED: RESPONSE TO MARCUS AND NAGEL

It is a riddle, wrapped in a mystery, inside an enigma.
– Winston Churchill

Marcus and Nagel (M&N; this volume) frame their commentary around the question, "What constitutes psychopathy?" Inherent to this longstanding question is the premise that psychopathy is "one thing." Yet there is abundant evidence now that psychopathy is non-unitary. Contemporary assessment instruments (see Patrick, 2018, chapters 3, 9–10, 20) quantify it in terms of distinct subdimensions (factors or facets), and cluster analyses of high scorers on these instruments have revealed distinct variants or subtypes – differentiated especially by presence versus absence of anxiousness or negative affectivity (Patrick, 2018, ch. 13). Additionally, recent years have seen growing interest in the topic of "successful psychopathy" (Patrick, 2018, ch. 24), as a counterpoint to the dominant historic focus on psychopathy in criminal offenders.

The variegated nature of psychopathy is considered in the triarchic model and it provides a useful reference point for addressing issues raised by M&N. If psychopathy is multifaceted and different variants exist, then issues of "necessity" and "sufficiency" become moot. For example, certain features important to a clinical diagnosis of psychopathy (e.g., reckless, irresponsible behavior; lack of planfulness; persistent violation of norms/rules/laws) are less relevant to the concept of successful psychopathy. And even among clinical cases, variation is clearly evident. As noted by M&N, Cleckley's hospital patients exhibited disinhibition and boldness in particular, whereas disinhibition and meanness are more salient in historic accounts of criminal psychopathy (Patrick, 2018, ch. 1). Further, criminal psychopathy itself includes distinct variants – one marked by reckless, irresponsible behavioral deviancy in the absence of emotional turmoil ("primary" variant), and the other by deviancy of this type accompanied by high negative affectivity ("secondary" variant). What is considered central to one variant of psychopathy may be peripheral or irrelevant to another variant.

M&N question whether disinhibitory tendencies are central to (necessary for) a diagnosis of psychopathy. When it comes to clinical descriptions and clinical diagnostic criteria, reckless-irresponsible behavioral deviancy is invariably represented. Indeed, Karpman characterized both primary and secondary psychopathy as involving behavioral deviance in the form of unreliability, irresponsibility, deceitfulness, fraudulence, thievery, and failure to learn from mistakes; it is for this reason he considered both variants to be clinically psychopathic. His primary/secondary typology was advanced to highlight differing etiologic pathways for behavior of this kind and implications of this for treatment and prognosis.

M&N identify certain aspects of our discussion of the construct of disinhibition that may be confusing to some readers. When the triarchic model refers to disinhibition as an essential part of clinical presentations of psychopathy, it uses the term in the broad phenotypic sense of reckless, irresponsible behavioral deviancy (as Karpman ascribed to both primary and secondary criminal psychopathy). All historic descriptions of psychopathy as a clinical condition include reference to persistent behavioral deviancy of this kind. However, historic and contemporary experts in the field generally agree that the presence of persistent behavioral deviancy does not itself qualify an individual for a diagnosis of psychopathy. In line with this, the triarchic model proposes that persistent behavioral deviancy must be accompanied by affective-interpersonal detachment – in the form of boldness, meanness, or both – to be diagnosable as psychopathy. Again, the reference here is to observable-phenotypic features of psychopathy such as glibness, persuasiveness, overconfidence or arrogance, emotional insensitivity, absence of remorse, and lack of empathic concern.

Importantly, the triarchic model also considers disinhibition, boldness, and meanness as *dispositions* with linkages to distinct biobehavioral systems, and it provides descriptions of individuals who epitomize high levels of each, unto itself. For example, individuals high in biobehavioral disinhibition exhibit difficulties in regulating emotion and restraining impulses in connection with reckless-irresponsible behavioral deviancy. They are also prone to substance abuse, internalizing problems, and suicidal behavior, and show impaired performance and brain responding in cognitive tasks (Patrick, 2018, chs. 6 and 18). However, only a subset of clinically psychopathic individuals – those whose behavioral deviancy arises primarily from biobehavioral disinhibition (or what has been termed externalizing proneness ([/liability]; Patrick, 2018, chs. 6 and 18) – will exhibit these characteristics. Others will exhibit reckless, irresponsible deviancy in part, or wholly, for other reasons. This idea of alternative pathways to "psychopathic behavior" (i.e., phenotypic disinhibitory deviance), introduced by Karpman, has been strongly emphasized in contemporary developmental theories of psychopathy (Patrick, 2018, chs. 19–20) and empirical research on psychopathy subtypes (Patrick, 2018, ch. 13).

However, many mysteries surround the nature of constitutional and environmental factors contributing to (or protecting against) the emergence of psychopathic behavior across time and developmental stages. The question of which attributes contribute to distinct subdimensions and variants (subtypes) of psychopathy, and in what combinations, is one that cannot be addressed fully through questionnaire or interview assessments of phenotypic features. It will also need to be addressed in terms of basic biobehavioral dispositions, and etiologic influences that give rise to them (Patrick, 2018, ch. 18), over the course of development (Patrick, 2018, chs. 5, 7, 19, 31).

CONSIDERING THE BASES FOR REPETITIVE, INSISTENT CRITICISMS: AN EMPATHIC RESPONSE TO LYNAM'S CRITIQUE

Before you criticize a man, walk a mile in his shoes. That way, when you criticize him, you'll be a mile away and have his shoes.
— Steve Martin

Professor Lynam's commentary (this volume) reiterates points made in prior works he and his collaborators have published since the 2012 meta-analysis he cites. One of these is that boldness is irrelevant to psychopathy because it relates to healthy outcomes and is weakly and inconsistently predictive of antisocial behavior. This issue has been addressed extensively in the literature (for relevant citations, see Patrick, 2018, chs. 1, 3, 8, 24) and, given space constraints, we do not readdress it here – except to say that the boldness construct is clearly represented in prominent historic conceptualizations of psychopathy and many contemporary inventories for assessing it (Patrick, 2018, chs. 1 and 8).

Other points that Lynam raises are readily addressable. He cites evidence that much of the variance in subscales of

the Triarchic Psychopathy Measure can be accounted for by FFM trait scores – but fails to mention that much of the variance in his FFM-based psychopathy prototype can be accounted for by the triarchic model facets (Drislane, Brislin, Jones, & Patrick, 2018; Poy, Segarra, Esteller, López, & Moltó, 2014). He suggests that the triarchic model deemphasizes the role of antisocial deviancy in psychopathy, when (per our response to M&N) the model identifies reckless-irresponsible behavioral deviancy as an essential feature of clinical psychopathy. He also suggests that the triarchic model "undersells" the importance of meanness (callousness) in psychopathy, when in fact the model places considerable emphasis on this construct – identifying it as central to historic descriptions of psychopathy in adult criminal offenders and contemporary accounts of psychopathy in youth.

The triarchic model was formulated to address disputes that have plagued the psychopathy area for many years and it is meant to be inclusive of differing perspectives on psychopathy. Given the ecumenical focus of the model, we have endeavored to understand the roots of persistent, vigorous criticisms of the model by Lynam and his collaborators. One source for their criticisms appears to lie in strong allegiance to the FFM personality framework: Lynam was prominent in advancing an FFM-personality based approach to characterizing psychopathy (see, e.g., Patrick, 2018, ch. 11), and so it is natural to question why an alternative trait-descriptive framework is useful. Our answer is twofold: (1) the triarchic model constructs were directly deduced from the conceptual-empirical literature on psychopathy and (2) the triarchic constructs are explicitly biobehavioral (Patrick, 2018, ch. 18), and correspond to dimensions of an emerging biobehavioral model of general psychopathology (Patrick, Iacono, & Venables, 2019). While compatible with the FFM, the triarchic model is potentially advantageous for particular purposes – e.g., interfacing psychopathy dimensions with neurobiological concepts/measures and etiologic models for other forms of psychopathology.

Another ostensible basis for Lynam et al.'s criticisms of the triarchic model is that Lynam views psychopathy through the lens of adult offender studies and developmental research on conduct problems in youth. The focus of these literatures is on the understanding, prediction, and amelioration of antisocial behavior – in particular, persistent and aggressive forms. The triarchic model acknowledges that constructs of meanness and disinhibition are particularly important to criminal and delinquent expressions of psychopathy (e.g., Patrick, 2018, ch. 1). However, the model is open to the possibility that other expressions of psychopathy exist – including a clinical variant marked by charm, persuasiveness, and insouciance along with reckless-irresponsible deviance, and non-clinical ("successful") variants in which boldness and meanness are most salient (Patrick, 2018, chs. 1, 18, 24).

REFERENCES

Drislane, L. E., Brislin, S. J., Jones, S., & Patrick, C. J. (2018). Interfacing five-factor model and triarchic conceptualizations of psychopathy. *Psychological Assessment, 30*(6), 834–840.

Patrick, C. J. (2018). *Handbook of Psychopathy* (2nd ed.). New York: Guilford Press.

Patrick, C. J., Iacono, W. G., & Venables, N. C. (2019). Incorporating neurophysiological measures into clinical assessments: Fundamental challenges and a strategy for addressing them. *Psychological Assessment*. Advance online publication. doi: 10.1037/pas0000713

Poy, R., Segarra, P., Esteller, À., López, R., & Moltó, J. (2014). FFM description of the triarchic conceptualization of psychopathy in men and women. *Psychological Assessment, 26*, 69–76.

12 Narcissistic and Histrionic Personality Disorders

SINDES DAWOOD, LEILA Z. WU, CHLOE F. BLITON, AND AARON L. PINCUS

The personality disorders with the most research (Antisocial, Borderline) were grouped in Cluster B (dramatic, erratic) of the *Diagnostic and Statistical Manual of Mental Disorders 3rd Edition* (DSM-III; American Psychological Association, 1980) and its subsequent revisions. Narcissistic Personality Disorder (NPD) and Histrionic Personality Disorder (HPD), the remaining DSM Cluster B disorders, are both covered in this chapter. This pairing is an interesting one because of their historical similarities yet discrepant contemporary trajectories. NPD and HPD are among the oldest characterizations of personality pathology in psychiatry and psychology. Both have roots in early psychoanalytic theory (Freud, 1914, 1931; Reich, 1949) and remain prominent in contemporary psychodynamic theory and practice (Fonagy & Luyten, 2012, Lingiardi & McWilliams, 2015; McWilliams, 2011; Ronningstam, 2011a). In parallel, narcissistic and histrionic personalities were also incorporated into descriptive psychiatry (Decker, 2013; Schneider, 1923).

Since their appearance in the DSM-III however, the trajectory of NPD and HPD as basic forms of personality pathology have diverged. Clinical interest in understanding, assessing, and treating narcissistic patients remains strong and is growing (Hinrichs, 2016; Ogrodniczuk, 2013; Pincus, Cain, & Wright, 2014). Consistent with clinical interests, research on narcissism in all its forms is at an all-time high (Miller, Lynam, Hyatt, & Campbell, 2017; Pincus, Roche, & Good, 2015). In stark contrast, clinical interest in understanding, assessing, and treating histrionic patients has waned and empirical research focusing on histrionic personality pathology is relatively scant and arrested (Bornstein, Denckla, & Chung, 2015). Some even conclude that "The concept of HPD is dead" (Blashfield, Reynolds, & Stennett, 2012, p. 623; see also Bakkevig & Karterud, 2010). For HPD to remain relevant in contemporary personality disorder classification these circumstances must change.

More generally, personality disorder classification and diagnosis are in flux. The DSM-5 (American Psychiatric Association, 2013) contains two distinct systems for personality disorder diagnosis. The *categorical* personality disorder model found in Section II reprints the DSM-IV-TR (American Psychiatric Association, 2000) diagnostic criteria without change. This is unfortunate, as it reflects none of the research on personality disorders conducted in the years since DSM-IV's original publication in 1994. The *hybrid categorical/dimensional* Alternative Model for Personality Disorders (AMPD; Skodol, 2012) was developed by the DSM-5 Personality and Personality Disorders Workgroup as part of the manual's revision process. The AMPD was approved by the DSM-5 Task Force, but the Board of Trustees of the American Psychiatric Association chose to place it in Section III for emerging measures and models as an "official" alternative that can receive the DSM-5 code of Other Specified Personality Disorder [301.89] (Zachar, Krueger, & Kendler, 2016). Similar disagreements emerged during the revision of personality disorder diagnosis for the International Classification of Diseases 11th edition (ICD-11) as it evolved toward a model like the DSM-5 AMPD (Herpertz et al., 2017; Hopwood et al., 2018; Hopwood et al., 2019; Krueger, 2016; Tyrer et al., 2011, 2014).

Beyond the DSM-5 and ICD-11 diagnostic systems, many forms of personality pathology, such as psychopathy (Hare & Neumann, 2008) and pathological narcissism (Pincus & Lukowitsky, 2010) are also conceptualized and assessed with purely *dimensional and multidimensional* models or by profiles of extreme scores on general personality trait dimensions such as the Five-Factor Model (Widiger & Costa, 2013). In this chapter, we review NPD and HPD from these three perspectives: Categorical (DSM-5 Section II), Hybrid Categorical/Dimensional (DSM-5 Section III), and Dimensional (pathological and normal traits).

NARCISSISTIC PERSONALITY PATHOLOGY

This section presents three conceptualizations of narcissistic personality pathology. First, we review the DSM-5 Section II categorical NPD diagnosis including its prevalence, stability, comorbidity, and empirical research base.

Then we review DSM-5 Section III AMPD hybrid NPD diagnosis, including a description of the model and a review of its clinical applications to NPD. Finally, we review a pair of dimensional approaches to pathological narcissism, including the grandiosity/vulnerability model and the Five-Factor Model.

Categorical NPD (DSM-5 Section II)

NPD was first introduced in DSM-III reflecting the body of literature on narcissism prior to 1980. DSM-III criteria mainly reflected grandiose attitudes and behaviors (e.g., grandiose sense of self-importance) with some attention to self and emotion regulation (e.g., idealized and devalued views of self and others) and deflation following criticism (Pincus et al., 2015). In an effort to improve reliability and reduce the overlap among DSM PD criteria sets, the NPD diagnosis from DSM-III to DSM-5 underwent notable changes: adding a number of criteria explicitly emphasizing grandiosity (e.g., arrogant, haughty behaviors and/or attitudes; frequently infers others are envious of him/her) and eliminating criteria and text describing dysregulation and vulnerability (e.g., shameful reactivity or humiliation in response to narcissistic injury, alternating states of idealization and devaluation) (Gunderson, Ronningstam, & Smith, 1995).

As the DSM-5 Section II personality disorder criteria remain unchanged from DSM-IV-TR, the current diagnostic criteria continue to reflect chronic expressions of excessive grandiosity and a somewhat narrow conceptualization of NPD as pathological grandiosity (Pincus, 2011). DSM-5 Section II describes NPD as a pervasive pattern of grandiosity (in fantasy or behavior), a constant need for admiration, and a lack of empathy, beginning by early adulthood and present in a variety of contexts, operationalized as nine diagnostic criteria paraphrased here: (i) an inflated sense of self-worth; (ii) preoccupation with fantasies of unlimited influence, achievement, intelligence, attractiveness, or romance; (iii) belief that one is distinctive and elite and should only associate with others of similar stature; (iv) excessive needs for respect, appreciation, and praise; (v) sense of privilege; (vi) willingness to take advantage of others for personal gain; (vii) lack of compassion; (viii) jealousy of others; and (ix) exhibition of conceited behaviors and attitudes. A patient must meet clinical threshold for a minimum of five of these criteria to be diagnosed with NPD. Thus, the DSM-5 Section II diagnosis of NPD reflects chronic expressions of excessive grandiosity. Consistent with this, a confirmatory factor analysis of these NPD criteria supported a one-factor solution (Miller, Hoffman, Campbell, & Pilkonis, 2008). Self-esteem vulnerability and emotional dysregulation are only mentioned in the "Associated Features Supporting Diagnosis" section where clinicians are also cautioned that patients with NPD may not outwardly exhibit vulnerable characteristics. DSM-5 Section II diagnostic criteria are mainly limited to observable presentations of narcissism and omit the underlying features that maintain and unify heterogeneous clinical presentations of narcissism (Caligor, Levy, & Yeomans, 2015).

Prevalence

Prevalence rates of NPD in the general population range from 0 percent to 5.3 percent (Ekselius, Tillfors, Furmark, & Fredrikson, 2001; Mattia & Zimmerman, 2001; Torgersen, Kringlen, & Cramer, 2001). A nationally representative epidemiological study found that the lifetime prevalence (i.e., cumulative assessment across all time points) of NPD is 6.2 percent (Stinson et al., 2008). Overall, NPD exhibits the lowest prevalence rate of any DSM personality disorder; however, this is inconsistent with the frequency of patients with narcissistic personality pathology reported in clinical practice (Cain, Pincus, & Ansell, 2008). Prevalence estimates among clinical samples range from 1.3 percent to 22 percent (e.g., Grilo et al., 1998; Zimmerman, Rothschild, & Chelminski, 2005). Among personality disorders, NPD typically has among the lowest correlation between clinical interviews and self-report ratings (Oltmanns & Turkheimer, 2006), possibly due to a lack of insight into how behavior is perceived by others (Carlson & Oltmanns, 2015) or a disregard for the negative impact of their behavior on others (Carlson, 2013). This might particularly impact the accuracy of typical population-based epidemiological assessments, as individuals with NPD may lack the insight or willingness to disclose narcissistic attitudes or difficulties (or even participate in such assessments).

Stability

Examination of the temporal stability of NPD varies depending on whether clinical interview or self-report is employed. Ronningstam, Gunderson, and Lyons (1995) employed the Diagnostic Interview for Narcissism (DIN; Gunderson, Ronningstam, & Bodkin, 1990) on 20 patients diagnosed with NPD over a three-year period. They found only modest diagnostic stability, with only 33 percent of the patients continuing to meet the DIN criteria for NPD at follow-up. The three-year stability of DSM-III-R diagnoses (50 percent) and DSM-IV diagnoses (46 percent) were slightly higher. Lenzenweger, Johnson, and Willett (2004) conducted individual growth curve analyses of interviewer-rated PD features over a four-year period in a sample of 250 participants. Results revealed significant variability in PD features, including NPD features, over time. Nestadt and colleagues (2010) interviewed 294 participants on two occasions, 12 to 18 years apart and found that NPD had among the lowest temporal stability levels (ICC = 0.10), and NPD traits at baseline did not significantly predict those same traits at follow-up. Self-reported NPD symptoms yielded a higher level of stability. Ball, Rounsaville, Tennen, and Kranzler (2001) reported a one-year temporal stability coefficient of 0.42 for the self-reported DSM-III-R NPD features in a clinical sample of

182 substance abusing inpatients. Samuel and colleagues (2011) examined the two-year rank order and mean level stability of PDs using self-report and interview based assessments. They found the rank order stability for NPD was higher for self-report than for interview ratings, and the mean level decrease in symptoms over time was smaller for the self-report compared to the interview ratings. Supporting previous findings, Vater et al. (2014) found a two-year remission rate for NPD diagnoses of 52 percent. Even with self-report measures, the temporal stability of DSM Section II NPD diagnosis remains quite modest.

Comorbidity

Numerous studies indicate that NPD exhibits the highest rates of comorbidity with antisocial and histrionic personality disorders, and is also commonly comorbid with borderline and schizotypal personality disorders (Levy, Chauhan, Clarkin, Wasserman, & Reynoso, 2009; Widiger, 2011). NPD also co-occurs with symptom syndromes, specifically bipolar 1 disorder, anxiety disorders, substance abuse disorder, posttraumatic stress disorder, and major depression (Clemence, Perry, & Plakun, 2009; Simonsen & Simonsen, 2011; Stinson et al., 2008).

DSM-5 Section II NPD Research

Due in part to the low prevalence of NPD, substantive research employing even modest samples of patients diagnosed with NPD is extremely rare. Most of this work has focused on examining empathy deficits and self-esteem in NPD. The best research of this nature involves a well-diagnosed sample of NPD patients in Germany. The investigators (Ritter et al., 2011) used both self-report and experimental methods to assess empathy and found that, compared to controls and patients with borderline personality disorder, NPD patients exhibited deficits in emotional empathy (i.e., an observer's emotional response to another person's emotional state) but not cognitive empathy (i.e., the ability to take another person's perspective and to represent others' mental states). This distinction could explain the NPD patient's tendency to successfully exploit others. In another study of these NPD patients (Schulze et al., 2013), the investigators used brain imaging techniques and found that, relative to controls, NPD patients had smaller gray matter volume in the left anterior insula. Importantly, gray matter volume in this area is positively correlated with self-reported emotional empathy. Supporting these conclusions, Nenadic and colleagues (2015) used voxel-based morphometry to identify structural issues in the brains of six patients diagnosed with NPD and found gray matter deficits in the right prefrontal and bilateral medial prefrontal regions. Frontal gray matter loss is associated with emotion dysregulation and deficits in coping behaviors. Complementary whole-brain analyses yielded smaller gray matter volume in fronto-paralimbic brain regions comprising the rostral and median cingulate cortex as well as dorsolateral and medial

parts of the prefrontal cortex, all of which are implicated in empathic functioning (Schulze et al., 2013).

Consistent with these findings, another group of investigators (Marissen, Deen, & Franklen, 2012), using a small independent clinical sample of NPD patients, found that they generally performed worse on a facial emotion recognition task compared to controls. In addition to this general deficit in emotion recognition, patients with NPD showed a specific deficit for emotions representing fear and disgust.

Empirical studies of self-esteem in NPD patients demonstrate mixed results. Investigators have found evidence supporting that, despite the grandiosity emphasized in the diagnostic criteria, NPD patients have lower explicit self-esteem than controls (Vater, Ritter, et al., 2013; Vater, Schröder-Abé, et al., 2013). However, Marissen and colleagues (Marissen, Brouwer, Hiemstra, Deen, & Franken, 2016) found that implicit and explicit self-esteem did not differ between NPD patients and control groups (e.g., patients with other PDs and healthy controls). This makes sense considering NPD is commonly comorbid with anxiety disorders, mood disorders, and posttraumatic stress disorder.

Finally, current research efforts have focused on the role of shame in individuals with NPD. Notably, Ritter and colleagues (2014) investigated the association of NPD and explicit and implicit shame as measured by self-report and performance measures, respectively. A small group of patients diagnosed with NPD reported higher levels of explicit shame than patients diagnosed with borderline personality disorder and healthy controls. Implicit shame-self associations (versus anxiety-self associations) were significantly stronger in NPD patients than in the control groups. Findings support continuing investigation of shame related processes in NPD.

As NPD exhibits high rates of co-occurrence with personality, anxiety, mood, and substance use disorders, novel research has explored the mechanisms driving comorbidity. Eaton and colleagues (2017) used a nationally representative sample to model NPD's transdiagnostic comorbidity structures through multivariate associations. Findings indicate that NPD is more strongly associated with a latent distress factor (versus a latent fear factor) within an internalizing–externalizing model. Furthermore, they concluded that NPD is composed of unique facets; however, it remains unclear whether shared variance and comorbidity represents a general factor of pathology overlapping with other disorders or an NPD-specific manifestation of unique symptoms. Hörz-Sagstetter and colleagues (2017) identified unique patterns of functioning among patients diagnosed with comorbid NPD and borderline personality disorder and patients only diagnosed with borderline personality disorder suggesting that comorbid NPD may serve as a buffer against anxiety and other Axis I disorders and reduce number of hospitalizations. However, within the context of a BPD diagnosis, NPD may also increase the co-occurrence of severe personality pathology including paranoia, antisocial personality features, and distortions of reality. Taken together, NPD exhibits unique associations with other disorders, and the basis for, and impact of such relationships must be further investigated.

Research on treatment of NPD is limited to case studies. There are no published randomized clinical psychotherapy trials, naturalistic studies of psychotherapy, or empirical evaluations of community-based interventions for NPD (Dhawan, Kunik, Oldham, & Coverdale, 2010; Levy, Reynoso, Wasserman, & Clarkin, 2007). Thus, there are no empirically validated treatments for NPD; however, extensions of empirically validated treatments such as dialectical behavior therapy (Reed-Knight & Fischer, 2011) and transference focused psychotherapy (Stern, Diamond, & Yeomans, 2017), are being developed.

Hybrid Dimensional/Categorical NPD (DSM-5 Section III AMPD)

The American Psychiatric Association officially recognizes the AMPD as an *Alternative Model* that complements the DSM-5 Section II PD diagnoses and has practical relevance for clinicians. Diagnosis with the AMPD requires fulfilling seven criteria for personality disorder. The first two, Criteria A (level of personality functioning) and Criteria B (maladaptive personality traits) are the most innovative. Criteria A involves clinician-rated assessment of severity of disturbances in selffunctioning (identity and self-direction) and interpersonal functioning (empathy and intimacy), reflecting impairments in regulatory and relational processes common to all personality disorders. Severity itself is an important clinical dimension, having significant implications for treatment planning (e.g., Caligor et al., 2015; Hopwood, Malone, et al., 2011; Pincus, Dowgwillo, & Greenberg, 2016; Yeomans, Clarkin, & Kernberg, 2015). Criteria B involves clinician and/or self-rated assessment of pathological personality traits which are organized into five broad trait domains (Negative Affectivity, Detachment, Antagonism, Disinhibition, Psychoticism) composed of 25 specific trait facets, reflecting individual differences in the expression of core personality impairments. Criteria C through G cover issues of pervasiveness, stability, early emergence, and discrimination from other mental disorders, effects of substances, and developmental stage or sociocultural environment. See the DSM-5 website for full descriptions and available assessment instruments.

What makes the AMPD a hybrid model is that it permits the diagnosis of six specific personality disorders (antisocial, avoidant, borderline, narcissistic, obsessive-compulsive, and schizotypal). For each personality disorder, specific criteria are provided for dimensional ratings of severity of personality impairments and specific elevations on maladaptive trait dimensions are specified. Maladaptive personality patterns not covered by these six

criterion sets (e.g., personality disorders such as paranoid, schizoid, histrionic, and dependent) are diagnosed as Personality Disorder – Trait Specified (PD-TS). In a PD-TS diagnosis, Criterion A threshold is met and the specific clinically significant pathological trait elevations are stated in lieu of an overarching category (e.g., PD-TS with suspiciousness, restricted affectivity, and hostility may support the diagnosis of "paranoid personality disorder"). The Trait Specified diagnosis alleviates the problem of the highly common and ambiguous DSM-IV "Personality Disorder Not Otherwise Specified" diagnosis (Verheul, 2005) by providing a more clinically useful description of patients that do not fit well into the available categories. Also, categorical diagnoses can be augmented by additional notable trait elevations when indicated.

NPD in the DSM-5 AMPD

The DSM-5 AMPD diagnostic criteria for NPD are paraphrased in Table 12.1. These criteria improve upon the overly narrow DSM-5 Section II NPD diagnosis by including criteria for self and interpersonal impairments (Criterion A) and explicitly specifying that grandiosity may be overt or covert (see also Skodol, Morey, Bender, & Oldham, 2015). This provides the clinician with diagnostic criteria that exhibit greater fidelity with the varied presentations of pathological narcissism seen in clinical practice (Kealy & Rasmussen, 2012; McWilliams, 2011; Pincus et al., 2014). Although there are not yet empirical studies employing samples of patients diagnosed with DSM-5 AMPD personality disorders, it is notable that NPD is commonly discussed in the emerging literature detailing clinical applications of the AMPD. In fact, nearly all recent articles included at least one case of NPD (Bach, Markon, Simonsen, & Krueger, 2015; Schmeck, Schlüter-Müller, Foelsch, & Doering, 2013; Waugh et al., 2017); and four articles focused specifically on issues related to the diagnosis of AMPD NPD (Caligor et al., 2015; Morey & Stagner, 2012; Pincus et al., 2016; Skodol et al., 2015).

Research findings and clinical practitioners agree that the core feature of NPD is pathological grandiosity (Ackerman, Hands, Donnellan, Hopwood, & Witt, 2017; Pincus & Lukowitsky, 2010). The DSM-5 Section II NPD diagnosis and the DSM-5 AMPD NPD diagnosis also converge on this. However, the former criteria set is mainly limited to a narrow group of generally overt grandiose behaviors that result in low diagnostic prevalence (Pincus et al., 2015) and failure to capture actual clinical presentations of treatment seeking narcissistic patients (Caligor et al., 2015; Pincus et al., 2014; Skodol et al., 2015). In contrast, the AMPD Criteria A (regulatory and relational processes) and B (maladaptive traits) allow clinicians to accurately diagnose NPD in a wider range of cases, reducing false negatives and improving treatment recommendations. Meeting threshold for DSM-5 AMPD NPD Criteria A in combination with elevated grandiosity (and possibly attention-seeking) conceptualized as maladaptive traits (Criteria B) can capture a wider range of grandiose clinical

Table 12.1 Paraphrased criteria for narcissistic personality disorder in the DSM-5 alternative model of personality disorders (Section III)

A.   Moderate or greater impairment in personality functioning, manifested by characteristic difficulties in two or more of the following four areas:

    1. **Identity**: Excessive reliance on others for self-concept and self-regard; self-evaluation is excessively exaggerated or devalued, or vacillating between extremes; affective instability mirrors fluctuations in self-regard.

    2. **Self-direction**: Aims based on gaining approval from others; perfectionistic achievement standards in order to see self as superior or excessively lax achievement standards based on a sense of privilege; often lacks insight regarding reasons for their behavior.

    3. **Empathy**: Impaired ability to notice or relate to the feelings and needs of others; overly focused on reactions of others, but only as it relates to self; disproportionately magnifies or minimizes own impact on others.

    4. **Intimacy**: Relationships largely self-serving and serve to promote self-regard; reciprocal functioning limited by lack of authentic curiosity in and concern for others' experiences and excessive needs for status, victory, and admiration from others.

B.   Elevations on the following pathological personality traits:

    1. **Grandiosity** (a facet of Antagonism): Feelings of entitlement, either overt or covert; self-centeredness; firmly holding to the belief that one is better than others; condescension toward others.

    2. **Attention seeking** (a facet of Antagonism): Excessive attempts to attract and be the focus of the attention of others; admiration seeking

---

presentations at varying levels of severity. Narcissistic grandiosity may be chronic but covert, chronic and overt, or oscillating with vulnerable self-states (Pincus et al., 2016).

In addition to recognizing the variations in expressions of grandiosity, three suggestions for revising the diagnosis of NPD to "re-incorporate" features of narcissistic vulnerability have appeared in the literature. One suggestion is to revise the DSM criteria to include features reflecting narcissistic vulnerability (e.g., Ronningstam, 2009). An alternative proposal is to consider narcissistic vulnerability as a specifier for NPD diagnoses (e.g., NPD with vulnerable features) similar to specifiers used for other diagnoses (Miller, Gentile, Wilson, & Campbell, 2013). A third alternative is to consider pathological narcissism a facet of general personality pathology, representing a core feature of all PDs rather than a specific personality disorder diagnosis (Morey, 2005; Morey & Stagner, 2012). However, this suggestion removes a very useful clinical diagnosis (Ronningstam, 2011b) and previously elicited significant negative reaction by the clinical community when the initial DSM-5 PD proposal suggested deleting NPD from the nosology (Skodol, 2012).

We agree with Skodol and colleagues (2015) that the DSM-5 AMPD NPD diagnosis appears to be a viable approach that is worthy of further study and refinement. Possible revisions to the DSM-5 AMPD NPD diagnosis to better account for narcissistic vulnerability could include expanding Criterion B beyond antagonism to include the facets of anhedonia or depressivity or the domain of negative affectivity. These could be required for diagnosis or they could be used to define a vulnerable specifier. Of course, such elevations would need to be carefully considered and distinguished from other possible comorbid diagnoses associated with negative affectivity.

Dimensional Approaches to Pathological Narcissism

In this section, we review two popular dimensional conceptualizations of pathological narcissism, the Grandiosity/Vulnerability model and its research base, and the Five-Factor Model trait perspective.

Narcissistic Grandiosity and Vulnerability Model

Narcissism can be defined as an individual's tendency to use a variety of self-regulation, affect-regulation, and interpersonal processes to maintain a positive – and possibly inflated – self-image. Thus, it is necessarily a complex personality construct involving (a) needs for recognition and admiration, (b) motivations to overtly and covertly seek out self-enhancement experiences from the social environment, (c) strategies to satisfy these needs and motives, and (d) abilities to manage self-enhancement failures and social disappointments (Morf, 2006; Morf, Horvath, & Torchetti, 2011; Morf & Rhodewalt, 2001).

Recent efforts to synthesize the corpus of description, theory, and research on pathological narcissism across the disciplines generated a contemporary model (Figure 12.1) that conceptualizes pathological narcissism as a combination of maladaptive self-enhancement motivation (Grandiosity) and impaired self, emotion, and interpersonal regulation (Vulnerability) in response to self-enhancement failures and lack of recognition and admiration from others (Cain et al., 2008; Pincus & Lukowitsky, 2010; Pincus et al., 2015). Put another way, narcissistic

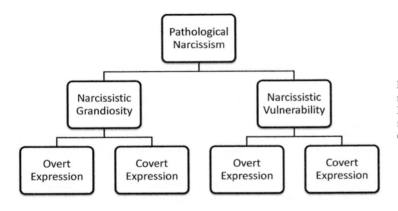

Figure 12.1 The hierarchical structure of pathological narcissism. By permission from Pincus, A. L., & Lukowitsky, M. R. (2010). Pathological narcissism and narcissistic personality disorder. *Annual Review of Clinical Psychology*, 6, p. 431.

individuals have notable difficulties transforming narcissistic needs (recognition and admiration) and impulses (self-enhancement motivation) into mature and socially appropriate ambitions and conduct (Kohut, 1977; Stone, 1998), and this heightens their sensitivity to the daily ups and downs of life and relationships (e.g., Besser & Priel, 2010; Besser, Zeigler-Hill, Weinberg, & Pincus, 2016; Ziegler-Hill & Besser, 2013). Such narcissistic vulnerability is reflected in experiences of anger, envy, aggression, helplessness, emptiness, low self-esteem, shame, avoidance of interpersonal relationships, and even suicidality (Kohut & Wolf, 1978; Krizan & Johar, 2012; Roche, Pincus, Lukowitsky, Ménard, & Conroy, 2013; Ronningstam, 2005).

As seen in Figure 12.1, narcissistic grandiosity and vulnerability together make up the higher order construct of pathological narcissism and are moderately intercorrelated (Wright, Lukowitsky, Pincus, & Conroy, 2010; Zeigler-Hill, Enjaian, & Essa, 2013). Expressions of narcissistic grandiosity and vulnerability may be chronic with each suppressing the other, or they may oscillate over time within the same person (Gore & Widiger, 2016; Hyatt et al., 2018; Pincus et al., 2016; Pincus & Wright, in press). Nevertheless, they exhibit convergent and divergent patterns of relationships across personality traits, internalizing and externalizing problems, self-esteem, self-conscious emotions, core affect, interpersonal functioning, and psychotherapy (Dowgwillo, Dawood, & Pincus, 2016; Pincus & Roche, 2011).

Research on Grandiosity and Vulnerability

Narcissistic grandiosity and vulnerability demonstrate distinct and substantially meaningful patterns of correlations across impulsive and perfectionistic traits, and omnibus models of general personality traits. Grandiosity is positively related to positive urgency and sensation seeking, while vulnerability is positively related to both positive and negative urgency components of impulsivity (Miller et al., 2010). Both grandiosity and vulnerability are positively associated with socially prescribed perfectionism and perfectionistic self-promotion; however, grandiosity is also associated with other-oriented

perfectionism while vulnerability is associated with non-disclosure of imperfection (Smith et al., 2016). In terms of Five-Factor Model personality traits, grandiosity is negatively correlated with neuroticism and agreeableness, and positively related to extraversion; vulnerability is similarly negatively correlated with agreeableness but is positively related to neuroticism and negative correlated with extraversion (Miller et al., 2010). Similar patterns are found in relation to the HEXACO personality model with the notable addition that both grandiosity and vulnerability are negatively related to honesty-humility (Bresin & Gordon, 2011).

Narcissistic grandiosity and vulnerability exhibit distinct and meaningful patterns of associations with internalizing problems and symptoms in both normal and clinical samples. This has been most extensively studied with depressive symptoms (Dawood & Pincus, 2018a; Ellison, Levy, Cain, Ansell, & Pincus, 2013; Erkoreka & Navarro, 2017; Kealy, Tsai, & Ogrodniczuk, 2012; Marčinko et al., 2014; Miller et al., 2010; Tritt, Ryder, Ring, & Pincus, 2010). In addition, narcissistic grandiosity and vulnerability are associated with suicide attempts and borderline personality disorder symptoms (Miller et al., 2010; Pincus et al., 2009), suicidal ideation (Jaksic, Marcinko, Hanzek, Rebernjak, & Ogrodniczuk, 2017), and non-suicidal self-injury (Dawood, Schroeder, Donnellan, & Pincus, 2018).

Narcissistic grandiosity and vulnerability also exhibit distinct and meaningful patterns of associations with externalizing problems and symptoms in both normal and clinical samples. Numerous laboratory-based and correlational studies (Lobbestael, Baumeister, Feibig, & Eckel, 2014; Reidy, Foster, & Zeichner, 2010; Widman & McNulty, 2010) show that grandiosity is positively associated with all forms of aggression (e.g., reactive, proactive, unprovoked, sexual), as well as violent behavior and self-reported homicidal thoughts in psychotherapy inpatients and outpatients (Ellison et al., 2013; Goldberg et al., 2007). In contrast, vulnerability is associated with self-reported aggression, but not with aggressive behavior assessed in the laboratory. Grandiosity is also associated with increased criminal behavior and gambling (e.g., Miller et al., 2010), as well as alcohol and drug use (e.g., Buelow & Brunell, 2014). Moreover, vulnerability interacted with self-reported childhood sexual abuse to predict overt and cyber stalking in men (Ménard & Pincus, 2012).

Narcissistic grandiosity and vulnerability exhibit distinct associations with self-esteem, self-conscious emotions, and core affect. Vulnerability is negatively related with self-esteem, whereas grandiosity is positively correlated with self-esteem (Maxwell, Donnellan, Hopwood, & Ackerman, 2011; Miller et al., 2010; Pincus et al., 2009). Zeigler-Hill and Besser (2013) found that vulnerability is uniquely associated with day-to-day fluctuations in feelings of self-worth. Vulnerability is positively associated with shame and hubris, negatively associated with authentic pride, and unrelated to guilt. In contrast, grandiosity is positively correlated with guilt and unrelated to pride and shame (Pincus, 2013). Different facets of pathological narcissism also predict the within-person severity, within-person vacillation, and within-person instability of shame experienced over time (Dawood & Pincus, 2018b). Vulnerability is positively correlated with negative affectivity and envy, and negatively correlated with positive affectivity, while grandiosity is only positively related to positive affectivity (Krizan & Johar, 2012). Finally, high levels of pathological narcissism predicted strong experimental effects for the implicit priming of self-importance (Fetterman & Robinson, 2010).

Narcissistic grandiosity and vulnerability are also associated with specific types of interpersonal problems. Grandiosity is associated with predominantly vindictive, domineering, and intrusive problematic behaviors (Ogrodniczuk, Piper, Joyce, Steinberg, & Duggal, 2009; Pincus et al., 2009). Similarly, vulnerability is associated with vindictive interpersonal problems but also shows positive associations with exploitable and avoidant problems (Pincus et al., 2009). Grandiosity and vulnerability also exhibit meaningful associations with interpersonal sensitivities, with grandiosity associated with sensitivity to others' remoteness, antagonism, and control, and vulnerability associated with sensitivity to others' remoteness, control, attention-seeking, and affection (Hopwood, Ansell, et al., 2011).

Narcissistic grandiosity and vulnerability also show differential associations with the utilization of psychiatric treatment. For instance, Ellison and colleagues (2013) found that narcissistic grandiosity was negatively correlated with treatment utilization (telephone-based crisis services, partial hospitalizations, inpatient admissions, taking medications) and positively correlated with outpatient therapy no-shows. Narcissistic vulnerability was positively correlated with use of telephone-based crisis services, inpatient admissions, and outpatient therapy sessions attended and cancelled. Results indicating that narcissistic vulnerability is positively associated with treatment utilization support the view that narcissistic patients are likely to present for services when they are in a vulnerable self-state (Pincus et al., 2014).

NPD and the Five-Factor Model

Theorists and researchers have suggested that the Five-Factor Model (FFM; Costa & McCrae, 1992) of normal personality structure can be used to both conceptualize and assess NPD (e.g., Campbell & Miller, 2013). The lens through which narcissism can be understood from the perspective of the FFM is by expert opinions, as well as empirical research. For instance, mental health clinicians (Samuel & Widiger, 2004) and academic researchers (Lynam & Widiger, 2001) have independently reported a nearly identical FFM trait profile for a prototypical case of NPD. The traits considered to be most prototypical and descriptive of NPD include low levels of agreeableness (e.g., low modesty, altruism, trust, tender-mindedness), low and high levels of extraversion (e.g., low warmth, high excitement seeking, high assertiveness), and mixed levels of neuroticism (e.g., low self-consciousness, high angry hostility). Miller, Lynam, Siedor, Crowe, and Campbell (2018) extended this research by examining how lay people use the FFM to rate a narcissistic individual (based on their own conceptualization of narcissism) across different age, gender, and occupational categories. Results showed that, across all categories, lay people emphasize the same FFM traits as clinicians and researchers. Moreover, meta-analytic reviews on FFM and NPD (e.g., Samuel & Widiger, 2008; Saulsman & Page, 2004) also confirm low agreeableness and high extraversion as central traits of NPD.

Given that most FFM-based personality disorder research relies on questionnaires that assess normal range personality traits, researchers have begun to develop FFM inventories that explicitly assess traits descriptive of the DSM personality disorders (see Widiger, Lynam, Miller, & Oltmanns, 2012). Thus, the Five Factor Narcissism Inventory (FFNI; Glover, Miller, Lynam, Crego, & Widiger, 2012) was created to assess the general personality traits most relevant to NPD, narcissistic grandiosity, and narcissistic vulnerability from an FFM perspective. The facets of the FFNI were identified based on expert consensus ratings and empirical findings. They include FFNI neuroticism (Reactive Anger, Shame, Indifference, Need for Admiration), FFNI extraversion (Exhibitionism, Authoritativeness, Thrill Seeking), FFNI openness (Grandiose Fantasies), FFNI antagonism (Cynicism/Distrust, Manipulativeness, Exploitativeness, Entitlement, Lack of Empathy, Arrogance), and FFNI conscientiousness (Acclaim Seeking). Glover et al. (2012) described how grandiose and vulnerable dimensions could be scored using the FFNI scales. Studies have shown that the FFNI grandiose and vulnerable narcissism scales manifest good convergent and discriminant associations with existing measures of narcissism, Dark Triad personality traits, interpersonal traits, externalizing and internalizing behaviors and symptoms, and romantic and attachment styles (see Miller, Gentile, & Campbell, 2013; Miller, Gentile, et al., 2013).

Recently, Miller and colleagues (2016) identified three factors across two samples in their factor analyses of the

15 FFNI facets. The first factor, labeled interpersonal antagonism (i.e., low agreeableness), included the subscales of manipulativeness, entitlement, empathy, arrogance, distrust, reactive anger, and thrill seeking. The second factor, labeled neuroticism, comprised a need for admiration, shame, and low indifference (i.e., high self-consciousness). The third factor, labeled agentic extraversion, consisted of the subscales of grandiose fantasies, acclaim seeking, exhibitionism, and authoritativeness. They found that existing measures of NPD are correlated with all three FFNI dimensions. Moreover, measures of narcissistic grandiosity and vulnerability were strongly correlated with FFNI interpersonal antagonism, but differentially related to the other two FFNI factors. Measures of narcissistic grandiosity (but not vulnerability) were correlated with FFNI agentic extraversion, while measures of narcissistic vulnerability (but not grandiosity) were correlated with FFNI neuroticism.

HISTRIONIC PERSONALITY PATHOLOGY

This section presents three conceptualizations of histrionic personality pathology. First, we review the DSM-5 Section II categorical HPD diagnosis including its prevalence, stability, comorbidity, and empirical research base. Then we review the DSM-5 Section III AMPD hybrid HPD diagnosis. Finally, we review a pair of dimensional approaches to histrionic pathology, including the dimensional assessment of histrionism and the Five-Factor Model.

Categorical HPD (DSM-5 Section II)

Prior to HPD's official introduction to the DSM-III, "emotionally unstable personality" appeared in DSM-I, and some consider this diagnosis a precursor to the current HPD diagnosis (e.g., Smith & Lilienfeld, 2012). In 1968, "hysterical personality" appeared in DSM-II focusing on the criteria of clinging to others, impressionistic speech, and over-the-top displays of emotion. Histrionic personality disorder first officially appeared in the DSM-III with an emphasis on dramatic, seductive, and attention seeking behaviors, manipulative suicidal attempts and gestures, and irrational, angry outbursts. Given that DSM-III's HPD criteria significantly overlapped with borderline personality disorder criteria, DSM-IV aimed at reducing the co-occurrence of the disorders and removed the criteria of angry outbursts and manipulative suicidal behaviors from the HPD diagnosis (Pfohl, 1991). After maneuvering criteria to reduce overlap with other personality disorders (see Bakkevig & Karterud, 2010), DSM-5 Section II describes HPD as a pervasive pattern of excessive emotionality and attention seeking, beginning by early adulthood and present in a variety of contexts operationalized as eight diagnostic criteria paraphrased here: (i) the need to be the center of attention; (ii) inappropriate and

sexually seductive behavior; (iii) highly changeable and superficial expressions of emotion; (iv) use of physical appearance to attract attention; (v) generalized and vague speech; (vi) dramatic, over-the-top expressions of emotion; (vii) suggestibility; and (viii) views relationships as closer and warmer than they really are. A patient must meet clinical threshold for a minimum of five of these criteria to be diagnosed with HPD.

Prevalence

Using DSM-III, DSM-III-R, and DSM-IV diagnostic criteria, prevalence rates for histrionic personality disorder vary from 0 percent to 3.2 percent in community samples and 1 percent to 6 percent in psychiatric samples (see Bakkevig & Karterud, 2010 for a review). More recent studies estimate roughly equivalent rates in community settings (0.2–2.9 percent) and higher rates in clinical settings ranging (10–15 percent) (Bornstein et al., 2015; Smith & Lilienfeld, 2012). Notably, studies using standardized interviews to assess for HPD find a prevalence estimate of 2–3 percent in the general population.

Stability

Samuel and colleagues (2011) investigated the stability of HPD as a categorical diagnosis. The Diagnostic Interview for DSM-IV Personality Disorders (Zanarini, Frankenburg, Sickel, & Yong, 1996) and Schedule for Nonadaptive and Adaptive Personality SNAP-2 (Clark, Simms, Wu, & Casillas, 2008) were administered to participants in the Collaborative Longitudinal Personality Disorders Study (CLPS) at baseline and after two years. Across the categorical diagnoses, HPD estimates decreased after two years. The rank order values for HPD stability as assessed by the SNAP-2 and DIPD-IV were 0.45 and 0.21, respectively.

Comorbidity

HPD shares a complex association with personality disorders due to diagnostic overlap. Numerous studies employing odds ratios analyses suggest that HPD is highly comorbid with all personality disorders (e.g., Lenzenweger, Lane, Loranger, Kessler, 2007; Trull, Jahng, Tomko, Wood, & Sher, 2010). Notably, comorbidity levels are highest for other Cluster B and dependent personality disorders (Bakkevig & Karterud, 2010). Due to the similarity in diagnostic criteria including attention seeking behaviors and manipulativeness, HPD commonly co-occurs with borderline personality disorder. Furthermore, HPD and NPD both describe a dysfunctional pattern of excessive attention-seeking leading to increased levels of comorbidity (Blagov & Westen, 2008; Smith & Lilienfeld, 2012). Similarly, HPD and antisocial personality disorder (ASPD) are both characterized by reckless, impulsive, and manipulative behaviors (Cale & Lilienfeld, 2002). Taken together, some theorists suggest that histrionism is a specific subtype of borderline personality disorder (Blavog & Westen, 2008; Westen & Heim, 2003) or NPD (Bakkevig and Karterud, 2010), or a gender biased, female manifestation of ASPD (Ford & Widiger, 1989). Finally, over-reliance on others and the need for approval drive the co-occurrence of HPD with dependent personality disorder (Bornstein et al., 2015).

HPD exhibits moderate to high comorbidity rates with dissociative disorders (Boon & Draijer, 1993), major depression (Dyck et al., 2001), dysthymia (Pepper et al., 1995), and anxiety disorders (Blashfield & Davis, 1993). The presence of HPD may impact the course and severity of other forms of psychopathology. For example, patients with comorbid bipolar disorder and HPD had significantly more suicide attempts than patients with bipolar disorder but not HPD (Garno, Goldberg, Ramirez & Ritzler, 2005).

HPD Research

Due in part to the low prevalence rate and high rates of co-occurrence with other personality disorders, research employing samples diagnosed with HPD is limited. However, the potential for gender bias in the HPD diagnosis is a pivotal issue receiving decent empirical attention (Bornstein et al., 2015). DSM-5 Section II notes that HPD may occur more frequently in females than in males. Historically, HPD has been considered as a feminine disorder with increased prevalence rates in women (Grant et al., 2004; Torgersen et al., 2001) as the HPD criteria closely align with physical appearance and seductive, suggestive behaviors. However, some feminist perspectives suggest that the inclusion of stereotypical feminine characteristics in the DSM diagnosis reflects negative attitudes and assumptions of traditionally feminine interaction styles (Gould, 2011). Clinicians seem to agree that women use seduction as a means of fulfilling their needs more than men (Stone, 1993). Theorists have postulated that HPD and ASPD share diagnostic overlap in the domains of impulsivity, manipulation, and behavioral disinhibition (Blagov, Fowler, & Lilienfeld, 2007; Cale & Lilienfeld, 2002). Empirical evidence suggests that co-occurring HPD and ASPD in men is often viewed as simply ASPD (Bornstein et al., 2015). This echoes a broader tendency to diagnose HPD more frequently in women and ASPD more frequently in men when presented with case examples depicting antisocial behavior for both genders (Ford & Widiger, 1989).

Culture may also play an important role in HPD diagnosis, but empirical evidence is lacking. Few studies have investigated the association between HPD diagnoses and culture (Makaremi, 1990). However, prevalence rates among different cultural groups suggest inequity (Mullins-Sweatt, Wingate, & Lengel, 2012). Lower rates of HPD have been found in Asian cultures possibly due to socialization practices and the disapproval of outwardly sexual behavior (Johnson, 1993). Conversely, HPD is more frequently diagnosed in Latino cultures where emotional expression is encouraged (Padilla, 1995). More research is needed to clarify the role of culture in HPD prevalence rates.

Hybrid Dimensional/Categorical HPD (DSM-5 Section III AMPD)

In the hybrid DSM-5 AMPD, HPD is not included as a categorical diagnosis due to lack of sufficient empirical research and waning clinical interest. However, clinicians can use Personality Disorder – Trait Specified (PD-TS) to note the presence of histrionic personality traits (Criteria B) combined with moderate or greater impairment in personality functioning (Criteria A). The AMPD Criteria B traits most consistent with descriptions of HPD are attention seeking, separation insecurity, manipulativeness, emotional lability, intimacy avoidance (low), and restricted affectivity (low). One significant limitation of the DSM-5 AMPD trait model is that it lacks coverage of maladaptive interpersonal warmth (Pincus, 2011; Wright et al., 2012). This is a core feature of both HPD and dependent personality disorder, both of which were not retained as categorical diagnoses in the AMPD. Thus, a PD-TS trait profile for HPD may be limited in the current version of the AMPD.

Dimensional Approaches to Histrionism

Excluding scales and interviews constructed to assess DSM HPD criteria, only one contemporary dimensional measure of histrionism, the Brief Histrionic Personality Scale, is currently available (BHPS; Ferguson & Negy, 2014). The BHPS includes two facets, seductiveness and attention-seeking, which are correlated with self-report measures of HPD and extraversion. However, we could find no additional research using the BHPS or alternative dimensional measures of histrionic personality.

HPD and the Five-Factor Model

As with NPD, theorists and researchers have suggested that the FFM of normal personality structure provides utility in conceptualizing and assessing HPD. In a meta-analysis conducted by Saulsman and Page (2004), HPD displayed a weighted effect size of 0.42 with the factor extraversion. These results were echoed in Samuel and Widiger's (2008) meta-analysis which exhibited a weighted effect size of 0.33 with extraversion. Within clinical settings, private practitioners described HPD cases as high in the extraversion facets of gregariousness and excitement-seeking (Samuel & Widiger, 2004). The prototypical presentation of HPD includes high levels on all facets of extraversion (e.g., warmth, gregariousness, assertiveness, activity, excitement seeking, and positive emotions) and the facets feelings and actions (openness) and trust (agreeableness) paired with low levels of the facets self-consciousness (neuroticism) and deliberation (conscientiousness) (Gore, Tomiatti, & Widiger, 2011; Lynam & Widiger, 2001).

More recently, a Five-Factor Histrionic Inventory (FFHI; Tomiatti, Gore, Lynam, Miller, & Widiger, 2012) was developed to assess the general personality traits most relevant to HPD. The facets include FFHI neuroticism (rapidly shifting emotions, melodramatic-emotionality), FFHI extraversion (attention seeking, intimacy seeking, social butterfly, flirtatiousness, vanity), FFHI agreeableness (touchy feely suggestibility, impressionistic thinking), FFHI openness (romantic fantasies), and FFHI conscientiousness (disorderliness). Tomiatti and colleagues (2012) reported good psychometric qualities, adequate convergent validity for 11 out of the 13 FFHI scales, and incremental validity over their respective NEO-PI-R facet scales for 12 out of 13 scales in accounting for variance in responses to the PDQ-4 HPD scale. However, we could find no other research employing the FFHI to empirically examine questions pertaining to histrionic personality functioning.

FUTURE DIRECTIONS FOR NPD AND HPD

Because the state of personality disorder classification and diagnosis is in significant flux, we chose to review three prominent conceptualizations of NPD and HPD that are currently employed in clinical and research contexts, rather than reifying a single perspective. In considering the categorical DSM-5 Section II, hybrid DSM-5 AMPD, and dimensional approaches, we find conceptualization of NPD is advancing in promising ways, whereas the future of HPD seems unclear and less promising.

A major concern regarding DSM-IV NPD (and thus DSM-5 Section II NPD) raised a decade ago was that the diagnostic criteria focused too narrowly on observable grandiosity and were not consistent with clinical conceptualizations of pathological narcissism and patterns of comorbidity that included experiences of emotional dysregulation, shame, depression, withdrawal, depletion, and suicidality (Cain et al., 2008; Pincus & Lukowitsky, 2010). With the obvious exception of DSM-5 Section II NPD, the two other conceptualizations reviewed here address this concern. The DSM-5 AMPD recognizes that grandiosity can be overt or covert, assesses vulnerability through Criteria A's regulatory and relational impairments, and assesses grandiosity though Criteria B's antagonistic trait elevations. Contemporary dimensional models are operationalized by measures like the FFNI and Pathological Narcissism Inventory (Pincus et al., 2009) that assess both narcissistic grandiosity and narcissistic vulnerability. As the field advances, particularly regarding research on temporal processes and mechanisms (e.g., Wright, 2014; Wright & Edershile, 2018; Wright et al., 2017), an emergent and comprehensive model of narcissistic personality pathology that integrates personality structure (i.e., traits) and personality dynamics (i.e., temporal processes and mechanisms) appears within reach (Hopwood, Zimmerman, Pincus, & Krueger, 2015).

HPD is one of the least studied personality disorders across disciplines (Blashfield & Intoccia, 2000), resulting in a meaningful but sparse body of literature. HPD is also a controversial diagnosis with regard to its convergent and discriminate validity, its contentious history with roots in hysteria, concerns about gender bias, and a lack of treatment approaches and outcomes (Bornstein et al., 2015; Bornstein & Malka, 2009; Morey, Alexander, & Boggs, 2005). For these reasons, HPD was deleted from the DSM-5 AMPD (Skodol, 2012) and research and clinical interest has continued to wane. Sociocultural factors such as more liberal attitudes and norms for personal and sexual expression may have an impact on conceptions of disorder severity or even the disorder itself. Before declaring that HPD is dead (Blashfield et al., 2012), we see two promising avenues for advancing conceptualization of HPD. First, the DSM-5 AMPD could develop Criteria A descriptors and a pathological trait profile for HPD. The latter is hampered somewhat by the lack of Criteria B traits reflecting maladaptive warmth.

A potentially more promising approach is to increase research using the FFHI. This measure's profile of traits overcomes the current DSM-5 AMPD limitation, assessing a broad array of problematic traits related to extraversion and agreeableness. Overall, the FFHI appears to cover all the major elements of histrionic personality pathology and we encourage additional research using this measure. If nothing is done in the next decade, it is unlikely that HPD will continue as a clinical diagnosis outside of psychodynamic practice.

REFERENCES

Ackerman, R. A., Hands, A. J., Donnellan, M. B., Hopwood, C. J., & Witt, E. A. (2017). Experts' views regarding the conceptualization of narcissism. *Journal of Personality Disorders, 31*, 346–361.

American Psychiatric Association. (1980). *Diagnostic and Statistical Manual of Mental Disorders* (3rd ed.). Washington, DC: American Psychiatric Association.

American Psychiatric Association. (2000). *Diagnostic and Statistical Manual of Mental Disorders* (4th ed., Text Revision). Washington, DC: American Psychiatric Association.

American Psychiatric Association. (2013). *Diagnostic and Statistical Manual of Mental Disorders* (5th ed.). Arlington, VA: American Psychiatric Publishing.

Bach, B., Markon, K., Simonsen, E., & Krueger, R. (2015) Clinical utility of the DSM-5 Alternative Model of Personality Disorders: Six cases from practice. *Journal of Psychiatric Practice, 21*, 1–23.

Bakkevig, J. F., & Karterud, S. (2010). Is the Diagnostic and Statistical Manual of Mental Disorders, histrionic personality disorder category a valid construct? *Comprehensive Psychiatry, 51*, 462–470.

Ball, S. A., Rounsaville, B. J., Tennen, H., & Kranzler, H. R. (2001). Reliability of personality disorder symptoms and personality traits in substance-dependent inpatients. *Journal of Abnormal Psychology, 110*, 341–352.

Besser, A., & Priel, B. (2010). Grandiose narcissism versus vulnerable narcissism in threatening situations: Emotional reactions to achievement failure and interpersonal rejection. *Journal of Social and Clinical Psychology, 29*, 874–902.

Besser, A., Zeigler-Hill, V., Weinberg, M., & Pincus, A. P. (2016). Do great expectations lead to great disappointments? Pathological narcissism and the evaluation of vacation experiences. *Personality and Individual Differences, 89,* 75–79.

Blagov, P. S., Fowler, K. A., & Lilienfeld, S. O. (2007). Histrionic personality disorder. In W. O'Donohue, K. A. Fowler, & S. O. Lilienfeld (Eds.), *Personality Disorders: Toward the DSM-V* (pp. 203–232). Thousand Oaks, CA: Sage.

Blagov, P. S., & Westen, D. (2008). Questioning the coherence of histrionic personality disorder: Borderline and hysterical personality subtypes in adults and adolescents. *Journal of Nervous and Mental Disease, 196,* 785–797.

Blashfield, R. K., & Davis, R. T. (1993). Dependent and histrionic personality disorders. In P. B. Sutker & H. E. Adams (Eds), *Comprehensive Handbook of Psychopathology* (pp. 395–409). New York: Plenum.

Blashfield, R. K., & Intoccia, V. (2000). *Growth of the literature on the topic of personality disorders. American Journal of Psychiatry, 157,* 472–473.

Blashfield, R. K., Reynolds, S. M., & Stennett, B. (2012). The death of histrionic personality disorder. In T. A. Widiger (Ed.), *The Oxford Handbook of Personality Disorders* (pp. 603–627). New York: Oxford University Press.

Boon, S., & Draijer, N. (1993). The differentiation of patients with MPD or DDNOS from patients with a cluster B personality disorder. *Dissociation, 6,* 126–135.

Bornstein, R. F., Denckla, C. A., & Chung, W. J. (2015). Dependent and histrionic personality disorders. In P. H. Blaney, R. F. Krueger, & T. Millon (Eds.), *Oxford Textbook of Psychopathology* (3rd ed., pp. 659–680). New York: Oxford University Press.

Bornstein, R. F., & Malka, I. L. (2009). Dependent and histrionic personality disorders. In P. H. Blaney, & T. Millon (Eds.), *Oxford Textbook of Psychopathology* (pp. 602–621). New York: Oxford University Press.

Bresin, K., & Gordon, K. H. (2011). Characterizing pathological narcissism in terms of the HEXACO model of personality. *Journal of Psychopathology and Behavioral Assessment, 33,* 228–235.

Buelow, M. T., & Brunell, A. B. (2014). Facets of narcissistic grandiosity predict involvement in health-risk behaviors. *Personality and Individual Differences, 69,* 193–198.

Cain, N. M., Pincus, A. L., & Ansell, E. B. (2008). Narcissism at the crossroads: Phenotypic description of pathological narcissism across clinical theory, social/personality psychology, and psychiatric diagnosis. *Clinical Psychology Review, 28,* 638–656.

Cale, E. M., & Lilienfeld, S. O. (2002). Sex differences in psychopathy and antisocial personality disorder: A review and integration. *Clinical Psychology Review, 22,* 1179–1207.

Caligor, E., Levy, K. N., & Yeomans, F. E. (2015). Narcissistic personality disorder: Diagnostic and clinical challenges. *American Journal of Psychiatry, 172,* 415–422.

Campbell, W. K., & Miller, J. D. (2013). Narcissistic Personality Disorder (NPD) and the Five-Factor Model: Delineating NPD, grandiose narcissism, and vulnerable narcissism. In T. A. Widiger & P. T Costa (Eds.), *Personality Disorders and the Five-Factor Model of Personality* (3rd ed., pp. 133–146). Washington, DC: APA.

Carlson, E. N. (2013). Honestly arrogant or simply misunderstood? Narcissists' awareness of their narcissism. *Self and Identity, 12,* 259–277.

Carlson, E. N., & Oltmanns, T. F. (2015). The role of metaperception in personality disorders: Do people with personality problems know how others experience their personality? *Journal of Personality Disorders, 29,* 449–467.

Clark, L. A., Simms, L. J., Wu, K. D., & Casillas, A. (2008). *Manual for the Schedule for Adaptive and Nonadaptive Personality (SNAP-2).* Minneapolis, MN: University of Minnesota Press.

Clemence, A. J., Perry, J. C., & Plakun, E. M. (2009). Narcissistic and borderline personality disorders in a sample of treatment refractory patients. *Psychiatric Annals, 39,* 175–184.

Costa, P. T., & McCrae, R. R. (1992). *Revised NEO Personality Inventory (NEO-PI-R) and NEO Five Factor Inventory (NEO-FFI) Professional Manual.* Odessa, FL: Psychological Assessment Resources.

Dawood, S., & Pincus, A. L. (2018a). Pathological narcissism and the severity, variability, and instability of depressive symptoms. *Personality Disorders: Theory, Research, and Treatment, 9,* 144–154.

Dawood, S., & Pincus, A. L. (2018b). A prospective study of pathological narcissism and shame. *Manuscript under review.*

Dawood, S., Schroeder, H. S., Donnellan, M. B., & Pincus, A. L. (2018). Pathological narcissism and non-suicidal self-injury. *Journal of Personality Disorders, 32,* 87–108.

Decker, H. S. (2013). *The Making of DSM-III: A Diagnostic Manual's Conquest of American Psychiatry.* New York: Oxford University Press.

Dhawan, N., Kunik, M. E., Oldham, J., & Coverdale, J. (2010). Prevalence and treatment of narcissistic personality disorder in the community: A systematic review. *Comprehensive Psychiatry, 51,* 333–339.

Dowgwillo, E. A., Dawood, S., & Pincus, A. L. (2016). The dark side of narcissism. In V. Zeigler-Hill & D. Marcus (Eds.), *The Dark Side of Personality* (pp. 25–44). Washington, DC: American Psychological Association.

Dyck, I. R., Phillips, K. A., Warshaw, M. G., Dolan, R. T., Shea, M. T., Stout, R. L., . . . Keller, M. B. (2001). Patterns of personality pathology in patients with generalized anxiety disorder, panic disorder with and without agoraphobia, and social phobia. *Journal of Personality Disorders, 15,* 60–71.

Eaton, N. R., Rodriguez-Seijas, C., Krueger, R. F., Campbell, W. K., Grant, B. F., & Hasin, D. S. (2017). Narcissistic personality disorder and the structure of common mental disorders. *Journal of Personality Disorders, 31,* 449–461.

Ekselius, L., Tillfors, M., Furmark, T., & Fredrikson, M. (2001). Personality disorders in the general population: DSM-IV and ICD-10 defined prevalence as related to sociodemographic profile. *Personality and Individual Differences, 30,* 311–320.

Ellison, W. D., Levy, K. N., Cain, N. M., Ansell, E. B., & Pincus, A. L. (2013). The impact of pathological narcissism on psychotherapy utilization, initial symptom severity, and early-treatment symptom change: A naturalistic investigation. *Journal of Personality Assessment, 95,* 291–300.

Erkoreka, L., & Navarro, B. (2017). Vulnerable narcissism is associated with severity of depressive symptoms in dysthymic patients. *Psychiatry Research, 257,* 265–269.

Ferguson, C. J., & Negy, C. (2014). Development of a brief screening questionnaire for histrionic personality symptoms. *Personality and Individual Differences, 66,* 124–127.

Fetterman, A. K., & Robinson, M. D. (2010). Contingent self-importance among pathological narcissists: Evidence from an implicit task. *Journal of Research in Personality, 44,* 691–697.

Fonagy, P., & Luyten, P. (2012). Psychodynamic models of personality disorders. In T. A. Widiger (Ed.), *The Oxford Handbook of Personality Disorders* (pp. 345–371). New York: Oxford University Press.

Ford, M. R., & Widiger, T. A. (1989). Sex bias in the diagnosis of histrionic and antisocial personality disorders. *Journal of Consulting and Clinical Psychology, 57,* 301–305.

Freud, S. (1914). On narcissism. In J. Strachey (Ed. and Trans.), *The Standard Edition of the Complete Psychological Works of Sigmund Freud* (Vol. XIV, pp. 66-102). London: Hogarth Press.

Freud, S. (1931). *Libidinal types.* In J. Strachey (Ed. and Trans.), *The Standard Edition of the Complete Psychological Works of Sigmund Freud* (Vol. XXII, pp. 310–333). London: Hogarth Press.

Garno, J. L., Goldberg, J. F., Ramirez, P. M., & Ritzler, B. A. (2005). Bipolar disorder with comorbid cluster B personality disorder features: Impact on suicidality. *Journal of Clinical Psychiatry, 66,* 339–345.

Glover, N., Miller, J. D., Lynam, D. R., Crego, C., & Widiger, T. A. (2012). The five factor narcissism inventory: A five-factor measure of narcissistic personality traits. *Journal of Personality Assessment, 94,* 500–512.

Goldberg, B. R., Serper, M. R., Sheets, M., Beech, D., Dill, C., & Duffy, K. G. (2007). Predictors of aggression on the psychiatric inpatient service: Self-esteem, narcissism, and theory of mind deficits. *Journal of Nervous and Mental Disease, 195,* 436–442.

Gore, W. L., Tomiatti, M., & Widiger, T. A. (2011). The home for histrionism. *Personality and Mental Health, 5,* 57–72.

Gore, W. L., & Widiger, T. A. (2016). Fluctuation between grandiose and vulnerable narcissism. *Personality Disorders: Theory, Research, and Treatment, 7,* 363–371.

Gould, C. S. (2011). Why the histrionic personality disorder should not be in the DSM: A new taxonomic and moral analysis. *International Journal of Feminist Approaches to Bioethics, 4*(1), 26–40.

Grant, B. F., Hasin, D. S., Stinson, F. S., Dawson, D. A., Chou, S. P., Ruan, W., & Pickering, R. P. (2004). Prevalence, correlates, and disability of personality disorders in the United States: results from the National Epidemiologic Survey on Alcohol and Related Conditions. *Journal of Clinical Psychiatry, 65,* 948–958.

Grilo, C. M., McGlashan, T. H., Quinlan, D. M., Walker, M. L., Greenfeld, D., & Edell, W. S. (1998). Frequency of personality disorders in two age cohorts of psychiatric inpatients. *American Journal of Psychiatry, 155,* 140–142.

Gunderson, J., Ronningstam, E., & Bodkin, A. (1990). The diagnostic interview for narcissistic patients. *Archives of General Psychiatry, 47,* 676–680.

Gunderson, J., Ronningstam, E., & Smith, L. E. (1995). Narcissistic personality disorder. In J. Livesley (Ed.), *The DSM-IV Personality Disorder Diagnoses* (pp. 201–212). New York: Guilford Press.

Hare, R. D., & Neumann, C. S. (2008). Psychopathy as a clinical and empirical construct. *Annual Review of Clinical Psychology, 4,* 217–246.

Herpertz, S. C., Huprich, S. K., Bohus, M., Chanen, A., Goodman, M., Mehlum, L., … Sharp, C. (2017). The challenge of transforming the diagnostic system of personality disorders. *Journal of Personality Disorders, 31,* 577–589.

Hinrichs, J. (2016). Inpatient therapeutic assessment with narcissistic personality disorder. *Journal of Personality Assessment, 98,* 111–123.

Hopwood, C. J., Ansell, E. A., Pincus, A. L., Wright, A. G. C., Lukowitsky, M. R., & Roche, M. J. (2011). The circumplex structure of interpersonal sensitivities. *Journal of Personality, 79,* 707–740.

Hopwood, C. J., Kotov, R., Krueger, R. F., Watson, D., Widiger, T. A., Althoff, R. R., … Zimmermann, J. (2018). The time has come for dimensional personality disorder diagnosis. *Personality and Mental Health, 12,* 82–86.

Hopwood, C. J., Krueger, R. F., Watson, D., Widiger, T. A., Althoff, R. R., Ansell, E. B., … Zimmermann, J. (2019). Commentary on "The challenge of transforming the diagnostic system for personality disorders." *Journal of Personality Disorders,* online commentary: https://guilfordjournals.com/doi/abs/10.1521/pedi_2019_33_00

Hopwood, C. J., Malone, J. C., Ansell, E. B., Sanislow, C. A., Grilo, C. M., McGlashan, T. H., … Morey, L. C. (2011). Personality assessment in DSM-5: Empirical support for rating severity, style, and traits. *Journal of Personality Disorders, 25,* 305–320.

Hopwood, C. J., Zimmermann, J., Pincus, A. L., & Krueger, R. F. (2015). Connecting personality structure and dynamics: Towards a more evidence based and clinically useful diagnostic scheme. *Journal of Personality Disorders, 29,* 431–448.

Hörz-Sagstetter, S., Diamond, D., Clarkin, J. F., Levy, K. N., Rentrop, M., Fischer-Kern, M., … Doering, S. (2017). Clinical characteristics of comorbid narcissistic personality disorder in patients with borderline personality disorder. *Journal of Personality Disorders, 32*(4), 1–14.

Hyatt, C. S., Sleep, C. E., Lynam, D. R., Widiger, T. A., Campbell, W. K., & Miller, J. D. (2018). Ratings of affective and interpersonal tendencies differ for grandiose and vulnerable narcissism: A replication and extension of Gore & Widiger. *Journal of Personality, 86*(3), 422–434.

Jaksic, N., Marcinko, D., Hanzek, M. S., Rebernjak, B., & Ogrodniczuk, J. S. (2017). Experience of shame mediates the relationship between pathological narcissism and suicidal ideation in psychiatric outpatients. *Journal of Clinical Psychology, 73,* 1670–1681.

Johnson, F. A. (1993). *Dependency and Japanese Socialization.* New York: New York University Press.

Kealy, D., & Rasmussen, B. (2012). Veiled and vulnerable: The other side of grandiose narcissism. *Clinical Social Work Journal, 40,* 356–366.

Kealy, D., Tsai, M., & Ogrodniczuk, J. S. (2012). Depressive tendencies and pathological narcissism among psychiatric outpatients. *Psychiatry Research, 196,* 157–159.

Kohut, H. (1977). *The Restoration of the Self.* New York: International Universities Press.

Kohut, H., & Wolf, E. S. (1978). The disorders of the self and their treatment: An outline. *International Journal of Psychoanalysis, 59,* 413–425.

Krizan, Z., & Johar, O. (2012). Envy divides the two faces of narcissism. *Journal of Personality, 80,* 1415–1451.

Krueger, R. F. (2016). The future is now: Personality disorder and the ICD-11. *Personality and Mental Health, 10,* 118–119.

Lenzenweger, M. F., Johnson, M. D., & Willett, J. (2004). Individual growth curve analysis illuminates stability and change in personality disorder features: The longitudinal study of personality disorders. *Archives of General Psychiatry, 61,* 1015–1024.

Lenzenweger, M. F., Lane, M. C., Loranger, A. W., & Kessler, R. C. (2007). DSM-IV personality disorders in the National Comorbidity Survey Replication. *Biological Psychiatry, 62*(6), 553–564.

Levy, K. N., Chauhan, P., Clarkin, J. F., Wasserman, R. H., & Reynoso, J. S. (2009). Narcissistic pathology: Empirical approaches. *Psychiatric Annals, 39*(4), 203–213.

Levy, K. N., Reynoso, J. S., Wasserman, R. H., & Clarkin, J. F. (2007). Narcissistic personality disorder. In W. O'Donohue, K. A. Fowler, & S. O. Lilienfeld (Eds.), *Personality Disorders: Toward the DSM-V* (pp. 233–277). Thousand Oaks, CA: Sage.

Lingiardi, V., & McWilliams, N. (2015). The psychodynamic diagnostic manual–2nd edition (PDM-2). *World Psychiatry, 14,* 237–239.

Lobbestael, J., Baumeister, R. F., Feibig, T., & Eckel, L. A. (2014). The role of grandiose and vulnerable narcissism in self-reported and laboratory aggression and testosterone reactivity. *Personality and Individual Differences, 69,* 22–27.

Lynam, D. R., & Widiger, T. A. (2001). Using the five-factor model to represent the DSM-IV personality disorders: An expert consensus approach. *Journal of Abnormal Psychology, 110,* 401–412.

Makaremi, A. (1990). Histrionic disorder among Iranian high school and college students. *Psychological Reports, 66*(3), 835–838.

Marčinko, D., Jakšić, N., Ivezić, E., Skočić, M., Surányi, Z., Lončar, M., ... Jakovljević, M. (2014). Pathological narcissism and depressive symptoms in psychiatric outpatients: Mediating role of dysfunctional attitudes. *Journal of Clinical Psychology, 70,* 341–352.

Marissen, M. A., Deen, M. L., & Franken, I. H. (2012). Disturbed emotion recognition in patients with narcissistic personality disorder. *Psychiatry Research, 198,* 269–273.

Marissen, M. A., Brouwer, M. E., Hiemstra, A. M., Deen, M. L., & Franken, I. H. (2016). A masked negative self-esteem? Implicit and explicit self-esteem in patients with Narcissistic Personality Disorder. *Psychiatry Research, 242,* 28–33.

Mattia, J., & Zimmerman, M. (2001). Epidemiology. In W. J. Livesley (Ed.), *The Handbook of Personality Disorders* (pp. 107–123). New York: Guilford Press.

Maxwell, K., Donnellan, M. B., Hopwood, C. J., & Ackerman, R. A. (2011). The two faces of Narcissus? An empirical comparison of the Narcissistic Personality Inventory and the Pathological Narcissism Inventory. *Personality and Individual Differences, 50,* 577–582.

McWilliams, N. (2011). *Psychoanalytic Diagnosis* (2nd ed.). New York: Guilford Press.

Ménard, K. S., & Pincus, A. L. (2012). Predicting overt and cyber stalking perpetration by male and female college students. *Journal of Interpersonal Violence, 27,* 2183–2207.

Miller, J. D., Dir, A., Gentile, B., Wilson, L., Pryor, L. R., & Campbell, W. K. (2010). Searching for a vulnerable dark triad: Comparing factor 2 psychopathy, vulnerable narcissism, and borderline personality disorder. *Journal of Personality, 85,* 1529–1564.

Miller, J. D., Gentile, B., & Campbell, W. K. (2013). A test of the construct validity of the Five-Factor Narcissism Inventory. *Journal of Personality Assessment, 95,* 377–387.

Miller, J. D., Gentile, B., Wilson, L., & Campbell, W. K. (2013). Grandiose and vulnerable narcissism and the DSM-5 pathological personality trait model. *Journal of Personality Assessment, 95,* 284–290.

Miller, J. D., Hoffman, B., Campbell, W. K., & Pilkonis, P. A. (2008). An examination of the factor structure of DSM-IV narcissistic personality disorder criteria: One or two factors? *Comprehensive Psychiatry, 49,* 141–145.

Miller, J. D., Lynam, D. R., Hyatt, C. S., & Campbell, W. K. (2017). Controversies in narcissism. *Annual Review of Clinical Psychology, 13,* 291–315.

Miller, J. D., Lynam, D. R., McCain, J. L., Few, L. R., Crego, C., Widiger, T. A., & Campbell, W. K. (2016). Thinking structurally about narcissism: An examination of the Five-Factor Narcissism Inventory and its components. *Journal of Personality Disorders, 30,* 1–18.

Miller, J. D., Lynam, D. R, Siedor, L., Crowe, M., Campbell, W. K. (2018). Consensual lay profiles of narcissism and their connection to the Five-Factor Narcissism Inventory. *Psychological Assessment, 30,* 10–18.

Morey, L. C. (2005). Personality pathology as pathological narcissism. In M. Maj, H. S. Akiskal, J. E. Mezzich, & A. Okasha (Eds.), *Evidence and Experience in Psychiatry, Volume 8: Personality Disorders* (pp. 328–331). New York: John Wiley.

Morey, L. C., Alexander, G. M., & Boggs, C. (2005). Gender and personality disorder. In J. Oldham, A. Skodol, & D. Bender (Eds.), *Textbook of Personality Disorders* (pp. 541-554). Washington, DC: American Psychiatric Press.

Morey, L. C., & Stagner, B. H. (2012). Narcissistic pathology as a core personality dysfunction: Comparing the DSM-IV and the DSM-5 proposal for narcissistic personality disorder. *Journal of Clinical Psychology, 68,* 908–921.

Morf, C. C. (2006). Personality reflected in a coherent idiosyncratic interplay of intra- and interpersonal self-regulatory processes. *Journal of Personality, 76,* 1527–1556.

Morf, C. C., Horvath, S., & Torchetti, T. (2011). Narcissistic self-enhancement: Tales of (successful?) self-portrayal. In M. D. Alicke & C. Sedikides (Eds.), *Handbook of Self-Enhancement and Self-Protection* (pp. 399–424). New York: Guilford Press.

Morf, C., & Rhodewalt, F. (2001). Unraveling the paradoxes of narcissism: A dynamic self-regulatory processing model. *Psychological Inquiry, 12,* 177–196.

Mullins-Sweatt, S. N., Wingate, L. R., & Lengel, G. J. (2012). Histrionic personality disorder: Diagnostic and treatment considerations. In P. K. Lundberg-Love, K. L. Nadal, & M. A. Paludi (Eds.) *Women and Mental Disorders* (pp. 57–73). Santa Barbara, CA: Praeger.

Nenadic, I., Güllmar, D., Dietzek, M., Langbein, K., Steinke, J., & Gaser, C. (2015). Brain structure in narcissistic personality disorder: A VBM and DTI pilot study. *Psychiatry Research: Neuroimaging, 231,* 184–186.

Nestadt, G., Di, C., Samuels, J. F., Bienvenu, O. J., Reti, I. M., Costa, P., ... Bandeen-Roche, K. (2010). The stability of DSM personality disorders over twelve to eighteen years. *Journal of Psychiatric Research, 44,* 1–7.

Ogrodniczuk, J. S. (2013). *Understanding and Treating Pathological Narcissism.* Washington, DC: American Psychological Association.

Ogrodniczuk, J. S., Piper, W. E., Joyce, A. S, Steinberg, P. I., & Duggal, S. (2009). Interpersonal problems associated with narcissism among psychiatric outpatients. *Journal of Psychiatric Research, 43,* 837–842.

Oltmanns, T. F., & Turkheimer, E. (2006). Perceptions of self and others regarding pathological personality traits. In R. F. Krueger & J. L. Tackett (Eds.), *Personality and Psychopathology* (pp. 71–111). New York: Guilford Press.

Padilla, A. M. (1995). *Hispanic Psychology: Critical Issues in Theory and Research.* Newbury Pak, CA: Sage.

Pepper, C. M., Klein, D. N., Andersom, R. L., Riso, L. P., Ouimette, P. C., & Lizardi, H. (1995). DSM-lll-R Axis II comorbidity in dysthymia and major depression. *American Journal of Psychiatry, 152,* 239–247.

Pfohl, B. (1991). Histrionic personality disorder: A review of available data and recommendations for DSM-IV. *Journal of Personality Disorders, 5,* 150–166.

Pincus, A. L. (2011). Some comments on nomology, diagnostic process, and narcissistic personality disorder in the DSM-5 proposal for personality and personality disorders. *Personality Disorders: Theory, Research, and Treatment, 2*, 41–53.

Pincus, A. L. (2013). The Pathological Narcissism Inventory. In J. Ogrodniczuk (Ed.), *Understanding and Treating Pathological Narcissism* (pp. 93–110). Washington, DC: American Psychological Association.

Pincus, A. L., Ansell, E. B., Pimentel, C. A., Cain, N. M., Wright, A. G. C., & Levy, K. N. (2009). Initial construction and validation of the Pathological Narcissism Inventory. *Psychological Assessment, 21*, 365–379.

Pincus, A. L., Cain, N. M., & Wright, A. G. C. (2014). Narcissistic grandiosity and narcissistic vulnerability in psychotherapy. *Personality Disorders: Theory, Research, and Treatment, 5*, 439–443.

Pincus, A. L., Dowgwillo, E. A., & Greenberg, L. (2016). Three cases of narcissistic personality disorder through the lens of the DSM-5 alternative model for personality disorders. *Practice Innovations, 1*, 164–177.

Pincus, A. L., & Lukowitsky, M. R. (2010). Pathological narcissism and narcissistic personality disorder. *Annual Review of Clinical Psychology, 6*, 421–446.

Pincus, A. L., & Roche, M. J. (2011). Narcissistic grandiosity and narcissistic vulnerability. In W. K. Campbell & J. D. Miller (Eds.), *Handbook of Narcissism and Narcissistic Personality Disorder* (pp. 31–40). Hoboken, NJ: John Wiley.

Pincus, A. L., Roche, M. J., & Good, E. W. (2015). Narcissistic personality disorder and pathological narcissism. In P. H. Blaney, R. F. Krueger, & T. Millon (Eds.), *Oxford Textbook of Psychopathology* (3rd ed., pp. 791–813). New York: Oxford University Press.

Pincus, A. L., & Wright, A. G. C. (in press). Narcissism as the dynamics of grandiosity and vulnerability. In S. Doering, H.-P. Hartmann, & O. F. Kernberg (Eds.), *Narzissmus: Grundlagen – Störungsbilder – Therapie* (2nd ed.). Stuttgart: Schattauer Publishers.

Reed-Knight, B., & Fischer, S. (2011). Treatment of narcissistic personality disorder symptoms in a dialectical behavior therapy framework. In J. D. Miller & W. K. Campbell (Eds.), *The Handbook of Narcissism and Narcissistic Personality Disorder: Theoretical Approaches, Empirical Findings, and Treatments* (pp. 466–475). Hoboken, NJ: John Wiley.

Reich, W. (1949). *Character Analysis*. New York: Farrar, Straus & Giroux.

Reidy, D. E., Foster, J. D., & Zeichner, A. (2010). *Narcissism and unprovoked aggression. Aggressive Behavior, 36*, 414–422.

Ritter, K., Dziobek, I., Preissler, S., Ruter, A., Vater, A., Fydrich T., ... Roepke, S. (2011). Lack of empathy in patients with narcissistic personality disorder. *Psychiatry Research, 187*, 241–247.

Ritter, K., Vater, A., Rüsch, N., Schröder-Abé, M., Schütz, A., Fydrich, T., ... Roepke, S. (2014). Shame in patients with narcissistic personality disorder. *Psychiatry Research, 215*(2), 429–437.

Roche, M. J., Pincus, A. L., Lukowitsky, M. R., Ménard, K. S., & Conroy, D. E. (2013). An integrative approach to the assessment of narcissism. *Journal of Personality Assessment, 95*, 237–248.

Ronningstam, E. (2005). *Identifying and Understanding the Narcissistic Personality*. New York: Oxford University Press.

Ronningstam, E. (2009). Narcissistic personality disorder: Facing DSM-V. *Psychiatric Annals, 39*, 111–121.

Ronningstam, E. (2011a). Psychoanalytic theories on narcissism and narcissistic personality. In W. K. Campbell & J. D. Miller (Eds.), *The Handbook of Narcissism and Narcissistic Personality*

Disorder: Theoretical Approaches, Empirical Findings, and Treatments (pp. 41–55). Hoboken, NJ: John Wiley.

Ronningstam, E. (2011b). Narcissistic personality disorder in DSM-V: In support of retaining a significant diagnosis. *Journal of Personality Disorders, 25*, 248–259.

Ronningstam, E., Gunderson, J., & Lyons, M. (1995). Changes in pathological narcissism. *American Journal of Psychiatry, 152*, 253–257.

Samuel, D. B., Hopwood, C. J., Ansell, E. B., Morey, L. C., Sanislow, C. A., Markowitz, J. C., ... Grilo, C. M. (2011). Comparing the temporal stability of self-report and interview assessed personality disorder. *Journal of Abnormal Psychology, 120*, 670–680.

Samuel, D. B., & Widiger, T. A. (2004). Clinicians' personality descriptions of prototypic personality disorders. *Journal of Personality Disorders, 18*, 286–308.

Samuel, D. B., & Widiger, T. A. (2008). A meta-analytic review of the relationships between the five-factor model and DSM-IV-TR personality disorders: A facet level analysis. *Clinical Psychology Review, 28*, 1326–1342.

Saulsman, L. M., & Page, A. C. (2004). The five-factor model and personality disorder empirical literature: A meta-analytic review. *Clinical Psychology Review, 23*, 1055–1085.

Schmeck, K., Schlüter-Müller, S., Foelsch, P., & Doering, S. (2013). The role of identity in the DSM-5 classification of personality disorders. *Child and Adolescent Psychiatry and Mental Health, 7*, 1–11.

Schneider, K. (1923). *Psychopathic Personalities*. London: Cassell.

Schulze, L., Dziobek, I., Vater, A., Heekeren, H. R., Bajbouj, M., Renneberg, B., ... Roepke, S. (2013). Gray matter abnormalities in patients with narcissistic personality disorder. *Journal of Psychiatric Research, 47*, 1363–1369.

Simonsen, S., & Simonsen, E. (2011). Comorbidity between narcissistic personality disorder and Axis I diagnoses. In W. K. Campbell & J. D. Miller (Eds.), *The Handbook of Narcissism and Narcissistic Personality Disorder: Theoretical Approaches, Empirical Findings, and Treatments* (pp. 239–247). Hoboken, NJ: John Wiley.

Skodol, A. E. (2012). Personality disorders in DSM-5. *Annual Review of Clinical Psychology, 8*, 317–344.

Skodol, A. E., Morey, L. C., Bender, D. S., & Oldham, J. M. (2015). The alternative DSM-5 model of personality disorders: A clinical application. *American Journal of Psychiatry, 172*, 606–613.

Smith, M. M., Sherry, S. B., Chen, S., Saklofske, D. H., Flett, G. L., & Hewitt, P. L. (2016). Perfectionism and narcissism: A meta-analytic review. *Journal of Research in Personality, 64*, 90–101.

Smith, S. F., & Lilienfeld, S. O. (2012). Histrionic personality disorder. In V. S. Ramachandran (Ed), *Encyclopedia of Human Behavior* (pp. 312–315). Amsterdam: Elsevier.

Stern, B. L., Diamond, D., & Yeomans, F. E. (2017). Transference-focused psychotherapy (TFP) for narcissistic personality: Engaging patients in the early treatment process. *Psychoanalytic Psychology, 34*, 381–396.

Stinson, F. S., Dawson, D. A., Goldstein, R. B., Chou, S. P., Huang, B., Smith, S. M., ... Grant, B. F. (2008). Prevalence, correlates, disability, and comorbidity of DSM-IV narcissistic personality disorder: Results from the Wave 2 National Epidemiologic Survey on Alcohol and Related Conditions. *Journal of Clinical Psychiatry, 69*, 1033–1045.

Stone, M. H. (1993). *Abnormalities of Personality*. New York: W. W. Norton.

Stone, M. H. (1998). Normal narcissism: An etiological and ethological perspective. In E. Ronningstam (Ed.), *Disorders of Narcissism: Diagnostic, Clinical, and Empirical Implications* (pp. 7–28). Washington, DC: American Psychiatric Publishing.

Tomiatti, M., Gore, W. L., Lynam, D. R., Miller, J. D., & Widiger, T. A. (2012). A five-factor measure of histrionic personality traits. In A. M. Columbus (Ed.), *Advances in Psychology Research* (Vol. 87, pp. 113–138). Hauppauge, NY: Nova Science Publishers.

Torgersen, S., Kringlen, E., & Cramer, V. (2001). The prevalence of personality disorders in a community sample. *Archives of General Psychiatry*, 58(6), 590–596.

Tritt, S. M., Ryder, A. G., Ring, A. J., & Pincus, A. L. (2010). Pathological narcissism and the depressive temperament. *Journal of Affective Disorders*, 122, 280–284.

Trull, T. J., Jahng, S., Tomko, R. L., Wood, P. K., & Sher, K. J. (2010). Revised NESARC personality disorder diagnoses: Gender, prevalence, and comorbidity with substance dependence disorders. *Journal of Personality Disorders*, 24(4), 412–426.

Tyrer, P., Crawford, M., Mulder, R., Blashfield, R., Farnam, A., Fossati, A., . . . Reed, G. M. (2011). The rationale for the reclassification of personality disorder in the 11th Revision of the International Classification of Diseases. *Personality and Mental Health*, 5, 246–259.

Tyrer, P., Crawford, M., Sanatinia, R., Tyrer, H., Cooper, S., Muller-Pollard, C., . . . Weich, S. (2014). Preliminary studies of the ICD-11 classification of personality disorder in practice. *Personality and Mental Health*, 8, 254–263.

Vater, A., Ritter, K., Schröder-Abé, M., Schutz, A., Lammers, C. H., Bosson, J. K., & Roepke, S. (2013). When grandiosity and vulnerability collide: Implicit and explicit self-esteem in patients with narcissistic personality disorder. *Journal of Behavior Therapy and Experimental Psychiatry*, 44, 37–47.

Vater, A., Ritter, K., Strunz, S., Ronningstam, E. F., Renneberg, B., & Roepke, S. (2014). Stability of narcissistic personality disorder: Tracking categorical and dimensional rating systems over a two-year period. *Personality Disorders: Theory, Research, and Treatment*, 5, 305–313.

Vater, A., Schröder-Abé, M., Ritter, K., Renneberg, B., Schulze, L., Bosson, J. K., & Roepke, S. (2013). The Narcissistic Personality Inventory: A useful tool for assessing pathological narcissism? Evidence from patients with narcissistic personality disorder. *Journal of Personality Assessment*, 95, 301–308.

Verheul, R. (2005). Clinical utility of dimensional models for personality pathology. *Journal of Personality Disorders*, 19, 283–302.

Waugh, M., Hopwood, C. J., Krueger, R. F., Morey, L. C., Pincus, A. L., & Wright, A. G. C. (2017). Psychological assessment with the DSM-5 alternative model for personality disorders: Tradition and innovation. *Professional Psychology: Research and Practice*, 48, 79–89.

Westen, D., & Heim, A. K. (2003). Disturbances of self and identity in personality disorders. In M. R. Leary & J. P. Tangney (Eds.), *Handbook of Self and Identity* (pp. 643–666). New York: Guilford Press.

Widiger, T. A. (2011). The comorbidity of narcissistic personality disorder with other DSM-IV personality disorders. In W. K. Campbell & J. D. Miller (Eds.), *Handbook of Narcissism and Narcissistic Personality Disorder: Theoretical Approaches, Empirical Findings, and Treatment* (pp. 248–260). Hoboken, NJ: John Wiley.

Widiger, T. A., & Costa P. T. (Eds.) (2013). *Personality Disorders and the Five-Factor Model of Personality* (3rd ed.). Washington, DC: American Psychological Association.

Widiger, T. A., Lynam, D. R., Miller, J. D., & Oltmanns, T. F. (2012). Measures to assess maladaptive variants of the five-factor model. *Journal of Personality*, 94, 450–455.

Widman, L., & McNulty, J. K. (2010). Sexual narcissism and the perpetration of sexual aggression. *Archives of Sexual Behavior*, 39, 926–939.

Wright, A. G. C. (2014). Integrating trait-and process-based conceptualizations of pathological narcissism in the DSM-5 era. In A. Besser (Ed.), *Handbook of Narcissism: Diverse Perspectives* (pp. 153–174). Hauppauge, NY: Nova Science Publishers.

Wright, A. G. C., & Edershile, E. A. (2018). Issues resolved and unresolved in pathological narcissism. *Current Opinion in Psychology*, 21, 74–79.

Wright, A. G. C., Lukowitsky, M. R., Pincus, A. L., & Conroy, D.E. (2010). The higher-order factor structure and gender invariance of the pathological narcissism inventory. *Assessment*, 17, 467–483.

Wright, A. G. C., Pincus, A. L., Hopwood, C. J., Thomas, K. M., Markon, K. E., & Krueger, R. F. (2012). An interpersonal analysis of pathological personality traits in DSM-5. *Assessment*, 19, 263–275.

Wright, A. G. C., Stepp, S. D., Scott, L. N., Hallquist, M. N., Beeney, J. E., Lazarus, S. A., & Pilkonis, P. A. (2017). The effect of pathological narcissism on interpersonal and affective processes in social interactions. *Journal of Abnormal Psychology*, 126, 898–910.

Yeomans, F. E., Clarkin, J. F., & Kernberg, O. F. (2015*). Transference-Focused Psychotherapy for Borderline Personality Disorder: A Clinical Guide*. Arlington, VA: American Psychiatric Publishing.

Zachar, P., Krueger, R. F., & Kendler, K. S. (2016). Personality disorder in DSM-5: An oral history. *Psychological Medicine*, 46, 1–10.

Zanarini, M. C., Frankenburg, F. R., Sickel, A. E., & Yong, L. (1996). *The Diagnostic Interview for DSM-IV Personality Disorders (DIPD-IV)*. Belmont, MA: McLean Hospital.

Zeigler-Hill, V., & Besser, A. (2013). A glimpse behind the mask: Facets of narcissism and feelings of self-worth. *Journal of Personality Assessment*, 95, 249–260

Zeigler-Hill, V., Enjaian, B., & Essa, L. (2013). The role of narcissistic personality features in sexual aggression. *Journal of Social and Clinical Psychology*, 32, 186–199.

Zimmerman, M., Rothschild, L., & Chelminski, I. (2005). The prevalence of DSM-IV personality disorders in psychiatric outpatients. *American Journal of Psychiatry*, 162, 1911–1918.

12a A Call for Scientific Caution: Commentary on Narcissistic and Histrionic Personality Disorders

BRANDON WEISS AND W. KEITH CAMPBELL

The chapter on narcissistic personality disorder by Dawood, Wu, Bliton, and Pincus is well done and we agree with many of the authors' key descriptions and arguments. At the same time, we believe there are important points to be made regarding their description of the disorder. The primary area of divergence from our perspective is their focus on narcissistic personality pathology, and narcissistic personality disorder (NPD) in particular, as a largely monolithic and unified construct. As a result, their description of the nomological network around NPD occurs with limited attention to potential distortions resulting from heterogeneity across scales that putatively measure NPD, overstatement of NPD's vulnerable character, and insufficient concern for the influence of sampling on results. We address these three issues below and argue that a view of narcissism that is appropriately cautious about potential theoretical bias moors our craft closer to the headlands of truth and shelters us from the idiot wind of inflated scientific confidence.

NPD IS NOT A NARROW CONSTRUCT

The first issue with the target authors' chapter and the field more broadly relates to the multiple conceptualizations and corresponding assessments of NPD in the literature. Variability in the measurement of NPD makes any conclusions about the functioning of NPD misleading in the absence of earnest qualification. Since 2010, an average of 357 peer-reviewed articles have been published per year in which narcissism is discussed in the Abstract, amounting to a substantial change from previous years (e.g., 219 in 1990, and 173 in 2000) (Miller, Lynam, Hyatt, & Campbell, 2017). This growing interest has accompanied a corresponding increase in available measures that assess NPD. The majority of these measures are self-report inventories (e.g., Pathological Narcissism Inventory [PNI], Pincus et al., 2009; Personality Diagnostic Questionnaire-4, Hyler, 1994), while interview-based measures are common as well. Some of the clearest evidence of variability in the NPD construct across measures is contained in Samuel and Widiger's (2008)

correlational study which observed how NPD's relations with Five-Factor Model (FFM) personality domains vary across the most widely used scales of NPD. Considerable variability can be seen across relations with all FFM domains, but particularly in relation to Neuroticism and Extraversion. Saulsman and Page (2004) demonstrated similar findings in a meta-analysis of correlations between NPD and personality. Across 18 samples in which at least seven different NPD measures were used, effect size estimates of relations between measures of NPD and Neuroticism, Extraversion, and Agreeableness, domains that are most related to NPD (e.g., Samuel & Widiger, 2008), were remarkably variable (Saulsman & Page, 2004, Table 2). For example, the standard deviations of sample effect size estimates approached .30 (in terms of units of Pearson r) for relations between NPD and Neuroticism, and .23 between NPD and Extraversion.

Of note, there are at least three contributors to the variability in these effect size estimates across measures of NPD. The first regards the potential effect of *method variance* on results. Across undergraduate, community, and psychiatric samples, weak to moderate convergence has been observed between self-report measures of NPD (e.g., PDQ-4) and interview-based measures (e.g., Hopwood et al., 2013). These results raise the importance of efforts to modify self-report measures, such that they bear greater convergence with interview measures; and examine where correlates with NPD diverge by measure type.

Second, *differences in content* in the wording of items on particular measures can produce outsized differences in the meaning and interpretation of items by respondents. Consider the difference between the *Diagnostic and Statistical Manual of Mental Disorders-5* (DSM-5; APA, 2013) NPD criterion "... is interpersonally exploitative, i.e., takes advantage of others to achieve his or her own ends" and the Millon Clinical Multiaxial Inventory-III (MCMI-III; Millon, Millon, & Davis, 1994) item designed to reflect it: i.e., "I don't blame anyone who takes advantage of someone who allows it." Although these items both describe attitudes towards exploitative behavior, the latter is notably passive whereas the former is active.

Third, measures vary in *vulnerable content* – that is, the proportion of vulnerable aspects of narcissism in the scale – may unduly bias results towards stronger relations between NPD and external correlates containing vulnerability (e.g., shame). Even fairly similar items may be sufficiently dissimilar to produce differences in interpretation by respondents. Note the difference between these two items within the Grandiose Fantasies subscale of the PNI: "I want to amount to something in the eyes of the world"; "I often fantasize about being admired and respected." Although these items are treated as being representative of pathological grandiosity, the former item evokes a sense of unredeemed inadequacy, which is redolent of narcissistic vulnerability and may be more related to a need for validation than status or gain. Indeed, the grandiose dimension of the PNI, as well as other measures of pathological narcissism and NPD (e.g., PDQ-4, MCMI-III), contain negative emotionality/fragility (i.e., vulnerability) that differs from other measures (Miller, McCain, et al., 2014).

DIFFERING CONCEPTUALIZATIONS OF NPD

The second issue in the target authors' chapter involves the predetermining influence of the authors' particular conceptualization of narcissism on conclusions about relations to external correlates. Differences between measures on the dimension of vulnerability can be linked to disagreement on conceptualizations of narcissism. The authors of the target chapter regard NPD as a self-regulatory disorder in which grandiose and vulnerable states oscillate in narcissistic individuals. Grandiose and vulnerable states are thought to stem from a common etiology, namely "intensely felt needs for validation and admiration," which motivate the seeking out of self-enhancement experiences (grandiose) as well as "self-, emotion-, and behavioral dysregulation (vulnerable) when these needs go unfulfilled or ego threats arise" (p. 32; Pincus & Roche, 2011). This conceptualization is not without empirical support, with studies finding that grandiose narcissism is linked to greater reactivity of self-esteem to adverse interpersonal events (e.g., Rhodewalt, Madrian, & Cheney, 1998); that narcissistic antagonism may be associated with fluctuation between grandiosity and shame (Oltmanns & Widiger, 2018); and that grandiosity may covary with vulnerability at high levels of grandiosity (Jauk & Kaufman, 2018). However, when researchers who subscribe to a conceptualization of NPD involving oscillating grandiose and vulnerable states favor measures that include a greater proportion of items reflecting a need for validation, understanding, and vulnerability to negative emotionality, such as the PNI, this decision can bias the magnitude of relations with external correlates involving internalizing features (e.g., suicidality).

It would have been important for the target authors to acknowledge that many researchers do not regard extant empirical support for oscillating grandiose and vulnerable states to be adequately compelling. These researchers dispute that grandiose and vulnerable narcissistic states co-occur within individuals at a rate that would warrant considering them manifestations of the same underlying disorder. Their view is based on evidence suggesting that grandiose and vulnerable states do not meaningfully co-occur in the same individuals (Miller, Widiger, & Campbell, 2014); vulnerable states exhibited by grandiosely narcissistic individuals seem limited to reactive anger rather than internalizing-related emotions such as shame or distress (e.g., Hyatt et al., 2018); grandiose and vulnerable narcissism are associated with very different childhood histories (e.g., Miller et al., 2011); and grandiosity shows substantial within-person stability from day to day (e.g., Wright & Simms, 2016). The DSM largely reflects this conceptualization. Factor analyses of NPD symptoms indicate that the DSM-IV (and DSM-5) NPD criteria set is primarily consistent with grandiose narcissism (Fossati et al., 2005).

As a further example of lack of clarity on this issue, the empirical evidence is mixed with respect to where NPD is located within the structure of common mental disorders, with some findings suggesting that NPD may be characterized as an *externalizing* disorder (e.g., Kendler et al., 2011), others failing to find support for meaningful relations (e.g., Røysamb et al., 2011), and still others indicating that NPD is a *distress* disorder with stronger relations to *internalizing*, despite non-trivial relations to *externalizing*, and uniquely high disorder-specific variance that is not easily accounted for (Eaton et al., 2017). Unfortunately, the target authors included only the latter finding in their review.

LOCATING AND SAMPLING NPD

The third issue with the target authors' chapter and the literature more broadly involves how to address the substantial effect of sampling on researchers' understanding of NPD. The target authors feature a preponderance of evidence from patient samples linking NPD to states of shame, lower explicit self-esteem, anxiety and mood disorders, emotion dysregulation, deficits in coping behaviors, and suicidality (e.g., Vater et al., 2013). However, it is important to consider the degree to which researchers' reliance on small (i.e., $n < 60$) psychiatric samples containing disproportionally high concentrations of individuals with vulnerable features exerts a predetermining influence on the external correlates we investigate.

Traits that are generally thought to be most strongly and consensually related to NPD (e.g., grandiosity, domineering, manipulativeness) are often found to be higher in community samples than inpatient samples (e.g., Morf et al. 2017, Table 7), a phenomenon that may be driven in part by a higher likelihood of terminating psychotherapy among individuals with higher grandiosity (e.g.,

Ellison, Levy, Cain, Ansell, & Pincus, 2013). In contrast, research participants found in clinical samples tend to be substantially higher in traits that are relatively uncharacteristic of grandiose narcissism, such as depressiveness and anhedonia. Indeed, clinical samples tend to demonstrate high comorbidity with disorders that share a core of neuroticism (e.g., 53 percent for BPD [Vater et al., 2013]). One exception to this pattern is Stinson et al.'s (2008) large community sample that found NPD to be associated with internalizing disorders, though the measure used has not been adequately assessed. These selection concerns make interpreting research from clinical samples, especially inpatient samples (e.g., Vater et al. 2013), particularly challenging, as clinical samples of narcissism are likely to overrepresent vulnerable aspects and bias empirical results.

CONCLUSION

The target authors' chapter provides a thorough description of NPD's conceptualization across a variety of models and literatures. Nevertheless, we believe it is important for researchers to be appropriately attentive to sources of bias that can unnecessarily distort our assumed body of knowledge. A key source of bias is the field's persistent disagreement about the structure and content of NPD and variability in its assessment. We support a more focused description of narcissism that places NPD as a disorder of antagonism in line with expert-based characterizations (e.g., Ackerman, Hands, Donnellan, Hopwood, & Witt, 2017) and FFM–NPD relations (e.g., Samuel & Widiger, 2008). The inclusion of specifiers would allow for the delineation of more grandiose and vulnerable forms of narcissism. Such a model would allow for individuals who exhibit co-occurring states of grandiose and vulnerable to be described with both specifiers. Nevertheless, the model we describe is a trait system, and thus would not easily describe a pattern of oscillating states. It is our view that data have not yet sufficiently demonstrated hypothesized self-regulatory psychodynamics in prototypical narcissism, particularly with respect to oscillation between grandiosity and vulnerability involving internalizing-related emotions such as shame and distress, although we regard this hypothesis worthy of continued examination. Longitudinal studies that examine fluctuations in grandiose and vulnerable states over temporally short increments are critical, as will be insights from physics-based systems models combined with trace data (e.g., Flack, 2012).

REFERENCES

Ackerman, R. A., Hands, A. J., Donnellan, M. B., Hopwood, C. J., & Witt, E. A. (2017). Experts' views regarding the conceptualization of narcissism. *Journal of Personality Disorders, 31,* 346–361.

American Psychiatric Association. (2013). Diagnostic and Statistical Manual of Mental Disorders (5th ed.). Arlington, VA: American Psychiatric Publishing.

Eaton, N. R., Rodriguez-Seijas, C., Krueger, R. F., Campbell, W. K., Grant, B. F., & Hasin, D. S. (2017). Narcissistic personality disorder and the structure of common mental disorders. *Journal of Personality Disorders, 31,* 449–461.

Ellison, W. D., Levy, K. N., Cain, N. M., Ansell, E. B., & Pincus, A. L. (2013). The impact of pathological narcissism on psychotherapy utilization, initial symptom severity, and early-treatment symptom change: A naturalistic investigation. *Journal of Personality Assessment, 95,* 291–300.

Flack, J. C. (2012). Multiple time-scales and the developmental dynamics of social systems. Philosophical Transactions of the Royal Society B, *367,* 1802–1810.

Fossati, A., Beauchaine, T. P., Grazioli, F., Carretta, I., Cortinovis, F., & Maffei, C. (2005). A latent structure analysis of Diagnostic and Statistical Manual of Mental Disorders, narcissistic personality disorder criteria. Comprehensive Psychiatry, *46,* 361–367.

Hopwood, C. J., Donnellan, M. B., Ackerman, R. A., Thomas, K. M., Morey, L. C., & Skodol, A. E. (2013). The validity of the Personality Diagnostic Questionnaire–4 Narcissistic Personality Disorder Scale for assessing pathological grandiosity. Journal of Personality Assessment, *95,* 274–283.

Hyatt, C. S., Sleep, C. E., Lynam, D. R., Widiger, T. A., Campbell, W. K., & Miller, J. D. (2018). Ratings of affective and interpersonal tendencies differ for grandiose and vulnerable narcissism: A replication and extension of Gore & Widiger. Journal of Personality, *86*(3), 422–434.

Hyler, S. E. (1994). Personality Diagnostic Questionnaire 4 (PDQ-4). New York: New York State Psychiatric Institute.

Jauk, E., & Kaufman, S. B. (2018). The higher the score, the darker the core: The nonlinear association between grandiose and vulnerable narcissism. Frontiers in Psychology, *9,* 1–14.

Kendler, K. S., Aggen, S. H., Knudsen, G. P., Røysamb, E., Neale, M. C., & Reichborn-Kjennerud, T. (2011). The structure of genetic and environmental risk factors for syndromal and subsyndromal common DSM-IV axis I and all axis II disorders. American Journal of Psychiatry, *168,* 29–39.

Miller, J. D., Hoffman, B. J., Gaughan, E. T., Gentile, B., Maples, J., & Campbell, W. K. (2011). Grandiose and vulnerable narcissism: A nomological network analysis. *Journal of Personality, 79,* 1013–1042.

Miller, J. D., Lynam, D. R., Hyatt, C. S., & Campbell, W. K. (2017). Controversies in narcissism. *Annual Review of Clinical Psychology, 13,* 291–315.

Miller, J. D., McCain, J., Lynam, D. R., Few, L. R. Gentile, B., MacKillop, J., & Campbell, W. K. (2014). A comparison of the criterion validity of popular measures of narcissism and narcissistic personality disorder via the use of expert ratings. Psychological Assessment, *26,* 958–969.

Miller, J. D., Widiger, T. A., & Campbell, W. K. (2014). Vulnerable narcissism: Commentary for the special series 'Narcissistic personality disorder: New perspectives on diagnosis and treatment'. Personality Disorders: Theory, Research, and Treatment, *5,* 450–451.

Millon, T., Millon, C., & Davis, R. D. (1994). MCMI–III Manual. Minneapolis, MN: National Computer Systems.

Morf, C. C., Schürch, E., Küfner, A., Siegrist, P., Vater, A., Back, M., … Schröder-Abé, M. (2017). Expanding the nomological net of the Pathological Narcissism Inventory: German validation and extension in a clinical inpatient sample. Assessment, *24,* 419–443.

Oltmanns, J. R., & Widiger, T. A. (2018). Assessment of fluctuation between grandiose and vulnerable narcissism: Development and initial validation of the FLUX scales. Psychological Assessment, 30, 1612–1624.

Pincus, A. L., Ansell, E. B., Pimentel, C. A., Cain, N. M., Wright, A. G. C., & Levy, K. N. (2009). Initial construction and validation of the Pathological Narcissism Inventory. *Psychological Assessment*, *21*, 365–379.

Pincus, A. L., & Roche, M. J. (2011). Narcissistic grandiosity and narcissistic vulnerability. In W. K. Campbell & J. D. Miller (Eds.), *Handbook of Narcissism and Narcissistic Personality Disorder* (pp. 31–40). Hoboken, NJ: John Wiley.

Rhodewalt, F., Madrian, J. C., & Cheney, S. (1998). Narcissism, self-knowledge organization, and emotional reactivity: The effect of daily experiences on self-esteem and affect. Personality and Social Psychology Bulletin, *24*, 75–87.

Røysamb, E., Kendler, K. S., Tambs, K., Ørstavik, R. E., Neale, M. C., Aggen, S. H., ... Reichborn-Kjennerud, T. (2011). The joint structure of DSM-IV Axis I and Axis II disorders. Journal of Abnormal Psychology, *120*, 198–209.

Samuel, D. B., & Widiger, T. A. (2008). A meta-analytic review of the relationships between the five-factor model and DSM-IV-TR personality disorders: A facet level analysis. *Clinical Psychology Review*, *28*, 1326–1342.

Saulsman, L. M., & Page, A. C. (2004). The five-factor model and personality disorder empirical literature: A meta-analytic review. *Clinical Psychology Review*, *23*, 1055–1085.

Stinson, F. S., Dawson, D. A., Goldstein, R. B., Chou, S. P., Huang, B., Smith, S. M., ... Grant, B. F. (2008). Prevalence, correlates, disability, and comorbidity of DSM-IV narcissistic personality disorder: Results from the Wave 2 National Epidemiologic Survey on Alcohol and Related Conditions. *Journal of Clinical Psychiatry*, *69*, 1033–1045.

Vater, A., Schröder-Abé, M., Ritter, K., Renneberg, B., Schulze, L., Bosson, J. K., & Roepke, S. (2013). The Narcissistic Personality Inventory: A useful tool for assessing pathological narcissism? Evidence from patients with narcissistic personality disorder. *Journal of Personality Assessment*, *95*, 301–308.

Wright, A. G. C., & Simms, L. J. (2016). Stability and fluctuation of personality disorder features in daily life. Journal of Abnormal Psychology, *125*, 641–656.

12b Beyond Nucleus Diagnostic Conceptualizations: Commentary on Narcissistic and Histrionic Personality Disorders

ELSA RONNINGSTAM AND TIFFANY RUSSELL

Narcissistic personality disorder, NPD, and histrionic personality disorder, HPD, are presently undergoing major changes in status, as well as clinical and empirical credibility and utility. While NPD has gained increased attention, HPD is facing difficulties foremost due to cultural and functional specifics. The chapter by Dawood, Wu, Bliton, and Pincus (this volume) provides a most timely and valuable overview of recent research and reconceptualizations that can broaden the clinical identification of these personality disorders. Studies of NPD, in particular, show significant advances in identifying multifactorial components that impact narcissistic symptoms and personality function.

In this commentary, we discuss issues that significantly influence narcissistic personality function and clinical presentation beyond the nucleus diagnostic conceptualization of NPD. We will also address some additional factors that affect level of functioning, sense of agency and control, and the Dark Triad with aggression and violence.

Clinicians treating patients with pathological narcissism (PN) or NPD in different settings and modalities are often struggling with these patients' unexpected and varied presentations and fluctuations. Clinicians as well as patients' negative reactions can readily evoke transference-countertransference enactments with risk for early dropout (Ellison, Levy, Cain, Ansell, & Pincus, 2013; Gamache, Savard, Lemelin, Côté, & Villeneuve, 2018; Kacel, Ennis, & Pereira, 2017). All this has contributed to an inequitable negative view of NPD with questions about its treatability (Kernberg, 2007).

Incorporating a dimensional approach as outlined in DSM-5 Section III AMPD substantiates the clinical complexity of NPD, which is influencing patients' engagement in and ability to benefit from treatment (Ronningstam, 2014). Dawood et al. (this volume) acknowledge that the dimensional diagnostic approach can help clinicians to identify a wider range of PN and NPD, and describe NPD in terms that can be more informative and helpful for the patients. The Personality Inventory for the DSM-5 (PID-5; Krueger, Derringer, Markon, Watson, & Skodol, 2012) is a

dimensional personality instrument corresponding with the AMPD, and including the five personality domains (Negative Affectivity, Antagonism, Psychoticism, Disinhibition, and Detachment). The Antagonism domain captures interpersonal challenges found in both grandiose and vulnerable narcissism. Facets of Negative Affectivity and Psychoticism account for dysregulation, contingent self-esteem, and entitlement rage seen in vulnerable narcissistic personality functioning (Wright et al., 2013). Consequently, PID-5 may also provide a way to integrate additional constructs like the Dark Triad and its more vulnerable counterpart into the diagnostic assessment and clinical applications of NPD

Dawood and colleagues' (this volume) review of research highlights different aspects of NPD functioning related to range of personality functioning: the inter-correlation between grandiose versus vulnerable, and overt external versus covert internal expressions of pathological narcissism, as well as co-occurrence with other psychiatric conditions. Recent research studies have provided a more comprehensive conceptualization of pathological narcissism (i.e., pointing to neuropsychological and neurological deficits as well as significant indicators of functioning across multiple domains including self-esteem emotion regulation, attachment patterns, and agency). These new facts and perspectives can guide clinical interventions beyond the trait-based conceptualization, and offer a more reliably explanatory connection between personality functioning, clinical presentations, and the diagnosis of NPD (Ronningstam, 2014, 2017).

Significant efforts are ongoing to improve assessment to capture co-occurrence and fluctuations between grandiose and vulnerable core features in NPD. However, this area still needs empirical attention and clinical reformulations as its multifactorial complexity goes far beyond the intersection between overt and covert aspects of the grandiosity–vulnerability oscillation as suggested by the authors. Stability versus oscillation between high competent and low impaired functioning, primarily related to ability to work and relate, represents one such range factor with major implications for the grandiosity–vulnerability balance. The concept of agency (Fonagy, Gergely, Jurist, & Target, 2002) and its relationship to narcissism has been connected to narcissistic personality functioning. Sense of agency is influenced by perceived accomplishments, perfectionism, and sense of control (internal and external), as well as by self-criticism, psychological trauma, and fear, and it plays a significant role in the individuals' assessment. Sense of agency can be especially consequential for people whose self-worth is fragile and ability for interpersonal relativeness compromised. Loss of sense of agency and control, with accompanying failure to sustain self-enhancement or live up to standards can escalate intense or determined suicidal ideations (Links & Prakash, 2013; Ronningstam, Weinberg, & Maltsberger, 2008).

The authors review research identifying comorbidity in NPD and mechanisms driving the co-occurrence of specific symptoms such as anxiety, mood disorder, and substance use. This is also of significant clinical importance, as the interaction between pathological narcissistic personality patterns and such comorbid conditions can have major impact on diagnosis and treatment of either or both conditions. Specific symptoms can paradoxically, when co-occurring with NPD, temporarily enhance internal control, self-esteem, competence, and achievements related to more grandiose strivings, and shield against insecurity and vulnerability Those include mood elevation in bipolar disorder, or the explicit psychological or physiological impact of a certain substance in substance use disorder (Benton, 2009). Consequently, such interaction will reduce motivation for treatment. Especially the co-interaction between elevated mood and narcissism can be confusing as patients' insecurity, fear of failure, or avoidance suddenly can switch into confidence and high aspirations with disruptions of treatment. The importance of longitudinal perspective on this interactions is highlighted by the finding that during manic and hypomanic episodes most bipolar patients exhibit a majority of NPD trait criteria, whereas only 11 percent of euthymic bipolar patients fulfill the diagnosis of NPD (Stormberg, Ronningstam, Gunderson, & Tohen, 1998).

AGGRESSION AND VIOLENCE

Aggression has long been considered a core aspect of pathological narcissism and NPD, either as an inherited constitutional drive (Kernberg, 1992), or a prime reaction to frustration, threats, and/or humiliation (Kohut, 1972). Narcissistic self-esteem regulation with self-enhancement and vulnerability is connected with a range of aggression, both internal and self-directed as well as external and interpersonal, including irritability, criticism, resentment, vindictiveness, rage, and hatred (Rhodewalt & Morf, 1998).

Severe aggression and violence associated with the Dark Triad is another area of research that needs further integration in the overall conceptualization of NPD. The Dark Triad (i.e., psychopathy, grandiose narcissism, and Machiavellianism; Paulhus & Williams, 2002) has received considerable attention in social and personality research, though the findings are rarely integrated into clinical science and practice. While each of the "dark" personalities contribute distinctive traits to the triad (e.g., narcissistic grandiosity), the cluster shares a common *dark core* of callousness and manipulativeness. These traits seem to account for the moderate inter-correlation between these personalities (Jones & Figueredo, 2013) and explain aspects of Cluster B comorbidity with greater specificity. Building on this concept of the Dark Triad, Miller and colleagues (Miller et al., 2010) proposed a *vulnerable* Dark Triad comprised of vulnerable narcissism, borderline personality disorder, and Hare's (1991) factor 2 psychopathy (i.e., irresponsible, impulsive, and sensation-seeking behaviors). This model would thus include interpersonal antagonism, emotional dysregulation, and vulnerability, which is a "dark" core of traits commonly found in clinical settings. However, additional work is required to determine more precisely the aspects that each personality type contributes to a vulnerable Dark Triad.

Narcissism is also related to sexual violence. Psychological reactivity, or an increased desire for something forbidden, may be related to sexual aggression in men with high levels of narcissism, as they are particularly reactive when denied something they desire. This reactivity seems interconnected with entitlement and an underlying sense of insecurity (Baumeister, Catanese, & Wallace, 2002; Bushman, Bonacci, van Dijk, & Baumeister 2003; Zeigler-Hill, Enjaian, & Essa, 2013). Entitlement in men can predict trait anger, negative attitudes towards women, sexual dominance, and a preference for impersonal sex (i.e., unrestricted sociosexuality; LeBreton, Baysinger, Abbey, & Jacques-Tiura, 2013). Narcissistic traits also indirectly predicted sexual violence in men (Russell & King, 2017), as well as sexual aggression and coercion in women (Russell, Doan, & King, 2017).

FEAR AND TRAUMA

Fear in NPD can readily be connected with Axis I anxiety or social phobia rather than with specific narcissistic dynamics and challenges. Such challenges can involve concrete external events as well as internal subjective or emotional experiences related to losing internal control, not measuring up or failing, and losing status, affiliation, or power. Overwhelming and consuming experience of fear can cause lapses in decisions, or force drastic decisions with seemingly immediate short-term gains. Considered a self-regulatory factor (Bélanger, Lafrenière, Vallerand, & Kruglanski, 2013) fear of losing control is related to narcissistic core features, such as self-enhancement with ambitions, competition, perfectionism, and aspirations. In addition, avoidance and procrastination, and even risk-taking efforts can all enable ignorance or modulation of fear (Ronningstam & Baskin-Sommers, 2013)

Trauma has also been connected to NPD in trauma associated narcissistic symptoms (TANS) (Simon, 2002). Those are caused primarily by an *internal* self-experience or by the *subjective* experience of an external event that threatens the continuity, coherence, stability, and well-being of the self. Sense of failing competence, with loss of self-esteem, standards, and self-worth, or loss of affiliation and connections to others, become overwhelming, intolerable, and even terrifying. Efforts to understand and find meaning in the experience fall short and the usual narcissistic self-regulatory and defensive strategies fail (Maldonado, 2006). Narcissistic psychological trauma related to losses, inconsistencies, and neglect can be implicit, somatized, and psychophysiologically contained in the body leading to difficult-to-regulate emotions and interpersonal relatedness. When such trauma co-occurs with depression it can be associated with self-organizing negativity (negative self-narrative; Ginot, 2012) linked to narcissistic self-esteem and identity (e.g., "I am the most hated member of my family" or " the most degraded staff at my workplace"). When combined with avoidance, this can perpetuate both underlying narcissistic pathology as well as the major psychiatric condition. In such interactions, it can be difficult to identify the co-occurring and usually covert or hidden narcissistic pathology that tends to perpetuate depressive symptoms. Consequently, such co-occurring conditions can be misdiagnosed as the impact of NPD remains unidentifiable.

SUICIDE

Suicidality can serve narcissistic functions, both when kept as an intention or fantasy that helps to sustain internal control ("I know that I can end my life if things do not go my way"), and when leading to actions in an effort to escape unbearable circumstances related to loss, failure, or humiliation. Suicide can also serve as a way to retaliate as the underlying narcissistic investment in the meaning and consequences of suicide can motivate and have an empowering effect. NPD related suicides are characterized by absence of depression, rage-shame escalation, and high lethality (Ronningstam, Weinberg, Goldblatt, Schechter, & Herbstman, 2018). Paradoxically suicide can serve to preserve self-regard, superiority, and triumph over defeat, to achieve sadistic control over others, or as an exit from uncontrollable situations (Kernberg, 1992, 2007)

CONCLUSION

There is significant value in the integration of different modalities of research on narcissism and NPD across multiple areas in psychology and psychiatry with longstanding clinical and psychoanalytic accounts. Integrating the hybrid AMPD can keep some of the original conceptualizations of narcissistic pathology on the cutting edge of psychological and neuropsychological science. Our prime aim is overall to optimally enhance our understanding and treatment of this complex personality condition, and Dawood and colleagues' chapter (this volume) represents an important step in that direction.

REFERENCES

Baumeister, R. F., Catanese, K. R., & Wallace, H. M. (2002). Conquest by force: A narcissistic reactance theory of rape and sexual coercion. *Review of General Psychology*, 6(1), 92–135.

Bélanger, J. J., Lafrenière, M.-A. K., Vallerand, R. J., & Kruglanski, A. W. (2013). Driven by fear: The effect of success and failure information on passionate individuals' performance. *Journal of Personality and Social Psychology*, 104(1), 180–195.

Benton, S. A. (2009). *Understanding the High-Functioning Alcoholic*. Plymouth: Rowman & Littlefield.

Bushman, B. J., Bonacci, A. M., van Dijk, M., & Baumeister, R. F. (2003). Narcissism, sexual refusal, and aggression: Testing a narcissistic reactance model of sexual coercion. *Journal of Personality and Social Psychology*, 84(5), 1027–1040.

Ellison, W. D., Levy, K. N., Cain, N. M., Ansell, E. B., & Pincus, A. L. (2013). The impact of pathological narcissism on psychotherapy utilization, initial symptom severity, and early treatment symptom change: A naturalistic investigation. *Journal of Personality Assessment*, 95(3), 291–300.

Fonagy, P., Gergely, G., Jurist, E., & Target, M. (2002). *Affect Regulation, Mentalization and the Development of the Self*. New York: Other Press.

Gamache, D., Savard, C., Lemelin., S, Côté, A., & Villeneuve, É. (2018). Premature termination of psychotherapy in patients with borderline personality disorder: A cluster-analytic study. *Journal of Nervous and Mental Disease*, 206(4), 231–238.

Ginot, E. (2012). Self-narratives and dysregulated affective states: The neuropsychological links between self-narratives, attachment, affect, and cognition. *Psychoanalytic Psychology*, 29(1), 59–80.

Hare, R. D. (1991). *The Hare Psychopathy Checklist–Revised*. Toronto: Multi-Health Systems.

Jones, D. N., & Figueredo, A. J. (2013). The core of darkness: Uncovering the heart of the dark triad. *European Journal of Personality*, 27(6), 521–531.

Kacel, E. L., Ennis, N., & Pereira, D. B. (2017). Narcissistic personality disorder in clinical health psychology practice: Case studies of comorbid psychological distress and life-limiting illness. *Behavioral Medicine*, 43(3), 156–164.

Kernberg, O. (1992). *Aggression in Personality Disorders and Perversions*. New Haven, CT: Yale University Press.

Kernberg, O. F. (2007). The almost untreatable narcissistic patient. *Journal of the American Psychoanalytic Association*, 55(2), 503–539.

Kohut, H. (1972). Thoughts on narcissism and narcissistic rage. *The Psychoanalytic Study of the Child*, 27, 360–400.

Krueger, R. F., Derringer, J., Markon, K. E., Watson, D., & Skodol, A. E. (2012). Initial construction of a maladaptive personality trait model and inventory for DSM-5. *Psychological Medicine*, 42(9), 1879–1890.

LeBreton, J. M., Baysinger, M. A., Abbey, A., & Jacques-Tiura, A. J. (2013). The relative importance of psychopathy-related traits in predicting impersonal sex and hostile masculinity. *Personality and Individual Differences, 55*(7), 817–822.

Links, P. S., & Prakash, A. (2013). Strategic issues in the psychotherapy of patients with narcissistic pathology. *Journal of Contemporary Psychotherapy, 44*, 97–107.

Maldonado, J. L. (2006). Vicissitudes in adult life resulting from traumatic experiences in adolescence. *International Journal of Psychoanalysis, 87*, 1239–1257.

Miller, J. D., Dir, A., Gentile, B., Wilson, L., Pryor, L. R., & Campbell, W. K. (2010). Searching for a vulnerable dark triad: Comparing factor 2 psychopathy, vulnerable narcissism, and borderline personality disorder. *Journal of Personality, 78*, 1529–1564.

Paulhus, D. L., & Williams, K. M. (2002). The dark triad of personality: Narcissism, Machiavellianism, and psychopathy. *Journal of Research in Personality, 36*, 556–563.

Rhodewalt, F., & Morf, C. C. (1998). On self-aggrandizement and anger: A temporal analysis of narcissism and affective reactions to success and failure. *Journal of Personality and Social Psychology, 74*, 672–685.

Ronningstam, E. (2014). Beyond the diagnostic traits: A collaborative exploratory diagnostic process for dimensions and underpinnings of narcissistic personality disorder. *Personality Disorders: Theory, Research, and Treatment, 5*, 434–438.

Ronningstam, E. (2017). Intersect between self-esteem and emotion regulation in narcissistic personality disorder: Implications for alliance building and treatment. *Borderline Personality Disorder and Emotion Dysregulation, 4*, 1–13.

Ronningstam, E., & Baskin-Sommers, A. (2013). Fear and decision-making in narcissistic personality disorder: A link between psychoanalysis and neuroscience. *Dialogues in Clinical Neuroscience, 15*, 191–201.

Ronningstam, E., Weinberg, I., Goldblatt, M, Schechter, M., & Herbstman, B. (2018). Suicide and self-regulation in narcissistic personality disorder. *Psychodynamic Psychiatry, 46*, 491–510.

Ronningstam, E., Weinberg, I., & Maltsberger, J. (2008). Eleven deaths of Mr. K: Contributing factors to suicide in narcissistic personalities. *Psychiatry: Interpersonal and Biological Processes, 71*, 169–182.

Russell, T. D., Doan, C. M., & King, A. R. (2017). Sexually violent women: The PID-5, everyday sadism, and adversarial sexual attitudes predict female sexual aggression and coercion against male victims. *Personality and Individual Differences, 111*, 242–249.

Russell, T. D., & King, A. R. (2017). Distrustful, conventional, entitled, and dysregulated: PID-5 personality facets predict hostile masculinity and sexual violence in community men. *Journal of Interpersonal Violence*, https://doi.org/10.1177/0886260517689887

Simon, R. I. (2002). Distinguishing trauma-associated narcissistic symptoms from posttraumatic stress disorder: A diagnostic challenge. *Harvard Review of Psychiatry, 10*, 28–36.

Stormberg, D., Ronningstam, E., Gunderson, J., & Tohen, M. (1998). Brief communication: Pathological narcissism in bipolar patients. *Journal of Personality Disorders, 12*, 179–185.

Wright, A. G. C., Pincus, A. L., Thomas, K. M., Hopwood, C. J., Markon, K. E., & Krueger, R. F. (2013). Conceptions of narcissism and the DSM-5 pathological personality traits. *Assessment, 20*, 339–352.

Zeigler-Hill, V., Enjaian, B., & Essa, L. (2013). The role of narcissistic personality features in sexual aggression. *Journal of Social and Clinical Psychology, 32*, 186–199.

12c Clinical Personality Science of Narcissism Should Include the Clinic: Author Rejoinder to Commentaries on Narcissistic and Histrionic Personality Disorders

AARON L. PINCUS, SINDES DAWOOD, LEILA Z. WU, AND CHLOE F. BLITON

Twenty-five years ago, Benjamin (1994a) presented an extended view of how her Structural Analysis of Social Behavior (SASB) model and theory could bridge personality theory and clinical psychology. This was followed by commentaries from a range of eminent scholars. Benjamin (1994b) divided the commentaries into those whose authors believed it necessary for clinical personality science to reciprocally inform and be informed by the clinical enterprise and those whose authors were dismissive of clinical complexity and promoted their preferred trait models. A quarter century later, a similar dichotomy is evident here.

CLINICAL COMPLEXITY OF NARCISSISM

Like Benjamin, Ronningstam is a clinical scientist and master clinician who has been treating patients with personality disorders continuously for decades. Her work consistently provides a bridge between clinical personality science and practice (e.g., Ronningstam, 2005, 2016). Her current commentary with Russell expands the clinical portrait of narcissism beyond what was presented in our chapter. We are reminded that the clinical presentation and treatment of narcissism is complex and serious, including risks for aggression, violence, and suicide, as well as complications due to fear and trauma, and related dark personality traits. We completely agree with these observations and concerns and recognize the list of risks and complications is even longer (Dowgwillo, Dawood, & Pincus, 2016). The portrait of narcissism Ronningstam and Russell paint here is clinically informed, dynamic, and complex. All Ronningstam's work articulating the complexity of narcissism suggests that to successfully build a bridge to the clinic, clinical personality science needs to integrate narcissistic structure (i.e., its fundamental traits) with narcissistic patients' dynamic intra- and interpersonal processes and maintenance mechanisms (Ackerman, Donnellan, & Wright, 2019; Pincus & Wright, in press). This is because personality processes and mechanisms are the key targets of psychotherapeutic intervention.

QUIT MAKING CALLS AND JOIN THE FIELD OF CONTEMPORARY CLINICAL PERSONALITY SCIENCE

Faced with the complexity of narcissistic phenomena observed in the clinic and the need to integrate structure and dynamics in advancing the utility of clinical science, Weiss and Campbell call for scientific caution. Notably, in response to Hopwood's (2018) target article making the same assertions for the clinical science of personality disorders more generally, Campbell's frequent collaborators made a similar call for "parsimony, proof, and prudence" (Miller & Lynam, 2018, p. 568). We would encourage these academic researchers to stop avoiding clinical complexity, and instead, take advantage of the advances in research methods, analytics, and technology to build a truly meaningful bridge between clinical personality science and practice. Their corpus of work to date has generally failed in this regard because profiles of trait elevations, correlations between trait and personality disorder scales, and expert trait ratings of prototypical personality disorders are not the clinical entities seen in the consulting room (Pincus, 2018).

Weiss and Campbell make three broad critiques of our chapter. First, they criticize us for synthesizing research on narcissism across related but not identical conceptualizations and measures. This is a straw man argument applicable to research on virtually all clinical (e.g., depression) and personality (e.g., impulsivity) constructs. The field certainly must reduce the heterogeneity in conceptualizing and assessing narcissism. Until then caution is needed, but without synthesis there is no cumulative science. Second, they critique the view that grandiosity and vulnerability may oscillate in narcissistic personalities. At its core, this is an anti-clinical stance. Those who regularly provide treatment and supervision for personality disordered patients have little argument with this perspective (e.g., Gore & Widiger, 2016), and longitudinal research on narcissistic states is emerging (Dowgwillo, Dawood, Bliton, & Pincus, 2018; Edershile & Wright, in press). The authors also misunderstand our position on oscillation. We assert that narcissistic patients may be chronically grandiose, chronically vulnerable, or oscillating (Pincus, Dowgwillo, & Greenberg, 2016). Perhaps certain presentations are more prominent in certain contexts. Third, they criticize us for examining narcissism in clinical contexts. Although we agree that expressions of narcissism may differ in treatment seeking outpatients compared to individuals in forensic or community contexts, we aim to develop a clinical personality science of narcissism that actually bridges to the clinic, not just another corner of the academy (Benjamin, 1994b).

REFERENCES

Ackerman, R. A., Donnellan, M. B., & Wright, A. G. C. (2019). Current conceptualizations of narcissism. *Current Opinion in Psychiatry*, *32*, 32–37.

Benjamin, L. S. (1994a). SASB: A bridge between personality theory and clinical psychology. *Psychological Inquiry*, *5*, 273–316.

Benjamin, L. S. (1994b). The bridge is supposed to reach the clinic, not just another corner of the academy. *Psychological Inquiry*, *5*, 336–343.

Dowgwillo, E. A., Dawood, S., Bliton, C. F., & Pincus, A. L. (2018). *Within-person covariation of narcissistic grandiosity and vulnerability in daily life*. Paper presented at the Society for Personality Assessment annual meeting, Washington, DC, March.

Dowgwillo, E. A., Dawood, S., & Pincus, A. L. (2016). The dark side of narcissism. In V. Zeigler-Hill & D. Marcus (Eds.), *The Dark Side of Personality: Science and Practice in Social, Personality, and Clinical Psychology* (pp. 25–44). Washington, DC: American Psychological Association.

Edershile, E. A., & Wright, A. G. C. (in press). Grandiose and vulnerable narcissistic states in interpersonal situations. *Self and Identity*.

Gore, W. L., & Widiger, T. A. (2016). Fluctuation between grandiose and vulnerable narcissism. *Personality Disorders: Theory, Research, and Treatment*, *7*, 363–371.

Hopwood, C. J. (2018). Interpersonal dynamics in personality and personality disorders. *European Journal of Personality*, *32*, 499–524.

Miller, J. D., & Lynam, D. R. (2018). A call for parsimony, proof, and prudence: A response to Hopwood. *European Journal of Personality*, *32*, 568–569.

Pincus, A. L. (2018). Bringing personality traits from bench to bedside. *European Journal of Personality*, *32*, 572–573.

Pincus, A. L., Dowgwillo, E. A., & Greenberg, L. (2016). Three cases of narcissistic personality disorder through the lens of the DSM-5 alternative model for personality disorders. *Practice Innovations*, *1*, 164–177.

Pincus, A. L., & Wright, A. G. C. (in press). Narcissism as the dynamics of grandiosity and vulnerability. In S. Doering, H.-P. Hartmann, & O. F. Kernberg (Eds.), *Narzissmus: Grundlagen – Störungsbilder – Therapie* (2nd ed.). Stuttgart: Schattauer Publishers.

Ronningstam, E. (2005). *Identifying and Understanding the Narcissistic Personality*. New York: Oxford University Press.

Ronningstam, E. (2016). Pathological narcissism and narcissistic personality disorder: Recent research and clinical implications. *Current Behavioral Neuroscience Reports*, *3*, 34–42.

13 Cluster C Anxious-Fearful Personality Pathology and Avoidance

CHARLES A. SANISLOW AND ANNA DARRE HECTOR

INTRODUCTION

Cluster C of the DSM-5 (APA, 2013), known as the *anxious-fearful* group of personality disorders, consists of the diagnoses Avoidant Personality Disorder (AVPD), Dependent Personality Disorder (DPD), and Obsessive-Compulsive Personality Disorder (OCPD). When the cluster groupings were first introduced in the DSM-III (APA, 1980), there was a fourth diagnosis, Passive Aggressive Personality Disorder (PAPD), which was retained in the DSM-III-R (APA, 1987), relegated to research status in the DSM fourth editions with the subtitle Negativistic Personality Disorder (APA, 1994, 2000), and then dropped in the DSM-5 (APA, 2013). To describe the core characteristics of anxious-fearful psychopathology, features of the DSM-5 Section II diagnoses, Passive Aggressive Personality Disorder (PAPD), and the Alternative Model of Personality Disorders (AMPD) in Section III of the DSM-5 are considered, with an emphasis on avoidant behavior.

The first section of this chapter describes the AVPD and related Cluster C personality diagnoses as set forth in Section II of DSM-5 (APA, 2013). We also discuss anxious-fearful personality pathology as conceptualized in the Alternative Model of Personality Disorders (AMPD; APA, 2013). The background and development of these definitions are considered to provide historical context for how the prototype of this kind of psychopathology has been understood, especially how associated features/symptoms have been lumped and split. This broader vision for how characterological anxious-fearful distress has been defined should provide perspective for future directions. Questions are raised concerning stability continuities and comorbidities, within-disorder heterogeneity, and ways that Cluster C diagnoses relate to clinical (non-personality) disorders and to avoidant behaviors. These questions prompt consideration of cross-cutting (i.e., transdiagnostic) dimensions, including trait-based

The authors are grateful to Marcia K. Johnson for her helpful suggestions for this chapter and insightful discussions about the subject herein.

constructs, along with well-studied constructs such as rejection sensitivity, perfectionism, dependency, shame and guilt. Additionally, alternative research approaches such as the National Institute of Mental Health (NIMH) Research Domain Criteria (RDoC) may be helpful in clarifying internal mechanisms of anxious-fearful psychopathology. We conclude with some thoughts about future directions, including some new ideas about how to represent personality disorders, traits, and mechanisms in the context of interpersonal relationships.

It is both an interesting and exciting time to be writing about DSM personality disorders. It is interesting because the field of psychopathology is in a state of flux, and definitions are more like targets under development than static, natural kinds. To illustrate, despite the substantial effort that went into a major revision of the characterization of the personality disorders for the most recent, fifth edition of the DSM (APA, 2013), the updated diagnostic structure for personality disorders reflects remaining disagreement about the best diagnostic structure. It is an exciting time because dialogue in the literature can stimulate novel ways to think of where to go next. Other chapters in this volume address questions about revisions and evidence for competing models and revisions, and this chapter will limit discussion to relevant historical context for the evolution of disorders in the anxious-fearful cluster. The aim is to help understand how the present Section II and III conceptualizations came to be, and to provide insights for how best to proceed going forward.

Noteworthy changes for the DSM-5 included the elimination of the Axis I/II distinction, and a new section for an alternative model of personality disorders. In the main section for all mental disorder diagnoses (including personality disorders), *Section II*, the structure and criteria of the personality disorder diagnoses (including the three clusters) remained unchanged from DSM-IV, ostensibly for purposes of clinical continuity. To accommodate the recommendation of the Personality Disorders Workgroup for the Alternative Model of Personality Disorders (AMPD), the American Psychiatric Association (APA) Board of Trustees created a new, unique section, *Section*

III solely for the AMPD. This broke from past traditions in revisions where diagnoses not fully embraced by consensus or supported by research were placed in the section labeled *Conditions for Further Study*. Thus, the AMPD became a clinically viable alternative, arguably on equal footing with the Section II personality disorder diagnoses (see Skodol, Morey, Bender, & Oldham, 2015). In the DSM-5 Section II personality disorder criteria, the three-cluster structure from the DSM-IV remains, with AVPD, DPD, and OCPD in Cluster C (APA, 2013). For the AMPD, in Section III, the cluster structure was abandoned, and the DPD diagnosis was eliminated, suggesting that only AVPD and OCPD will be included if the alternative in its present form replaces the model.

IN SEARCH OF THE CORE: HISTORY OF ANXIOUS-FEARFUL AND AVOIDANT PATHOLOGY

Going back to early, pre-DSM roots in describing avoidant personality pathology, Hoch (1910) pointed to a reclusive character pattern, a person who was marked by tendencies to be shy, reticent, and reclusive, and to live in a world of fantasy. Around the same time, Bleuler (1911/1950, p. 391) used the label "schizoid" to describe a socially avoidant personality, a person who is "shut-in" and "comfortably dull and at the same time sensitive." Kretschmer (1925) later divided schizoid concept into two subtypes, anaesthetic or hyperaesthetic. The anaesthetic subtype described individuals who seemed affectively insensitive, dull, and lacking in spontaneity, akin to the DSM-III schizoid personality disorder (SPD), whereas the hyperaesthetic subtype individuals seemed affectively excitable, anxious, shy, and sensitive, akin to DSM-III AVPD. For a psychoanalytical conception of what she termed a detached personality type, Horney used the descriptions "socially avoidant" (1945) and "interpersonally avoidant" (1950).

In the first DSM (APA, 1952), personality disorders were divided into three groupings that were different from the current clusters. They were *Personality Pattern Disturbance*, *Personality Trait Disturbance*, and *Sociopathic Personality Disturbances* (APA, 1952).[1] The modern anxious-fearful cluster has roots in the first and second groupings, with the disorder Schizoid Personality in the DSM-I Personality Pattern Disturbance grouping. In the DSM-I Personality Trait Disturbance grouping were Passive-Aggressive Personality, which included a "passive-dependent type" with features of indecisiveness and clingy dependency, and Compulsive Personality, characterized by "chronic, excessive, or obsessive concern with adherence to standards of conscience or of conformity" (APA, 1952, p. 37). (The Sociopathic grouping included

antisocial and dyssocial reactions, sexual deviations, and alcohol and drug addictions.)

In the next edition of the DSM (DSM-II; APA, 1968), the higher-order groupings were eliminated, and the personality disorders were lumped together in a single group (with sexual deviations and addictions segregated to their own respective groupings outside of the personality disorders). The descriptions for the four Cluster C predecessors largely remained the same, except for Passive-Aggressive Personality, where the passive-dependent subtype was dropped. The other notable change was that Obsessive was added to the title of Compulsive Personality. These early versions of the modern anxious-fearful concept groupings notably differed in their various psychoanalytical theoretical formulations.

It was Millon (1969) who broke from psychoanalytic theory, instead drawing from personality psychology and social learning theory, and his rationale to split SPD and AVPD was eventually adopted in the DSM-III (APA, 1980). His proposal to distinguish avoidant from schizoid was not without controversy, however. Response from the psychiatric community was that the distinction was unwarranted and based on an incomplete understanding of Kretschmer's (1925) psychoanalytically informed personality subtypes. Specifically, the criticism was that the anaesthetic and hyperaesthetic concepts were at either end of a single dimensional continuum, and thus it was inappropriate to break this continuous distribution (Livesley & West, 1986; Livesley, West & Tanney, 1985). This criticism was responded to by the psychologists working with the chair of the DSM-IV (Allen Frances) with research that showed the AVPD criteria set hung more closely with other anxious-fearful disorders (e.g., DPD), and was distinct from schizoid (Trull, Widiger, & Frances, 1987). Among the ironies in this dust-up was that Millon's model (1973) was dimensional, but was used to frame the DSM-III (APA, 1980) personality disorders in categorical terms.

As discussion about changes for the diagnostic manual brewed during the late 1960s and early 1970s, and relevant research findings accumulated in the lead up to the transformative DSM-III in 1980, there were developments taking place in personality psychology that would greatly influence the conceptualization of the personality disorders. Also notable was Millon's empirical work with the development of his personality measure, the Millon Clinical Multiaxial Inventory (MCMI; Millon, 1977). The MCMI influenced the structure for the then forthcoming DSM-III, separating clinical disorders from personality disorders, and including the personality disorders avoidant, dependent, obsessive-compulsive, and passive-aggressive (among others) that were to appear the DSM-III. However, the MCMI had only two higher-order groupings for personality disorders: severe personality pathology (borderline, schizotypal, and paranoid), and clinical personality patterns (the remaining personality disorders, AVPD, DPD, OCPD, and PAPD among them).

---

[1] This excludes a fourth grouping for transient, situational disorders, later represented outside of personality disorders as *Adjustment Disorders* from DSM-III onward.

In the DSM-III (APA, 1980), personality disorders were classified on a separate Axis II to draw attention to their importance, and the modern three-cluster groupings were first described, although the clusters were not formally separated by headings until the DSM-III-R (APA, 1987). In DSM-III (APA, 1980) and DSM-III-R (APA, 1987), the Anxious-Fearful cluster included AVPD, OCPD, DPD, and PAPD. In the DSM-IV (APA, 1994) (and the DSM-IV-TR (APA, 2000) (text revision)), PAPD was dropped from Axis II Cluster C and moved to a research section, "Criteria Sets and Axes Provided for Further Study" (APA, 1994).

A significant higher-level change in the DSM-5 was the elimination of the Axis I/II distinction that separated personality disorders from clinical disorders. An unanticipated result of the original motivation to place personality disorders on a separate axis was that clinicians tended to focus their primary diagnosis on Axis I, and gave short shrift to personality disorders, according them second class status (Sanislow & McGlashan, 1998). Strong lobbying from special interest groups argued that not giving personality disorders equal footing with the major mental disorders by not placing them on the same axis gave insurance companies license to deny reimbursement for treatment on the rationale they were character problems and not "real" illnesses. The elimination of the separate axis for personality disorders may have also reflected the development of empirically supported treatments for them. Another factor was better understanding of the neurobiology. Also, prospective studies showed that remissions from personality disorders were more common than had been assumed, and thus potentially more treatable (Sanislow et al., 2009; Zanarini, Frankenburg, Hennen, Reich, & Silk, 2006).

In the DSM-5 Section II (the main diagnostic section for all clinical and personality disorders), personality disorders are categorically defined. For the anxious-fearful cluster, AVPD, DPD, and OCPD were retained (as noted, PAPD disappeared from the conditions warranting further study, with no mention of why in the section where changes to the manual are described). In the new Section III, AMPDs are dimensionally represented, several personality disorders are not included, and the higher-order cluster grouping is dropped as well (instead, the disorders are listed alphabetically). Among the anxious-fearful disorders, only AVPD and OCPD are retained.

One reason for these shifts may be the high rates of co-occurring personality disorders (Blashfield, McElroy, Pfohl, & Blum, 1994; Oldham et al., 1995; Stuart et al., 1998), especially among those who are more severely disturbed (McGlashan et al., 2000). Additionally, the cluster structure has not been supported by studies examining co-variance structures of the symptoms (Bell & Jackson, 1992; Fossati et al., 2000; Lenzenweger, Lane, Loranger, & Kessler, 2007; Sanislow et al., 2002). Another attempt to address these problems is reflected in the eleventh edition of the International Classification of Disease (ICD-11), where the Working Group has recommended that personality disorders be described in general terms with only a few subtype specifiers and more of an emphasis on severity. Their rationale included in part the high rates of observed comorbidity as well as the goal of clinical utility (Bach & First, 2018; Reed, 2018).

DSM-5 SECTION II CLUSTER C CATEGORIES

As is characteristic of the requisite general definition required for the diagnosis of any DSM-5 personality disorder, features for each of the Cluster C disorders focus on the self, and on relationships with others (see "General Definition of Personality Disorders," APA, 2013, pp. 646–647). They include enduring patterns (at least two) of disruptions in cognition, affect, interpersonal functioning, and/or impulse control. By definition, personality disorders are stable, present across personal circumstances and social situations, and of long duration beginning around late adolescence. Echoing the "Harmful" part of Wakefield's (1992) Harmful Dysfunction model (the harm), "personality disorders lead to clinical significant distress or impairment in social, occupational, or other areas of functioning" (APA, 2013, p. 646). The dysfunctional internal mechanism part of Wakefield's model is notably absent from the DSM-5 definition. The three DSM-5 Cluster C disorders (AVPD, DPD, OCPD), along with the now defunct PAPD diagnosis, are briefly described in the following.

Avoidant Personality Disorder (AVPD)

The DSM-5 Section II criteria for AVPD are shown in Table 13.1. The DSM-5 Section II diagnostic criteria for AVPD include "pervasive fear of social inhibition, feelings of inadequacy, and hypersensitivity to negative evaluation," view of the self as "socially inept, personally unappealing, or inferior to others," and "preoccupation with being criticized or rejected in social situations" (APA, 2013, pp. 672–673). The "avoidance" in AVPD is considered distinct from social avoidance seen in other DSM-5 personality disorders (such as schizotypal and schizoid) by a sense of isolating or avoiding others because those with AVPD show a "longing to be active participants in social life" (APA, 2013, p. 673), and AVPD socially avoidant behaviors are due to fears of rejection and inadequacy (see also Sanislow, Bartolini, & Zoloth, 2012; Sanislow, da Cruz, Gianoli, & Reagan, 2012).

Dependent Personality Disorder (DPD)

The DSM-5 Section II describes the core of DPD (see Table 13.2) as characterized by the "excessive need to be taken care of" which can cause "submissive and clinging behavior" (APA, 2013, p. 675). Those afflicted with DPD are observed to lack self-confidence and report feeling "uncomfortable or helpless when alone because of fears

Table 13.1 DSM-5 Section II Avoidant Personality Disorder Diagnostic Criteria (APA, 2013, pp. 672–673)

A pervasive pattern of social inhibition, feelings of inadequacy, and hypersensitivity to negative evaluation, beginning by early adulthood and present in a variety of contexts, as indicated by four (or more) of the following:

(1) Avoids occupational activities that involve significant interpersonal contact, because of fears of criticism, disapproval, or rejection.

(2) Is unwilling to get involved with people unless certain of being liked.

(3) Shows restraint within intimate relationships because of the fear of being shamed or ridiculed.

(4) Is preoccupied with being criticized or rejected in social situations.

(5) Is inhibited in new interpersonal situations because of feelings of inadequacy.

(6) Views self as socially inept, personally unappealing, or inferior to others.

(7) Is unusually reluctant to take personal risks or to engage in any new activities because they may prove embarrassing.

Table 13.2 DSM-5 Section II Dependent Personality Disorder Diagnostic Criteria (APA, 2013, p. 675)

A pervasive and excessive need to be taken care of that leads to a submissive and clinging behavior and fears of separation, beginning by early adulthood and present in a variety of contexts, as indicated by five (or more) of the following:

(1) Has difficulty making everyday decisions without an excessive amount of advice and reassurance from others.

(2) Needs others to assume responsibility for most major areas of his or her life.

(3) Has difficulty expressing disagreement with others because of fear of loss of support or approval. (**Note:** Do not include realistic fears of retribution.)

(4) Has difficulty initiating projects or doing things on his or her own (because of a lack of self-confidence in judgment or abilities rather than a lack of motivation or energy).

(5) Goes to excessive lengths to obtain nurturance and support from others, to the point of volunteering to do things that are unpleasant.

(6) Feels uncomfortable or helpless when alone because of exaggerated fears of being unable to care for himself or herself.

(7) Urgently seeks another relationship as a source of care and support when a close relationship ends.

(8) Is unrealistically preoccupied with fears of being left to take care of himself or herself.

of being unable to care for him or herself" (APA, 2013, pp. 675–676). As a result, these individuals have difficulty making decisions, taking accountability for their own actions, and expressing opinions that may differ from those of their peers (APA, 2013, p. 675). In contrast to AVPD, those with DPD may go to "excessive lengths to obtain nurturance and support from others" at the expense of their own happiness and report feeling extreme discomfort being alone (APA, 2013, p. 675). Those with AVPD instead show reclusive behavior due to fears of rejection, despite a desire for interpersonal relationships.

Obsessive Compulsive Personality Disorder (OCPD)

OCPD is the last of the three anxious-fearful personality disorders in DSM-5 Section II (see Table 13.3). It is described as a "pervasive pattern of preoccupation with orderliness, perfectionism, and mental and interpersonal

control at the expense of flexibility, openness, and efficiency" (APA, 2013, p. 678). This need for control leads individuals to focus their efforts on planning, which can distract them from successful and efficient completion of the task at hand. In contrast to overreliance on others (DPD) and the active avoidance of others (AVPD), an emphasis on work and productivity comes at the expense of interpersonal relationships. Those with OCPD tend to have greater interest in work than in leisure activities or developing relationships.

Passive Aggressive Personality Disorder (PAPD) (Negativistic Personality Disorder)

As noted earlier, PAPD is not in the DSM-5. However, it is covered here even though it was phased out, first to a condition warranting further study in DSM-IV and then dropped altogether with the publication of DSM-5. The

Table 13.3 DSM-5 Section II Obsessive Compulsive Personality Disorder Diagnostic Criteria (APA, 2013, pp. 678–679)

A pervasive pattern of preoccupation with orderliness, perfectionism, and mental and interpersonal control, at the expense of flexibility, openness, and efficiency, beginning by early adulthood and present in a variety of contexts, as indicated by four (or more) of the following:

(1)	Is preoccupied with details, rules, lists, order, organization, or schedules to the extent that the major point of the activity is lost.
(2)	Shows perfectionism that interferes with task completion (e.g., is unable to complete a project because his or her own overly strict standards are not met).
(3)	Is excessively devoted to work and productivity to the exclusion of leisure activities and friendships (not accounted for by obvious economic necessity).
(4)	Is overconscientious, scrupulous, and inflexible about matters of morality, ethics, or values (not accounted for by cultural or religious identification).
(5)	Is unable to discard worn-out or worthless objects even when they have no sentimental value.
(6)	Is reluctant to delegate tasks or to work with others unless they submit to exactly his or her way of doing things.
(7)	Adopts a miserly spending style toward both self and others; money is viewed as something to be hoarded for future catastrophes.
(8)	Shows rigidity and stubbornness.

eradication of PAPD was not without objections (e.g., Blashfield & Intoccia, 2000; Wetzler & Morey, 1999), and psychometric research has supported its validity (e.g., Hopwood et al., 2009; see also Morey, Hopwood, & Klein, 2007). Moreover, significant rates of diagnostic co-occurrence of DSM-III-R PAPD with the other Cluster C personality disorders were noted, especially with AVPD (33.3 percent) and DPD (30.6 percent), less so with OCPD (16.7 percent); of interest, PAPD frequently co-occurs with other personality disorders outside of Cluster C, including BPD (66.1 percent), Narcissistic (50.0 percent), Histrionic (33.3 percent), Antisocial (25.0 percent), and Paranoid (30.6 percent) (Morey, 1988), suggesting the cross-cutting nature of the essence of PAPD of personality pathology.

Given the transient status of PAPD as a personality disorder, it should come as no surprise that not only has the diagnosis undergone significant revisions, but the concept has changed as well. Passive-aggressive was first used clinically to describe soldiers who acted out their desire not to comply with orders by passive non-compliance in the War Department Technical Bulletin, 203,[2] where it was classified under the rubric of "Immaturity Reactions" (War Department, 1946). The term passive-aggressive is also burdened by its folk meaning and a tendency for the term to be invoked colloquially, but the pathology is much

more pernicious than commonly understood. Since its early conceptualization, PAPD was mainly couched in the psychoanalytic framework for both DSM-I and II. Those early formulations described unconscious psychodynamics involving an inability to modulate oral aggression arising from ambivalence toward the caregiver – metaphorically biting the hand that feeds you (e.g., Abraham, 1924; Fenichel, 1945). Kernberg (1976) theorized that a less than fully integrated superego was only able to primitively modulate the ego. In more contemporary cognitive theory, PAPD was thought to be rooted in beliefs related to power and autonomy, leaving PAPD individuals feeling vulnerable to the demands of others (Pretzer & Beck, 1996).

From DSM-III in 1980 to the exile of PAPD from the personality disorder diagnostic section to the research section in DSM-IV in 1994 until it was eliminated in DSM-5 in 2013, there were many changes in the diagnostic criteria stemming in large part from conceptual disagreements about the disorder. In the DSM-III (APA, 1980), PAPD retained its focus on resistance to demands for performance through some combination of two or more of the following: procrastination, dawdling, stubbornness, intentional inefficiency, or forgetfulness (APA, 1980, p. 329). For DSM-III-R (APA, 1987), features of anger were incorporated to the idea of resistance, including terms such as "sulky," "irritable," "argumentative," "resents," "scorns" (APA, 1987, pp. 357–358). Millon (1993) detailed his rationale to broaden the category of PAPD to make it more clinically significant. His rationale grew in part out of the discontent of the DSM-IV Workgroup that criticized the DSM-III-R diagnosis as being too narrow. Millon embraced the recommendation that the scope be enlarged to "... encompass non-dynamic behavioral, cognitive, and

---

[2] The War Department Technical Bulletin 203, released October 10, 1945, and reproduced in the *Journal of Clinical Psychology* (War Department, 1946) provided a nomenclature of psychiatric disorders and reactions, and was the precursor to the first edition of the DSM. In addition to the diagnosis *passive-aggressive*, there also was a related disorder, *passive-dependent* that foreshadowed DPD. Working in the Office of the Surgeon General, William C. Menninger (who later became a Brigadier General) chaired the committee that produced the document.

affective features that the historical clinical literature indicates often co-exist in syndromal form with passive-aggressive element" (Millon, 1993, p. 83; see Frances & Widiger, 1987). Rather than reformulate the PAPD construct, it was decided to introduce a new category to replace PAPD, and to locate it in the Appendix for further evaluation for continued use by both clinicians and researchers (Millon, 1993). The resulting diagnosis emphasized the expression of anger and irritability, including "sullen and argumentative," "envy and resentful," "exaggerated and persistent complaints," and "hostile defiance" (APA, 1994, p. 735).

Benjamin (1993) disagreed with the emphasis of expression of anger that found its way into DSM-IV with Millon's (1993) urging, and argued that the element of masochism in PAPD should not be ignored. Benjamin further argued that PAPD merited clinical attention because the very nature of this kind of personality pathology could undermine treatment. In her book, *Interpersonal Diagnosis and Treatment of Personality Disorders*, she provided the following descriptive prototype of passive-aggressive interpersonal process:

[A passive-aggressive] may dislike the therapist's treatment idea, but go along with it anyway. The silliness and uselessness of the plan will soon become "apparent" through its lack of effectiveness. Similarly, suicidal acts may be escalated because of the perceived need to escape pain and suffering, but they will also be revengeful in some way. In other words, the self is attacked, but at the same time so is someone else. *The anger is not direct, and it is masochistic.* (Benjamin, 1993, p. 268, emphasis added)

Given the element of inward-directed anger, Benjamin (1993) warned that if self-destructive behaviors of PAPD are not explicitly addressed in treatment, efforts that are aimed solely at addressing a comorbid condition are likely to fail. Indeed, the error of not targeting PAPD behavior could offer one explanation for the long lamented difficulties treating more severe borderline and narcissistic personality pathologies. To illustrate, she offered a case example where a patient's self-harm behavior (cutting) was rooted in PAPD interpersonal dynamics (Benjamin, 1993). The observation is astute in light of reports that the borderline personality disorder criterion "Self-Harm" is frequently over-weighted by clinicians when making a borderline personality disorder diagnosis (Morey & Benson, 2016; Morey & Ochoa, 1989).

DSM-5 SECTION III ALTERNATIVE MODEL OF PERSONALITY DISORDERS (AMPD)

As with Section II, there is a general set of gateway criteria to qualify for any of the Section III personality disorder diagnoses. Each of the Section III personality disorders has a specific prototype rating system that explicitly directs focus on aspects of self, and on aspects of interpersonal relationships. The prototype ratings are augmented by an accompanying trait-based system for each personality disorder. In contrast to Section II personality disorders, each of the Section III alternative disorders is posed in terms of dimensions. Though the alternative disorders are similar, they also include a separate rating for functioning to more explicitly focus on impairment. "Personality functioning and personality traits also can be assessed whether or not the individual has a personality disorder – a feature that provides clinically useful information about all individuals" (APA, 2013, p. 816).

In the AMPD, only two Cluster C disorders have been retained, AVPD and OCPD. The AMPD diagnostic scheme constitutes a sort of hybrid multidimensional prototype rating of personality disorder, with two kinds of criteria, the first for personality functioning, and the second for pathological traits. The elements of personality functioning include *self* (identity, direction) and *interpersonal* (empathy, intimacy), and the elements of traits were selected from an admixture of trait models, but perhaps most clearly echo the work by Harkness and McNulty (1994; see other chapters in this volume for more detail).

In the DSM-5 Section III alternative model (see Table 13.4), AVPD functional problems in *self* include low self-esteem based on seeing oneself as socially inept, unappealing, or inferior, and suffering excessive feelings of shame. Unrealistic standards can lead to reluctance to pursue goals, take risks, or engage in new activities involving interpersonal contact. *Interpersonally*, there is a preoccupation with criticism or rejection, distortion of others' views as negative, reluctance to get involved in social activities certain of being liked and fear of being shamed or ridiculed leads to diminished reciprocation in relationships (APA, 2013, p. 765).

For OCPD, the DSM-5 Section III alternative model (see Table 13.5) stipulates that, in regard to *self*, identity and self-worth are derived through productivity (APA, 2013, p. 768), and the diagnosis is characterized by a "rigid perfectionism" (APA, 2013, p. 768). *Interpersonally*, these individuals show "difficulty understanding and appreciating the ideas, feelings, or behaviors of others" and relationships take a back seat to work, and are further compromised by "rigidity and stubbornness" (APA, 2013, p. 768).

AVOIDANCE BEHAVIORS: MALADAPTIVE COPING

For both AVPD and OCPD, relationships are avoided and problematic (see Table 13.6). While AVPD patients are hesitant to engage with others due to a fear of rejection, OCPD patients struggle with empathy and value work over personal relationships, and avoid others based on their perceived incompetence. Even though DPD and PAPD are not in the AMPD Section III, OCPD characteristics of difficulty completing tasks appear similar on the surface. However, for OCPD, it is "rigidity" and an inability to compromise that gets in the way, whereas DPD individuals

Table 13.4 DSM-5 Section III Avoidant Personality Disorder Diagnostic Criteria (APA, 2013, pp. 765–766)

Criteria A and B for Avoidant Personality Disorder in the DSM-5 Section III AMPD Model for Personality Disorders:

A. Moderate or greater impairment in personality functioning, manifest by characteristic difficulties in two or more of the following four areas:

   (1) **Identity:** Sense of self derived predominantly from work or productivity; constricted experience and expression of strong emotions.

   (2) **Self-direction:** Difficulty competing tasks and realizing goals, associated with rigid and unreasonably high and inflexible internal standards of behavior; overly conscientious and moralistic attitudes.

   (3) **Empathy:** Difficult understanding and appreciating the ideas, feelings, or behaviors of others.

   (4) **Intimacy:** Relationships seen as secondary to work and productivity; rigidity and stubbornness negatively affect relationships with others.

B. Three or more of the following four pathological personality traits, one of which must be (3) Anxiousness:

   (1) **Anxiousness** (an aspect of **Negativity Affectivity**): Intense feelings of nervousness, tenseness, or panic, often in reaction to social situations; worry about the negative effects of past unpleasant experiences and future negative possibilities; feeling fearful, apprehensive, or threatened by uncertainty; fears of embarrassment.

   (2) **Withdrawal** (an aspect of **Detachment**): Reticence in social situations; avoidance of social contacts and activity; lack of initiation of social contact.

   (3) **Anhedonia** (an aspect of **Detachment**): Lack of enjoyment from, engagement in, or energy for life's experiences; deficits in the capacity to feel pleasure or take interest in things.

   (4) **Intimacy** (an aspect of **Detachment**): Avoidance of close or romantic relationships, interpersonal attachments, and intimate sexual relationships.

are prone to get stuck because they are unable to make decisions on their own. As described earlier for the case of PAPD, the act of avoidance is more masochistic, a punishment of the self, rather than driven by an expression of hostility toward the other, the latter merely on the receiving end of collateral damage.

COMORBIDITY WITH CLINICAL DISORDERS

The dissolution of Axis I/II so that the personality disorder categories were migrated to the same section as the clinical disorders (those formally on Axis I) reflected consensus of the field that there exists a continuity between personality disorders and clinical disorders, evidenced in part by frequent association of pathological features spanning this division. This raises the proposition that certain co-occurring clinical personality diagnoses may be linked in continuous fashion on a dimension of severity. For two Cluster C personality disorders, AVPD and OCPD, a number of studies provide evidence that this might be the case.

AVPD and OCPD Clinical Disorders Comorbidity

AVPD frequently co-occurs with a spectrum of anxiety and, to a lesser extent, with depressive disorders. Most prominent for anxiety disorders is Social Phobia (SP), which was introduced in the DSM-III. Also important is the more broadly defined successor, Social Anxiety

Disorder (SAD), which was introduced in the DSM-IV to replace SP.[3] This is largely unsurprising because criteria of this disorder pair are similar to AVPD in many ways. The occurrence of either panic disorder or social phobia was reported to be to up to eight to nine times more likely for those diagnosed with AVPD (Skodol et al., 1995). In a clinical sample of outpatients presenting for treatment for depression, one-third of the sample met DSM-III-R criteria for either AVPD or social phobia, or both disorders (Alpert et al., 1997).

Zimmerman and colleagues (Zimmerman, Rothschild, & Chelminski, 2005) reported that AVPD occurred in 20.3 percent of the cases of major depressive disorder, 26.1 percent of the cases of generalized anxiety disorder, and 21.8 percent of the cases of panic disorder in an outpatient sample. In the Collaborative Longitudinal Personality Study (CLPS; McGlashan et al., 2000) reported comorbidities for treatment-seeking patients who were cell-assigned to the AVPD group.[4] For DSM-IV anxiety disorders, social phobia (38.2 percent), posttraumatic stress disorder (28.0

---

[3] In the DSM-IV, Social Phobia was subtitled Social Anxiety Disorder; for DSM-5, Social Anxiety Disorder had the subtitle Social Phobia.

[4] Cell assignment to one of the four CLPS index personality disorders required diagnosis from a structured interview, and an additional confirmation using either the DSM-IV scoring algorithm of the Schedule of Non-Adaptive and Adaptive Personality, or a blind Prototype Rating completed by the referring clinician; thus, occurrence of the four primary personality disorders in CLPS exceeded the number for the cell-assigned disorders (Skodol et al., 2005).

Table 13.5 DSM-5 Section III Obsessive Compulsive Personality Disorder Diagnostic Criteria (APA, 2013, pp. 768–769)

Criteria A and B for Obsessive Compulsive Personality Disorder in the DSM-5 Section III AMPD Model for Personality Disorders:

A. Moderate or greater impairment in personality functioning, manifest by characteristic difficulties in two or more of the following four areas:

    (1) *Identity:* Low self-esteem associated with self-appraisal as socially inept, personally unappealing, or inferior; excessive feelings of shame or inadequacy.

    (2) *Self-direction:* Unrealistic standards for behavior associated with reluctance to pursue goals, take personal risks, or engage in new activities involving interpersonal contact.

    (3) *Empathy:* Preoccupation with, and sensitivity to, criticism or rejection, associated with distorted inference of others' perspectives as negative.

    (4) *Intimacy:* Reluctance to get involved with people unless being certain of being liked; diminished mutuality within intimate relationships because of fear of being shamed or ridiculed.

B. Three or more of the following four pathological personality traits, one of which must be (1) Rigid Perfectionism:

    (1) *Rigid Perfectionism* (an aspect of extreme **Conscientiousness** [the opposite pole of Disinhibition*]): Rigid insistence on everything being flawless, perfect, and without errors or faults, including one's own and others' performance; sacrificing of timeliness to ensure correctness in every detail; believing that there is only one right way to do things; difficulty changing ideas and/or viewpoint; preoccupation with details, organization, and order.

    (2) *Perseveration* (an aspect of **Negative Affectivity**): Persistence at tasks long after the behavior has ceased to be functional or effective; continuance of the same behavior despite repeated failures.

    (3) *Intimacy avoidance* (an aspect of **Detachment**): Avoidance of close or romantic relationships, interpersonal attachments, and intimate sexual relationships.

    (4) *Restricted affectivity* (an aspect of **Detachment**): Little reaction to emotionally arousing situations; constricted emotional experience and expression; indifference or coldness.

Note: *Detachment was changed to "Disinhibition" in an August 2015 update by the American Psychiatric Association because "Disinhibition" was the opposite pole of conscientiousness. https://psychiatryonline.org/pb-assets/dsm/update/DSM5Update_October2017.pdf (accessed August 12, 2018).

Table 13.6 Avoidance behaviors and core anxiety/fear for Anxious-Fearful Personality Disorders

Personality disorder	Avoidance behaviors	Anxiety or fear
Avoidant	Relationships and intimacy	Being revealed as inept
Dependent	Assertiveness and agency	Being a not good person
Obsessive-compulsive	Intimacy and communion	Being imperfect
Passive-aggressive	Obligations and responsibilities	Being taken advantage of

Note: Avoidant *behaviors* may instrumentally be invoked in the service of reducing anxiety or fear, but are more likely to instead have the adverse effect of reinforcing (or not extinguishing) anxiety and fear.

percent), panic disorder (22.9 percent), and generalized anxiety disorder (21.7 percent) frequently co-occurred with AVPD.

Among CLPS AVPD patients, 44.6 percent met criteria for alcohol abuse or dependence, and 32.5 percent for abuse or dependence of another substance (cases for these percentages are not mutually exclusive). Given the well-established overlap between depressive disorders and substance use disorders (e.g., Swendsen & Merikangas, 2000), depressive disorders are another connecting node, linking AVPD and other clinical disorders. Among Axis I disorders most frequently occurring with AVPD in the CLPS sample was major depressive disorder (81.5 percent) and dysthymic disorder (21.7 percent) (McGlashan et al., 2000). In a sample of older adults undergoing treatment for major depressive disorder, 11.8 percent of the patients were comorbid DSM-IV AVPD (Devanand, 2002).

Some more recent studies examining AVPD and social phobia have focused on relational problems and have added abandonment fears to the anxiety associated with close relationships (Eikenæs, Pedersen & Wilberg, 2016). In studies framed by comparisons of categorical diagnostic groupings, there is less support for a continuum model (e.g., Boone et al., 1999; Lampe & Sunderland, 2015). However, while there continues to be an interest in preserving the notion of categorical definitions for social-related anxiety, evidence for dimensional qualities is too strong to ignore (e.g., Chambless, Fydrich, & Rodebaugh, 2008; Crome, Baillie, Slade & Ruscio, 2010; Ralevski et al. 2005; Skocic, Jackson, & Hulbert, 2015; van Velzen, Emmelkamp, & Scholing, 2000).

For OCPD, Obsessive Compulsive Disorder (OCD) would seem a logical connection. Unlike AVPD and SP, however, the criteria for the disorders are less similar, the core of OCPD centered around combination of perfectionism and experiential avoidance, whereas OCD entails repetitive, ritualistic thoughts and behaviors. Nonetheless, a number of researchers have examined the continuities between the two disorders, and there is some evidence that they are on a continuum of severity. Some research has identified latent dimensions (e.g., severity) that cut across OCPD and sometimes co-occurring disorders such as depressive, anxiety, and tic disorders, but also posited the presence of subtype groupings that they argue are distinct (Nestadt et al., 2003). Others have similarly argued that those diagnosed with both OCPD and OCD represent a specific, more severe subtype of OCD (e.g. Coles, Pinto, Mancebo, Rasmussen, & Eisen, 2008; Garyfallos et al., 2010). The preponderance of research, however, suggests the presence of core dimension of severity between OCPD and OCD (e.g., Gordon, Salkovskis, Oldfield & Carter, 2013; Lochner et al., 2011). OCPD does have associations with other clinical disorders, in particularly eating disorders (e.g., Serpell, Livingstone, Neiderman, & Lask, 2002; Thornton & Russell, 1997). Not surprisingly, features of these disorders share the common element of striving for perfection.

In sum, AVPD frequently co-occurs with a spectrum of anxiety and depressive disorders. The frequency of co-occurrence with depressive disorders varies widely and is likely somewhat dependent on the sample. Among anxiety disorders, social phobia is noteworthy because features of that disorder are similar in many respects to AVPD criteria, but also because of the dimension that runs from normal shyness to a disabling social reclusiveness. For OCPD, the relation with OCD as well as various forms of eating disorders is notable, particularly the features of perfectionism and experiential avoidance. With CLPS data, analysis of a subset of OCPD symptoms revealed a unique link to OCD (Eisen et al., 2006). Other research has identified a dimension of "self-control" anchored on either end by impulsivity (OCD) and over control (OCPD) as a salient cross-cutting feature bridging the two categorical diagnoses (Pinto, Steinglass, Greene, Weber, & Simpson, 2014). Treatment outcome research using exposure with response prevention for OCD found poorer outcomes were associated with the OCPD-related

feature perfectionism. Evidence for dimensional conceptualizations may be most compelling when intermediate phenotypes or components of the diagnoses are the focus of study. Overall, these sorts of findings raise questions about the specificity and coverage of the categorical diagnostic definitions.

Findings such as these thematically suggest that well-studied cross-cutting dimensions offer another way to break free from categorical comparisons and identify higher-order constructs that might better correspond to basic trait models. Examples might include: self-esteem (e.g., Gyurak, & Ayduk, 2007; Lynum, Wilberg & Karterud, 2008), rejection sensitivity (e.g., Ayduk, Gyurak, & Luerssen, 2008; Downey & Feldman, 1996; Kross, Egner, Ochsner, Hirsh, & Downey, 2007), perfectionism, dependency (Blatt, D'Afflitti, & Quinlan, 1976; Hewitt & Flett, 1991), and experience avoidance (e.g., Wheaton & Pinto, 2017). Clearly, many of these dimensions cut across not only clinical disorder–personality disorder boundaries, but also run through various personality disorders, including other, non-Cluster C disorders.

Pathoplasticity

Personality disorders and clinical disorders may also be related via the concept of pathoplasticity. Pathoplasticity is theoretically agnostic about the presence of a shared etiology and instead emphasizes "the influence of one condition on the presentation or course of the other" (Shea et al., 2004, p. 500). In other words, the presence of one disorder impacts the course and treatment outcome of the other, but they do not necessarily stem from the same pathology. With CLPS data, Shea and colleagues (2004) found a significant association for the longitudinal associations of AVPD and Axis I anxiety disorders. This finding suggested a continual interplay of AVPD with social phobia and obsessive-compulsive disorder over the course of time (Shea et al., 2004). In contrast, major depressive disorder was more related to borderline personality disorder than AVPD when controlling for depressed mood.

Using the same CLPS data, Warner and colleagues (2004) tested the relations of personality traits to DSM-IV-TR symptoms using a cross-lagged structural modeling approach. The changes in avoidant personality traits defined with the Five-Factor Model using an approach devised by Lynam and Widiger (2001) preceded changes in the AVPD criteria. The Warner results provided a conceptual link between personality traits and personality disorders implied by the DSM, and support for the addition of personality traits in the DSM-5.

These comorbidities and dimensional associations raise a question related to the AMPD approach to bifurcate personality traits and the more traditional personality disorder self–other definitional features. Why would personality traits not have similar implications for clinical disorder diagnoses more broadly? If, for instance, AVPD and SP/SAD, or OCPD and OCD are indeed continua of severity, why would trait-level specifications be limited only to the personality disorder portion of the continuum? Another alternative would be to define the symptomatic pathology in personality disorders in much the same way as the clinical disorders, and to construct trait models based on personality psychology to identify constellations that would pose risk or resilience in the course of mental disorders more generally. In any event, these potentially contiguous dimensions that cut across the traditionally separate clinical and personality disorders raise the issue of where to carve nature between "disorders" and "traits" (cf. Gangestad & Snyder, 1985).

BIOLOGICAL MECHANISMS

One criticism of the DSM-5 Personality Disorders Workgroup was the lack of consideration of biologically-based and temperamental models of personality disorder diagnoses, or at least published consideration of the pros and cons of such models (see special issue of *Journal of Personality Disorders*). Notably absent was Cloninger's Seven Factor Model of Temperament and Character (Cloninger, Svrakic, & Przybeck, 1993) as well as the Psychobiological Model offered by Siever and Davis (1991). This is especially salient because there has been a burgeoning interest in the biological and neuroscientific study of personality disorders, although much has been directed at borderline personality disorder (Campbell et al., 2007; Donegan et al., 2003; Etkin, Prater, Hoeft, Menon, & Schatzberg, 2010; Schmidt & Jetha, 2009). Some of these biological studies addressed personality disorders in the anxious-fearful cluster (e.g., AVPD; Denny et al., 2015), but most often, reports of these disorders are from studies where one has been employed as a contrast condition (e.g., AVPD serving as contrast group to borderline, relative to normal controls; Herpertz et al., 2000).

The Siever and Davis model (1991) was prescient in that it posited intermediate phenotypes that had been well studied outside of the context of the DSM framework, thereby not constraining the dimensional qualities of the construct on the basis of study inclusion rules that might limit meaningful variance. Their constructs were *cognitive/perceptual organization, impulsivity/aggression, affective instability*, and *anxiety/inhibition*, and they emphasized that these biological dimensions cut across Axis I/II, that is, both clinical and personality disorders (Siever & Davis, 1991). However, there was not good one-to-one correspondence to the various personality disorders (see Shea et al., 2004), and this may be one reason why they were not included. On the other hand, those dimensions themselves were supported by a preponderance of biological and genetic evidence, and it may be that it was the DSM that was the limiting factor when attempting to clarify the relation to the dimensions and personality disorder categories (see

Cuthbert, 2005; Eaton, Krueger, South, Simms, & Clark, 2011).

Nonetheless, given advances in integrative neuroscience, the potential to further tease apart the mechanisms of personality pathology could offer rewards for better treatment targets. Some personality researchers have attempted to link five-factor traits to structural features of the brain (e.g., DeYoung et al., 2010; Grazioplene, Chavez, Rustichini, & DeYoung, 2016).

Example: Using the NIMH RDoC to Research Anxious-Fearful-Avoidant Pathology

Clearly, there are many commonalities in the neural structures and pathways involved in behaviors among Cluster C personality disorders, and the NIMH RDoC offers a framework to organize the relations of these systems and behaviors (Sanislow et al., 2010). For example, an obvious domain is Negative Valence, which includes constructs for anxiety and fear. Yet other midbrain pathways are involved in processing fear/threat stimuli as well as social bonding, and connections to regions of cortex such as OFC and vmPFC. But there are complicated behaviors that need to be accounted for to understand the clinical problems with anxious-fearful-avoidant pathology. In the RDoC, the domain "positive valence systems" is defined as "responsible for responses to positive motivational situations or contexts, such as reward seeking, consummatory behavior, and reward/habit learning" (RDoC Matrix Website). The construct "approach motivation," which lies in this domain, may provide a useful framework for thinking about AVPD and the mechanisms that underlie it. The RDoC approach describes motivation as the "mechanisms/processes that regulate the direction and maintenance of approach behavior influenced by pre-existing tendencies, learning, memory, stimulus characteristics, and deprivation states," towards "innate or acquired cues, implicit or explicit goals" (RDoC Matrix Website). Taken together with the description of approach motivation put forth in RDoC, establishing meaningful social relationships can be seen as a goal for AVPD patients, but the need to address systems involved in the anticipation of anxiety provoked by potential social interactions is important. On the other hand, regulating that anxiety by avoiding social interaction can inhibit these patients from seeking these goals, promoting further social withdrawal.

The sub-constructs of approach motivation outlined in the RDoC further describe behavioral patterns associated with AVPD. For example, "reward valuation" refers to the ability to estimate the likelihood of an outcome as well as its value, and focuses on the notion of "calibration" through personal biases and experiences (RDoC Matrix Website). In this way, individuals with AVPD can be seen as predisposed to view the likelihood of a positive social interaction as low, leading them to become withdrawn. Similarly, "action selection" describes the way cost/benefit computations occur in a decision-making context (RDoC Matrix Website). In this view, those suffering AVPD might be seen as prone to repeatedly making maladaptive choices based on their errant analyses.

Beyond approach motivation, connecting the symptoms of AVPD with RDoC may help clarify neural and psychological mechanisms of AVPD, as well as those in other Cluster C personality disorders. Much of the neural circuitry that supports relevant aspects of approach motivation is also relevant to other important constructs in RDoC that pertain to AVPD. For example, the amygdala is related to expectancy, reward prediction error, action selection within approach motivation, and is also tied to affiliation and attachment within social processes. In addition, the RDoC notes other midbrain areas, such as striatum, substantia nigra/ventral tegmental area (VTA), and nucleus accumbens (NAcc), which are involved in approach motivation and certain fear and anxiety responses. The RDoC also implicates higher cortical structures, such as orbitofrontal cortex (OFC) and the pathways linking the limbic system and cortex in relevant processes. This suggests that disrupted activity in certain midbrain or cortical structures, or the connections between them, may play a role in AVPD, along with physiological changes associated with the stress response, for example, changes in heart rate and skin conductance. For the person suffering AVPD, the cognitive control of emotion may be accomplished through avoidance behaviors.

There are also parallels between DSM-5 symptoms and RDoC constructs for other Cluster C personality disorders. In the case of DPD, the RDoC indicates similar physiology may be affected as in AVPD, despite different symptoms. As noted, the DSM-5 describes DPD as an "excessive need to be taken care of" which can cause "submissive and clinging behavior" (APA, 2013, p. 675). Dependent patients lack self-confidence and feel "uncomfortable or helpless when alone because of fears of being unable to care for him or herself" (APA, 2013, pp. 675–676). As a result, these individuals are indecisive, avoid responsibility for their actions, and they are reluctant to express opinions that may differ from those of their peers (APA, 2013, p. 675).

Unlike those with AVPD, DPD individuals may go to "excessive lengths to obtain nurturance and support from others" at the expense of their own happiness and feel extreme discomfort being alone (APA, 2013, p. 675). AVPD patients instead show reclusive behavior due to fears of rejection, despite a desire for interpersonal relationships. These differences may reflect shared underlying mechanisms for the two diagnoses. The RDoC shows similar parallels for the DPD symptoms – within the negative valence systems domain, acute threat and potential threat reflect the "activation of the brain's defensive motivational system" in situations of "perceived danger," whether that threat is something specific or more "ambiguous" (RDoC Matrix Website). Action selection, within the positive valence systems, also proves useful in describing DPD symptoms, particularly with respect to seeking out

relationships and support from others through "excessive" means (RDoC Matrix Website; APA, 2013, p. 675). Further, social processes involving affiliation and attachment outlined in RDoC suggest the way disruptions in this area may lead to "over-attachment," which closely relates to "submissive and clinging behavior" and excessive reliance on others that characterizes DPD (APA, 2013, p. 675).

RDoC is useful for analyzing DPD symptoms from the DSM-5 grouping, and potentially connecting them to the physiological mechanisms that appear in DPD as well as similar symptoms in other DSM-5 constructs. Similar to AVPD, midbrain structures involved in fear/stress responses and social attachments, as well as reward pathways seem to be affected, such as hypothalamus, amygdala, bed nucleus of the stria terminalis (BNST), and NAcc, as well as higher cortical structures involved in processing these responses, including vmPFC and OFC (RDoC). Similar pathways are also implicated to other aspects of the disorder as well – amygdala is implicated in action selection and in processes of social attachment and bond formation. Neurotransmitters involved in these systems also show similarities across RDoC, particularly those associated with affiliation and attachment like oxytocin and vasopressin, and in fear and reward pathways, like dopamine. In addition, the autonomic nervous system is closely linked to fear and stress responses, which mirrors the anxiety characteristic of AVPD patients, albeit with a different basis. Other RDoC constructs, such as agency within the social processes domain, also seem to be affected, but the neural structures implicated in these processes have not yet been fully established.

Similar to AVPD and DPD, OCPD symptoms align closely with constructs in the RDoC pertaining to threat and reward processing, as well as social affiliations and attachments. OCPD patients show anger or frustration when tasks are not completed in the way they feel is best. This lack of control (and deviance from "flawless" ideals) can be threatening, and acute stress responses may be activated. More generally, reward systems may be activated that support the pursuit of perfectionism, and explain rigid behavior in these patients. Disruptions in social attachments and affiliations seem to be at work in this disorder as well, particularly in the way that perfectionism and productivity take precedence over relationships.

A critical distinguishing feature of social behaviors in OCPD (compared to AVPD or DPD) is a decreased ability to understand the emotions of others and to express intimate feelings. Many of these behaviors are described under the construct perception of others, within social processes. The physiological underpinnings of these processes are not fully established, but hormones associated with attachment like oxytocin and vasopressin as well as certain cortical structures, such as medial prefrontal cortex (mPFC), may be implicated. In addition, habit formation described in RDoC recalls symptoms of OCPD, such as hoarding and focus on "details, rules, lists, order, organization, or schedules" (APA, 2013, p. 678). Such behaviors may be mediated by similar midbrain structures (substantia nigra (SN), VTA, and striatum), as well as cortical areas (mPFC) involved in planning.

CONCLUDING THOUGHTS

The historical vantage point of this chapter highlights a sundry of lumping, splitting, re-grouping, and reorganizing of the salient types of clinical problems related to chronic kinds of anxiety, fear, and avoidance in attempts at formal classification dating back to the turn of the last century. As discussed, there have been different ideas about how these problems come about, and varying ideas about the underlying dynamics, whether views of those mechanisms are shaped by a psychoanalytic, psychological, behavioral, or biological approaches. But, strikingly, conceptions of this kind of personality pathology have largely remained the same even though various groupings and divisions have come and gone, in some instances, more than once.

Clearly there are many forces at work, including guild interests of psychiatry and psychology, and divisions and cross-alliances within and between camps (see Volume 26, Number 6 of the *Journal of Personality Disorders* for illustrations). There are scientific issues, too. Other chapters in this volume discuss the merits of competing models, factors that are no doubt relevant for efforts going forward. It is also important to keep in mind the different goals of clinical utility and research validity in formulating clinical tools for diagnosis and carrying out research on the structure or mechanisms of personality pathology (Skodol, 2012). The goal of clinical diagnosis is practical, and not primarily an academic enterprise. The "caseness" of a categorical diagnosis helps clinicians to recognize a prototype of a set of problems and to begin to think about a treatment plan, to communicate to third party payers, including documenting disability. The goal of clinical research is to achieve valid conceptions of psychopathology. Clarifying the mechanisms – psychological *and* biological – and how they are manifest in the interpersonal processes that are the space of personality is the challenge (see Carson, 1989). Transdiagnostic constructs and alternative research strategies such as RDoC offer possibilities to see things in a different light. Our review of the anxious-fearful-avoidant pathologies shows us that research constrained to some variant of the DSM structure may get us no farther than a reshuffled deck of cards.

REFERENCES

Abraham, K. (1924). The influence of oral eroticism on character formation. In *Selected Papers on Psychoanalysis* (English translation, 1927). London: Hogarth Press.

Alpert, J. E., Uebelacker, L. A., McLean, N. E., Nierenberg, J. A., Pava, J. J., Worthington III, J. R., ... Fava, M. (1997). Social phobia, avoidant personality disorder, and atypical depression: Co-occurrence and clinical implications. *Psychological Medicine, 27*, 627–633.

American Psychiatric Association. (1952). *Diagnostic and Statistical Manual of Mental Disorders*. Washington, DC: American Psychiatric Association.

American Psychiatric Association. (1968). *Diagnostic and Statistical Manual of Mental Disorders* (2nd ed.). Washington, DC: American Psychiatric Association.

American Psychiatric Association. (1980). *Diagnostic and Statistical Manual of Mental Disorders* (3rd ed.). Washington, DC: American Psychiatric Association.

American Psychiatric Association. (1987). *Diagnostic and Statistical Manual of Mental Disorders* (revised 3rd ed.). Washington, DC: American Psychiatric Association.

American Psychiatric Association. (1994). *Diagnostic and Statistical Manual of Mental Disorders* (4th ed.). Washington, DC: American Psychiatric Association.

American Psychiatric Association. (2000). *Diagnostic and Statistical Manual of Mental Disorders* (4th ed., Text Revision). Washington, DC: American Psychiatric Association.

American Psychiatric Association. (2013). *Diagnostic and Statistical Manual of Mental Disorders* (5th ed.). Arlington, VA: American Psychiatric Publishing.

Ayduk, O., Gyurak, A., & Luerssen, A. (2008). Individual differences in the rejection–aggression link in the hot sauce paradigm: The case of rejection sensitivity. *Journal of Experimental Social Psychology, 44*, 775–782.

Bach, B., & First, M. B. (2018). Application of the ICD-11 classification of personality disorders. *BMC Psychiatry*. https://doi.org/10.1186/s12888–01801908-3

Bell, R. C., & Jackson, H. J. (1992). The structure of personality disorders in DSM-III. *Acta Psychiatrica Scandinavica, 85*, 279–287.

Benjamin, L. S. (1993). *Interpersonal Diagnosis and Treatment of Personality Disorders* (2nd ed.). New York: Guilford Press.

Blashfield, R. K., & Intoccia, V. (2000). Growth of the literature on the topic of personality disorders. *American Journal of Psychiatry, 167*, 472–473.

Blashfield, R. K., McElroy, R. A., Pfohl, B., & Blum, N. (1994). Comorbidity and the prototype model. *Clinical Psychology: Science and Practice, 1*, 96–99.

Blatt, S. J., D'Afflitti, J. P., & Quinlan, D. M. (1976). Experiences of depression in normal young adults. *Journal of Abnormal Psychology, 85*, 383–389.

Bleuler, E. (1911/1950). *Dementia Praecox or the Group of Schizophrenias* (Trans. J. Zinkin). New York: International Universities Press.

Boone, M. L., McNeil, D. W., Masia, C. L., Turk, C. L., Carter, L. E., Ries, B. J., & Lewin, M. R. (1999). Multimodal comparisons of social phobia subtypes and avoidant personality disorder. *Journal of Anxiety Disorders, 13*, 271–292.

Campbell, D. W., Sareen, J., Paulus, M. P., Goldin, P. R., Stein, M. B., & Reiss, J. P. (2007). Time-varying amygdala response to emotional faces in generalized social phobia. *Biological Psychiatry, 62*, 455–463.

Carson, R. C. (1989). Personality. *Annual Review of Psychology, 40*, 227–248.

Chambless, D. L., Fydrich, T., & Rodebaugh, T. L. (2008). Generalized social phobia and avoidant personality disorder: Meaningful distinction or useless duplication? *Depression and Anxiety, 25*, 8–19.

Cloninger, C. R., Svrakic, D. R., & Przybeck, T. R. (1993). A psychobiological model of temperament and character. *Archives of General Psychiatry, 50*, 975–990.

Coles, M. E., Pinto, A., Mancebo, M. C., Rasmussen, S. A., & Eisen, J. L. (2008). OCD with comorbid OCPD: A subtype of OCD? *Journal of Psychiatric Research, 42*, 289–296.

Crome, E., Baillie, A., Slade, T., & Ruscio, A. M. (2010). Social phobia: Further evidence of dimensional structure. *Australian and New Zealand Journal of Psychiatry, 44*, 1012–1020.

Cuthbert, B. N. (2005). Dimensional models of psychopathology: Research agenda and clinical utility. *Journal of Abnormal Psychology, 14*, 565–569.

Denny, B. T., Fan, J, Liu, X., Ochsner, K. N., Guerreri, S., Mayson, S. J., ... Koenigsberg, H. W. (2015). Elevated amygdala activity during reappraisal anticipation predicts anxiety in avoidant personality disorder. *Journal of Affective Disorders, 172*, 1–7.

Devanand, D. P. (2002). Comorbid psychiatric disorders in late life depression. *Biological Psychiatry, 52*, 236–242.

DeYoung, C. G., Hirsh, J. B., Shane, M. S., Papademetris, X., Rajeevan, N., & Gray, J. R. (2010). Testing predictions from personality neuroscience: Brain structure and the Big Five. *Psychological Science, 21*, 820–828.

Donegan, N. H., Sanislow, C. A., Blumberg, H. P., Fulbright, R. K., Lacadie, C., Skudlarski, P., ... Wexler, B. E. (2003). Amygdala hyperreactivity in borderline personality disorder: Implications for emotional dysregulation. *Biological Psychiatry, 54*, 1284–1293.

Downey, G., & Feldman, S. I. (1996). Implications of rejection sensitivity for intimate relationships. *Journal of Personality and Social Psychology, 70*, 1327–1343.

Eaton, N. R., Krueger, R. F., South, S., Simms, L., & Clark, L. A. (2011). Contrasting prototypes and dimensions in the classification of personality pathology: Evidence that dimensions, but not prototypes, are robust. *Psychological Medicine, 41*, 1151–1163.

Eikenæs, I., Pedersen, G., & Wilberg, T. (2016). Attachment styles in patients with avoidant personality disorder compared with social phobia. *Psychology and Psychotherapy: Theory, Research and Practice, 89*, 245–260.

Eisen, J. L., Coles, M. E., Shea, M. T., Pagano, M. E., Stout, R. L.., Yen, S. ... Rasmussen, S. A. (2006). Clarifying the convergence between obsessive compulsive personality disorder criteria and obsessive compulsive disorder. *Journal of Personality Disorders, 20*, 294–305.

Etkin, A., Prater, K. E., Hoeft, F., Menon, V., & Schatzberg, A. F. (2010). Failure of anterior cingulate activation and connectivity with the amygdala during implicit regulation of emotional processing in generalized anxiety disorder. *American Journal of Psychiatry, 167*, 545–554.

Fenichel, O. (1945). *The Psychoanalytical Theory of the Neurosis*. New York: W. W. Norton.

Fossati, A., Maffei, C., Bagnato, M., Battaglia, M., Donati, D., Donini, M., ... Prolo, F. (2000). Patterns of covariation of DSM-IV personality disorders in a mixed psychiatric sample. *Comprehensive Psychiatry, 41*, 206–215.

Frances, A., & Widiger, T. (1987). A critical review of four DSM-III personality disorders. In G. Tischer (Ed.), *Diagnosis and Classification in Psychiatry*. New York: Cambridge University Press.

Gangestad, S., & Snyder, M. (1985). "To carve nature at its joints": On the existence of discrete classes in personality. *Psychological Review, 92*, 317–349.

Garyfallos, G., Katsigiannopoulos, K., Adamopoulou, A., Papazisis, G., Karastergiou, A., & Bozikas, V. P. (2010). Comorbidity of obsessive-compulsive disorder with obsessive-compulsive personality disorder: Does it imply a specific subtype of obsessive-compulsive disorder? *Psychiatry Research, 177*, 156–160.

Gordon, O. M., Salkovskis, P. M., Oldfield, V. B., & Carter, N. (2013). The association between obsessive compulsive disorder and obsessive compulsive personality disorder: Prevalence and clinical presentation. *British Journal of Clinical Psychology, 52*, 300–315.

Grazioplene, R. G., Chavez, R. S., Rustichini, A., & DeYoung, C. G. (2016). White matter correlates of psychosis-linked traits support continuity between personality and psychopathology. *Journal of Abnormal Psychology, 125*, 1135–1145.

Gyurak, A., & Ayduk, O. (2007). Defensive physiological reactions to rejection: The effect of self-esteem and attentional control on startle responses. *Psychological Science, 18*, 886–892.

Harkness, A. R., & McNulty, J. L. (1994). The Personality Psychopathology Five (PSY-5): Issue from the pages of a diagnostic manual instead of a dictionary. In S. Strack & M. Lorr (Eds.), *Differentiating Normal and Abnormal Personality* (pp. 291–315). New York: Springer.

Herpertz, S. C., Schwenger, U. B., Kunert, H. J., Lukas, G., Gretzer, U., Nutzmann, L., ... Sass, H. (2000). Emotional responses in patients with borderline as compared with avoidant personality disorder. *Journal of Personality Disorders, 14*, 339–351.

Hewitt, P. L., & Flett, G. L. (1991). Perfectionism in the self and social contexts: Conceptualization, assessment, and association with psychopathology. *Journal of Personality and Social Psychology, 60*, 456–470.

Hoch, A. (1910). Constitutional factors in the dementia praecox group. *Review of Neurology and Psychiatry, 8*, 463–474.

Hopwood, C. J., Morey, L. C., Markowitz, J. C., Pinto, A., Skodol, A. E., Gunderson, J. G., ... Sanislow, C. A. (2009). The construct validity of passive-aggressive personality disorder. *Psychiatry, 72*, 256–268.

Horney, K. (1945). *Our Inner Conflicts*. New York: W. W. Norton.

Horney, K. (1950). *Neurosis and Human Growth*. New York: W. W. Norton.

Kernberg, O. F. (1976). *Object Relations Theory and Clinical Psychoanalysis*. New York: Jason Aronson.

Kretschmer, E. (1925). *Physique and Character: An Investigation of the Nature of Constitution and Temperament*. London: Kegan Paul.

Kross, E., Egner, T., Ochsner, K., Hirsh, J., & Downey, G. (2007). Neural dynamics of rejection sensitivity. *Journal of Cognitive Neuroscience, 19*, 945–956.

Lampe, L., & Sunderland, M. (2015). Social phobia and avoidant personality disorder: Similar but different? *Journal of Personality Disorders, 29*, 115–130.

Lenzenweger, M. F., Lane, M. C., Loranger, A. W., & Kessler, R. C. (2007). DSM-IV personality disorders in the National Comorbidity Survey Replication. *Biological Psychiatry, 62*, 553–564.

Livesley, W. J., & West, M. (1986). The DSM-III distinction between schizoid and avoidant personality disorders. *Canadian Journal of Psychiatry, 31*, 59–61.

Livesley, W. J., West, M., & Tanney, A. (1985). Historical comment on DSM-III schizoid and avoidant personality disorders. *American Journal of Psychiatry, 142*, 1344–1347.

Lochner, C., Serebro, P., van der Merwe, L., Hemmings, S., Kinnear, C., Seedat, S., & Stein, D. J. (2011). Comorbid obsessive-compulsive personality disorder in obsessive-compulsive disorder (OCD): A marker of severity. *Progress in Neuro-Psychopharmacology & Biological Psychiatry, 35,* 1087–1092.

Lynam, D. R., & Widiger, T. A. (2001). Using the five factor model to represent the DSM-IV personality disorders: An expert consensus approach. *Journal of Abnormal Psychology, 110,* 401–412.

Lynum, L. I., Wilberg, T., & Karterud, S. (2008). Self-esteem in patients with borderline and avoidant personality disorders. *Scandinavian Journal of Psychology, 49,* 469–477.

McGlashan, T. H., Grilo, C. M., Skodol, A. E., Gunderson, J. G., Shea, M. T., Morey, L. C., ... Stout, R. L. (2000). The Collaborative Longitudinal Personality Disorders Study: baseline Axis I/II and II/II diagnostic co-occurrence. *Acta Psychiatrica Scandinavica, 102,* 256–264.

Millon, T. (1969). *Modern Psychopathology: A Biosocial Approach to Maladaptive Learning and Functioning.* Philadelphia: W. B. Saunders.

Millon, T. (1973). *Theories of Psychopathology and Personality* (2nd ed.). Philadelphia: W. B. Saunders.

Millon, T. (1977). *Millon Clinical Multiaxial Inventory Manual* (2nd ed.). Minneapolis: National Computer Systems.

Millon, T. (1993). Negativistic (passive-aggressive) personality disorder. *Journal of Personality Disorders, 7,* 78–85.

Morey, L. C. (1988). Personality disorders in DSM-III and DSM-III-R: Convergence, coverage, and internal consistency. *American Journal of Psychiatry, 145,* 573–577.

Morey, L. C., & Benson, K. T. (2016). An investigation of adherence to diagnostic criteria, revisited: Clinical diagnosis of the DSM-IV/DSM-5 Section II personality disorders. *Journal of Personality Disorders, 30,* 130–144.

Morey, L. C., Hopwood, C. J., & Klein, D. (2007). Depressive, passive-aggressive, and sadistic personality disorders. In W. O'Donohue, K. A. Fowler, & S. O. Lilienfeld (Eds.), *Personality Disorders: Toward the DSM-V* (pp. 353–374). Thousand Oaks, CA: Sage Publications.

Morey, L. C., & Ochoa, E. S. (1989). An investigation of adherence to diagnostic criteria: Clinical diagnosis of the DSM-III personality disorders. *Journal of Personality Disorders, 3,* 180–192.

Nestadt, G., Addington, A., Samuels, J., Liang, K., Bienvenu, O. J., Riddle, M., ... Cullen, B. (2003). The identification of OCD-related subgroups based on comorbidity. *Biological Psychiatry, 53,* 914–920.

Oldham, J. M., Skodol, A. E., Kellman, H. D., Hyler, S. E., Doidge, N., Rosnick, L., & Gallaher, P. E. (1995). Comorbidity of axis I and axis II disorders. *American Journal of Psychiatry, 152,* 571–578.

Pinto, A., Steinglass, J. E., Greene, A. L., Weber, E. U., & Simpson, H. B. (2014). Capacity to delay reward differentiates obsessive-compulsive disorder and obsessive-compulsive personality disorder. *Biological Psychiatry, 75,* 653–659.

Pretzer, J. L., & Beck, A. T. (1996). A cognitive theory of personality disorders. In J. F. Clarkin and M. F. Lenzenweger (Eds.), *Major Theories of Personality Disorder* (pp. 36–105). New York: Guilford Press.

Ralevski, E., Sanislow, C. A., Grilo, C. M., Skodol, A. E., Gunderson, J. G., Shea, M. T., ... McGlashan, T. H. (2005). Avoidant personality disorder and social phobia: Distinct enough to be separate disorders? *Acta Psychiatrica Scandinavica, 112,* 208–214.

Reed, G. M. (2018). Progress in developing classification of personality disorders for ICD-11. *World Psychiatry, 17,* 227–229.

Sanislow, C. A., Bartolini, E., & Zoloth, E. C. (2012). Avoidant personality disorder. In V. S. Ramachandran (Ed.), *Encyclopedia of Human Behavior* (2nd ed., pp. 257–266). San Diego, CA: Academic Press.

Sanislow, C. A., da Cruz, K., Gianoli, M. O., & Reagan, E. R. (2012). Avoidant personality disorder, traits, and type. In T. A. Widiger (Ed.), *The Oxford Handbook of Personality Disorders* (pp. 549–565). New York: Oxford University Press.

Sanislow, C. A., Little, T. D., Ansell, E. B., Grilo, C. M., Daversa, M., Markowitz, J. C., ... McGlashan, T. H. (2009). Ten-year stability and latent structure of the DSM-IV schizotypal, borderline, avoidant, and obsessive-compulsive personality disorders. *Journal of Abnormal Psychology, 118,* 507–519.

Sanislow, C. A., & McGlashan, T. H. (1998). Treatment outcome of personality disorders. *Canadian Journal of Psychiatry, 43,* 237–250.

Sanislow, C. A., Morey, L. C., Grilo, C. M., Gunderson, J. G., Shea, M. T., Skodol, A. E., ... McGlashan, T. H. (2002). Confirmatory factor analysis of DSM-IV schizotypal, borderline, avoidant, and obsessive-compulsive personality disorders: Findings from the Collaborative Longitudinal Study of Personality Disorders. *Acta Psychiatrica Scandinavica, 105,* 28–36.

Sanislow, C. A., Pine, D. S., Quinn, K. J., Kozak, M. J., Garvey, M. A., Heinssen, R. K. ... Cuthbert, B. N. (2010). Developing constructs for psychopathology research: Research Domain Criteria. *Journal of Abnormal Psychology, 119,* 631–639.

Schmidt, L. A., & Jetha, M. K. (2009). Temperament and affect vulnerability: Behavioral, electrocortical, and neuroimaging perspectives. In M. de Haan & M. R. Gunnar (Eds.), *Handbook of Developmental Social Neuroscience* (pp. 305–323). New York: Guilford Press.

Serpella, L., Livingstone, A., Neidermanb, M., & Laska, B. (2002). Anorexia nervosa: Obsessive-compulsive disorder, obsessive-compulsive personality disorder, or neither? *Clinical Psychology Review, 22,* 647–669.

Shea, M. T., Stout, R. L., Yen, S., Pagano, M. E., Skodol, A. E., Morey, L. C., ... Zanarini, M. C. (2004). Associations in the course of personality disorders and axis I disorders over time. *Journal of Abnormal Psychology, 113,* 499–508.

Siever, L. J., & Davis, K. L. (1991). A psychobiological perspective on the personality disorders. *American Journal of Psychiatry, 148,* 1647–1658.

Skocic, S., Jackson, H., & Hulbert, C. (2015). Beyond DSM-5: An alternative approach to assessing social anxiety disorder. *Journal of Anxiety Disorders, 30,* 8–15.

Skodol, A. E. (2012). Personality disorders in DSM-5. *Annual Review of Clinical Psychology, 8,* 317–344.

Skodol, A. E., Gunderson, J. G., Shea, M. T., McGlashan, T. H., Morey, L. C., Sanislow, ... Stout, R. L. (2005). The Collaborative Longitudinal Personality Disorders Study (CLPS): Overview and implications. *Journal of Personal Disorders, 19,* 487–504.

Skodol, A. E., Morey, L. C., Bender, D. S., & Oldham, J. M. (2015). The alternative model for personality disorders: A clinical application. *American Journal of Psychiatry, 172,* 606–613.

Skodol, A. E., Oldham, J. M., Hyler, S. E., Stein, D. J., Hollander, E., Gallaher, P. E., & Lopez, A. E. (1995). Patterns of anxiety and personality disorder comorbidity. *Journal of Psychiatric Research, 29,* 361–367.

Stuart, S., Pfohl, B., Battaglia, M., Bellodi, L., Grove, W., & Cadoret, R. (1998). The cooccurrence of DSM-III-R personality disorders. *Journal of Personality Disorders, 12,* 302–315.

Swendsen, J. D., & Merikangas, K. R. (2000). The comorbidity of depression and substance use disorders. *Clinical Psychology Review, 20*, 173–189.

Thornton, C., & Russell, J. (1997). Obsessive compulsive comorbidity in the dieting disorders. *International Journal of Eating Disorders, 21*, 83–87.

Trull, T. J., Widiger, T. A., & Frances, A. (1987). Covariation of criteria sets for avoidant, schizoid, and dependent personality disorders. *American Journal of Psychiatry, 144*, 767–771.

van Velzen, C. J. M., Emmelkamp, P. M. G., & Scholing, A. (2000). Generalized social phobia versus avoidant personality disorder: Differences in psychopathology, personality traits, and social and occupational functioning. *Journal of Anxiety Disorders, 14*, 395–411.

Wakefield, J. C. (1992). Disorder as harmful dysfunction: A conceptual critique of *DSM-III-R*'s definition of mental disorder. *Psychological Review, 99*, 232–247.

War Department. (1946). Nomenclature of psychiatric disorders and reactions: War Department Technical Bulletin, Medical 203. *Journal of Clinical Psychology, 2*, 289–296.

Warner, M. B., Morey, L. C., Finch, J. F., Gunderson, J. G., Skodol, A. E., Sanislow, C. A., ... Grilo, C. M. (2004). The longitudinal relationship of personality traits and disorders. *Journal of Abnormal Psychology, 113*, 217–227.

Wetzler, S., & Morey, L.C. (1999). Passive-aggressive personality disorder: The demise of a syndrome. *Psychiatry, 62*, 49–59.

Wheaton, M. G., & Pinto, A. (2017). The role of experiential avoidance in obsessive-compulsive personality disorder traits. *Personality Disorders: Theory, Research, and Treatment, 8*, 383–388.

Zanarini, M. C., Frankenburg, F. R., Hennen, J., Reich, D. B., & Silk, K. R. (2006). Prediction of the 10-year course of borderline personality disorder. *American Journal of Psychiatry, 163*, 827–832.

Zimmerman, M., Rothschild, L., & Chelminski, I. (2005). The prevalence of DSM-IV personality disorders in psychiatric outpatients. *American Journal of Psychiatry, 162*, 1911–1918.

13a Epidemiological, Factor-Analytic, and Cognitive Factors in the Position of Obsessive-Compulsive Personality Disorder among the Cluster C Personality Disorders: Commentary on Cluster C Anxious-Fearful Personality Pathology and Avoidance

ARNOUD ARNTZ

The chapter by Sanislow and Hector gives an excellent overview of the history of the Cluster C personality disorders (PDs). Currently, three PDs are assumed to be part of this cluster. However, one of them, Obsessive-Compulsive PD (OCPD), seems to deviate from the others in a range of areas. In support of this assertion, I will discuss research varying from epidemiological to information processing studies. Following Sanislow and Hector's suggestion to go beyond variants of the DSM structure by using transdiagnostic constructs, this commentary addresses three key points including: (1) contributions of epidemiology research with a focus on differences between obsessive-compulsive personality disorder (OCPD) and other PDs; (2) factor-analytic evidence for the DSM cluster structure of PDs; and (3) the role of cognitive processes and structures.

EPIDEMIOLOGY: THE STRANGE POSITION OF OCPD COMPARED TO OTHER PDs

Epidemiological research has documented peculiar characteristics of OCPD. First, whereas in the general population most if not all PDs are associated with indices of poorer social-economic functioning, this appears to be not the case for OCPD. On the contrary, in the general population OCPD is associated with higher educational level, higher income, socioeconomic status, and is not associated with unfortunate living situations (Torgersen, 2012). Moreover, in contrast to the data supporting the point made by Sanislow and Hector that OCPD is characterized by severe interpersonal problems such as a lack of empathy, there is no evidence at all that OCPD is associated with poorer marital functioning, more divorce, or more living without a partner (Torgersen, 2012). Third, a similar picture emerges across studies with respect to quality of life and level of functioning, with no association between OCPD and these variables in the general population. Fourth, whereas prevalences in the general population (in Western countries) are about 2.5 percent for Avoidant PD (AVPD), 1 percent for Dependent PD (DEPD)

and 2 percent for OCPD, the prevalences in *clinical samples* show a very different picture: about 25 percent for AVPD and 15 percent for DEPD, but only 10 percent for OCPD. Thus, whereas the clinical vs. general prevalence ratios are 10:1 and 15:1 for AVPD and DEPD, the ratio is only 5:1 for OCPD (data from Torgersen, 2012). Thus, unexpectedly small numbers of people with OCPD seek help in mental healthcare, again indicating the relatively good functioning of many people with OCPD.

These findings question whether OCPD as defined by the DSM criteria is a disorder at all. Indeed, many of the OCPD traits as currently defined, and associated characteristics, match well with the current values of Western societies, such as putting ratio above emotion or social considerations, perfectionism, productivity, control, hard working, and taking high responsibility (e.g., Pfohl & Blum, 1995). This suggests that there is not so much deviation of OCPD traits from cultural norms. Interestingly, one usually sees OCPD patients after they decompensated because of working too hard, e.g., with an initial clinical presentation of depression or burnout. Alternatively, epidemiological studies among the general population might have overestimated the prevalence of OCPD, e.g., by not validly assessing whether the traits cause dysfunction –although this argument would hold for all PDs.

Following from questions about the role and level of functional impairment in OCPD, we next move to discuss the ways in which OCPD also has a *status aparte* from the other PDs at the level of cluster structure.

FACTOR-ANALYTIC EVIDENCE FOR THE DSM CLUSTER STRUCTURE OF PDs

How does OCPD fit within the cluster structure that the DSM hypothesizes? To answer this, a second order principal component analysis (PCA) was done on a SCID-II trait score data set of $n = 2165$ patients and non-patients (34.3 percent men; M age = 33.04, range 16–66, SD = 11.05). This data set is an extension of one that was previously used for taxometric analyses (Arntz et al.,

Table 13.a.1 Factor loadings of SCID-II trait scores per PD on components after oblimin rotation

PD Scale	Component		
	1	2	3
Avoidant		.79	
Dependent		.86	
Obsessive-Compulsive		.45	
Paranoid	.43	.32	.35
Schizotypal	.64		
Schizoid	.82		
Histrionic			.76
Narcissistic			.73
Borderline		.31	.60
Anti-social			.63

Note: Loadings < .25 are not presented. Loadings > .40 printed bold.

Table 13.a.2 Component correlation matrix

Component	1	2	3
1	1.00		
2	.22	1.00	
3	.23	.13	1.00

2009). In that study good evidence was found for a factor structure following the DSM-IV classification of PDs, and for a dimensional rather than a categorical nature of the PD traits of six PDs (including the three Cluster C PDs).

For the present PCA, 1–2–3 trait scores were summed per PD to get a dimensional score per PD, and a first PCA was run to inspect the scree plot to decide on how many components to extract. Next, a PCA was run with this number of components followed with oblimin rotation, thus allowing for correlation between components. For the first analysis, the Depressive and the Negativistic (= Passive Aggressive) PDs were excluded, as not being fully acknowledged in the DSM-IV.

There were three components with eigenvalue > 1 and the scree plot indicated three components. These explained 58 percent of the variance. The factor loadings after oblimin rotations are given in Table 13.a.1. As can be seen, the first component reflects Cluster A, the second Cluster C, and the third Cluster B. There are three additional cross-loadings, though they are all ≤ .35: the Paranoid scale also loads on components 2 and 3, thus shares variance with clusters B and C; and the Borderline scale loads on component 2, i.e., shares variance with Cluster C. Nevertheless, *grosso modo* the clusters are quite convincingly recovered in the data. Table 13.a.2 presents the correlations between the components, which are very modest, giving further evidence for relatively independent clusters.

When Depressive and Negativistic PD scales were added, results were very similar: again three components appeared, corresponding with the three PD-clusters. Depressive PD loaded solely on the Cluster C factor (.75), Negativistic PD on both Cluster B (.51) and C (.32).

The three clusters hypothesized by the DSM model of PDs were well recovered in the data as second order factors. The three cross-loadings were rather small in size, and fit with clinical observations and research (e.g., Arntz, Weertman, & Salet, 2011) that Borderline PD shows phenomena that overlap with Cluster C, such high fear, guilt and shame feelings, feelings of inferiority, and rejection sensitivity, and that many patients with Paranoid PD are less "psychotic" than the other Cluster A PDs, and share features with Cluster B and Cluster C patients – for example, their treatment response to Cluster B and C based treatment models is quite good (e.g., Bamelis, Evers, Spinhoven, & Arntz, 2014).

Replicating previous studies discussed by Sanislow and Hector, the results also show that Negativistic (Passive-Aggressive) PD loaded on both Cluster B and C, notably even stronger on Cluster B. Thus, passive-aggressive traits might be more characteristic of Cluster B PD pathology than of Cluster C, perhaps related to the relatively strong presence of anger in the criteria (Sanislow and Hector, this volume). Another remarkable finding is that Obsessive-Compulsive PD (OCPD) does not load highly on the second order Cluster C factor. Unlike Paranoid PD, which also shows a limited loading on its hypothesized cluster, there are no cross-loadings that help us to explain. This suggests that OCPD differs from other PDs in Cluster C in ways that cannot be explained by characteristics that belong to Cluster A or B. Indeed, it has been questioned before whether a fourth general factor underlies OCPD (de Reus & Emmelkamp, 2012). I will now address how OCPD has its own characteristics from the point of view of cognitive models of PDs.

COGNITIVE PROCESSES AND STRUCTURES

Cognitive models of PDs hypothesize that schemas that steer information processing underlie the PD. At least part of schemas can be represented in beliefs that people may be aware of, which they then can evaluate as to how strongly they believe them. Indeed, studies indicated that different PDs are characterized by specific sets of beliefs as assessed with self-report, including all Cluster C PDs (Arntz, Dreessen, Schouten, & Weertman, 2004; Beck et al., 2001). An important information processing bias is interpretational bias. One study indeed found evidence for interpretational biases in Borderline, Avoidant, and Dependent PD, but *not* in OCPD, when assessing choice and believability of preformulated interpretations of ambiguous scenarios (Arntz et al., 2011). Moreover, the interpretations hypothesized to be specific for OCPD turned out to be very popular and highly believable among non-patients. This suggests that the way OCPD patients tend to view situations is not strongly deviating from what is normal in Western culture. Open responses to ambiguous scenarios were also investigated, and here OCPD showed increased responses expressing compulsiveness and worry, as well as reduced flexibility and acceptance, compared to non-patients. These categories point more to processing peculiarities in OCPD than to characteristic *content* of interpretations. Moreover, OCPD was not related to open responses related to avoidance and self-criticism, neither to guilt and fear of judgment; whereas the other Cluster C PDs showed elevated scores on these types of open responses. In sum, this interpretation study suggested that OCPD is not so much characterized by typical interpretational content, compared to non-patients, but rather by deviating cognitive styles of rigidity, compulsiveness, and worry.

However, this interpretation study can be criticized for at least two reasons. First, response options for healthy interpretations were missing in the closed format part, to prevent socially desirable answers. However, this might have led the non-patients to opt for the relatively least dysfunctional options, those hypothesized to be specific for OCPD. Second, interpretational processes may take place at an automatic level, and explicit assessment might therefore miss important biases. Indeed, a study into implicit cognitive biases in OCPD found evidence for biases that people are not necessarily aware of, with OCPD being associated with self-views of being responsible, conscientious, disciplined, etc., and views of other people as being irresponsible, lazy, undisciplined, etc. (Weertman, Arntz, de Jong, & Rinck, 2008). Interestingly, this tendency to view others in derogatory ways, and the self as superior in these areas is not what one would expect in a Cluster C PD. Is there further evidence that OCPD shows a cognitive profile that is atypical for people from the anxious-fearful cluster?

A study investigating profiles in schema modes of six PDs indeed indicates a very different constellation in OCPD than in the other Cluster C PDs (Bamelis et al., 2014). (Schema modes refer to a construct describing the momentary cognitive-emotional-behavioral state the person is in, resulting from the way a person copes with an activated schema.) For instance, whereas AVPD and DEPD show increased vulnerable child modes, reflecting an emotional vulnerable state that would be common in children when they are in emotional need, OCPD did not show any association with such modes (despite that theory assumes an association, and despite associations between OCPD and childhood emotional abuse, dysfunctional parenting experiences, etc. (e.g., de Reus &

Emmelkamp, 2012; Lobbestael, Arntz, & Bernstein, 2010)). Moreover, whereas a punitive internalization of caregivers characterized AVPD and DEPD, it was a demanding internalization that characterized OCPD. A powerful use of an overcompensating style of coping with schema activation is expected to lead to successful keeping vulnerable child modes out of awareness. Indeed, whereas AVPD and DEPD were characterized by avoidant types of coping, OCPD was characterized by overcompensating. Interestingly, overcompensating to keep vulnerable schemas out of awareness is characteristic of Narcissistic, Histrionic, and Anti-Social PDs – that are usually viewed as quite distinct from Cluster C PDs.

In sum, studies of cognitive models of PDs have indicated quite a difference in cognitive processes and structures between OCPD and the other Cluster C PDs. Superficially, there seems to be little difference between OCPD and non-patients when one examines conscious interpretations, whereas there is a clear distinction between the other Cluster C PDs and non-patients. However, there appear to be distinctive styles in OCPD, characterized by lack of flexibility, problems with accepting problematic situations, compulsiveness and worry. When one examines implicit measures, OCPD is clearly different from non-patients, with superior views of the self and inferior views of others. Lastly, OCPD seems associated with keeping vulnerable feelings out of awareness by an overcompensating style of control and perfectionism, which is unique among Cluster C PDs.

CONCLUSIONS

Research into epidemiology, factor-analytic structures, and cognitive models all indicated that OCPD has a position that is different from the other Cluster C PDs. In the general population, there is little indication that OCPD is associated with (highly) problematic dysfunctioning. Given the general prevalence, the prevalence in clinical sample is, compared to other PDs, unexpectedly low.

Examining findings from factor-analytic studies, the association between OCPD and the second order Cluster C factor is rather weak. As a result, it has been proposed that a distinct latent trait not subsumed by the three clusters underlies OCPD. Considering the results of studies into cognitive models, we see again evidence for a relatively weak distinction between normality and OCPD when it comes to interpretations. However, a specific overcompensating style of dealing with vulnerable feelings might create a superficially similarity with "normal" Western beliefs and values. Nevertheless, the degree to which perfectionism, control, responsibility, conscientiousness and the like are used as compensating strategies is excessive and creates the risk of burnout and depression.

Building on the points raised, the somewhat narcissistic way in which OCPD is characterized by superior self- and derogatory other views is very different from what is commonly seen in the other Cluster C PDs. Thus, anxiety, fear, and avoidance seem to play a much less central role in OCPD than in AVPD and DEPD, whereas a more over-compensating style seems to be much more central.

However, other processes than discussed so far might contribute to a distinct position of OCPD. For instance, it has been proposed that OCPD develops from another compensating dynamic, using control and obsession for details to deal with cognitive disorganization caused by executive control deficits (Aycicegi-Dinn, Caldwell-Harris, & Dinn, 2009).

Clearly, further research into cognitive processes and structures will further advance our understanding of the differences and commonalities between OCPD and the other Cluster C PDs. That said, there might be a need for a refined formulation of OCPD traits so that a better distinction can be made between functional and dysfunctional forms of this personality dimension, thus allowing for a better understanding of its role as a Cluster C PD.

REFERENCES

Arntz, A., Bernstein, D., Gielen, D., van Nieuwenhuyzen, M., Penders, K., Haslam, N., & Ruscio, J. (2009). Taxometric evidence for the dimensional structure of Cluster C, paranoid, and borderline personality disorders. *Journal of Personality Disorders*, 23(6), 606–628.

Arntz, A., Dreessen, L., Schouten, E., & Weertman, A. (2004). Beliefs in personality disorders: A test with the personality disorder belief questionnaire. *Behaviour Research and Therapy*, 42(10), 1215–1225.

Arntz, A., Weertman, A., & Salet, S. (2011). Interpretation bias in Cluster C and borderline personality disorders. *Behaviour Research and Therapy*, 49(8), 472–481.

Aycicegi-Dinn, A., Caldwell-Harris, C. L., & Dinn, W. M. (2009). Obsessive-compulsive personality traits: Compensatory response to executive function deficit? *International Journal of Neuroscience*, 119, 600–608.

Bamelis, L. L. M., Evers, S. M. A. A., Spinhoven, P., & Arntz, A. (2014). Results of a multicentered randomised controlled trial of the clinical effectiveness of schema therapy for personality disorders. *American Journal of Psychiatry*, 171, 305–322.

Beck, A. T., Butler, A. C., Brown, G. K., Dahlsgaard, K. K., Newman, C. F., & Beck, J. S. (2001). Dysfunctional beliefs discriminate personality disorders. *Behaviour Research and Therapy*, 39(10), 1213–1225.

de Reus, R. J. M. & Emmelkamp, P. M. G. (2012). Obsessive-compulsive personality disorder: A review of current empirical findings. *Personality and Mental Health*, 6(1), 1–21.

Lobbestael, J., Arntz, A., & Bernstein, D. P. (2010). Disentangling the relationship between different types of childhood maltreatment and personality disorders. *Journal of Personality Disorders*, 24(3), 285–295.

Pfohl, B., & Blum, N. (1995). Obsessive-compulsive personality disorder. In W. J. Lively (Ed.), *The DSM-IV Personality Disorders* (pp. 261–276). New York: Guilford Press.

Torgersen, S. (2012). Epidemiology. In T. A. Widiger (Ed.), *The Oxford Handbook of Personality Disorders* (pp. 186–205). New York: Oxford University Press.

Weertman, A., Arntz, A., de Jong, P. J., & Rinck, M. (2008). Implicit self- and other-associations in obsessive-compulsive personality disorder traits. *Cognition and Emotion*, 22(7), 1253–1275.

13b Examining Cluster C Personality Pathology Using an Interpersonal Lens: Commentary on Cluster C Anxious-Fearful Personality Pathology and Avoidance

NICOLE M. CAIN

The chapter by Sanislow and Hector (this volume) provided an excellent overview of Cluster C personality pathology with a particular focus on anxiety, fear, and avoidant behaviors. The authors were comprehensive in describing the evolution of anxious-fearful and avoidant personality pathology throughout the various editions of the DSM, as well as highlighting important changes in how DSM-5 (APA, 2013) Section III, the Alternative Model for Personality Disorders (AMPD), assesses Cluster C pathology. The section on using NIMH RDoC to investigate anxious-fearful-avoidant pathology was particularly relevant to personality disorder (PD) researchers and highlighted several ways that Cluster C pathology fits within the RDoC matrix. One of the unifying themes of the chapter was the emphasis on social processes and the relationship between social functioning and Cluster C pathology. I offer comments intended to extend and elaborate on this theme by arguing that interpersonal theory provides a valuable lens through which to view Cluster C pathology.

Sanislow and Hector (this volume) highlighted that individuals diagnosed with Cluster C PDs are likely to view others as a source of frustration and tend to report significant interpersonal problems and distress. Diagnostic criteria reflect the salience of interpersonal dysfunction across all PD diagnoses and clinicians of all theoretical orientations who treat personality pathology (e.g., Benjamin, 2003; Clarkin, Yeomans, & Kernberg, 2006; Linehan, 1993), including Cluster C, are inevitably faced with threats to the therapeutic alliance, dissolution of important relations, as well as damage to the patient's life caused by entrenched maladaptive interpersonal behaviors. Thus, it is not surprising that interpersonal difficulties are a critical feature of personality pathology, leading Hopwood and colleagues (Hopwood, Wright, Ansell, & Pincus, 2013) to argue that PDs are fundamentally interpersonal in nature.

Interpersonal theory asserts that the most important expressions of personality and psychopathology occur in phenomena involving more than one person, the interpersonal situation (Sullivan, 1953). Pincus and Ansell (2013) noted that the interpersonal situation is the experience of a pattern of relating self with other associated with varying levels of anxiety (or security) in which learning takes place that significantly influences the development of self-concept and social behavior. The interpersonal situation is intimately tied to the genesis, development, maintenance, and mutability of personality and PD through the continuous patterning and repatterning of interpersonal experience (social learning) in an effort to satisfy fundamental human motives (e.g., agency and communion) in ways that increase security and self-esteem (positively reinforcing) and avoid anxiety (negatively reinforcing). Over time, this social learning leads to the development of mental representations of self and others (Blatt, Auerbach, & Levy, 1997) as well as enduring patterns of adaptive or maladaptive interpersonal behavior (Benjamin, 2003; Hopwood, 2018; Pincus, 2005).

Agency and communion provide helpful dimensions for conceptualizing interpersonal situations and their mental representations (Pincus, 2005; Wiggins, 2003). Agency is manifested in strivings for power and mastery, while communion is found in strivings for intimacy and connection with others. These meta-concepts also form the interpersonal circumplex (IPC; Leary, 1957), with the underlying dimensions of dominance-submission (agency) on the vertical axis and nurturance-coldness (communion) on the horizontal axis. The IPC has been used to describe both adaptive and maladaptive interpersonal behavior and to describe a person's typical way of relating to others, i.e., their interpersonal style.

Applying the IPC to Cluster C pathology, Cain and colleagues (Cain, Ansell, Simpson, & Pinto, 2015) examined the specific types of interpersonal problems and interpersonal sensitivities associated with obsessive-compulsive PD (OCPD). As noted by Sanislow and Hector (this volume), individuals with OCPD find it difficult to relax and are preoccupied with work to the detriment of social relations. These individuals are often also characterized as rigid and controlling, which can lead to hostility toward others. In a clinical sample of adult outpatients diagnosed with OCPD, Cain et al. found that these individuals reported hostile-dominant interpersonal problems and sensitivity to warm-dominant behavior in others. This interpersonal pattern suggests that individuals with OCPD are overly controlling, vindictive, and cold in their interpersonal relationships, while also being sensitive to or irritated by warm, communal approach behaviors by others. These results suggest that interpersonal warmth in particular is an interpersonal irritant for individuals with OCPD. It is likely that warm, communal behavior in others frustrates the interpersonal motives (Horowitz et al., 2006) of patients with OCPD, which involve being more emotionally restrained, rigid, and controlling in relationships. This interpersonal pattern is consistent with the description of the avoidance behavior commonly observed in OCPD provided by Sanislow and Hector (this volume). These individuals are likely to emphasize work and productivity at the expense of intimacy and connection with others.

Sanislow and Hector (this volume) also note that OCPD is associated with deficits in empathy. Cain and colleagues (2015) used the Interpersonal Reactivity Index (IRI; Davis, 1980) to investigate different facets of empathy in individuals with OCPD. Results showed that individuals with OCPD reported low levels of perspective taking as compared to healthy controls. Perspective taking is the ability to spontaneously adopt the psychological viewpoint of others. In contrast, there were no significant differences between individuals with OCPD and healthy controls on empathic concern. Empathic concern involves sympathy and concern for the unfortunate circumstances of others, a more affective component of empathy. These results suggest that individuals with OCPD may have the *capacity* to experience sympathy and concern for others and may be able to intuit the appropriate affective response to another person, similar to healthy controls, but are limited in their *ability* to subsequently demonstrate the appropriate emotional response in a social situation or adopt the other person's point of view.

Interpersonal theory also allows us to move past static individual differences to investigate more dynamic aspects of personality pathology (Cain & Ansell, 2015; Hopwood, 2018), such as pathoplasticity. As noted by Sanislow and Hector (this volume), pathoplasticity refers to the mutually influencing, non-etiological relationship between psychopathology and another psychological system (Shea et al., 2004). Interpersonal pathoplasticity emphasizes that the expression of certain maladaptive behaviors, symptoms, and mental disorders tend to occur in the larger context of an individual's interpersonal functioning. In this way, interpersonal style has the potential for influencing the content and focus of symptoms and will likely shape the responses and coping strategies individuals employ when presented with psychological and social stressors (Cain & Ansell, 2015).

Related to Cluster C pathology, Alden and Capreol (1993) examined interpersonal pathoplasticity in a sample of outpatients diagnosed with avoidant personality disorder (AVPD). Results showed that AVPD was associated with two distinct interpersonal subtypes, an exploitable AVPD subtype and a cold AVPD subtype. Patients in the exploitable AVPD subtype reported interpersonal problems with being overly warm and submissive, while patients in the cold AVPD subtype reported problems with being withdrawn and isolated in their relationships. Interestingly, patients in the exploitable AVPD subtype benefited from both graduated exposure and interpersonal skills training interventions targeting their social avoidance, while patients in the cold AVPD subtype only benefited from graduated exposure for their avoidance behaviors. These results suggest the importance of examining interpersonal motivation (Horowitz et al., 2006) to understand social avoidance in AVPD. Those patients in the exploitable AVPD subtype may be more responsive to interpersonal skills training given their motivation for intimacy and connection, while those in the cold AVPD subtype may be using self-protective motives to avoid social rejection and may initially react poorly to interventions aimed at maximizing social closeness. The patients in the cold AVPD group may be more prone to treatment noncompliance or dropout to protect themselves from rejection by others. Treatment may need to use a graduated exposure model to slowly decrease fears about social rejection before a more interpersonally focused skills approach could be useful. These results were subsequently replicated by Cain and colleagues (Cain, Pincus, & Grosse Holtforth, 2010) in a sample of outpatients diagnosed with social phobia, a disorder which shares many clinical features with AVPD as noted by Sanislow and Hector (this volume). Cain et al. found two interpersonal subtypes in social phobia, a friendly-submissive subtype similar to the exploitable AVPD subtype and a cold-submissive subtype similar to the cold AVPD subtype. As expected, the friendly-submissive social phobia subtype reported significantly lower social anxiety and significantly higher well-being and satisfaction at post-treatment than those in the cold-submissive social phobia subtype.

In addition to investigations of pathoplasticity, interpersonal theory also uses agency and communion to model both stability and variability in self–other processes. These self–other patterns are referred to as interpersonal signatures (Fournier, Moskowitz, & Zuroff, 2009; Hopwood, 2018). Research on interpersonal signatures is based on the seminal work of Mischel and Shoda (1995) on the cognitive-affective processing system (CAPS), which argues that individuals encode the psychological features of a given situation through a complex configuration of within-person structures and processes (i.e., cognitive-affective units) that include competencies, expectancies, values, and goals. This complex system of interrelated structures and processes gives rise to stable, but situation-contingent *if … then* dispositions or behavioral signatures, such that each individual demonstrates stable levels of behavior within situations and stable patterns of behavior across situations. Within interpersonal theory, the situations in which cognitive and affective processing are primarily observed are interpersonal in nature along the dimensions of agency and communion.

Wang and colleagues (2014) investigated the interpersonal signature associated with high dependency by examining intra-individual variability in interpersonal and emotional functioning over a seven-day period in a sample of undergraduate students. They found that for participants with higher dependency, perceiving others as submissive and unfriendly was associated with decreased positive emotion. Wang et al. note that experiencing others as more submissive may run counter to dependency needs, suggesting to the highly dependent individual that they may need to be more autonomous. This likely evokes uncertainty and dysregulation, thus decreasing positive affect. Conversely, a more agentic and communal other would be consistent with dependency needs and likely to contribute to feeling secure and satisfied within the relationship. This interpersonal signature is consistent with the description of dependent personality disorder (DPD) provided by Sanislow and Hector (this volume), highlighting that those with DPD often have difficulty with asserting themselves and desire being taken care of by others.

Wang and colleagues (2014) also found that in those with high dependency, perceiving others as dominant and unfriendly was associated with being more quiet and passive in the interaction. This pattern of becoming less activated by dominant, unfriendly others may serve to help those with high dependency to maintain relationships with these more dominant others. This type of relationship would be consistent with the need to rely on stronger, more competent others, even if the relationship is also unpleasant. Research has shown that higher dependency is associated with perceiving dominance in others as also friendly (Roche, Pincus, Hyde, Conroy, & Ram, 2013), and perhaps this perception serves to help those with high dependency maintain relationships with dominant-unfriendly others. Future research should continue to examine interpersonal signatures in Cluster C pathology.

In sum, Sanislow and Hector (this volume) argue for moving beyond DSM structure to understand Cluster C pathology. I agree, and have offered comments illustrating how interpersonal theory can play a central role in advancing the assessment and treatment of Cluster C pathology. Interpersonal theory provides a useful framework for understanding the complex social processes that signify personality pathology. A thorough assessment of interpersonal functioning in Cluster C pathology will allow us to more specifically target the interpersonal difficulties associated with these anxious-dependent-avoidant pathologies.

REFERENCES

Alden, L. E., & Capreol, M. J. (1993). Avoidant personality disorder: Interpersonal problems as predictors of treatment response. *Behavior Therapy, 24,* 357–376.

American Psychiatric Association. (2013). Diagnostic and Statistical Manual of Mental Disorders (5th ed.). Arlington, VA: American Psychiatric Publishing.

Benjamin, L. S. (2003). *Interpersonal Reconstructive Therapy: Promoting Change in Nonresponders.* New York: Guilford Press.

Blatt, S. J., Auerbach, J. S., & Levy, K. N. (1997). Mental representations in personality development, psychopathology, and the therapeutic process. *Review of General Psychology, 1,* 351–374.

Cain, N. M., & Ansell, E. B. (2015). An integrative interpersonal framework for personality pathology. In S. Huprich (Ed.), *Personality Disorders: Toward Theoretical and Empirical Integration in Diagnosis and Assessment* (pp. 345–362). Washington, DC: American Psychological Association.

Cain, N. M., Ansell, E. B., Simpson, H. B., & Pinto, A. (2015). Interpersonal functioning in obsessive-compulsive personality disorder. *Journal of Personality Assessment, 97,* 90–99.

Cain, N. M., Pincus, A. L., & Grosse Holtforth, M. (2010). Interpersonal subtypes in social phobia: Diagnostic and treatment implications. *Journal of Personality Assessment, 92,* 514–528.

Clarkin, J. F., Yeomans, F. E., & Kernberg, O. F. (2006). *Psychotherapy for Borderline Personality: Focusing on Object Relations.* Washington, DC: American Psychiatric Publishing.

Davis, M. (1980). A multidimensional approach to individual differences in empathy. *JSAS Catalog of Selected Documents in Psychology, 10,* 85.

Fournier, M., Moskowitz, D. S., & Zuroff, D. (2009). The interpersonal signature. *Journal of Research in Personality, 43,* 155–162.

Hopwood, C. J. (2018). Interpersonal dynamics in personality and personality disorder. *European Journal of Personality, 32,* 499–524.

Hopwood, C. J., Wright, A. G., Ansell, E. B., & Pincus, A. L. (2013). The interpersonal core of personality pathology. *Journal of Personality Disorders, 27,* 270–295.

Horowitz, L. M., Wilson, K. R., Turan, B., Zolotsev, P., Constantino, M. J., & Henderson, L. (2006). How interpersonal motives clarify the meaning of interpersonal behavior: A revised circumplex model. *Personality and Social Psychology Review, 10,* 67–86.

Leary, T. (1957). *Interpersonal Diagnosis of Personality.* New York: Ronald Press.

Linehan, M. M. (1993). *Cognitive-Behavioral Treatment for Borderline Personality Disorder.* New York: Guilford Press.

Mischel, W., & Shoda, Y. (1995). A cognitive-affective system theory of personality: Reconceptualizing situations, dispositions, dynamics, and invariance in personality structure. *Psychological Review, 102,* 246–268.

Pincus, A. L. (2005). A contemporary integrative interpersonal theory of personality disorders. In J. Clarkin & M. Lenzenweger (Eds.), *Major Theories of Personality Disorder* (2nd ed., pp. 282–331). New York: Guilford Press.

Pincus, A. L., & Ansell, E. B. (2013). Interpersonal theory of personality. In J. Suls & H. Tennen (Eds.), *Handbook of Psychology, Volume 5: Personality and Social Psychology* (2nd ed., pp. 141–159). Hoboken, NJ: Wiley.

Roche, M. J., Pincus, A. L., Hyde, A. L., Conroy, D. E., & Ram, N. (2013). Within-person co-variation of agentic and communal perceptions: Implications for interpersonal theory and assessment. *Journal of Research in Personality, 47,* 445–452.

Shea, M. T., Stout, R. L., Yen, S., Pagano, M. E., Skodol, A. E., Morey, L. C., … Zanarini, M. C. (2004). Associations in the course of personality disorders and Axis I disorders over time. *Journal of Abnormal Psychology, 113,* 499–508.

Sullivan, H. S. (1953). *The Interpersonal Theory of Psychiatry.* New York: W. W. Norton.

Wang, S., Roche, M. J., Pincus, A. L., Conroy, D. E., Rebar, A. L., & Ram, N. (2014). Interpersonal dependency and emotion in everyday life. *Journal of Research in Personality, 53,* 5–12.

Wiggins, J. S. (2003). *Paradigms of Personality Assessment.* New York: Guilford Press.

13c Processes, Mechanisms, and Progress: Author Rejoinder to Commentaries on Cluster C Anxious-Fearful Personality Pathology and Avoidance

CHARLES A. SANISLOW AND ANNA DARRE HECTOR

Commentaries on our chapter by Cain and Arntz raise compelling questions about the status quo as related to the Cluster C personality disorders. In response, we have taken the opportunity to clarify our perspective and elaborate our central thesis suggesting that an integration of mechanisms would open possibilities for new kinds of progress.

Cain (this volume) provided a persuasive argument for the validity and utility of interpersonal theory to enhance our understanding – and treatment – of anxious fearful pathology, and made a compelling case for interpersonal theory as vital to understand and treat anxious-fearful personality disorders. We agree. Cain illustrated the value of interpersonal theory for identifying pathognomonic patterns of maladaptive behavior, and for implementing treatment strategies. In our chapter, we made an appeal to integrate *internal* (psychological and biological) mechanisms into the study of personality pathology, elaborated ways that this might be done, and argued that this would move the field farther than another reorganization of symptoms. While we embrace Cain's argument for interpersonal processes, we also want to draw attention to elements of the person in the interpersonal situation. We do so with a focus on both interpersonal theory and mechanisms.

Cain traced the roots of interpersonal theory back to Sullivan (1953). Sullivan championed the idea of understanding human behavior and its aberrations through the lens of interpersonal process, and he realized the resulting empirical advantage towards efforts to identify pathologies and to change them for the better. In the predominant psychoanalytic thinking of his era, his focus on overt behavior was a radical departure from the then contemporary object relations theory. Sullivan was also a pragmatist because he targeted the treatment of pathology where it was manifested, in life and the therapy context. Moreover, he was ahead of his time because he connected interpersonal transactions to the internal mechanisms that humans brought to interaction. Key among the concepts introduced by Sullivan was his notion of *parataxic* distortions that served to minimize anxiety and facilitate

development – for better or worse – by creating expectancies and instances of selective inattention (Sullivan, 1953). Essentially, he was tapping mental operations that would decades later be elaborated by mainstream concepts in cognitive psychology (Carson, 1982).

Arntz (this volume) marshaled evidence based on structural models that challenged the structural organization of Cluster C, assembling evidence that obsessive-compulsive personality disorder (OCPD) is a misfit. We generally agree with this distinction, and findings from the Collaborative Longitudinal Personality Study including factor analysis (Sanislow et al., 2002) and comorbidities across clusters (McGlashan et al., 2000), support Arntz's contention. We hasten to add, however, that limiting focus to the symptom level to improve diagnosis is likely to have the unintended consequence of keeping us in the weeds. Structural models of psychopathology symptoms have value for identifying compelling symptom clusters, but validation requires spelling out connections to internal mechanisms (Sanislow, 2016).

Arntz does move on to make connections to internal mechanisms by reporting features of cognitive schemas that distinguish OCPD from other Cluster C personality disorders. Namely, OCPD patients tend to overcompensate to defend against vulnerable feelings, in contrast to other Cluster C sufferers who tend to rely on avoidance strategies. It may be matters of grain size or focus that there is lack of agreement in the extent to which different sorts of maladaptive behaviors share in common the avoidance (i.e., defense) of some form of anxiety. OCPD may appear to be adaptable because overcompensation can be functional for some individuals. Regardless, our goal is not to defend the cluster structure of the DSM. Rather, we emphasize the importance of developmental processes in determining how a common dysfunctional internal mechanism may give rise to varied outcomes (Cichetti & Rogosch, 1996).

In this light, we reiterate our assertion that there is considerable promise in expanding focus to transdiagnostic constructs and processes that have utility for anchors of personality that relate to maladaptive behavior. For example, Downey and Feldman (1996) suggest that rejection sensitive (RS) individuals are more likely to perceive rejection and ill intent in ambiguous social situations, both with strangers and romantic partners. This assumption of malicious intent by others may help explain why some RS individuals exhibit aggressive behaviors. Downey describes the process as a self-fulfilling prophecy to ensure rejection by romantic partners (Downey, Freitas, Michaelis, & Khouri, 1998). Further, *interpersonal mechanisms* (external, as opposed to internal) provide an opportunity to capitalize on the power of the interpersonal approach for better understand and treating Cluster C personality disorders. Critchfield, Benjamin & Levenick (2015) remind us that multiple diagnoses are the rule and not the exception for personality disordered patients, and thus present complications for treatment. Using Benjamin's (2003) Interpersonal Reconstructive Therapy (IRT) approach, they identified interpersonal prototypes that cut across multiple personality disorders, including obsessive compulsive, passive aggressive, and borderline, and demonstrated specificity and sensitivity of cross-cutting interpersonal processes that transcended DSM diagnoses.

All things considered, we do not view the higher order organization of Cluster C as an ultimate truth, nor do we view personality disorder diagnoses themselves as natural kinds. We do think that the frequency of diagnostic co-occurrence among personality disturbed individuals complicates matters. The reality that successful forms of psychotherapeutic treatment are not targeted at a personality disorder diagnoses per se but rather at maladaptive patterns of behavior, as suggested by Cain, or at dysfunctional cognitive schemas, as suggested by Arntz, support the utility of valid, cross-cutting mechanisms. Our chapter argued that incorporating basic internal mechanisms and their dysfunction into research – whether with RDoC or with other approaches – will be necessary to move beyond another rearrangement of symptoms and traits and to allow us to live meaningfully outside the cluster. Our rejoinder reiterates our view, and, motivated by our commentators, we add that *person* (mechanism) and *situation* (interpersonal processes) are inseparable (Cain), and that

an awareness and articulation of grain size will serve us well as we go forward (Arntz).

REFERENCES

Benjamin, L. S. (2003). *Interpersonal Reconstructive Therapy*. New York: Guilford Press.

Carson, R. C. (1982). Self-fulfilling prophecy, maladaptive behavior, and psychotherapy. In J. C. Anchin and D. J. Kiesler (Eds.), *Handbook of Interpersonal Psychotherapy* (pp. 64–77). New York: Pergamon.

Cicchetti, D., & Rogosch, F. A. (1996). Equifinality and multifinality in developmental psychopathology. *Development and Psychopathology, 8,* 597–600.

Critchfield, K. L., Benjamin, L. S., & Levenick, K. (2015). Reliability, sensitivity, and specificity of case formulations for comorbid profiles in interpersonal reconstructive therapy: Addressing mechanisms of psychopathology. *Journal of Personality Disorders, 29,* 547–573.

Downey, G., & Feldman, S. I. (1996). Implications of rejection sensitivity for intimate relationships. *Journal of Personality and Social Psychology, 70*(6), 1327–1343.

Downey, G., Freitas, A. L., Michaelis, B., & Khouri, H. (1998). The self-fulfilling prophecy in close relationships: Rejection sensitivity and rejection by romantic partners. *Journal of Personality and Social Psychology, 75*(2), 545–560.

McGlashan, T. H., Grilo, C. M., Skodol, A. E., Gunderson, J. G., Shea, M. T., Morey, L. C., . . . Stout, R. L. (2000). The Collaborative Longitudinal Personality Disorders Study: Baseline Axis I/II and II/II diagnostic co-occurrence. *Acta Psychiatrica Scandinavica, 102,* 256–264.

Sanislow, C. A. (2016). Connecting psychopathology metastructure and mechanisms. *Journal of Abnormal Psychology, 125,* 1158–1165.

Sanislow, C. A., Morey, L. C., Grilo, C. M., Gunderson, J. G., Shea, M. T., Skodol, A. E., . . . McGlashan, T. H. (2002). Confirmatory factor analysis of DSM-IV schizotypal, borderline, avoidant, and obsessive-compulsive personality disorders: Findings from the Collaborative Longitudinal Study of Personality Disorders. *Acta Psychiatrica Scandinavica, 105,* 28–36.

Sullivan, H. S. (1953). *The Interpersonal Theory of Psychiatry*. New York: W. W. Norton.

PART IV ASSESSMENT

14 Methods and Current Issues in Dimensional Assessments of Personality Pathology

CHLOE M. EVANS, TREVOR F. WILLIAMS, AND LEONARD J. SIMMS

The purpose of this chapter is to review the current state of the dimensional assessment of personality disorder (PD), which is part of a broader paradigm shift in how psychopathology in general is conceptualized and measured; this shift is referred to by Kotov and colleagues (2017) as the "quantitative classification movement" (see also a recent chapter by Williams & Simms, in press, who describe the quantitative classification paradigm in the context of traditional and alternative classification paradigms). Briefly, a quantitative-dimensional model conceptualizes psychopathology as lying on a continuum with normal psychological functioning, such that psychopathology is quantitatively, as opposed to qualitatively, different from psychological health. This movement has elevated empirical relations between symptoms over clinical intuitions, leading to models that reject traditional diagnoses and emphasize the continuity of psychological functioning

A dimensional classification schema is especially relevant to the domain of personality pathology for at least two reasons. First, there is extensive evidence that PD symptoms vary continuously between clinical samples and the general population, suggesting a shared, dimensional latent structure (e.g., Livesley, Schroeder, Jackson, & Jang, 1994). Second, a dimensional model would potentially ameliorate the well-documented limitations of the categorical model of PD in the various editions of the *Diagnostic and Statistical Manual of Mental Disorders* (DSM), such as excessive comorbidity, within-disorder heterogeneity, arbitrary disorder thresholds, and poor coverage of the full range of aberrant personality functioning (e.g., Clark, 2007). Simply treating the ten current categorical PD diagnoses as dimensional would not address the limitations in this second point (e.g., comorbidity); thus, researchers have begun to focus on well-supported PD trait and dysfunction models (Morey, Bender, & Skodol, 2013; Widiger & Trull, 2007). This shift to trait and dysfunction models has positioned PD researchers as leaders in the shift to a quantitative, dimensional model of psychopathology (Krueger, 2013).

We begin with a review of the most widely accepted and commonly used measures of maladaptive personality traits, as well as dimensional assessment measures of psychosocial dysfunction associated with these traits. Although there are many points of continuity among these measures, we structure our discussion around their differences, as this may illuminate areas for further research and discussion. Important differences among measures include theoretical origin, method of scale construction, degree of correspondence with well-known trait dimensions, attention received in the empirical literature, and degree of bipolarity (vs. unipolarity) of the underlying dimensions. We also consider the clinical utility of the reviewed measures.

In the second part of this chapter, we review some of the more contentious issues at the forefront of dimensional assessment of personality pathology. First, we discuss the current state of the empirical literature surrounding whether and how personality traits can be psychometrically distinguished from personality dysfunction. Second, we touch upon the incremental utility of adaptive trait assessment above and beyond maladaptive trait assessment in clinical contexts. Third, we explore the question of whether traits are maladaptive at one pole (i.e., maladaptively unipolar) or both poles (i.e., maladaptively bipolar). Fourth, we discuss the similarities and differences in facet-level structure across trait models, in contrast to the general agreement that can be found at the broader domain level. Finally, we argue that multi-method assessment is a crucial component of dimensional personality assessment, and suggest that divergence among sources is not problematic, but clinically useful.

REVIEW OF PD TRAIT MEASURES

The assessment of maladaptive personality traits has a long and rich history, as evidenced by the number of measures reviewed here. We have organized our discussion of these measures (as well as an accompanying summary presented in Table 14.1) around theoretical origin, resulting in three categories: (1) measures rooted directly in the Five-Factor Model (FFM), (2) maladaptive

Table 14.1 Key features of dimensional assessments

Measure	Citations	Construction	Structure	Scales & Items	Scale Polarity	Response Options	Formats	Availability	Norms	Languages	Clinical Features
Five Factor Model											
Five Factor Form	17	Created descriptive anchors for each FFM facet	FFM	5 Domains (6 facets each), 30 Facets (single-items)	Bipolar	5-point scale (maladaptive low to maladaptive high)	Full	http://stephaniesweatt.wixsite.com/ okstateppl/projects	Community	English	b
Five Factor Model Score Sheet	13	Created descriptive anchors for each FFM facet	FFM	5 Domains (6 facets each), 30 Facets (single-items)	Bipolar	7-point scale (problematic, very low to problematic, very high)	Full	Few et al. (2010)	Outpatient	English	b
Structured Interview for the Five Factor Model of Personality	74	Developed and evaluated interview questions for each FFM facet	FFM	5 Domains (6 facets each), 30 Facets (4 items each)	Bipolar	3-point scale (0-absent, 1-present, no impairment, 2-present, impairment)	Full	Psychological Assessment Resources	Manual	English, French	a, b, c, d, and f
Five Factor Model of PD											
Five Factor Borderline Inventory	32	Developed scales for BPD-relevant FFM facets	Untested	12 Facets (120 items)	Unipolar	5-point scale (disagree strongly to agree strongly)	Full and Short	http://stephaniesweatt.wixsite.com/ okstateppl/projects	Community	English	b
FFOCI	25	Developed scales for OCPD-relevant FFM facets	Untested	12 Facets (120 items)	Unipolar	5-point scale (strongly disagree to strongly agree)	Full, Short	http://samppl.psych.purdue.edu/ ~dbsamuel/research.html	mTurk	English, Chinese	b, c
FFSI	32	Developed scales for STPD-relevant FFM facets	Untested	9 Facets (90 items)	Unipolar	5-point scale (strongly disagree to strongly agree)	Full	widiger@email.uky.edu	None	English	c

FFNI	44	Developed scales for NPD relevant FFM facets	Antagonism, Neuroticism, & Agentic Extraversion; Grandiose Narcissism & Vulnerable Narcissism	15 Facets (148 items)	Unipolar	5-point scale (strongly disagree to strongly agree)	Full, Informant, Short	http://psychology.uga.edu/directory/josh-miller	Student	English, Italian-Short Form (Fossati, Somma, Borroni, & Miller, 2017)	a, c
EPA	99	Developed scales for Psychopathy-relevant FFM facets	Antagonism, Emotional Stability, Disinhibition, & Narcissism	18 Facets (178 items)	Unipolar	5-point scale (disagree strongly to agree strongly)	Full, Short, Super Short	http://psychology.uga.edu/directory/josh-miller	None	English	a, c, and e
FFDI	24	Developed scales for DPD-relevant FFM facets	Untested	12 Facets (120 items)	Unipolar	5-point scale (strongly disagree to strongly agree)	Full	widiger@email.uky.edu	None	English	c
FFHI	11	Developed scales for HPD-relevant FFM facets	Untested	10 Facets (100 items)	Unipolar	Unknown	Full	widiger@email.uky.edu	None	English	-
FFAvA	12	Developed scales for AVPD-relevant FFM facets	Untested	10 Facets (70 items)	Unipolar	5-point scale (disagree strongly to agree strongly)	Full	dlynam@purdue.edu	None	English	-
Pathological Trait Models											
SNAP-2	212	Content- and factor-analytic studies of PD criteria and related features	Negative Affectivity, Positive Affectivity, Disinhibition vs. Constraint	15 traits (390 items)	Mixed	True or False	Full, Short	Contact Lee Anna Clark, lclark6@nd.edu	Manuel	English	a, b, c, d, e, f
DAPP-BQ	264	Literature review, expert opinion, and interviews of PD clients	18 primary traits/dimensions	69 sub-traits (between two and seven per dimension)		5 pt-scale (Very Unlike Me to Very Like Me)	DAPP-BQ, DAPP-BQ-A, DAPP-BQ-SF, DAPP-DQ	http://www.sigmaassessmentsystems.com/assessments/dimensional-assessment-of-personality-pathology-basic-questionnaire/	Community, clinical	English, French, Spanish, Portuguese	a, b, c, d, e, f

Table 14.1 (cont.)

Measure	Citations	Construction	Structure	Scales & Items	Scale Polarity	Response Options	Formats	Availability	Norms	Languages	Clinical Features
MMPI PSY-5-RF	189	Replicated rational selection used to match item to theoretical constructs	Aggressiveness, Psychoticism, Disconstraint, Negative Emotionality, and Positive Emotionality	5 Domains (104 items)	Unipolar	True or False	MMPI-2 and MMPI-2-RF	University of Minnesota Press	Manual	English, Dutch, Chinese, Spanish, Arabic, Farsi, French, Greek, Hebrew, Hmong, Icelandic, Italian, Japanese, Korean, Norwegian, Russian, Thai, Turkish, Vietnamese	a, b, c, d, e, f
PID-5	336	PD trait literature review and bottom-up factor analyses	Negative Affectivity, Detachment, Psychoticism, Antagonism, and Disinhibition	25 Facets (220 items)	Unipolar	4-point scale (Very False of Often False to Very True or Often True)	Full, Short-100, Short-25, Informant, Child	https://www.psychiatry.org/psychiatrists/practice/dsm/educational-resources/assessment-measures	Community, Clinical	English, Dutch, Norwegian, German, Arabic, Portuguese, French, Spanish	a, b, c, d
CAT-PD	66	PD trait literature review and bottom-up factor analyses	Based on a PSY-5 organizing scheme	33 Facets (216 items + 30 for the optional validity scales)	Unipolar	5-point scale (Very Untrue of Me to Very True of Me)	Full-Adaptive, Full-Static, Informant, Interview	Contact Len Simms, ljsimms@buffalo.edu		English, Dutch, Norwegian, Spanish	a, b, c, d, e
PAI (PID-5 scoring)	1	Stepwise regression using PAI scales as predictors of PID-5 facets	Negative Affectivity, Detachment, Psychoticism, Antagonism, and Disinhibition	25 Facets (344 items)	Unipolar	4-point scale (Not at all true to Very true)	Adult & Adolescent	https://www.parinc.com/products/pkey/287	Morey, 1991 and Busch et al., 2017	Spanish	a, b, e
General Personality Functioning											
MDPF	39	Conceptual generation followed by 2 rounds of factor analysis	2 higher-order factors: non-coping, non-cooperativeness	10 items per each higher-order factor	NA	4-pt scale (definitely false – definitely true)	Full only	Parker et al., 2004	Italian community sample	English, Italian (Fossati et al., 2017)	b, d

Measure	Citations	Development approach	Domains	Items/Facets		Response scale	Versions	Source	Sample	Languages	Notes
SIPP	101	Expert-guided rational-intuitive approach	5 higher-order domains: self-control, identity integration, relational capacities, social concordance, responsibility	16 lower order facets, between 2 and 5 facets per domain, between 7 and 8 items per facet	NA	4-pt (I fully agree, I partly agree, I partly disagree, I fully agree)	Full, Short Form (SIPP-SF 64 items)	https://www.deviersprong.nl/over-de-viersprong/over-de-viersprong-onderzoek/onderzoekslijn-diagnostiek/onderzoekslijn-assessment-en-indicatiestelling/sipp-main-menu/	PD, Outpatient, Community	English, Dutch, Norwegian, Argentinian, Italian	a, b, c, d, f
GAPD	8 citations for Hentschel & Livesley, 2013; 3 empirical studies prior to Hentschel & Livesley, 2013	Literature review, assessment interviews, and therapy sessions informed the writing of items to assess adaptive failure constructs	(1) Self-Pathology, (2) Interpersonal Dysfunction	original 114-item version shortened to 85-item version (Hentschel & Livesley, 2013). Only items that differentiated between criterion groups (PD vs. no PD) were retained. 8 subscales (4 self-pathology, 4 interpersonal pathology)		5-pt (1 = very unlike me – 5 = very like me)	Full only	Livesley (2006)	Canadian Community Sample & Dutch Clinical Sample	English, Dutch (Berghuis, 2007), German (Hentschel & Livesley, 2003)	b
LPFS-BF 2.0	None, but 7 for the original LPFS-BF	Conceptually generated by 4 clinical psychologists to capture LPFS. One item per facet	2 higher-order domains (self and interpersonal functioning); 4 subdomains (self: identity, self-direction; interpersonal: empathy, intimacy)	12 facets (3 per subdomain)		4-pt (1 = very false or often false, 4 = very true or often true)	self-report	Bach & Hutsebaut, 2018	Outpatient, inpatient	Dutch, English	a, c
LPFS-SR	0	Conceptually generated to capture LPFS. One item per clause	2 higher-order domains (self and interpersonal functioning); 4 subdomains (self: identity, self-direction; interpersonal: empathy, intimacy)	80 items		4-pt (1 = totally false, not at all true, 4 = very true)	self-report	Morey, 2017 supplemental material	MTurk sample	English	a, b, c, d

Table 14.1 (*cont.*)

Measure	Citations	Construction	Structure	Scales & Items	Scale Polarity	Response Options	Formats	Availability	Norms	Languages	Clinical Features
DLOPFQ	1	Experts individually conceptually generated items to assess the LPFS constructs. Items agreed upon among experts were retained	2 higher-order domains (self and interpersonal functioning); 4 subdomains (self: identity, self-direction; interpersonal: empathy, intimacy) 2 further subdomains per each subscale (Work/School and Social (close) Relationships)	132 items (66 questions asking about work/school contexts and the same 66 questions asking about Social Relationships context		6-pt Likert (1 = strongly disagree to 6 = strongly agree)	self-report	huprichst@udmercy.edu	Psychiatric and medical outpatient sample	English	a, c
IIP-64/IIP-C	512	Intake interviews, circumplex analysis (Alden et al., 1990), further psychometric pruning (final items chosen based on communalities and scale loadings	2 higher-order dimensions: (1) dominance, (2) nurturance	8 scales: Domineering (PA), Vindictive (BC), Cold (DE), Socially Avoidant (FG), Nonassertive (HI), Exploitable (JK), Overly Nurturant (LM), Intrusive (NO)		5-pt Likert scale (0 = not at all to 4 = extremely)	IIP-32 (Short Circumplex)	available for purchase at https://www.mindgarden.com/113-inventory-of-interpersonal-problems	Manual	English, Finnish, Greek, Malay, Polish, Spanish	a, b, c, f

Note: Citations are based on Web of Science searches from February–May of 2018. Clinical features are coded as follows: a = published factor structure, b = available norms, c = all scale alphas > .70, d = retest reliability evidence, e = presence of validity scales, and f = interpretive materials available (case studies, manuals, etc.).

extensions of the FFM keyed to most traditional PDs, known collectively as the Five-Factor Model of Personality Disorder (FFM-PD), and (3) pathological personality trait measures.

FIVE FACTOR MODEL MEASURES

FFM measures do not assess pathological traits *per se*; rather, they are based on the assumption that extremely low or high levels of the five FFM normative-range personality traits – neuroticism, extraversion, agreeableness, conscientiousness, and openness – constitute personality pathology and are associated with psychosocial dysfunction. The FFM has its roots in two distinct traditions. First, any discussion of the FFM is incomplete if it fails to acknowledge the conceptual links between the FFM and the lexically-based Big Five literature (e.g., Goldberg, 1993). That said, clinical applications of the FFM largely have their roots in the work of Costa and McCrae, who formalized the FFM as the five broad traits listed above and their nested 30 subordinate facets. Although the NEO family of measures were designed to measure normal-range variants of personality, they deserve discussion in this section because the NEO has been the basis of a large literature linking FFM traits and personality pathology (e.g., Widiger, Trull, Clarkin, Sanderson, & Costa, 2002). The full NEO-FFM model first emerged in the revised NEO Personality Inventory (NEO-PI-R; Costa & McCrae, 1992). A minor revision was published in 2015 (NEO-PI-3; McCrae, Costa, & Martin, 2005; McCrae & Costa, 2010), but the NEO-FFM has remained remarkably consistent and robust for over 25 years. Notably, the work of Tom Widiger and his colleagues and students has greatly enhanced our understanding of PD traits, using the FFM model as a foundation. Most relevant to our purpose here, Widiger has developed several FFM-based measures designed to explicitly extend the normal-range NEO traits into the maladaptive range, presumably making them more amenable to clinical research and practice. We now discuss the most prominent of these FFM measures.

The Five Factor Form

The Five Factor Form (FFF; Rojas & Widiger, 2014) is a recent measure of the FFM designed to explicitly assess adaptively *and* maladaptively high and low levels of each FFM facet (Rojas & Widiger, 2018). The FFF consists of one item for each FFM facet, each rated on a five-point scale including the following anchors: 1 (*maladaptive low*), 2 (*normal low*), 3 (*neutral*), 4 (*normal high*), and 5 (*maladaptive high*). In addition, each item also includes exemplar descriptors of both the maladaptive and normal-range options. For example, for the facet of Warmth, 1 = "*cold, distant*" and 2 = "*formal-reserved*" on the low end, and 4 = "*affectionate, warm*" and 5 = "*intense attachments*" on the high end. Thus, options 1 and 5 reflect maladaptively low

and high manifestations of warmth, respectively, whereas options 2 and 4 reflect normal-range variations in warmth. Although only limited research has been published on the FFF thus far, some early work has demonstrated evidence for its convergent and discriminant validity relative to a range of measures, including other FFM measures (e.g., Rojas & Widiger, 2018). That said, the explicit adaptive-maladaptive structure of the FFM has shown only mixed support thus far in the literature and deserves further scrutiny (Rojas, 2017).

The Five Factor Model Score Sheet

The Five Factor Model Score Sheet (FFMSS; Widiger & Spitzer, 2002) is a conceptually generated, brief clinician-rated measure of the FFM with one item per facet (Few et al., 2010). With respect to reliability of the FFMSS, there is empirical evidence for the adequate internal consistency of four of five FFMSS domains, with the exception of Neuroticism (α = .61; Few et al., 2010). With respect to validity, the FFMSS has demonstrated good convergence with maladaptive trait measures (e.g., the Schedule for Nonadaptive and Adaptive Personality [SNAP; Clark, 1993]) as well as expert-generated PD prototypes (Few et al., 2010). Further, the FFMSS demonstrated significant incremental validity relative to the DSM-IV PD criteria in the prediction of psychosocial dysfunction across domains (e.g., romantic relationships, occupational functioning; Few et al., 2010).

The Structured Interview for the Assessment of the Five-Factor Model of Personality (SIFFM)

The SIFFM (Trull & Widiger, 1997) is a semi-structured interview measure of the FFM whose 120 items are evenly distributed across the 30 NEO facets, such that there are four items per facet (Trull et al., 1998). The SIFFM was developed in hopes of capitalizing on the psychometric advantages of the interview method over self-report (e.g., allows for clinical observation, responses may be clarified by elicitation of examples; Trull et al., 1998). In addition, an interview measure presumably facilitates research examining the associations between personality traits and PDs, given that the PDs are commonly assessed via interview (Trull et al., 1998). The SIFFM fulfills many of our criteria for clinical utility (see Table 14.1 Note), including a published factor structure, acceptable internal consistency, and acceptable test-retest reliability (Trull et al., 1998). Further, the SIFFM domains converge in a theoretically predictable way with the NEO-PI-R and PID-5 domains, as well as peer ratings of FFM traits (Helle, Trull, Widiger, & Mullins-Sweatt, 2017; Trull et al., 1998). Finally, there is evidence that the SIFFM accounts for significant variance in PD symptoms after controlling for general personality pathology (Trull, Widiger, & Burr, 2001).

FFM-PD Measures

Eight measures are associated with the FFM-PD, one each corresponding to the DSM-5 Section II PDs, with the exception of Paranoid PD and Schizoid PD. The theoretical origin of these measures can ultimately be traced back to the FFM, but not as directly as the FFM measures reviewed above. Rather, these measures follow from an additional postulate that the FFM can account for the ten categorical PD diagnoses (e.g., Widiger et al., 2002). As such, the FFM-PD measures do not directly assess normative personality traits, nor are they intended to capture the full breadth of the FFM (i.e., assessing all five factors). Rather, each measure is limited to those facets of the FFM that have shown empirical relevance to a given PD based on extant research (e.g., Bagby & Widiger, 2018).

The number of facets per measure ranges from 9 for the Five Factor Schizotypal Inventory (FFSI; Edmundson, Lynam, Miller, Gore, & Widiger, 2011) to 18 for the Elemental Psychopathy Assessment (EPA; Lynam et al., 2011). Two FFM-PD measures – the Five Factor Narcissism Inventory (FFNI; Glover, Miller, Lynam, Crego, & Widiger, 2012) and the EPA – have a factor analytically derived domain-level structure, whereas the remainder of FFM-PD measures are scored and interpreted only at the facet level. Notably, neither the FFNI nor the EPA has a higher-order domain structure that is perfectly aligned with the FFM (see Table 14.1 for details). Thus, unlike the three FFM-derived measures described above, it is unclear how exactly the FFNI and EPA measures fit within the broader FFM framework and rich empirical tradition of the full FFM.

Space constraints do not permit a full description of each FFM-PD measure; interested readers are referred to a recent special issue of *Psychological Assessment* that focuses on the measures within this collection (Bagby & Widiger, 2018). However, it is notable that the FFM-PD measures vary in the extent to which they have been used in empirical research (citations ranging from 11 for the Five Factor Histrionic Inventory [FFHI; Tomiatti, Gore, Lynam, Miller, & Widiger, 2012] to 99 for the EPA). In terms of clinical utility, these measures fulfill between zero (FFHI, Five Factor Avoidant Assessment) and three (EPA) of our clinical utility criteria. Moreover, it is unclear how this collection of measures is meant to be used in clinical work, since collectively these measures include too many items and numerous overlapping scales to be efficiently used by practicing clinicians. Work is needed to integrate these eight measures into a single, efficient FFM-PD measure.

PATHOLOGICAL TRAIT MODEL-DERIVED MEASURES

In contrast to the previously reviewed measures, some PD trait measures have been developed to directly assess the traits presumed to underlie the PD criteria listed in the various editions of the DSM. Such measures have emerged in the literature over the last 25 years, with increasing evidence of structural consensus and clinical utility.

Schedule for Nonadaptive and Adaptive Personality-2

The SNAP (Clark, 1993) and its second edition (SNAP-2; Clark, Simms, Wu, & Casillas, 2002) were developed to provide a means for assessing trait dimensions relevant to the diagnosis of personality pathology. The SNAP-2 includes 390 items and measures three broad temperament dimensions corresponding to a Big Three personality model (i.e., negative temperament, positive temperament, and disinhibition vs. constraint), as well as 12 lower-order facets that were developed via an iterative series of factor- and content-analytic procedures applied to PD diagnostic criteria and related features. The clinical utility of the measure is strong, as it includes a comprehensive set of validity scales (including a set of scales keyed to the DSM PDs for clinicians who desire a bridge between categorical and trait-dimensional PD conceptualizations), has strong community and clinical norms, and has considerable evidence in support of its reliability and validity (e.g., see Simms & Clark, 2006).

The Dimensional Assessment of Personality Pathology – Basic Questionnaire (DAPP-BQ)

The DAPP-BQ (Livesley & Jackson, 2009) is similar to the SNAP in that it was developed as an early attempt to represent and measure the traits presumably underlying personality pathology. The DAPP-BQ includes 290 items and measures 18 lower-order traits nested within 4 higher-order dimensions – Emotional Dysregulation, Dissocial Behavior, Inhibition, and Compulsivity. Items were conceptually generated to capture the DSM-III PD criteria (Bagge & Trull, 2003). All 18 of the DAPP-BQ trait scales have documented evidence of internal consistency across clinical and non-clinical samples, as well as test-retest reliability (e.g., van Kampen, 2002). Further, the DAPP-BQ has demonstrated convergent validity with respect to PD symptoms (e.g., Bagge & Trull, 2003) and normal-range personality traits (e.g., van Kampen, 2002). These features, as well as the existence of automated administration and interpretation services, make the DAPP-BQ a measure with reasonable clinical utility. However, the lack of validity scales arguably is a limitation of the DAPP-BQ in high-stakes testing contexts.

Personality Psychopathology Five MMPI-2-RF Scales (PSY-5)

The PSY-5 model (Harkness & McNulty, 1994, 2007) – which includes the five broad traits of Aggressiveness, Psychoticism, Constraint, Negative Emotionality, and Positive Emotionality – is notable because it represents both a measure of broad traits thought to be relevant to adaptive and maladaptive personality and a model of such traits that has gained traction in recent years as the basis for the alternative model of personality disorder (AMPD; as published in Section III of DSM-5) and numerous measures of AMPD traits (to be reviewed below). As a measure, the PSY-5 first appeared as a cohesive set of scales developed for the Minnesota Multiphasic Personality Inventory-2 (MMPI-2). More recently, the PSY-5 scales have been refined for the restructured forms of the MMPI-2 (MMPI-2-RF; Ben-Porath & Tellegen, 2008). Items initially were chosen from the full MMPI-2 item pool via replicated rational selection, followed by rational and psychometric pruning (Harkness, McNulty, & Ben-Porath, 1995). The scales have demonstrated good reliability, as well as convergent validity with respect to the PID-5 and various external criteria (e.g., Harkness et al., 2013). The PSY-5 scales have good clinical utility to the extent that they are embedded in a widely used and researched measure; thus, all of the features that make the MMPI-2-RF useful in clinical settings (e.g., strong norms, validity scales) can be applied to the PSY-5 scales. In addition to being a set of MMPI-2-RF scales, the PSY-5 model bears a strong resemblance to the structural model underlying the AMPD and its derivative measures described below. However, the lack of PSY-5 facet scales sets an upper limit on its usefulness.

Personality Inventory for DSM-5 (PID-5)

The PID-5 (Krueger, Derringer, Markon, Watson, & Skodol, 2012) is the official measure of the AMPD as represented in Section III of DSM-5. It includes 220 self-report items that assess the 25 maladaptive traits of the AMPD. Traits are distributed across five higher-order domains that are isomorphic with the PSY-5 model: Negative Affectivity, Detachment, Antagonism, Disinhibition, and Psychoticism (Krueger et al., 2012). Items were conceptually generated by expert consensus and psychometrically pruned over two rounds of data collection (Krueger et al., 2012). The PID-5 has demonstrated adequate to good convergent and discriminant validity with respect to normal-range trait measures, other maladaptive trait measures, and the traditional DSM-IV PD categories (e.g., Wright & Simms, 2014; Yam & Simms, 2014). Moreover, the measure has demonstrated adequate test-retest reliability and a replicable factor structure (e.g., Al-Dajani, Gralnick, & Bagby, 2016). The PID-5's status as the official measure of the AMPD and its large research base are features that improve its clinical utility; however, the lack of integrated validity scales limits its usefulness in high-stakes contexts.

Personality Assessment Inventory PID-5 Scoring (PAI-PID-5)

The Personality Assessment Inventory (PAI; Morey, 1991) is a self-report measure consisting of 344 items nested within 22 full scales and 31 subscales that assess a broad range of psychopathology constructs, including personality pathology. Most relevant to the present chapter, Busch, Morey, and Hopwood (2017) published a scoring algorithm by which the PAI scale scores could be used to assess the AMPD traits via multiple regression. Results indicated that PAI-estimated AMPD traits were adequately correlated with PID-5-estimated AMPD trait profiles and reproduced the five factors of the AMPD with good fidelity (Busch et al., 2017). The primary advantage of using the PAI to estimate AMPD traits is that the PAI has a robust research literature and includes features that improve its clinical utility (e.g., strong norms and validity scales), thus making it more heavily used in clinical settings.

Comprehensive Assessment of Traits Relevant to Personality Disorder-Static Form (CAT-PD-SF)

The CAT-PD-SF (Simms et al., 2011) was developed to identify a comprehensive model and efficient measure of PD traits. Although developed independently, the CAT-PD facets are similar to those represented in the AMPD. The CAT-PD-SF is a brief measure drawn from the full CAT-PD item pool. The CAT-PD project yielded 33 facet scales measuring an integrative set of PD traits. These scales were formed following data collection through an iterative series of factor- and content-analytic procedures. The full CAT-PD scales are long by design (1366 total items; M scale length = 44 items $\pm$ 12) so as to be amenable for computerized adaptive testing. However, a static form (CAT-PD-SF) was developed using a combination of statistical and content validity considerations to facilitate quick and standardized assessment across studies and in clinical settings. The static form measures all 33 traits using 216 items. In addition, a 246-item version exists that includes validity scales. The static scales demonstrate good internal consistency, test-retest reliability, and evidence of convergent and discriminant validity (e.g., Wright & Simms, 2014), and have been used in a growing number of PD trait studies. Notably, the CAT-PD has been shown to tap additional variance relevant to PD not directly assessed by the PID-5, such as self-harm and antisocial behavior (e.g., Evans & Simms; 2018; Yalch & Hopwood, 2016).

PERSONALITY DYSFUNCTION MEASURES

The assessment of personality dysfunction is a younger and less developed area of research than that of personality trait assessment (Ro & Clark, 2009). However, there has been an increased focus on conceptualizing and measuring personality dysfunction in recent years in the wake of the publication of DSM-5, particularly in response to AMPD's inclusion of a clinician rating scale of self and interpersonal dysfunction (i.e., the Levels of Personality Functioning Scale [LPFS; APA, 2013]). Reviewed below (and summarized in Table 14.1) are seven prominent personality dysfunction measures, four of which predate the LPFS, and three of which have been developed with the express purpose of operationalizing the LPFS.

In addition, seven of the most prominent measures of impairment in personality functioning are included in Table 14.1. The theoretical origin, method of construction, and structure of each measure are reviewed below, and reliability and validity are briefly evaluated.

Inventory of Interpersonal Problems-Circumplex (IIP-64/IIP-C). The IIP-64 (Alden, Wiggins, & Pincus, 1990) is one of many adaptations of the original 127-item Inventory of Interpersonal Problems developed by Horowitz and colleagues in 1988 (see Hughes & Barkham, 2005, for a review). The IIP-64 most directly assesses interpersonal problems that characterize personality dysfunction, whereas the remaining measures assess both self and interpersonal problems. It consists of two higher-order dimensions (Dominance and Nurturance) and eight scales (Domineering, Vindictive, Cold, Socially Avoidant, Nonassertive, Exploitable, Overly Nurturant, and Intrusive).

Measure of Disordered Personality Functioning Scale (MDPF). The MDPF (Parker et al., 2004) is not linked to any particular theory of personality dysfunction; rather, the initial phase of item construction was informed by a comprehensive literature review (Parker et al., 2002) from which the research team identified 17 constructs central to the definition of personality dysfunction. The 141 items initially written to assess these constructs where whittled (via several rounds of factor analysis) to 20 items loading onto two higher-order factors: Non-Coping and Non-Cooperativeness, which refer to self and interpersonal dysfunction, respectively (Parker et al., 2004).

General Assessment of Personality Disorder (GAPD). The GAPD (Livesley, 2006) is an 85-item self-report measure intended to assess self and interpersonal pathology as defined by Livesley's adaptive failure model of PD (Berghuis, Kamphuis, & Verheul, 2012). Its structure is hierarchical, such that eight subfacets are nested within two higher-order facets (i.e., Self Pathology and Interpersonal Pathology; Hentschel & Livesley, 2013). The four subfacets that load onto Self Pathology are Differentiation, Integration, Consequences of Self Pathology, and Self-Directedness (Hentschel & Livesley, 2013). The four subfacets that load onto Interpersonal Pathology are Attachment/Intimacy, Affiliation, Prosocial Behavior, and Cooperativeness. An initial 144-item pool was conceptually generated on the basis of both a literature review and therapy sessions with individuals with a PD (Hentschel & Livesley, 2013). Subsequently, items that failed to differentiate between individuals with and without a PD in pilot testing were eliminated (Hentschel & Livesley, 2013).

Severity Indices of Personality Problems (SIPP). The SIPP (Verheul et al., 2008) is a 118-item self-report measure that was developed using an expert-guided, rational-intuitive approach to measure five higher-order domains of personality functioning: Self-Control, Identity Integration, Relational Capacities, Social Concordance, and Responsibility (Verheul et al., 2008). However, it is important to note that four of the five higher-order domains seem to correspond with the four subdomains of the Levels of Personality Functioning Scale (LPFS) described in the AMPD in DSM-5. Specifically, SIPP Self-Control is conceptually consistent with LPFS Self-Direction, SIPP Identity Integration maps onto LPFS Identity, SIPP Relational Capacities maps onto LPFS Intimacy, and SIPP Social Concordance is conceptually similar to LPFS Empathy. There is considerable evidence for the clinical readiness of the SIPP-118, including a replicated factor structure and adequate test-retest reliability, internal consistency, and convergent and discriminant validity (see Verheul et al., 2008, for more details).

LPFS-Based Measures. All three measures reviewed below share the factor structure of the LPFS, with four lower-order domains (Identity, Self-Direction, Empathy, Intimacy) that are nested within two higher-order domains (i.e., Identity and Self-Direction onto Self-Functioning, and Empathy and Intimacy onto Interpersonal Functioning).

Levels of Personality Functioning Scale – Brief Form 2.0 (LPFS-BF 2.0). The LPFS-BF 2.0 (Bach & Hutsebaut, 2018) was developed as a PD screen by a team of four clinicians, and consists of 12 items corresponding to each of the 12 LPFS scoring criteria (Hutsebaut, Feenstra, & Kamphuis, 2016). Among several of its strengths are the wide availability of the LPFS-BF-2.0 and empirical support for its convergent validity (e.g., LFPS-BF Self-Functioning is associated with SIPP Identity Integration, LPFS Interpersonal Functioning is associated with SIPP Relational Capacities and Social Concordance; Hutsebaut et al., 2016). Further, there is empirical support for the utility of the LPFS-BF in differentiating those with versus without PDs in a clinical sample (Hutsebaut et al., 2016).

Level of Personality Functioning Scale – Self-Report (LPFS-SR). The LPFS-SR (Morey, 2017), an 80-item measure developed by Les Morey, consists of one item per "information unit" in the LPFS scoring criteria. One unique aspect of this measure is that its scoring scheme weighs items according to the LPFS severity level to which they correspond, such that items that reflect moderate impairment are weighted +1.5, whereas items that reflect severe impairment are weighted +2.5 (Morey, 2017). One particular strength of the LPFS-SR is its high level of test-retest reliability, albeit over a relatively short time interval (i.e., approximately 15 days). Hopwood, Good, and Morey (2018) reported test-retest reliabilities of .90, .89, and .91 for self-functioning, interpersonal functioning, and the total score, respectively.

DSM-5 Levels of Personality Functioning Questionnaire (DLOPFQ). The DLOPFQ (Huprich et al., 2018) was developed from a larger pool of items written independently by experts to assess the constructs underlying the LPFS; the final 66 items were those agreed upon by the experts as a team (Huprich et al., 2018). Each of the 66 items is asked twice; respondents are asked to report on how true each item is for them in the context of work/school and then in the context of social relationships (Huprich et al., 2018). Explicit consideration of cross-situational variability is a potential unique strength of the DLOPFQ; however, Huprich and colleagues (2018) failed to detect meaningful cross-situational differences in item responses in a mixed sample, calling into question the utility of this distinction.

CURRENT TOPICS IN DIMENSIONAL ASSESSMENT OF PERSONALITY PATHOLOGY

Can Traits and Dysfunction Be Distinguished?

Despite the existence of separate measures to assess PD traits and personality dysfunction, as described above, recent literature has openly questioned whether such traits and impairments are psychometrically differentiable (see Widiger et al., 2019, for a review). There are a number of reasons why researchers and clinicians may wish to assess personality traits separately from dysfunction. First, one might argue that PD assessment should be consistent with the PD diagnostic system, in which extreme traits/features and psychosocial dysfunction both are required to diagnose personality pathology (Livesley et al., 1994; Leising & Zimmermann, 2011). Second, the malleability of personality dysfunction (which tends to vary more over time than personality traits) makes it a promising target for treatment (e.g., Bastiaansen, De Fruyt, Rossi, Schotte, & Hofmans, 2013; Skodol, 2011). Third, dysfunction has been shown to index the severity of personality pathology (e.g., Hopwood et al., 2011; Morey et al., 2013), which, in turn, predicts treatment outcomes more strongly than traits. Fourth, it is likely that dysfunction and traits inform different treatment decisions; namely, dysfunction may indicate the level of care required (e.g., inpatient vs. outpatient), whereas traits may guide selection of a particular therapeutic technique or modality (Bastiaansen et al., 2013).

However, it is unclear whether it is possible to assess PD traits and personality dysfunction distinctly. Indeed, evidence indicates that maladaptive personality trait measures tend to overlap substantially with a range of personality dysfunction measures (e.g., Berghuis, Kamphuis, & Verheul, 2014; Hentschel & Pukrop, 2014; Mullins-Sweatt & Widiger, 2010) and that such findings are consistent with conceptual overlap, rather than measurement redundancy. For instance, Zimmerman and colleagues (2015) performed a joint factor analysis of 60 individual LPFS descriptions and scales of the PID-5 informant version and found a significantly better fit for a model in which trait and dysfunction indicators were allowed to load on the same factors. Although some trait domains emerged relatively purely (Disinhibition,

Psychoticism) in the best-fitting model, negative affectivity traits and self-dysfunction loaded together, and antagonistic traits loaded on an interpersonal dysfunction factor (Zimmerman et al., 2015). Finally, Calabrese and Simms (2014), in a ten-day prospective study of PD and related impairments, found that baseline dysfunction ratings failed to predict daily dysfunction above and beyond maladaptive personality traits, calling into question the distinction between PD traits and dysfunction.

In general, research examining the incremental validity of maladaptive traits and dysfunction in predicting personality pathology has found that maladaptive personality traits evidence significant incremental validity relative to dysfunction, whereas the opposite pattern has not held (e.g., Berghuis et al., 2014; Hentschel & Pukrop, 2014). However, it is important to note that the degree to which traits and dysfunction overlap varies across both dysfunction subdomain and PD type. For instance, in one recent study of incremental validity at the PD level of analysis (Bastiaansen et al., 2013), SIPP Identity Integration incrementally predicted borderline PD above PD traits, SIPP Self-Control incrementally predicted antisocial PD and borderline PD, SIPP Relational Functioning incrementally predicted schizoid PD, and SIPP Responsibility incrementally predicted antisocial PD. However, such findings are preliminary, and future work would do well to clarify and confirm the associations between particular types of personality dysfunction and particular PDs.

Development of the LPFS was informed by extant clinician-rated personality dysfunction measures and secondary data analysis (Zimmerman et al., 2015). Therefore, empirical validation is necessary, and results have been mixed. Empirical findings generally have been supportive of the structural validity of the LPFS, with a handful of notable exceptions. First, Zimmerman and colleagues' (2015) confirmatory factor analyses of LPFS ratings indicated that self-reflective functioning, currently an aspect of Self-Direction, also is significantly associated with interpersonal functioning. They also found that the Interpersonal Functioning domain captures Empathy significantly better than Intimacy, suggesting a three-domain structure (Self Functioning, Prosocial Functioning, Relational Functioning) as a viable alternative (Zimmerman et al., 2015). Second, Bastiaansen and colleagues (2013) suggested that the emotion regulation aspect of Identity, which overlaps extensively with the Criterion B Emotional Lability trait, should be eliminated in service of incremental validity. Finally, little empirical support has been offered to justify the disorder-specific impairment descriptors included in the AMPD. Correlational analyses indicated that disorder-specific impairments were uniformly moderately associated with all trait- and criterion-specified PDs, rather than being uniquely associated with any single PD (Anderson & Sellbom, 2018).

In sum, although some desire a way to conceptualize and measure personality dysfunction separately from PD traits, it remains to be seen whether these two related aspects of personality pathology can be psychometrically disentangled. Further, whether dysfunction evidences incremental validity relative to PD traits in the prediction of personality pathology remains an open question.

THE ROLE OF ADAPTIVE PERSONALITY TRAITS

Although this chapter's focus is on assessing personality pathology, some researchers and therapists have argued that adaptive personality traits and personal strengths are also clinically important (Cheavens, Strunk, Lazarus, & Goldstein, 2012; Costa & McCrae, 1992; Padesky & Mooney, 2012). Indeed, given the complexity of individual differences, it is likely that even individuals with severe personality pathology have some strengths or adaptive traits (e.g., Miller, 1991). Adaptive personality traits may serve protective functions, lead to positive life outcomes, and perhaps facilitate therapeutic interventions (Miller, Pilkonis, & Mulvey, 2006; Ozer & Benet-Martinez, 2006). Furthermore, given the overlap of PD impairment and maladaptive personality traits noted above (e.g., Berghuis et al., 2014; Hentschel & Pukrop, 2014; Mullins-Sweatt & Widiger, 2010), adaptive traits may provide relatively unique information about individuals (Hopwood et al., 2011).

For example, trait conscientiousness – which is part of the Big Five/FFM model – is related to positive life outcomes, such as educational achievement, job performance, and health (Bakker, Demerouti, & ten Brummelhuis, 2012; Bogg & Roberts, 2004; Poropat, 2009). Furthermore, considerable psychotherapy research suggests that it predicts positive treatment outcomes (Anderson & McLean, 1997; Bottlender & Soyka, 2005). Although there is limited research on mechanisms that may explain this association, some work suggests that more conscientious individuals feel more engaged early in treatment (Samuel, Bucher, & Suzuki, 2018), are more likely to complete therapy homework (Miller, 1991), and are more likely to attend sessions (Miller et al., 2006). Many of the assessments in Table 14.1 have scales for assessing maladaptively low conscientiousness; however, only a handful explicitly assess adaptively high conscientiousness (i.e., FFF, FFMSS, SIFFM). That said, some recent research rooted in item response theory suggests that even measures that primarily assess personality pathology (e.g., PID-5) can provide substantial information about adaptively high conscientiousness (e.g., Suzuki, Samuel, Pahlen, & Krueger, 2015).

In contrast to conscientiousness, low agreeableness (e.g., callousness) is generally viewed as maladaptive, whereas high agreeableness is considered adaptive. Research indicates that high agreeableness is related to positive therapy outcomes (Canuto, Meiler-Mititelu, Herrmann, Giannakopoulos, & Weber, 2008; Ogrodniczuk, Piper, Joyce, McCallum, & Rosie, 2003) and that this relation may be explained by more dramatic improvements in

therapeutic alliance over time (e.g., Hirsh, Quilty, Bagby, & McMain, 2012). These findings are consistent with research showing that therapeutic alliance is a crucial factor in effective psychotherapy (e.g., Flückiger, Del Re, Wampold, Symonds, & Horvath, 2012) and that agreeableness more generally promotes positive interpersonal relations (Ozer & Benet-Martinez, 2006; Williams & Simms, 2016). Similar to conscientiousness, most measures in Table 14.1 do not explicitly aim to assess adaptive high agreeableness; however, these maladaptivity-focused measures likely still provide considerable information about adaptive agreeableness (Suzuki et al., 2015). Although other adaptive traits have been shown to have clinical relevance (e.g., openness to experience; Miller et al., 2006), the above examples of agreeableness and conscientiousness provide useful illustrations. Further research is needed on the role of adaptive traits in PD assessments and how such information can be integrated into broader PD models.

MALADAPTIVE UNIPOLARITY VS. BIPOLARITY

The examples in the preceding section on adaptive traits imply that one extreme, or "pole," of a trait dimension is maladaptive (e.g., low conscientiousness) and the opposing pole is adaptive (e.g., high conscientiousness); however, whether traits are maladaptive at one pole (i.e., maladaptively unipolar) or at both (i.e., maladaptively bipolar) is presently a matter of disagreement (e.g., Samuel & Tay, 2018; Williams & Simms, in press). It is important to resolve this debate, as it has implications for the representation of traits in diagnostic systems (Krueger et al., 2011; Samuel, 2011) and may influence how the measures in Table 14.1 are interpreted (e.g., whether low scores on PID-5 detachment are considered maladaptive). Despite the importance of this topic, it is under-researched and beset by a number of conceptual difficulties.

The "scale polarity" column in Table 14.1 represents what is typically claimed about each measure. Aside from the fact that the polarity of scales is often not discussed, it is often the case that conclusions about polarity are based on whether traits are measured by indicators (e.g., items) that appear to be conceptual opposites (e.g., exhibitionism vs. social withdrawal) that are maladaptive. Although informative, inferences about constructs based on scale characteristics (e.g., item-total correlations) may be limited; a construct validity perspective (Cronbach & Meehl, 1955) would suggest that a better understanding of maladaptive bipolarity could be reached through examining how traits relate to external impairment and psychopathology variables. For instance, meta-analyses of FFM and AMPD relations to common mental disorders (e.g., Hopwood, Thomas, Markon, Wright, & Krueger, 2012; Kotov, Gamez, Schmidt, & Watson, 2010) and PDs (Fowler et al., 2015; Samuel & Widiger, 2008) generally support maladaptive unipolarity, with the exceptions of a moderate (i.e., $r = .33$) correlation between histrionic PD and extraversion, as well as a small association (i.e., $r = .24$) between conscientiousness and obsessive-compulsive PD. A similar picture emerges when relations to general impairment (e.g., low well-being) are considered, as FFM and AMPD traits tend to relate to poor functioning at one trait pole (Calabrese & Simms, 2014; Ro & Clark, 2013). Thus, these literatures suggest some evidence of maladaptive bipolarity for conscientiousness and extraversion, although the relation for extraversion to histrionic PD may be complex and primarily accounted for by low agreeableness (Gore, Tomiatti, & Widiger, 2011).

An additional conceptual problem with explorations of trait polarity is the focus on linear relations with psychopathology and impairment. As some researchers have noted (Samuel, 2011; Williams & Simms, in press), if a trait is related to impairment at both poles and is adaptive in the middle of the dimension, then the form of its relation to impairment would be U-shaped (i.e., curvilinear). Thus, correlations and linear regression would need to be supplemented by polynomial regressions or other appropriate analyses. Few studies have examined curvilinear relations between traits and psychopathology or impairment. One of the first explicit studies of such relations (Carter, Guan, Maples, Williamson, & Miller 2016) found a curvilinear relation between conscientiousness and well-being, although the decrement in well-being at high levels of conscientiousness was minor relative to the lack of well-being associated with low conscientiousness. Recently, Williams and Simms (in press), examined curvilinear relations of FFM and AMPD domains with a range of psychopathology and general impairment variables, but found no evidence of maladaptive bipolarity in models focused on these relations. Although there have been mixed findings for maladaptive bipolarity when examining curvilinear relations, recent statistical advances (e.g., ideal point scoring; Carter et al., 2016) and methodological considerations (e.g., more deliberate sampling; Samuel & Tay, 2018) may increase the likelihood of uncovering curvilinear relationships.

As a whole, whether personality traits are maladaptively bipolar has been understudied in the PD literature. More focused research on this topic may improve our understanding of trait models and the measures developed to assess them; however, until then, researchers and clinicians will need to carefully consider the bipolarity of the scales they use. The designations in Table 14.1 provide a starting point for such thinking, but should be supplemented by examining recent research on these measures.

MULTISOURCE ASSESSMENT

The "Formats" column in Table 14.1 lists methods reflecting varied information sources: the self, an informant (parent, spouse, peer, etc.), and trained assessors (clinicians). Although self-reports are the most frequently used assessment information source and provide valid data on personality pathology (as evidenced by convergent validity with important outcomes; Dawood & Pincus, 2016; Ozer & Benet-Martinez, 2006; Yen et al., 2009), theory and research suggest the limitations of self-report measures as stand-alone assessments of personality pathology (Hopwood & Bornstein, 2014; Carlson, Vazire, & Oltmanns, 2013). In fact, both informant-reports (Oltmanns & Turkheimer, 2009) and interviews (Stepp, Trull, Burr, Wolfenstein, & Vieth, 2005) provide unique and valid information about personality pathology, above and beyond self-report assessments. Researchers and clinicians should carefully consider the value and limitations of individual methods of assessment, as well as how multiple sources of information can be combined.

Beyond recognizing the value of multiple assessment methods, it is useful to consider whether the relative value of a source depends upon the construct being assessed and why this might be, as this allows theoretical and empirical principles to guide multi-method assessment. One set of principles comes from Vazire's (2010) Self–Other Knowledge Asymmetry model, which proposes that the relative validity of self- and informant-reports is a function of a trait's (a) observability (e.g., involves overt behavior) and (b) evaluativeness (e.g., is socially desirable). Specifically, when assessing PD-related features, self-reports are likely to provide more valid information on less observable traits (e.g., neuroticism), whereas informants can contribute substantial unique information on evaluative traits that are relatively observable (e.g., agreeableness; Carlson et al., 2013). However, it is important to note that the self–informant relationship also influences the validity of ratings, such that intimate informants (spouses, close family, etc.) can also provide valid information about less observable traits (Connelly & Ones, 2010). Limited research exists on factors that influence the relative value of clinician reports (Galione & Oltmanns, 2014); however, they are likely (a) improved by the use of structured instruments and (b) most useful when self-reports cannot be relied upon due a lack of insight regarding the consistency and impairment associated with a particular PD dimension (e.g., Trull et al., 1998).

Ultimately, multiple sources of information may be useful for assessing PD dimensions; however, the integration of such data can prove complicated when sources disagree. It is beyond the scope of this chapter to fully treat this topic (see Hopwood & Bornstein, 2014); however, it is worth recognizing several considerations relevant to both clinicians and researchers. First, reports from a single source reflect both shared and unique information, as well as error. It follows from this that statistically combining or averaging across sources will remove source-specific error, as well as unique and valid information provided by individual sources (Galione & Oltmanns, 2014). Second, it may be important to consider the reasons for discrepancies across sources, as these discrepancies can provide information about personality pathology as well (Mosterman & Hendriks, 2011). Finally, it is worth noting that not all measures in Table 14.1 have formats for multiple sources. Given this, it is important that clinicians and researchers consider their needs for multi-method data as they choose measures for studies and clinical assessments.

WORKING TOWARD A CONSENSUAL SET OF PD FACETS

The measures described above can be understood as residing within a broader higher-order structural model of normal and abnormal personality traits. The FFM represents five higher-order dimensions with roots in the normal-range personality literature. The PSY-5 includes a similar set of maladaptive personality dimensions that are keyed in the direction of their most maladaptive poles. Despite some apparent dissimilarities between these higher-order models (e.g., the FFM includes openness, whereas the PSY-5 includes the domain of psychoticism), a growing literature has shown that measures representing each higher-order model can be represented in the same structural model (e.g., Samuel, Simms, Clark, Livesley, & Widiger, 2010; Wright & Simms, 2014).

Historically, there has been much less consistency across models with respect to their lower-order facets. Widiger and Simonsen (2005, 2006), for example, summarized 18 faceted PD models and organized the facets rationally into a five-factor scheme based on the FFM/PSY-5. Well over 100 facets were organized in this way, suggesting that different measures have proposed many different ways to conceptualize the narrower facets that give rise to the broad domains of PD traits. Several themes were apparent from their collection of facets. First, within each broad domain, there was substantial overlap across similarly named traits (e.g., sociability and social closeness on the one hand and aloofness, detachment, and social avoidance on the other all appeared to tap quite similar aspects of interpersonal behavior in the extraversion-introversion domain). Second, some lower-order facets were listed across multiple domains (e.g., alienation, entitlement, social closeness, dependency), which was likely due to different conceptualizations of these traits across models. Widiger and Simonsen (2006, p. 15) concluded "that an important goal of future research will be the identification of a common ground among alternative dimensional models of personality disorder."

So, where do we stand, more than a decade later, with respect to Widiger and Simonsen's (2006) conclusion? As noted earlier in this chapter, several new faceted PD measures have been developed (e.g., PID-5, CAT-PD, and the collection of FFM-PD measures), leading to mixed progress with respect to a consensual lower-order facet structure for personality pathology. On a positive note, the CAT-PD and PID-5 measures, despite arising through relatively independent processes, are quite similar at the facet-level: Of the PID-5's 25 facets, the CAT-PD has a direct one-to-one match for 24 of them (PID-5 deceptiveness is folded into CAT-PD manipulativeness). However, the CAT-PD also includes several additional facets that are arguably important to the broad assessment of personality pathology (self-harm, norm-violation, etc.) and that have demonstrated incremental validity relative to the PID-5 (Evans & Simms, 2018; Yalch & Hopwood, 2016). Moreover, the FFM-PD measures include many different facets whose connections with the PID-5 and CAT-PD models are less easily described (e.g., Timorousness). Complicating the connections with the FFM-PD facets is that the eight FFM-PD measures often include overlapping facets that have been conceptualized differently to best represent the given PD they were designed to represent.

Thus, although progress has been made with respect to identifying a consensual facet structure for personality pathology, much more work is needed. One recent development may hasten this process: the Hierarchical Taxonomy of Psychopathology (HiTOP; Kotov et al., 2017) consortium – whose mission it is to develop a consensual dimensional psychiatric classification system – is in the process of developing measures to represent the full domain of psychopathology dimensions, including those related to PDs. This process, if successful, should further hone our understanding of the lower-order facets of personality pathology.

SUMMARY, CONCLUSIONS, AND FUTURE DIRECTIONS

In this chapter, we have summarized the prominent dimensional measures of traits and impairment related to personality pathology. Much progress has been made in the dimensional assessment of personality traits that are presumed to underlie PD, including significant progress toward a consensual facet structure for PD traits. However, the distinctions made in the literature between PD traits and PD functioning/impairment have resulted in two related sets of measures whose interconnections have only become a recent focus in the literature. An important task for the PD literature is to address whether PD traits and impairment are indeed differentiable aspects of personality pathology, as this question has important implications for the measures reviewed here, as well as the broader conceptualization of personality pathology in our classification systems.

Another task for the PD community to address is that of clinical utility. We have attempted in Table 14.1 and throughout the text to note the features of the reviewed measures that serve the interests of clinical utility. Dimensional PD measures appear to vary considerably in terms of whether they include such features. Measures attached to existing batteries, such as the MMPI-2-RF and PAI, are in the best position to have immediate clinical impact given that these measures already have enjoyed considerable traction in applied practice. Conversely, more modern measures, such as the PID-5 and CAT-PD, may have a longer road to travel to become useful clinical instruments. All too often, researchers focus on developing research measures only and neglect adding the features that might make them more useful in clinical settings. This is true of some of the measures reviewed here, especially the measures of PD functioning/impairment, which largely lack adequate norms or clear interpretive guidelines.

Notably, clinical psychologists and related practitioners are often relatively adherent to the measures they initially elected to use in their clinical practice. For example, numerous reviews have documented that practicing clinicians continue to favor measures such as like the MMPI-2, Rorschach Inkblot Method, and Thematic Apperception Test, despite the information provided in reviews like this and the literature more broadly that more modern measures are available that provide a more nuanced and evidence-based way to assess personality pathology (e.g., Piotrowski, 1999). Why might this be? Although a full treatment of this question is beyond the scope of this chapter, it is clear that current PD researchers will need to do more than they are currently doing to counter this phenomenon. Adding features to tests to improve their clinical utility (e.g., strong norms, validity scales, interpretive materials, scoring services) is an important and necessary first step to improve the state of clinical PD assessment. However, more is probably needed, including efforts to interact directly with clinicians in workshops and continuing education activities, as well as to influence the methods emphasized in training programs for psychologists and allied mental health professionals.

In sum, there is no shortage of ways to assess the features of personality pathology through a dimensional lens. Researchers in this domain would do well to continue working toward integration across models (e.g., HiTOP) and building clinically useful measures of dimensional PD features.

REFERENCES

Al-Dajani, N., Gralnick, T. M., & Bagby, R. M. (2016). A psychometric review of the Personality Inventory for DSM-5 (PID-5): Current status and future directions. *Journal of Personality Assessment, 98*(1), 62–81.

Alden, L. E., Wiggins, J. S., & Pincus, A. L. (1990). Construction of circumplex scales for the Inventory of Interpersonal Problems. *Journal of Personality Assessment, 55*(3–4), 521–536.

American Psychiatric Association. (2013). *Diagnostic and Statistical Manual of Mental Disorders* (5th ed.). Arlington, VA: American Psychiatric Publishing.

Anderson, J. L., & Sellbom, M. (2018). Evaluating the DSM-5 Section III personality disorder impairment criteria. *Personality Disorders: Theory, Research, and Treatment, 9*(1), 51–61.

Anderson, K. W., & McLean, P. D. (1997). Conscientiousness in depression: Tendencies, predictive utility, and longitudinal stability. *Cognitive Therapy and Research, 21*(2), 223–238.

Bach, B., & Hutsebaut, J. (2018). Level of Personality Functioning Scale – Brief Form 2.0: Utility in capturing personality problems in psychiatric outpatients and incarcerated addicts. *Journal of Personality Assessment, 100*(6), 660–670.

Bagby, R. M., & Widiger, T. A. (2018). Five Factor Model personality disorder scales: An introduction to a special section on assessment of maladaptive variants of the five-factor model. *Psychological Assessment, 30*(1), 1–9.

Bagge, C. L., & Trull, T. J. (2003). DAPP-BQ: Factor structure and relations to personality disorder symptoms in a non-clinical sample. *Journal of Personality Disorders, 17*(1), 19–32.

Bakker, A. B., Demerouti, E., & ten Brummelhuis, L. L. (2012). Work engagement, performance, and active learning: The role of conscientiousness. *Journal of Vocational Behavior, 80*, 555–564.

Bastiaansen, L., De Fruyt, F., Rossi, G., Schotte, C., & Hofmans, J. (2013). Personality disorder dysfunction versus traits: Structural and conceptual issues. *Personality Disorders: Theory, Research, and Treatment, 4*(4), 293–303.

Ben-Porath, Y. S., & Tellegen, A. (2008). *MMPI-2-RF (Minnesota Multiphasic Personality Inventory- 2 Restructured Form) Manual for Administration, Scoring, and Interpretation*. Minneapolis, MN: University of Minnesota Press.

Berghuis, H. (2007).*General Assessment of Personality Disorder (GAPD). Version 2007*. Amersfoort: Symfora groep.

Berghuis, H., Kamphuis, J. H., & Verheul, R. (2012). Core features of personality disorder: Differentiating general personality dysfunctioning from personality traits. *Journal of Personality Disorders, 26*, 1–13.

Berghuis, H., Kamphuis, J. H., & Verheul, R. (2014). Specific personality traits and general personality dysfunction as predictors of the presence and severity of personality disorders in a clinical sample. *Journal of Personality Assessment, 96*(4), 410–416.

Bogg, T., & Roberts, B. W. (2004). Conscientiousness and health-related behaviors: A meta-analysis of the leading behavioral contributors to mortality. *Psychological Bulletin, 130*(6), 887–919.

Bottlender, M., & Soyka, M. (2005). Impact of different personality dimensions (NEO Five-Factor Inventory) on the outcome of alcohol-dependent patients 6 and 12 months after treatment. *Psychiatry Research, 136*, 61–67.

Busch, A. J., Morey, L. C., & Hopwood, C. J. (2017). Exploring the assessment of the DSM-5 Alternative Model for Personality Disorders with the Personality Assessment Inventory. *Journal of Personality Assessment, 99*(2), 211–218.

Calabrese, W. R., & Simms, L. J. (2014). Prediction of daily ratings of psychosocial functioning: Can ratings of personality disorder traits and functioning be distinguished? *Personality Disorders: Theory, Research, and Treatment, 5*(3), 314–322.

Canuto, A., Meiler-Mititelu, C., Herrmann, F., Giannakopoulos, P., & Weber, K. (2008). Impact of personality on termination of short-term group psychotherapy in depressed elderly outpatients. *International Journal of Geriatric Psychiatry, 23*, 22–26.

Carlson, E. N., Vazire, S., & Oltmanns, T. F. (2013). Self–other knowledge asymmetries in personality pathology. *Journal of Personality, 81*(2), 155–170.

Carter, N. T., Guan, L., Maples, J. L., Williamson, R. L., & Miller, J. D. (2016). The downsides of extreme conscientiousness for psychological well-being: The role of obsessive-compulsive tendencies. *Journal of Personality*, *84*(8), 510–522.

Cheavens, J. S., Strunk, D. R., Lazarus, S. A., & Goldstein, L. A. (2012). The compensation and capitalization models: A test of two approaches to individualizing the treatment of depression. *Behavior Research and Therapy*, 50, 699–706.

Clark, L. A. (1993). *Manual for the Schedule for Nonadaptive and Adaptive Personality (SNAP)*. Minneapolis: University of Minnesota Press.

Clark, L. A. (2007). Assessment and diagnosis of personality disorder: Perennial issues and an emerging reconceptualization. *Annual Review of Clinical Psychology*, *58*, 227–257.

Clark, L. A., Simms, L. J., Wu, K. D., & Casillas, A. (2002). *Schedule for Nonadaptive and Adaptive Personality (2nd ed.): Manual for Administration, Scoring, and Interpretation*. Unpublished test manual.

Connelly, B. S., & Ones, D. S. (2010). An 'other' perspective on personality: Meta-analytic integration of observers' accuracy and predictive validity. *Psychological Bulletin*, *136*(6), 1092–1122.

Costa, P. T., & McCrae, R. R. (1992). Normal personality assessment in clinical practice: The NEO Personality Inventory. *Psychological Assessment*, *4*(1), 5–13.

Cronbach, L. J., & Meehl, P. E. (1955). Construct validity in psychological tests. *Psychological Bulletin*, *52*(4), 281–302.

Dawood, S., & Pincus, A. L. (2016). Multi-surface interpersonal assessment in a cognitive-behaviors therapy context. *Journal of Personality Assessment*, *98*(5), 449–460.

Edmundson, M., Lynam, D. R., Miller, J. D., Gore, W. L., & Widiger, T. A. (2011). A Five-Factor measure of schizotypal personality traits. *Assessment*, *18*(3), 321–334.

Evans, C., & Simms, L. J. (2018). Assessing inter-model continuity between the Section II and Section III conceptualization of borderline personality disorder in DSM-5. *Personality Disorders: Theory, Research, and Treatment*, *9*, 290–296.

Few, L. R., Miller, J. D., Morse, J. Q., Yaggi, K. E., Reynolds, S. K., & Pilkonis, P. A. (2010). Examining the reliability and validity of clinician ratings on the Five-Factor Model Score Sheet. *Assessment*, *17*(4), 440–453.

Flückiger, C., Del Re, A. C., Wampold, B., Symonds, D., & Horvath, A. O. (2012). How central is the alliance in psychotherapy? A multilevel longitudinal meta-analysis. *Journal of Counseling Psychology*, *59*(1), 10–17.

Fossati, A., Somma, A., Borroni, S., & Miller, J. D. (2017). Assessing dimensions of pathological narcissism: Psychometric properties of the Short Form of the Five-Factor Narcissism Inventory in a sample of Italian university students. *Journal of Personality Assessment*, *100*, 250–258.

Fowler, J. C., Sharp, C., Kalpakci, A., Madan, A., Clapp, J., Allen, J. G., Frueh, B. C., & Oldham, J. M. (2015). A dimensional approach to assessing personality functioning: Examining personality trait domains utilizing DSM-IV personality disorder criteria. *Comprehensive Psychiatry*, *56*, 75–84.

Galione, J., & Oltmanns, T. F. (2014). Multimethod assessment of traits. In C. J. Hopwood & R. F. Bornstein (Eds.), *Multimethod Clinical Assessment* (pp. 21–50). New York: Guilford Press.

Glover, N., Miller, J. D., Lynam, D. R., Crego, C., & Widiger, T. A. (2012). The Five-Factor Narcissism Inventory: A Five-Factor measure of narcissistic personality traits. *Journal of Personality Assessment*, *94*(5), 500–512.

Goldberg, L. R. (1993). The structure of phenotypic personality traits. *American Psychologist*, *48*, 26–34.

Gore, W. L., Tomiatti, M., & Widiger, T. A. (2011). The home for histrionism. *Personality and Mental Health*, 5, 57–72.

Harkness, A. R., & McNulty, J. L. (1994). The personality psychopathology five (PSY-5): Issues from the pages of a diagnostic manual instead of a dictionary. In S. Strack and M. Lorr (Eds.), *Differentiating Normal and Abnormal Personality* (pp. 291–315). New York: Springer.

Harkness, A. R., & McNulty, J. L. (2007). Restructured versions of the MMPI-2 Personality Psychopathology Five (PSY-5) Scales. *Paper presented at the meeting of the American Psychological Association*, San Francisco, CA.

Harkness, A. R., McNulty, J. L., & Ben-Porath, Y. S. (1995). The Personality Psychopathology Five (PSY-5): Constructs and MMPI-2 scales. *Psychological Assessment*, *7*(1), 104–114.

Harkness, A. R., McNulty, J. L., Finn, J. A., Reynolds, S. M., Shields, S. M., & Arbisi, P. (2013). The MMPI-2-RF Personality Psychopathology Five (PSY-5-RF) scales: Development and validity research. *Journal of Personality Assessment*, *96*(2), 140–150.

Helle, A. C., Trull, T. J., Widiger, T. A., & Mullins-Sweatt, S. N. (2017). Utilizing interview and self-report assessment of the Five-Factor Model to examine convergence with the Alternative Model for Personality Disorders. *Personality Disorders: Theory, Research, and Treatment*, *8*(3), 247–254.

Hentschel, A. G., & Livesley, W. J. (2013). The General Assessment of Personality Disorder (GAPD): Factor structure, incremental validity of self-pathology, and relations to DSM-IV personality disorders. *Journal of Personality Assessment*, *95*(5), 479–485.

Hentschel, A. G., & Pukrop, R. (2014). The essential features of personality disorder in DSM-5: The relationship between Criteria A and B. *Journal of Nervous and Mental Disease*, *202*(5), 412–418.

Hirsh, J. B., Quilty, L. C., Bagby, R. M., & McMain, S. F. (2012). The relationship between agreeableness and the development of the working alliance in patients with Borderline Personality Disorder. *Journal of Personality Disorders*, *26*(4), 616–627.

Hopwood, C. J., & Bornstein, R. F. (Eds.) (2014). *Multimethod Clinical Assessment*. New York: Guilford Press.

Hopwood, C. J., Good, E. W., & Morey, L. C. (2018). Validity of the DSM-5 Levels of Personality Functioning Scale–Self Report. *Journal of Personality Assessment*, *100*(6), 650–659.

Hopwood, C. J., Malone, J. C., Ansell, E. B., Sanislow, C. A., Grilo, C. M., McGlashan, T. H., ... Morey, L. C. (2011). Personality assessment in DSM-5L: Empirical support for rating severity, style, and traits. *Journal of Personality Disorder*, *25*(3), 305–320.

Hopwood, C. J., Thomas, K. M., Markon, K. E., Wright, A. G. C., & Krueger, R. F. (2012). DSM-5 personality traits and DSM-IV personality disorders. *Journal of Abnormal Psychology*, *121*(2), 424–432.

Hughes, J., & Barkham, M. (2005). Scoping the Inventory of Interpersonal Problems, its derivatives and short forms: 1988–2004. *Clinical Psychology and Psychotherapy*, *12*, 475–496.

Huprich, S. K., Nelson, S. M., Meehan, K. B., Siefert, C. J., Haggerty, G., Sexton, J., ... Baade, L. (2018). *Introduction of the DSM-5 Levels of Personality Functioning Questionnaire*. Personality Disorders: Theory, Research, and Treatment, *9*(6), 553–563.

Hutsebaut, J. Feenstra, D. J., & Kamphuis, J. H. (2016). Development and preliminary psychometric evaluation of a brief self-report questionnaire for the assessment of the DSM-5 Level of Personality Functioning Scale: The LPFS Brief Form (LPFS-

BF). *Personality Disorders: Theory, Research, and Treatment, 7* (2), 192–197.

Kotov, R., Gamez, W. Schmidt, F., & Watson, D. (2010). Linking 'big' personality traits to anxiety, depressive, and substance use disorders: A meta-analysis. *Psychological Bulletin, 136*(5), 768–821.

Kotov, R., Krueger, R. F., Watson, D., Achenbach, T. M., Althoff, R. R., Bagby, R. M., ... Zimmerman, M. (2017). The Hierarchical Taxonomy of Psychopathology (HiTOP): A dimensional alternative to traditional nosologies. *Journal of Abnormal Psychology, 4*, 454–477.

Krueger, R. F. (2013). Personality disorders are the vanguard of the post-DSM-5.0 era. *Personality Disorders: Theory, Research, and Treatment, 4*, 355–362.

Krueger, R. F., Derringer, J., Markon, K. E., Watson, D., & Skodol, A. E. (2012). Initial construction of a maladaptive personality trait model and inventory for DSM-5. *Psychological Medicine, 42*, 1879–1890.

Krueger, R. F., Eaton, N. R., Clark. L. A. Watson, D., Markon, K. E. Derringer, J., ... Livesley, W. J. (2011). Deriving an empirical structure of personality pathology for DSM-5. *Journal of Personality Disorders, 25*(2), 170–191.

Leising, D., & Zimmermann, J. (2011). An integrative conceptual framework for assessing personality and personality pathology. *Review of General Psychology, 15*(4), 317–330.

Livesley, W. J. (2006). *General Assessment of PD (GAPD). Unpublished manuscript, Department of Psychiatry*, University of British Columbia, Vancouver, BC, Canada.

Livesley, W. K., & Jackson, D. N. (2009). *Manual for the Dimensional Assessment of Personality Pathology–Basic Questionnaire (DAPP-BQ)*. Port Huron, MI: Sigma Assessment Systems.

Livesley, W. J., Schroeder, M. L., Jackson, D. N., & Jang, K. L. (1994). Categorical distinctions in the study of personality disorder: Implications for classification. *Journal of Abnormal Psychology, 103*, 6–17.

Lynam, D. R., Gaughan, E. T., Miller, J. D., Miller, D. J., Mullins-Sweatt, S., & Widiger, T. A. (2011). Assessing the basic traits associated with psychopathy: Development and validation of the Elemental Psychopathy Assessment. *Psychological Assessment, 23*(1), 108–124.

McCrae, R. R., & Costa Jr., P. T. (2010). *NEO Inventories Professional Manual*. Lutz, FL: Psychological Assessment Resources.

McCrae, R. R., Costa Jr., P. T., & Martin, T. A. (2005). The NEO-PI-3: A more readable Revised NEO Personality Inventory. *Journal of Personality Assessment, 84*(3), 261–270.

Miller, J. D., Pilkonis, P. A., & Mulvey, E. P. (2006). Examining the contributions of Axis II psychopathology and the Five Factor Model of personality. *Journal of Personality Disorders, 20*(4), 369–387.

Miller, T. R. (1991). The psychotherapeutic utility of the Five-Factor Model of personality: A clinician's experience. *Journal of Personality Assessment, 57*(3), 415–433.

Morey, L. C. (1991). *Professional Manual for the Personality Assessment Inventory*. Odessa, FL: Psychological Assessment Resources.

Morey, L. C. (2017). Development and initial evaluation of a self-report form of the DSM-5 Level of Personality Functioning Scale. *Psychological Assessment*. Advance online publication. http://dx.doi.org/10.1037/pas00004

Morey, L. C., Bender, D. S., & Skodol, A. E. (2013). Validating the proposed *Diagnostic and Statistical Manual of Mental Disorders,*

5th Edition, severity indicator for personality disorder. *Journal of Nervous and Mental Disease, 201*(9), 729–735.

Mosterman, R. M., & Hendriks, A. A. J. (2011). Self–other disagreement in personality assessment: Significance and prognostic value. *Clinical Psychology and Psychotherapy, 18*, 159–171.

Mullins-Sweatt, S. N., & Widiger, T. A. (2010). Personality-related problems in living: An empirical approach. *Personality Disorders: Theory, Research, and Treatment, 1*(4), 230–238.

Ogrodniczuk, J. S., Piper, W. E., Joyce, A. S., McCallum, M., & Rosie, J. S. (2003). NEO-Five Factor personality traits as predictors of response to two forms of group psychotherapy. *International Journal of Group Psychotherapy, 53*(4), 417–442.

Oltmanns, T. F., & Turkheimer, E. (2009). Person perception and personality pathology. *Current Directions in Psychological Science, 18*, 32–36.

Ozer, D. J., & Benet-Martinez, V. (2006). Personality and the prediction of consequential outcomes. *Annual Review of Psychology, 57*, 401–421.

Padesky, C. A., & Mooney, K. A. (2012). Strengths-based cognitive-behavioral therapy: A four-step model to build resilience. *Clinical Psychology and Psychotherapy, 19*, 283–290.

Parker, G., Both, L., Olley, A., Hadzi-Pavlovic, D., Irvine, P., & Jacobs, G. (2002). Defining disordered personality functioning. *Journal of Personality Disorders, 16*(6), 503–522.

Parker, G., Hadzi-Pavlovic, D., Both, L., Kumar, S., Wilhelm, K., & Olley, A. (2004). Measuring disordered personality functioning: To love and to work reprised. *Acta Psychiatrica Scandinavica, 110*(3), 230–239.

Piotrowski, C. (1999). Assessment practices in the era of managed care: Current status and future directions. *Journal of Clinical Psychology, 55*(7), 787–796.

Poropat, A. E. (2009). A meta-analysis of the Five-Factor Model of personality and academic performance. *Psychological Bulletin, 135*(2), 322–338.

Ro, E., & Clark. L. A. (2009). Psychosocial functioning in the context of diagnosis: Assessment and theoretical issues. *Psychological Assessment, 21*(3), 313–324.

Ro, E., & Clark, L. A. (2013). Interrelations between psychosocial functioning and adaptive- and maladaptive-range personality traits. *Journal of Abnormal Psychology, 122*(3), 822–835.

Rojas, S. L. (2017). *Dismantling the Five Factor Form*. Dissertation, University of Kentucky.

Rojas, S. L., & Widiger, T. A. (2014). Convergent and discriminant validity of the Five Factor Form. *Assessment, 21*(2), 143–157.

Rojas, S. L., & Widiger, T. A. (2018). Convergent and discriminant validity of the Five Factor Form and the Sliderbar Inventory. *Assessment, 25*(2), 222–234.

Samuel, D. B. (2011). Assessing personality in the *DSM-5*: The utility of bipolar constructs. *Journal of Personality Assessment, 93*(4), 390–397.

Samuel, D. B., Bucher, M. A., & Suzuki, T. (2018). A preliminary probe of personality predicting psychotherapy outcomes: Perspectives from therapists and their clients. *Psychopathology, 51* (2), 122–129.

Samuel, D., Simms, L. J., Clark, L. A., Livesley, J., & Widiger, T. A. (2010). An item response theory integration of normal and abnormal personality scales. *Personality Disorders: Theory, Research, and Treatment, 1*, 5–21.

Samuel, D. B., & Tay, L. (2018). Aristotle's golden mean and the importance of bipolarity for personality models: A commentary on "Personality Traits and Maladaptivity: Unipolarity vs. Bipolarity." *Journal of Personality*.

Samuel, D. B., & Widiger, T. A. (2008). A meta-analytic review of the relationships between the five-factor model and *DSM-IV-TR* personality disorders: A facet level analysis. *Clinical Psychology Review, 28*, 1326–1342.

Simms, L. J., & Clark, L. A. (2006). The Schedule for Nonadaptive and Adaptive Personality (SNAP): A dimensional measure of traits relevant to personality and personality pathology. In S. Strack (Ed.), *Differentiating Normal and Abnormal Personality* (2nd ed., pp. 431–450). New York: Springer.

Simms, L. J., Goldberg, L. R., Roberts, J. E., Watson, D., Welte, J., & Rotterman, J. H. (2011). Computerized Adaptive Assessment of Personality Disorder: Introducing the CAT-PD Project. *Journal of Personality Assessment, 93*, 380–389.

Skodol, A. E. (2011). Scientific issues in the revision of personality disorders for DSM-5. *Personality and Mental Health, 5*, 97–111.

Stepp, S. D., Trull, T. J., Burr, R. M., Wolfenstein, M., & Vieth, A. Z. (2005). Incremental validity of the Structured Interview for the Five-Factor Model of Personality (SIFFM). *European Journal of Personality, 19*(4), 343–357.

Suzuki, T., Samuel, D. B., Pahlen, S., & Krueger, R. F. (2015). *DSM-5* Alternative Personality Disorder Model traits as maladaptive extreme variants of the Five-Factor Model: An item-response theory analysis. *Journal of Abnormal Psychology, 124*(2), 343–354.

Tomiatti, M., Gore, W. L., Lynam, D. R., Miller, J. D., & Widiger, T. A. (2012). A five-factor measure of histrionic personality traits. In A. M. Columbus (Ed.), *Advances in Psychology Research* (Vol. 87, pp. 113–138). Hauppauge, NY: Nova Science.

Trull, T. J., & Widiger, T. A. (1997). *Structured Interview for the Five-Factor Model of Personality (SIFFM): Professional Manual*. Odessa, FL: Psychological Assessment Resources.

Trull, T. J., Widiger, T. A., & Burr, R. (2001). A structured interview assessment of the Five-Factor Model of personality: Facet-level relations to the Axis II personality disorders. *Journal of Personality, 69*(2), 175–198.

Trull, T. J., Widiger, T. A., Useda, J. D., Holcomb, J., Doan, B., Axelrod, S. R., ... Gershuny, B. S. (1998). A structured interview for the assessment of the Five-Factor Model of personality. *Psychology Assessment, 10*(3), 229–240.

van Kampen, D. (2002). The DAPP-BQ in the Netherlands: Factor structure and relationship with basic personality dimensions. *Journal of Personality Disorders, 16*(3), 235–254.

Vazire, S. (2010). Who know what about a person? The Self–Other Knowledge Asymmetry (SOKA) Model. *Journal of Personality and Social Psychology, 98*(2), 281–300.

Verheul, R., Andrea, H., Berghout, C. C., Dolan, C., Busschbach, J. J. V., van der Kroft, P. J. A., ... Fonagy, P. (2008). Severity Indices of Personality Problems (SIPP-118): Development, factor structure, reliability, and validity. *Psychological Assessment, 20*(2), 23–34.

Widiger, T. A., Bach, B., Chmielewski, M., Clark, L. A., DeYoung, C. G., Hopwood, C. J., ... Thomas, K. M. (2019). Criterion A of the AMPD in HiTOP. *Journal of Personality Assessment, 101*(4), 345–355.

Widiger, T. A., & Simonsen, E. (2005). Alternative dimensional models of personality disorder: Finding a common ground. *Journal of Personality Disorders, 19*(2), 110–130.

Widiger, T. A., & Simonsen, E. (2006). Alternative dimensional models of personality disorder: Finding a common ground. In T. A. Widiger, E. Simonsen, P. J., Sirovatka, & D. A. Regier (Eds.), *Dimensional Models of Personality Disorders: Refining the Research Agenda for DSM-V* (pp. 1–21). Washington, DC: American Psychiatric Association.

Widiger, T. A., & Spitzer, R. L. (2002). *Five-Factor Model Score Sheet*. Unpublished measure.

Widiger, T. A., & Trull, T. J. (2007). Plate tectonics in the classification of personality disorder: Shifting to a dimensional model. *American Psychologist, 62*(2), 71–83.

Widiger, T. A., Trull, T. J., Clarkin, J. F., Sanderson, C. J., & Costa, P. T., Jr. (2002). A description of the DSM-IV personality disorders with the five-factor model of personality. In P. T. Costa, Jr., & T. A. Widiger (Eds.), *Personality Disorders and the Five-Factor Model of Personality* (2nd ed., pp. 89–99). Washington, DC: American Psychological Association.

Williams, T. F., & Simms, L. J. (2016). Personality disorder models and their coverage of interpersonal problems. *Personality Disorders: Theory, Research, and Treatment, 7*, 15–27.

Williams, T. F., & Simms, L. J. (in press). Conceptual foundations of descriptive psychopathology and observational designs. In A. G. C. Wright & M. N. Hallquist (Eds.), *Handbook of Research Methods in Clinical Psychology*. New York: Cambridge University Press.

Wright, A. G. C., & Simms, L. J. (2014). On the structure of personality disorder traits: Conjoint analyses of the CAT-PD, PID-5, and NEO-PI-3 trait models. *Personality Disorders: Theory, Research, and Treatment, 5*, 43–54.

Yalch, M. M & Hopwood, C. J. (2016). Convergent, discriminant, and criterion validity of *DSM-5* traits. *Personality Disorders: Theory, Research, and Treatment, 7*, 394–404.

Yam, W. H., & Simms, L. J. (2014). Comparing criterion- and trait-based personality disorder diagnoses in DSM-5. *Journal of Abnormal Psychology, 123*, 802–808.

Yen, S., Shea, M. T., Sanislow, C. A., Skodol, A. E., Grilo, C. M., Edelen, M. O., ... Gunderson, J. G. (2009). Personality traits as prospective predictors of suicide attempts. *Acta Psychiatrica Scandinavica, 120*, 222–229.

Zimmerman, J., Bohnke, J. R., Eschstruth, R., Mathews, A., Wenzel, K., & Leising, D. (2015). The latent structure of personality functioning: Investigating Criterion A from the Alternative Model for Personality Disorders in DSM-5. *Journal of Abnormal Psychology, 124*(3), 532–548.

14a The Clinical Utility and Applications of Dimensional Assessments of Personality Pathology: Commentary on Methods and Current Issues in Dimensional Assessments of Personality Pathology

ASHLEY C. HELLE, NEIL A. MEYER, JIWON MIN, AND STEPHANIE N. MULLINS-SWEATT

In their chapter, Evans, Williams, and Simms (this volume) review current measures and methods of assessing personality pathology from a dimensional perspective. The focus of their chapter is two-fold: (1) discussing prominent dimensional measures of traits and impairment and reviewing the clinical utility of these measures, and (2) reviewing timely issues at the center of personality trait assessment, including trait bipolarity, multi-method assessment, and the assessment of dysfunction. Our focus for this commentary is to emphasize the clinical usefulness of these measures. We strongly agree with Evans and colleagues that an important task for the personality disorder (PD) community is to establish the clinical usefulness of measures in order to increase their utility to practitioners.

Transitioning dimensional models into practice is an important and challenging endeavor for the field. The authors discussed relevant concerns and potential roadblocks to this implementation, such as the length of many measures. For example, the Five-Factor Model Personality Disorder (FFMPD) measures (e.g., Five Factor Borderline Inventory, Elemental Psychopathy Assessment) collectively would be quite lengthy, as each full-length measure has more than 100 items. We agree that administration of all of these measures with one client could be logistically problematic and have limited utility within a general therapy setting. Many of the validated FFMPD measures have newly developed and validated short-forms (e.g., Five Factor Obsessive Compulsive Inventory; Griffin et al., 2018), which can improve the ease of usage for practitioners and the experience for clients. Additionally, a number of other dimensional measures (e.g., CAT-PD-Static Form, PID-5) are considerably shorter. In fact, the FFMPD scales themselves can be administered modularly in order to recreate the constructs within the DSM-5 Alternative Model (see Crego, Oltmanns, & Widiger, 2018).

The road to implementation of evidence-based assess-

ment (i.e., utilizing empirically derived personality assessments in practice) can be particularly challenging when attempting to balance various goals of multiple parties. This is a multi-step process, involving the empirical development and validation of the original assessments and then their short-forms, assessment of clinical utility and needs of clients and practitioners, and dissemination and implementation (an area that is often neglected in the assessment realm). This disconnect between the notion of maintaining the empirical structure of a model and implementing core aspects of clinical utility into measure development and application is understandable, given that both validity concerns and clinical utility are competing priorities. It is perhaps noteworthy that these competing concerns mirror those seen when developing diagnostic manuals (Mullins-Sweatt, Lengel, & DeShong, 2016). Responding to and incorporating aspects of feasibility, acceptability, and utility into the empirical development and application of personality assessment is a key aspect of successful implementation and a timely concern, given the integration of primary care health integration models of mental health treatment.

THE ROLE OF ADAPTIVE TRAITS TO TREATMENT

Evans et al. state, "Further research is needed on the role of adaptive traits in PD assessments and how such information can be integrated into broader PD models" (p. 340 in the previous chapter). This is an important point, as maintaining adaptive traits within personality assessment and the application of these models to treatment is consistent with literature related to personality traits and mental health treatment more generally (Lengel, Helle, DeShong, Meyer, & Mullins-Sweatt, 2016). One benefit of including adaptive traits in assessments is the ability to address the stigmatized nature of pathological traits, particularly within mental health and PDs. Within psychopathology and psychiatric diagnoses, PDs are highly stigmatized, as they have been described as disorders of one's "personality" or "who you are." As Widiger and Costa

Ashley Helle's work on this chapter was supported by National Institute on Alcohol Abuse and Alcoholism Grant T32 AA–13526 (PI: Kenneth Sher).

(2012) describe, the inclusion of normal or adaptive traits can be beneficial in personality assessment. We believe that in addition to the robust empirical support for a general trait model, the inclusion of general traits can not only decrease stigma, but assist with the therapeutic assessment process and feedback and treatment planning. For example, a study on client preferences for personality trait feedback found that individuals found adaptive and maladaptive trait feedback to be useful, accurate, and relevant (Lengel & Mullins-Sweatt, 2017).

UTILITY OF BIPOLARITY WITHIN DIMENSIONAL ASSESSMENT MEASURES

We agree that bipolarity should continue to be an area of careful consideration – both in research and in applied use of these measures. As Evans et al. discuss, advances in statistical techniques and methodological approaches can improve our ability to detect the actual presence of and correlates of (including impairment) traits at each end of the "pole." For example, the use of ecological momentary assessment may assist in more accurately capturing behaviors and daily life impairment associated with traits that may be related to high "internalizing" versus the externalizing that is often viewed as the more obvious maladaptive end of the pole. Likewise, with new technologies, we can further assess associated impairment through the use of broader ambulatory assessment to determine health and physiological correlates that may be more strongly associated with these traits (e.g., high conscientiousness and cardiovascular effects) when externalizing behaviors are not as central to the trait or research question of interest.

One challenge with the issue of trait bipolarity relates to assessment (as discussed) and realities of clinical and policy implementation. A structure that includes trait bipolarity has the potential to be challenging for diagnoses, leading to downstream issues with healthcare reimbursement, and thus, presenting a barrier for practitioners. Whereas we agree with Evans et al. that this should not be a reason to not utilize these traits, we recognize some of the legitimate logistical concerns that may exist and agree with the authors that further research is warranted in this area.

INCREMENTAL UTILITY OF DYSFUNCTION

Evans et al. provide a succinct summary of literature describing whether traits and dysfunction can or should be distinguished. They conclude that the question of whether dysfunction provides incremental validity over personality traits and whether traits and dysfunction can be psychometrically differentiated requires further research. Specifically, the authors provided a number of studies that call into question the ability to distinguish between PD traits and personality dysfunction, which we

will expand upon here by providing additional studies not included in the Evans et al. chapter.

Wygant and colleagues (2016) found that personality impairment criteria for antisocial personality disorder (ASPD) from the DSM-5 alternative model of personality disorder (AMPD) had incremental validity over the PD traits in predicting PCL-R psychopathy and SCID-II ASPD. Liggett, Sellbom, and Carmichael (2017) also found similar results when examining obsessive-compulsive personality disorder (OCPD) criteria from AMPD; specifically, that the impairment criteria had incremental validity above and beyond the PD traits when operationalizing OCPD. The inconclusive findings when examining whether personality trait and dysfunction can be distinct underscores the necessity of further research.

Additionally, when discussing the utility of personality dysfunction, it is imperative to consider incremental validity over traits in predicting external criteria. Creswell and colleagues (Creswell, Bachrach, Wright, Pinto, & Ansell, 2016) found that personality dysfunction did not have incremental validity over personality traits when predicting problematic alcohol use. On the other hand, Roche (2018) found that both traits and dysfunction provided incremental validity over each other in predicting a trans-theoretical model of personality organization (TTM; Blais, 2010). Clearly, additional research exploring the utility of personality traits and dysfunction with regard to external criteria is needed.

OTHER ISSUES IN ASSESSMENT

Evans et al. discuss the importance of multiple sources of assessment when assessing personality pathology. We strongly agree and want to further highlight research that has documented the importance of utilizing structured and semi-structured assessments when using multiple sources. For example, Samuel et al. (2013) found incremental validity in the prediction of psychosocial functioning over five years for PD diagnoses made by client self-report assessments and semi-structured interviews over naturalistic therapist diagnoses. As a result, they cautioned against the use of PD diagnoses by clinicians, noting that they were outperformed by semi-structured interviews in all cases and by patient self-reports in almost all cases. However, it is important to note that more recent research has found higher agreement between patient self-report and therapist informant report of dimensional PD symptoms, suggesting more convergence than previously suggested by the literature (Samuel, Suzuki, Bucher, & Griffin, 2018).

MOVING FORWARD AND BRIDGING THE GAP

The authors highlight an important gap in the implementation of much of what has been discussed in the literature. The research-to-practice gap that occurs is not unique to psychopathology (or, more specifically, personality trait) assessment research or treatment. This can be seen across diagnoses and within many disciplines (e.g., medicine, psychology). When practice and research are segregated, the dilemma no longer becomes what model or measure to use, but how to ensure that these two necessary entities communicate, share ideas, and implement the best evidence-based practices. Evans et al. speak to this, stating, "However, more is probably needed, including efforts to interact directly with clinicians in workshops and continuing education activities, as well as to influence the methods emphasized in training programs for psychologists and allied mental health professionals" (p. 343 in the previous chapter).

Over a decade of research provides evidence that dimensional models indeed provide sufficient clinical utility (e.g., Blais, 1997; Samuel & Widiger, 2004, 2006; Verheul, 2005) and more in-depth information about an individual's specific personality profile (Widiger & Trull, 2007). Whereas empirical support should theoretically "carry more weight" than practitioners' preferences for the models or measures to use, measures must be known about, feasible, and acceptable in order to improve dissemination and implementation. Direct interaction, training, feedback, and participation from practitioners are essential at multiple levels (e.g., graduate level training, routine updated trainings in practices). Research has indicated that experts and clinicians agree that PDs can be conceptualized as maladaptive variants of personality traits (e.g., Bernstein, Iscan, Maser, & Boards of the Directors of ARPD and ISSPD, 2007) and that clinicians often prefer dimensional models to categorical models on many aspects of clinical utility (e.g., Morey, Skodol, & Oldham, 2014). However, this support has been equivocal, and there are aspects of clinical utility (e.g., communication with other professionals) on which dimensional models are rated similarly to extant models (Morey et al., 2014). It is areas like this in which training and bridging the gap could assist the field in moving forward. In conclusion, we highlight agreement with Evans et al. that continuing to improve the dimensional assessment of PD is a worthwhile endeavor. As part of this work, researchers must continue to consider the usefulness and incremental validity of such assessments in order to improve their training, implementation, and use.

REFERENCES

Bernstein, D. B., Iscan, C., Maser, J., & Boards of the Directors of ARPD and ISSPD (2007). Opinions of personality disorder experts regarding the DSM-IV personality disorders classification system. *Journal of Personality Disorders, 21*, 536–551.

Blais, M. A. (1997). Clinician ratings of the five-factor model of personality and the DSM-IV personality disorders. *Journal of Nervous and Mental Disease, 185*, 388–393.

Blais, M. A. (2010). The common structure of normal personality and psychopathology: Preliminary exploration in a non-patient sample. *Personality and Individual Differences, 48*, 322–326.

Crego, C., Oltmanns, J. R., & Widiger, T. A. (2018). FFMPD scales: Comparisons with the FFM, PID-5, and CAT-PD-SF. *Psychological Assessment, 30*, 62–73.

Creswell, K. G., Bachrach, R. L., Wright, A. G., Pinto, A., & Ansell, E. (2016). Predicting problematic alcohol use with the DSM-5 alternative model of personality pathology. *Personality Disorders: Theory, Research, and Treatment, 7*(1), 103–111.

Griffin, S. A., Suzuki, T., Lynam, D. R., Crego, C., Widiger, T. A., Miller, J. D., & Samuel, D. B. (2018). Development and examination of the Five-Factor Obsessive-Compulsive Inventory–Short Form. *Assessment, 25*(1), 56–68.

Lengel, G. J., Helle, A. C., DeShong, H. L., Meyer, N. A., & Mullins-Sweatt, S. N. (2016). Translational applications of personality science for the conceptualization and treatment of psychopathology. *Clinical Psychology: Science and Practice, 23*(3), 288–308.

Lengel, G. J., & Mullins-Sweatt, S. N. (2017). The importance and acceptability of general and maladaptive personality trait computerized assessment feedback. *Psychological Assessment, 29*(1), 1–12.

Liggett, J., Sellbom, M., & Carmichael, K. L. (2017). Examining the DSM-5 section III criteria for obsessive-compulsive personality disorder in a community sample. *Journal of Personality Disorders, 31*(6), 790–809.

Morey, L. C., Skodol, A. E., & Oldham, J. M. (2014). Clinician judgments of clinical utility: A comparison of DSM-IV-TR personality disorders and the alternative model for DSM-5 personality disorders. *Journal of Abnormal Psychology, 123*, 398–405.

Mullins-Sweatt, S. N., Lengel, G. J., & DeShong, H. L. (2016). The importance of considering clinical utility in the construction of a diagnostic manual. *Annual Review of Clinical Psychology, 12*, 133–155.

Roche, M. J. (2018). Examining the alternative model of personality disorder in daily life: Evidence for incremental validity. *Personality Disorders: Theory, Research, and Treatment, 9*(6), 574–583.

Samuel, D. B., Sanislow, C. A., Hopwood, C. J., Shea, M. T., Skodol, A. E., Morey, L. C., ... & Grilo, C. M. (2013). Convergent and incremental predictive validity of clinician, self-report, and structured interview diagnoses for personality disorders over 5 years. *Journal of Consulting and Clinical Psychology, 81*(4), 650–659.

Samuel, D. B., Suzuki, T., Bucher, M. A., & Griffin, S. A. (2018). The agreement between clients' and their therapists' ratings of personality disorder traits. *Journal of Consulting and Clinical Psychology, 86*(6), 546–555.

Samuel, D. B., & Widiger, T. A. (2004). Clinicians' personality descriptions of prototypic personality disorders. *Journal of Personality Disorders, 18*, 286–308.

Samuel, D. B., & Widiger, T. A. (2006). Clinicians' judgments of clinical utility: A comparison of the DSM-IV and five-factor models. *Journal of Abnormal Psychology, 115*, 298–308.

Verheul, R. (2005). Clinical utility of dimensional models for personality pathology. *Journal of Personality Disorders, 19*, 283–302.

Widiger, T. A., & Costa, P. T. (2012). Integrating normal and abnormal personality structure: The five-factor model. *Journal of Personality, 80*, 1471–1506.

Widiger, T. A., & Trull, T. J. (2007). Plate tectonics in the classification of personality disorder: Shifting to a dimensional model. *American Psychologist, 62*, 71–83.

Wygant, D. B., Sellbom, M., Sleep, C. E., Wall, T. D., Applegate, K. C., Krueger, R. F., & Patrick, C. J. (2016). Examining the DSM-5 alternative personality disorder model operationalization of antisocial personality disorder and psychopathy in a male correctional sample. *Personality Disorders: Theory, Research, and Treatment, 7*(3), 229–239.

14b   New and Continuing Developments in the Assessment of Personality Disorders: Commentary on Methods and Current Issues in Dimensional Assessments of Personality Pathology

MICHAEL CARNOVALE AND R. MICHAEL BAGBY

Evans, Williams, and Simms (this volume) have written an impressively comprehensive and contemporary review of the various instruments and methods designed to assess dimensional personality pathology. These authors review a wide range of tests and cover most of the issues that are critical areas of concern or discussion in the field. This chapter will surely serve as a key reference for clinicians and researchers interested in the assessment of personality pathology. It should be emphasized, however, that the field of dimensional personality pathology is moving and evolving at a breathtaking pace, which is especially the case since the introduction of the Alternative Model of Personality Disorders (AMPD) in Section III of the fifth edition of the *Diagnostic and Statistical Manual of Mental Disorders* (DSM-5) (American Psychiatric Association, 2013), and we would anticipate yet another review will be needed in short order.

In this commentary, we: (a) expand on several topics covered by Evans et al. that we believe are especially relevant to clinical applicability/utility (i.e., multisource assessment, validity scales, and norms), and (b) identify and discuss other topics that we believe are relevant to the assessment of dimensional personality pathology that were not directly addressed in their chapter (i.e., longitudinal assessment, other newer measures).

MULTIPLE SOURCES OF INFORMATION

The use of multiple sources of information in the assessment of personality pathology is clearly an important issue. Specifically, Evans et al. point out the potential of self-reports' validity being compromised by a lack of insight, and the potential of informant reports and clinical interviews providing incremental validity. There are, however, many questions that we believe future research should address within this topic.

First, with the use of informant-reports in clinical practice, is merely one informant adequate, or is it more advantageous to have multiple informants? At a psychometric level, it is likely the case that the use of multiple informants increases the reliability of the assessment of a target's dimensional personality pathology, but it may be less pragmatic to actually solicit reports from multiple informants (or even one informant) in practice. Further, is there a specific *kind* of an informant that may provide the most useful information regarding a target's personality pathology (e.g., a romantic partner compared to a parent or close friend)?

Second, and relatedly, how can systematic measurement error (i.e., response biases) in informant-reports be taken into account? For example, with the use of one particular informant, it may be the case that this informant especially likes the target, which may therefore compromise the validity of this informant's ratings of the target (e.g., presenting the target in a favorable light; Leising, Erbs, & Fritz, 2010).

Third, are clinician-rated instruments compromised if there is a lack of insight from a patient, or if there is evidence that a patient is engaging in non-credible responding on self-report instruments? Specifically, as certain clinician-rated instruments heavily rely on the responses of the patients themselves, it is reasonable to expect that the information provided by the clinician-rated instruments may be accordingly affected.

Fourth, there is some uncertainty if meta-perception-based reports (i.e., asking a target how they believe other people see them) can be useful in the assessment of personality pathology (e.g., Carlson & Barranti, 2016). It may be the case that framing assessment items from a different point of view may overcome response biases inherent in typically framed self-reported items (i.e., worded in first-person), and may provide a more pragmatic alternative to informant-reports. Specifically, if there is evidence to suggest that the use of meta-perceptions provides equivalent incremental validity as informant-reports, it may be easier for a clinician to administer a meta-perception-based measure than to solicit an informant to complete a measure.

Finally, as mentioned by Evans et al., what are the patterns of discrepancy between self-reports, informant-reports, and clinician-rated instruments that could be expected in the context of assessing personality pathology? Is it the case that self-reports tend to have higher mean scores than informant-reports (e.g., Sleep, Lamkin, Lynam, Campbell, & Miller, 2018)? Is it the case that those with more severe personality pathology tend to diverge from informant-reports more than those with less severe personality pathology? It is clear that much more research needs to be done in this area in order to potentially inform clinical practice in the assessment of personality pathology.

ABSENCE OF VALIDITY SCALES

A second issue of clinical relevance noted by Evans et al. is the absence of validity scales in many of the instruments assessing personality pathology. Validity scales typically assess three types of test protocol validity: inconsistent responding, non-credible over-reporting, and non-credible under-reporting. Out of the more than 20 scales listed in Table 14.1 in Evans et al., only six include validity scales, and even fewer have validity scales that assess both forms of non-credible reporting and inconsistent responding. We believe this a remarkable shortcoming. Although an over-reporting (Sellbom, Dhillon, & Bagby, 2018) and response inconsistency scales (Bagby & Sellbom, 2018; Keeley, Webb, Peterson, Roussin, & Flanagan, 2016) have been developed for the Personality Inventory for DSM-5 (PID-5), an under-reporting scale has yet to be developed and validated for this measure. While many personality and some clinical researchers may eschew the notion of validity scales for a variety of different reasons, clinicians expect them and the clinical utility of any measure that includes validity scales is enhanced (Hopwood & Sellbom, 2013). As suggested in the previous section on multisource assessment, it may also be useful to investigate the inclusion of validity scales for informant-based measures.

NEED FOR NORMATIVE DATA

We are also in agreement with Evans et al. that, for any instrument assessing personality pathology, it would be useful to gather normative data in order to generate T-scores for a given examinee, and therefore increase clinical utility. Although a number of the measures outlined by Evans et al. have associated normative data, there are also many measures outlined that have yet to gather normative data. With respect to the PID-5 scoring of the Personality Assessment Inventory (PAI) in particular, Evans et al. suggest that an advantage of using the PAI relative to many other instruments discussed is that the PAI has strong norms. We agree that the PAI *does* contain strong norms for its established subscales, but at the same time, we would argue that it is premature to promote the PID-5 scoring of the PAI based on this reason alone. That is, we believe new normative data must be collected based on responses to these new PID-5-based subscales in order

to realize its clinical utility with respect to the ability to derive T-scores.

TRACKING PERSONALITY PATHOLOGY ACROSS TIME

One issue that was given limited attention by Evans et al. was the extent to which each measure could be used to track personality pathology traits across time (e.g., over the course of treatment). In general, only a relatively small amount of research has been conducted regarding the longitudinal assessment of personality pathology (for a review, see Morey & Hopwood, 2013), and regarding the capacity of most of the scales reviewed for longitudinal assessment (e.g., Wright, Hopwood, Skodol, & Morey, 2016). Moreover, most of this research has focused on more "panel" style longitudinal data (e.g., yearly assessments), and less research has focused on more *intensive* longitudinal data (i.e., daily diary methods, ecological momentary assessments; Roche, 2018; Wright & Simms, 2016), especially in the context of treatment.

Two possible measures that may be feasible to use to track personality pathology in the context of treatment are the brief 25-item version of the PID-5 (PID-5-BF; see Roche, 2018 for the use of the PID-5-BF in daily diary research) and the recently developed Personality Dynamics Diary (PDD; Zimmermann et al., 2019). The PID-5-BF retains the five broader domains of the full PID-5, whereas the PDD contains nine subscales that assess various trait expressions. Of note, Zimmermann et al. (2019) found some support for the clinical utility of the PDD from the perspective of patients and therapists.

It would also be interesting to extend the use of informant-reports in the context of intensive longitudinal assessments. For example, can informant-reports provide useful information regarding the symptom course of a patient during treatment, beyond self-reports? As well, and more broadly, would it be feasible and useful to collect information regarding a patient's behaviors across different types of contexts, from both self-reports and informant-reports? Overall, it is clear that more research has to be done in order to examine the feasibility and clinical utility of certain scales for tracking personality pathology across time.

NEW MEASURES WITH CONSIDERABLE POTENTIAL

While Evans et al. reviewed an extensive list of measures, there are two newer measures that were not reviewed that may hold significant potential to improve existing dimensional assessment. First, the Structured Clinical Interview for the DSM-5 Alternative Model for Personality Disorders (SCID-5-AMPD; First, Skodol, Bender, & Oldham, 2018), as the name suggests, is a structured interview that contains three modules designed to assess the AMPD. Module I involves a more structured assessment of the Level of Personality Functioning Scale (i.e., Criterion A of the

AMPD), Module II involves the assessment of the 25 maladaptive personality facets and the five maladaptive personality domains of the AMPD (analogous to the scales that can be derived from the PID-5), and Module III involves the assessment of the six personality disorders that were retained and modified in the AMPD. As of the writing of this commentary, there have been two studies examining the reliability and validity of Module I of the SCID-5-AMPD (Buer Christensen et al., 2018; Kampe et al., 2018). It would be informative for future research to further examine the psychometric properties of the SCID-5-AMPD, as well as for the potential addition of norms for this measure to increase clinical utility.

Second, the recent Personality Inventory for ICD-11 (PiCD; Oltmanns & Widiger, 2018) is a self-reported measure designed to assess the dimensional trait model of personality pathology in the 11th edition of the World Health Organization's *International Classification of Diseases*. Structurally, the PiCD contains five subscales: (a) Negative Affective, (b) Detachment, (c) Dissocial, (d) Disinhibition, and (e) Anankastic. It is evident that four of these five domains are conceptually similar to the Negative Affect, Detachment, Antagonism, and Disinhibition domains, respectively, from the AMPD (Oltmanns & Widiger, 2018). There is preliminary evidence for the reliability and validity of the PiCD (Oltmanns & Widiger, 2018), and as this classification for personality disorders has been accepted by the World Health Organization (Mulder & Tyrer, 2019), there is also likely to be more research and examinations of its clinical utility (Bagby & Widiger, in press).

POTENTIAL DOWNSIDES IN THE EXPANSIVE GROWTH OF MEASURES

One final, and arguably the most important, concern we would like to discuss is the potentially problematic existence of such a large number of measures. In general, we agree with Evans et al. regarding the need for a consensual set of personality pathology features, and we believe it may be difficult to determine the relative utility of each measure and to ultimately decide on one or two measures in the context of research or in clinical practice. In the research context, we believe it's important that the field of dimensional personality pathology accumulate data sets that are reasonably comparable across sites, and that results from published studies have a common metric to evaluate outcomes (which also has implications for evaluating replicability). This seems to be a challenging task given the proliferation of existing measures. In clinical practice, one should be using the most empirically supported approaches, but it may be difficult for the busy clinician to navigate the vast assessment literature to compare all of the measures at a nuanced level. Therefore, we believe much research has to be done comparing these measures in terms of their relative psychometric

properties (e.g., Crego, Oltmanns, & Widiger, 2018), and their relative clinical utility (e.g., prediction of treatment course/outcomes, preferential treatment selection). Further, it may be useful to conduct multi-trait/multi-method studies in order to examine the presence of "jingle/jangle" fallacies among similarly conceptualized or differentially conceptualized subscales (i.e., to test convergent and discriminant validity, or conceptual overlap; Ziegler, Booth, & Bensch, 2013). As mentioned by Evans et al., perhaps a unified approach among a large number of researchers, such as through the HiTOP initiative, is a step forward toward construct clarification and consensus, and in turn, measurement consensus.

REFERENCES

American Psychiatric Association. (2013). *Diagnostic and Statistical Manual of Mental Disorders* (5th ed.). Arlington, VA: American Psychiatric Publishing.

Bagby, R. M., & Sellbom, M. (2018). The validity and clinical utility of the Personality Inventory for DSM-5 Response Inconsistency Scale. *Journal of Personality Assessment, 100*(4), 398–405.

Bagby, R. M., & Widiger, T. A. (in press). The assessment of ICD-11 personality disorders: Introduction to the special section. *Psychological Assessment*.

Buer Christensen, T., Paap, M. C. S., Arnesen, M., Koritzinsky, K., Nysaeter, T.-E., Eikenaes, I., . . . Hummelen, B. (2018). Interrater reliability of the Structured Clinical Interview for the DSM-5 Alternative Model of Personality Disorders Module I: Level of Personality Functioning Scale. *Journal of Personality Assessment, 100*(6), 630–641.

Carlson, E. N., & Barranti, M. (2016). Metaperceptions: Do people know how others perceive them? In J. A. Hall, M. S. Mast, & T. V. West (Eds.), *The Social Psychology of Perceiving Others Accurately* (pp. 165–182). New York: Cambridge University Press.

Crego, C., Oltmanns, J. R., & Widiger, T. A. (2018). FFMPD scales: Comparisons with the FFM, PID-5, and CAT-PD-SF. *Psychological Assessment, 30*(1), 62–73.

First, M. B., Skodol, A. E., Bender, D. S., & Oldham, J. M. (2018). *User's Guide for the Structured Clinical Interview for the DSM-5 Alternative Model for Personality Disorders (SCID-5-AMPD)*. Arlington, VA: American Psychiatric Association Publishing.

Hopwood, C. J., & Sellbom, M. (2013). Implications of DSM-5 personality traits for forensic psychology. *Psychological Injury and Law, 6*(4), 314–323.

Kampe, L., Zimmermann, J., Bender, D., Caligor, E., Borowski, A.-L., Ehrenthal, J. C., . . . Hörz-Sagstetter, S. (2018). Comparison of the Structured DSM-5 Clinical Interview for the Level of Personality Functioning Scale with the Structured Interview of Personality Organization. *Journal of Personality Assessment, 100*(6), 642–649.

Keeley, J. W., Webb, C., Peterson, D., Roussin, L., & Flanagan, E. H. (2016). Development of a Response Inconsistency Scale for the Personality Inventory for DSM-5. *Journal of Personality Assessment, 98*(4), 351–359.

Leising, D., Erbs, J., & Fritz, U. (2010). The letter of recommendation effect in informant ratings of personality. *Journal of Personality and Social Psychology, 98*(4), 668–682.

Morey, L. C., & Hopwood, C. J. (2013). Stability and change in personality disorders. *Annual Review of Clinical Psychology, 9*, 499–528.

Mulder, R., & Tyrer, P. (2019). Diagnosis and classification of personality disorders: Novel approaches. *Current Opinion in Psychiatry, 32*(1), 27–31.

Oltmanns, J. R., & Widiger, T. A. (2018). A self-report measure for the ICD-11 dimensional trait model proposal: The personality inventory for ICD-11. *Psychological Assessment, 30*(2), 154–169.

Roche, M. J. (2018). Examining the alternative model for personality disorder in daily life: Evidence for incremental validity. *Personality Disorders, 9*(6), 574–583.

Sellbom, M., Dhillon, S., & Bagby, R. M. (2018). Development and validation of an Overreporting Scale for the Personality Inventory for DSM-5 (PID-5). *Psychological Assessment, 30*(5), 582–593.

Sleep, C. E., Lamkin, J., Lynam, D. R., Campbell, W. K., & Miller, J. D. (2018). Personality disorder traits: Testing insight regarding presence of traits, impairment, and desire for change. *Personality Disorders: Theory, Research, and Treatment.* Advance online publication.

Wright, A. G. C., Hopwood, C. J., Skodol, A. E., & Morey, L. C. (2016). Longitudinal validation of general and specific structural features of personality pathology. *Journal of Abnormal Psychology, 125*(8), 1120–1134.

Wright, A. G. C., & Simms, L. J. (2016). Stability and fluctuation of personality disorder features in daily life. *Journal of Abnormal Psychology, 125*(5), 641–656.

Ziegler, M., Booth, T., & Bensch, D. (2013). Getting entangled in the nomological net. *European Journal of Psychological Assessment, 29*(3), 157–161.

Zimmermann, J., Woods, W. C., Ritter, S., Happel, M., Masuhr, O. Jaeger, U., ... Wright, A. G. C. (2019). Integrating structure and dynamics in personality assessment: First steps toward the development and validation of a personality dynamics diary. *Psychological Assessment, 31*(4), 516–531.

14c The Importance of Multiple Sources, Longitudinal Assessment, and Clinical Utility: Author Rejoinder to Commentaries on Methods and Current Issues in Dimensional Assessments of Personality Pathology

CHLOE M. EVANS, TREVOR F. WILLIAMS, AND LEONARD J. SIMMS

We thank the commentators (Carnovale & Bagby, this volume; Helle, Meyer, Min, & Mullins-Sweatt, this volume) for their feedback on our chapter, which we believe significantly enhances our original discussion of the dimensional assessment of personality pathology. In response, we would like to expand upon three issues (mentioned in either one or both commentaries) that we anticipate will be key areas for the personality assessment literature to resolve in the near future: multi-source assessment, longitudinal assessment, and clinical utility.

MULTI-SOURCE ASSESSMENT

First, we were pleased to see general agreement regarding the potential importance of obtaining information on an individual's personality from multiple sources. In addition, both commentaries also emphasized the need for additional research on multi-source personality data and how it should be interpreted. In particular, topics such as the choice of informant, measuring informant biases (e.g., socially desirable responding), potential biases in structured interviews (e.g., reliance on honest interviewees), between-source discrepancies, and the promise of meta-perceptual reports are important avenues for basic research. Beyond this, however, Carnovale and Bagby (this volume) raise important questions regarding the applied practicality of contacting one or more informants for a personality assessment; we believe the issue of practicality is worth further discussion.

Although it is true that gathering data from informants as part of an assessment is potentially burdensome, it is worth noting, for example, that such burden is less controversial within the domain of attention deficit hyperactivity disorder (ADHD). In ADHD assessments, parents, teachers, coworkers, and peers may all become involved in the assessment and provide relevant data (e.g., Seixas, Weiss, & Müller, 2012). This is supported by research documenting the unique contributions that these additional sources make (e.g., Sibley et al., 2012). Given the strength of personality assessment research indicating the

value of informant-reports (Connelly & Ones, 2010; Oltmanns & Turkheimer, 2009), perhaps a normative shift is necessary. Put otherwise, although additional research is needed to develop the precise tools and practices for efficient multi-source personality assessment, work also is needed to disseminate and implement such multi-source methods in applied settings.

LONGITUDINAL ASSESSMENT

Second, we would like to reiterate the importance of longitudinal assessment of personality pathology, as discussed by Carnovale and Bagby. As research continues to demonstrate that personality pathology is less stable than previously assumed (e.g., Morey & Hopwood, 2013), it makes good sense that personality assessment measures are capable of capturing dynamic processes that unfold over time (and across contexts). Given that the within-person processes measured by longitudinal assessment typically are the targets of treatment (as opposed to between-person variance captured by cross-sectional assessment), and given that longitudinal assessment is required to monitor treatment progress, the ability of an assessment measure to capture change over time should be considered when evaluating its clinical utility.

In response to the need for longitudinal personality assessment, Zimmermann and colleagues (2019) recently developed the Personality Dynamics Diary (PDD), a 32-item self-report measure that assesses daily behavioral manifestations of personality traits as well as the environmental contexts that may influence trait expression. Somewhat surprisingly, therapists who piloted the PDD indicated that information gleaned from the measure provided little incremental utility in treatment planning beyond the initial assessment (Zimmermann et al., 2019). In addition, the most commonly cited reason that therapists declined to pilot the PDD was fear of overburdening clients with a daily measure (Zimmermann et al., 2019). Thus, despite the potential relevance of longitudinal measurement to the treatment of personality pathology, work remains to convince clinicians of these measures' clinical utility. Specifically, researchers will need to demonstrate that the incremental utility of longitudinal assessment outweighs any anticipated client burden (although it is notable that clients in Zimmermann et al.'s study did not find daily completion of the PDD particularly onerous). Further, the development of clear guidelines linking certain longitudinal data patterns to specific treatment interventions likely will facilitate dissemination efforts.

CLINICAL UTILITY

Finally, we appreciate the added comments by both commentaries regarding the need for greater clinical utility in the dimensional PD assessment literature and in clinical applications more generally. As noted in our chapter, features like validity scales, adequate norms, and proper interpretive and training materials largely are lacking for modern dimensional PD measures, especially those within the PD functioning domain. Clearly, much more is needed if we wish to influence the way practitioners interact with and adopt PD assessment methods that are rooted in modern conceptualizations of PD.

Professional inertia likely serves as one of many impediments to change in this domain. However, little systematic data exist on this point. In our lab, we currently are studying the factors that influence how clinicians make decisions about psychological assessment and classification, including in the PD realm. We've started running focus groups and later will follow-up with a more systematic national survey of mental health practitioners. Our results thus far are far from complete or definitive, but our early inspections of the qualitative data suggest that we may face a very steep climb if we truly wish to influence the assessment behavior of mental health practitioners. The pressures exerted on clinicians – e.g., billing/reimbursement policies, demands for brief assessments, and the need to see increasing numbers of clients – leave many clinicians adopting suboptimal measures (or none at all!) in the service of more efficient service. We hope our work on this project, when complete, will permit the field to better understand these pressures and adopt practices that will better engage clinicians who face such pressures.

One factor that may be especially detrimental to clinical utility is the dizzying array of PD models and measures available for use. Efforts to consolidate this work (e.g., see HiTOP consortium; Kotov et al., 2017) hopefully will serve to catalyze research and measurement work in the service of a single transdiagnostic model of psychopathology and thus, perhaps, clarify the modern work for clinicians who might have been inclined to adopt it but have been put off by the lack of unity in the field.

REFERENCES

Connelly, B. S., & Ones, D. S. (2010). An other perspective on personality: Meta-analytic integration of observers' accuracy and predictive validity. *Psychological Bulletin*, *136*(6), 1092–1122.

Kotov, R., Krueger, R. F., Watson, D., Achenbach, T. M., Althoff, R. R., Bagby, R. M., ... Zimmerman, M. (2017). The Hierarchical Taxonomy of Psychopathology (HiTOP): A dimensional alternative to traditional nosologies. *Journal of Abnormal Psychology*, *4*, 454–477.

Morey, L. C., & Hopwood, C. J. (2013). Stability and change in personality disorders. *Annual Review of Clinical Psychology*, *9*, 499–528.

Oltmanns, T. F., & Turkheimer, E. (2009). Person perception and personality pathology. *Current Directions in Psychological Science*, *18*(1), 32–36.

Seixas, M., Weiss, M., & Müller, U. (2012). Systematic review of national and international guidelines on attention-deficit hyperactivity disorder. *Journal of Psychopharmacology*, *26*(6), 753–765.

Sibley, M. H., Pelham Jr, W. E., Molina, B. S., Gnagy, E. M., Waschbusch, D. A., Garefino, A. C., ... Karch, K. M. (2012). Diagnosing ADHD in adolescence. *Journal of Consulting and Clinical Psychology*, *80*(1), 139–150.

Zimmermann, J., Woods, W. C., Ritter, S., Happel, M., Masuhr, O. Jaeger, U., ... Wright, A. G. C. (2019). Integrating structure and dynamics in personality assessment: First steps toward the development and validation of a personality dynamics diary. *Psychological Assessment*, *31*(4), 516–531.

15 Categorical Assessment of Personality Disorders: Considerations of Reliability and Validity

JANINE D. FLORY

DSM-5 was published in 2013 and although there was widespread consensus on the shortcomings of the existing paradigm for diagnosing personality disorders (PDs) (First et al., 2002) the revised manual included (a) no changes to the text or structure of the existing ten personality disorders categories, plus PD not otherwise specified and (b) a proposed alternative dimensional model designated in a separate section of DSM-5 entitled "Emerging Measures and Models" (Section III). This was a disappointing outcome to many who see the value in a dimensional classification approach and the pathway to further future revision has been documented in numerous publications (Krueger, 2013; Skodol, Morey, Bender, & Oldham, 2013; Widiger, 2013).

There have been multiple efforts to understand why even a compromise hybrid classification was not adopted. The view that a major shift would be disruptive to clinical practice and research (Gunderson, 2013) appeared to have substantial influence. In a parallel effort, the committee that is revising the International Classification of Diseases-11 Mental or Behavioral Disorders section on PDs has proposed a dimensional approach (Tyrer, Crawford, & Mulder, 2011). Here, too, there is debate about a proposed dimensional approach to supplant or augment the existing categorical diagnoses (Herpertz et al., 2017; Hopwood et al., 2018) and the final product is expected for release in 2019.

The well-known and widely accepted limitations of the existing ten DSM-5 categories for capturing personality dysfunction in a clinically informative and valid manner include the common co-occurrence of two or more categorical diagnoses within individuals, heterogeneity within each diagnostic category (i.e., two people with the same diagnosis may share only one symptom), unclear boundaries between normal and abnormal personality functioning, and incomplete coverage of personality dysfunction (Morey, Benson, Busch, & Skodol, 2015; Widiger & Trull, 2007). These drawbacks are not unique to personality disorders, as there are many psychiatric diagnoses that lend themselves to the use of dimensional conceptualization (Haslam, Holland, & Kuppens, 2012) and co-occurrence of psychiatric disorders within individuals is common. However, this seems to be particularly salient for personality dysfunction as there is widespread acceptance of the view that personality traits adhere to a universal, dimensional structure that is heritable and observed cross-culturally (Widiger & Costa, 2012). Further, the latent structure of personality is similar in clinical and non-clinical samples (O'Connor, 2002). On the other hand, the frequently cited advantages of the categorical method of diagnosis include clinical utility, facilitation of communication among providers, public policy stakeholders, and reimbursement entities; and they provide an international language for describing personality dysfunction and for developing assessment tools (Herpertz et al., 2017; Kendell & Jablensky, 2003).

A review of categorical and dimensional approaches for diagnosis of PDs was presented by Miller and colleagues (Miller, Few, & Widiger, 2012) and provides a still timely and comprehensive review. Readers are referred to this work for a full account of all published interviews and questionnaires that measure DSM-III-R to DSM-IV-TR PDs. Because this chapter was written and published just prior to the publication of DSM-5, the review also provides an important bridge between the two manuals and includes a description of proposals for changes to PD diagnostic procedures for DSM-5. The proposed changes included the possibility of deleting some diagnoses from the DSM altogether (e.g., dependent, narcissistic, schizoid, histrionic, and paranoid); the use of a prototype matching procedure; the addition of personality functioning rating scales to consider self and other functioning, which are key constructs that signify impairment; and the use of personality trait profiles. As is now known, none of these approaches were adopted in the main part of DSM-5, but some aspects were included in Section III as noted above.

SELF-REPORT SCALES FOR DIAGNOSIS OF PERSONALITY DISORDERS

Although there is a tendency to conflate the categorical approach with interviews and the dimensional approach with self-report (Strickland et al., 2019) and assume that only interviews can be used to obtain a categorical diagnosis of PDs, there are more than 20 self-report scales that have been developed to make provisional or likely diagnoses of the PDs. Eleven of these scales diagnose all ten PDs included in DSM-IV-TR/DSM-5. A brief discussion of the use of self-report scales for diagnosing personality disorders is presented here. For further discussion and information about scoring procedures, readers are referred to the review by Miller and colleagues (Miller et al., 2012) which also includes original sources for the inventories and scales.

Self-report scales that are used to diagnose personality disorders include those that are atheoretical (e.g., Structured Clinical interview for DSM-IV Axis II Personality Disorders [SCID-II]; First, Gibbon, Spitzer, Williams, & Benjamin, 1997), listing each diagnostic criterion as it appears in the DSM and those that are embedded within comprehensive personality inventories (e.g., Schedule for Nonadaptive and Adaptive Personality [SNAP], Clark, 1993; Revised NEO Personality Inventory [NEO-PI-R], Costa & Macrae, 1992; Millon Clinical Multiaxial Inventory [MCMI-III], Millon, Millon, & Davis, 1997; and Minnesota Multiphasic Personality Inventory [MMPI-2], Butcher et al., 2001). The latter inventories provide information about personality traits or temperament embedded within a theoretical model of personality in addition to PD diagnoses, or in the case of the MMPI-2, other facets of psychopathology. The major advantage to using self-report inventories is the relative ease and low cost of obtaining diagnoses. Moreover, some instruments include validity scales to offset the biases inherent to self-assessment.

When using self-report scales to diagnose PDs, it is important to remember that extreme scores do not necessarily equal impairment. By definition, PDs (and by extension, all psychiatric diagnoses) require that symptoms or traits are associated with functional impairment and/or distress. Thus, the optimal use of dimensional self-report scales should include an assessment of self and other functioning. These aspects are incorporated into the DSM-5 alternative model and include well-accepted characteristics of adaptive personality functioning. The elements associated with a coherent sense of self include a consideration of identity (e.g., self-esteem, boundaries between self and other, emotion regulation) and self-direction (e.g., pursuit of goals, prosocial behavior, self-reflection). With respect to interpersonal functioning, this includes empathy (comprehension and tolerance of other perspectives) and intimacy (e.g., desire and capacity for closeness, mutual regard for others). Because it might be difficult for people to rate their own impairment, the use of clinician ratings might be useful in augmenting self-reported personality. In 2018, First and colleagues (First, Skodol, Bender, & Oldham, 2018) published a structured clinical interview to assess the DSM-5 alternative model for personality disorders. This interview includes two

modules and the first module (Bender, Skodol, First, & Oldham, 2018) includes an assessment of view of self and quality of interpersonal relationships. Buer Christensen and colleagues (Buer Christensen et al., 2018) published an inter-rater reliability study of this interview showing good to excellent rater reliability; test-retest reliability was less reliable for some sub-domains, but this might reflect actual changes in functioning rather than poor agreement over time.

Given that the PDs described in DSM-5 are unchanged from DSM-IV-TR, the chapter by Miller and colleagues (Miller et al., 2012) is particularly helpful for people who are new to PD assessment in that it provides thorough descriptions of the most commonly used self-report scales (and structured interviews, reviewed below). The descriptions include information about the number of items on the scales and interviews, whether they cover one or more DSM formulations and the key disadvantages/advantages of each instrument. Moreover, a large portion of the chapter is devoted to an exhaustive presentation of convergent validity associations for PD scores using (1) self-report scales compared to other self-reports and (2) self-report scales compared to dimensional scores derived from interviews. Almost without fail, Miller and colleagues noted that there was higher convergence between two self-rated scores than between self-report and interview-based dimensional assessments. The lower convergence between self-rated versus interview-based scores is likely due to at least two factors including method (in)variance and the expected discrepancy between self-rated traits and those rated by a clinician.

Notably, both comparisons yielded the conclusion there is little to no agreement between measures designed to diagnose OCPD. For both comparisons (self-report versus self-report and self-report versus interview), avoidant PD showed the highest convergence. It should be noted that disagreement across assessment instruments may reflect lack of agreement regarding conceptualization of the PD in addition to, or instead of, measurement differences. Also presented in Miller et al.'s (2012) chapter is a table of comparisons between interview assessed PDs, which is notably less comprehensive owing to the general lack of research comparing PD diagnoses derived from structured interviews. This point will be highlighted again below.

STRUCTURED INTERVIEWS FOR DIAGNOSIS OF PERSONALITY DISORDERS

Although unstructured diagnostic interviews represent the most common practice in the clinical setting, these interviews vary between and within clinicians as the goal is often to come to any diagnosis quickly for treatment planning, including choosing an intervention that can address symptoms. Five semi-structured interviews have been developed and are used widely to diagnose the DSM-IV-TR/DSM-5 personality disorders. A sixth interview was published in 2018 and is designed to assess the DSM-5 Alternative Model for Personality Disorders (First et al., 2018). This section will present and evaluate the most commonly used interviews that have empirical support and have been used to derive categorical diagnoses of PDs. Rater reliability characteristics of these interviews for diagnosing categories will be presented, in alphabetical order, followed by a general discussion of the validity of categorical diagnoses. The use of these interviews in epidemiological samples to describe prevalence will also be noted.

The *Alcohol Use Disorder and Associated Disabilities Interview Schedule* (AUDADIS) was administered as part of the National Institute on Alcohol Abuse and Alcoholism's National Epidemiologic Survey on Alcohol and Related Conditions (NESARC) in two waves: 2001–2002 (Wave 1) and 2004–2005 (Wave 2). NESARC is a representative sample of nearly 50,000 civilian adults in the United States and was designed to assess current and past alcohol consumption and other mood, anxiety, and personality disorders as operationalized for DSM-IV (Hasin & Grant, 2015). Seven personality disorders were assessed at Wave 1 and the remaining three were assessed at Wave 2. In contrast to the other interviews for PD diagnosis described in this chapter, the AUDADIS was administered by lay interviewers after extensive training (Grant et al., 2004). Diagnostic criteria are queried in the order they appear in the DSM-IV. Following a positive response, respondents were asked whether the item reflected how they "felt or acted most of the time throughout their life regardless of the situation or whom they were with" to assess whether a given PD symptom represented a long-term pattern. Additionally, each positive response was followed by a question about whether the symptom caused problems at work, school or with other people to assess functional impairment. To meet criteria for a categorical diagnosis, the requisite number of items had to be endorsed and at least one item had to be associated with impairment.

The population targeted by NESARC includes non-institutionalized adults in the United States. Of general relevance for the US population with PDs, the sample included people in boarding and rooming houses, non-transient hotels and shelters, college housing and group homes. For the reliability study, groups of 400 subsamples were randomly contacted to complete the reliability study. PDs were assessed at only one of the eight regional offices: Antisocial PD was assessed from the regional office in Los Angeles and the other PDs were assessed from the Kansas City office. Gender distributions were approximately equal in these two regions, but the Los Angeles sample was approximately 40 percent Hispanic. The Kansas City regional office sample was predominantly white, non-Hispanic. Retest reliability was assessed for Wave 1 interview items two to three months after the initial interview and the kappa values ranged from .40 (Histrionic PD) to .67 (Antisocial PD) (Grant et al., 2003), mostly reflecting a moderate level of agreement. It is not clear from the

description of this reliability study whether the kappa reflects inter-rater agreement or whether the same interviewer administered both assessments, which would reflect intra-rater consistency, or alternatively, temporal stability.

The *Diagnostic Interview for DSM-IV Personality Disorders* (DIPD-IV) is a semi-structured interview developed by Zanarini and colleagues (Zanarini, Frankenburg, Sickel, & Yong, 1996) to assess DSM-IV-TR PDs. The interview includes 252 questions to assess the 11 PDs (including PD not otherwise specified), which are assessed in the order presented in DSM-IV-TR. Respondents are asked yes/no questions followed by open-ended questions to determine how to rate each criterion on a 3-point scale (0 = absent or clinically insignificant; 1 = present but uncertain of clinical significance; 2 = present and clinically significant). The time frame for the items is the past two years. Inter-rater and retest reliability characteristics were reported by Zanarini and colleagues (Zanarini, Frankenburg, Chauncey, & Gunderson, 1987) on the initial version of the interview, based on DSM-III PDs in a clinical sample. Forty-three inpatients were assessed by three raters at a single time-point; a separate set of 54 patients were assessed one week apart, by two different raters. Approximately half of the sample was female and all of the people in the study were white. With respect to rater reliability, only one inter-rater coefficient was below .75 (paranoid personality disorder) and the other coefficients ranged from .87 to 1.0 (antisocial, avoidant). Retest reliability retest coefficients ranged from .46 (passive aggressive PD) to .85 (borderline PD).

The DIPD-IV was used to assess PDs in the Collaborative Longitudinal Personality Disorders Study (CLPS) (Gunderson et al., 2000), which is a cohort of nearly 700 treatment-seeking adults recruited across a range of clinical sites and followed over time. The sample included treatment-seeking adults who met DSM-IV-TR diagnostic criteria for one of five PDs, including schizotypal PD, borderline PD, avoidant PD, and obsessive-compulsive PD or a comparison group of patients with major depressive disorder, but no PD. Median inter-rater characteristics in a subset of this cohort were reported by Zanarini and colleagues (2000) and ranged from .58 (paranoid PD) to .71 (obsessive-compulsive PD); antisocial PD ratings were highest (1.0). Retest kappa coefficients ranged from .39 (paranoid PD) to 1.0 (narcissistic PD). The demographic characteristics were not reported for this reliability study, but were selected from the larger CLPS study, which included 64 percent women and was 76 percent white (Gunderson et al., 2000). Participants in the reliability study were selected based on "availability," which suggests that the sample might include people with less severe pathology. There are no estimates of rater reliability for several of the PDs, as the coefficients were only calculated if the PD was diagnosed in at least five people. Despite incomplete coverage of all of the PD categories, results reported with this cohort have provided useful information about the longitudinal course of personality, including the relationship between change in dimensions versus diagnostic categories (Samuel et al., 2011).

The *International Personality Disorder Examination* (IPDE) (Loranger et al., 1994) was developed as part of a joint project between the National Institutes of Health and the World Health Organization. Originally developed for the assessment of PDs according to the DSM-III-R and the International Classification of Diseases, Tenth Revision (ICD-10), the interview was revised for DSM-IV-TR. The interview assesses 11 DSM-IV-TR and 10 ICD-10 PDs and was developed in field trials administered in 11 countries across North America, Europe, Africa, and Asia with the aim of diagnosing PDs in different languages and cultures. The Personality Disorder Examination (PDE) was the basis for the IPDE and is described by Loranger et al. (1991). The IPDE includes 157 items rated on a scale of 0 (absent or within normal range), 1 (present to an accentuated degree), or 2 (pathological, meets criterion) and the behavior or trait must be present for five or more years. The interview procedure also includes the IPDE Screening Questionnaire, which is a 77-item T/F self-report scale. Based upon review of the screening questionnaire, the IPDE interview can be administered. The questions are arranged in topical sections that assess background characteristics and aspects about work, self, and interpersonal relationships.

Loranger et al. (1994) reported inter-rater reliability and temporal stability characteristics in a large multi-site international sample of 716 patients. Twenty percent of the interviews were independently rated by a silent observer and 34 percent were reassessed after an average of six months. The sample included approximately equal numbers of men and women and some participants were psychiatric inpatients at the time of assessment. Demographic information was not reported in the published report, but respondents resided in Asia (India and Japan), Africa (Kenya), the United States, and Europe. Kappa statistics for rater reliability and temporal stability were only calculated if at least 5 percent of the sample met diagnostic criteria. Inter-rater agreement for three PDs that met this minimum frequency were between .70 and .80 (dependent, avoidant, and borderline PD), but histrionic PD agreement was low (.34). Temporal stability for these four PD diagnoses ranged from .45 to .70.

The *Structured Interview for DSM-IV Personality Disorders* (SIDP-IV) (Pfohl, 1995) consists of 337 questions that cover the ten DSM-IV Axis PDs as well as four optional PDs: Mixed Personality Disorder (i.e., PDNOS), Self-Defeating, Depressive, and Negativistic Personality Disorders. The initial version of the interview was developed for DSM-III (Pfohl, Stangl, & Zimmerman, 1983) and the interview was revised for DSM-III-R (Pfohl, Blum, Zimmerman, & Stangl, 1989). The questions of the SIDP-IV are organized into topical sections that assess different aspects of potential functional impairment, including interests and activities, work style, close

relationships, social relationships, emotions, observational criteria (rated by interviewer based on a respondent's behavior during the interview), self-perception, perception of others, stress and anger, and social conformity. The authors of the interview argue that this structure is conducive to establishing rapport. They also describe the questions as "non-pejorative" in that they do not directly use the wording from DSM, which might be off-putting to a respondent. All items are rated on a scale of 0 (not present) to 3 (strongly present). To assess the necessary condition of temporal stability, respondents are also asked whether a trait has been prominent for most of the last five years. The authors also recommend that a close friend or relative be interviewed for additional information (informant interview).

With respect to inter-rater reliability of the SIDP-IV, Damen, De Jong, and Van der Kroft (2004) published a study of 50 Dutch men and women who were seeking treatment for opioid use disorder. The interview was translated from English into Dutch and two raters conducted all of the interviews; both were present for every interview in an observer/rater design and they were blind to each other's ratings. The authors computed kappa coefficients for each item of the interview and reported that 78 percent of the items had an agreement level > .75. One item (preoccupation with fantasies of unlimited success, power, brilliance, beauty, or ideal love from the Narcissistic PD criteria) had a kappa below .40 and three items could not be determined due to low variability in the ratings. Kappa coefficients for the categorical diagnoses ranged from .65 to 1.0 (mean = .86). Jane, Pagan, Turkheimer, Fiedler, and Oltmanns (2006) also conducted a rater-reliability study with the SIDP-IV, interviewing more than 400 US Air Force recruits selected from a sample of more than 2000. The PD sample included people who scored highly on self-report measures of personality pathology and others who were nominated by peers as having problematic personality characteristics. A third of the sample (60 percent male) was randomly selected from the larger group as control participants. The interviews were tape recorded and rated by a second rater who was blind to the interviewer's ratings. In this detailed report, the authors present intra-class coefficients for each item as well as a narrative summary of the items that showed the highest and lowest concordance for each personality disorders. Race and ethnicity characteristics were not reported for the sample. Intra-class coefficients for the categorical diagnoses ranged from .35 (Narcissistic PD) to .85 (Dependent PD); Schizoid PD did not occur in this sample, and only one person was diagnosed with Schizotypal PD.

The *Structured Clinical Interview for DSM-5 Personality Disorders* (SCID-5-PD) (First, Williams, Benjamin, & Spitzer, 2016) is a 302-item interview developed for the assessment of DSM-5 personality disorders. This is a recent revision of the SCID-II, which was originally developed for DSM-III and revised for DSM-III-R and DSM-IV.

Although the diagnostic criteria were not changed from DSM-IV to DSM-5, the authors of the SCID-II reviewed and revised several items for clarity. Note that this group also developed an interview for the assessment of the DSM-5 Alternative Model for Personality Disorders (First et al., 2018). The SCID-5-PD includes assessment procedures for the 11 DSM-IV Personality Disorders (including PDNOS), presented in the order they appear in the DSM-5. The SCID-5 Personality Questionnaire can be used as a screening instrument, administered prior to interview. The rater reviews the responses and only queries positive responses to the self-report T/F questionnaire. Training materials are available from the authors, including a taped recording of a sample interview using DSM-IV-TR materials so that a new rater can check his or her ratings against a reference interview. As with the other interviews in the SCID portfolio, there is a computer-assisted version. Results from eight reliability studies using DSM-III-R and DSM-IV criteria are summarized in the SCID-5-PD user's guide (First et al., 2016). Sample sizes ranged from 31 to 284 and the studies were conducted in the United States, Japan, Italy, and the Netherlands. Kappa coefficients vary widely across groups, with some reliability coefficients as low as .02. However, a review of these studies indicates that the studies conducted with the DSM-IV and DSM-5 versions show acceptable to excellent reliability for categorical diagnoses. Finally, Somma and colleagues (2016) conducted a rater reliability study in 104 patients using the Italian translation of the SCID-5-PD and obtained kappa coefficients in the range of .82 (any PD) to 1.0 on all but two PD diagnoses (avoidant and dependent PD), which were .66 and .58, respectively.

VALIDITY OF CATEGORICAL DIAGNOSES DERIVED FROM STRUCTURED INTERVIEWS

If an assessment method does not measure a construct reliably, there is no reason to assess the validity of the methodology. Given that the interviews described above have all established moderate to high levels of reliability for at least some diagnoses, it is then a reasonable question to ask whether the categorical diagnoses derived from the interviews are valid.

In exploring the validity of the tests above, several lines of evidence can be examined. First, a comparison of two interviews can be conducted to evaluate whether there is agreement with respect to the diagnoses that are made. This type of head-to-head comparison has rarely been conducted and/or published. O'Boyle and Self (1990) administered the PDE (the precursor to the IPDE) and the SCID II for DSM-III-R to 20 adults with depression and observed poor agreement between the interviews. In contrast, Pilkonis and colleagues (1995) reported a comprehensive and systematic examination of reliability and validity characteristics of the PDE and the SIDP-III-R in a sample of 108 treatment-seeking adults. The process of

rater training and making a best-estimate diagnosis by consensus was described; a process that uses "longitudinal, expert and all data" (LEAD) to come to diagnostic consensus (Kranzler, Kadden, Babor, & Rounsaville, 1994; Pilkonis, Heape, Ruddy, & Serrao, 1991). The inter-rater reliability coefficient for any PD diagnosis in this study was .55 (78 percent agreement) for the PDE and .58 (81 percent agreement) for the SIDP-III-R. They note that the high prevalence of personality dysfunction in the sample constrained the reliability of the categorical diagnoses. Rater reliability coefficients for dimensional scores for the two interviews ranged from .85 to .92 on the PDE and from .82 to .90 on the SIDP-R. With respect to validity, the authors designated clinical consensus among several raters as the "gold standard" of diagnosis. Agreement between group consensus and diagnoses derived from either of the two interviews was low as both methods underestimated the presence versus absence of a personality disorder. The authors concluded by describing the advantages of using dimensional scores derived from the ratings of individual criteria to enhance reliability and validity of the ratings.

A second form of convergent validity is attained by examining correlations between interview-derived categories and self-report scales of normal and/or abnormal personality. As noted above, Miller et al. (2012) compiled results from this literature and show that the correlations are generally low to moderate. While this can be interpreted as low convergent validity for diagnostic categories, this is not the only explanation. Low association between clinician-rated and self-rated items has been observed for other forms of psychopathology (e.g., PTSD) (Forbes, Creamer, & Biddle, 2001) and suggests that the two methods tap different things or alternatively, that first order correlations may not be the most optimal means for examining agreement between clinicians and patients (Monson et al., 2008). Clinicians make informed judgments about temporal stability and level of impairment when asking about whether a characteristic is present or not. Experienced clinicians or diagnosticians make determinations about ratings and/or symptom severity based on a highly contextualized view of psychopathology. Further, clinicians make decisions regarding differential diagnosis related to comorbid conditions that an individual rating his or her own behavior might not consider. For some traits (e.g., Narcissism), the individual may lack insight into whether there is functional impairment associated with the trait and/or not understand the source of such impairment.

A third means of evaluating the validity of diagnostic categories is the examination of sensitivity and specificity rates, which provide information about false positives (being diagnosed with a PD when there is no PD) and false negatives (not being diagnosed with a PD when a PD diagnosis is warranted). Very few studies have reported sensitivity and specificity for categorical diagnoses of PD. The utility of the SCID-II personality questionnaire as a screener for the diagnosis of PD using structured interviews has been examined in three studies (Ekselius, Lindstrom, von Knorring, Bodlund, & Kullgren, 1994; Jacobsberg, Perry, & Frances, 1995; Nussbaum & Rogers, 1992). All three studies reported a low rate of false negatives.

PREVALENCE OF CATEGORICAL PERSONALITY DISORDERS IN LARGE COHORTS

The AUDADIS was developed for use in the NESARC cohort (Hasin & Grant, 2015) and has not been used to assess PDs in other samples or cohorts. However, NESARC is a nationally representative sample of the US population and is the largest cohort to date with interview-assessed PDs. Limited data sets are available for investigators, making this an important and useful resource for examining PDs and comorbidity with alcohol use and mood and anxiety disorders. It has been noted that the practice of only requiring that a single item be associated with impairment may have resulted in false positives. The prevalence estimate for any personality disorder diagnosis in this sample was 21.5 percent. In a reanalysis of the data, Trull and colleagues (Trull, Jahng, Tomko, Wood, & Sher, 2010) made a categorical diagnosis only if there was impairment associated with all the requisite number of criteria in a specific diagnostic category; as expected, observed rates were lower for all categories and were more in line with previously published epidemiological studies (i.e., 6–15 percent and see below). Trull and colleagues also noted that the use of two separate data collection waves should ideally be modeled in analyses as method variance may account for observed patterns of covariation between symptoms and/or categories.

As noted above, the NESARC cohort is a large, nationally representative sample, but the regional centers that collected the data for the reliability subsamples did not all assess PDs. All but one of the PDs was assessed in a single Midwestern regional office, while Antisocial PD was assessed only on the west coast. Very little research has been devoted to documenting race and ethnicity with respect to the prevalence of PDs, despite the impact that cultural factors have on self-concept, worldview, and interpersonal behavior (McGilloway, Hall, Lee, & Bhui, 2010). Given the importance of identity and interpersonal functioning in defining personality dysfunction, these factors warrant further study and inclusion in research designed to document prevalence of PDs. None of the reliability studies cited here had demographically representative samples and some studies did not even report the demographic characteristics of the sample. Thus, bias in sampling related to inadequate representation of population race and ethnicity prevalence should be considered as another potential source of error in establishing true estimates of reliability of the diagnoses.

The IPDE has been administered in several large samples to determine the prevalence of DSM PDs, including a subsample of the National Comorbidity Study-Replication (NCS-R) (Lenzenweger, Lane, Loranger, & Kessler, 2007). The prevalence of any DSM-IV PD in this US cohort was 11.9 percent. Benjet and colleagues (Benjet, Borges, & Medina-Mora, 2008) administered the IPDE DSM-IV screening questionnaire in a true prevalence epidemiological study to more than 2300 adults in Mexico and reported a prevalence rate of 6.1 percent for any PD. The SID-P-III-R was administered in a representative sample in Norway to more than 2000 adults (Torgersen et al., 2008), showing a true prevalence rate of 13.4 percent. The SCID II was administered in two longitudinal cohorts, both designed to document the developmental transition from adolescence to adulthood. The prevalence of any DSM-III-R PD in these two cohorts was 15.7 percent (Cohen, Crawford, Johnson, & Kasen, 2005) and 12.7 percent (Johnson, Cohen, Kasen, Skodol, & Oldham, 2008). The latter prevalence rate includes depressive and passive-aggressive PD. Additionally, the SCID II was used to estimate the prevalence of DSM-III-R PDs in a family study in Germany, reporting a rate of any PD at 10 percent.

CONCLUSIONS

Reliability

A categorical diagnosis of any PD can generally be assessed in a reliable manner using the structured interviews described above, although there are some exceptions as noted above. Several conclusions can be made from the above review. First, the makeup of the sample will greatly affect reliability. The relative proportion of PD rates, the presence of comorbidities, recruitment strategies (e.g., from clinical settings versus population-based), and demographic makeup of the sample can all greatly affect the rate of PD in a sample and this will impact on whether a PD can be assessed reliably. For example, when a sample is representative of the population, the rate of any PD will be low. A low number of disagreements between any two raters will not have a large impact on reliability. In contrast, when the sample is treatment seeking and has a high base rate of personality dysfunction, the same low number of disagreements can lead to low reliability coefficients. Second, some PD diagnoses can be more reliably assessed than others. Jane and colleagues (Jane et al., 2006) have argued that the items and diagnoses with the highest level of rater agreement are those that are easily observable and/or reportable and that do not require a high degree of insight on the part of the interviewee. This conclusion is supported by the above review, which notes that reliability coefficients for histrionic, paranoid, and narcissistic PDs are lower than .60 in several studies, regardless of the interview that was used to assess PDs.

Third, "dimensionalizing" categories can enhance reliability. Most of the reliability studies described above report findings for both categorical diagnoses and for dimensional scores that are obtained by summing responses to the interview items. Other than the AUDADIS, all the interviews described above use a 3- or 4-point ordinal scale for rating each interview item. These values can be summed within PD categories to obtain a dimensional score that reflects symptom severity or alternatively, the clinician's confidence in making the rating for each criterion. In all cases, the use of summed scores resulted in appreciably higher reliability coefficients. This method of adding dimensionality to categorical diagnoses has been recommended to strengthen the reliability of PD diagnoses (Helzer, Kraemer, & Krueger, 2006). Research groups who study "discrete" groups based on interview-assessed categories are encouraged to also report dimensional scores for descriptive purposes. These dimensional scores will greatly enhance the ability to compare results across studies and research groups. These dimensional scores lend themselves to a more powerful examination of social and biological correlates and other indices of convergent and divergent validity.

Finally, in addition to reporting summed scores along with dichotomous groups, it is incumbent upon research groups that use interviews (or self-reports) to create dichotomous groups for study to report rater reliability among their own raters and provide details about the consensus process. A description of how temporal stability and functional impairment was determined is critical.

Categories and Dimensions Together

The combination of categories and dimensional traits can be particularly informative for researchers and clinicians who examine PDs over time. The early definitional view of PDs that they are immutable from early adulthood and set a lifelong course of dysfunction has been altered by longitudinal and treatment research (and clinical practice) showing that recovery from PD is possible. As noted above, several self-report scales have been developed to provide both categorical and dimensional measures of PD, and some provide dimensional measures of personality or temperament. There is a distinct advantage to using such a measure instead of a structured interview that only queries/scores maladaptive behavior and traits. In 2007, Clark proposed that PDs can be reconceptualized as representing "change within relative stability" (Clark, 2007). That is, single observation assessments of these sentinel behaviors that signal dysfunction to self and other are inherently more difficult to assess reliably, whereas traits and PD diagnoses will render more stable coefficients. Thus, extreme trait measures in the absence of a PD diagnosis might signal vulnerability to episodic dysfunction. The interview measures, in contrast, even when summed across categories, provide only information about abnormal behavior without conferring information about normative variation in personality. When feasible, the use of such a measure with a structured interview in a research study can also provide information about convergent validity using multi-method assessments.

Finally, as can be seen from this review, there are a relatively large number of self-reports and interviews that have been used to assess PDs according to the categorical model. While this demonstrates a robust interest in this area of investigation, research establishing inter-rater reliability across instruments is somewhat dated and incomplete. The shift from a categorical conceptualization and assessment of PDs to the alternative model is (hopefully) an iterative process and future research and clinical practice that incorporates both approaches will represent progress in assessment and conceptualization of personality disorders.

REFERENCES

American Psychiatric Association. (2000). *Diagnostic and Statistical Manual of Mental Disorders (4th ed., Text Revision)*. Washington, DC: American Psychiatric Association.

American Psychiatric Association. (2013). *Diagnostic and Statistical Manual of Mental Disorders* (5th ed.). Arlington, VA: American Psychiatric Publishing.

Bender, D., Skodol, A. E., First, M. B., & Oldham, J. M. (2018). *Structured Clinical Interview for the DSM-5 Alternative Model for Personality Disorders: Module I*. Washington, DC: American Psychiatric Press.

Benjet, C., Borges, G., & Medina-Mora, M. E. (2008). DSM-IV personality disorders in Mexico: Results from a general population survey. *Revista Brasileira de Psiquiatria, 30*(3), 227–234.

Buer Christensen, T., Paap, M. C. S., Arnesen, M., Koritzinsky, K., Nysaeter, T. E., Eikenaes, I., ... Hummelen, B. (2018). Inter-rater reliability of the Structured Clinical Interview for the DSM-5 Alternative Model of Personality Disorders Module I: Level of Personality Functioning Scale. *Journal of Personality Assessment, 100*(6), 630–641.

Butcher, J. N., Graham, J. R., Ben-Porath, Y. S., Tellegen, A., Dahlstrom, W. G., & Kaemmer B. (2001). *Minnesota Multiphasic Personality Inventory–2*. Minneapolis: University of Minnesota Press.

Clark, L. A. (1993). *Manual for the Schedule for Nonadaptive and Adaptive Personality (SNAP)*. Minneapolis: University of Minnesota Press.

Clark, L. A. (2007). Assessment and diagnosis of personality disorder: Perennial issues and an emerging reconceptualization. *Annual Review of Psychology, 58*, 227–257.

Cohen, P., Crawford, T. N., Johnson, J. G., & Kasen, S. (2005). The children in the community study of developmental course of personality disorder. *Journal of Personality Disorders, 19*(5), 466–486.

Costa, P. T., & McCrae, R. R. (1992). *Revised NEO Personality Inventory (NEO-PI-R) and NEO Five Factor Inventory (NEO-FFI) Professional Manual*. Odessa, FL: Psychological Assessment Resources.

Damen, K. F., De Jong, C. A., & Van der Kroft, P. J. (2004). Interrater reliability of the structured interview for DSM-IV personality in an opioid-dependent patient sample. *European Addiction Research*, *10*(3), 99–104.

Ekselius, L., Lindstrom, E., von Knorring, L., Bodlund, O., & Kullgren, G. (1994). SCID II interviews and the SCID Screen questionnaire as diagnostic tools for personality disorders in DSM-III-R. *Acta Psychiatrica Scandivavica*, *90*(2), 120–123.

First, M. B., Bell, C. C., Cuthbert, B., Krystal, J. H., Malison, R., Offord, D. R., Reiss, D., Shea, T., Widiger, T, & Wisner, K. L. (2002). Personality disorders and relational disorders: A research agenda for addressing crucial gaps in DSM. In D. J. Kupfer, M. B. First, & D. A., Regier (Eds.), *A Research Agenda for DSM-V* (pp. 123–199). Washington, DC: American Psychiatric Press.

First, M. B., Gibbon, M., Spitzer, R. L., Williams, J. B. W., & Benjamin, L. S. (1997). *Structured Clinical Interview for DSM-IV Axis II Personality Disorders (SCID-II)*. Washington, DC: American Psychiatric Press.

First, M. B., Skodol, A. E., Bender, D. S., & Oldham, J. M. (2018). *User's Guide for the SCID-5-AMPD: Structured Clinical Interview for the DSM-5 Alternative Model for Personality Disorders*. Arlington, VA: American Psychiatric Association.

First, M. B., Williams, J. B. W., Benjamin, L. S., & Spitzer, R. L. (2016). *Structured Clinical Interview for DSM-5 (SCID-5): User's Guide*. Arlington, VA: American Psychiatric Association.

Forbes, D., Creamer, M., & Biddle, D. (2001). The validity of the PTSD checklist as a measure of symptomatic change in combat-related PTSD. *Behaviour Research and Therapy*, *39*(8), 977–986.

Grant, B. F., Dawson, D. A., Stinson, F. S., Chou, P. S., Kay, W., & Pickering, R. (2003). The Alcohol Use Disorder and Associated Disabilities Interview Schedule-IV (AUDADIS-IV): Reliability of alcohol consumption, tobacco use, family history of depression and psychiatric diagnostic modules in a general population sample. *Drug and Alcohol Dependence*, *71*(1), 7–16.

Grant, B. F., Hasin, D. S., Stinson, F. S., Dawson, D. A., Chou, S. P., Ruan, W. J., & Pickering, R. P. (2004). Prevalence, correlates, and disability of personality disorders in the United States: Results from the national epidemiologic survey on alcohol and related conditions. *Journal of Clinical Psychiatry*, *65*(7), 948–958.

Gunderson, J. G. (2013). Seeking clarity for future revisions of the personality disorders in DSM-5. *Personality Disorders: Theory, Research, and Treatment*, *4*(4), 368–376.

Gunderson, J. G., Shea, M. T., Skodol, A. E., McGlashan, T. H., Morey, L. C., Stout, R. L., ... Keller, M. B. (2000). The Collaborative Longitudinal Personality Disorders Study: Development, aims, design, and sample characteristics. *Journal of Personality Disorders*, *14*(4), 300–315.

Hasin, D. S., & Grant, B. F. (2015). The National Epidemiologic Survey on Alcohol and Related Conditions (NESARC) Waves 1 and 2: Review and summary of findings. *Social Psychiatry and Psychiatric Epidemiology*, *50*(11), 1609–1640.

Haslam, N., Holland, E., & Kuppens, P. (2012). Categories versus dimensions in personality and psychopathology: A quantitative review of taxometric research. *Psychological Medicine*, *42*(5), 903–920.

Helzer, J. E., Kraemer, H. C., & Krueger, R. F. (2006). The feasibility and need for dimensional psychiatric diagnoses. *Psychological Medicine*, *36*(12), 1671–1680.

Herpertz, S. C., Huprich, S. K., Bohus, M., Chanen, A., Goodman, M., Mehlum, L., ... Sharp, C. (2017). The challenge of transforming the diagnostic system of personality disorders. *Journal of Personality Disorders*, *31*(5), 577–589.

Hopwood, C. J., Kotov, R., Krueger, R. F., Watson, D., Widiger, T. A., Althoff, R. R., ... Zimmermann, J. (2018). The time has come for dimensional personality disorder diagnosis. *Personality and Mental Health*, *12*(1), 82–86.

Jacobsberg, L., Perry, S., & Frances, A. (1995). Diagnostic agreement between the SCID-II screening questionnaire and the Personality Disorder Examination. *Journal of Personality Assessment*, *65*(3), 428–433.

Jane, J. S., Pagan, J. L., Turkheimer, E., Fiedler, E. R., & Oltmanns, T. F. (2006). The interrater reliability of the Structured Interview for DSM-IV Personality. *Comprehensive Psychiatry*, *47*(5), 368–375.

Johnson, J. G., Cohen, P., Kasen, S., Skodol, A. E., & Oldham, J. M. (2008). Cumulative prevalence of personality disorders between adolescence and adulthood. *Acta Psychiatrica Scandinavica*, *118*(5), 410–413.

Kendell, R., & Jablensky, A. (2003). Distinguishing between the validity and utility of psychiatric diagnoses. *American Journal of Psychiatry*, *160*(1), 4–12.

Kranzler, H. R., Kadden, R. M., Babor, T. F., & Rounsaville, B. J. (1994). Longitudinal, expert, all data procedure for psychiatric diagnosis in patients with psychoactive substance use disorders. *Journal of Nervous and Mental Disease*, *182*(5), 277–283.

Krueger, R. F. (2013). Personality disorders are the vanguard of the post-DSM-5.0 era. *Personality Disorders: Theory, Research, and Treatment*, *4*(4), 355–362.

Lenzenweger, M. F., Lane, M. C., Loranger, A. W., & Kessler, R. C. (2007). DSM-IV personality disorders in the National Comorbidity Survey Replication. *Biological Psychiatry*, *62*(6), 553–564.

Loranger, A. W., Lenzenweger, M. F., Gartner, A. F., Susman, V. L., Herzig, J., Zammit, G. K., ... Young, R. C. (1991). Trait-state artifacts and the diagnosis of personality disorders. *Archives of General Psychiatry*, *48*(8), 720–728.

Loranger, A. W., Sartorius, N., Andreoli, A., Berger, P., Buchheim, P., Channabasavanna, S. M., ... Regier, D. A. (1994). The International Personality Disorder Examination: The World Health Organization/Alcohol, Drug Abuse, and Mental Health Administration international pilot study of personality disorders. *Archives of General Psychiatry*, *51*(3), 215–224.

McGilloway, A., Hall, R. E., Lee, T., & Bhui, K. S. (2010). A systematic review of personality disorder, race and ethnicity: prevalence, aetiology and treatment. *BMC Psychiatry*, *10*, 33.

Miller, J. D., Few, L. R., & Widiger, T. A. (2012). Assessment of personality disorders and related traits: Bridging DSM-IV-TR and DSM-5. In T. A. Widiger (Ed.), *The Oxford Handbook of Personality Disorders* (pp. 108–140). New York: Oxford University Press.

Millon, T., Millon, C., & Davis, R. (1997). *MCMI-III Manual* (2nd ed.). Minneapolis: National Computer Systems.

Monson, C. M., Gradus, J. L., Young-Xu, Y., Schnurr, P. P., Price, J. L., & Schumm, J. A. (2008). Change in posttraumatic stress disorder symptoms: Do clinicians and patients agree? *Psychological Assessment*, *20*(2), 131–138.

Morey, L. C., Benson, K. T., Busch, A. J., & Skodol, A. E. (2015). Personality disorders in DSM-5: Emerging research on the alternative model. *Current Psychiatry Reports*, *17*(4), 558.

Nussbaum, D., & Rogers, R. (1992). Screening psychiatric patients for Axis II disorders. *Canadian Journal of Psychiatry*, *37*(9), 658–660.

O'Boyle, M., & Self, D. (1990). A comparison of two interviews for DSM-III-R personality disorders. *Psychiatry Research*, *32*(1), 85–92.

O'Connor, B. P. (2002). The search for dimensional structure differences between normality and abnormality: A statistical review of published data on personality and psychopathology. *Journal of Personality and Social Psychology, 83*(4), 962–982.

Pfohl, B. (1995). *Structured Interview for DSM-IV Personality (SIDP-IV)*. Iowa City, IA: University of Iowa College of Medicine.

Pfohl, B., Blum, N., Zimmerman, M., & Stangl, D. (1989). *Structured Interview for DSM-III-R Personality: SIDP-R*. Iowa City, IA: University of Iowa.

Pfohl, B., Stangl, D., & Zimmerman, M. (1983). *Structured Interview for DSM-III Personality (SIDP)*. Iowa City, IA: University of Iowa Hospitals and Clinics.

Pilkonis, P. A., Heape, C. L., Proietti, J. M., Clark, S. W., McDavid, J. D., & Pitts, T. E. (1995). The reliability and validity of two structured diagnostic interviews for personality disorders. *Archives of General Psychiatry, 52*(12), 1025–1033.

Pilkonis, P. A., Heape, C. L., Ruddy, J., & Serrao, P. S. (1991). Validity in the diagnosis of personality disorders: The use of the LEAD standard. *Psychological Assessment, 3*, 46–54.

Samuel, D. B., Hopwood, C. J., Ansell, E. B., Morey, L. C., Sanislow, C. A., Markowitz, J. C., ... Grilo, C. M. (2011). Comparing the temporal stability of self-report and interview assessed personality disorder. *Journal of Abnormal Psychology, 120*(3), 670–680.

Skodol, A. E., Morey, L. C., Bender, D. S., & Oldham, J. M. (2013). The ironic fate of the personality disorders in DSM-5. *Personality Disorders: Theory, Research, and Treatment, 4*(4), 342–349.

Somma, A., Fossati, A., Terrinoni, A., Williams, R., Ardizzone, I., Fantini, F., ... Ferrara, M. (2016). Reliability and clinical usefulness of the personality inventory for DSM-5 in clinically referred adolescents: A preliminary report in a sample of Italian inpatients. *Comprehensive Psychiatry, 70*, 141–151.

Strickland, C. M., Hopwood, C. J., Bornovalova, M. A., Rojas, E. C., Krueger, R. F., & Patrick, C. J. (2019). Categorical and dimensional conceptions of personality pathology in DSM-5: Toward a model-based synthesis. *Journal of Personality Disorders, 33*(2), 185–213.

Torgersen, S., Czajkowski, N., Jacobson, K., Reichborn-Kjennerud, T., Roysamb, E., Neale, M. C., & Kendler, K. S. (2008). Dimensional representations of DSM-IV cluster B personality disorders in a population-based sample of Norwegian twins: A multivariate study. *Psychological Medicine, 38*(11), 1617–1625.

Trull, T. J., Jahng, S., Tomko, R. L., Wood, P. K., & Sher, K. J. (2010). Revised NESARC personality disorder diagnoses: Gender, prevalence, and comorbidity with substance dependence disorders. *Journal of Personality Disorders, 24*(4), 412–426.

Tyrer, P., Crawford, M., & Mulder, R. (2011). Reclassifying personality disorders. *Lancet, 377*(9780), 1814–1815.

Widiger, T. A. (2013). A postmortem and future look at the personality disorders in DSM-5. *Personality Disorders: Theory, Research, and Treatment, 4*(4), 382–387.

Widiger, T. A., & Costa, P. T., jr. (2012). Integrating normal and abnormal personality structure: The Five-Factor Model. *Journal of Personality, 80*(6), 1471–1506.

Widiger, T. A., & Trull, T. J. (2007). Plate tectonics in the classification of personality disorder: Shifting to a dimensional model. *American Psychologist, 62*(2), 71–83.

Zanarini, M. C., Frankenburg, F. R., Chauncey, D. L., & Gunderson, J. G. (1987). The Diagnostic Interview for Personality Disorders: Interrater and test-retest reliability. *Comprehensive Psychiatry, 28*(6), 467–480.

Zanarini, M. C., Frankenburg, F. R., Sickel, A. E., & Yong, L. (1996). *The Diagnostic Interview for DSM Personality Disorders (DIPD)*. Belmont, MA: McLean Hospital.

Zanarini, M. C., Skodol, A. E., Bender, D., Dolan, R., Sanislow, C., Schaefer, E., ... Gunderson, J. G. (2000). The Collaborative Longitudinal Personality Disorders Study: Reliability of axis I and II diagnoses. *Journal of Personality Disorders, 14*(4), 291–299.

15a Categories, Constructs, and the Assessment of Personality Pathology: Commentary on Categorical Assessment of Personality Disorders

ROBERT F. BORNSTEIN

The past decade has been a time of great controversy in the study of personality pathology. Although recent editions of the *Diagnostic and Statistical Manual of Mental Disorders* (DSM-5; American Psychiatric Association [APA], 2013) and *International Classification of Diseases* (ICD-10; World Health Organization [WHO], 2004) conceptualized personality disorders (PDs) categorically, both manuals are moving toward a system wherein personality pathology will be described via scores on an array of trait dimensions. Both manuals will likely incorporate a five-dimensional model, although the traits that comprise these dimensions differ in ICD-11 and DSM-5.1. In ICD-11 personality functioning is captured by scores on dissociality, detachment, negative affectivity, anankastia (obsessiveness), and disinhibition (see Tyrer, Reed, & Crawford, 2015).

Based on initial work examining the Alternative Model for Personality Disorders (AMPD) in DSM-5 it appears that DSM-5.1 will employ a slightly different set of core traits: negative affectivity, detachment, disinhibition, antagonism, and psychoticism. In line with the structure of the Five-Factor Model (FFM), the five AMPD trait domains comprise 25 narrower facets (e.g., the domain of disinhibition comprises the facets of irresponsibility, impulsivity, distractibility, risk taking, and rigid perfectionism).

These shifts are substantial, but the concepts that underlie them are not new: there has long been disagreement regarding whether personality pathology is best conceptualized categorically or dimensionally (see Bornstein, 2019, for an historical overview). The tone of this debate has changed, however, becoming more polarized in recent years. Some researchers argue that findings supporting dimensional conceptualizations of personality pathology are so compelling it is time to jettison PD categories altogether and move to a trait-based diagnostic framework (Hopwood et al., 2018; Widiger, Gore, Crego, Rojas, & Oltmanns, 2017). Others maintain that categorical and dimensional PD models both have certain advantages, and that integrative frameworks combining features of both perspectives hold great promise in conceptualizing and diagnosing PDs (Herpertz et al., 2017; Silk, 2015). The dimensional-categorical debate continues, and however the diagnostic manuals evolve it is

unlikely that extant PD categories will disappear from the clinical literature anytime soon.

With this ongoing controversy as context, Flory (this volume) provides a sophisticated, balanced, and compelling review of evidence bearing on the reliability and validity of diagnostic interviews for PDs – a contrast to many of the divisive writings that have appeared in this area in recent years. Flory emphasizes three strategies for evaluating the validity of categorical diagnoses assessed via structured interview: (1) comparison of two interviews designed to assess the same PD construct; (2) correlations between interview ratings and patient self-reports; and (3) sensitivity and specificity rates (i.e., proportions of false positives and false negatives) associated with different diagnostic interviews. As Flory notes, each of these validation strategies yields important information, but none can provide definitive evidence that one interview is clearly superior to others. Clinical consensus among several expert raters using Longitudinal Expert All Data (LEAD) procedures is the closest thing to a "gold standard" against which results from PD interviews and questionnaires can be compared (see Aboraya, France, Young, Curci, & LePage, 2005).

MEASURES, MODELS, AND CONCEPTUAL FRAMEWORKS

Beyond summarizing evidence regarding the reliability and validity of widely-used interview measures, Flory's review illuminates a number of broader issues that are central to the evaluation of contemporary PD frameworks, but often go unnoticed. Two broader issues that stand out are: (a) distinguishing categories and constructs from the measures used to quantify them; and (b) distinguishing overarching conceptual frameworks from narrower assessment rubrics.

Distinguishing Categories and Constructs from the Measures Used to Quantify Them

Beginning with the seminal work of Cronbach and Meehl (1955), psychometricians have grappled with the paradoxical reality that it is not possible to disentangle completely the evidence bearing on a psychological construct from the validity of measures used to quantify that construct. Cronbach and Meehl's cogent observations regarding construct validity apply to a broad array of psychological concepts (see Messick, 1995); in the present context these observations suggest that it is important to distinguish the utility of a diagnostic category (and the construct underlying that category) from the validity of measures that assess that category and its underlying construct. Although the PD interviews reviewed by Flory (this volume) vary with regard to the strength of their reliability and validity evidence, the psychometric soundness (or lack of soundness) of these measures does not allow definitive conclusions to be drawn regarding the conceptual rigor or clinical utility of the PD categories they assess.

Distinguishing Overarching Conceptual Frameworks from Narrower Assessment Rubrics

Flory (this volume) notes that one obstacle to progress in recent years has been an unintended conflation of model and measure: most PD interviews assess constructs derived from the categorical perspective, whereas dimensional PD assessments are typically based on patient self-reports. A different sort of conflation has characterized the ongoing dimensional-categorical debate, with critics on both sides citing flaws in a specific assessment rubric to dismiss the overarching perspective from which that rubric was derived. Thus, many critiques of the categorical perspective on PDs are in fact critiques of particular instantiations of the categorical perspective (typically DSM or ICD categories); flaws in DSM or ICD diagnostic criteria are then used to argue against categorical PD models *in toto* (see Verheul, 2005). Similarly, limitations in a particular dimensional framework (most often the FFM) are sometimes used to argue against the utility of dimensional PD models in general (Kernberg & Caligor, 2005). Just as it is important to distinguish PD categories and constructs from the measures used to assess them, it is important to distinguish the clinical utility of a specific categorical or dimensional framework (e.g., DSM or FFM) from the categorical and dimensional perspectives, broadly construed.

BEYOND SELF-REPORT IN THE STUDY OF PERSONALITY PATHOLOGY

People have limited introspective access to their own internal states. Moreover, they are notoriously poor judges of their behavioral predispositions and cannot predict accurately how they will respond in various contexts and settings (see Dunning, Heath, & Suls, 2018; Wilson, 2009). Across a broad array of domains in psychology the correlation (r) between self-report and expressed behavior ranges from about .2 to .3 (Meyer et al., 2001). Similar modest correlations are obtained when self-reports and peer reports of personality pathology are compared (Oltmanns & Turkheimer, 2009). These findings have noteworthy implications for conceptualizing and assessing PDs.

Flory (this volume) correctly notes that meta-analytic findings from O'Connor (2002) have been accepted as evidence that "the latent structure of personality is similar in clinical and non-clinical samples." Flory's interpretation of these results is in line with that of most clinicians and clinical researchers. It is important to keep in mind, however, that 34 of the 37 personality and psychopathology measures in O'Connor's meta-analysis were questionnaires. This illustrates a widespread problem in the contemporary PD literature: researchers often interpret findings regarding self-reported behavior as if these results reflected actual behavior. A more accurate summary of O'Connor's meta-analytic results might be that the latent structure of *self-reported* personality is similar in clinical and non-clinical samples. The degree to which parallel patterns would emerge when personality is assessed using other methods is open to question.

People's unavoidable introspective limitations – limitations which are magnified in many forms of personality pathology – constrain researchers' ability to validate PD interview data with information derived from questionnaires or other interviews. As a result, a different assessment strategy is needed. A complete understanding of personality pathology – at the level of the individual patient as well as at the broader level of conceptual framework – requires that patient self-reports be complemented with evidence from other sources (e.g., expressed behavior, informant-reports, performance-based test data). When clinical constructs are assessed using multiple methods, results obtained using different methods typically yield divergent results (see Hopwood & Bornstein, 2014, for examples); such multi-method test score divergences are both empirically informative and clinically meaningful (Bornstein, 2011, 2017).

These limitations inherent in patients' self-reports do not mean that self-report PD data are irrelevant. On the contrary, self-reports are an important aspect of PD assessment, providing crucial perspective regarding how patients with various forms of personality pathology perceive and present themselves. That being said, rigorous validation of PD measures, categories, and diagnostic rubrics requires assessing PD related behavior *in vivo*, rather than relying exclusively on questionnaire and interview data. Recent studies using ambulatory assessment techniques have employed this approach successfully. For example, Roche and colleagues (Roche, Jacobson, & Pincus, 2016) assessed links between personality impairment and interpersonal functioning in college students over 14 days, finding that changes in behavior were triggered by cognitive and affective dynamics (e.g., negative emotions, cognitive distortions) that would be expected to impact interpersonal functioning as conceptualized by the AMPD. Approaching this issue from a categorical rather than dimensional perspective, Hepp and colleagues (Hepp, Lane, Wycoff, Carpenter, & Trull, 2018) found that across 21 days of behavior sampling, negative interpersonal events (e.g., rejection, conflict) triggered theoretically-related affective responses (e.g., hostility) more strongly in patients with borderline PD than in non-borderline controls.

Along somewhat different lines, to demonstrate convincingly that a personality trait or underlying dynamic plays a role in particular form of personality pathology, researchers must use experimental manipulations to prime key traits, or hypothesized PD dynamics. Following these manipulations researchers can assess the impact of primes on responding. For example, to demonstrate that antagonism plays a causal role in borderline pathology (see APA, 2013, pp. 766–767), lexical primes can be used to activate antagonism in participants who show high versus low levels of borderline features. Exposure to these primes should lead to increased emotional dysregulation and decreased capacity for mentalization in borderline PD participants, but not in participants with low levels of borderline pathology, nor in those with PDs theoretically unrelated to antagonism (e.g., avoidant, histrionic). Similarly, lexical primes can be used to prime helplessness schemas in dependent and nondependent participants, allowing the differential impact of these primes to be assessed. Using this procedure Bornstein and colleagues (Bornstein, Ng, Gallagher, Kloss, & Regier, 2005) demonstrated that a perception of oneself as powerless and ineffectual is central to the dynamics of dependent PD.

TOWARD AN INTEGRATIVE PERSPECTIVE ON PERSONALITY PATHOLOGY

The increasing polarization which has characterized the categorical-dimensional PD debate in recent years obscures the fact that these two perspectives have more in common than is usually acknowledged. After all, clinicians cannot render categorical PD diagnoses without first making a series of dimensional symptom ratings (e.g., determining whether a patient's grandiosity is severe enough to be clinically significant). Similarly, to employ dimensional PD ratings effectively in clinical settings clinicians must employ severity thresholds that distinguish normal from pathological functioning.

In pointing toward future research in this area Flory offers a clear and substantive recommendation to help bridge the gap between the categorical and dimensional perspectives on PDs, proposing that, "Research groups who study 'discrete' group-based interview-assessed categories are encouraged to also report dimensional scores for descriptive purposes. These dimensional scores will greatly enhance the ability to compare results across studies and research groups" (p. 362 in the previous chapter). This is an excellent

suggestion; in recent years there have been several proposals for integrating categorical and dimensional PD data in ways that accentuate the strengths of each (e.g., Helzer, Kraemer, & Krueger, 2006; Hopwood et al., 2011). The future of PD diagnosis may lie in integrative models which combine dimensional and categorical data to facilitate clinical decision-making and treatment planning.

REFERENCES

Aboraya, A., France, C., Young, J., Curci, K., & LePage, J. (2005). The validity of psychiatric diagnosis revisited. *Psychiatry, 9,* 48–55.

American Psychiatric Association. (2013). *Diagnostic and Statistical Manual of Mental Disorders* (5th ed.). Arlington, VA: American Psychiatric Publishing.

Bornstein, R. F. (2011). Toward a process-focused model of test score validity: Improving psychological assessment in science and practice. *Psychological Assessment, 23,* 532–544.

Bornstein, R. F. (2017). Evidence based psychological assessment. *Journal of Personality Assessment, 99,* 435–445.

Bornstein, R. F. (2019). The trait-type dialectic: Construct validity, clinical utility, and the diagnostic process. *Personality Disorders: Theory, Research, and Treatment, 10,* 199–209.

Bornstein, R. F., Ng, H. M., Gallagher, H. A., Kloss, D. M., & Regier, N. G. (2005). Contrasting effects of self-schema priming on lexical decisions and Interpersonal Stroop Task performance: Evidence for a cognitive/interactionist model of interpersonal dependency. *Journal of Personality, 73,* 731–761.

Cronbach, L. J., & Meehl, P. E. (1955). Construct validity in psychological tests. *Psychological Bulletin, 52,* 281–302.

Dunning, D., Heath, C., & Suls, J. M. (2018). Reflections on self-reflection: Contemplating flawed self-judgments in the clinic, classroom, and office cubicle. *Perspectives on Psychological Science, 13,* 185–189.

Helzer, J. E., Kraemer, H. C., & Krueger, R. F. (2006). The feasibility and need for dimensional psychiatric diagnoses. *Psychological Medicine, 36,* 1671–1680.

Hepp, J., Lane, S. P., Wycoff, A. M., Carpenter, R. W., & Trull, T. J. (2018). Interpersonal stressors and negative affect in individuals with borderline personality disorder and community adults in daily life: A replication and extension. *Journal of Abnormal Psychology, 127,* 183–189.

Herpertz, S. C., Huprich, S. K., Bohus, M., Chanen, A., Goodman, M., Mehlum, L., ... Sharp, C. (2017). The challenge of transforming the diagnostic system of personality disorders. *Journal of Personality Disorders, 31,* 577–589.

Hopwood, C. J., & Bornstein, R. F. (Eds.) (2014). *Multimethod Clinical Assessment.* New York: Guilford Press.

Hopwood, C. J., Kotov, R., Krueger, R. F., Watson, D., Widiger, T. A., Althoff, R. R., ... Zimmermann, J. (2018). The time has come for dimensional personality disorder diagnosis. *Personality and Mental Health, 12,* 82–86.

Hopwood, C. J., Malone, J. C, Ansell, E. B., Sanislow, C. A., Grilo, C. M., Pinto, A. ... Morey, L. C. (2011). Personality assessment in DSM-5: Empirical support for rating severity, style, and traits. *Journal of Personality Disorders, 25,* 305–320.

Kernberg, O. F., & Caligor, E. (2005). A psychoanalytic theory of personality disorders. In J. F. Clarkin & M. F. Lenzenweger

(Eds.), *Major Theories of Personality Disorder* (2nd ed., pp. 114–156). New York: Guilford Press.

Messick, S. (1995). Validity of psychological assessment: Validation of inferences from persons' responses and performances as inquiry into score meaning. *American Psychologist, 50,* 741–749.

Meyer, G. J., Finn, S. E., Eyde, L. D., Kay, G. G., Moreland, K. L., Dies, R. R. ... Reed, G. M. (2001). Psychological testing and psychological assessment: A review of evidence and issues. *American Psychologist, 56,* 128–165.

O'Connor, B. P. (2002). The search for dimensional structure differences between normality and abnormality: A statistical review of published data on personality and psychopathology. *Journal of Personality and Social Psychology, 83,* 962–982.

Oltmanns, T. F., & Turkheimer, E. (2009). Person perception and personality pathology. *Current Directions in Psychological Science, 18,* 32–36.

Roche, M. J., Jacobson, N. C., & Pincus, A. L. (2016). Using repeated daily assessments to uncover oscillating patterns and temporally-dynamic triggers in structures of psychopathology:

Applications to the DSM-5 alternative model of personality disorders. *Journal of Abnormal Psychology, 125,* 1090–1102.

Silk, K. R. (2015). The value of retaining personality disorder diagnoses. In S. K. Huprich (Ed.), *Personality Disorders: Toward Theoretical and Empirical Integration* (pp. 23–41). Washington, DC: American Psychological Association.

Tyrer, P., Reed, G. M., & Crawford, M. J. (2015). Classification, assessment, prevalence, and effect of personality disorder. *Lancet, 385,* 717–726.

Verheul, R. (2005). Clinical utility of dimensional models for personality pathology. *Journal of Personality Disorders, 19,* 283–302.

Widiger, T. A., Gore, W. L., Crego, C., Rojas, S. L., & Oltmanns, J. R. (2017). Five factor model and personality disorder. In T. A. Widiger (Ed.), *The Oxford Handbook of the Five-Factor Model* (pp. 449–478). New York: Oxford University Press.

Wilson, T. D. (2009). Know thyself. *Perspectives on Psychological Science, 4,* 384–389.

World Health Organization. (2004). *International Classification of Diseases (ICD-10).* Geneva: WHO.

15b The Need for a More Rigorous Approach to Diagnostic Reliability: Commentary on Categorical Assessment of Personality Disorders

MICHAEL CHMIELEWSKI AND MAYSON TRUJILLO

Flory (this volume) presents an overview of categorical personality disorders (PDs) and briefly discusses some of their well-established problems. Specifically, categorical PDs have excessive diagnostic comorbidity, extreme heterogeneity, and arbitrary boundaries with normality. As Flory notes, these problems are not unique to personality disorders. In fact, categorical diagnoses for nearly all forms of psychopathology appear to be less reliable and valid than commonly believed (Chmielewski, Clark, Bagby, & Watson, 2015; Regier et al., 2013). In addition, the categorical PD model also suffers from poor convergent and discriminant validity, excessive use of the not otherwise specified diagnosis, and low diagnostic stability (for reviews see Clark, 2007; Hopwood et al., 2018; Widiger & Samuel, 2005; Widiger & Trull, 2007)

Flory then relates several commonly touted advantages of categorical PDs, including clinical utility, facilitating communication, reimbursement, public policy, and a common international language. However, such claims are not universally accepted. As Hopwood et al. (2018) argue, the clinical utility of categorical PDs, is at best, questionable, as most categorical PDs do not have validated interventions. It is also debatable whether categorical PDs have an advantage in terms of providing a universal language and facilitating communication. Clinicians already use dimensional models in their practice and the majority of clinicians and researchers support moving away from categorical models to dimensional models (Bernstein, Iscan, Maser, & Boards of the Directors of ARPD and ISSPD, 2007; Helzer, Wittchen, Krueger, & Kraemer, 2008; Nelson, Huprich, Shankar, Sohnleitner, & Paggeot, 2017; Widiger & Samuel, 2005).

This debate notwithstanding, the purported advantages of the categorical PD model hinge on diagnoses being reliable. In other words, a patient should receive the same diagnosis regardless of the hospital or clinic they attend. Likewise, researchers examining specific categorical PDs must be recruiting similar patients into their studies. To the extent that this does not occur, patient care is compromised; potential mechanisms or risk factors (e.g., neurobiological, genetic, trait, cognitive, and environmental) will be elusive; modeling the natural course of personality pathology or identifying what leads to changes in diagnostic status becomes nearly impossible; the effectiveness and efficacy of new treatments cannot be accurately determined; and research findings will be unlikely to replicate (Chmielewski et al., 2015; Chmielewski, Ruggero, Kotov, Liu, & Krueger, 2017; Chmielewski & Watson, 2009; Clarke et al., 2013; Nathan & Langenbucher, 1999). Finally, claims of a "common language" become nearly impossible to support when everyone is, unknowingly, interpreting the language differently. In sum, the claimed advantages require that different diagnosticians, conducting separate independent interviews, come to the same PD diagnosis.

Unfortunately, there is the tendency to give, at best, cursory attention to this critical issue in the literature. Although this is common, we believe it is detrimental to the continued advancement of science. Instead, we argue it is essential to evaluate the assessment of personality disorders with the same scientific rigor we evaluate interventions, search for underlying mechanisms, and test hypotheses.

TAKING A MORE RIGOROUS APPROACH TO DIAGNOSTIC RELIABILITY

We fully agree with Flory that it is essential researchers report the level of diagnostic reliability in their specific studied sample (this is far too rare in the literature), as well as details about interviewer training, additional patient information made available, and how consensus was reached. However, these are only initial steps. Here we focus on two additional issues that are critical for a more serious approach to diagnostic reliability: (1) how should diagnostic reliability be assessed and (2) how reliable should diagnoses be?

Most kappa estimates for PDs come from the audio/video recording method in which one clinician conducts the interviews and provides diagnoses and a second clinician then independently provides diagnoses based on

369

recordings of the interviews. This method inflates reliability estimates for several reasons (Chmielewski et al., 2015; Kraemer, Kupfer, Clarke, Narrow, & Regier, 2012). When interviewing clinicians determine a patient does not meet diagnostic criteria for a PD, they do not ask about any remaining symptoms (this is true for semi-structured interviews because most use "skip outs"). This forces the second clinician to agree that no diagnosis is present because they do not have the symptom information necessary to confer a diagnosis. It is also impossible for the second clinician to clarify interview items, probe patient responses, or ask more in-depth questions about specific symptoms. It is possible that each clinician would have obtained different information if separate interviews were conducted. Moreover, for a variety of reasons (i.e., transient states, comfort with interviewer, clinician skill), patients may volunteer different information to one clinician versus another if separate interviews were conducted. In other words, the audio/video recording method artificially constrains the information to be identical and does not allow for truly independent ratings. As such, it is a poor proxy for whether or not patients would receive the same diagnosis at different hospitals or clinics and whether researchers are studying similar patients (Chmielewski et al., 2015; Kraemer et al., 2012).

A more realistic and ecologically valid estimate of diagnostic reliability is provided by the test-retest method (Chmielewski et al., 2015; Kraemer et al., 2012). In this method, two independent interviewers, with no knowledge of the patients' diagnostic status, independently conduct separate interviews over an interval short enough that true change in diagnostic status is highly unlikely. Conceptually, this is similar to dependability estimates for self-report measures (Chmielewski et al., 2017; Chmielewski & Watson, 2009; Gnambs, 2014; McCrae, Kurtz, Yamagata, & Terracciano, 2011). High levels of test-retest diagnostic reliability/dependability are essential when assessing personality and personality pathology. Indeed, these analyses are critical for establishing the validity of PD assessments and provide a compelling way to determine which models of personality pathology are more valid.

BASING EXPECTATIONS ON THE NATURE OF THE CONSTRUCT AND BENCHMARKS

There is a tendency in the literature to interpret nearly any kappa coefficient, regardless of its magnitude, as evidence of "adequate" reliability. At best, general guidelines or "rules of thumb" are referenced. As defined in the DSM-5, personality pathology must have "an enduring pattern," be "pervasive and inflexible," and be "stable over time" (American Psychiatric Association, 2013, p. 645). It is important to acknowledge that if categorical PDs "carved nature at the joint" and the measures/interviews assessing them did so without measurement error, then test-retest diagnostic reliability would be 1.0. We acknowledge that

achieving this goal is not practical because of the ubiquitous nature of measurement error. However, we propose that evaluating estimates of diagnostic reliability in terms of how much they deviate from the expectations set by the DSM-5 definition provides a more meaningful context for evaluating assessments and prevents the practice of interpreting any reliability estimate as acceptable.

We propose that estimates of dependability for measures of "normal" personality traits serve as ideal minimal benchmarks for test-retest diagnostic reliability. This is because "normal" personality traits and categorical PDs are both defined by stable patterns of thoughts, feelings, and behaviors. A recent meta-analysis of dependability estimates for Big Five personality measures reported a median dependability of .82 (Gnambs, 2014). Interview measures of Big Five traits have demonstrated similar levels of dependability (Big Five Domains, ICC = .81 to .93; Trull et al., 1998). These benchmarks are not unrealistic or arbitrary; they represent what can be achieved given typical assessment and measurement tools. As such, we believe they represent minimal acceptable standards for the test-retest reliability/dependability of personality pathology measures and interviews.

In Flory's review the majority of categorical PDs demonstrated test-retest diagnostic reliability that was substantially below 1.0. In fact, the grand mean kappa of all PDs was only .61; with mean kappas for specific diagnoses ranging from .40 (paranoid) to .75 (borderline). Moreover, these values failed to reach benchmark standards from the normal personality literature.

ADVANCING CLINICAL SCIENCE

Taking a more rigorous approach to diagnostic reliability leads to a fundamentally different conclusion than that reached by Flory. Indeed, the reliability of categorical PDs using these interviews appears to be far lower than the DSM-5 conceptualization would indicate. Moreover, they demonstrate substantial levels of measurement error when a more rigorous approach to reliability is taken. This represents critical problems for the categorical PD model. As expressed by Hopwood et al. (2018, p. 83), "We are concerned about the implications of retaining a categorical system that has been so thoroughly shown to be empirically and clinically problematic."

As noted by Flory, diagnostic reliability is required for diagnostic validity. However, the role of test-retest diagnostic reliability/dependability is even more critical for the validity of personality pathology because stability is the core feature of PD. As Blashfield and Livesley (1991, p. 265) note, "short-term stability must be expected" and "Failure to demonstrate stability . . . raises questions about validity." The fact that all the interviews reviewed by Flory demonstrated poor test-retest reliability/dependability suggests the fault is not with the interviews themselves. Rather, it is clear that the limits of what can be achieved by the categorical PD model have been reached.

Flory makes the important point that dimensionalizing the categorical PDs results in substantially higher levels of reliability. Indeed, even though the interviews were all developed to assess categorical PDs, dimensional scores created by summing symptoms from these measures achieved test-retest reliability/dependability that was substantially closer to 1.0 (grand mean r/ICC = .72; mean r/ICC range = .61 to .79) and approached benchmarks from the personality literature; this mirrors meta-analyses from the broader psychopathology literature demonstrating that dimensionalizing categorical DSM diagnoses results in a 15 percent increase in reliability and an 37 percent increase in criterion validity (Markon, Chmielewski, & Miller, 2011). Nevertheless, dimensionalizing categorical PDs fails to address the lack of discriminant validity across disorders and the extremely heterogeneous nature of the symptoms included within PDs. In addition, dimensionalizing the current PDs does not allow for research into which elements might be more or less stable over time, which, as Flory notes, is an important area for future research.

The DSM-5 also includes maladaptive personality traits within Section III of the manual, which offer several advantages over the categorical PD model or dimensional representations of it. These pathological traits eliminate comorbidity and heterogeneity (Krueger & Markon, 2014); capture the important variance in the categorical PD model (Hopwood, Thomas, Markon, Wright, & Krueger, 2012; Miller, Few, Lynam, & MacKillop, 2015); are strongly associated with dimensional models which have considerable research documenting their genetic underpinnings, cross-cultural validity, course, and correlates (De Fruyt et al., 2013; Quilty, Ayearst, Chmielewski, Pollock, & Bagby, 2013; Suzuki, Griffin, & Samuel, 2016; Widiger & Trull, 2007); have important links to functioning and other clinical constructs (Chmielewski et al., 2017; Hopwood et al., 2013); and have potential to guide treatment (Hopwood et al., 2018; Hopwood, Zimmermann, Pincus, & Krueger, 2015). Moreover, the DSM-5 pathological traits demonstrate test-retest dependability (mean domain dependability r = .83 to .88) that exceed the categorical PD model and are equal to the aforementioned benchmarks (Chmielewski et al., 2017; Suzuki et al., 2016).

In sum, assessments of categorical PDs fail to achieve levels of diagnostic reliability indicated by their operationalization in DSM-5 and fail to reach benchmarks demonstrated by assessments of personality traits. If the goal is to provide optimal patient care and to advance clinical science, then adopting a trait-based dimensional model of personality pathology is necessary.

REFERENCES

American Psychiatric Association. (2013). *Diagnostic and Statistical Manual of Mental Disorders* (5th ed.). Arlington, VA: American Psychiatric Publishing.

Bernstein, D. B., Iscan, C., Maser, J., & Boards of the Directors of ARPD and ISSPD (2007). Opinions of personality disorder experts regarding the DSM-IV personality disorders classification system. *Journal of Personality Disorders*, 21(5), 536–551.

Blashfield, R. K., & Livesley, W. J. (1991). Metaphorical analysis of psychiatric classification as a psychological test. *Journal of Abnormal Psychology*, 100(3), 262–270.

Chmielewski, M., Clark, L. A., Bagby, R. M., & Watson, D. (2015). Method matters: Understanding diagnostic reliability in DSM-IV and DSM-5. *Journal of Abnormal Psychology*, 124(3), 764–769.

Chmielewski, M., Ruggero, C. J., Kotov, R., Liu, K., & Krueger, R. F. (2017). Comparing the dependability and associations with functioning of the DSM-5 Section III trait model of personality pathology and the DSM-5 Section II personality disorder model. *Personality Disorders: Theory, Research, and Treatment*, 8(3), 228–236.

Chmielewski, M., & Watson, D. (2009). What is being assessed and why it matters: The impact of transient error on trait research. *Journal of Personality and Social Psychology*, 97(1), 186–202.

Clark, L. A. (2007). Assessment and diagnosis of personality disorder: Perennial issues and an emerging reconceptualization. *Annual Review of Psychology*, 58, 227–257.

Clarke, D. E., Narrow, W. E., Regier, D. A., Kuramoto, S. J., Kupfer, D. J., Kuhl, E. A., ... Kraemer, H. C. (2013). DSM-5 field trials in the United States and Canada, Part I: Study design, sampling strategy, implementation, and analytic approaches. *American Journal of Psychiatry*, 170(1), 43–58.

De Fruyt, F., De Clercq, B., Bolle, M. D., Wille, B., Markon, K., & Krueger, R. F. (2013). General and maladaptive traits in a Five-Factor Framework for DSM-5 in a university student sample. *Assessment*, 20(3), 295–307.

Gnambs, T. (2014). A meta-analysis of dependability coefficients (test–retest reliabilities) for measures of the Big Five. *Journal of Research in Personality*, 52, 20–28.

Helzer, J. E., Wittchen, H.-U., Krueger, R. F., & Kraemer, H. C. (2008). Dimensional options for DSM-V: The way forward. In J. E. Helzer, H. C. Kraemer, R. F. Krueger, H.-U. Wittchen, P. J. Sirovatka, & D. A. Regier (Eds.), *Dimensional Approaches in Diagnostic Classification: Refining the Research Agenda for DSM-V* (pp. 115–127). Arlington, VA: American Psychiatric Association.

Hopwood, C. J., Kotov, R., Krueger, R. F., Watson, D., Widiger, T. A., Althoff, R. R., ... Blais, M. A. (2018). The time has come for dimensional personality disorder diagnosis. *Personality and Mental Health*, 12(1), 82–86.

Hopwood, C. J., Thomas, K. M., Markon, K. E., Wright, A. G. C., & Krueger, R. F. (2012). DSM-5 personality traits and DSM–IV personality disorders. *Journal of Abnormal Psychology*, 121(2), 424–432.

Hopwood, C. J., Wright, A. G., Krueger, R. F., Schade, N., Markon, K. E., & Morey, L. C. (2013). DSM-5 pathological personality traits and the personality assessment inventory. *Assessment*, 20(3), 269–285.

Hopwood, C. J., Zimmermann, J., Pincus, A. L., & Krueger, R. F. (2015). Connecting personality structure and dynamics: Towards a more evidence-based and clinically useful diagnostic scheme. *Journal of Personality Disorders*, 29(4), 431–448.

Kraemer, H. C., Kupfer, D. J., Clarke, D. E., Narrow, W. E., & Regier, D. A. (2012). DSM-5: How reliable is reliable enough? *American Journal of Psychiatry*, 169(1), 13–15.

Krueger, R. F., & Markon, K. E. (2014). The role of the DSM-5 personality trait model in moving toward a quantitative and empirically based approach to classifying personality and psychopathology. *Annual Review of Clinical Psychology*, *10*, 477–501.

Markon, K. E., Chmielewski, M., & Miller, C. J. (2011). The reliability and validity of discrete and continuous measures of psychopathology: A quantitative review. *Psychological Bulletin*, *137*(5), 856–879.

McCrae, R. R., Kurtz, J. E., Yamagata, S., & Terracciano, A. (2011). Internal consistency, retest reliability, and their implications for personality scale validity. *Personality and Social Psychology Review*, *15*(1), 28–50.

Miller, J. D., Few, L. R., Lynam, D. R., & MacKillop, J. (2015). Pathological personality traits can capture DSM-IV personality disorder types. *Personality Disorders: Theory, Research, and Treatment*, *6*(1), 32–40.

Nathan, P. E., & Langenbucher, J. W. (1999). Psychopathology: Description and classification. *Annual Review of Psychology*, *50*, 79–107.

Nelson, S. M., Huprich, S. K., Shankar, S., Sohnleitner, A., & Paggeot, A. V. (2017). A quantitative and qualitative evaluation of trainee opinions of four methods of personality disorder diagnosis. *Personality Disorders: Theory, Research, and Treatment*, *8*(3), 217–227.

Quilty, L. C., Ayearst, L., Chmielewski, M., Pollock, B. G., & Bagby, R. M. (2013). The psychometric properties of the Personality Inventory for DSM-5 in an APA DSM-5 field trial sample. *Assessment*, *20*(3), 362–369.

Regier, D. A., Narrow, W. E., Clarke, D. E., Kraemer, H. C., Kuramoto, S. J., Kuhl, E. A., & Kupfer, D. J. (2013). DSM-5 field trials in the United States and Canada, Part II: Test-retest reliability of selected categorical diagnoses. *American Journal of Psychiatry*, *170*(1), 59–70.

Suzuki, T., Griffin, S. A., & Samuel, D. B. (2016). Capturing the DSM-5 Alternative Personality Disorder Model Traits in the Five-Factor Model's nomological net. *Journal of Personality*, *85*(2), 220–231.

Trull, T. J., Widiger, T. A., Useda, J. D., Holcomb, J., Doan, B. T., Axelrod, S. R., ... & Gershuny, B. S. (1998). A structured interview for the assessment of the Five-Factor Model of Personality. *Psychological Assessment*, *10*(3), 229–240.

Widiger, T. A., & Samuel, D. B. (2005). Diagnostic categories or dimensions? A question for the Diagnostic and Statistical Manual of Mental Disorders–Fifth Edition. *Journal of Abnormal Psychology*, *114*(4), 494–504.

Widiger, T. A., & Trull, T. J. (2007). Plate tectonics in the classification of personality disorder: Shifting to a dimensional model. *American Psychologist*, *62*(2), 71–83.

15c Balancing Hopeful and Pessimistic Views of the Future of Categorical Assessment: Author Rejoinder to Commentaries on Categorical Assessment of Personality Disorders

JANINE D. FLORY

The commentaries by Bornstein (this volume) and Chmielewski and Trujillo (this volume) of my review and critique of categorical approaches for diagnosing personality disorders (PDs) are appreciated. Both respectfully take issue with the continued singular conceptualization of PDs as discrete categories. This is not at odds with my review as my intent was not to "take sides" on a contentious debate but to provide an overview of existing methods for diagnosing PDs as categories and to make recommendations for future research given the reality of DSM-5.

Bornstein (this volume) expands upon the observation that models and measures are often conflated and critiques of instruments (e.g., a structured interview) might be better characterized as a critique of a categorical model of pathology (i.e., DSM) and vice versa. I frequently remind myself not to make the same error. Bornstein also notes the limitations of conclusions drawn from research that is solely based on self-report, as people generally lack context and insight when rating their own behaviors and traits. The recommendation to use specific language indicating the source of information when reporting results about personality pathology is sound. I would add that large-scale personality research that uses self-rated constructs is often conducted in university settings with college students, calling into question the generalizability of the findings to clinical and community samples.

Bornstein echoes a recurring call for multi-modal assessment of PDs, including informant reports, expressed behavior and performance-based test data. He provides some intriguing data using such methods to advance the study of borderline PD and dependent PD. Bornstein ends with the sanguine observation that the dimensional and categorical perspectives have much in common and that an integrative approach will advance research and clinical practice. I share this hopeful view.

Chmielewski and Trujillo (this volume) take a more pessimistic view of the continued use of diagnostic categories and call for greater rigor in establishing reliable methods for diagnosis. I could not agree more with this appeal as it aligns with my position in the chapter that the state of the science in establishing reliable methods of assessment using interviews lags other areas of PD research. Research that uses multi-modal assessments to establish reliable diagnostic methods, including interviews and self-reports as well as informant reports, biological markers, and expressed behaviors is almost non-existent. To quote Clark, "single-point-in-time and single-source-of-information assessment should not be expected to yield entirely valid PD diagnoses" (Clark, 2007, p. 244). And yet, the type of work that is almost universally recommended for advancing the field is not an easy or inexpensive research endeavor. Neither is research designed to conceptualize treatable conditions based on multiple dimensions of personality and functioning, which requires large-n research, especially if biological, ecological, and informant measures are included. Collaboration and open communication among research groups is essential to carry out this important work.

Chmielewski & Trujillo (this volume) describe ways to increase rigor when establishing reliability including using the test-retest method of rater reliability rather than the audio/video recording method in which a second-rater listens to or watches a previously recorded interview. The argument is that the listener is tipped off by skip-out questions and knows when the original interviewer has made a yes/no decision about a particular diagnostic criterion. The use of retest interviews can be burdensome to interviewees, however, and increases the expense of a research study. A cheaper, less burdensome alternative is to audio/video record an interview asking all questions with no skip-outs. The authors also helpfully suggest setting benchmarks for reliability based on estimates for normative personality traits. Chmielewski & Trujillo end with a less hopeful view of the future utility of establishing reliability for categorical diagnoses and firmly advocate for continued shift to dimensional conceptualization and assessment of PDs.

Although not a specific focus of the chapter, I would add that the process of refining and understanding how to diagnose PDs will also be advanced by treatment development. At present, it is rare that dimensions or categories direct treatment selection or planning for PDs. In contrast, measurement-based care is being implemented in treatment protocols for mood and anxiety disorders and substance use disorders (Lewis et al., 2019). The need for consensus on assessment of key dimensional constructs that inform PD diagnosis should include consideration of how assessments can inform treatment selection and track recovery and potential for relapse.

In closing, the process of identifying optimal methods for diagnosing PDs is still a work in progress. As I have noted in the chapter, researchers and clinicians who work with other DSM categories have also struggled with how to define and assess disorder. For example, the diagnosis of PTSD has expanded from 12 diagnostic criteria in DSM-III to 20 in DSM-5, shifting the relative importance of the symptom clusters along the way. And while the Clinician Administered PTSD Scale (CAPS) is universally accepted as the gold-standard interview for the diagnosis of PTSD, the DSM-IV version of the interview had more than nine scoring rules for determining whether a symptom was a symptom (Weathers, Keane, & Davidson, 2001). The interview has been revised for DSM-5 and scoring has been simplified (Weathers et al., 2018), but there is a generation of research using the earlier definitions of the disorder and interview with established cut points that no longer apply.

The shift from a categorical to a dimensional paradigm is an iterative journey that requires cooperation between camps who have different conceptual views and use different methodologies. We have come a long way from conceptualization of personality and PDs as immutable traits and disorders that are environmentally mediated. There is widespread recognition that PDs develop from a complex interplay between environmental, cultural, and inherited and biological factors. From the ground, it is hard see this as a shifting of the tectonic plates (Widiger & Trull, 2007), but I believe there is reason to be hopeful that shifting will continue in a productive direction.

REFERENCES

Clark, L. A. (2007). Assessment and diagnosis of personality disorder: Perennial issues and an emerging reconceptualization. *Annual Review of Psychology, 58*, 227–257.

Lewis, C. C., Boyd, M., Puspitasari, A., Navarro, E., Howard, J., Kassab, H., … Kroenke, K. (2019). Implementing measurement-based care in behavioral health: A review. *JAMA Psychiatry, 76*, 324–335.

Weathers, F. W., Bovin, M. J., Lee, D. J., Sloan, D. M., Schnurr, P. P., Kaloupek, D. G., … Marx, B. P. (2018). The Clinician-Administered PTSD Scale for DSM-5 (CAPS-5): Development and initial psychometric evaluation in military veterans. *Psychological Assessment, 30*(3), 383–395.

Weathers, F. W., Keane, T. M., & Davidson, J. R. (2001). Clinician-administered PTSD scale: A review of the first ten years of research. *Depression and Anxiety, 13*(3), 132–156.

Widiger, T. A., & Trull, T. J. (2007). Plate tectonics in the classification of personality disorder: Shifting to a dimensional model. *American Psychologist, 62*(2), 71–83.

16 Assessment of Mechanisms in Personality Disorders

SHEILA E. CROWELL, PARISA R. KALIUSH, AND ROBERT D. VLISIDES-HENRY

INTRODUCTION

Mechanisms are processes or events that produce or catalyze change, underlie or drive an observed phenomenon, or explain why an outcome occurred (Hedström & Ylikoski, 2010; Kazdin, 2007). Not surprisingly, personality disorder and other psychopathology researchers are extremely interested in identifying mechanisms, given that much of what we study involves mental processes that are difficult to observe. For mental health practitioners, the search for mechanisms is of critical importance. Biological mechanisms associated with psychopathology may hold promise for psychiatric medication management (e.g., MacKinnon & Pies, 2006) and may be alterable with behavioral interventions (e.g., Perroud et al., 2013). Identifying psychosocial and contextual mechanisms contributing to high-risk outcomes could inform psychotherapeutic treatments or prevention efforts (Kazdin, 2007). In short, the identification of mechanistic processes that underlie change, allows for more targeted and effective therapies that can be tailored to the unique requirements of those who are in greatest need. Furthermore, assessing mechanisms during treatment could help us better understand why some therapies are effective or ineffective.

The search for mechanisms in personality disorders (PDs) is especially important. First, PDs are chronic, pervasive, costly, and a source of significant distress for those affected and their loved ones (Lieb, Zanarini, Schmahl, Linehan, & Bohus, 2004). Second, many PDs are difficult to treat and/or researchers have not conducted necessary basic research or appropriate clinical trials to establish effective intervention targets, especially for Cluster A (Bamelis, Evers, Spinhoven, & Arntz, 2014). Third, many PDs are relatively rare compared to other psychiatric diagnoses (American Psychiatric Association, 2013; Tyrer, Reed, & Crawford, 2015), which makes it difficult to conduct treatment-outcome studies without costly multisite efforts that are challenging to fund. Finally, PDs, with the possible exception of borderline personality disorder (BPD), are among the most poorly understood psychiatric conditions, even though these diagnoses are a significant source of both morbidity and mortality (Kolla et al., 2016).

Therefore, it is urgent that we advance current understanding of PDs by identifying processes that underlie the emergence and maintenance of personality pathology and drive treatment outcomes.

Despite its promise, mechanistic research is diminished by several limiting factors. As a concept, the word "mechanism" is used often and is occasionally misused in the literature. This is likely due to poor understanding of what defines a mechanism. Further, most study designs are inadequate to test mechanistic theories and the dominant analytic techniques are similarly ill-suited for establishing causal processes. In order to remedy this situation, researchers must deploy more complex study designs (e.g., longitudinal, multiple levels of analysis, random assignment) and learn more sophisticated analytic techniques (see e.g., Markon & Jonas, 2016). Finally, mechanistic research cannot occur in the absence of a theory – ideally one which has withstood many empirical challenges and the test of Occam's razor. Thus, overly complex and/or atheoretical findings that introduce a potential mechanism must be viewed with skepticism.

In this chapter, we seek to clarify the definition of a mechanism with attention to these limiting factors and common problems as they relate to PDs. Next, we highlight dominant mechanistic theories in PD research and briefly describe methodological and analytic approaches that are well-suited to test these theories. Then, we examine empirical studies of biological, contextual, and biosocial mechanisms of risk for PDs with a critical eye. We propose that mechanistic research is critical for understanding, preventing, and treating PDs and that PD researchers should define, assess, and evaluate potential mechanisms with great care.

TERMINOLOGY, CONCEPTS, AND THEORIES

Defining Mechanisms

The concept of a mechanism has a long history in the psychiatric literature. Freud (e.g., Freud & Breuer, 1893,

p. 26) described the psychological reaction to severe trauma as "the mechanism of psychically acquired hysteria" and a causal factor in the etiology of hysterical symptoms. Thus, even early use of the term implied causality. This understanding continues to more recent definitions of a mechanism as "the cogs and wheels of the causal process through which the outcome to be explained was brought about" (Hedström & Ylikoski, 2010, p. 50). As Hedström and Ylikoski describe, there are four key elements that define a mechanism. First, a mechanism can be identified by the phenomenon or effect it produces. In other words, a mechanism includes all of the parts, operations, and their organization that, taken together, yield an observed outcome.

Second, a mechanism involves elements of a causal process that *increase the probability* of that observed outcome. In this regard, Hedström and Ylikoski take a more liberal definition of a mechanism than do other authors (e.g., Mahoney, 2001), who propose that a mechanism must be *sufficient* to produce the outcome of interest. Thus, Hedström and Ylikoski assume that mechanistic processes likely include some random elements that could produce different outcomes, particularly in the social sciences.

Third, a mechanism has structure, and "when a mechanism-based explanation opens the black box, it discloses this structure" (Hedström & Ylikoski, 2010, p. 51). Thus, a mechanistic description reveals how the outcome occurs, which includes the participating entities as well as their properties, activities, and relations. Importantly, once these components of a mechanism are revealed, it is possible to delve into a series of subsequent investigations into each of the component parts and their role in the mechanistic process (e.g., one might ask whether it is possible to prevent or change the outcome by altering certain components).

Finally, there is a hierarchy inherent in mechanisms and the scientific disciplines that seek to elucidate mechanistic processes. Consequently, what we define as a mechanism in the social and psychological sciences invariably includes elements that would be broken down further by other scientific disciplines. This progression continues down to the most elemental physical processes that can be reduced no further. Importantly, it is not necessary to elucidate every component of the causal process in order to identify and study a psychological mechanism. Even if we are unable – or neglect to delineate – each of the component entities and activities, a mechanistic account serves as a framework for understanding how an outcome came to be.

Key Concepts

Importance of Theory

The search for a mechanism requires rigorous gathering of empirical evidence in order to differentiate a verifiable

mechanistic explanation from "mechanism-based storytelling" (Hedström & Ylikoski, 2010, p. 53). As a result, the process of establishing a mechanism is lengthy and begins with theory. This theory serves as one account of processes within the black box while simultaneously hypothesizing that other competing explanations are less plausible. Over time, theories are refined and mechanistic explanations reveal new black boxes that we must open and examine. Freud's mechanistic account provides a good example. He advanced a theory that trauma is the causal mechanism of most acquired anxiety and, furthermore, through hypnosis and other techniques, it is possible to identify traumas and/or other repressed conflicts that are the source of current distress (Freud & Breuer, 1893). This prompted research into associations between trauma exposure and psychiatric symptoms, such as cases of "shell shock" during the First World War (Myers, 1915), and combat fatigue during the Second World War (Saul, 1945).

As the field advanced, scientists asked more sophisticated questions and began to test animal models of stress exposure. For example, Garattini, Giacalone, and Valzelli (1967) found that mice who were kept in isolation for four weeks became aggressive relative to those raised communally. At the end of the four-week experiment, these mice were injected with tranylcypromine (a monoamine oxidase inhibitor [MAO]) and their brains were analyzed to examine how serotonin (5HT) and the serotonin metabolite 5HIAA were processed. The authors found an increase in 5HT turnover among isolated relative to communal mice, which they implied was a potential mechanism linking isolation stress with later aggressive behavior. Psychological research on posttraumatic stress disorder (PTSD) also progressed and researchers began to ask the question of *who* develops PTSD following a traumatic event. Not surprisingly, meta-analytic findings revealed considerable heterogeneity among those with a PTSD diagnosis, their pretrauma histories, and trauma-concurrent stressors/supports (Brewin, Andrews, & Valentine, 2000). Current research on mechanisms linking trauma exposure to PTSD is focused on a number of biological and social risk factors, including genes, epigenetic regulation, inflammation, psychophysiology, neurocircuitry, prior trauma or childhood family adversity, preexisting mental disorders, and lack of social support (see e.g., Admon, Milad, & Hendler, 2013; Bromet, Atwoli, Kawakami, & Navarro-Mateu, 2017; McLaughlin & Lambert, 2017; Shalev, Liberzon, & Marmar, 2017). Thus, the black box of how trauma leads to psychopathology, and for whom, is becoming more transparent and nuanced.

Design and Analytic Considerations

A mechanistic theory provides a causal hypothesis of how several elements, processes, and activities operate together to produce – or increase the probability of – an outcome. However, it is a challenge to test causal theories in PDs and other complex psychological disorders.

Thankfully, modern research has transcended early theories involving simple etiological causes, such as a single gene for psychopathy (although psychopathy is highly heritable; Larsson, Andershed, & Lichtenstein, 2006; Viding, Blair, Moffitt, & Plomin, 2005) or trauma as the root of BPD (although trauma is a known risk factor for BPD; Lieb et al., 2004). Instead of searching for *the* cause of PDs, researchers now seek to understand pieces of a complex causal puzzle in which many elements contribute, probabilistically, to the end result. This requires drawing careful conclusions from well-designed experiments.

Historically, researchers have sought to test causal theories using statistical methods (Kazdin, 2007). However, statistics alone are insufficient for identifying causal processes unless certain design considerations are met, such as random assignment to experimental or control conditions, careful control of confounding variables, and manipulation of the independent variable (see e.g., Crowell et al., 2017). In PD research, this is most often accomplished within clinical trials. For example, in one clinical trial of treatment for BPD (Clarkin, Levy, Lenzenweger, & Kernberg, 2007), participants were randomized to three different interventions that were similar in the amount of contact provided, quality of providers, and several other variables. The results revealed that targeting specific clinical problems in therapy led to changes in key outcomes for some therapies over others. Transference focused therapy, for example, was uniquely effective at reducing irritability and verbal and direct assault. The authors hypothesized that repeatedly focusing on self-control in the context of the therapist–patient relationship may have been a mechanism by which this change occurred.

Similarly, Gratz and colleagues (Gratz, Bardeen, Levy, Dixon-Gordon, & Tull, 2015) examined changes in emotion dysregulation as a mechanism of change in a group therapy targeting emotion regulation deficits. They found that reductions in emotion dysregulation mediated the effects of group therapy on BPD symptoms, such as self-inflicted injury. Clinical trials offer a powerful opportunity to test mechanistic theories because they allow random assignment to an enhanced experience (given that random assignment to stressful environments is unethical). However, this design often involves many synergistic elements and processes – individual therapy, group therapy, medication management, therapist–client match, client preferences for treatment style – making it difficult to disentangle key components contributing to change (see e.g., Ahn & Wampold, 2001). Other common designs include random assignment to different tasks or examining within-person changes to laboratory stressors such as conflict or rejection (e.g., Crowell et al., 2005, 2017). These designs allow for a more microanalytic approach to testing mechanistic theories. A limitation of these approaches is that they only allow for tests of proximal causes within a larger causal sequence.

A wide range of analytic and statistical approaches have been developed and used to test causal theories. The most common include mediation analysis, structural equation modeling, and other multivariate approaches (e.g., Joreskog, Sorbom, & Magidson, 1979; Lowry & Gaskin, 2014; Preacher & Hayes, 2004). More recently, researchers have introduced dynamic causal modeling – a Bayesian approach – and convergent cross mapping – a dynamic systems technique designed to detect causal relationships within time-series data (Clark et al., 2015; Stephan et al., 2010). However, we must evaluate the causal promises of these methods with a critical eye, remembering that answers will only be meaningful in the context of a well-reasoned question and study design. Indeed, in one of the most widely cited articles on causal modeling, Bentler (1980, p. 420) states that the word "cause" is not intended to convey any philosophical meaning beyond "a hypothesized unobserved process" and that other terms, such as process or system modeling would work equally well. Thus, just like the theories they are designed to test, statistical methods that underlie mechanism-based research are both fraught and full of promise.

Mechanistic Theories and Personality Disorders

Clearly, there are many challenges inherent to defining, studying, and testing mechanisms. If we accept the broadest definitions of the term, a mechanism can be examined at almost any level of analysis and can include almost any combination of elements within a causal sequence of events. This opens up a veritable gold mine of research questions for scientists interested in understanding how PDs emerge, are maintained, and change over time or with treatment. The risk, however, is that we have identified a term that means everything and, as a result, is meaningless. Thus, if we seek to advance PD research, we must ground our mechanistic work in testable (and falsifiable) theories.

There are several theories currently at the forefront of PD research. A majority of these are based on dimensional, trait-based conceptualizations of personality and PDs. Dimensional theorists seek to explain psychopathology in terms of broad, transdiagnostic traits, such as internalizing/externalizing and the Five-Factor Model (Kotov et al., 2017; Krueger & Markon, 2014; Wright et al., 2012). This perspective holds great promise for mechanistic research, since underlying mechanisms of risk likely cut across diagnostic categories (Beauchaine & McNulty, 2013; Kotov et al., 2017). Indeed, as Kupfer, First, and Regier (2002, p. xviii) noted, "not one laboratory marker has been found to be specific in identifying any of the DSM-defined syndromes. Epidemiologic and clinical studies have shown extremely high rates of comorbidities among the disorders, undermining the hypothesis that the syndromes represent distinct etiologies." This observation, along with research over the past 15 years, suggests that common traits underlie many DSM diagnoses, including PDs (Caspi et al., 2014; Cuthbert & Insel, 2013; Kotov et al., 2017). For PD theorists, however, connections between general personality structure and diagnosable PDs are especially clear because PDs appear to represent an extreme variant of normative personality dimensions (Crowell & Kaufman, 2016; Miller, Lyman, Widiger, & Leukefeld, 2001; Widiger & Simonsen, 2005).

In addition to dimensional approaches, PD researchers have increasingly focused on etiology and developmental precursors to PDs (Bornovalova, Lejuez, Daughters, Rosenthal, & Lynch, 2005; Crowell, Beauchaine, & Linehan, 2009; De Fruyt & De Clercq, 2014). This work also emerges from a trait-based conceptualization of psychopathology with a specific emphasis on early biologically-based temperament, parent–child relationships (e.g., attachment, interaction patterns), and biology × environment interactions. As with dimensional approaches, a major focus of this work is on emotional processes, such as emotion dysregulation, and mechanisms that underlie its development, including research on emotional instability, poor emotional awareness, mood-dependent impulsive behavior, emotional lability, and other forms of dysregulated emotions and behavior. Thus, although there are a range of potential mechanisms that are relevant to PD research, emotional processes are a focus of this review.

BIOLOGICAL MECHANISMS

Researchers use a number of techniques to test biological mechanisms of PDs and PD development, including neuroimaging, psychophysiological, neurotransmitter activity, genetic, and epigenetic processes. Understandably, each of these methods can only elucidate a few components of the many complex mechanisms that underlie PDs. For example, neuroimaging techniques are useful for revealing biological responses that occur during emotion dysregulation (Doll et al., 2013). Even though imaging and many other biological techniques can only reveal part of a mechanistic process, biomarkers serve as potential targets in treatment research and help scientists understand emotional and psychological processes at another level of analysis.

Neuroimaging

Researchers have used functional magnetic resonance imaging (fMRI), MRI, and electroencephalography (EEG) to examine emotional processes in the moment. Specifically, those with PDs tend to have distinct activation of brain areas related to emotional processing. For instance, Doll and colleagues (2013) used fMRI to examine connectivity between the default mode network, salience network, and central executive network. They hypothesize that connections between these brain networks form a foundation for emotion regulation. Specifically, these areas are activated by emotions, cognitions, and

behaviors – thus, connectedness allows for appropriate coordination of neural activity. The researchers found that those with BPD (compared to controls) had abnormal connectivity between the networks, suggesting a possible mechanism for emotion dysregulation. Other researchers have shown that connectivity between neural regions is important for emotion regulation. For those with schizotypal PD, there appears to be altered frontotemporal activity and connectivity between these areas and other neural regions (Fervaha & Remington, 2013).

In addition to neural pathways, activity in specific regions may also be associated with emotion dysregulation. The amygdala is an important region for emotions (particularly fear) and their regulation, ultimately making it a candidate mechanism of PDs. A smaller amygdala with reduced functioning has been associated with psychopathy (Moul, Killcross, & Dadds, 2012). From this, one may tentatively conclude that limited emotion regulation might underlie risk for psychopathy. Researchers have also found that the anterior cingulate cortex (ACC) and amygdala of those with BPD displayed heightened activity (compared to controls), both at rest and in response to fearful faces (Mitchell, Dickens, & Picchioni, 2014). Relatedly, MacKinnon and Pies (2006) reviewed structural MRI techniques and found that women with BPD had reduced hippocampal volume and elevated blood oxygen levels in the amygdala compared to controls. In a review, Susman (2006) discussed how abnormal amygdala functioning might mediate the relation between early-life trauma and emotion dysregulation. Finally, Hajcak, MacNamara, and Olvet (2010) have used EEG to determine that the specific event-related potentials (ERP) P300 and the late positive potential (LPP) are linked to emotion regulation. Future research should examine how these brain regions might be *causally* linked to emotion dysregulation and PDs.

Mixed neurological findings also have been found in children and adolescents, though the literature is still emerging. Goodman, Mascitelli, and Triebwasser (2013) compared the neurobiology literature on adult-onset and adolescent-onset BPD. However, they found minimal data on brain abnormalities in adolescent-onset BPD compared to controls. That is, there were no clear differences in ACC, amygdala, and hippocampus size and functionality or ERP P300. In another review, Brunner, Henze, Richter, and Kaess (2015) also did not find any structural or functional differences but they do report clear differences in limbic system gray matter volume and functionality for children with BPD, suggesting differences in emotion regulation from an early age. These limbic gray matter changes could be due to an interaction with early-life stress and abuse (Ensink, Biberdzic, Normandin, & Clarkin, 2015). Other reviews have found similarly mixed results in regards to brain structures, EEG findings, and gray matter differences (Winsper et al., 2016), though some older articles still need to be replicated (see e.g., Deckel, Hesselbrock, & Bauer, 1996). Thus, there is a clear need for further research on neurobiological mechanisms of youth PDs.

These studies all support the hypothesis that diminished amygdala size and functioning may play a mechanistic role in PDs, though this may be limited to adults. However, due to study design limitations, sample sizes, and lack of replication of key findings, we cannot be certain that we have identified key components of the mechanistic pathway (see also van Zutphen, Siep, Jacob, Goebel, & Arntz, 2015 for a critical review of imaging findings in BPD). Nevertheless, these findings bring us closer to a better understanding of emotional processes in PDs.

Neurochemistry

Researchers have found that neurochemical and hormonal abnormalities are associated with emotion dysregulation. Although a thorough review is beyond the scope of this chapter, neurotransmitter and neuroendocrine dysfunction are a major focus of PD research (for a review, see e.g., Bridgett, Burt, Edwards, & Deater-Deckard, 2015). Briefly, monoamine oxidase-A and -B (MAO-A, MAO-B) are a group of enzymes that catalyze monoamines. Low levels of MAO-B have been found in antisocial personality disorder (ASPD) and BPD (Zuckerman & Kuhlman, 2000). In a study by Kolla and colleagues (2016), researchers found that MAO-A levels in the prefrontal cortex and ACC were elevated among those with BPD compared to control individuals.

There is also an extensive literature linking neurotransmitter function, psychopathology, and PDs (for reviews, see e.g., Kenna et al., 2012; Martin, Ressler, Binder, & Nemeroff, 2010). Researchers have found that serotonin is critical for regulating emotions, particularly aggression, with reduced serotonin levels predicting greater frequency of antisocial behaviors (Trull, Stepp, & Durrett, 2003). Lee (2006) found that serotonin and GABA interact with one another to affect amygdala activation and impair self-regulation. Susman (2006) found that attenuation of the serotonergic system, abnormalities in the gamma aminobutyric (GABA) system, and reduced cortisol levels were all linked to antisocial behaviors and ASPD. Finally, alterations in vasopressin and oxytocin may mediate the established link between early-life trauma and PD development (Heinrichs, von Dawans, & Domes, 2009). Thus, neurotransmitters appear to play a central role in self-regulation, psychopathology, and PDs (see also, Strauman, 2017).

Additionally, HPA axis activation (i.e., corticotropin releasing factor [CRF] and cortisol) is related to emotion dysregulation and has been a focus of research on depression and anxiety (Pagliaccio et al., 2015; Stetler & Miller, 2011). Lee (2006) found that CRF, serotonin, and GABA levels interact with one another to affect amygdala activity, ultimately hampering regulatory capacity. In one review, Hostinar, Sullivan, and Gunnar (2014) found a literature consensus that cortisol levels can be regulated through social support, though this process was ultimately moderated by levels of oxytocin, vasopressin, and sympathetic neurotransmitters (e.g., norepinephrine, epinephrine). In one interesting animal study, Butler and colleagues (Butler, Ariwodola, & Weiner, 2014) found that socially isolated rats showed disrupted HPA axis function, anxiety-like behaviors, and were more likely to develop a preference for and over-use of EtOH (alcohol). Thus, HPA-axis dysfunction is one potential link in the causal chain from social isolation to alcohol abuse and other forms of psychopathology, which has clear relevance for PDs (Butler, Karkhanis, Jones, & Weiner, 2016; Crowell, 2016; Mushtaq, Shoib, Shah, & Mushtaq, 2014).

While some have found no differences in cortisol activity for adolescents with BPD (Winsper et al., 2016), other reviews have shown attenuated cortisol reactivity to stress in adolescents (Brunner et al., 2015; Ensink et al., 2015; Goodman et al., 2013), again evidencing the inconsistency in the biological findings for PD youths. Few other neurochemical differences have been found, as most authors report either a lack of clear differences between PD youth and control youths or simply a dearth of literature (e.g., Brunner et al., 2015).

Other Physiology

A variety of other physiological processes and markers have been linked to regulatory capacity and PDs. For example, those with BPD tend to have lower cholesterol and leptin levels compared with controls (Trull et al., 2003). In a comprehensive review, Thayer and Sternberg (2006) found that reduced vagal tone (i.e., low heart rate variability [HRV]/respiratory sinus arrhythmia [RSA]), an established marker of regulatory capacity, is linked to greater levels of inflammatory markers (e.g., interleukin-6) and cortisol and reduced levels of glucose. This review suggests that unhealthy physiology (e.g., inflammation, cortisol) is associated with emotion dysregulation, which in turn is associated with psychopathology and PDs. Further, in a meta-analysis, Koenig, Kemp, Feeling, Thayer, and Kaess (2016) compared resting state HRV in BPD individuals compared to controls. The results showed a dosage effect of BPD symptoms on HRV, with lower HRV being related to more BPD traits. The autonomic nervous system is also involved in antisocial symptoms. Those with ASPD and incarcerated individuals tend to have reduced autonomic arousal (i.e., less heart rate reactivity) compared to controls (Susman, 2006). In the same review, the author found that children who display risk for ASPD have reduced HRV when challenged compared to controls, suggesting a lack of regulatory capacity. In sum, a variety of physiological markers are related to emotion dysregulation and PDs.

There is an extensive literature on youth psychopathology and psychophysiological indices of risk (see

Beauchaine, 2001). However, few researchers have attempted to link these findings to theories of PD development. In one study, Raine and colleagues found that low resting heart rate at age 3 was a significant predictor of aggression and antisocial behaviors at age 11 (Raine, Venables, & Mednick, 1997). In our own work, we have also examined how peripheral physiology is associated with PD risk. For instance, we found that self-injuring adolescents scored higher on measures of emotion dysregulation, externalizing psychopathology, and BPD symptoms, and also had attenuated electrodermal responding (EDR) compared to depressed adolescents (Crowell et al., 2012). This suggests that EDR may be one mechanism of risk for impulsivity and externalizing traits among girls at risk for BPD, although further research is needed. When examining dyads consisting of depressed adolescents and their mothers, we found that depressed and self-injuring adolescents showed moment-to-moment withdrawal in RSA in response to aversive maternal behaviors and their mothers showed a similar pattern in response to adolescent aversive behaviors. In contrast, control adolescents and their mothers showed RSA increases in response to aversive behaviors, which possibly reflects better emotion regulation in the face of interpersonal stress (Crowell et al., 2014). Although many participants in these studies had only subthreshold PD traits, research with high-risk adolescents is important for bridging the gap between early vulnerability factors and a later PD diagnosis.

Genetics

Researchers have examined a variety of candidate genes and genetic factors that underlie emotion dysregulation and PDs. Many of these genes are related to the production, transport, and degradation of neurotransmitters (e.g., MAO-A, serotonin), but sex chromosomes also appear to play a role. For example, the male sex chromosome puts males at greater risk for aggressive behaviors (Eme, 2007). Those with a variation of the MAO-A production gene such that there is reduced MAO-A production tend to be at greater risk for aggression, conduct disorder, and ASPD (Lee, 2006; Susman, 2006). Researchers have also found that BPD, depression, and emotional lability co-aggregate in families (MacKinnon & Pies, 2006), potentially suggesting a common genetic pathway. Canli, Ferra, and Duman (2009) showed that genetic variations resulting in less production of 5-HTTLPR, COMT, and MAO-A are linked to top-down cortical emotion modulation – that is, prefrontal involvement in emotion regulation. The effects of genes may be differentially impactful throughout the lifespan. For instance, Bornovalova, Hicks, Iacono, and McGue (2009) found that the heritability of BPD is slightly higher for those aged 14–24 than for older adults. Genes have been linked clearly to temperaments that might predispose the youth to PD risk (Brunner et al., 2015; Ensink et al., 2015). Additionally, a few candidate

genes may put children and adolescents at risk for BPD symptoms, including the short 5-HTTLPR (similar to adults), the oxytocin receptor, and FKBP5 (Winsper et al., 2016). In a recent study, Bornovalova and colleagues (2018) found that genetic differences primarily accounted for the comorbidity between BPD and substance use disorders, while BPD comorbidity with other disorders was largely due to environmental influences. This study furthers understanding of the common genetic (or epigenetic) mechanisms to psychiatric comorbidity in PDs.

Epigenetics

Researchers studying epigenetic processes typically examine genetic methylation, the process by which gene function is more or less activated, although specific effects vary greatly by gene, situation, and amount of methylation (Bird, 2002). Perhaps unsurprisingly, methylation of the MAO-A and MAO-B genes appears to be related to emotion dysregulation and PD risk. Dammann and colleagues (2011) showed that MAO-A and MAO-B methylation predicted BPD risk for females only. Furthermore, hypermethylation of the MAO-A promoter may lead to downregulation of MAO-A, ultimately predicting reduced serotonin concentration and ASPD risk (Checknita et al., 2015). The methylation of other genes has also been linked to emotion dysregulation: S-COMT methylation has predicted BPD (Dammann et al., 2011) and methylation of the oxytocin receptor gene has predicted callousness and lack of sociality (Kumsta, Hummel, Chen, & Heinrichs, 2013).

CONTEXTUAL AND ENVIRONMENTAL MECHANISMS

There are countless contextual and environmental risk factors, ranging from childhood abuse (see e.g., Belsky et al., 2012) to low socioeconomic status (see e.g., Cohen et al., 2008), that are associated with development and maintenance of PDs. Researchers sometimes describe these as *mechanisms*; however, not all risk factors meet the definition of a mechanism. Potential contextual and environmental mechanisms must be linked to theories of change and/or processes that underlie the emergence of PDs. Research exploring contextual and environmental mechanisms of risk are crucial for informing psychosocial prevention and intervention (Crowell et al., 2013). However, research to date is limited by difficulties determining what constitutes a mechanism in the social sciences and challenges with determining causality among associated variables, especially if they are assessed concurrently. Also, some authors use contextual and environmental mechanisms interchangeably, which can confuse interpretation of findings and limit our ability to apply findings to prevention and intervention efforts. To limit this confusion, we describe contextual and environmental mechanisms separately. We define contextual mechanisms as processes in an individual's local, daily environment that directly influence their health and well-being. These processes are malleable and shift frequently (e.g., parenting behaviors). In contrast, environmental mechanisms are more stable and encompass broader societal factors, such as neighborhood violence and socioeconomic status (SES).

Contextual Mechanisms

Early Maternal Withdrawal

There are an increasing number of prospective studies examining the influences of early caregiving interactions on the development of psychopathology. Primarily, this research focuses on early mother–infant interaction patterns, and addresses such constructs as early separation, disrupted communication, and disorganized attachment. Maternal withdrawal to infant attachment cues emerges repeatedly as a strong predictor of BPD and conduct disorder symptoms, as well as suicidality and self-injury in adolescence (Lyons-Ruth, 2008; Lyons-Ruth, Bureau, Easterbrooks, Obsuth, & Hennighausen, 2013; Lyons-Ruth, Bureau, Holmes, Easterbrooks, & Brooks, 2013; Steele & Siever, 2010; Stepp, Lazarus, & Byrd, 2015). Maternal withdrawal is characterized by a general lack of interaction with an infant, including a lack of greeting and comforting, delayed or cursory responding, redirecting the infant's attention from the mother to toys, and engaging primarily in distanced interactions (e.g., interacting from across the room; Lyons-Ruth, Bureau, Easterbrooks, et al., 2013).

Interestingly, maternal withdrawal to infant attachment cues has surfaced as a stronger predictor of adolescent borderline and conduct disorder symptoms than has maternal negative-intrusive behavior, despite consistent links between negative-intrusive behavior and abuse, and abuse and borderline pathology (Lyons-Ruth, 2008). For instance, Lyons-Ruth, Bureau, Holmes, et al. (2013) found that maternal withdrawal during an infant attachment assessment at 18 months accounted for the relation between clinician referral due to concerning quality of care and offspring borderline and conduct disorder features around age 18 years. The effect of maternal withdrawal on later offspring borderline and conduct disorder features was independent of, and additive to, the severity of childhood abuse (Lyons-Ruth, Bureau, Holmes, et al., 2013). Thus, child abuse is an important risk factor in the development of personality disorders, but it is more likely that abusive experiences interact with early maternal interactions (i.e., environment × environment interaction), rather than acting alone, to confer risk for pathology (Caspi et al., 2002; Fruzzetti, Shenk, & Hoffman, 2005; Neuhaus & Beauchaine, 2017).

Extended maternal separation has also been identified as a potential mechanism in the development of PDs (Chanen & Kaess, 2012; Crawford, Cohen, Chen, Anglin, & Ehrensaft, 2009; Steele & Siever, 2010). Specifically, extended maternal separation (i.e., more than one month)

from the infant during the first five years was found to be a significant predictor of offspring borderline personality pathology among a large random community sample (Crawford et al., 2009). Not only did extended early maternal separation predict the presence of adolescent borderline symptoms, it predicted significantly slower declines of these symptoms as the offspring progressed through normative maturation and socialization processes (Crawford et al., 2009). Interestingly, separation due to divorce or death was not predictive of offspring borderline symptoms (Crawford et al., 2009). Thus, it is difficult to determine if the separation itself catalyzed the development of personality pathology. Because separation due to other reasons, such as mothers leaving for personal reasons or infants being sent away for extended stays with relatives, was predictive of borderline symptoms, it is more likely that extended separation is a risk factor when it is due to maternal withdrawal (i.e., lack of maternal investment in caregiving).

Invalidating Interaction Patterns

Invalidating parent–child interactions are characterized by parental rejection or minimization of children's emotional expressions, especially those that are overwhelming for the family to manage (Crowell, Yaptangco, & Turner, 2016; Linehan, 1993). This intolerance toward a child's emotional expression communicates to the child that their experiences are unreasonable, and that they must cope independently with their distress (Linehan, 1993). Consequently, the child does not learn basic emotion regulation skills, and instead uses increasingly labile interaction patterns to garner support and validation from caregivers (Crowell et al., 2009). This feedback loop of invalidation and extreme emotional lability may recur over many years, disrupting family relationships and increasing the child's risk for PD development (Crowell et al., 2009, 2013, 2016; Linehan, 1993).

Hallquist, Hipwell, and Stepp (2015) prospectively investigated invalidating parenting, poor self-control (e.g., inability to control temper during arguments), and negative emotionality among girls aged 5–14 years as predictors of BPD at 14–17 years of age. These researchers found that all three factors were predictive of borderline personality symptoms at age 14 (Hallquist et al., 2015). Importantly, results revealed a reciprocal effect of poor self-control and invalidating parenting on each other in their prediction of borderline personality symptoms at age 14 (Hallquist et al., 2015). These findings highlight the importance of studying bidirectional parent–child influences on the development of personality pathology, and support the theory that invalidating interaction patterns are prominent mechanisms in the development of emotion dysregulation and PDs.

Coercive Interaction Patterns

Coercion theory (Patterson, 1982) was developed separately from Linehan's (1993) invalidating environment theory, but also involves reinforcement of extreme negative affectivity and emotion dysregulation (Beauchaine, Klein, Crowell, Derbidge, & Gatzke-Kopp, 2009; Crowell et al., 2016; Dishion, Duncan, Eddy, Fagot, & Fetrow, 1994; Snyder, Schrepferman, & St. Peter, 1997). During coercive interactions, parents of emotionally aroused children match or exceed the child's aversiveness, who, in turn, matches or exceeds the arousal of their parent (Beauchaine et al., 2009). This escalation continues until the antagonistic interaction terminates, negatively reinforcing aggression, emotional lability, and autonomic arousal (Beauchaine et al., 2009). Individuals who are raised within coercive environments may not acquire the basic skills of discriminating and labeling emotions or managing strong emotions, which increases risk for PDs (Fruzzetti et al., 2005).

Initially, coercion theory was developed and tested among adolescent males who displayed externalizing behavior problems and were at risk for developing antisocial PD (see e.g., Patterson, DeBaryshe, & Ramsey, 1990). However, we have examined coercive mother–child interaction patterns among self-injuring adolescents at risk for developing BPD (Crowell et al., 2013). Each mother–child dyad engaged in a ten-minute discussion about a topic of conflict, and trained research assistants coded the interactions for parental invalidation and conflict escalation as well as aversive utterances. We found that mothers of self-injuring adolescents primarily matched or escalated conflict, and would de-escalate conversations only after extreme adolescent behavior. These coercive responses contrasted with control mothers who primarily matched at the lowest level of adolescent aversiveness and de-escalated more intense utterances, regardless of adolescent behavior. Thus, we found emerging evidence of coercive parent–child interactions among emotionally dysregulated and self-injuring adolescents at risk for PD development.

Invalidation and Coercion among Adults

Adults with PD diagnoses, especially BPD, often have distressing interpersonal histories, and demonstrate continued difficulty in forming healthy relationships (see Crowell, 2016 for a review). Thus, there is an urgent need to use more sophisticated research designs and statistical analyses to investigate invalidating and coercive interaction patterns among adults with PDs. Much of research on adults with PDs focuses on individual-level factors, neglecting potential dynamic contextual influences, such as invalidating or coercive interaction patterns with romantic partners, which may serve as mechanisms underlying maintenance of PD symptoms (Chen et al., 2004; Crowell, 2016). There is growing consensus in the field of PD research that PDs demonstrate more heterotypic continuity than stability across development (Sharp & Romero, 2007; Skodol et al., 2002), which highlights the need for more longitudinal research on contextual

mechanisms of PDs in adulthood (Conway, Hammen, & Brennan, 2015).

Environmental Mechanisms

Neighborhood Effects

Traditionally, neighborhood environments have been considered indirect influences in developmental pathways to personality pathology, and therefore would not be deemed mechanisms. Indeed, there are countless interwoven factors (e.g., socioeconomic status, violence exposure, pollution) associated with neighborhoods, making it nearly impossible to detect a causal relation between one factor and PD development (Caspi, Taylor, Moffitt, & Plomin, 2000). Caspi et al. (2000) conducted a nationwide study of 2-year-old twins, and found that children in deprived neighborhoods (i.e., those characterized by low car availability, greater number of single parents, and high unemployment rates) were at significantly greater risk for demonstrating emotional and behavior problems than were those in higher SES neighborhoods. Further, these neighborhood effects accounted for variability in behavior and emotional problems above and beyond genetic liability (Caspi et al., 2000). Research demonstrates consistently that children who are impulsive and raised in high-risk neighborhoods are more likely to engage in antisocial behaviors (Lynam et al., 2000; Neuhaus & Beauchaine, 2017). Thus, there is clearly an effect of neighborhood on the development of emotion dysregulation and possibly PDs. However, the exact mechanisms that catalyze development of personality pathology warrant further investigation.

Peer Group Affiliation

Peer group affiliation is often related to an individual's neighborhood and has been shown to influence the development of personality pathology (Beauchaine et al., 2009; Dishion, McCord, & Poulin, 1999; Ingoldsby & Shaw, 2002; Nelson & Dishion, 2004; Piehler & Dishion, 2008). Certain neighborhoods may foster harmful peer group affiliations that subsequently predict delinquency, substance use, violence, and adult maladjustment (Beauchaine et al., 2009). Dishion and colleagues explored these associations and found that rejection and isolation from peers in grade school was predictive of adult antisocial behaviors, even after controlling for early academic performance and presence of antisocial behaviors (Nelson & Dishion, 2004; Piehler & Dishion, 2008). Also, Dishion et al. (1999) found that peer group interventions can inadvertently become iatrogenic when they foster "deviancy training" among high-risk adolescents. Snyder et al. (2008) found that, among boys and girls, peer "deviancy training" in kindergarten predicted conduct disorder symptoms by third grade, and acted independently of several factors, including peer coercion, child impulsivity, and child verbal ability. These contagion effects from deviant peer affiliation have been observed among self-injuring and emotionally dysregulated youth at risk for BPD as well (Beauchaine et al., 2009; Putnam & Silk, 2005). Research on peer group affiliation offers a promising avenue for psychosocial prevention and intervention of PDs, and highlights the importance of examining several related constructs when delineating environmental mechanisms in PD development.

BIOLOGY–ENVIRONMENT INTERACTIONS

Research examining both biological vulnerabilities and contextual/environmental risk factors has revealed a synergistic rather than additive effect on PD development (Beauchaine et al., 2009). In fact, biology × environment interactions may be present even in the absence of significant main effects (Beauchaine et al., 2009). Advanced research methods foster the examination of complex interaction models and have promoted the emergence of the biosocial model of PDs. Marsha Linehan (1993) outlined a leading biosocial theory of BPD. She hypothesized that BPD is a disorder of emotion dysregulation, which emerges when a biologically vulnerable child is faced with specific environmental risks (see also Crowell et al., 2009). As personality pathology seems to demonstrate heterotypic continuity from childhood to adulthood (Sharp & Romero, 2007; Skodol et al., 2002), it is crucial that researchers investigate biology × environment interactions across development.

Prenatal and Infancy

Prenatal adversity, epigenetic programming, and infant temperament are important processes in the onset and development of psychopathology, including PDs (Gartstein & Skinner, 2018). Epigenetics involves alterations in gene function, without changing gene structure, that occur in response to environmental exposures (Bird, 1986) – it is the molecular mechanism driving environmental influences on phenotypic outcomes associated with physical and mental health (Gartstein & Skinner, 2018). One of the most commonly studied forms of epigenetics is DNA methylation – that is, the addition of a small methyl group to a cytosine nucleotide-phosphate-guanine nucleotide (CpG) sequence which has the capacity to activate or deactivate genes (Gartstein & Skinner, 2018). Prenatal exposure to maternal stress and depression predicts greater NR3C1 (glucocorticoid receptor) gene methylation and stress, resulting in heightened HPA (cortisol) responsivity, in infants (Monk, Spicer, & Champagne, 2012; Oberlander et al., 2008). These findings point to NR3C1 methylation as a mechanism by which early events affect later-life stress and emotional lability, which is consistent with a stress and emotion dysregulation pathway to PD risk. Epigenetic mechanisms also mediate environmental influences on infant temperament (e.g., negative

emotionality, extraversion, effortful control; Gartstein & Skinner, 2018). Temperament is highly heritable and directly associated with internalizing and externalizing behaviors that become more salient in infancy (Beauchaine, 2015; Bornovalova et al., 2013). Interestingly, researchers are finding that infant temperament may serve as a genetic mediator, or mechanism, driving the relation between abuse experiences and PD development (Bornovalova et al., 2013).

Childhood and Adolescence

In addition to examining infant temperament as a mediator in the relation between early abuse experiences and PD development, researchers have found that children genetically predisposed to lower production of serotonin and COMT tend to be at greater risk for harsher discipline by parents (Bridgett et al., 2015). They described these findings in both interaction and evocative terms – children naturally producing less serotonin and COMT tend to have poorer emotion regulation, evoking harsher responses from parents. This biological vulnerability then interacts with parental stress levels to result in harsher disciplining. Trait impulsivity, which is associated with an early temperamental trait of behavioral disinhibition (Bornovalova et al., 2013), is not inherently pathological or a sufficient predictor of PD development (Bornovalova, Gratz, Delaney-Brumsey, Paulson, & Lejuez, 2006; Sharma, Markon, & Clark, 2014), but may confer risk for eventual borderline and antisocial PD symptoms when interacting with environmental risk factors. For example, Lynam et al. (2000) found that impulsive 13-year-old boys were at greater risk for juvenile offending at age 17 in poor versus high SES neighborhoods, indicating that impulsivity was associated with antisocial behaviors only when paired with poor neighborhoods (i.e., those defined by census-SES data as high poverty).

Young Adulthood and Adulthood

Research on the biology × environment interactions conferring risk for PD development and maintenance into adulthood lacks cohesion with work done on infant temperament and adolescent PD development. In general, longitudinal studies on biological vulnerabilities and environmental conditions contributing to adult PDs are sparse (Conway et al., 2015), and authors rarely outline viable mechanisms, as they mainly focus on individual-level factors (Crowell, 2016). Nonetheless, there is some research exploring biosocial mechanisms in PD development among young adults and adults. For example, Stepp, Scott, Jones, Whalen, and Hipwell (2016) assessed negative affectivity (i.e., a temperamental trait) among at-risk girls across three years (ages 16–18) and found a significant interaction between negative affectivity and family adversity to predict BPD symptoms; specifically, exposure to adversity strengthened the relation between negative affectivity and BPD symptoms. Also, Perroud et al. (2011) retrospectively assessed childhood maltreatment and sexual abuse experiences among adults and found that NR3C1 methylation interacted with not only prenatal risk, but childhood abuse to predict greater HPA axis activity and, ultimately, BPD risk. Finally, in one novel study, Knoblich and colleagues (2018) examined epigenetic changes among women with BPD following treatment with Dialectical Behavior Therapy (DBT) and found an interesting epigenome × treatment interaction: patients with higher methylation of APBA3 and MCF2 responded better to DBT treatment. Although preliminary, this study introduces a unique approach to epigenetic research in adults with PDs.

LIMITATIONS AND FUTURE DIRECTIONS

There are many limitations of the current literature. First, most studies focus on borderline and antisocial PDs, with relatively fewer examining Cluster A and C diagnoses. Second, there is an overwhelming focus on emotional processes, slightly less research on mechanisms underlying risky or impulsive behavior (e.g., Lawrence, Allen, & Chanen, 2010), or cognitive and attentional mechanisms (e.g., Posner et al., 2002), and even less research on mechanisms of identity-related or interpersonal distress (however, see Kaufman & Crowell, 2018; Lejuez et al., 2003). Third, there is little continuity between child, adolescent, and adult studies and few lifespan developmental theories (e.g., Hughes, Crowell, Uyeji, & Coan, 2012). This limits our understanding of early precursors for adult personality pathology or adult outcomes of child PD risk. Fourth, as with other psychopathology research, there is ongoing need for replications of mechanistic findings, systematic reviews, and meta-analyses. Finally, there are too few studies examining mechanisms of treatment response in transdiagnostic samples. As the field moves toward a more dimensional understanding of psychopathology, it may be possible to examine key PD features across diagnostic groups, including but not limited to avoidance, emotion dysregulation, impulsivity, scrupulosity, withdrawal, and suspiciousness. Thus, our understanding of PDs will only grow along with the broader focus on dimensions of risk. Future research should continue to address these limitations in order to expand and refine our mechanistic understanding of PDs.

In conclusion, mechanism-based work holds great promise for refining theories of PD etiology, inspiring new directions in research, and improving treatment. However, it is important for the field to be thoughtful in how we identify and test mechanisms. Many studies rely on simple statistical tests (e.g., mediation with cross-sectional data) or propose novel biomarkers that have not yet been studied rigorously (e.g., candidate gene studies). Unfortunately, some of these studies advance potential PD mechanisms in the absence of theory. This makes it difficult to place empirical findings within a broader theoretical framework and replicate key components of the theory. In order to improve and expand mechanistic research, it is important to take stock of current findings and delve into each new black box – carefully identifying as many component parts as possible. Given the significant suffering associated with PDs, we must leave no stone unturned in search of factors that underlie PD risk or drive treatment outcomes.

REFERENCES

Admon, R., Milad, M. R., & Hendler, T. (2013). A causal model of post-traumatic stress disorder: Disentangling predisposed from acquired neural abnormalities. *Trends in Cognitive Sciences*, 7, 337–347.

Ahn, H.-n., & Wampold, B. E. (2001). Where oh where are the specific ingredients? A meta-analysis of component studies in counseling and psychotherapy. *Journal of Counseling Psychology*, 48, 251–257.

American Psychiatric Association. (2013). *Diagnostic and Statistical Manual of Mental Disorders* (5th ed.). Arlington, VA: American Psychiatric Publishing.

Bamelis, L. L. M., Evers, S. M. A. A., Spinhoven, P., & Arntz, A. (2014). Results of a multicenter randomized controlled trial of the clinical effectiveness of schema therapy for personality disorders. *American Journal of Psychiatry*, 171, 305–322.

Beauchaine, T. P. (2001). Vagal tone, development, and Gray's motivational theory: Toward an integrated model of autonomic nervous system functioning in psychopathology. *Development and Psychopathology*, 13, 183–214.

Beauchaine, T. P. (2015). Future directions in emotion dysregulation and youth psychopathology. *Journal of Clinical Child and Adolescent Psychology*, 44, 875–896.

Beauchaine, T. P., Klein, D. N., Crowell, S. E., Derbidge, C., & Gatzke-Kopp, L. (2009). Multifinality in the development of personality disorders: A biology × sex × environment interaction model of antisocial and borderline traits. *Development and Psychopathology*, 21, 735–770.

Beauchaine, T. P., & McNulty, T. (2013). Comorbidities and continuities as ontogenic processes: Toward a developmental spectrum model of externalizing psychopathology. *Development and Psychopathology*, 25, 1505–1528.

Belsky, D. W., Caspi, A., Arseneault, L., Bleidorn, W., Fonagy, P., Goodman, M., ... Moffitt, T. E. (2012). Etiological features of borderline personality related characteristics in a birth cohort of 12-year-old children. *Development and Psychopathology*, 24, 251–265.

Bentler, P. M. (1980). Multivariate analysis with latent variables: Causal modeling. *Annual Review of Psychology*, 31, 419–456.

Bird, A. P. (1986). CpG-rich islands and the function of DNA methylation. *Nature*, 321, 209–213.

Bird, A. P. (2002). DNA methylation patterns and epigenetic memory. *Genes and Development*, 16, 6–21.

Bornovalova, M. A., Gratz, K. L., Delaney-Brumsey, A., Paulson, A., & Lejuez, C. W. (2006). Temperamental and environmental risk factors for borderline personality disorder among inner-city substance users in residential treatment. *Journal of Personality Disorders*, 20, 218–231.

Bornovalova, M. A., Hicks, B. M., Iacono, W. G., & McGue, M. (2009). Stability, change, and heritability of borderline personality disorder traits from adolescence to adulthood: A longitudinal twin study. *Development and Psychopathology, 21*, 1335–1353.

Bornovalova, M. A., Huibregtse, B. M., Hicks, B. M., Keyes, M., McGue, M., & Iacono, W. (2013). Tests of a direct effect of childhood abuse on adult borderline personality disorder traits: A longitudinal discordant twin design. *Journal of Abnormal Psychology, 122*, 180–194.

Bornovalova, M. A., Lejuez, C. W., Daughters, S. B., Rosenthal, M. Z., & Lynch, T. R. (2005). Impulsivity as a common process across borderline personality and substance use disorders. *Clinical Psychology Review, 25*, 790–812.

Bornovalova, M. A., Verhulst, B., Webber, T., McGue, M., Iacono, W. G., & Hicks, B. M. (2018). Genetic and environmental influences on the codevelopment among borderline personality disorder traits, major depression symptoms, and substance use disorder symptoms from adolescence to young adulthood. *Development and Psychopathology, 30*, 49–65.

Brewin, C. R., Andrews, B., & Valentine, J. D. (2000). Meta-analysis of risk factors for posttraumatic stress disorder in trauma-exposed adults. *Journal of Consulting and Clinical Psychology, 68*, 748–766.

Bridgett, D. J., Burt, N. M., Edwards, E. S., & Deater-Deckard, K. (2015). Intergenerational transmission of self-regulation: A multidisciplinary review and integrative conceptual framework. *Psychological Bulletin, 141*, 602–654.

Bromet, E. J., Atwoli, L., Kawakami, N., & Navarro-Mateu, F. (2017). Post-traumatic stress disorder associated with natural and human-made disasters in the World Mental Health Surveys. *Psychological Medicine, 47*, 227–241.

Brunner, R., Henze, R., Richter, J., & Kaess, M. (2015). Neurobiological findings in youth with borderline personality disorder. *Scandinavian Journal of Child and Adolescent Psychiatry and Psychology, 3*, 22–30.

Butler, T. R., Ariwodola, O. J., & Weiner, J. L. (2014). The impact of social isolation on HPA axis function, anxiety-like behaviors, and ethanol-drinking. *Frontiers in Integrative Neuroscience, 7*, 102–112.

Butler, T. R., Karkhanis, A. N., Jones, S. R., & Weiner, J. L. (2016). Adolescent social isolation as a model of heightened vulnerability to comorbid alcoholism and anxiety disorders. *Alcoholism: Clinical and Experimental Research, 40*, 1202–1214.

Canli, T., Ferra, J., & Duman, E. A. (2009). Genetics of emotion regulation. *Neuroscience, 164*, 43–54.

Caspi, A., Houts, R. M., Belsky, D. W., Goldman-Mellor, S. J., Harrington, H., Isreal, S., … Moffitt, T. E. (2014). The p factor: One general psychopathology factor in the structure of psychiatric disorders? *Clinical Psychological Science, 2*, 119–137.

Caspi, A., McClay, J., Moffitt, T. E., Mill, J., Martin, J., Craig, I. W., … Poulton, R. (2002). Role of genotype in the cycle of violence in maltreated children. *Science, 297*, 851–854.

Caspi, A., Taylor, A., Moffitt, T. E., & Plomin, R. (2000). Neighborhood deprivation affects children's mental health: Environmental risks identified in a genetic design. *Psychological Science, 11*, 338–342.

Chanen, A. M., & Kaess, M. (2012). Developmental pathways to borderline personality disorder. *Current Psychiatry Reports, 14*, 45–53.

Checknita, D., Maussion, G., Labonté, B., Comai, S., Tremblay, R. E., Vitaro, F., … Turecki, G. (2015). Monoamine oxidase A gene promoter methylation and transcriptional downregulation in an offender population with antisocial personality disorder. *British Journal of Psychiatry, 206*, 216–222.

Chen, H., Cohen, P., Johnson, J. G., Kasen, S., Sneed, J. R., & Crawford, T. N. (2004). Adolescent personality disorders and conflict with romantic partners during the transition to adulthood. *Journal of Personality Disorders, 18*, 507–525.

Clark, A. T., Ye, H., Isbell, F., Deyle, E. R., Cowles, J., Tilman, G., & Sugihara, G. (2015). Spatial convergent cross mapping to detect causal relationships from short time series. *Ecology, 96*, 1174–1181.

Clarkin, J. F., Levy, K. N., Lenzenweger, M. F., & Kernberg, O. F. (2007). Evaluating three treatments of borderline personality disorder: A multiwave study. *American Journal of Psychiatry, 164*, 922–928.

Cohen, P., Chen, H., Gordon, K., Johnson, J., Brook, B., & Kasen, S. (2008). Socioeconomic background and the developmental course of schizotypal and borderline personality disorder symptoms. *Development and Psychopathology, 20*, 633–650.

Conway, C. C., Hammen, C., & Brennan, P. A. (2015). Adolescent precursors of adult borderline personality pathology in a high-risk community sample. *Journal of Personality Disorders, 29*, 316–333.

Crawford, T. N., Cohen, P. R., Chen, H., Anglin, D. M., & Ehrensaft, M. (2009). Early maternal separation and the trajectory of borderline personality disorder symptoms. *Development and Psychopathology, 21*, 1013–1030.

Crowell, S. E. (2016). Biting the hand that feeds: Current opinion on the interpersonal causes, correlates, and consequences of borderline personality disorder. *F1000 Research, 5*, 2796–2803.

Crowell, S. E., Baucom, B. R., McCauley, E., Potapova, N. V., Fitelson, M., Barth, H., … Beauchaine, T. P. (2013). Mechanisms of contextual risk for adolescent self-injury: Invalidation and conflict escalation in mother–child interactions. *Journal of Clinical Child and Adolescent Psychology, 42*, 467–480.

Crowell, S. E., Baucom, B. R., Yaptangco, M., Bride, D., Hsiao, R., McCauley, E., & Beauchaine, T. P. (2014). Emotion dysregulation and dyadic conflict in depressed and typical adolescents: Evaluating concordance across psychophysiological and observational measures. *Biological Psychology, 98*, 50–58.

Crowell, S. E., Beauchaine, T. P., Hsiao, R. C., Vasilev, C. A., Yaptangco, M., Linehan, M. M., & McCauley, E. (2012). Differentiating adolescent self-injury from adolescent depression: Possible implications for borderline personality development. *Journal of Abnormal Child Psychology, 40*, 45–57.

Crowell, S. E., Beauchaine, T. P., & Linehan, M. (2009). A biosocial developmental model of borderline personality: Elaborating and extending Linehan's theory. *Psychological Bulletin, 135*, 495–510.

Crowell, S. E., Beauchaine, T. P., McCauley, E., Smith, C. J., Stevens, A. L., & Sylvers, P. (2005). Psychological, autonomic, and serotonergic correlates of parasuicide among adolescent girls. *Development and Psychopathology, 17*, 1105–1127.

Crowell, S. E., Butner, J. E., Wiltshire, T. J., Munion, A. K., Yaptangco, M., & Beauchaine, T. P. (2017). Evaluating emotional and biological sensitivity to maternal behavior among self-injuring and depressed adolescent girls using nonlinear dynamics. *Clinical Psychological Science, 5*, 272–285.

Crowell, S. E., & Kaufman, E. A. (2016). Borderline personality disorder and the emerging field of developmental neuroscience. *Personality Disorders: Theory, Research, and Treatment, 7*, 324–333.

Crowell, S. E., Yaptangco, M., & Turner, S. L. (2016). Coercion, invalidation, and risk for self-injury and borderline personality traits. In T. J. Dishion & J. J. Snyder (Eds.), *The Oxford Handbook of Coercive Relationship Dynamics* (pp. 182–193). New York: Oxford University Press.

Cuthbert, B. N., & Insel, T. R. (2013). Toward the future of psychiatric diagnosis: The seven pillars of RDoC. *BMC Medicine, 11*, 126–133.

Dammann, G., Teschler, S., Haag, T., Altmüller, F., Tuczek, F., & Dammann, R. H. (2011). Increased DNA methylation of neuropsychiatric genes occurs in borderline personality disorder. *Epigenetics, 6*, 1454–1462.

De Fruyt, F., & De Clercq, B. (2014). Antecedents of personality disorder in childhood and adolescence: Toward an integrative developmental model. *Annual Review of Clinical Psychology, 10*, 449–476.

Deckel, A. W., Hesselbrock, V., & Bauer, L. (1996). Antisocial personality disorder, childhood delinquency, and frontal brain functioning: EEG and neuropsychological findings. *Journal of Clinical Psychology, 52*, 639–650.

Dishion, T. J., Duncan, T. E., Eddy, J. M., Fagot, B. I., & Fetrow, R. (1994). The world of parents and peers: Coercive exchanges and children's social adaptation. *Social Development, 3*, 255–268.

Dishion, T. J., McCord, J., & Poulin, F. (1999). When interventions harm: Peer groups and problem behavior. *American Psychologist, 54*, 755–764.

Doll, A., Sorg, C., Manoliu, A., Wöller, A., Meng, C., Förstl, H., . . . Riedl, V. (2013). Shifted intrinsic connectivity of central executive and salience network in borderline personality disorder. *Frontiers in Human Neuroscience, 7*, 1–13.

Eme, R. F. (2007). Sex differences in child-onset, life-course-persistent conduct disorder: *A review of biological influences*. Clinical Psychology Reviews, 27, 607–627.

Ensink, K., Biberdzic, M., Normandin, L., & Clarkin, J. (2015). A developmental psychopathology and neurobiological model of borderline personality disorder in adolescence. *Journal of Infant, Child, and Adolescent Psychotherapy, 14*, 46–69.

Fervaha, G., & Remington, G. (2013). Neuroimaging findings in schizotypal personality disorder: A systematic review. *Progress in Neuro-Psychopharmacology and Biological Psychiatry, 43*, 96–107.

Freud, S., & Breuer, J. (1893). On the psychical mechanism of hysterical phenomena: A preliminary communication. In S. Freud *Selected Papers on Hysteria and Other Psychoneuroses* (Trans. A. A. Brill, 1912). New York: The Journal of Nervous and Mental Disease Publishing Company. Available at www.bartleby.com/280/1.html

Fruzzetti, A. E., Shenk, C., & Hoffman, P. D. (2005). Family interaction and the development of borderline personality disorder. *Development and Psychopathology, 17*, 1007–1030.

Garattini, S., Giacalone, E., & Valzelli, L. (1967). Isolation, aggressiveness and brain 5-hydroxytryptamine turnover. *Journal of Pharmacy and Pharmacology, 19*, 338–339.

Gartstein, M. A., & Skinner, M. K. (2018). Prenatal influences on temperament development: The role of environmental epigenetics. *Development and Psychopathology, 30*, 1269–1303.

Goodman, M., Mascitelli, K., & Triebwasser, J. (2013). The neurobiological basis of adolescent-onset borderline personality disorder. *Journal of the Canadian Academy of Child and Adolescent Psychiatry, 22*, 212–219.

Gratz, K. L., Bardeen, J. R., Levy, R., Dixon-Gordon, K. L., & Tull, M. T. (2015). Mechanisms of change in an emotion regulation group therapy for deliberate self-harm among women with borderline personality disorder. *Behaviour Research and Therapy, 65*, 29–35.

Hajcak, G., MacNamara, A., & Olvet, D. M. (2010). Event-related potentials, emotion, and emotion regulation: An integrative review. *Developmental Neuropsychology, 35*, 129–155.

Hallquist, M. N., Hipwell, A. E., & Stepp, S. D. (2015). Poor self-control and harsh punishment in childhood prospectively predict borderline personality symptoms in adolescent girls. *Journal of Abnormal Psychology, 124*, 549–564.

Hedström, P., & Ylikoski, P. (2010). Causal mechanisms in the social sciences. *Annual Review of Sociology, 36*, 49–67.

Heinrichs, M., von Dawans, B., & Domes, G. (2009). Oxytocin, vasopressin, and human social behavior. *Frontiers in Neuroendocrinology, 30*, 548–557.

Hostinar, C. E., Sullivan, R. M., & Gunnar, M. R. (2014). Psychobiological mechanisms underlying the social buffering of the hypothalamic-pituitary-adrenocortical axis: A review of animal models and human studies across development. *Psychological Bulletin, 140*, 256–282.

Hughes, A. E., Crowell, S. E., Uyeji, L., & Coan, J. A. (2012). A developmental neuroscience of borderline pathology: Emotion dysregulation and social baseline theory. *Journal of Abnormal Child Psychology, 40*, 21–33.

Ingoldsby, E. M., & Shaw, D. S. (2002). Neighborhood contextual factors and early-starting antisocial pathways. *Clinical Child and Family Psychology Review, 5*, 21–55.

Joreskog, K. G., Sorbom, D., & Magidson, J. (1979). *Advances in Factor Analysis and Structural Equation Models*. New York: University Press of America.

Kaufman, E. A., & Crowell, S. E. (2018). Biological and behavioral mechanisms of identity pathology development: An integrative review. *Review of General Psychology, 22*, 245–263.

Kazdin, A. E. (2007). Mediators and mechanisms of change in psychotherapy research. *Annual Review of Clinical Psychology, 3*, 1–27.

Kenna, G. A., Roder-Hanna, N., Leggio, L., Zywiak, W. H., Clifford, J., Edwards, S., . . . Swift, R. M. (2012). Association of the 5-HTT gene-linked promoter region (5-HTTLPR) polymorphism with psychiatric disorders: Review of psychopathology and pharmacotherapy. *Pharmacogenomics and Personalized Medicine, 5*, 19–35.

Knoblich, N., Gundel, F., Brückmann, C., Becker-Sadzio, J., Frischholz, C., & Nieratschker, V. (2018). DNA methylation of APBA3 and MCF2 in borderline personality disorder: Potential biomarkers for response to psychotherapy. *European Neuropsychopharmacology, 28*, 252–263.

Koenig, J., Kemp, A. H., Feeling, N. R., Thayer, J. F., & Kaess, M. (2016). Resting state vagal tone in borderline personality disorder: A meta-analysis. *Progress in Neuro-Pharmacology and Biological Psychiatry, 64*, 18–26.

Kolla, N. J., Chiuccariello, L., Wilson, A. A., Houle, S., Links, P., Bagby, R. M., . . . Meyer, J. H. (2016). Elevated monoamine oxidase-A distribution volume in borderline personality disorder is associated with severity across mood symptoms, suicidality, and cognition. *Biological Psychiatry, 79*, 117–126.

Kotov, R., Krueger, R. F., Watson, D., Achenbach, T. M., Althoff, R. R., Bagby, R. M., . . . Zimmerman, M. (2017). The Hierarchical Taxonomy of Psychopathology (HiTOP): A dimensional alternative to traditional nosologies. *Journal of Abnormal Psychology, 126*, 454–477.

Krueger, R. F., & Markon, K. E. (2014). The role of the DSM-5 personality trait model in moving toward a quantitative and empirically based approach to classifying personality and psychopathology. *Annual Review of Clinical Psychology, 10,* 477–501.

Kumsta, R., Hummel, E., Chen, F. S., & Heinrichs, M. (2013). Epigenetic regulation of the oxytocin receptor gene: Implications for behavioral neuroscience. *Frontiers in Neuroscience, 7,* 1–6.

Kupfer, D. J., First, M. B., & Regier, D. A. (2002). Introduction. In D. J. Kupfer, M. B. First, & D. A. Regier (Eds.), *A Research Agenda for DSM-V* (pp. xv–xxiii). Washington, DC: American Psychiatric Association.

Larsson, H., Andershed, H., & Lichtenstein, P. (2006). A genetic factor explains most of the variation in the psychopathic personality. *Journal of Abnormal Psychology, 115,* 221–230.

Lawrence, K. A., Allen, J. S., & Chanen, A. M. (2010). Impulsivity in borderline personality disorder: Reward-based decision-making and its relationship to emotional distress. *Journal of Personality Disorders, 24,* 785–799.

Lee, R. (2006). Childhood trauma and personality disorder: Toward a biological model. *Current Psychiatry Reports, 8,* 43–52.

Lejuez, C. W., Daughters, S. B., Nowak, J. A., Lynch, T., Rosenthal, M. Z., & Kosson, D. (2003). Examining the inventory of interpersonal problems as a tool for conducting analogue studies of mechanisms underlying borderline personality disorder. *Journal of Behavior Therapy and Experimental Psychiatry, 34,* 313–324.

Lieb, K., Zanarini, M. C., Schmahl, C., Linehan, M. M., & Bohus, M. (2004). Borderline personality disorder. *Lancet, 364,* 453–461.

Linehan, M. (1993). *Cognitive-Behavioral Treatment of Borderline Personality Disorder.* New York: Guilford Press.

Lowry, P. B., & Gaskin, J. (2014). Partial least squares (PLS) structural equation modeling (SEM) for building and testing behavioral causal theory: When to choose it and how to use it. *IEEE Transactions on Professional Communication, 57,* 123–146.

Lynam, D. R., Caspi, A., Moffitt, T. E., Wikström, P. H., Loeber, R., & Novak, S. (2000). The interaction between impulsivity and neighborhood context on offending: The effects of impulsivity are stronger in poorer neighborhoods. *Journal of Abnormal Psychology, 109,* 563–574.

Lyons-Ruth, K. (2008). Contributions of the mother–infant relationship to dissociative, borderline, and conduct symptoms in young adulthood. *Infant Mental Health Journal, 29,* 203–218.

Lyons-Ruth, K., Bureau, J., Easterbrooks, M. A., Obsuth, I., & Hennighausen, K. (2013). Parsing the construct of maternal insensitivity: Distinct longitudinal pathways associated with early maternal withdrawal. *Attachment and Human Development, 15,* 562–582.

Lyons-Ruth, K., Bureau, J., Holmes, B., Easterbrooks, A., & Brooks, N. H. (2013). Borderline symptoms and suicidality/self-injury in late adolescence: Prospectively observed relationship correlates in infancy and childhood. *Psychiatry Research, 206,* 273–281.

MacKinnon, D. F., & Pies, R. (2006). Affective instability as rapid cycling: Theoretical and clinical implications for borderline personality and bipolar spectrum disorders. *Bipolar Disorders, 8,* 1–14.

Mahoney, J. (2001). Beyond correlational analysis: Recent innovations in theory and method. *Sociological Forum, 16,* 575–593.

Markon, K. E., & Jonas, K. G. (2016). Structure as cause and representation: Implications of descriptivist inference for structural modeling across multiple levels of analysis. *Journal of Abnormal Psychology, 125,* 1146–1157

Martin, E. I., Ressler, K. J., Binder, E., & Nemeroff, C. B. (2010). The neurobiology of anxiety disorders: Brain imaging, genetics, and psychoneuroendocrinology. *Clinics in Laboratory Medicine, 30,* 865–891.

McLaughlin, K. A., & Lambert, H. K. (2017). Child trauma exposure and psychopathology: Mechanisms of risk and resilience. *Current Opinion in Psychology, 14,* 29–34.

Miller, J. D., Lyman, D. R., Widiger, T. A., & Leukefeld, C. (2001). Personality disorders as extreme variants of common personality dimensions: Can the five factor model adequately represent psychopathy? *Journal of Personality, 69,* 253–276.

Mitchell, A. E., Dickens, G. L., & Picchioni, M. M. (2014). Facial emotion processing in borderline personality disorder: A systematic review and meta-analysis. *Neuropsychology Review, 24,* 166–184.

Monk, C., Spicer, J., & Champagne, F. A. (2012). Linking prenatal maternal adversity to developmental outcomes in infants: The role of epigenetic pathways. *Development and Psychopathology, 24,* 1361–1376.

Moul, C., Killcross, S., & Dadds, M. R. (2012). A model of differential amygdala activation in psychopathy. *Psychological Review, 119,* 789–806.

Mushtaq, R., Shoib, S., Shah, T., & Mushtaq, S. (2014). Relationship between loneliness, psychiatric disorders and physical health: A review on the psychological aspects of loneliness. *Journal of Clinical and Diagnostic Research, 8,* 1–4.

Myers, C. S. (1915). A contribution to the study of shell shock: Being an account of three cases of loss of memory, vision, smell, and taste, admitted into the Duchess of Westminster's war hospital, Le Touquet. *Lancet, 185,* 316–320.

Nelson, S. E., & Dishion, T. J. (2004). From boys to men: Predicting adult adaptation from middle childhood sociometric status. *Development and Psychopathology, 16,* 441–459.

Neuhaus, E., & Beauchaine, T. P. (2017). Impulsivity and vulnerability to psychopathology. In T. P. Beauchaine & S. P. Hinshaw (Eds.), *Child and Adolescent Psychopathology* (pp. 178–212). Hoboken, NJ: John Wiley.

Oberlander, T. F., Weinberg, J., Papsdorf, M., Grunau, R., Misri, S., & Devlin, A. M. (2008). Prenatal exposure to maternal depression, neonatal methylation of human glucocorticoid receptor gene (NR3C1) and infant cortisol stress responses. *Epigenetics, 3,* 97–106.

Pagliaccio, D., Luby, J. L., Bogdan, R., Agrawal, A., Gaffrey, M. S., Belden, A. C., … Barch, D. M. (2015). Amygdala functional connectivity, HPA axis genetic variation, and life stress in children and relations to anxiety and emotion regulation. *Journal of Abnormal Psychology, 124,* 817–833.

Patterson, G. R. (1982). *Coercive Family Processes* (Vol. 3). Eugene, OR: Castalia Publishing Company.

Patterson, G. R., DeBaryshe, B., & Ramsey, E. (1990). A developmental perspective on antisocial behavior. *American Psychologist, 44,* 329–335.

Perroud, N., Paoloni-Giacobino, A., Prada, P., Olié, E., Salzmann, A., Nicastro, R., … Malafosse, A. (2011). Increased methylation of glucocorticoid receptor gene (NR3C1) in adults with a history of childhood maltreatment: A link with the severity and type of trauma. *Translational Psychiatry, 1*, 1–9.

Perroud, N., Salzmann, A., Prada, P., Nicastro, R., Hoeppli, M-E., Furrer, S., ... Malafosse, A. (2013). Response to psychotherapy in borderline personality disorder and methylation status of the BDNF gene. *Translational Psychiatry, 3*, e207–e214.

Piehler, T. F., & Dishion, T. J. (2008). Interpersonal dynamics within adolescent friendships: Dyadic mutuality, deviant talk, and patterns of antisocial behavior. *Child Development, 78*, 1611–1624.

Posner, M. I., Rothbart, M. K., Vizueta, N., Levy, K. N., Evans, D. E., Thomas, K. M., & Clarkin, J. F. (2002). Attentional mechanisms of borderline personality disorder. *Proceedings of the National Academy of Sciences USA, 99*, 16366–16370.

Preacher, K. J., & Hayes, A. F. (2004). SPSS and SAS procedures for estimating indirect effects in simple mediation models. *Behavior Research Methods, Instruments, and Computers, 36*, 717–731.

Putnam, K. M., & Silk, K. R. (2005). Emotion dysregulation and the development of borderline personality disorder. *Development and Psychopathology, 17*, 899–925.

Raine, A., Venables, P. H., & Mednick, S. A. (1997). Low resting heart rate at age 3 years predisposes to aggression at age 11 years: Evidence from the Mauritius Child Health Project. *Journal of the American Academy of Child and Adolescent Psychiatry, 36*, 1457–1464.

Saul, L. J. (1945). Psychological factors in combat fatigue: With special reference to hostility and the nightmares. *Psychosomatic Medicine, 7*, 257–272.

Shalev, A., Liberzon, I., & Marmar, C. (2017). Post-traumatic stress disorder. *The New England Journal of Medicine, 376*, 2459–2469.

Sharma, L., Markon, K. E., & Clark, L. A. (2014). Toward a theory of distinct types of "impulsive" behaviors: A meta-analysis of self-report and behavioral measures. *Psychological Bulletin, 140*, 374–408.

Sharp, C., & Romero, C. (2007). Borderline personality disorder: A comparison between children and adults. *Bulletin of the Menninger Clinic, 71*, 85–114.

Skodol, A. E., Siever, L. J., Livesley, W. J., Gunderson, J. G., Pfohl, B., & Widiger, T. A. (2002). The borderline diagnosis II: Biology, genetics, and clinical course. *Biological Psychiatry, 51*, 951–963.

Snyder, J., Schrepferman, L., McEachern, A., Barner, S., Johnson, K., & Provines, J. (2008). Peer deviancy training and peer coercion: Dual processes associated with early-onset conduct problems. *Child Development, 79*, 252–268.

Snyder, J., Schrepferman, L., & St. Peter, C. (1997). Origins of antisocial behavior: Negative reinforcement and affect dysregulation of behavior as socialization mechanisms in family interaction. *Behavior Modification, 21*, 187–215.

Steele, H., & Siever, L. (2010). An attachment perspective on borderline personality disorder: Advances in gene–environment considerations. *Current Psychiatry Reports, 12*, 61–67.

Stephan, K. E., Penny, W. D., Moran, R. J., den Ouden, H. E. M., Daunizeau, J., & Friston, K. J. (2010). Ten simple rules for dynamic causal modeling. *NeuroImage, 49*, 3099–3109.

Stepp, S. D., Lazarus, S. A., & Byrd, A. L. (2015). A systematic review of risk factors prospectively associated with borderline personality disorder: Taking stock and moving forward. *Personality Disorders: Theory, Research, and Treatment, 7*, 316–323.

Stepp, S. D., Scott, L. N., Jones, N. P., Whalen, D. J., & Hipwell, A. P. (2016). Negative emotional reactivity as a marker of vulnerability in the development of borderline personality disorder symptoms. *Development and Psychopathology, 28*, 213–224.

Stetler, C., & Miller, G. E. (2011). Depression and hypothalamic-pituitary-adrenal activation: A quantitative summary of four decades of research. *Psychosomatic Medicine, 73*, 114–126.

Strauman, T. J. (2017). Self-regulation and psychopathology: Toward an integrative translational paradigm. *Annual Review of Clinical Psychology, 13*, 497–523.

Susman, E. J. (2006). Psychobiology of persistent antisocial behavior: Stress, early vulnerabilities and the attenuation hypothesis. *Neuroscience and Biobehavioral Reviews, 30*, 376–389.

Thayer, J. F., & Sternberg, E. (2006). Beyond heart rate variability: Vagal regulation of allostatic systems. *Annals of the New York Academy of Sciences, 1088*, 361–372.

Trull, T. J., Stepp, S. D., & Durrett, C. A. (2003). Research on borderline personality disorder: An update. *Current Opinion in Psychiatry, 16*, 77–82.

Tyrer, P., Reed, G. M., & Crawford, M. J. (2015). Classification, assessment, prevalence, and effect of personality disorder. *Lancet, 385*, 21–27.

van Zutphen, L., Siep, N., Jacob, G. A., Goebel, R., & Arntz, A. (2015). Emotional sensitivity, emotion regulation and impulsivity in borderline personality disorder: A critical review of fMRI studies. *Neuroscience and Biobehavioral Reviews, 51*, 64–76.

Viding, E., Blair, R. J. R., Moffitt, T. E., & Plomin, R. (2005). Evidence for substantial genetic risk for psychopathy in 7-year-olds. *Journal of Child Psychology and Psychiatry, 46*, 592–597.

Widiger, T. A., & Simonsen, E. (2005). Alternative dimensional models of personality disorder: Finding a common ground. *Journal of Personality Disorders, 19*, 110–130.

Winsper, C., Marwaha, S., Lereya, S. T., Thompson, A., Eyden, J., & Singh, S. P. (2016). A systematic review of the neurobiological underpinnings of borderline personality disorder (BPD) in childhood and adolescence. *Reviews in the Neurosciences, 27*, 827–847.

Wright, A. G. C., Thomas, K. M., Hopwood, C. J., Markon, K. E., Pincus, A. L., & Krueger, R. F. (2012). The hierarchical structure of DSM-5 pathological personality traits. *Journal of Abnormal Psychology, 121*, 951–957.

Zuckerman, M., & Kuhlman, M. (2000). Personality and risk-tasking: Common biosocial factors. *Journal of Personality, 68*, 999–1029.

16a Parts, Wholes, and Explanations of Personality and Its Pathologies: Commentary on Assessment of Mechanisms in Personality Disorders

KRISTIAN E. MARKON

The breadth of mechanistic explanations covered by Crowell, Kaliush, and Vlisides-Henry (this volume) is striking. The theories and accompanying evidence span a variety of causal mechanisms (biological, environmental, and interactions thereof) and different levels of analysis (from the molecular to the ecological). As a whole, these explanatory accounts have little in common other than being mechanistic and involving variables related to personality disorder. Given this breadth, it's not surprising that Crowell et al. preface their chapter with a discussion of what, exactly, a mechanism is – with so many different theoretical accounts under the umbrella of mechanistic explanation, it is critical to define its boundaries.

Someone unfamiliar with this area of study might wonder why it's unclear what a mechanistic theory is, and what other non-mechanistic theories of personality pathology might be considered. In other scientific disciplines, such as physics or chemistry, it might be difficult to identify an explanation that is not mechanistic. The definition of a mechanistic account as outlined by Crowell and colleagues – involving a hierarchically constituted structure whose elements causally increase the probability of some outcome – seems uncontroversial enough, so why is it necessary to clarify?

One reason is that behavioral etiology is complex, with the longstanding, unusual patterns of behavior that constitute personality disorder arguably being especially complex. This complexity leads to the chain of associations from explanans and explanandum being blurred by fuzzy probabilistic associations. Crowell et al. touch on this issue, as they do the related problem of study designs in behavioral research being causally underpowered due to ethical, economic, and other challenges. In short, it is often difficult to conclusively establish causality mechanistically for a variety of reasons; because of this, personality disorder researchers and theorists are often left with non-mechanistic accounts lacking the causality component of the definition outlined by the authors. Within personality disorder research, and the behavioral sciences more broadly, we can often predict better than we can isolate the necessary mediating components of the prediction.

Another reason for ambiguity about the meaning of mechanism, though, is that the boundaries between explanans and explanandum are often unclear. Certainly this is not always the case: MAO-A-related genotypes discussed by Crowell et al. are relatively clearly defined, for example, and are clearly distinguished from physically aggressive behavior *per se*. Often, however, boundaries between explanatory variables are less clear, either due to conceptual ambiguities in how different types of variables are related, or due to fuzziness in differences between constructs of the same type.

Consider, for example, associations between functional neural disconnectivity and emotion dysregulation (reviewed by Crowell et al., this volume). Is it more appropriate to say disconnectivity between certain neural structures mechanistically explains emotionally dysregulated state, or is it more appropriate to state that such disconnectivity is a physical instantiation of emotionally dysregulated state? In some ways it is a difference that doesn't matter, as in either case some decomposable physical process is being invoked to predict a mental state. In other ways, though, the difference is critical to questions about what is meant by a mechanism, and what is needed to provide a complete biological account of a psychological process. The relationship between neural state and psychological state involves complex questions about mind–brain mappings that do not necessarily arise in discussing the relationship between other mechanistic explanations, such as the influence of parenting behavior on child psychopathology. In a typical mechanistic explanation, there are antecedent causes and descendent effects. However, in the case of mind–brain relationships at some level the psychological phenomena are coincident with and one and the same as the physical substrates. Can an effect be its cause?

Other types of fuzzy construct boundaries become relevant to mechanistic explanations as well. *Weak emergence* accounts of personality and personality pathology have been of increasing interest, for example (Baumert et al., 2017). In these accounts, psychological, mentalistic phenomena are not related to one another due to some common etiologic factor, continuous or discrete, internal or external. Rather, they are related through direct influences on one another. In this type of account, for example, borderline splitting directly causes emotional instability or vice versa; the two phenomena are not associated because of some shared process, liability, or disease state. Weak emergence accounts can be thought of as a type of dynamic model in some ways, in that associations between mental structures or states are explained in terms of mutual direct causal relationships between them, as well as with other phenomena such as relationship variables.

Weak emergence accounts do not necessarily involve variables at different levels of scientific analysis, such as mental states and their physical substrates; current accounts often involve mental processes influencing one another, isolated from underlying physical processes. In this sense, mental–physical cause–effect questions are not as directly salient. Weak emergence accounts do, however, still raise questions about whether causes and effects can be distinguished in such paradigms, and whether or not they are mechanistic explanations at all. At some level, for example, one might question whether or not splitting can entirely be distinguished from emotional instability, in that some variation in emotional response is presumably involved in splitting. It might then be asserted that emotional instability causes splitting, but given that emotional response is decomposable into cognitive and other components, might the social cognitive components of splitting not constitute part of a varying emotional response? Are both better thought of as being manifestations of some shared processes or patterns? What is the difference between that and mutual direct causation between cognitive and other components of emotional response? Are "splitting" and "emotional lability" imprecise constructs to use in describing personality pathology? When causes and effects are both inferred mental states, it becomes difficult to delineate boundaries between them, raising questions about whether or not weak emergence accounts are properly thought of as mechanistic *per se*.

One frequent response to the dilemma of whether or not a given set of constructs is reasonable in a causal explanation is to invoke experimental manipulation (Costantini & Perugini, 2018). If a putative cause can be manipulated and has an effect, according to this rationale, it provides a mechanistic explanation. So, for example, if splitting is manipulated (via randomly assigned psychotherapy for example), and influences emotional instability, it provides an account by which the former causes the latter. Conversely, if emotional instability is manipulated (via pharmacological intervention, for example), and influences splitting, the former causes the latter. If something can be manipulated, boundary problems become moot.

The problem with this reasoning, however, is in the assumption that a manipulation is acting through the pathway that was hypothesized, and not through some other pathway. Specifically, that the independent variable

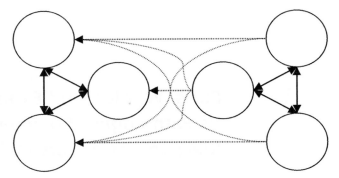

Figure 16.a.1 Path diagram for hypothetical causal system

is what is assumed, and that an experimental manipulation operates in the way that is intended. Presumably, unique and shared effects on measured variables can be modeled and estimated – for example, the effect of a therapeutic intervention targeting splitting can be parsed into components actually unique to splitting, and those unique to, as well as shared with, emotional lability. However, the question of unmodeled pathways still looms large in such scenarios. Parsing associations of experimental manipulations into unique and shared components, after all, does little to establish the nature of those unique and shared components, even when there is an experimental manipulation. When a chemical is introduced experimentally into a solution, we have a reasonably good understanding of what is being introduced; in a psychological intervention, in contrast, the active components are relatively unclear and often nonspecific (Baskin, Tierney, Minami, & Wampold, 2003).

The success of experimental designs in the behavioral sciences indicates that it is possible to explore issues of causality and mechanism with mental, psychological variables. With personality and other broadband individual difference variables, however, the effects involved span relatively long timescales, and the scope is relatively broad. This is especially challenging when faced with the sorts of unusual behavior encountered in personality pathology. With personality pathology, behavioral patterns might be so unusual as to be unique to a specific individual, and extreme enough as to call into question the ecological validity of experimentally manipulated analogue variables (for instance, experimentally induced aggression in a laboratory versus severe, cruel physical violence). How to definitively link relatively concrete, specific definable mechanisms to trait-like timescales and broad pervasive patterns is currently unclear. Research indicates that personality can be changed (Roberts et al., 2017), but the precise intra-individual pathways and mechanisms by which this occurs are not always well-established.

Consider the hypothetical path diagram in Figure 16.a.1, for example, where stronger paths are illustrated with solid lines and weaker paths are illustrated with dotted paths. The set of three variables on the right forms a system, and the set on the left forms a system; all three variables on the right affect those on the left. Under certain conditions, one might discuss the set of variables on the right in terms of a unitary construct, and the set on the left in terms of a unitary construct. The paths from right to left, moreover, suggest that, in this scenario, the superordinate construct on the right would be said to cause that on the left. The conundrum, however, is what are the conditions under which this is the case? When can one substitute the system in Figure 16.a.1 with two constructs, one of which is causing the other? As the solid paths approach perfect association, this substitution is probably actually necessary, but what happens as the associations weaken? What about experimental manipulation of the variables on the right?

As mechanistic accounts of personality pathology are elaborated, it is likely that challenges pertaining to levels of analysis and boundaries between variables will increasingly be encountered. Related research on how to best integrate structural models with experimental and other causally informative designs is almost certainly needed to better characterize the nature of mechanisms involved in personality pathology: establishing some sort of causality is itself challenging, but establishing the nature of those causes is even more challenging. In many ways, these challenges are inevitable, reflecting the nature of scientific progress as theories become more elaborated and are shaped in response to empirical study. However, they also in part reflect challenges unique to the study of psychological variables, especially as they play out over broad timescales and dimensions of human experience and behavior. As progress in the field continues, we will undoubtedly change the constructs of focus, honing them and exploring the causal pathways involved in personality disorder outcomes to better approximate the processes uncovered.

REFERENCES

Baskin, T. W., Tierney, S. C., Minami, T., & Wampold, B. E. (2003). Establishing specificity in psychotherapy: A meta-analysis of structural equivalence of placebo controls. *Journal of Consulting and Clinical Psychology*, 71(6), 973–979.

Baumert, A., Schmitt, M., Perugini, M., Johnson, W., Blum, G., Borkenau, P., ... Wrzus, C. (2017). Integrating personality structure, personality process, and personality development. *European Journal of Personality*, 31(5), 503–528.

Costantini, G., & Perugini, M. (2018). A framework for testing causality in personality research: Testing causality in personality research. *European Journal of Personality*, 32(3), 254–268.

Roberts, B. W., Luo, J., Briley, D. A., Chow, P. I., Su, R., & Hill, P. L. (2017). A systematic review of personality trait change through intervention. *Psychological Bulletin*, 143(2), 117–141.

16b Genetic and Environmental Mechanisms in BPD over the Lifespan: Commentary on Assessment of Mechanisms in Personality Disorders

MARINA A. BORNOVALOVA, ALEXANDRIA M. CHOATE, AND HAYA FATIMAH

The last 20 years have seen substantial advances in estimating genetic/temperamental and environmental contributions to the development and maintenance of borderline personality disorder (BPD). Stressful life events (SLEs) and other environmental contributions to BPD have been studied extensively and the importance of these SLEs is captured quite well in the chapter by Crowell, Kaliush, and Vlisides-Henry (this volume). However, the *transactions* which are reciprocal effects between the person and his or her environment are empirically overlooked despite the fact that such transactions are at the heart of many theories of psychopathology. In this commentary, we argue that a look at the broader personality and psychopathology literature suggests indirect evidence for transactional mechanisms in BPD and the important role transactional processes play in the development and maintenance of the disorder.

STUDIES OF CHILD AND ADOLESCENT FACTORS: ETIOLOGICAL TRANSACTIONAL PROCESSES

Environmental events are not entirely environmental. Studies of BPD etiology and maintenance traditionally separate personal (temperamental, genetic) and environmental (trauma, stressful life events, parenting factors) into two distinct "boxes." Environmental factors contributing to BPD include (but are not limited to): trauma, stressful life events (SLEs), and parenting styles – especially punishment (lack of), warmth, negativity, and control (Schuppert, Albers, Minderaa, Emmelkamp, & Nauta, 2012). However, studies using the classical twin design report that these putatively environmental factors show at least partial genetic contribution. For example, Kendler and Baker (2007) conducted a systematic review of genetic influences on environmental factors and found parenting to be largely heritable, with heritability estimates highest for parental warmth (34–37 percent), and lower for

This work was supported by DA032582 (NIDA). No conflict of interest exists for any of the authors

measures of control and negativity (12–17 percent). Family environment (support, cohesion, expressiveness, control, independence) was also 18–30 percent heritable. This general pattern held regardless of whether the child or parent reported on parenting behavior. On the other hand, childhood trauma – another correlate of BPD – does not seem to be particularly heritable; there is at best very modest heritability for emotional abuse, and little to no heritability of physical and sexual abuse (Bornovalova et al., 2013; Jaffee et al., 2004; but see Richmond-Rakerd et al., 2019 and Schaefer et al., 2018 for converse findings).

Generally, the heritability of environmental factors suggests both active and evocative gene–environment correlations (Scarr & McCartney, 1983). These correlations are direct analogs of the transactional processes in BPD. Evocative gene–environment correlations (rGE) result from the environment (e.g., parenting) differentially responding to genetically influenced characteristics of the child. Evocative rGE captures a transactional process between offspring and their parents: for instance, parents may respond to the child's difficult temperament with harsh and negative parenting. Conversely, active rGE occurs when a child actively selects environments that are correlated with his or her genetically influenced characteristics ("niche-picking"); active rGE is less relevant to transactions with parents, but is relevant to the general adolescent social context (e.g., peer selection).

Personality likely contributes to the heritability of parenting in BPD. One way to unpack processes driving rGE is to examine the genetic correlation of the environmental variable of interest (e.g., parenting) and another variable (e.g., BPD, normal personality traits. No studies yet document the genetic correlation between BPD traits and parenting factors, but the normal personality literature is informative. Krueger, Markon, and Bouchard (2003) reported a small phenotypic (~.16) but large genetic (.77) correlation between personality traits of negative emotionality and retrospectively reported parental acceptance, conflict, and control. The genetic correlation between the trait-constraint (impulsivity reversed) and parenting was .64.

Non-twin longitudinal studies directly provide evidence for the offspring's personality contributions to parenting. Whalen et al. (2014) coded transactions between mothers and daughters in the laboratory and found dyadic negative escalation to be predictive of increased BPD symptoms over time. Similar effects were found in a study of children and their biological mothers suggesting maladaptive mother–child interactions mediate the longitudinal transmission of maternal BPD symptoms to their offspring (Reinelt et al., 2014). Finally, a large longitudinal study examined the developmental trajectories of BPD symptoms in relation to parenting. Time-specific elevations in BPD symptoms predicted increases in harsh punishment and low warmth (but not vice versa). Child impulsivity and negative emotionality as well as caregiver psychopathology predicted parenting trajectories, whereas only child characteristics were predictive of BPD trajectories (Stepp et al., 2014).

Personality may mediate the relationship between BPD and heritable non-family social experiences. We know little about the non-family social context of children and adolescents with BPD features. Yet, although the biosocial models do not explicitly describe the social lives of adolescents at risk for BPD, one would expect that patterns developed in the context of the family would partially translate into non-family contexts. Notably, number of friends, social support, and bullying are moderately to highly heritable in adolescence (Bowes et al., 2013) and show genetic correlations with personality and psychopathology. For instance, Connolly and Beaver (2016) found the heritability of bullying victimization to be ~70 percent. Bullying victimization correlated with child delinquency and child depression/anxiety, and common genetic factors partially mediated these relationships. In a sample of late adolescents, Billig, Hershberger, Iacono, and McGue (1996) reported trait-constraint to have a high genetic correlation (.69) with non-independent/non-family SLEs. Non-twin studies provide support as well: Jensen-Campbell et al. (2002) reported that neuroticism was correlated with perceived peer acceptance, whereas agreeableness was significantly associated with peer-reported acceptance and friendship.

STUDIES OF ADULT FACTORS: MAINTENANCE/ EXACERBATION TRANSACTIONAL PROCESSES

Development and maintenance of BPD do not end in adolescence, and neither do the transactions between the person and his or her environment. New pathogenic or maintenance factors are also possible and are implicitly predicted by the biosocial model. For instance, the model makes predictions regarding the carry-over effects of patterns learned and reinforced in childhood into interpersonal, romantic, and social relationships. It likewise makes predictions for lifestyle choices that increase the probability of experiencing stressful life events.

Fortunately, the literature describing how BPD actively transacts with its environment in adulthood is slowly accumulating.

BPD is associated with social difficulties and stressful life events in adulthood. While BPD symptoms are associated with a range of negative outcomes, these effects may not be specific to BPD. In a four-year longitudinal study, Daley, Burge, and Hammen (2000) reported that BPD symptoms predicted four-year romantic dysfunction (e.g., romantic chronic stress, conflicts, partner satisfaction, abuse, and unwanted pregnancy), and less partner-reported satisfaction. However, these associations were not unique to BPD, but accounted for by general personality pathology. SLEs also appear to be correlated with BPD features: in two studies of middle-aged adults, BPD features predicted negative life events – especially dependent and interpersonal life events – even after adjusting for depression and other personality disorders (Gleason, Powers, & Oltmanns, 2012; Powers, Gleason, & Oltmanns, 2013).

Adult environmental events are also heritable. Numerous twin studies have documented the contribution of active and evocative gene–environment correlations to life events common to those with BPD including marital difficulties, divorce, SLEs, and trauma in adulthood. Divorce shows a weighted mean heritability of 35 percent, with heritability of marital satisfaction, conflict, and warmth ranging from 13 percent for conflict to 28 percent for satisfaction (Kendler & Baker, 2007). Personality characteristics of negative emotionality, constraint, aggression, positive emotionality, and optimism have significant genetic correlations with divorce and marital problems in the expected direction (Chipuer, Plomin, Pedersen, McClearn, & Nesselroade, 1993; Jocklin, McGue, & Lykken, 1996; Spotts et al., 2005). SLEs appear to be similarly heritable (17–31 percent), with reporting of high-risk (62 percent) and military trauma (47 percent) demonstrating genetic contributions as well (Kendler & Baker, 2007; Lyons et al., 1993; Richmond-Rakerd et al., 2019).

Personality contributes to heritable adult life events. In a large longitudinal twin study, genetic factors were found to partially contribute to negative controllable and less controllable life events, though the majority of this contribution was environmental (Kandler, Bleidorn, Riemann, Angleitner, & Spinath, 2012). Neuroticism and agreeableness had a moderate, genetically mediated effect on future SLEs, whereas the effects from life events on personality were environmentally mediated. Evidence from molecular data also provide evidence for genetic influences on adverse life experiences: 30 percent of variance in reported SLEs including dependent (illness, death, and being robbed) – and independent (unemployment, separation, financial problems, and legal matters) – life events were explained by single nucleotide polymorphisms (SNPs). When traits of neuroticism and behavioral disinhibition were ruled out, genetic contributions to SLEs disappeared (Powers et al., 2013).

WORKING THEORETICAL MODEL: GENETIC CONTROL OF EXPOSURE TO THE ENVIRONMENT IN BPD

Kendler and Eaves (1986) describe a model of depression – termed "genetic control over exposure to the environment" – that may be useful for testing person–environment transactions in BPD over the lifespan. This model posits that genes can act on the liability to psychiatric illness by predisposing individuals to select themselves into high-risk environments. Kendler, Karkowski, and Prescott (1999) documented that relative to individuals without a history of depression, individuals with depressive disorders experience more SLEs. These events are at least partially dependent on one's genetic liability. Hammen (2006) and Joiner (2000) suggest processes by which individuals with depression generate interpersonal and dependent life events. These include poor interpersonal problem-solving, negative feedback and excessive reassurance seeking, interpersonal conflict avoidance, and blame maintenance. Although genetic control over environmental exposure is nested within the biosocial theory, there are benefits for model multiplication. First, invoking Kendler and Eaves' model places BPD in the context of general psychopathology and invites tests of whether effects are specific to BPD. Second, this model provides a well-developed body of methodological and empirical literature using both phenotypic and genetically informative designs. This literature can then serve as a metaphorical trail of breadcrumbs for tests of the same phenomena in BPD.

We extend this model to BPD by positing that (i) the traits of neuroticism, agreeableness, and conscientiousness at least partially mediate the relationship of BPD with the experience of negative parenting, interpersonal stress, and SLEs, and this mediation is genetic in origin. In childhood and adolescence, BPD – partially through these traits – contributes to environmental stressors (e.g., experience of being bullied), as well as reduced parental warmth and increased negativity. In adulthood, these traits contribute to increased exposure to interpersonal and dependent life events. (ii) This transactional process continues to develop throughout the lifespan with different trait combinations contributing to a wide array of social processes such peers vs. family influence. (iii) The effects of the person on the environment may not be specific to BPD, but instead may be indicative of a general liability to interpersonal, personality, and affective dysfunction.

FUTURE DIRECTIONS

Many gaps remain in our understanding of transactional processes in BPD across the lifespan. Foremost, there is a clear need for direct tests of BPD and its transactions with the environment – and the mechanisms driving those transactions. These transactions should be studied outside as well as within the family and throughout the lifespan. It is important to note that personality disorders – especially when conceptualized as an extensions of normal personality – are likely to be polygenic, and candidate gene studies are unlikely to be fruitful. For now, researchers studying the genetic basis of BPD would be best served by using existing twin and adoptive datasets or genome-wide association studies from very large data sets. Multimorbidity should be modeled in molecular studies as well. Such questions can be examined within existing longitudinal and/or genetically informative epidemiological studies that routinely collect data on normal personality traits. These normal personality traits can be subsequently scored to provide a proxy of BPD features. Finally, given evidence for the direct effects of adverse environments on BPD features, detection of the individual-based contributing factors to environmental exposure can aid prevention efforts that can target these malleable traits. In turn, this may reduce the risk of environmental stressor exposure in vulnerable individuals.

REFERENCES

Billig, J. P., Hershberger, S. L., Iacono, W. G., & McGue, M. (1996). Life events and personality in late adolescence: Genetic and environmental relations. *Behavior Genetics*, 26(6), 543–554.

Bornovalova, M. A., Huibregtse, B. M., Hicks, B. M., Keyes, M., McGue, M., & Iacono, W. (2013). Tests of a direct effect of childhood abuse on adult borderline personality disorder traits: A longitudinal discordant twin design. *Journal of Abnormal Psychology*, 122(1), 180–194.

Bowes, L., Maughan, B., Ball, H., Shakoor, S., Ouellet-Morin, I., Caspi, A., . . . Arseneault, L. (2013). Chronic bullying victimization across school transitions: The role of genetic and environmental influences. *Development and Psychopathology*, 25(2), 333–346.

Chipuer, H., Plomin, R., Pedersen, N. L., McClearn, G. E., & Nesselroade, J. R. (1993). Genetic influence on family environment: The role of personality. *Developmental Psychology*, 29(1), 110–118.

Connolly, E. J., & Beaver, K. M. (2016). Considering the genetic and environmental overlap between bullying victimization, delinquency, and symptoms of depression/anxiety. *Journal of Interpersonal Violence*, 31(7), 1230–1256.

Daley, S. E., Burge, D., & Hammen, C. (2000). Borderline personality disorder symptoms as predictors of 4-year romantic relationship dysfunction in young women: Addressing issues of specificity. *Journal of Abnormal Psychology*, 109(3), 451–460.

Gleason, M. E., Powers, A. D., & Oltmanns, T. F. (2012). The enduring impact of borderline personality pathology: Risk for threatening life events in later middle-age. *Journal of Abnormal Psychology*, 121(2), 447–457.

Hammen, C. (2006). Stress generation in depression: Reflections on origins, research, and future directions. *Journal of Clinical Psychology*, 62(9), 1065–1082.

Jaffee, S. R., Caspi, A., Moffitt, T. E., Polo-Tomas, M., Price, T. S., & Taylor, A. (2004). The limits of child effects: Evidence for genetically mediated child effects on corporal punishment but not on physical maltreatment. *Developmental Psychology*, 40(6), 1047–1058.

Jensen-Campbell, L. A., Adams, R., Perry, D. G., Workman, K. A., Furdella, J. Q., & Egan, S. K. (2002). Agreeableness, extraversion, and peer relations in early adolescence: Winning friends and deflecting aggression. *Journal of Research in Personality*, *36*(3), 224–251.

Jocklin, V., McGue, M., & Lykken, D. T. (1996). Personality and divorce: A genetic analysis. *Journal of Personality and Social Psychology*, *71*(2), 288–299.

Joiner Jr, T. E. (2000). Depression's vicious scree: Self-propagating and erosive processes in depression chronicity. *Clinical Psychology: Science and Practice*, *7*(2), 203–218.

Kandler, C., Bleidorn, W., Riemann, R., Angleitner, A., & Spinath, F. M. (2012). Life events as environmental states and genetic traits and the role of personality: A longitudinal twin study. *Behavior Genetics*, *42*(1), 57–72.

Kendler, K. S., & Baker, J. H. (2007). Genetic influences on measures of the environment: A systematic review. *Psychological Medicine*, *37*(5), 615–626.

Kendler, K. S., & Eaves, L. J. (1986). Models for the joint effect of genotype and environment on liability to psychiatric illness. *American Journal of Psychiatry*, *143*(3), 279–289.

Kendler, K. S., Karkowski, L. M., & Prescott, C. A. (1999). Causal relationship between stressful life events and the onset of major depression. *American Journal of Psychiatry*, *156*(6), 837–841.

Krueger, R. F., Markon, K. E., & Bouchard Jr, T. J. (2003). The extended genotype: The heritability of personality accounts for the heritability of recalled family environments in twins reared apart. *Journal of Personality*, *71*(5), 809–833.

Lyons, M. J., Goldberg, J., Eisen, S. A., True, W., Tsuang, M. T., Meyer, J. M., & Henderson, W. G. (1993). Do genes influence exposure to trauma? A twin study of combat. *American Journal of Medical Genetics*, *48*(1), 22–27.

Powers, A. D., Gleason, M. E., & Oltmanns, T. F. (2013). Symptoms of borderline personality disorder predict interpersonal (but not independent) stressful life events in a community sample of older adults. *Journal of Abnormal Psychology*, *122*(2), 469–474.

Reinelt, E., Stopsack, M., Aldinger, M., Ulrich, I., Grabe, H. J., & Barnow, S. (2014). Longitudinal transmission pathways of borderline personality disorder symptoms: From mother to child? *Psychopathology*, *47*(1), 10–16.

Richmond-Rakerd, L. S., Trull, T. J., Gizer, I. R., McLaughlin, K., Scheiderer, E. M., Nelson, E. C., ... Heath, A. C. (2019). Common genetic contributions to high-risk trauma exposure and self-injurious thoughts and behaviors. *Psychological Medicine*, *49*(3), 421–430.

Scarr, S., & McCartney, K. (1983). How people make their own environments: A theory of genotype→ environment effects. *Child Development*, *54*(2), 424–435.

Schaefer, J. D., Moffitt, T. E., Arseneault, L., Danese, A., Fisher, H. L., Houts, R., ... Caspi, A. (2018). Adolescent victimization and early-adult psychopathology: Approaching causal inference using a longitudinal twin study to rule out noncausal explanations. *Clinical Psychological Science*, *6*(3), 352–371.

Schuppert, H. M., Albers, C. J., Minderaa, R. B., Emmelkamp, P. M., & Nauta, M. H. (2012). Parental rearing and psychopathology in mothers of adolescents with and without borderline personality symptoms. *Child and Adolescent Psychiatry and Mental Health*, *6*(1), 29.

Spotts, E. L., Lichtenstein, P., Pedersen, N., Neiderhiser, J. M., Hansson, K., Cederblad, M., & Reiss, D. (2005). Personality and marital satisfaction: A behavioural genetic analysis. *European Journal of Personality*, *19*(3), 205–227.

Stepp, S. D., Whalen, D. J., Scott, L. N., Zalewski, M., Loeber, R., & Hipwell, A. E. (2014). Reciprocal effects of parenting and borderline personality disorder symptoms in adolescent girls. *Development and Psychopathology*, *26*(2), 361–378.

Whalen, D. J., Scott, L. N., Jakubowski, K. P., McMakin, D. L., Hipwell, A. E., Silk, J. S., & Stepp, S. D. (2014). Affective behavior during mother–daughter conflict and borderline personality disorder severity across adolescence. *Personality Disorders: Theory, Research, and Treatment*, *5*(1), 88–96.

16c Complexity and Transactions: Author Rejoinder to Commentaries on Assessment of Mechanisms in Personality Disorders

PARISA R. KALIUSH, ROBERT D. VLISIDES-HENRY, AND SHEILA E. CROWELL

Markon (this volume) as well as Bornovalova, Choate, and Fatimah (this volume) provide thoughtful remarks on our chapter. Markon raises important points regarding the complexity of mechanistic research – namely, difficulties defining clear boundaries between hypothesized causes and effects. For example, he questions the mechanistic influences of neural disconnectivity on the development of emotion dysregulation, proposing that such neural phenomena may be physical manifestations of dysregulated emotional states rather than components of a causal process. He also introduces *weak emergence* as a way to conceptualize development of personality disorders (PDs). Weak emergence accounts for macroscopic phenomena (e.g., borderline personality disorder) that derive from lower-order parts (e.g., invalidating relationships) but cannot be reduced to simple explanations due to complexity and the lengthy timescales over which mechanistic pathways develop (Baumert et al., 2017).

Bornovalova and colleagues also address difficulties explaining the development of PDs. They argue that mechanistic research rarely extends beyond simple unidirectional relations (e.g., candidate genes to environments). In actuality, it is more likely that these phenomena exert reciprocal influences across time, and "genetic" or "environmental" factors are not as distinct as traditionally conceptualized. For instance, parenting has heritability estimates ranging from 12 to 37 percent (Kendler & Baker, 2007). Bornovalova and colleagues describe a theoretical perspective, "genetic control over exposure to the environment" (i.e., gene–environment correlation), which may prove more fruitful for testing reciprocal influences on PD development across the lifespan. We agree that grounding mechanistic research in theory is vital to disentangling elements of complex mechanistic processes (Hedström & Ylikoski, 2010).

In response to these rich commentaries, we delve briefly into the complexity and transactional nature of mechanisms in PD development. Specifically, we discuss nonlinear dynamical systems and psychopathology research. Dynamical systems models allow researchers to examine persons and/or variables across time (see e.g., Granic,

O'Hara, Pepler, & Lewis, 2007; Pezard & Nandrino, 2001). Behaviors, traits, and other individual differences are assumed to have "attractors" and "repellers" (Granic et al., 2007; Kenrick et al., 2002). That is, across time one would expect some degree of stability in key characteristics as a person continuously repels from, or is attracted to, certain points. For example, a person may show some stability in their emotions, behaviors, or physiology around a mean (i.e., their set point). However, the theory also assumes that people are "open systems," subject to frequent "perturbations" or disruptions, which pull them away from their typical set point. For instance, a person's level of negative affect may be relatively stable and attracted (i.e., drawn back) to a moderate level. External factors (e.g., a fight with peers or a fun gathering) can perturb this system, temporarily shifting the set point toward higher or lower negative affect. When human characteristics are conceptualized as longitudinal open systems, researchers attend to a system's stability and attractor/repeller points. Ultimately, one can argue from a dynamical systems perspective that current approaches to assessing personality disorder mechanisms present an incomplete picture of the dynamics of psychopathology over time.

In our chapter, we highlighted the complexity of PD assessment and multiple coexisting mechanisms. Yet only recently have dynamical systems approaches been applied to clinical research (see e.g., Gelfand & Engelhart, 2012). Unlike other areas of psychological science, the clinical implications behind dynamical systems research may lend to more nuanced interpretations of mechanisms. For example, our lab used nonlinear dynamics to characterize emotional and biological sensitivity among self-injuring, depressed, and control adolescent girls and their mothers during a 10-minute conflict discussion (Crowell et al., 2017). As hypothesized, we found that self-injuring adolescents were more sensitive – behaviorally and psychophysiologically – to their mothers' conflict behaviors than depressed or control adolescents. In addition, we found that adolescents' behaviors did not "drive" their mothers' responses. Thus, we used a dynamical systems approach to complement a key developmental theory: that vulnerability for self-injury is greatest among adolescents who are more sensitive to family environments (Crowell, Beauchaine, & Linehan, 2009). Although we did not assess every possible mechanism, we sought to link our mechanistic research to theory and feasible treatment targets.

Moving forward, researchers should acknowledge implications associated with studying mechanisms in PDs. As noted in our original chapter, the notion of causality is implicit to mechanistic research. However, testing causal theories is often beyond the capacity of our methodological and statistical approaches. As highlighted in both commentaries, there are complexities that hinder current understanding of PD development and mechanistic pathways. We hypothesize that delving deeper into dynamical systems theory, weak emergence, and complex gene–environment associations will enrich our understanding and treatment of PDs.

REFERENCES

Baumert, A., Schmitt, M., Perugini, M., Johnson, W., Blum, G., Borkenau, P., ... Wrzus, C. (2017). Integrating personality structure, personality process, and personality development. *European Journal of Personality*, *31*, 503–528.

Crowell, S. E., Beauchaine, T. P., & Linehan, M. M. (2009). A biosocial developmental model of borderline personality: Elaborating and extending Linehan's theory. *Psychological Bulletin*, *135*, 495–510.

Crowell, S. E., Butner, J. E., Wiltshire, T. J., Munion, A. K., Yaptangco, M., & Beauchaine, T. P. (2017). Evaluating emotional and biological sensitivity to maternal behavior among self-injuring and depressed adolescent girls using nonlinear dynamics. *Clinical Psychological Science*, *5*, 272–285.

Gelfand, L., & Engelhart, S. (2012). Dynamical systems theory in psychology: Assistance for the lay reader is required. *Frontiers in Psychology*, *3*, 1–3.

Granic, I., O'Hara, A., Pepler, D., & Lewis, M. D. (2007). A dynamic systems analysis of parent–child changes associated with successful "real-world" interventions for aggressive children. *Journal of Abnormal Child Psychology*, *35*, 845–857.

Hedström, P., & Ylikoski, P. (2010). Causal mechanisms in the social sciences. *Annual Review of Sociology*, *36*, 49–67.

Kendler, K. S., & Baker, J. H. (2007). Genetic influences on measures of the environment: A systematic review. *Psychological Medicine*, *37*, 615–626.

Kenrick, D. T., Maner, J. K., Butner, J., Li, N. P., Becker, D. V., & Schaller, M. (2002). Dynamical evolutionary psychology: Mapping the domains of the new interactionist paradigm. *Personality and Social Psychology Review*, *6*, 347–356.

Pezard, L., & Nandrino, J. L. (2001). Dynamic paradigm in psychopathology: "Chaos Theory," from physics to psychiatry. *L'Encephale*, *27*, 260–268.

PART V TREATMENT

17 Cognitive Behavioral Approaches

M. ZACHARY ROSENTHAL, KRISTIN P. WYATT, AND KIBBY MCMAHON

INTRODUCTION

Cognitive and behavioral psychotherapies for the treatment of personality disorders have been developed and evaluated for over 30 years. Although some of the better established treatments are manualized interventions with specific brand names (e.g., dialectical behavior therapy; Linehan, 1993), others more generally have been labeled as cognitive, behavioral, or cognitive-behavioral. In this chapter, we refer collectively to these treatments as cognitive behavioral therapies (CBTs). Despite being commonly used to denote a particular kind of psychotherapeutic approach, cognitive behavioral therapy (CBT) is not a single or uniform treatment protocol for psychiatric disorders in general, or personality disorders specifically. Instead, the plural form of CBT (i.e., CBTs) refers to a family of interventions bound together by empirically supported principles of behavioral, emotional, and cognitive change grounded in learning theories and basic science. There are hundreds of randomized controlled trials using different CBT protocols to treat individuals across the lifespan, in different cultures and treatment settings, using varying formats (e.g., group, couples, and individual) and technologies (e.g., apps, virtual reality, telephone), and for a long list of specific psychiatric disorders. CBT is not one intervention. The family of CBTs form a class, type, or category of related treatments.

When conceptualized this way, CBTs for all psychiatric disorders refer to a group of interventions including traditional or so-called first-wave behavior therapies (e.g., those that discount the causative role of changing cognition and other private unobservable events, such as systematic desensitization; Wolpe, 1961), as well as second-wave (e.g., those that emphasize the importance of changes in the content of cognition as causative, such as cognitive therapy; Beck, 1991) and "third-wave" therapies (e.g., those that emphasize the importance of changing the context of how one experiences cognition and other private events, without relying on changing the content of such experiences, such as acceptance- and mindfulness-based therapies; Hayes, Strosahl, & Wilson, 1999, 2012;

Linehan, 1993). There are important differences among the first, second, and third waves of CBTs. For example, traditional cognitive therapy is based on information processing theory, which asserts that cognitive schemas develop as a means of organizing experiences in normal cognitive development, and that such schemas will reflect key concepts of self and others, thereby influencing decisions and actions (Beck, 1991). Therapists using this approach help patients develop skills to identify and change maladaptive patterns of learned schemas and related behaviors. In contrast, interventions in acceptance and commitment therapy do not include direct skills training procedures to change cognition and behavior, but instead are designed to disrupt verbal relationships among stimuli through experiential learning (ACT, Hayes et al., 1999, 2012). Despite the particulars in the differences among CBT protocols, these approaches arguably are more similar than different, and can be considered together as a collection of modern or contemporary CBTs used across psychiatric disorders and other problems related to mental health.

In this chapter, we begin by providing a detailed overview of the CBTs that have been developed, manualized, and investigated for the treatment of individuals with personality disorders. These treatments have been variably labeled as empirically supported or evidence-based and have a specific brand name referring to a specific set of interventions. Accordingly, we refer to these as "branded" cognitive and behavioral treatments.

Unfortunately, there are very few branded CBTs for personality disorders. This could be due to a host of factors. Chief among them may be the lack of research that has been conducted to develop, evaluate, and disseminate psychotherapies for personality disorders. Such psychotherapy outcome research takes a long time and is expensive. However, this is not unique to CBTs and generally is true for the treatment of most mental health problems. Several additional considerations may help to explain why there are so few well-studied and established treatments for personality disorders in particular.

Personality disorders are characterized by longstanding patterns of dysfunctional intra-personal and interpersonal behavior pervasive across contexts. Accordingly, it may take longer to treat patients diagnosed with personality disorders than those with many other conditions, irrespective of the treatment approach. Individuals with personality disorders commonly are diagnosed with other co-occurring disorders (e.g., such as anxiety, mood, and substance use disorders; Grant et al., 2005; Trull, Jahng, Tomko, Wood, & Sher, 2010) and are high utilizers of mental health resources (Bender et al., 2001), making it costly and difficult to develop treatment protocols for personality disorders that can be applied across co-occurring conditions. In addition, personality disorders and related interpersonal dysfunction are associated with poor response to traditional psychotherapies (for a discussion on this, see Beck, Davis, & Freeman, 2015). Taken together, a primary reason for so few well-studied treatments for personality disorders may be the prohibitive amount of time and costs associated with conducting such research.

In addition to there being a very small number of empirically supported manualized treatment protocols for personality disorders, the majority of rigorously conducted treatment outcome research has been restricted to borderline personality disorder (BPD). Put differently, there are several established CBTs for BPD, but little to no manualized CBT protocols with strong empirical support for other personality disorders. At the same time, clinicians using CBTs are faced with the challenge of treating patients across personality disorder diagnoses, even in the absence of clearly delineated specific CBT protocols. Whether it is patients meeting criteria for paranoid, narcissistic, obsessive-compulsive, or any other personality disorder diagnosis, across all three clusters of personality disorders, clinicians need guidance even in the absence of well-established branded treatment protocols.

Still another challenge for clinicians is the absence of well-established CBTs for patients who may not meet full criteria for a personality disorder diagnosis (or other diagnosis), but may have significant impairment and distress associated with chronic and enduring personality dysfunction. Indeed, the validity of personality disorders as categorical diagnoses may be called into question due to the heterogeneity of symptoms within diagnoses, the co-occurrence of personality disorders with other disorders, and the use of a polythetic diagnostic approach. Despite several decades of research and calls for the use of dimensional models of personality dysfunction, dimensional models of treating personality dysfunction have not taken hold in mainstream clinical practice. There are no well-established CBTs for transdiagnostic patients with personality dysfunction characterized by, for example, high emotional instability, low agreeableness, and low conscientiousness.

In sum, (a) there are few branded and well-studied CBTs for personality disorders, (b) the most well-studied of them are for BPD, and (c) clinicians using CBTs need guidance in how to treat patients across personality disorder diagnoses and those with personality dysfunction who do not meet full criteria for a diagnosis. Accordingly, after first reviewing branded CBTs in detail, we outline how clinicians can use empirically supported principles of change to formulate a flexible and personally-tailored cognitive behavioral treatment for patients across personality disorders and problems with personality dysfunction not meeting full diagnostic criteria for any specific personality disorder diagnosis.

BRANDED COGNITIVE AND BEHAVIORAL TREATMENTS FOR PERSONALITY DISORDERS

Within the family of contemporary CBTs, a few treatment protocols have been specifically developed for personality disorders. These treatments include dialectical behavior therapy, schema-focused therapy, and cognitive therapy for personality disorders. The following sections include an overview of these treatments, including their rationale and structure, and their supporting treatment outcome research.

Dialectical Behavior Therapy

Dialectical behavior therapy (DBT), originally a treatment for suicidal and self-injurious behavior and with more recent support for multiple problems beyond BPD (e.g., transdiagnostic emotion dysregulation, Neacsiu, Eberle, Kramer, Wiesmann, & Linehan, 2014; bipolar disorder, Goldstein et al., 2015), has become the gold-standard treatment for BPD. At its core, DBT is a combination of traditional behavior therapy and cognitive therapy interventions, contemplative mindfulness-based spiritual practices, and a dialectical philosophy (Linehan, 1993). Using dialectics, a flexible perspective of viewing the world that allows for synthesis of the valid aspects of seemingly opposite viewpoints, DBT synthesizes acceptance- and change-focused cognitive behavioral principles and interventions. Across behavioral, cognitive, emotional, and interpersonal areas of functioning, psychopathology in BPD is viewed as the cause or consequence of pervasive problems with emotion dysregulation. In DBT, symptoms of BPD are thought to develop over time from a reciprocal and recurrent transaction between a pervasively invalidating environment and biological systems underlying emotional sensitivity, reactivity, and delayed recovery following emotional arousal (biosocial theory, Linehan, 1993; for reviews of empirical support see Crowell, Beauchaine, & Linehan, 2009; Domes, Schulze, & Herpertz, 2009; Kaiser, Jacob, Domes, & Arntz, 2017; Rosenthal et al., 2008). Like a tennis match, the back and forth of biology and environment transactionally impact each other over time. From a DBT perspective, beginning early in life, biological systems underlying emotional arousal impact and are impacted by the social environment. At the same time, the environment influences these same biological systems. Over time and with pervasive invalidation of one's private experiences, emotional functioning becomes impaired, changing how the environment responds to the individual, which, in turn, affects the underlying emotional systems regulating emotions, reciprocally impacting how behaviors are expressed in the environment, and so on.

DBT features four primary modes of treatment to target the multiple problems and skills deficits associated with emotion dysregulation: (1) individual therapy to maintain motivation in treatment and apply skills taught to clinically-relevant behavioral patterns, (2) group skills training to acquire new cognitive and behavioral skills, (3) telephone coaching to enhance the generalization of behavioral skills learned during group and individual therapy, and (4) therapist consultation team to treat the therapist and promote adherent application of DBT (Linehan, 1993).

In individual therapy, therapists use acceptance and change principles to hierarchically target: (1) life-threatening behaviors (e.g., self-injurious behavior), (2) therapy-interfering behaviors (i.e., anything interfering with the process of therapy), and (3) quality of life-interfering behaviors (e.g., problems with anxiety, mood, sleep, substance use, etc.; Linehan, 1993). Given that DBT is behavior therapy-based, individual therapy uses behavior analytic assessment and problem-solving that emphasizes directly addressing functions a problem behavior is hypothesized to serve (e.g., self-injurious behavior can function to regulate emotional arousal or communicate distress to others). In addition to function-specific targeting, change strategies of stimulus control, contingency management, exposure, and skills training are used and infused with acceptance (e.g., mindfulness) and dialectical (e.g., using a devil's advocate approach to explore multiple perspectives and enhance cognitive flexibility) strategies.

In DBT, individual therapy sessions begin with the review of a self-monitoring sheet, called a "diary card," in an effort to set session targets in line with the treatment hierarchy, and to efficiently review events from the past week, therapy homework, and use of skills. A behavioral analysis is typically then conducted by examining the observable events and unobservable private experiences (e.g., thoughts, feelings, physical sensations, etc.) that occurred before, during, and after the problem behavior. What emerges from these behavioral analyses, commonly called "chain" analyses, is that primary links in the chain of events surrounding problem behaviors are identified and considered as possible targets for change. Over time, chain analyses with the same patient reveal patterns of proximal causation and functions for problem behaviors. Skills are discussed and, whenever reasonable, role-played, modeled, and rehearsed in-session. The therapist uses contingency management and clarification to shape

the patient's behavior into being more skillful during session, and a collaborative plan is made to generalize the skills from individual therapy into the expected daily events in the patient's life. As an example, if a patient self-injured in the past week, a chain analysis would be done to identify the function of the self-injury, relevant skills would be explored and practiced during session to prevent future self-injury, and the patient and therapist together would problem-solve when and how to use which specific skills to prevent self-injury over the next week.

In DBT group skills training, therapists teach new behaviors in a class format, with mindfulness practice, review of skills practice from the past week, and teaching of new skills each session. Skills modules taught are mindfulness, emotion regulation, distress tolerance, and interpersonal effectiveness, all of which correspond to skills deficits observed in BPD (Linehan, 2014). Typically, there are two DBT skills group co-leaders, with one attending during the group to therapy-interfering behaviors and other group process issues, and the other leading the mindfulness, homework review, and teaching functions. To enhance effective communication between patients and individual therapists, DBT skills group co-leaders encourage patients to speak directly with their individual therapists about how to personally tailor DBT skills learned during group, and to use DBT skills to help resolve any interpersonal problems patients might have with their therapist or others.

Telephone consultation to patients is used throughout the week to assist patients in practicing effectively asking for help in applying the skills to their real-world environments. This serves to promote generalization of behavioral skills, in conjunction with outside of session practice exercises (i.e., therapy homework) from both individual and group therapies. In this way, when DBT patients have difficulty using skills in their daily environments, they are encouraged to call their individual therapist for skills coaching. The therapist responds with brief (5–10 minutes) problem-solving and coaching on the use of specific DBT skills. If a patient calls when a therapist is not available, the therapist calls back within 24 hours, but typically much sooner. If a patient has self-harmed within the past 24 hours, the therapist invokes the "24-hour rule," and does not assist with skills coaching in order to prevent inadvertently reinforcing dysfunctional behavior.

Finally, the fourth primary mode of DBT is therapist consultation team. This weekly meeting includes all members of the DBT treatment team, and has the primary function of providing support, problem-solving, ongoing learning, and feedback to therapists to enhance fidelity to the treatment model. Because DBT is a team-based intervention, in order to be conducting individual DBT one must be a part of a therapist consultation team. During team meetings, there is a clear and consistent structure, with a team leader, an observer of processes out of adherence to the DBT model, and a note-taker to record key decisions made by the team. Each meeting involves a mindfulness practice, didactics, review and problem-solving of therapist needs (e.g., feeling demoralized, tired, or cynical), and an emphasis on balancing change with validation and acceptance during review of patient care needs. Indeed, therapist consultation team is not a staffing-meeting-as-usual. If a therapist is judgmental, off-topic, or defensive, for example, the team attends to these behaviors and helps the therapist be less judgmental, more targeted, or less defensive. Therapist consultation team is a critical component to a healthy DBT program, as it is a context for therapists to regain morale, develop new approaches to recurring and seemingly intransigent patient problems, and ensure the other three primary modes of DBT are being done with fidelity to the model.

The application of DBT to BPD has been thoroughly studied. Fourteen randomized controlled trials (RCTs) of standard DBT have been conducted in six countries examining effects in individuals with BPD or BPD traits (e.g., Linehan et al., 2006; Mehlum et al., 2014), and additional less rigorous studies have been performed (e.g., Rathus & Miller, 2002; Rizvi, Hughes, Hittman, & Vieira Oliveira, 2017). In response to this extensive work, Division 12 of the American Psychological Association has labeled the empirical support for application of DBT for BPD as strong (see Chambless et al., 1998 for expanded definition of "well-established treatments"), indicating that a minimum of two independent research groups using strong group designs have found that DBT is equivalent to another established treatment and/or statistically superior to another treatment or placebo.

Amongst these RCTs, several demonstrate that standard DBT led to improvements on common outcome variables, including improvements in parasuicidal behavior (suicidal behavior and non-suicidal self-injury variables; Carter, Willcox, Lewin, Conrad, & Bendit, 2010; Clarkin, Levy, Lenzenweger, & Kernberg, 2007; Linehan, Armstrong, Suarez, Allmon, & Heard, 1991; Linehan et al., 1999, 2006, 2015; McMain et al., 2009; Mehlum et al., 2014; Pistorello, Fruzzetti, MacLane, Gallop, & Iverson, 2012; Verheul et al., 2003), depression (Clarkin et al, 2007; Koons et al., 2001; Linehan et al., 1991, 2006, 2015; McMain et al., 2009; Mehlum et al., 2014), use of hospital-based crisis services (Koons et al., 2001; Linehan et al., 1991, 2006, 2015; McMain et al., 2009), and suicidal ideation (Koons et al., 2001; Linehan et al., 1991, 2006; Mehlum et al., 2014).

However, in these randomized studies, DBT outperformed the comparison treatment condition only some of the time. For example, DBT has been shown to reduce parasuicidal behavior more than usual care treatments in some trials (Linehan et al., 1991; Mehlum et al., 2014; Pistorello et al., 2012). Other studies have found that DBT was superior to the comparison group in decreasing non-suicidal self-injury, but not suicidal behavior (Linehan et al., 2015; Verheul et al., 2003), or vice versa (Linehan et al., 2006). Lastly, several studies reported that DBT did not differ significantly from other treatment conditions on parasuicide outcomes (Carter et al., 2010;

Linehan et al., 1999; Linehan et al., 2002; McMain et al., 2009). For depression outcomes, some investigators have found DBT to yield reductions superior to other treatments (Pistorello et al., 2012; interviewer-rated only: Mehlum et al., 2014; self-report only: Koons et al., 2001), whereas others found control treatments to perform similarly to DBT (Andreasson et al., 2016; Linehan et al., 1991, 2006; McMain et al., 2009). Only two (Linehan et al., 1991, 2006) of seven studies (Koons et al., 2001; Linehan et al., 1999, 2002; McMain et al., 2009; Mehlum et al., 2014) reported that DBT reduced hospitalizations significantly more than comparison treatments. Lastly, of the studies that found DBT to reduce suicidal ideation, DBT only outperformed usual care in one (Mehlum et al., 2014). DBT has also demonstrated significantly greater improvements in BPD symptoms (Pistorello et al., 2012), hopelessness (Koons et al., 2001), anger expression (Koons et al., 2001), drug use (Linehan et al. 1999, 2002), social adjustment (Pistorello et al., 2012), and therapy-interfering attendance behaviors (Linehan et al., 1991) than other treatments.

Several meta-analyses have been conducted to synthesize these findings across studies. Four meta-analytic reviews examined DBT specifically and outcomes for BPD, whereas others have examined samples beyond personality disorders (the interested reader is referred to Hawton et al., 2016; Ost, 2008; and Ougrin, Tranah, Stahl, Moran, & Asarnow, 2015). Two groups of researchers compared DBT to treatment-as-usual (TAU) across studies, each using five RCTs (Panos, Jackson, Hasan, & Panos, 2014; Stoffers et al., 2012). Stoffers and colleagues (2012) reported that DBT outperformed TAU on parasuicidality, general mental health, and anger, with significant moderate to large effect sizes, whereas DBT did not differentially reduce attrition compared to TAU. Panos et al. (2014) found that DBT led to significantly better outcomes than TAU in reducing suicide attempts and suicidal behavior, though effects on depression symptoms were not superior to TAU and impact on attrition was only marginally better in DBT. In addition, Cristea and colleagues (2017) examined 12 DBT RCTs in a review of psychotherapies for BPD. They found that among psychotherapies, DBT and psychodynamic approaches were the only treatments with significantly better outcomes than control treatments for all BPD-relevant outcomes, including suicidal and parasuicidal behaviors and BPD symptoms, with DBT demonstrating small to moderate effect sizes. In another meta-analytic study examining DBT for BPD, eight RCTs and eight non-randomized and/or non-controlled studies were used to compare pre- and post-treatment outcomes (Kliem, Kröger, & Kosfelder, 2010). DBT was observed to yield moderate global effects, with significant moderate effects for suicidal and parasuicidal behaviors. One conclusion that can be made when synthesizing the results from these meta-analytic reviews is that the most consistent effects of DBT have been in the reduction of parasuicidal and suicidal behaviors.

Notably, recent studies highlight the importance of the skills training component of DBT in the treatment of BPD. Specifically, in BPD samples, DBT skills use mediates improvements in non-suicidal self-injury and depression (Neacsiu, Rizvi, & Linehan, 2010). Additionally, DBT interventions with active skills components (i.e., standard DBT and DBT skills group with case management) have been found to yield significantly greater reductions in self-injury and quicker improvements in depression and anxiety during treatment than DBT individual therapy only without any skills (Linehan et al., 2015).

Three RCTs have been conducted examining the effects of DBT in personality disorders, including but not limited to BPD. Feigenbaum and colleagues (2012) examined the effects of DBT as compared to TAU in Cluster B personality disorders. In each treatment group, over 90 percent of participants met full criteria for BPD, and over 35 percent met criteria for avoidant personality disorder. Paranoid personality disorder was observed in 40 percent of subjects in the DBT group, as compared to 13 percent in TAU, and all other PDs represented less than 15 percent of sample. Both groups demonstrated significant improvements in general clinical outcomes, parasuicidal behavior, and anger expression. Priebe et al. (2012) also examined DBT versus TAU in individuals with any personality disorder and self-harm behavior, in a clinic with a high rate of BPD diagnoses. The authors did not report data on personality disorder diagnoses. DBT was found to yield significantly faster reductions in self-harm behavior than TAU, though other comparisons were non-significant. Lastly, a study of older depressed adults with a personality disorder compared 24 weeks of DBT with medication management to medication management only, with obsessive-compulsive personality disorder best represented in this sample, followed by avoidant and borderline personality disorders, respectively (Lynch et al., 2007). The DBT group demonstrated more cases of and faster rates of remission, and demonstrated greater decreases in interpersonal sensitivity and aggression compared to medication management alone. Given the paucity of data from controlled clinical trials examining personality disorders in general (and not BPD specifically or primarily), firm conclusions cannot be drawn about the efficacy of DBT for all personality disorders.

Schema Focused Therapy

Schema focused therapy (SFT), sometimes referred to as schema focused cognitive therapy, is a treatment protocol specifically developed for personality disorders or other difficult-to-treat problems that do not respond to traditional cognitive behavioral therapies (Young, 1990; Young, Klosko, & Weishaar, 2003). The focus of this therapy is addressing early maladaptive schemas (EMS), which are conceptualized as longstanding emotional and cognitive patterns that cause maladaptive behaviors. An overarching goal of treatment is insight related to schemas in order to engage in adaptive ways of coping with daily life events. The following discussion gives a brief overview of maladaptive schemas, coping styles, and their etiology.

Within the model used in SFT, EMS are longstanding maladaptive patterns of thoughts, behaviors, and emotions thought to have originally developed to help individuals cope with unmet needs in their childhood environment. In this conceptual model, the basic emotional needs in childhood are: (1) secure attachment to others, (2) autonomy, (3) freedom to express valid needs and emotions, (4) spontaneity and play, and (5) realistic limits and self-control. Consistent frustration of these needs in childhood leads to patterns of thinking, feeling, and behaving that may have been functional within the childhood environment, but are no longer effective in adulthood. In SFT, there are 18 schemas classified into five categories, based on the hypothesized unmet needs in childhood: (1) disconnection and rejection, (2) impaired autonomy and performance, (3) impaired limits, (4) other-directedness, and (5) overvigilance and inhibition. For example, a schema within the disconnection and rejection category is "abandonment/instability," which stems from a chronic frustration of the need for secure attachment in childhood. Due to this unmet need for secure attachment, it is hypothesized that the individual develops a belief that emotional support from others is unreliable. When this individual encounters signs of instability in adulthood, this schema will be activated, triggering intense negative emotions and maladaptive coping behaviors. Such coping behaviors are further categorized into three broad maladaptive coping styles: (1) schema surrender, which refers to accepting the schema as true and behaving in ways that are consistent with the schema, (2) schema avoidance, which refers to avoiding contexts or stimuli that would activate the schema, or (3) schema overcompensation, wherein the individual behaves in ways that are opposite of the schema. These coping behaviors are thought to manifest as the personality disorder traits or maladaptive interpersonal behaviors that interfere with the quality of patients' lives.

SFT is delivered through individual therapy in the assessment phase and change phases of treatment. The goal of the assessment phase is to gain awareness and insight into the origin and associated maladaptive coping styles relevant to key EMS. Assessment is achieved through thorough discussions with the therapist and the use of self-report questionnaires. These assessments ultimately inform the case conceptualization developed collaboratively between the therapist and patient.

After a case conceptualization is formulated, the treatment proceeds to the change phase, which includes cognitive, experiential, and behavioral pattern-breaking techniques. Cognitive techniques guide patients through challenging thoughts and beliefs related to their schemas. The goal of these techniques is to train patients to learn that dysfunctional thoughts and beliefs are not true.

Experiential techniques, such as imagery and role-play with the therapist, are designed to activate the schemas during the therapy session and trigger the emotional responses typically associated with schemas. The function of these techniques is to help patients emotionally confront the figures that did not meet their needs in childhood. For example, therapists lead patients through exercises where they imagine difficult memories from childhood and bring awareness and effective communication of their anger towards neglectful or abusive caregivers. These exercises facilitate externalizing of schemas, so that it is easier for patients to be aware of and challenge schemas instead of passively believing them. Behavioral pattern-breaking involves helping patients identify and modify maladaptive coping behaviors so that they can engage in healthier coping behaviors when schemas are activated. For example, the therapist will help patients target problems expressing emotions to others, generate alternative methods of expressing emotions that are more effective, and guide the patients through practicing these new behaviors through imagery or role-play exercises.

The therapeutic relationship between the patient and the therapist has an important role in the change phase of SFT. For example, there is an emphasis on meeting the patient's frustrated childhood needs through empathy and limited reparenting from the therapist, which the patient is encouraged to internalize as an adaptive healthy adult schema. Using the case conceptualization, the SFT therapist provides empathy, emotional support, and appropriate interpersonal boundaries that help redress the patient's unmet needs. The therapist provides limited reparenting through the therapeutic relationship (e.g., responding contingently to observe limits around patient and therapist behaviors during sessions) and through imagery, in which patients may imagine themselves as vulnerable children while the therapist engages in an empathetic, supportive dialogue with those figures. Through these dialogues, SFT aims to help patients learn to relate to their schemas with insight and compassion and to regulate their behaviors, thoughts, and emotions more effectively when elicited by such schemas.

Techniques in SFT are generalized outside of the therapy setting into the patients' lives through behavioral homework assignments and flash-cards that remind patients of their schemas and their planned responses (e.g., the evidence against their schemas or adaptive coping behaviors). Ultimately, the goal of SFT is a change in schemas, in which EMS are activated less frequently or intensely and patients engage in healthier coping behaviors when schemas are activated.

Previous research has demonstrated the efficacy of SFT for BPD (Farrell, Shaw, & Webber, 2009; Gisen-Bloo et al., 2006). For example, a study in the Netherlands treated 86 patients with either SFT or transference focused psychotherapy (TFT) twice a week for three years. Throughout the treatment period, 45 percent of the patients in the SFT condition recovered fully from BPD, compared to only 24 percent of those who received TFT (Gisen-Bloo et al., 2006). In a one-year follow up after treatment, 52 percent of the patients in the SFT condition fully recovered from BPD compared to 29 percent in the TFT condition (Gisen-Bloo et al., 2006).

SFT has some empirical support as a treatment for personality disorders more broadly. For example, a multi-center randomized controlled trial in the Netherlands compared the effects of SFT to clarification oriented therapy and TAU in 323 patients with mixed personality disorders (Bamelis, Evers, Spinhoven, & Arntz, 2014). This study found that more patients in the SFT condition compared to the two control conditions recovered from personality disorders three years after treatment began. Other empirical studies have found that SFT delivered in a group format is efficacious in treating BPD (Farrell et al., 2009), as well as other Cluster B (Zorn, Roder, Thommen, Müller, & Tschacher, 2007) and Cluster C (Hoffart, Versland, & Sexton, 2002) personality disorders. Across studies, research has provided preliminary evidence that SFT is efficacious for treating personality disorders in both individual and group formats. However, because the strongest evidence for this treatment is within BPD, more empirical research is needed to conclusively determine the efficacy of SFT across all personality disorders. In addition, given the limited amount of research conducted using SFT for BPD, definitive conclusions cannot yet be made about SFT compared to DBT, a more rigorously studied and well-established treatment for BPD.

Cognitive Therapy and Other CBTs

DBT and SFT are two branded CBTs that were specifically developed and tested as treatments for personality disorders. However, other researchers have adapted the broad framework of cognitive therapy to treat personality disorders. In 1990, Aaron Beck and colleagues developed a cognitive approach for personality disorders at a time when there were no manualized and empirically supported treatments for personality disorders (Beck , 1991). Beck's framework is based on the model that personality traits develop to fulfill important survival functions in specific environments. Similar to the model in SFT, in order to fulfill these functions, individuals develop core schemas, which refer to cognitive structures or sets of beliefs that include attitudes, assumptions, or expectations. These schemas are nested within networks of learned emotional, cognitive, and behavioral patterns that determine specific responses to challenges in the environment to fulfill survival goals. In personality disorders, these schemas and modes are adaptive for survival in certain environments, such as within childhood, but are overdeveloped and too rigid to adapt over time to different environments. For example, a mode that motivates an individual towards aggressive competition can be adaptive in childhood environments, but could contribute to the development of antisocial personality disorder symptoms.

Therapeutic techniques that identify, challenge, and modify dysfunctional beliefs form the basis of cognitive therapy. The goal of cognitive therapy for personality disorders is to reduce the intensity and availability of maladaptive schemas and strengthen more adaptive schemas (Beck, 1991). Consistent with SFT, the process of cognitive therapy for personality disorders includes assessment and change phases. Stemming from the initial assessment phase, the cognitive therapist develops a case conceptualization collaboratively with the patient. The developmental narrative, current life problems, and therapeutic relationship are three important sources of data for understanding, predicting, and effectively responding to the patient's dysfunctional beliefs. For example, maladaptive schemas may be evident during therapy as early as the initial evaluation session via patient thoughts that occur in the moment (e.g., "automatic thoughts") and are communicated to the therapist. These automatic thoughts (e.g., "this is going to sound stupid . . .") reflect or can give rise to verbalized conditional assumptions (e.g., "if someone criticizes me, it means they know I'm inferior") or to core beliefs within a schema about the patient's sense of self, others, or future (e.g., "I am always inferior"). During the assessment phase of treatment, therapists listen carefully for imperative words such as "should" or "must" that span multiple contexts in a patient's life, as they are common indicators of dysfunctional schemas. The therapist and patient collaboratively develop a case conceptualization by carefully discussing current life problems, the developmental history of such problems, as well as thoughts that arise during session.

The change phase of cognitive therapy involves helping patients become more facile at identifying and challenging maladaptive automatic thoughts, assumptions, and schema with ways of thinking that lead to more adaptive behaviors (Beck et al., 1990). A central therapeutic approach in cognitive therapy is questioning the patient about thoughts that occurred during problematic situations and tracing them back to underlying schemas. The therapist can draw upon many different techniques in this process, including but not limited to the use of Socratic questioning, a thought record or other homework to practice challenging automatic thoughts between clinic visits, problem-solving, or experiential exercises. Beck et al. (1990) recommended experiential exercises for personality disorders to elicit schemas and associated behavioral responses. As with SFT, experiential exercises in cognitive therapy include role-play between the therapist and the patient, reliving old childhood experiences, and imagery. For example, the therapist can prompt the patient to close her or his eyes, visualize a recent difficult situation, and reflect on the thoughts present at that time. The therapist would assist the patient in identifying and challenging any problematic ways of thinking that are elicited during such exercises.

As an example, when a patient becomes aware of relevant maladaptive schemas, the therapist can guide the patient through reality testing, evaluating the evidence for and against the schema. Testing the "truth" of the maladaptive schemas functions to weaken their ability to trigger other maladaptive patterns, such as dysfunctional coping behaviors. Eventually, the therapist can help the patient by modifying maladaptive beliefs with thoughts that are better grounded in evidence and reason and trigger more positive affect and adaptive behaviors. For example, patients can learn to modify their negative, generalized assumptions (e.g., "they criticized me, which means I'm inferior") to more benign interpretations that are specific to the situation (e.g., "they commented on a small mistake I made, which means that they are paying attention to my work and may be identifying areas of improvement"). More generally, as in SFT, the cognitive therapist treating personality disorders can flexibly and creatively use different techniques both to (a) increase insight into how core schemas are activated and contribute to current life problems and (b) develop more flexible cognitive and behavioral response patterns when dysfunctional ways of thinking occur.

Empirical research has provided some evidence for the efficacy of cognitive therapy for personality disorders. Similar to SFT and DBT, cognitive therapy adapted for personality disorders was found to be efficacious for BPD (Brown, Newman, Charlesworth, Crits-Christoph, & Beck, 2004; Cottraux et al., 2009; Davidson et al., 2006; Davidson, Tyrer, Norrie, Palmer & Tyrer, 2010). For example, one randomized controlled trial with 106 patients with BPD compared the effects of TAU combined with cognitive therapy to TAU alone (Davidson et al., 2006). This study found that two years after treatment, the cognitive therapy plus TAU condition led to a significant reduction in anxiety, dysfunctional beliefs, and number of suicidal acts compared to TAU alone.

As with DBT and SFT, relatively fewer studies have tested the effects of cognitive therapy on personality disorders beyond BPD. The studies that have investigated cognitive therapy across personality disorders have variability in the range of specific interventions used, with some emphasizing traditional cognitive change interventions and others using behavior therapy interventions as part of a more general cognitive behavioral approach. That is, cognitive therapy as a specific approach can be differentiated from the broader category of cognitive behavioral therapies for personality disorders, with the latter including a wide range of empirically supported behavioral and cognitive change interventions targeting a host of psychological processes (e.g., emotion regulation, behavioral dyscontrol, interpersonal dysfunction). For example, studies have found that behavioral therapy including exposure-based procedures may be efficacious in treating avoidant personality disorder (APD; Alden, 1989; Alden & Capreol, 1993). Another study with 62 patients with APD found that at a six-month follow-up, only 9 percent of patients randomized to a CBT condition were still diagnosed with APD, compared to 36 percent of patients randomized to a brief dynamic therapy group (Emmelkamp et al., 2006). This body of research suggests that cognitive behavioral approaches may be efficacious for the treatment of APD. However, as noted earlier in regards to DBT and SFT, more research is needed to reach definitive conclusions about the effects of cognitive therapy or other treatment protocols within the family of CBTs for patients with APD or other personality disorders outside of BPD.

Although DBT, SFT, and cognitive therapy have the largest number of rigorously controlled studies for the treatment of BPD, a few additional cognitive behavioral approaches have been developed and applied in the treatment of BPD. These include an emotion regulation group intervention developed by Gratz and Gunderson (2006) and systems training for emotional predictability and problem solving (STEPPS) developed by Blum and colleagues in 2005 (Blum et al., 2008), both of which are delivered in group format and are notably shorter than DBT.

Emotion regulation group therapy (ERGT) is designed as an intervention to target emotion regulation difficulties in BPD, and draws heavily on behavior therapy, DBT (Linehan, 1993), ACT (Hayes et al., 1999, 2012), and emotion-focused therapy (Gratz & Gunderson, 2006; Greenberg, 2015). In this treatment, participants learn about the function of self-harm behaviors and learn skills to increase emotional awareness, clarity, and acceptance, and behavior change (e.g., non-avoidance, alternatives to impulsive behavior) to promote values-consistent behaviors. Of note, many of these skills overlap with those taught during the emotion regulation module in DBT skills training (Linehan, 2014). Gratz and colleagues (Gratz, Tull, & Levy, 2014) conducted a randomized controlled trial comparing ERGT to a waitlist control condition among women with BPD and self-harm behavior. Individuals receiving ERGT demonstrated significant reductions in deliberate self-harm behavior and other self-destructive behaviors, emotion dysregulation, BPD symptoms, quality of life, and stress and depression symptoms, with medium to large effect sizes (Gratz et al., 2014). This study not only supports the promise for using ERGT but also suggests that a brief group skills-based intervention for BPD is feasible, acceptable, and can be efficacious.

STEPPS is a group-delivered intervention that includes psychoeducation and skill training by integrating cognitive therapy, behavioral skills, and a systems-based approach to improving interpersonal relationships. Examples of skills include: "distancing, communicating, challenging, distracting, and problem management … goal setting, healthy eating behaviors, sleep hygiene, regular exercise, leisure activities, health monitoring (e.g., medication adherence), avoiding self-harm, and interpersonal effectiveness" (Blum et al., 2008, p. 469). Notably,

many of these skills overlap with those in the skill training modules of distress tolerance, emotion regulation, and interpersonal effectiveness modules of DBT (Linehan, 2014).

Among studies examining STEPPS as a treatment approach, Blum and colleagues (2008) compared STEPPS plus TAU to TAU alone in the treatment of BPD. STEPPS yielded significantly greater improvements than TAU in BPD symptoms, as well as impulsivity, negative affect, and global functioning and mood. Additional randomized trials demonstrate similar results (Van Wel et al., 2009), as do less rigorous studies in samples with BPD (Black et al., 2008) and co-occurring ASPD and BPD (Black, Simsek-Duran, Blum, McCormick, & Allen, 2016).

STEPPS incorporates family members and partners in psychoeducation around BPD. However, this is not unique among empirically supported cognitive behavioral interventions for BPD. For example, DBT has been adapted for adolescents and young adults by incorporating family members in skills training and individual therapy as needed (Miller, Rathus, & Linehan, 2006). In these adaptations, multi-family skills training groups are used, which include both the patient and at least one family member learning DBT skills. In addition, within standard DBT for adults, family members are encouraged to periodically attend individual therapy sessions (no more than one per month) to enhance alignment in skills training between the patient and family members.

DBT, SFT, and cognitive therapy share similar theoretical models, but are distinct in their approach and emphasis. Because all three branded treatments are within the family of CBTs, they are all founded on the premise that individuals develop certain patterns of thoughts, behaviors, and emotions in early life environments, but that such learned patterns are not effective within their current environments. Because thoughts, behaviors, and emotions are interrelated and can influence each other, CBTs aim to modify one of these three phenomena to change problematic patterns of behavior. SFT is the most similar to the traditional cognitive therapy model, except it arguably places more emphasis on experiential exercises, the therapeutic relationship, and the role of childhood experiences. Perhaps more importantly, the SFT model includes specific types of schemas, modes, and coping styles that can manifest transdiagnostically across personality disorders and other more episodic disorders. Both cognitive therapy and SFT involve monitoring and challenging core schemas and their associated problematic behaviors. In both therapies, exercises that trigger strong emotional reactions are indicative that patients have accessed and may be able to use learned skills to modify core schemas. Additionally, the overarching goal of both treatments is to reduce how often dysfunctional schemas are triggered and to increase newer and more adaptive responses when such schemas are elicited.

DBT deviates most from the other two branded cognitive behavioral treatment protocols. Indeed, DBT was developed, in part, in response to gaps in traditional cognitive therapy, such as the prioritized emphasis on changing behavior and ways of thinking in the absence of guidelines for validation and acceptance of patients (Linehan, 1993). Because patients may respond aversively to the common cognitive therapy technique of challenging the truth of automatic thoughts, assumptions, or underlying schemas, DBT places more emphasis on the balance of acceptance and change. Change strategies in DBT include cognitive modification techniques directly adapted from Beck's cognitive therapy, but are used alongside mindfulness and acceptance strategies to help patients learn a broad repertoire of skills to respond to unpleasant thoughts and emotions.

Notably, all three branded CBTs for personality disorders have the strongest empirical support for BPD. Of these treatments, DBT is the only one specifically developed for BPD. Importantly, there is a distinct lack of CBTs developed for other personality disorders, such as paranoid, antisocial, obsessive-compulsive, and narcissistic personality disorders (Trull et al., 2010). Considering this gap in the field, clinicians treating symptoms of other personality disorders can draw upon the principles of change within the family of CBTs to target cognitive, behavioral, or affective processes underlying these symptoms.

WITHOUT A BRANDED EMPIRICALLY SUPPORTED PROTOCOL: PRINCIPLES OF CHANGE FROM CBTs

There are few evidence-based treatments with strong empirical support for personality disorders, even fewer that are cognitive behavioral, and, among the CBTs, fewer still that have not been evaluated only or primarily for patients with BPD. Without a branded and well-researched CBT intervention, clinicians who wish to use a cognitive behavioral approach need to flexibly tailor treatments using strategies, processes, and principles of change from empirically supported CBTs. This work includes an assessment of ways in which one's learning history may have contributed to the development and maintenance of the presenting problems. It also includes functional analysis as a primary tool to understand and gain insight into the context and function of primary problem behaviors and ongoing life stressors. As with the CBTs previously reviewed, a general approach also would include the collaborative and iterative development of a case conceptualization that includes mutually agreed upon cognitive and behavioral targets for change. However, which interventions should be used, for whom, and in what sequence?

We suggest that interventions selected are extensions of the case conceptualization, tailored to the individual patient, and drawn from the literature on CBTs for other disorders and problem behaviors. Approaches used across behavior therapies and cognitive therapies, for example, should be considered. We have already reviewed cognitive modification and skills training approaches used in CBTs for personality disorders. Standard behavior therapy approaches used across treatments for a range of disorders, such as stimulus control procedures, shaping, and contingency management, also can be considered for use when appropriate in the management of personality disorders. Exposure-based procedures are another example of interventions that can be considered when treating patients with personality disorders.

Exposure-Based Procedures

Exposure is a well-established therapeutic strategy used to promote new learning in response to emotionally evocative stimuli, including long-term reductions in emotional arousal and avoidance behaviors (e.g., Bouton, 1988; Craske et al., 2008). Traditional exposure models, long-established for treating anxiety and associated disorders (e.g., Malleson, 1959; Watson & Marks, 1971), involve repeated and/or prolonged presentation of feared or aversive stimuli and representations of those stimuli that evoke emotional reactivity and expression, while blocking fear-based behavioral urges of avoidance and escape. These strategies are used with the goal of reducing anxiety intensity and avoidance behaviors over time in contexts with the evocative stimuli, and have been implemented using a variety of modalities to contact the feared stimuli, including imaginal, *in vivo* (real-life), narrative, interoceptive, and virtual reality (e.g., Craske, Rowe, Lewin, & Noriega-Dimitri, 1997; Foa, Steketee, Turner, & Fischer, 1980; Reger et al., 2016). Evidence for these approaches in the treatment of anxiety and posttraumatic stress disorder is robust for exposure-focused treatments, as well as multi-component cognitive behavioral treatments that emphasize exposure (e.g., Abramowitz, 1996; Barlow, Craske, Cerny & Klosko, 1989; Choy, Fyer, & Lipsitz, 2007).

Evidence examining application of traditional exposure approaches in personality disorder specific samples is limited, with some studies examining outcomes for obsessive compulsive personality disorder (OCPD), APD, and BPD. For example, Sadri and colleagues (2017) examined the application of exposure and response prevention in a sample with co-occurring OCPD and obsessive compulsive disorder (OCD), finding noted improvements in OCD symptoms post-treatment (Sadri et al., 2017). Although this result is promising, other studies have found that OCPD severity and presence can impede efficacy of exposure for OCD symptoms, with perfectionism significantly contributing to less improvement (Pinto, Liebowitz, Foa, & Simpson, 2011). These findings may suggest that perfectionism as a class of behaviors may be particularly important to target in this population with exposure or other interventions, with some studies suggesting that exposure-based treatment effectively reduces perfectionism in socially anxious individuals (Ashbaugh et al., 2007). For example, non-reinforced exposure to imperfection in a patient with OCPD related to impression management could include crafting an email that is imperfect (e.g., misspelled words, communication of objectives without much clarity, leaving off an important recipient). The CBT therapist would help the patient by blocking urges to fix the errors or imperfections, encouraging the patient to allow the imperfect email to be sent without correcting the imperfections. Similarly, in this example, the therapist could encourage the patient to communicate via email or in other ways with spontaneity, and without effortful and distressing scrutiny. Having been exposed to such imperfect communication multiple times without adverse outcomes, the distress associated with such impression management would be expected to decrease and give rise to an increasingly diverse and flexible behavioral repertoire.

For APD, several researchers have observed the overlap in symptomology and presentation between social anxiety disorder (social phobia) and APD (e.g., Carter & Wu, 2010; Lampe & Sunderland, 2015; Tillfors, Furmark, Ekselius, & Fredrikson, 2004; Turner, Beidel, & Townsley, 1992). There has been debate about the utility of the distinction between these disorders (e.g., Lampe & Sunderland, 2015), considering the high rates of generalized social anxiety disorder reported amongst individuals with APD (36–100 percent; Cox, Pagura, Stein, & Sareen, 2009; Herbert, Hope & Bellack, 1992) and other studies reporting non-significant differences in amounts of APD in generalized social phobia as compared to non-generalized social phobia (Dyck et al., 2001). Despite data pointing to differences between social phobia and APD, including greater functional impairment (Huppert, Strunk, Ledley, Davidson, & Foa, 2008; Marques et al. 2012), depression symptoms (Huppert et al., 2008), social fear, and avoidance (Kose et al., 2009) for individuals with generalized social phobia with (vs. without) APD, and greater similarities between generalized social phobia and APD than specific social phobia (Carter & Wu, 2010), many researchers have contended that there is no significant difference (e.g., Hope, Herbert, & White, 1995; Widiger, 1992).

Among the studies of exposure-based treatment for social anxiety disorder, only a few have explicitly included APD. Among these studies, Hope and colleagues (1995) and Brown, Heimberg, and Juster (1995) included APD in their sample of social phobia and examined cognitive behavioral group therapy (a multi-component treatment with emphasis on exposure) for social phobia (Heimberg, 1991). Both studies concluded that APD was not a predictor of treatment outcome. Brown et al. (1995) observed that the number of individuals meeting criteria for APD significantly decreased from pre- to post-treatment. Hope et al. (1995) found that individuals with APD did not benefit differently than individuals without APD on self-report measures of social anxiety and improvement ratings, though socially phobic APD individuals reported higher distress during a behavioral approach task than subjects with social phobia without APD. Huppert et al. (2008) found that APD influenced the rate of change, wherein individuals with APD (randomly assigned to a multi-component group CBT using exposure-based procedures, medication alone, combined treatment, or placebo) responded more quickly early in treatment than socially anxious subjects without APD. Using a more exposure-focused group treatment, Feske, Perry, Chambless, Renneberg, and Goldstein (1996) found that individuals with APD improved significantly over treatment, though demonstrated less improvement than non-APD subjects at post-treatment and follow-up time points.

Taken together, the evidence across these studies suggests that exposure-based procedures are reasonable candidate interventions to consider when using a non-manualized CBT-based protocol for the treatment of APD. For example, non-reinforced exposure to contexts and stimuli associated with imperfection may be considered for individuals with OCPD. Exposure to cues associated with social anxiety and avoidance of interpersonal contexts may be helpful for patients with APD. Such approaches can be informed by the previously identified evidence-based treatment protocols for social anxiety disorder. For patients with dependent personality disorder, exposure-based procedures can be considered as one way to help patients learn to tolerate the anxiety associated with behaving with more autonomy and less dependency. In such a case, a hierarchy of fearful situations associated with increasing anxiety and dependency can be collaboratively generated, with the patient being exposed imaginally and in vivo to gradually more anxiety-evocative contexts and cues. Indeed, across Cluster C personality disorder diagnoses, exposure-based approaches may help reduce anxious distress and avoidance, creating opportunities for new learning to occur, and, over time, for more flexible and context sensitive responses to life stressors.

Beyond applications of exposure to anxiety, treatment developers in the 1990s began applying exposure-based procedures to other emotions. Some researchers emphasized three components of exposure therapies: cue exposure, response prevention, and acting opposite to emotion-based urges (e.g., Barlow, Allen & Choate, 2016; Linehan, 1993, 2014; McMain, Korman, & Dimeff, 2001), whereas others have emphasized decreasing experiential avoidance across emotions (e.g., Hayes et al., 1999, 2012) or behavioral inhibition of problematic emotion-based urges (response prevention) and activation of alternative skillful behaviors (acting opposite; approach behavior) with somewhat less emphasis on subjectively experiencing the distressing affective state (Lejuez, Hopko, Acierno, Daughters, & Pagoto, 2011).

With the exception of DBT, these approaches have not been directly examined in personality disorders. However, exposure-based interventions have been applied to the emotions of shame, anger, disgust, and depression in a number of research studies. Directly germane to personality disorders, Rizvi and Linehan (2005) used an opposite action intervention (Linehan, 2014) over the course of eight to ten sessions, alongside DBT skills group, to target the reduction of shame in a sample of individuals with BPD. In this study, opposite action included cue exposure (i.e., presenting the trait or behavior about which the individual feels ashamed), blocking shame-based action tendencies (e.g., sustained eye contact, representing or maintaining exposure to shame cues despite urges to avoid or escape from them), and engaging in behaviors (including changing body posture, facial expression) opposite to the shame-based action tendencies. Importantly, these procedures were only used when shame was not justified, as defined by behavior that did not violate the participant's values and would not result in rejection by others if known. Rizvi and Linehan observed significant decreases in self-reported shame from pre- to post-treatment, with reductions specifically in event-specific shame. Given that shame has been found to predict self-injurious behaviors in BPD (Brown, Linehan, Comtois, Murray, & Chapman, 2009), application of exposure in this manner may be especially important in the treatment of BPD.

Studies also have investigated the effects of exposure on disgust in psychiatric samples characterized by difficulties with disgust. In one study, individuals with body dysmorphic disorder who engaged in mirror exposures viewing themselves demonstrated significant reductions in disgust (Nezirolgu, Hickey, & McKay, 2010). In another study examining disgust in contamination-based OCD, researchers found significant decreases in disgust after exposure to disgust-inducing stimuli (Broderick, Grisham, & Weidemann, 2013). Similarly, another study observed marked reductions in disgust during intensive exposure-based treatment for OCD (Athey et al., 2015). These findings may be particularly applicable to OCPD, given the overlap in symptoms between OCD and OCPD (Garyfallos et al., 2010), and in BPD, in light of findings indicating that high pathogen disgust has been associated with more BPD features (Standish, Benfield, Bernstein, & Tragesser, 2014).

Exposure-based procedures as applied to problems related to anger also have begun to be investigated. Because high levels of trait anger in BPD and ASPD predict physical aggression (Kolla, Meyer, Bagby, & Brijmohan, 2017), cognitive behavioral therapies for these personality disorders may benefit by using exposure-based interventions to reduce anger. Some studies have used exposure techniques as part of other more primary interventions (e.g., self-statements; Tafrate & Kassinove, 1998) or as a brief mood induction (Lobbestael, Arntz, Cima, & Chakhssi, 2009). The use of exposure-based procedures for problems with the regulation of anger may be germane to the treatment of anger in BPD and antisocial personality disorder, both of which are associated with similar anger

problems (e.g., Bateman, O'Connell, Lorenzini, Gardner, & Fonagy, 2016). Others, such as Grodnitzky and Tafrate (2000), applied a group-based imaginal exposure intervention in a sample of individuals with anger problems and observed significant reductions on several anger measures. It is important to note that there is no rationale for using exposure-based interventions as a single method for the treatment of anger across personality disorders. Nonetheless, exposure procedures can be considered when using a cognitive behavioral case conceptualization-based approach to treat a patient with personality disorder symptoms that include anger regulation problems.

The impact of exposure-based interventions on a range of affective states beyond anger has also been examined in the context of the treatment of posttraumatic stress disorder (PTSD). For example, in a sample of individuals with BPD and PTSD, researchers found that over the course of prolonged exposure treatment, participants reported significant reductions in emotions beyond fear/anxiety, including general distress, guilt, shame, and disgust (Harned, Ruork, Liu, & Tkachuck, 2015). Further, in a sample of individuals with PTSD, Langkaas and colleagues observed decreases in internalized anger, hostility, guilt, and trauma-related shame following exposure-based trauma treatment (Langkaas et al., 2017). These findings lend further support to the hypothesis that exposure-based procedures may have beneficial impacts across emotions, and thus may be helpful in treating problem behaviors occurring in response to emotional distress across personality disorders.

Lastly, indirect support for the use of exposure-based procedures can be derived from studies that have explored attempts to control unwanted private experiences in personality disorders. Many studies have investigated avoidance, emotional suppression, and emotional inhibition in personality disorders (Bijttebier & Vertommen, 1999; Cheavens et al., 2005; Kruedelbach, McCormick, Schulz, & Grueneich, 1993; Lynch, Robins, Morse, & Krause, 2001; Rosenthal, Cheavens, Lejuez, & Lynch, 2005). Bijttebier and Vertommen (1999) observed use of avoidant coping strategies among psychiatric inpatients with diagnoses of paranoid, schizoid, schizotypal, borderline, and avoidant personality disorders. Further, experiential avoidance specifically has been associated with a range of personality disorders, including borderline (Chapman, Specht, & Cellucci, 2005), avoidant, dependent (Spinhoven, Bamelis, Molendijk, Haringsma, & Arntz, 2009), and obsessive-compulsive (Spinhoven et al., 2009; Wheaton & Pinto, 2017) personality disorders. Although we are not aware of any studies that have examined experiential avoidance in paranoid, schizoid, or schizotypal personality disorders, a greater tendency to avoid unwanted and unpleasant private experiences has been associated with higher frequency of paranoid ideation amongst individuals with psychotic disorders (Castilho et al., 2017). Given that one of the primary aims of exposure is to reduce avoidance behaviors, findings related to the role of experiential avoidance in personality disorders underscore the importance of considering exposure-based approaches when treating these patients.

THIRD WAVE BEHAVIOR THERAPIES FOR PERSONALITY DISORDERS: BEYOND DBT

Although not developed and tested for personality disorders specifically, acceptance and commitment therapy (ACT; Hayes et al., 1999, 2012), mindfulness based cognitive therapy (MBCT; Segal, Williams & Teasdale, 2013), and functional analytic psychotherapy (FAP; Kohlenberg & Tsai, 1991) are third wave cognitive behavioral therapies that may be considered when treating patients with personality disorders.

ACT is designed to increase patients' psychological flexibility and present-moment focus to facilitate adaptive behaviors in line with patients' long-term values. This treatment uses several principles of change in service of these goals, including exposure and mindfulness to target experiential avoidance (Hayes et al., 1999, 2012). A few recent studies have explored the use of group ACT interventions with personality disorders (Clarke, Kingston, James, Bolderston, & Remington, 2014; Morton, Snowdon, Gopold, & Guymer, 2012). One study found that the addition of an ACT intervention to TAU led to significant improvements in BPD symptoms compared to treatment as usual (Morton et al., 2012). Although no published studies have demonstrated its efficacy with other personality disorders, providers may draw upon ACT interventions to treat problems with experiential avoidance and cognitive rigidity in patients with personality disorders.

Similar to ACT, MBCT targets experiential avoidance through present-moment awareness and acceptance. As MBCT was originally developed as a group treatment for major depression, it combines traditional cognitive therapy techniques with mindfulness skills to help patients bring awareness to negative thought patterns and develop adaptive coping strategies in response to them. The benefits of mindfulness include changes in attentional control (Bishop et al., 2004) and reduced experiential avoidance (Hayes et al., 1999, 2012), which may effectively treat problematic cognition and behavior in personality disorders. One quasi-experimental study found an eight-week MBCT program adapted for BPD led to increases in attentional control and mindfulness (Sachse, Keville, & Feigenbaum, 2011). Another study found that a mindfulness intervention reduced anxiety and negative affect among participants with high trait interpersonal dependency (McClintock & Anderson, 2013), pointing to the hypothesis that such techniques may be beneficial in patients with dependent personality disorder. As previously detailed, DBT is a well-established mindfulness-based psychotherapy for BPD. However, clinicians wishing to use a contemporary CBT approach in the absence of a specific branded treatment protocol for personality disorders can consider using mindfulness exercises from ACT or MBCT as part of the treatment plan.

FAP may also be useful for treating personality disorders, as it was originally developed as a behavioral treatment for patients with interpersonal difficulties. FAP aims to target and change problematic interpersonal behaviors within the therapeutic relationship by reinforcing adaptive in-session behaviors (Tsai, Yard, & Kohlenberg, 2014; Tsai et al. 2009). Only one single-case study has evaluated the efficacy of FAP for personality disorders, finding that narcissistic and histrionic behaviors decreased over a brief course of FAP (Callaghan, Summers & Weidman, 2003). The findings from this study suggest that these decreases could be attributed to the therapist responding contingently to patient problem behaviors and improvements. Therefore, narcissistic and histrionic behaviors may be able to be targeted and changed using contingency management and other basic principles of behavior change. Although considerably more empirical research is needed to determine the efficacy of FAP for the treatment of personality disorders, we suggest that a case conceptualization-based intervention for personality disorders include the use of therapist contingency management of relevant interpersonal behaviors. This includes, for example, explicit orientation to and implementation of contingency management and behavior change strategies in response to real-time clinically relevant behaviors during therapy sessions.

SUMMARY

In this chapter, we have focused on the use of branded CBT protocols and interventions drawn from the family of contemporary CBTs that can be used in the treatment of patients with personality disorders. Most empirical research investigating CBTs for personality disorders have been evaluated for use with BPD. These include DBT, SFT, and cognitive therapy. Only DBT was developed specifically for BPD, and, to date (based on the available treatment outcome research), DBT remains the gold standard approach for the outpatient treatment of BPD. Because far less treatment research has been done outside of BPD, clinicians using cognitive behavioral approaches in the treatment of personality disorders are encouraged to collaboratively build a CBT-based case conceptualization and treatment plan with patients. This would include the use of similar strategies, techniques, and procedures used in other CBTs, tailored to the individual and to the specific psychological processes being targeted. In this way, and in the absence of manualized and well-established protocols for all personality disorders, patients can receive treatment from CBT therapists that is coherently organized (i.e., not eclectic), grounded in empirically supported methods of behavior change (e.g., functional analysis, contingency management, stimulus control, shaping, skill training, cognitive modification, exposure-based procedures, mindfulness and acceptance-based procedures), and flexibly tailored to the individual needs of each patient.

REFERENCES

Abramowitz, J. S. (1996). Variants of exposure and response prevention in the treatment of obsessive-compulsive disorder: A meta-analysis. *Behavior Therapy*, 27(4), 583–600.

Alden, L. (1989). Short-term structured treatment for avoidant personality disorder. *Journal of Consulting and Clinical Psychology*, 57(6), 756–764.

Alden, L. E., & Capreol, M. J. (1993). Avoidant personality disorder: Interpersonal problems as predictors of treatment response. *Behavior Therapy*, 24(3), 357–376.

Andreasson, K., Krogh, J., Wenneberg, C., Jessen, H. K., Krakauer, K., Gluud, C., ... Nordentoft, M. (2016). Effectiveness of dialectical behavior therapy versus collaborative assessment and management of suicidality treatment for reduction of self-harm in adults with borderline personality traits and disorder: A randomized observer-blinded clinical trial. *Depression and Anxiety*, 33(6), 520–530.

Ashbaugh, A., Antony, M. M., Liss, A., Summerfeldt, L. J., McCabe, R. E., & Swinson, R. P. (2007). Changes in perfectionism following cognitive-behavioral treatment for social phobia. *Depression and Anxiety*, 24(3), 169–177.

Athey, A. J., Elias, J. A., Crosby, J. M., Jenike, M. A., Pope, H. G., Hudson, J. I., & Brennan, B. P. (2015). Reduced disgust propensity is associated with improvement in contamination/washing symptoms in obsessive-compulsive disorder. *Journal of Obsessive-Compulsive and Related Disorders*, 4, 20–24.

Bamelis, L. L., Evers, S. M., Spinhoven, P., & Arntz, A. (2014). Results of a multicenter randomized controlled trial of the clinical effectiveness of schema therapy for personality disorders. *American Journal of Psychiatry*, 171(3), 305–322.

Barlow, D. H., Allen, L. B., & Choate, M. L. (2016). Toward a unified treatment for emotional disorders. *Behavior Therapy*, 47(6), 838–853.

Barlow, D. H., Craske, M. G., Cerny, J. A., & Klosko, J. S. (1989). Behavioral treatment of panic disorder. *Behavior Therapy*, 20(2), 261–282.

Bateman, A., O'Connell, J., Lorenzini, N., Gardner, T., & Fonagy, P. (2016). A randomized controlled trial of mentalization-based treatment versus structured clinical management for patients with comorbid borderline personality disorder and antisocial personality disorder. *BMC Psychiatry*, 16, 304.

Beck, A. T. (1991). Cognitive therapy: A 30-year retrospective. *American Psychologist*, 46(4), 368–375.

Beck, A. T., Davis, D. D., & Freeman, A. (Eds.) (2015). *Cognitive Therapy of Personality Disorders*. New York: Guilford Press.

Bender, D. S., Dolan, R. T., Skodol, A. E., Sanislow, C. A., Dyck, I. R., McGlashan, T. H., ... Gunderson, J. G. (2001). Treatment utilization by patients with personality disorders. *American Journal of Psychiatry*, 158(2), 295–302.

Bijttebier, P., & Vertommen, H. (1999). Coping strategies in relation to personality disorders. *Personality and Individual Differences*, 26, 847–856.

Bishop, S. R., Lau, M., Shapiro, S. L., Carlson, L., Anderson, N. D., & Carmody, J. (2004). Mindfulness: A proposed operational definition. *Clinical Psychology: Science and Practice*, 11, 230–241.

Black, D. W., Blum, N., Eichinger, L., McCormick, B., Allen, J., & Sieleni, B. (2008). STEPPS: Systems Training for Emotional Predictability and Problem Solving in women offenders with borderline personality disorder in prison: A pilot study. *CNS Spectrums*, 13(10), 881–886.

Black, D. W., Simsek-Duran, F., Blum, N., McCormick, B., & Allen, J. (2016). Do people with borderline personality disorder complicated by antisocial personality disorder benefit from the STEPPS treatment program? *Personality and Mental Health*, 10(3), 205–215.

Blum, N., St. John, D., Pfohl, B., Stuart, S., McCormick, B., Allen, J., ... Black, D. W. (2008). Systems Training for Emotional Predictability and Problem Solving (STEPPS) for outpatients with borderline personality disorder: A randomized controlled trial and 1-year follow-up. *American Journal of Psychiatry*, 165(4), 468–478.

Bouton, M. E. (1988). Context and ambiguity in the extinction of emotional learning: Implications for exposure therapy. *Behaviour Research and Therapy*, 26(2), 137–149.

Broderick, J., Grisham, J. R., & Weidemann, G. (2013). Disgust and fear responding in contamination-based obsessive-compulsive disorder during pictorial exposure. *Behavior Therapy*, 44(1), 27–38.

Brown, E. J., Heimberg, R. G., & Juster, H. R. (1995). Social phobia subtype and avoidant personality disorder: Effect on severity of social phobia, impairment, and outcome of cognitive behavioral treatment. *Behavior Therapy*, 26(3), 467–486.

Brown, G. K., Newman, C. F., Charlesworth, S. E., Crits-Christoph, P., & Beck, A. T. (2004). An open clinical trial of cognitive therapy for borderline personality disorder. *Journal of Personality Disorders*, 18(3), 257–271.

Brown, M. Z., Linehan, M. M., Comtois, K. A., Murray, A., & Chapman, A. L. (2009). Shame as a prospective predictor of self-inflicted injury in borderline personality disorder: A multimodal analysis. *Behaviour Research and Therapy*, 47(10), 815–822.

Callaghan, G. M., Summers, C. J., & Weidman, M. (2003). The treatment of histrionic and narcissistic personality disorder behaviors: A single-subject demonstration of clinical improvement using functional analytic psychotherapy. *Journal of Contemporary Psychotherapy*, 33(4), 321–339.

Carter, G. L., Willcox, C. H., Lewin, T. J., Conrad, A. M., & Bendit, N. (2010). Hunter DBT project: Randomized controlled trial of dialectical behaviour therapy in women with borderline personality disorder. *Australian & New Zealand Journal of Psychiatry*, 44(2), 162–173.

Carter, S. A., & Wu, K. D. (2010). Symptoms of specific and generalized social phobia: An examination of discriminant validity and structural relations with mood and anxiety symptoms. *Behavior Therapy*, 41(2), 254–265.

Castilho, P., Martins, M. J., Pinto, A. M., Viegas, R., Carvalho, S., & Madeira, N. (2017). Understanding the effect of attachment styles in paranoid ideation: The mediator role of experiential avoidance. *Journal of Contextual Behavioral Science*, 6(1), 42–46.

Chambless, D. L., Baker, M. J., Baucom, D. H., Beutler, L. E., Calhoun, K. S., Crits-Christoph, P., ... Johnson, S. B. (1998). Update on empirically validated therapies, II. *The Clinical Psychologist*, 51(1), 3–16.

Chapman, A. L., Specht, M. W., & Cellucci, T. (2005). Borderline personality disorder and deliberate self-harm: Does experiential avoidance play a role? *Suicide and Life-Threatening Behavior*, 35(4), 388–399.

Cheavens, J. S., Rosenthal, M. Z., Daughters, S. D., Novak, J., Kossen, D., Lynch, T. R., & Lejuez, C. W. (2005). An analog investigation of the relationships among perceived parental criticism, negative affect, and borderline personality disorder features: The role of thought suppression. *Behavior Research and Therapy, 43*, 257–268.

Choy, Y., Fyer, A. J., & Lipsitz, J. D. (2007). Treatment of specific phobia in adults. *Clinical Psychology Review, 27*, 266–286.

Clarke, S., Kingston, J., James, K., Bolderston, H., & Remington, B. (2014). Acceptance and commitment therapy group for treatment-resistant participants: A randomized controlled trial. *Journal of Contextual Behavioral Science, 3*(3), 179–188.

Clarkin, J. F., Levy, K. N., Lenzenweger, M. F., & Kernberg, O. F. (2007). Evaluating three treatments for borderline personality disorder: A multiwave study. *American Journal of Psychiatry, 164*(6), 922–928.

Cottraux, J., Note, I. D., Boutitie, F., Milliery, M., Genouihlac, V., Yao, S. N., ... Djamoussian, D. (2009). Cognitive therapy versus Rogerian supportive therapy in borderline personality disorder. *Psychotherapy and Psychosomatics, 78*(5), 307–316.

Cox, B. J., Pagura, J., Stein, M. B., & Sareen, J. (2009). The relationship between generalized social phobia and avoidant personality disorder in a national mental health survey. *Depression and Anxiety, 26*(4), 354–362.

Craske, M. G., Kircanski, K., Zelikowsky, M., Mystkowski, J., Chowdhury, N., & Baker, A. (2008). Optimizing inhibitory learning during exposure therapy. *Behaviour Research and Therapy, 46*(1), 5–27.

Craske, M. G., Rowe, M., Lewin, M., & Noriega-Dimitri, R. (1997). Interoceptive exposure versus breathing retraining within cognitive-behavioural therapy for panic disorder with agoraphobia. *British Journal of Clinical Psychology, 36*(1), 85–99.

Cristea, I. A., Gentili, C., Cotet, C. D., Palomba, D., Barbui, C., & Cuijpers, P. (2017). Efficacy of psychotherapies for borderline personality disorder: A systematic review and meta-analysis. *JAMA Psychiatry, 74*(4), 319–328.

Crowell, S. E., Beauchaine, T. P., & Linehan, M. M. (2009). A biosocial developmental model of borderline personality: Elaborating and extending Linehan's theory. *Psychological Bulletin, 135*(3), 495–510.

Davidson, K., Norrie, J., Tyrer, P., Gumley, A., Tata, P., Murray, H., & Palmer, S. (2006). The effectiveness of cognitive behavior therapy for borderline personality disorder: Results from the borderline personality disorder study of cognitive therapy (BOSCOT) trial. *Journal of Personality Disorders, 20*(5), 450–465.

Davidson, K. M., Tyrer, P., Norrie, J., Palmer, S. J., & Tyrer, H. (2010). Cognitive therapy v. usual treatment for borderline personality disorder: Prospective 6-year follow-up. *British Journal of Psychiatry, 197*(6), 456–462.

Domes, G., Schulze, L., & Herpertz, S. C. (2009). Emotion recognition in borderline personality disorder: A review of the literature. *Journal of Personality Disorders, 23*(1), 6–19.

Dyck, I. R., Phillips, K. A., Warshaw, M. G., Dolan, R. T., Shea, M. T., Stout, R. L., ... Keller, M. B. (2001). Patterns of personality pathology in patients with generalized anxiety disorder, panic disorder with and without agoraphobia, and social phobia. *Journal of Personality Disorders, 15*(1), 60–71.

Emmelkamp, P. M., Benner, A., Kuipers, A., Feiertag, G. A., Koster, H. C., & van Apeldoorn, F. J. (2006). Comparison of brief dynamic and cognitive–behavioural therapies in avoidant personality disorder. *British Journal of Psychiatry, 189*(1), 60–64.

Farrell, J. M., Shaw, I. A., & Webber, M. A. (2009). A schema-focused approach to group psychotherapy for outpatients with borderline personality disorder: A randomized controlled trial. *Journal of Behavior Therapy and Experimental Psychiatry, 40*(2), 317–328.

Feigenbaum, J. D., Fonagy, P., Pilling, S., Jones, A., Wildgoose, A., & Bebbington, P. E. (2012). A real-world study of the effectiveness of DBT in the UK National Health Service. *British Journal of Clinical Psychology, 51*(2), 121–141.

Feske, U., Perry, K. J., Chambless, D. L., Renneberg, B., & Goldstein, A. J. (1996). Avoidant personality disorder as a predictor for treatment outcome among generalized social phobics. *Journal of Personality Disorders, 10*(2), 174–184.

Foa, E. B., Steketee, G., Turner, R. M., & Fischer, S. C. (1980). Effects of imaginal exposure to feared disasters in obsessive-compulsive checkers. *Behaviour Research and Therapy, 18*(5), 449–455.

Garyfallos, G., Katsigiannopoulos, K., Adamopoulou, A., Papazisis, G., Karastergiou, A., & Bozikas, V. P. (2010). Comorbidity of obsessive-compulsive disorder with obsessive-compulsive personality disorder: Does it imply a specific subtype of obsessive-compulsive disorder? *Psychiatry Research, 177*(1), 156–160.

Giesen-Bloo, J., Van Dyck, R., Spinhoven, P., Van Tilburg, W., Dirksen, C., Van Asselt, T., ... Arntz, A. (2006). Outpatient psychotherapy for borderline personality disorder: Randomized trial of schema-focused therapy vs Transference-Focused Psychotherapy. *Archives of General Psychiatry, 63*(6), 649–658.

Goldstein, T. R., Fersch-Podrat, R. K., Rivera, M., Axelson, D. A., Merranko, J., Yu, H., ... Birmaher, B. (2015). Dialectical behavior therapy for adolescents with bipolar disorder: Results from a pilot randomized trial. *Journal of Child and Adolescent Psychopharmacology, 25*(2), 140–149.

Grant, B. F., Hasin, D. S., Stinson, F. S., Dawson, D. A., Chou, S. P., Ruan, W. J., & Huang, B. (2005). Co-occurrence of 12-month mood and anxiety disorders and personality disorders in the US: Results from the National Epidemiologic Survey on Alcohol and Related Conditions. *Journal of Psychiatric Research, 39*(1), 1–9.

Gratz, K. L., & Gunderson, J. G. (2006). Preliminary data on an acceptance-based emotion regulation group intervention for deliberate self-harm among women with borderline personality disorder. *Behavior Therapy, 37*(1), 25–35.

Gratz, K. L., Tull, M. T., & Levy, R. (2014). Randomized controlled trial and uncontrolled 9-month follow-up of an adjunctive emotion regulation group therapy for deliberate self-harm among women with borderline personality disorder. *Psychological Medicine, 44*(10), 2099–2112.

Greenberg, L. S. (2015). *Emotion-Focused Therapy: Coaching Clients to Work through Their Feelings* (2nd ed.). Washington, DC: American Psychological Association.

Grodnitzky, G. R., & Tafrate, R. C. (2000). Imaginal exposure for anger reduction in adult outpatients: A pilot study. *Journal of Behavior Therapy and Experimental Psychiatry, 31*(3–4), 259–279.

Harned, M. S., Ruork, A. K., Liu, J., & Tkachuck, M. A. (2015). Emotional activation and habituation during imaginal exposure for PTSD among women with borderline personality disorder. *Journal of Traumatic Stress, 28*(3), 253–257.

Hawton, K., Witt, K. G., Salisbury, T. L. T., Arensman, E., Gunnell, D., Hazell, P., ... van Heeringen, K. (2016). Psychosocial interventions following self-harm in adults: A systematic review and meta-analysis. *Lancet Psychiatry, 3*(8), 740–750.

Hayes, S. C., Strosahl, K. D., & Wilson, K. G. (1999). *Acceptance and Commitment Therapy: An Experiential Approach to Behavior Change.* New York: Guilford Press.

Hayes, S. C., Strosahl, K. D., & Wilson, K. G. (2012). *Acceptance and Commitment Therapy: The Process and Practice of Mindful Change* (2nd ed.). New York: Guilford Press.

Heimberg, R. G. (1991). *A Manual for Conducting Cognitive-Behavioral Group Therapy for Social Phobia* (2nd ed.). Unpublished manuscript available from the Center for Stress and Anxiety Disorders, Pine West Plaza, Bldg. 4, Washington Avenue Extension, Albany, NY 12205.

Herbert, J. D., Hope, D. A., & Bellack, A. S. (1992). Validity of the distinction between generalized social phobia and avoidant personality disorder. *Journal of Abnormal Psychology, 101*(2), 332–339.

Hoffart, A., Versland, S., & Sexton, H. (2002). Self-understanding, empathy, guided discovery, and schema belief in schema-focused cognitive therapy of personality problems: A process–outcome study. *Cognitive Therapy and Research, 26* (2), 199–219.

Hope, D. A., Herbert, J. D., & White, C. (1995). Diagnostic subtype, avoidant personality disorder, and efficacy of cognitive-behavioral group therapy for social phobia. *Cognitive Therapy and Research, 19*(4), 399–417.

Huppert, J. D., Strunk, D. R., Ledley, D. R., Davidson, J. R., & Foa, E. B. (2008). Generalized social anxiety disorder and avoidant personality disorder: Structural analysis and treatment outcome. *Depression and Anxiety, 25*(5), 441–448.

Kaiser, D., Jacob, G. A., Domes, G., & Arntz, A. (2017). Attentional bias for emotional stimuli in borderline personality disorder: A meta-analysis. *Psychopathology, 49*(6), 383–396.

Kliem, S., Kröger, C., & Kosfelder, J. (2010). Dialectical behavior therapy for borderline personality disorder: A meta-analysis using mixed-effects modeling. *Journal of Consulting and Clinical Psychology, 78*(6), 936–951.

Kohlenberg, R. J., & Tsai, M. (1991). *Functional Analytic Psychotherapy: Creating Intense and Curative Therapeutic Relationships.* New York: Plenum Press.

Kolla, N. J., Meyer, J. H., Bagby, R. M., & Brijmohan, A. (2017). Trait anger, physical aggression, and violent offending in antisocial and borderline personality disorders. *Journal of Forensic Sciences, 62*(1), 137–141.

Koons, C. R., Robins, C. J., Tweed, J. L., Lynch, T. R., Gonzalez, A. M., Morse, J. Q., ... Bastian, L. A. (2001). Efficacy of dialectical behavior therapy in women veterans with borderline personality disorder. *Behavior Therapy, 32*(2), 371–390.

Kose, S., Solmaz, M., Celikel, F. C., Citak, S., Ozturk, M., Tosun, M., ... Sayar, K. (2009). Comorbidity of avoidant personality disorder in generalized social phobia and its impact on psychopathology. *Klinik Psikofarmakoloji Bülteni, 19*, 340–346.

Kruedelbach, N., McCormick, R. A., Schulz, S. C., & Grueneich, R. (1993). Impulsivity, coping styles, and triggers for craving in substance abusers with borderline personality disorders. *Journal of Personality Disorders, 7*, 214–222.

Lampe, L., & Sunderland, M. (2015). Social phobia and avoidant personality disorder: Similar but different? *Journal of Personality Disorders, 29*(1), 115–130.

Langkaas, T. F., Hoffart, A., Øktedalen, T., Ulvenes, P. G., Hembree, E. A., & Smucker, M. (2017). Exposure and non-fear emotions: A randomized controlled study of exposure-based and rescripting-based imagery in PTSD treatment. *Behaviour Research and Therapy, 97*, 33–42.

Lejuez, C. W., Hopko, D. R., Acierno, R., Daughters, S. B., & Pagoto, S. L. (2011). Ten year revision of the brief behavioral activation treatment for depression: Revised treatment manual. *Behavior Modification, 35*(2), 111–161.

Linehan, M. M. (1993). *Cognitive-Behavioral Treatment of Borderline Personality Disorder.* New York: Guilford Press.

Linehan, M. M. (2014). *DBT Skills Training Manual* (2nd ed.). New York: Guilford Press.

Linehan, M. M., Armstrong, H. E., Suarez, A., Allmon, D., & Heard, H. L. (1991). Cognitive-behavioral treatment of chronically parasuicidal borderline patients. *Archives of General Psychiatry, 48*(12), 1060–1064.

Linehan, M. M., Comtois, K. A., Murray, A. M., Brown, M. Z., Gallop, R. J., Heard, H. L., ... Lindenboim, N. (2006). Two-year randomized controlled trial and follow-up of dialectical behavior therapy vs therapy by experts for suicidal behaviors and borderline personality disorder. *Archives of General Psychiatry, 63*(7), 757–766.

Linehan, M. M., Dimeff, L. A., Reynolds, S. K., Comtois, K. A., Welch, S. S., Heagerty, P., & Kivlahan, D. R. (2002). Dialectical behavior therapy versus comprehensive validation therapy plus 12-step for the treatment of opioid dependent women meeting criteria for borderline personality disorder. *Drug and Alcohol Dependence, 67*(1), 13–26.

Linehan, M. M., Korslund, K. E., Harned, M. S., Gallop, R. J., Lungu, A., Neacsiu, A. D., ... Murray-Gregory, A. M. (2015). Dialectical behavior therapy for high suicide risk in individuals with borderline personality disorder: A randomized clinical trial and component analysis. *JAMA Psychiatry, 72*(5), 475–482.

Linehan, M. M., Schmidt, H., Dimeff, L. A., Craft, J. C., Kanter, J., & Comtois, K. A. (1999). Dialectical behavior therapy for patients with borderline personality disorder and drug-dependence. *American Journal on Addictions, 8*(4), 279–292.

Lobbestael, J., Arntz, A., Cima, M., & Chakhssi, F. (2009). Effects of induced anger in patients with antisocial personality disorder. *Psychological Medicine, 39*(4), 557–568.

Lynch, T. R., Cheavens, J. S., Cukrowicz, K. C., Thorp, S. R., Bronner, L., & Beyer, J. (2007). Treatment of older adults with co-morbid personality disorder and depression: A dialectical behavior therapy approach. *International Journal of Geriatric Psychiatry, 22*(2), 131–143.

Lynch, T. R., Robins, C. J., Morse, J. Q., & Krause, E. D. (2001). A mediation model relating affect intensity, emotion inhibition, and psychological distress. *Behavior Therapy, 32*, 519–536.

Malleson, N. (1959). Panic and phobia: A possible method of treatment. *Lancet, 1*, 225–227.

Marques, L., Porter, E., Keshaviah, A., Pollack, M. H., Van Ameringen, M., Stein, M. B., & Simon, N. M. (2012). Avoidant personality disorder in individuals with generalized social anxiety disorder: What does it add? *Journal of Anxiety Disorders, 26*(6), 665–672.

McClintock, A. S., & Anderson, T. (2015). The application of mindfulness for interpersonal dependency: Effects of a brief intervention. *Mindfulness, 6*(2), 243–252.

McMain, S., Korman, L. M., & Dimeff, L. (2001). Dialectical behavior therapy and the treatment of emotion dysregulation. *Journal of Clinical Psychology, 57*(2), 183–196.

McMain, S. F., Links, P. S., Gnam, W. H., Guimond, T., Cardish, R. J., Korman, L., & Streiner, D. L. (2009). A randomized trial of dialectical behavior therapy versus general psychiatric management for borderline personality disorder. *American Journal of Psychiatry, 166*(12), 1365–1374.

Mehlum, L., Tørmoen, A. J., Ramberg, M., Haga, E., Diep, L. M., Laberg, S., ... Grøholt, B. (2014). Dialectical behavior therapy for adolescents with repeated suicidal and self-harming behavior: A randomized trial. *Journal of the American Academy of Child & Adolescent Psychiatry*, *53*(10), 1082–1091.

Miller, A. L., Rathus, J. H., & Linehan, M. M. (2006). *Dialectical Behavior Therapy with Suicidal Adolescents*. New York: Guilford Press.

Morton, J., Snowdon, S., Gopold, M., & Guymer, E. (2012). Acceptance and commitment therapy group treatment for symptoms of borderline personality disorder: A public sector pilot study. *Cognitive and Behavioral Practice*, *19*(4), 527–544.

Neacsiu, A. D., Eberle, J. W., Kramer, R., Wiesmann, T., & Linehan, M. M. (2014). Dialectical behavior therapy skills for transdiagnostic emotion dysregulation: A pilot randomized controlled trial. *Behaviour Research and Therapy*, *59*, 40–51.

Neacsiu, A. D., Rizvi, S. L., & Linehan, M. M. (2010). Dialectical behavior therapy skills use as a mediator and outcome of treatment for borderline personality disorder. *Behaviour Research and Therapy*, *48*(9), 832–839.

Neziroglu, F., Hickey, M., & McKay, D. (2010). Psychophysiological and self-report components of disgust in body dysmorphic disorder: The effects of repeated exposure. *International Journal of Cognitive Therapy*, *3*(1), 40–51.

Öst, L. G. (2008). Efficacy of the third wave of behavioral therapies: A systematic review and meta-analysis. *Behaviour Research and Therapy*, *46*(3), 296–321.

Ougrin, D., Tranah, T., Stahl, D., Moran, P., & Asarnow, J. R. (2015). Therapeutic interventions for suicide attempts and self-harm in adolescents: Systematic review and meta-analysis. *Journal of the American Academy of Child & Adolescent Psychiatry*, *54*(2), 97–107.

Panos, P. T., Jackson, J. W., Hasan, O., & Panos, A. (2014). Meta-analysis and systematic review assessing the efficacy of dialectical behavior therapy (DBT). *Research on Social Work Practice*, *24*(2), 213–223.

Pinto, A., Liebowitz, M. R., Foa, E. B., & Simpson, H. B. (2011). Obsessive compulsive personality disorder as a predictor of exposure and ritual prevention outcome for obsessive compulsive disorder. *Behaviour Research and Therapy*, *49*(8), 453–458.

Pistorello, J., Fruzzetti, A. E., MacLane, C., Gallop, R., & Iverson, K. M. (2012). Dialectical behavior therapy (DBT) applied to college students: A randomized clinical trial. *Journal of Consulting and Clinical Psychology*, *80*(6), 982–994.

Priebe, S., Bhatti, N., Barnicot, K., Bremner, S., Gaglia, A., Katsakou, C., ... Zinkler, M. (2012). Effectiveness and cost-effectiveness of dialectical behaviour therapy for self-harming patients with personality disorder: A pragmatic randomised controlled trial. *Psychotherapy and Psychosomatics*, *81*(6), 356–365.

Rathus, J. H., & Miller, A. L. (2002). Dialectical behavior therapy adapted for suicidal adolescents. *Suicide and Life-Threatening Behavior*, *32*(2), 146–157.

Reger, G. M., Koenen-Woods, P., Zetocha, K., Smolenski, D. J., Holloway, K. M., Rothbaum, B. O., & ... Gahm, G. A. (2016). Randomized controlled trial of prolonged exposure using imaginal exposure vs. virtual reality exposure in active duty soldiers with deployment-related posttraumatic stress disorder (PTSD). *Journal of Consulting and Clinical Psychology*, *84*(11), 946–959.

Rizvi, S. L., Hughes, C. D., Hittman, A. D., & Vieira Oliveira, P. (2017). Can trainees effectively deliver dialectical behavior therapy for individuals with borderline personality disorder? Outcomes from a training clinic. *Journal of Clinical Psychology*, *73*(12), 1599–1611.

Rizvi, S. L., & Linehan, M. M. (2005). The treatment of maladaptive shame in borderline personality disorder: A pilot study of "opposite action." *Cognitive and Behavioral Practice*, *12*(4), 437–447.

Rosenthal, M. Z., Cheavens, J. S., Lejuez, C. W., & Lynch, T. R. (2005). Thought suppression mediates the relationship between negative affect and borderline personality disorder symptoms. *Behaviour Research and Therapy*, *43*(9), 1173–1185.

Rosenthal, M. Z., Gratz, K. L., Kosson, D. S., Cheavens, J. S., Lejuez, C. W., & Lynch, T. R. (2008). Borderline personality disorder and emotional responding: A review of the research literature. *Clinical Psychology Review*, *28*(1), 75–91.

Sachse, S., Keville, S., & Feigenbaum, J. (2011). A feasibility study of mindfulness-based cognitive therapy for individuals with borderline personality disorder. *Psychology and Psychotherapy: Theory, Research and Practice*, *84*(2), 184–200.

Sadri, S. K., McEvoy, P. M., Egan, S. J., Kane, R. T., Rees, C. S., & Anderson, R. A. (2017). The relationship between obsessive compulsive personality and obsessive compulsive disorder treatment outcomes: Predictive utility and clinically significant change. *Behavioural and Cognitive Psychotherapy*, *45*(5), 524–529.

Segal, Z. V., Williams, J. M. G., & Teasdale, J. D. (2013). *Mindfulness-Based Cognitive Therapy for Depression* (2nd ed.). New York: Guilford Press.

Spinhoven, P., Bamelis, L., Molendijk, M., Haringsma, R., & Arntz, A. (2009). Reduced specificity of autobiographical memory in Cluster C personality disorders and the role of depression, worry, and experiential avoidance. *Journal of Abnormal Psychology*, *118*(3), 520–530.

Standish, A. J., Benfield, J. A., Bernstein, M. J., & Tragesser, S. (2014). Characteristics of borderline personality disorder and disgust sensitivity. *The Psychological Record*, *64*(4), 869–877.

Stoffers, J. M., Voellm, B. A., Rücker, G., Timmer, A., Huband, N., & Lieb, K. (2012). Psychological therapies for people with borderline personality disorder. *The Cochrane Library*. doi: 10.1002/14651858.CD005652.pub2

Tafrate, R. C., & Kassinove, H. (1998). Anger control in men: Barb exposure with rational, irrational, and irrelevant self-statements. *Journal of Cognitive Psychotherapy*, *12*(3), 187–211.

Tillfors, M., Furmark, T., Ekselius, L., & Fredrikson, M. (2004). Social phobia and avoidant personality disorder: One spectrum disorder? *Nordic Journal of Psychiatry*, *58*(2), 147–152.

Trull, T. J., Jahng, S., Tomko, R. L., Wood, P. K., & Sher, K. J. (2010). Revised NESARC personality disorder diagnoses: Gender, prevalence, and comorbidity with substance dependence disorders. *Journal of Personality Disorders*, *24*(4), 412–426.

Tsai, M., Kohlenberg, R. J., Kanter, J. W., Kohlenberg, B., Follete, W. C., & Callaghan, G. M. (2009). *A Guide to Functional Analytic Psychotherapy: Awareness, Courage, Love and Behaviorism*. New York: Springer.

Tsai, M., Yard, S., & Kohlenberg, R. J. (2014). Functional analytic psychotherapy: A behavioral relational approach to treatment. *Psychotherapy*, *51*(3), 364–371.

Turner, S. M., Beidel, D. C., & Townsley, R. M. (1992). Social phobia: A comparison of specific and generalized subtypes and avoidant personality disorder. *Journal of Abnormal Psychology*, *101*(2), 326–331.

Van Wel, E. B., Bos, E. H., Appelo, M. T., Berendsen, E. M., Willgeroth, F. C., & Verbraak, M. M. (2009). The efficacy of the systems training for emotional predictability and problem solving (STEPPS) in the treatment of borderline personality disorder: A randomized controlled trial. *Tijdschrift Voor Psychiatrie, 51*(5), 291–301.

Verheul, R., Van Den Bosch, L. M., Koeter, M. W., De Ridder, M. A., Stijnen, T., & Van Den Brink, W. (2003). Dialectical behaviour therapy for women with borderline personality disorder. *British Journal of Psychiatry, 182*(2), 135–140.

Watson, J. P., & Marks, I. M. (1971). Relevant and irrelevant fear in flooding: A crossover study of phobic patients. *Behavior Therapy, 2*(3), 275–293.

Wheaton, M. G., & Pinto, A. (2017). The role of experiential avoidance in obsessive-compulsive personality disorder traits. *Personality Disorders: Theory, Research and Treatment, 8*(4), 383–388.

Widiger, T. A. (1992). Generalized social phobia versus avoidant personality disorder: A commentary on three studies. *Journal of Abnormal Psychology, 101*(2), 340–343.

Wolpe, J. (1961). The systematic desensitization treatment of neuroses. *Journal of Nervous and Mental Disease, 132*(3) 189–203.

Young, J. E. (1990). *Cognitive Therapy for Personality Disorders: A Schema-Focused Approach*. Sarasota, FL: Professional Resource Exchange,

Young, J. E., Klosko, J. S., & Weishaar, M. E. (2003). *Schema Therapy: A Practitioner's Guide*. New York: Guilford Press.

Zorn, P., Roder, V., Thommen, M., Müller, D., & Tschacher, W. (2007). Evaluation of a new integrative therapy program for patients with personality disorder-results of a multi-center study. *European Psychiatry, 22*, S59–S60.

17a Applying a Cognitive-Behavioral, Principle-Based Approach to the Treatment of Personality Disorders: Commentary on Cognitive Behavioral Approaches

CHRISTOPHER D. HUGHES AND SHIREEN L. RIZVI

Rosenthal, Wyatt, and McMahon (this volume) have written an impressive chapter that outlines well the difficulties faced by CBT clinicians treating clients with personality disorders, and the empirically supported, "branded" CBT interventions available for clinicians. In addition to providing an overview to CBT as applied to personality disorders, the authors paid specific attention to three treatments: dialectical behavior therapy (DBT), schema focused therapy (SFT), and cognitive therapy. We wholeheartedly agree with the authors' recommendation that, when treating clients with personality disorders without specific established protocols, a collaboratively constructed, CBT principle-based case conceptualization and treatment plan is warranted. In fact, given the complex, heterogeneous, and pervasiveness of the dysfunctions related to personality disorders, it seems that flexible and individualized principle-based CBT approaches may even be preferable to protocol-based treatments. We recognize that developing and implementing such interventions can be a daunting task for clinicians. Therefore, the following commentary aims to briefly review and expand upon some relevant aspects of personality disorders that present challenges for clinicians, and to outline the steps we recommend clinicians follow in their treatment of personality-disordered clients.

In addition to the problems detailed by Rosenthal and colleagues, there are other factors that are likely to contribute to the difficulty faced by CBT clinicians treating clients with personality disorders. First, the screening and assessment of personality disorders is often not a part of routine clinical care, leaving them undiagnosed in many clinical settings (Bender et al., 2001; Tyrer, Reed, & Crawford, 2015). This is likely, at least in part, a symptom of the lack of evidence-based treatments for most personality disorders (i.e., clinicians may be less inclined to assess for a problem they feel ill equipped to address), as well as a reluctance to give a diagnosis due to the stigma related to personality disorders among mental health providers and in the general community (Sheehan, Nieweglowski, & Corrigan, 2016).

Second, the ten DSM-5 personality disorders are heterogeneous, with hundreds of distinct constellations of symptoms possible within any single personality disorder (APA, 2013). The interpersonal and intra-personal difficulties associated with personality disorders vary widely – not only across different personality disorders but also within each specific disorder. For example, the interpersonal problems of an individual with paranoid personality disorder would look quite different from those of someone with dependent personality disorder. Furthermore, one individual meeting criteria for BPD may experience interpersonal problems stemming from efforts to avoid abandonment, whereas another may not, instead experiencing greater interpersonal problems related to dysfunctional expressions of anger. Given their vast heterogeneity, it seems implausible that any one intervention could effectively address all the possible needs of clients with personality disorder diagnoses. Therefore, it seems that any effective personality disorder treatment would require a wide range of interventions that can be applied in a flexible and idiographic manner to address each individual's unique set of problems. An approach to treatment requiring clinicians to select relevant, empirically supported methods of behavior change would also require a principle-based framework to ensure that it remains organized and structured, and to prevent therapist drift or theoretical eclecticism (see Tolin, 2016). In fact, the CBTs for personality disorders detailed by Rosenthal and colleagues (DBT, SFT, and cognitive therapy) are more akin to this approach than they are to protocol-based CBTs for other disorders.

A third important factor to consider, touched on by Rosenthal and colleagues, is comorbidity. As Rosenthal and colleagues pointed out, personality disorders are highly comorbid with anxiety, mood, and substance use disorders. Furthermore, co-occurrence among the different personality disorders is also common (Lenzenweger, Lane, Loranger, & Kessler, 2007). Therefore, treatments that are transdiagnostic and/or modular in nature may be more useful than disorder-specific interventions when treating personality disorders and their likely comorbidities (see Lungu & Linehan, 2016, for a description of DBT as a modular treatment).

Fourth, compounding the issues of comorbidity and lack of routine assessment is the fact that clients with personality disorders often do not present to treatment seeking help for personality disorder behaviors, but for other disorders, such as depression, anxiety, and/or substance use. By definition, the complex constellation of pathology in personality disorders is longstanding and consistent across various contexts. Therefore, individuals with personality disorders may view those symptoms as part of life (never having known anything different), and instead seek treatment for the later-onset and/or episodic problems related to their comorbid disorders (Tyrer, Mitchard, Methuen, & Ranger, 2003).

These issues of comorbidity and heterogeneity, although perhaps more pronounced in personality disorders, are not unique to these disorders. Whereas many non-personality disorders have manualized CBTs, the difficulties translating them from the randomized clinical trials in which they were developed to 'real-world' clinical practice have been discussed in numerous papers (e.g., Kendall & Beidas, 2007; Nock, Goldman, Wang, & Albano, 2004). Further, although many empirically supported CBT protocols have been developed and widely utilized, CBT is, at its core, a principle-driven treatment; CBT clinicians, guided by their case conceptualization, implement empirically derived techniques to modify the specific cognitions and behaviors hypothesized to be maintaining the client's presenting problems (Beck, 2011; Tolin, 2016). Generally, the recommendation for clinicians delivering CBT in "uncharted clinical territories" is to make modifications to branded CBTs based on relevant research and broader CBT principles, while treating each case as a scientific experiment by collecting and analyzing data from the case to test the effectiveness of the modified treatment (Nock et al., 2004). We agree with Rosenthal and colleagues that a similar approach can be applied to the treatment of personality disorders in the absence of branded CBTs. The remainder of this chapter outlines the components we believe can be used to guide CBT clinicians treating personality disorders in a manner that is flexible enough to be tailored to each client's unique set of problems while remaining grounded in research and adherent to the principles of CBT.

ASSESSMENT

Clinicians need a comprehensive understanding of each of their client's problems and how they relate to one another. Assessment often begins with diagnostic clinical interviews and self-report measures. However, because personality disorders are so heterogeneous and (other than BPD) lack evidence-based CBTs, knowing the specific personality disorder(s) for which a client meets criteria provides little guidance for intervention selection. Therefore, an assessment of the client's presenting problems (difficulties with emotion regulation, interpersonal dysfunction, experiential avoidance, etc.) and overall levels of functioning within specific domains (e.g., work, interpersonal, recreation, etc.) is likely to prove useful to clinicians. During the initial assessment, the clinician should also take a comprehensive history of the client's treatment experiences, assessing their helpfulness, as well as what the client did and did not like about each. Finally, clinicians should assess what the client wants to get out of treatment, setting the stage for identifying treatment goals/targets.

CASE CONCEPTUALIZATION

Following the initial assessment, clinicians should work with clients to organize their problems into one coherent clinical picture, forming the basis of the case conceptualization. This goes beyond simply listing their diagnoses, or even all of their problems, to identifying how their problems relate to and interact with one another. This process can help identify clients' core problems – the ones that are contributing to the greatest amount of impairment and/or distress in their lives.

TRANSLATING GOALS/PROBLEMS INTO TREATMENT TARGETS

Next, clinicians should help clients translate their problems/goals for treatment (e.g., improve depression) into behaviorally specific, operationalized targets for treatment (e.g., increase daily positive affect, decrease time spent ruminating, etc.). This will facilitate both the selection of interventions aimed to address the problems and the assessment of their utility in terms of reduction in problems and progress towards goals. During this process, clinicians should be careful to set targets collaboratively and avoid imposing their own goals on the client.

CREATING A TARGET HIERARCHY

Clinicians should then work with clients to prioritize treatment targets, creating a hierarchy by determining the specific goals the client is interested in working towards first (with an emphasis on prioritizing those targets that will have the biggest impact on improving the client's life). This structure will help clinicians and clients organize and prioritize the multiple, complex, and interrelated problems they wish to address, keeping treatment structured from week to week in the absence of a session-by-session protocol. It is important to note that the target hierarchy is not grouped by disorder, but based on transdiagnostic, behaviorally specific targets. For example, rather than "(1) decrease specific phobia of insects, (2) decrease social anxiety, (3) improve academic performance, (4) increase positive affect, etc." a more effective target hierarchy could condense those targets into "(1) decrease avoidance of anxiety provoking situations, including environments with insects, social interactions, and studying for school, and (2) increase daily positive affect and pleasant events."

INTERVENTION SELECTION AND IMPLEMENTATION

Once the highest order target has been identified, clinicians must work with clients to conduct a functional analysis of the behavior to develop a comprehensive understanding of the problem. Understanding the problem behavior in relation to its antecedents and consequences, often using recent experiences as illustrative examples, facilitates the identification of the problem's maintaining factors (Rizvi & Ritschel, 2014). Clinicians can then use this understanding to select appropriate CBT interventions that are most likely to lead to the desired changes, based on research and broader CBT principles. Once the intervention is selected and implemented, its utility must be evaluated through continual tracking and assessment of problems and check-ins with clients to monitor changes in target behaviors over time. Based on these assessments, clinicians can determine what adjustments should be made to the treatment plan to more effectively address treatment targets, or repeat the previous steps to determine which target to address next and how to do so.

In the absence of a protocol to follow over the course of treatment, it is paramount to treat each case as an experiment – generating and testing hypotheses (assessment and treatment planning), gathering and analyzing data (self-monitoring, symptom tracking, check-ins), and adjusting theory based on data (modify/update treatment plan based on relative utility of interventions used). This process allows clinicians to flexibly create an idiographic treatment package tailored to each client's specific needs that is based on existent empirically supported CBT interventions and guided by broader CBT principles, thereby preventing treatment from drifting into intuition-driven, theoretical eclecticism.

THE THERAPEUTIC RELATIONSHIP

A significant component to any therapy is establishing and maintaining a positive therapeutic alliance. This may be particularly critical when working with clients with personality disorders, given the interpersonal difficulties at the core of many of these disorders. As interpersonal conflict is likely to arise within treatment, clinicians should work to address ruptures head on, using them as an opportunity to model effective skills use in resolving interpersonal problems. This approach may be facilitated by setting the foundation for doing so at the outset of treatment by acknowledging that conflicts are likely to arise, asking the client about past experiences and problems

with therapy and therapists, and planning for how both parties can bring up and address problems when they arise.

CONCLUSION

In the absence of evidence-based treatments for the broad range of personality disorders, we believe that the above outlined methodology represents a CBT-grounded approach to personality disorder treatment. Ideally, researchers will develop and assess the efficacy of CBT interventions for individuals with personality disorders that future clinicians can integrate into their work. For example, Radically Open DBT (RO-DBT; Lynch, 2018), although requiring further research, has shown promise in addressing various disorders of overcontrol (e.g., obsessive compulsive personality disorder). Although it would be virtually impossible to create specific protocols for every combination of personality and comorbid disorders, transdiagnostic and/or modular CBT packages that can be idiographically tailored and applied to the wide variety of clients with personality disorders may be the most promising. The treatments outlined by Rosenthal and colleagues, as well as the principles described here, could serve as the foundation upon which future researchers and clinicians can create new empirically driven CBTs for clients with personality disorders.

REFERENCES

American Psychiatric Association. (2013). *Diagnostic and Statistical Manual of Mental Disorders* (5th ed.). Arlington, VA: American Psychiatric Publishing.

Beck, J. S. (2011). *Cognitive Behavior Therapy: Basics and Beyond*. New York: Guilford Press.

Bender, D. S., Dolan, R. T., Skodol, A. E., Sanislow, C. A., Dyck, I. R., McGlashan, T. H., ... Gunderson, J. G. (2001). Treatment utilization by patients with personality disorders. *American Journal of Psychiatry*, 158(2), 295–302.

Kendall, P. C., & Beidas, R. S. (2007). Smoothing the trail for dissemination of evidence-based practices for youth: Flexibility within fidelity. *Professional Psychology: Research and Practice*, 38(1), 13–20.

Lenzenweger, M. F., Lane, M. C., Loranger, A. W., & Kessler, R. C. (2007). DSM-IV personality disorders in the National Comorbidity Survey Replication. *Biological Psychiatry*, 62(6), 553–564.

Lungu, A., & Linehan, M. M. (2016). Dialectical behavior therapy: A comprehensive multi-and transdiagnostic intervention. In C. M. Nezu & A. M. Nezu (Eds.), *The Oxford Handbook of Cognitive and Behavioral Therapies* (pp. 200–214). New York: Oxford University Press.

Lynch, T. R. (2018). *Radically Open Dialectical Behavior Therapy: Theory and Practice for Treating Disorders of Overcontrol*. Oakland, CA: New Harbinger Publications.

Nock, M. K., Goldman, J. L., Wang, Y., & Albano, A. M. (2004). From science to practice: The flexible use of evidence-based treatments in clinical settings. *Journal of the American Academy of Child & Adolescent Psychiatry*, 43(6), 777–780.

Rizvi, S. L., & Ritschel, L. A. (2014). Mastering the art of chain analysis in dialectical behavior therapy. *Cognitive and Behavioral Practice*, *21*(3), 335–349.

Sheehan, L., Nieweglowski, K., & Corrigan, P. (2016). The stigma of personality disorders. *Current Psychiatry Reports*, *18*(1), 11.

Tolin, D. F. (2016). *Doing CBT: A Comprehensive Guide to Working with Behaviors, Thoughts, and Emotions*. New York: Guilford Press.

Tyrer, P., Mitchard, S., Methuen, C., & Ranger, M. (2003). Treatment rejecting and treatment seeking personality disorders: Type R and type S. *Journal of Personality Disorders*, *17*(3), 263–268.

Tyrer, P., Reed, G. M., & Crawford, M. J. (2015). Classification, assessment, prevalence, and effect of personality disorder. *Lancet*, *385*(9969), 717–726.

17b Implementation Challenges in Real World Settings: Commentary on Cognitive Behavioral Approaches

ANDREA L. GOLD AND SHIRLEY YEN

In their review of cognitive and behavioral approaches for personality disorders (PDs), Rosenthal, Wyatt, and McMahon (this volume) provide an excellent, comprehensive summary of cognitive behavioral therapies (CBTs) and related research spanning over 30 years. The authors conceptualize CBTs as a family of interventions collectively defined by their application of empirically supported principles stemming from basic science to promote behavioral, emotional, and cognitive change. Although the evidence supporting cognitive and behavioral approaches to the treatment of PDs is relatively sparse compared to the abundant literature on randomized controlled trials (RCTs) for mood and anxiety disorders, it is nonetheless encouraging to see the breadth of CBTs for PDs.

As reviewed in this chapter, interventions showing some empirical support for the treatment of PDs include dialectical behavior therapy (DBT), schema focused therapy (SFT), cognitive therapy for personality disorders, emotion regulation group therapy (ERGT), and systems training for emotional predictability and problem solving (STEPPS). However, as the authors acknowledge, most of this work is restricted to borderline personality disorder (BPD), and strong empirical support for other PDs is lacking. There are many reasons why cognitive and behavioral psychotherapy development has been limited to BPD. Of note, BPD is unique among the PDs in terms of its inclusion of suicidal behaviors or non-suicidal self-injury (NSSI) as a diagnostic criterion, which translates into higher rates of suicide attempts and risk for psychiatric hospitalizations within this population. In the community, the presence of suicidal and self-injurious behaviors among individuals with BPD reflects a higher level of risk and associated healthcare costs, as well as heightened urgency for intervention and priority for clinical research (Bender et al., 2001; Yen et al., 2003; Zanarini, Frankenburg, Khera, & Bleichmar, 2001; Zanarini et al., 2008). Similarly, this diagnostic criterion of BPD provides an outcome variable that is easier to measure and operationalize relative to the criteria for other PDs. Indeed, the focus within DBT treatment research on specific behavioral outcomes, such as the frequency of NSSI

events and suicide attempts and the use of hospital-based crisis services, facilitates outcome assessment and increases the likelihood of observable improvements. In this sense, it is understandable that outcome research for BPD has outpaced other PDs. More work is needed to evaluate how and when CBTs promote clinical improvements across PD diagnoses. Indeed, despite the fact that other PDs are also associated with high rates of suicide and suicidal behaviors (Ansell et al., 2015; Giner et al., 2013; Links, Gould, & Ratnayake, 2003), as well as significant impairment and disability (Skodol et al., 2005), they are disproportionately understudied with respect to treatment.

Similar to the way in which BPD stands out among all PDs as having the most treatment outcome research, the authors note that DBT stands out among established CBTs as the "gold standard" BPD treatment. DBT clearly appears to be the most widely implemented intervention when it comes to CBTs for PDs. Why might this be the case? One possibility is that DBT has the most empirical support for its utility, ranging from RCTs (Koons et al., 2001; Linehan, Armstrong, Suarez, Allmon, & Heard, 1991; Linehan et al., 2006) and meta-analyses (Kliem, Kröger, & Kosfelder, 2010; Panos, Jackson, Hasan, & Panos, 2014) to quasi-experimental research (Bohus et al., 2004; Rathus & Miller, 2002) and program evaluation studies (Bohus et al., 2000; Comtois, Elwood, Holdcraft, Smith, & Simpson, 2007; Yen, Johnson, Costello, & Simpson, 2009). Moreover, DBT has ample training programs, including the Behavioral Tech organization that helps clinicians establish and monitor DBT programs. Additionally, the DBT-Linehan Board of Certification (DBT-LBC) evaluates and identifies providers and programs that deliver DBT with fidelity to the model, serving to confirm that implementation adheres to the evidence-based research. At the same time, the DBT-LBC is a relatively new organization, founded within the last five years. Thus, many implementations of DBT in the community reflect adaptations of the outpatient model investigated in RCTs, but with varying degrees of modifications. Indeed, treating PDs in real world settings often requires clinicians to make necessary adaptations to fit the needs of the clinic or community. For example, DBT has been adapted to match levels of care available in the environment, including residential, inpatient, partial hospital, and intensive-outpatient levels of care, as well as outpatient services provided in community mental health centers and Veterans Affairs medical centers.

Moreover, DBT-based interventions are sometimes implemented ahead of the science. For example, DBT clinics geared toward adolescents developed before the completion of efficacy trials. The first DBT-A RCT (Mehlum et al., 2014) was published over half a decade following the publication of the first DBT-A treatment guide (Miller, Rathus, & Linehan, 2006) and concurrently with the DBT-A treatment handbook (Rathus & Miller, 2014). The second RCT for DBT-A, a multi-site study, was only recently published (McCauley et al., 2018) – over a decade following the initial treatment guide. Furthermore, brief guides describing the follow-up to standard DBT-A treatments, the so-called phase 2 or graduate group treatments have been published for adolescents (Miller et al., 2006; Rathus & Miller, 2014) and implemented in clinical communities without the research to demonstrate their efficacy.

These repeated trends for DBT applications for adolescents to be implemented ahead of the science clearly suggest a dire need for adolescent interventions that cannot wait for the science. As evidenced in Rosenthal et al.'s review, studies of cognitive behavioral approaches to PDs tend to focus on adults. Yet, in the case of BPD, there is ample evidence it can be reliably diagnosed in adolescence, and the DSM-5 (APA, 2013) allows for the diagnosis before adulthood. Indeed, the National Education Alliance for BPD (NEA.BPD) recently began a global initiative to support collaborative work advancing developmental approaches to BPD: the Global Alliance for the Prevention and Intervention of BPD (GAP; www.borderlinepersonalitydisorder.com/what-is-gap/). Clearly, clinicians are faced with challenges surrounding the presentation of PD symptoms, particularly BPD, in high-risk adolescent populations, and cognitive and behavioral intervention efforts for this population must take into account developmental perspectives, family systems, and pediatric approaches.

Even when cognitive and behavioral approaches to treating PDs are available, there may be challenges to implementing them. First, diagnostic heterogeneity – a problem for any PD – is a particular problem when considering treatments targeting all PDs. Comorbidity appears to be the rule rather than the exception, reflecting comorbidity among multiple PDs (Hyler, Kellman, Oldham, & Skodol, 1992) and with disorders other than PDs, such as mood and anxiety disorders (Kaufman & Charney, 2000). Indeed, oftentimes what brings individuals with PD diagnoses into treatment is their comorbid depression or anxiety. Although comorbidity leads to challenges in treatment implementation, CBTs reflect a family of interventions that may be particularly well suited to handle such heterogeneous and comorbid clinical presentations. CBTs for both PDs and mood and anxiety disorders reflect and apply the same principles, such as exposure, cognitive restructuring, and behavioral activation. This allows clinicians to flexibly deploy and tailor CBTs to address a range of symptom presentations. Although the authors note that CBTs for transdiagnostic personality dysfunction are not yet established, such work is under development (Mulder & Chanen, 2013) and has a precedent in existing CBT approaches, such as the Unified Protocol for emotional disorders developed by Barlow and colleagues (Barlow et al., 2017). Furthermore, although implementing CBTs for PDs in the context of psychiatric comorbidity is further compounded by the issue of dual diagnosis (or comorbid substance use disorders), DBT has addressed this issue through the adaptation of DBT for substance using populations (Linehan et al., 1999), which may present a model for other CBTs.

As the authors note, there are few "branded CBTs" for PDs, particularly for PDs other than BPD. This may be due to a host of factors that make it exceedingly challenging to conduct psychotherapy development and outcome research for PDs. For example, a longer time course is often needed to address the more pervasive and longstanding patterns of maladaptive intra- and interpersonal behaviors associated with PDs relative to other psychiatric disorders. Treatment settings such as Veterans Affairs medical centers may be in an ideal position to conduct such work, given the presence of large systems and interdisciplinary treatment teams that allow longer courses of treatment in the absence of barriers linked to insurance. Indeed, treatment of PDs requires time and resources; thus, affordability is a barrier for many patients in need of treatment. It is thus not a surprise that much of the research on treatments for PDs has been conducted outside of the United States, where healthcare costs and barriers to healthcare are generally lower. Given that adaptations for DBT and other types of CBTs are often required to match the needs of the clinic or community, an investment in effectiveness research beyond DBT for BPD is necessary to develop, evaluate, and disseminate promising interventions.

In conclusion, although it is promising that there are several CBTs for PDs, the focus of research has been predominantly on BPD and DBT. Although evidence for the effectiveness of DBT is accumulating, there is a need to reach a broader spectrum of PD patients. A CBT targeting common symptom presentations may be a promising approach, and is in need of further development and research.

REFERENCES

American Psychiatric Association. (2013). *Diagnostic and Statistical Manual of Mental Disorders* (5th ed.). Arlington, VA: American Psychiatric Publishing.

Ansell, E. B., Wright, A. G., Markowitz, J. C., Sanislow, C. A., Hopwood, C. J., Zanarini, M. C., . . . Grilo, C. M. (2015). Personality disorder risk factors for suicide attempts over 10 years of follow-up. *Personality Disorders: Theory, Research, and Treatment, 6*(2), 161–167.

Barlow, D. H., Farchione, T. J., Sauer-Zavala, S., Latin, H. M., Ellard, K. K., Bullis, J. R., . . . Cassiello-Robbins, C. (2017). *Unified Protocol for Transdiagnostic Treatment of Emotional Disorders: Therapist Guide.* New York: Oxford University Press.

Bender, D. S., Dolan, R. T., Skodol, A. E., Sanislow, C. A., Dyck, I. R., McGlashan, T. H., . . . Gunderson, J. G. (2001). Treatment utilization by patients with personality disorders. *American Journal of Psychiatry, 158*, 295–302.

Bohus, M., Haaf, B., Simms, T., Limberger, M. F., Schmahl, C., Unckel, C., . . . Linehan, M. M. (2004). Effectiveness of inpatient dialectical behavioral therapy for borderline personality disorder: A controlled trial. *Behaviour Research and Therapy, 42*(5), 487–499.

Bohus, M., Haaf, B., Stiglmayr, C., Pohl, U., Bohme, R., & Linehan, M. (2000). Evaluation of inpatient dialectical-behavioral therapy for borderline personality disorder: A prospective study. *Behaviour Research and Therapy, 38*(9), 875–887.

Comtois, K. A., Elwood, L., Holdcraft, L. C., Smith, W. R., & Simpson, T. L. (2007). Effectiveness of dialectical behavior therapy in a community mental health center. *Cognitive and Behavioral Practice, 14*(4), 406–414.

Giner, L., Blasco-Fontecilla, H., Perez-Rodriguez, M. M., Garcia-Nieto, R., Giner, J., Guija, J. A., . . . De Leon, J. (2013). Personality disorders and health problems distinguish suicide attempters from completers in a direct comparison. *Journal of Affective Disorders, 151*(2), 474–483.

Hyler, S. E., Kellman, H., Oldham, J., & Skodol, A. (1992). Diagnosis of DSM-III-R personality disorders by two structured interviews: Patterns of comorbidity. *American Journal of Psychiatry, 149*, 213–220.

Kaufman, J., & Charney, D. (2000). Comorbidity of mood and anxiety disorders. *Depression and Anxiety, 12*(S1), 69–76.

Kliem, S., Kröger, C., & Kosfelder, J. (2010). Dialectical behavior therapy for borderline personality disorder: A meta-analysis using mixed-effects modeling. *Journal of Consulting and Clinical Psychology, 78*(6), 936–951.

Koons, C. R., Robins, C. J., Tweed, J. L., Lynch, T. R., Gonzalez, A. M., Morse, J. Q., . . . Bastian, L. A. (2001). Efficacy of dialectical behavior therapy in women veterans with borderline personality disorder. *Behavior Therapy, 32*(2), 371–390.

Linehan, M. M., Armstrong, H. E., Suarez, A., Allmon, D., & Heard, H. L. (1991). Cognitive-behavioral treatment of chronically parasuicidal borderline patients. *Archives of General Psychiatry, 48*(12), 1060–1064.

Linehan, M. M., Comtois, K. A., Murray, A. M., Brown, M. Z., Gallop, R. J., Heard, H. L., . . . Lindenboim, N. (2006). Two-year randomized controlled trial and follow-up of dialectical behavior therapy vs therapy by experts for suicidal behaviors and borderline personality disorder. *Archives of General Psychiatry, 63*(7), 757–766.

Linehan, M. M., Schmidt, H., III, Dimeff, L. A., Craft, J. C., Kanter, J., & Comtois, K. A. (1999). Dialectical behavior therapy for patients with borderline personality disorder and drug-dependence. *American Journal on Addictions, 8*(4), 279–292.

Links, P. S., Gould, B., & Ratnayake, R. (2003). Assessing suicidal youth with antisocial, borderline, or narcissistic personality disorder. *Canadian Journal of Psychiatry, 48*(5), 301–310.

McCauley, E., Berk, M. S., Asarnow, J. R., Adrian, M., Cohen, J., Korslund, K., . . . Linehan, M. M. (2018). Efficacy of dialectical behavior therapy for adolescents at high risk for suicide: A randomized clinical trial. *JAMA Psychiatry, 75*(8), 777–785.

Mehlum, L., Tørmoen, A. J., Ramberg, M., Haga, E., Diep, L. M., Laberg, S., . . . Sund, A. M. (2014). Dialectical behavior therapy for adolescents with repeated suicidal and self-harming behavior: A randomized trial. *Journal of the American Academy of Child & Adolescent Psychiatry, 53*(10), 1082–1091.

Miller, A. L., Rathus, J. H., & Linehan, M. M. (2006). *Dialectical Behavior Therapy with Suicidal Adolescents.* New York: Guilford Press.

Mulder, R., & Chanen, A. M. (2013). Effectiveness of cognitive analytic therapy for personality disorders. *British Journal of Psychiatry, 202*, 89–90.

Panos, P. T., Jackson, J. W., Hasan, O., & Panos, A. (2014). Meta-analysis and systematic review assessing the efficacy of dialectical behavior therapy (DBT). *Research on Social Work Practice, 24*(2), 213–223.

Rathus, J. H., & Miller, A. L. (2002). Dialectical behavior therapy adapted for suicidal adolescents. *Suicide and Life-Threatening Behavior, 32*(2), 146–157.

Rathus, J. H., & Miller, A. L. (2014). *DBT® Skills Manual for Adolescents.* New York: Guilford Press.

Skodol, A. E., Grilo, C. M., Pagano, M. E., Bender, D. S., Gunderson, J. G., Shea, M. T., . . . McGlashan, T. H. (2005). Effects of personality disorders on functioning and well-being in major depressive disorder. *Journal of Psychiatric Practice, 11*(6), 363–368.

Yen, S., Johnson, J., Costello, E., & Simpson, E. B. (2009). A 5-day dialectical behavior therapy partial hospital program for women with borderline personality disorder: Predictors of outcome from a 3-month follow-up study. *Journal of Psychiatric Practice, 15*(3), 173–182.

Yen, S., Shea, M. T., Pagano, M., Sanislow, C. A., Grilo, C. M., McGlashan, T. H., . . . Morey, L. C. (2003). Axis I and axis II disorders as predictors of prospective suicide attempts: Findings from the collaborative longitudinal personality disorders study. *Journal of Abnormal Psychology, 112*(3), 375–381.

Zanarini, M. C., Frankenburg, F. R., Khera, G. S., & Bleichmar, J. (2001). Treatment histories of borderline inpatients. *Comprehensive Psychiatry, 42*(2), 144–150.

Zanarini, M. C., Frankenburg, F. R., Reich, D. B., Fitzmaurice, G., Weinberg, I., & Gunderson, J. G. (2008). The 10-year course of physically self-destructive acts reported by borderline patients and axis II comparison subjects. *Acta Psychiatrica Scandinavica, 117*(3), 177–184.

17c Further Considerations about Cognitive Behavioral Therapies and Personality Disorders: Author Rejoinder to Commentaries on Cognitive Behavioral Approaches

M. ZACHARY ROSENTHAL, KRISTIN P. WYATT, AND KIBBY MCMAHON

We appreciate the thoughtful commentaries about our chapter written by Gold and Yen and, separately, Hughes and Rizvi. Each pair of authors raises many excellent points about the challenges associated with drawing upon the available body of scientific research when using cognitive and behavioral therapies to treat individuals with personality disorders (PDs). Both commentaries converge on the recommendation that clinicians using cognitive behavioral therapies for patients with PDs consider using principle-driven, modular, and transdiagnostic approaches. In this brief rejoinder, we highlight and extend upon several particular comments made in both commentaries.

The authors have highlighted the limitations of the current established CBTs for PDs. For example, therapies that have demonstrated efficacy for mainly one PD are often used for other populations without sufficient empirical justification. Gold and Yen (this volume) note that DBT is the most well-studied treatment specifically for BPD. Due to its efficacy for BPD, it has been adapted for use in other populations. At times, this has occurred ahead of the pace of scientific research directly testing and supporting the efficacy within such populations. The authors note, for example, how DBT for adolescents (DBT-A) was disseminated to clinicians prior to results from rigorously conducted randomized controlled clinical trials demonstrating its efficacy (Mehlum et al., 2014). DBT-A is not alone. There are other adaptations from standard DBT (and other treatments) that have been (or are currently being) disseminated to clinicians early in the process of such approaches being directly empirically investigated.

In the absence of an evidence base for manualized interventions with strong empirical support for these other populations, what is the clinician to do when such patients present for help? We believe that branded but understudied adaptations of CBT protocols for PDs, such as DBT, have taken hold because these interventions: (a) are grounded in transdiagnostically relevant empirically supported principles of change, and (b) offer hope and a treatment plan to clinicians who otherwise may lack hope or clarity about a treatment plan. On the one hand, it makes sense why established CBT protocols have been adapted and disseminated in the absence of extensive research studies directly testing the newly adapted approach. In some ways, these adaptations are in line with procedures we have argued for in our chapter: using case conceptualization to guide selection of empirically supported procedures corresponding to the relevant clinical processes and contexts. On the other hand, we wish to emphasize the importance of clinicians being aware of and communicating to patients the limitations in the science underlying the treatment they are offering.

Looking forward, the high comorbidity and complexity of personality pathology call for a new approach to treatment. We have argued in our chapter that a reasonable approach is to move beyond branded manualized treatments to empirically supported principles of change with a case conceptualization that organizes treatment targets, processes, and outcomes. Like Gold and Yen, Hughes and Rizvi also share interesting insights in their commentary on this new approach. We appreciate the high specificity of the suggestions provided (e.g., structured case formulation, target hierarchy), in that these suggestions more clearly operationalize ways to enact empirically supported principle-driven treatment. Hughes and Rizvi's commentary on the need for behaviorally specific targets of change is especially germane to a principle-driven approach. We agree that this may be particularly difficult to do when treating PD populations, given the heterogeneity of clinical presentations, therapeutic goals, and therapy-interfering interpersonal behaviors that can inadvertently delay treatment progress.

We also welcome their highlighting the advantages of a modular approach to the treatment of personality dysfunction, with flexible and tailored interventions using empirically supported cognitive and behavioral principles and processes. This approach is especially timely, given current national healthcare trends in payer reform that emphasize a shift to value-based care using a population health framework. More specifically, insurers and payers (e.g., Medicare, Medicaid, commercial payers) are transitioning from fee-for-service to fee-for-value and risk-based models of care. Within these value-based care models, clinicians will increasingly be required by payers to take financial risk by demonstrating value across the patients they treat. With regard to PDs, one implication of this shift is that clinicians will increasingly be incentivized with financial risk and reward to provide measurable improvements in treatment for the lowest possible cost to the payer.

As payers change to value-based models of reimbursement, it will be increasingly important to identify low-cost and flexible interventions that target specific, transdiagnostic forms of personality dysfunction. A modular approach, as suggested by Hughes and Rizvi, might include the systematic use of screening tools that capture transdiagnostic personality dysfunction and stratify patients into those needing time-limited versus longerterm care pathways. This approach could be considered a more resource-lean, lower cost way to engage specific psychological process targets (e.g., disinhibition, psychological flexibility) known to underlie personality dysfunction and to be amenable to change using empirically supported modules of interventions. Such an approach would offer measurement-based care and enhance access to services for more people by utilizing a time-limited approach.

In sum, the current "branded" CBTs for PDs are often resource heavy and are limited in their ability to meet the complexity, heterogeneity, and pervasiveness of personality dysfunction in clinical populations. We agree with the rest of the authors that we should consider modular, principle-driven approaches to conceptualization and treatment. With these approaches, we can better distinguish those patients who need to be treated with these comprehensive protocols from those who would instead benefit from a streamlined adaptation targeted to specific processes of change.

REFERENCES

Mehlum, L., Tørmoen, A. J., Ramberg, M., Haga, E., Diep, L. M., Laberg, S., ... Grøholt, B. (2014). Dialectical behavior therapy for adolescents with repeated suicidal and self-harming behavior: A randomized trial. *Journal of the American Academy of Child & Adolescent Psychiatry*, 53(10), 1082–1091.

18 Psychoanalytic/Psychodynamic Approaches to Personality Disorders

PETER FONAGY, ANTHONY BATEMAN, PATRICK LUYTEN, ELIZABETH ALLISON, AND CHLOE CAMPBELL

INTRODUCTION

Historically, psychoanalytic thinking played a major role in identifying and defining personality disorders (PDs), in particular, by recognizing PDs as a collection of diagnoses that require a specific clinical approach. From Adolph Stern's (1938) influential description of his work with borderline patients, and the concept of the schizoid personality developed by Ronald Fairbairn (1940/1952) and others (e.g., Guntrip, 1968), personality pathology has acquired – and retained – a core position in psychoanalytic thinking. Psychoanalysis has traditionally focused on personality features associated with psychopathology, rather than symptoms that arise from and perpetuate psychological problems (Clarkin, Fonagy, & Gabbard, 2010). Now, at a time when psychodynamic treatment is just one part of a large, diverse field of psychological interventions, PD remains an area of pathology in which psychodynamic thinking is influential and psychodynamic interventions have shown effectiveness (Cristea et al., 2017; Leichsenring & Rabung, 2008).

We will begin this chapter with a brief overview of the psychodynamic approach to PDs. Next, we will describe some of the major contemporary psychodynamic approaches to PDs, their respective models, and the evidence for their effectiveness. Finally, we will describe more recent developments in our thinking in relation to PD, and how connecting this with theoretical developments in the area of a general psychopathology or "p" factor (Caspi et al., 2014) has led us to reconsider our views in relation to the conceptualization of PDs and their treatment.

The particular challenges presented by therapeutic work with individuals with PD have required psychoanalysts to reconsider their work in creative ways – for example, the limitations of a drive-focused, intra-psychic model in the context of working with severely disturbed patients has contributed to a shift towards a more interpersonal, object-relational and developmental approach. This position of being forced to think differently – in terms of both theory and technique – inspired Stern's (1938) paper on

what at the time was termed the "borderline group of neuroses," its original meaning being on the borderline between neurosis and psychosis. The intricacies of comorbidity, complexity, and chronicity associated with PD continue to represent a significant challenge to how clinicians work, and have driven ongoing discussions about the structure of psychopathology (Skodol et al., 2011). Psychodynamic thinking has made some vital contributions to the ways in which we now understand PD. However, the psychodynamic approach has also had its limitations; indeed, it might be argued that one of the reasons PD has stimulated so much intellectual interest in the psychoanalytic literature lies in the challenges that clinicians have faced when working with people with a diagnosis of PD.

DIFFERENT PSYCHOANALYTIC TRADITIONS AND APPROACHES TO PERSONALITY DISORDER

The Kleinian–Bionian Model

One of the models of PD that is perhaps most commonly held by psychoanalysts derives from the work of Melanie Klein and Wilfred Bion. In essence, this model posits that personality pathology is driven by the dominance of the *paranoid–schizoid position*, which causes the individual to split objects into good (idealized, loving) and bad (persecutory, frightening, hateful). The model also posits that psychological health depends on the individual being able to retain (with relative stability) the *depressive position*, which is characterized by a more balanced and developmentally mature capacity to recognize and tolerate the presence of both bad and good together in one object, and to identify and correct one's own tendency to split representations of self and others in an unrealistic and distorting way.

In the classic Kleinian model, the tendency toward the paranoid–schizoid position is considered to be primarily constitutional in origin, reflecting the individual's overwhelming destructive impulses – described as "envy" by

427

Klein (1957) – being turned upon the object, who provides love and sustenance. Bion elaborated this theory further by suggesting that environmental processes might exacerbate this constitutional tendency. For Bion, the primary environmental factor at work was the caregiver's limited capacity for *reverie*, a concept used by Bion (1967) to describe a caregiver's ability to tolerate and contain their child's primitive and often difficult thoughts and feelings, and reflect them back to the child in a contained and manageable form.

In relation to the symptoms and characteristics of PDs, this model proposes that persecutory anxiety – that is, the sense of an overwhelming threat from a bad object – results in a sense of fragmentation and even annihilation of the self. These symptoms are characteristic of severe PD, and are particularly pertinent in the context of recent work suggesting that borderline PD (BPD), which is perhaps most archetypically associated with these symptoms, may capture the core of personality pathology or be representative of all PDs (Sharp et al., 2015). In this model, chronic depression, such as manifests in depressive PD but also in most if not all PDs, is considered to be an outcome of the individual being unable to escape their fear of harming the loved object and thus repressing all aggression, resulting in feelings of self-persecution. Narcissistic pathology is thus considered to be a defense against envy and dependence; here, the individual makes use of the other in highly destructive ways, leading to two possible forms of narcissism: *thin-skinned*, in which the individual demands constant reassurance, and *thick-skinned*, in which the individual presents a hostile, often arrogant and self-isolating stance in relation to others (Rosenfeld, 1971).

The work of the Kleinian school of writers has substantially enriched our understanding of emotional development and psychological functioning, while the work of Bion created a bridge between the two (previously separated) areas of cognitive development and personality pathology. The influence of some of Bion's thinking can be seen in recent mentalizing approaches to PDs (described later in this chapter), for example, with parallels being evident between the notion of the function of reverie (in Bion's thinking) and the role of the caregiver's mirroring in helping the child tolerate and ultimately be able to think about his/her own thoughts and feelings, and then others' (in mentalizing theory). In contrast, there are undoubtedly points of divergence between Kleinian thinking and more contemporary work. One notable example derives from the fact that many Kleinians are skeptical about or even somewhat hostile toward the place of empirical investigation in psychoanalysis, whereas the pragmatic and intellectual value of the pursuit of empirical testing is a driving principle of modern psychodynamic therapies. Furthermore, growing understanding of neuropsychology, the role of genetics in mental health and disorder, and the complexity of gene–environment interactions and epigenetics has left the classical Kleinian model appearing, by contrast, prone to over-specification and excessively causally linear in relation to the links between early experience and psychopathology in later life.

The British Object Relations Perspective

As mentioned in the introduction, Ronald Fairbairn was one of the early leading psychoanalytic figures in the field of PD. One of the key shifts, which was driven in the first instance by Fairbairn, was a new focus on the individual's need for the other and a connection with the other *per se*, rather than the things (e.g., sustenance, libidinal gratification) provided by others. This represented quite a radical change of emphasis in psychoanalytic thinking from psychic structure to psychic content.

Fairbairn (1952b) proposed that the infant has a primary drive for contact – that is, to create object relations. If this need for intimacy is not adequately met, the intolerable experience of a rejecting or unsatisfying caregiver is defensively split and internalized separately from the main, idealized representation of the caregiver and the self in relation to the caregiver. According to this viewpoint, the coexistence of these incompatible representations – the so-called schizoid condition – gives rise to psychological disorder (Fairbairn, 1952b).

One of Fairbairn's major contributions was the suggestion that severe early traumas are stored in memories that are "frozen" or dissociated from a person's central ego or functional self (Fairbairn, 1944). The experience of privation, for example, makes the infant view his/her love as bad and destructive, which in turn causes him/her to withdraw from emotional contact with the outer world, and ultimately creates a highly disturbed experience of external reality. Schizoid personality (Fairbairn, 1940/1952, 1952a) arises out of the baby's feeling that his/her love for the mother will destroy her and that it therefore has to be inhibited, along with all intimacy. The ego is split and neither the other nor the self is perceived as a whole person. These individuals hide their love and protect themselves from the love of others. To this theory, Winnicott (1965a) added the idea of a falseness in self-presentation that becomes truly maladaptive only in the context of an intimate interpersonal relationship: this was where the concept of the "false self" originated. Guntrip (1968) further added that the rejection by a hostile object leads to a "hunger" for objects that at the same time are feared.

Winnicott (1965b) also argued that borderline patients employ a number of the same defenses as psychotic patients. Winnicott (1960) notes that these patients have no sense that others – including the therapist – have lives of their own. Such patients respond with intense anger if their sense of omnipotence is threatened. These observations have been confirmed by research showing that BPD patients have a specific deficit in mental-state awareness in the context of attachment relationships (Fonagy & Target, 1996).

Winnicott, and object relational formulations more generally, did not completely reject the role of constitutional factors in psychopathology, but they often exclusively emphasized the role of the early environment. Such an emphasis is clearly incompatible with the results of behavioral genetic studies that have since taken place (e.g., Plomin & McGuffin, 2003). By contrast, the Freudian tradition showed greater respect for constitutional factors and the role of genetics in, for example, symptom choice and vulnerability to environmental stress. Research on the genetics of PD has in fact shown that PD is highly heritable (Bornovalova, Hicks, Iacono, & McGue, 2009; Distel et al., 2008; Kendler et al., 2008; Torgersen et al., 2008).

The major weakness of Winnicott's theory – which the entire British object relations tradition displays – is its potentially somewhat naïve reconstruction of infancy in the adult mind, leading to often somewhat metaphorical descriptions that are clinically immensely useful, but fail to do justice to the complexity of psychological development. In the face of the evidence (e.g. Rutter, Kim-Cohen, & Maughan, 2006), the argument for a linear development from infancy to adulthood cannot be maintained. In fact, longitudinal studies have suggested that personality is subject to reorganization throughout the complex trajectory of development, based on significant positive and negative influences (Lyons-Ruth & Jacobvitz, 2008; Lyons-Ruth, Yellin, Melnick, & Atwood, 2005).

Kohut and Self Psychology

Heinz Kohut's central idea, developed most fully in the 1970s, was that an essential developmental need for the infant, in the context of his/her helplessness and lack of physical self-mastery, is the experience of an understanding, supportive caregiver (Kohut, 1971, 1977; Kohut & Wolf, 1978). Kohut further proposed that this need for understanding – empathy was a key term in his writing – persists throughout the lifespan. In the early years of life, the caregiver's support and empathy helps support the development of the child's experience of selfhood. This process of self formation is in the first instance supported by the caregiver treating the child as a self in his/her own right, by identifying and recognizing the child's affects and helping the child to tolerate and think about them. Kohut describes the caregiver as acting as a *selfobject* – the person in the environment who performs functions for the self. The caregiver begins this process with the infant by providing empathic and mirroring responses. The child's experience of having his/her affects integrated and presented back to him/her in this way allows the child to achieve a healthy developmental stage characterized by a sense of their own grandiosity, which in turn acts as a defense against vulnerability. The infant's normal stage of "grandiosity" becomes, in healthy development, integrated with more connected, realistic ambitions, via the idealized identification of a selfobject. The self-cohesion provided by the selfobject's empathic and supportive care enables the child to develop the capacity for self-regulation and a stable sense of self-esteem.

In Kohut's model, psychopathology arises from the fear of losing one's sense of who one is. Deficiencies in the facilitating experiences provided by the selfobject can lead to a primary psychic defect and an inadequately developed sense of self. According to this model, PD is the result of a weakened sense of self that is susceptible to temporary fragmentation. Kohut was particularly interested in narcissistic PD, and his thinking in relation to PDs initially focused on narcissistic personality, which he interpreted as a developmental arrest at the stage of the grandiose exhibitionistic self, which has not been tempered by integrative and mirroring responses from the caregiver. This failure on the part of the caregiver causes an arrest in the movement from the grandiose exhibitionistic self to realistic ambition, and from the idealization of the parental imago to the formation of a healthier ego ideal. Repression of the grandiose self leads, according to Kohut, to low self-esteem, vague depression, and lack of initiative (Rosenfeld's [1971] "thin-skinned" narcissism). When splitting dominates, the grandiose self manifests as boastfulness, arrogance, and a dismissive attitude that is out of touch with reality (Rosenfeld's "thick-skinned" narcissism). Fundamentally, both forms of narcissism are characterized by low self-esteem, hypersensitivity to criticism, and the need to continue to be mirrored. According to this theory, violent behavior by narcissistic individuals is triggered by a threat to the self that is experienced as a sense of shame, which generates an overwhelming need to inflict injury on the shaming person and repair the narcissistic injury (Gilligan, 1997). In this self-psychology model, BPD is conceptualized as the outcome of an incapacity to retain access psychologically to soothing selfobjects; this creates an inner emptiness and a failure of integrated self-organization that results in an overwhelming annihilative panic when faced with the possibility of a threat to a relationship.

The Structural Object Relations Model

Otto Kernberg has been a highly influential thinker in the field of PD. His initial contribution was to succeed in integrating the ego psychology and object relations traditions (see Kernberg, 1975, 1980a, 1980b, 1984, 1992). Kernberg's theory positions affect as the primary motivational system. Accordingly, the representation of the relationship between self and object is driven by an "engine" of associated affects (Kernberg, 1982). This triad of self, object, and affect (which Kernberg termed an *object relations unit or dyad*) constitutes the basic building blocks of one's personality.

Kernberg delineated a developmental trajectory that was strongly influenced by the work of Jacobson and

Mahler (Jacobson, 1953a, 1953b; Mahler, Pine, & Bergman, 1975), but with less rigidly prescribed timing. According to this trajectory, in the very first stage (named "infantile autism," taking place in the first month or so of life) the infant does not differentiate between the self and the object. During the second stage ("symbiosis"), good and bad object representations are split by the ego to protect good images from the destructive power of bad images. In the third year of life, the polarized good and bad representations slowly become more integrated "separation-individuation," enabling the formation of total object representations and self-representations, which constitutes the fourth stage – "object constancy" (Kernberg, 1980b). If this integration fails, splitting remains the principal mechanism of defense.

In PD, split or part-object relations are formed under the impact of diffuse and overwhelming affective states. These affects activate persecutory relations between the self and object. From this perspective, BPD, for example, is characterized by: (1) ego weakness (poor affect tolerance, impulse control, and little sublimatory capacity); (2) primitive defenses, including splitting; (3) identity diffusion; (4) intact reality testing, but a propensity to shift toward primary process thinking; and (5) pathological internalized object relations. Influenced by Kleinian theory, Kernberg relates these features to the intensity of destructive and aggressive affects and the relative weakness of the ego structures available to deal with them.

Projective identification – which is pervasive in BPD – is seen as the by-product of an absence of differentiation between self and object. Projective identification is seen as resulting from massive primitive denial, ensuring that an individual can ignore his/her good feelings towards the object, leaving bad feelings to dominate his/her consciousness. This gives rise to the extreme and repeated oscillation between contradictory self-concepts – as, for example, victim or victimizer, dominant or submissive – that is characteristic of BPD (Kernberg, Selzer, Koenigsberg, Carr, & Appelbaum, 1989). Transient psychotic episodes can occur because self and object representations are readily fused; however, because reality testing remains adequate, these episodes do not persist. Self-destructiveness, self-injurious behavior, and suicidal gestures are thought to coincide with intense phases of rage against the object (Kernberg, 1987). Moreover, these gestures can establish control over the individual's environment because they provoke feelings of guilt. Self-injury is also seen as protecting the individual from identity diffusion.

In Kernberg's model, people with BPD have not achieved the developmental capacity to integrate the good and bad self and object images into a single representation. Kernberg leaves open to question the reasons why an individual may not achieve this stage; his model does not rely on a simple environmental explanation centering around suboptimal early experiences. Kernberg's thinking is thus in agreement with emerging evidence about the powerful role of genetic factors in BPD. There are other ways in which Kernberg's work has a richness and openness that keeps it from being superseded by contemporary developments. One key element – which differentiates Kernberg's work from the Kleinian background from which it has emerged – is his engagement with empiricism: Kernberg's commitment to research has rendered both his theory and his therapeutic techniques testable. The development with his colleagues of a systematic treatment approach based on his views, transference-focused psychotherapy (TFP; described later in this chapter), has involved translating object relations theory into a clinical practice that is realistic and testable.

We would also suggest that Kernberg's (1975) designation of borderline personality organization (BPO) constitutes a creative response to the clinical dilemmas presented by the failure of PDs, or of traditional Axis I diagnoses, to remain in their categorical "boxes" in the lived experience of psychopathology. The BPO is characterized by identity diffusion caused by "the failure of psychological integration resulting from the predominance of aggressive internalized object relations over idealized ones" (Kernberg, Yeomans, Clarkin, & Levy, 2008, p. 603) and can be present in PDs, notably narcissistic PD and antisocial PD (particularly in their more severe forms), as well as in some forms of depression. As mentioned above, a recent study has suggested that BPD features may represent the core of personality pathology (Sharp et al., 2015), the implications of which – that BPD criteria may be associated with a general psychopathology severity factor – are intriguingly consistent with Kernberg's suggestion that BPO represents more than the narrow diagnostic category of BPD (Kernberg, 1967).

The Interpersonal–Relational Approach

The interpersonal–relational approach represents an area in which a psychoanalytic contribution to PD has developed more recently. This approach has roots in the interpersonal psychiatry school of Harry Stack Sullivan (1953), in particular, the view that subjectivity is intrinsically interpersonal (Mitchell, 1988). In this respect, there is also an overlap with the interpersonalist emphasis of Kohut's self psychology, discussed earlier (Kohut, 1977). An area where the interpersonal–relational and the object relations schools differ is that the interpersonalist approach regards pathology as being embedded in relational matrixes, whereas object relations tends to understand pathology in terms of an individual's developmental arrest.

According to the interpersonal model, the purpose of therapy is to help the patient develop a more richly varied relational world (Mitchell, 1991). Because the interpersonal–relational approach focuses on interpersonal patterns rather than psychiatric nosology, its formulations tend to avoid labels such as "depression," "personality disorder," or "narcissism." The individual is seen not as having problems, but as having problematic *relationships*. From this point of view, diagnostic labels reify interpersonal problems and would take attention away from a therapeutic focus on the individual's relationship difficulties (e.g., Fairfield, Layton, & Stack, 2002).

Mentalizing Theory

A more recent psychoanalytic approach has emerged out of the confluence of attachment theory and research on mentalizing and, more recently, contemporary evolutionary thought. *Mentalizing* refers to one's understanding of the behavior of both oneself and others in terms of thoughts, feelings, wishes, and desires (Bateman & Fonagy, 2016). From this perspective, mental disorders in general can be viewed as the mind misinterpreting its own experience of itself, and, by extension, its experience of others (Bateman & Fonagy, 2010).

The mentalizing model was first developed in the framework of a large research study, which found that, while the security of infant attachment was strongly predicted by the parents' security of attachment during pregnancy (Fonagy, Steele, Steele, Moran, & Higgitt, 1991), it was predicted even more strongly by the parents' capacity to understand their childhood relationships with their own parents in terms of states of mind, which can be best described as mentalizing or *reflective functioning* (Fonagy et al., 1991). This study began a program of empirical research, treatment development, and theoretical work focused on the concept of mentalizing, which was postulated to emerge in the context of early attachment relationships, as a fundamental determinant of self-organization and affect regulation.

The mentalizing approach to BPD is fundamentally developmental. It focuses on attachment disruptions and related impairments in mentalizing or the capacity to develop second-order representations (i.e., representations of representations). The theory of mentalizing postulates that one's understanding of others depends on whether one's own mental states were adequately understood by caring, attentive, non-threatening adults in early life. Problems with affect regulation, attentional control, and self-control stemming from dysfunctional attachment relationships (Agrawal, Gunderson, Holmes, & Lyons-Ruth, 2004; Lyons-Ruth et al., 2005; Sroufe, Egeland, Carlson, & Collins, 2005) are thus thought to be mediated via a failure to develop a robust capacity to mentalize (Bateman & Fonagy, 2010).

This is not a straightforwardly environmental position; rather, the interaction between genetic predisposition and early (and later) influences on the development of the capacity to mentalize is thought to be of key importance in the development of BPD (Fonagy & Luyten, 2016). Our ideas about mentalizing are thus situated within a broader developmental approach that emphasizes the elements of interaction and diathesis–stress that are implicated in the emergence of BPD.

In recent years, proponents of mentalizing theory have taken the argument a step further to incorporate another important function of attachment relationships and, later on, the broader sociocultural environment. This is the development of *epistemic trust*, that is, trust in the authenticity and personal relevance of interpersonally transmitted knowledge. Epistemic trust enables social learning and salutogenesis (the capacity to benefit from positive social input) in an ever-changing social and cultural context (Fonagy, Luyten, & Allison, 2015). This thinking is largely based on Csibra and Gergely's (2009) theory of *natural pedagogy*. Human beings are faced with a major "learnability" problem: they are born into a world that is filled with objects and customs whose function or use is *epistemically opaque* (i.e., cannot easily be deduced from their appearance).

Humans have evolved to both teach and learn new and relevant cultural information rapidly. Human communication is specifically adapted to allow the transmission of epistemically opaque information; the communication of such knowledge is enabled by an epistemically trusting relationship. Epistemic trust allows the recipient of information being conveyed to them to relax their natural *epistemic vigilance* – a phenomenon that is self-protective and naturally occurring because it is not in anyone's interest to believe everything they are told indiscriminately. Relaxation of epistemic vigilance allows an individual to accept that *what they are being told matters to them* (Sperber et al., 2010).

These views do not diminish the importance of attachment, but place theories concerning the role of attachment in a somewhat different perspective. In terms of psychopathology, we suggest that the most significant implication of the developmental triad of attachment, mentalizing, and epistemic trust lies in the consequences of a breakdown in epistemic trust. We suggest that many, if not all, types of psychopathology might be characterized by a temporary or permanent disruption of epistemic trust and the social learning process it enables. It is here that attachment processes may be crucial.

An infant whose channels for learning about the social world have been disrupted – that is, one whose social experiences with his/her caregivers have led to a breakdown in epistemic trust – is left in a state of uncertainty and permanent epistemic vigilance. All humans seek social knowledge, but when such reassurance and input is sought from others, the content of their communication may be rejected, its meaning might be misunderstood, or it may be (mis)interpreted as having hostile intent. From this perspective, many forms of mental disorder might be considered manifestations of failures of social communication arising from epistemic mistrust, epistemic hypervigilance, or outright *epistemic freezing* – a complete inability to trust others as a source of knowledge about the world, which may be characteristic of many individuals with marked histories of trauma and personality problems. For example, someone who was traumatized in childhood has little reason to trust others and will reject information from others that does not fit with their pre-existing beliefs. Therapists may think of such people as "hard to reach," but they are simply showing an adaptation to a social environment in which information from attachment figures was likely to be misleading or actively intended to be damaging. Hence, from this perspective, PDs are seen not as disorders of personality, but as understandable adaptations to the environment, even if they ultimately are counterproductive in terms of the functioning of the individual.

CONTEMPORARY PSYCHODYNAMIC TREATMENTS

There is a growing evidence for a range of contemporary psychodynamic treatments (for a review, see Leichsenring et al., 2015). Among the most researched are Transference-Focused Therapy, Mentalization-Based Treatment, and general psychiatric management.

Transference-Focused Psychotherapy

Transference-focused psychotherapy (TFP) was developed within an object relations theoretical framework of borderline pathology. The conceptualization of the pathology in TFP is not just based on the specific criteria of DSM-III (and more recent editions of the DSM) but more broadly on the concept of BPO, with major structural deficits in representations of self and others and the use of primitive defenses such as splitting (as described earlier in this chapter). The basic assumption and starting point of TFP for BPD is that typical self–object relations are activated in the therapeutic relationship. These can then be subsequently worked through using clarification, confrontation, and interpretation, particularly of the transference (hence the name of this treatment). The focus is specifically on the split internal representations of self and others that are typical of BPD patients. For instance, BPD patients often mentally represent others as either persecutors or idealized rescuers, and their self-representation is characterized by marked identity diffusion. Treatment is focused on the patient's present life rather than the past. The goals of treatment are to reduce harmful actions by the patient and to develop a therapeutic relationship in which the patient can come to reflect on his/her active and reactive perceptions of self and others, including within the relationship with the therapist and with important others currently in the patient's life. Techniques of clarification, confrontation, and interpretation in the here-and-now are used to expand the patient's awareness of his/her conceptions of self and others, especially in "hot," conflictual situations when affect dysregulation is strong. The sequence of clarification, confrontation, and interpretation aims to provide a context in which the patient does not simply

continue with his/her incoherent, contradictory sense of self and others, but can reflect rather than react, and start to reappraise dominant themes of self–other situations.

TFP is a manualized intervention (Clarkin, Yeomans, & Kernberg, 2006) that was first developed as a highly structured, twice-weekly individual treatment for patients with BPO. More recently, modified versions of TFP have been developed for work with patients with narcissistic pathology and patients with more severe personality pathology (Yeomans & Diamond, 2010).

TFP typically evolves through a series of stages. Initially, the focus is on contract setting, including agreement about boundaries of treatment and the role of the clinician in managing self-destructive behaviors, and making an initial evaluation of the patient. These initial steps provide a secure base from which to further explore the patient's dominant object relational patterns. Next, these dominant object relational patterns are investigated in detail through the use of clarification, confrontation, and interpretation. This stage of treatment focuses on how self–object patterns are activated in the transference relationship. Gradually, these self–object patterns are clarified, and the patient is increasingly confronted with the self–object poles, typical of BPD patients, that are lived out in the transference relationship (e.g., victim and aggressor), and their oscillations between these poles – and this oscillation is linked to their typical patterns of relating to others. These relational patterns are then connected to the patient's developmental history in a way that explores the potential defensive functions of their self–object representations. This process is thought to decrease the need for splitting, omnipotent control, and projective identification; to lead to more differentiated and integrated representations of self and other; and to improve reflective functioning (i.e., mentalizing) and affect regulation.

The therapeutic stance in TFP is more active than in "traditional" psychoanalytic treatments, although there is an emphasis on technical neutrality and the use of the countertransference to trace typical self–object dyads. As an example, if the therapist feels terrorized by the patient's relentless criticism of him/her, he/she uses this feeling in an attempt to clarify, confront, and/or interpret the two poles of the underlying self–object dyad and its defensive functions. The patient might "terrorize" the therapist (who then feels as if he/she is the victim of a relentless perpetrator) because the patient fears that the therapist is bored with him/her and therefore wants to end the treatment. By becoming a perpetrator out of fear of becoming a victim, the patient reverses the roles: instead of being a victim, he/she becomes a perpetrator. In the later and more advanced stages of treatment, the therapist might also interpret the patient's underlying but disavowed wish to be cared for by a perfect, idealized caregiver, a key feature of TFP.

Evidence Base

There is a growing evidence base for the effectiveness of TFP. A one-year randomized clinical trial (RCT) with a sample of 90 individuals with BPD compared the effectiveness of TFP, dialectical behavior therapy (DBT), and psychodynamic supportive therapy (PST). Significant improvements in anxiety, depression, global functioning, and social adjustment were observed for each treatment group. In addition, TFP and DBT were associated with significant reductions in suicidality, and TFP and PST were associated with reductions in impulsivity (Clarkin, Levy, Lenzenweger, & Kernberg, 2007). This study found that TFP alone was associated with significant reductions in irritability and verbal and direct assault, and with positive changes in levels of reflective functioning and attachment style (Levy et al., 2006).

The effectiveness of TFP as a treatment for BPD was further evaluated in a comparison with schema-focused therapy (SFT) in a three-year RCT. In this study, which had 88 participants, TFP was associated with improvements across all domains assessed, although the dropout rate was higher for TFP, and SFT was superior to TFP with respect to reduction in BPD manifestations, general psychopathologic dysfunction, and change in SFT/TFP personality concepts (Giesen-Bloo et al., 2006). A more recent study of TFP versus treatment by experienced community psychotherapists, with a sample of 104 women with BPD, found that TFP was significantly more effective in terms of BPD symptoms, psychosocial functioning, personality organization, rates of suicide attempts, and psychiatric inpatient admissions. TFP also had a significantly lower participant dropout rate (Doering et al., 2010). In the TFP condition, there were significant improvements in mentalizing, and improvements in reflective function were significantly correlated with improvements in personality organization (Fischer-Kern et al., 2015).

Mentalization-Based Treatment

Mentalization-based treatment (MBT) is, essentially, a therapy that places mentalizing processes at the center of the therapy process, rather than directly focusing on object representations. At the core of MBT is the idea that the therapy works through the therapist establishing an enduring attachment relationship with the patient, while continuously stimulating mentalizing in the patient. The objective is for the patient to discover more about how they think and feel about themselves and others, how these thoughts and feelings influence their behavior, and how distortions in understanding themselves and others lead to maladaptive actions – albeit ones intended to maintain stability and manage incomprehensible feelings.

MBT was originally developed in the 1990s for the treatment of adults with BPD in a partial (day) hospital setting (Bateman & Fonagy, 1999). MBT has subsequently evolved into a more widely applied approach that has been used in work with patients with a range of PDs (most notably antisocial PD) and other mental health disorders (e.g., eating disorders, depression) in a range of treatment settings, and with adolescents as well as adults. As such, a program of MBT does necessarily always have the same shape. However, the structure of treatment is broadly replicated across the different contexts in which it is applied. The original outpatient program involved patients attending 5 days per week for a maximum period of 18–24 months (Bateman, 2005; Bateman & Fonagy, 1999). For the treatment of PDs, MBT now most commonly consists of an 18-month outpatient program comprising weekly individual sessions of 50 minutes and weekly group sessions of 75 minutes (Bateman & Fonagy, 2009).

The structure of MBT for PDs normally consists of three phases. The first comprises an assessment of the patient's mentalizing capacities and personality function, contracting and engaging the patient in treatment, and identifying any problems that might interfere with treatment. Specific elements of this phase include giving a diagnosis, providing psychoeducation, establishing a hierarchy of therapeutic aims, stabilizing the patient's social and behavioral problems, reviewing the patient's medication, and defining a pathway of actions to be taken in the event of a crisis.

The second phase consists initially of individual therapy, followed by the introduction of group therapy alongside the individual sessions. There is a fairly firm insistence in MBT that consistent attendance of both the individual and group sessions is necessary in order for the patient to be able to continue on the program, and that simply attending for individual treatment (as is most often the case for patients who do not attend all of their sessions) is not an option. During this second phase of the program, the main work of seeking to develop more robust mentalizing skills is undertaken.

The final phase of MBT, which normally begins at 12 months of treatment when there is a further 6 months remaining, involves preparing the patient for the end of treatment. Typically, at this point, many of the most obvious and worrying aspects of BPD symptomatology, such as impulsive behavior and affective instability, have diminished. However, patients may still struggle with interpersonal and social/vocational functioning, and may experience considerable difficulty in their general functioning and ability to form constructive relationships. Therefore, assuming that symptomatic and behavioral problems are well controlled, this final phase focuses on the interpersonal and social aspects of functioning. The final phase must also involve consideration of the end of treatment and the feelings of separation and loss that might be associated with such an ending. This is not just about facilitating the end of treatment; working on these issues may be of great value in consolidating the gains made in therapy. A final component of this phase is to collaboratively develop with the patient a follow-up treatment plan. There is no prescribed follow-up treatment in MBT, but this plan may, depending on the patient's needs and preferences, consist of couples therapy, group therapy, outpatient maintenance treatment, or educational/vocational counseling connected with returning to education or work.

The fundamental aim of MBT is to re-establish mentalizing when it is lost and maintain mentalizing when it is present. The MBT clinician focuses on the patient's subjective sense of self. To do so, they need to (1) identify and work with the patient's mentalizing capacities, (2) represent internal states in themselves and in the patient, (3) focus on these internal states, and (4) sustain this focus in the face of constant challenges from the patient over a significant period of time. To achieve this level of focus, mentalizing techniques need to be (1) offered in the context of an attachment relationship, (2) consistently applied over time, and (3) used to reinforce the therapist's capacity to retain mental closeness with the patient.

In agreement with the mentalization-based theoretical model of BPD described earlier, MBT is aimed at gently expanding the patient's mentalizing capacities while paying attention to the stability of his/her sense of self, and managing the interpersonal intimacy between therapist and patient and helping the patient maintain a level of arousal that ensures his/her engagement in the process. The well managed (i.e., not too intense and not too detached) attachment relationship between the patient and therapist optimizes the level of arousal. In MBT, the aim and the actual outcome of an intervention on the patient's immediate emotional and cognitive state are thought to be more important than the insight gained from interpreting particular defenses or understanding aspects of the transference relationship, although of course such insights emerge during treatment. The therapist assesses and attends to breaks in mentalizing, which are assumed to represent a break in the patient's continuity of experience of their mind. When these occur, the therapist's task is to "rewind" to the moment before the break in subjective continuity occurred. The therapist then explores the current emotional context in the session by identifying the momentary affective state between patient and therapist. Identifying the therapist's own contribution to the break in mentalizing – and showing humility in relation to this and taking responsibility for it – is often key.

As should be clear, the focus is on the process rather than the content. At the heart of MBT practice is the concept of the therapist's *mentalizing stance*. Typically, the mentalizing stance includes the following components: (1) humility deriving from a sense of "not knowing"; (2) patience in taking time to identify differences in perspectives; (3) explicit legitimizing and accepting of different perspectives; (4) active questioning of the patient about his/her experience, asking for detailed descriptions of experience ("what" questions) rather than explanations ("why" questions); and (5) careful eschewing of the need to "help" the patient to understand what makes no sense (e.g., by saying explicitly that something is unclear). This last aspect in particular sets MBT apart from predominantly insight-oriented therapies. The MBT therapist is there to help the patient learn about the complexities of the patient's thoughts and feelings about him/herself and others, how that relates to his/her responses, and how "errors" in understanding him/herself and others lead to actions. It is not for the therapist to "tell" the patient about how he/she feels, what he/she thinks, how he/she should behave, or what the underlying conscious or unconscious reasons for his/her difficulties are.

The key features that facilitate the therapeutic aim of MBT – the recovery of more robust mentalizing – may be seen in terms of the following structural properties of the treatment: (1) an extensive effort to maintain engagement in treatment (validation in conjunction with emphasis on the need to address behaviors that interfere with therapy, such as alcohol or substance abuse or self-harm); (2) utilization of a model of pathology that is explained to the patient; (3) an active stance by the therapist, that is, an explicit intent to validate and demonstrate empathy, generate a strong attachment relationship, and create epistemic trust (a sense in the patient that the therapist's views of the world can be trusted as relevant to the patient); (4) a focus on emotion processing and the connection between actions and feelings (e.g., how suicidal wishes link to feelings of abandonment); (5) a genuine inquiry into patients' mental states (behavioral analysis, clarification, confrontation); (6) adoption of a structure of treatment that suggests increased activity, proactivity, and self-agency (avoiding the use of an expert stance, and encouraging collaboration with the patient and a "sit side-by-side" therapeutic attitude); (7) acceptance of a defined structure for the nature of the relationship between patient and therapist that is robust to distortions by the patient's emotional dysregulation (i.e., what is crucial is that the therapist is able to think without having to withdraw from exchanges or fall back on "mindless" rules established by prior contract or precedent); (8) therapeutic work is supported by the structure provided by a manual, and adherence to that structure is sustained by supervision; (9) the therapist and the entire therapeutic milieu reflect commitment to the mentalization-based approach and underscore the importance the therapist attaches to the patient's thoughts and feelings. Enabling mentalizing and developing epistemic trust and the capacity for salutogenesis that results from the restoration of these capacities, is perhaps a component of other effective therapies for BPD, as we shall discuss more fully below.

What is avoided in mentalization-based treatment (MBT) is the use of complex descriptions of mental states and behaviors that go beyond the patient's ability to process while in states of high arousal. This cautious approach to transference interpretation in MBT underlines a further aspect of treatment, namely, the level of training required to deliver a treatment effectively without iatrogenic effects. Dynamic therapies have often been criticized for their complexity and difficulty to implement well without a long period of training. MBT was developed as a research-based treatment to be implemented by generic mental health professionals, and this may account for its perhaps over-cautious approach. MBT is concerned to avoid the possible harmful effects of overzealous and clumsy transference interpretation. In other words, transference interpretation is a complex technique that is not easily learned and may specifically risk harm in patients with BPD if used inappropriately. Three days' basic training is provided and supervision is offered in the workplace as practitioners see patients for treatment. Current results suggest that reasonable outcomes may be achievable within this framework of mental health services without lengthy specialist training. This supports the general utility of MBT.

Evidence Base

There is an ample evidence base for MBT, beginning with an RCT of an 18-month program for 44 patients with BPD in a partial hospital setting (Bateman & Fonagy, 1999, 2001), which found significant and enduring changes in mood states and interpersonal functioning. Outcome measures included frequency of suicide attempts and acts of self-injury, number and duration of inpatient admissions, service use, and self-reported depression, anxiety, general symptom distress, interpersonal function, and social adjustment. Relative to treatment as usual (TAU), the benefits were large, with a number needed to treat of approximately two. The benefits were also observed to increase during the follow-up period of 18 months. The day hospital MBT program has been investigated in a series of outcome studies, culminating in an eight-year follow-up study (Bateman & Fonagy, 2008), the longest follow-up of treatment for BPD conducted to date. Compared with TAU, MBT was associated with fewer suicide attempts, emergency room visits and inpatient admissions, less medication and outpatient treatment utilization, and lower impulsivity. At follow-up, far fewer patients in the MBT group than the TAU group met criteria for BPD (13 percent vs. 87 percent). In addition to symptomatic improvement, patients in the MBT group showed greater improvement in interpersonal and occupational functioning.

Similarly, in an RCT involving 134 patients, an intensive outpatient MBT program proved more effective than structured clinical management for BPD at the end of the 18-month treatment period (Bateman & Fonagy, 2009), particularly for patients with more than two PD diagnoses (Bateman & Fonagy, 2013). Compared with TAU, the outpatient treatment resulted in lower rates of suicidal behavior and non-suicidal self-injury, as well as fewer hospitalizations. The MBT group also showed improved social adjustment, coupled with diminished depression, symptom distress, and interpersonal distress. An RCT in Denmark investigating the efficacy of MBT versus a less intensive, manualized supportive group therapy program in patients diagnosed with BPD found that MBT was superior to the comparison treatment on

clinician-rated Global Assessment of Functioning (Jørgensen et al., 2013). These results were sustained 18 months later in a naturalistic follow-up (Jørgensen et al., 2014). In another study from Denmark (Petersen et al., 2010), a cohort of patients treated with partial hospitalization followed by group MBT showed significant improvements after treatment of on average two years on a range of measures, including Global Assessment of Functioning, hospitalizations, and vocational status, with further improvement at two-year follow-up.

A naturalistic study by Bales et al. (2012) in the Netherlands investigated the effectiveness of an 18-month manualized program of MBT in 45 patients with severe BPD. Treatment was associated with significant positive change in symptom distress, social and interpersonal functioning, and personality pathology and functioning, with moderate to large effect sizes. However, this study is limited by the lack of a control group. Another study by the same group (Bales et al., 2015) used propensity score matching to ascertain the best matches for 29 MBT patients from within a larger ($n = 175$) group who received other specialized psychotherapeutic treatments. Generally moderate improvement across all domains was found in the group receiving other psychotherapeutic treatment, while effect sizes were consistently large for MBT, with Cohen's d for reduction in psychiatric symptoms of −1.06 and −1.42 at 18 and 36 months, respectively, and Cohen's d ranging from 0.81 to 2.08 for improvement in areas of personality functioning. However, between-condition differences in effects should be viewed with caution because of the non-randomized study design and the variations in treatment dose received by participants.

More recently, research has been undertaken to assess the effectiveness of MBT in different diagnostic contexts. An RCT in the UK (Robinson et al., 2016) compared MBT for eating disorders (MBT-ED) against specialist supportive clinical management for patients with eating disorders and symptoms of BPD. There was a high dropout rate in this study (only 15 of the 68 participants eligible for randomization [22 percent] completed the 18-month follow-up), making results difficult to interpret, but MBT-ED was associated with greater reductions in Shape Concern and Weight Concern on the Eating Disorder Examination, relative to the control treatment. Another recent RCT of MBT for individuals with comorbid antisocial PD and BPD found that MBT was effective in reducing anger, hostility, paranoia, and frequency of self-injurious behavior and suicide attempts, and brought about improvements in negative mood, general psychiatric symptoms, interpersonal problems, and social adjustment (Bateman, O'Connell, Lorenzini, Gardner, & Fonagy, 2016).

CONCLUSION: GOING FORWARD

Recent meta-analyses have suggested that there are now several forms of psychological therapy for BPD and other types of PDs that are of some value (Cristea et al., 2017; Leichsenring, Leibing, Kruse, New, & Leweke, 2011; Stoffers et al., 2012). What is more, these meta-analyses have suggested that there is little substantial difference in effectiveness between specialized and non-specialized treatment approaches, at least in the treatment of BPD (Cristea et al., 2017). Meta-analytic findings so far thus clearly suggest that there is no single treatment method – psychodynamic or otherwise – that can claim exclusive therapeutic potency.

These findings are congruent with the recent emphasis in psychoanalytic approaches to PD on epistemic trust – that psychopathology is a form of disordered social cognition, perpetuated by the obstacles to communication that these social cognitive difficulties create. What is called "psychotherapy" may simply be, from this perspective, a recent variant of an activity that has been part of the repertoire of communicative behavior for a very long time – turning to other people's thoughts to help us make sense of our own. For individuals with PDs, the loss of epistemic trust is a powerful obstacle to this process of beneficially accessing other people's minds in order to reinstate the capacity to tolerate and understand one's own mind. This may lead to a new view on the mechanisms of change in the treatment of individuals with personality problems, and particularly with regard to their so-called hard-to-reach or treatment-resistant character (Fonagy et al., 2015).

Effective modes of psychological treatment for PDs that now exist all involve, in our opinion, three distinct processes of communication that cumulatively render them effective (Fonagy & Luyten, 2016):

- *Communication System 1: The teaching and learning of content*

  The different therapeutic schools belong to this system. They may be effective primarily because they involve the therapist conveying to the patient a model for understanding the mind that the patient can understand, as it includes a convincing recognition and identification of his/her own state. This feeling of being recognized and understood may in itself lower the patient's epistemic vigilance.

- *Communication System 2: The re-emergence of robust mentalizing*

  When the patient is once again open to social communication in contexts that had previously been marred by epistemic hypervigilance, he/she begins to show increased interest in the therapist's mind and the therapist's use of thoughts and feelings, which stimulates and strengthens the patient's capacity for mentalizing. Improvements in mentalizing or social cognition may thus be a common factor in different interventions.

- *Communication System 3: The re-emergence of social learning*

  The relaxation of the patient's epistemic hypervigilance achieved via the first two systems of

communication enables the patient to become more open to social learning. This allows the patient to apply his/her new mentalizing and communicative capabilities to wider social encounters, outside the consulting room. This final part of the process depends upon the patient having a sufficiently benign social environment to allow him/her to gain the necessary experiences to validate and bolster his/her improved mentalizing, and to continue to facilitate the relaxation of epistemic mistrust, in the wider social world.

These three systems of communication, we suggest, provide a framework for investigating the effectiveness of psychotherapies. Beyond the therapeutic treatment itself, the model also directs attention to the social environment, and to interventions that may directly target environmental factors that could contribute to the origin and maintenance of psychopathology, and those factors that could have the potential to support recovery and the patient's capacity to benefit from benign aspects of his/her environment. This widening of the view of what determines therapeutic outcomes to include the social environment beyond the consulting room represents a challenge to the potential omnipotence of all psychological therapies, but perhaps more archetypally, to the therapeutic primacy of the psychoanalytic relationship.

What role do these speculations leave for the psychoanalytic approach in particular? We suggest that its future may lie in helping us make sense of how we think about PD, how we conceptualize psychopathology, and what it is that makes treatment effective. This is not simply an intellectual exercise: traditional diagnostic categories, and the treatments accordingly assigned to them, are increasingly viewed as failing to recognize the complexity of mental health presentations throughout the lifespan (Skodol et al., 2011). These issues are particularly pertinent in the field of PD, in which recurrence, comorbidity, and complexity are very common (O'Connor, 2005; O'Connor & Dyce, 1998). The psychoanalytic approach encompasses a uniquely sophisticated model of the mind, which, if applied with intellectual openness rather than rigid orthodoxy, can tolerate the categorical complexity of personality-disordered states.

REFERENCES

Agrawal, H. R., Gunderson, J., Holmes, B. M., & Lyons-Ruth, K. (2004). Attachment studies with borderline patients: A review. *Harvard Review of Psychiatry, 12*(2), 94–104.

Bales, D., Timman, R., Andrea, H., Busschbach, J. J., Verheul, R., & Kamphuis, J. H. (2015). Effectiveness of day hospital mentalization-based treatment for patients with severe borderline personality disorder: A matched control study. *Clinical Psychology & Psychotherapy, 22*(5), 409–417.

Bales, D., van Beek, N., Smits, M., Willemsen, S., Busschbach, J. J., Verheul, R., & Andrea, H. (2012). Treatment outcome of 18-month, day hospital mentalization-based treatment (MBT) in patients with severe borderline personality disorder in the Netherlands. *Journal of Personality Disorders*, 26(4), 568–582.

Bateman, A. (2005). Day hospital treatment of borderline personality disorder. In M. C. Zanarini (Ed.), *Borderline Personality Disorder* (pp. 281–304). Boca Raton, FL: Taylor & Francis.

Bateman, A., & Fonagy, P. (1999). Effectiveness of partial hospitalization in the treatment of borderline personality disorder: A randomized controlled trial. *American Journal of Psychiatry*, 156(10), 1563–1569.

Bateman, A., & Fonagy, P. (2001). Treatment of borderline personality disorder with psychoanalytically oriented partial hospitalization: An 18-month follow-up. *American Journal of Psychiatry*, 158(1), 36–42.

Bateman, A., & Fonagy, P. (2008). Eight-year follow-up of patients treated for borderline personality disorder: Mentalization-based treatment versus treatment as usual. *American Journal of Psychiatry*, 165(5), 631–638.

Bateman, A., & Fonagy, P. (2009). Randomized controlled trial of outpatient mentalization-based treatment versus structured clinical management for borderline personality disorder. *American Journal of Psychiatry*, 166(12), 1355–1364.

Bateman, A., & Fonagy, P. (2010). Mentalization based treatment for borderline personality disorder. *World Psychiatry*, 9(1), 11–15.

Bateman, A., & Fonagy, P. (2013). Impact of clinical severity on outcomes of mentalisation-based treatment for borderline personality disorder. *British Journal of Psychiatry*, 203, 221–227.

Bateman, A., & Fonagy, P. (2016). *Mentalization-Based Treatment for Personality Disorders: A Practical Guide*. New York: Oxford University Press.

Bateman, A., O'Connell, J., Lorenzini, N., Gardner, T., & Fonagy, P. (2016). A randomised controlled trial of mentalization-based treatment versus structured clinical management for patients with comorbid borderline personality disorder and antisocial personality disorder. *BMC Psychiatry*, 16, 304. doi:10.1186/s12888-016-1000-9

Bion, W. R. (1967). *Second Thoughts*. London: Heinemann.

Bornovalova, M. A., Hicks, B. M., Iacono, W. G., & McGue, M. (2009). Stability, change, and heritability of borderline personality disorder traits from adolescence to adulthood: A longitudinal twin study. *Development and Psychopathology*, 21(4), 1335–1353.

Caspi, A., Houts, R. M., Belsky, D. W., Goldman-Mellor, S. J., Harrington, H., Israel, S., ... Moffitt, T. E. (2014). The p factor: One general psychopathology factor in the structure of psychiatric disorders? *Clinical Psychological Science*, 2(2), 119–137.

Clarkin, J. F., Fonagy, P., & Gabbard, G. O. (Eds.) (2010). *Psychodynamic Psychotherapy for Personality Disorders: A Clinical Handbook*. Washington, DC: American Psychiatric Publishing.

Clarkin, J. F., Levy, K. N., Lenzenweger, M. F., & Kernberg, O. F. (2007). Evaluating three treatments for borderline personality disorder: A multiwave study. *American Journal of Psychiatry*, 164(6), 922–928.

Clarkin, J. F., Yeomans, F. E., & Kernberg, O. F. (2006). *Psychotherapy for Borderline Personality: Focusing on Object Relations*. Washington, DC: American Psychiatric Publishing.

Cristea, I. A., Gentili, C., Cotet, C. D., Palomba, D., Barbui, C., & Cuijpers, P. (2017). Efficacy of psychotherapies for borderline personality disorder: A systematic review and meta-analysis. *JAMA Psychiatry*, 74(4), 319–328.

Csibra, G., & Gergely, G. (2009). Natural pedagogy. *Trends in Cognitive Sciences*, 13(4), 148–153.

Distel, M. A., Trull, T. J., Derom, C. A., Thiery, E. W., Grimmer, M. A., Martin, N. G., ... Boomsma, D. I. (2008). Heritability of borderline personality disorder features is similar across three countries. *Psychological Medicine*, 38(9), 1219–1229.

Doering, S., Horz, S., Rentrop, M., Fischer-Kern, M., Schuster, P., Benecke, C., ... Buchheim, P. (2010). Transference-focused psychotherapy v. treatment by community psychotherapists for borderline personality disorder: Randomised controlled trial. *British Journal of Psychiatry*, 196(5), 389–395.

Fairbairn, W. R. D. (1940/1952). Schizoid factors in the personality. In *An Object-Relations Theory of the Personality* (pp. 3–28). New York: Basic Books (original work published 1940).

Fairbairn, W. R. D. (1944). Endopsychic structure considered in terms of object-relationships. *International Journal of Psychoanalysis*, 25, 70–93.

Fairbairn, W. R. D. (1952a). *An Object-Relations Theory of the Personality*. New York: Basic Books.

Fairbairn, W. R. D. (1952b). *Psychoanalytic Studies of the Personality*. London: Tavistock.

Fairfield, S., Layton, L., & Stack, C. (Eds.) (2002). *Bringing the Plague: Toward a Postmodern Psychoanalysis*. New York: Other Press.

Fischer-Kern, M., Doering, S., Taubner, S., Hörz, S., Zimmermann, J., Rentrop, M., ... Buchheim, A. (2015). Transference-focused psychotherapy for borderline personality disorder: Change in reflective function. *British Journal of Psychiatry*, 207(2), 173–174.

Fonagy, P., & Luyten, P. (2016). A multilevel perspective on the development of borderline personality disorder. In D. Cicchetti (Ed.), *Developmental Psychopathology, Volume 3: Maladaptation and Psychopathology* (3rd ed., pp. 726–792). New York: John Wiley & Sons.

Fonagy, P., Luyten, P., & Allison, E. (2015). Epistemic petrification and the restoration of epistemic trust: A new conceptualization of borderline personality disorder and its psychosocial treatment. *Journal of Personality Disorders*, 29(5), 575–609.

Fonagy, P., Steele, M., Steele, H., Moran, G. S., & Higgitt, A. C. (1991). The capacity for understanding mental states: The reflective self in parent and child and its significance for security of attachment. *Infant Mental Health Journal*, 12(3), 201–218.

Fonagy, P., & Target, M. (1996). Playing with reality: I. Theory of mind and the normal development of psychic reality. *International Journal of Psycho-Analysis*, 77(Pt 2), 217–233.

Giesen-Bloo, J., van Dyck, R., Spinhoven, P., van Tilburg, W., Dirksen, C., van Asselt, T., ... Arntz, A. (2006). Outpatient psychotherapy for borderline personality disorder: Randomized trial of schema-focused therapy vs transference-focused psychotherapy. *Archives of General Psychiatry*, 63(6), 649–658.

Gilligan, J. (1997). *Violence: Our Deadliest Epidemic and its Causes*. New York: Grosset/Putnam.

Guntrip, H. (1968). *Schizoid Phenomena, Object Relations and the Self*. London: Hogarth Press.

Jacobson, E. (1953a). The affects and their pleasure-unpleasure qualities in relation to the psychic discharge processes. In R. Loewenstein (Ed.), *Drives, Affects, Behavior* (Vol. 1, pp. 38–66). New York: International Universities Press.

Jacobson, E. (1953b). *On the Psychoanalytic Theory of Affects: Depression*. New York: International Universities Press.

Jørgensen, C. R., Bøye, R., Andersen, D., Døssing Blaabjerg, A. H., Freund, C., Jordet, H., & Kjølbye, M. (2014). Eighteen months post-treatment naturalistic follow-up study of mentalization-based therapy and supportive group treatment of borderline personality disorder: Clinical outcomes and functioning. *Nordic Psychology, 66*(4), 254–273.

Jørgensen, C. R., Freund, C., Boye, R., Jordet, H., Andersen, D., & Kjolbye, M. (2013). Outcome of mentalization-based and supportive psychotherapy in patients with borderline personality disorder: A randomized trial. *Acta Psychiatrica Scandinavica, 127*(4), 305–317.

Kendler, K. S., Aggen, S. H., Czajkowski, N., Roysamb, E., Tambs, K., Torgersen, S., ... Reichborn-Kjennerud, T. (2008). The structure of genetic and environmental risk factors for DSM-IV personality disorders: A multivariate twin study. *Archives of General Psychiatry, 65*(12), 1438–1446.

Kernberg, O. F. (1967). Borderline personality organization. *Journal of the American Psychoanalytic Association, 15*(3), 641–685.

Kernberg, O. F. (1975). *Borderline Conditions and Pathological Narcissism.* New York: Jason Aronson.

Kernberg, O. F. (1980a). *Internal World and External Reality: Object Relations Theory Applied.* New York: Jason Aronson.

Kernberg, O. F. (1980b). Some implications of object relations theory for psychoanalytic technique. In H. Blum (Ed.), *Psychoanalytic Explorations of Technique: Discourse on the Theory of Therapy* (pp. 207–239). New York: International Universities Press.

Kernberg, O. F. (1982). Self, ego, affects, and drives. *Journal of the American Psychoanalytic Association, 30*(4), 893–917.

Kernberg, O. F. (1984). *Severe Personality Disorders: Psychotherapeutic Strategies.* New Haven, CT: Yale University Press.

Kernberg, O. F. (1987). A psychodynamic approach. *Journal of Personality Disorders, 1*(4), 344–346.

Kernberg, O. F. (1992). *Aggression in Personality Disorders and Perversions.* New Haven, CT: Yale University Press.

Kernberg, O. F., Selzer, M. A., Koenigsberg, H. W., Carr, A. C., & Appelbaum, A. H. (1989). *Psychodynamic Psychotherapy of Borderline Patients.* New York: Basic Books.

Kernberg, O. F., Yeomans, F. E., Clarkin, J. F., & Levy, K. N. (2008). Transference focused psychotherapy: Overview and update. *International Journal of Psychoanalysis, 89*(3), 601–620.

Klein, M. (1957). *Envy and gratitude. In* Envy and Gratitude and Other Works. The Writings of Melanie Klein (Vol. 3, pp. 176–235). London: Hogarth Press.

Kohut, H. (1971). *The Analysis of the Self.* New York: International Universities Press.

Kohut, H. (1977). *The Restoration of the Self.* New York: International Universities Press.

Kohut, H., & Wolf, E. S. (1978). The disorders of the self and their treatment: An outline. *International Journal of Psycho-Analysis, 59*, 413–426.

Leichsenring, F., Leibing, E., Kruse, J., New, A. S., & Leweke, F. (2011). Borderline personality disorder. *Lancet, 377*(9759), 74–84.

Leichsenring, F., Luyten, P., Hilsenroth, M., Abbass, A., Barber, J., Keefe, J., ... Steinert, C. (2015). Psychodynamic therapy meets evidence-based medicine: A systematic review using updated criteria. *The Lancet Psychiatry, 2*(7), 648–660.

Leichsenring, F., & Rabung, S. (2008). Effectiveness of long-term psychodynamic psychotherapy: A meta-analysis. *JAMA, 300* (13), 1551–1565.

Levy, K. N., Meehan, K. B., Kelly, K. M., Reynoso, J. S., Weber, M., Clarkin, J. F., & Kernberg, O. F. (2006). Change in attachment patterns and reflective function in a randomized control trial of transference-focused psychotherapy for borderline

personality disorder. *Journal of Consulting and Clinical Psychology, 74*(6), 1027–1040.

Lyons-Ruth, K., & Jacobvitz, D. (2008). Attachment disorganization: Genetic factors, parenting contexts, and developmental transformation from infancy to adulthood. In J. Cassidy & P. R. Shaver (Eds.), *Handbook of Attachment: Theory, Research, and Clinical Applications* (2nd ed., pp. 666–697). New York: Guilford Press.

Lyons-Ruth, K., Yellin, C., Melnick, S., & Atwood, G. (2005). Expanding the concept of unresolved mental states: Hostile/helpless states of mind on the Adult Attachment Interview are associated with disrupted mother–infant communication and infant disorganization. *Development and Psychopathology, 17* (1), 1–23.

Mahler, M. S., Pine, F., & Bergman, A. (1975). *The Psychological Birth of the Human Infant: Symbiosis and Individuation.* New York: Basic Books.

Mitchell, S. A. (1988). *Relational Concepts in Psychoanalysis: An Integration.* Cambridge, MA: Harvard University Press.

Mitchell, S. A. (1991). Contemporary perspectives on the self: Toward an integration. *Psychoanalytic Dialogues, 1*, 121–147.

O'Connor, B. P. (2005). A search for consensus on the dimensional structure of personality disorders. *Journal of Clinical Psychology, 61*(3), 323–345.

O'Connor, B. P., & Dyce, J. A. (1998). A test of models of personality disorder configuration. *Journal of Abnormal Psychology, 107*(1), 3–16.

Petersen, B., Toft, J., Christensen, N. B., Foldager, L., Munk-Jorgensen, P., Windfeld, M., ... Valbak, K. (2010). A 2-year follow-up of mentalization-oriented group therapy following day hospital treatment for patients with personality disorders. *Personality and Mental Health, 4*(4), 294–301.

Plomin, R., & McGuffin, P. (2003). Psychopathology in the postgenomic era. *Annual Review of Psychology, 54*, 205–228.

Robinson, P., Hellier, J., Barrett, B., Barzdaitiene, D., Bateman, A., Bogaardt, A., ... Fonagy, P. (2016). The NOURISHED randomised controlled trial comparing mentalisation-based treatment for eating disorders (MBT-ED) with specialist supportive clinical management (SSCM-ED) for patients with eating disorders and symptoms of borderline personality disorder. *Trials, 17*, 549. doi:10.1186/s13063-016-1606-8

Rosenfeld, H. (1971). A clinical approach to the psychoanalytic theory of the life and death instincts: An investigation into the aggressive aspects of narcissism. *International Journal of Psycho-Analysis, 52*(2), 169–178.

Rutter, M., Kim-Cohen, J., & Maughan, B. (2006). Continuities and discontinuities in psychopathology between childhood and adult life. *Journal of Child Psychology and Psychiatry, 47*(3-4), 276–295.

Sharp, C., Wright, A. G., Fowler, J. C., Frueh, B. C., Allen, J. G., Oldham, J., & Clark, L. A. (2015). The structure of personality pathology: Both general ('g') and specific ('s') factors? *Journal of Abnormal Psychology, 124*(2), 387–398.

Skodol, A. E., Clark, L. A., Bender, D. S., Krueger, R. F., Morey, L. C., Verheul, R., ... Oldham, J. M. (2011). Proposed changes in personality and personality disorder assessment and diagnosis for DSM-5 Part I: Description and rationale. *Personality Disorders: Theory, Research, and Treatment, 2*(1), 4–22.

Sperber, D., Clement, F., Heintz, C., Mascaro, O., Mercier, H., Origgi, G., & Wilson, D. (2010). Epistemic vigilance. *Mind & Language, 25*(4), 359–393.

Sroufe, L. A., Egeland, B., Carlson, E. A., & Collins, W. A. (2005). *The Development of the Person: The Minnesota Study of Risk and Adaptation from Birth to Adulthood*. New York: Guilford Press.

Stern, A. (1938). Psychoanalytic investigation of and therapy in the borderline group of neuroses. *Psychoanalytic Quarterly, 7* (4), 467–489.

Stoffers, J. M., Vollm, B. A., Rucker, G., Timmer, A., Huband, N., & Lieb, K. (2012). Psychological therapies for people with borderline personality disorder. *Cochrane Database of Systematic Reviews, 8*(8) [Article CD005652]. doi:10.1002/14651858. CD005652.pub2

Sullivan, H. S. (1953). *The Interpersonal Theory of Psychiatry*. New York: W. W. Norton.

Torgersen, S., Czajkowski, N., Jacobson, K., Reichborn-Kjennerud, T., Roysamb, E., Neale, M. C., & Kendler, K. S. (2008). Dimensional representations of DSM-IV cluster B personality disorders in a population-based sample of Norwegian twins: A multivariate study. *Psychological Medicine, 38*(11), 1617–1625.

Winnicott, D. W. (1960). The theory of the parent–infant relationship. *International Journal of Psycho-Analysis, 41*, 585–595.

Winnicott, D. W. (1965a). Ego distortion in terms of true and false self. In *The Maturational Processes and the Facilitating Environment* (pp. 140–152). New York: International Universities Press.

Winnicott, D. W. (1965b). *The Maturational Processes and the Facilitating Environment*. New York: International Universities Press.

Yeomans, F., & Diamond, D. (2010). Transference-focused psychotherapy and borderline personality disorder. In J. F. Clarkin, P. Fonagy, & G. O. Gabbard (Eds.), *Psychodynamic Psychotherapy for Personality Disorders: A Clinical Handbook* (pp. 209–238). Washington, DC: American Psychiatric Publishing.

18a Contemporary Psychodynamic Treatments: Commentary on Psychoanalytic/Psychodynamic Approaches to Personality Disorders

KENNETH N. LEVY

Fonagy and colleagues (this volume) are to be commended for a wonderfully rich and nuanced presentation of contemporary psychodynamic treatments (PDTs) for personality disorders. This is no easy feat as psychodynamics approaches with a long history are not monolithic and are quite diverse. Fonagy and colleagues begin their chapter with a brief overview of the psychodynamic approach to PDs, followed by an elaboration of the contributions from the major traditions within the psychodynamic perspective. Although they focus on models, this section provides a rich historical perspective as well.

Following their overview in the first section of the chapter, they focus on two of the primary contemporary psychodynamic approaches to PDs, with a particular focus on mentalization-based treatment (MBT) and transference-focused psychotherapy (TFP). In this section, Fonagy and colleagues provide a nice explication of the respective models, and a detailed consideration of the evidence for their effectiveness. It is important, as they note, that on the basis of numerous randomized controlled trials (RCTs) and comprehensive meta-analyses, the evidence for psychodynamic treatments for personality disorders is as strong as the evidence for treatments from other orientations (some have suggested that because there are more studies of DBT than other treatments, that there is more empirical evidence for DBT than other treatments; however, another way of thinking about it is that because there are more studies of DBT, we can be more confident in its effect size, which is no different than what is found for other treatments, including PDTs).

Fonagy and colleagues then close by articulating a model based on their more recent thinking and the findings in the literature regarding the equivalence of outcomes for various treatments irrespective of theoretical orientation. Although I was disappointed that the authors did not take up the implications of a general psychopathology or "p" factor as fully as I expected, I found this closing section to be an interesting, timely, and integrative conceptualization. It provides a valuable pearl with which to end the chapter.

In reading the chapter, I asked myself, who is the reader that this chapter is written for? Most of the chapter is written, as I think the editors intended, for a broad audience ranging from psychopathologists and clinicians at all stages of their career including those in training for these positions. This is a challenging task, and the chapter delivers the kind of information that would be of value to all individuals across the broad target audience. As one example, the reader of this chapter will derive an excellent understanding of the contemporary models for treating BPD and its corresponding evidence.

This success notwithstanding, in order to meet the needs of a broad audience the historical review could have benefited from more explication. Although such history is important and often neglected, the main points can be obscured by the use of psychoanalytic language that might be foreign to such readers (e.g., objects). It would be useful to provide clarification of what the terms mean and/or elaboration of how they evolved. As such, I felt this section missed the opportunity to educate those less familiar with the psychodynamic model and the value of such an approach. Below I highlight some of the points that I think could have had more emphasis in stressing the unique contributions and utility of a psychodynamic approach.

Psychodynamic approaches to personality disorders, although diverse, all share certain basic tenets. Arguably there may be additional tenets for consideration, but I will focus on the following: (1) that early childhood relationships with caregivers play an important role in shaping how we experience and view subsequent relationships (this is the idea of transference); (2) that some mental processes, such as motives, desires, and memories, are not readily available to awareness or conscious introspection (the idea of the unconscious); (3) people are sometimes motivated to keep threatening thoughts or feelings out of awareness (this is the idea of defense); and (4) the importance of individual or personal meaning (this is the idea of psychic reality and explains why two people can experience the same event very differently or why an event can be traumatic to one person but not another).

The idea that early childhood relationships with caregivers play an important role in shaping how individuals experience and view subsequent relationships is not unique to psychodynamic approaches. However, more unique to the PDT approach is that the representations (schemas or internal working models) built up slowly over years through these interactions with others and the environment result in what Freud called transference. Transference is simply the tendency in which represented aspects of important and formative relationships (e.g., with parents) are attributed to other people. This process of transference can be conscious, but also is often unconscious or implicit (Levy & Scala, 2012). Within any interaction, there are individual differences in transference in terms of the degree, extent, rigidity, and awareness of transference. Transference can be in line with reality or reality-based, in that it is based on aspects of the individual or the situation that can pull for transference. It can also be evoked – that is, people encountered can act in ways to elicit reactions and behaviors that are consistent with one's transference tendencies. The amount of transference can vary as a function of the individual, the target, and the situation. Lastly, an important feature of transference is that some aspects are not only unconscious but are related to conflicts and defensive processes. In healthier individuals, initial transference reactions quickly give way to the more reality-based aspects of the real relationship (Gelso, 2010; Gill, 1979). In less psychologically healthy individuals transferences are often inconsistent with the social reality and are rigidly held despite evidence to the contrary. While transference is not necessarily the focus in treatment in all psychodynamic approaches as it is in TFP, most psychodynamic approaches, including supportive ones and MBT, track and attend to transferential processes (Appelbaum, 2007; Bateman & Fonagy, 2007; Gabbard, 2007) because awareness of these processes can assist with the managing of the patient–therapist relationship.

Thus, to summarize from above, the concept of transference is not simply a jargon filled term referring to a vestige of an obsolete model but it is a concept that has clinical utility both diagnostically (and phenomenologically in the moment for both the patient and the therapists) and for conceptualizing treatment dynamics, whether or not one is engaged in tracking the transference like in MBT or a supportive dynamic therapy, or the therapist is engaged in the process of interpreting it as it relates to thoughts, feelings, and behaviors in the patient, such as the case in TFP.

Moreover, from a psychodynamic approach, mental representations not only serve as templates for viewing later relationships, but they have certain qualities. For instance, in comparison to CBT approaches, psychodynamic theory emphasizes the structural aspects more than the content or valance of the representations. These structural aspects include not only the organization of the representations but include the developmental aspects of

representation. This developmental focus is important because it means that not all representations are encoded or can be retrieved through the same mechanism across individuals or even within individuals. Thus, there are inter- and intra-individual differences that must be accounted for. Structural aspects of representation also include the affective components of representation. For example, much like Marcel Proust, Kernberg (2001) stresses that every representation has an affect attached to it and every affect has representations associated with it. This means attending to the affect provides a window to the representations associated with emotion – representations that can be explicated and understood. Likewise, as Fonagy and colleagues contend, representations of emotional experience affect mental states and vice versa (what Fonagy, Jurist, and their respective colleagues refer to as mentalized affectivity; Fonagy et al., 2004; Greenberg, Kolasi, Hegsted, Berkowitz, & Jurist, 2017; Jurist, 2005).

Beyond the developmental, affective, and structural aspects of representations discussed above, the psychodynamic approach is unique in that it not only recognizes the conscious phenomenological aspects of experience but also the implicit or unconscious aspects of representation. In recent years, cognitive-behavioral (de Jong, 2002; Teachman & Allen, 2007; Teachman & Woody, 2002; Teachman, Woody, & Magee, 2006) and even behavioral approaches (if one considers experiential avoidance an implicit process) have begun to recognize and even focus on implicit processes but not quite in the same way as from a psychodynamic perspective. Implicit processes are not simply automatic, quick, reflexive processes outside of awareness but can involve motivational influences and defensive processes (LeBreton, Moeller, Johnson, & Levy, in press).

Another issue that deserves elaboration is that Fonagy and colleagues limited the focus of their review to MBT and TFP. On the one hand, this makes sense given the prominence of these two treatments within the psychodynamic world, in the personality disorder literature, their recognition among treatment guidelines, and in psychiatric and psychology training (Sansone, Kay, & Anderson, 2013). On the other hand, as a more general chapter on psychodynamic treatments, it is important to at least identify that other important approaches exist including Dynamic Deconstructive Psychotherapy (DDP; Gregory, Delucia-Deranja, & Mogle, 2010), Psychodynamic Supportive Therapy; Appelbaum, 2007), and Gunderson's Good Psychiatric Management (GPM; Gunderson & Links, 2015; McMain et al., 2009). Granted, the current articulation of the GPM model while consistent with a psychodynamic approach (for example, seeing emotion dysregulation as activated by defensive processes in reaction to an attachment based interpersonal hypersensitivity), is organized in a psychoeducational structure. Nonetheless, in the RCT (McMain et al., 2009) examining DBT as compared to GPM, the psychotherapy utilized was based on Gunderson's psychodynamic approach

(Gunderson & Links, 2008), which shares many principles and a structure that is similar to aspects of MBT and TFP. Thus, although these approaches may not deserve the same space devoted to them as TFP and MBT, they do deserve mention to ensure the reader gets a perspective that is broad and inclusive of the wide range of work done in this domain of treatment for PDs.

The final point I would like to make specific to Fonagy and colleagues' concluding section (this volume) concerns the convergence of a psychodynamic model of personality disorders, particularly Kernberg's, with the findings of a general psychopathology or "p" factor (Caspi & Moffitt, 2018), the Alternative Model for Personality Disorders (AMPD), the recent findings within assessment of personality pathology about general ('g') and specific ('s') factors (Sharp et al., 2015), and the Cognitive Affective Personality System (CAPS) model (Mischel & Shoda, 1995; for reviews, see Clarkin, Levy, & Ellison, 2010; Huprich & Nelson, 2015). This convergence provides validity for the psychodynamic model and shows its clinical utility. These convergences also show that rather than being an old antiquated model deserving to be jettisoned from contemporary consideration, the psychodynamic model is theoretically and clinical useful and has been absorbed, knowingly as in the case of the alternative model and the p factor, and maybe unknowingly in the case of the CAPS model.

First articulated in the late 1960s, Kernberg proposed a model for understanding a range of personality disorders along two dimensions – severity and internalizing vs. externalizing (Kernberg, 1967; Kernberg & Caligor, 2005). Various personality disorders could be arrayed along this two-dimensional space. Consistent with recent research (Sharp et al., 2015; Wright, Hopwood, Skodol, & Morey, 2016), Kernberg conceptualized the severity dimension in terms of level of borderline functioning. This conceptualization is also consistent with the AMPD in Section III of the DSM in that borderline pathology is of central heuristic value for representing what is common to all personality pathology (Criterion A). The progression from lower levels of severity in personality pathology to higher levels of severity is tied to more impaired and maladaptive self–other representations and functioning. Thus, in Kernberg's model, the central BPD symptoms – abandonment fears, unstable relationships that alternate between idealization and devaluation, affect instability, identity disturbance, paranoid ideation, and chronic feelings of emptiness, and angry outburst – arise from an individual's impaired and distorted internal images of self and other, what Kernberg called identity diffusion. The data from Sharp et al. and Wright et al. are consistent with this idea. So is recent data from our lab (Scala et al., 2018) where in an intensive repeated measurement design examining BPD patients as compared to anxiety disordered patients over a 21-day period, we found, as many might predict, that affect regulation deficits in terms of negative affect predicted suicidal urges. However, this relationship was only found when patients were in identity diffuse mental states. Although BPD patients scored significantly higher and experienced more identity disturbance, negative affect, and suicidal urges than those with anxiety disorders, the process worked similarly across both groups.

In summary, Fonagy and colleagues (this volume) have provided an important explication of the contemporary psychodynamic treatments for borderline personality disorder with a focus on transference-focused psychotherapy and mentalization-based treatment. I have tried to highlight and elaborate the theory behind these models and show that rather than being outdated and irrelevant, contemporary psychodynamic models are consistent with evidence from general psychopathological models. The psychodynamic model, with its focus on the developmental psychopathology of self–other representations, conscious and unconscious mental processes such as defense and transference, and the importance of psychic reality have much to offer and the resulting treatments have shown comparable efficacy.

REFERENCES

Appelbaum, A. H. (2007). Supportive psychotherapy. In J. M. Oldham, A. E. Skodol, & D. S. Bender (Eds.), *The American Psychiatric Publishing Textbook of Personality Disorders* (pp. 311–326). Washington, DC: American Psychiatric Publishing.

Bateman, A., & Fonagy, P. (2007). The use of transference in dynamic psychotherapy. *American Journal of Psychiatry, 164,* 853-855.

Caspi, A., & Moffitt, T. E. (2018). All for one and one for all: Mental disorders in one dimension. *American Journal of Psychiatry, 175,* 831–844.

Clarkin, J. F., Levy, K. N., & Ellison, W. D. (2010). Personality disorders. In L. M. Horowitz & S. Strack (Eds.), *Handbook of Interpersonal Psychology: Theory, Research, Assessment, and Therapeutic Interventions* (pp. 383–403). New York: John Wiley.

de Jong, P. J. (2002). Implicit self-esteem and social anxiety: Differential self-favouring effects in high and low anxious individuals. *Behaviour Research and Therapy, 40,* 501–508.

Fonagy, P., Gergely, G., & Jurist, E. L. (2004). *Affect Regulation, Mentalization and the Development of the Self.* New York: Other Press.

Gabbard, G. (2007). Do all roads lead to Rome? Findings on Borderline Personality Disorder (editorial). *American Journal of Psychiatry, 164,* 853–855.

Gelso, C. J. (2010). *The Real Relationship in Psychotherapy: The Hidden Foundation of Change.* Washington, DC: American Psychological Association.

Gill, M. M. (1979). The analysis of the transference. *Journal of the American Psychoanalytic Association, 27,* 263–289.

Greenberg, D. M., Kolasi, J., Hegsted, C. P., Berkowitz, Y., & Jurist, E. L. (2017). Mentalized affectivity: A new model and assessment of emotion regulation. *PLoS ONE,* 12(10), e0185264.

Gregory, R. J., Delucia-Deranja, E., & Mogle, J. A. (2010). Dynamic deconstructive psychotherapy versus optimized community care for borderline personality disorder co-occurring with alcohol use disorders: 30-month follow-up. *Journal of Nervous and Mental Disease, 198,* 292–298.

Gunderson, J. G., & Links, P. (2008). *Borderline Personality Disorder: A Clinical Guide.* Washington, DC: American Psychiatric Press.

Gunderson, J. G., & Links, P. (2014). *Handbook of Good Psychiatric Management for Borderline Personality Disorder.* Washington, DC: American Psychiatric Press.

Huprich, S. K., & Nelson, S. M. (2015). Advancing the assessment of personality pathology with the cognitive-affective processing system. *Journal of Personality Assessment, 97,* 467–477.

Jurist, E. (2005). Mentalized affectivity. *Psychoanalytic Psychology, 22*(3), 426–444.

Kernberg, O. F. (1967). Borderline personality organization. *Journal of the American Psychoanalytic Association, 15*(3), 641–685.

Kernberg, O. F. (2001). Object relations, affects, drives: Toward a new synthesis. *Psychoanalytic Inquiry, 21*(5), 604–619.

Kernberg, O. F., & Caligor, E. (2005). A psychoanalytic theory of personality disorders. In M. Lenzenweger & J. F. Clarkin (Eds.), *Major Theories of Personality Disorder* (2nd ed., pp. 114–156). New York: Guilford Press.

Levy, K. N., & Scala, J. W. (2012). Transference, transference interpretations, and transference-focused psychotherapies. *Psychotherapy, 49*(3), 391–403.

LeBreton, J. M., Moeller, A., Johnson, B. N., & Levy, K. N. (in press). Conceptualizing and measuring the implicit personality. In D. Wood, S. J. Read, P. D. Harms, & A. Slaughter (Eds.), *Emerging Approaches to Measuring and Modeling the Person and Situation.*

McMain, S. F., Links, P. S., Gnam, W. H., Guimond, T., Cardish, R. J., Korman, L., & Streiner, D. L. (2009). A randomized trial of dialectical behavior therapy versus general psychiatric management for borderline personality disorder. *American Journal of Psychiatry, 166*(12), 1365–1374.

Mischel, W., & Shoda, Y. (1995). A cognitive-affective system theory of personality: Reconceptualizing situations, dispositions, dynamics, and invariance in personality structure. *Psychological Review, 102,* 246–268.

Sansone, R. A., Kay, J., & Anderson, J. L. (2013). Resident didactic education in borderline personality disorder: Is it sufficient? *Academic Psychiatry, 37,* 287–288.

Scala, J. W., Levy, K. N., Johnson, B. N., Kivity, Y., Ellison, W. D., Pincus, A. L., ... Wilson, S. J. (2018). The role of negative affect and self-concept clarity in predicting self-injurious urges using ecological momentary assessment. *Journal of Personality Disorders, 32,* 36–57.

Sharp, C., Wright, A. G., Fowler, J. C., Frueh, B. C., Allen, J. G., Oldham, J., & Clark, L. A. (2015). The structure of personality pathology: Both general ('g') and specific ('s') factors? *Journal of Abnormal Psychology, 124*(2), 387–398.

Teachman, B. A., & Allen, J. P. (2007). Development of social anxiety: Social interaction predictors of implicit and explicit fear of negative evaluation. *Journal of Abnormal Child Psychology, 35,* 63–78.

Teachman, B. A., & Woody, S. R. (2002). Automatic processing in spider phobia: Implicit fear associations over the course of treatment. *Journal of Abnormal Psychology, 112,* 100–109.

Teachman, B. A., Woody, S. R., & Magee, J. (2006). *Implicit and explicit appraisals of the importance of intrusive thoughts. Behaviour Research and Therapy, 44,* 785–805.

Wright, A. G. C., Hopwood, C. J., Skodol, A. E., & Morey, L. C. (2016). *Longitudinal validation of general and specific structural features of personality pathology. Journal of Abnormal Psychology, 135,* 1120–1134.

18b Consideration of Commonalities in Distinct Models of Treatment for Individuals with Borderline Personality Disorder: Commentary on Psychoanalytic/ Psychodynamic Approaches to Personality Disorders

NICHOLAS SALSMAN AND LAURENCE Y. KATZ

The chapter from Fonagy, Bateman, Luyten, Allison, and Campbell (this volume) on psychoanalytic/psychodynamic approaches to personality disorder and their description of mentalization-based treatment (MBT) delineates a number of striking similarities with the principles of dialectical behavior therapy (DBT, Linehan, 1993). These two treatments are very different and there is no evidence suggesting equivalence, but the common principles may be indicative of areas of shared understanding of best practices in the treatment of individuals with borderline personality disorder (BPD). The differences between the two treatments may also illuminate empirical questions needing further exploration. The amassed empirical support for each of these approaches reflects that these treatments can work for individuals with BPD. Examining the commonalities and differences among them may offer ideas about critical elements of any effective treatment of BPD.

COMMON STRUCTURAL PROPERTIES OF MBT AND DBT

Fonagy et al. describe nine structural properties of MBT, which have significant overlap with structural properties of DBT. The first principle describes maintaining client engagement through the use of a combination of validation with "the need to address behaviors that interfere with therapy such as alcohol or substance abuse or self-harm" (p. 434 in the previous chapter). In their MBT manual, Bateman and Fonagy (2016) elucidate how from the initial sessions, the therapist and client work together to agree to reduce self-harm and consistently target this behavior through analysis of self-harm behavior and generation of ways to change. This first structural property of MBT suggests that it is important for treatment providers to combine two distinct approaches. DBT practitioners strive to continually synthesize acceptance and change. Treatment providers are expected to synthesize these two distinct approaches in every moment of the treatment. On the acceptance side DBT practitioners utilize validation,

teach and practice acceptance skills, and employ mindfulness. These acceptance-based techniques are balanced with change-focused interventions, such as change oriented skills, contingency management, and cognitive modification, to help clients change their destructive behaviors. Both treatments emphasize the importance of validating clients' experiences while also helping them to change critical actions.

The second structural property of MBT is to have a model of pathology that is described to the patient. Adherents of DBT follow this principle as well through the utilization of the biosocial model (see Crowell, Beauchaine, & Linehan, 2009 for an explanation of this theory). In DBT, this model, based in research, guides therapist action, helps to remove blame and judgment, and increases the likelihood of validation of self and others. The biosocial model describes how problems like the symptoms of BPD develop as an individual's biologically based emotional vulnerability transacts with an invalidating environment, i.e., the person does the best that they can to adapt within the environment. Similarly, Fonagy et al. state that from the MBT perspective, "personality disorders are not seen as disorders of personality, but as understandable adaptations to the environment, even if they ultimately are counterproductive in terms of the functioning of the individual" (p. 432 in the previous chapter). Both of these models offer validating and non-judgmental explanations for the problems experienced by people with BPD, which effectively inform treatment.

The third structural property of MBT described by the authors is that therapists actively develop a strong therapeutic relationship with validation. The relationship between therapist and a chronically suicidal client in DBT is considered critical. Linehan (1993, p. 154) states, "Indeed, the strength of the relationship is what keeps such a patient (and often the therapist as well) in the therapy. At times, if all else fails, the strength of the relationship will keep a patient alive during a crisis." Validation strategies are considered to be a critical set of strategies that are used consistently throughout DBT to engage the client, maintain the relationship, and re-

regulate emotion. There is an assumption in DBT that the therapeutic relationship is a real relationship between equals. Linehan (1997) describes six levels of validation, with the highest level being radical genuineness, where the therapist engages with the client as their genuine self, not adopting a persona or playing a role with insincere mannerisms of how a therapist should act. Fonagy et al. (this volume) list the sixth structural property of MBT as, "adoption of a structure of treatment that suggests increased activity, proactivity, and self-agency (avoiding the use of an expert stance, and encouraging collaboration with the patient and a 'sit side-by-side' therapeutic attitude)" (p. 434 in the previous chapter). The importance of a collaborative relationship built with validation highlights that having a human-to-human connection may be a critical element of treatment. The seventh structural property of MBT describes the importance of a robust relationship between therapist and client. DBT therapists are called to explicitly target behaviors of the client or therapist that interfere with the treatment. This principle creates a structure that is explicitly designed to foster a robust relationship. Thus, both MBT and DBT place immense importance on actively building a therapeutic relationship that is genuine, validating, and able to withstand significant tension.

The fourth structural property of MBT is, "a focus on emotion processing and the connection between actions and feelings" and the fifth structural property is "a genuine inquiry into patients' mental states (behavioral analysis, clarification, confrontation)" (Fonagy et al., this volume, p. 434 in the previous chapter). DBT is an emotion-focused treatment and it conceptualizes BPD as a disorder of emotion regulation. The treatment teaches individuals to practice experiencing their emotions without avoidance or holding on to their emotions. Actions such as self-injury and suicidal behaviors are assessed through a process of behavioral chain analysis and these behaviors and their determinants are understood through examining links consisting of emotions, thoughts, actions, physical sensations, and environmental events. Through the therapist and client developing a mutual understanding of the behaviors and their determinants, solutions specifically targeting problematic links can be developed. The centrality of emotions and systematic analysis of how actions, internal experiences and the environment transact are principles that are shared by both treatments.

The eighth structural property of MBT described by the authors is that treatment providers structure their interventions based on a manual and supervision is used to sustain adherence to the manual. The ninth structural property of MBT is that everyone involved with the therapeutic milieu is committed to MBT and strengthens validation of the patient's emotions and thoughts. These structural properties highlight a team approach to MBT. In DBT, all DBT providers including individual therapists and group leaders meet weekly for a consultation team. This consultation team is set up to accomplish two main

goals: (1) to monitor and maintain the adherence of the members of the team to the DBT principles described by Linehan (1993, 2015) and (2) to enhance therapist motivation. The team approach in DBT is sometimes thought of as a community of providers treating a community of clients. In the weekly team meeting, providers remind themselves of the mutual agreements of the team members, including an agreement called the phenomenological empathy agreement, where therapists are called to understand patients' and each other's behaviors from a non-pejorative and validating perspective. Both MBT and DBT build structures into treatment in order to increase adherence to the treatment principles and utilize a community of providers to reinforce the principles with clients.

SKILLS TRAINING IN THE TREATMENT OF INDIVIDUALS WITH PERSONALITY DISORDERS

The authors cite Fonagy and Luyten (2016) in hypothesizing about three communication systems that are present in effective treatments for individuals with personality disorders. These three systems are "the teaching and learning of content," "the re-emergence of robust mentalizing," and "the re-emergence of social learning." These systems point to the central importance of skills training in effective treatment. Language, methodology, and content of skills training differ greatly in MBT and DBT and these differences may point to empirical questions about the impact of different skills and the need to study mechanisms of change in these treatments to inform necessary treatment components. Nonetheless, the underlying principle of engaging in skills training as a critical part of treatment is present in both therapies. Linehan (2015) describes three phases of learning in skills training: knowledge acquisition, skills strengthening, and skills generalization. These three phases have some striking parallels with the three communication systems. Knowledge acquisition involves using didactic strategies to convey the information that is a necessary, but not sufficient, prerequisite of practicing the skills. This phase has parallels to the system of "teaching and learning content." The second phase of learning, skills strengthening, involves practicing the skills in order to translate knowledge into action. This practice is necessary to allow skills to become more robust, as indicated by Fonagy et al. (this volume). Bateman and Fonagy (2016) indicate that the setting of therapy serves the function of increasing skills. The third phase of learning, skills generalization, involves learning to apply skills in all relevant contexts. Fonagy et al. (this volume) say of the third communication system, "This allows the patient to apply his/her new mentalizing and communicative capabilities to wider social encounters, outside the consulting room" (p. 436 in the previous chapter). Thus, what clients learn in treatment must then be generalized to life outside of treatment.

THE ROLE OF INSIGHT IN MBT AND DBT

In both MBT and DBT, insight is not prioritized as an outcome that needs to come first. Fonagy et al. (this volume) state:

In MBT, the aim and the actual outcome of an intervention on the patient's immediate emotional and cognitive state is thought to be more important than the insight gained from interpreting particular defenses or understanding aspects of the transference relationship, although of course such insights emerge during treatment. (p. 434 in the previous chapter)

In DBT, an emphasis often is placed first on changing behavior and then having insight follow. In response to criticism that DBT focuses only on symptoms and does not treat underlying causes, Bedics, Atkins, Comtois, and Linehan (2012) conducted an analysis to examine if and how DBT produces intra-psychic change in comparison to treatment by non-behavioral experts in the context of a randomized controlled trial with suicidal individuals with BPD. Their analyses revealed that individuals in DBT had significantly greater increases on the introject affiliation measure from Lorna Benjamin's Structural Analysis of Social Behavior (Benjamin, 1974) than individuals in treatment by non-behavioral experts. These analyses revealed that in DBT, although emphasis may often be placed first on behavioral change, the process of change leads to significant changes in how people perceive themselves. This de-emphasis of insight as a primary agent of change then frees the therapeutic dyad to prioritize elements of treatment such as emotional experiencing. As Fonagy et al (this volume) state, when there are breaks in mentalizing, the therapist attends to those moments and, "explores the current emotional context in the session by identifying the momentary affective state between patient and therapist" (p. 435 in the previous chapter).

THE IMPORTANCE OF FLEXIBILITY AMONG TREATMENT PROVIDERS

In MBT and DBT emphasis is placed on adherence to the principles of the treatment manuals, and nonetheless both treatments emphasize the need for flexible application of these principles. In principle-based treatment, there are few if any situations where there is only one correct intervention. Thus, practitioners of these principle-based treatments should be able to apply principles without rigidity. Fonagy et al. (this volume) state, "The psychoanalytic approach encompasses a uniquely sophisticated model of the mind, which, if applied with intellectual openness rather than rigid orthodoxy, can tolerate the categorical complexity of personality-disordered states" (p. 436 in the previous chapter). In DBT, flexibility is critical in the delivery of treatment. Responding in the moment to a client who is struggling with intense emotion dysregulation requires mindfulness on the part of the therapist and effective problem-solving. In describing dialectical strategies in DBT using the metaphor of ballroom dancing, Linehan (1993) states:

"Dancing" with the patient often requires the therapist to move quickly from strategy to strategy, alternating acceptance with change, control with letting go, confrontation with support, the carrot with the stick, a hard edge with softness, and so on in rapid succession. (p. 203)

Rigid orthodoxy will prevent a person from engaging effectively and genuinely in the therapeutic process with individuals with BPD.

CONCLUSION

The psychoanalytic approaches, including MBT, are quite distinct from DBT. The differences range from key divergence in overarching theory to significant variation in the interventions utilized in moment-to-moment interactions. It is our belief that having distinct, empirically validated approaches to treating individuals with BPD will serve the greatest good. There is no one treatment that works for everyone suffering from BPD. Therefore, the availability of varied treatments is likely to increase the proportion of individuals with BPD who are treated with an effective intervention.

Nonetheless, the goal of this commentary is to identify some commonalities in principles shared between MBT and DBT, which may be indicative of best practices when treating individuals with BPD. Some candidates for what may be best practices include approaching treatment with a balanced combination of validation and change-based strategies which directly target severe behaviors such as suicidal behaviors and non-suicidal self-injury; providing a compassionate model of the pathology; actively building a strong, genuine, and validating therapeutic relationship; a central focus on emotions and how they are related to actions; use of a team-based approach that promotes adherence to the treatment model; teaching skills that address the model of pathology; and promoting flexibility within the treatment approach to address the complexities of the clients' problems. We would hypothesize that within these commonalities are some necessary, but not sufficient conditions for effective treatment of individuals with BPD. Further research on mechanisms of change is needed to develop a more complete understanding. Examining other empirically supported treatments may help to clarify if they too include these commonalities. It may also be helpful to understand how and why other treatments deviate from these principles.

REFERENCES

Bateman, A., & Fonagy, P. (2016). *Mentalization-Based Treatment for Personality Disorders*. New York: Oxford University Press.

Bedics, J., Atkins, D. C., Comtois, K. A., & Linehan, M. M. (2012). Treatment differences in the therapeutic relationship and introject during a 2-year randomized controlled trial of Dialectical Behavior Therapy versus nonbehavioral psychotherapy experts for borderline personality disorder. *Journal of Consulting and Clinical Psychology, 80*, 66–77.

Benjamin, L. S. (1974). Structural analysis of social behavior. *Psychological Review, 81*, 392–425.

Crowell, S. E., Beauchaine, T. P., & Linehan, M. M. (2009). A biosocial developmental model of borderline personality: Elaborating and extending Linehan's theory. *Psychological Bulletin, 135*, 495–510.

Fonagy, P., & Luyten, P. (2016). A multilevel perspective on the development of borderline personality disorder. In D. Cicchetti (Ed.), *Developmental Psychopathology, Volume 3: Maladaptation and Psychopathology* (3rd ed., pp. 726–792). New York: John Wiley.

Linehan, M. (1993). *Cognitive-Behavioral Treatment of Borderline Personality Disorder*. New York: Guilford Press.

Linehan, M. (1997). Validation and psychotherapy. In A. C. Bohart & L. S. Greenberg (Eds.), *Empathy Reconsidered: New Directions in Psychotherapy* (pp. 353–392). Washington, DC: American Psychological Association.

Linehan, M. (2015). *DBT Skills Training Manual* (2nd ed.). New York: Guilford Press.

18c Further Development of Three Key Issues: Author Rejoinder to Commentaries on Psychoanalytic/ Psychodynamic Approaches to Personality Disorders

PETER FONAGY, ANTHONY BATEMAN, PATRICK LUYTEN, ELIZABETH ALLISON, AND CHLOE CAMPBELL

We are delighted to have two expert and enlightening commentaries on our chapter and we broadly concur with both in the issues raised. Given space limitations, this rejoinder takes up a few key issues raised for further development, including (a) the full range of available psychodynamic treatments, (b) the added value of a dimensional approach, and (c) the role of transference.

THE FULL RANGE OF AVAILABLE PSYCHODYNAMIC TREATMENTS

As Levy (this volume) points out, we did not cover the full range of psychodynamic treatments available for personality disorder, such as Dynamic Deconstructive Psychotherapy, Psychodynamic Supportive Therapy, and Good Psychiatric Management (GPM). Psychodynamic understanding and relational processes form a central part of GPM for BPD, which is now manualized (Gunderson & Links, 2014). GPM is a structured treatment based on supportive dynamic psychotherapy. The underlying theory is that interpersonal sensitivity is at the core of the disorder. As a result, considerable emphasis is placed on forming a working and relational therapeutic alliance and focusing on interpersonal sensitivities of the patient. Management of self-destructive behaviors and impulsivity, and help with emotional regulation is undertaken pragmatically using medication, reassurance, psychoeducation, and crisis management. An RCT comparing GPM with dialectical behavior therapy (DBT) showed no differences between treatments on any outcomes at the end of treatment or at two-year follow-up (McMain, Guimond, Streiner, Cardish, & Links, 2012; McMain et al., 2009).

The value of giving a full account of the range of possible treatments for BPD is underscored by the findings of Cristea and colleagues' meta-analysis, which found roughly equal treatment effect sizes for all bona fide psychotherapeutic interventions (Cristea et al., 2017). The fact there is now a variety of approaches that are effective in the treatment of BPD – not many years ago regarded as a condition that was almost impossible to treat – is, as Salsman and Katz (this volume) remark, a state of affairs to be celebrated. Some interventions will be more acceptable and/or effective than others for different individuals. Embracing a heterodoxy of approaches and thinking about intervention choices in a way that is tailored to best meet the needs of the patient is an issue that is gaining increasing traction as a result of growing challenges to the categorical diagnostic approach to psychopathology. It is being compellingly argued that problems such as comorbidity (Copeland, Shanahan, Erkanli, Costello, & Angold, 2013; Kessler, Chiu, Demler, Merikangas, & Walters, 2005; Merikangas et al., 2010) and lack of clarity around severity and what this might mean for disease boundaries (Zimmermann, Morgan, & Stanton, 2018) reflect the distinct possibility that existing categories lack validity. These issues – of comorbidity and severity – are, of course, of particular clinical relevance in the treatment of PD.

ADDED VALUE OF A DIMENSIONAL APPROACH

A dimensional approach to psychopathology is being increasingly considered more clinically useful as well as more conceptually and empirically valid (Beauchaine & Cicchetti, 2016; Forbes, Tackett, Markon, & Krueger, 2016). The emerging body of evidence on the general psychopathology factor (the "p" factor) also supports the empirical validity of the dimensional approach (Caspi & Moffitt, 2018). As suggested by Levy, more could have been said in our original text on the key topical research area of the p factor. We have written extensively about this elsewhere (Fonagy, Luyten, Allison, & Campbell, 2017a, 2017b). Recent research indeed points to a general vulnerability for persistent distressing conditions characterized by a lack of emotional stability running the gamut of diagnostic conditions not fully accounted for by associations at the spectral level (Sharp et al., 2015).

One of the significant benefits of a dimensional approach to psychopathology is that it supports and advances the case for a more flexible and tailored approach to psychopathology by undermining the tendency to regard a patient as a mere manifestation of a diagnostic category. As Salsman and Katz elegantly point out, flexibility in thinking about treatment according to individual needs is essential if we are to hope that patients do not withdraw "from engaging effectively and genuinely in the therapeutic process."

There are many additional valuable points that we would like to follow up in the rich and thoughtful commentaries provided by Levy and Salsman and Katz; unfortunately space does not allow us to do so. However, we would particularly like to acknowledge Levy's point about the use of jargon. The chapter could indeed have benefited from a more restrained use of psychoanalytic language, and we regard this comment as a well-placed reminder of this occupational hazard/indulgence of the psychoanalytic world.

THE ROLE OF TRANSFERENCE

A further point we would like to mention is the role of transference, as discussed by Levy. The concept of transference is problematic and multi-layered, and restricting it to unconscious experiences is a controversial issue even within the psychoanalytic world. Our position has always been that transference is key to mentalizing relationships, most particularly the one in the here-and-now with the therapist, which is likely to be critical to achieving significant therapeutic gain. Implicitly all therapeutic approaches address the issue, in terms of aspects of relational processes that interfere with therapy, as in DBT, or as something that informs about childhood experience and its current representation in the patient's mind, as in classical psychoanalysis. In all these contexts, addressing and working with the therapeutic relationship serves to increase the psychosocial literacy of the patient in terms of learning about other minds as well as their own. In that sense, we would suggest that all psychodynamic therapeutic modalities focus on the clinician–patient relationship in the hope that doing so will contribute to the patient's well-being. While patterns of relationships – whether in therapy, from childhood, or outside therapy – might be pointed to, a difference between the more classical psychodynamic approach and MBT-informed approaches is that the purpose of this relationship focus is not primarily to provide insight or explanation to the patient. Rather, it is in the service of stimulating and strengthening mentalizing, and of adopting a thoughtful, inquisitive stance in relation to mental states in self and others.

REFERENCES

Beauchaine, T. P., & Cicchetti, D. (2016). A new generation of comorbidity research in the era of neuroscience and Research Domain Criteria. *Development and Psychopathology*, 28(4 Pt 1), 891–894.

Caspi, A., & Moffitt, T. E. (2018). All for one and one for all: Mental disorders in one dimension. *American Journal of Psychiatry*, 175(9), 831–844.

Copeland, W. E., Shanahan, L., Erkanli, A., Costello, E. J., & Angold, A. (2013). Indirect comorbidity in childhood and adolescence. *Frontiers in Psychiatry*, 4, 144.

Cristea, I. A., Gentili, C., Cotet, C. D., Palomba, D., Barbui, C., & Cuijpers, P. (2017). Efficacy of psychotherapies for borderline personality disorder: A systematic review and meta-analysis. *JAMA Psychiatry*, 74(4), 319–328.

Fonagy, P., Luyten, P., Allison, E., & Campbell, C. (2017a). What we have changed our minds about: Part 1. Borderline personality disorder as a limitation of resilience. *Borderline Personality Disorder and Emotional Dysregulation*, 4, 11. doi:10.1186/s40479-017-0061-9

Fonagy, P., Luyten, P., Allison, E., & Campbell, C. (2017b). What we have changed our minds about: Part 2. Borderline personality disorder, epistemic trust and the developmental significance of social communication. *Borderline Personality Disorder and Emotional Dysregulation*, 4, 9. doi:10.1186/s40479-017-0062-8

Forbes, M. K., Tackett, J. L., Markon, K. E., & Krueger, R. F. (2016). Beyond comorbidity: Toward a dimensional and hierarchical approach to understanding psychopathology across the life span. *Development and Psychopathology*, 28(4 Pt 1), 971–986.

Gunderson, J. G., & Links, P. (2014). *Handbook of Good Psychiatric Management for Borderline Personality Disorder*. Washington, DC: American Psychiatric Press.

Kessler, R. C., Chiu, W. T., Demler, O., Merikangas, K. R., & Walters, E. E. (2005). Prevalence, severity, and comorbidity of 12-month DSM-IV disorders in the National Comorbidity Survey Replication. *Archives of General Psychiatry*, 62(6), 617–627.

McMain, S. F., Guimond, T., Streiner, D. L., Cardish, R. J., & Links, P. S. (2012). Dialectical behavior therapy compared with general psychiatric management for borderline personality disorder: Clinical outcomes and functioning over a 2-year follow-up. *American Journal of Psychiatry*, 169(6), 650–661.

McMain, S. F., Links, P. S., Gnam, W. H., Guimond, T., Cardish, R. J., Korman, L., & Streiner, D. L. (2009). A randomized trial of dialectical behavior therapy versus general psychiatric management for borderline personality disorder. *American Journal of Psychiatry*, 166(12), 1365–1374.

Merikangas, K. R., He, J. P., Burstein, M., Swanson, S. A., Avenevoli, S., Cui, L., . . . Swendsen, J. (2010). Lifetime prevalence of mental disorders in U.S. adolescents: Results from the National Comorbidity Survey Replication–Adolescent Supplement (NCS-A). *Journal of the American Academy of Child & Adolescent Psychiatry*, 49(10), 980–989.

Sharp, C., Wright, A. G. C., Fowler, J. C., Frueh, B. C., Allen, J. G., Oldham, J., & Clark, L. (2015). Borderline personality pathology as the 'g' factor of personality disorder. *Journal of Abnormal Psychology*, 124(2), 387–398.

Zimmermann, M., Morgan, T. A., & Stanton, K. (2018). The severity of psychiatric disorders *World Psychiatry*, 17(3), 258–275.

19 Using DSM-5 and ICD-11 Personality Traits in Clinical Treatment

BO BACH AND JENNIFER PRESNALL-SHVORIN

This chapter provides a guideline for how maladaptive personality traits may inform treatment planning and therapy for individuals with personality problems and disorders. As reviewed elsewhere in this handbook, both the DSM-5 and ICD-11 have moved towards dimensional trait models of personality disorders that are substantially coherent with the universal Five-Factor Model of Personality (see Table 19.2). Importantly, the DSM-5 and ICD-11 trait domains have been replicated across different cultures (e.g., Bach, Sellbom, Kongerslev, et al., 2017; Lotfi, Bach, Amini, & Simonsen, 2018; Pires, Sousa Ferreira, & Gonçalves, 2017). Accordingly, this chapter primarily will focus on maladaptive traits according to the DSM-5 Section III and the ICD-11, which we anticipate will provide considerable worldwide utility for using those new diagnostic systems in treatment planning.

As therapists, we wish to maximize the possibility of successful outcomes in treatment while minimizing unnecessary discomfort and negative effects, which can be challenging when working with personality disordered patients. On one hand, we want to enable treatment compliance and motivate energetic patient efforts. On the other hand, we want to address the core issues that are driving the clinical problems. Our goal in this chapter is to discuss how to consider personality traits in the service of accommodating both of these needs in a clinical setting.

The last 70 years of research on individual differences suggest that personality trait assessment should be included in treatment planning independent of therapeutic framework (Allport, 1961; Cattell, 1943; Eysenck, 1947; Harkness & Lilienfeld, 1997). In the absence of personality trait formulations, therapists may misunderstand that signs and symptoms conceptualized as "presenting complaints" or "targets of treatment" may be manifestations of maladaptive personality traits. The essential role of traits in conceptions of disordered personality is already recognized in the DSM-IV/5 definition of personality disorder as characterized by inflexible and maladaptive *traits*. However, DSM-IV/5 personality disorder categories are implicitly composed of heterogeneous trait configurations (Bach, Anderson, & Simonsen, 2017;

Morey, Benson, & Skodol, 2016; Presnall, 2013). Each DSM-IV/5 personality disorder category appears to be a compound assortment of maladaptive personality traits, which essentially complicates empirically based treatment (Lynam & Widiger, 2001). For example, when treating borderline personality disorder, we do not know for sure whether we are dealing with separation/abandonment anxiety, aggression/hostility, or impulsivity/risk taking. Thus, for a more meaningful and more focused treatment, we need to direct our attention to the homogeneous building blocks of personality psychopathology, or *traits* (Widiger & Clark, 2000). Accordingly, it should be obvious that therapies for personality disorders would focus on managing and treating specific maladaptive traits instead of heterogeneous categories. In other words, therapists should treat specific problems (e.g., emotional lability) and not diagnoses (e.g., borderline personality disorder). In addition to a large body of research showing that traits influence our reactions to events in general (Kotov, Gamez, Schmidt, & Watson, 2010; Roberts, Kuncel, Shiner, Caspi, & Goldberg, 2007), it has also been shown that traits shape our responses to treatment (Bagby, Gralnick, Al-Dajani, & Uliaszek, 2016). Importantly, a systematic review of the literature shows that traits are not only robust predictors of important life outcomes, but appear to be amenable to intervention (Roberts, Luo, et al., 2017). However, most current treatments barely mention this matter. Instead, the psychodynamic and cognitive behavior therapy literature usually refers to enduring features of attachment styles, defense mechanisms, schemas, and self–other narratives, which are either manifestations of or otherwise associated with traits (e.g., Bach & Bernstein, 2019; Fossati et al., 2015; Granieri et al., 2017; Hopwood, Schade, Krueger, Wright, & Markon, 2013).

As summarized in Table 19.1, personality traits can be used in treatment in a number of ways (Bagby et al., 2016; Harkness & Lilienfeld, 1997).

The recommendations for DSM-5 and ICD-11 informed treatment presented in this chapter are generally supported by research derived from universal five-factor traits (Widiger & Costa, 2013), the Dimensional Assessment of

Table 19.1 Six ways mental health care may benefit from considering patient traits
1. Provide a context for establishing a favorable treatment alliance with the patient
2. Guide therapists in tailoring treatment to personality
3. Provide a framework for understanding basic traits that are hardwired (and should be accepted) versus maladaptive trait expressions that are changeable (and should be treated)
4. Improve the patient's self-knowledge, insight, and motivation for treatment
5. Promote psychoeducation about how personality traits serve to maintain symptoms
6. Encourage patients to broaden their desired treatment goals beyond symptom improvement

Personality Pathology (Livesley, 2003), the Schedule for Nonadaptive and Adaptive Personality (Clark, 1993), and the Minnesota Multiphasic Personality Inventory – Personality Psychopathology 5 (Harkness & McNulty, 2006), which all describe different aspects and levels of the Five-Factor Model (Widiger & Simonsen, 2005). In recent years, hundreds of studies have provided empirical support for the DSM-5 traits (Al-Dajani, Gralnick, & Bagby, 2016; Miller, Sleep, & Lynam, 2018) as measured with the Personality Inventory for DSM-5 (PID-5; Krueger, Derringer, Markon, Watson, & Skodol, 2012). Essentially, all of the aforementioned measures have shown substantial convergence with the DSM-5 and ICD-11 trait domains (Anderson et al., 2013; Bach, Sellbom, Skjernov, & Simonsen, 2018; Bastiaens et al., 2016; Clark et al., 2015; Gore & Widiger, 2013; Oltmanns & Widiger, 2018). However, not all the specific ideas discussed below have been empirically validated, such as how to structure a therapeutic alliance with a patient characterized by detachment.

PRE-TREATMENT ASSESSMENT OF TRAITS

Before a therapist can take traits into account, there must be an appropriate and feasible method of trait assessment. In regards to the maladaptive traits described in DSM-5 and ICD-11, we recommend using at least one of several approaches. First, the PID-5 may be employed as a self-report form (Krueger et al., 2012) or informant report form (Markon, Quilty, Bagby, & Krueger, 2013). Likewise, the ICD-11 traits may be measured using the Personality Inventory for ICD-11 (PiCD; Oltmanns & Widiger, 2018). Another solution is to use a simple algorithm for deriving the five ICD-11 domains from PID-5 trait facets (Bach, Sellbom, Kongerslev, et al., 2017). For a more thorough assessment, the patient may be administered the Structured Clinical Interview for DSM-5 – Alternative Model of

Personality Disorder – Module II (SCID-AMPD; Skodol, First, Bender, & Oldham, 2018), which may also yield the five ICD-11 domains by using the aforementioned algorithm for that purpose (Bach, Sellbom, Kongerslev, et al., 2017). Finally, the traits may simply be rated by the therapist based on observations, unstructured questions, and/or other clinical information (Morey, Krueger, & Skodol, 2013). We refer to Miller et al. (2018) for an updated empirical review of the maladaptive traits described in DSM-5 Section III, and to Bach, Markon, Simonsen, and Krueger (2015) and Bach and First (2018) for clinical illustrations.

WHICH ASPECTS OF TRAITS SHOULD WE SEEK TO CHANGE?

An important distinction in this chapter is that traits should not be confused with the impairment they may cause, which is consistent with the well-known distinction by Allport (1961) that personality *is* something and personality *does* something. This also aligns with McCrae and Costa's (1995) distinction between *basic tendencies* and *characteristic adaptions*. For example, a patient who is prone to becoming anxious (i.e., trait anxiousness) could fashion many alternative adaptations in his or her everyday life to avoid or temporarily reduce anxiety, including social withdrawal, substance or alcohol use, self-help reading, exercise, or meditation. A similar distinction has been proposed by Leising and Zimmermann (2011), who describe *personality dispositions* that may become problematic as separate from the possible *negative consequences* of those personality patterns. For example, an individual may have a trait disposition to experience fear that results in frequently feeling stressed out and becoming socially isolated. Likewise, in the DSM-5 Section III system (American Psychiatric Association [APA], 2013) and the ICD-11 system (World Health Organization [WHO], 2019), personality disorders are conceptualized in terms of both stylistic traits and their related functional impairment/severity. Accordingly, a patient may have prominent features of negative affectivity, which may involve *mild* impairment in self and interpersonal functioning (e.g., some distress without serious dysfunction) or *severe* impairment in self and interpersonal functioning (e.g., hatred, self-harm, and/or psychotic-like perceptions under stress). Finally, this is comparable to the rationale provided in the Sociogenomic Trait Intervention Model (STIM), which focuses on changing trait-related states in a way that ensures the changes are enduring. However, only if these state changes become internalized, extended, and automatic would they qualify as changes in traits (Roberts, Hill, & Davis, 2017).

A basic clinical principle is that traits tend to be resistant to change, whereas characteristic adaptations or functional impairment may be less resistant to change. Therefore, treatment should target what personality *does* to the patient (i.e., characteristic adaptions), as we cannot really change what it *is* (i.e., basic tendencies). Not even 20 years on the couch can turn a high anxiousness Woody Allen-like character into a low anxiousness person. Instead, the patient may be helped to find new adaptive ways of coping that fits her or his traits, which offers better potential for constructive growth and more healthy relationships. In other words, one must learn to live well with oneself. Accordingly, the patient's level of impairment may be elucidated in terms of how much the traits impact the patient's ability to live a fulfilling life. In line with this, traits are important to address because their maladaptive expressions influence the clinical portrait. For example, emotional lability, anxiousness, and impulsivity affect how the patient responds to stress, challenges, and daily tasks. Clinical practice should therefore focus attention on understanding the traits while changing their consequences. This is consistent with Wachtel's (1973) suggestion that psychotherapeutic interventions should be targeted toward the choices of current environmental stimuli, rather than toward the underlying dispositions. From this perspective, lasting therapeutic change usually depends on modulating the impact of the traits and not getting rid of them, which will be further explained in the following.

HOW THERAPISTS MAY BENEFIT FROM CONSIDERING PATIENT TRAITS

As summarized in Table 19.1, psychotherapists may make use of patient trait information in several ways. In this section, we provide guidelines for how to use traits to establish a favorable treatment alliance, improve self-knowledge and insight for patients (including therapeutic assessment), and inform psychoeducation as well as the focus and implementation of treatment.

Using Traits to Establish a Favorable Treatment Alliance

As a precondition of effective treatment of the patient's problems, the therapist must establish a favorable alliance with the patient (Martin, Garske, & Davis, 2000). Most therapists intuitively adapt their personal style to the patient's personality traits. However, once a framework of personality traits is established, the therapist can do this more consciously and with more confidence (Gartstein, Putnam, Aron, & Rothbart, 2016). For each of the five DSM-5 and ICD-11 trait domains, we therefore present a tailored approach to forming the alliance in the "Guidelines for Specific Trait Domains."

Personality Traits as a Source of Self-Knowledge and Insight

It is vital for patients to understand their own self, as one must learn to live well with oneself (Gartstein et al., 2016). For example, individuals who acknowledge their own weaknesses and accurately perceive how others view them appear to be more liked by others (e.g., Oltmanns, Gleason, Klonsky, & Turkheimer, 2005). In other words, the insights gained from personality assessment may potentially improve relationships, which are often impaired among those with personality disorders.

The approach of collaborative therapeutic assessment is ideally suited for promoting self-knowledge (Fischer & Finn, 2008). In this procedure, patients can first be asked to identify questions about themselves that they would like the assessment to address. Subsequently, the test results can be used to answer the patient's questions after the assessment while also discussing the accuracy of the test profile and its interpretations. For example, are the traits demonstrated in everyday life and how? This approach not only relies on the validity/accuracy of the test results but also takes advantage of the profile as a framework for discussion of the patient's mental health issues in general. As a particularly powerful achievement, therapeutic assessment may also help patients develop a more compassionate understanding of themselves.

Using Traits in Psychoeducation

When working with traits, an essential goal is to help patients accept that traits are part of their biological heritage – and therefore something they must own – without conveying the idea that traits cannot be changed into something more adaptive. Personality traits are not fate, and knowing about them can actually lead to greater freedom. As previously emphasized, the patient must learn to live well with oneself. This balanced communication with the patient is achieved by educating the patient about how the environment influences traits, so that the patient understands that it is possible to adjust the way traits are expressed. Some aspects of traits are mostly hardwired, whereas others are more changeable. A particularly useful way of building this acceptance is to encourage patients to identify ways in which their traits may be beneficial (e.g., Figure 19.4 and Figure 19.6). As a part of this process, the therapist must teach the patient about what traits actually look like "in action." The most common traits probably emerged sometime in human history because they involved an adaptive advantage. They helped our remote ancestors solve adaptive problems in their environment and survive long enough to pass on their genes. For example, the disinhibition facet of impulsivity (see Figure 19.4) may have served as a productive feature when adaptive (e.g., quickly hunting down an animal) and a problematic feature when maladaptive (e.g., neglecting long-term consequences). This way of presenting the information suggests that traits are not naturally maladaptive; instead, they are only maladaptive when individuals have learned to express them in ways that cause dysfunction or lack the flexibility that applies to adaptive trait functioning (Livesley, 2003). Taken together, this kind of psychoeducation often facilitates change in and of itself. The patient does not have to change a global quality that he or she feels is a fundamental part of the self, but rather more specific aspects of his or her behavior.

Even apparently problematic traits such as emotional lability and anxiousness can be useful. For example, a male patient with high levels of depressivity and anxiousness that led to periods of misery and dysphoria learned to be more tolerant of these feelings when he recognized that they contributed to his work. He was an aspiring artist, and the despair and melancholy added a dimension to his paintings that was not present when his mood was less depressed. Previously, he feared the feelings of melancholy and dejection, and whenever his mood dropped, he would ruminate over problems instead of taking advantage of it. Once he realized that the feelings could be used creatively, he ruminated less and painted more, which in return had the impact of moderating his sadness.

As another example, a troubled writer and poet had extremely labile moods and was unsteady in her productivity due to emotional lability, impulsivity, eccentricity, and some unusual beliefs and experiences. Like the previous patient, she feared mood changes, but she also feared alienation and exclusion from society because of her way of being. She therefore regularly told herself that she could not handle this life and therefore had to kill herself. She did not attempt to kill herself, but used self-harm as a way of coping with the pain and disillusion. After some time, her emotional lability settled enough for her to realize that her vulnerable traits, eccentric style, and unusual perceptions actually helped her write peculiar but impressive avant-garde literature that was highly recognized among intellectuals. Consequently, instead of feeling despair, she began to appreciate the freshness, depth, spontaneity, and originality that her personality added to life. This development helped her to tolerate her emotional lability, which indirectly had a settling effect that reduced the impairment caused by this lability.

Finally, it is generally easier to acknowledge the adaptive significance of traits when the context is taken into account because traits are context-dependent. Therefore, a particular trait may be valuable in some situations but not in others. For example, the trait domain of detachment may be problematic in social situations (e.g., at parties), but it could be useful in other settings in which it is an advantage to be self-reliant, cool headed, capable of self-absorption, and have little need for interpersonal contact (e.g., an academic researcher or a "HGV" truck driver). Understanding this usefulness of otherwise maladaptive traits helps therapists and patients not to evaluate traits in all-or-none terms.

Using Traits to Inform Focus of Treatment

Psychotherapists need to work with traits in two ways. First, treatment must be tailored to fit patients' salient traits in addition to their psychopathology and presenting problems. For example, patients with trait features of negative affectivity as well as antagonism/dissociality and/or disinhibition are usually "too reactive." Consequently, an important task for therapists is to contain their behavior and reduce their reactivity by teaching them to both tolerate and regulate it. The opposite applies to patients with features of detachment and anankastia, as these patients are less emotionally responsive. Thus, the therapeutic task is to increase their emotional activity and liberty while also accepting their trait nature.

Secondly, as previously emphasized, treatment needs to focus on changing maladaptive traits into more adaptive traits, without seeking to get rid of the basic traits. Accordingly, treatment should focus on modulating trait expression by helping the patient to find more healthy or constructive ways to express or manage basic traits. Such management or modulation particularly makes sense when we look at how the environment influences trait expression. In other words, the environment may amplify or reduce the expression of the genetic trait dispositions (Livesley, 2003). This premise implies that it is possible to change the expression of maladaptive traits by modifying the environment. Accordingly, it may reduce maladaptive trait behavior in some patients if they are encouraged to evade certain situations and relationships that evoke these behaviors. Therapists often do this intuitively; for example, by helping patients to detect and prevent risk situations for self-harm such as spending too much time alone. This approach involves understanding that the highly emotionally labile patient will probably always be emotionally labile and experience mood swings, although the magnitude of these swings may be dampened by teaching the patient how to regulate emotions. Likewise, the detached patient with restricted affectivity and intimacy avoidance is unlikely to become even modestly extraverted and attention-seeking, but may be helped to feel more comfortable in relating to other people. A concrete implication of this approach is that some patients may benefit from receiving help in finding or generating environments that allow them to express their core traits in more functional and satisfying ways. This strategy particularly applies to patients at the extreme end of a trait continuum. For example, detached patients are best helped by encouraging them to create a fulfilling way of living that is consistent with their basic stylistic traits and needs, rather than attempting to modify traits that are "hardwired" and extremely resistant to change.

GUIDELINES FOR SPECIFIC DSM-5 AND ICD-11 TRAIT DOMAINS

In this section, we provide ideas for the treatment of specific trait domains in the DSM-5 Section III and the ICD-11 models of personality disorders, including negative affectivity, detachment, antagonism/dissociality,

Table 19.2 Alignment among DSM-5, ICD-11, and FFM traits

DSM-5	ICD-11	FFM
Negative Affectivity	Negative Affectivity	High Neuroticism
Detachment	Detachment	Low Extraversion
Antagonism	Dissociality	Low Agreeableness
Disinhibition	Disinhibition	Low Conscientiousness
(low Disinhibition)	Anankastia	High Conscientiousness
Psychoticism	(Schizotypal/ Dissociation)	High Openness

disinhibition, anankastia, and psychoticism. As shown in Table 19.2, the DSM-5 and ICD-11 trait domains are highly concordant and align with maladaptive extremes of universal five-factor traits. Based on a comprehensive review of the literature, it is assumed that the first two domains of negative affectivity (high neuroticism) and detachment (low extraversion) are most amenable to treatment (Roberts, Luo, et al., 2017).

Negative Affectivity

This domain is essentially the same as elevated neuroticism and comprises the opposite pole of emotional stability. It is not a coincidence that negative affectivity is presented here as the first domain, as it may lead to a number of obvious consequences including emotional crises, deliberate self-harm, and suicidality (Livesley, 2003). Patients with negative affectivity are typically characterized by anxiousness, emotional lability, low self-esteem, and depressivity, as well as their interpersonal (e.g., submissiveness) and behavioral (e.g., avoidance or self-harm) manifestations. The emotional dysregulation and anxiousness related to negative affectivity tend to disrupt cognition in the form of perseveration, separation insecurity, and suspiciousness, and interfere with interpersonal behavior in the form of hostility and submissiveness (APA, 2013; WHO, 2019). Consistent with the WHO characterization of non-specific psychological distress, negative affectivity is associated with elevated levels of emotional suffering that are shared with a wide range of disorders (without being specific to any single disorder) and predict a range of mental and physical problems and may tax one's ability to cope (Phillips, 2009).

Whereas negative affectivity is a component of nearly all personality disorders (with perhaps the exception of schizoid and antisocial/psychopathy), the presentation of the facets of negative affectivity may differ. The facet of

anxiousness may appear as social anxiousness, evaluation apprehension, and distrust-related anxiety as seen in avoidant and schizotypal disorders. Emotional lability and depressivity may be confined to affective dysregulation and feelings of shame and hopelessness, as seen in borderline personality disorder. The facet of hostility may manifest as the reactive anger of narcissistic personality disorder, dysregulated anger of borderline personality disorder, or the intimidating rage of antisocial personality disorder. The overall goal of treating negative affectivity is to help the patient find more adaptive expressions of this trait as illustrated in Figure 19.1.

Establishing a Therapeutic Relationship

The patient with prominent features of negative affectivity may also be characterized as the neurotic patient around whom many of the technical features of classic psychoanalysis were developed. Due to transference, the patient tends to link such neurotic features to the therapist: "Does the therapist really care about me or think about me between sessions?" Trait facets of submissiveness and separation insecurity in particular may influence the patient–therapist relationship. Depending on the configuration of counter-transference, the therapist may be overly nursing ("come to me, and let me soothe you") or sadistic/abusive ("get it together, pantywaist").

A more contemporary approach to building a successful alliance with patients characterized by negative affectivity involves (1) educating the patient about his or her willingness to experience anxiety and (2) encouraging the patient to regard the relationship with the therapist as simply providing more examples of how the patient is constantly scanning for cues of threats to self-esteem. In line with most traditional therapeutic approaches, the therapist aims to reduce such anxiety because it interferes with healthy information processing. For example, in response to a therapist's casual statement that a patient's suit is well tailored, the patient may anxiously wonder whether the therapist is saying "you need disguise because you are fat." Accordingly, interventions aimed at reducing the influence of anxiety and related difficulties may involve the therapist listening to how the patient listens to or perceives other's remarks (i.e., "listening to listening").

Treatment Goals for Negative Affectivity

Because emotional distress has historically been a chief component in patients' presenting complaints, virtually all modes of psychotherapy target aspects of negative affectivity to some degree (Widiger & Trull, 1992). For example, traditional Beckian cognitive therapy targets negative automatic thinking and beliefs often related to emotional disorders (Beck, 1983), dialectical behavior therapy targets emotional dysregulation (Linehan & Dexter-Mazza, 2008), acceptance and commitment therapy focuses on acceptance of negative affect (Hayes, 2004), and compassion focused therapy targets problematic cognitions and emotions related to anxiety, anger, trauma, shame, and self-criticism by means of

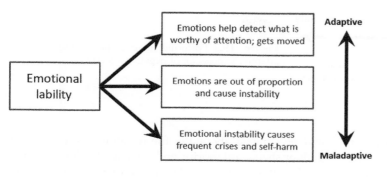

Figure 19.1 From maladaptive to adaptive expression of negative affectivity

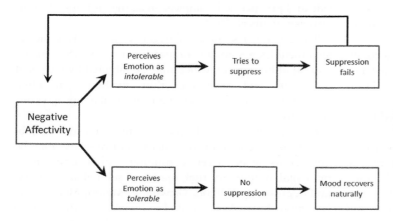

Figure 19.2 A rationale for focusing on negative affectivity in the treatment of emotional disorder

compassionate mind training (Gilbert, 2014). Transference-focused psychotherapy assumes that enhanced emotional control results from the resolution of structural impairments to personality that involve fragmented object relationships that are addressed in the context of the interaction between therapist and patient (Clarkin, Yeomans, & Kernberg, 2006). Mentalization based treatment assumes that emotion regulation increases with improved mentalizing capacity and epistemic trust (Bateman & Fonagy, 2016). Finally, schema therapy assumes that emotional suffering is reduced by fostering emotional fulfillment of the patient's inner "vulnerable child," including modification of underlying schemas, such as defectiveness and vulnerability to harm, through corrective emotional experiences (Young, Klosko, & Weishaar, 2003).

An implicit or explicit aim for most therapies seems to be to change the patient from anxious to non-anxious or mistrustful to trusting (e.g., Beck, Davis, & Freeman, 2015; Linehan & Dexter-Mazza, 2008). However, it may be false advertisement to claim that increased awareness of automatic appraisals will eventuate in the extinction of thoughts associated with negative affectivity. In fact, the single greatest misconception that patients (and many therapists) hold about therapy is that a high negative affectivity person can be turned into a low negative affectivity person. Instead, genetically influenced traits of negative affectivity may be modified by environmental manipulation, but only within certain limits. Accordingly, the patient can learn to identify and deal with automatic appraisals in a healthier manner. For example, he or she can learn to select new adaptations to the experience of anxiety or sadness. Yet, as previously mentioned, this is not the same as turning a Woody Allen-like patient with prominent negative affectivity into a patient with low negative affectivity. Figure 19.1 illustrates how the negative affectivity facet of emotional lability potentially may be expressed in a more adaptive manner. In general, it has been suggested that patients with negative affectivity may benefit from treatment that focuses more globally on emotion regulation and stress management skills (Bagby et al., 2016; Barlow, Sauer-Zavala, Carl, Bullis, & Ellard, 2014). Below, we present some examples of specific approaches and techniques that may be utilized to target problems related to negative affectivity.

The Unified Protocol is a specific transdiagnostic cognitive-behavioral approach designed for a range of emotional disorders that share the underlying trait of negative affectivity (Barlow et al., 2011), including mood and anxiety disorders and avoidant and borderline personality disorders (Sauer-Zavala, Bentley, & Wilner, 2016). The Unified Protocol approach targets negative affectivity by extinguishing distress in response to the experience of strong emotions. As illustrated in Figure 19.2, reduction of aversive reactions to emotions by improving tolerance is

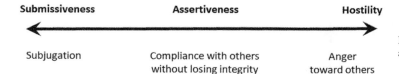

Figure 19.3 Fostering assertiveness ensures more adaptive expression of negative affectivity

thought to lead to less reliance on the maladaptive, avoidant emotion-regulation strategies that exacerbate symptoms. In the end, this is expected to lead to fewer negative emotions (Barlow et al., 2011; Sauer-Zavala et al., 2016). In other words, improvement of negative reactions to emotional stimuli reduces the intensity and frequency of forthcoming experiences and is thereby thought to enhance the adaptivity of negative affectivity.

Patients with prominent features of negative affectivity are not just chronically unhappy, anxious, or worried, but can easily be pushed over the edge when things actually do go wrong in their lives. Because of this chronic state of reactivity to challenging events, mindfulness-based treatment has been identified as an intervention that may be of particular value for helping individuals with negative affectivity cope with such challenges (Drake, Morris, & Davis, 2017). Accordingly, the patient is trained in practicing mindfulness by consciously, curiously, and acceptingly focusing attention on present thoughts, feelings, and bodily sensations without judgment or efforts to avoid or fight these experiences. In practice, patients are encouraged not to judge aspects of negative affectivity as negative, but to instead take a gentle, inquisitive attitude, which reduces racing thoughts, rumination, and worry (Dimidjian & Linehan, 2008) and changes the impact of negative emotions and sensations on the patient. Drake and colleagues (2017) found that even patients with the highest levels of negative affectivity can learn to cope with challenging life situations by drawing on mindfulness-based coping strategies. In other words, mindfulness may be viewed as a learned trait or skill that explains why some individuals with negative affectivity are less distressed than others. Mindfulness also comprises an essential part of the Unified Protocol and dialectical behavioral therapy.

The emotional lability facet of negative affectivity is a core feature of borderline personality disorder (Bach, Sellbom, Bo, & Simonsen, 2016), and involves instability of mood and emotions, including emotions that are intense, easily aroused, and/or out of proportion to circumstances. Patients experiencing emotional lability may often use maladaptive coping strategies, such as substance abuse, binge eating, self-harm, or other behaviors that function to avoid or suppress emotions. Dialectical behavioral therapy was developed to address this core feature by enhancing emotion regulation skills in terms of distress tolerance, acceptance, and mindful awareness (Linehan & Dexter-Mazza, 2008).

The depressivity facet of negative affectivity also deserves particular psychotherapeutic attention. This facet involves feelings of being down, hopeless, miserable, and pessimistic about the future, along with pervasive guilt or shame, inferiority, and suicidal ideation or behavior. Compassion focused therapy may be an efficient treatment to address the shame and self-criticism in patients with high levels of depressivity by helping the patient feel safe and practice self-compassion as the antithesis to self-criticism (Gilbert, 2014).

The anxiousness facet of negative affectivity typically also includes a somatic component (e.g., muscle tension and rapid heart rate), which may be targeted by means of relaxation and stress-reduction methods, including breathing exercises and neuromuscular progressive relaxation.

Interpersonal facets of negative affectivity, such as submissiveness, separation insecurity, and hostility, may be targeted using assertiveness training to change the environmental reinforcers that maintain self-defeat, anxiety, and depressivity (Millon, Grossman, Millon, Meagher, & Ramnath, 2004). As illustrated in Figure 19.3, this may be conceptualized as an assertive balance between submissiveness at one maladaptive pole and hostility at another maladaptive pole. The goal of this approach is to train patients to take care of their own needs in an adaptive manner by being sufficiently compliant when most appropriate, and saying no or protesting when most appropriate.

In general, negative affectivity is substantially related to most maladaptive schemas of emotional disorders as defined in the schema therapy model (Bach & Bernstein, 2019; Schmidt, Joiner Jr., Young, & Telch, 1995; Thimm, 2010). For example, the facet of separation insecurity aligns with the schema of abandonment, whereas the facet of submissiveness aligns with the schema of subjugation (Bach & Bernstein, 2019). Due to such schemas, patients with negative affectivity are likely to feel vulnerable, lonely, abandoned, distressed, and deprived from having their emotional needs met, which are sustained by the absence of healthy coping strategies. Consequently, patients with prominent features of negative affectivity may benefit from the schema-focused approaches used in schema therapy, such as enhancement of the patient's healthy adult function that must protect and soothe the vulnerable part of the patient (where negative affect and related schemas are experienced).

Detachment

This domain is essentially associated with extremely low extraversion (i.e., maladaptive introversion), and patients

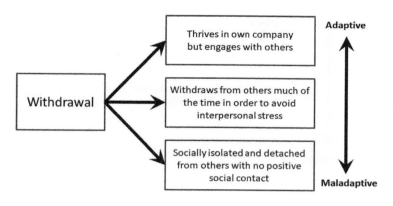

Figure 19.4 From maladaptive to adaptive expression of detachment

with such features may describe themselves as shy, introverted, avoidant, or a "loner." Others may view them as cold, unsociable, unexcitable, and uninterested. Detachment is typically characterized by facets of withdrawal, restricted affectivity, anhedonia, intimacy avoidance, and sometimes suspiciousness (APA, 2013; WHO, 2019). In terms of low FFM extraversion, this typically involves low levels of warmth, gregariousness, excitement seeking, positive emotion, and activity (Costa & McCrae, 1992). Patients with detachment may initiate therapy due to feeling as if they are missing out on something in life; however, they will likely be reticent to aggressively pursue interpersonal interactions or novel activities. They may have a select few friends, acquaintances, or colleagues who have expressed concern, distress, or frustration with their detached, withdrawn, and unassertive behavior, contributing external pressure that leads to treatment-seeking. The overall goal of treating detachment is to help the patient find more adaptive expressions of this trait as illustrated in Figure 19.4.

Establishing a Therapeutic Relationship

Therapists like to be appreciated by their patients and to obtain a sense of progress and personal competency from sessions. Such appreciation and progress is often mirrored in the facial expressions of positive affectivity. Consequently, patients with prominent features of detachment (i.e., restricted affectivity) tend to frustrate therapists' own "narcissistic" needs for appreciation and approval. Even insightful and psychologically sharp observations by the therapist may not trigger any facial markers of interest, and therapist jokes seem to fall flat. Thus, unless the therapist takes these trait features into account, he or she may get upset or disappointed with such patients. The worst case of such therapeutic narcissism may cause the therapist to have unexplained rage at the difficult patient who fails to appreciate how brilliant the therapist is. In such cases, it is important for therapists to understand that patients are not to be used as "positive feedback machines." Instead, a good and healthy alliance with the patient should begin with a decision by the therapist not to use the patient to meet his or her own narcissistic needs.

Furthermore, the therapist must also understand that a low level of positive affectivity does not mean that the patient is psychologically flat or that his or her life is intellectually poor (Harkness & McNulty, 2006).

Therapies vary in the extent to which they require the patient or therapist to speak and interact. A patient with prominent features of detachment is often a person of few words. Depending on the therapeutic and theoretical framework, this may be misinterpreted as a deficit or as a sign that a more talkative and happy part inside the patient is "repressed" or has been "shut down." Eventually, such approaches to the detached patient may result in early dropout. Likewise, highly enthusiastic healthcare staff should not "get in the face" of the detached patient in an attempt to make the patient more engaged in social activities. Staff may misinterpret the lack of response from the detached patient as disrespect and start "pushing" the patient to get a response, until the patient eventually does react! Such mechanisms of detached personality warrant particular consideration when working with forensic and substance use patients (Harkness & McNulty, 2006).

Treatment Goals for Detachment

Individual therapists can assist patients in setting appropriate goals and expectations, understanding the nature of detachment and the responses it evokes in others, and clarifying the specific negative impact of detachment in patients' lives. Figure 19.4 shows how the detachment facet of withdrawal potentially may be expressed in a less maladaptive manner. Therapy with patients characterized by detachment may target related core beliefs involving a lack of interest in relationships, mistrust, independence, and interpersonal ambivalence (Hopwood et al., 2013).

Behavioral therapy and skills training, including approaches such as behavioral activation (Lejuez, Hopko, Acierno, Daughters, & Pagoto, 2011), could also serve a primary role in treating patients with detachment. In order to begin behavioral therapy, it is critical to understand the specific deficits of detachment that are most detrimental to the patient's successful functioning, as well as the reinforcers that are maintaining maladaptive behaviors. Typical social reinforcers (such as attention or

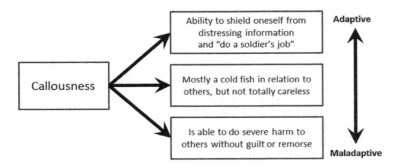

Figure 19.5 From maladaptive to adaptive expression of antagonism/dissociality

physical touch) are unlikely to be effective for patients with detachment, so it is imperative that the therapist and the patient work together to determine what will foster more adaptive behaviors of detachment. In the case of a therapy such as behavioral activation, this includes the consideration of values before moving into the determination of activities to be undertaken as part of the therapy.

Finally, and perhaps most important, patients with low hedonic capacity due to detachment may feel secondary guilt because they do not feel what they are "supposed" to feel about social interactions. Therefore, a primary intervention may be to help detached patients feel more comfortable being who they are. This involves the therapist understanding the patient, and then helping the patient understand, appreciate, and accept him- or herself (Fischer & Finn, 2008). This trait also has implications for the treatment environment in general. In certain cases, it may be best to help the patient feel safe by means of familiar "isolation" from too much social stimuli and enthusiasm. This is consistent with Nidotherapy-based management of schizoid personality disorders (Tyrer, 2002).

Antagonism or Dissociality

This domain is associated with extremely low agreeableness, and is probably the domain that therapists would most prefer to avoid. Facets of this domain include callousness, manipulativeness, deceitfulness, grandiosity, attention seeking, hostility, and sometimes low submissiveness and low anxiousness (APA, 2013; WHO, 2019). In terms of low FFM agreeableness, this domain typically involves lack of altruism, compliance, modesty, and tendermindedness (Costa & McCrae, 1992). The overall goal of treating antagonism/dissociality is to help the patient find more adaptive expressions of this trait as illustrated in Figure 19.5.

Establishing a Therapeutic Relationship

From the outset of therapy, patients presenting with antagonism or dissociality will be resistant to therapists'

efforts to establish rapport, will oppose most forms of assessment, will be frequently evasive or dishonest, and will explain that other people are the cause of their problems. They may be referred through the justice system or by their employer, or may be seeking therapy in order to obtain some secondary gain (e.g., lawsuit settlement and child custody). However, if accompanied by features of negative affectivity, the antagonism/dissociality may be an externalizing voice of something more vulnerable inside the patient that longs for understanding, comfort, and stability (Bach & Bernstein, 2019).

Within the therapeutic relationship, these patients may engage in the same manipulation, dishonesty, arrogance, and defiance that they exhibit in other relationships. Therapists must therefore avoid engaging in power struggles or responding defensively when challenged; this must be combined with a healthy dose of skepticism. There is a constant tension between the therapist attempting to model trust, straightforwardness, and empathy, while remaining alert to the patient's dishonesty and manipulativeness. Therapists who are considering initiating treatment with individuals low in agreeableness should reflect upon their ability to confront unpleasant behaviors without defensiveness or moral judgment (Harkness & McNulty, 2006).

A patient high on this domain may attempt to dominate and control the therapist. By predicting such domination tactics to the patient, the therapist may equalize the relationship. If the patient subsequently attempts to control and dominate, this will only reveal the therapist's expertise. The therapist can also try to sublimate or contain the patient's need for control within the therapy by identifying options and giving choices to the patient. Explicit attempts to share control with the patient also addresses the potential counter-transferential revenge-based impulses to control and dominate the patient.

To establish a working alliance with the patient, it is essential to show insight and sensitivity to the patient's worldview. Finding an appropriate balance between advocating changes and validating the patient is a constant clinical task. Patients high on antagonism/dissociality are typically highly competitive and may seek to outperform others, especially when the trait facet of grandiosity applies to the patient. Therefore, "morally correct" confrontations in which mutuality and cooperativeness are seen as morally superior may threaten the alliance. The patient may simply be prone to view the therapist as naïve and uncool.

Treatment Goals for Antagonism/Dissociality

Therapists must maintain realistic expectations regarding treatment outcomes for this domain, which is highly consistent with the treatment of antisocial and narcissistic personality disorders. Although such individuals may seem resistant to intervention, they are not untreatable (Behary & Dieckman, 2012; Bernstein, Arntz, & de Vos, 2007; Ronningstam, 2010; Salekin, 2002). Therapeutic techniques, such as cognitive-behavioral or interpersonal therapy, should employ rational and utilitarian arguments that focus on the benefits of prosocial behavior. For example, if a patient is self-centered, defiant, and arrogant and struggling to obtain employment, the therapist should illustrate why altruism, compliance, and modesty would be attractive to an employer.

If episodes of recent aggression or antagonistic behavior are presented in the clinical session, the therapist can acknowledge the benefits of using aggression before a more comprehensive analysis of the costs. Afterwards, the therapist can move on with psychoeducation about interpersonal influence and management theory as more useful alternatives to mere aggression: the mafia boss Tony Soprano meets Abraham Maslow. Consequently, a reasonable goal for therapy can be structured around the patient first developing an awareness of the costs of using an antagonistic/dissocial strategy (Harkness & McNulty, 2006; Livesley, 2003). Then, the therapist can treat the patient as having a skill deficit by training in more appropriate strategies of interpersonal influence. Figure 19.5 shows how the antagonism/dissociality facet of callousness potentially may be expressed in a less maladaptive manner. If the aforementioned approach succeeds and a quality alliance is established, the therapist can move on with more in-depth treatment of characterological features by means of schema therapy (Behary & Dieckman, 2012; Bernstein et al., 2007), mentalization based treatment (Bateman & Fonagy, 2016), or transference focused therapy (Stern, Diamond, & Yeomans, 2017), among others.

Antisocial and narcissistic personality disorders can be said to comprise severe forms of antagonism/dissociality, and modified versions of schema therapy have been developed for such features (Behary & Dieckman, 2012; Bernstein et al., 2007). The schema therapy model for psychopathy only addresses aspects that are thought to be linked with insecure attachment styles and/or trauma, and not solely innate neurobiological factors (Bernstein et al., 2007). The treatment typically focuses on schemas related to insufficient self-control and a sense of having special rights, which are also related to frequently acting

cruel and selfish. This is further accentuated by excessive reference to others for admiration as an attempt to regulate one's own self-esteem. Moreover, antagonistic individuals often experience anger when their needs are not met, which may be expressed as highly demanding and hostile behavior. As an attempt to maintain social dominance and a sense of superiority, they may strategically bully, dominate, or hurt others. Finally, antagonistic individuals may also be extremely alert to potential threats to social dominance or superiority (Bach & Bernstein, 2019). Essentially, the schema therapist must confront and bypass antagonistic overcompensating modes (e.g., "predator mode" and "self-aggrandizer mode"), gain access to an underlying vulnerable or angry part of the patient, and enhance the patient's healthy adult functions (Young et al., 2003).

DISINHIBITION

This domain is essentially associated with low conscientiousness. Patients with such features are typically characterized by facets of irresponsibility, impulsivity, distractibility, risk taking, and lack of perseverance and ability to follow rules (APA, 2013; WHO, 2019). In terms of low conscientiousness, this domain typically involves low ability to keep order, low dutifulness, low self-discipline, low competence, and low achievement striving (Costa & McCrae, 1992). The overall goal of treating disinhibition is to help the patient find more adaptive expressions of disinhibition as illustrated in Figure 19.6.

Establishing a Therapeutic Relationship

Establishing an alliance with the disinhibited patient can be tricky, but is doable when offering the patient a real understanding of the disinhibited personality. Disinhibited patients are not likely to have sought therapy under their own motivation. Instead, a family member or friend may have called for the appointment and transported the patient to therapy (assuming treatment is not compulsory due to legal concerns). They may appear unkempt, although not necessarily unclean. When describing the nature of their problems, they may be vague and unfocused, which makes it difficult to write up a focused case-formulation and treatment plan.

The therapist should avoid acting like a school principal or an authoritarian parent, which may only be obnoxious to the patient. Instead, remember that spontaneity and novelty will be attractive to the patient, whereas triviality and predictability may drive the patient away. Be prepared to listen to and tolerate greater risk taking and less awareness of long-term consequences. Seek to build a relationship with the patient around the goal of helping him or her to live with a disinhibited personality, rather than shaming the patient into inhibition or anankastia (Harkness & McNulty, 2006).

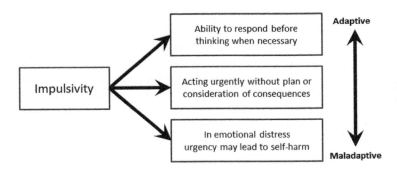

Figure 19.6 From maladaptive to adaptive expression of disinhibition

Treatment Goals for Disinhibition

Behavioral therapy is one obvious treatment for problems related to disinhibition (Safren, 2006). The therapist should identify what is rewarding or punishing for the patient, which must be strong enough to effectively change the likelihood that a behavior will take place. The patient and therapist should then discuss the patient's behaviors that are creating the most severe negative consequences, which will serve as the first behavioral targets. In addition to directly modifying behaviors, the therapist should assist the patient in changing her or his environment to create an effective reward and punishment system that is naturally maintained by the environment, keeping in mind that feelings of mastery and accomplishment are unlikely to be effective reinforcers for these patients. Figure 19.6 shows how the disinhibition facet of impulsivity potentially may be expressed in a less maladaptive manner.

Family systems therapy may also be an appropriate option for the treatment of disinhibition (Brown, 1999). Families and friends will have established ways of interacting with the patient, which are likely to play a role in maintaining behavior. For example, some families treat the patient as the "scapegoat." Positive changes in the patient are viewed skeptically by the family and the system functions most smoothly when the patient can be blamed for negative situations. The therapist will work with the family to identify these patterns of interaction, and to change possible reinforcers that have served to maintain the patient's behaviors.

A primary goal of treating maladaptive disinhibition is to help the patient learn to live with a disinhibited personality. In many clinical settings, a disinhibited personality may be equated with ADHD, which is consistent with research showing that disinhibition facets of distractibility and impulsivity capture ADHD (Sellbom, Bach, & Huxley, 2018; Smith & Samuel, 2017). In any case, this involves helping the patient find safer and more healthy adaptations that still fit with the patient's need for excitement, risk taking, and novelty. However, there are currently no known interventions for turning high disinhibition into low disinhibition, which should also be kept in mind when planning the treatment. Overall, the therapist should help the patient realize how this hardwired feature of disinhibition consistently influences various aspects of life, including relationships, financial problems, short time horizon, distractibility, alcohol- and drug use, and boredom. Such a personality-based case conceptualization might help the patient understand the underlying disposition and life pattern (Sellbom et al., 2018). After some time, the patient can start to appreciate and distinguish features of disinhibition from the adaptations he or she has developed. This has a clear advantage over a pathological diagnostic formulation. Consistent with clinical management of ADHD, patients with disinhibition may benefit form learning certain skills for everyday life as if they had ADHD (Safren, 2006).

Anankastia

This domain is essentially associated with maladaptive low disinhibition and maladaptive high conscientiousness, which causes the patient to have extremely high standards of thought and behavior and a tendency to rigidly persevere around conventionality and organization. Patients with such features are typically characterized by aspects of rigid perfectionism along with emotional and behavioral constraint, including concern with following rules and meeting obligations, deliberativeness, rigid perseveration, stubbornness, and rigid control of emotional expression (WHO, 2019). In terms of maladaptive high FFM conscientiousness, this domain may involve excessive orderliness, dutifulness, achievement striving, and self-discipline (Costa & McCrae, 1992). Anankastia is substantially associated with obsessive-compulsive personality disorder, which in the ICD-10 is labeled F60.5 anankastic personality disorder. Sometimes individuals with narcissistic personality disorder may also demonstrate the acclaim-seeking aspect of maladaptive high achievement-striving, which is consistent with Millon's bureaucratic compulsive subtype of obsessive-compulsive personality disorder (Millon et al., 2004). The overall goal of treating anankastia is to help the patient find more adaptive expressions of perfectionism as illustrated in Figure 19.7.

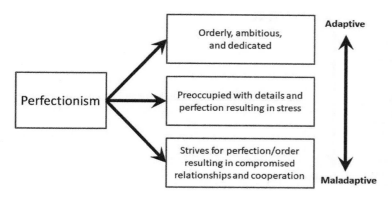

Figure 19.7 From adaptive to maladaptive expression of anankastia

Establishing a Therapeutic Relationship

The overwhelming preoccupation with orderliness, perfectionism, and control of their lives, emotional expressions, and relationships means that most types of treatment are going to be, at best, difficult. Treatment options that do not fit within the patient's scheme will likely be quickly rejected rather than attempted. Treatment is complicated if patients do not accept that they are anankastic, or believe that their thoughts or behaviors are in some sense correct and therefore should not be changed. However, patients with anankastia who do decide to initiate therapy are likely to be successful, as they will be diligent about completing homework, consistent in their attendance, and are unlikely to prematurely terminate treatment (Harkness & McNulty, 2006).

Anankastic patients may be most comfortable with clearly structured therapy. Therefore, the anankastic patient may also respond better with specific goals and an active therapist providing direction, guidance, sets of rules, and reasonable advice. In other words, therapists should strive to be on time, remember the plan, and keep the structure of the session. In that way, the therapist creates a common "tradition" for a patient who yearns to be traditional. Moreover, homework helps structure the therapeutic work outside the session. However, after a positive alliance has been established, it may be worthwhile to tone down the structure and predictability in order to help the patient become a bit more tolerant of imperfection, flexibility, and emotional spontaneity in relationships. Accordingly, therapist mistakes and insufficiencies may cause ruptures in therapy that eventually reveal important issues that should be dealt with.

Treatment Goals for Anankastia

Because the domain of anankastia is somewhat the opposite of disinhibition, the target of treatment is also somewhat the opposite, as it would actually help most anankastic patients to have some more disinhibition. Thus, a reasonable clinical target is to help the patient find healthy adaptations for an anankastic or highly conscientious personality. Some patients with anankastia may recognize that their disordered personality is leading to

negative life consequences and will identify those as the target for therapy. Others may seek therapy in order to treat the consequences themselves, such as neglected and failed relationships or physical and emotional exhaustion.

One important aspect of treatment is to have patients examine and properly identify *feeling states*, rather than just intellectualizing or distancing themselves from their emotions. Patients characterized by anankastia often are not in touch with their emotional states as much as their thoughts. It may be helpful to lead the patient away from *describing* situations, events, and daily happenings and instead talk about how these elements made the patient *feel*. Although a group therapy modality may be helpful and effective, most people with anankastia will not be able to withstand the minimum social contact necessary to gain a healthy group dynamic. They may quickly become ostracized by the group for pointing out other people's deficits and "wrong-headed" ways of doing things. In such settings, the anankastic patient may also take the role as the wise co-therapist (Gabbard & Newman, 2007; Simon, 2015).

Because of its organization, straightforward approach, and homework component, cognitive behavioral treatment is likely to appeal to patients with anankastia. In the cognitive portion, therapists can assist anankastic patients in examining their faulty beliefs regarding perfection, order, and control. Behaviorally, the therapist should make strong use of shaping within the context of homework assignments (Simon, 2015).

Psychodynamic therapy may also be effective in treating anankastia, focusing on early dynamics that may have established or maintained their preoccupation with order, perfection, and achievement and how these dynamics are continuing in adult life. Analytically, the patient would ultimately be working to reshape and quiet an over-active superego (Gabbard & Newman, 2007).

Schema therapy has been shown to be an effective treatment for Cluster C personality disorders, including the obsessive-compulsive type (Arntz, 2012; Hopwood & Thomas, 2014), and, thus, might also be particularly effective in the treatment of anankastia. The schema therapist may target the unrelenting standards schema as a

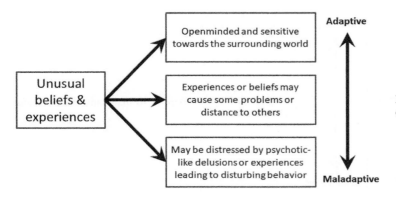

Figure 19.8 From maladaptive to adaptive expressions of psychoticism

driving force behind the anankastic style. Moreover, the therapist and the patient may analyze whether the anankastic personality is a manifestation of an internalized demanding authority (i.e., an echo of demanding parental messages from upbringing that are still very dominant in the patient's life) or a perfectionistic over-controller coping mode. In the former, the patient may feel that the only right way to be is to be perfect or high-achieving, keep everything in order, strive for high status, be humble, put others' needs before one's own, or be efficient and avoid wasting time. Such anankastic features often involve extreme conscientiousness, including excessive standards and responsibility, which therefore also implicate a self-sacrifice schema and a compliant surrenderer coping mode. Consequently, the patient typically feels that it is wrong to express feelings or to act spontaneously. The maladaptive anankastia may also be a product of a perfectionistic over-controller mode, however, which may have been developed to protect the self from a perceived or real threat (e.g., misfortune, criticism, losing control) by means of perseveration and extreme control. In either case, the target of schema therapy is to understand the patient's real needs and help him or her to have them met in an adaptive manner. This involves building up a more flexible healthy adult mode (i.e., a new internalized "good" parent) that can outmatch the dysfunctional modes related to anankastia and "take care" of an underlying vulnerable child mode in an authentic manner (Arntz, 2012).

The aforementioned therapeutic approaches may be further strengthened using compassion-focused therapy (Gilbert, 2014) focusing on exchanging self-criticism (i.e., internalized critical/demanding authority) with self-compassion (i.e., acceptance and compassion from an internalized "good" authority). Moreover, modified versions of dialectical behavior therapy for obsessive-compulsive personality features and disorders of emotional over-control target the rigidity, inhibited emotional expression, and stubbornness characterizing anankastic features (Lynch, Hempel, & Dunkley, 2015; Miller & Kraus, 2007). Finally, the previously mentioned STIM has been adapted to a specific treatment approach for

problems related to Conscientiousness (Roberts, Hill, & Davis, 2017).

Psychoticism

Historically, factor analysis of personality structure has yielded a fifth domain entitled unconventionality, openness, oddity, or psychoticism (Chmielewski, Bagby, Markon, Ring, & Ryder, 2014). Accordingly, the variance comprised by this domain may appear somewhat diverse, including features ranging from unusual/creative perspectives on life to psychotic-like experiences. This domain includes facets such as cognitive and perceptual dysregulation, eccentricity, and unusual beliefs and experiences. In terms of extremely high FFM openness, this domain may involve having an extraordinary imagination along with the ability to fantasize, show interest in abstractions and aesthetics, have original ideas, and think in different ways. The overall goal of treating psychoticism is to help the patient find more adaptive expressions of psychotic-like features as illustrated in Figure 19.8.

Establishing a Therapeutic Relationship

First of all, patients with high psychoticism should be recognized for the adaptations they've achieved under the extraordinary conditions of being prone to schizotypal, psychotic-like, quasi-psychotic, or dissociative features, including depersonalization (e.g., feeling like a robot not in control of own speech or movements) and derealization (e.g., feelings of being alienated from or unfamiliar with surroundings). For example, patients with psychoticism must manage social interaction even though they do not experience the world like most others do. The ability to trust their own perceptions, something most people take for granted, may fail. Additionally, patients with psychoticism may be seen by others as odd, bizarre, mad, or strange, which may have led to alienating and discouraging experiences. Thus, the therapist should highlight and encourage the healthy functioning of the patient, including the social adaptation that has been achieved despite deviating cognitions and perceptual dysregulation. Praising this achievement may form an important basis for a working alliance (Harkness & McNulty, 2006). The therapist must also keep in mind that a patient with elevated psychoticism, according to interview-ratings or self-report, has acknowledged that his or her thinking and perception are unusual. Consequently, the patient might also be prepared to talk about psychoticism. However, many therapists have fears about the malignancy of the topic (e.g., latent delusions), which may weaken the alliance with and reinforce the alienation of the patient.

Treatment Goals for Psychoticism

Miscommunication and misperception are enemies of good social functioning. Therefore, it can be beneficial to provide the patient with skills in reality checking, emotion recognition, and separating fact from beliefs. For example, it may be helpful for the patient if the therapist frequently checks what the patient got out of a certain communication during the therapy session. Moreover, the therapist can help the patient make good decisions about communicating with others about unusual thinking (Harkness & McNulty, 2006), which may include social cognition training (Henderson, 2013).

In cases where facets of unusual beliefs and experiences and eccentricity are predominant due to schizotypal features, it may be useful to take advantage of existing treatment approaches for schizotypal and related disorders. For example, cognitive therapy may adjust distorted thought patterns and give the patient a set of coping skills to alleviate tension and anxiety in social situations (Renton & Mankiewiecz, 2015). This also may include targeting core beliefs, schemas, and modes related to mistrust, isolation, and alienation that are thought to be associated with psychotic or pre-psychotic features (Bach & Bernstein, 2019; Hopwood et al., 2013).

In cases where the perceptual dysregulation facet is predominant due to dissociative phenomena or transient psychotic-like episodes in borderline personality disorder, a trauma-focused approach to dissociation and/or complex posttraumatic stress disorder might be relevant (Kulkarni, 2017). It has been suggested that therapist awareness of the frequency and severity of dissociation in borderline personality disorder is essential to safety planning in relation to suicidal risk management (Korzekwa, Dell, & Pain, 2009). Thus, as a potential suicidal or parasuicidal risk factor, perceptual dysregulation may explicitly reflect intrusive traumas that are linked to dissociation or psychotic-like experiences in some patients (Bach & Fjeldsted, 2017). The mercurial nature of emotions associated with psychotic-like experiences in borderline personality disorder has also been the subject of the mindfulness and emotion regulation components of dialectical behavior therapy (Linehan & Dexter-Mazza, 2008). These techniques may target the perceptual dysregulation facet of psychoticism, and could potentially be applied to unusual beliefs and experiences. In particular, the observing and describing skills of mindfulness may assist patients with psychoticism in thinking more concretely,

and the emotion regulation skills focusing on reducing emotional vulnerability (i.e., basic self-care skills with an emphasis on balance, including treat physical illness, balance eating, avoid mood-altering drugs, balance sleep, get exercise, and build mastery) may be effective for treating perceptual dysregulation and associated sensitivity.

CONCEPTUALIZING AND TREATING PATIENTS WITH MULTIPLE TRAITS

The least sophisticated way of interpreting and using personality traits in treatment is to take one trait domain or facet at a time and only consider what that particular feature indicates about the patient. Such a simplistic approach forfeits the more finely detailed information that would be derived from an integrative and multidimensional view of all trait domains and facets in combination.

Consider, for instance, two patients for whom negative affectivity constitutes the most prominent feature. One patient may be characterized by a secondary trait of antagonism/dissociality, and thus exhibit externalizing anger or overcompensating grandiosity due to vulnerability related to dysregulated emotions or self-esteem. By contrast, the second patient may be characterized by a secondary trait of detachment, suggesting that the negative affectivity may be coped with through internalizing features of depressivity, withdrawal, and anxiousness (which looks very different from the first patient). Accordingly, the ideal way of using a trait system in treatment is to allow any one finding to be adjusted and expanded by any other finding. Taken together, the clinical implications of secondary traits are vital and may have substantial consequences for treatment planning and targets of treatment.

Although this is a goal worth striving for, those who evaluate personality traits as a part of treatment planning operate in a way that represents a compromise between the simplistic interpretations based on single-trait elevations and the ideal report that takes into account every prominent trait dimension at the same time. At times, one may have a clear idea of how the meaning and clinical implications of one trait is altered by the presence of another trait. Those who routinely evaluate and use the trait system have ready-made interpretations and solutions for treatment planning. An interpretation that included the two most prominent traits is most appropriate when only two traits are elevated or when there is a sizeable gap between the scores obtained on the second highest trait and the third. Therapists using trait subfacets, such as the 25 facets of the DSM-5 Section III trait system, should typically take into consideration the three most prominent facets (a "top three" interpretation). However, some elements of the fourth or the fifth elevations are occasionally added in cases where those traits or facets offer information that appears to be of particular relevance for treatment planning.

As previously explained, the categorical personality disorders are mostly composed of different constellations of overlapping trait domains (APA, 2013). For example, a constellation of negative affectivity and detachment captures avoidant personality disorder, which may therefore be treated using approaches for this diagnostic category (e.g., Arntz, 2012). The same applies to a constellation of antagonism/dissociality and disinhibition capturing antisocial personality disorder (e.g., Bateman & Fonagy, 2016; Bernstein et al., 2007), as well as psychoticism and detachment capturing schizotypal personality disorder (e.g., Renton & Mankiewicz, 2015). Pure detachment can be treated as schizoid personality disorder (Renton & Mankiewicz, 2015), and pure anankastia can be treated as obsessive-compulsive personality disorder (e.g., Simon, 2015). However, anankastia with detachment as a secondary trait may be treated as a puritanical or inhibited type, anankastia with negative affectivity may be treated as a conscientious or worried type, and anankastia with antagonism/dissociality may be treated as a bureaucratic, narcissistic, or sadistic type (Millon et al., 2004). In many cases, the presence of anankastia may also be considered a protective factor in terms of the orderliness and ability to work on demanding tasks found in low disinhibition. Borderline personality disorder is more complex and heterogeneously comprised of different potential domains. Some milder cases may only be characterized by negative affectivity in terms of emotional lability, separation insecurity, anxiousness, and depressivity, whereas some more severe cases may be characterized by the same negative affectivity features accompanied by disinhibition (e.g., impulsivity), antagonism/dissociality (e.g., hostility), and psychoticism (e.g., perceptual dysregulation). As evident from the aforementioned trait content, different configurations of borderline personality disorder have substantial implications for treatment planning and targets of treatment. Problems such as self-injury or suicidal behavior are more challenging to deal with in the latter case. In general, the presence of secondary psychoticism, reflective of chaotic thinking, dissociation, or alienation, may indicate severe distress and is very likely to be trauma-related. This particularly applies to combinations of negative affectivity and psychoticism.

Sometimes, patients also have very divergent facet scores within the same domain. Consider, for example, one male patient who has been prone to impulsive outbursts and cheeky actions since childhood, often resulting in humiliating and shameful reprimands from authorities and sometimes resulting in physical abuse from his stepfather and mother. Although he cannot help being verbally impulsive on different occasions, he is also very anxious about what will happen. Consequently, his score on impulsivity is very high, while his score on risk taking is very low. This constellation has clinical implications in terms of focusing on how to accept and regulate his innate impulsivity, while simultaneously dealing with his learned shame and fear of wrongdoing that causes him to be tense and afraid of taking any risks in social situations.

CONCLUSION

This chapter provided an overview of how the empirically derived trait dimensions included in DSM-5 and ICD-11 may be useful for establishing a favorable treatment alliance, increasing the patient's self-knowledge, providing psychoeducation, planning realistic treatment goals, and matching therapy to the patient's personality. A conclusive key message is that practitioners should not treat traits *per se* but the maladaptive expressions of traits. We encourage therapists to start working from this trait perspective and suggest that future developments of evidence-based psychotherapy manuals are tailored to the empirically derived trait domains described in this chapter. Such an approach could include more attention to the homogeneous building blocks of pathological *traits* (e.g., emotional lability) than to the heterogeneous categories of specific mental disorders (e.g., borderline personality disorder). So far, this has already been initiated with the Unified Protocol targeting a range of emotional disorders that are driven by underlying traits of negative affectivity, including avoidant, dependent, and borderline personality disorder features. Likewise, future randomized controlled trials should evaluate the clinical significance of focusing on these domains in contrast to the traditional heterogeneous diagnostic categories.

REFERENCES

Al-Dajani, N., Gralnick, T. M., & Bagby, R. M. (2016). A psychometric review of the Personality Inventory for DSM-5 (PID-5): Current status and future directions. *Journal of Personality Assessment, 98*(1), 62–81.

Allport, G. W. (1961). *Pattern and Growth in Personality*. New York: Holt, Rinehart & Winston.

American Psychiatric Association. (2013). *Diagnostic and Statistical Manual of Mental Disorders* (5th ed.). Arlington, VA: American Psychiatric Publishing.

Anderson, J. L., Sellbom, M., Bagby, R. M., Quilty, L. C., Veltri, C. O. C., Markon, K. E., & Krueger, R. F. (2013). On the convergence between PSY-5 domains and PID-5 domains and facets: Implications for assessment of DSM-5 personality traits. *Assessment, 20*(3), 286–294.

Arntz, A. (2012). Schema Therapy for Cluster C Personality Disorders. In M. van Vreeswijk, J. Broersen, & M. Nadort (Eds.),*The Wiley-Blackwell Handbook of Schema Therapy: Theory, Research, and Practice* (pp. 397–414). Malden, MA: Wiley-Blackwell.

Bach, B., Anderson, J., & Simonsen, E. (2017). Continuity between interview-rated personality disorders and self-reported DSM-5 traits in a Danish psychiatric sample. *Personality Disorders: Theory, Research, and Treatment, 8*(3), 261–267.

Bach, B., & Bernstein, D. P. (2019). Schema therapy conceptualization of personality functioning and traits in ICD-11 and DSM-5. *Current Opinion in Psychiatry, 32*(1), 38–49.

Bach, B., & First, M. B. (2018). Application of the ICD-11 classification of personality disorders. *BMC Psychiatry, 18*(1), 351.

Bach, B., & Fjeldsted, R. (2017). The role of DSM-5 borderline personality symptomatology and traits in the link between childhood trauma and suicidal risk in psychiatric patients. *Borderline Personality Disorder and Emotion Dysregulation*, 4(1), 12. http://doi.org/10.1186/s40479-017-0063-7

Bach, B., Markon, K., Simonsen, E., & Krueger, R. F. (2015). Clinical utility of the DSM-5 Alternative Model of Personality Disorders. *Journal of Psychiatric Practice*, 21(1), 3–25.

Bach, B., Sellbom, M., Bo, S., & Simonsen, E. (2016). Utility of DSM-5 section III personality traits in differentiating borderline personality disorder from comparison groups. *European Psychiatry*, 37(9), 22–27.

Bach, B., Sellbom, M., Kongerslev, M., Simonsen, E., Krueger, R. F., & Mulder, R. (2017). Deriving ICD-11 personality disorder domains from DSM-5 traits: Initial attempt to harmonize two diagnostic systems. *Acta Psychiatrica Scandinavica*, 136(1), 108–117.

Bach, B., Sellbom, M., Skjernov, M., & Simonsen, E. (2018). ICD-11 and DSM-5 personality trait domains capture categorical personality disorders: Finding a common ground. *Australian & New Zealand Journal of Psychiatry*, 52(5), 425–434.

Bagby, R. M., Gralnick, T. M., Al-Dajani, N., & Uliaszek, A. A. (2016). The role of the Five-Factor Model in personality assessment and treatment planning. *Clinical Psychology: Science and Practice*, 23(4), 365–381.

Barlow, D. H., Farchione, T. J., Fairholme, C. P., Ellard, K. K., Boisseau, C. L., Allen, L. B., & Ehrenreich-May, J. T. (2011). *Unified Protocol for Transdiagnostic Treatment of Emotional Disorders: Therapist Guide*. New York: Oxford University Press.

Barlow, D. H., Sauer-Zavala, S., Carl, J. R., Bullis, J. R., & Ellard, K. K. (2014). The nature, diagnosis, and treatment of neuroticism. *Clinical Psychological Science*, 2(3), 344–365.

Bastiaens, T., Claes, L., Smits, D., De Clercq, B., De Fruyt, F., Rossi, G., ... De Hert, M. (2016). The construct validity of the Dutch Personality Inventory for DSM-5 Personality Disorders (PID-5) in a clinical sample. *Assessment*, 23(1), 42–51.

Bateman, A., & Fonagy, P. (2016). *Mentalization Based Treatment for Personality Disorders: A Practical Guide*. New York: Oxford University Press.

Beck, A. T. (1983). Cognitive therapy of depression: New perspectives. In P. J. Clayton and J. E. Barrett (Eds.), *Treatment of Depression: Old Controversies and New Approaches* (pp. 265–290). New York: Raven.

Beck, A. T., Davis, D. D., & Freeman, A. (2015). *Cognitive Therapy of Personality Disorders* (3rd ed.). New York: Guilford Press.

Behary, W. T., & Dieckman, E. (2012). Schema therapy for narcissism: The art of empathic confrontation, limit-setting, and leverage. In W. K. Campbell & J. D. Miller (Eds.), *The Handbook of Narcissism and Narcissistic Personality Disorder: Theoretical Approaches, Empirical Findings, and Treatments*. New York: John Wiley & Sons.

Bernstein, D. P., Arntz, A., & de Vos, M. (2007). Schema focused therapy in forensic settings: Theoretical model and recommendations for best clinical practice. *International Journal of Forensic Mental Health*, 6(2), 169–183.

Brown, J. (1999). Bowen family systems theory and practice: Illustration and critique. *Australian and New Zealand Journal of Family Therapy*, 20(2), 94–103.

Cattell, R. B. (1943). The description of personality: Basic traits resolved into clusters. *Journal of Abnormal and Social Psychology*, 38(4), 476–506.

Chmielewski, M., Bagby, R. M., Markon, K., Ring, A. J., & Ryder, A. G. (2014). Openness to experience, intellect, schizotypal personality disorder, and psychoticism: Resolving the controversy. *Journal of Personality Disorders*, 28(4), 483–499.

Clark, L. A. (1993). *SNAP, Schedule for Nonadaptive and Adaptive Personality: Manual for Administration, Scoring, and Interpretation*. Minneapolis: University of Minnesota Press.

Clark, L. A., Vanderbleek, E., Shapiro, J., Nuzum, H., Allen, X., Daly, E., ... Ro, E. (2015). The brave new world of personality disorder-trait specified: Effects of additional definitions on coverage, prevalence, and comorbidity. *Psychopathology Review*, 2(1), 52–82.

Clarkin, J. F., Yeomans, F. E., & Kernberg, O. F. (2006). *Psychotherapy for Borderline Personality: Focusing on Object Relations*. Washington, DC: American Psychiatric Publishing.

Costa, P. T., & McCrae, R. R. (1992). Normal personality assessment in clinical practice: The NEO Personality Inventory. *Psychological Assessment*, 4(1), 5–13.

Dimidjian, S., & Linehan, M. M. (2008). Mindfulness practice. In W. T. O'Donohue (Ed.), *Cognitive Behavior Therapy: Applying Empirically Supported Techniques in Your Practice* (2nd ed., pp. 327–336). Hoboken, NJ: John Wiley & Sons.

Drake, M. M., Morris, D. M., & Davis, T. J. (2017). Neuroticism's susceptibility to distress: Moderated with mindfulness. *Personality and Individual Differences*, 106, 248–252.

Eysenck, H. J. (1947). *Dimensions of Personality*. London: Routledge & Kegan Paul.

Fischer, C. T., & Finn, S. E. (2008). Developing the life meaning of psychological test data: Collaborative and therapeutic approaches. In R. P. Archer & S. R. Smith (Eds.), *Personality Assessment* (pp. 379–404). New York: Routledge.

Fossati, A., Krueger, R. F., Markon, K. E., Borroni, S., Maffei, C., & Somma, A. (2015). The DSM-5 Alternative Model of Personality Disorders from the perspective of adult attachment. *Journal of Nervous and Mental Disease*, 203(4), 252–258.

Gabbard, G. O., & Newman, C. F. (2007). Psychotherapy of obsessive-compulsive personality disorder. In G. O. Gabbard, J. Beck, & J. Holmes (Eds.), *Oxford Textbook of Psychotherapy* (pp. 329–338). New York: Oxford University Press.

Gartstein, M. A., Putnam, S. P., Aron, E. N., & Rothbart, M. K. (2016). Temperament and personality. In S. Maltzman (Ed.), *The Oxford Handbook of Treatment Processes and Outcomes in Psychology: A Multidisciplinary, Biopsychosocial Approach* (pp. 11–41). New York: Oxford University Press.

Gilbert, P. (2014). The origins and nature of compassion focused therapy. *British Journal of Clinical Psychology*, 53(1), 6–41.

Gore, W. L., & Widiger, T. A. (2013). The DSM-5 dimensional trait model and five-factor models of general personality. *Journal of Abnormal Psychology*, 122(3), 816–821.

Granieri, A., La Marca, L., Mannino, G., Giunta, S., Guglielmucci, F., & Schimmenti, A. (2017). The relationship between defense patterns and DSM-5 maladaptive personality domains. *Frontiers in Psychology*, 1–12. http://doi.org/10.3389/fpsyg.2017.01926

Harkness, A. R., & Lilienfeld, S. O. (1997). Individual differences science for treatment planning: Personality traits. *Psychological Assessment*, 9(4), 349–360.

Harkness, A. R., & McNulty, J. L. (2006). An overview of personality: The MMPI-2 Personality Psychopathology Five (PSY-5) Scales. In J. N. Butcher (Ed.), *MMPI-2: A Practitioner's Guide* (pp. 73–97). Washington, DC: American Psychological Association.

Hayes, S. (2004). Acceptance and commitment therapy and the new behavior therapies: Mindfulness, acceptance, and relationship. In S. C. Hayes, V. M. Follette, & M. M. Linehan (Eds.), *Mindfulness and Acceptance: Expanding the Cognitive-Behavioral Tradition* (pp. 1–29). New York: Guilford Press.

Henderson, A. R. (2013). The impact of social cognition training on recovery from psychosis. *Current Opinion in Psychiatry, 26* (5), 429–432.

Hopwood, C. J., Schade, N., Krueger, R. F., Wright, A. G. C., & Markon, K. E. (2013). Connecting DSM-5 personality traits and pathological beliefs: Toward a unifying model. *Journal of Psychopathology and Behavioral Assessment, 35*(2), 162–172.

Hopwood, C. J., & Thomas, K. M. (2014). Schema therapy is an effective treatment for avoidant, dependent and obsessive-compulsive personality disorders. *Evidence Based Mental Health, 17*(3), 90–91.

Korzekwa, M. I., Dell, P. F., & Pain, C. (2009). Dissociation and borderline personality disorder: An update for clinicians. *Current Psychiatry Reports, 11*(1), 82–88.

Kotov, R., Gamez, W., Schmidt, F., & Watson, D. (2010). Linking "big" personality traits to anxiety, depressive, and substance use disorders: A meta-analysis. *Psychological Bulletin, 136*(5), 768–821.

Krueger, R. F., Derringer, J., Markon, K. E., Watson, D., & Skodol, A. E. (2012). Initial construction of a maladaptive personality trait model and inventory for DSM-5. *Psychological Medicine, 42* (9), 1879–1890.

Kulkarni, J. (2017). Complex PTSD: A better description for borderline personality disorder? *Australasian Psychiatry, 25*(4), 333–335.

Leising, D., & Zimmermann, J. (2011). An integrative conceptual framework for assessing personality and personality pathology. *Review of General Psychology, 15*(4), 317–330.

Lejuez, C. W., Hopko, D. R., Acierno, R., Daughters, S. B., & Pagoto, S. L. (2011). Ten year revision of the brief behavioral activation treatment for depression: Revised treatment manual. *Behavior Modification, 35*(2), 111–161.

Linehan, M. M., & Dexter-Mazza, E. T. (2008). Dialectical behavior therapy for borderline personality disorder. In D. H. Barlow (Ed.), *Clinical Handbook of Psychological Disorders: A Step-by-Step Treatment Manual* (4th ed., pp. 365–420). New York: Guilford Press.

Livesley, W. J. (2003). *Practical Management of Personality Disorder.* New York: Guilford Press.

Lotfi, M., Bach, B., Amini, M., & Simonsen, E. (2018). Structure of DSM-5 and ICD-11 personality domains in Iranian community sample. *Personality and Mental Health.* http://doi.org/10.1002/pmh.1409

Lynam, D. R., & Widiger, T. A. (2001). Using the Five-Factor Model to represent the DSM-IV personality disorders: An expert consensus approach. *Journal of Abnormal Psychology, 110*(3), 401–412.

Lynch, T. R., Hempel, R. J., & Dunkley, C. (2015). Radically open-dialectical behavior therapy for disorders of over-control: Signaling matters. *American Journal of Psychotherapy, 69* (2), 141–162.

Markon, K. E., Quilty, L. C., Bagby, R. M., & Krueger, R. F. (2013). The development and psychometric properties of an informant-report form of the Personality Inventory for DSM-5 (PID-5). *Assessment, 20*(3), 370–383.

Martin, D. J., Garske, J. P., & Davis, M. K. (2000). Relation of the therapeutic alliance with outcome and other variables: A meta-analytic review. *Journal of Consulting and Clinical Psychology, 68*(3), 438–450.

McCrae, R. R., & Costa, P. T. (1995). Trait explanations in personality psychology. *European Journal of Personality, 9*(4), 231–252.

Miller, J. D., Sleep, C., & Lynam, D. R. (2018). DSM-5 alternative model of personality disorder: Testing the trait perspective captured in Criterion B. *Current Opinion in Psychology, 21*, 50–54

Miller, T. W., & Kraus, R. F. (2007). Modified dialectical behavior therapy and problem solving for obsessive-compulsive personality disorder. *Journal of Contemporary Psychotherapy, 37*(2), 79–85.

Millon, T., Grossman, S., Millon, C., Meagher, S., & Ramnath, R. (2004). *Personality Disorders in Modern Life* (2nd ed.). Hoboken, NJ: John Wiley & Sons.

Morey, L. C., Benson, K. T., & Skodol, A. E. (2016). Relating DSM-5 section III personality traits to section II personality disorder diagnoses. *Psychological Medicine, 46*(3), 647–655.

Morey, L. C., Krueger, R. F., & Skodol, A. E. (2013). The hierarchical structure of clinician ratings of proposed DSM-5 pathological personality traits. *Journal of Abnormal Psychology, 122* (3), 836–841.

Oltmanns, T. F., Gleason, M. E. J., Klonsky, E. D., & Turkheimer, E. (2005). Meta-perception for pathological personality traits: Do we know when others think that we are difficult? *Consciousness and Cognition, 14*(4), 739–751.

Oltmanns, J. R., & Widiger, T. A. (2018). A self-report measure for the ICD-11 dimensional trait model proposal: The Personality Inventory for ICD-11. *Psychological Assessment, 30*(2), 154–169.

Phillips, M. R. (2009). Is distress a symptom of mental disorders, a marker of impairment, both or neither? *World Psychiatry, 8*(2), 91–92.

Pires, R., Sousa Ferreira, A., & Gonçalves, B. (2017). The factor structure of the Portuguese version of the personality inventory for DSM-5 (PID-5). *European Psychiatry, 41*, S259.

Presnall, J. R. (2013). Disorders of personality: Clinical treatment from a Five-Factor Model perspective. In T. A. Widiger & P. T. Costa (Eds.), *Personality Disorders and the Five-Factor Model of Personality* (3rd ed., pp. 409–432). Washington, DC: American Psychological Association.

Renton, J. C., & Mankiewicz, P. D. (2015). Paranoid, schizotypal, and schizoid personality disorder. In A. T. Beck, D. D. Davis, & A. Freeman (Eds.), *Cognitive Therapy of Personality Disorders* (pp. 244–275). New York: Guilford Press.

Roberts, B. W., Hill, P. L., & Davis, J. P. (2017). How to change conscientiousness: The sociogenomic trait intervention model. *Personality Disorders: Theory, Research, and Treatment, 8*(3), 199–205.

Roberts, B. W., Kuncel, N. R., Shiner, R., Caspi, A., & Goldberg, L. R. (2007). The power of personality: The comparative validity of personality traits, socioeconomic status, and cognitive ability for predicting important life outcomes. *Perspectives on Psychological Science, 2*(4), 313–345.

Roberts, B. W., Luo, J., Briley, D. A., Chow, P. I., Su, R., & Hill, P. L. (2017). A systematic review of personality trait change through intervention. *Psychological Bulletin, 143*(2), 117–141.

Ronningstam, E. (2010). Narcissistic personality disorder: A current review. *Current Psychiatry Reports, 12*(1), 68–75.

Safren, S. A. (2006). Cognitive-behavioral approaches to ADHD treatment in adulthood. *Journal of Clinical Psychiatry, 67*(8), 46–50.

Salekin, R. T. (2002). Psychopathy and therapeutic pessimism: Clinical lore or clinical reality? *Clinical Psychology Review, 22* (1), 79–122.

Sauer-Zavala, S., Bentley, K. H., & Wilner, J. G. (2016). Trans-diagnostic treatment of borderline personality disorder and comorbid disorders: A clinical replication series. *Journal of Personality Disorders*, 30(1), 35–51.

Schmidt, N. B., Joiner Jr., T. E., Young, J. E., & Telch, M. J. (1995). The schema questionnaire: Investigation of psychometric properties and the hierarchical structure of a measure of maladaptive schemas. *Cognitive Therapy and Research*, 19(3), 295–321.

Sellbom, M., Bach, B., & Huxley, E. (2018). Related personality disorders located within an elaborated externalizing psychopathology spectrum. In J. E. Lochman & W. Matthys (Eds.), *The Wiley Handbook of Disruptive and Impulse-Control Disorders* (pp. 103–124). Chichester: John Wiley & Sons.

Simon, K. M. (2015). Obsessive-compulsive personality disorder. In A. T. Beck, D. D. Davis, & A. Freeman (Eds.), *Cognitive Therapy of Personality Disorders* (3rd ed., pp. 203–222). New York: Guilford Press.

Skodol, A. E., First, M. B., Bender, D. S., & Oldham, J. M. (2018). Module II: Structured clinical interview for personality traits. In M. B. First, A. E. Skodol, D. S. Bender, & J. M. Oldham (Eds.), *Structured Clinical Interview for the DSM-5 Alternative Model for Personality Disorders (SCID-AMPD)*. Arlington, VA: American Psychiatric Association.

Smith, T. E., & Samuel, D. B. (2017). A multi-method examination of the links between ADHD and personality disorder. *Journal of Personality Disorders*, 31(1), 26–48.

Stern, B. L., Diamond, D., & Yeomans, F. E. (2017). Transference-focused psychotherapy (TFP) for narcissistic personality: Engaging patients in the early treatment process. *Psychoanalytic Psychology*, 34(4), 381–396.

Thimm, J. C. (2010). Personality and early maladaptive schemas: A five-factor model perspective. *Journal of Behavior Therapy and Experimental Psychiatry*, 41(4), 373–380.

Tyrer, P. (2002). Nidotherapy: A new approach to the treatment of personality disorder. *Acta Psychiatrica Scandinavica*, 105(6), 469–471.

Wachtel, P. L. (1973). Psychodynamics, behavior therapy, and the implacable experimenter: An inquiry into the consistency of personality. *Journal of Abnormal Psychology*, 82(2), 324–334.

Widiger, T. A., & Clark, L. A. (2000). Toward DSM-V and the classification of psychopathology. *Psychological Bulletin*, 126 (6), 946–963.

Widiger, T. A., & Costa P. T. (Eds.) (2013). *Personality Disorders and the Five-Factor Model of Personality* (3rd ed.). Washington, DC: American Psychological Association.

Widiger, T. A., & Simonsen, E. (2005). Alternative dimensional models of personality disorder: Finding a common ground. *Journal of Personality Disorders*, 19(2), 110–130.

Widiger, T. A., & Trull, T. J. (1992). Personality and psychopathology: An application of the Five-Factor Model. *Journal of Personality*, 60(2), 363–393.

World Health Organization. (2019). *ICD-11 Clinical Descriptions and Diagnostic Guidelines for Mental and Behavioural Disorders*. Geneva: World Health Organization.

Young, J. E., Klosko, J. S., & Weishaar, M. E. (2003). *Schema Therapy: A Practitioner's Guide*. New York: Guilford Press.

19a A Functional Understanding of the Relationship between Personality and Clinical Diagnoses and Implications for Treatment Planning: Commentary on Using DSM-5 and ICD-11 Personality Traits in Clinical Treatment

SHANNON SAUER-ZAVALA

In their compelling chapter, Bach and Presnall-Shvorin provide a comprehensive reminder of the importance of considering patients' personality profiles when building a therapeutic alliance and selecting treatment approaches. Although, as the authors note, the notion of using personality to inform treatment is not new (e.g., Allport, 1961; Cattell, 1943; Eysenck, 1947; Harkness & Lilienfeld, 1997), they provide a practical guide to understanding how various maladaptive manifestations of the Five-Factor Model (FFM; e.g., Costa & McCrae, 1992) affect alliance and suggest how existing treatment approaches map on to several FFM domains.

A conceptual point that warrants further discussion is the authors' assertion that there is a clear distinction between personality traits themselves and their phenotypic expression that, in extreme cases, constitutes a clinical disorder (e.g., Allport, 1961; Leising & Zimmermann, 2011). They further note that personality cannot be altered in response to treatment, and that the problematic, observable manifestations of traits should be the focus of care. Unfortunately, the characteristic thoughts and behaviors associated with traits often correspond to *Diagnostic and Statistical Manual* (DSM) disorders, resulting in an unwieldy proliferation of treatment approaches geared toward each discrete diagnosis. For example, within their treatment recommendations for negative affectivity, Bach and Presnall-Shvorin describe seven distinct treatment models that correspond to the facets of neuroticism (e.g., for emotional lability, provide dialectical behavior therapy; for depressivity, provide self-compassion training). Although an examination of personality profiles at the facet level allows for increased treatment specificity over DSM classification, it also likely results in a large training burden for clinicians who must become familiar with numerous interventions in order to provide coverage for the FFM.

Despite these challenges, the FFM may still provide a useful frame for streamlining treatment planning that reaches beyond a descriptive taxonomy. An understanding of the core, functional processes that underscore evolution from trait to disorder may point to a limited number of treatment elements with bidirectional impact on both traits and their phenotypic manifestations. A proposal for developing functional models of DSM disorders based on the FFM is provided in the following commentary; neuroticism and its associated disorders will be used as the illustrative example, followed by a summary of how presented principles may be applied to additional dimensions of personality.

A FFM-BASED FUNCTIONAL MODEL OF DISORDERS

Neuroticism predicts a range of public health problems, including a variety of mental disorders and their co-occurrence (Clark, Watson, & Mineka, 1994; Henriques-Calado, Duarte-Silva, Junqueira, Sacoto, & Keong, 2014; Khan, Jacobson, Gardner, Prescott, & Kendler, 2005; Krueger & Markon, 2006; Sauer-Zavala & Barlow, 2014; Trull & Sher, 1994; Weinstock & Whisman, 2006). Moving past a descriptive taxonomy, a functional model characterizing the processes through which neurotic temperament evolves into the distress and interference associated with a broad range of DSM disorder symptoms can be used to develop robust treatment elements that may simultaneously address disorder symptoms along with neuroticism itself. Specifically, there is ample support for the notion that disorders falling along the traditional neurotic spectrum (e.g., anxiety disorders, depressive disorders) result from three interacting components (see: Barlow, Sauer-Zavala, Carl, Bullis, & Ellard, 2014; Sauer-Zavala & Barlow, 2014): (1) the trait-like tendency to experience negative emotions (neuroticism), (2) aversive reactions to these emotional experiences when they occur, and (3) subsequent attempts to suppress or otherwise avoid them. Although avoidant strategies may be effective in the short term, there is compelling evidence to suggest that suppressed emotions return with greater frequency and intensity (e.g., Campbell-Sills, Barlow, Brown, & Hofmann, 2006), maintaining emotional disorder symptoms in the long term (Purdon, 1999).

Emerging research suggests that treatments explicitly designed to address this functional model are associated with promising reductions in a range of clinical presentations, as well as neuroticism itself (e.g., Armstrong & Rimes, 2016; Carl, Gallagher, Sauer-Zavala, Bentley, & Barlow, 2014; Rapee, Kennedy, Ingram, Edwards, & Sweeney, 2005, 2010). An examination of the components included in these treatments suggests commonalities. Specifically, all three provide psychoeducation on the adaptive function of emotions and encourage an approach oriented stance toward these experiences. Reduced avoidant coping in the face of strong emotions limits the paradoxical rebound effects that maintain both negative affectivity and DSM disorder symptoms. Targeting underlying functional processes in this manner is consistent with the National Institute of Mental Health's Research Domain Criteria (RDoC) initiative that tasks researchers to look beyond diagnoses to identify core processes implicated in the development and maintenance of symptoms across a range of disorders (Insel et al., 2010).

With regard to heterogeneity in presentations within high levels of neuroticism (e.g., high self-consciousness, low depressivity), a comprehensive functional model may help clinicians conceptualize these differences. For example, social withdrawal associated with depressivity, discomfort with somatic sensations associated with anxiousness, and non-suicidal self-injury associated with mood lability may all be conceptualized as aversive, avoidant reactions to emotional experiences per the functional model described above – perhaps warranting only minor variations on a unified treatment approach. As a result, clinicians with a strong understanding of this functional model of neurotic spectrum disorders can address varied clinical presentations with a streamlined treatment approach. Thus, treating neuroticism itself with a limited number of treatment strategies, rather than its individual facets or downstream clinical correlates, may represent a more efficient and cost-effective means of addressing the wide swath of public health problems associated with this trait.

Of course, it is important to note that neurotic spectrum disorders represent just one functional class of psychopathology, and it may be possible to identify additional broad classes characterized by their own unique shared mechanisms. Specifically, a similar perspective can be taken with regard to addressing the clinical disorders that may arise from falling at the extreme poles on the other four dimensions of the FFM. For example, low levels of extraversion have been shown to confer added risk, beyond neuroticism, for depressive disorders, social anxiety, and agoraphobia (e.g., Brown, Chorpita, & Barlow, 1998), whereas high levels of this trait (along with high levels of openness) are associated with bipolar disorder (Bagby et al., 1996; Quilty, Sellbom, Tackett, & Bagby, 2009). Similarly, maladaptive variants (both high and low levels) of agreeableness, conscientiousness, and openness have each been linked to specific forms of psychopathology (Widiger, Lynam, Miller, & Oltmanns, 2012). Some theoretical and empirical work has already been done to establish functional models accounting for the relationship between traits and DSM disorder symptoms, along with suggesting corresponding streamlined interventions strategies (e.g., extraversion: Carl, Soskin, Kerns, & Barlow, 2013; conscientiousness: Roberts, Hill, & Davis, 2017). Overall, these efforts may result in fewer diagnostic categories, along with a smaller number of more broad-based psychological interventions.

CONCLUSIONS

Identifying shared functional mechanisms that apply to broader groups of disorders may inform more efficient strategies designed to explicitly target the processes that maintain symptoms across diagnostic boundaries. It is possible that the FFM may provide a framework for understanding and addressing the majority of psychopathology included in the DSM system, along with the traits themselves. The bulk of the literature elucidating how personality features evolve into clinical diagnoses has been conducted in the context of neuroticism. However, understanding the functional processes that account for how the other FFM traits evolve into the distress and impairment that characterize a mental disorder is an important step in identifying effective treatment strategies that may move these personality features. Using the FFM as the basis for intervention selection may result in a limited number of treatment elements, each mapping on to one of the five dimensions of temperament that confer risk for a wide swath of psychopathology. In other words, this dimensional approach to *treatment* may lead to a more manageable number of evidence-based treatment components, reducing therapist training burden while also providing coverage to the full range of DSM disorders.

REFERENCES

Allport, G. (1961). *Pattern and Growth in Personality*. Oxford: Holt, Reinhart & Winston.

Armstrong, L., & Rimes, K. A. (2016). Mindfulness-based cognitive therapy for neuroticism (stress vulnerability): A pilot randomized study. *Behavior Therapy*, *47*(3), 287–298.

Bagby, R. M., Young, L. T., Schuller, D. R., Bindseil, K. D., Cooke, R. G., Dickens, S. E., ... Joffe, R. T. (1996). Bipolar disorder, unipolar depression and the Five-Factor Model of personality. *Journal of Affective Disorders*, *41*(1), 25–32.

Barlow, D. H., Sauer-Zavala, S., Carl, J. R., Bullis, J. R., & Ellard, K. K. (2014). The nature, diagnosis, and treatment of neuroticism: Back to the future. *Clinical Psychological Science*, *2*(3), 344–365.

Brown, T. A., Chorpita, B. F., & Barlow, D. H. (1998). Structural relationships among dimensions of the DSM-IV anxiety and mood disorders and dimensions of negative affect, positive affect, and autonomic arousal. *Journal of Abnormal Psychology*, *107*(2), 179–192.

Campbell-Sills, L., Barlow, D. H., Brown, T. A., & Hofmann, S. G. (2006). Effects of suppression and acceptance on emotional responses of individuals with anxiety and mood disorders. *Behaviour Research and Therapy*, 44(9), 1251–1263.

Carl, J. R., Gallagher, M. W., Sauer-Zavala, S. E., Bentley, K. H., & Barlow, D. H. (2014). A preliminary investigation of the effects of the unified protocol on temperament. *Comprehensive Psychiatry*, 55(6), 1426–1434.

Carl, J. R., Soskin, D. P., Kerns, C., & Barlow, D. H. (2013). Positive emotion regulation in emotional disorders: A theoretical review. *Clinical Psychology Review*, 33(3), 343–360.

Cattell, R. B. (1943). The description of personality: Basic traits resolved into clusters. *Journal of Abnormal and Social Psychology*, 38(4), 476–506.

Clark, L. A., Watson, D., & Mineka, S. (1994). Temperament, personality, and the mood and anxiety disorders. *Journal of Abnormal Psychology*, 103(1), 103–116.

Costa, P. T., & McCrae, R. R. (1992). Normal personality assessment in clinical practice: The Neo Personality Inventory. *Psychological Assessment*, 4(1), 5–13.

Eysenck, H. J. (1947). *Dimensions of Personality*. London: Routledge & Kegan Paul.

Harkness, A. R., & Lilienfeld, S. O. (1997). Individual differences science for treatment planning: Personality traits. *Psychological Assessment*, 9(4), 349–360.

Henriques-Calado, J., Duarte-Silva, M. E., Junqueira, D., Sacoto, C., & Keong, A. M. (2014). Five-factor model personality domains in the prediction of Axis II personality disorders: An exploratory study in late adulthood women non-clinical sample. *Personality and Mental Health*, 8(2), 115–127.

Insel, T., Cuthbert, B., Garvey, M., Heinssen, R., Pine, D. S., Quinn, K., ... Wang, P. (2010). Research domain criteria (RDoC): Toward a new classification framework for research on mental disorders. *American Journal of Psychiatry*, 167(7), 748–751.

Khan, A. A., Jacobson, K. C., Gardner, C. O., Prescott, C. A., & Kendler, K. S. (2005). Personality and comorbidity of common psychiatric disorders. *British Journal of Psychiatry*, 186, 190–196.

Krueger, R. F., & Markon, K. E. (2006). Understanding psychopathology: Melding behavior genetics, personality, and quantitative psychology to develop an empirically based model. *Current Directions in Psychological Science*, 15(3), 113–117.

Leising, D., & Zimmermann, J. (2011). An integrative conceptual framework for assessing personality and personality pathology. *Review of General Psychology*, 15(4), 317–330.

Purdon, C. (1999). Thought suppression and psychopathology. *Behaviour Research and Therapy*, 37(11), 1029–1054.

Quilty, L. C., Sellbom, M., Tackett, J. L., & Bagby, R. M. (2009). Personality trait predictors of bipolar disorder symptoms. *Psychiatry Research*, 169(2), 159–163.

Rapee, R. M., Kennedy, S., Ingram, M., Edwards, S., & Sweeney, L. (2005). Prevention and early intervention of anxiety disorders in inhibited preschool children. *Journal of Consulting and Clinical Psychology*, 73(3), 488–497.

Rapee, R. M., Kennedy, S. J., Ingram, M., Edwards, S. L., & Sweeney, L. (2010). Altering the trajectory of anxiety in at-risk young children. *American Journal of Psychiatry*, 167(12), 1518–1525.

Roberts, B. W., Hill, P. L., & Davis, J. P. (2017). How to change conscientiousness: The sociogenomic trait intervention model. *Personality Disorders: Theory, Research, and Treatment*, 8(3), 199–205.

Sauer-Zavala, S., & Barlow, D. H. (2014). The case for borderline personality disorder as an emotional disorder: Implications for treatment. *Clinical Psychology: Science and Practice*, 21(2), 118–138.

Trull, T. J., & Sher, K. J. (1994). Relationship between the five-factor model of personality and Axis I disorders in a nonclinical sample. *Journal of Abnormal Psychology*, 103(2), 350–360.

Weinstock, L. M., & Whisman, M. A. (2006). Neuroticism as a common feature of the depressive and anxiety disorders: A test of the revised integrative hierarchical model in a national sample. *Journal of Abnormal Psychology*, 115(1), 68–74.

Widiger, T. A., Lynam, D. R., Miller, J. D., & Oltmanns, T. F. (2012). Measures to assess maladaptive variants of the five-factor model. *Journal of Personality Assessment*, 94(5), 450–455.

19b The Need for Mechanistic Models to Translate Traits from Bench to Bedside: Commentary on Using DSM-5 and ICD-11 Personality Traits in Clinical Treatment

WHITNEY R. RINGWALD, ELIZABETH A. EDERSHILE, WILLIAM C. WOODS, AND AIDAN G. C. WRIGHT

Bach and Presnall-Shvorin's proposal for trait-informed treatment represents an important step towards translating emergent, empirically driven models of personality pathology into clinical applications. Given the problematically large gap between the bench and bedside in personality psychopathology, connecting the two, as Bach and Presnall-Shvorin suggest, is imperative. In support of their effort to refine interventions by systematic consideration of individual differences, we wish to emphasize the necessity of integrating stable and dynamic features of personality by identifying underlying mechanistic processes. Many of the authors' recommendations are predicated on assumed relationships between traits and associated behavioral manifestations, and we suggest that a unifying, mechanistic model would clarify and validate these recommendations. In this commentary, we present promising theoretical frameworks, relevant research, and needed future directions for our mutual imperative to improve available treatments through scientific understanding. In particular, scientific models that articulate the processes occurring between dispositional and behavioral manifestations are needed (e.g., DeYoung, 2015; Fleeson & Jayawickreme, 2015; Wright, 2011).

We share the same concerns with current categorical diagnostic nosologies expressed by Bach and Presnall-Shvorin, and agree with their endorsement of a dimensional model of personality traits. Factor analytic studies of personality pathology structure have consistently produced variants of the five-factor maladaptive trait model put forth by Bach and Presnall-Shvorin, and have failed to support traditional, discrete criterion clusters (e.g., Aslinger, Manuck, Pilkonis, Simms, & Wright, 2018; Conway, Hammen, & Brennan, 2012; O'Connor, 2005; Wright et al., 2012). Defining pathological traits dimensionally more accurately accounts for marked heterogeneity in symptom presentation and begins to resolve issues of comorbidity among personality disorders (Hopwood et al., 2018). A dimensional approach to conceptualizing personality pathology is substantiated by evidence of concordance between established basic trait models and maladaptive trait models. Situating maladaptive traits into a broader understanding of personality provides a fruitful foundation for future research.

As stated by the authors, because traits represent general behavioral tendencies, they are relevant for understanding the daily life of an individual and, therefore, necessitate treatment considerations. Indeed, in research using intensive, repeated measurements of behavior and affect, dispositional traits are associated with daily trait-related manifestations with considerable specificity (Fleeson, 2001; Wright & Simms, 2016). Bach and Presnall-Shvorin's theoretical stance is based on an understanding that traits are more probabilistic than deterministic and are not maladaptive *per se*; rather, the maladaptive behavioral manifestations of a trait are the most appropriate therapeutic targets.

This intuitively compelling notion that there are both relatively fixed aspects of personality and aspects that are more variable and amenable to change has recently been quantitatively evaluated and supported. A series of factor analyses suggest that the structure of personality pathology is comprised of a general PD "severity" factor and statistically independent personality "styles" (Hopwood et al., 2011; Jahng et al., 2011; Oltmanns, Smith, Oltmanns, & Widiger, 2018; Sharp et al., 2015; Williams, Scalco, & Simms, 2018; Wright, Hopwood, Skodol, & Morey, 2016). Further, general PD severity is strongly associated with psychosocial outcomes and declines rapidly over time in naturalistic studies, whereas PD style is less predictive of outcomes (c.f., Jahng et al., 2011) and tends to be more stable over time (Woods, Edershile, Wright, & Lenzenweger, 2019; Wright et al., 2016). These data suggest, as the authors put forth, that not every trait is an equal candidate for intervention, and identification of those dimensions of personality that contribute to dysfunction and can be modified will allow clinicians to direct resources more effectively. At the same time, identifying those dimensions of personality that represent mostly fixed individual differences, so-called specific or stylistic factors, can inform treatment planning in terms of expectations, goals, and interventions. That these specific factors are not nearly as predictive of psychiatric distress as the general PD factor (Hopwood et al., 2011; Williams et al., 2018; Wright et al., 2016; but see Jahng et al., 2011) suggests an approach to treatment that regards individual differences as intrinsic assets rather than solely liabilities.

Understanding psychopathology in terms of static descriptions of averaged tendencies provides an incomplete account limited in predictive power and clinical utility (Beltz, Wright, Sprague, & Molenaar, 2016; Scott et al., 2017; Wright, Beltz, Gates, Molenaar, & Simms, 2015). Human behavior, emotion, the transactional relationships between people and between a person and her or his environment, and the complex psychological mechanisms that mediate these relationships, are *dynamic* processes. Knowing a person's traits describes a likely collection of behavioral responses but says nothing reliable about why and when that person will engage in those behaviors and, therefore, reveals little about fundamental aspects of human experience and what contributes to the dysfunctional patterns that bring a client to treatment.

It is reasonable to infer the motivations or phenomenology associated with different traits as these authors have done, and, as a measure of central tendency, these trait-informed inferences may prove to be accurate much of the time. However, we propose that, absent a comprehensive mechanistic model that links traits to trait-relevant behavior, such conclusions regarding causal processes are confined to speculation and could inhibit therapeutic progress. To illustrate how these limitations could unfold in the clinical setting, we present a brief case example.

Imagine Patient X who is profoundly fearful of rejection and abandonment. To prevent the seemingly inevitable pain and conflict of relationships, she now completely avoids them. This patient has had no close friendships or romantic partners for years and expresses no interest in developing intimacy. She appears high in the trait of detachment. Therefore, based on trait-informed model logic, the focus of treatment would be helping her "accept" her lack of normative interest in relationships. Yet, this patient is naturally oriented towards relationships and craves connection, but has adapted her behavior to protect herself. Her detachment serves a regulatory function that is unaccounted for by a descriptive, trait-level assessment but would be an indispensable insight for her treatment provider. Indeed, her characteristic behavior reflects her relationship insecurity, a separate trait from a different domain.

As demonstrated by this example, a model of psychopathology that moves beyond description to one that elucidates underlying causal processes is needed to complete a clinical portrait. This would also accommodate the many cases where observed maladaptive behavior and motivating goals align. Whereas we find many of the recommended approaches put forth by Bach and Presnall-Shvorin to be sensible and likely effective in many cases, greater impact could be achieved with a cohesive theoretical and empirical rationale to account for the mechanistic relationship between traits and trait-relevant expressions.

As the authors suggest, the identified maladaptive traits correspond to putatively extreme variants of basic traits (e.g., Widiger & Trull, 2007), yet extremity is not a precondition for dysfunction. Evaluation of impairment cannot be made on the basis of traits alone but must be qualified by specific domains of dysfunction. We propose integrating insights from a framework such as the cybernetic theory of personality and psychopathology (DeYoung, 2015; DeYoung & Krueger, 2018) to operationalize causation and meaningfully define maladaptation.

A complete review of this theory can be found elsewhere (DeYoung & Krueger, 2018), but we will highlight how this model could complement and extend Bach and Presnall-Shvorin's recommendations for treatment. DeYoung and Krueger propose that psychopathology be defined by the failure of characteristic adaptations to move a person towards her or his psychological goals. Characteristic adaptations are those interpretations and strategies that a person develops in response to the demands of life to meet her or his needs. Returning to the case of Patient X, the patient had adapted to her experiences of rejection and perceived abandonment by disengaging from relationships. Conceptualizing her personality mechanistically would allow a clinician to identify that her withdrawal behavior functions to meet her psychological goal of avoiding pain at the expense of failing to meet concurrent goals of companionship. Disentangling dysfunctional mechanisms from personality traits provides a system for specifying the appropriate point of intervention. In cybernetic terms, a clinician would help the example patient replace her current, problematic characteristic adaptations with ones that minimize the conflict between her psychological goals. For instance, she may work on improving emotion regulation to attenuate her responses to perceived slights so that relationships are more satisfying – an approach that differs from that indicated from an exclusively surface-level trait-informed treatment.

Measuring latent, dynamic features of clinical phenomena to empirically substantiate these theoretically coherent and face-valid ideas has proven elusive but will be necessary for clarifying personality structure in a way that is useful for guiding treatment recommendations. We enthusiastically support individualizing treatment and assert that these efforts cannot solely rely on references to population averages (i.e., individual differences in traits), but require idiographic data (Wright et al., 2019). A promising methodological approach for capturing the function of individual behavior is the use of ambulatory assessment (Stone & Shiffman, 1994). Through repeated measurement of participants' emotions, cognitions, and actions in their daily life, a more ecologically valid, personalized characterization of personality expression can be achieved. Such rich, contextualized data can also reveal environmental contingencies of pathological responses, which, as underscored by Bach and Presnall-Shvorin, are important in trait-informed treatment.

For instance, using ecological momentary assessment, Wright et al. (2017) examined the links among participants' self-reported affect, behavior, and perceptions of others' behavior to identify specific social circumstances that prompt narcissistic behavior. Namely, people higher in narcissistic features tend to respond more aggressively to perceived dominance in others – a response mediated by negative affect, suggesting a regulatory function. These data provide a far more nuanced and clinically meaningful account of personality pathology than can be provided by trait-level descriptions.

The extensive body of work on personality traits continues to be relevant; indeed, trait models have been shown to strongly predict most major life outcomes (Ozer & Benet-Martinez, 2006). However, empirical advances that allow for more granular characterization at the within-person level will make possible a hierarchical, mechanistic model of personality that can more accurately differentiate between what personality *is* and what it *does*. Building on the trait-informed model with greater understanding of the function of trait expressions and those contextual variables that maintain pathology can lead to better assessment methods and more meaningful diagnostic schemata. Further, given the extensive work on personality traits, understanding dynamic processes and how these processes relate to trait dimensions will make for a rich body of literature, maximizing possibilities to connect this literature to clinical application. As for Bach and Presnall-Shvorin's important imperatives to increase patient participation and strengthen therapeutic rapport, appreciation for the function of maladaptive behavior is integral for validating the patient's experience and deciding on treatment goals.

Assimilation of traits and dynamic processes of personality into a single framework would provide a generalizable structure flexible enough to adapt extant treatment approaches to individual problems. A fuller understanding of causal mechanisms could potentially bolster efforts to identify agents of change in different therapeutic models and make treatment more efficient. Bach and Presnall-Shvorin conceptually match interventions to personality trait expressions – a task we suggest could be made more systematic through cybernetic evaluation and an appreciation of the basic structure of personality processes. We wish to acknowledge the significance of the authors' contributions towards translating dimensional trait models into treatment and hope to support their effort by encouraging incorporation of dynamic elements of personality for even greater precision in the treatment of psychopathology.

REFERENCES

Aslinger, E. N., Manuck, S. B., Pilkonis, P. A., Simms, L. J., & Wright, A. G. C. (2018). Narcissist or narcissistic? Evaluation of the latent structure of narcissistic personality disorder. *Journal of Abnormal Psychology, 127*(5), 496–502.

Beltz, A. M., Wright, A. G. C., Sprague, B. N., & Molenaar, P. C. (2016). Bridging the nomothetic and idiographic approaches to the analysis of clinical data. *Assessment, 23*(4), 447–458.

Conway, C., Hammen, C., & Brennan, P. (2012). A comparison of latent class, latent trait, and factor mixture models of DSM-IV borderline personality disorder criteria in a community setting: Implications for DSM-5. *Journal of Personality Disorders, 26*(5), 793–803.

DeYoung, C. G. (2015). Cybernetic big five theory. *Journal of Research in Personality, 56*, 33–58.

DeYoung, C. G., & Krueger, R. F. (2018). A cybernetic theory of psychopathology. *Psychological Inquiry, 29*(3), 117–138.

Fleeson, W. (2001). Toward a structure- and process-integrated view of personality: Traits as density distributions of states. *Journal of Personality and Social Psychology, 80*(6), 1011–1027.

Fleeson, W., & Jayawickreme, E. (2015). Whole trait theory. *Journal of Research in Personality, 56*, 82–92.

Hopwood, C. J., Kotov, R., Krueger, R. F., Watson, D., Widiger, T. A., Althoff, R. R., … Bornovalova, M. A. (2018). The time has come for dimensional personality disorder diagnosis. *Personality and Mental Health, 12*(1), 82–86.

Hopwood, C. J., Malone, J. C., Ansell, E. B., Sanislow, C. A., Grilo, C. M., McGlashan, T. H., … Morey, L. C. (2011). Personality assessment in DSM-5: Empirical support for rating severity, style, and traits. *Journal of Personality Disorders, 25*, 305–320.

Jahng, S., Trull, T. J., Wood, P. K., Tragesser, S. L., Tomko, R., Grant, J .D., … Sher, K. J. (2011). Distinguishing general and specific personality disorder features and implications for substance dependence comorbidity. *Journal of Abnormal Psychology, 120*, 656–669.

O'Connor, B. P. (2005). A search for consensus on the dimensional structure of personality disorders. *Journal of Clinical Psychology, 61*(3), 323–345.

Oltmanns, J. R., Smith, G. T., Oltmanns, T. F., & Widiger, T. A. (2018). General factors of psychopathology, personality, and personality disorder: Across domain comparisons. *Clinical Psychological Science, 6*(4), 581–589.

Ozer, D. J., & Benet-Martinez, V. (2006). Personality and the prediction of consequential outcomes. *Journal of Personality, 57*, 401–421.

Scott, L. N., Wright, A. G., Beeney, J. E., Lazarus, S. A., Pilkonis, P. A., & Stepp, S. D. (2017). Borderline personality disorder symptoms and aggression: A within-person process model. *Journal of Abnormal Psychology, 126*(4), 429–440.

Sharp, C., Wright, A. G. C., Fowler, J. C., Frueh, B. C., Allen, J. G., Oldham, J., & Clark, L. A. (2015). The structure of PD: Both general ('g') and specific ('s') factors? *Journal of Abnormal Psychology, 124*, 387–398.

Stone, A. A., & Shiffman, S. (1994). Ecological momentary assessment (EMA) in behavioral medicine. *Annals of Behavioral Medicine, 16*(3), 199–202.

Widiger, T. A., & Trull, T. J. (2007). Plate tectonics in the classification of personality disorder: Shifting to a dimensional model. *American Psychologist, 62*(2), 71–83.

Williams, T. F., Scalco, M. D., & Simms, L. J. (2018). The construct validity of general and specific dimensions of PD. *Psychological Medicine, 48*(5), 834–848.

Woods, W. C., Edershile, E. A., Wright, A. G. C., & Lenzenweger, M. F. (2019). Illuminating ipsative change in personality disorder and normal personality: A multimethod examination from a prospective longitudinal perspective. *Personality Disorder: Theory, Research, and Treatment, 10*(1), 80–86.

Wright, A. G. C. (2011). Quantitative and qualitative distinctions in personality disorder. *Journal of Personality Assessment*, *93*(4), 370–379.

Wright, A. G. C., Beltz, A. M., Gates, K. M., Molenaar, P., & Simms, L. J. (2015). Examining the dynamic structure of daily internalizing and externalizing behavior at multiple levels of analysis. *Frontiers in Psychology*, *6*, 1914.

Wright, A. G. C., Gates, K. M., Arizmendi, C., Lane, S. T., Woods, W. C., & Edershile, E. A. (2019). Focusing personality assessment on the person: Modeling general, shared, and person specific processes in personality and psychopathology. *Psychological Assessment*, *31*(4), 502–515.

Wright, A. G. C., Hopwood, C. J., Skodol, A. E., & Morey, L. C. (2016). Longitudinal validation of general and specific structural features of PD. *Journal of Abnormal Psychology*, *125*, 1120–1134.

Wright, A. G. C., & Simms, L. J. (2016). Stability and fluctuation of personality disorder features in daily life. *Journal of Abnormal Psychology*, *125*(5), 641–656.

Wright, A. G. C., Stepp, S. D., Scott, L. N., Hallquist, M. N., Beeney, J. E., Lazarus, S. A., & Pilkonis, P. A. (2017). The effect of pathological narcissism on interpersonal and affective processes in social interactions. *Journal of Abnormal Psychology*, *126*(7), 898–910.

Wright, A. G. C., Thomas, K. M., Hopwood, C. J., Markon, K. E., Pincus, A. L., & Krueger, R. F. (2012). The hierarchical structure of DSM-5 pathological personality traits. *Journal of Abnormal Psychology*, *121*, 951–957.

19c

Simplicity and Dynamics of the ICD-11 Trait Qualifiers in Relation to Treatment: Author Rejoinder to Commentaries on Using DSM-5 and ICD-11 Personality Traits in Clinical Treatment

BO BACH

Sauer-Zavala and Ringwald, Edershile, Woods, and Wright raise some important points about trait-informed treatment, particularly with regard to the importance of simplicity and trait dynamics for clinical treatment. In this rejoinder, I briefly propose how these issues may be addressed within the realm of ICD-11 classification of PDs, including the five trait qualifiers expressing specific styles of personality dysfunction (Reed, 2018).

Sauer-Zavala underscores the importance of simplicity by focusing on the five higher-order domains (e.g., Neuroticism or Negative Affectivity) without getting sidetracked by the various subfacets and corresponding treatment approaches (which involve a large training burden for clinicians). Consistent with this point, the ICD-11 trait qualifiers are aimed at capturing essential maladaptive features of the FFM domains without providing any code for subfacets. The ICD-11 model was developed to be useful across all WHO member countries by providing a manageable number of trait qualifiers and corresponding treatment components, which may, eventually, reduce the therapist training burden. This aligns with the vision of the WHO Personality Disorder Working Group "that any classification system of PDs for the ICD-11 must be usable and useful for health care workers in lower-resource settings who are not highly trained specialist mental health professionals" (Reed, 2018, p. 227). Thus, from a WHO perspective, simplicity seems obvious, although it may also frustrate some clinicians who appreciate the palette of ten PD types or 25 subfacets. Therefore, the simple coding of one, two, or three ICD-11 trait qualifiers (after classification of severity) may only serve as the first step in a process that leads to the development of a clinical management plan. For clinicians with sufficient resources, a second step may involve elaboration of the trait domain coding by means of 25 clinically informative DSM-5 Alternative Model of Personality Disorders (AMPD) subfacets (Bach et al., 2017) or dynamic conceptualizations (Bach & Kongerslev, 2018).

Ringwald et al. highlight the importance of taking dynamic elements of traits into account (including the mechanistic relationship between traits and trait-relevant expressions), which they argue is valuable for effective clinical conceptualization and treatment. The ICD-11 diagnostic guidelines appear to take such dynamic aspects of trait qualifiers into account. For example, the ICD-11 model suggests that individuals with Negative Affectivity sometimes vacillate between a range of emotions in a short period of time. Additionally, individuals with Negative Affectivity may exhibit low self-esteem in several ways, for example: (a) *avoidance* of situations that are judged too difficult; (b) *dependency* on others for advice, help, and direction; (c) *envy* of others' abilities and indicators of success; and (d) *suicidal ideation* due to believing themselves to be useless (WHO, 2019). These four multi-causal response patterns comprise different situational and motivational expressions of Negative Affectivity, often resulting in different treatment implications.

Dynamic aspects of trait qualifiers may also involve specific constellations of co-occurring traits. For example, the ICD-11 guideline states that individuals with Negative Affectivity, who are also characterized by Dissociality, are more likely to experience "externalized" features of Negative Affectivity (e.g., anger, hostility, contempt), whereas those who are characterized by co-occurring Detachment are more likely to experience "internalized" features of Negative Affectivity (e.g., anxiety, depression, pessimism, guilt). Moreover, according to the ICD-11 guideline, individuals with Negative Affectivity often exhibit negativistic attitudes, which may be expressed differently depending on the individual's other traits. Negativistic individuals high on Detachment are most likely to blame themselves for poor outcomes, whereas those high on Dissociality are most likely to blame others for offering such bad ideas (WHO, 2019). Thus, rather than being narrowly or categorically defined, the ICD-11 trait qualifiers allow for various constellations and potential manifestations across situations and interpersonal dynamics. Whereas the trait profiles of two patients may be very similar, their behavior, interpersonal dynamics, and indicated treatments may be very dissimilar.

The aforementioned trait dynamics are also acknowledged in the ICD-11 definition of core PD dysfunction

(WHO, 2019). Accordingly, an individual may be characterized as having difficulty maintaining positive self-esteem in one situation (e.g., self-contempt), while having an unrealistically positive self-view in another situation (e.g., entitlement), which may even be observed during one session of therapy. Moreover, poor emotion regulation may cause an individual to give up easily in one situation but to persist unreasonably in pursuit of goals that have no chance of success in others. Finally, certain interpersonal conflicts may cause the individual to surrender to others (e.g., in an attempt to achieve others' love and protection), whereas others may result in fits of temper (e.g., when the individual's own needs have been suppressed for too long).

Taken together, the ICD-11 trait qualifiers provide a parsimonious framework that is manageable across all WHO member countries, while also allowing for the assessment of features of personality trait dynamics. The field of PDs needs to move on from questions about which traits exist to questions about how the traits function. However, future psychometric development is needed to operationalize this for research and clinical practice. For example, it could be useful to develop an instrument that takes different situational expressions of ICD-11 trait qualifiers into account across different life settings (e.g.,

in social surroundings, in intimate relationships, and when under stress or pressure). In line with this, Ringwald et al.'s proposal of integrating insights from the cybernetics theory of personality and psychopathology seems fascinating and worthwhile, and hopefully we will see such integration in relation to DSM-5 AMPD and ICD-11 trait qualifiers within the near future.

REFERENCES

Bach, B., & Kongerslev, M. T. (2018). Personality dynamics in schema therapy and the forthcoming ICD-11 classification of personality disorder. *European Journal of Personality*, *32*(5), 527–528.

Bach, B., Sellbom, M., Kongerslev, M., Simonsen, E., Krueger, R. F., & Mulder, R. (2017). Deriving ICD-11 personality disorder domains from DSM-5 traits: Initial attempt to harmonize two diagnostic systems. *Acta Psychiatrica Scandinavica*, *136*(1), 108–117.

Reed, G. M. (2018). Progress in developing a classification of personality disorders for ICD-11. *World Psychiatry*, *17*(2), 227–228.

World Health Organization. (2019). *ICD-11 Clinical Descriptions and Diagnostic Guidelines for Mental and Behavioural Disorders*. Geneva: World Health Organization.

20 Brief Therapeutic Approaches for Personality Disorders

KATHERINE L. DIXON-GORDON, LINDSEY C. CONKEY, AND SHERRY E. WOODS

INTRODUCTION

Personality disorders (PDs) are longstanding patterns of maladaptive cognition, affect, and behavior that lead to substantial distress and impairment (American Psychiatric Association, 2013). These disorders affect approximately 9 percent of the population (4.4–14.8 percent; Quirk et al., 2016; Samuels et al., 2002). Relative to these modest prevalence rates, PDs incur disproportionately great societal costs. Individuals who suffer from PDs use more treatment resources (Quirk et al., 2016), rely more heavily on disability and social services (Østby et al., 2014), and have reduced life expectancies (Fok et al., 2012). The fifth revision of the *Diagnostic and Statistical Manual of Mental Disorders* (DSM-5) delineates ten distinct forms of PDs that are classified into three clusters based on similar patterns of maladaptive behaviors (American Psychiatric Association, 2013). Schizoid, paranoid, and schizotypal PDs are classified in Cluster A and involve odd or eccentric patterns of behavior. Antisocial, borderline, narcissistic, and histrionic PDs are classified in Cluster B, and involve dramatic and impulsive patterns of behavior. Avoidant, dependent, and obsessive-compulsive PDs are classified in Cluster C, and involve anxious or fearful patterns of behavior. In addition to these categorical distinctions that distinguish the presence or absence of PDs based on diagnostic thresholds, PDs may also be observed on a continuum (Trull, Distel, & Carpenter, 2011). Consequently, the DSM-5 provides an alternative model that characterizes PDs as maladaptive variants of normative personality dimensions.

The presence of PDs often complicates the treatment process, a particularly concerning problem since these disorders occur at high rates (up to 45 percent) in clinical settings (Zimmerman, Rothschild, & Chelminski, 2005). The presence of PDs often indicates a more severe symptom presentation. For instance, patients with emotional disorders and co-occurring PDs were more severely depressed at intake than their counterparts without PDs (Lis & Myhr, 2016). Additionally, PDs have been associated with greater treatment drop-out (Schindler, Hiller, & Witthöft, 2013), and Cluster B PD traits specifically have been linked to poorer working alliance in treatment (Olesek et al., 2016). These factors may have fueled some of the historical concerns about the amenability of PDs to treatment (Lewis & Appleby, 1988).

The late twentieth century welcomed the emergence of several psychotherapies for PDs (see Dixon-Gordon, Turner, & Chapman, 2011). The most well-studied of these treatments have predominately focused on borderline PD, including dialectical behavior therapy (DBT; Linehan, 1993), mentalization-based therapy (MBT; Fonagy & Bateman, 2008), and schema-focused therapy (SFT; Giesen-Bloo et al., 2006). Apart from these borderline PD-specific treatments, meta-analytic evidence supports the efficacy of PD psychotherapies broadly when compared to treatment-as-usual (TAU; Budge et al., 2013). The implementation and reach of these treatments has so far been limited, due in part to their length (one to three years) and intensity (two to six hours per week). Public healthcare systems often lack the resources to develop and sustain PD treatment programs (Carmel, Rose, & Fruzzetti, 2013; National Collaborating Centre for Mental Health, 2009). Although longer-term treatment is recommended for patients with PDs (Crits-Christoph & Barber, 2007), promoting uptake of evidence-based strategies would be enhanced by an understanding of patient populations, settings, and services in which briefer treatments are effective. Briefer programs would be less costly, easier to implement and sustain, and more accessible to larger numbers of patients. In an effort to address this public need, researchers have focused their efforts on developing and assessing the utility of brief interventions.

The following review will detail recent advances in brief treatments for PDs. As such, the objectives of the present review are to: (1) provide a summary of the extant literature on briefer treatments for PDs, and (2) provide recommendations for future research and clinical practice.

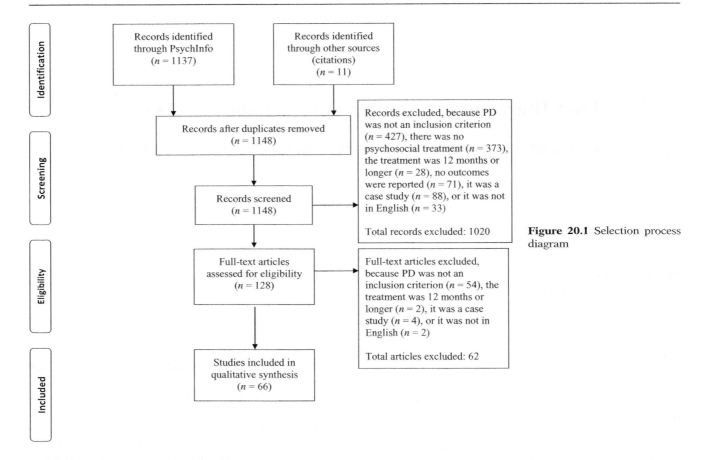

Figure 20.1 Selection process diagram

AN UPDATE OF BRIEF PSYCHOSOCIAL TREATMENTS FOR PDs

The present chapter provides an update on the empirical literature related to brief treatments of PDs.[1] In line with treatment guidelines, we focused on psychosocial therapies for PDs (National Collaborating Centre for Mental Health, 2009). To ensure that these treatments were designed to target the problems associated with PDs, we focus herein on trials that were specifically designed for PD samples. Of note, this approach excluded trials that examined PDs as potential moderators of treatment response for other conditions. Although brief treatments have been defined with many durations (e.g., 1–40 sessions; Center for Substance Abuse Treatment, 1999), given the lengthy duration of many existing PD treatments, we

have reviewed interventions involving less than one year of therapy. See Figure 20.1 for our selection process and excluded articles. A total of 66 articles are summarized below. The studies included in the final review are presented in Table 20.1. Only a minority of these studies were randomized controlled trials (RCTs; $n = 25$). Nearly half focused on borderline PD ($n = 32$). We have organized this literature broadly by treatment approach.

Dynamic Approaches

A recent surge in research on psychodynamic treatments has yielded support for time-limited versions of these treatments for PDs. Building off prior work (Davanloo, 1980), short-term dynamic psychotherapy (STDP) draws on traditional psychoanalytic theory and emphasizes an active role of the therapist through elicitation of affect and use of the therapeutic relationship. Several RCTs have compared brief (i.e., 40 sessions) STDP to other treatments for PD. For instance, patients with any PD randomized to receive STDP reported significant improvements in patient-identified target complaints and symptom severity ($N = 49$; Hellerstein et al., 1998). In addition, after completing STDP, patients with a Cluster C PD ($N = 50$) exhibited improvements in general psychiatric symptoms, PD symptoms, interpersonal problems (Svartberg, Stiles, & Seltzer, 2004), social adjustment ($N = 81$; Winston et al., 1991, 1994), emotional and identity symptoms (Berggraf

[1] This review involved a search of PsychInfo; search terms were: [(brief or "short-term") AND (treatment or intervention or therapy or "dialectical behavior") AND ("personality disorder" or "personality disorders")]. We also identified articles that were cited within any reviewed full-text to ensure comprehensive coverage of this area. To be included in this review, research needed to be (1) an empirical primary source, (2) peer-reviewed literature, (3) written or translated into the English language, (4) published prior to the date the most recent search was conducted for the present manuscript (December 4, 2017), (5) conducted in human samples, (6) quantitative, (7) a study of a sample that included PD symptoms (defined dimensionally or categorically) as an inclusion criterion for the sample, and (8) a study of a brief (i.e., <1 year) psychosocial therapeutic approach.

Table 20.1 Summary of studies meeting inclusion criteria

Reference	Sample	Diagnosis	Treatment	Length	Design
Dynamic					
(Amianto et al., 2011)	N = 35	BPD	SB-APP+STM (n = 18) vs. STM (n = 17)	12 months	RCT with 1-year follow-up
(Andreoli et al., 2016)	N = 170	BPD and depression	AP-Clinicians (n = 70) vs. AP-Nurses (n = 70) vs. TAU (n = 30)	3 months, 2x a week	RCT with 3-month follow-up
(Berggraf et al., 2014), secondary analyses of (Svartberg et al., 2004)	N = 47	Cluster C PD	STDP (n = 23) vs. cognitive therapy (n = 24)	40 sessions	RCT
(Hellerstein et al., 1998)	N = 49	PD	STDP (n = 25) vs. BSP (n = 24) – other arms of this trial were not reported	40 sessions	RCT with 6-month follow-up
(Horn, Verhuel, et al., 2015)	N = 134	PD	STIP-TA (n = 67) vs. other psychotherapies (n = 67)	3 months	Non-randomized controlled trial
(Muran et al., 2005)	N = 128	Cluster C PD or PDNOS	STDP (n = 16) vs. CBT (n = 19) vs. BRT (n = 21)	30 weekly sessions	Non-randomized controlled trial
(Ryle & Golynkina, 2000)	N = 27	BPD	Cognitive analytic therapy	24 sessions	Uncontrolled trial
(Schanche et al., 2011), secondary analyses of (Svartberg et al., 2004)	N = 50	Cluster C PD	STDP (n = 25) vs. cognitive therapy (n = 25)	40 sessions	RCT
(Svartberg et al., 2004)	N = 50	Cluster C PD	STDP (n = 25) vs. cognitive therapy (n = 25)	40 sessions	RCT with 2-year follow-up
(Ulvenes et al., 2012), secondary analyses of (Svartberg et al., 2004)	N = 46	Cluster C PD	STDP (n = 23) vs. cognitive therapy (n = 23)	40 sessions	RCT
(Vinnars et al., 2005)	N = 156	PD	Manualized dynamic supportive-expressive psychotherapy (n = 80) vs. community dynamic therapy (n = 76)	40 sessions	RCT with 1-year follow-up
(Westerman et al., 1995) secondary analyses of Winston et al., 1991	N = 59	PD, primarily Cluster C	BAP (n = 21) vs. STDP (n = 21) vs. waitlist (n = 17)	40 weeks BAP/STDP, 15 week waitlist	RCT with 1.5-year follow-up for subsample (n = 38)
(Winston et al., 1991)	N = 47	PD, primarily Cluster C	BAP (n = 17) vs. STDP (n = 15) vs. waitlist (n = 17)	40 weeks BAP/STDP, 20-week waitlist	RCT
(Winston et al., 1994)	N = 81	PD, primarily Cluster C	BAP (n = 30) vs. STDP (n = 25) vs. waitlist (n = 26)	40 weeks BAP/STDP, 15-week waitlist	RCT with 1.5-year follow-up for subsample (n = 38)

Table 20.1 (*cont.*)

Reference	Sample	Diagnosis	Treatment	Length	Design
Cognitive-behavioral					
(Alden, 1989)	$N = 76$	APD	CBT exposure vs. CBT exposure and interpersonal skills training vs. CBT exposure and interpersonal skills with a focus on close relationships vs. waitlist	10 weeks	RCT with 3-month follow-up
(Andreasson et al., 2016)	$N = 108$	BPD	DBT ($n = 57$) vs. CAMS ($n = 51$)	16 weeks	RCT
(Blum et al., 2002)	$N = 52$	BPD	STEPPS	20 weeks	Uncontrolled trial
(Bohus et al., 2000)	$N = 24$	BPD inpatients	Inpatient DBT	3 months	Uncontrolled trial
(Bohus et al., 2004)	$N = 50$	BPD inpatients	Inpatient DBT ($n = 31$) vs. waitlist ($n = 19$)	3 months	Non-randomized controlled trial
(Bos et al., 2010)	$N = 79$	BPD	STEPPS ($n = 42$) vs. TAU ($n = 37$)	18 weeks	RCT
(Chugani et al., 2013)	$N = 19$	Cluster B PD diagnosis or traits	DBT skills training ($n = 11$) vs. TAU ($n = 8$)	11 weeks	Non-randomized controlled trial
(Davidson et al., 2009)	$N = 52$	ASPD +aggression	CBT+TAU ($n = 25$) vs. TAU ($n = 27$)	6 or 12 months	RCT
(Davidson et al., 2014)	$N = 20$	PD (with recent episode of self-harm)	MACT ($n = 14$) vs. TAU ($n = 11$)	6 sessions	RCT
(Dixon-Gordon et al., 2015)	$N = 19$	BPD	DBT emotion regulation ($n = 7$) vs. DBT interpersonal effectiveness ($n = 6$) vs. psychoeducation ($n = 6$)	6 sessions	RCT
(Doyle et al., 2013)	$N = 126$	ASPD traits	ETS ($n = 70$) vs. TAU ($n = 26$)	5 weeks	Non-randomized controlled trial
(Emmelkamp et al., 2006)	$N = 62$	APD	CBT ($n = 21$) vs. BDT ($n = 23$) vs. waitlist ($n = 18$)	20 weeks	RCT
(Evans et al., 1999)	$N = 32$	Recent self-harm and Cluster B PD traits	MACT ($n = 18$) vs. TAU ($n = 16$)	Max 6 months + bibliotherapy	RCT
(Feliu-Soler et al., 2014)	$N = 35$	BPD	DBT mindfulness skills training + GPM ($n = 18$) vs. GPM ($n = 17$)	10 weeks	RCT
(Gratz & Gunderson, 2006)	$N = 22$	BPD females with recent and recurrent self-injury	ERGT ($n = 12$) vs. TAU ($n = 10$)	14 weeks	RCT

Table 20.1 (*cont.*)

Reference	Sample	Diagnosis	Treatment	Length	Design
(Gratz & Tull, 2011)	$N = 23$	BPD females with recent and recurrent self-injury	ERGT	14 weeks	Uncontrolled trial
(Gratz et al., 2014)	$N = 61$	BPD females with recent and recurrent self-injury	ERGT immediately ($n = 31$) vs. waitlist+later ERGT ($n = 30$)	14 weeks	RCT with uncontrolled 9-month follow-up
(Harvey et al., 2010)	$N = 38$	BPD	STEPPS	20 weeks	Uncontrolled trial
(Huband et al., 2007)	$N = 176$	PD	Problem-solving group sessions ($n = 87$) vs. waitlist ($n = 89$)	16 sessions	RCT
(Kleindienst et al., 2008), Secondary analyses from (Bohus et al., 2004)	$N = 60$	BPD	Inpatient DBT ($n = 40$) vs. waitlist+TAU ($n = 20$)	3 months with 21-month follow-up	Uncontrolled trial
(Kröger et al., 2013)	$N = 1423$	BPD	Inpatient DBT	3 months	Uncontrolled trial
(McMain et al., 2017)	$N = 84$	BPD and recent self-injury	DBT skills ($n = 42$) vs. waitlist ($n = 42$)	20 weeks	RCT
(Meaney-Tavares & Hasking, 2013)	$N = 17$	BPD	DBT skills-training sessions	8 sessions	Uncontrolled trial
(Pasieczny & Connor, 2011)	$N = 90$	BPD	DBT ($n = 43$) vs. waitlist+TAU ($n = 47$)	6 months	Non-randomized controlled trial
(Perroud et al., 2010)	$N = 447$	PD (94% BPD)	Intensive DBT	3-4 weeks	Uncontrolled trial
(Rizvi et al., 2017)	$N = 50$	BPD	DBT	6 months	Uncontrolled trial
(Sahlin et al., 2017)	$N = 95$	Women with BPD or BPD features and recurrent self-injury	ERGT	14 weeks	Uncontrolled naturalistic trial with 6-month follow-up
(Soler et al., 2009)	$N = 59$	BPD	Brief DBT skills ($n = 29$) vs. standard group ($n = 30$)	13 weeks	RCT
(Soler et al., 2012)	$N = 59$	BPD	DBT-mindfulness group + GPM ($n = 40$) vs. GPM alone ($n = 19$)	8 sessions	RCT
(Springer et al., 1996)	$N = 31$	PD	Brief DBT inpatient ($n = 16$) vs. wellness activity-control ($n = 15$)	10 daily-sessions	RCT
(Stanley et al., 2007)	$N = 20$	BPD	Brief DBT	6 months	Uncontrolled trial

Table 20.1 (*cont.*)

Reference	Sample	Diagnosis	Treatment	Length	Design
(Thylstrup et al., 2015); (Thylstrup et al., 2017)	$N = 176$	ASPD and substance use	ILC ($n = 96$) vs. TAU ($n = 80$)	6 sessions, 11 weeks	RCT with 15-month follow-up
(Yen et al., 2009)	$N = 50$	BPD	Brief inpatient DBT	5 days	Uncontrolled trial with 3-month follow-up
(Weinberg et al., 2006)	$N = 30$	BPD and recurrent NSSI	MACT ($n = 15$) vs. TAU ($n = 15$)	6 sessions	RCT with 6-month follow-up
Integrative					
(Ball et al., 2005)	$N = 52$	PD in homeless adults	DFST ($n = 26$) vs. substance abuse counseling ($n = 26$)	6 months	RCT
(Ball, 2007)	$N = 30$	PD	DFST ($n = 15$) vs. 12FT ($n = 15$)	6 months	RCT
(Nenadić et al., 2017)	$N = 9$	BPD or Cluster C PD	GST	12–15 weeks	Uncontrolled trial
(Pabst et al., 2011)	$N = 21$	BPD+PTSD	Narrative exposure	$Mean_{sessions} = 14$ (11–19)	Uncontrolled trial with 6-month follow-up
(Prunetti et al., 2013)	$N = 51$	PD (71%BPD)	CET	3 weeks	Uncontrolled trial with 3-month follow-up
(Renner et al., 2013)	$N = 26$	Cluster B or C PD or features	Schema CBT	20 sessions	Uncontrolled trial
(Skewes et al., 2015)	$N = 8$	PD ($n = 7$ APD)	GST	20 sessions	Uncontrolled trial with 6-month follow-up
Multi-component Programs					
(Amianto et al., 2011)	$N = 35$	BPD	SB-APP+STM ($n = 18$) vs. STM ($n = 17$)	12 months	RCT with 1-year follow-up
(Bartak et al., 2010)	$N = 371$	Cluster C PD	Long-term outpatient treatment ($n = 68$), short day hospital treatment ($n = 77$), long-term day hospital treatment ($n = 74$), short inpatient treatment ($n = 59$), long-term inpatient treatment ($n = 93$)	Various	Non-randomized naturalistic trial
(Gratz et al., 2006)	$N = 36$	BPD	Integrative, step-down treatment program for BPD	Hospitalization average of 8 weeks; outcomes measured at 1- and 3-months	Uncontrolled trial

Table 20.1 (*cont.*)

Reference	Sample	Diagnosis	Treatment	Length	Design
(Horn, Bartak, et al., 2015)	N = 205	PDNOS	Short-term outpatient (n = 17), long-term outpatient (n = 50), short-term day-hospital (n = 26), long-term day-hospital (n = 36), short-term inpatient (n = 52), long-term inpatient (n = 36)	Various (short-term <6 months, long-term >6 months)	Non-randomized naturalistic trial
(Ogrodniczuk et al., 2011)	N = 197	PD	Day treatment program including art, exercise, vocational, interpersonal, and cognitive behavioral groups	18 weeks	Uncontrolled trial
(Petersen et al., 2008)	N = 66	PD	Day treatment including individual and group psychodynamic and cognitive therapy (n = 38) vs. TAU +waitlist (n = 28)	5 months	Non-randomized controlled trial
(Sollberger et al., 2015)	N = 44	BPD inpatients	DST (n = 32) vs. TAU (n = 12)	12 weeks	Non-randomized controlled trial

Note: 12FT = 12 step facilitation therapy; AP = abandonment psychotherapy; APD = avoidant personality disorder; ASPD = antisocial personality disorder; BAP = brief adaptive psychotherapy; BDT = brief dynamic therapy; BPD = borderline personality disorder; BRT = brief relational therapy; BSP = brief supportive psychotherapy; CBT = cognitive behavioral therapy; CET = cognitive evolutionary therapy; CAMS = collaborative assessment and management of suicidality; DFST = dual-focused schema therapy; DST = structured disorder-specific inpatient treatment; ERGT = emotion regulation group therapy; ETS = enhanced thinking skills intervention; GPM = general psychiatric management; GST = group schema therapy; ILC = impulsive learning counseling; MACT = manual-assisted cognitive therapy; NSSI = non-suicidal self-injury; PD = personality disorder; PDNOS = personality disorder not otherwise specified; RCT = randomized controlled trial; SBPP = Sequential Brief Adlerian Psychodynamic Psychotherapy; STDP = short term dynamic psychotherapy; STIP-TA = short-term inpatient psychotherapy based on transactional analysis; STM = structured team management; STEPPS = systems training for emotional predictability and problem solving; TAU = treatment as usual.

et al., 2014), and self-compassion (Schanche, Stiles, McCullough, Svartberg, & Nielsen, 2011). In addition, both STDP and brief adaptive therapy demonstrated superiority to a waitlist control (Winston et al., 1991, 1994), but this waitlist was only 15–20 weeks in duration, confounding the treatment conditions with time. There were no other significant differences between STDP and comparison conditions. Given the lack of a matched control condition, the efficacy of STDP warrants further study.

In terms of specificity, there is little evidence that STDP outperforms other treatments for PDs. No significant differences emerged between STDP and brief supportive psychotherapy (Hellerstein et al., 1998), brief adaptive therapy (a more cognitively oriented dynamic treatment; Winston et al., 1994), or cognitive therapy (Berggraf et al., 2014; Schanche et al., 2011; Svartberg et al., 2004). Among patients with a Cluster C PD or PD not otherwise specified (N = 128), a 30-session STDP with weekly half-hour sessions had a higher proportion of treatment drop-outs relative to brief relational therapy in a non-randomized controlled trial, and a lower rate of patients who achieved reliable improvements in interpersonal functioning than

the CBT condition (Muran, Safran, Samstag, & Winston, 2005).

Examinations of the processes associated with outcomes in STDP shed light on putative mechanisms of this treatment. In secondary analyses evaluating process in STDP (Ulvenes et al., 2012; Westerman, Foote, & Winston, 1995), there was evidence of differential processes across treatments. Whereas avoidance of affect was associated with less symptom reduction in STDP, it was associated with more symptom reduction in cognitive therapy (Ulvenes et al., 2012). In addition, the strength of the therapeutic alliance was associated with outcome in STDP (Westerman et al., 1995).

Other trials have compared a range of other dynamic approaches to TAU for PDs. For instance, an RCT compared supportive-expressive dynamic psychotherapy, a time-limited (i.e., 40-session) manualized treatment designed to alter maladaptive interpersonal patterns characteristic of PDs, to TAU for patients with PDs (N = 156; Vinnars, Barber, Norén, Gallop, & Weinryb, 2005). Although there were no between-group differences in PD severity, psychiatric symptoms, or global functioning post-treatment, the supportive-expressive treatment was associated with significantly fewer visits to community mental health centers than TAU at the one-year follow-up. In addition, a non-randomized trial compared the utility of a three-month inpatient psychotherapy program based on transactional analysis (involving both psychodynamic and cognitive behavioral principles and tailored for personality pathology) to TAU (Horn, Verhuel, et al., 2015). Patients with PDs (N = 67) were matched with patients in other Dutch treatment programs. Patients in the treatment condition improved significantly more in terms of general psychiatric symptoms and quality of life, and had higher recovery rates (68 percent vs. 48 percent in the control). Effect sizes were large, and improvements persisted over the three-year follow-up period. These data offer preliminary support for the potential utility of these brief dynamic interventions, although replication is needed.

Several dynamic interventions were designed to treat borderline PD in particular. Some of these studies compared time-limited dynamic treatments to a less resource-intensive control condition. For instance, one RCT compared abandonment psychotherapy as delivered by certified psychotherapists to the same treatment delivered by nurses and to TAU (Andreoli et al., 2016). Abandonment psychotherapy is a three-month, twice-weekly manualized intervention designed to target abandonment fears characteristic of borderline PD by cultivating emotional understanding and insight about maladaptive patterns. Integrating principles of MBT and DBT, this approach also directly targets therapy interfering and safety-interfering behaviors. Among patients with an admission due to self-injury who met criteria for major depression and borderline PD (N = 170), the experimental conditions did not significantly differ, and both resulted in reduced suicidal ideation, suicide attempts, and a lower likelihood of a psychiatric hospitalization at the three-month follow-up, relative to TAU. Therefore, formal training in psychotherapy does not appear to be associated with better outcomes, further increasing the accessibility of this treatment.

Likewise, another study compared a time-limited psychodynamic treatment, Sequential Brief Adlerian Psychodynamic Psychotherapy (SB-APP), to a less resource-intensive clinician-training condition for participants with borderline PD (N = 35) and a history of high treatment use (Amianto et al., 2011). In 40 weekly sessions, SB-APP focuses on strengthening identity, increasing validation of the self and emotions, and reducing idealization. Based on the notion that one aspect of effective treatments for PDs involves providing staff with training in a cohesive view of the disorder, SB-APP was compared to staff simply receiving supervised team management. All patients demonstrated improvements in global functioning and reductions in anger. The SB-APP showed greater decreases in borderline PD symptoms, including suicide attempts, feelings of emptiness, impulsivity, and relationship disturbance, than the control condition. Thus, individual

psychotherapy contributed more than additional clinician training and support.

Finally, cognitive analytic therapy is a dynamic treatment that aims to diagram and reflect on the fragmented emotion-dependent "self-states" experienced by individuals with borderline PD (Ryle & Golynkina, 2000). In an uncontrolled trial of 24 sessions of cognitive analytic therapy for patients with borderline PD (N = 27), 52 percent of patients no longer met PD criteria following treatment (Ryle & Golynkina, 2000). This study remains to be replicated.

Together, the 14 studies reviewed in this section document nine trials examining brief dynamic treatments for PDs (see Table 20.1). Although patients receiving treatment in most of these controlled trials exhibited within-group symptom improvements, only a handful outperformed comparison conditions. The transactional analysis inpatient program (Horn, Verhuel, et al., 2015) and STDP (Winston et al., 1991, 1994) resulted in greater improvement in symptoms and functioning than TAU for PDs. Abandonment psychotherapy (Andreoli et al., 2016) and SB-APP (Amianto et al., 2011) outperformed TAU or an enhanced staff-training, respectively, in reducing suicide attempts and symptoms of borderline PD. None of these results have been replicated, providing only preliminary support for the efficacy of these treatments. Although many studies of STDP fell within our initial search criteria, it is worth noting that several trials allowed for variable duration of treatment and were therefore not included in the present study. Thus, this review likely underestimates the evidence base of STDP.

Cognitive-Behavioral Approaches

The time-limited, problem-focused nature of cognitive behavioral therapy (CBT) lends itself to briefer applications for PDs. Generally, these approaches aim to modify dysfunctional patterns of thinking and behaving by providing psychoeducation, managing contingencies, and improving self-management and social skills deficits (e.g., Doyle et al., 2013; Huband, McMurran, Evans, & Duggan, 2007; Linehan, 1993). Given the prominence of interpersonal problems across PDs, improving social skills in this population was expected to alleviate many of the symptoms and functional impairments associated with a range of PDs (Huband et al., 2007). Based on this premise, Huband and colleagues developed a 16-session problem-solving group therapy as both a brief intervention and a prelude to additional treatment (Huband et al., 2007). In an RCT comparing this intervention to a waitlist control for patients with PDs (N = 176), those who received the intervention had significantly better problem-solving skills, overall higher social functioning, and lower anger expression than controls, although there were no differences in utilization of mental health services.

Preliminary evidence suggests that brief cognitive-behavioral treatments are useful for the treatment of avoidant PD. One RCT compared 20 sessions of CBT to a brief dynamic therapy or a waitlist control for patients with avoidant PD (N = 62; Emmelkamp et al., 2006). Although both active conditions led to decreases over treatment in social anxiety, avoidance, and both avoidant and obsessive-compulsive PD symptoms (albeit not dependent PD symptoms), CBT outperformed the brief dynamic treatment on all these outcomes. These improvements were maintained at a six-month follow-up.

In an effort to identify the relative efficacy of different cognitive-behavioral interventions for avoidant PD, an RCT compared a no-treatment control condition to ten weeks of group therapy containing effective elements of treatments for interpersonal problems for patients with avoidant PD (N = 76; Alden, 1989). In particular, this study compared the no-treatment control to three different 10-week groups focused on (1) graduated exposure only; (2) exposure plus interpersonal skill training; or (3) exposure, interpersonal skills, and the development of intimacy in close relationships. The treatment conditions demonstrated greater improvement than the control condition across interviewer-rated and self-report measures of social inhibition, anxiety, self-esteem, and relational functioning. Further, the intimacy condition outperformed the other social skills condition with regard to the frequency of and satisfaction with social activities (although there were no significant differences between the exposure condition and the other group treatment conditions). The improvements found across the treatment conditions were maintained over the three-month follow-up. Despite these improvements and the fact that half of the participants rated their specific targets as "improved," few participants (9 percent) rated these targets as completely satisfactory, and symptom scores remained in the clinical range. Thus, although even brief CBT is effective in reducing avoidance and improving social activities for avoidant PD, particularly if the treatment directly targets close relationships, full remission of symptoms was rarely seen.

Two controlled trials have evaluated brief cognitive behavioral interventions for antisocial PD. One pilot RCT directly compared 6 or 12 months of CBT to TAU for males with antisocial PD and a recent act of aggression (N = 52; Davidson et al., 2009). No differences emerged at the 12-month follow-up with respect to anxiety, depression, alcohol abuse, anger, acts of aggression, or social functioning. The authors noted that patients who received 6 months of CBT showed greater improvement in social functioning than those who received TAU, although this difference was non-significant. Another approach, enhanced thinking skills, consists of 20 group sessions over five weeks that teach impulse control, flexible thinking, interpersonal problem-solving, and reasoning (Doyle et al., 2013). In a non-randomized controlled trial for inmates with antisocial PD (N = 126; 49 completers), ETS outperformed

the waitlist TAU in reducing anger and antisocial PD symptoms and improving problem-solving.

Another RCT examined a psychoeducation-based adjunctive treatment to a substance use treatment program for antisocial PD. Patients with antisocial PD (N = 176) were randomly assigned to receive six sessions of impulsive lifestyle counseling (ILC) psychoeducation over 11 weeks or TAU (Thylstrup, Schrøder, Fridell, & Hesse, 2017; Thylstrup, Schrøder, & Hesse, 2015). Across both groups, patients reported a decrease in aggression, although no significant difference emerged between conditions. However, relative to TAU, ILC was associated with increased abstinence (Thylstrup et al., 2017) and decreased drug use in the three-month follow-up (Thylstrup et al., 2015). Together, these studies suggest the utility of even shorter-term cognitive-behavioral interventions in reducing some of the symptoms of antisocial PD.

The vast majority of brief cognitive-behavioral treatments were developed to focus on Cluster B PDs, particularly borderline PD. In some cases, these treatments were also evaluated for patients with a range of PDs. For instance, an adjunctive manual-assisted cognitive therapy (MACT) that focuses on understanding the precipitants and advantages and disadvantages of problem behaviors and provides psychoeducation about adaptive coping strategies was originally evaluated for borderline PD, but has been implemented for a range of other PDs. One RCT examined the utility of a six-session adjunctive MACT or TAU only for patients with borderline PD and recent self-injury (N = 30; Weinberg, Gunderson, Hennen, & Cutter, 2006). The MACT condition resulted in significantly greater decreases in the frequency of non-suicidal self-injury during treatment, as well as greater decreases in self-injury severity and frequency over the six-month follow-up. There were no significant differences in change in suicidal ideation. Another study expanded the application of MACT to a sample of inpatients with PDs (N = 20) who were admitted to the hospital for an episode of self-injury (Davidson, Brown, James, Kirk, & Richardson, 2014). Patients who received six sessions of MACT reported lower anxiety, depression, and suicidal ideation than those who received TAU at the three-month follow-up. There were no significant differences in alcohol use, and differences in the frequency of self-injury over the treatment period were not reported.

Further enhancing the accessibility of MACT, an RCT compared a modified MACT protocol involving fewer sessions (i.e., 0–6) plus MACT-based bibliotherapy to TAU for patients with a Cluster B PD and a history of self-injury (N = 34; Evans et al., 1999). Participants in the MACT condition were given a manual and the option of attending up to six sessions; however, participants attended an average of only 2.7 sessions, and five participants did not attend any sessions. Even with this lower level of care, the MACT condition had significantly greater reductions in depressive symptoms and non-significantly reduced suicidal acts and costs of care. This approach may therefore be a model for increasing accessibility of care in other skills-based interventions.

Many studies have examined briefer cognitive-behavioral interventions for borderline PD and its associated problem behaviors. Systems training for emotional predictability and problem solving (STEPPS) is a manualized group-based cognitive-behavioral skills program developed for individuals with borderline PD (Blum, Pfohl, John, Monahan, & Black, 2002). In two uncontrolled studies, participants with borderline PD (N = 52; Blum et al., 2002; N = 38; Harvey, Black, & Blum, 2010) reported significant improvements in mood, clinical symptoms, and PD symptoms after 20 weeks of STEPPS. Another RCT comparing 18 weeks of STEPPS to TAU for patients with borderline PD (N = 79; Bos, van Wel, Appelo, & Verbraak, 2010) found that participants in the STEPPS condition had significantly greater improvements in general and borderline PD-specific symptomology as well as quality of life; however, there were no differences in impulsive behaviors or instances of non-suicidal self-injury. Further, although treatment gains were maintained at six-month follow-up, there were no significant group differences in recovery rates (i.e., overall psychological distress below the clinical cut-off).

Based on empirical research suggesting that self-injury primarily functions to regulate intense distress, emotion regulation group therapy (ERGT) was developed to enhance emotion regulation among women with prominent borderline PD symptoms and recurrent self-injury (Gratz & Gunderson, 2006). Specifically, this group-based, time-limited treatment targets one particularly concerning aspect of borderline PD – non-suicidal self-injury – and its proposed underlying mechanism of emotion regulation difficulties. Over 14 weekly group sessions, ERGT focuses on providing psychoeducation and skills training focused on increasing understanding of the functions of self-injury, increasing emotional awareness and understanding, teaching adaptive emotion regulation strategies, and encouraging willingness to experience emotions in the service of long-term goals. An uncontrolled trial found that ERGT resulted in reductions in self-injury, symptoms of BPD, depression, and anxiety, and improvements in vocational functioning in a sample of women with borderline PD and recent, recurrent self-injury (Gratz & Tull, 2011). A preliminary RCT compared ERGT to TAU for women with borderline PD and recent, recurrent self-injury (Gratz & Gunderson, 2006). ERGT outperformed TAU in reducing self-injury, emotion dysregulation, and symptoms of borderline PD, anxiety, and depression. Findings were replicated in a larger RCT among women with threshold or subthreshold borderline PD and recent, recurrent self-injury (N = 61), and gains were maintained over a nine-month follow-up (Gratz, Tull, & Levy, 2014). In addition, a naturalistic uncontrolled trial for women with borderline PD symptoms and self-injury (N = 95) from outpatient clinics across Sweden revealed that ERGT

resulted in improvements in self-injury, other self-destructive behaviors, emotion dysregulation, and psychiatric symptoms (Sahlin et al., 2017). Of particular note, clinicians in this study had no prior exposure to ERGT, aside from completing a brief workshop and related readings. Despite the short-term nature of this treatment, gains were maintained over the six-month follow-up. The replication of these findings across multiple trials provides among the most consistent support for the efficacy of a brief treatment for borderline PD. Furthermore, the implementation of this treatment by clinicians with minimal prior experience in naturalistic settings underscores the probable effectiveness of this treatment. Additional work is needed to ascertain whether ERGT includes specific ingredients that will outperform other bona fide treatments for borderline PD.

Dialectical behavior therapy (DBT) is a comprehensive treatment that balances cognitive behavioral strategies of change with the acceptance-based philosophy of Zen Buddhism (Linehan, 1993). This approach typically involves one year of weekly group skills training to teach mindfulness, interpersonal effectiveness, emotion regulation, and distress tolerance skills, along with weekly individual psychotherapy and telephone coaching. The complex, resource-intensive nature of DBT has prompted many clinicians to implement briefer versions of this treatment program. DBT has been streamlined in many ways by different groups; for instance, by truncating the duration of treatment or providing only one mode of treatment (e.g., just the skills group). Empirical evaluations of these abbreviated forms of DBT are just emerging.

Data from uncontrolled trials suggest that shortened versions of DBT may be useful for borderline PD. For instance, six months of DBT for patients with borderline PD yielded improvements in depression, self-injury (N = 20; Stanley, Brodsky, Nelson, & Dulit, 2007; N = 50; Rizvi, Hughes, Hittman, & Vieira Oliveira, 2017), suicidal ideation (Stanley et al., 2007), emotion regulation, symptoms of borderline PD, and overall adjustment (Rizvi et al., 2017). Despite the brief nature of these treatments, effect sizes were comparable to other trials of DBT (Rizvi et al., 2017). Further supporting the feasibility of short-term DBT, one of these trials relied on training clinicians as study therapists (Rizvi et al., 2017), suggesting that beneficial treatment provision does not require extensive experience.

Controlled trials likewise support the utility of abbreviated standard DBT for borderline PD. An RCT evaluated six months of DBT compared to TAU plus a waitlist for Australian females with borderline PD (N = 73; Carter, Willcox, Lewin, Conrad, & Bendit, 2010). There were no differences between groups on the primary outcomes of self-injury or treatment utilization, although both groups had significant reductions in these metrics. However, the DBT group improved significantly more than the control group on measures of disability and quality of life. In a slightly larger sample, patients with borderline PD (N = 90) were randomized to either six months of standard outpatient DBT or a waitlist control (Pasieczny & Connor, 2011). The DBT condition showed a greater reduction in self-injury (suicidal and non-suicidal) and treatment use (e.g., emergency department and psychiatric admissions and days of hospitalization) than the waitlist control. However, several other findings from this RCT warrant consideration. In particular, additional DBT was offered as indicated and, in this case, additional gains were achieved, suggesting that more treatment could confer greater benefit. In addition, patients who had intensively trained therapists demonstrated greater reductions in self-injury, suggesting that DBT may not be as effective when administered by someone without extensive training in and experience with the treatment.

In addition to reducing the duration of treatment, the week-to-week time commitment of DBT has also been streamlined by focusing on only the DBT group skills training component. As such, an RCT compared 20 weeks of DBT skills training groups to a waitlist control for patients with borderline PD and recent self-injurious behaviors (N = 84), with a 12-week follow-up (McMain, Guimond, Barnhart, Habinski, & Streiner, 2017). Findings revealed that the DBT arm had greater reductions in suicidal and non-suicidal self-injury and anger, as well as greater improvements in distress tolerance and emotion regulation. Another RCT compared 13 weeks of standalone DBT group skills training to standard group therapy for patients with borderline PD (N = 59; Soler et al., 2009). The DBT group had greater decreases in reported depression, anxiety, and borderline PD symptoms of anger and affect lability.

In another adaptation of standard DBT, an intensive program condensed the standard format of one weekly 2-hour group session to four weekly 2–4 hour group sessions for three to four weeks in an uncontrolled study of outpatients with a PD (N = 447; predominantly borderline PD; N = 418; Perroud, Uher, Dieben, Nicastro, & Huguelet, 2010). Despite the relatively high (19.9 percent) drop-out rates, there were significant pre- to post-treatment improvements in depression, hopelessness, and symptom distress. Of note, a substantial proportion of the sample (N = 103) underwent a second course of DBT, and although hopelessness and depression did not improve in this round, symptom distress was significantly further reduced.

Another truncated form of DBT has been compared to an established short-term treatment for suicidality, collaborative assessment and management of suicidality (CAMS; Andreasson et al., 2016). Patients with two or more borderline PD criteria and a recent suicide attempt (N = 108) were randomized to either 16 weeks of DBT or CAMS. CAMS is a flexible, atheoretical approach to target and manage suicidality in a collaborative and empathic manner. No significant differences emerged in borderline PD symptoms, depression, non-suicidal self-injury, or suicidal behavior frequencies. As such, this brief form of DBT was not superior to another established treatment for suicidality.

The short-term nature of inpatient hospitalization has also led to an increased need for abbreviated forms of DBT in inpatient contexts. An uncontrolled naturalistic trial evaluated the utility of three months of DBT for inpatients with borderline PD (N = 24; Bohus et al., 2000). This abbreviated model of DBT involves (1) developing a functional analysis of target behaviors, (2) providing psychoeducation, (3) providing training in emotion regulation and distress tolerance skills, (4) managing contingencies of target behaviors, and (5) engaging in discharge planning. Results suggested decreases in self-injury frequency, dissociation, depression, anxiety, and overall symptoms over the course of treatment. In a non-randomized controlled trial, this three-month inpatient DBT program was compared to a waitlist control for inpatients with borderline PD (N = 50; Bohus et al., 2004). Results revealed that DBT outperformed the waitlist comparison in reducing depression symptoms, anxiety symptoms, general psychiatric symptom severity, and self-injury and enhancing interpersonal functioning, with 42 percent of participants exhibiting clinically-significant improvements in general psychiatric symptom severity. Furthermore, these improvements were sustained over the 21-month follow-up (Kleindienst et al., 2008). A large-scale naturalistic trial of three months of DBT for inpatients with borderline PD (N = 1423) also found significant improvements in depression, borderline PD, and general psychopathology symptoms and global functioning (Kröger, Harbeck, Armbrust, & Kliem, 2013).

Two studies have examined even more condensed formats of DBT in inpatient contexts. In an uncontrolled trial, a five-day inpatient DBT program for patients with borderline PD (N = 50) yielded improvements in general psychopathology, depression, hopelessness, anger expression, and dissociation over a three-month period (Yen, Johnson, Costello, & Simpson, 2009). Additionally, an RCT examined an abbreviation of DBT to ten daily sessions compared to an activity control "wellness and living" group for inpatients with a PD (N = 31; Springer, Lohr, Buchtel, & Silk, 1996). Although all participants demonstrated significant decreases in depression, hopelessness, and suicidal ideation, there were no between-group differences. Given the absence of any documentation of superiority over comparison conditions, there is no evidence that such condensed inpatient forms of DBT are efficacious.

Abbreviated formats of standard DBT have also been developed to accommodate the time demands imposed by the semester structure of universities and colleges. An uncontrolled trial examined the utility of eight two-hour DBT group skills-training sessions for college students with borderline PD (N = 17; Meaney-Tavares & Hasking, 2013). Participants demonstrated significant reductions in depression, borderline PD symptoms, and self-blame, although no significant change in anxiety was seen. Another trial included a non-randomized TAU control condition, and examined the relative utility of an 11-week

DBT skills training class for college students with Cluster B PDs or PD traits (N = 19; Chugani, Ghali, & Brunner, 2013). Those in DBT showed significantly greater increases in skills use and decreases in maladaptive coping than the TAU group. Although both conditions demonstrated decreases in emotion regulation difficulties, there was no significant difference between conditions. Evidence of the superiority of DBT skills training over a non-randomized TAU control condition, albeit preliminary, provides suggestive support for the possible utility of brief DBT skills training for PD traits in college students.

Another strategy for abbreviating DBT is to focus on specific skills modules. A non-randomized controlled trial assigned consecutive hospital patients with borderline PD (N = 35) to either general psychiatric management (GPM) alone or GPM plus a 10-week DBT mindfulness skills training group (DBT-M; Feliu-Soler et al., 2014). No differences were found in terms of self-reported mindfulness or laboratory-assessed biological or subjective indices of emotional reactivity. However, the DBT-M condition resulted in greater improvements in observer-rated depressive symptomology and psychiatric severity. Another RCT revealed that eight sessions of DBT mindfulness group plus GPM outperformed GPM alone in improving impulsivity on a behavioral task among patients with borderline PD (N = 59; Soler et al., 2012). In another small pilot RCT, women with borderline PD (N = 19) were assigned to six weeks of group therapy involving DBT interpersonal effectiveness skills, DBT emotion regulation skills, or psychoeducation (Dixon-Gordon, Chapman, & Turner, 2015). The emotion regulation condition resulted in significantly greater reductions in self-injury than the other conditions. Although preliminary, these findings support the utility of specific DBT skills modules, namely mindfulness and emotion regulation, in the reduction of BPD-relevant symptoms.

Taken together, these 33 studies describe 31 trials of CBT for PDs (see Table 20.1), particularly borderline PD (n = 23) and related problems (i.e., self-injury; n = 2). Over half of the trials (n = 21) were controlled. The only trials that were replicated focused on borderline PD. Although 17 studies evaluated variations of DBT, many of these implementations were idiosyncratic, and only a few of the trials of these versions were replicated. The three-month inpatient DBT program showed promising results in uncontrolled trials (Bohus et al., 2000; Kröger et al., 2013), and outperformed a waitlist condition in reducing self-injury and depression, anxiety, and general psychiatric symptoms and increasing global functioning. (Bohus et al., 2004). Likewise, six months of DBT yielded improvements in self-injury in both uncontrolled trials (Rizvi et al., 2017; Stanley et al., 2007) and when compared to waitlist controls (McMain et al., 2017; Pasieczny & Connor, 2011). Controlled studies also demonstrated the superiority of MACT to TAU in reducing self-injury (Weinberg et al., 2006), suicidal behaviors (Evans et al., 1999), and suicidal ideation (Davidson et al., 2014)

among patients with Cluster B PDs and self-injury. In addition, both uncontrolled (Harvey et al., 2010) and controlled (Bos et al., 2010) evaluations of STEPPS support its utility in reducing symptoms of borderline PD. Finally, open trials of ERGT reveal improvements in self-injury, borderline PD and other psychiatric symptoms, and emotion regulation difficulties from pre- to post-treatment (Gratz & Tull, 2011; Sahlin et al., 2017), and RCTs demonstrate the superiority of ERGT to TAU in reducing self-injury, emotion regulation difficulties, and other symptoms of borderline PD and depression, and improving quality of life (Gratz & Gunderson, 2006; Gratz et al., 2014).

Integrative Approaches

Several interventions for PDs integrate principles from diverse theoretical orientations. For instance, schema-focused therapy (SFT) is an integrative approach informed by cognitive-behavioral, attachment, and psychodynamic perspectives (Giesen-Bloo et al., 2006) and is predicated on the theory that a failure to meet early attachment needs results in maladaptive relational and intra-personal schemas. SFT targets these deficits through limited reparenting, experiential imagery and dialogue, cognitive restructuring, and behavioral exercises. An uncontrolled trial aimed to examine the utility of 12–15 sessions of group SFT among inpatients with borderline PD or Cluster C PDs (N = 9; Nenadić, Lamberth, & Reiss, 2017). Patients who underwent this brief group showed significant reductions in symptom severity and maladaptive schema modes. Of note, effect sizes (ds = 0.69–0.86) were judged to be smaller than other applications of this treatment. Likewise, two uncontrolled trials demonstrated the utility of a 20-session group SFT for patients with a Cluster B PD, Cluster C PD, or prominent PD features (N = 26; Renner et al., 2013) and patients with Cluster C PDs (N = 8; Skewes, Samson, Simpson, & van Vreeswijk, 2015) in reducing general symptom severity, maladaptive schemas, and dysfunctional coping.

In recognition of the frequent co-occurrence of PD and substance use disorders, efforts have been made to combine SFT and relapse prevention strategies for drug dependence, resulting in dual-focus schema therapy. In one RCT, homeless adults with a PD (N = 52) were randomized to six months of dual-focus schema therapy or substance abuse counseling three times weekly, but high drop-out (N = 40) precluded an evaluation of the efficacy of the intervention (Ball, Cobb-Richardson, Connolly, Bujosa, & O'Neall, 2005). In another RCT, outpatients with a PD and methadone-maintained opioid dependence (N = 30) were randomized to either six months of dual-focus schema therapy or 12-Step Facilitation Therapy (Ball, 2007). Across both conditions, patients reported decreases in alcohol problems, psychiatric symptoms, and dysphoria. Dual-focus schema therapy yielded a steeper decline and overall less substance use than the 12-Step condition, whereas the 12-Step condition had greater decreases in dysphoria. Although promising, dual-focus schema therapy did not demonstrate clear superiority over the comparator in these trials.

Interpersonal group psychotherapy is another integrative treatment for borderline PD that focuses on providing a context for interpersonal interactions, and works to clarify and develop boundaries, allow for grief, and encourage more balanced views of self in relation to others (Munroe-Blum & Marziali, 1995). This manualized treatment consists of 30 1 ½ hour sessions (25 weekly, then 5 biweekly). An RCT for patients with borderline PD (N = 110) compared interpersonal group psychotherapy to individual TAU (individual dynamic psychotherapy). Although patients showed improvements in depression, general symptoms, and social adjustment, there were no significant between-group differences at post-treatment or one-year follow-up. Consequently, extant data do not currently support the efficacy of this treatment for PDs.

Cognitive evolutionary therapy focuses on enhancing meta-cognitive functioning and highlighting the evolutionary functional influences on meta-cognition. In an inpatient setting including patients with a PD (N = 51; 71 percent borderline; 35 percent avoidant PD), participants underwent three weeks of cognitive evolutionary therapy including 20 hours a week of both individual and group therapy, as well as some skills training from DBT (Prunetti, Bosio, Bateni, & Liotti, 2013). Significant improvements were observed in general psychiatric symptom severity, depression, anxiety, paranoia, interpersonal sensitivity, subsequent hospital admissions, and attendance in outpatient therapy. Without a control condition, however, the efficacy of cognitive evolutionary therapy remains unclear.

Narrative exposure therapy is an exposure-based treatment that aims to change the autobiographical associations of event memories thought to underlie borderline PD (Pabst et al., 2011). One uncontrolled feasibility study examined the utility of narrative exposure therapy for women with borderline PD and co-occurring posttraumatic stress disorder (PTSD) without a stabilization period (N = 12; n = 10 completers). From pre-treatment to the six-month follow-up, significant reductions were found in depression, PTSD symptoms, and dissociation, whereas the reductions in borderline PD symptoms were non-significant. Consequently, although these data provide preliminary support for the utility of this treatment for PTSD, they are not particularly promising with regard to PD symptoms.

These seven trials constitute a variety of integrative approaches for PDs (see Table 20.1). Four of these treatments were informed by SFT, which was associated with improvements in PD symptoms (Nenadić et al., 2017; Skewes et al., 2015) and symptom distress (Renner et al., 2013) in uncontrolled trials. In addition, relative to a 12-Step condition, dual-focused schema therapy demonstrated improvements in substance use outcomes (Ball, 2007), suggesting this may be a promising, potentially efficacious treatment with some specific ingredients that outperform other active treatments for PD and substance use. Replication in controlled trials will instill more confidence in these results.

Multi-Component Programmatic Approaches

Although the interventions offered in psychiatric programs are often heterogeneous, it is fruitful to consider how varied lengths of such programs may affect outcomes in PDs. Indeed, several studies of PD treatment programs suggest that significant improvements can be seen much sooner than one year. One such uncontrolled naturalistic trial of a day-treatment program involving a range of groups (vocational, cognitive-behavioral, art, etc.) for patients with PDs (N = 197, 125 completers) revealed significant improvements in interpersonal problems, social adjustment, general psychiatric severity, dysfunctional behaviors, and overall quality of life after only 18 weeks of treatment (Ogrodniczuk et al., 2011). Likewise, another intensive outpatient treatment program designed for patients with prominent borderline PD features or a borderline PD diagnosis (N = 36) yielded significant improvements with large effect sizes in borderline PD-relevant behaviors and symptoms after three months (Gratz, Lacroce, & Gunderson, 2006). Specifically, improvements were seen in emotion regulation, self-injury, symptom severity, and quality of life at one month, and significant changes with large effect sizes were observed in all outcome variables except for self-injury between one and three months. Despite demonstrating improvements in some domains, there were no significant changes in global functioning or quality of life, and the majority of the sample did not reach normative levels of functioning. These studies provide preliminary evidence for the utility of these relatively brief, heterogeneous programs, but the absence of control conditions precludes any conclusions regarding their efficacy.

Two non-randomized controlled studies evaluated the utility of specialized treatment programs relative to control conditions. One of these studies compared outcomes among PD patients (N = 66) enrolled in a Danish day-treatment to a waitlist-control (Petersen et al., 2008). The day treatment comprised five months of both psychodynamic and cognitive therapy in group and individual settings for 11 hours each week. Those who received the intervention demonstrated lower rates of psychiatric hospitalizations and suicide attempts than the waitlist, as well as significant decreases in symptom severity and global functioning (albeit not interpersonal functioning). Similarly, a 12-week, structured, disorder-specific inpatient treatment combining psychodynamic treatment with DBT skills training was compared in a non-randomized controlled trial to inpatient TAU for patients with borderline PD (N = 44; Sollberger et al., 2015). The disorder-specific condition showed significant decreases in identity diffusion and instability and depression. Both of these programs demonstrated utility for PDs over control conditions.

A non-randomized naturalistic study compared outcomes for patients (N = 205) across six different treatment modalities (Horn, Bartak, et al., 2015). Specifically, short- (≤6 months) and long- (>6 months) term outpatient treatment, short- and long-term day-hospital treatment, and short- and long-term inpatient treatment. Outcomes were assessed yearly up to 60 months after baseline, and participants in all treatment modalities showed improvements in symptom severity and social functioning. At the one-year follow-up, short-term and long-term outpatient treatments outperformed inpatient treatment in reducing psychiatric symptom severity, but these differences became non-significant over time. Thus, these treatments showed comparable benefits by the follow-up. Likewise, another non-randomized naturalistic study compared these treatment modalities for patients with Cluster C PDs (Bartak et al., 2010). All groups showed improved psychiatric symptoms and psychosocial functioning one year later; short-term inpatient treatment (<6 months) showed more improvement than the other groups.

Despite their heterogeneity, these six studies underscore the utility of brief, multi-componential treatment programs for PDs (see Table 20.1). The two controlled trials suggest that disorder-specific treatments result in greater reductions in PD symptoms than TAU (Sollberger et al., 2015) or waitlist-controls (Petersen et al., 2008).

DISCUSSION

This emerging literature documenting brief interventions for PDs constitutes a dramatic shift in the approach to treating these disorders. The advent of efficacious treatments for PDs (e.g., Fonagy & Bateman, 2008; Linehan, 1993) has cast off prior beliefs about the intractability of PDs. Moreover, prior recommendations that PDs require longer-term treatments than other disorders (Crits-Christoph & Barber, 2007) have been confronted by pragmatic demands from under-resourced communities. Consequently, accumulating research has been dedicated to developing briefer, more accessible interventions for patients with PDs.

The present review has yielded encouraging results. Interventions lasting less than one year have yielded promising outcomes in the treatment of PDs, underscoring the utility of even relatively brief psychosocial interventions for these disorders. It is worth noting that the effect sizes from some of these treatments (e.g., DBT) were comparable to longer forms of the treatment (Rizvi et al., 2017). These interventions cut across theoretical orientations (e.g., Hellerstein et al., 1998; Rizvi et al., 2017; Winston et al., 1994), suggesting that the effectiveness of brief

treatments is not circumscribed to a particular approach. These findings are consistent with work identifying trans-theoretical aspects of effective treatments for borderline PD (Weinberg, Ronningstam, Goldblatt, Schechter, & Maltsberger, 2011). Specifically, research indicates that longer borderline PD treatments share a structured time-limited approach based on a biopsychosocial model, elements of safety planning, attention to treatment motivation and compliance, a focus on the here and now, an emphasis on the therapeutic relationship, and a group component. Many of these transtheoretical features may also contribute to the utility of briefer treatments for PDs.

The pressure for increased access to treatments for PDs may also be addressed by reducing the resources needed to deliver such treatments. For instance, data from some of these trials suggest that interventions delivered by trainees (Rizvi et al., 2017) or nurses (Andreoli et al., 2016) were beneficial, increasing the accessibility of treatments. Similarly, the group-based nature of many of these brief psychotherapies (e.g., Blum et al., 2002; Gratz & Gunderson, 2006) further facilitates patient access.

The brief nature of these treatments necessitates a precise and strategic approach to targeting the problems central to PDs. It is worth noting that many of these possibly efficacious briefer treatments for PDs directly targeted proposed mechanisms hypothesized to underlie the presenting problems, most prominently emotion regulation and interpersonal functioning. Consistent with the notion that emotion regulation difficulties underlie many of the problem behaviors in borderline PD (Gratz & Gunderson, 2006; Linehan, 1993), briefer treatments that focus on enhancing mindfulness of emotions and emotion regulation generally outperformed comparison conditions. For example, predicated on the notion that the self-injury characteristic of borderline PD serves an emotion regulatory function, both ERGT (Gratz & Gunderson, 2006; Gratz & Tull, 2011; Gratz et al., 2014; Sahlin et al., 2017) and MACT (Davidson et al., 2014; Evans et al., 1999; Weinberg et al., 2006) directly focus on enhancing adaptive emotion regulation capacities. Likewise, training in DBT emotion regulation (Dixon-Gordon et al., 2015) and mindfulness (Feliu-Soler et al., 2014; Soler et al., 2012) skills outperformed comparison conditions. In addition, in line with views that interpersonal difficulties contribute to many PDs (Westerman et al., 1995), interpersonally-focused treatments were efficacious for avoidant PD (Alden, 1989), and a strong therapeutic relationship emerged as a prospective mechanism of STDP (Westerman et al., 1995). A clearer understanding of the mechanisms of action of larger, more comprehensive treatments for PDs may suggest other avenues for further streamlining treatments for these disorders. This review also highlights important directions for future research. First, many of the evaluations of brief treatments were uncontrolled, and among those that included control groups, few have been replicated. Only a few treatments have garnered sufficient empirical support to be considered efficacious for the treatment of PDs. Among these include STDP, especially for Cluster C PDs, although there is not yet evidence for the specificity of this treatment for PDs relative to factors common to many forms of psychotherapy (Hellerstein et al., 1998; Winston et al., 1994). Likewise, a number of cognitive-behavioral interventions have been shown to be efficacious for borderline PD and/or self-injury in controlled trials, including ERGT (Gratz & Gunderson, 2006; Gratz et al., 2014), six-month DBT (McMain et al., 2017; Pasieczny & Connor, 2011), and MACT (Davidson et al., 2014; Evans et al., 1999; Weinberg et al., 2006). However, many of the abbreviations of PD treatments such as DBT were idiosyncratic truncations of treatments. Further work evaluating similar versions of abridged treatments would bolster the confidence in these initial results.

Second, most treatment development efforts have thus far focused on borderline PD and other Cluster B disorders. Although these efforts are reasonable in light of the tremendously high rate of treatment utilization among those with borderline PD, even relative to other PDs (Ansell, Sanislow, McGlashan, & Grilo, 2007), there remains scarce work on brief treatments for other PDs. Therefore, additional research is needed on efficacious treatments for mixed PD presentations and other PDs.

Third, findings from some of these studies underscore the need for longer interventions in some cases. For instance, effect sizes in some of these briefer treatments were judged to be smaller than longer versions of these treatments (e.g., Nenadić et al., 2017). In addition, when patients opted to undergo additional courses of DBT after the briefer treatments, they derived further benefits (Pasieczny & Connor, 2011; Perroud et al., 2010). Accordingly, although even short-term treatments may stabilize acute symptoms, many patients may require longer term treatment. Yet, only a few studies have compared the cost and clinical utility of different durations or "doses" of treatments (Davidson et al., 2009). Whereas two trials found continued improvement with longer durations of therapy for borderline PD (Pasieczny & Connor, 2011; Perroud et al., 2010), another trial did not find significant differences in patients who received 6 versus 12 months of treatment (Davidson et al., 2009). Since bona fide interventions may yield considerable benefit early on, differences between different "doses" of treatment are likely to be small and trials will need to be powered for equivalence (Christensen, 2007). Only a few studies to date have confronted the most important question facing these abbreviated treatments: namely, is it worth it? Economic evaluations will be an important component of future comparisons of durations of treatment.

Likewise, research will need to investigate moderators to determine who is likely to benefit most from briefer versus longer treatments. Such work has the potential to inform an empirical examination of a stepped care model (Paris, 2013, 2015). In this model, patients with positive prognostic indicators could be offered a brief streamlined intervention first, whereas those who require more intensive intervention could be identified early and matched with appropriate programs. Those who do not derive sufficient benefit from brief front-line interventions could then be offered a "stepped up" treatment.

The arrival of streamlined treatments has the potential to revolutionize PD treatment and management. Given the enormous toll these disorders pose to individuals, the health system, and society (Quirk et al., 2016; Zimmerman et al., 2005), more efficient and accessible treatments have the potential to address an urgent public health need. Attention to increased accessibility must be balanced by an acknowledgment that many of these patients will require more comprehensive or longer treatments. A stepped care approach addressing both of these needs may represent a path forward.

REFERENCES

Alden, L. (1989). Short-term structured treatment for avoidant personality disorder. *Journal of Consulting and Clinical Psychology*, 57(6), 756–764.

American Psychiatric Association. (2013). *Diagnostic and Statistical Manual of Mental Disorders* (5th ed.). Arlington, VA: American Psychiatric Publishing.

Amianto, F., Ferrero, A., Pierò, A., Cairo, E., Rocca, G., Simonelli, B., . . . Fassino, S. (2011). Supervised team management, with or without structured psychotherapy, in heavy users of a mental health service with borderline personality disorder: A two-year follow-up preliminary randomized study. *BMC Psychiatry*, 11 (1), 181. https://doi.org/10.1186/1471-244X-11-181

Andreasson, K., Krogh, J., Wenneberg, C., Jessen, H. K. L., Krakauer, K., Gluud, C., . . . Nordentoft, M. (2016). Effectiveness of dialectical behavior therapy versus collaborative assessment and management of suicidality treatment for reduction of self-harm in adults with borderline personality traits and disorder: A randomized observer-blinded clinical trial. *Depression and Anxiety*, 33(6), 520–530.

Andreoli, A., Burnand, Y., Cochennec, M.-F., Ohlendorf, P., Frambati, L., Gaudry-Maire, D., . . . Frances, A. (2016). Disappointed love and suicide: A randomized controlled trial of "abandonment psychotherapy" among borderline patients. *Journal of Personality Disorders*, 30(2), 271–287.

Ansell, E. B., Sanislow, C. A., McGlashan, T. H., & Grilo, C. M. (2007). Psychosocial impairment and treatment utilization by patients with borderline personality disorder, other personality disorders, mood and anxiety disorders, and a healthy comparison group. *Comprehensive Psychiatry*, 48(4), 329–336.

Ball, S. A. (2007). Comparing individual therapies for personality disordered opioid dependent patients. *Journal of Personality Disorders*, 21(3), 305–321.

Ball, S. A., Cobb-Richardson, P., Connolly, A. J., Bujosa, C. T., & O'Neall, T. W. (2005). Substance abuse and personality disorders in homeless drop-in center clients: Symptom severity and psychotherapy retention in a randomized clinical trial. *Comprehensive Psychiatry*, 46(5), 371–379.

Bartak, A., Spreeuwenberg, M. D., Andrea, H., Holleman, L., Rijnierse, P., Rossum, B. V., . . . Emmelkamp, P. M. G. (2010). Effectiveness of different modalities of psychotherapeutic treatment for patients with cluster C personality disorders: Results of a large prospective multicentre study. *Psychotherapy and Psychosomatics, 79*(1), 20–30.

Berggraf, L., Ulvenes, P. G., Øktedalen, T., Hoffart, A., Stiles, T., McCullough, L., & Wampold, B. E. (2014). Experience of affects predicting sense of self and others in short-term dynamic and cognitive therapy. *Psychotherapy, 51*(2), 246–257.

Blum, N., Pfohl, B., John, D. S., Monahan, P., & Black, D. W. (2002). STEPPS: A cognitive-behavioral systems-based group treatment for outpatients with borderline personality disorder: A preliminary report. *Comprehensive Psychiatry, 43*(4), 301–310.

Bohus, M., Haaf, B., Simms, T., Limberger, M. F., Schmahl, C., Unckel, C., . . . Linehan, M. M. (2004). Effectiveness of inpatient dialectical behavioral therapy for borderline personality disorder: A controlled trial. *Behaviour Research and Therapy, 42*(5), 487–499.

Bohus, M., Haaf, B., Stiglmayr, C., Pohl, U., Bohme, R., & Linehan, M. M. (2000). Evaluation of inpatient dialectical-behavioral therapy for borderline personality disorder: A prospective study. *Behaviour Research and Therapy, 38*, 875–887.

Bos, E. H., van Wel, E. B., Appelo, M. T., & Verbraak, M. J. P. M. (2010). A randomized controlled trial of a Dutch version of Systems Training for Emotional Predictability and Problem Solving for borderline personality disorder. *Journal of Nervous and Mental Disease, 198*(4), 299–304.

Budge, S. L., Moore, J. T., Del Re, A. C., Wampold, B. E., Baardseth, T. P., & Nienhuis, J. B. (2013). The effectiveness of evidence-based treatments for personality disorders when comparing treatment-as-usual and bona fide treatments. *Clinical Psychology Review, 33*(8), 1057–1066.

Carmel, A., Rose, M., & Fruzzetti, A. E. (2013). Barriers and solutions to implementing dialectical behavior therapy in a public behavioral health system. *Administration and Policy in Mental Health and Mental Health Research Services, 18*(9), 1199–1216.

Carter, G. L., Willcox, C. H., Lewin, T. J., Conrad, A. M., & Bendit, N. (2010). Hunter DBT project: Randomized controlled trial of dialectical behaviour therapy in women with borderline personality disorder. *The Australian and New Zealand Journal of Psychiatry, 44*(2), 162–173.

Center for Substance Abuse Treatment. (1999). Brief interventions and brief therapies for substance abuse. In *Treatment Improvement Protocol Series* (Vol. 34). Rockville, MD: Substance Abuse and Mental Health Services Administration.

Christensen, E. (2007). Methodology of superiority vs. equivalence trials and non-inferiority trials. *Journal of Hepatology, 46*(5), 947–954.

Chugani, C. D., Ghali, M. N., & Brunner, J. (2013). Effectiveness of short term dialectical behavior therapy skills training in college students with cluster B personality disorders. *Journal of College Student Psychotherapy, 27*(4), 323–336.

Crits-Christoph, P., & Barber, J. P. (2007). Psychological treatments for personality disorders. In P. E. Nathan & J. M. Gorman (Eds.), *A Guide to Treatments That Work* (3rd ed., pp. 641–658). New York: Oxford University Press.

Davanloo, H. (1980). *Short-Term Dyanmic Psychotherapy.* New York: Jason Aronson.

Davidson, K. M., Brown, T. M., James, V., Kirk, J., & Richardson, J. (2014). Manual-assisted cognitive therapy for self-harm in personality disorder and substance misuse: A feasibility trial. *Psychiatric Bulletin, 38*(3), 108–111.

Davidson, K. M., Tyrer, P., Tata, P., Cooke, D., Gumley, A., Ford, I., . . . Crawford, M. J. (2009). Cognitive behaviour therapy for violent men with antisocial personality disorder in the community: An exploratory randomized controlled trial. *Psychological Medicine, 39*(4), 569–577.

Dixon-Gordon, K. L., Chapman, A. L., & Turner, B. J. (2015). A preliminary pilot study comparing dialectical behavior therapy emotion regulation skills with interpersonal effectiveness skills and a control group treatment. *Journal of Experimental Psychopathology, 6*(4), 369–388.

Dixon-Gordon, K. L., Turner, B. J., & Chapman, A. L. (2011). Psychotherapy for personality disorders. *International Review of Psychiatry, 23*(3), 282–302.

Doyle, M., Khanna, T., Lennox, C., Shaw, J., Hayes, A., Taylor, J., . . . Dolan, M. (2013). The effectiveness of an enhanced thinking skills programme in offenders with antisocial personality traits. *Journal of Forensic Psychiatry and Psychology, 24*(1), 1–15.

Emmelkamp, P. M. G., Benner, A., Kuipers, A., Feiertag, G. A., Koster, H. C., & Van Apeldoorn, J. (2006). Comparison of brief dynamic and cognitive-behavioural therapies in avoidant personality disorder. *British Journal of Psychiatry, 189*, 60–64.

Evans, K., Tyrer, P., Catalan, J., Schmidt, U., Davidson, K., Dent, J., . . . Thompson, S. (1999). Manual-assisted cognitive-behaviour therapy (MACT): A randomized controlled trial of a brief intervention with bibliotherapy in the treatment of recurrent deliberate self-harm. *Psychological Medicine, 29*(1), 19–25.

Feliu-Soler, A., Pascual, J. C., Borràs, X., Portella, M. J., Martín-Blanco, A., Armario, A., . . . Soler, J. (2014). Effects of dialectical behaviour therapy-mindfulness training on emotional reactivity in borderline personality disorder: Preliminary results. *Clinical Psychology and Psychotherapy, 21*(4), 363–370.

Fok, M. L.-Y., Hayes, R. D., Chang, C. K., Stewart, R., Callard, F. J., & Moran, P. (2012). Life expectancy at birth and all-cause mortality among people with personality disorder. *Journal of Psychosomatic Research, 73*(2), 104–107.

Fonagy, P., & Bateman, A. (2008). The development of borderline personality disorder: A mentalizing model. *Journal of Personality Disorders, 22*(1), 4–21.

Giesen-Bloo, J., van Dyck, R., Spinhoven, P., Van Tilburg, W., Dirksen, C. D., Van Asselt, T., . . . Arntz, A. (2006). Outpatient psychotherapy for borderline personality disorder: Randomized trial of schema-focused therapy vs transference-focused psychotherapy. *Archives of General Psychiatry, 63*, 649–658.

Gratz, K. L., & Gunderson, J. G. (2006). Preliminary data on an acceptance-based emotion regulation group intervention for deliberate self-harm among women with borderline personality disorder. *Behavior Therapy, 37*(1), 25–35.

Gratz, K. L., Lacroce, D. M., & Gunderson, J. G. (2006). Measuring changes in symptoms relevant to borderline personality disorder following short-term treatment across partial hospital and intensive outpatient levels of care. *Journal of Psychiatric Practice, 12*(3), 153–159.

Gratz, K. L., & Tull, M. T. (2011). Extending research on the utility of an adjunctive emotion regulation group therapy for deliberate self-harm among women with borderline personality pathology. *Personality Disorders: Theory, Research, and Treatment, 2*(4), 316–326.

Gratz, K. L., Tull, M. T., & Levy, R. (2014). Randomized controlled trial and uncontrolled 9-month follow-up of an adjunctive emotion regulation group therapy for deliberate self-harm among women with borderline personality disorder. *Psychological Medicine, 44*(10), 2099–2112.

Harvey, R., Black, D. W., & Blum, N. (2010). Systems Training for Emotional Predictability and Problem Solving (STEPPS) in the United Kingdom: A preliminary report. *Journal of Contemporary Psychotherapy*, 40, 225–232.

Hellerstein, D. J., Rosenthal, R. N., Pinsker, H., Samstag, L. W., Muran, J. C., & Winston, A. (1998). A randomized prospective study comparing supportive and dynamic therapies: Outcome and alliance. *Journal of Psychotherapy Practice and Research*, 7 (4), 261–271.

Horn, E. K., Bartak, A., Meerman, A. M. M. A., Rossum, B. V, Ziegler, U. M., Thunnissen, M., … Verheul, R. (2015). Effectiveness of psychotherapy in personality disorders not otherwise specified: A comparison of different treatment modalities. *Clinical Psychology and Psychotherapy*, 22(5), 426–442.

Horn, E. K., Verhuel, R., Thunnissen, M., Delimon, J., Soons, M., Meerman, A. M. M. A., … Busschbach, J. J. V. (2015). Effectiveness of short-term inpatient psychotherapy based on transactional analysis with patients with personality disorders: A matched control study using propensity score. *Journal of Personality Disorders*, 29(5), 663–683.

Huband, N., McMurran, M., Evans, C., & Duggan, C. (2007). Social problem-solving plus psychoeducation for adults with personality disorder. *British Journal of Psychiatry*, 190, 307–314.

Kleindienst, N., Limberger, M. F., Schmahl, C., Steil, R., Ebner-Priemer, U. W., & Bohus, M. (2008). Do improvements after inpatient dialectical behavioral therapy persist in the long term? *Journal of Nervous and Mental Disease*, 196(11), 847–851.

Kröger, C., Harbeck, S., Armbrust, M., & Kliem, S. (2013). Effectiveness, response, and dropout of dialectical behavior therapy for borderline personality disorder in an inpatient setting. *Behavior Research and Therapy*, 51, 411–416.

Lewis, G., & Appleby, L. (1988). Personality disorder: The patients psychiatrists dislike. *British Journal of Psychiatry*, 153 (1), 44–49.

Linehan, M. M. (1993). *Cognitive-Behavioral Treatment of Borderline Personality Disorder*. New York: Guilford Press.

Lis, E., & Myhr, G. (2016). The effect of borderline personality pathology on outcome of cognitive behavior therapy. *Journal of Psychiatric Practice*, 22(4), 270–282.

McMain, S. F., Guimond, T., Barnhart, R., Habinski, L., & Streiner, D. L. (2017). A randomized trial of brief dialectical behaviour therapy skills training in suicidal patients suffering from borderline disorder. *Acta Psychiatrica Scandinavica*, 135(2), 138–148.

Meaney-Tavares, R., & Hasking, P. (2013). Coping and regulating emotions: A pilot study of a modified Dialectical Behavior Therapy. *Journal of American College Health*, 61(5), 303–309.

Munroe-Blum, H., & Marziali, E. (1995). A controlled trial of short-term group treatment for borderline personality disorder. *Journal of Personality Disorders*, 9(3), 190–198.

Muran, J. C., Safran, J. D., Samstag, L. W., & Winston, A. (2005). Evaluating an alliance-focused treatment for personality disorders. *Psychotherapy: Theory, Research, Practice, Training*, 42 (4), 532–545.

National Collaborating Centre for Mental Health. (2009). *Borderline Personality Disorder: Treatment and Management*. British Psychology Society and the Royal College of Psychiatrists.

Nenadić, I., Lamberth, S., & Reiss, N. (2017). Group schema therapy for personality disorders: A pilot study for implementation in acute psychiatric in-patient settings. *Psychiatry Research*, 253, 9–12.

Ogrodniczuk, J. S., Lynd, L. D., Joyce, A. S., Grubisic, M., Piper, W. E., & Steinberg, P. I. (2011). Predicting response to day treatment for personality disorder. *Canadian Journal of Psychiatry*, 56(2), 110–117.

Olesek, K. L., Outcalt, J., Dimaggio, G., Popolo, R., George, S., & Lysaker, P. H. (2016). Cluster B personality disorder traits as a predictor of therapeutic alliance over time in residential treatment for substance use disorders. *Journal of Nervous and Mental Disease*, 204(10), 736–740.

Østby, K. A., Czajkowski, N., Knudsen, G. P., Ystrom, E., Gjerde, L. C., Kendler, K. S., … Reichborn-Kjennerud, T. (2014). Personality disorders are important risk factors for disability pensioning. *Social Psychiatry and Psychiatric Epidemiology*, 49(12), 2003–2011.

Pabst, A., Schauer, M., Bernhardt, K., Ruf, M., Goder, R., Rosentraeger, R., … Seeck-Hirschner, M. (2011). Treatment of patients with borderline personality disorder and comorbid posttraumatic stress disorder using narrative exposure therapy: A feasibility study. *Psychotherapy and Psychosomatics*, 81(1), 61–63.

Paris, J. (2013). Stepped care: An alternative to routine extended treatment for patients with borderline personality disorder. *Psychiatric Services*, 64(10), 1035–1037.

Paris, J. (2015). Stepped care and rehabilitation for patients recovering from borderline personality disorder. *Journal of Clinical Psychology*, 71(8), 747–752.

Pasieczny, N., & Connor, J. (2011). The effectiveness of dialectical behaviour therapy in routine public mental health settings: An Australian controlled trial. *Behaviour Research and Therapy*, 49 (1), 4–10.

Perroud, N., Uher, R., Dieben, K., Nicastro, R., & Huguelet, P. (2010). Predictors of response and drop-out during intensive dialectical behavior therapy. *Journal of Personality Disorders*, 24(5), 634–650.

Petersen, B., Toft, J., Christensen, N. B., Foldager, L., Munk-Jorgensen, P., Lien, K., & Valbak, K. (2008). Outcome of a psychotherapeutic programme for patients with severe personality disorders. *Nordic Journal of Psychiatry*, 62(6), 450–456.

Prunetti, E., Bosio, V., Bateni, M., & Liotti, G. (2013). Three-week inpatient Cognitive Evolutionary Therapy (CET) for patients with personality disorders: Evidence of effectiveness in symptoms reduction and improved treatment adherence. *Psychology and Psychotherapy: Theory, Research and Practice*, 86(3), 262–279.

Quirk, S. E., Berk, M., Chanen, A. M., Koivumaa-Honkanen, H., Brennan-Olsen, S. L., Pasco, J. A., & Williams, L. J. (2016). Population prevalence of personality disorder and associations with physical health comorbidities and health care service utilization: A review. *Personality Disorders: Theory, Research, and Treatment*, 7(2), 136–146.

Renner, F., van Goor, M., Huibers, M., Arntz, A., Butz, B., & Bernstein, D. (2013). Short-term group schema cognitive-behavioral therapy for young adults with personality disorders and personality disorder features: Associations with changes in symptomatic distress, schemas, schema modes and coping styles. *Behaviour Research and Therapy*, 51(8), 487–492.

Rizvi, S. L., Hughes, C. D., Hittman, A. D., & Vieira Oliveira, P. (2017). Can trainees effectively deliver dialectical behavior therapy for individuals with borderline personality disorder? Outcomes from a training clinic. *Journal of Clinical Psychology*, 73 (12), 1599–1611.

Ryle, A., & Golynkina, K. (2000). Effectiveness of time-limited cognitive analytic therapy of borderline personality disorder: Factors associated with outcome. *British Journal of Medical Psychology*, 73(Pt 2), 197–210.

Sahlin, H., Bjureberg, J., Gratz, K. L., Tull, M. T., Hedman, E., Bjärehed, J., ... Hellner, C. (2017). Emotion regulation group therapy for deliberate self-harm: A multi-site evaluation in routine care using an uncontrolled open trial design. *BMJ Open*, 7 (10), 1–12. https://doi.org/10.1136/bmjopen-2017-016220

Samuels, J., Eaton, W. W., Bienvenu, O. J., Brown, C. H., Costa, P. T., & Nestadt, G. (2002). Prevalence and correlates of personality disorders in a community sample. *British Journal of Psychiatry*, 180, 536–542.

Schanche, E., Stiles, T. C., McCullough, L., Svartberg, M., & Nielsen, G. H. (2011). The relationship between activating affects, inhibitory affects, and self-compassion in patients with Cluster C personality disorders. *Psychotherapy*, 48(3), 293–303.

Schindler, A., Hiller, W., & Witthöft, M. (2013). What predicts outcome, response, and drop-out in CBT of depressive adults? A naturalistic study. *Behavioural and Cognitive Psychotherapy*, 41(3), 365–370.

Skewes, S. A., Samson, R. A., Simpson, S. G., & van Vreeswijk, M. (2015). Short-term group schema therapy for mixed personality disorders: A pilot study. *Frontiers in Psychology*, 6, 1–9.

Soler, J., Pascual, J. C., Tiana, T., Cebrià, A., Barrachina, J., Campins, M. J., ... Pérez, V. (2009). Dialectical behaviour therapy skills training compared to standard group therapy in borderline personality disorder: A 3-month randomised controlled clinical trial. *Behaviour Research and Therapy*, 47(5), 353–358.

Soler, J., Valdepérez, A., Feliu-Soler, A., Pascual, J. C., Portella, M. J., Martín-Blanco, A., ... Pérez, V. (2012). Effects of the dialectical behavioral therapy-mindfulness module on attention in patients with borderline personality disorder. *Behaviour Research and Therapy*, 50(2), 150–157.

Sollberger, D., Gremaud-Heitz, D., Riemenschneider, A., Agarwalla, P., Benecke, C., Schwald, O., ... Dammann, G. (2015). Change in identity diffusion and psychopathology in a specialized inpatient treatment for borderline personality disorder. *Clinical Psychology and Psychotherapy*, 22(6), 559–569.

Springer, T., Lohr, N. E., Buchtel, H. A., & Silk, K. R. (1996). A preliminary report of short-term cognitive-behavioral group therapy for inpatients with personality disorders. *Journal of Psychotherapy Practice and Research*, 5(1), 57–71.

Stanley, B., Brodsky, B., Nelson, J. D., & Dulit, R. (2007). Brief dialectical behavior therapy (DBT-B) for suicidal behavior and non-suicidal self injury. *Archives of Suicide Research*, 11(4), 337–341.

Svartberg, M., Stiles, T. C., & Seltzer, M. H. (2004). Randomized, controlled trial of the effectiveness of short-term dynamic psychotherapy and cognitive therapy for cluster C personality disorders. *American Journal of Psychiatry*, 161, 810–817.

Thylstrup, B., Schrøder, S., Fridell, M., & Hesse, M. (2017). Did you get any help? A post-hoc secondary analysis of a randomized controlled trial of psychoeducation for patients with antisocial personality disorder in outpatient substance abuse treatment programs. *BMC Psychiatry*, 17(1), 7. https://doi.org/10.1186/s12888-016-1165-2

Thylstrup, B., Schrøder, S., & Hesse, M. (2015). Psycho-education for substance use and antisocial personality disorder: A randomized trial. *BMC Psychiatry*, 15(1), 283. https://doi.org/10.1186/s12888–015-0661-0

Trull, T. J., Distel, M. A., & Carpenter, R. W. (2011). DSM-5 borderline personality disorder: At the border between a dimensional and a categorical view. *Current Psychiatry Reports*, 13(1), 43–49.

Ulvenes, P. G., Berggraf, L., Hoffart, A., Stiles, T. C., Svartberg, M., McCullough, L., & Wampold, B. E. (2012). Different processes for different therapies: Therapist actions, therapeutic bond, and outcome. *Psychotherapy*, 49(3), 291–302.

Vinnars, B., Barber, J. P., Norén, K., Gallop, R., & Weinryb, R. M. (2005). Manualized supportive-expressive psychotherapy versus therapy for patients with personality disorders: Bridging efficacy and effectiveness. *American Journal of Psychiatry*, 162 (17), 1933–1940.

Weinberg, I., Gunderson, J. G., Hennen, J., & Cutter Jr., C. J. (2006). Manual assisted cognitive treatment for deliberate self-harm in borderline personality disorder patients. *Journal of Personality Disorders*, 20(5), 482–492.

Weinberg, I., Ronningstam, E., Goldblatt, M. J., Schechter, M., & Maltsberger, J. T. (2011). Common factors in empirically supported treatments of borderline personality disorder. *Current Psychiatry Reports*, 13(1), 60–68.

Westerman, M. A., Foote, J. P., & Winston, A. (1995). Change in coordination across phases of psychotherapy and outcome: Two mechanisms for the role played by patients' contribution to the alliance. *Journal of Consulting and Clinical Psychology*, 63 (4), 672–675.

Winston, A., Laikin, M., Pollack, J., Samstag, L. W., McCullough, L., & Muran, J. C. (1994). Short-term psychotherapy of personality disorders. *American Journal of Psychiatry*, 151(2), 190–194.

Winston, A., Pollack, J., McCullough, L., Flegenheimer, W., Kestenbaum, R., & Trujillo, M. (1991). Brief psychotherapy of personality disorders. *Journal of Nervous and Mental Disease*, 179(4), 188–193.

Yen, S., Johnson, J., Costello, E., & Simpson, E. B. (2009). A 5-day dialectical behavior therapy partial hospital program for women with borderline personality disorder: Predictors of outcome from a 3-month follow-up study. *Journal of Psychiatric Practice*, 15(3), 173–182.

Zimmerman, M., Rothschild, L., & Chelminski, I. (2005). The prevalence of DSM-IV personality disorder in psychiatric outpatients. *American Journal of Psychiatry*, 162, 1911–1918.

20a What Knowledge Is Lacking on Brief Interventions for Personality Disorders and Why: Commentary on Brief Therapeutic Approaches for Personality Disorders

LARS MEHLUM

Although emotional and behavioral symptoms of personality disorder (PD) vary considerably across specific disorders, impairment and suffering caused by affective, cognitive, and interpersonal dysfunction in people with PD is, by definition, severe. Since those who are affected often have extensive use of health and social services and less than average productivity, the costs of these disorders to society are very large (Soeteman, Hakkaart-van Roijen, Verheul, & Busschbach, 2008). However, PDs, even the most challenging forms such as borderline personality disorder (BPD), are treatable conditions; over the last decades, several empirically validated psychotherapeutic approaches have emerged, giving rise to treatment optimism in clinicians and hope in patients and their families (see Rosenthal, Wyatt, & McMahon, Chapter 17 this volume; Fonagy, Bateman, Luyten, Allison, & Campbell, Chapter 18 this volume). Furthermore, economic evaluations have shown that these treatments have good potential for significant cost savings, since they are more effective and, contrary to what is often believed, usually less expensive than traditional treatments when all costs are taken into consideration (Haga, Aas, Groholt, Tormoen, & Mehlum, 2018; Meuldijk, McCarthy, Bourke, & Grenyer, 2017).

Still, most evidence-based psychotherapeutic approaches for PD are lengthy (one to three years) and intensive (several sessions per week), and they rely heavily on access to extensively trained and highly skilled therapists. These are resource requirements that can hardly be met by treatment providers in the average routine clinical setting, even in high-income countries. And, even in cases where economic and human resources are not an issue, lengthy and intensive treatments may still be infeasible for large proportions of people in need of treatment, who may not be able to match the high level of patient compliance and commitment required. These major obstacles to large-scale implementation of evidence-based treatments for PD constitute some of the background for the attempts to develop brief interventions or abbreviated versions of existing approaches that have emerged over recent years.

Dixon-Gordon and coworkers' comprehensive review of advances made in the field of brief treatments for PDs clearly demonstrates that there is not a lack of creative approaches to developing such treatments. However, despite this creativity, the relatively high amount of research in this field, and some promising results that have emerged, we still have many unresolved questions. In this commentary, we will discuss some of the questions and challenges that seem to remain for the task of developing and validating brief interventions for PD.

BRIEF INTERVENTIONS FOR PD: IS THIS A REALISTIC APPROACH?

Most of the brief treatments that have been proposed so far seem to be based on the assumption that long-term treatments could be shortened or simplified while still retaining approximately the same effectiveness. However, given the way we conceptualize PD as an inflexible, pervasive, and enduring pattern of experiencing or behaving that deviates markedly from common expectations causing significant distress and impairment, what are the odds we are going to succeed in developing interventions for such disorders that are both effective and brief? These are not episodic or time limited syndromes and they typically do not affect only some mental functions; they affect most areas of functioning. Many patients with PD, particularly those who have BPD, are perceived by their clinicians as "multi-problem" patients with an extremely large number of life problems and treatment needs. These are some of the reasons why patients with PDs are usually regarded as hard to treat and thus requiring high doses of treatment. However, *more* treatment or *longer lasting* or *more intensive* treatment does not necessarily mean *more effective* treatment.

The problem is that to develop brief treatments with approximately the same or even better effects as the longer or more intensive interventions, we would need more knowledge than we currently have on how treatments produce change and growth. Without knowing the mechanisms of therapeutic change and treatment component(s) responsible for this change, modifying treatments to make them briefer and less resource demanding – while still retaining the same treatment effects – is a risky business. Conversely, with a better understanding of which treatment elements are key to change, we could probably concentrate our efforts on delivering only these elements and thus save resources.

The most extensively researched treatment for BPD, at least in terms of number of randomized controlled trials published, is Dialectical Behavior Therapy (DBT), but it is only recently that high-quality dismantling or component studies have emerged. In their recent comparison of different DBT treatment modalities, Linehan and coworkers demonstrated that interventions that included skills training were more effective than DBT without this treatment modality (Linehan et al., 2015). For some patients, this could mean that important treatment needs (e.g., reductions in suicidal and self-injurious behaviors) could possibly be met through skills training alone or skills training combined with a brief initial number of individual therapy sessions. Support for this is found in a number of less sophisticated studies of skills training of varying length as a stand-alone intervention; these are highlighted in Dixon-Gordon et al.'s review.

This leads us to the question of not only what are the most effective, and thus indispensable, treatment components, but what treatment components work best for whom. Treatment trials have, to date, largely been able to demonstrate overall effectiveness of the interventions in relatively heterogeneous clinical samples. Studies with samples large enough to allow for analysis of treatment moderators will likely give us more precise information on who is benefiting the most from the treatments. For some patients, certain outcomes of certain aspects of the treatment will probably be even better than for the average patient group, whereas for others it will probably be weaker, absent, or even negative. There is a great need to tailor and optimize treatments to individual patients, but to do so we need more knowledge.

The need to avoid harming patients through our interventions is another important concern. Since psychotherapeutic interventions are powerful tools, there is a real danger that some patients will have side-effects or adverse outcomes. As pointed out by Fonagy and Bateman (2006), patients with BPD are particularly vulnerable to side-effects of treatments that activate their attachment system. Most treatments regard such activation necessary for a therapeutic relationship to evolve and for the patient to improve her or his psychological functioning in interpersonal relationships. But, in the context of brief treatments for BPD – where attachment would typically soon be followed by separation – the treatment should, as a consequence, include strategies to protect patients against the potential dangers of attachment system overactivation.

BRIEF INTERVENTIONS: SHOULD THEY HAVE A DIFFERENT FOCUS?

Since we may lack much of the knowledge needed to realistically expect brief treatment approaches to PD to be comparable to longer term treatments in their effectiveness, a relevant question is whether the focus for brief treatments should be entirely or partly different from the original or longer term treatments. Brief treatments could focus on stabilizing the patient to make other and/or subsequent treatments feasible. Brief treatments could, for example, include strategies to improve patients' distress tolerance and interpersonal functioning just enough to allow them to tolerate receiving and benefiting from other help. These interventions could focus on building or maintaining some supportive social relationships or staying employed. People with PD often have treatment interfering behaviors that reduce their capacity for staying in treatment or responding to the treatment. Brief interventions could have a limited focus on reducing such behaviors. Or, rather than targeting the PD itself, brief interventions could focus on symptoms and problems often experienced by people with PD, such as depressive symptoms, substance abuse, anxiety, or other co-occurring conditions. Effectively delivering treatments for these symptoms and problems to people with PD may necessitate development of strategies that are different from those required for treatment of people without PD. Brief interventions for PD could build on positive experiences from e-mental health tools developed for other psychiatric disorders, such as depression, through the use of therapist guided internet-based self-help interventions. Brief interventions could also focus on teaching patients coping skills and helping them practice these skills through the use of interactive web-based computer programs.

An important additional focus for brief interventions for "hard to treat" patients with PD is to address the negative transactions that often evolve between clinicians and patients and, thus, the stigma still experienced by many people with PD when seeking treatment. Clinicians' notions of what is "hard to treat" in these patients could, in reality, be less strongly associated with the PD itself and more strongly associated with certain learned illness behaviors or adaptations patients have made to their environments, secondary effects of the disorder, or even iatrogenic effects of past treatments. Brief interventions aimed at avoiding these perils would have a potential of substantially improving the treatment gains for many patients with PD across a wide range of treatment settings.

FUTURE RESEARCH DIRECTIONS

Dixon-Gordon et al.'s review leaves a clear impression that, despite the multitude of approaches to developing brief interventions for PD, too many studies have lacked the adequate research design, methodological rigor, and statistical power to provide any firm conclusions about treatment effects. Too often, "brief treatment" seems to have been paired with "brief study," creating more confusion than clarity. Furthermore, there is currently no agreement as to what should be the criteria for determining treatment response or remission in PD. A lack of consensus regarding core outcome measures makes systematic reviews and meta-analyses more difficult. There is also a lack of conceptual clarity; most studies published so far have been unclear about what brief interventions really mean. Is it low-dose we are talking about, or treatment of brief duration?

Obviously, there is a need for carefully designed studies of brief interventions that are clearly defined as to the level of the disorder they aim to treat (i.e., the PD itself or its associated symptoms and/or problems), the aspect of the disorder they will focus on, the mechanism(s) of change they will utilize, the specific patient group the treatment will target, and the treatment response criteria with which the outcome will be evaluated. Since the main rationale for developing and evaluating such brief interventions for PD is to save resources and make treatments accessible to more people, an aspect of economic and implementation evaluation should probably always be included in future empirical studies. As virtually no brief intervention for PD has been convincingly replicated so far, future studies should preferably be conducted in a collaborative way to facilitate replications. This calls for stronger national and international collaborations between clinical researchers. Recently, PD researchers in Europe have formed an alliance to address the need for speeding up research on and dissemination of PD-specific treatments on this continent (Mehlum et al., 2018). This alliance organizes training seminars for young PD clinical researchers to promote high-quality research in more European countries, and offers workshop conferences for clinicians to speed up the dissemination of evidence-based treatments in underserved regions. Finally, the alliance organizes research congresses and offers members and affiliates opportunities to develop their research collaborations on specific topics through an increasing number of thematic sections. Hopefully, such alliances will lead to a more systematic building of the evidence base needed to deliver evidence-based and affordable treatments in a sustainable way to the people who need them.

REFERENCES

Fonagy, P., & Bateman, A. (2006). Progress in the treatment of borderline personality disorder. *British Journal of Psychiatry*, *188*, 1–3.

Haga, E., Aas, E., Groholt, B., Tormoen, A. J., & Mehlum, L. (2018). Cost-effectiveness of dialectical behaviour therapy vs. enhanced usual care in the treatment of adolescents with self-harm. *Child and Adolescent Psychiatry and Mental Health*, *12*, 22. doi:10.1186/s13034-018-0227-2

Linehan, M. M., Korslund, K. E., Harned, M. S., Gallop, R. J., Lungu, A., Neacsiu, A. D., ... Murray-Gregory, A. M. (2015). Dialectical behavior therapy for high suicide risk in individuals with borderline personality disorder: A randomized clinical trial and component analysis. *JAMA Psychiatry*, *72*(5), 475–482.

Mehlum, L., Bateman, A., Dalewijk, H. J., Doering, S., Kaera, A., Moran, P. A., ... Bohus, M. (2018). Building a strong European alliance for personality disorder research and intervention. *Borderline Personality Disorder and Emotion Dysregulation*, *5*, 7. doi:10.1186/s40479-018-0082-z

Meuldijk, D., McCarthy, A., Bourke, M. E., & Grenyer, B. F. (2017). The value of psychological treatment for borderline personality disorder: Systematic review and cost offset analysis of economic evaluations. *PLoS One*, *12*(3), e0171592. doi:10.1371/journal.pone.0171592

Soeteman, D. I., Hakkaart-van Roijen, L., Verheul, R., & Busschbach, J. J. (2008). The economic burden of personality disorders in mental health care. *Journal of Clinical Psychiatry*, *69*(2), 259–265.

20b Short- and Long-Term Personality Disorder Treatment Studies Should Inform One Another: Commentary on Brief Therapeutic Approaches for Personality Disorders

BRANDON T. UNRUH

Given my day job as a personality disorder (PD) specialist delivering the major long-term borderline PD treatments in adapted forms in a short-term residential PD treatment program, Dixon-Gordon, Conkey, and Woods' exhaustive review (this volume) of studies on PD treatments with a duration of less than one year poses important questions about how best to shape and reshape the aims, structure, and techniques of PD treatments. This commentary aims to show that the growing work on short-term interventions summarized here pushes the state of PD treatment forward in two directions that are increasingly important given the limitations of long-term treatments: enhancing treatment accessibility and improving our understanding of how PDs change.

SHORT-TERM PD TREATMENT STUDIES WILL IMPROVE TREATMENT ACCESSIBILITY

Dixon-Gordon and colleagues contextualize their review of short-term PD treatment studies by summarizing how the implementation of empirically validated long-term PD treatments has been limited by their duration and cost, as well as the magnitude of time required by both clinicians (to establish and maintain adherence) and patients (to attend multiple treatment sessions per week). The authors are right to remind us that the public health demand is not being met by our current approach to disseminating PD treatments.

The authors suggest several ways in which the best of the short-term PD treatment studies can pave the way for improvements in accessibility. These strategies include: emphasizing more cost-effective group-based interventions, empowering an expanded workforce inclusive of clinicians with less specialized or advanced training, and honing in on the areas of emotion regulation and interpersonal functioning that appear to be particularly relevant targets for PDs. The authors suggest that future research directions should include testing incrementally smaller durations or "doses" of treatments and identifying moderators predictive of which patients will do well with shorter treatment durations and which will require longer or more specialized treatments.

The conclusions and suggestions made by Dixon-Gordon and colleagues match up well with evolving principles of generalist PD treatment as outlined in Good Psychiatric Management (GPM; Gunderson & Links, 2014) and emerging GPM-oriented stepped-care models (Choi-Kain, Albert, & Gunderson, 2016). The GPM model – itself an eclectic blend of psychodynamic, behavioral, and supportive case management techniques with empirical understandings of the origins and features of borderline PD – offers a clear conceptual framework for the authors' proposal of how short-term PD interventions may be codified and sequenced into an algorithm guiding the selection of "first-line" PD treatments.

For example, in GPM, the length and intensity of treatment is titrated according to the patient's pace of functional progress. Adjunctive treatments may be added, or primary treatment sessions may become more frequent, when a specific goal is being productively addressed. When the patient does not progress, GPM recommends a consultation to evaluate barriers to progress, as well as a possible referral to one of the longer-term specialist treatments, such as Dialectical Behavior Therapy (DBT), Mentalization-Based Treatment (MBT), or Transference-Focused Psychotherapy (TFP), if indicated. These longer-term specialist PD treatments take the treatment out of the hands of generalist clinicians, as they require implementing a more elaborated theoretical orientation, structural organization, and set of techniques over an extended period of time. Learning and delivering these treatments adherently requires a level of investment in training, supervision, and infrastructure that is unrealistic for most clinicians treating borderline PD and, thus, is best reserved for aspiring borderline PD specialists (Unruh & Gunderson, 2016).

In contrast, GPM employs simpler, more time-limited interventions that are increased or decreased across various intensities and levels of care based on the patient's symptoms, functioning, level of engagement and progress, and comorbidities. However, GPM currently lacks precise, empirically driven rationales for when to recommend specific adjunctive interventions or shifts within the focus of the treatment over time. For example, when should a patient who started weekly case management sessions three months ago be referred to an adjunctive DBT skills group, mentalization group, or psychodynamic interpersonal group? Should this patient remain in the adjunctive group for three, six, or nine months (or longer) if progress is not being made before they are stepped up to a more intense or longer-term treatment modality? GPM leaves these decisions up to clinician judgment and accumulated anecdotal wisdom, emphasizing the pragmatism of "doing what works" and the flexibility to run with the strengths of the clinician and opportunities within the clinical system at hand.

Of the major longer-term treatments, GPM is thus the most accessible for most clinicians, clinical systems, and patients. This is important because longitudinal studies suggest that most PD patients receive a great deal of treatment over many years that is not empirically validated (Zanarini, Frankenburg, Reich, Conkey, & Fitzmaurice, 2015) or provided by PD specialists.

For these reasons, further studies on longer-term specialized treatments are not likely to yield improved guidelines for the kinds of interventions most PD patients will receive. "Dismantling" studies, wherein various elements of long-term treatments are isolated and evaluated in comparison with one another, are helpful but rare. And, when longer-term treatments *are* compared head-to-head, the comparison is between two elaborate systems of theory and technique, rather than individual interventions accessible to generalist clinicians and their patients.

In contrast, Dixon-Gordon and colleagues' review highlights that shorter-term treatment studies are moving forward by testing specific interventions of limited duration and intensity, which could be readily appropriated by generalists as part of GPM's stepped-care model. Briefer permutations of the long-term specialized treatments are being repurposed, combined, and sequenced, and then tested in novel shorter-term configurations: a DBT skills training group is compared with DBT skills group plus individual DBT; GPM is compared with GPM plus a DBT mindfulness group; a mentalizing group is offered following a DBT skills group; and various "doses" of DBT formats are tried at differing session frequencies and overall treatment durations. These shorter-term treatment studies may answer questions long posed and left unanswered by long-term treatment studies, including which particular DBT elements are most effective, whether elements of DBT and MBT can be effectively combined, and which group interventions are best across modalities.

Short-term treatment studies may thus be an ideal experimental "cauldron" in which to isolate, mix, compare, and contrast specific, relatively simple, time-limited interventions that can be sequenced into empirical algorithms within a "first-line" generalist framework such as GPM.

SHORT-TERM PD TREATMENT STUDIES WILL HELP US BETTER UNDERSTAND EARLY CHANGE PROCESSES

Dixon-Gordon and colleagues highlight certain short-term PD treatments as particularly effective, noting that some have effect sizes similar to those achieved by some longer-term PD treatments. Notably, the most effective short-term treatments bear the same kinds of ties as longer-term treatments to particular theoretical orientations, technical approaches, and models of change. For example, emotion regulation group therapy was developed to enhance emotion regulation "based on empirical research suggesting self-injury primarily functions to regulate intense distress"; short-term dynamic psychotherapy bears strong marks of psychoanalytic theory and technique; manual-assisted cognitive therapy relies heavily on cognitive interventions; and six-month DBT shares clear-cut theoretical and technical features with its parent treatment. All major long-term specialist treatments for BPD are similarly linked with differing theories of how BPD originates and is perpetuated, and with different treatment aims and purported mechanisms of change (Gunderson, Fruzzetti, Unruh, & Choi-Kain, 2018).

However, if these short-term interventions are used to flesh out a "first-line" generalist treatment program that would precede referral to long-term specialist treatments, can we really expect generalist clinicians to learn and effectively implement them? How many different packages of theory, structure, and technique can be learned and delivered by the average clinician not specializing in PDs? Indeed, Dixon-Gordon and colleagues rightly argue that future directions in short-term PD treatment research should attempt to identify effective transtheoretical clinical strategies that can "cut across theoretical orientations."

Here is where the process of fine-tuning short-term PD treatments may benefit from conclusions drawn from research on longer-term approaches. First, we know that most patients benefit similarly from generalist and specialist treatments. Head-to-head comparisons of specialized PD treatments with manualized generalist treatments (such as DBT versus good psychiatric management or MBT versus structured clinical management) show little substantive difference in outcome for most patients (Cristea et al., 2017). This implies that the more specific elements of each treatment are less important than shared nonspecific structural or process elements (Fonagy, Luyten, & Bateman, 2017).

What do we know about common active ingredients in long-term PD treatments? Current hypotheses about shared change processes invoke commonality at two levels. Some studies highlight *systemic and structural factors*, such as basic elements of the treatment frame or therapist stance. Weinberg, Ronningstam, Goldblatt, Schechter, and Maltsberger (2010) concluded that major evidence-based treatments for PDs share a clear treatment framework, high attention to affect, a focus on the treatment relationship, an active therapist, and exploratory and change-oriented interventions. Further, since their analysis, the evolution of most major PD treatments has resulted in increasing overlap in their structural factors. Specifically, most major PD treatments now explicitly encourage support for the therapist by way of team consultation or peer supervision; crisis planning and specific protocols for addressing suicidal, self-harming, and treatment-interfering behavior; delivery of psychoeducation; a designated pre-treatment or contracting phase; and attention to functioning outside of therapy. Although the mechanisms by which these structural elements address borderline PD psychopathology are unclear, one possibility is that they work through *containment* of typical challenging emotional experiences arising in both patients and clinicians working together in the face of borderline PD-related interpersonal difficulties.

Shared change processes are also posited to occur at the level of *mental state factors*, such as in emotion regulation or reflective functioning. One example is the process of "epistemic trust" that has become integrated into MBT as its conceptualization of borderline PD has broadened to incorporate research on social cognition and learning theory. This model posits that successful borderline PD treatment within any modality requires patients to come to believe in the trustworthiness of clinicians and in the personal relevance of what is being communicated within the treatment. Arriving at this position of epistemic trust is considered a necessary precondition for any new learning about the social world to take hold and then generalize beyond the treatment context. According to this model, epistemic trust is ideally established through clinicians' attention to mentalizing processes within psychotherapy no matter what particular technique or theoretical school is followed (Fonagy, Luyten, & Allison, 2015).

This model posits an interpersonal and intra-psychic process of change common to all long-term borderline PD treatments, despite divergent elements within each treatment that appear to have greater specificity. It may be that the elements most specific to each treatment send ostensive cues that effectively engage certain individuals and foment disconnection for others. For example, the didactic classroom elements of DBT skills group and the mnemonics used for skills acquisition may appeal to the desire of some patients for tangible skills and solutions from treatment, whereas other patients may experience DBT as too structured or directive and feel more comfortable with MBT's more exploratory group culture. Other patients may be drawn to TFP's frank portrayals of less experience-near elements of interpersonal process (such as hypothesized split-off aggression). It is possible to see how different patients might arrive through divergent treatment modalities at a similar position of trust in, regard for, and commitment to a treatment that has become a personally relevant and trustworthy source of knowledge about self and others. Could this model derived from long-term treatment studies be applied to understanding mechanisms of short-term treatments?

Dixon-Gordon and colleagues appropriately couch their conclusions about short-term treatments as a whole tentatively, pointing out that only a few are proven effective according to accepted standards of empirical validation. However, I believe the comprehensiveness of their review positions them to venture even bolder hypotheses that may guide future research. Among the short-term treatments they have identified as most effective, what elements are actually shared at the structural and organizational level? More speculatively, what common processes of change might exist at the level of mental states? Do the treatments that work do so through containment – i.e., by providing a sense of safety and structure that prevents treatment-interfering behavior? Do they more effectively establish epistemic trust by better capturing the attention and trust of the individuals they intend to treat? Are they better at helping patients understand the mental states underlying their own behavior and that of others? Many more hypotheses could be proposed and considered. I am interested in hearing Dixon-Gordon and colleagues' further speculation about what transtheoretical change processes could underlie the approaches that appear to work most effectively in the short term, despite their varying theoretical underpinnings and techniques.

For PD treatments that work in any duration and at any level of care, improving their accessibility to patients and our understanding of how they work will depend on continued efforts to investigate both longer-term and short-term treatments. Clinicians and researchers investigating these treatments on either side of the duration divide must remain united in dialogue by the shared quest to identify elements that tie all treatments that work together. Whereas longer-term treatment studies lend themselves to the analysis of larger-scale structural and technical elements leading to fuller remission of symptoms, it may be that changes observed within shorter-term treatment studies more directly enhance our understanding of how most patients with PDs can begin to recover.

REFERENCES

Choi-Kain, L. W., Albert, E. B., & Gunderson, J. G. (2016). Evidence-based treatments for borderline personality disorder: Implementation, integration, and stepped care. *Harvard Review of Psychiatry*, 24(5), 342–356.

Cristea, I. A., Gentili, C., Cotet, C. D., Palomba, D., Barbui, C., & Cuijpers, P. (2017). Efficacy of psychotherapies for borderline personality disorder: A systematic review and meta-analysis. *JAMA Psychiatry*, 74(4), 319–328.

Fonagy, P., Luyten, P., & Allison, E. (2015). Epistemic petrification and the restoration of epistemic trust: A new conceptualization of borderline personality disorder and its psychosocial treatment. *Journal of Personality Disorders*, 29(5), 575–609.

Fonagy, P., Luyten, P., & Bateman, A. (2017). Treating borderline personality disorder with psychotherapy: Where do we go from here? *JAMA Psychiatry*, 74(4), 316–317.

Gunderson, J. G., Fruzzetti, A., Unruh, B., & Choi-Kain L. (2018). Competing theories of borderline personality disorder. *Journal of Personality Disorders*, *32*(2), 148–167.

Gunderson, J. G., & Links, P. (2014). *Handbook of Good Psychiatric Management for Borderline Personality Disorder*. Arlington, VA: American Psychiatric Publishing.

Unruh, B. T., & Gunderson, J. G. (2016). "Good enough" psychiatric residency training in borderline personality disorder: Challenges, choice points, and a model generalist curriculum. *Harvard Review of Psychiatry*, *24*(5), 367–377.

Weinberg, I., Ronningstam, E., Goldblatt, M. J., Schechter, M., & Maltsberger, J. T. (2010). Common factors in empirically supported treatments of borderline personality disorder. *Current Psychiatry Reports*, *13*(1), 60–68.

Zanarini, M. C., Frankenburg, F. R., Reich, D. B., Conkey, L. C., & Fitzmaurice, G. M. (2015). Treatment rates for patients with borderline personality disorder and other personality disorders: A 16-year study. *Psychiatric Services*, *66*(1), 15–20.

20c   Next Steps: Author Rejoinder to Commentaries on Brief Therapeutic Approaches for Personality Disorders

KATHERINE L. DIXON-GORDON, LINDSEY C. CONKEY, AND SHERRY E. WOODS

We welcomed the opportunity to read our colleagues' (Drs. Mehlum and Unruh) perspectives regarding our review of brief therapeutic approaches for personality disorders (PDs). These experts identified notable implications of the growing evidence base, and remaining questions for both research and treatment.

IDENTIFYING MECHANISMS OF CHANGE

Both Drs. Mehlum and Unruh point to the importance of understanding the factors that contribute to change in briefer treatments for PDs. As noted by Dr. Unruh, these briefer treatments share conceptualizations of mechanisms with their parent treatments. Turning to the extant data, we can identify some of what Dr. Unruh refers to as the *structural/systematic* aspects of the treatment, or the *ingredients* that produce change. Of note, the structure of the effective treatments ranged from individual and group outpatient psychotherapy to inpatient programs.

Among these common ingredients is a focus on explicit education to enhance emotion regulation. This focus is evident across a number of treatments, ranging from the enhanced thinking skills to teach impulse control for antisocial PD (Doyle et al., 2013) to emotion regulation skills training in dialectical behavior therapy for borderline PD (e.g., Rizvi, Hughes, Hittman, & Vieira Oliveira, 2017). Indeed, standalone emotion regulation-focused groups have consistently demonstrated efficacy for borderline PD (Dixon-Gordon, Chapman, & Turner, 2015; Gratz & Gunderson, 2006). Another common element seen across theoretical approaches is a focus on interpersonal functioning, ranging from fostering balanced views of the self in relation to others (Munroe-Blum & Marziali, 1995), to teaching interpersonal skills for borderline PD (Rizvi et al., 2017), to facilitating interpersonal exposure for avoidant PD (Alden, 1989). Another shared aspect of these treatments that may separate them from treatment as usual is their insistence that treatment can work. This alone may constitute a critical mechanism of change, given that treatment credibility and expectancies have been shown to be predictors of treatment outcomes (Keuroghlian, Frankenburg, & Zanarini, 2013), and may be especially important for the frequently-stigmatized population of PD patients.

Although many of these treatment ingredients are theorized to target processes within the patient (referred to by Dr. Unruh as *mental state factors*), this has not been directly tested in many cases. Future studies would benefit from multimodal assessments of these putative within-patient change processes.

UNDERSTANDING MODERATORS OF TREATMENT OUTCOME

It is conceivable that distinct processes account for change across distinct outcomes. Thus, as noted by Dr. Mehlum, we also must consider the question of which treatments are best for *whom*. Given that patients with PDs often present with multiple problems, there are also the questions of which treatment elements are best for *which outcomes* and *when*. Different outcomes may be achievable at different timeframes, with some treatment goals lending themselves to briefer treatments. For instance, helping clients reduce out-of-control behaviors may be a nearer-term goal than improving their sense of self-worth. Indeed, one key short-term outcome to consider in this regard is the reduction of crisis behaviors that lead to hospitalization, since hospitalizations predict poor treatment response in longer-term treatments (Coyle, Shaver, & Linehan, 2018). It is also worth considering that short-term treatments may require new targets, such as preparing for the imminent conclusion of therapy, as noted by Dr. Mehlum. We recommend that future studies include repeated measures to depict the dose–response relationship across outcomes. Likewise, it is critical that we understand the long-term effects of short-term treatments.

MOVING FORWARD

There is a pressing need to increase access to PD treatments that work. A stepped-care model akin to emerging good psychiatric management-oriented models (Choi-Kain, Albert, & Gunderson, 2016) may provide such a framework; however, we still require data to make evidence-based treatment recommendations for who needs further treatment and when. A clearer understanding of the mechanisms and moderators of treatment response over time would begin to address this gap.

REFERENCES

Alden, L. (1989). Short-term structured treatment for avoidant personality disorder. *Journal of Consulting and Clinical Psychology, 57*(6), 756–764.

Choi-Kain, L. W., Albert, E. B., & Gunderson, J. G. (2016). Evidence-based treatments for borderline personality disorder: Implementation, integration, and stepped care. *Harvard Review of Psychiatry, 24*(5), 342–356.

Coyle, T. N., Shaver, J. A., & Linehan, M. M. (2018). On the potential for iatrogenic effects of psychiatric crisis services: The example of dialectical behavior therapy for adult women with borderline personality disorder. *Journal of Consulting and Clinical Psychology, 86*(2), 116–124.

Dixon-Gordon, K. L., Chapman, A. L., & Turner, B. J. (2015). A preliminary pilot study comparing dialectical behavior therapy emotion regulation skills with interpersonal effectiveness skills and a control group treatment. *Journal of Experimental Psychopathology, 6*(4), 369–388.

Doyle, M., Khanna, T., Lennox, C., Shaw, J., Hayes, A., Taylor, J., . . . Dolan, M. (2013). The effectiveness of an enhanced thinking skills programme in offenders with antisocial personality traits. *Journal of Forensic Psychiatry and Psychology, 24*(1), 1–15.

Gratz, K. L., & Gunderson, J. G. (2006). Preliminary data on an acceptance-based emotion regulation group intervention for deliberate self-harm among women with borderline personality disorder. *Behavior Therapy, 37*(1), 25–35.

Keuroghlian, A. S., Frankenburg, F. R., & Zanarini, M. C. (2013). The relationship of chronic medical illnesses, poor health-related lifestyle choices, and health care utilization to recovery status in borderline patients over a decade of prospective follow-up. *Journal of Psychiatric Research, 47*(10), 1499–1506.

Munroe-Blum, H., & Marziali, E. (1995). A controlled trial of short-term group treatment for borderline personality disorder. *Journal of Personality Disorders, 9*(3), 190–198.

Rizvi, S. L., Hughes, C. D., Hittman, A. D., & Vieira Oliveira, P. (2017). Can trainees effectively deliver dialectical behavior therapy for individuals with borderline personality disorder? Outcomes from a training clinic. *Journal of Clinical Psychology, 73*(12), 1599–1611.

21 Recent Developments in the Pharmacologic Management of Personality Disorders

PAUL S. LINKS, PHILIPPE BOURSIQUOT, AND MADISON LINKS

INTRODUCTION

Case Example

Ms. A., a 28-year-old separated woman with panic disorder and borderline personality disorder, had been exposed over her years of treatment to multiple medications including sertraline, aripiprazole, valproic acid, gabapentin, paroxetine, venlafaxine, risperidone, fluoxetine, citalopram, topiramate, and desvenlafaxine. In spite of her multiple exposures and general experience that medications had not been useful, the patient still attended the consult to request a new medication that might be helpful for her symptoms.

This case example illustrates that patients with borderline personality disorder will request and are often prescribed multiple medications over the course of their disorder. However, the use of medication in the management of borderline personality disorder and other personality disorders is highly controversial. The United Kingdom National Institute for Healthcare and Excellence (NICE, 2015) states that medications are "not to be used" in the management of borderline personality disorder; although they could be utilized to treat comorbid psychiatric disorders. The NICE treatment guidelines are known to be stringent and directly contrast with the American Psychiatric Association guidelines that recommend a symptom targeted approach to the pharmacologic management of patients with borderline personality disorder (APA, 2001). The Australian guidelines from 2012 do not recommend medications as primary interventions but suggest time-limited use for specific symptoms and as adjuncts to psychological therapies (National Health and Medical Research Council, 2012). In spite of the controversy and the need for further research, medication can play a role in the management of symptoms and in improving the functioning of patients with borderline personality disorder and other personality disorders.

Regardless of clinical guidelines, prescribing combinations and high doses of medication are endemic in clinical practice. Zanarini and colleagues (Zanarini, Frankenberg, Hennen, & Silk, 2004) empirically demonstrated that poly-pharmacy was very common and found that over six years of follow-up, 40 percent of patients with borderline personality disorder had been taking three or more concurrent psychotropic medications, 20 percent had been taking four or more, and 10 percent had been taking five or more medications. As a preliminary test of the efficacy and safety of poly-pharmacy, Zanarini and colleagues (Zanarini, Frankenberg, & Parachini, 2004) compared fluoxetine, olanzapine, and the combination of the two medications in 45 women with borderline personality disorder without current major depressive disorder. The study demonstrated that olanzapine was more effective than either fluoxetine alone or their combination for impulsive aggressiveness and dysphoria, and suggested that the support for poly-pharmacy "was limited." Based on a survey of the use of psychotropic medication in patients cared for in the United Kingdom mental health services, Paton and colleagues (Paton, Crawford, Bhatti, Patel, & Barnes, 2015) reported that 82 percent of patients with personality disorders alone were prescribed at least one psychotropic medication, as were 94 percent of patients with personality disorders and at least one comorbid psychiatric diagnosis. The Emotionally Unstable Personality Disorder (EUPD), the ICD-10 equivalent of borderline personality disorder, was the most common personality disorder diagnosis and in spite of the NICE guidelines, 87 percent of patients with EUPD alone were prescribed at least one psychotropic medication and two-thirds were receiving at least two different classes of psychotropic medication. Crawford et al. (2011) in a separate survey had found evidence that patients cared for by a specialist personality disorder service were less likely to be prescribed psychotropic medication than patients seen within a general adult psychiatric service. However, even in psychosocial randomized controlled clinical trials involving patients with borderline personality disorder that tried to set up ideal conditions, patients were still exposed to two different medications on average (McMain et al., 2009) over the course of treatment.

In this chapter, recent research evidence is reviewed regarding the use of medication for patients with personality disorders. The bulk of the research has been done with patients with borderline personality disorder and this research will be discussed by each drug type. For other personality disorders, less empirical research exists but the evidence again is reviewed by drug type. The review will also make mention of some novel approaches that require further research. These novel approaches highlight possible neuropathological mechanisms underlying personality disorders and may open up new avenues for managing these patients. We will conclude by discussing the limitations of the current research and summarize the principles of our pharmacologic approach.

REVIEW METHODOLOGY

A literature search was conducted using the McMaster University Health Sciences Library online catalogue search tool. Parameters of the literature search involved sources limited to peer-reviewed journal articles published between January 1, 2008 and November 19, 2017. In addition, the Health Sciences Library website has a health related article database that was used to find sources. The databases used to search for articles included: OVID, Pubmed, Clinical Key, Cochrane Library, DynaMed Plus, and PsychINFO. The keywords and phrases used for the literature search included the following: personality disorders, borderline personality disorder, pharmacology, pharmacotherapy, drugs, medications, anti-depressants, anti-convulsants, anti-psychotics, anxiolytics, and emotionally unstable personality disorder. The reference lists of sources found via the initial search were scanned to find the titles of additional articles. Fifty-two references were identified by our search methods and the authors in preparing this chapter reviewed all of these articles. Updating the search as of December 31, 2017, six additional articles were identified and reviewed.

BORDERLINE PERSONALITY DISORDER

Antipsychotic Medications

Based on the major meta-analytic studies and recent reviews done since 2009 (Hancock-Johnson, Griffiths, & Picchioni, 2017; Ingenhoven, Lafay, Rinne, Passchier, & Duivenvoorden, 2010; Lieb, Völlm, Rücker, Timmer, & Stoffers, 2010; Mercer, Douglass, & Links, 2009; Nose, Cipriani, Biancosino, Grassi, & Barbui, 2006; Stoffers & Lieb, 2015), antipsychotic medications are superior to placebo in managing certain symptoms in patients with borderline personality disorder. Antipsychotic medications seem useful in lessening anger, impulsivity, aggression, and the cognitive perceptual disturbances found in patients with borderline personality disorder. Many of the second and third generation antipsychotics have been used with patients with

borderline personality disorder; however, all of the studies utilized small samples and were of short duration. The one exception is the study by Zanarini and colleagues (Zanarini et al., 2011) that tested olanzapine versus placebo in a large randomized controlled trial involving 451 outpatients. In this study, 5–10 mg of olanzapine was superior to placebo in lessening borderline personality symptoms. During an open label extension study, the placebo participants improved in a fashion similar to the patients previously treated with olanzapine once active drug was started (Zanarini et al., 2012). Although benefits were evident, the adverse effects of olanzapine were found to be considerable, including somnolence, fatigue, and increased appetite and weight.

Another major study compared quetiapine ER versus placebo in an eight-week randomized controlled trial involving 95 participants. This research compared quetiapine ER 300 mg per day to quetiapine ER 150 mg per day to placebo. Black et al. (2014) found a large effect size for the low-dose quetiapine ER versus placebo on borderline symptoms ($d = -0.79$). The moderate dose versus placebo comparison was not significant, and there were no significant differences between the quetiapine groups. On secondary outcomes including verbal and physical aggression, both quetiapine doses were superior to placebo. However, side effects were common particularly with the moderate dose quetiapine ER. The side effects such as sedation predicted participants' discontinuation of the study. This study had fairly stringent exclusion criteria for comorbid disorders so further studies are clearly indicated to generalize the findings to the majority of patients with borderline personality disorder who present with multiple comorbid disorders.

Rohde and colleagues (Rohde, Polcwiartek, Correll, & Nielsen, 2017) studied the effects of exposure to clozapine on naturalistic outcomes in patients with borderline personality disorder using Danish national registries and a two-year mirror-image model. Within the sample of 25,916 patients with borderline personality disorder, 4.27 percent (1107) received at least one clozapine prescription. The mean dose of clozapine was 286 mg (95% CI [244,327]) and the mean follow-up was 529.67 days. After adjusting for secular trends and removing patients with comorbid schizophrenia, schizoaffective, or bipolar disorder, treatment with clozapine was associated with a significant decrease in admissions and significant reductions in psychiatric bed-days in patients with "specific" borderline personality disorder. There was no evidence that exposure was associated with an increase in serious adverse side effects such as agranulocytosis, cardiomyopathy, myocarditis, and neuroleptic malignant syndrome. Among all patients with borderline personality disorder, clozapine treatment was related to a significant reduction in the number of patients performing self-harm or overdosing. These observational data are consistent with earlier case series that suggested benefits of clozapine treatment on psychotic symptoms, self-harm behaviors, suicidal ideation, impulsivity, use of restraints, and overall functioning in patients with borderline personality disorder (Beri & Boydell, 2014).

In summary, antipsychotic medications appear to have some usefulness for symptoms of borderline personality disorder such as anger, impulsive aggression, and the cognitive perceptual features. The Cochrane review raised one potential concern suggesting that olanzapine had a clear tendency to cause more suicidal ideation and self-harm in comparative trials. However, this finding does not appear to be a consistent observation but a caution worth noting that needs further study. Overall, antipsychotic medication at low doses can have some value but the risks versus the benefits have to be carefully weighed. Tolerability continues to be a major issue in using antipsychotic medications among patients with borderline personality disorder.

Mood Stabilizers

Mood stabilizers have shown particular promise in treating patients with borderline personality disorder. These medications have been found to have benefits for anger, impulsivity, and perhaps also for affective instability symptoms of borderline personality disorder (Hancock-Johnson et al., 2017; Ingenhoven et al., 2010; Lieb et al., 2010; Mercer et al., 2009; Nose et al., 2006; Stoffers & Lieb, 2015) Various mood stabilizers have been utilized including valproic acid, lamotrigine, and topiramate. Lamotrigine seems to be effective for reducing anger, impulsivity, and perhaps also depression. Reich and colleagues (Reich, Zanarini, & Bieri, 2009), for example, carried out a 12-week randomized controlled trial of flexible dose lamotrigine versus placebo in patients with borderline personality disorder. These patients were chosen for having evidence of severe affective instability and the study's primary outcomes were related to measures of affective instability. The lamotrigine group ($n = 15$) versus the placebo group ($n = 13$) demonstrated significant reductions in affective instability and impulsivity. However, two caveats to note related to this research were that the mean dose of lamotrigine was only 106.7 mg per day and that 3/15 (20 percent) of the lamotrigine participants developed rashes. In practice, this medication is generally well tolerated, but because of the dangers of the Stevens-Johnson syndrome, the medication has to be slowly titrated over weeks to the therapeutic dose range. Therefore, lamotrigine would not be an appropriate medication to use to try to stabilize a patient with borderline personality disorder in crisis. Omega-3 fatty acids (eicosapentaenoic acid [EPA], docosahexaenoic acid [DHA]) have also been evaluated in patients with borderline personality disorder and they may have modest benefit on mood symptoms usually focusing on EPA plus DHA in the range of 1–2 g per day (Hancock-Johnson et al., 2017; Stoffers & Lieb, 2015).

In summary, mood stabilizers can be useful for some with borderline personality disorder and there is evidence to support their use. Most of the trials have been of short duration, although there is a recent investigation of the long-term effectiveness of lamotrigine in patients with borderline personality disorder. Crawford et al. (2018) undertaking a multi-site randomized controlled trial of lamotrigine (up to 200 mg per day) versus placebo in a sample of 252 patients with 3, 6, and 12-month follow-up and found no benefits. The outcome measures were extensive and covered symptoms, self-harm, quality of life, and cost-effectiveness. The results of this study are highly compelling, and are discussed in chapter 21c. Again, mood stabilizers have significant side effects (particularly for women in the childbearing years) and the risks versus benefits must be carefully evaluated.

Antidepressants

The meta-analytic and systematic reviews of pharmacologic treatment in patients with borderline personality disorder suggest that antidepressants have a limited role in the management of these patients (Hancock-Johnson et al., 2017; Ingenhoven et al., 2010; Lieb et al., 2010; Mercer et al., 2009; Nose et al., 2006; Stoffers & Lieb, 2015). There is some evidence that anger, depression, and perhaps affective instability can be symptom targets when using these medications. For example, a recent pilot study of duloxetine in patients with borderline personality disorder suggested that impulsivity, anger, and affective instability were improved (Bellino, Paradiso, Bozzatello, & Bogetto, 2010). However, there is no robust evidence supporting the efficacy of antidepressants in treating borderline personality disorder. Most often, antidepressants are used to treat comorbid depression or anxiety disorders. The use of antidepressants for comorbid disorders is justified; however, the patient has to be realistic about the expected outcomes. For example, we know that the longitudinal course of comorbid depression in patients with borderline personality disorder is more influenced by having the underlying borderline personality disorder resolved than focusing on the comorbid depression (Gunderson & Links, 2014).

Methylphenidate

Attention deficit disorder is often found to be comorbid with borderline personality disorder and this raises the question about prescribing stimulants such as methylphenidate for patients with borderline personality disorder. No randomized controlled trial evidence examining the use of methylphenidate in patients with borderline personality disorder was found for this review; however, there are two studies that are of relevance to this question. An open label prospective study in 14 adolescent females with borderline personality disorder and attention deficit hyperactivity disorder (ADHD) examined several outcomes related to prescribing up to 60 mg per day of methylphenidate (Golubchik, Sever, Zalsman, & Weizman, 2008). The study excluded adolescents with psychosis or substance abuse diagnoses. The findings indicated that ADHD and aggressive symptoms were improved; however, interestingly, in three of the patients, self-harming behaviors were eliminated after exposure to methylphenidate (Golubchik et al., 2008). There was no worsening of the borderline personality symptoms and no development of psychoses. The study requires replication but suggests that, for certain patients, aggressive and self-harming behavior may be helped by methylphenidate. A second prospective naturalistic study compared patients with borderline personality disorder with and without ADHD on methylphenidate to patients with borderline personality disorder and ADHD not on methylphenidate (Prada et al., 2015). All of these patients were going through an intensive Dialectical Behavior Therapy (DBT) program during the course of the investigation. Patients with borderline personality disorder and ADHD on methylphenidate showed significant improvement compared to patients with borderline personality disorder and ADHD not on methylphenidate on motor impulsiveness, overall impulsiveness, ADHD severity, state anger, and depression severity. In addition, the study suggested that patients who had their ADHD symptoms treated with methylphenidate were more available and able to benefit from the DBT program. Again, the study suggests that methylphenidate may have a role in making patients with borderline personality disorder and ADHD better able to participate in psychosocial interventions. This research illustrates that the outcomes of pharmacological interventions should include changes in functioning beyond just symptom improvement.

In summary, methylphenidate prescribed in slowly released preparations may prove useful in patients with borderline personality disorder and comorbid ADHD. When diagnosing ADHD in patients with borderline personality disorder, the clinician should try to confirm the ADHD diagnosis in childhood using collateral and/or school records. Stimulant medications prescribed for adult patients with borderline personality disorder and comorbid ADHD can be helpful, and the benefits should be particularly apparent through improvements in functioning in their treatment programs, school, or work settings.

Novel Approaches

Opioid antagonists such as naltrexone have been tested in female patients with borderline personality disorder in terms of their impact on dissociative symptoms; however, the research showed non-significant effects of naltrexone on dissociative symptoms. The role of naltrexone in modifying dissociation and self-injurious behavior in patients with borderline personality disorder remains controversial but deserves further study (Moghaddas, Dianatkhah, Ghaffari, & Ghaeli, 2017). Clonidine has been used to decrease inner tension and hyperarousal and may be useful in patients with borderline personality disorder and comorbid posttraumatic stress disorder (PTSD; Hancock-Johnson et al., 2017; Stoffers & Lieb, 2015). Doxazosin, a long-acting alpha-1-antagonist that produces fewer orthostatic side effects than prazosin, was studied using a retrospective chart review in inpatients admitted with borderline personality disorder and/or PTSD (Roepke et al., 2017). The results demonstrated that doxazosin reduced nightmares in patients who took the medication over a 12-week period with a medium pre-post effect size (d = 0.78). The authors concluded that doxazosin appears to be a viable option to prazosin in treating trauma-associated nightmares. However, further randomized controlled trials are clearly needed to clarify the role of these medications in patients with borderline personality disorder and comorbid PTSD.

As patients with borderline personality disorder demonstrate dysfunctional interpersonal relationships, several medications have been advanced as possible approaches to improve prosocial behavior. Oxytocin in normal participants has been shown to promote group trust and cooperation and improve social cognitive abilities such as emotional recognition (Amad, Thomas, & Perez-Rodriguez, 2015). Therefore, oxytocin was believed to have possible benefits for improving deficits in mentalizing and the bias to negatively-valenced social stimuli that are found in patients with borderline personality disorder. At this point, there are no clinical trials of oxytocin in patients with borderline personality disorder and most of the studies that have been done have examined laboratory outcomes related to prosocial behavior (Amad et al., 2015). These studies showed a mixture of results in patients with borderline personality disorder, with some evidence that oxytocin can improve hypersensitivity to social threats but contradictory findings that oxytocin may lessen trust and cooperative behaviors in certain social dilemmas. These mixed results may be explained by the social salience hypothesis (Shamay-Tsoory et al., 2009), which suggests that oxytocin may modulate the salience to both positive- and negative-valenced social emotions and, therefore, in certain contexts may lead to contradictory outcomes. Although interest remains in studying the role of oxytocin in patients with borderline personality disorder, all of these findings come from laboratory studies and this research has not controlled for various confounders such as gender differences, menstrual cycle effects, and medication interactions.

Research is underway to determine whether medication could modify the social pain patients with borderline personality disorder experience with actual or perceived social rejection. A recent randomized controlled trial tested the efficacy of exogenous opioids to reduce separation distress and the risk of suicide in adult severely suicidal patients (Yovell et al., 2016). This study tested buprenorphine up to 0.8 mg versus placebo in severely suicidal adult patients without substance abuse to determine whether the medication would reduce suicide ideation and the probability of suicide risk. These patients were not selected for having borderline personality disorder; however, more than half of the participants met criteria for the disorder. Over the four-week trial, buprenorphine versus placebo led to significant reductions in suicidal ideation and in the suicide probability scale. The study also found a reduction in depressive symptoms, but this reduction was smaller than the impacts on suicide risk. Based on these results, the mechanism of action was felt to be through reducing social pain associated with rejection and abandonment versus impacting and reducing depressive symptoms. The study was limited by a high dropout rate, short duration of follow-up, and a need to further study the safety of buprenorphine. However, this research indicates a unique line of inquiry to determine whether modifying social pain can reduce suicidal crises in patients with borderline personality disorder.

Other medications that have been implicated in modifying social pain include acetaminophen and marijuana (Deckman, DeWall, Way, Gilman, & Richman, 2014; DeWall et al., 2010). Roberts and colleagues (Roberts, Krajbich, Cheavens, Campo, & Way, 2018) carried out a randomized controlled trial in undergraduates to determine whether acetaminophen would increase trust behavior in students high in borderline personality disorder features. Participants received an acute dose of 1000 mg of acetaminophen or placebo and then completed an economic trust game. The findings demonstrated that participants with high borderline personality disorder features evidenced less trusting behaviors than participants with low borderline personality disorder features; however, the acute administration of acetaminophen reduced the behavioral distrust of the participants with high borderline personality disorder features. The authors speculated that acetaminophen increased trust in participants with high borderline personality disorder features by reducing negative affect about the possibility of social rejection regardless of expectations. Deckman et al. (2014) used data from cross-sectional, longitudinal, and experimental study designs to test whether marijuana reduced the pain of social exclusion. Based on four separate studies, the authors concluded that marijuana – similar to acetaminophen – activated cannabinoid 1 receptors and could buffer both social and physical pain.

Transcranial magnetic stimulation has been studied in patients with borderline personality disorder through several case reports. A few case reports utilizing a focus in the dorsal lateral prefrontal cortex have suggested that transcranial magnetic stimulation may have an impact on borderline symptoms such as anger and affective instability (Arbabi, Hafizi, Ansari, Oghabian, & Hasani, 2013; Cailhol et al., 2014). Feffer and colleagues (Feffer, Peters, Bhui, Downar, & Giacobbe, 2017) used a focus on the dorsal medial prefrontal cortex and documented improvement in depressive rather than borderline symptoms in three cases of patients with borderline personality disorder. Transcranial magnetic stimulation deserves further study in patients with borderline personality disorder, particularly with regard to its impact on mood and affective instability.

PHARMACOTHERAPY IN OTHER PERSONALITY DISORDERS

Compared to borderline personality disorder, there is a relative dearth of evidence-based directives with respect to pharmacological interventions for other personality disorders (Ripoll, Triebwasser, & Siever, 2011). The available literature provides guidance for mainly two additional personality disorders: schizotypal and avoidant. Also, contrary to borderline personality disorder, much less evidence supports the use of mood stabilizers for other personality disorders.

Antipsychotic Medications

Both typical and atypical antipsychotics have been studied – and found beneficial – in schizotypal personality disorder (Bateman, Gunderson, & Mulder, 2015; Herpertz et al., 2007; Mazza, Marano, & Janiri, 2016; Roepke et al., 2008). This stems mostly from small, open-label studies (Bateman et al., 2015). Koenigsberg et al. (2003) reported one of the few randomized controlled trials in patients with schizotypal personality disorder. Koenigsberg et al. hypothesized that risperidone would be useful for both the positive and negative symptoms of the disorder. Twenty-one schizotypal patients were involved in the randomized controlled trial. They were treated with risperidone up to a maximum dose of 2 mg per day. Results of the study revealed significant effects on both positive and negative psychotic symptoms. Using a 30 percent change in scores as a response rate, four of seven patients exposed to risperidone were considered responders versus none in the placebo arm. Overall, the benefits of antipsychotic medication pertained to modifying the psychotic-like symptoms, but also the cognitive deficits that are mostly associated with schizotypal personality disorder.

Antidepressants

Herpertz et al. (2007), on the basis of the clinical resemblance and continuum between social phobia and avoidant personality disorder, suggested extrapolating the findings pertaining to the pharmacological interventions for social phobia to treatment options for avoidant personality disorder. As such, on the basis of randomized controlled trials conducted in patients with social phobia, selective serotonin reuptake inhibitors, as well as the selective norepinephrine reuptake inhibitor venlafaxine, can be first-line pharmacological agents for the treatment of avoidant personality disorder. There is also a role for phenelzine, although the side effect profile makes this a less appealing choice. The presence of avoidant personality disorder was noted in some of these studies (4 of 26), with similar or even greater benefit from moclobemide (3 studies) and sertraline (1 randomized controlled trial) in samples with the two conditions rather than social phobia alone. Unfortunately, pharmacological treatment suggestions related specifically to avoidant personality disorder are based on case series rather than randomized controlled trials (Deltito & Stam, 1989).

Novel Approaches

A randomized placebo-controlled double-blind trial (McClure et al., 2010) showed that pergolide, a D_1 and D_2 dopamine agonist, reduced several cognitive deficits in patients with schizotypal personality disorder. The domains that improved during the trial were visuo-spatial working memory, executive functioning, verbal learning, and memory. Although pergolide has since been removed from the market due to concerns around induction of valvular heart disease, future research in this domain may identify agents with similar properties and benefits.

Intranasal oxytocin has also been tested in patients with antisocial personality disorder (Alcorn, Rathnayaka, Swann, Moeller, & Lane, 2015). In this small study ($n = 6$), male participants received intranasal oxytocin, and human aggression was monitored with the point subtraction aggression paradigm. The results were not conclusive, but this new approach, along with some more robust findings in borderline personality disorder, may suggest the utility of further study in other personality disorders.

LIMITATIONS

Although there is research evidence supporting the value of medication over placebo for certain symptom targets in patients with borderline personality disorder, this research has many limitations. Most of the studies have samples with an overrepresentation of women, and the number of men with borderline personality disorder involved in these studies is limited. Overall, the sample sizes in the studies are small, trial durations are short, and often there have been extensive exclusions of participants with clinical or non-personality disorder psychiatric comorbidities that make the generalizing of findings problematic. The quality of the studies is often questionable, creating a risk of biases. The study of personality disorders has been severely hampered by the limits of the measures of the psychopathology characteristic of these disorders. It may well be that impulsive aggressiveness is the best-measured aspect of personality disorder pathology and we have been able to demonstrate change in this because

of its measurable behavioral component. There is a lack of definition of the affective and cognitive aspects of personality disorders. Not only do we have to refine the definition of the various aspects of psychopathology, but we also need to develop responsive measurements that can capture change through pharmacological interventions. These measurement issues need to be addressed so that we may demonstrate beyond behavior that we are able to effect changes in affect and cognition.

Finally, as patients with borderline personality disorder are often exposed to medication, there has been insufficient attention given to the side effects and reasons for withdrawal in previous pharmacologic trials. An important outcome of pharmacological trials should be an improvement in work, family, and other aspects of role performance. In the future, pharmacological trials should include indicators of quality of life so they can be used as measures of effectiveness of pharmacological interventions and provide a broader assessment of the impact of pharmacological interventions beyond symptom reduction and side effects. Certainly more research on the psychopharmacologic management of patients with personality disorder is warranted and needs to be supported.

PATIENTS' EXPERIENCE OF MEDICATION

Clinicians, besides considering the research evidence for using medication, must understand patients' experience of being prescribed medication. Rogers and Acton (2012) used qualitative methods and thematic analysis to capture the experiences of seven patients with a diagnosis of a personality disorder treated within a specialist service. The patients spoke about their recovery pathways and how they often felt that they were not involved in treatment decisions, including whether they wanted medication to be a part of their recovery plans. Some patients felt that medication was not necessary for their recovery, whereas others saw medication as important to their recovery. The patients reported more opportunity to have input in their treatment when they were treated by a specialty service (Rogers & Acton, 2012).

The clinician needs to ask about the patient's perceptions of medication treatment particularly because most of the medications are associated with adverse effects. As many young people are diagnosed with personality disorders, their exposure to medications can lead to an increased risk of obesity and the development of metabolic syndromes that can impact their lifetime morbidity, mortality, and quality of life. All personality disorder clusters have been shown to have a robust relationship with obesity, and in the McLean Study of Adult Development, the rate of obesity rose among patients with borderline personality disorder from 17 percent at baseline to 28 percent at six-year follow-up (Dixon-Gordon, Conkey, & Whalen, 2018)

In addition to taking time to understand patients' perceptions of the role of medications in their recovery, the clinician must understand the psychodynamic and interpersonal exchanges associated with the pharmacotherapy relationship. Kenneth Silk (1996, p. 124) cautioned "understanding what medication means to the patient is crucial because whenever medication is introduced into any therapy, it has repercussions on the transference process." Perhaps this is nowhere truer than when prescribing for the patient with borderline personality disorder. Pills and prescriptions can be loaded with meanings, affected by the patient's attachment history, and affected by how the patient regards him- or herself in illness and as a receiver of care. Understanding what purpose and meaning medication holds – not only for the patient but also for the involved clinician(s) – can help to minimize and make use of transference/relationship feelings, direct psychoeducation about personality disorders and the role of medication, and assess clearly the impact of any one medication change. The clinician's self-worth and anxieties regarding being competent and/or in control can become magnified in the context of a therapeutic relationship with the borderline personality disorder patient who feels helpless, hopeless, out of control or too controlled, and acts out these meanings – in part – via their expectations of and adherence to medication.

In structuring our thinking of how to examine the meanings and dynamics of the pharmacotherapy relationship alongside the effect of a medication adjustment, Gunderson (2001) identified the need to assess what positive and negative attributions the patient has towards medication and towards the prescribing clinician. Building upon this notion, two dimensions or axes can be addressed (Table 21.1). The first axis tracks the "outcome" or treatment response. The second axis examines the transference/relationship issues and quality of the therapeutic relationship. Using this model assumes two things: (1) the patient is basically compliant with medication and (2) the therapist's expectations regarding the effectiveness of the medication are in accordance with existing evidence.

Where there is a negative rapport and apparent negative response to medication both subjectively and objectively, the patient – and clinician – may begin to attach several negative meanings to the medication and therapy. The patient who experiences difficult side effects or gets no relief may feel they are being "experimented upon" and question the genuineness of the clinician's concern. Many patients with borderline personality disorder will feel paranoid and persecuted at times, and may view medication as the clinician's covert means of trying to control them. Increased non-adherence of the patient to the regime may be a warning sign. At the same time, some clinicians, particularly those who feel rushed or pressed for time, may respond with feeling thwarted and that their effort has been deliberately sabotaged; in other words, they too feel as persecuted as the patient. Warning signs

Table 21.1 Therapeutic outcomes and pitfalls

		Attributions	
		Negative Relationship	Positive Relationship
Treatment Response	Negative	Feeling controlled, persecuted, thwarted	Won't stop ineffective medication; may abuse them.
		Non-compliant patient; avoidant therapist	Secret non-compliance & stockpiling
		Patient as "untreatable" versus therapist feeling "incompetent"	
	Positive	All improvement attributed to medication. Therapy is dismissed, and possibly avoided. Patient potential to improve only half accessed.	Therapist &/or medications idealized short term. Symptom chasing

of this reaction might include avoidance of the patient, cutting time, changing or cancelling appointments, or being increasingly inflexible. These efforts by the clinician to try to gain more control are just what the patient fears. The patient's complaints may then be inadequately assessed and misattributed solely to their "personality." Other negative attributions or meanings that may be attached to the medication and therapy include being untreatable, helpless, dependent, and/or viewed as incompetent.

In another scenario, the patient may have a negative treatment response but still maintain a basically positive rapport with the pharmacotherapist. In some circumstances, the patient may not want to stop a medication even though it appears to be causing disconcerting side effects or is of questionable benefit. In such circumstances, the medication regime may have some positive meaning or association, perhaps to a previous soothing or valued therapist. Such a patient could possibly resort to abusing these medications in seeking the soothing memory of the old therapist, perhaps misattributing treatment failure as their own "incurability" and hopelessness. Additionally, a patient may think that compliance is essential, even though there is subjectively and objectively little benefit, in order to maintain the current clinician's approval. Another possible outcome in this scenario is the patient's secret non-compliance and stockpiling of medication. The patient will need careful coaching to have them evaluate if their need is actually being met through such behaviors.

In a third scenario, one might have a positive treatment response yet the rapport remains negative. Whereas symptom relief will usually enhance the patient–clinician relationship, medication and therapy can continue to hold a great deal of negative meaning that can be projected into the relationship. Feelings and perceptions of being mentally ill or "disordered," vulnerable, or controlled can remain at play. The patient may accept that medication has some value but downplay the relationship, taking on the stance of "You're not such a great doctor but I'm hanging in there just for the meds." The clinician who consequently feels rejected and helpless may, once again, want to avoid the patient with the consequence being that the therapeutic relationship is left to dwindle; dynamic issues do not get addressed and the patient's distress related to interpersonal issues remains.

In a fourth and final scenario, the response to medication is positive and the therapeutic rapport is also positive. Even in this circumstance, pitfalls exist. The meanings the patient – and clinician – attribute to medication need to be understood. A primary pitfall is that the clinician and/or medication may become idealized and this may be short-lived. Without a clear understanding of what change medication has effected alongside the therapy relationship, life stressors, and the patient's acquisition and use of new coping skills, these positive gains may be incorrectly attributed to medication. A downturn in the patient's mood that becomes attributed solely to the medication "not working anymore" might result in the once idealized clinician making greater and greater efforts to eliminate the symptom. Symptom chasing, polypharmacy, over-involvement, and therapy exhaustion are all possible consequences.

CLINICAL APPROACH

To ensure that pharmacotherapy does more good than harm, we suggest that clinicians adopt the following approach when prescribing medications to patients with personality disorders. When treating a patient with a personality disorder, the clinician is often clear when aggressive treatment is needed and when to first prescribe pharmacotherapy. The difficulty according to Soloff (2000) is when to settle for "modest gains" and then maintain and eventually stop the current regime. As a result, clinical outcomes should be measurable and related to the patients' functioning. When medications are to be considered, the clinician should create a partnership with the patient in choosing the medication, discussing the options, and then monitoring and evaluating the outcome.

Table 21.2 Pharmacological summary

Drug type	Summary	Example
Mood stabilizers	Broadest effectiveness, but only modest effectiveness for depression/mood stabilization. More useful for anger/impulsivity	Lamotrigine Dose: 150–200 mg per day Major side effect: Stevens-Johnson syndrome
Antipsychotics	Second broadest effectiveness. Side effects encourage time-limited trials	Quetiapine Dose: 150–300 mg per day Major side effects: somnolence, fatigue and increased appetite and weight
Antidepressants	Uncertain value, used for comorbid disorders especially for depression/ anxiety	Fluoxetine Dose: 20–40 mg per day Major side effect: increased agitation/ suicidality
Anti-anxiety	Benzodiazepines: habit forming, sometimes disinhibiting. Relatively contraindicated; trauma-related anxiety – clonidine; prazosin	Prazosin Dose: 3–10 mg per day Major side effect: hypotension

Encourage patients to investigate the medications using appropriate online resources or reading materials. Often, patients can be directly engaged in deciding how best to measure the outcomes of interest. In addition, symptoms that might be possible side effects of the medication should be monitored at baseline and over the course of the medication trial.

Some useful principles to follow when managing patients with personality disorders are avoiding polypharmacy, regularly reviewing the value of long-term medications, treating comorbid clinical or non-personality psychiatric disorders as a priority (especially if they interfere with functioning or participation in psychosocial treatment), and eschewing medication changes during crisis episodes. Crisis management skills ultimately will be much more useful in crisis episodes versus a possible placebo response to a new medication. If the patient fails to respond to a medication, the agreement should be to taper and stop the first medication before beginning another medication (unless a cross-taper is feasible). If the patient has negative attitudes towards the medications or their use, as indicated above, these feelings need to explored and understood. Whenever medications are to be considered, the patient and clinician must evaluate and monitor the risks versus the benefits. Finally, the patient must understand that medications are adjunctive agents, whereas psychosocial interventions appear to be the primary approach to treatment.

SUMMARY

Good psychiatric care of patients with personality disorders still supports the use of medication for specific symptoms and to foster certain outcomes in patients with personality disorders (see Table 21.2; Gunderson & Links, 2014). Unfortunately, most of the trials involve patients with borderline personality disorder and, thus, we know much less about how to use medications for other personality disorders or how effective medication would be for specific pathological personality traits regardless of diagnosis. Pharmacotherapy should still be considered as an adjunct to evidence-based psychosocial interventions, and the clinician must carefully weigh the risks versus benefits of prescribing psychotropic medication. Certainly more research and pharmacological trials are indicated and several novel approaches suggest that new neuropathological mechanisms are worthy of further study. In the future, collaborative networks of researchers should be established that would allow the testing of pharmacological agents in larger, representative samples using state-of-the-art clinical trials. In addition, specific protocols could test an algorithm approach to the treatment of personality disorders based on systemized protocols.

REFERENCES

Alcorn, J. L., Rathnayaka, N., Swann, A. C., Moeller, F. G., & Lane, S. D. (2015). Effects of intranasal oxytocin on aggressive responding in antisocial personality disorder. *The Psychological Record*, 65(4), 691–703.

Amad, A., Thomas, P., & Perez-Rodriguez, M. M. (2015). Borderline personality disorder and oxytocin: Review of clinical trials and future directions. *Current Pharmaceutical Design*, 21. doi:10.2174/1381612821666150619093019

American Psychiatric Association. (2001). Practice guideline for the treatment of patients with borderline personality disorder. *American Journal of Psychiatry*, 158, 1–52.

Arbabi, M., Hafizi, S., Ansari, S., Oghabian, M. A., & Hasani, N. (2013). High frequency TMS for the management of borderline personality disorder: A case report. *Asian Journal of Psychiatry*, 6(6), 614–617.

Bateman, A., Gunderson, J., & Mulder, R. (2015). Treatment of personality disorder. *Lancet*, 385(9969), 735–743.

Bellino, S., Paradiso, E., Bozzatello, P., & Bogetto, F. (2010). Efficacy and tolerability of duloxetine in the treatment of

patients with borderline personality disorder: A pilot study. *Journal of Psychopharmacology*, 24, 333–339.

Beri, A., & Boydell, J. (2014). Clozapine in borderline personality disorder: A review of the evidence. *Annals of Clinical Psychiatry*, 26, 139–144.

Black, D. W., Zanarini, M. C., Romine, A., Shaw, M., Allen, J., & Schulz, S. C. (2014). Comparison of low and moderate dosages of extended-release quetiapine in borderline personality disorder: A randomized, double-blind, placebo-controlled trial. *American Journal of Psychiatry*, 171(11), 1174–1182.

Cailhol, L., Roussignol, B., Klein, R., Bousquet, B., Simonetta-Moreau, M., Schmitt, L., ... Birmes, P. (2014). Borderline personality disorder and rTMS: A pilot study. *Psychiatry Research*, 216, 155–157.

Crawford, M. J., Kakad, S., Rendel, C., Mansour, N. A., Crugel, M., Liu, K. W., ... Barnes, T. R. (2011). Medication prescribed to people with personality disorders: The influence of patient factors and treatment setting. *Acta Psychiatrica Scandinavica*, 124(5), 396–402.

Crawford, M. J., Sanatinia, R., Barrett, B., Cunningham, G., Dale, O., Ganguli, P., Lawrence-Smith, G., Leeson, V.C., Lemonsky, F., Lykomitrou-Matthews, G., Montgomery, A.A., Morriss, R., Munjiza, J., Paton, C., Skorodzien, I., Singh, V., Tan, W., Tyrer, P., & Reilly, J. G. (2018). Lamotrigine for people with borderline personality disorder: a RCT. *Health Technology Assessment* (Winchester, England), 22(17), 1–68. https://doi.org/10.3310/hta22170.

Deckman, T., DeWall, C. N., Way, B., Gilman, R., & Richman, S. (2014). Can marijuana reduce social pain? *Social Psychological and Personality Science*, 5(2), 131–139.

Deltito, J. A., & Stam, M. (1989). Psychopharmacological treatment of avoidant personality disorder. *Comprehensive Psychiatry*, 30(6), 498–504.

DeWall, C. N., MacDonald, G., Webster, G. D., Masten, C. L., Baumeister, R. F., Powell, C., ... Eisenberger, N. I. (2010). Acetaminophen reduces social pain: Behavioral and neural evidence. *Psychological Science*, 21(7), 931–937.

Dixon-Gordon, K. L., Conkey, L. C., & Whalen, D. J. (2018). Recent advances in understanding physical health problems in personality disorders. *Current Opinion in Psychology*, 21, 1–5.

Feffer, K., Peters, S. K., Bhui, K., Downar, J., & Giacobbe, P. (2017). Successful dorsomedial prefrontal rTMS for major depression in borderline personality disorder: Three cases. *Brian Stimulation*, 10, 716–717.

Golubchik, P., Sever, J., Zalsman, G., & Weizman, A. (2008). Methylphenidate in the treatment of female adolescents with cooccurrence of attention deficit/hyperactivity disorder and borderline personality disorder: A preliminary open-label trial. *International Clinical Psychopharmacology*, 23(4), 228–231.

Gunderson, J. G. (2001). *Borderline Personality Disorder: A Clinical Guide*. Washington, DC: American Psychiatric Publishing.

Gunderson, J. G., & Links, P. S. (2014). *Handbook of Good Psychiatric Management for Borderline Personality Disorder*. Washington, DC: American Psychiatric Publishing.

Hancock-Johnson, E., Griffiths, C., & Picchioni, M. (2017). A focused systematic review of pharmacologic treatment for borderline personality disorder. *CNS Drugs*, 31, 345–356.

Herpertz, S. C., Zanarini, M., Schulz, C. S., Siever, L., Lieb, K., Möller, H., ... WFSBP Task Force on Personality Disorders (2007). World Federation of Societies of Biological Psychiatry (WFSBP) Guidelines for Biological Treatment of Personality Disorders. *The World Journal of Biological Psychiatry*, 8(4), 212–244.

Ingenhoven, T., Lafay, P., Rinne, T., Passchier, J., & Duivenvoorden, H. (2010). Effectiveness of pharmacotherapy for severe personality disorders: Meta-analyses of randomized controlled trials. *Journal of Clinical Psychiatry, 71*(1), 14–25.

Koenigsberg, H. W., Reynolds, D., Goodman, M., New, A. S., Mitropoulou, V., Trestman, R. L., ... Siever, L. J., (2003). Risperidone in the treatment of schizotypal personality disorder. *Journal of Clinical Psychiatry, 64*, 628–634.

Lieb, K., Völlm, B., Rücker, G., Timmer, A., & Stoffers, J. M. (2010). Pharmacotherapy for borderline personality disorder: Cochrane systematic review of randomised trials. *British Journal of Psychiatry, 196*, 4–12.

Mazza, M., Marano, G., & Janiri, L. (2016). An update on pharmacotherapy for personality disorders. *Expert Opinion on Pharmacotherapy, 17*(15), 1977–1979.

McClure, M. M., Harvey, P. D., Goodman, M., Triebwasser, J., New, A., Koenigsberg, H. W., ... Siever, L. J. (2010). Pergolide treatment of cognitive deficits associated with schizotypal personality disorder: Continued evidence of the importance of the dopamine system in the schizophrenia spectrum. *Neuropsychopharmacology, 35*(6), 1356–1362.

McMain, S. F., Links, P. S., Gnam, W. H., Guimond, T., Cardish, R. J., Korman, L., & Streiner, D. L. (2009). A randomized trial of dialectical behavior therapy versus general psychiatric management for borderline personality disorder. *American Journal of Psychiatry, 166*(12), 1365–1374.

Mercer, D., Douglass, A. B., & Links, P. S. (2009). Meta-analyses of mood stabilizers, antidepressants and antipsychotics in the treatment of borderline personality disorder: Effectiveness for depression and anger symptoms. *Journal of Personality Disorders, 23*(2), 156–174.

Moghaddas, A., Dianatkhah, M., Ghaffari, S., & Ghaeli, P. (2017). The potential role of naltrexone in borderline personality disorder. *Iran Journal of Psychiatry, 12*, 142–146.

National Health and Medical Research Council. (2012). *Clinical Practice Guideline for the Management of Borderline Personality Disorder*. National Health and Medical Research Council, Canberra, Australia.

National Institute for Health and Clinical Excellence. (2015). *Borderline Personality Disorder: Recognition and Management*. www.nice.org.uk/guidance/cg78/resources/borderline-personality-disorder-recognition-and-management-pdf-975635141317

Nose, N., Cipriani, A., Biancosino, B., Grassi, L., & Barbui, C. (2006). Efficacy of pharmacotherapy against core traits of borderline personality disorder: Meta-analysis of randomized controlled trials. *International Clinical Psychopharmacology, 21*, 345–353.

Paton, C., Crawford, M. J., Bhatti, S. F., Patel, M. X., & Barnes, T. R. E. (2015). The use of psychotropic medication in patients with emotionally unstable personality disorder under the care of UK Mental Health Services. *Journal of Clinical Psychiatry, 76* (4), e512–e518.

Prada, P., Nicastro, R., Zimmermann, J., Hasler, R., Aubry, J.-M., & Perroud, N. (2015). Addition of methylphenidate to intensive dialectical behaviour therapy for patients suffering from comorbid borderline personality disorder and ADHD: A naturalistic study. *ADHD Attention Deficit and Hyperactivity Disorders, 7*(3), 199–209.

Reich, D. B., Zanarini, M. C., & Bieri, K. A. (2009). A preliminary study of lamotrigine in the treatment of affective instability in borderline personality disorder. *International Clinical Psychopharmacology, 24*, 270–275.

Ripoll, L. H., Triebwasser, J., & Siever, L. J. (2011). Evidence-based pharmacotherapy for personality disorders. *International Journal of Neuropsychopharmacology, 14*(9), 1257–1288.

Roberts, I. D., Krajbich, I., Cheavens, J. S., Campo, J. V., & Way, B. M. (2018). Acetaminophen reduces distrust in individuals with borderline personality disorder features. *Clinical Psychological Science, 6*(1), 145–154.

Roepke, S., Danker-Hopfe, H., Repantis, D., Behnia, B., Bernard, F., Hansen, M.-L., & Otte, C. (2017). Doxazosin, an alpha-1-adrenergic-receptor antagonist for nightmares in patients with posttraumatic stress disorder and/or borderline personality disorder: A chart review. *Pharmacopsychiatry, 50*, 26–31.

Roepke, S., Merkl, A., Dams, A., Ziegenhorn, A., Anghelescu, I., Heuser, I., & Lammers, C. (2008). Preliminary evidence of improvement of depressive symptoms but not impulsivity in Cluster B personality disorder patients treated with quetiapine: An open label trial. *Pharmacopsychiatry, 41*, 176–181.

Rogers, B., & Acton, T. (2012). "I think we're all guinea pigs really": A qualitative study of medication and borderline personality disorder. *Journal of Psychiatric and Mental Health Nursing, 19*, 341–347.

Rohde, C., Polcwiartek, C., Correll, C. U., & Nielsen, J. (2017). Real-world effectiveness of clozapine for borderline personality disorder: Results from a 2-year mirror-image study. *Journal of Personality Disorders, 31*, 1–15.

Shamay-Tsoory, S. G., Fischer, M., Dvash, J., Harari, H., Perach-Bloom, N., & Levkovitz, Y. (2009). Intranasal administration of oxytocin increases envy and schadenfreude (gloating). *Biological Psychiatry, 66*(9), 864–870.

Silk, K. R. (1996). Rational pharmacotherapy for patients with personality disorders. In P. S. Links (Ed.), *Clinical Assessment and Management of Severe Personality Disorders* (pp. 109–142). Washington, DC: American Psychiatric Publishing.

Soloff, P. H. (2000). Psychopharmacology of borderline personality disorder. *Psychiatric Clinics of North America, 23*, 169–192.

Stoffers, J. M., & Lieb, K. (2015). Pharmacotherapy for borderline personality disorder: Current evidence and recent trends. *Current Psychiatry Reports, 17*, 534–545.

Yovell, Y., Bar, G., Mashiah, M., Baruch, Y., Briskman, I., Asherov, J., ... Panksepp, J. (2016). Ultra-low-dose buprenorphine as a time-limited treatment for severe suicidal ideation: A randomized controlled trial. *American Journal of Psychiatry, 173*, 491–498.

Zanarini, M. C., Frankenberg, F. R., Hennen, J., & Silk, K. R. (2004). Mental health service utilization by borderline personality disorder patients and Axis II comparison subjects followed prospective for 6 years. *Journal of Clinical Psychiatry, 65*, 28–36.

Zanarini, M. C., Frankenberg, F. R., & Parachini, E. A. (2004). A preliminary randomized trial of fluoxetine, olanzapine and the olanzapine-fluoxetine combination in women with borderline personality disorder. *Journal of Clinical Psychiatry, 65*, 903–907.

Zanarini, M. C., Schulz, S. C., Detke, H. C., Tanaka, Y., Zhao, F., Lin, D., ... Corya, S. (2011). A dose comparison of olanzapine for the treatment of borderline personality disorder: A 12-week randomized, doubleblind, placebo-controlled study. *Journal of Clinical Psychiatry, 72*, 1353–1362.

Zanarini, M. C., Schulz, S., Detke, H., Zhao, F., Lin, D., Pritchard, M., ... Corya, S. (2012). Open-label treatment with olanzapine for patients with borderline personality disorder. *Journal of Clinical Psychopharmacology, 32*, 398–402.

21a New Efforts towards Evidence-Informed Practice and Practice-Informed Research: Commentary on Recent Developments in the Pharmacologic Management of Personality Disorders

JUTTA STOFFERS-WINTERLING AND KLAUS LIEB

In their chapter, Links et al. gave an overview of the major findings and recent research on the topic of drug treatments for borderline personality disorder (BPD) and other personality disorders. The authors discuss the limitations of research in this area and the role of medications within the therapeutic relationship, and then give clinical recommendations.

We would like to share some thoughts about the relevance and value of current research on BPD drug treatment. Our point of view mainly comes from evidence-based medicine (EBM). In a famous article, David Sackett and colleagues defined the practice of EBM as "integrating individual clinical expertise with the best available external clinical evidence i.e., clinically relevant research" (Sackett, Rosenberg, Gray, Haynes, & Richardson, 1996, p. 71). But how relevant is research for BPD treatment in reality? What would relevant research mean in this field? And what can be done to enhance the value of future evaluation studies?

We are aware of a clear gap between current clinical practice and the corresponding evidence. For example, as Links et al. report, most people with a diagnosis of BPD are prescribed psychotropic drugs (i.e., around 80–90 percent of patients take approximately 2.7 psychotropic drugs concurrently; Bridler et al., 2015; Zanarini, Frankenburg, Reich, Harned, & Fitzmaurice, 2015). The high rate of medication use is not at all reflected by corresponding research. As the authors point out, there is only one randomized controlled trial (RCT) that investigated polypharmacy systematically (Zanarini, Frankenburg, & Parachini, 2004), and its findings do not support this practice. This is a good example of the disconnect between research and clinical practice.

Another example of the mismatch of research and clinical practice is the case of quetiapine. Although it is the single drug most often used in the field, it has only been investigated by a single placebo-controlled RCT in BPD so far (Black et al., 2014). Obviously, the lack of any high-quality supporting evidence did not keep practitioners from prescribing this medication; prescription rates of approximately 30 percent were observed at times when still not a single RCT of quetiapine was available (Bridler et al., 2015). Now that one RCT is available, replication trials are urgently needed to foster the robustness of the findings and our confidence in them; however, we are only aware of one other industry-sponsored RCT (the findings of which have never been published (NCT00254748, n.d.) and another independently funded RCT that was discontinued because the investigators had major problems in recruiting quetiapine-naïve participants (ACTRN12615000705583, n.d.). Obviously, for the case of quetiapine, clinical practice has outrun treatment evaluation research.

The field of BPD treatment research is a very busy one, but not all new RCT studies make relevant contributions. For example, olanzapine is the one drug that is clearly dominating RCT research. Overall, there are 12 RCTs involving olanzapine (Stoffers & Lieb, 2015). The findings are far from convincing as Link et al. report, with only moderate beneficial effects linked to considerable adverse effects. Still, four new olanzapine RCTs, involving another 223 participants, have become available since publication of the Cochrane review: one compares olanzapine to a first-generation antipsychotic (haloperidol; Shafti & Shahveisi, 2010), two compare it to other second-generation antipsychotics (i.e., asenapine and aripiprazole; see Bozzatello, Rocca, Uscinska, & Bellino, 2017 and Shafti & Kaviani, 2015, respectively), and another one compares olanzapine to the SSRI antidepressant sertraline (Jariani, Saaki, Nazari, & Birjandi, 2010). These trials are of limited value because they ask and investigate questions that are of minimal relevance: What can we learn from the comparison of one medication with small beneficial effects and clear adverse effects (olanzapine) to alternate medications that have never been tested in placebo-controlled trials before (asenapine, sertraline), or to drugs with available but questionable evidence of effectiveness (aripiprazole), or to a drug that no one would ever seriously regard as an alternative (haloperidol)? The findings of these studies can only suggest which medication is associated with fewer adverse effects, but this must not be mistaken as support for their overall usefulness.

The EBM community has become aware of the research–practice gap, which has been recorded across all biomedical research (Chalmers & Glasziou, 2009). Though it is clear that research should reflect and inform issues relevant to consumers (i.e., clinicians, patients, and care providers; Sackett et al., 1996), the question of why research that might transform healthcare is not being produced more successfully deserves closer examination. Chalmers and Glasziou (2009) have identified and systemized stages throughout the research process during which avoidable misallocation of resources may appear, including (1) formulating relevant research questions, (2) elaborating an appropriate research design, (3) regulating and managing research efficiently, (4) making research information accessible, and (5) reporting of research findings. In response, the REWARD alliance was established (Macleod et al., 2014), with the aim of improving the value of research by suggesting strategies to regulate, design, conduct, manage, and analyze research appropriately, as well as to facilitate the reporting and dissemination of research findings (http://rewardalliance.net).

Yet, which research questions are of value and should be prioritized? To find this out, already existing evidence must be considered before designing new projects. Both published and ongoing research is systematically synthesized in sources such as Cochrane Collaboration reviews (www.cochranelibrary.com/) or up-to-date evidence-based treatment guidelines (NHMRC, 2013; NICE, 2009). Taking into account these sources, it is possible to draw conclusions about relevant questions, including "Which encouraging pilot findings need replication?" and "Which questions or comparisons are simply redundant?"

Still too often, economic factors drive decisions about research topics, study designs, and comparators in order to bring new products to market ("seeding trials") or to expand market shares. In contrast, public funding organizations and other non-industry sponsors facilitate setting research priorities independently from the prospects for commercial profit. We are currently aware of two such projects that are of enormous value for the field. First, there is an ongoing placebo-controlled RCT of aripiprazole (ACTRN12616001192471, n.d.). Its findings will make an important contribution to the field because, to date, there is only one small placebo-controlled RCT available reporting very large effects (Nickel et al., 2006), but its trustworthiness has been doubted (NICE, 2009). Another outstanding example of a valuable contribution is the recently published placebo-controlled RCT of lamotrigine by Crawford and colleagues (Crawford et al., 2015; Crawford et al., 2018a). Before, there were only two RCTs available, each including 27 participants who were followed up for 8 and 12 weeks (Reich, Zanarini, & Bieri, 2009; Tritt et al., 2005). This single new placebo-controlled RCT adds observations from 276 participants followed up for one year. It was sufficiently powered to detect clinically meaningful effects, but could not find any. These are robust findings in which we can have great confidence,

and they have the potential to transform the prescribing habits for lamotrigine (as depicted in Table 21.2 of Links et al.'s chapter) and maybe even mood stabilizers in general (Gunderson & Choi-Kain, 2018) – if they are adequately disseminated and recognized. The chances of this are good, as the study findings and even raw data are freely available for the public (EudraCT Number 2012-003136-23, n.d.; Crawford et al., 2018b).

While updating the Cochrane Collaboration review (Stoffers-Winterling et al., 2018), we found study registrations and protocols available for almost all newly eligible RCTs, which facilitates judgment of reporting completeness and accuracy. This was not the case for the majority of trials included in the preceding Cochrane review (Stoffers et al., 2010). Without a doubt, this is the result of the "equator network" (www.equator-network.org/; Simera et al., 2010), an initiative that aims at improving transparent and accurate reporting of health research. Now, study registration is obligatory for publication of trials in high impact journals (De Angelis et al., 2004).

Finally, two initiatives should be mentioned here that come from the EBM community and aim to increase the value of research: First, the AllTrials campaign that advocates for the full publication of study results from all clinical trials (Brown, 2013), and resulted in the development of an internet-based tool for identifying unpublished results of registered trials (http://fdaaa.trialstracker.net/). Second, the James Lind Alliance (Petit-Zeman, Firkins, & Scadding, 2010; www.jla.nihr.ac.uk/) that facilitates priority setting partnerships (PSP) wherein patients, clinicians, and care providers are brought together with the aim of identifying and prioritizing questions about the effects of treatments, and formulating relevant research questions.

Despite some shortcomings outlined by Links et al., we are aware of the first results of initiatives that aim at closing the research–practice gap, including the recent study of Crawford (Crawford, et al., 2018a, 2018b). Not only is this study a fine and encouraging example of a new culture of high-quality, relevant research, it has the potential to directly improve health, which is what clinical trials are supposed to do.

REFERENCES

ACTRN12615000705583. (n.d.). Evaluation of quetiapine as an adjunct treatment to psychotherapy for borderline personality disorder. Retrieved September 16, 2018, from www.anzctr.org.au/ACTRN12615000705583.aspx

ACTRN12616001192471. (n.d.). VERBATIM: A randomised controlled trial of aripiprazole for the treatment of auditory verbal hallucinations in borderline personality disorder. Retrieved September 16, 2018, from www.anzctr.org.au/Trial/Registration/TrialReview.aspx?id=371038

EudraCT Number 2012-003136-23. (n.d.). EudraCT Number 2012-003136-23 – Clinical trial results – EU Clinical Trials Register. Retrieved August 14, 2018, from www.clinicaltrialsregister.eu/ctr-search/trial/2012-003136-23/results

NCT00254748. (n.d.). Verkes Borderline Study: The effect of quetiapine on borderline personality disordered patients. Retrieved September 16, 2018, from https://ClinicalTrials.gov/show/NCT00254748

Black, D. W., Zanarini, M. C., Romine, A., Shaw, M., Allen, J., & Schulz, S. C. (2014). Comparison of low and moderate dosages of extended-release quetiapine in borderline personality disorder: A randomized, double-blind, placebo-controlled trial. *American Journal of Psychiatry*, *171*(11), 1174–1182.

Bozzatello, P., Rocca, P., Uscinska, M., & Bellino, S. (2017). Efficacy and tolerability of asenapine compared with olanzapine in borderline personality disorder: An open-label randomized controlled trial. *CNS Drugs*, *31*(9), 809–819.

Bridler, R., Häberle, A., Müller, S. T., Cattapan, K., Grohmann, R., Toto, S., ... Greil, W. (2015). Psychopharmacological treatment of 2195 in-patients with borderline personality disorder: A comparison with other psychiatric disorders. *European Neuropsychopharmacology: The Journal of the European College of Neuropsychopharmacology*, *25*(6), 763–772.

Brown, T. (2013). It's time for AllTrials registered and reported. In The Cochrane Collaboration (Ed.), *Cochrane Database of Systematic Reviews*. Chichester: John Wiley & Sons. https://doi.org/10.1002/14651858.ED000057

Chalmers, I., & Glasziou, P. (2009). Avoidable waste in the production and reporting of research evidence. *Lancet*, *374*(9683), 86–89.

Crawford, M. J., Sanatinia, R., Barrett, B., Byford, S., Cunningham, G., Gakhal, K., ... Reilly, J. G. (2015). Lamotrigine versus inert placebo in the treatment of borderline personality disorder: Study protocol for a randomized controlled trial and economic evaluation. *Trials*, *16*, 308. https://doi.org/10.1186/s13063-015-0823-x

Crawford, M. J., Sanatinia, R., Barrett, B., Cunningham, G., Dale, O., Ganguli, P., ... Reilly, J. G. (2018a). The clinical effectiveness and cost-effectiveness of lamotrigine in borderline personality disorder: A randomized placebo-controlled trial. *American Journal of Psychiatry*. https://doi.org/10.1176/appi.ajp.2018.17091006

Crawford, M. J., Sanatinia, R., Barrett, B., Cunningham, G., Dale, O., Ganguli, P., ... Reilly, J. G. (2018b). Lamotrigine for people with borderline personality disorder: A RCT. *Health Technology Assessment (Winchester, England)*, *22*(17), 1–68. https://doi.org/10.3310/hta22170.

De Angelis, C., Drazen, J. M., Frizelle, F. A., Haug, C., Hoey, J., Horton, R., ... International Committee of Medical Journal Editors (2004). Clinical trial registration: A statement from the International Committee of Medical Journal Editors. *The New England Journal of Medicine*, *351*(12), 1250–1251.

Gunderson, J. G., & Choi-Kain, L. W. (2018). Medication management for patients with borderline personality disorder. *American Journal of Psychiatry*, *175*(8), 709–711.

Jariani, M., Saaki, M., Nazari, H., & Birjandi, M. (2010). The effect of olanzapine and sertraline on personality disorder in patients with methadone maintenance therapy. *Psychiatria Danubina*, *22*(4), 544–547.

Macleod, M. R., Michie, S., Roberts, I., Dirnagl, U., Chalmers, I., Ioannidis, J. P. A., ... Glasziou, P. (2014). Biomedical research: Increasing value, reducing waste. *Lancet*, *383*(9912), 101–104.

National Health and Medical Research Council, Canberra, Australia [NHMRC]. (2013). *Clinical Practice Guideline for the Management of Borderline Personality Disorder*. Retrieved August 27, 2018 from www.nhmrc.gov.au/guidelines/publications/mh25.

National Institute for Health and Care Excellence, UK [NICE]. (2009). *NICE Clinical Guideline 78. Borderline Personality Disorder: Treatment and Management. Full Guideline (January 2009)*. Retrieved August 27, 2018 from www.nice.org.uk/guidance/cg78.

Nickel, M. K., Muehlbacher, M., Nickel, C., Kettler, C., Pedrosa, G. F., Bachler, E., ... Kaplan, P. (2006). Aripiprazole in the treatment of patients with borderline personality disorder: A double-blind, placebo-controlled study. *American Journal of Psychiatry*, *163*(5), 833–838.

Petit-Zeman, S., Firkins, L., & Scadding, J. W. (2010). The James Lind Alliance: Tackling research mismatches. *Lancet*, *376* (9742), 667–669.

Reich, D. B., Zanarini, M. C., & Bieri, K. A. (2009). A preliminary study of lamotrigine in the treatment of affective instability in borderline personality disorder. *International Clinical Psychopharmacology*, *24*(5), 270–275.

Sackett, D. L., Rosenberg, W. M., Gray, J. A., Haynes, R. B., & Richardson, W. S. (1996). Evidence based medicine: What it is and what it isn't. *BMJ*, *312*(7023), 71–72.

Shafti, S., & Kaviani, H. (2015). A comparative study on olanzapine and aripiprazole for symptom management in female patients with borderline personality disorder. *Klinik Psikofarmakoloji Bülteni/Bulletin of Clinical Psychopharmacology*, *25*(1), 38–43.

Shafti, S., & Shahveisi, B. (2010). Olanzapine versus haloperidol in the management of borderline personality disorder: A randomized double-blind trial. *Journal of Clinical Psychopharmacology*, *30*(1), 44–47.

Simera, I., Moher, D., Hirst, A., Hoey, J., Schulz, K. F., & Altman, D. G. (2010). Transparent and accurate reporting increases reliability, utility, and impact of your research: Reporting guidelines and the EQUATOR Network. *BMC Medicine*, *8*, 24. https://doi.org/10.1186/1741-7015-8-24

Stoffers, J. M., & Lieb, K. (2015). Pharmacotherapy for borderline personality disorder: Current evidence and recent trends. *Current Psychiatry Reports*, *17*(1), 534–545.

Stoffers, J., Völlm, B. A., Rucker, G., Timmer, A., Huband, N., & Lieb, K. (2010). Pharmacological interventions for borderline personality disorder. *Cochrane Database of Systematic Reviews*, *6* [CD005653]. https://doi.org/10.1002/14651858.CD005653.pub2

Stoffers-Winterling, J. M., Storebø, O. J., Völlm, B. A., Mattivi, J. T., Nielsen, S. S., Kielsholm, M. L., ... Lieb, K. (2018). Pharmacological interventions for people with borderline personality disorder. *Cochrane Database of Systematic Reviews*, *2*. https://doi.org/10.1002/14651858.CD012956

Tritt, K., Nickel, C., Lahmann, C., Leiberich, P. K., Rother, W. K., Loew, T. H., & Nickel, M. K. (2005). Lamotrigine treatment of aggression in female borderline-patients: A randomized, double-blind, placebo-controlled study. *Journal of Psychopharmacology*, *19*(3), 287–291.

Zanarini, M. C., Frankenburg, F. R., & Parachini, E. A. (2004). A preliminary, randomized trial of fluoxetine, olanzapine, and the olanzapine-fluoxetine combination in women with borderline personality disorder. *Journal of Clinical Psychiatry*, *65*(7), 903–907.

Zanarini, M. C., Frankenburg, F. R., Reich, D. B., Harned, A. L., & Fitzmaurice, G. M. (2015). Rates of psychotropic medication use reported by borderline patients and Axis II Comparison subjects over 16 years of prospective follow-up. *Journal of Clinical Psychopharmacology*, *35*(1), 63–67.

21b Considerations Regarding the Pharmacological Management of Personality Disorders: Commentary on Recent Developments in the Pharmacologic Management of Personality Disorders

LUIS C. FARHAT AND MARC N. POTENZA

The chapter by Links et al. (this volume) reviews the current state of understanding regarding medication management for personality disorders (PDs). The authors note that, compared to many other psychiatric disorders (especially those termed Axis I disorders in earlier editions of the *Diagnostic and Statistical Manual*; American Psychiatric Association, 2013), there are relatively few (if any) well validated pharmacotherapies for PDs, with most of the research focused on individuals with borderline personality disorder (BPD). The authors discuss limitations of many of the studies in this area, including the use of small sample sizes and uncontrolled designs, and note inconsistencies in recommendations regarding the extent to which medications are advised for administration in clinical settings. Whereas the United Kingdom National Institute for Healthcare and Excellence (NICE, 2015) does not recommend the use of psychopharmacologic agents in the treatment of individuals with BPD, the American Psychiatric Association supports the use of medications in a symptom-driven approach (APA, 2001). Further, medications may be used to treat other disorders that commonly co-occur with PDs. Indeed, the frequent co-occurrence of PDs with other psychiatric disorders may, in part, explain the observations in clinical practice settings that most people with PDs are prescribed pharmacotherapies.

In this commentary, we expand upon the important points raised by the authors regarding patient involvement in pharmacotherapy, consideration of adverse effects and quality of life, and the importance of therapeutic alliance in these processes. We also review some of the limitations of clinical trials for medications for PDs to date, and explore reasons why empirically supported pharmacotherapies for PDs may be lagging behind those for many other psychiatric disorders. Additionally, we discuss how some of these limitations may interfere with the aggregation and interpretation of study results, as well as the translation of findings to clinical settings. Finally, we hypothesize how different approaches, such as targeting symptom domains or focusing on co-occurring disorders (using gambling disorder as an example), could be potentially beneficial to the development of efficacious pharmacotherapies for PDs.

Historically, PDs were considered, at least by some, to be largely stable constructs. As such, PDs were considered Axis II disorders, differing from Axis I conditions that were thought to be more amenable to change, particularly with medications. This conceptualization may, in part, explain why there have been relatively fewer systematic large-scale pharmacotherapy randomized clinical trials for PDs than for most Axis I disorders.

Nonetheless, Links et al. (this volume) note that a broad range of classes of medications (mood stabilizers, antipsychotics, antidepressants, anxiolytics, and others) have been examined for PDs, especially borderline personality disorder (BPD), with many studies showing some positive findings, particularly within specific symptom domain categories. However, they also note multiple concerns with medication management of PDs (e.g., high drop-out and non-compliance rates; adverse effects that may impact quality of life). These represent important factors that must be taken into consideration when weighing the pros and cons of medications; for example, whereas antipsychotics like olanzapine may help specific symptoms in BPD, adverse effects relating to weight gain may lead to metabolic syndrome and poorer quality of life. As such, having a good therapeutic relationship that actively involves the patient in the pharmacotherapeutic process is extremely important in the treatment of individuals with PDs, as discussed in greater detail by Links et al.

As described by Links et al., most trials reviewed in the chapter show some promising results in the treatment of PDs, particularly with respect to specific symptom domains in BPD. However, existing trials of PDs often have several important methodological limitations that may hamper how their results are translated or transferred into clinical settings (Bateman, Gunderson, & Mulder, 2015).

Researchers may face challenges when determining the target characteristics of the samples to be studied in clinical trials. Like other psychiatric disorders, PDs are heterogeneous conditions. Wright et al. (2013) stated that heterogeneity in BPD is likely to influence how treatments may best be delivered and the outcomes of these treatments. Patients with PDs usually have more than one psychiatric diagnosis. For example, Zimmerman and Mattia (1999) found that 69.5 percent of individuals with BPD had three or more DSM-IV Axis I disorders, and 47.4 percent presented with four or more such diagnoses. Whereas researchers acknowledge heterogeneity related to comorbidities and try to control for this variability through statistical means, inclusion/exclusion criteria, and other approaches, the resulting approach may limit generalizability to clinical settings. Further, although some statistical approaches may be appropriate for disorders characterized by low rates of comorbidity and heterogeneity, they may not be as useful for disorders that are highly heterogeneous, such as PDs (Joyce, Kehagia, Tracy, Proctor, & Shergill, 2017).

Another strategy researchers may employ to reduce heterogeneity is to define inclusion criteria involving specific severity thresholds. For example, Black et al. (2014) only included BPD patients with total scores of 9 or more on the Zanarini Rating Scale for BPD (ZAN-BPD; Zanarini et al., 2003). Although this strategy has some benefits, it may only account for quantitative differences between patients. As many possible combinations of responses to a scale result in the same total score, PD trials may enroll participants who experience different aspects of PD psychopathology, and this difference may be overlooked. Therefore, such qualitative differences may not be properly addressed and may complicate findings and their interpretation. This effect has been termed *weak aggregation* (Joyce, Tracy, & Shergill, 2017).

Heterogeneity related to co-occurring disorders may also represent an opportunity to test and develop treatment algorithms. For example, consider gambling disorder, a condition for which there is currently no indicated medication. Based on existing data from pharmacotherapy trials that have selected patients based on patterns of co-occurring disorders, pharmacotherapy recommendations stemming from the presence or absence of specific disorders may be generated (Bullock & Potenza, 2012) and updated based on subsequent findings (e.g., de Brito et al., 2017; Grant et al., 2014; Grant, Potenza, Kraus, & Petrakis, 2017). This approach of employing pharmacological interventions based on co-occurring disorders is likely to resonate with prescribing physicians trained to evaluate patients systematically for the presence or absence of specific disorders.

Another important consideration involves the outcome measures employed in PD trials. Currently, there are no universally accepted instruments to report changes in PD psychopathology. For example, the ZAN-BPD was initially developed as an interview-based instrument, and, more recently, a self-report version was published (Zanarini, Weingeroff, Frankenburg, & Fitzmaurice, 2015). The ZAN-BPD evaluates changes in BPD psychopathology, and it has become well accepted as an important instrument to report improvement in BPD psychopathology in clinical trials (Black et al., 2014; Zanarini et al., 2011). Nevertheless, other recent trials have employed different outcome measures. For example, Rohde and colleagues (Rohde, Polcwiartek, Correll, & Nielsen, 2017) evaluated how their intervention influenced the number of psychiatric admissions, psychiatric bed-days, concomitant medications, serious adverse effects, and intentional self-harm or overdose. Meanwhile, a study by Bellino and colleagues (Bellino, Paradiso, Bozzatello, & Bogetto, 2010) used another measure, the BPD Severity Index (BPDSI; Arntz et al., 2003). The use of different outcome measures complicates comparison of results across trials. Consensus statements regarding how best to assess treatment outcome, as have been generated for studies of gambling disorder (Walker et al., 2006), may help in harmonizing measures across studies.

How improvements in outcome measures reported in trials relate to clinical well-being and quality of life is also complicated. One standard approach compares changes in endpoint scores between the active and control groups. If the difference is significant, efficacy is proposed. However, a statistical difference does not necessarily correspond to a significant clinical response. This is also a concern for other psychiatric conditions, and may explain why other disorders, such as trichotillomania (Houghton et al., 2015), do not have indicated pharmacologic treatment options.

Adverse effects also warrant consideration. One of the largest randomized clinical trials to date of a medication for BPD involved olanzapine, with some positive effects noted in specific symptom domains. However, the use of second-generation antipsychotics like olanzapine may result in significant weight gain, metabolic syndrome, and cardiovascular morbidity and mortality (Newcomer, 2007). Given that many individuals with BPD demonstrate weight gain over time, adverse effects such as these are important to monitor. Likewise, valproic acid and other anticonvulsants may have teratogenic effects (Ornoy, 2009); thus, given that most patients with BPD are women (American Psychiatric Association, 2013; Ten Have et al., 2016), clinicians should consider the risks and benefits of these medications, as well as possible alternatives. In light of these adverse effects, quality of life measures are important to administer and discuss with patients on an ongoing basis.

The issues described above may be addressed using different approaches. A current debate involves the relative utility of dimensional versus categorical approaches to psychopathology, with the research domain criteria (RDoC) approach representing an important example of the former (Insel et al., 2010). The *Diagnostic and Statistical Manual of Mental Disorders, Fourth Edition* (DSM-IV, American Psychiatric Association, 1994, p. 633) stated that "an alternative to the categorical approach is the dimensional perspective that Personality Disorders represent maladaptive variants of personality traits that merge imperceptibly into normality and into one another." Consistent with this statement, several groups have proposed changes to PD assessment. Trull and colleagues (Trull, Tragesser, Solhan, & Schwartz-Mette, 2007) called attention to problems of the categorical diagnosis, such as poor stability of the PD diagnosis over time and high rates of heterogeneity among individuals with the same PD diagnosis. They proposed that a dimensional model would provide higher inter-rater reliability in assessing PD symptomatology and account for the aforementioned heterogeneity and deficits in diagnostic stability over time. Moreover, after evaluating several dimensional models for conceptualizing personality and PDs, they concluded that, despite their differences, these models overlapped in multiple ways. Widiger and Trull (2007) also discussed problems associated with categorical diagnoses of PDs and proposed that PDs be conceptualized within the dimensional Five-Factor Model. Others have supported this approach, with one survey finding that four out of five experts believe that PDs should be examined from a dimensional perspective (Bernstein, Iscan, & Masner, 2007).

PD clinical trials are increasingly integrating dimensional constructs, for example, by evaluating how risperidone may be safe and efficacious in the treatment of specific aspects of impulsivity in BPD. This approach should be expanded further – not only to relevant constructs within BPD, but also to dimensions specific to other PDs in respective trials of medications for these disorders. How researchers and clinicians in this field may best utilize both dimensional and categorical approaches to treatment development is an important and timely consideration that will likely have significant impact.

In conclusion, psychopharmacologic treatment of PDs is an emerging area that is presently difficult to evaluate, due to the limitations of the trials conducted to date. As additional data are generated using approaches that permit greater harmonization across studies, employ larger sample sizes, consider heterogeneities, and incorporate dimensional as well as categorical measures, it is hoped that there may be more safe and effective pharmacological treatments for people with PDs.

REFERENCES

American Psychiatric Association. (1994). *Diagnostic and Statistical Manual of Mental Disorders* (4th ed.). Washington, DC: American Psychiatric Association.

American Psychiatric Association. (2001). Practice guideline for the treatment of patients with borderline personality disorder. *American Journal of Psychiatry, 158*, 1–52.

American Psychiatric Association. (2013). *Diagnostic and Statistical Manual of Mental Disorders* (5th ed.). Arlington, VA: American Psychiatric Publishing.

Arntz, A., Van den Hoorn, M., Cornelis, J., Verheul, R., van den Bosch, W. M., & de Bie, A. J. (2003). Reliability and validity of the borderline personality disorder severity index. *Journal of Personality Disorders, 17*, 45–59.

Bateman, A. W., Gunderson, J., & Mulder, R. (2015). Treatment of personality disorder. *Lancet, 385*, 735–743.

Bellino, S., Paradiso, E., Bozzatello, P., & Bogetto, F. (2010). Efficacy and tolerability of duloxetine in the treatment of patients with borderline personality disorder: A pilot study. *Journal of Psychopharmacology, 24*, 333–339.

Bernstein, D. P., Iscan, C., & Masner, J. (2007). Opinions of personality disorder experts regarding the DSM-IV personality disorders classifications system. *Journal of Personality Disorders, 21*(5), 536–551.

Black, D. W., Zanarini, M. C., Romine, A., Shaw, M., Allen, J., & Schulz, S. C. (2014). Comparison of low and moderate dosages of extended-release quetiapine in borderline personality disorder: A randomized, double-blind, placebo controlled trial. *American Journal of Psychiatry, 171*(11), 1174–1182.

Bullock, S. A., & Potenza, M. N. (2012). Pathological gambling: Neuropsychopharmacology and treatment. *Current Psychopharmacology, 1*(1), 67–85.

de Brito, A. M., de Almeida Pinto, M. G., Bronstein, G., Carneiro, E., Faertes, D., Fukugawa, V., ... Tavares, H. (2017). Topiramate combined with cognitive restructuring for the treatment of gambling disorder: A two-center, randomized, double-blind clinical trial. *Journal of Gambling Studies, 33*(1), 249–263.

Grant, J. E., Odlaug, B. L., Chamberlain, S. R., Potenza, M. N., Schreiber, L. R., Donahue, C. B., & Kim, S. W. (2014). A randomized, placebo-controlled trial of N-acetylcysteine plus imaginal desensitization for nicotine-dependent pathological gamblers. *Journal of Clinical Psychiatry, 75*(1), 39–45.

Grant, J. E., Potenza, M. N., Kraus, S. W., & Petrakis, I. L. (2017). Naltrexone and disulfiram treatment response in veterans with alcohol dependence and co-occurring problem-gambling features. *Journal of Clinical Psychiatry, 78*(9), e1299–e1306.

Houghton, D. C., Capriotti, M. R., De Nadai, A. S., Compton, S. N., Twohig, M. P., Neal-Barnett, A. M., ... Woods, D. W. (2015). Defining treatment response in trichotillomania: A signal detection analysis. *Journal of Anxiety Disorder, 36*, 44–51.

Insel, T., Cuthbert, B., Garvey, M., Heinssen, R., Pine, D.S., Quinn, K., ... Wang, P. (2010). Research domain criteria (RDoC): Toward a new classification framework for research mental disorders. *American Journal of Psychiatry, 167*(7), 748–751.

Joyce, D. W., Kehagia, A. A., Tracy, D. K., Proctor, J., & Shergill, S. S. (2017). Realising stratified psychiatry using multidimensional signatures and trajectories. *Journal of Translational Medicine, 15*, 15. doi:10.1186/s12967-016-1116-1

Joyce, D. W., Tracy, D. K., & Shergill, S. S. (2017). Are we failing clinical trials? A case for strong aggregate outcomes. *Psychological Medicine, 48*(2), 177–186.

National Institute for Health and Care Excellence, UK [NICE]. (2015). *Borderline Personality Disorder: Recognition and Management.* www.nice.org.uk/guidance/cg78/resources/borderline-personality-dosrder-recognition-and-management-pdf-975635141317

Newcomer, J. W. (2007). Antipsychotic medications: Metabolic and cardiovascular risk. *Journal of Clinical Psychiatry, 68*(4), 8–13.

Ornoy, A. (2009). Valproic acid in pregnancy: How much are we endangering the embryo and fetus? *Reproductive Toxicology, 28*(1), 1–10.

Rohde, C., Polcwiartek, C., Correll, C. U., & Nielsen, J. (2017). Real-world effectiveness of clozapine for borderline personality disorder: Results from a 2-year mirror-image study. *Journal of Personality Disorders, 31*, 1–15.

Ten Have, M., Verheul, R., Kaasenbrood A., van Dorsselaer S., Tuithof, M., & Kleinjan, M. (2016). Prevalence rates of borderline personality disorder symptoms: A study based on the Netherlands Mental Health Survey and Incidence Study–2. *BMC Psychiatry, 16*, 249.

Trull, T. J., Tragesser, S. L., Solhan, M., & Schwartz-Mette, R. (2007). Dimensional models of personality disorder: Diagnostic and Statistical Manual of Mental Disorders Fifth Edition and beyond. *Current Opinion in Psychiatry, 20*(1), 52–56.

Walker, M., Toneatto, T., Potenza, M. N., Petry, N., Ladouceur, R., Hodgins, D. C., … Blaszczynski, A. (2006). A framework for reporting outcomes in problem gambling treatment research: The Banff, Alberta Consensus. *Addiction, 101*(4), 504–511.

Widiger, T. A., & Trull, T. J. (2007) Plate tectonics in the classification of personality disorder: Shifting to a dimensional model. *American Psychologist, 62*(2), 71–83.

Wright, A. G. C., Hallquist, M. N., Morse, J. Q., Scott, L. N., Stepp, S. D., Nolf, K. A., & Pilkonis, P. A. (2013). Clarifying interpersonal heterogeneity in borderline personality disorder using latent mixture modeling. *Journal of Personality Disorder, 27*(2), 125–143.

Zanarini, M. C., Schulz, S. C., Detke, H. C., Tanaka, Y., Zhao, F., Lin, D., … Corya, S. (2011). A dose comparison of olanzapine for the treatment of borderline personality disorder: A 12-week randomized, doubleblind, placebo-controlled study. *Journal of Clinical Psychiatry, 72*, 1353–1362.

Zanarini, M. C., Vujanovic, A. A., Parachini, E. A., Boulanger, J. L., Frankernburg, F. R., & Hennen, J. (2003). Zanarini Rating Scale for Borderline Personality Disorder (ZAN-BPD): A continuous measure of DSM-IV borderline psychopathology. *Journal of Personality Disorders, 17*(3), 233–242.

Zanarini, M. C., Weingeroff, J. L., Frankenburg, F. R., & Fitzmaurice, G. M. (2015). Development of the self-report version of the Zanarini Rating Scale for Borderline Personality Disorder. *Personality and Mental Health, 9*(4), 243–249.

Zimmerman, M., & Mattia, J.I. (1999). Axis I diagnostic comorbidity and borderline personality disorder. *Comprehensive Psychiatry, 40*(4), 245–252.

21c Directions for Future Drug Trial Research: Author Rejoinder to Commentaries on Recent Developments in the Pharmacologic Management of Personality Disorders

PAUL S. LINKS, PHILIPPE BOURSIQUOT, AND MADISON LINKS

The two excellent commentaries have greatly enriched the discussion of the pharmacological management of patients with personality disorders (PDs) and particularly the direction that future drug trial research must take.

Stoffers-Winterling and Lieb (this volume) stressed the need for quality research that closes the gap between evidence and practice. The recently completed trial by Crawford and colleagues (2018) stands out as a reference point for trial methodology that will advance our understanding of pharmacological management of patients with PDs. They completed a multi-site randomized controlled trial comparing lamotrigine (up to 200 mg/day) versus placebo with treatment as usual in 276 patients with borderline personality disorder (BPD) and, most uniquely, completed assessments at 3-, 6-, and 12-month follow-ups. The primary outcome of the study was the improvement in BPD symptoms as measured by the total score of the Zanarini Rating Scale for Borderline Personality Disorder (ZAN-BPD). The study also included a breadth of secondary outcomes, such as depression, self-harm, use of alcohol and other drugs, social functioning, quality of life, and cost-effectiveness of the intervention. The study, although well-conceived, suffered because only 33.7 percent of participants were compliant with medications throughout the trial. Overall, the trial demonstrated no significant differences between the lamotrigine and comparison groups in BPD symptoms at 12 months, as well as no significant differences in any of the secondary outcomes, including cost and health-related quality of life. Furthermore, an analysis of the effect of treatment adherence revealed no relationship between greater medication adherence and better outcomes. The authors concluded that there was no benefit of treating patients with BPD with lamotrigine.

Although we agree with Stoffers-Winterling and Lieb (this volume) that the Crawford et al. study represents a high-water mark for pharmacological trials done in patients with PDs, two caveats should be made regarding the results. First, almost all of the participants had "complex" PDs, which means that patients had coexisting personality problems in addition to BPD and were recruited from secondary care mental health services. Therefore, the findings may not generalize to less complex and severe patients with BPD. In keeping with the two earlier randomized controlled trials that recruited samples from primary care clinics or using community advertisements, lamotrigine may have value for less complex and severe patients with BPD. Second, the earlier randomized controlled trials suggested that lamotrigine may have a role in lessening anger, impulsivity, and affective instability (as measured by the ZAN-BPD). Unfortunately, the ZAN-BPD may not be an adequate measure to capture change in these aspects of borderline personality pathology. For example, the ZAN-BPD is a clinician-administered scale that rates the nine criteria of BPD on a severity scale from no symptoms to severe symptoms. If clinicians were to rate affective instability on patients' single report of their mood variability or cross-sectional observations, then this rating is likely to be unreliable and invalid (Links et al., 2007). Future trials assessing affective instability should include various methods such as experience sampling methodology or laboratory assessments to capture this feature of borderline pathology.

Farhat and Potenza (this volume) discussed the need to be able to aggregate and compare across trials and the need for harmonization of outcome measures. As discussed above, although the ZAN-BPD has become an important measure to report improvement in BPD symptoms in clinical studies, the assessment of symptom improvement is insufficient to determine meaningful interventions for patients with PDs. Farhat and Potenza called for including measures that capture "clinical well-being and quality of life" and more attention to recording adverse effects. Changing functional outcomes remains one of the most challenging issues related to our current evidence-based treatment approaches for patients with PDs, as previous psychosocial intervention trials have shown an inability to improve functional outcomes despite being effective in the treatment of symptoms. For example, in their randomized controlled trial comparing Dialectical Behavior Therapy to General Psychiatric Management, McMain and colleagues (McMain, Guimond,

Streiner, Cardish, & Links, 2012) found no significant improvement in the percentage of participants either working or attending school from the beginning of the trial to the end of the follow-up period (60.3 percent at the beginning of treatment versus 51.8 percent at the end of the follow-up period). Similarly, 39.7 percent of participants were receiving psychiatric disability benefits before therapy and 38.8 percent were receiving this support at the end of the follow-up period. In general, interventions for patients with PDs have not focused on rehabilitation and improving the patient's functioning. The measurement of functional outcomes in clinical trials is also problematic. Summarizing across existing randomized controlled trials of psychotherapy interventions for BPD, we found that 14 different measures of functioning or quality of life had been employed. The need to harmonize our approach to measuring functional improvement remains a priority for future intervention research.

We fully agree with our commentators that research into pharmacological interventions for patients with PDs needs to advance by (1) using superior methodology as per Crawford et al. (2018), (2) developing a consensus on the best measures, (3) incorporating dimensional models of personality pathology, (4) accounting for patient heterogeneities, and (5) creating partnerships between patients, clinicians, and care providers in order to develop a meaningful research agenda going forward.

REFERENCES

Crawford, M. J., Sanatinia, R., Barrett, B., Cunningham, G., Dale, O., Ganguli, P., ... Reilly, J. G. (2018). Lamotrigine for people with borderline personality disorder: A RCT. *Health Technology Assessment*, 22, 1–68.

Links, P. S., Eynan, R., Heisel, M. J., Barr, A., Korzekwa, M., McMain, S., & Ball, J. S. (2007). Affective instability and suicidal ideation and behavior in patients with borderline personality disorder. *Journal of Personality Disorders*, 21, 72–86.

McMain, S. F., Guimond, T., Streiner, D. L., Cardish, R. J., & Links, P. S. (2012). Dialectical behavior therapy compared with general psychiatric management for borderline personality disorder: Clinical outcomes and functioning over a 2-year follow-up. *American Journal of Psychiatry*, 169, 650–661.

Index

(Italicized 'f' and 't' after page numbers refer to figures and tables, respectively)